A CONCORDANCE

TO THE

POEMS OF ROBERT HERRICK

A CONCORDANCE

TO THE

POEMS OF ROBERT HERRICK

COMPILED AND EDITED

BY

MALCOLM MacLEOD

FORMERLY INSTRUCTOR IN ENGLISH IN THE UNIVERSITIES OF VIRGINIA AND MISSOURI

HASKELL HOUSE PUBLISHERS LTD.

Publishers of Scarce Scholarly Books

NEW YORK, N. Y. 10012

1971

First Published 1936

HASKELL HOUSE PUBLISHERS LTD.
Publishers of Scarce Scholarly Books
280 LAFAYETTE STREET
NEW YORK, N. Y. 10012

Library of Congress Catalog Card Number: 76-92974

Standard Book Number 8383-0991-7

Printed in the United States of America

TO THE MEMORY OF MY MOTHER

PREFACE

TEXT.—The Concordance is based upon F. W. Moorman's Oxford English Texts Edition of Robert Herrick's poems, published by the Oxford University Press, Oxford, 1915. This edition aims to reproduce the original text of the *Hesperides* and *Noble Numbers* as it appeared in 1648; to collate the text with manuscripts, music-books, and anthologies contemporaneous with Herrick; to include, with collations, ten additional poems that were not printed in the volume of 1648.

The following erroneously numbered lines of the basic text are correctly indicated in the Concordance:

Page 174	*The parting Verse, or charge to his supposed Wife when he travelled*	50 for 30
Page 252	*To Electra*	5 for 4
Page 325	*Of Love*	5 for 4
Page 335	*The pillar of Fame*	5 for 4
Page 371	*His wish to God*	5 for 3

QUOTATIONS.—With the exception of rare instances in which the final word of a line is hyphenated, a single line of poetry constitutes a citation.

CONCORDANCE-TITLES.—On account of both the large number of poems and the repetition of titles assigned to the various pieces, it has seemed best to designate the poems numerically. They are numbered progressively from 1-1130 in the *Hesperides*; 1-272 in the *Noble Numbers*; 1-10 in the Additional Poems. The letter H., N., or A. shows in which of the three groups a poem occurs.

EXPLANATION OF REFERENCES.—The following line may be taken as an illustration:

Ye have been fresh and green, ...110. H.274, 1

The number 110 indicates the page of the basic text on which the line is found. H.274 refers the reader back to the list of numerical titles at the front of the Concordance, where it will be observed that H.274 is in the *Hesperides* and that its verbal equivalent is *To Meddowes*. Finally, the number 1 is that of the line in the poem.

The lines illustrating any concordance-word are arranged primarily in their order by pages; secondly, by the sequence of numerical titles on the page; thirdly, by the number of the line within the poem.

OMISSIONS.—These words are not represented in the Concordance:

am	hers	them
and	my	they
are	ours	we
been	theirs	

Since they have no metrical significance in the line, the following dialogue guides are not included:

85.	H.213	Mirtillo, Amintas, Amarillis, Chorus
130.	H.329	Chorus
159.	H.421	Montano, Silvio, Mirtillo, Chorus
183.	H.492	Endimion Porter, Lycidas Herrick
220.	H.633	Chorus: Sacerdotum, Juvenum, Senum, Virginum, Pastorum, Matronarum, Omnium
243.	H.716	Chorus, Lallage
248.	H.730	Charon, Phylomel
280.	H.870	Herrick, Julia
305.	H.984	Lacon, Thyrsis
309.	H.1001	Question, Answer
323.	H.1068	Herrick, Amarillis
342.	N.17	Verse, Verse Chorus
364.	N.96	Chorus
365.	N.97	Chorus
366.	N.98	Chorus
367.	N.102	Star, Chorus
373.	N.123	Chorus

The lines given below are not cited in the Concordance because they are composed of words that are either entirely omitted or are not individually illustrated in the Partial Lists.

May by	11. H.20, 8
For me	11. H.20, 12
Why I so	12. H.26, 2
And I to thee	29. H. 87, 5
Then thou shalt be	87. H.214, 11
And where	111. H.280, 3
Will be	111. H.280, 11
That I will be	162. H.426, 23
And this	198. H.544, 29
That she,	220. H.633, 10
As thee,	220. H.633, 11
May be	220. H.633, 12
To these	246. H. 724, 25
Which are	246. H.724, 29
For if you	307. H.988, 4
That we	307. H.988, 7
I must	308. H.993, 1
Will I	308. H.993, 11
I will	308. H.993, 14
But this	308. H.993, 19
And he	308. H.993, 25
Whom we	308. H.993, 26
Wee may	308. H.993, 29
And who shall not	317. H.1035, 11
I sho'd not be	363. N.92, 4
With Thine, or Thee,	363. N.92, 5
So by this	414. A.5, 11

PARTIAL LISTS.—In this Concordance, as in others, purposes of economy have necessitated the arbitrary selection of certain words that are illustrated only in part.

a	it	thee
an	i'th'	their
art (verb)	I've	then
as	may	these
at	me	thine
aye	might (auxiliary)	this
be	mine (pronoun)	those
but	must	thou
by	myself	thy
can	no (adverb)	'tis
can't	nor	to
co'd	not	to'th'
could	of	unto
did (auxiliary)	on	upon
do (auxiliary)	or	very
for	o'th'	was
from	our	were
had	out	what
has	own	when
hath	's	whenas
have	shall	where
he	shalt	which
he'll	she	who
her	she'd	whom
he's	she'll	whose
him	she's	why
his	sho'd	will
I	should	with
I'	so	wo'd
if	t'	would
I'll	't	y'
I'm	th'	ye
in	th'are	you
into	that	your
is	the	yours

As a further device toward compression, typical uses of the following words are noted, and all of the remaining occurrences may be found in an appended list of numerical references unaccompanied by quotations.

all	no
canst	that's
hast	'twas
we'll	

VARIANTS.—It has seemed advisable to avoid the reconstruction of lines for which there are in most cases several readings, a process that might conceivably counteract Professor Moorman's labor of collation. Such variant concordance-words are, therefore, rendered thus:

Shakespeare — — — — — — — — —, ...443. var. H.475, 51

If the line is one of several under a given concordance-word, only the dashes and reference numbers appear.

Where an alternate word is clearly the misspelling of a satisfactory variant, such a word is omitted. Two examples are *sroaking* for *stroking* (434. var. H.293, 35) and *spinters* for *spinster's* (440. var. H.443, 101).

The readings of the Firth Manuscript (pages 451-453) have been compared with those of the Critical Appendix to preclude repetition. Variants between an inserted passage given in the Critical Appendix and the Firth Manuscript but not in the textual version of the poem will of course lead the reader back to the Critical Appendix for all the readings of a line.

The version of *Oberon's Feast* (H.293) given in its entirety in the Critical Appendix on pages 434-435 requires particular mention. It has been collated with Professor Moorman's accepted reading of the poem and with the list of variants pointed out by him. The words not occurring in either of these are listed. A variant word in a line closely corresponding to one in the text is shown as a variant of that line regardless of differences in the order of the lines in the poems. When a reference to a line from this reprinted poem concludes with a number and a letter, the number indicates the line of the accepted reading from which the second version differs, and the letter shows the position of this line in the second printing of the poem. Again, a reference ending with a letter instead of a line-number means that the line is in only the reprinted poem, which proceeds from lines *a* to *ff*.

INSERTIONS.—The Critical Appendix presents several passages that do not appear in the text proper. In the Concordance these are considered insertions and the lines involved are given the number of the line in the text after which the insertion comes. Besides bearing this number, they are also lettered from *a* to show their position in the interpolated passage. Variant words to these lines are also designated as insertions. A typical line is:

Why then goe forward, sweet Auspicious Bride, ...431. ins. H.283, 50a

SPELLING.—In alphabetizing entries, the general editorial policy has been to modernize the spelling of concordance-words. The appearance of the words in their quotations is of course unchanged.

Names have for the most part been left as they stand in the text except when the modern spelling is necessary for clearness, as with (Ben) *Jonson,* which is printed *Johnson* in the poetry. The cross-references should minimize confusion in this respect.

In lieu of reproducing the more difficult manuscript abbreviations, the following three words have been expanded:

appear 413. A.4, 3
everlasting 413. A.4, 11
part 405. A.1, 38

The numbers 3 and 1,000 are listed under *three* and *thousand.*

CROSS-REFERENCES.—On account of the irregularity of Seventeenth Century spelling, an effort has been made to furnish ample cross-references.

Obsolete words whose spelling in the text varies from that of the dictionaries have usually been placed under the accepted spelling with a cross-reference from the less desirable form.

Words hyphenated in Herrick but now spelled singly carry a cross-reference from the second element to the complete word.

A matter of especial difficulty has been the grouping of words that are given as two in Herrick but which are to-day one. From the standpoint of the original it seems preferable to refer the reader back from the complete word to one of its parts.

ACKNOWLEDGMENTS.—Although this Concordance has been principally the work of one compiler and editor, I should like to express my gratitude to those who have been most actively interested during the stages of its preparation:

Professor Lane Cooper of Cornell University, who has encouraged the project with both advice and friendly offers of further aid.

Those of my former students at the University of Missouri who so competently assisted in the execution of a limited number of concordance-slips.

Mr. C. A. Wiese of the Banta Publishing Company, for his patient coöperation.

Margaret McClure MacLeod, for her comprehensive interest and valued help.

Professor Archibald Anderson Hill of the University of Virginia, to whom I am particularly indebted for his time, suggestions, and able counsel.

T. Ruth Spencer, whose generosity in financing the book is only another manifestation of her devotion through the years.

MALCOLM MACLEOD

University, Virginia
November, 1932

A LIST
of the
NUMERICAL TITLES USED IN THIS CONCORDANCE
with the corresponding titles and page-numbers in the Oxford English Texts Edition of Herrick, published by the Oxford University Press, (Oxford, 1915)

NOTE

In the basic text the poems are grouped as follows: *Hesperides* (pages 1-335); *Noble Numbers* (pages 337-403); Additional Poems (pages 404-419).

The poems in this Concordance are numbered progressively from H. 1 to H. 1130 in the *Hesperides;* from N. 1 to N. 272 in the *Noble Numbers;* from A. 1 to A. 10 in the Additional Poems.

In the few cases where two poems of the same title occur on a page, the title is followed by (1) and (2) to indicate which comes first on the page. An instance is *Another* on page 6 of the text.

The dedication to *The Fairie Temple:* or, *Oberons Chappell* is numbered H. 223a; the body of the poem is referred to as H. 223.

The independent concluding couplets of the *Hesperides* and *Noble Numbers,* without titles in the text, are here designated as H. 1130 and N. 272 respectively.

HESPERIDES

HIS NOBLE NUMBERS:
OR,
HIS PIOUS PIECES

ADDITIONAL POEMS
NOT INCLUDED IN HESPERIDES OR NOBLE NUMBERS

ERRATA

(The first numbers refer to page and column.)

READ:

15 –2 **Bank,** 165. H.443, 26; of mosse *for* or moose.
20 –1 **Belickling** *for* **Belicking.**
21 –2 **Betickling** *for* **Beticling.**
39 –2 **Clean** *for* **Cleane.**
41 –2 **Cock's-tread** *for* **Cocks-tread.**
42 –1 **Come,** 36. H.106, 50; suck *for* such.
42 –2 **Codling's** *for* **Codlin's.**
46 –2 **Convenient**—var. H.443, 89 *for* var. H.443, 88.
49 –1 **Cross-track**—man' *for* man.
55 –2 **Denounced,** 46. H.128, 47; thee *for* three.
58 –2 **Discease**—**Disease** *for* **Decease.**
58 –2 **Dish,** 363. N.93, 6; from *for* frim.
58 –2 **Dishes,** 119. H.293, 5; feast *for* feat.
61 –2 **Done,** 395. N.244, 4; the like *for* like.
63 –1 **Doubt,** 168. H.443, 121; no *for* not.
70 –1 **End**—425. var. H.197, 14 *for* var. 425. H.197, 14.
71 –1 **Enthrall**—14. H.34, 6 *for* 14. 8.34, 6.
71 –1 **Epithalamie**—**See Epithalamium** *for* **See Epithalamion.**
71 –1 **Epithalamium** *for* **Epithalamion.**
83 –2 **First,** 242. H.713, 18; Urn *for* Urne.
87 –2 **For,** 152. H.390, 1; be *for* to.
91 –2 **From's**—Natiue *for* Nature.
96 –1 **Glass,** 75. H.193, 26; they *for* thy.
113 – 1 **Here,** 28. H.84, 6; he *for* be.
115 – 2 **Heys** *for* **Heyes.**
116 – 1 **Hispid** *for* **Hisped.**
123 – 2 **Induct** *for* **Induced.**
155 – 2 **Marmelet** *for* **Marmalet.**
155 – 2 **Masque** *for* **Mask.**
165 – 1 **Murders** *for* **Murder's.**
165 – 2 **Must,** 133. H.336, 25; on *for* one.
165 – 2 **Mutius**—mighty *for* might.
167 – 2 **Nectarel** *for* **Nectarell.**
187 – 1 **Pannicles** *for* **Panicles.**
190 – 2 **Perfume,** 89. H.219, 13; with *for* will.
201 – 1 **Puplike** *for* **Pup-like.** Insert **See Public.**
202 – 1 **Quarrelets** *for* **Quarelets.**
204 – 2 **Rectress** *for* **Rectoress.**
205 – 2 **Remains,** 277. H.852, 4; Or *for* Of.
212 – 1 **Safety's** *for* **Safeties.** Follows **Safety.**
226 – 2 **Sing,** 5. H.1, 6; sing of *for* sing.
232 – 1 **Soft-maiden's-blush** *for* **Soft-maidens-blush.**
234 – 2 **Sour,** 395. N.246, 5; Yet *for* Let.
235 – 1 **Spartaness**—sprightly *for* slightly.
235 – 2 **Speaks,** 130. H.329, 18; speaks *for* speake.
240 – 2 **Stirring**—Substitute: **Stirring** the waters, I am come; and here,
246 – 2 **Sweats**—102. H.253, 8 *for* 102. N.253, 8.
248 – 1 **Swelling,** 139. H.348, 2; Plump *for* Pump.
249 – 2 **Taste,** 46. H.128, 51; but not **taste** thee *for* but not **taste.**
251 – 1 **Tells,** 180. H.478, 7; are *for* art.
277 – 1 **Vestiment** *for* **Vestment.**
277 – 1 **Vestiments** *for* **Vestments.**
277 – 1 **Vice**—239. H.698, 1 *for* 239. N.698, 1.
280 – 2 **Wassailing,** 368. N.102, 22; wee'l *for* wee l.
283 – 1 **Weeping,** 159. H.421, 7; him *for* his.
294 – 2 **Work**—389. N.214, 1 for 3 9. N.214, 1.
295 – 2 **Worshipper** *for* **Worshiper.**
296 – 1 **Wrath,** 340. N.7, 2; perturbation *for* peturbation.
297 – 2 **Yet,** 97. H.233, 3; you'l *for* you l.
299 – 1 **Younker** *for* **Yonker.** Should be in column 2.

ORDER

1 –1 **Abide**—151. H.387, 5 precedes 237. H.685, 8.
7 –1 **Along**—418. A.9, 41 follows 417. A.8, 37.
13 –2 **Aunt**—Citation should be under **Ant,** p. 8, col. 2.
17 –1 **Bear**—437. var. H.336, 126 should be under **Beer,** p. 18, col. 2.
22 –1 **Bewray**—Citation should illustrate concordance-word **Beray** inserted on p. 20, col. 2.
25 –1 **Bodies**—157. H.414, 6 should illustrate concordance-word **Bodice** inserted above.
25 –2 **Born**—78. H.197, 49 should be under **Borne.**
26 –2 **Bouzing**—Citation should illustrate **Bousing.**
34 –2 Reverse order of **Capacious** and **Capable.**
38 –1 **Chin**—134. H.336, 92 should be first citation under **Chine.**
41 –1 **Coats**—5. H.2, 5 should illustrate concordance-word **Cotes** inserted on p. 47, col. 1.
54 –2 **Decease**—316. H.1028, 21 should be under **Disease** on p. 58, col. 2.
55 –1 **Deeds**—55. H.149, 89 should be under **Deads** on p. 53, col. 2.
55 –1 **Defends**—333. H.1117, 2 and 370. N.109, 1 should illustrate concordance-word **Defensive** inserted below.
55 –2 **Denied**—391. N.226, 1 should illustrate concordance-word **Deniest** inserted below.
58 –1 **Dinasty** should read **Dynasty.** Citation i lustrating **Dynasty** should be inserted on p. 66, col. 1.
66 –2 **Eager**—442 var. H.575, 20 and 443. var. H.580, 10 (p. 67, col. 1) should be under **Each** on p. 66, col. 2.
71 –2 **Ere**—184. H.492, 26 precedes 201. H.556, 4.
90 –1 **Free**—129. H.324, 2 and 129. H.324, 3 precede 133. H.336, 37.
153 – 1 **Makes**—170. H.452, 3 should be under **Makest** in col. 2.
155 – 1 **Maquerel**—Citation should illustrate concordance-word **Mackerel** inserted on p. 150, col. 2.
158 – 2 **Men's**—424. var. H.164, 4 should be under **Men** above.
164 – 1 **Mounds**—261. H.781, 8 and 323. H.1068, 7 should illustrate concordance-word **Maunds** on p. 156, col. 1.
187 – 1 **Pale**—404. A.1, 13 should be under **Pair** above.
200 – 1 **Prove**—351. N.48, 7 should be in col. 2 following 327. N.1082, 2.
205 – 1 **Reeks**—56. H.149, 117 should illustrate concordance-word **Reaks** inserted on p. 204, col. 1.
205 – 1 **Reined** should follow **Reigns.**
228 – 2 **Sleight**—342. N.16, 1 should be under **Slight** on p. 229, col. 1.
236 – 2 **Spirit**—427. var. H.197, 49 should illustrate concordance-word **Spiritful** inserted below.
239 – 2 **Stench**—Citation should illustrate concordance-word **Stanch** inserted on p. 238, col. 1.
241 – 2 **Straight**—65. H.172, 18 should illustrate concordance-word **Strait** on p. 242, col. 1.
248 – 1 **Tabbies** should precede **Tabernacle.**
255 – 2 **Thence**—200. H.551, 5 should follow 193. H.524, 3.
256 – 1 **There**—226. H.649, 2 should be under **Therewithal** on p. 257, col. 2.
259 – 1 **Thirty**—151. H. 385, 5 should illustrate concordance-word **Thirty-five** inserted below.
264 – 1 **Time's**—450. var. A.9, 19 should be under **Times** below.
270 – 1 **Trout-flies'**—92. H.223, 72 should illustrate concordance-word **Trout-fly's** inserted below.
271 – 2 **Turns**—450. var. A.9, 58 should be under **Turned** above.

281 – 1 **Watched**—92. H.223, 73 should be under **Watchet** below.
290 – 2 **Wilt**—26. H.79, 9 should illustrate concordance-word **Will't** inserted above.
293 – 2 **Wonder**—372. N.118, 5 should precede 384. N.183, 1.
293 – 2 **Wonderous** should read **Wondrous.** The entry should be on p. 294, col. 1.
294 – 1 **Word's**—26. H.79, 10 should be under **Words** below.

DELETE:

2 – 1 **Accept**—repeated 88. H.218, 8.
8 – 2 **Another**—426. var. H.197, 40.
8 – 2 **Ant**—452. ins. H.443, 45e.
17 – 1 **Bears**—447. var. A.1, 6.
26 – 2 **Bousing—See Bouzing.**
35 – 1 **Castor's** and citation.
36 – 2 **Charge**—449. var. A.3, 54.
55 – 1 **Deity**—452. var. H.443, 99.
69 – 2 **Enchasing**—452. var. H.443, 60.
74 – 1 **Express**—432. var. H.283, 68.
104 – 1 **Guilt**—436. ins. H.336, 48g.
106 – 1 **Handmaid**—449. var. A.3, 100.
150 – 2 **Mackarell See Maquerel.**
156 – 1 **Maunds—See Mounds.**
166 – 2 **Name**—449. var. A.8, 13.
178 – 1 **O'ercome**—435. var. H.293, 33aa.
204 – 2 **Rectresse See Rectoress.**
208 – 2 **Rind**—448. var. A.1, 98.
223 – 1 **Shortest**—432. var. H.283, 72.
228 – 2 **Sleight** and citation. Substitute **Sleight See Slight.**
239 – 2 **Stench** and citation. Substitute **Stench See Stanch.**
291 – 1 **Wing**—448. var. A.3, 22.

INSERT:

3 – 1 **Afar See Far.**
48 – 2 **Crewels See Cruels.**
78 – 1 **Far-fetched See Far, Fetched.**
94 – 2 **Giltheads** – – – – – – – – –, . .436. ins. H.366, 48g.
115 – 1 **Hereabout See Here.**
149 – 2 **Love-vexed See Vexed.**
153 – 2 **Malkin See Maukin.**
192 – 2 **Pips See Peeps.**
200 – 1 **Public—See Puplike.**
203 – 2 **Raspis See Respasses.**
244 – 2 **Such-like See Such.**
281 – 1 **Watched—See Watchet.**

A CONCORDANCE TO THE POEMS OF ROBERT HERRICK

A (Partial List) See George-A-Green, Sweet-slugabed.
Of sacred * Orgies flyes, A round, A round..........7. H.8, 8
A telling what rare sights h'ad seen:.............13. H.27, 8
Love and my selfe (beleeve me) on a day......17. H.44, 1
Ile leave thy heart a dying....................27. H.81, 36
Or some full flame, which with a pride aspires,....45. H.128, 17
Help! O help! your Boy's a dying..............50. H.139, 5
When tuckt up she a hunting goes;...............51. H.142, 14
She must no more a Maying:.................56. H.149, 114
Still a falling, yet I see.........................62. H.162, 5
Few Beads are best, when once we goe a Maying..68. H.178, 28
But my Corinna, come, let's goe a Maying.......68. H.178, 42
Many a green-gown has been given;............69. H.178, 51
Many a jest told of the Keyes betraying........69. H.178, 55
This night, and Locks pickt, yet w'are not a Maying.
69. H.178, 56
Come, my Corinna, come, let's goe a Maying.....69. H.178, 70
When next he came a pilfring so,..............71. H.182, 29
And seeing it, I made a stay..................73. H.187, 5
And perfume the aire a while:....................74. H.189, 2
But on a sudden, all was chang'd and gone....81. H.202, 3
Old Time is still a flying:......................84. H.208, 2
The higher he's a getting;........................84. H.208, 6
Rest but a while here, by this bank of Lillies,....86. H.213, 10
And many a dapper Chorister..................92. H.223, 104
Many a trifle too, and trinket,................93. H.223, 123
Sho'd I a jot the better see?....................97. H.235, 4
Lest a handsome anger flye,....................98. H.238, 13
Like a Lightning, from her eye,................98. H.238, 14
Fall gently, gently, and a while him keep........99. H.244, 5
That strik'st a stilnesse into hell:...............103. H.254, 2
Love on a day (wise Poets tell)................105. H.260, 1
But on a sudden all were gone.................107. H.263, 16
Or that this Yonker keeps so strict a Lent,.....122. H.305, 3
A little while from Tramplers free;...........123. H.306, 10
The gardens-glory liv'd a while,...............126. H.318, 4
As sure a Mattins do's to him belong,..........128. H.321, 5
Seldome or never, knows a wain,...............143. H.369, 2
It keeps a growth in thee; and so will runne...147. H.377, 43
Just upon five and thirty pounds a yeare.........151. H.385, 4
He'l turn a Papist, rancker then before.........151. H.385, 6
Many a Teaster by his game, and bets........154. H.400, 2
'Tis but as day a kindling:....................154. H.404, 2
Were there not a Matter known,...............163. H.433, 1
Many a Counter, many a Die,.................166. H.443, 51
But you may stay yet here a while,............176. H.467, 4
Long time w'ave here been a toying:............195. H.534, 3
Be ever and ever a spending;..................195. H.534, 9
Broomsted a lamenesse got by cold and Beere;..201. H.555, 1
Then feast, and coy't a little; then to bed.......216. H.618, 8
Which had a juice in it:......................222. H.635, 2
Gander (they say) doth each night pisse a Bed:..223. H.636, 2
Of a Pease, that 'gins to chit,.................223. H.638, 13
At noone of Night are a working...............225. H.643, 18
Never man yet had a regredience................228. H.656, 2
Flies no thought higher then a fleece:..........229. H.662, 12
Like to a Deaw, or melted Frost...............233. H.670, 27
'Gainst thou go'st a mothering.................236. H.684, 2
With eating many a miching Mouse............246. H.724, 24
Ph. A deale of Love, and much, much Griefe together.
248. H.730, 14
Who for a long sad time has weeping stood,.....251. H.745, 3
Come while the Log is a teending............263. H.784, 12
The while the meat is a shredding;.............263. H.784, 15
To fill the Paste that's a kneading.............263. H.784, 18
He is a serving, who's a Trencher-man..........265. H.796, 4
And old, old Age is a farre off:..................267. H.806, 3
Are a turning:...............................308. H.993, 24
If the Maides a spinning goe.................315. H.1026, 5
No more shall I a long thy christall glide,......315. H.1028, 7
When as the roof's a tottering:................318. H.1036, 4
(As with a Magick) laid them all agen:.......326. H.1080, 18
Of sugered rush a glads him with.........434. ins. H.293, 41d
Abashed Be bold my Booke, nor be abasht, or feare
212. H.603, 1
Abate Sometimes 'two'd blaze, and then abate,....67. H.175, 11
Age shall not wrong thee; or one jot abate......280. H.869, 3
Abbey-lubbers I, and their Abby-Lubbers too:..93. H.223, 108
Abdomen The Abdomen of a Bee;................223. H.638, 9
Abel Speak, did the Bloud of Abel cry............387. N.203, 1
The bloud of Abel was a thing.................388. N.204, 1
Aberrations Some Aberrations in my Poetry;........32. H.95, 2
From aberrations to live free;..................357. N.72, 17
Abhor But stinking breath, I do as hell abhorre it.
210. H.588, 2
I abhor the slimie kisse,.........................282. H.878, 1
Abhorre, and spew out all Neutralities............353. N.54, 4
Justly our dearest Saviour may abhorre us,......388. N.209, 1
Abide Which is His Shade, who can abide His Flame!
237. H.685, 8
But thou kind Prew did'st with my Fates abide,..151. H.387, 5
Abilities On our part, wanting all abilities.........356. N.71, 4
Able So long as I am able......................235. H.674, 15
Lord, I confesse, that Thou alone art able........357. N.73, 1
Abode Last, let us make our best abode,..........111. H.278, 5
Shall never shrink, where making thine abode,...143. H.365, 11
Jove, joy'st when guests make their abode......147. H.377, 62
Abound Then so t'abound,........................368. N.104, 7
But where sin swells, there let Thy grace abound..398. N.261, 6
Abounds Hell is the place where whipping-cheer abounds,
372. N.120, 1
About See 'Bout
Then shall my Ghost not walk about, but keep......9. H.14, 17
Of Wife) about I'le lead;..........................13. H.31, 8
About her spotlesse neck she knit................14. H.34, 3
About her head I writhing hung,...............16. H.41, 9
My curles about her neck did craule,.............16. H.41, 14
A Lawne about the shoulders thrown............28. H.83, 3
About thy neck a Carkanet is bound,..............30. H.88, 5
About thy wrist, the rich *Dardanium............30. H.88, 8
About the sweet bag of a Bee,....................31. H.92, 1
Sighs numberlesse he cast about,.................42. H.119, 5
Throwing about his wild, and active fires........45. H.128, 18
About the Arch of either eye;....................46. H.130, 8
No Furies, here about,........................56. H.149, 103
I saw about her spotlesse wrist,..................64. H.169, 1
About this Urne, wherein thy Dust is laid,.......73. H.186, 18
In the wild aire, when thou hast rowl'd about,....87. H.215, 3
While we this Trentall sing about thy Grave......89. H.219, 2
Here goe about for to recite...................91. H.223, 34
Guesse cuts his shooes, and limping, goes about....98. H.239, 1
About the Cart, heare, how the Rout...........101. H.250, 15
And roule about, and in their motions burne.....113. H.283, 38
About the Roofe a Syren in a Sphere;.........115. H.283, 102
The sheet about, like flakes of snow............116. H.283, 150
That Milk-maids make about the hearth,......126. H.319, 12
Then as ye sit about your embers,..............127. H.319, 37
About your eares; and lay upon...............127. H.319, 43
Why I tye about thy wrist,.....................128. H.322, 1
And as it shines, it throwes a scent about,......131. H.331, 7
Sphering about the wassail cup,...............136. H.336, 148
So smells the Breath about the hives,............145. H.375, 7
Or flash about the spacious Theater............150. H.382, 10
The Fringe about this, are those Threds........167. H.443, 106
About him, when the Taverns shot's to pay.......173. H.463, 2
Yet, ere twelve Moones shall whirl about.........178. H.476, 7
Then no gazing more about,.....................180. H.482, 3
And I, about the Cup shall see..................185. H.495, 3
Letcher was Carted first about the streets,........195. H.532, 1
About whose Throne the crowd of Poets throng..206. H.575, 29
Here about, but has his eyes,...................221. H.633, 30
Will whirle about, and blow them thence at last...226. H.650, 4
About the Cover of this Book there went........227. H.652, 7
But walk'st about thine own dear bounds,......230. H.662, 15
About the Bed, there sighing stood.............237. H.686, 3
By ruffling winds, about the world.............245. H.720, 16
I keep, that playes about my House,............246. H.724, 22
A Gyges Ring they beare about them still,.......250. H.737, 1
He tacks about, and now he doth profess.........266. H.800, 5
Singing about my everlasting fire................294. H.938, 4
A rowle of Parchment Clunn about him beares,...295. H.941, 1
This line about, live Thou throughout the world;..298. H.955, 2
About their House, their clamorous I, or No:....303. H.975, 4
A crawling Vine about Anacreon's head:.......313. H.1017, 2
Since when (me thinks) my braines about doe swim.
313. H.1017, 13
And set about with Lillies;.....................323. H.1068, 6
When (God knowes) I'm tost about,.............348. N.41, 33
Bell-man of Night, if I about shall go............349. N. 43, 1
To gird my loynes about.........................352. N.53, 11
A wing about thy Sepulcher!.....................361. N.83, 68
Cast Holy Water all about,......................365. N.97, 4
Where round about Thou seest but all things vaine,
371. N.113, 3
It clings about; so I by Thee..................371. N.114, 4
So long as I about Thee craule?.................371. N.114, 6
Though ills stand round about me;.............373. N.122, 10
All set about with Lillies......................375. N.123, 80
— — — — — — — — —, ...430. var. H.283, 14
Lyes here about, and as we guesse.......440. ins. H 443, 45r
Abouts Lies here abouts; and for to pave........166. H.443, 53
Above See 'Bove
Thrice, and above, blest (my soules halfe) art thou.
34. H.106, 1
'Tis thou, above Nectar, O Divinest soule!........45. H.128, 19
Above an houre since; yet you not drest,........68. H.178, 8
Mine aged limbs above my chaire:...........135. H.336, 108
You, above all Those Sweets of Westminster:...137. H.341, 10
Above they are the Angels spiced wine..........226. H.645, 2
What State above, what Symmetrie below,.......297. H.947, 9
But chang'd above,.........................314. H.1024, 17
God is above the sphere of our esteem,.............340. N.4, 1
Fit for the place above;..........................352. N.53, 10
Above the rest................................359. N.83, 4

How soberly above the rest....................375. N.123, 64
Which heats those ravisht Soules above:.........395, N.246, 2
Aboue the entrance there is written this...........406. A.1, 73
Shewes like the Heavens aboue ye Moone,........413. A.4, 13
— — — — — — — — — — —, ...423. var. H.128, 23
Abroad Or flie abroad to seeke for woe...........6. H.2, 20
Come, we'll abroad; and let's obay..............68. H.178, 39
But walke abroad, yet wisely well..............174. H.465, 13
— — — — — — — — — — — —, ...423. var. H.128, 18
Absence (In my short absence) to unsluce a teare:.14. H.35, 10
By thy short absence, to desire and love thee?....77. H.197, 24
In my short absence; yet behold..............174, H.465, 19
Absent But being absent, Love lies languishing..13. H.30, 2
Where Mirth and Friends are absent when we Dine
197. H.541, 3
Absolute God gives to none so absolute an Ease,..387. N.199, 1
Absolution Since Absolution you can give to them
322. H.1062, 9
Abstinence Is the defensive vertue, Abstinence...333. H. 1117, 2
Absyrtus-like Absyrtus-like all torne confusedly:..300. H.960, 2
Abundance Gemms in abundance upon you:......68. H.178, 20
Blessings, in abundance come,..................124. H.314, 1
Abundant You'l do my Neice abundant honour...257, H.764, 10
Abundant plagues I late have had,..............354. N.57, 1
Accept To accept such coynes as these;..........88. H.218, 8
To accept such coynes as these;..............88. H.218, 8
These accept, and Ile be free,..................129. H.324, 3
If Jove wo'd speake, he wo'd accept of thine.....301, H.966, 14
As to accept my companie,......................399. N.265, 4
T'accept each Heart,..........................401. N.268, 33
Acceptance Acceptance it might find of thee.......214. H.613, 4
Reade acceptance by the smoake..............280. H.870, 18
But the acceptance, that must be,............351. N.47, 57
Access I write of Youth, of Love, and have Accesse.5. H.1, 5
By your accesse; (O you the best of Kings!)....25. H.77, 10
Which when I saw, I made accesse............51. H.142, 17
Permit my Book to have a free accesse........137. H.341, 11
Tell that Brave Man, fain thou wo'dst have access
301. H.963, 1
Temptations hurt not, though they have accesse:..359, N.79, 1
Accite See Excite
Accompany Thee spend a sigh, t'accompany my teare.
42. H.122, 6
Accomplish Chor. Long live the King; and to accomplish this,
300. H.961, 19
Accomplished My solemne Vowes have here accomplished:
23. H.72, 2
Nor wil't be long, ere this accomplish'd be;......26. H.79, 9
And Rites were all accomplished;............237. H.686, 14
Accompts See Accounts
According Mans fortunes are according to his paines.
253. H.752, 2
According to Thy liking........................363. N.92, 12
Account Account of such a flock of sheep;......133. H.336, 44
Last night I drew up mine Account,........369. N.107, 1
But like a Person of some high account:........398. N.263, 16
Accounted To be accounted inside cleane:........250. H.738, 2
Accounts All accompts must come to cleere:......373. N.121, 8
Accursed The Death accurs't....................401. N.268, 4
Accusation If Accusation onely can draw blood,..194. H.528, 1
Accuse Accuse thy feet......................375. N.123, 69
Accustomed That, I was accustom'd to............10. H.19, 4
Ache That Heart to bleed, your's ne'r will ake...11. H.20, 11
Which though they furre, will neither ake, or rot..46. H.129, 2
I held Love's head while it did ake;..........188. H.509, 1
My head doth ake,...........................210. H.591, 1
Aches And weather by our aches, grown........134. H.336, 87
Acknowledger Acknowledger of you............228. H.657, 13
Aclock See O'clock
Acorn Dryed, hony-combs, Browne Achorne cupps
439. ins. H.443, 45j
Acquaintance To sweet acquaintance there......271. H.824, 16
Acquire And look how all those heavenly Lamps acquire
3. Ded.H., 5
Acre That an Acre hath of Nose:..................11. H.21, 6
Acrimonious Whose acrimonious humour bites him here.
98. H.239, 4
Acron See Acorn
— — — — — — — — — — —, ...452. ins. H.443, 45j
Act See Overact
There is an Act that will more fully please:......24. H.74, 10
A sleep, untill the act be done................57. H.149, 142
For men did strut, and stride, and stare, not act.
150. H.382, 6
Here was not with the act combin'd...........175. H.465, 62
(And hang the head when as the Act is done)..196. H.537, 2
Next we will act, how young men wooe;........215. H.616, 19
Hast thou begun an act? ne're then give o're:...236. H.680, 1
The sweetest solace is to act no sin............341. N.13, 2
In Prayer the Lips ne're act the winning part,....346. N.35, 1
Lord! let me never act that beggars part,.......347. N.39, 3
Sin is an act so free, that if we shall..........389. N.218, 1
That must this day act the Tragedian,..........398. N.263, 20
Not those poor Theeves that act their parts with Thee:
399. N.263, 23
Those act without regard, when once a King,..399. N.263, 24
And thence proceed, to act Thy Passion........399. N.263, 29
Why then, go on to act: Here's wonders to be done,
401. N.268, 7
Act when Thou wilt,..........................401. N.268, 10
To raise an Act to full astonishment;..............415. A.7, 8
not halfe so much the Act, as end........421. ins. H.106, 42b
Prophan'd in Speech, or done an act that's fowle
426. ins. H.197, 29a
Acted And that's the part to be acted..........247. H.727, 12
When once the sin has fully acted been,.........346. N.37, 1
Acting But to the acting of this private Play:......24. H.74, 12
When we obey, by acting what we heare.........346. N.36, 3
Action To quick action, or the warme soft side....45. H.128, 5
For Lust and action; on he'l go,..............165. H.443, 11
That makes the Action, good, or ill............175. H.465, 64
Or to the good, or evill action..................214. H.614, 4
Base in action as in clothes:..................255. H.761, 12
To do ten Bad, for one Good Action..........339. N.1, 6
The Lawes of Action, will both sigh, and weep;.399. N.263, 37
Actions Blast these-like actions, or a thing that's worse;
79. H.197, 84
And his actions high be told..................108. H.266, 19
Shall make thy actions with their ends to meet.
128. H.320, 8
Brave men can't die; whose Candid Actions are..168. H.444, 5
— — — — — — — — — — — —, ...427. ins. H.197, 48c
Active The active Sea-horse, & with pride,........30. H.90, 2
Throwing about his wild, and active fires.........45. H.128, 18
The soule, like lightning, and as active too.......45. H.128, 28
O! give them active heat.......................57. H.149, 125
Then let thy active hand scu'd o're thy Lyre:....67. H.176, 3
Thou mak'st me ayrie, active to be born,......78. H.197, 49
Fill each part full of fire, active to doe........79. H.197, 79
It is an active flame, that flies,...............130. H.329, 8
Following with love and active heate thy game,..301. H.966, 7
Awake! the while the active Finger...........364. N.96, 6
Though Thou beest all that Active Love,......395. N.246, 1
An active spiritt full marrow, and what's good;
426. ins. H.197, 48d
— — — — — — — — — — — —, ...427. var. H.197, 49
Act's The first Act's doubtfull, (but we say)......94. H.225, 9
Acts See Quarter-acts
He Acts the Crime, that gives it Cherishing.......10. H.17, 2
Comely Acts well; and when he speaks his part,..266. H.799, 1
His own He acts not, but anothers part:.........343. N.22, 2
These were thy Acts, and thou shalt have......375. N.123, 85
'Ad See Had
Adam But nothing so; The Dinner Adam had,....273. H.835, 3
Add Then to that twenty, adde an hundred more:..24. H.74, 4
Adde a Cypresse-sprig thereto,..................89. H.220, 3
To adde a nobler Planet to the seven?..........112. H.283, 6
Adde to that thirty five, but five pounds more,...151. H.385, 5
We'l from our owne, adde far more years to his.
300. H.961, 20
Adde sugar, nutmeg and ginger,..............317. H.1035, 21
Add still to those............................363. N.92, 10
Add but a bit of flesh, to boyle:...............377. N.130, 2
Will add a power, to keep me innocent;........397. N.255, 2
Added To him that has, there shall be added more;..22. H.64, 3
Adders' — — — — — — — —, ...435. var. H.293, 44o
Addled Only, if one prove addled, that he eates....204. H.568, 3
Address And to the Bag-pipe all addresse;......127. H.319, 47
Both addresse to sacrifice:......................280. H.870, 2
Shall stand for euer, though I doe addresse.......412. A.3, 97
Adds And adds perfumes unto the Wine, which thou
148. H.377, 81
State at a distance adds to dignities.............236. H.682, 2
Adieu Adieu, mine Host, Adieu,..................27. H.81, 35
Love and they'l thank you for't. Adieu.........70. H.180, 8
With a teare; and so Adieu......................89. H.220, 4
Howsoever, cares, adue;......................191. H.519, 5
Live long, Lacon, so adew....................306. H.984, 41
And though we bid adieu to day,.............324. H.1068, 23
My frolick Youths adieu;....................328. H.1091, 6
Ah Dorcas, Dorcas! now adieu................374. N.123, 31
Admirable As that in all that admirable round,....307. H.992, 3
Admiration Thee with the eye of admiration?......45. H.128, 38
Worthy the Publique Admiration:..............297. H.947, 4
Confus'd in utter Admiration...................326. H.1080, 10
With admiration both of them and thee,............415. A.7, 4
Admire Thee and their lips espous'd; while I admire,
46. H.128, 50
As Love shall helpe me, I admire..............272. H.828, 9
Admired To make but One (and that's thy selfe) admir'd.
121. H.301, 6
O Thing admir'd! there did appeare............237. H.687, 5
And no lesse prais'd, then of the maides admir'd.
299, H.956, 10
And be of all admired, Tomasin................304. H.979, 2
Admiredly But yet how more admir'dly bright.....270. H.819, 6
Admit It seem'd by this time to admit the touch;..47. H.131, 5
Admit I Cloe put away,........................70. H.181, 19
No mixture did admit.........................75. H.193, 16
Me, me, forsaken, here admit..................170. H.449, 26

Of Love he sho'd **admit**......................222. H.635, 4
Not a wimbling Tongue **admit**:...................282. H.878, 6
Admits When feare **admits** no hope of safety, then
333. H.1118, 1
Whome love **admitts** to this Hesperides...........405. A.1, 70
Admitted To be **admitted** there...................54. H.149, 38
Ado To clense his eyes, Tom Brock makes much **adoe**,
110. H.273, 1
'Tis with very much **ado**;........................182. H.489, 6
Knit them with knots (with much **adoe** unty'd)..291. H.920, 2
Adopted **Adopted** some; none got by theft.......236. H.681, 4
Adoption Number, Your owne, by free **Adoption**;
107. H.264, 4
Are Gods, of them, but by **Adoption**............379. N.143, 4
Heire-ship be lesse, by our **adoption**:...........395. N.248, 2
Adoration — — — — — — — — —, ...423. var. H.128, 38
Adore Thee to **adore** thy God, the first of all...363. N.94, 2
Not to **adore** that, but to worship Thee.......371. N.115, 10
Adored **Adored** Cesar! and my Faith is such,......62. H.161, 13
Adorn See **Re-adorn**
Adorned **Adorn'd** this smoother Mead..........110. H.274, 16
Adratick See **Adriatic**
Adriatic Rough as th' **Adratick** sea, yet I........70. H.181, 23
Adue See **Adieu**
Adulce Some mirth, t'**adulce** mans miseries?......233, H.670, 6
Adulterate — — — — — — —, ...424. var. H.128, 53
Adulteries She'l runne to all **adulteries**.........287. H.899, 10
To barr out bolde **Adulteryes**,..................408. A.2, 36
Adulterous (Bred from the dung-hils, and **adulterous** rhimes,)
155. H.405, 13
Adultery One slit's enough to let **Adultry** in.....44. H.126, 4
In hot **Adult'ry** with another Wine?...........78. H.197, 40
Betrayes the Hearts **Adulterie**...................254. H.755, 2
Advance Their silv'rie flames **advance**,..........55. H.149, 57
Advent Thy second **Advent**, that must be........397. N.257, 3
Adventer See **Adventure**
Adventure Tel them, now they must **adventer**,....56. H.149, 99
Adverse **Adverse** and prosperous Fortunes both work on
349. N.44, 1
Adversity **Adversity** then breeds the discontent....235. H.676, 2
Adversity hurts none, but onely such............239. H.697, 1
Advice For pitties sake give your **advice**,...........8. H.13, 3
And from thy Compasse taking small **advice**,......36. H.106, 81
Take mine **advise**, and go not neere............279. H.868, 1
Danger to give the best **advice** to Kings.........318. H.1037, 2
Still take **advice**; though counsels when they flye.318. H.1039, 1
Advise See **Advice**
Aegyptians See **Egyptians**
Aequall See **Equal**
Æsculapius **Æsculapius**! come and bring.........122. H.302, 3
Æson **Æson** had (as Poets faine)..................10. H.19, 9
Affairs Nor are thy daily and devout **affaires**......36. H.106, 63
Of tardidation in the Lords **Affaires**............378. N.137, 6
Affect Lyd. While thou no other didst **affect**,......70. H.181, 5
They much **affect** the Papacie:..................93. H.223, 110
Affectedness See **Ill-affectedness**
Affection For whose **affection**, Lydia, I..........70. H.181, 11
And double my **affection** on thee; as doe those,..78. H.197, 43
Not for **affection** to her, or her Bed;...........129. H.326, 2
Faith, and **Affection**: which will never slip...252. H.745, 19
Affection will **affection** move,...................252. H.746, 7
For to let **Affection** in.........................253. H.750, 9
Not an **Affection**, but a Deitie...................380. N.148, 2
No other, then Christs full **Affection**............383, N.174, 2
Without the least hope of **affection**............392. N.230, 26
Then full **affection**, enter here..................402. N.269, 9
Affection's You say, to me-wards your **affection's** strong;
51. H.143, 1
Affections And all **Affections** are forgot,..........190. H.515, 17
Him and his **affections** ever.....................209. H.587, 4
Afflictions **Afflictions** they most profitable are......343. N.24, 1
Afflictions bring us joy in times to come,........349. N.45, 1
Afflicts God n'ere **afflicts** us more then our desert,..341. N.10, 1
Afford Comforts you'l **afford** me some:............74. H.191, 6
Jove may **afford** us thousands of reliefs;.........153. H.397, 1
What sweets the Country can **afford**............192. H.521, 3
Can with the smallest cost **afford**...............200. H.552, 2
His thumb-nailes-par'd, **afford** him sperrables.....226. H.648, 2
All these, and more, shall then **afford**............239. H.696, 11
Earth **afford** ye flowers to strew.............306. H.984, 43
Give, if thou canst, an Almes; if not, **afford**,......356. N.71, 1
Affording **Affording** salve of Soveraigntie..........377. N.129, 4
Affords I kenn my home; and it **affords** some ease,
352. N.51, 9
The web **affords** now nothing;................374. N.123. 37
Affright With those deeds done by day, which n'er **affright**
35. H.106, 37
The suddenness did me **affright**;................116. H.284, 5
Keeping no currish Waiter to **affright**,..........147. H.377, 47
And those sounds that us **affright**..............177. H.473, 5
The Quarter-day do's ne'r **affright**.............200. H.552, 11
Since Ghost ther's none to **affright** thee.........217. H.619, 10
And, lying down, have nought t' **affright**........231. H.662, 74
Ring the Saints-Bell, to **affright**................258. H.769, 8
Affrighted **Affrighted** shall come,................225. H.643, 23
If ye feare to be **affrighted**....................323. H.1065, 1
Then the Foe will fly **affrighted**.............324. H.1069, 8
Affrighting **Affrighting**..........................377. N.128, 16
Affrightment To wonder and **affrightment**: Thou art He,
398. N.263, 21
Afore Goe thou **afore**; and I shall well............33. H.98, 5
Afraid Be you more warie, then **afraid**........49. H.136, 15
She need not be **afraid**:.......................56. H.149, 94
Here, for to make the face **affraid**;............148. H.377, 78
And night's **afraid** of the sounding...........334. H.1122, 18
Afresh Let's kisse **afresh**, as when we first begun....24. H.74, 8
Spring up **afresh**; when all these mists are spent,
52. H.146, 11
Africa — — — — — — — —, ...449. var. A.3, 74
After Of Heaven, and hope to have it **after** all.......5. H.1, 14
'Twill not be long (Perilla) **after** this,..........9. H.14, 5
To live some few-sad-howers **after** thee:..........11. H.22, 2
Then **after** her comes smiling May..............23. H.70, 3
And **after** sorrowes spent, I slept:..............51. H.142, 4
At last, I find, (**after** my much to doe).........61. H.161, 5
(**After** a dew, or dew-like shower)..............71. H.182, 3
Meet **after** long divorcement by the Iles:......77. H.197, 2
The Sea-scourg'd Merchant, **after** all his toile,....77. H.197, 16
When, **after** these, h'as paid his vows,..........93. H.223, 135
If **after** rude and boystrous seas,.................94. H.225, 1
Pressing before, some coming **after**,............101. H.250, 17
Run **after** with their breeches rent.............101. H.250, 25
But turne soone **after** calme, as Balme, or Oile...105. H.259, 4
After short prayers, they set on bread;.......119. H.293, 8
That tost up, **after** Fox-i'th'hole:..............126. H.319, 14
So likewise **after** our disseace,.................139. H.353, 3
After the rare Arch-Poet Johnson dy'd,.........150. H.382, 1
Me weare the Willow; **after** that,..............161. H.425, 7
Shall now, or ever **after** come................165. H.442, 14
After the Feast (my Shapcot) see,............165. H.443, 1
And **after** they have shown their pride,........176. H.467, 16
After that, in the mould.......................197. H.540, 3
Till **after** I had handled them;.................203. H.562, 4
That's tost up **after** Fox i' th' Hole.............231. H.662, 57
When **after** many Lusters thou shalt be........231. H.664, 1
First, crack the strings, and **after** that,........240. H.705, 11
Made it for ever **after** red.....................241. H.706, 4
After a thousand Lusters hurld,...............245. H.720, 15
And **after** that, lay downe some silver pence,...245. H.723, 9
I follow'd **after** to descrie....................247. H.729, 5
Who **after** his transgression doth repent,......268. H.809, 1
Will, **after** ease, a richer harvest yeild:........292. H.922, 2
A cleare will come **after** a cloudy day..........293. H.930, 2
As dearest Peace, **after** destructive Warre:......300. H.961, 2
After our long, and peevish sicknesses.........300. H.961, 4
Since **after** death comes glory, Ile not haste.....314. H.1022, 2
After leaves, the tree must fall.................321. H.1058, 2
Enspir'd by th' Sun-beams **after** dews & showers.
326. H.1080, 14
Soone **after**, he for beere so scores his wheat,....327. H.1086, 3
After a day, or two, or three,................328. H.1090, 4
He sayes his fore and **after** Grace for it:......332. H.1112, 2
After thy labour take thine ease..............334. H.1123, 1
Draw me, but first, and **after** Thee I'le run,....358. N.77, 14
Sins first dislik'd, are **after** that belov'd...........362. N.85, 2
After true sorrow for our sinnes, our strife......362. N.91, 1
Chor. And **after** us (distressed)................375. N.123, 87
After this life, the wages shall..................380. N.149, 1
Not **after** one sort, there excruciate all:........391. N.227, 2
Howeuer **after** tymes will praise,...............407. A.2, 15
After-grace Might me excite to fore, and **after-grace**.
371. N.115, 8
After-times See **After**
Again Baths that made him young **againe**:.........10. H.19, 10
Because his Tongue was ty'd **againe**...............13. H.27, 10
And stroak'd the stripes, and I was whole **agen**.....16. H.40, 6
Asswag'd, and he was well **again**...............18. H.46, 10
These eyes of mine shall see you mix **agen**.........26. H.79, 6
And back **again**, (tortur'd with fears) doth fly,..36. H.106, 67
With weather foule, then faire **againe**............47. H.133, 13
Trouble Death to lay **agen**......................52. H.145, 6
But they left Hope-seed to fill up **againe**.........52. H.146, 8
And make me smooth as Balme, and Oile **againe**...67. H.176, 6
Once lost, can ne'r be found **againe**:............69. H.178, 64
And love **againe** love-cast-off Lydia?............70. H.181, 20
Let's kisse, and kisse **agen**;.....................74. H.192, 5
Lost in the wild sea, once **againe**:..............79. H.198, 8
Kisse, and sigh, so part **agen**...................82. H.203, 14
Like to a slumbring Bride, awake **againe**.........99. H 244, 8
But for to make it spring **againe**...............102. H.250, 55
Since Clouds disperst, Suns guild the Aire **again**...105. H.259, 2
And consume, and grow **again** to die,........115. H.283, 138
Ne'r to be found **againe**........................125. H.316, 20
But they fill up their Ebbs **again**:..............133. H.336, 20
The Ages fled, Ile call **agen**:..................134. H.336, 80
To those, and then **agen** to thee................136. H.336, 137
This year **again**, the medows Deity.............140. H.354, 2
Till I shall come **again**, let this suffice,..........146. H.377, 1
Where both may feed, and come **againe**;........146. H.377, 12
Her Resurrection ha's **again** with Thee.........150. H.382, 20
I shall quite dislike **agen**......................155. H.407, 6
And dales **again**: Mir. No I will languish still;..159. H.421, 36

Unlesse you skin **again** each part..............164. H.442, 10
And no **again**, and so deny,..................174. H.465, 35
Lean-horn'd, before I come **again**............176. H.465, 78
To spring **againe** another yeare.................189. H.514, 8
Did soon draw in **agen**.........................194. H.525, 5
And as He shuts, close up to Maids **again**.......196. H.537, 4
Wound up **again**: Once down, He's down for ever..202. H.558, 2
But if that golden Age wo'd come **again**,........214. H.612, 7
Give me my earthen Cups **again**,................222. H.635, 9
I return your Almes **agen**......................224. H.638, 28
But when that is gone; **Again**,................227. H.651, 3
Never **againe** to have ingression here:............227. H.652, 2
Crowne it **agen agen**;..........................227. H.653, 5
That brave Spirit comes **agen**..................242. H.714, 12
To get thy Steerling, once **again**,............244. H.716, 37
By poares and cavernes back **agen**.............245. H.720, 8
A sullen day will cleere **againe**.................247. H.725, 8
Others shall spring up in their place **agen**:......256. H.763, 12
What wo'd she give to get that soule **agen**?.....266. H.801, 4
Cheerfull day shall spring **agen**.................276. H.850, 8
Which quencht, then lay it up **agen**,...........285. H.893, 3
Or come **agen**:................................289. H.911, 12
But this I know, should Jupiter **agen**..........301. H.966, 11
For me embalm'd to live **againe**;...............313. H.1020, 6
Never **againe** shall I with Finnie-Ore..........315. H.1028, 11
But when **again** sh'as got her healthfull houre,..320. H.1054, 5
And, from a Priest, turne Player once **again**....325. H.1076, 4
(As with a Magick) laid them all **agen**:........326. H.1080, 18
Or fetch me back that Cloud **againe**,............340. N.3, 9
To pay **agen**,.................................346. N.38, 11
Back, back **again**; each thing is done..........366. N.97, 24
knowne, 'not thay giue **againe**, thay take....422. ins. H.106, 92f
Against My puling Pipe to beat **against** thine eare:.17. H.42, 2
Saile **against** Rocks, and split them too;..........31. H.90, 8
Strong **against** future harme:..................55. H.149, 88
Against you come, some Orient Pearls unwept:..68. H.178, 22
A man prepar'd **against** all ills to come,........128. H.323, 1
That's counter-proofe **against** the Farms mishaps,.128. H.323, 5
For which their cryes might beate **against** thine eares,
149. H.377, 125
Thus, though the Rooke do's raile **against** the sin,
163. H.439, 3
To shore the Feeble up, **against** the strong;....201. H.557, 11
Physitians fight not **against** men; but these.....226. H.646, 1
Against thy Heifer, I will here...............243. H.716, 13
Against diseases here the strongest fence......333. H.1117, 1
Against the wicked, in another world...........357. N.74, 4
Against thy purer Essence? For that fault . . .
426. ins. H.197, 29b
Agast See Aghast
Age **Age** cals me hence, and my gray haires bid come,
9. H.14, 3
When **age** or Chance has made me blind,........32. H.98, 1
When my date's done, and my gray **age** must die;
40. H.112, 1
That **Age** is best, which is the first,.............84. H.208, 9
The gripings of the chine by **age**;.............134. H.336, 92
Oft as your field, shall her old **age** renew,....140. H.355, 13
Sleeping the lucklesse **Age** out, till that she....150. H.382, 19
One Cordelion had that **Age** long since;......170. H.451, 15
Then, when Thou see'st thine **Age** all turn'd to gold,
181. H.483, 9
Borne I was to meet with **Age**,................191. H.519, 1
But if that golden **Age** wo'd come again,.......214. H.612, 7
But **Age** hath brought me right to Bed.........216. H.617, 6
And turn the iron **Age** to Gold..............233. H.670, 29
For, I'm grown old; &, with mine **age**, grown poore:
258. H.768, 2
The present **Age** will tell the world thou art....267. H 804, 11
And old, old **Age** is a farre off:................267. H.806, 3
Me in mine **Age**, or forraign Funerals,.........269. H.818, 2
Age shall not wrong thee; or one jot abate.....280. H.869, 3
My selfe now live: this **age** best pleaseth mee...292. H.927, 2
O Yeares! and **Age**! Farewell:...................354. N.58, 1
I would to God, that mine old **age** might have..371. N.115, 1
But on our **Age** most sweet Indulgences.........383. N.175, 2
And quafe it to the Prophets of our **Age**;........412. A.3, 88
And when an other **age** shall bring..............418. A.9, 31
Aged The growth, and down-fall of her **aged** trees: 23. H.69, 2
Ye see the **aged** Vessell crown'd:..............94. H.225, 6
The **Aged** point out, This is she,.............114. H.283, 64
Which crept into each **aged** Sire..............135. H.336, 104
Mine **aged** limbs above my chaire:..........135. H.336, 108
Ile drink the **aged** Cecubum,..................208. H.582, 3
The Hector over **Aged** Exeter;..................251. H.745, 2
Yet with the bench of **aged** sires,..............303. H.973, 11
Can I be gamesome (**aged** now)................329. H.1093, 2
— — — — — — — — — — —, ...437. var. H.336, 112
Agen See Again
Ages The **Ages** fled, Ile call agen:.............134. H.336, 80
Nor thinke these **Ages** that do hoarcely sing....155. H.405, 5
Aghast And In a Whirl-wynd twirld her home, **agast**
410. A.3, 25
Ago As I did, not long **ago**,....................131. H.332, 3
Agony A Coadjutor in the **Agonie**...............382. N.163, 2
Agree Since Coats, and Hamlets, best **agree**..........5. H.2, 5
Till they co'd not **agree**,.........................105. H.258, 2
Or both of them, that do **agree**................142. H.362, 3
That they no better do **agree**...................163. H.434, 3
Some this, some that, but all in this **agree**,....288. H.907, 9
How heart and hand do all **agree**,..............365. N.97, 9
Agreed See 'Greed
Lets call for Hymen if **agreed** thou art;........261. H.781, 1
Agrees What Gesture, Courtship; Comliness **agrees**,
148. H.377, 95
Ague Now an **Ague**, then a Fever,..............103. H.253, 9
And swore I'de got the **ague** of the house.....262. H.783, 20

Ah **Ah** my Perilla! do'st thou grieve to see..........9. H.14, 1
And found (**Ah** me!) this flesh of mine........17. H.41, 22
But **ah**! if empty dreames so please,............20. H.56, 9
Ah my Anthea! Must my heart still break?......24. H.74, 1
Ah cruell Sea! and looking on't,..................42. H.119, 9
Ah! what is then this curious skie,............48. H.133, 16
Alas! I call; but **ah**! I see....................50. H.140, 11
Ah me! I try; and trying, prove,...............60. H.157, 3
Ah! then too late, close in your chamber keeping,
63. H.164, 12
But **ah**! I co'd not: sho'd it move............67. H.175, 21
Then, **Ah**! Then, where is your grace,..........74. H.189, 5
Ah, cruell Love! must I endure................74. H.191, 1
Whether I wo'd; but (**ah**!) I know not how,..84. H.210, 7
Ah then consider! What all this implies;......131. H.330, 14
Ah Posthumus! Our yeares hence flye,........132. H.336, 1
Ah woe is me, woe, woe is me,................156. H.412, 9
Mirt. **Ah**! Amarillis, farewell mirth and pipe;....159. H.421, 8
Ah! Lycidas, come tell me why................183. H.492, 1
But **ah**! what sweets smelt every where,......237. H.686, 11
But **ah**! it hapned as he made................265. H.798, 7
Ah Ben!......................................289. H.911, 1
It (**Ah**!) too late repents me..................296. H.946, 9
Ah cruell maides! Ile goe my way,............312. H.1014, 5
But (**ah**!) by starres malignant crost,........313. H.1020, 3
Ah Biancha! now I see,.......................307. H.991, 1
And **ah**! the Poore,............................374. N.123, 18
Ah Dorcas, Dorcas! now adieu..................374. N.123, 31
But, **ah**, alas! the Almond Bough,..............375. N.123, 51
Ah! Sions Daughters, do not feare..............400. N.266, 7
— — — — — — — — —, ...431. ins. H.283, 60c
Aha **Aha** my boyes! heres wheat for Christmas Pies!
327. H.1086, 2
Ai See Ay
Aid Saint Ben to **aide** me........................212. H.604, 4
Aids Now Autumne's come, when all those flowrie **aids**
114. H.283, 92
Ail Say, what is't that thou do'st **aile**?..........305. H.984, 9
Aim By studying to know vertue; and to **aime**..35. H.106, 7
All conditions I **aime** at.......................209. H.585, 3
All thoughts, but such as **aime** at getting Princes,77. H.197, 8
Air As shews the **Aire**, when with a Rain-bow grac'd;
40. H.114, 1
And as she stood, the wanton **Aire**..............51. H.142, 11
Aire coyn'd to words, my Julia co'd not heare;..58. H.150, 3
Which wantons with the Love-sick **aire**:.........61. H.160, 6
Fresh-quilted colours through the **aire**:..........67. H.178, 4
And perfume the **aire** a while:.................74. H.189, 2
Into the boundlesse **aire**:......................75. H.193, 21
In the wild **aire**, when thou hast rowl'd about,..87. H.215, 3
Like to a dreadfull Comet in the **Aire**:.........87. H.215, 6
(Made rivall with the **aire**)...................103. H.255, 2
Since Clouds dispert, Suns guild the **Aire** again..105. H.259, 2
ing the Chafte **Aire** with fumes of Paradise.....112. H.283, 16
As is the **Air**, and let us be..................133. H.336, 38
So smells the **Aire** of spiced wine;............145. H.375, 5
The passive **Aire** such odour then assum'd,....157. H.414, 7
What gives it hanging in the **Aire**............167. H.443, 105
As the **aire** that circles me:..................183. H.490, 18
Let Poets feed on **aire**, or what they will;......186. H.498, 7
To blast the **Aire**, but Amber-greece and Gums..205. H.575, 6
So double gilds the **Aire**, as that no night......206. H.575, 15
Those counter-changed Tabbies in the **ayre**,....207. H.576, 3
Onely to kisse that **Aire**,......................231. H.663, 7
(As is that **ayre** that circles thee)..............233. H.670, 18
I'le strike thee such a nimble **Ayre**,..........243. H.716, 32
With which the **aire** is full:...................257. H.767, 2
To cloath thy words in gentle **Ayre**.............408. A.2, 54
I'th **ayre**, a greater Text of light...............413. A.4, 19
Print thy lips into the **ayre**,...................414. A.5, 10
Cha. I will be gentle as that **Air** which yeelds....416. A.8, 7
It ever dangling smil'd i' th' **aire**...............418. A.9, 26
— — — — — — — — —, ...439. var. H.443, 39
Air-like And **Aire-like**, leave no pression to be seen
250. H.737, 7
Airs Sweet **Aires** move here; and more divine..166 H.443, 39
As **aires** doe breathe, or winds doe blow:......282. H.881, 8
Airy As **ayrie** as the leaves of gold;............66. H.175, 2
Thou mak'st me **ayrie**, active to be born,......78. H.197, 49
And all those **airie** silks to flow,.................202. H.560, 15
Their **ayry** coulors to discerne,..................418. A.9, 56
Ake See Ache
Akin Next in an Arch, **akin** to this,..............90. H.223, 15
Alack **Alack** and welladay!....................156. H.412, 10

Alack for grief!.......306. H 984, 36
Alas Alas! If kissing be of plagues the worst,....33. H.101, 3
Alas for pitty! and for us.......48. H.136, 4
Alas! said she, my Wag! if this.......50. H.139, 12
Alas! the heat and death's the same;.......50. H.140, 5
Alas! I call; but ah! I see.......50. H.140, 11
Alas for me! that I have lost.......72. H.185, 8
Alas,.......100. H.246, 5
Alas you have not known that shower,.......104. H.257, 6
Since now (alas).......144. H.371, 4
Yet out alas! the deaths the same,.......155. H 406, 5
Alas! we blesse, but see none here.......179. H.476, 25
Ph. Alas for me! Ch. Shame on thy witching note,
248. H.730, 11
None of these; but out, alas!.......305. H.984, 10
Alas I can't, for tell me how.......329. H.1093, 1
Alas! I cannot pay a jot; therefore.......368. N.103, 7
But, ah, alas! the Almond Bough,.......375. N.123, 1
Alcestis Loving Alcestis there we find:.......283. H.885, 4
Alchemist At thy unequal'd Play, the Alchymist:.150. H.382, 16
Alchymist See Alchemist
Alcinous Orchards like to Alcinous,.......436. ins. H.336, 48d
Ale See Whitsun-ale
Our browner Ale into the cruse:.......135. H.336, 126
Can hold of Beere and Ale an Ocean;.......171. H 454, 2
That brings us either Ale or Beere;.......179. H.476, 26
Not made of Ale, but spiced Wine:.......193. H.521, 48
With North-down Ale doth troule here,.......235. H.674, 10
Drencht in Ale, or drown'd in Beere.......255. H.761, 20
He'l sell her Eyes, and Nose, for Beere and Ale..272. H.829, 4
Punchin by Beere and Ale, spreads so.......273. H.832, 4
A drought of wine, ale, beere (at all).......291. H.919, 6
With store of ale too;.......317. H.1035, 22
And though with ale ye be whet here;.......317. H.1035, 27
Ale-dyed Till that we see our cheekes Ale-dy'd....219. H.629, 3
Ale-shop Place in the Ale-shop.......320. H.1051, 8
Alias But alias call'd here Fatuus ignis.......91. H.223, 31
Alike Alike i'th' dust.......190. H.515, 32
All are alike faire, when no spots we see.......209. H.586, 2
Pleasing alike; alike both singular:.......209. H.586, 4
Then please alike the Pewter and the Plate;....209. H.586, 7
In every part alike compleat.......243. H.716, 9
Your Fate, and Ours, alike Victorious are.......271. H.823, 2
Thus have, or have not, all alike is good,.......332. H.1112, 5
And bring t'th' heart destruction both alike....333. H.1120, 6
With zeale alike, as 'twas begun;.......366. N.97, 25
Not shar'd alike be unto all.......380. N.149, 2
Alive Yet, Porter, while thou keep'st alive,.......72. H.185, 15
Our Barke; yet she will keepe alive.......134. H.336, 60
Alive, as Noble Westmorland;.......218. H.626, 11
All Of Heaven, and hope to have it after all.......5. H.1, 14
Made all that touch't her with her scent,.......9. H.15, 11
To my pretty Witchcrafts all:.......10. H.19, 2
A teare at all for that:.......12. H.23, 6
And had told all; but did refraine,.......13. H.27, 9
Stately Iulia, prime of all;.......15. H.39, 3
(Faire Destinies all three).......18. H.47, 6
All the yeere, where Cherries grow.......20. H.53, 8
Night to the Record! that was all.......20. H.56, 8
And come all to Buckittings:.......21. H.61, 4
Ile wish I might turne all to eare,.......22. H.68, 2
Ride on with all white Omens; so, that where..25. H.77, 11
And all with showrs wet through,.......26. H.81, 11
Ere I wo'd love at all.......28. H.85, 8
Were thy streames silver, or thy rocks all gold...29. H.86, 6
Thy men; and rockie are thy wayes all over.......29. H.86, 8
Content makes all Ambrosia.......37. H.106, 116
And that is all.......43. H.123, 15
And seeing her not dead, but all disleav'd;.......46. H.130, 11
And all because, Faire Maid, thou art.......47. H.132, 9
All such as are not soft like them.......47. H.132, 14
Ye coole, and comfort all, but me.......50. H.140, 12
All bolts, all barres, all gates shall cleave; as when
52. H.146, 14
Armes, and hands, and all parts else,.......53. H.147, 7
To tell all prosp'rous chance.......55. H.149, 58
Shapelesse the world (as when all Chaos was)...59. H.154, 8
When all your world of Beautie's gone.......61. H.160, 10
And Leaves did heale, all sick of humane seed:..61. H.161, 2
I live for ever; let the rest all lye.......63. H.165, 3
Or fret at all.......65. H.172, 11
And all confus'd, I there did lie.......67. H.175, 17
That, that he took, and that was all.......71. H.182, 26
E'en all almost:.......72. H.185, 9
Doth all at once impaire,.......75. H.193, 23
A meere Botch of all and some.......76. H.195, 4
Ne'r shine upon me; May my Numbers all.....79. H 197, 89
But on a sudden, all was chang'd and gone.......81. H 202, 3
Dead thee to th' most, if not destroy thee all...82. H.204, 12
Amar. With all white luck to you. Mirt. But say, What news
85. H.213, 3
The drooping Kingdome suffers all.......89. H.219, 8
You first of all crown'd her; she must of due,....94. H 224, 9
(Clad, all, in Linnen, white as Lillies.).......101. H.250, 12
Drink frollick boyes, till all be blythe.......102. H.250, 43
Little thou't love, or not at all.......103. H.253, 18
Thou art to all lost love the best,.......106. H.262, 1
That Verse, of all the Verses here, shall be....107. H.264, 5
I could wish you all, who love,.......117. H.289, 1
I co'd wish, ye all, who frie.......117. H.289, 9
But all this while his eye is serv'd,.......119. H.293, 13
Mercie secure ye all, and keep.......121. H.299, 5
My Masters all, Good day to you.......121. H.299, 8
My Crosse; my Cord; and all farewell.......123. H.306, 4
If not requite, yet thank ye all.......123. H.306, 12
How rich a man is, all desire to know;.......130. H.323, 1
Between the lips, (all cherrie-red,).......130. H.329, 5
Ah then consider! What all this implies;.......131. H.330, 14
Lips she has, all Rubie red,.......138. H.342, 5
Turn'd all to Mell, and Manna there for thee.....143. H.370, 4
Shall run, as rivers, all throughout thy soyl.....144. H.370, 6
All over-archt with Oringe flowers;.......145. H.375, 12
As men, turne all to eares.......151. H.388, 8
Short lot, or not, to be content with all.......153. H.396, 2
Jolly and Jillie, bite and scratch all day,.......156. H.411, 1
The reason is, though all the day they fight,.....156. H.411, 3
And all the while my part shall be to weepe;...159. H.421, 37
Is it because his money all is spent?.......160. H.423, 2
So like to this, nay all the rest.......164. H.440, 9
That of my skin, I all am stript;.......164. H.442, 7
I've paid Thee, what I promis'd; that's not All;
168. H.444, 1
And mak'st all hell.......170. H.452, 3
Passe all we must the fatall Ferry:.......172. H.457, 2
I am of all bereft;.......173. H.460, 1
Bankt all with Lillies, and the Cream.......179. H.476, 14
Then, when Thou see'st thine Age all turn'd to gold,
181. H.483, 9
The All, and End.......189. H.515, 6
And having danc't ('bove all the best).......192. H.521, 33
And shame-fac't Plum, (all simp'ring there)...192. H.521, 38
Having but seven in all; three black, foure white.
195. H.531, 2
Some parts may perish; dye thou canst not all:..200. H.554, 1
All times unto their frenzies; Thou shalt there..206. H.575, 47
Beumont and Fletcher, Swans, to whom all eares
206. H.575, 51
(The Sun once set) all of one colour are....207 H.576, 4
Now tis in's Hand, he gives no Almes at all.....207. H.577, 4
To most of men, but most of all to me:.......210. H.590, 2
Yet we must all.......211. H.596, 14
But by the Muses sweare, all here is good,.......212. H.603, 3
Who all the day themselves doe please,.......231. H.662, 72
Let her Lucrece all day be,.......232. H.665, 15
I'le eat and drink up all here.......235. H.674, 18
Twice two fell out, all rotten at the root.......247. H.728, 2
Ch. And is that all? I'm gone. Ph. By love I pray thee,
248. H.730, 17
With all wise speed for execution.......252. H.749, 2
Bids ye all be free;.......263. H.784, 5
Cloth'd all with incorrupted light;.......270. H.819, 5
All has been plundered from me, but my wit;..272. H.830, 1
Thou art all turn'd isicle?.......273. H.836, 2
All is well; now next to these.......280. H.870, 13
By his Probossis that he is all nose.......284. H.886, 2
Till they be all over wet,.......284. H.891, 3
That surfeit tooke by bread, the worst of all...286. H.895, 2
She'l runne to all adulteries.......287. H.899, 10
He wished me all Good speed.......295. H.942, 8
Who fli'st at all heights: Prose and Verse run'st through;
298. H.955, 7
(His teeth all out) to rince and wash his gummes.
301. H.965, 2
And be of all admired, Tomasin.......304. H.979, 2
Down with the Holly, Ivie, all,.......304. H.980, 3
Me, and my sad Play-mates all,.......306. H.984, 39
And all confused multitude:.......312. H.1016, 4
For all the Divell helps, will be a poore man...315. H.1025, 2
Give S. Distaffe all the right,.......315. H.1026, 11
When the great Crack not Crushes one, but all.
319. H.1045, 2
Or fear of it, but Love keeps all in awe.).......326. H.1080, 20
Love's of it self, too sweet; the best of all.......327. H.1084, 1
The way of all Flesh is,.......328. H.1091, 3
Thus have, or have not, all alike is good,.......332. H.1112, 5
All saving health, and help for me.......342. N.17, 8
God is all fore-part; for, we never see.......342. N.18, 1
God will have all, or none; serve Him, or fall..353. N.54, 1
God co'd have made all rich, or all men poore;....356. N.69, 1
O thou, the wonder of all dayes!.......359. N.83, 1
On our meat, and on us all. Amen.......364. N.95, 6
Cast Holy Water all about,.......365. N.97, 4
The Altars all on fier be;.......365. N.97, 7
Come pitie us, all ye, who see.......373. N.123, 1
Our eyes out all together.......373. N.123, 10
The Place that filleth All in all.......385. N.185, 2
Have, have ye no regard, all ye.......400. N.266, 1
A place desir'd of all but got by theis.......405. A.1, 69
But all we wither and our Light.......413. A.4, 10
To be with juice of Cedar washt all over;.......415. A.7, 6
And so to Bed: Pray wish us all Good Rest.....419. A.10, 8
List of references:......3. Ded.H, 5; 3. Ded.H, 7; 3, Ded.H,

9; 7. H.6, 2; 7. H.6, 5; 7. H.9, 7; 8. H.10, 7; 8. H.11, 7; 9. H.15, 8; 12. H.23, 7; 12. H.26, 11; 14. H.35, 7; 16. H.39, 11; 16. H.41, 17; 17. H.44, 8; 20. H.55, 1; 21. H.57, 1; 21. H.61, 8; 21. H.62, 6; 23. H.69, 1; 23. H.69, 5; 23. H.70, 8; 23. H.71, 5; 24. H.74, 11; 25. H.76, 4; 25. H.78, 7; 26. H.81, 7; 29. H.86, 4; 31. H.90, 6; 36. H.106, 62; 37. H.106, 90; 40. H.114, 4; 40. H.115, 6; 40. H.115, 8; 41. H.117, 3; 41. H.117, 9; 42. H.119, 6; 44. H.124, 3; 46. H.128, 40; 46. H.129, 6; 46. H.130, 5; 47. H.132, 10; 47. H.133, 8; 48. H.133, 15; 49. H.136, 30; 50. H.140, 4; 52. H.145, 2; 52. H.146, 11; 53. H.147, 10; 55. H.149, 63; 56. H.149, 107; 57. H.149, 159; 58. H.151, 1; 58. H.152, 1; 59. H.152, 12; 59. H.155, 5; 60. H. 158, 1; 61. H.160, 4; 62. H.161, 7; 62. H.161, 8; 62. H.162, 2; 62. H.162, 12; 64. H.168, 8; 65. H.170, 5; 67. H.177, 4; 68. H.178, 10; 69. H.178, 67; 69. H.179, 3; 72. H.185, 1; 72. H.185, 11; 74. H.191, 4; 75. H.193, 30; 76. H.194, 2; 76. H.194, 5; 77. H.197, 8; 77. H.197, 16; 80. H.201, 24; 81. H.201, 49; 81. H.202, 6; 84. H.209, 8; 85. H.211, 9; 85. H.213, 2; 86. H.213, 15; 86. H.213, 38; 88. H.216, 19; 88. H.218, 6; 90. H.222, 2; 91. H.223, 26; 91. H.223, 40; 94. H.224, 5; 94. H.226, 1; 94. H.226, 4; 100. H.247, 3; 101. H.250, 8; 101. H.250, 34; 101. H.250, 37; 102. H.250, 49; 103. H.253, 11; 103. H.255, 8; 103. H.256, 1; 103. H.256, 4; 107. H.263, 16; 107. H.263, 21; 113. H.283, 21; 114. H.283, 92; 114. H.283, 98; 116. H.283, 151; 116. H.283, 152; 116. H.283, 154; 116. H.283, 157; 117. H.286, 4; 118. H.291, 15; 118. H.292, 2; 121. H.299, 3; 121. H.300, 1; 121. H.301, 1; 121. H.301, 2; 121. H.301, 4; 124. H.313, 5; 124. H.313, 7; 124. H.313, 11; 125. H.314, 10; 127. H.319, 47; 128. H.323, 1; 129. H.323, 12; 131. H.330, 5; 131. H.331, 2; 132. H.333, 10; 132. H.335, 3; 132. H.336, 10; 133. H.336, 56; 136. H.336, 149; 137. H.341, 6; 137. H.341, 10; 138. H.343, 4; 140. H.354, 12; 140. H.356, 4; 142. H.363, 3; 143. H.366, 1; 144. H.372, 1; 145. H.375, 9; 147. H.377, 59; 148. H.377, 90; 149. H.377, 129; 149. H.377, 136; 149. H.380, 2; 150. H.382, 5; 150. H.382, 17; 151. H.386, 5; 151. H.387, 4; 151. H.387, 8; 151. H.388, 2; 151. H.388, 4; 152. H.389, 2; 152. H.392, 1; 153. H.395, 5; 154. H.403, 6; 155. H.405, 12; 155. H.405, 14; 155. H.405, 18; 157. H.415, 8; 163. H.432, 2; 163. H.437, 2; 165. H.442, 12; 165. H.443, 12; 166. H.443, 33; 166. H.443, 38; 167. H.443, 108; 169. H.449, 15; 169. H.449, 19; 169. H. 449, 21; 169. H.449. 25: 170. H. 450, 2; 170. H.450, 3; 170. H.451, 1; 170. H.451, 3; 171. H.452, 8; 172. H.456, 9; 174. H.465, 7; 174. H.465, 10; 176. H.465, 80; 177. H.473, 7; 179. H.476, 24; 179. H.476, 27; 179. H.476, 30; 180. H.480, 2; 182. H.487, 1; 184. H.492, 35; 186. H.497, 10; 187. H.506. 10; 189. H.514, 5; 189. H.515, 2; 190. H.515, 15; 190. H.515, 17; 190. H.515, 27; 190. H.515, 30; 190. H.515, 31; 190. H.515, 36; 191. H.518, 2; 193. H.521, 50; 195. H.533, 2; 196. H.539, 4; 197. H.539, 12; 197. H.542, 1; 199. H.549, 4; 201. H.557, 4; 202. H.558, 3; 202. H.558, 4; 202. H.560, 15; 205. H.575, 11; 208. H.583, 1; 209. H.585, 3; 209. H.586, 1; 209. H.586, 2; 214. H.612, 3; 215. H.616, 16; 220. H.633, 4; 221. H.633, 53; 222. H.633, 60; 222. H.634, 15; 223. H.635, 15; 223. H.637, 2; 224. H.639, 2; 229. H.660, 3; 229. H.661, 2; 230. H.662, 14; 232. H.665, 10; 232. H.667, 1; 232. H.668, 6; 235. H.674, 12; 235. H.676, 1; 236. H.681, 5; 237. H.686, 8; 237. H.686, 12; 237. H.686, 14; 238. H.690, 8; 238. H.690, 12; 239. H.695, 12; 239. H.696, 11; 239. H.698, 1; 241. H.712, 2; 242. H.713, 10; 242. H.715, 2; 244. H.719, 6; 245. H.722, 2; 246. H.725, 1; 247. H.726, 1; 247. H.727, 11; 248. H.730, 18; 248. H.730, 23; 250. H.737, 4; 250. H.739, 3; 252. H.748, 2; 254. H.756, 15; 255. H.761, 19; 256. H.763, 13; 257. H.767, 3; 257. H.767, 7; 258. H.767, 11; 259. H.771, 4; 263. H.785, 5; 265. H.794, 6; 266. H.800, 1; 266. H.800, 6; 266. H.802, 1; 267. H.804, 1; 267. H.804, 5; 267. H.807, 1; 272. H.826, 2; 272. H.827, 1; 276. H.849, 1; 280. H.869, 2; 280. H.870, 8; 282. H.877, 2; 282. H.881, 4; 283. H.885, 1; 284. H.886, 1; 284. H.891, 6; 285. H.894, 2; 286. H.895, 1; 286. H.897, 6; 286. H.897, 7; 286. H.897, 8; 286. H.897, 9; 286. H.897, 11; 286. H.898, 9; 287. H.899, 4; 288. H.907, 9; 288. H.909, 2; 290. H.913, 2; 291. H.919, 6; 292. H.924, 1; 292. H.926, 2; 292. H.928, 1; 294. H.936, 3; 295. H.940, 2; 295. H.941, 2; 296. H.946, 5; 296. H.946, 11; 298. H.955, 3; 299. H.958, 2; 300. H.960, 2; 302. H.968, 10; 305. H.981, 1; 305. H.982, 4; 307. H.992, 3; 309. H.996, 5; 310. H.1002, 4; 311. H.1011, 1; 312. H.1016, 6; 316. H.1028, 17; 316. H.1028, 20; 318. H.1036, 2; 318. H.1040, 2; 318. H.1041, 2; 319. H.1050, 2; 320. H.1051, 16; 324. H.1071, 3; 326. H.1080, 12; 326. H. 1080, 18; 327. H.1082, 4; 328. H.1088, 8; 328. H.1091, 8; 330. H.1099, 3; 330. H.1100, 3; 331. H.1104, 1; 334. H.1124, 2; 335. H.1129, 12; 339. N.2, 7; 339. N.2, 9; 339. N.3, 3; 341. N.15, 5; 342. N.16, 1; 342. N.20, 2; 343. N.27, 1; 346. N.36, 2; 348. N.41, 38; 348. N.41, 43; 349. N.44, 4; 350. N.47, 29; 351. N.47, 51; 353. N. 54, 4; 353. N.56, 1; 354. N.58, 6; 355. N.65, 6; 356. N.68, 4; 356. N.69, 3; 356. N.69, 4; 356. N.71, 4; 357. N.72, 10; 357. N.73, 3; 357. N.74, 3; 359. N.83, 5; 360. N.83, 13; 360. N.83, 14; 360. N.83, 17; 360. N.83, 48; 361. N.83, 62; 361. N.83, 73; 362. N.88, 2; 363. N.93, 6; 363. N.94, 2; 364. N.96, 12; 364. N.96, 24; 365. N.96, 28; 365. N.96, 32; 365. N.97, 9; 365. N.97, 10; 366. N.97, 21; 366. N.98, 11; 366. N.98, 24; 367. N.102, 7; 368. N.102, 17; 368. N.103, 4; 369. N.106, 4; 370. N.108, 7; 371. N.112, 1; 371. N.113, 3; 371. N.114, 5; 372. N.118, 4; 373. N.121, 8; 375. N.123, 61; 375. N.123, 74; 375. N.123, 80; 376. N.125, 8; 376. N.127, 4; 377. N.128, 15; 377. N.129, 8; 378. N.131, 2; 378. N.134, 2; 378. N.137, 4; 378. N.137, 5; 379. N.139, 1; 379. N.145, 2; 380. N.149, 2; 380. N.151, 2; 382. N.166, 1; 383. N. 171, 2; 383. N.173, 2; 384, N.179, 4; 388. N.207, 1; 389. N.214, 5; 389. N.218, 2; 390. N.221, 1; 390. N.222, 2; 391. N.226, 1; 391. N.227, 2; 392. N.229, 1; 393. N.235, 1; 394. N.238, 1; 394. N.239, 4; 395. N.246, 1; 395. N.246, 3; 399. N.263, 22; 399. N.264, 2; 400. N.267, 2; 400. N.267, 10; 401. N.268, 5; 401. N.268, 13; 402, N.269, 15; 402; N. 269, 17; 403. N.272, 1; 406. A.1, 71; 409. A.2, 99; 411. A.3, 35; 413. A.4, 20; 416. A.8, 14; 416. A.8, 19; 426. var. H. 197, 47; 426. ins. H.197, 48a; 426. ins. H.197, 48c; 427. ins. H.197, 77a; 428. var. H. 197, 84; 431. ins. H.283, 60m; 434. ins. H.293, 41e; 435. ins. H.293, ee; 436. ins. H.336, 48b; 437. var. H.336, 135; 438. var. H. 412, 4; 441. var. H.465, 28; 443. var. H.580, 4; 443. var. H.580, 8.

Allay With hope you would **allay** the same:.......157. H.413, 2
Sweetnesse to **allay** my sowre...................204. H.569, 11
— — — — — — — —, ...433. var. H.293, 28

All-filling And as all-present, so **all-filling** too.....394. N.237, 2

All-flayed To be **all-flayd** with whipping-cheere,..399. N.265, 8

All-honored Haile holy, and **all-honour'd** Tomb,....402. N.269, 1

Allied And to all flowers **ally'd** in blood,............7. H.9, 7

Allotted To mortall men great loads **allotted** be,..242. H.715, 1

Allow Do'st rather poure forth, then **allow**......148. H.377, 82
Fresh strowings **allow**.........................256. H.762, 1

All-present God is **all-present** to what e're we do,..394. N.237, 1
And as **all-present**, so all-filling too.............394. N.237, 2

All's But when **all's** hush't, Case then a fish more mute, 303. H.975, 7
Gray or white, **all's** one to me..................330. H.1098, 4
Of all the House: the best of **all's** the Heart.....356. N.68, 4
Chor. **All's** gone, and Death hath taken........374. N.123, 27
All's now fledd saue this alone..................418. A.9, 23

All-sufferance God is **all-sufferance** here; here He doth show 357. N.74, 1

All-tempting See **Tempting**

Allure The lovely shoulders now **allure** the eye....406. A.1, 95

Allurement Then nature for a sweet **allurement** setts 404. A.1, 19

Alluring This, this **alluring** Hook might be......193. H.521, 45
Alluring me, and tempting so:................202. H.560, 16
Man to th' **alluring** object gives his will.........392. N.230, 32

Alma Let's go (my **Alma**) yet e're we receive,.....355. N.65, 7

Almighty See **Mighty**
Almighty God me grant;.......................369. N.104, 15
O thou **Allmightye** Nature, who did'st giue.......410. A.3, 29
— — — — — — — — —, ...437. var. H. 336, 135

Almond And **Almond** blossoms, that do mix......145. H.375, 13
As Blossomes of the **Almond** Tree..............203. H.562, 6
But, ah alas! the **Almond** Bough...............375. N.123, 51

Almonds With paste of **Almonds**, Syb her hands doth scoure; 203 H.561, 1
To paste of **Almonds** turn'd by thee:............267. H.805, 4

Almost Ye Roses **almost** withered;.....................7. H.9, 2
Of Roses, **almost** smothered:......................20. H.56, 2
And rude (**almost**) as rudest Salvages............29. H.86, 12
To' th' (**almost**) sev'n and fortieth yeare...........41. H.116, 2
E'en all **almost**:..72. H.185, 9
Their number (**almost**) infinite,.................91. H.223, 35
Past one aclock, and **almost** two,..................121. H.299, 7
Almost to be Lunatick:.................................122. H.302, 2
Unto an **almost** nothing; then,................134. H.336, 79
Dull to my selfe, and **almost** dead to these......214. H.612, 1
(Amongst mine honour'd) Thee (**almost**) the last: 256. H.763, 2
The bound (**almost**) now of my book I see......313. H.1019, 1
By the clock 'tis **almost** One.....................373. N.121, 14
When I behold Thee, **almost** slain,..............400. N.267, 1

Alms My **Almnes** is such:........................171. H.455, 6
Now tis in's Hand, he gives no **Almes** at all......207. H.577, 4
He gives an **almes**, and chides them from his doore. 220. H.632, 2
Give an **Almes** to one that's poore,...........223. H.638, 2
For an **Almes**; then give me such.............223. H.638, 22
I return your **Almes** agen......................224. H.638, 28
Instead of **almes**, sets dogs upon the poor.........238. H.694, 2
He askt an **almes**; I gave him bread,............295. H.942, 5
For loves sake asking **almes** of thee?............312. H.1014, 2
He who asks **almes** in that so sacred Name,.......347. N.39, 5
Give, if thou canst, an **Almes**; if not, afford,......356. N.71, 1

Almshouse Some one poore **Almes-house**; there to lie, or stir, 371. N.115, 3

Aloft Where build **aloft**; and being fixt by These,..185. H.496, 9
Thou dwel'st **aloft**, and I want wings to flie.......352. N.52, 2
Bearing **aloft** this rich round world of wonder.....405. A.1, 46
aloft, and like two armies, come..........432. ins. H.283, 140d

Alone Who are my Works Creator, and **alone**......3. Ded.H., 3
Onely Herrick's left **alone**,......................16. H.39, 12
Touch not the Tyrant; Let the Gods **alone**........32. H.97, 5
'Tis thou, **alone**, who with thy Mistick Fan,......45. H 128, 23
Sitting **alone** (as one forsook)...................51. H.142, 1
Let me **alone** to fit the mind.......................59. H.153, 4
If not, (as banisht) I will live **alone**............60. H.156, 5
I have one, and she **alone**,.......................62. H.162, 10
Then when it grew **alone**;..........................75. H.193, 7
Survey this Chappell, built, **alone**,................90. H.223a, 3
Your poore estates, **alone**......................110. H.274, 20

Lying alone,....114. H.283, 75
Leech boasts, he has a Pill, that can alone,....125. H.315, 1
I have now; yet I alone,....157. H.415, 7
I co'd never walke alone;....183. H.490, 13
With all the rest; while thou alone....184. H.492, 35
Co'd reade the Intext but my selfe alone....227. H.652, 6
From him, who all alone sits there,....263. H.785, 5
There really alone;....279. H.863, 14
Burr is a smell-feast, and a man alone,....296. H.944, 1
Thou art that man of men, the man alone,....297. H.947, 3
Lost to the world; lost to my selfe; alone....298. H.954, 1
Case is a Lawyer, that near pleads alone,....303. H.975, 1
Lord, I confesse, that Thou alone art able....357. N.73, 1
A prayer, that is said alone,....381. N.158, 1
Predestination is the Cause alone....389. N.215, 1
Sin is the cause of death; and sin's alone....390. N.219, 1
God has foure keyes, which He reserves alone;...390. N.224, 1
Even Thou alone, the bitter cup....400. N.267, 8
All's now fledd saue this alone....418. A.9, 23
— — — — — — — — — —, ...450. var. A.9, 5
Along Death with it still walkes along....418. A.9, 41
Along with you my teare....43. H.123, 2
Sho'd wend along his Baby-ship to see?....86. H.213, 26
Amint. And I will beare along with you....86. H.213, 39
Will goe with you along....125. H.316, 10
But you, my Lord, are One, whose hand along..141. H.359, 13
May (Great Augustus) goe along with You....300. H.961, 18
No more shall I a long thy christall glide,....315. H.1028, 7
Along, come along,....320. H.1051, 1
Thy Father brought with him along....360. N.83, 25
Bring Him along, most pious Priest,....365. N.97, 11
Along the dark, and silent night,....372. N.121, 1
Along with it some tempting blandishment....389. N.217, 2
A breath of balm along the Elizean fields....416. A.8, 8
Chorus. We sail along, to visit mortals never;....417. A.8, 37
Aloud He cry'd aloud, Help, help the wound:....18. H.46, 4
Already Is lopt already; and the rest but stand....203. H.565, 2
Already coin'd to pay for it....218. H.626, 7
Already tame, and all thine owne?....282. H.881, 4
allready spillt, her rayes must gleame....430. ins. H.283, 20d
Also Will, with my Willow-wreath also,....161. H.425, 11
And the Elves also,....217 H.619, 3
The Pea also....317. H.1035, 5
Altar See Virgin-altar
Altar of Incense, I smell there....59. H.155, 4
Neere to the Altar stands the Priest,....91. H.223, 50
The Altar is not here foure-square,....91. H.223, 54
(Just in the middle of the Altar)....92. H.223, 70
He lowly to the Altar bows:....93. H.223, 136
As a fir'd Altar, is each stone,....113. H.283, 23
Next to the Altar humbly kneele, and thence,....128. H.320, 5
Kisse the Altar, and confess....138. H.346, 9
Upon his Altar, men shall read thy lines;....143. H.366, 2
No Planke from Hallowed Altar, do's appeale..149. H.377, 127
And thy brest the Altar, whence....158. H.417, 3
Let's to the Altar of perfumes then go,....168. H.445, 3
And a new Altar;....213. H.604, 10
Altar cleane, no fire prophane?....280. H.870, 6
Let us to the Altar go....303. H.974, 4
Over the golden Altar now is spread,....355. N.65, 3
(The Altar of our love) thy Stone....359. N.83, 12
Upon thine Altar! then return,....361. N.83, 77
Then, like a perfum'd Altar, see....366. N.98, 10
Upon an Altar rear'd by Him, and crown'd....369. N.105, 7
And fowle thy Altar, Charme some Into froggs,....412. A.3, 91
And see o^r Alter burne....413. A.4, 32
What though your laden Altar now has wonne
432. ins. H.283, 70a
Altar's Burns for the Altars ornament....92. H.223, 96
The Altar's ready; Fire to consume....102. H.251, 3
Altars As Beasts unto the Altars go....161. H.425, 9
The next, because her Altars did not shine....197. H.539, 9
Then I'le your Altars strew....228. H.657, 10
Shall I say her Altars be....273. H.836, 3
And to thee Altars raise,....281. H.874, 14
Thee and thine Altars emptie....296. H.946, 24
A thousand Altars smoake; a thousand thighes...300. H.961, 7
That sho'd you stirre, we and our Altars too....300. H.961, 17
The Altars all on fier be;....365. N.97, 7
for your approach, yet see their Altars pine?
431. ins. H.283, 60f
Alter Visage of them can alter him;....215. H.615, 4
Alteration The alteration is in us, not Him....340. N.7, 4
Alternative Where Joyes and Griefs have Turns Alternative.
264. H.792, 2
Although See Though
Shall move t'wards you; although I see....49. H.136, 34
Although the Pile be all perfume....50. H.140, 4
Draw I co'd once (although not stocks or stones,..84. H.210, 5
We are not poore; although we have....133. H.336, 41
Although not archt, yet weather proofe,....133. H.336, 52
Thus faire and cleane you are, although there be..189. H.511, 5
Although ye have a stock of wit,....218. H.626, 6
Although with some, yet little paine:....233. H.670, 10
In our high art, although we can't excell,....234. H.673, 10
Women, although they ne're so goodly make it,...235. H.675, 1
Rich or poore although it be;....253. H.750, 2
Although he has no riches,....259. H.772, 17
Although our suffering meet with no reliefe,....333. H.1119, 1
Although we cannot turne the fervent fit....356. N.67, 1
— — — — — — — — — —, ...428. var. H.238, 10
Altogether Is halfe, or altogether innocent....268. H.809, 2
on you is altogether lost,....432. ins. H.283, 70d
Always The happy fortune will not alwayes last...218. H.621, 2
Amarillis Sweet Amarillis, by a Spring's....46. H.130, 1
But dear Amintas, and sweet Amarillis,....86. H.213, 9
Mirt. Ah! Amarillis, farewell mirth and pipe;....159. H.421, 8
Dear Amarillis! Mon. Hark! Sil. mark: Mir. this earth
grew sweet....159. H.421, 11
Where, Amarillis, Thou didst set thy feet....159. H.421, 12
And dainty Amarillis,....184. H.492, 30
May find your Amarillis....323. H.1068, 8
Amazed As Hell, and Earth, and Heav'n may stand amaz'd.
399. N.263, 31
At which amaz'd, and pondring on the food,....262. H.783, 17
Amber Melting melodious words, to Lutes of Amber..22. H.67, 4
Treading on Amber, with their silver-feet:....26. H.79, 8
You see how Amber through the streams....75. H.193, 17
Rich beads of Amber here....80. H.201, 8
In Amber, or some Chrystall shell,....88. H.216, 14
And Amber; Spice-....112. H.283, 15
Butter of Amber, Cream, and Wine, and Oile...144. H.370, 5
Of Amber chaf't between the hands,....145. H.375, 16
Of Amber quick was buried....186. H.497, 12
Of Amber cleanly buried:....269. H.817, 2
And Bake the floure of Amber for thy bread....269. H.818, 6
And plaister'd round with Amber....345. N.33, 24
— — — — — — — — — —, ...426. var. H.197, 27
Ambergris Of Balme, of Oyle, of Spice, and Amber-Greece.
5. H.1, 8
Give them the scent of Amber-Greece:....20. H.54, 2
To blast the Aire, but Amber-greece and Gums....205. H.575, 6
Ambers Musks and Ambers more from her:....59. H.155, 8
These Musks, these Ambers, and those other smells
157. H.414, 3
When a warm tongue do's with such Ambers meet.
269. H.816, 4
Ambition In Man, Ambition is the common'st thing;.21. H.58, 1
That slippery all Ambition is....229. H.661, 2
Ambition's No, thy Ambition's Master-piece....229. H.662, 11
Ambitious Which with ambitious humblenes stands vnder
405. A.1, 45
Hence rise those twoe ambitious hills that looke...406. A.1, 81
Amble Those smooth-pac't Numbers, amble every where;
141. H.359, 10
Ambler The wanton Ambler chanc'd to see....12. H.27, 3
Ambrose But Mary cal'd then (as S. Ambrose saith).
386. N.192, 4
(S. Ambrose sayes) without the Thorn:....396. N. 251, 2
Ambrosia Content makes all Ambrosia....37. H.106, 116
Which full of Nectar and Ambrosia is,....186. H.498, 4
Ambrosia-like Ambrosia-like, or Nectarell:....20. H.54, 4
Amen Kissing the Omen, said Amen:....73. H.187, 7
To say, Amen....87. H.214, 8
Both to the Cocks-tread say Amen;....179. H.476, 20
On our meat, and on us all. Amen....364. N.95, 6
To Voices, say, Amen....369. N.106, 16
Amend The bad to punish, and the good t'amend..343, N.26, 2
Amidst Amidst the deepes;....134. H.336, 61
Yo^r name amidst the sacred smoke....413. A.4, 30
— — — — — — — — — —, ...429. var. H.263, 1
Amintas But dear Amintas, and sweet Amarillis,....86. H.213, 9
Amiss Wo't thou not smile, or tell me what's amisse?
78. H.197, 33
There's no constraint to do amisse,....390. N.225, 1
Ammonites He slew the Ammonites, we know,....360. N.83, 27
Among And with rich clusters (hid among....16. H.41, 10
(Among the rest)....43. H.123, 22
Cupid as he lay among....50. H.139, 1
You are the Queen all flowers among,....88. H.216, 19
Among the Mirtles, as I walkt,....106. H.263, 1
Among ye, striving for her lace:....114. H.283, 84
Among thy Fancies, tell me this,....130. H.329, 1
Among the Elves, (if mov'd) the stings....165. H.443, 16
flies curious wings; and these among....166. H.443, 69
Among your Mirtles to be writ:....170. H.449, 27
Of those mild Men, thou art to live among:....172. H.456, 6
Next to which Two; among the City-Powers,....176. H.466, 3
One chiefe transgression is among the rest,....197. H.539, 7
Among which Holies, be Thou ever known,....199. H. 545, 7
Among which glories, (crown'd with sacred Bayes,
206. H.575, 49
The holy Sisters some among....237. H.686, 9
'Tis said, as Cupid danc't among....241. H.706, 1
Among disasters that discention brings,....260. H.774, 1
Thee here among my righteous race:....278. H.859, 2
Tis much among the filthy to be clean;....318. H.1042, 1
Among these Tempests great and manifold....319. H.1044, 1
Among Gods Blessings, there is no one small....353. N.55, 2
Lies He the Lillie-banks among?....367. N.102, 3
The Bad among the Good are here mixt ever:....383. N.172, 1

Amongst But, **amongst** All encircled here, not one..94. H.224, 5
Sorrowes divided **amongst** many, lesse..........239. H.699, 1
That I **amongst** you live a Citizen..............242. H.713, 12
(**Amongst** mine honour'd) Thee (almost) the last:
256. H.763, 2
(**Amongst** the rest) both bright and singular;...267. H.804, 10
Amongst this scumme, the Souldier, with his speare,
398. N.263, 9
Amongest the thrice-three-sacred Virgins, fill....412. A.3, 86
— — — — — — — — — — —, ...429. var. H.263, 1
— — — — — — — — — — —, ...443. var. H.575, 49
— — — — — — — — — — —, ...452. var. H.443, 16
Amorous The soft and **am'rous** soule;............54. H.149, 26
Amount And found my Debits to **amount**........369. N.107, 2
Amour See D'amour
Amphion Some have Thee call'd **Amphion**; some of us,
288. H.907, 7
Amphion-like **Amphion-like**) men made of flesh and bones,
84. H.210, 6
Amphitheatre — — — — — — — —, ...443. var. H.575, 48
Ample May his **ample** Name be knowne.........108. H 266, 17
Like Sybels Leaves, throughout the **ample** world? 172. H.459, 4
Compar'd (in this my **ample** Orbe) to Him......236. H.685, 4
Am'rous See Amorous
An (Partial List)
Me thought, (last night) love in **an** anger came,....16. H.40, 1
Then to that twenty, adde **an** hundred more:......24. H.74, 4
Such **an** one, as will repeat......................62. H.162, 13
Their Christal natures to **an** union..............77. H.197, 4
Y'ave farced well, pray make **an** end;..........146. H.377, 24
Wherein t'ave had **an** enjoying.................195. H.534, 6
He gives **an** almes, and chides them from his doore.
220. H.632, 2
Give **an** Almes to one that's poore,............223. H.638, 2
For **an** Almes; then give me such.............223. H.638, 22
If thou hast found **an** honie-combe,.............288. H.909, 1
He askt **an** almes; I gave him bread,...........295. H.942, 5
Out of hell **an** horrour call,...................377. N.128, 14
Not **an** Affection, but a Deitie................380. N.148, 2
Sin is **an** act so free, that if we shall...........389. N.218, 1
Is it to fast **an** houre,........................391. N.228, 9
To such **an** height, to such a period rais'd,......399. N.263, 30
Which ope themselves to shewe **an** holy shrine....404. A.1, 26
— — — — — — — — — — —, ...434. var. H.293, 37
— — — — — — — — — — —, ...437. var. H.336, 79
— — — — — — — — — — —, ...450. var. A.9, 30
— — — — — — — — — — —, ...451. var. H.197, 78
Anacreon Rouze **Anacreon** from the dead;..........39. H.111, 9
Horace, **Anacreon** both had lost their fame,......45. H.128, 31
Anacreon......................................198. H.544, 8
Ile bring thee Herrick to **Anacreon**,............206. H.575, 32
Anacreon's A crawling Vine about **Anacreon's** head:
313. H.1017, 2
Anathema **Anathema** to it, and me..............229. H.660, 4
Ancestors Charg'd with the Armes of all his **Ancestors**:
295. H.941, 2
Ancestry Wrapt up in Seare-cloth with thine **Ancestrie**:
231. H.664, 2
By the dead bones of our deare **Ancestrie**........278. H.860, 8
Anchor Thus if our ship fails of her **Anchor** hold,..266. H.800, 7
And here my ship rides having **Anchor** cast.....334. H.1126, 2
Anchor-hold My ship has here one only **Anchor-hold**;
319. H.1044, 2
Anchus Where **Anchus** and rich Tullus blend....133. H.336, 26
Ancient Of **antient** honesty, may boast.........147. H.377, 42
Low, and of Thrones the **Ancient** Majesty.......325. H.1073, 4
And't **And't** shall doe so for thee..............108. H.267, 12
Angel To finde Bethesda, and an **Angel** there,......61. H.161, 3
The Tree, Bethesda, and the **Angel** too:.........61. H.161, 6
Shall by the mighty **Angell** be reveal'd:......256. H.763, 16
Tell me, white **Angell**; what is now become....403. N.271, 3
Angels O thou the drink of Gods, and **Angels**! Wine
45. H.128, 11
While Golden **Angels** (some have told to me)....86. H.213, 23
And **Angels** will be borne, while thou dost sing...102. H.252, 2
Angells are called Gods; yet of them, none.......379. N.143, 1
God, and good **Angells** guide Thee; and so blesse
399. N 263, 32
Angels' Above they are the **Angels** spiced wine.....226. H.645, 2
Anger Me thought, (last night) love in an **anger** came,
16. H.40, 1
Whereupon in **anger** flying......................50. H.139, 3
Lest a handsome **anger** flye,....................98. H.238, 13
Farre hence be all speech, that may **anger** move:.222. H.633, 60
For **anger** spat on thee her Looking-glasse:......249. H.732, 2
But the **anger** ends all here,.................255. H.761, 19
But heard with **anger**, we confesse the crime.....260. H.776, 2
Words beget **Anger**: **Anger** brings forth blowes:.287. H.901, 1
For which (me thought) in prittie **anger** she....313. H.1017, 11
Angler So that an **Angler**, for a daies expence,....282. H.879, 3
Angry By which, mine **angry** Mistresse might descry,
58. H.150, 5
Angry if Irene be............................204. H.566, 1
God when He's **angry** here with any one,.........340. N.7, 1
Animal See Plant-animal
Annoint See 'Noint
Remembring. to **anoint**..........................55. H.149, 86
A Sweating-Closset, to **annoint** the silke-......149. H.377, 121
Anon Wee'l see the Fairy-Court **anon**.............119. H.293, 6
What now we like, **anon** we disapprove:..........191. H.517, 1
Another When one is past, **another** care we hav....18. H.48, 1
Did rather choose to blesse **another** clime?........77. H.197, 22
In hot Adult'ry with **another** Wine?.............78. H.197, 40
Another snapt the Cherry.....................142. H.364, 8
To spring againe **another** yeare..................189. H.514, 8
To be **another** day re-worne,..................190. H.515, 41
When I behold **another** grace...................202. H.560, 5
These I co'd praise thee for beyond **another**,......210. H.590, 9
I'le play thee such **another** strain;.............244. H.716, 38
Against the wicked, in **another** world.............357. N.74, 4
God is more here, then in **another** place,.........387. N.197, 1
— — — — — — — — — — —, ...426. var. H.197, 40
Another's Merry at **anothers** hearth; y'are here...146. H.377, 29
Be lesse **anothers** Laurell, then thy praise.......297. H.947, 14
His own He acts not, but **anothers** part:.........343. N.22, 2
Answer They doe grow? I **answer**, There,...........19. H.53, 4
Though good things **answer** many good intents;..110. H.275, 1
I must **answer** (Sweet) thy part................186. H.500, 3
I will **answer**, These discover.................208. H.580, 11
And (Noble friend) this **answer** I must give:....312. H.1013, 2
Ant Much-more, provides, and hoords up like an **Ant**;
73. H.188, 1
Give me then an **Ant** to eate;...................223. H.638, 5
— — — — — — — — — — —, ...452. ins. H.443, 45e
Anthea If deare **Anthea**, my hard fate it be.........11. H.22, 1
Anthea, Herrick, and his Poetry.................11. H.22, 10
Anthea bade me tye her shooe;...................14. H.33, 1
Smooth **Anthea**, for a skin......................16. H.39, 5
And thou (**Anthea**) must withdraw from him......20. H.55, 2
Ah my **Anthea**! Must my heart still break?........24. H.74, 1
So looks **Anthea**, when in bed she lyes,...........34. H.104, 1
Come **Anthea**, know thou this,.................235. H.678, 1
Come **Anthea** let us two.......................255. H.761, 1
Tell me **Anthea**, dost thou fondly dread........262. H.781, 13
Anthea I am going hence......................277. H.854, 1
Anthea laught, and fearing lest excesse..........311. H.1006, 1
Sick is **Anthea**, sickly is the spring,...........320. H.1054, 1
The while my deer **Anthea** do's but droop,......320. H.1054, 3
Anthea's If I kisse **Anthea's** brest,.................59. H.155, 1
Anthonie See Antony
Antient See Ancient
Antique Of Persian Loomes, and **antique** Plate:..239. H.696, 10
Or **Antique** pledges, House or lande,..............407. A.2, 9
Antony As Cleopatra came to **Anthonie**;........79. H.197, 74
Was drunk to **Antonie**.........................240. H.705, 8
Any In **any** one, the least indecencie:.............10. H.16, 2
Not that I thinke, that **any** Dart,................10. H.20, 4
To give (if **any**, yet) but little sound..............15. H.38, 8
Nor **any** was preferr'd 'fore me..................70. H.181, 2
As **any** other, this can tell;......................24. H.73, 8
Colder yet then **any** one:.......................40. H.115, 12
Any noise, they both will wake,..................52. H.145, 4
Nor **any** bed to give the shew..................63. H.164, 10
More sweet then **any**...........................83. H.205, 8
Of **any** men that were..........................85. H.211, 12
Poore of the Parish, (if there's **any**)............92. H.223, 90
Co'd never since find **any** rest...................96. H.229, 6
That long I love not **any**.......................100. H.249, 8
As for to make this, that, or **any** one...........107. H.264, 3
Shark, when he goes to **any** publick feast,......118. H.292, 1
And sport it **any** way;.........................160. H.422, 11
That single may have **any**......................160. H.422, 16
Or **any** blow...................................161. H. 426, 2
For a wrought Purse; can **any** tell wherefore?....162. H.427, 2
And shall dispaire, that **any** art..................164. H.442, 8
Of **any** tackling can declare..................167. H.443, 104
Who writes sweet Numbers well as **any** can:....172. H.459, 2
If I **any** fret or vex,............................177. H.472, 3
Any one part that's dissonant in you:...........189. H.511, 2
He ever pickt (as yet) of **any** one..............204. H.568, 6
And of **any** wood ye see,.......................204. H.569, 15
To **any** one unsober syllable....................210. H.590, 8
Then if **any** Peece proves new,.................217. H.620, 10
And not by **any** sordid shift:....................221. H.633, 47
Any Orts the Elves refuse.....................223. H.638, 19
Strikes me dead as **any** stone?..................254. H.757, 6
My Passions **any** rest..........................272. H 828, 8
Ponder my words, if so that **any** be............290. H.914, 1
Then Case, as loud as **any** Serjant there,........303. H.975, 5
Here to **any**;...................................308. H.993, 3
Or **any** tone 314. H.1024, 10
Any part backward in the Deitie..................342. N.18, 2
With **any** thing unhallowed, here:...............366. N.98, 2
Wip't out few, (God knowes) if **any**............373. N.121, 10
For **any** ill; but, for the proof of Faith:.........380. N.150, 2
Anyone To thee, then unto **any one**:...........147. H.377, 70
God when He's angry here with **any one**,........340, N.7, 1
Anything As you, or **any thing**................125. H.316, 14
Nor dreads he **any thing**:......................259. H.772, 12
If **any thing** delight me for to print..............355. N.61, 1
— — — — — — — — — — —, ...427. var. H.197, 53
Anywhere Or peirce it **any where**;................11. H.20, 6

Apace We shall grow old apace, and die..........69. H.178, 59
Neglected beauty perisheth apace................97. H.234, 2
Will come on apace;..........................267. H.806, 5
Apart Neatly apart;..........................114. H.283, 95
Ape Ever gamesome as an ape:...............306. H.984, 29
Apollo 'Tis not Apollo can, or those thrice three..45. H.128, 29
And that Apollo shall so touch Your eare,........107. H.264, 2
Shalt lead, like young Apollo.................184. H.492, 36
But by Apollo! as I worship wit,..............234. H.673, 7
Less then Apollo, that ursurp'st such Three?....276. H.851, 6
Unshorn Apollo, come, and re-inspire...........280. H.871, 2
Be thou Apollo, or the type of him:............299. H.956, 12
Apollo sings, his harpe resounds; give roome,......415. A.7, 1
Apollo's Thy Fiers from me; but Apollo's curse...79. H.197, 83
Apollos Image side with Thee to blesse.......254. H.756, 11
Seemes like Apollo's when the morne he blesses....404. A.1, 2
— — — — — — — — — — — —, ...451. var. H.336, 48
Apostata — — — — — — — — —, ...431. var. H.283, 57
Apostate And till I turne Apostate to thy love,....79. H.197, 81
And turne Apostate: Love will................113. H.283, 57
I turne Apostate to the strict Comande....424. ins. H. 128, 46c
Apostles Apostles, way (unshackled) to goe out....52. H.146, 16
Apostles' Th' Apostles Mounts of the New Testament
381. N.157, 4
Appeal True, I confesse I left thee, and appeale...78. H.197, 41
No Planke from Hallowed Altar, do's appeale..149. H.377, 127
Appealed When to Thee I have appeal'd;........348. N.41, 47
Appear See Reappear
And those her lips doe now appeare................7. H.9, 11
A glorious forme appeare to me:................51. H.142, 6
But all faire signs appeare.....................56. H.149, 107
Onely, Ile not appeare to thee,.................58. H.152, 3
Me thinks that onely lustre doth appeare..........94. H.226, 3
Never my Book's perfection did appeare,..........99. H.245, 1
Why doe not all fresh maids appeare............103. H.256, 1
Your storme is over; Lady, now appeare........105. H.259, 7
But think on these, that are t'appeare,........127. H.319, 39
Look, how the Rainbow doth appeare..........139. H.353, 1
Sisters of Fate appeare to me..................153. H.399, 2
No shadowes great appeare;....................164. H.441, 6
Then will appeare a cheerfull Heaven...........188. H.508, 6
O Flame of Beauty! come, appeare, appeare.....191. H.516, 3
Thou shalt come forth, and then appeare........192. H.521, 31
Fled are the Frosts, and now the Fields appeare..224. H.642, 1
O Thing admir'd! there did appeare............237. H.687, 5
At last, i' th' noone of winter, did appeare......262. H.783, 13
Wilt thou appear, when thou art set.............270. H.819, 7
Appeare thou to mine eyes.....................271. H.824, 6
Do thou to me appeare;......................271. H.824, 14
Or Easters Eve appeare.........................285. H.892, 8
In all our high designments, 'twill appeare.......292. H.924, 1
Hence, hence prophane, and none appeare.........366. N.98, 1
Before Thy Virgin-Altar I appeare,............368. N.103, 2
His humane Nature did, in part, appeare:........389. N.214, 2
But let each p^r^sant Cheeke appear..............413. A.4, 3
Doth not to the sight appeare..................418. A.9, 48
Appears Thus, and thus it now appears..........17. H.43, 9
War, which before was horrid, now appears........25. H.77, 7
He tooke her; now the jest in this appeares,.......129. H.326, 5
Yet not a Lillie from the Bed appeares;.......180. H.477, 4
Appeares but in His Meaner Majestie...........236. H.685, 6
Appease Who, with his looks too, can appease......31. H.90, 4
This day, the Queen-Priest, thou are made t'appease
197. H.539, 5
Appetite To coole, not cocker Appetite...........35. H.106, 26
Not curious whether Appetite be fed,..........37. H.106, 107
With blasting eye, the appetite,................147. H.377 48
A more unconquer'd appetite.................167. H.443, 115
So as to rise still with an appetite............220. H.633, 19
And mad'st a promise that mine appetite........262. H.783, 2
Appetites Our witty appetites to please,....436. ins. H.336, 48f
Applaud If well the Dice runne, lets applaud the cast:
218. H.621, 1
The good applaud: the peccant lesse condemne,..322. H.1062, 8
Applause Give up the just applause to verse:...136. H.336, 136
Is Fame, (the breath of popular applause.)......169. H.448, 2
Three, unto whom the whole world give applause;
276. H.851, 7
Apple (If a wild Apple can be had)............135. H.336, 122
The blushing Apple, bashfull Peare,............192. H.521, 37
Apple or Plume is neately layd,...........439. ins. H.443, 45b
Of fragrant Apples, blushing Plums, or Peares:..205. H.575, 10
Apple's-core An Apples-core is hung up dry'd,...93. H.223, 126
Apply To wound my heart, and never to apply,....52. H.146, 19
And bid the Youth apply.......................56 H.149, 95
Your Finger to apply.........................221. H.633 36
The stakes are laid: let's now apply...........243. H.716 19
Some salve to every sore, we may apply;......274. H.841, 1
Approach That flow of Gallants which approach...239. H.696, 1
By Thine approach, each their beholding eye.....398. N.263, 14
for your approach, yet see their Altars pine?
431. ins. H.283, 60f
Approaching More and more approaching nigh....377. N.128, 6
Approve What I fancy, I approve,.................11. H.21, 1
Ile praise, and Ile approve....................160. H.422, 5
What is a Kisse? Why this, as some approve;....218. H.622, 1
Approved As the wise Cato had approv'd of thee...78. H.197, 64
But lost to that they most approv'd:...........180. H.478, 2
Apricocks And Apricocks, in youthfull yeares:....268. H.811, 4
Apricots See Apricocks
April Of April, May, of June, and July-Flowers......5. H.1, 2
First, April, she with mellow showrs...........23. H.70, 1
Blowne out of April; or some New-.............112. H.283, 3
When as her Aprill houre drawes neare,.........221. H.633, 58
Of this or that great Aprill day shall be,.......257. H.763, 19
(The generall Aprill of the worlde) dothe Come,...410. A.3, 34
Apron Her Apron gave (as she did passe)......251. H.740, 9
ΑΡΧΗ God is the ΑΡΧΗ and the ΤΕΛΟΣ too...403. N.272, 2
Aquinas Or Good at all, (as learn'd Aquinas saith.)
383. N.173, 2
Arabia Or rich Arabia did commix,............402. N.269, 16
Arabian Th' Arabian Dew besmears............80. H.201, 10
Arch About the Arch of either eye;..............46. H. 130, 8
Next in an Arch, akin to this,..................90. H.223, 15
No more is seen the Arch of Peace.............139. H.353, 4
Which cense this Arch; and here and there,......166. H.443, 45
Arched See Overarched
Although not archt, yet weather proofe,........133. H.336, 52
Architect But the foundacõn of this Architect....405. A.1, 43
Arch-like Arch-like, hold up, Thy Name's Inscription.
168 H.444, 4
Arch-poet After the rare Arch-Poet Johnson dy'd,.150. H.382, 1
Are See Y'are
Argues Argues a strong distemper of the mind....356. N.70, 2
Argus Thou sail'st with others, in this Argus here;.23. H.71, 1
Ariadne's It sparkles now like Ariadne's Crowne...264. H.789, 4
Aright Consider sorrowes, how they are aright:..268. H.810, 1
Arise The storme will arise,......................225. H.643, 19
Ark An Arke a Tabernacle is...................68. H.178, 34
Sleeps, laid within some Ark of Flowers,........367. N.102, 5
Arks With Wicker Arks did come...............110. H.274, 6
Arm Or Pelops Arme of Yvorie.................34. H.105, 6
Enthrall'd her Arme, as Prisoner.............64. H.169, 4
Armed With such an arm'd, but such an easie Foe,
216. H.618, 11
Armies aloft, and like two armies, come..432. ins. H.283, 140d
Armlet A curious Armelet........................18. H.47, 4
Arms To enflesh my thighs, and armes:..........10. H.19, 6
And armes and hands they did enthrall:........16. H.41, 15
Fold now thine armes; and hang the head,....47. H.132, 1
Armes, and hands, and all parts else,.........53. H.147, 7
The Armes to hugge it? throw, throw.........115. H.283, 117
Fold mine Armes, sob, sigh, or weep:..........182. H.490, 10
Or else by Armes.............................213. H.609, 5
Or fold mine armes, and sigh, because I've lost.222. H.634, 12
Charg'd with the Armes of all his Ancestors:..295. H.941, 2
The Coward then takes Armes, and do's the deed.
309. H.999, 2
From wch two armes like branches seem to spread
406. A.1, 97
That armes the forehead of the Vnicorne.....406. A.1, 104
Fould now thine armes, and in thy last looke reare
414. A.6, 7
Armsful And by the Armes-full (with a Brest unhid)
147. H.377, 37
Army — — — — — — — — —, ...437. var. H.336, 106
Aromatic Of Aromatike wine,....................80. H.201, 26
And for no less then Aromatick Wine........262. H.783, 9
Aromatical Richly Aromaticall..................59. H.155, 6
Aromatics To make rich these Aromatikes:......145. H.375, 14
With Musk-flies, are th' Aromaticks,..........166. H.443, 44
Here, all her rare Aromaticks................402. N.269, 17
Arose I pittifull arose,..........................26. H.81, 13
Around I'le drink to the Garlands a-round it:....239. H.695, 3
Arrant Of deep and arrant ignorance came in;...150. H.382, 14
Array In a more rich and sweet aray:..........23. H.70, 4
— — — — — — — — — — —, ...433. var. H.293, 28
Arrears For why sayes he, all debts and their arreares,
142. H.363, 3
Arrow And wedded string and arrow,............27. H.81, 30
No Arrow nockt, onely a stringlesse Bow:....357. N.74, 2
Arrows His Arrowes flie; and all his stones are hurl'd
357. N.74, 3
Arse See Erse
Cloy'd they are up with Arse; but hope, one blast
226. H.650, 3
She cocks out her Arse at the parting,.........333. H.1122, 3
Art (Partial List of Verb)
Come bring your sampler, and with Art,..........10. H.20, 1
Doe more bewitch me, then when Art..........28. H.83, 13
Rockie thou art; and rockie we discover.........29. H.86, 7
How rich and pleasing thou my Julia art........30. H.88, 1
(If mercifull, as faire thou art;................33 H.103, 6
That plague; because thou art content..........35. H.106, 22
Which Art, not Nature, makes so rare;......37. H.106, 112
Nor art thou so close-handed, but can'st spend..38. H.106, 129
Work'st more then Wisdome, Art, or Nature can,
45. H.128, 24
Herrick, thou art too coorse to love...........51. H.142, 22
To warme my Breast, when thou my Pulse art gone.
73. H.186, 16

Art quickens Nature; Care will make a face:...97. H.234, 1
Thou art a plant sprung up to wither never,....98. H.240, 1
Drest up with all the Country Art..........101. H.250, 8
Thou art to all lost love the best,............106. H.262, 1
Thou art my life, my love, my heart,...........109. H.267, 21
Nature and Art, one more..................115. H.283, 129
Thus, thou, that man art, whom the Fates conspir'd 121. H.301, 5
Thou my pretty Captive art?.................128. H.322, 5
Knap the thread, and thou art free:..........128. H.322, 8
The Painters art in thy Sciography?..........139. H.347, 2
Who art chief at marriages,..................141. H.360, 2
The first of Nature, and the next of Art:......153. H.394, 2
Art presupposes Nature; Nature shee..........153. H.394, 3
Since thou art gone, no more I mean to play,..159. H.421, 9
And shall dispaire, that any art.............164. H.442, 8
Why! yet to shew that thou art just,........169. H.446, 11
O Jealousie, that art.......................170. H.452, 1
Of those mild Men, thou art to live among:....172. H.456, 6
Though thou art young, thou canst say no,....174. H.465, 34
That so thou art, because thou must..........175. H.465, 39
Lastly, be mindfull (when thou art grown great) 181. H.483, 13
That art the cause Endimion;................183. H.492, 7
Can teach a man the Art of memory:..........186. H.501, 2
Come thou, who art the Wine, and wit........189. H.515, 1
Thou art of what I did intend...............189. H.515, 5
Thou art The Man, the onely Man best known,..194. H.526, 3
Goddesse, I begin an Art;...................195. H.530, 1
This day, the Queen-Priest, thou art made t'appease 197. H.539, 5
Dotes less on Nature, then on Art............202. H.560, 18
Colours, let Art supply.....................224. H.641, 2
In our high art, although we can't excell,....234. H.673, 10
Art discontent with me......................240. H.705, 4
He doth it with the sweetest tones of Art:....266. H.799, 2
'Tis the Chyrurgions praise, and height of Art..268. H.808, 1
But since th' art Printed, thou dost call........287. H.899, 3
Lord, I confesse, that Thou alone art able......357. N.73, 1
Fail'd in my part; O! Thou that art my deare,..398. N.261, 2
Thou art that Roscius, and that markt-out man,.398. N.263, 19
To wonder and affrightment: Thou art He,....398. N.263, 21
And God, as Thou art, comes to suffering.....399. N.263, 25
Who Mercie art,............................401. N.268, 32
Least thankes to Nature, most to Art......421. ins. H.106, 26b
— — — — — — — — — — —, ...426. ins. H.197, 48a
— — — — — — — — — — —, ...427. var. H.197, 59
Articles They have their Book of Articles:......92. H.223, 80
Artist And when, wise Artist, that thou hast,....48. H.133, 14
Artless Artlesse the Sceane was; and that monstrous sin 150. H.382, 13
When the artlesse Doctor sees................347. N.41, 13
Art's By Arts wise hand, but to this end........76. H.193, 46
The nails faln off by Whit-flawes: Art's.......166. H.443, 59
Arts For one to whom espous'd are all the Arts;..121. H.301, 2
Live you, great Mistresse of your Arts, and be..326. H.1080, 21
As (Partial List)
When such a Light as You are leads the way:....3. Ded.H, 2
Deerely I lov'd thee; as my first-borne child:........6. H.3, 2
As beames of Corrall, but more cleare............7. H.9, 12
As Goddesse Isis (when she went,................9. H.15, 9
And her grinders black as jet;................11. H.21, 12
As were (time past) thy holy Filitings:........11. H.22, 6
Kept as close as Danae was:....................14. H.36, 5
(As they were closely set)....................18. H.47, 2
Thus woe succeeds a woe; as wave a wave.....18. H.48, 2
As, could they hear, the Damn'd would make no noise. 22. H.67, 2
As blessed soules cann't heare too much:........22. H.68, 4
As any other, this can tell;..................24. H.73, 8
Let's kisse afresh, as when we first begun.......24. H.74, 8
But yet, though Love likes well such Scenes as these, 24. H.74, 9
As one, in long-lamented-widow-hood;.........25. H.77, 4
As in a flowrie Nunnery:......................25. H.78, 4
Which as a warme, and moistned spring,.......25. H 78, 9
As oft as Night is banish'd by the Morne,........26. H.80, 1
Brought him, (as Love professes)............27. H.81. 22
By me, o'r thee, (as justments to the dead)....27. H.82, 4
A people currish; churlish as the seas;........29. H 86, 11
And rude (almost) as rudest Salvages............29. H.86, 12
As the eternall monument of me...............30. H.89, 10
(If mercifull, as faire thou art;..................33. H.103, 6
True, I confesse; such Whites as these........34. H.105, 7
Got, not so beautifull, as chast:................35. H.106, 34
These, and sowre herbs, as dainty meat?.....37. H.106, 114
So much for want, as exercise:...............37. H.106, 118
As well as spare: still conning o'r this Theame,..38. H.106, 131
Draw him as like too, as you can,..............38. H.108, 5
Those Sundayes onely, when as Briefs are read .39. H.109, 2
As shews the Aire, when with a Rain-bow grac'd; 40. H.114, 1
When as Leander young was drown'd,........42. H.119, 1
Wept as he'd drowne the Hellespont,..........42. H.119, 10
Thou shed'st one teare, when as I went away;.42. H.122, 10
And strings my tears as Pearle...............43. H.123, 6
When as the Lilly marries with the Rose!........44. H.124, 2
To me, as blood to life and spirit: Neare,......45. H.128, 2
So neare, or deare, as thou wast once to me...45. H.128, 10
The soule, like lightning, and as active too.....45. H.128, 28
As is thy powerful selfe. Prethee not smile;....46. H.128, 45
To th'board, so hot, as none co'd touch the same: 47. H.131, 2
All such as are not soft like them............47. H.132, 14
But we as fearlesse of the Sunne,................48. H.136, 10
Continues cold, as is the night.................49. H.136, 31
From Fames black lips, as you from me.....49. H.136, 36
Cupid as he lay among.......................50. H.139, 1
Sitting alone (as one forsook)..................51. H.142, 1
Not so much Rose, as Wreathe...............51. H.144, 4
This, as I wish for, so I hope to see;.........52. H.146, 17
No; he's but Fore-man, as he was before.......53. H.148, 4
As Zephirus when he 'spires..................55. H.149, 67
As with a will repenting.....................55. H.149, 76
As she, so you'l be ripe for men..............56. H.149, 112
As with a heart possest:.....................57. H.149, 136
Breathe as the Damask Rose:.................57. H.149, 144
Or sweet, as is that gumme..................57. H.149, 145
As is the fish, or tonguelesse Crocadile.........58. H.150, 2
As Jove did, when he made his rapes:........58. H.152, 2
As he did once to Semele.....................58. H.152, 4
And kissing, so as none may heare,............59. H.152. 11
Shapelesse the world (as when all Chaos was)..59. H.154, 8
If not, (as banisht) I will live alone.............60. H.156, 5
And you must fade, as well as they..........61. H.159, 17
When as that Rubie, which you weare,........61. H.160, 7
Enthrall'd her Arme, as Prisoner.............64. H.169, 4
Or so, as Darknesse made a stay.............64. H.169, 7
As endless prove;..........................66. H.172, 29
And pure as Gold for ever....................66. H.172, 30
As ayrie as the leaves of gold;.................66. H.175, 2
As if to stir it scarce had leave:.................66. H.175, 6
As Lovers fall into a swoone:................67. H.175, 16
And make me smooth as Balme, and Oile againe..67. H.176, 6
When as a thousand Virgins on this day,........68. H.178, 13
And sweet as Flora. Take no care.............68. H.178, 17
As if here were those cooler shades of love.......68. H.178, 36
And sin no more, as we have done, by staying;..68. H.178, 41
As fast away as do's the Sunne:...............69. H.178, 62
And as a vapour, or a drop of raine............69. H.178, 63
Rough as th' Adratick sea, yet I..............70. H.181, 23
And thus surpriz'd (as Filchers use)..........71. H.182, 11
And as I prune my feather'd youth, so I....72. H.185, 19
Now as I doe; and but for thee,..............72. H.185, 24
As soone dispatcht is by the Night, as Day...73. H.186, 4
When as Cherries come in place?.............74. H.189, 6
So though y'are white as Swan, or Snow,......76. H.193, 49
Welcome as are the ends unto my Vowes:.......77. H.197, 14
Left in this rak't-up Ash-heap, as a mark.......78. H.197, 37
Thou mak'st me nimble, as the winged howers,..78. H.197, 51
As the wise Cato had approv'd of thee........78. H.197, 64
As Queenes, meet Queenes; or come thou unto me, 79. H.197, 73
As Cleopatra came to Anthonie;...............79. H.197, 74
When Pyramids, as men,.......................81. H.201, 47
As Men, the Heavens have their Hypocrisie?....81. H.202, 8
Bright as the Wise-men's Torch, which guided them 86. H.213, 21
As he is Prince, he's Shepherd too.............86. H.213, 44
As my last Remembrances.....................88. H.218, 9
When as the chosen seed shall spring..........89. H.219, 19
As Rome's Pantheon had not more...........90. H.223, 8
And, as Sir Thomas Parson tells,..............92. H.223, 79
A Laurel for her, (ever young as love).........94. H.224, 8
As your health or comes, or goes;..............96. H.232, 6
Numberlesse, as are your haires...............96. H.232, 8
As well as I....................................97. H.232, 18
Barre close as you can, and bolt fast too your doore, 97. H.233, 1
Mop-ey'd I am, as some have said,............97. H.235, 1
And burn thee 'up, as well as I...............98. H.238, 15
Like noyse-lesse Snow; or as the dew of night:..100. H.247, 2
Not all at once, but gently, as the trees........100. H.247, 3
As spotlesse pure, as it is sweet:..............101. H.250, 10
(Clad, all, in Linnen, white as Lillies.).........101. H.250, 12
As here a Custard, there a Pie,................101. H.250, 33
(As you) may have their fill of meat...........102. H.250, 46
As the Summers Corne has eares:..............102. H.253, 4
Wept out our heart, as well as eyes.............104. H.256, 14
Fresh, as their blood; and ever grow,..........104. H.256, 19
Just as the modest Morne...................104. H.257, 4
Or that ye have not seen as yet................104. H.257, 20
But turne soone after calme, as Balme, or Oile...105. H.259, 4
And beat ye so, (as some dare say)...........105. H.260, 7
For as these flowers, thy joyes must die,......107. H.263, 19
As to be the Chick of Jove......................108. H.266, 8
A heart as soft, a heart as kind,...............108. H.267, 5
Serv'd, but as Tapers, for to burne,............109. H.271, 5
As a fir'd Altar, is each stone,..................113. H.283, 23
You multiply, as doth a Fish..................113. H.283, 50
Ye Towre her up, as Danae was;..............116. H.283, 144
A shew, as if 't 'ad been a snake:................116. H.284, 4

AS

For mine own part I'de as lieve,..............117. H.285, 10
Cold as Ice, or coole as I......................117. H.289, 10
Browne as his Tooth. A little Moth,..........120. H.293, 41
Kept, as Danae in a Tower:..................120. H.297, 4
And as coy be, as you can,..................121. H.297, 13
As her little eyes did peep....................123. H.310, 4
As yet the early-rising Sun....................125. H.316, 3
As you, or any thing.........................125. H.316, 14
Or as the pearles of Mornings dew............125. H.316, 19
As Gilly flowers do but stay....................126. H.318, 1
So you sweet Lady (sweet as May)............126. H.318, 3
(Sweet as your selfe, and newly blown)........126. H.318, 8
As Daughters to the instant yeare:............127. H.319, 40
As sure a Mattins do's to him belong,..........128. H.321, 5
Of Chance, (as made up all of rock, and oake:)..129. H.323, 12
She weares as trophees of her honour..........131. H.330, 13
As when a Rain-bow in perfumes goes out.....131. H.331, 8
As Benjamin, and Storax, when they meet.....131. H.331, 10
As Fate do's lead or draw us; none,..........132. H.336, 6
As is the Air, and let us be..................133. H.336, 38
True Calenders, as Pusses eare................134. H.336, 89
Flutter and crow, as in a fit................135. H.336, 110
Plump as the cherry,.........................136. H.336, 139
Though not so fresh, yet full as merry........136. H.336, 140
As the crickit;...............................136. H.336, 141
Which is as white and hair-less as an egge.....139. H.349, 2
Oft as your field, shall her old age renew,......140. H.355, 13
Shall run, as rivers, all throughout thy soyl......144. H.370, 6
Till this world shall dissolve as men,..........146. H.376, 12
Welcome as thunder to our beere:............146. H.377, 30
As the old Race of mankind did,..............147. H.377, 38
But as thy meate, so thy immortall wine......147. H.377, 71
As the Canary Isles were thine:...............148. H.377, 84
So draw, and paint, as none may do the like,..150. H.384, 5
As well the Winters, as the Summers Tide:....151. H.387, 6
As men, turne all to eares.....................151. H.388, 8
For as my Heart, ene so mine Eye............154. H.402, 5
'Tis but as day a kindling:..................154. H.404, 2
When as a publick ruine bears down All.......155. H.405, 18
But yet get chilren (as the neighbours say.)....156. H.411, 2
(Sweet as the Vestrie of the Oracles.)........157. H.414, 4
As when to Jove Great Juno goes perfum'd.....157. H.414, 8
Wo'd I see Lawn, clear as the Heaven, and thin?
158. H.416, 1
Sil. Words sweet as Love it self. Montano, Hark.
159. H.421, 17
As Beasts unto the Altars go..................161. H.425, 9
(As Salust saith) co-incident to feare...........162. H.430, 2
Full as a Bee with Thyme, and Red,............165. H.443, 9
As Cherry harvest, now high fed.............165. H.443, 10
Lust ha's no eares; He's sharpe as thorn;......165. H.443, 13
Who as they lowe empearl with milk..........166. H.443, 41
His Moon-tann'd Mab, as somewhat sick,.......167. H.443, 84
And (Love knowes) tender as a chick.........167. H.443, 85
As a Drink-offering, to the dead:..............169. H.449, 20
See, see a Jemme (as rare as Bælus eye.).......172. H.459, 8
Thee live, as dead and in thy grave;..........174. H.465, 12
(As that chaste Queen of Ithaca..............174. H.465, 30
Thy thoughts as cold, as is thy sleep:..........175. H.465, 48
As one triumphant; when I find.............176. H.465, 79
As One,.......................................178. H.475, 4
As when the Beames..........................181. H.484, 6
As the aire that circles me:....................183. H.490, 18
Even as the meanest Flower...................184. H.493, 8
We two (as Reliques left) will have............190. H.515, 11
As is the mould:..............................190. H.515, 16
As lull'd asleep;..............................190. H.515, 38
As Robes laid by;............................190. H.515, 40
As if they started at Bo-peep,..................194. H.525, 4
As in Pictures we descry,.......................194. H.527, 8
As thou deserv'st, be proud; then gladly let....194. H.529, 1
And as He shuts, close up to Maids again.......196. H.537, 4
As Wine......................................198 H.544, 5
As in our clothes, so likewise he who lookes,....202. H.559, 1
I cannot pipe as I was wont to do,............205. H.573, 1
As Blossomes of the Almond Tree..............203. H.562, 6
I plaid with Love, as with the fire............203. H.563, 1
But ne'r so much as licks the speckled shells:..204. H.568, 2
With superstition, (as the Cream of meates.)....204. H.568, 4
Clean my Roomes, as Temples be,............204. H.569, 5
As in a Globe of Radiant fire, and grac't......207. H.575, 58
But stinking breath, I do as hell abhorre it.......210. H.588, 2
As when the Sweet Maria lived here:..........214. H.612, 10
As great men lead; the meaner follow on,......214. H.614, 3
Where merry as the Maids we'l be.............215. H.616, 2
As now a Satyr, then a Swan;................215. H.616, 17
And sigh, and kiss, as Lovers do:..............215. H.616, 20
As wearied Pilgrims, once possest.............216. H.617, 1
What is a Kisse? Why this, as some approve;..218. H.622, 1
Alive, as Noble Westmorland;................218. H.626, 11
Lungs (as some, say) ne'r sets him down to eate,
223. H.637, 1
Tread, Sirs, as lightly as ye can.............226. H.644, 1
Cob clouts his shooes, and as the story tells,....226. H.648, 1
Sound Teeth has Lucie, pure as Pearl, and small,
226. H.649, 1
Sweet as the blossomes of the Vine..........230. H.662, 34
Of short sweet grasse, as backs with wool.....230. H.662, 43
So little left, as if they ne'r had been:..........231. H.664, 4
Of teeth, as deaf as nuts, and all her own.......232. H.668, 6
(As is that ayre that circles thee).............233. H.670, 18
And that wee'l do; as men, who know,........233 H.670, 36
Me, as a fear'd infection:......................235. H.677, 6
Yet scarre-crow-like I'le walk, as one,..........235. H.677, 7
As Heaven had spent all perfumes there.......237. H.686, 12
And clos'd her up, as in a Tombe...............237. H.686, 16
As the Godhead doth indite...................242. H.714, 6
A Heifer smooth, and black as jet,..............243. H.716, 8
And wanton as a Kid as yet..................243. H.716, 10
As Kine, when they at milking meet...........243. H.716, 30
Over thine Oat, as Soveraigne................244. H.716, 40
As many Lawes and Lawyers do expresse......244. H.718, 1
As stones and salt gloves use to give, even so...248. H.731, 3
As my small Cruse best fits my little Wine......249. H.733, 3
As my small Jarre best fits my little Oyle.......249. H.733, 6
As my small stuffe best fits my little Shed.......249. H.733, 9
As my small Bell best fits my little Spire.......249. H.733, 12
As my small Pipe best fits my little note.........249. H.733, 15
As sweetly Lady, give me leave to tell ye,....249. H.733, 17
As colours steale into the Peare or Plum,......250. H.737, 6
She lookt as she'd been got with child..........251. H.740, 7
White as Zenobias teeth, the which the Girles..251. H.741, 1
(As other Townes and Cities were) for gold,....251. H.745, 6
Strikes me dead as any stone?................254. H.757, 6
Such as the Prince is, will his People be.........255. H.759, 2
Go to Feast, as others do.....................255. H.761, 2
Base in action as in clothes:..................255. H.761, 12
I cannot love, as I have lov'd before:........258. H.768, 1
Beere small as Comfort, dead as Charity........262. H.783, 16
As you doe give them Wassailing...........264. H.787, 4
Orpheus he went (as Poets tell)...............265. H.798, 1
(As Lamps for everlasting shining here:)........267. H.804, 8
As Julia looks when she doth dress............268. H.811, 9
As smooth, and nak't, as she that was..........271. H.824, 7
As purest Pearles, or Pebles do...............271. H.824, 11
As Lillies shrin'd in Christall, so............271. H.824, 13
As Love shall helpe me, I admire.............272. H.828, 9
Because as Plants by water grow,.............273. H.832, 3
Peapes he do's strut, and pick his Teeth, as if..273. H.835, 1
Was cheese full ripe with Teares, with Bread as sad.
273. H.835, 4
True Love is tonguelesse as a Crocodile..........274. H.837, 8
Faire as Eve in Paradice:....................274. H.838, 2
He weepes and sighs (as weary of his life.)....275. H.842, 2
Teares have their springs from joy, as well as woe.
275. H.842, 4
As if or'e washt in Hippocrene................277. H.857, 2
Jone as my Lady is as good i'th' dark...........279. H.864, 2
Those faces (sower as Vineger.)...............279. H.868, 2
(As in an other Rosamond.)..................281. H.876, 4
Caught my poore soule, as in a snare:..........281. H.876, 8
As aires doe breathe, or winds doe blow:.......282. H.881, 8
New things succeed, as former things grow old.
285. H.892, 22
(As to the breaking of a Bride-Cake) home:...286. H.898, 10
I freeze as fast, and shake for cold............290. H.915, 2
As some plants prosper best by cuts and blowes;
292. H.929, 3
Who, kissing, kill such Saints as these?........294. H.937, 6
As in the River Julia did,.....................294. H.939, 5
He toucht me so, as that I burn,.............295. H 942, 11
As Cadmus once a new way found,............297. H.948, 5
As dearest Peace, after destructive Warre:....300. H.961, 2
Welcome as slumbers; or as beds of ease.........300. H.961, 3
As to a still protecting Deitie..................300. H.961, 16
And as time past when Cato the Severe..........301. H.962, 1
Stood as he had been turn'd from flesh to stone:
301. H.962, 4
As my weake shoulders cannot beare...........303. H.973, 9
As when the disagreeing Commons throw......303. H.975, 3
Then Case, as loud as any Serjant there.........303. H.975, 5
Grow up in Beauty, as thou do'st begin,.........304. H.979, 1
Smooth in each limb as a die;................305. H.984, 20
Sharply pointed as a thorn:...................306. H.984, 22
Ever gamesome as an ape:....................306. H.984, 29
But yet harmless as a sheep...................306. H.984, 30
May fart for joy, as well as shout:............306. H.987, 2
As is your name, so is your comely face,.........307. H.992, 1
And as that part, so every portion else,.........307. H.992, 5
As one.......................................308. H.993, 7
As flowrie vestures doe descrie...............311. H.1010, 7
And as in meanes, in minde all torne.........312. H.1016, 6
Me thought I saw (as I did dreame in bed)....313. H.1017, 1
Ile live as one Regenerate...................313. H.1020, 8
To bath in thee (as thousand others doe.)......315. H.1028, 6
Must revell, as Queene, in the Court here.......317. H.1035, 6
As when ye innocent met here.................317. H.1035, 30
As big as a Cowle............................320. H.1051, 5
For as I will not sell ye,......................321. H.1055, 2
Or sho'dst thou prize me as a Dish............321. H.1056, 11
The first as Doctor, and the last as Knight.....322. H.1062, 12
For as farre as that doth light,..............322. H.1064, 5

This I am sure; I Ravisht stood, as one......326. H.1080, 9
And look as all were capable of Love:.........326. H.1080, 12
(As with a Magick) laid them all agen:........326. H.1080, 18
As if we sho'd for ever part?..................328. H.1090, 2
Which sits as Dew of Roses there:............328. H.1090, 9
As Inapostate, to the thing he heares,..........330. H.1100, 16
When Pimpes feat sweat (as they doe often use).332. H.1113, 1
And as our bad, more then our good Works are:..339. N.1, 2
And tast thou them as saltlesse there,............339. N.3, 5
Him, as He is, is labour without end...........340. N.8, 2
Lambs, by the Law, which God requires as due..341. N.9, 2
That powres in oyle, as well as wine............342. N.17, 10
God, as He is most Holy knowne;..............343. N.23, 1
Do with me, God! as Thou didst deal with John,
343. N.25, 1
As Gospell tells,...............................345. N.33, 14
As for to beg my bread from doore to doore;..347. N.39, 2
As to speak, Lord, say and hold...............347. N.40, 4
Low is my porch, as is my Fate,..............350. N.47, 11
Like as my Parlour, so my Hall...............350. N.47, 17
Even as monilesse, as He...................354. N.59, 14
As men do wane in thankfulnesse.............358. N.76, 2
Slowly her chariot drives, as if that she........358. N.77, 3
When a mans Faith is frozen up, as dead;......359. N.80, 1
Cold as Paddocks though they be,..............364. N.95, 3
With zeale alike, as 'twas begun;...............366. N.97, 25
But as Heavens publike and immortall Eye....371. N. 113, 5
Ghost-like, as in my meaner sepulcher;.........371. N.115, 4
And comely as the Chrysolite.................375. N. 123, 76
Or as a neat...................................375. N.123, 78
These hung, as honours o're thy Grave,........375. N.123, 86
God, as He's potent, so He's likewise known,..378. N.135, 1
As just Men are intitled Gods, yet none......379. N.143, 3
True rev'rence is (as Cassiodore doth prove)....380. N.147, 1
God tempteth no one (as S. Aug'stine saith)..380. N.150, 1
God (as the learned Damascen doth write)......381. N.161, 1
Jehovah, as Boëtius saith,.....................382. N.168, 1
Or Good at all, (as learn'd Aquinas saith.)....383. N.173, 2
Paradise is (as from the Learn'd I gather)....383. N.177, 1
For those, who did as malefactors die........384. N.180, 4
But, as they walk't here in their vestures white,.384. N.181, 4
As Sun-beames pierce the glasse, and streaming in,
385. N.184, 1
'Tis (as S. Bernard saith) but seemingly.......385. N.188, 4
The Virgin Marie was (as I have read)......385. N.190, 1
So long (it seem'd) as Maries Faith was small,....386. N.192, 1
But Mary cal'd then (as S. Ambrose saith).....386. N.192, 4
Sabbaths are threefold, (as S. Austine sayes:)..386. N.194, 1
Noah the first was (as Tradition sayes)..........386. N.195, 1
To burn, not shine (as learned Basil saith.)....387. N.202, 2
Ev'n as the sprinkled bloud cal'd on..........387. N.203, 3
Of ours, as is the rising of the wheat..........388. N.208, 6
Either as when (the learned Schoolemen say)....388. N.210, 2
The good by mercy, as the bad by paines.........389. N.212, 2
The sheet I sleep in, as my Winding-sheet......392. N.230, 18
To me, as to the gen'rall Doome,............393. N.232, 2
When as the Mountains quak'd for dread,.....393. N.232, 5
And as all-present, so all-filling too............394. N.237, 2
As when, in humane nature He works more...395. N.244, 3
'Tis never read there (as the Fathers say)......396. N.249, 5
As my little Pot doth boyle,...................397. N.258, 1
Not as a thief, shalt Thou ascend the mount,..398. N.263, 15
As Hell, and Earth, and Heav'n may stand amaz'd.
399. N.263, 31
I flie from Thee, as others did:................399. N.265, 2
To vanquish Hell, as here He conquer'd Death?..403. N.271, 6
Parting the paire, as wee may well suppose.....404. A.1, 13
As divers strings do singly disagree............406. A.1, 107
As In a more Conspicuous Text...............407. A.2, 32
His soule as to a bedd of spice..............408. A.2, 44
As in a bedd of Frankensence.................408. A.2, 46
That smooth as Oyle, sweet softe and Cleane..408. A.2, 55
As is the childish Bloome of Beane,...............408. A.2, 56
White handes as smooth, as Mercies, bring.......408. A.2, 59
Or lyke as woole meetes steele, giue way.........408. A.2, 69
(As wth a Tempeste) Nature through the worlde.410. A.3, 24
As Fame or Rumour, hath or Trumpe or Tongue.
411. A.3, 46
Soe wth like lookes, as once the Ministrell......411. A.3 67
Shall want a Hand-mayde, (as she ofte will vse)..412. A.3, 100
Thoughe as a seruant, yet a Mayde of Honor...412. A.3, 102
Smooth as the Childhood of the yeare..........413. A.4, 4
As faith can seale It you;....................414. A.5, 4
When as some kinde..........................414. A.5, 13
With as cold frost, as erst we meet with fire;......414. A.6, 10
With such white vowes as fate can nere dissever..414. A.6, 11
Cha. I will be gentle as that Air which yeelds...416. A.8, 7
But such as have been drown'd in this wilde sea,
417. A.8, 31
Know, to' th' hearing as the touch.............418. A.9, 50
These have their Fate, and wear away as Men;..419. A.10, 2
— — — — — — — — — — —, ...429. var. H.263, 22
or blend so as the sight..................431. ins. H.283, 50i
begin to pinke as weary that the warres...432. ins. H.283, 140b
— — — — — — — — — — —, ...437. var. H.336, 108
(As if it was a tribute paid)............439. ins. H.443, 45c
As Butter'd bred, the which the wild......439. ins. H.443, 45p
Of higher price, as halfe-iet-ringes........440. ins. H.443, 45s
— — — — — — — — — — —, ...441. var. H.465, 24

Ascend Not as a thief, shalt Thou ascend the mount,
398. N.263, 15
Why then begin, great King! ascend Thy Throne,
399. N.263, 28

Ascendant For an Ascendent throughly Auspicate:
300. H.961, 10

Ascended He that ascended in a cloud, shall come
382. N.162, 1

Ascent In the ascent of curious Lace,..........202. H.560, 6

Ashes That joynt to ashes sho'd be burnt,........28. H.85, 7
May blow my ashes up, and strike thee blind...49. H.138. 8
Of ashes, scarce suffice.........................81. H.201, 43
Or else to ashes he will waste.................113. H.283, 40
What needs she fire and ashes to consume,......178. H.474, 5
Here, her ashes, or her Urne..................276. H.848, 5
With ashes knead,...............................353. N.56, 8
— — — — — — — — — — —, ...426. var. H.197, 37
— — — — — — — — — — —, ...430. var. H.283, 28

Ash-heap Left in this rak't-up Ash-heap, as a mark
78. H.197, 37

Ash-heaps His soule to Ash-heaps in that rich perfume?
113. H. 283, 28
Of Ash-heapes, in the which ye use............127. H.319, 21
— — — — — — — — — — —, ...453. var. H.283, 39

Ash-pans They have their Ash-pans, & their Brooms
92. H.223, 101

Aside To get thine ends, lay bashfulnesse aside;......8. H.12, 1
Or laid aside forlorne;.........................106. H.262, 6
Makes holy these, all others lay aside:..........114. H.283, 98
To lay thy pen and ink aside?...................357. N.72, 12

Ask Who feares to aske, doth teach to be deny'd....8. H.12, 2
And ask why....................................12. H.26, 4
If so be, you ask me where.....................19. H.53, 3
They vow'd to ask the Gods....................31. H.92, 4
I'm sure she'll ask no more...................43. H.123, 36
But if thy whimpring looks doe ask me why?....46. H.128, 41
And ask, Where's now the colour, forme and trust
49. H.138, 4
Love bade me aske a gift,......................100. H.249, 1
Aske me, why I do not sing.................131. H.332, 1
If thou aske me (Deare) wherefore.............186. H.500, 1
Aske me why I send you here.................208. H.580, 1
Aske me why I send to you...................208. H.580, 3
Ask me why this flower do's show...............208. H.580, 7
Ask me why the stalk is weak..................208. H.580, 9
Won't for his tenth part ask you one.........208. H.581, 6
I dare not ask a kisse;........................231. H.663, 1
To ask our wages, e're our work be done.......241. H.708, 2
When These can aske, and Kings can give no more.
255. H.758, 4
Aske his Story, not this Stone...............289. H.910, 4
Aske me what hunger is, and Ile reply,..........293. H.931, 1
You aske me what I doe, and how I live?....312. H.1013, 1
If we may ask the reason, say;...............364. N.96, 11
Great things ask for, when thou dost pray,....381. N.158, 3
Ask not for gold, which metall is:............381. N.158, 6
In Gods commands, ne're ask the reason why;.397. N.260, 1
His spunge, and stick, do ask why Thou dost stay?
398. N.263, 11

Asked One ask'd me where the Roses grew?.....18. H.45, 1
I smiling, ask'd them what they did?...........18. H.47, 5
Some ask'd me where the Rubies grew?..........24. H.75, 1
Some ask'd how Pearls did grow, and where?...24. H.75, 5
I ask't thee oft, what Poets thou hast read,....66. H.174, 1
I askt my Lucia but a kisse;.................212. H.599, 1
Had I then askt her Maidenhead?.............212. H.599, 4
In the Vision I askt, why?....................219. H.628, 3
He askt an almes; I gave him bread,...........295. H.942, 5
When his Assignes askt him the reason why?...332. H.1114, 3
And askt me, when............................346. N.38, 9

Asking For loves sake asking almes of thee?......312. H.1014, 2

Asks He who asks almes in that so sacred Name,..347. N.39, 5

Asleep Lest Issue lye asleep.......................53. H.149, 18
Let Lullaby the pretty Prince asleep!..........86. H.213, 18
Charm me asleep, and melt me so............95. H. 227, 1
My paines asleep;.............................95. H.227, 17
Who, as soone, fell fast asleep,...............123. H.310, 3
My Organ fast asleep;........................144. H.371, 15
While all beauty lyes asleep..................170. H.450, 2
When as your Baby's lull'd asleep?............189. H.514, 2
As lull'd asleep;............................190. H.515, 38
Sung asleep with Lullabies:...................224. H.640, 2
And Lull asleepe.............................314. H.1024, 22
These Two asleep are: I'll but be Vndrest......419. A.10, 7

A-slumbering As Julia once a-slumb'ring lay,.......71. H.182, 1

Aspects By all Aspects that blesse............258. H.767, 11
All Aspects malevolent?.......................286. H.897, 6

Aspire See Re-aspire
They onely will aspire,........................81. H.201, 46

Aspires Or some full flame, which with a pride aspires,
45. H.128, 17

Aspiring Its humble selfe twixt twoe aspiring cloudes,
406. A.1, 84

Ass The Nagge (like to the Prophets **Asse**)......13. H.27, 6
To tire thy patient Oxe or **Asse**..................233. H.670, 3
Worship, and not to'th' **Asse** that carried her...330. H.1099, 6
An **Asse** unto Him, for an offering:...........384. N.179, 2
Assault not to this or that **assault**,........433. ins. H.283 140g
Assention By the **Assention** of thy Lawn, see All.154. H.403, 6
Assigns When his **Assignes** askt him the reason why?
332. H.1114, 3
Ass's soft-skin, or bath in **Asses** milke:.........149. H.377, 122
Assuage Then to **asswage**........................134. H.336, 91
Thou dost their wrath **asswage**..................373. N.122, 3
Assuaged **Asswag'd**, and he was well again.......18. H.46, 10
Assume Not only to your selves **assume**...........9. H.15, 5
And every thing **assume**.........................55. H.149, 65
Assumed The passive Aire such odour then **assum'd**,
157. H.414, 7
Assurance Till when, in such **assurance** live, ye may
38. H.106, 145
Assure Such let my life **assure** me, when my breath
392. N.230, 33
Assured This play, be **assur'd**,.................247. H.727, 7
Be yet **assur'd**, thou shalt have one..............334. H.1123, 5
Assures (As this looking-glasse **assures**)........418. A.9, 28
Astonished E'ne so my numbers will **astonisht** be
301. H.962, 5
Astonishment To raise an Act to full **astonishment**;
415. A.7, 8
Astride The Hag is **astride**,...................225. H.643, 1
At (Partial List)
Who with thy leaves shall wipe (**at** need)..........6. H.5, 1
Let us (though late) **at** last (my Silvia) wed;....8. H.10, 1
A teare **at** all for that:.........................12. H.23, 6
For tincture, wonder **at**..........................12. H.23, 8
At childish Push-pin (for our sport) did play:..17. H.44, 2
Playing for sport, **at** Cherry-pit:...............19. H.49, 2
And comming downe, shall make no noise **at** all...21. H.62, 6
(**At** first) infused with the same:...............24. H.73, 4
Two Cupids fell **at** odds;.........................31. H.92, 2
Wink **at** small faults, the greater, ne'rthelesse......32. H.95, 3
But thou **at** home, blest with securest ease,....36. H.106, 69
Buy'st Travell **at** the lowest price...............36. H.106, 82
Vice rules the Most, or All **at** Court:..........37. H.106, 90
He weares all day, and drawes those teeth **at** night.
46. H.129, 6
A Robin-Red-brest; who **at** view,................46. H.130, 4
At which poore Robin flew away:...............46. H.130, 10
When thou shalt laugh **at** my Religious dust;....49. H.138, 3
At which she smil'd; then with her hairs........50. H.139, 10
Such bashfulnesse **at** last........................54. H.149, 28
Open **at** your command;.........................57. H.149, 158
May Death yet come **at** last;....................58. H.149, 165
Noone-day and Midnight shall **at** once be seene:
59. H.154, 1
Trees, **at** one time, shall be both sere and greene:..59. H.154, 2
To shew **at** once, both night and day............64. H.169, 8
Or fret **at** all...................................65. H.172, 11
Where so much sirrop ran **at** waste..............71. H.182, 18
At which she smil'd; and bade him goe.........71. H.182, 27
And had no other pride **at** all,..................75. H.193, 30
At full their proper excellence;..................76. H.193, 38
Blush not **at** all for that; since we have set......76. H.194, 5
All thoughts, but such as aime **at** getting Princes,
77. H.197, 8
When her high carriage did **at** once present......79. H.197, 75
Play ye **at** Hide or Seek,.........................83. H.207, 7
At Noone of Day, was seene a silver Star,......86. H.213, 20
At most a fault, 'tis but a fault of love..........86. H.213, 28
At my returne,...................................87. H.214, 13
Something for Shew-bread, and **at** hand..........92. H.223, 69
I have Mirtle rods, (**at** will).....................98. H.238, 9
At Draw-Gloves we'l play,.......................99. H.243, 1
Roses **at** first were white,.......................105. H.258, 1
Reaching **at** heaven,.............................112. H.283, 5
(Just **at** the setting of the Sun)................123. H.306, 6
At my up-rising next, I shall,..................123. H.306, 11
No newes of Navies burnt **at** Seas;.............126. H.319, 1
That sleeps **at** home; and sayling there **at** ease,..128. H.323, 3
That sighs **at** others death; smiles at his own...129. H.323, 13
And my tongue **at** one time mute..............131. H.332, 6
Henceforth **at** such a rate,.......................137. H.340, 11
Who spurn'd **at** Envie; and co'd bring, with ease,
137. H.341, 5
Who art chief **at** marriages,.....................141. H.360, 2
The coblers getting time, is **at** the Last.........144. H.374, 2
Who hither **at** her wonted howers..............145. H.376, 5
Weathers, and never grudged **at**...............147. H.377, 64
While Reverence, waiting **at** the bashfull board,..148. H.377, 75
Driving these sharking trades, is out **at** heels.....153. H.398, 2
Raspe playes **at** Nine-holes; and 'tis known he gets
154. H.400, 1
Broke **at** the Losse of Maiden-heads:..........167. H.443, 107
Next, **at** that great Platonick yeere,............190. H.515, 47
As if they started **at** Bo-peep,.................194. H.525, 4
Then **at** th' opening of mine eyes,..............199. H.549, 3
All conditions I aime **at**........................209. H.585, 3
Jone, and my Lady have **at** that time one,......209. H.586, 5
And perish **at** the last..........................211. H.596, 16
Knock **at** a Starre with my exalted Head......214. H.612, 14
We'l venter (if we can) **at** wit:.................215. H.616, 4
If not, **at** Draw-gloves we will play;............215. H.616, 5
Playing **at** Questions and Commands:...........215. H.616, 8
And smiling **at** our selves, decree,..............216. H.616, 29
At noone of Night are a working...............225. H.643, 18
And can'st not mend, but carpe **at** it:...........229. H.660, 2
Love **at** no time idle is:.........................235. H.678, 2
But **at** push-pin (half the day:)..................235. H.678, 4
State **at** a distance adds to dignities...........236. H.682, 2
At Stool-ball, Lucia, let us play,.................238. H.690, 1
At trundling of the Ball,.........................238. H.690, 6
At Post and Paire, or Slam, Tom Tuck would play
238. H.693, 1
Twice two fell out, all rotten **at** the root.........247. H.728, 2
That either profits, or not hurts **at** all...........252. H.748, 2
Are the Junketts still **at** Wakes:.................255. H.761, 4
Who **at** a dead lift,..............................256. H.762, 13
And wonder **at** Those Things that thou dost know.
257. H.763, 22
Pusse and her Prentice both **at** Draw-gloves play;
260. H.773, 1
At last, i' th' noone of winter, did appeare......262. H.783, 13
We pray for showers (**at** our need)...........279. H.867, 5
Which wee, and times to come, shall wonder **at**..310. H.1002, 2
— — — — — — — — —, ...424. var. H.164, 10
Welcome **at** last unto the Threshold, Time..431. ins. H.283, 60k
— — — — — — — — — — — —, ...432. var. H.283, 84
— — — — — — — — — — — —, ...437. var. H.336, 116
Athenians Mercy, the wise **Athenians** held to be..380. N.148, 1
Atoms Conserves of **Atomes**, and the mites,..435. ins. H.293, cc
Attained Has not **attain'd** his Noone............125. H.316, 4
Attempt **Attempt** the end, and never stand to doubt;
311. H.1008, 1
Attempted Hast thou **attempted** greatnesse? then go on,
252. H.747, 1
Where War with rashnesse is **attempted**, there
268. H.813, 3
Attempts Shame checks our first **attempts**; but then 'tis prov'd
362. N.85, 1
Attend Pleasures, many here **attend** ye,..........125. H.314, 5
While sweet-breath Nimphs, **attend** on you this Day.
140. H.354, 8
The Shooting Starres **attend** thee;..............217. H.619, 2
Of black-bore-cats to **attend** her;..............333. H.1122, 9
Attendant Shame is a bad **attendant** to a State:...182. H.488, 1
Attended **Attended** with those desp'rate cares,....36. H.106, 64
Nor courts thou Her because she's well **attended**..201. H.557, 7
Attended thus (in a most solemn wise).........286. H.898, 3
Attending With the white Vestures, all **attending** Thee.
196. H.539, 4
The State of Poets there **attending** Thee:......324. H.1071, 2
Attending.......................................377. N.128, 20
Attends And Genius who **attends**................54. H.149, 43
Attent While other Rusticks, lesse **attent**........101. H.250, 23
Attica The smoake of his beloued **Attica**,........412. A.3, 74
Attilius Torments for high **Attilius**; and, with want,
370. N.108, 9
Augean To purifie this my **Augean** stable:........357. N.73, 2
Aught Pauls hands do give, nought else for **ought** we know.
248. H.731, 4
For **ought** that I could say.....................346. N.38, 6
Will blush to death, if **ought** be spi'd.........366. N.98, 13
Augmentation All serve to th' **Augmentation** of his good.
349. N.44, 4
Augustine God tempteth no one (as S. **Aug'stine** saith)
380. N.150, 1
Augustus May (Great **Augustus**) goe along with You.
300. H.961, 18
Aunt That which the **Aunt** did tast, not eate;
439. ins. H.443, 45e
Aurora See how **Aurora** throwes her faire..........67. H.178, 3
Or like vnto **Aurora** when shee setts..............404. A.1, 3
Auspicate For an Ascendent throughly **Auspicate**:
300. H.961, 10
Auspice All Rites well ended, with faire **Auspice** come
286. H.898, 9
Auspicious High with thine own **Auspitious** Destinies:
181. H.483, 2
Your eager Bridegroome with **auspitious** feet.....216. H.618, 2
Why then goe forward, sweet **Auspicious** Bride,
431. ins. H. 283, 50a
Austin Sabbaths are threefold, (as S. **Austine** sayes:)
386. N.194, 1
Confession twofold is (as **Austine** sayes,)......395. N.243, 1
Author So, that an **Author** needs no other Bayes.188. H.506, 11
If the chiefe **author** of the faction dyes;..........132. H.335, 2
Authority Due to the Merits, not **Authoritie**.......120. H.296, 2
Autumn's Now **Autumne's** come, when all those flowrie aids
114. H.283, 92
Avaunt Pale care, avant,.........................368. N.104, 10
Ave-Mary Ere **Ave-Mary** thou canst say..........271. H.824, 3
Avert But to **avert** the worst;..................55. H.149, 83
Avoid But **avoid** here...........................307. H.988, 12
But to instruct them, to **avoid** all snares........378. N.137, 5

But that held back by sin......................370. N.111, 4
Freely from them, and hold none back at all.....380. N.151, 2
To change, or call back, His past Sentences......389. N.216, 4
My lipps shall send a 1000 back to you...........414. A.5, 16
Thy thoughts to say, I backe am come....441. ins. H.465, 14b
Listen, while they call backe the former yeare,
443. var. H.575, 52
Backling — — — — — — — — —, ...440. var. H.443, 104
Backs Of short sweet grasse, as backs with wool..230. H.662, 43
Back-turning Back-turning slackens Resolution....252. H.747, 2
Backward Fore- or backward in her love:..........82. H.203, 8
Forward, or backward, side-ward, and what pace.148. H.377, 93
Backward he should not looke while he..........265. H.798, 5
Any part backward in the Deitie..................342. N.18, 2
Throwing his eye balls backward, to suruaye....411. A.3, 73
Bacon And Bacon, (which makes full the meale).101. H.250, 31
Bad See Bade
If good I'le smile, if bad I'le sigh for Thee.........6. H.3, 8
Good princes must be pray'd for: for the bad......32. H.97, 1
Or here so bad, but you may pardon them........64. H.168, 6
Lame, and bad times, with those are past,.......134. H.336, 82
Reward it is, that makes us good or bad.........139. H.351, 2
Mon. Bad are the times. Sil. And wors then they are we.
159. H.421, 1
Mon. Troth, bad are both; worse fruit, and ill the tree:
159. H.421, 2
And reckon this for fortune bad..............179. H.476, 38
Shame is a bad attendant to a State:............182. H.488, 1
Dash all bad Poems out of countenance........187. H.506, 10
O! Times most bad,...........................211. H.596, 1
Of both our Fortunes good and bad we find......257. H.765, 1
Since for one Bad, one Good I know:..........283. H.885, 2
For one Medea that was bad,...................283. H.885, 5
A Good and Bad. Sirs credit me...............283. H.885, 10
Bad are all surfeits: but Physitians call..........286. H.895, 1
Tis but a dog-like madnesse in bad Kings,.......292. H.929, 1
Must shun the bad, I, and suspect the best.......305. H.981, 2
Times bad...................................308. H.993, 22
And as our bad, more then our good Works are:....339. N.1, 2
To do ten Bad, for one Good Action...........339. N.1, 6
The bad to punish, and the good t'amend..........343. N.26, 2
I do believe, the bad must goe.................358. N.78, 7
The Bad among the Good are here mixt ever:....383. N.172, 1
The Good without the Bad are here plac'd never..383. N.172, 2
Draw out of bad a soveraigne good to man.......383. N.176, 2
To th' good and bad, in common, for two ends:..387. N.201, 2
The good by mercy, as the bad by paines.......389. N.212, 2
Departing hence, where Good and Bad souls go....416. A.8, 26
Bade I brake my bonds of Love, and bad thee goe,....6. H.3, 5
Anthea bade me tye her shooe;.................14. H.33, 1
I bade him not goe seek;.......................18. H.45, 2
But forthwith bade my Julia shew................18. H.45, 3
I smil'd; and bade him once more prove,.........64. H.166, 9
Untrusse, his Master bade him; and that word....65. H.171, 5
At which she smil'd; and bade him goe.........71. H.182, 27
But stay the time till we have bade Good night..73. H.186, 2
Love bade me aske a gift,......................100. H.249, 1
In a Dreame, Love bad me go..................219. H.628, 1
He bade me then that Neck-lace use;...........279. H.863, 9
Bælus' See, see a Jemme (as rare as Bælus eye.)..172. H.459, 8
Bag See Honey-bag
About the sweet bag of a Bee,....................31. H.92, 1
And gave the Bag between them...............31. H.92, 12
And take his bag; but thus much know,.........71. H.182, 28
And well bestrutted Bees sweet bagge:........119. H.293, 34
A Bag and Bottle thou shalt have;............192. H.521, 21
Bagpipe And to the Bag-pipe all addresse;......127. H.319, 47
Baiae Baiæ, nor keep.........................133. H.336, 43
Bait May baite his hooke, with maggots taken thence
282. H.879, 4
Bake And Bake the floure of Amber for thy bread..269. H.818, 6
Baked Of rosted warden, or bak'd peare,........145. H.375, 23
And this rawly bak't will bring................284. H.890, 5
Baker The Bran the Baker did his Breech bewray:.219. H.630, 2
Bald Has blear'd his eyes: Besides, his head is bald..33. H.99, 2
Be she bald, or do's she weare................253. H.750, 10
Baldwin Prewdence Baldwin (once my maid)......262. H.782, 2
Ball See Cowslip-ball, Eyeball, Fast-ball, Fust-ball, Fuz-ball-pudding, Stool-ball
Woe, woe to them, who (by a ball of strife)......26. H.79, 1
Then like a Globe, or Ball of Wild-fire, flie,......87. H.215, 9
This ball of Cow-slips, these she gave me here...159. H.421, 16
At trundling of the Ball,......................238. H.690, 6
Ballad-mongers Base Ballad-mongers, who vsurpe thy name
412. A.3, 90
Balls See Eyeballs, Fuz-balls
Their balls to Cindars: haste,..................113. H.283, 39
Balls of Cowslips, Daisie rings,...............306. H.984, 25
We Cowslip balls,............................361. N.83, 52
Throwing his eye balls backward, to suruaye......411. A.3, 73
Balm Of Balme, of Oyle, of Spice, and Amber-Greece..5. H.1, 8
Yet I bring Balme and Oile to heal your sore....52. H.146, 22
And make me smooth as Balme, and Oile againe...67. H.176, 6
You are like Balme inclosed (well).............88. H.216, 13
But turne soone after calme, as Balme, or Oile...105. H.259, 4
That breath the Balm, the myrrh, the Nard shal be,
129. H.327, 5
And 'noint with Tirian Balme; for when........133. H.336, 34
By pouring Balme and Oyle into her wounds.....201. H.557, 18
Sit smiling in the Meads; where Balme and Oile,.205. H.575, 3
Balm may thy Trees drop, and thy Springs runne oyle
269. H.818, 7
A soveraign balme found out to cure me........274. H.841, 4
In Gilead though no Balme be found,............342. N.17, 5
Let Balme, and Cassia send their scent..........361. N.83, 65
Bring'st, in Thy Blood, a Balm, that shall........366. N.98, 23
Pure Balm, that shall........................401. N.268, 12
A breath of balm along the Elizean fields...........416. A.8, 8
Balsam — — — — — — — — —, ...438. var. H.412, 26
Balsamum To bring him Lint, and Balsamum,......18. H.46, 6
To Thee, for curing Balsamum:..................377. N.129, 2
Band But therewithall I'le bring the Band,........370. N.107, 7
Bands Sudds Launders Bands in pisse; and starches them
98. H.237, 1
Say (if she's fretfull) I have bands..............98. H.238, 6
So smell those bracelets, and those bands......145. H.375, 15
With bands of Cow-slips bind him;............157. H.412, 26
The neck with bands..........................172. H.458, 12
Bane When with Neglect, (the Lovers bane)......106. H.262, 9
Or bring some bane..........................210. H.591, 5
Colde Hemlocke, or the Libbards bane....422. ins. H.106, 116b
Banes See Banns
Banish Banish consent, and 'tis no sinne........175. H.465, 56
Banished Banish'd from thee I live; ne'r to return,..19. H.52, 3
As oft as Night is banish'd by the Morne,........26. H.80, 1
If not, (as banisht) I will live alone............60. H.156, 5
— — — — — — — — —, ...437. var. H. 336, 74
Banishment To banishment....................144. H.371, 8
Into a long and irksome banishment;..........242. H.713, 14
Froms Natiue Cuntrye, into Banishm^t,..........411. A.3, 72
Bank Rest but a while here, by this bank of Lillies,
86. H.213, 10
Track they redeem a bank or moose..........165. H.443, 26
A Primrose Banke did cross her way,........288. H.908, 3
Banked Bankt all with Lillies, and the Cream....179. H.476, 14
Banks See Lily-banks, Primrose-banks
Glide by the banks of Virgins then, and passe..113. H.283, 41
When of the Banks their leave they take;........180. H.478, 6
Never make sick your Banks by surfeiting.....316. H.1028, 24
— — — — — — — — — —, ...442. var. H.575, 3
Banns O Frost! O Snow! O Haile forbid the Banes.
40. H.113, 2
Banquet (Invited to the Thesbian banquet) ta'ne..78. H.197, 66
Go to your banquet then, but use delight,......220. H.633, 18
Banquets Kisses are but dry banquets to a Feast.
265. H.797, 2
Baptime See Baptism
Bapti'me See Baptism
Baptism Were I to give thee Baptime, I wo'd chuse.28. H.84, 1
A Baptime o're the flowers......................95. H.227, 26
Which makes the Bapti'me; 'tis decreed,........365. N.97, 18
The strength of Baptisme, that's within;.........396. N.253, 1
Baptize Baptize me and thee, and so............303. H.974, 3
Bar Now barre the doors, the Bride-groom puts..56. H.149, 121
Barre close as you can, and bolt fast too your doore,
97. H. 233, 1
Prithee, when next thou do'st invite, barre State,.161. H.424, 3
That Bar, this Bend; that Fess, this Cheveron;..295. H.941, 4
To whose dismall Barre, we there..............373. N.121, 7
The Bench is then their place; and not the Barre..
376. N.126, 2
To barr out bolde Adulteryes,................. . 408. A.2, 36
Barbarous Tis worse then barbarous cruelty to show
199. H.550, 1
Barbels To lard the shambles: Barbels bred.....133. H.336, 46
Barber The Barber stopt his Nose, and ranne away.
323. H.1066, 4
Bards Those Bardes, and I, all in a Chorus sing,.324. H.1071, 3
Bare Then I co'd say, that house is bare,........358. N.75, 9
— — — — — — — — — —, ...450. var. A.9, 32
Bares See Bears
Barge In Barge (with boughes and rushes beautifi'd)
315. H.1028, 8
Bark If having run my Barque on ground,......94. H.225, 5
That my Barque may safely runne............129. H.325, 3
Our Barke; yet she will keepe alive............134. H.336, 60
My wearied Barke, O Let it now be Crown'd!..334. H.1127, 1
To bark, or bite, without Thee?..............373. N.122, 12
— — — — — — — — — —, ...424. var. H.164, 10
Barking Keeping the barking stomach wisely quiet,
35. H.106, 29
Barks — — — — — — — — —, ...436. var. H.336, 60
Barley Wheat, Barley, Rie, or Oats; what is't....376. N.127, 3
Barley-Breaks Y'ave had at Barly-breaks..........56. H.149, 118
The Virgins lost at Barley-breakes,.......440. ins. H.443, 45u
Barn Be ye to the Barn then born,... ....58. H.149, 169
Whose Field his feot is, and whose Barn his shooe?
270. H.822, 4
Barns To strut thy barnes with sheafs of Wheat...233. H.670, 21
Barque See Bark

But out of hope his wife might die to beare 'em. 72. H.184, 2
Amint. And I will beare along with you.......86. H.213, 39
To kisse, and beare away......................110. H.274, 7
Plumpe Bed beare up, and swelling like a cloud, 115. H.283, 112
Bear up the Magick bough, and spel:........136. H.336, 134
The saucie Subjects still will beare the sway.....138. H.345, 2
Trees never beare, unlesse they first do blow...180. H.477, 6
The vowes of those, that children beare:......221. H.633, 57
A Gyges Ring they beare about them still,.......250. H.737, 1
Other mens sins wee ever beare in mind;.......253. H.751, 1
If ill, then Kings, not Souldiers beare the blame. 260. H.774, 4
Wassaile the Trees, that they may beare........264. H.787, 1
Do's Fortune rend thee? Beare with thy hard Fate: 270. H.820, 1
No cowards must his royall Ensignes beare.......280. H.872, 2
Trees this year beare; next, they their wealth with-hold: 292. H.922, 3
To have friends to beare a part:..............302. H.968, 4
As my weake shoulders cannot beare..........303. H.973, 9
W'ave more to beare our charge, then way to go? 308. H.995, 2
Sometimes He strikes us more then flesh can beare; 341. N.10, 3
Besides my healthfull Ewes to beare............350. N.47, 47
Go prettie child, and beare this Flower........354. N.59, 1
Doth Jesus beare,...........................401. N.268, 2
(Heauen and my soule beare Record of my Vowe) 411. A.3, 48
I've more to beare my Chardge, then way to goe, 411. A.3, 54
Wee have noe vinyards which doe beare...436. ins. H.336, 48a
— — — — — — — — — — — —, ...437. var. H.336, 126
— — — — — — — — — — — —, ...447. var. A.1, 52
Beard And love to have my Beard..............65. H.170, 3
Bearded See Black-bearded
Beards But Beards of Mice, a Newt's stew'd thigh, 119. H.293, 37
Bearest Thou, thou that bear'st the sway.......281. H.874, 1
Bearing Bearing a Christall continent:.........187. H.504, 2
Bearing aloft this rich round world of wonder...405. A.1, 46
Bearing downe Time before you; hye......431. ins. H.283, 50c
Bears Prigg bears away the body and the sole..143. H.368, 4
When as a publick ruine bears down All.....155. H.405, 18
Where Fortune bears no sway o're things......190. H.515, 35
Where ev'ry tree & wealthy issue beares......205. H.575, 9
Tygers and Beares (I've heard some say)......252. H.746, 3
The King he beares the blame of all..........290. H.913, 2
A rowle of Parchment Clunn about him beares,.295. H.941, 1
Bares in it selfe a gracefull maiestye............404. A.1, 6
Beares vp twoe globes where loue and pleasure sitt, 405. A.1, 52
— — — — — — — — — — — —, ...447. var. A.1, 6
— — — — — — — — — — — —, ...453. var. H.283, 112
Beast No Beast, for his food,.................225. H.643, 13
Is the beast exempt from staine,..............280. H.870, 5
Of the holy Beast we bring..................280. H.870, 11
— — — — — — — — — — — —, ...445. var. H.730, 10
Beasts While leanest Beasts in Pastures feed,...77. H.196, 1
As Beasts unto the Altars go................161. H.425, 9
Nor Beasts (fond thing) but only humane soules. 248. H.730, 10
Not on the flesh of beasts, but on the seede 432. ins. H.283, 70f
Beat My puling Pipe to beat against thine eare:..17. H.42, 2
You have Pulses that doe beat................96. H.232, 9
Seas chafe and fret, and beat, and over-boile;..105. H.259, 3
And beat ye so, (as some dare say)..........105. H.260, 7
For which their cryes might beate against thine eares, 149. H.377, 125
Me thinks like mine, your pulses beat;.........157. H.413, 5
Beat with their num'rous feet, which by......165. H.443, 23
That my pulses high may beate................217. H.620, 3
Th' unequall Pulse to beat, as heretofore......254. H.756, 6
We know they dare not beate us;.............259. H.772, 8
Beat me, bruise me, rack me, rend me,.......351. N.48, 5
Lord, do not beat me,.........................351. N.49, 1
Know so long Treaties; beate the drumme.432. ins. H.283, 140c
Beaten In all that way no beaten path;..........372. N.118, 4
Beating Upon me beating ever:................353. N.56, 15
Beats Who's that (said I) beats there,............26. H.81, 5
Beats with a button'd-staffe the poore:........146. H.377, 14
Vertue best loves those children that she beates. 270. H.820, 4
Beaumont See Beamond
Beumont and Fletcher, Swans, to whom all eares 206. H.575, 51
Beauteous Then, beauteous Maid, you may retire;.49. H.136, 32
And beautious Bride we do confess y'are wise,..113. H.283, 51
Leaving a distance for the beawtious small....406. A.1, 89
Beauties These fresh beauties (we can prove)....15. H.37, 1
To all thy witching beauties, Goe, Away.......46. H.128, 40
Thee, and thy beauties; kisse, we will be friends, 78. H.197, 70

One night i' th' yeare, my dearest Beauties, come 222. H.634, 1
Sleep with thy beauties here, while we......375. N.123, 81
Beautified In Barge (with boughes and rushes beautifi'd) 315. H.1028, 8
Are beawtifi'd with faire fring'd canopies........404. A.1, 10
Beautiful Got, not so beautifull, as chast:........35. H.106, 34
Beautify And see your selfe to beautifie my Book; 94. H.226, 2
To beawtify the legg and foote withall..........406. A.1, 90
Beautifying Which for the better beawtifying shrowdes 406. A.1, 83
Beauty Beauty, no other thing is, then a Beame..33. H.102, 1
Of Womans beauty? and with hand more rude...49. H.138, 5
More beauty to commend......................75. H.193, 27
Neglected beauty perisheth apace...............97. H.234, 2
Then beauty turn'd to sowernesse............143. H.367, 2
While all beauty lyes asleep...................170. H.450, 2
O Flame of Beauty! come, appeare, appeare....191. H.516, 3
If Men can say that beauty dyes;............203. H.564, 1
For her beauty it was such..................274. H.838, 3
Leave others Beauty, to set up withall........299. H.958, 6
Grow up in Beauty, as thou do'st begin,......304. H.979, 1
A deale of beauty yet in thee...............375. N.123, 72
Next doth her chinne with dimpled beawty striue 405. A.1, 33
Whence beawty springs, and thus I kisse thy foot. 406. A.1, 112
Poor relique of the beawty, bone,..............418. A.9, 24
Of yor beawty death comes soone..............418. A.9, 46
— — — — — — — — — — — —, ...427. var. H.197, 70
— — — — — — — — — — — —, ...441. var. H.465, 18
Beauty's Beauti's no other but a lovely Grace...274. H.840, 1
Keepes line for line with Beauties Parallels.....307. H.992, 6
Her brest (a place for beawtyes throne most fitt) 405. A.1, 51
When all your world of Beautie's gone.......61. H.160, 10
Because See 'Cause
Because my Julia's lip was by,................12. H.23, 3
Because his Tongue was ty'd againe...........13. H.27, 10
You blame me too, because I cann't devise.....15. H.38, 3
And all, because they were possest..............25. H.78, 7
Ile write, because Ile give......................32. H.96, 1
That plague; because thou art content.........35. H.106, 22
Because he cannot sleep i'th' Church, free-cost..39. H.109, 4
And all because, Faire Maid, thou art..........47. H.132, 9
Or else because Grill's roste do's burn his Spit,..48. H.135, 3
And must we part, because some say,...........48. H.136, 1
Of these Reports; because you see.... ....49. H.136, 16
And Cruell Maid, because I see..................60. H.159, 1
Am I despis'd, because you say,..............63. H.164, 1
Because I doe..................................87. H.214, 3
Because I've liv'd so long a maid:...........97. H.235, 2
Because thou prizest things that are...........119. H.293, 3
Because y'are slow;..........................137. H.340, 4
Why weres he none? Because we may suppose,...154. H.401, 3
Is it because his money all is spent?..........160. H.423, 2
No, but because the Ding-thrift now is poore,...160. H.423, 3
That so thou art, because thou must.........175. H.465, 39
Because with Flowers her Temple was not drest: 197. H.539, 8
The next, because her Altars did not shine....197. H.539, 9
I did not sup, because no friends were there.....197. H.541, 2
Here we rejoyce, because no Rent............200. H.552, 7
Because we feed on no mans score:..........200. H.552, 14
Nor courts thou Her because she's well attended 201. H.557, 7
Because no fence,...........................213. H.609, 2
Or fold mine armes, and sigh, because I've lost 222. H.634, 12
Then you must like, because I love...........252. H.746, 8
Because as Plants by water grow,..............273. H.832, 3
No, but because he wo'd not have it seen,.....275. H.843, 3
Love, love me now, because I place..........278. H.859, 1
Because begot of my Immortall seed.........280. H.869, 6
Because thy selfe art comming to the Presse:..298. H.955, 10
Or else because th' art like a modest Bride....301. H.963, 3
Because his stock will not hold out for white...309. H.997, 2
Because not plac't here with the midst, or first...329. H.1092, 2
He said, because he got his wealth thereby.....332. H.1114, 4
Because I'me odious in thy sight,...............344. N.29, 9
Because the prettie Babe do's bleed...........366. N.98, 21
Because I send Thee all.......................376. N.125, 8
Because the Law forbad to sit and crie........384. N.180, 3
Because the wicked do partake of them:......387. N.201, 4
Because our flesh stood most in need of Him.....390. N.222, 4
because you feede.....................432. ins. H.283, 70e
Become By You become Immortall Substances...3. Ded.H, 10
What is become of me: there I................60. H.159, 5
Stray, to become lesse circular,..............134. H.336, 68
Tell me, white Angell; what is now become..403. N.271, 3
Becomes And more then well becomes the day?....48. H.136, 3
Bed See Bridal-bed, Bride-bed, Child-bed, Sweet-slugabed
And loving lie in one devoted bed..............8. H.10, 2
I dream'd we both were in a bed..............20. H.56, 1
The rest Ile speak, when we meet both in bed....24. H.74, 14

Looks like a Bride now, or a bed of flowers,....25. H.77, 5
So looks Anthea, when in bed she lyes,..........34. H.104, 1
Cuffe comes to Church much; but he keeps his bed
39. H.109, 1
And return him drunk to bed:................39. H.111, 10
Contented with the bed of one.................41. H.116, 8
The kisse of Virgins; First-fruits of the bed;..45. H.128, 7
To the bed, the bashfull Bride...............53. H.149, 10
To the bed, the bashfull Bride...............53. H.149, 20
To the bed, the bashfull Bride...............54. H.149, 30
To the bed, the bashfull Bride...............54. H.149, 40
The bed for luckie ends:....................54. H.149, 44
To the bed, the bashfull Bride...............54. H.149, 50
To the bed the bashfull Bride................55. H.149, 70
Watch, or did make the bed:..................56. H.149, 105
And now, Behold! the Bed or Couch........57. H.149, 131
And ravisht, plunge into the bed,............59. H.152, 9
Nor any bed to give the shew................63. H.164, 10
Nay! not so much as out of bed?............68. H.178, 9
And make my bed,...........................95. H.227, 6
Unto the bed the bashfull Bride;............109. H.271, 4
To bed, to bed, kind Turtles, now, and write...114. H.283, 71
To Bed; or her they'l tire,..................115. H.283, 109
Plumpe Bed beare up, and swelling like a cloud,
115. H.283, 112
The bed is ready, and the maze of Love.......115. H.283, 121
We'll call on Night, to bring ye both to Bed:...124. H.313, 10
May the Bed, and this short night,..........124. H.314, 3
Not for affection to her, or her Bed;.........129. H.326, 2
And makes more soft the Bridall Bed.........130. H.329, 7
The cole once spent, we'l then to bed,........136. H.336, 151
Tis Julia's Bed, and she sleeps there.........139. H.348, 3
Dear, in thy bed of Roses, then,.............146. H.376, 11
When out of bed my Love doth spring,......154. H.404, 1
I'th'bed of strawburies......................156. H.412, 16
Or here my Bed, or here my Grave...........158. H.420, 4
But in the Bridall Bed:.....................160. H.422, 12
His Bed, Male children shall beget...........162. H.429, 2
Halfe tipsie to the Fairie Bed,...............165. H.443, 4
And now the bed, and Mab possest...........168. H.443, 118
With this, that I am in thy bed...............175. H.465, 50
By holy Himen to the Nuptiall Bed............180. H.477, 2
Yet not a Lillie from the Bed appeares;........180. H.477, 4
Both Bed, and Bride.........................190. H.515, 10
Shall blesse thy Bed, and blesse thy Board.....192. H.521, 4
The soft sweet Mosse shall be thy bed,.........192. H.521, 5
But Age hath brought me right to Bed.......216. H.617, 6
Then feast, and coy't a little; then to bed.....216. H.618, 8
Sho'd see safe brought to Bed...............220. H.633, 17
Go then discreetly to the Bed of pleasure;......220. H.633, 24
Gander (they say) doth each night pisse a Bed:
223. H.636, 2
To have thy mind, and nuptiall bed,...........233. H.670, 11
About the Bed, there sighing stood..........237. H.686, 3
To the Bridall Bed,.........................239. H.695, 11
Must be the first man up, and last in bed:....259. H.771, 2
They draw their clothes off both, so draw to bed.
260. H.773, 4
And Genius waits to have us both to bed.......261. H.781, 6
It is no other then the Bed..................269. H.815, 3
Here she lyes (in Bed of Spice)................274. H.838, 1
Go to Bed, and care not when...............276. H.850, 7
And stealing still with love, and feare to Bed,..286. H.898, 15
Me thought I saw (as I did dreame in bed)..313. H.1017, 1
When I lie within my bed,...................347. N.41, 5
To make my bed soft in my sicknesses:........358. N.77, 9
Shall we ere bring coy Brides to bed;........360. N.83, 50
Sleep in thy peace, thy bed of Spice;.........361. N.83, 61
What though my bed be now my grave,........361. N.84, 3
And when the night perswades me to my bed,..392. N.230, 13
His soule as to a bedd of spice..............408. A.2, 44
As in a bedd of Frankensence...............408. A.2, 46
But Least I should forgett his bedd............409. A.2, 83
Thou bring'st vnto his bedd A frost..........409. A.2, 86
And so to Bed: Pray wish us all Good Rest....419. A.10, 8

Bedabbled When the bedabled Morne............112. H.283, 19
Bedabled with the dew........................156. H.412, 4
And prettily bedabled so,....................247. H.729, 2

Bedangling His Shirt bedangling from his knee,...295. H.942, 3

Bedewed Bedew'd with teares, are worne.........106. H.262, 8

Bediapered — — — — — — — —, ...421. var. H.106, 46

Bed-rid Wither'd with yeeres, and bed-rid Mumma lyes;
90. H.222, 1

Bed's Close to my Beds side she did stand......153. H.399, 3

Beds Charme then the chambers; make the beds for ease,
245. H.723, 11
Welcome as slumbers; or as beds of ease........300. H.961, 3
Or search the beds of Spices through,........367. N.102, 10
The Jewes their beds, and offices of ease,......386. N.193, 1

Bedstead No Fatal Owle the Bedsted keeps,.....56. H.149, 101

Bee Thus like a Bee, Love-gentle stil doth bring...16. H.40, 7
About the sweet bag of a Bee,..................31. H.92, 1
Roses, by a Bee was stung...................50. H.139, 2
Which Country people call a Bee..............50. H.139, 9
It chanc't a Bee did flie that way,............71. H.182, 2
Of flowers, ne'r suckt by th' theeving Bee:....86. H.213, 37
Fly to my Mistresse, pretty pilfring Bee,......100. H.248, 1
For pitty, Sir, find out that Bee,............156. H.412, 11
Full as a Bee with Thyme, and Red,..........165. H.443, 9
Nor Bee, or Hive you have be mute;........179. H.476, 17
Not Marshals Bee, which in a Bead............186. H.497, 11
The Abdomen of a Bee;......................223. H.638, 9
Stung by a fretfull Bee;......................272. H.828, 2
Love turn'd himselfe into a Bee,..............283. H.883, 9

Beef Of Flanks and Chines of Beefe doth Gorrell boast
89. H.221, 1
Foundation of your Feast, Fat Beefe:........101. H.250, 29
Where laden spits, warp't with large Ribbs of Beefe,
146. H.377, 9
His jawes had tir'd on some large Chine of Beefe.
273. H.835, 2

Beer See Bier
Prig now drinks Water, who before drank Beere:..71. H.183, 1
Call me The sonne of Beere, and then confine..79. H.197, 87
But 'tis no Gout (beleeve it) but hard Beere,..98. H.239, 3
There's that, which drowns all care, stout Beere;
101. H.250, 37
Welcome as thunder to our beere:............146. H.377, 30
No, no, thy bread, thy wine, thy jocund Beere..147. H.377, 57
Can hold of Beere and Ale an Ocean;........171. H.454, 2
That brings us either Ale or Beere;..........179. H.476, 26
Broomsted a lamenesse got by cold and Beere;..201. H.555, 1
And noses tann'd with Beere..................219. H.629, 4
Drencht in Ale, or drown'd in Beere...........255. H.761, 20
Beere small as Comfort, dead as Charity.......262. H.783, 16
Drink now the strong Beere,..................263. H.784, 13
Sold his old Mothers Spectacles for Beere:....272. H.829, 2
He'l sell her Eyes, and Nose, for Beere and Ale.
272. H.829, 4
Punchin by Beere and Ale, spreads so........273. H.832, 4
(When drunke with Beere) to light him home, i'th' dark.
273. H.834, 4
A drought of wine, ale, beere (at all).........291. H.919, 6
To Beer Drinkers............................320. H.1051, 6
To soure the Bread, and turn the Beer........321. H.1056, 9
Soone after, he for beere so scores his wheat,...327. H.1086, 3

Beer-broth From Beer-broth at all,.............320. H.1051, 16

Bee's And well bestrutted Bees sweet bagge:....119. H.293, 34

Beest Though thou beest young, kind, soft, and faire,
174. H.465, 3
On with thy worke, though thou beest hardly prest;
311. H.1009, 1
Far away, if thou beest by..................324. H.1069, 4
Though Thou beest all that Active Love,.......395. N.246, 1
If Thou beest taken, God forbid,.............399. N.265, 1
— — — — — — — — — —, ...441. var. H.465, 34

Bee-stock Soe good a soile bee-stocke and till,....409. A.2, 106

Beet Or Pea, or Bean, or Wort, or Beet,........200. H.552, 5
Makes those, and my beloved Beet,..........350. N.47, 35

Beetle See Idol-beetle-fly

Beets To taste boyl'd Nettles, Colworts, Beets, and eate
37. H.106, 113

Beeves Of Beeves for sacrifice;................250. H.736, 2
Of Beeves here ready stand for Sacrifice......300. H.961, 8

Befall That in warfare can befall..............151. H.386, 6

Befalls When ere I go, or what so ere befalls....269. H.818, 1

Befell What befell ye;..........................74. H.190, 4

Be-fool Ans. Love will be-foole ye:............309. H.1001, 6

Before The Gods protection, but the night before)..9. H.14, 12
Hony to salve, were he before did sting.........16. H.40, 8
Jems, then those two, that went before:........23. H.70, 6
War, which before was horrid, now appears......25. H.77, 7
I shall dislike, what once I lov'd before.........31. H.93, 4
But thrice three Moones before she dy'd.......41. H.116, 6
For which, before thy Threshold, we'll lay downe
41. H.117, 7
Of which, sweet Swans must drink, before they sing
45. H.128, 34
No; he's but Fore-man, as he was before......53. H.148, 4
Before, my deare Perilla, I will be............59. H.154, 9
Stand before you, my learn'd Diocesan?......64. H.168, 2
Before that we have left to dreame:............69. H.178, 48
Before we know our liberty...................69. H.178, 60
Prig now drinks Water, who before drank Beere:
71. H.183, 1
An Olive-branch before me lay:................73. H.187, 4
Grapes, before Herrick leaves Canarie Sack.....78. H.197, 48
Ships have been drown'd, where late they danc't before.
85. H.212, 2
Three dayes before the shutting in of May,....86. H.213, 13
And when before him we have laid our treasures,
87. H.213, 47
Pressing before, some coming after,............101. H.250, 17
To speak by Teares, before ye have a Tongue...104. H.257, 14
Play then they ever knew before..............115. H.283, 130
Paying before you praise; and cockring wit,....141. H.359, 15
Before I went...............................144. H.371, 7
Thou had'st the wreath before, now take the Tree;
150. H.383, 1
He'l turn a Papist, rancker then before.......151. H.385, 6
Lean-horn'd, before I come again.............176. H.465, 78
Those paines it lately felt before...............189. H.514, 4

But before that day comes,....................197. H.540, 5
And Charles here Rule, as he before did Raign;
214. H.612, 8
And warn'd before, wo'd not beware..........219. H.628, 12
No man despaires to do what's done before.....236. H.680, 2
Some starres were fixt before; but these are dim,
236. H.685, 3
Before thy swift Postilion;..................239. H.696, 4
I cannot love, as I have lov'd before:..........258. H.768, 1
'Twas rich before; but since your Name is downe,
264. H.789, 3
Before we can be aware of.....................267. H.806, 6
Before the Press scarce one co'd see..........287. H.899, 1
An injurie, before a benefite:...................292. H.923, 2
Ile come before...............................296. H.946, 23
That Teare shall scarce be dri'd before........328. H.1090, 10
I'm halfe return'd before I go.................328. H.1090, 13
Since Fame that sides with these, or goes before
329. H.1092, 3
Full, and fild-full, then when full-fild before....341. N.15, 6
Yet before the glasse be out,...................348. N.41, 35
Down before Baal, Bel, or Belial:...............353. N.54, 2
We offer here, before thy Shrine,..............360. N.83, 32
Before ye purge, and circumcise................366. N.98, 8
A King, before conception crown'd.............368. N.102, 18
Before Thy Virgin-Altar I appeare,............368. N.103, 2
Thy mercy-seat I'le lay before;...............369. N.107, 6
Before my last, but here a living grave,.........371. N.115, 2
He teares and tugs us, then he did before;....372. N.116, 2
Then ever, yet, the like was done before.......395. N.244, 4
Before Mans fall, the Rose was born..........396. N.251, 1
Long before this, the base, the dull, the rude,....398. N.263, 5
Before the last least sand of Thy ninth houre be run;
401. N.268, 8
Sinne made before............................401. N.268, 23
Of those god-full prophetts longe before........411. A.3, 42
Wth Joyes before, and Pleasures left behind:..411. A.3, 64
Some hours before I should have been his Bride..416. A.8, 16
Read it then before your lipp..................417. A.9, 13
bearing downe Time before you; hye......431. ins. H.283, 50c
Before unknowne; the blood of fleas.......435. ins. H.293, w
Then Jove and Chaos them before........437. var. H.336, 136
Befriend Like the sparks of fire, befriend thee...217. H.619, 5
Befringed Whose head befringed with bescattered tresses
404. A.1, 1
Beg I burn, I burn; and beg of you..........50. H.140, 1
I beg of Love, that ever I.....................64. H.169, 11
Ile beg, and buy it too........................160. H.422, 4
Never beg, or humbly wooe..................182. H.490, 11
I dare not beg a smile;.......................231. H.663, 2
I'le beg of thee first here to have mine Urn....242. H.713, 18
Ph. I'le beg a penny, or Ile sing so long,....248. H.730, 21
From scorne I begge of thee,..................281. H.874, 11
Beg for my Pardon Julia; He doth winne.......329. H.1095, 3
As for to beg my bread from doore to doore;..347. N.39, 2
Began Began to speak, and would have been......13. H.27, 7
The lid began to let out day;..................46. H.130, 9
Of Julia, and began to sip;..................71. H.182, 6
He thus began himselfe t'excuse:.............71. H.182, 12
Doll she so soone began the wanton trade;.....149. H.379, 1
Paul, he began ill, but he ended well;........387. N.200, 1
Judas began well, but he foulely fell:..........387. N.200, 2
— — — — — — — — — —, ...433. var. H.293, 24
Beget Is there no way to beget..................10. H.19, 7
In her wisdome co'd beget......................57. H.149, 150
Showrs or Sun-shines co'd beget.............108. H.266, 4
For to beget...............................135. H.336, 101
His Bed, Male children shall beget.............162. H.429, 2
Which may be done, if (Sir) you can beget....170. H.451, 5
Co'd a noble Verse beget;.....................217. H.620, 5
Words beget Anger: Anger brings forth blowes:.287. H.901, 1
And soe begett lust and temptation........430. ins. H.283, 20f
Begets Nature begets by th' Sun and showers,....103. H.256, 5
(Nature begets by th' Sun, and showers,)......166. H.443, 34
Love love begets, then never be...............252. H.746, 1
This begets the more delight,..................194. H.527, 6
Begetting See Life-begetting
Beggar Love, like a Beggar, came to me........295. H.942, 1
Shall I a daily Begger be,....................312. H.1014, 1
Jacob Gods Beggar was; and so we wait......383. N.171, 1
Beggar's Well will serve the Beggars use.......223. H.638, 20
Lord! let me never act that beggars part,......347. N.39, 3
Beggars (Though ne're so rich) all beggars at His Gate.
383. N.171, 2
Begin Begin to charme, and as thou stroak'st mine eares
67. H.176, 1
Begin to wooe:..............................87. H.214, 4
His kitling eyes begin to runne..............119. H.293, 24
Beginne with Jove; then is the worke halfe done;
128. H.321, 1
I beginne to waine in sight;..................180. H.482, 1
Goddesse, I begin an Art;....................195. H.530, 1
Then, then begin............................221. H.633, 38
Content, begin, and I will bet................243. H.716, 7
Chor. Why then begin, and let us heare......243. H.716, 16
Chor. Much time is spent in prate; begin,......243. H.716, 23
Begin with a kisse,..........................247. H.727, 1
Ch. Why then begin, and all the while we make
248. H.730, 23
When I touch, I then begin..................253. H.750, 8
To pray for me doe thou begin,..............277. H.854, 5
Wo'd I well my worke begin?..................286. H.897, 2
Grow up in Beauty, as thou do'st begin,........304, H.979, 1
Here we begin new life; while thousands quite..313. H.1019, 3
Begin then to chuse,..........................317. H.1035, 7
Stay me, by crowing, ere I do begin;............349. N.43, 4
But let no Christmas mirth begin................366. N.98, 7
Where shall I now begin to make, for one.......368. N.103, 5
Let me, though late, yet at the last, begin......392. N.230, 29
Why then begin, great King! ascend Thy Throne,
399. N.263, 28
Why then, Begin............................401. N.268, 14
In that you doe beginne, then end:......431. ins. H. 283, 60t
begin to pinke as weary that the warres..432. ins. H.283, 140b
Beginnest See Begin'st
Beginnings In godlinesse, not the beginnings, so..387. N.200, 3
Begins See 'Gins
Where love begins, there dead thy first desire:...281. H.873, 1
God loads, and unloads, (thus His work begins)...341. N.14, 1
Begin'st Consult ere thou begin'st, that done, go on
252. H.749, 1
Begot Because begot of my Immortall seed.......280. H.869, 6
Begs With all her Owle-ey'd issue begs a boon..116. H.283, 152
How Herrick beggs, if that he can-..............214. H.611, 3
Who begs to die for feare of humane need,......277. H.855, 1
Beguile Or smile more inly; lest thy looks beguile
46. H.128, 46
But let's not beguile.........................247. H.727, 5
More mildlie least thy temptinge lookes beguile
424. ins. H.128. 46e
Begun Let's kisse afresh, as when we first begun....24. H.74, 8
If well thou hast begun, goe on fore-right;......123. H.309, 1
And runnes most smoothly, when tis well begunne.
128. H.321, 2
On, as thou has begunne, brave youth, and get...150. H.384, 1
Ha's not as yet begunne.......................164. H.441, 2
Hast thou begun an act? ne're then give o're:....236. H.680, 1
With zeale alike, as 'twas begun;................366. N.97, 25
Behavior And 'gainst your chast behaviour there's no Plea,
189. H.511, 3
Civil Behaviour, and Religion..................199. H.545, 4
And unsmooth behaviour.......................204. H.569, 12
And with as firme behaviour I will meet........392. N.230, 17
Beheld You have beheld a smiling Rose..........75. H.193, 1
You have beheld, how they...................110. H.274, 5
Have ye beheld (with much delight)...........164. H.440, 1
Thou hast beheld those seas, and Countries farre;
330. H.1100, 5
I haue behelde two louers in a night.............410. A.3, 1
Behind And leave no scent behind ye:............83. H.207, 2
Looks forward, scornes what's left behind:......132. H.336, 14
His feet were helpt, and left his Crutch behind:..201. H.555, 3
None sees the fardell of his faults behind.........253. H.751, 2
No one least Branch there left behind:..........304. H.980, 6
And leave me here behind thee;................323. H.1068, 2
Wth Joyes before, and Pleasures left behind:......411. A.3, 64
Behold But now 'tis known, Behold; behold, I bring
27. H.82, 7
To my content, I never sho'd behold,............29. H.86, 5
Behold! how Hymens Taper-light..............54. H.149, 51
And now, Behold! the Bed or Couch..........57. H.149, 131
Thy Azure Robe, I did behold,................66. H.175, 1
Behold, Tibullus lies..........................81. H.201, 41
Behold this living stone,.......................85. H.211, 17
Behold that circummortall purity:...............96. H.230, 2
Ambo. Lets cheer him up. Sil. Behold him weeping ripe.
159. H.421, 7
In my short absence; yet behold..............174. H.465, 19
When I behold a Forrest spread...............202. H.560, 1
When I behold another grace..................202. H.560, 5
Behold them in a spacious Theater..............206. H.575, 48
Those strong-hoof'd Mules, which we behold,....239. H.696, 5
Behold, for us the Naked Graces stay............261. H.781, 7
Let me in my Glasse behold...................277. H.852, 2
I lately fri'd, but now behold..................290. H.915, 1
When flowing garments I behold...............311. H.1010, 1
Behold a suddaine Metamorphosis..............325. H.1076, 2
O then! for mercies sake, behold................344. N.29, 5
Behold I go,................................354. N.58, 2
And therewithall, behold, it hath................372. N.118, 3
When I behold Thee, almost slain,...............400. N.267, 1
Hence they have born my Lord: Behold! the Stone
403. N.271, 1
For now behold the golden Pompe is come,........415. A.7, 2
Beholder To the beholder, and the sufferer:........343. N.24, 2
Beholders But being so; then the beholders cry,...172. H.459, 7
Turnes the beholders into stone...............418. A.9, 58
Beholdest Here thou behold'st thy large sleek Neat
230. H.662, 35
Beholding From the beholding Death, and cruelties.
236. H.679, 2
By Thine approach, each their beholding eye....398. N.263, 14

Behung The leaves) her temples I behung:........16. H.41, 11
My locks behung with frost and snow:........134. H.336, 76
And all behung with these pure Pearls,........167. H.443, 108
Being But being absent, Love lies languishing.......13. H.30, 2
Which being done, the fretfull paine...............18. H.46, 9
Name it I would; but being blushing red,.........24. H.74, 13
Which being seen,..............................30. H.89, 6
Whose love growes more enflam'd, by being Foes..78. H.197, 44
And being ravisht thus,.........................81. H.201, 34
But being spent, the worse, and worst...........84. H.208, 11
That being ravisht, hence I goe..................95. H.227, 3
But being vanquisht quite,.....................105. H.258, 5
Set on your selfe, by being nice:...............113. H.283, 54
In his wide Codpiece, (dinner being done)........118. H.292, 5
But being poore, and knowing Flesh is deare,....122. H.305, 5
Where being laid, all Faire signes looking on,...124. H.313, 11
Leaving their Poet (being now grown old)......151. H.387, 3
Being here their ends deny'd....................152. H.391, 3
Bacchus, being full of Thee?...................157. H.415, 2
Or like a medow being lately mown............159. H.421, 21
Then being seated in that smoother Sphere,......172. H.456, 7
But being so; then the beholders cry...........172. H.459, 7
Where build aloft; and being fixt by These,......185. H.496, 9
Being drunke, who 'twas that Can'd his Ribs last night.
186. H.501, 4
For being too-too-kind?........................188. H.509, 8
For being comely, consonant, and free...........210. H.590, 1
But now 'tis clos'd; and being shut, & seal'd,....227. H.652, 11
Or Roses, being withered:....................233. H.670, 25
And (being to be sanctifi'd)....................237. H.686, 2
While we have our being here:.................238. H.691, 4
Which, on the white Rose being shed,...........241. H.706, 3
As for the rest, being too great a summe.......267. H.804, 13
And being cup-shot, more he co'd not doe.......313. H.1017, 10
And better Being, they receive from You.......326. H.1080, 26
Thou being dead,.............................374. N.123, 38
That being ignorant of that one, he may.........379. N.142, 3
But no more Woman, being strong in Faith;....386. N.192, 3
Being, oft here, the just mans portion.........387. N.201, 6
God hates the Duall Number; being known.......396. N.249, 1
The which with ruby rednes being tipt............404. A.1, 21
Bel Down before Baal, Bel, or Belial:............353. N.54, 2
Belial Down before Baal, Bel, or Belial:..........353. N.54, 2
Belicking — — — — — — — — — — —, ...434. ins. H.293, 41f
Belie Truggin now lives but to belye his name....283. H.882, 2
Belief I want beliefe; O gentle Silvia, be.........204. H.570, 3
Believe Love and my selfe (beleeve me) on a day...17. H.44, 1
And beleeve there be such things:..............36. H.106, 86
Beleeve me; you will most......................53. H.149, 15
But 'tis no Gout (beleeve it) but hard Beere,......98. H.239, 3
Since which (beleeve the rest).................105. H.258, 7
Beleeve young man all those were teares.........131. H.330, 5
Believe, Love speaks it not, but Lust;..........175. H.465, 40
Believe him not; for he forgot it quite,..........186. H.501, 3
But would to Love I could beleeve 'twas so!....279. H.866, 2
Believe it (dearest) ther's not one...........324. H.1068, 19
I do believe, that die I must,...................358. N.78, 1
I do believe, that when I rise,.................358. N.78, 3
I do believe, that I must come,..................358. N.78, 5
I do believe, the bad must goe..................358. N.78, 7
I do believe, the good, and I,...................359. N.78, 9
I do believe, I shall inherit....................359. N.78, 11
I do believe, the One in Three,................359. N.78, 13
I will believe, that then my body dies:..........392. N.230, 20
Most maye smile, beleiue will none,..............418. A.9, 36
— — — — — — — — — — — —, ...424. var. H.164, 2
Believest Sitt'st, and beleev'st that there be seas,..36. H.106, 70
— — — — — — — — — —, ...422. var. H.106, 86
Believe't — — — — — — — —, ...450. var. A.9, 36
Bell See Passing-bell, Saint's-bell
As my small Bell best fits my little Spire......249. H.733, 12
And the tinkling of my Bell,.....................372. N.121, 3
Which to effect, let ev'ry passing Bell..........392. N.230, 11
Bellies And find'st their bellies there as full......230. H.662, 42
To come with their own bellies unto feasts:....310. H.1005, 2
Bellman (The Bell-man of the night) proclaime the clock
207. H.575, 62
Bell-man of Night, if I about shall go.........349. N.43, 1
Nay tell the Bell-man of the Night had tould.....410. A.3, 17
Bellona Never since first Bellona us'd a Shield,..170. H.451, 11
Bells Their Beads of Nits, Bels, Books, & Wax..93. H.223, 115
Belly Her Belly, Buttocks, and her Waste..........16. H.41, 7
The belly chiefly; not the eye:.................35. H.106, 28
A little meat best fits a little bellie,............249. H.733, 16
His hungry belly borne by Legs Jaile-free.......332. H.1112, 4
Chor. Thy belly like a hill is,.................375. N.123, 77
Then comes the belly seated next belowe..........405. A.1, 59
Belong As sure a Mattins do's to him belong,....128. H.321, 5
Or other Rites that doe belong to me;..........219. H.627, 6
Two instruments belong unto our God;........394. N.241, 1
— — — — — — — — — — — —, ...438. var. H.357, 2
Belongs This not the least is, which belongs to Kings.
260. H.774, 2
In, or without; all, all belongs to Thee:.........368. N.103, 4
Belongs all gold superfluous......................394. N.239, 4
Beloved Love is most loth to leave the thing beloved.
73. H.186, 12
Our own beloved privacie:.....................200. H.552, 18
Whom one belov'd will not suffice,..............287. H.899, 9
Make way to my Beloved Westminster:......316. H.1028, 14
Makes those, and my beloved Beet,...............350. N.47, 35
Sins first dislik'd, are after that belov'd...........362. N.85, 2
The smoake of his beloued Attica,..............412. A.3, 74
Below That chiding streams betray small depth below.
15. H.38, 10
And looking down below,.........................27. H.81, 19
What trust to things below, when as we see,......81. H.202, 7
Teares, though th'are here below the sinners brine,
226. H.645, 1
Meane time like Earth-wormes we will craule below,
257. H.763, 21
What State above, what Symmetrie below,......297. H.947, 9
Then comes the belly seated next belowe..........405. A.1, 59
Bemoan Your frailties; and bemone ye;..........184. H.493, 10
Ben Saint Ben to aide me......................212. H.604, 4
And thou Saint Ben, shalt be..................213. H.604, 11
To drink to Thee my Ben....................227. H.653, 8
Ah Ben!...289. H.911, 1
My Ben...289. H.911, 11
Bench Luggs, by the Condemnation of the Bench,..79. H.199, 1
Yet with the bench of aged sires,..............303. H.973, 11
The Bench is then their place; and not the Barre..376. N.126, 2
Bend Oft bend the Bow, and thou with ease shalt do,
245. H.722, 1
That Bar, this Bend; that Fess, this Cheveron;..295. H.941, 4
Bending And bending, (yet it doth not break?)..208. H.580, 10
Each bending then, will rise a proper flower.....320. H.1054, 6
Beneath In Vaults beneath?.....................85. H.211, 14
Ch. What's thy request? Ph. That since she's now beneath
248. H.730, 15
Or'e which you'l walk, when I am laid beneath..312. H.1013, 4
Lighten my candle, so that I beneath...........358. N.77, 10
Beneath this Tree,...........................401. N.268, 37
Is He, from hence, gone to the shades beneath,..403. N.271, 5
Benedicite From Murders Benedicitie............121. H.299, 2
Who writ for many. Benedicite..................298. H.952, 4
Unlesse God gives the Benedicite................379. N.140, 2
Benediction Worthy thy Benediction;..............339. N.2, 8
Benefit An injurie, before a benefite:............292. H.923, 2
God to bestow a second benefit..................348. N.42, 2
Benighted Unto the lad benighted.................26. H.81, 16
When ye are (by chance) benighted:..........323. H.1065, 2
Benison Of living water by thy Benizon..........245. H.723, 4
Upon thee many a Benizon...................303. H.973, 18
For a Benizon to fall..........................364. N.95, 5
Benjamin As Benjamin, and Storax, when they meet.
131. H.331, 10
Bent Forthwith his bow he bent,..................27. H.81, 29
In either which a small tall bent.................92. H.223, 95
Bents Sweet Bents wode bow, to give my Love the day:
159. H.421, 24
Chains of sweet bents let us make,..............235. H.678, 5
Green Rushes then, and sweetest Bents,........285. H.892, 17
Benumb To benumme my hopes and me..........266. H.803, 6
Benumbs Benummes like the forgettfull floode......409. A.2, 88
Bepearled This Primrose, thus bepearl'd with dew?
208. H.580, 4
Bepimpled His cheeks be-pimpled, red and blue;...38. H.108, 7
Bepranked Be-pranckt with Ribbands, to this end,.193. H.521, 44
Bequeath Bequeath to me one parting kisse:......34. H.103, 16
Then, even then, I will bequeath my heart......73. H.186, 14
Which we will give Him; and bequeath.........365. N.96, 29
Bereaved Bereav'd,.............................308. H.993, 4
Bereft I am of all bereft;.......................173. H.460, 1
Yet, though now of Muse bereft,...............182. H.489, 9
God has a Right Hand, but is quite bereft........394. N.240, 1
Berkley Yet if thou wert not, Berkley, loyall proofe,
252. H.745, 13
Bernard 'Tis (as S. Bernard saith) but seemingly...385. N.188, 4
Berry See Strawberry
Bescattered Whose head befringed with bescattered tresses
404. A.1, 1
Beseech I doe beseech thee, ere we part,...........33. H.103, 5
Beset And all beset with flowers.................103. H.255, 8
Beset with Mirtles; whose each leafe drops Love..107. H.265, 4
Beset with stately Figures (every where)........185. H.496, 2
Smile, like a field beset with corne?............364. N.96, 15
Beshivered Beshiver'd into seeds of Raine;......340. N.3, 10
Beshrewed So with a blush, beshrew'd the deed...187. H.504, 6
Beside Beside their Fumigations,...............93. H.223, 120
And many Flowers beside;....................285. H.892, 14
The Lictors bundl'd up their rods: beside,........291. H.920, 1
Beside we must know,.........................317. H.1035, 4
Besides No part besides must of thy selfe be known,
30. H.83, 11
Has blear'd his eyes: Besides, his head is bald......33. H.99, 2
Besides, the childhood of the Day has kept,......68. H.178, 21
Besides, know this, I never sting................71. H.182, 19
And know, besides, ye must revoke............102. H.250, 47
Wods't thou know, besides all these,............103. H.253, 11
Besides (Ai me!) since she went hence to dwell,.159. H.421, 27

Besides I give Thee here a Verse that shall......168. H.444, 2
Besides us two, i' th' Temple here's not one......168. H.445, 1
High are These Statues here, besides no lesse....185. H.496, 7
Besides rare sweets, I had a Book which none...227. H.652, 5
Besides too, in a brave,......................259. H.772, 16
Besides, the most religious Prophet stands......262. H.781, 9
Teach me besides, what love wil do;..........325. H.1075, 5
Besides ye see me daily grow...............329. H.1093, 3
Besides my healthfull Ewes to beare...........350. N.47, 47
To guild thy Tombe; besides, these Caules,......360. N.83, 43
Death for stout Cato; and besides all these,......370. N.108, 7
Besmeared With Wine and Oile besmear'd.........65. H.170, 4
Besmear'd with Grapes; welcome he shall thee thither,
206. H.575, 37
Besmears Th' Arabian Dew besmears...........80. H.201, 10
Bespangling See Dew-bespangling
Besparkling — — — — — — — —, ...430. var. H.283, 36
Bespread A blush their cheeks bespred;..........105. H.258, 6
A Spinners circle is bespread,................167. H.443, 101
Best See Past-best
Since Coats, and Hamlets, best agree...............5. H.2, 5
By your accesse; (O you the best of Kings!).....25. H.77, 10
Charls the best Husband, while Maria strives......26. H.79, 3
To be, and is, the very best of Wives:..........26. H.79, 4
Best with those Virgin-Verses thou hast writ:........28. H.84, 4
I'le doe my best to win, when'ere I wooe:......31. H.91, 1
Let's doe our best, our Watch and Ward to keep....32. H.95, 5
A way that's best...........................43. H.123, 23
Slowly goes farre: The meane is best: Desire......51. H.143, 3
The best way how to loose the Zone...........56. H.149, 92
And lik'st the best? Still thou reply'st, The dead...66. H.174, 2
And to thy selfe be best this sentence knowne,....67. H.177, 3
Few Beads are best, when once we goe a Maying..68. H.178, 28
And pay no vowes to thee? who wast their best..78. H.197, 59
That Age is best, which is the first,............84. H.208, 9
And quickly give, The swiftest Grace is best.....87. H.213, 46
Thou art to all lost love the best,...............106. H.262, 1
Crosses doe still bring forth the best events.....110. H.275, 2
Last, let us make our best abode,...............111. H.278, 5
But if flames best like ye, then.................118. H.289, 11
By Time, and Counsell, doe the best we can,.....120. H.294, 1
Let Kings Command, and doe the best they may,..138. H.345, 1
This is your houre; and best you may command,...140. H.354, 9
And speak it with the best.....................144. H.371, 12
Best and more suppling piece he cuts, and by....147. H.377, 51
Love he that will; it best likes me,..............155. H.408, 1
The Grace, the Glorie, and the best............189. H.515, 3
Where all are best;...........................190. H.515, 30
And having danc't ('bove all the best)..........192. H.521, 33
Thou art The Man, the onely Man best known,..194. H.526, 3
Come thou in, with thy best part,..............195. H.530, 2
Who dead, deserve our best remembrances......209. H.584, 8
'Tis best to feed Love; but not over-fill:........220. H.633, 23
That the best compost for the Lands..........230. H.662, 23
Thou shalt thy Name have, and thy Fames best trust,
231. H.664, 5
A wager, who the best shall play,..............243. H.716, 2
Since both have here deserved best............243. H.716, 36
A little Saint best fits a little Shrine,...........249. H.733, 1
A little prop best fits a little Vine,.............249. H.733, 2
As my small Cruse best fits my little Wine.......249. H.733, 3
A little Seed best fits a little Soyle,............249. H.733, 4
A little Trade best fits a little Toyle:...........249. H.733, 5
As my small Jarre best fits my little Oyle.......249. H.733, 6
A little Bin best fits a little Bread,............249. H.733, 7
As my small stuffe best fits my little Shed......249. H.733, 9
A little Hearth best fits a little Fire,..........249. H.733, 10
As my small Bell best fits my little Spire.......249. H.733, 12
A little streame best fits a little Boat;........249. H.733, 13
A little lead best fits a little Float;............249. H.733, 14
As my small Pipe best fits my little note.........249. H.733, 15
A little meat best fits a little bellie,............249. H.733, 16
Of creatures, woman is the best..............250. H.739, 4
Happy Rusticks, best content.................255. H.761, 21
And by your self, the best....................258. H.767, 17
Vertue best loves those children that she beates...270. H.820, 4
The best of all the sacrificed meate;............272. H.826, 2
Truth is best found out by the time, and eyes;..287. H.902, 1
Of the Poets; but the Best....................289. H.910, 2
My selfe now live: this age best pleaseth mee....292. H.927, 2
As some plants prosper best by cuts and blowes;..292. H.929, 3
Give house-roome to the best; 'Tis never known..293. H.935, 1
Lines have, or sho'd have, thou the best canst show.
297. H.947, 10
The best and truest Chronicles of me...........304. H.978, 6
Must shun the bad, I, and suspect the best.......305. H.981, 2
Let's strive to be the best; the Gods, we know it,
309. H.1000, 1
Those ends in War the best contentment bring,..316. H.1029, 1
Danger to give the best advice to Kings.......318. H.1037, 2
Love's of it self, too sweet; the best of all......327. H.1084, 1
An equall mind is the best sauce for griefe......333. H.1119, 2
And is the best known, not defining Him...........340. N.4, 2
Those Saints, which God loves best,.............344. N.28, 1
To feed, or lodge, to have the best of Roomes:.....356. N.68, 2
Of all the House: the best of all's the Heart......356. N.68, 4

Be the best New-yeares Gift to all..............366. N.98, 24
Let thy obedience be the best Reply.............397. N.260, 2
— — — — — — — — — — — —, ...436. var. H.336, 17
— — — — — — — — — — — —, ...436. var. H.336, 40
— — — — — — — — — — — —, ...451. ins. H.197, 48b
Bestirs Bestirs his Hand, but starves in hand the Suite.
303. H.975, 8
Bestow Mirt. And I a Sheep-hook will bestow,....86. H.213, 42
Neither Silver to bestow.........................88. H.218, 2
More Ile bestow:..............................171. H.455, 10
God to bestow a second benefit..................348. N.42, 2
That Thou on Widdowes didst bestow..........374. N.123, 26
Bestowest O fruitfull Genius! that bestowest here..242. H.713, 7
Bestows God on our Youth bestowes but little ease;
383. N. 175, 1
Bestrew And with some flowrs my grave bestrew,..70. H.180, 7
That will with flowers the Tomb bestrew,........156. H.412, 7
Foure times bestrew thee ev'ry yeere............360. N.83, 36
Bestride Give me that man, that dares bestride.....30. H.90, 1
Bestroking Bestroaking Fate the while............113. H.283, 29
Bestrowted — — — — — — — —, ...435. var. H.293, 34 bb
Bestrutted And well bestrutted Bees sweet bagge:
119. H.293, 34
Bestuffed — — — — — — — — —, ...434. var. H.293, 34
Besweeted — — — — — — — — —, ...433. var. H.293, 22
Besweetened Brought and besweetned in a blew..119. H.293, 22
Beswetted — — — — — — — — —, ...433. var. H.293, 22
Bet That likewise I may pay the Bet,..........238. H.690, 11
Content, begin, and I will bet..................243. H.716, 7
Be't See Be
Be't to your praise, no peace was broken.......114. H.283, 90
Be't for my Bridall, or my Buriall..............232. H.667, 2
Well, or be't or be't not so,....................277. H.852, 5
Betake That high Enchantment I betake me now:.62. H.161, 10
Bethesda To finde Bethesda, and an Angel there,..61. H.161, 3
The Tree, Bethesda, and the Angel too:..........61. H.161, 6
Bethlehem To Gods sweet Babe, when borne at Bethlehem;
86. H.213, 22
Bethwack to Bethwack us;....................320. H.1051, 9
Beticling — — — — — — — — —, ...434. ins. H.293, 41f
Betide Please him, and then all good-luck will betide
124. H.313, 5
Betimes Betimes my Mattens say:................87. H.214, 2
To-morrow, Julia, I betimes must rise,...........102. H.251, 1
Let me Thy voice betimes i' th morning heare;..358. N.77, 12
Betray That chiding streams betray small depth below.
15. H.38, 10
Salutes with tears of joy; when fires betray......77. H.197, 17
But such the Drap'ry did betray.................288. H.908, 7
Betrayed Orecome, or halfe betray'd by Tiffanies:..34. H.104, 2
Our Sires betraid their Countrey and their King.
252. H.745, 10
Betraying Many a jest told of the Keyes betraying
69. H.178, 55
Betrays Which so betrayes her blood, as we discover
158. H.416, 3
Betrayes the Hearts Adulterie...................254. H.755, 2
Bets Many a Teaster by his game, and bets:......154. H.400, 2
Better Better 'twere my Book were dead,..........21. H.59, 5
Better tis that one shu'd fall,....................21. H.61, 7
In thy both Last, and Better Vow:...............34. H.106, 2
Smooth, faire, and fat; none better I can tell:....86. H.213, 6
Sho'd I a jot the better see?......................97. H.235, 4
Shall smile and smell the better by thy beads.....143. H.370, 2
That they no better do agree....................163. H.434, 3
'Tis better yet...............................172. H.458, 7
Better look the Roses red,......................194. H.527, 3
Of better to be had!............................211. H.596, 4
'Twas better there to toyle, then prove..........219. H.628, 5
Tap (better known then trusted) as we heare....272. H.829, 1
Farre better t'were for either to be mute,.......287. H.901, 5
Will be better for your Batch.................322. H.1063, 4
And better Being, they receive from You.......326. H.1080, 26
Better it is, premonish'd, for to shun............349. N.43, 5
All these, and better Thou dost send............351. N.47, 51
Better he starv'd, then but to tast one crumme...355. N.65, 10
'Tis better to be poore,........................368. N.104, 6
Which for the better beawtifying shrowdes........406. A.1, 83
As for thy birth, and better seeds...............407. A.2, 19
Hym for his better Cherrishing.................408. A.2, 60
— — — — — — — — — — — —, ...422. var. H.106, 71
— — — — — — — — — — — —, ...437. var. H.336, 126
— — — — — — — — — — — —, ...452. var. H.443, 93
Bettered The Rod (perhaps) was better'd by the name;
306. H.986, 3
Bettering Bettering them both, but by a double straine,
343. N.24, 3
Betty — — — — — — — — —, ...444. var. H.649, 1
Between Between thy Breasts (then Doune of Swans more white)...30. H.88, 9
And gave the Bag between them.................31. H.92, 12
Flasht out between the Middle and Extreame.....33. H.102, 2
Betweene whose glories, there my lips Ile lay,....96. H.230, 3
Between the lips, (all cherrie-red,)............130. H.329, 5
And oft between,.............................135. H.336, 115

Of Amber chaf't between the hands,..........145. H.375, 16
But still the envious Scene between............247. H.729, 7
Between Domitians Martiall then, and Thee.....301. H.966, 10
Between the finger, and the thumb;............356. N.66, 6
And in the milky vally that's betweene..........405. A.1, 55
— — — — — — — — — —, ...432. var. H.283, 106
Betwixt Betwixt us two no more Logomachie.....287. H.901, 4
— — — — — — — — — —, ...435. var. H.329, 5
Beucolicks See Bucolics
Beware Of my cure, doe you beware...........62. H.162, 17
And warn'd before, wo'd not beware...........219. H.628, 12
O beware! in time submit;....................273. H.836, 5
Scorch their plackets, but beware..............315. H.1026, 7
Bewash Let the Maides bewash the men.........315. H.1026, 10
Bewearied See Night-bewearied
Farre more then night bewearied............136. H.336, 152
Bewitch Doe more bewitch me, then when Art......28. H.83, 13
He fully quaffs up to bewitch................120. H.293, 52
All with temptation doth bewitch..............166. H.443, 38
Bewitched Of him bewitcht: then forthwith make..284. H.890, 3
Bewitching And to your more bewitching, see, the proud
115. H.283, 111
As much bewitching his desire............434. ins. H.293, 41f
Bewitchings — — — — — — — —, ...453. var. H.283, 111
Bewray That Bran the Baker did his Breech bewray:
219. H.630, 2
Beyond These I co'd praise thee for beyond another,
210. H.590, 9
What is beyond the mean is ever ill:..........220. H.633, 22
Ne're trauylde for beyonde the seas,.............409. A.2, 92
Beyound the fare-fetch Marchandize.............409. A.2, 94
Beyond its stinted Circle; giueing foode..........410. A.3, 31
Biancha Biancha, Let.................................29. H.87, 1
Ah Biancha! now I see,.......................307. H.991, 1
Then Biancha, I am gone......................307. H.991, 4
Then, Biancha, let me rest.....................307. H.991, 7
Bib Upon his Bibb, or Stomacher:................354. N.59, 6
Bible Reading Thy Bible, and my Book; so end..371. N.115, 12
Bice Thy Bice, thy Umber, Pink, and Lake;......38. H.108, 2
Bice laughs, when no man speaks; and doth protest
265. H.795, 1
Bid Age cals me hence, and my gray haires bid come,
9. H.14, 3
Thy frown (last night) did bid me goe;..........33. H.103, 3
But bid Good-night, and close their lids for ever...41. H.118, 8
And bid the Youth apply........................56. H.149, 95
Since that Love and Night bid enter...........56. H.149, 100
Of life, until ye bid............................58. H.149, 164
And bid the world Good-night....................85. H.211, 4
Bid me to live, and I will live................108. H.267, 1
Or bid me love, and I will give................108. H.267, 3
Bid that heart stay, and it will stay,...........108. H.267, 9
Or bid it languish quite away,..................108. H.267, 11
Bid me to weep, and I will weep,..............109. H.267, 13
Bid me despaire, and Ile despaire,............109. H.267, 17
Or bid me die, and I will dare.................109. H.267, 19
And so to bid goodnight?.......................176. H.467, 9
Shortly I shall bid goodnight:..................180. H.482, 2
Then bid Christmas sport good-night;.........315. H.1026, 12
And though we bid adieu to day,..............324. H.1068, 23
We bid the Creuse and Pannier too:..........374. N.123, 32
Of nature: bidd mee nowe fare well, or smile
424. ins. H.128, 46d
Biddest See Bid'st
Bids Then know, that Nature bids thee goe, not I.
46. H.128, 42
Jack kisses Jill, and bids her freely eate:........186. H.498, 2
Bids ye all be free;..........................263. H.784, 5
And what we blush to speake, she bids us write...275. H.846, 2
When that Death bids come away...............277. H.852, 8
Which got, the third, bids him a King come downe.
292. H.925, 2
Devotion bids me hither bring..................402. N.270, 3
Tis not my voice, but heauens, that bidds thee goe;
414. A.6, 2
— — — — — — — — — — —, ...422. var. H.106, 115
Bid'st Thou bidst me come; I cannot come; for why,
352. N.52, 1
Thou bidst me come away,......................352. N.53, 1
Then, if Thou bidst me pay, or go..............370. N.107, 11
Bier Clean washt, and laid out for the Beere;....374. N.123, 12
Big As big as a Cowle.........................320. H.1051, 5
Bigness Saint Will o'th' Wispe (of no great bignes)
91. H.223, 30
Bill Doves, 'two'd say, yee bill too long.........57. H.149, 140
Bring in her Bill, once more, the Branch of Peace.
225. H.642, 22
Bills See Star-chamber-bills
Bin An easie blessing to your Bin,..............178. H.476, 2
The Larder fills with meat; the Bin with bread..221. H.633, 45
A little Bin best fits a little Bread,.............249. H.733, 7
A little Byn,....................................350. N.47, 20
The Basket and the Bynn of Bread,............374. N.123, 15
Not Bin..391. N.228, 23
Chippinge, the mice filcht from the Binne,.439. ins. H.443, 45g
Bind With other Flowers, bind my Love..........98. H.238, 2
Of Pearle, and Gold, to bind her hands:........98. H.238, 7
Bind up his senses with your numbers, so,........99. H.244, 3
And bind.......................................100. H.246, 12
With bands of Cow-slips bind him;.............157. H.412, 26
Where Rust and Cobwebs bind the gate;.......179. H.476, 29
As to bind up her chaps when she is dead.......205. H.571, 4
And bind the paine;............................210. H.591, 4
Bind me but to thee with thine haire,..........293. H.934, 1
Bindeth 'Tis but silke that bindeth thee,.........128. H.322, 7
Binding (Binding the wheele of Fortune to his Sphere)
137. H.341, 4
Fetcht binding gellye of a starre...........434. ins. H.293, 41h
Bins Be evermore these Bynns replenished.......245. H.723, 6
Birch Are twigs of Birch, and willow, growing there:
39. H.110, 2
He vow'd Destruction both to Birch, and Men:..65. H.171, 2
When Yew is out, then Birch comes in,........285. H.892, 13
But had it been of Birch, the death's the same...306. H.986, 4
Bird I am a bird, and though no name I tell,......248. H.730, 7
The bastard Phenix; bird of Paradice;..........262. H.783, 8
Bird snatcht away from th' cryinge child,..439. ins. H.443, 45q
Birds See Summer-birds
I sing of Brooks, of Blossomes, Birds, and Bowers:..5. H.1, 1
The Purling springs, groves, birds, and well-weav'd Bowrs,
36. H.106, 45
With all luckie Birds to side...................57. H.149, 159
When all the Birds have Mattens seyd,..........68. H.178, 10
Birds chuse their Mates, and couple too, this day:
149. H.378, 2
To catch the pilfring Birds, not Men...........231. H.662, 69
When all Birds els do of their musick faile,......247. H.726, 1
Birth See Star-led-birth
I come to pay a Debt of Birth I owe...........27. H.82, 12
Mirt. And that his birth sho'd be more singular,..86. H.213, 19
Sung out his Birth with Heav'nly Minstralsie.....86. H.213, 24
The Calculation of thy Birth, Brave Mince...194. H.526, 6
Musique had both her birth, and death with Thee.
288. H.907, 10
What was thy Birth, thy starre that makes thee knowne,
299. H.956, 5
What was my Birth, to whom I was a Wife:....304. H.978, 2
Of Julia Herrick gave to me my Birth.........316. H.1028, 16
One Birth their Parents gave them; but their new,
326. H.1080, 25
Mans former Birth is grace-lesse; but the state.326. H.1080, 27
I sing Thy Birth, Oh JESU!.....................345. N.33, 2
Of Birth, a base................................345. N.33, 7
The Birth of this our heavenly King?............364. N.96, 3
'Tis He is borne, whose quickning Birth.........364. N.96, 19
The Birth is fruitlesse: Chor. Then the work God speed.
365. N.97, 19
Come, then, and gently touch the Birth..........366. N.98, 18
Or say, if this new Birth of ours...............367. N.102, 4
One Birth our Saviour had; the like none yet...384. N.182, 1
As for thy birth, and better seeds..............407. A.2, 19
Birthright Of His great Birth-right nothing derogate.
395. N.248, 4
Births By those ignoble Births, which shame the stem
251. H.745, 7
Bishop Next, like a Bishop consecrate my ground,.245. H.723, 7
Bishop't 'Tis Good Confirm'd; for you have Bishop't it.
64. H.168, 10
Bit A little Pipkin with a bit...................124. H.312, 5
Onely remaind a little bit,......................153. H.399, 8
E'en but a bit,...................................171. H.455, 12
Give for bread, a little bit.....................223. H.638, 12
A hope of my desired bit?.....................312. H.1014, 4
And eat with thee a savory bit,................321. H.1056, 5
Be they those that Homer bit,..................329. H.1096, 3
Flood, if he has for him and his a bit,..........332. H.1112, 1
And next, to take a bit..........................352. N.53, 7
Brought at the last to th' utmost bit,...........376. N.124, 3
Add but a bit of flesh, to boyle:.................377. N.130, 2
Bite Shake the Thyrse, and bite the Bayes:...... 39. H.111, 8
Thy Thyrse, and bite the Bayes.................81. H.201, 32
But though it scar'd, it did not bite............116. H.284, 6
Jolly and Jillie, bite and scratch all day,........156. H.411, 1
Nor Snake, or Slow-worme bite thee:..........217. H.619, 7
'Tis cowardice to bite the buried...............218. H.625, 2
Sent forth by them, our flesh to eate, or bite.....278. H.862, 4
Came a mad dog, and did bite,.................306. H.984, 34
To bark, or bite, without Thee?...............373. N.122, 12
Bite of themselves to scape away..........440. ins. H.443, 56b
Bites May every Ill, that bites, or smarts,............6. H.5, 3
Whose acrimonious humour bites him here.........98. H.239, 4
A hand to desp'rate, or a knife that bites......147. H.377, 53
Biting See Future-biting
Bits His choyce bitts with; then in a trice........119. H.293, 11
And with our Broth and bread, and bits; Sir, friend,
146. H.377, 23
Little bits, that nestle there..................224. H.638, 23
And all those other Bits, that bee..............350. N.47, 29
The Bits, the Morsells, and the deale...........374. N.123, 24
Some bitts of thimbles seeme to dresse...440. ins. H.443, 45aa
Bitten Saw Cupid bitten by a flea:................18. H.46, 2
A winged Snake has bitten me,................50. H.139, 8

Bitter So where He gives the bitter Pills, be sure,..344. N.31, 3
Shed for their Master many a bitter teare:......384. N.180, 10
What bitter cups had been your due,.........400. N.266, 14
Even Thou alone, the bitter cup...............400. N.267, 8
Bitterness Ther's in love, no bitterness..........138. H.346, 10
Thee in Thy severall parts of bitternesse;......399. N.263, 33
Black See Long-black-thumb-nail
And her grinders black as jet;.................11. H.21, 12
From Fames black lips, as you from me.........49. H.136, 36
First, in a Neech, more black than jet,..........90. H.223, 11
Where the bounds of black Death be:............96. H.231, 4
Black and rowling is her eye,...................138. H.342, 3
Black your haires are; mine are white;.........194. H.527, 5
Having but seven in all; three black, foure white..195. H.531, 2
Black I'm grown for want of meat;............223. H.638, 4
A Heifer smooth, and black as jet,.............243. H.716, 8
When the Black Dooms-day Bookes (as yet unseal'd)
256. H.763, 15
Dead all black contingencies:...................286. H.897, 8
Kisse my Brown wife, and black Posterity.......310. H.1003, 4
For my haires black colouring:..................330. H.1098, 2
Black-bearded For no black-bearded Vigil from thy doore
146. H.377, 13
Black-bore-cats Of black-bore-cats to attend her;.333. H.1122, 9
Blackest Of blackest silk, a curious twist 64. H.169, 2
Black-eyed To be but three, Black-ey'd, wee'l thinke y'are old.
173. H.462, 2
Blacks Sho'd I not put on Blacks, when each one here
288. H.907, 1
He who wears Blacks, and mournes not for the Dead,
319. H.1047, 1
The Muses will weare blackes, when I am dead..335. H.1128, 6
Blame You blame me too, because I cann't devise..15. H.38, 3
If ill, then Kings, not Souldiers beare the blame. 260. H.774, 4
We blame, nay we despise her paines............279. H.867, 1
The King he beares the blame of all............290. H.913, 2
Blameless With blamelesse carriage, I liv'd here,....41. H.116, 1
Blanch Blanch swears her Husband's lovely; when a scald
33. H.99, 1
But Blanch has not so much upon her head,......205. H.571, 3
Blandishment My Genius with a fuller blanishment?
78. H.197, 56
Along with it some tempting blandishment......389. N.217, 2
— — — — — — — — — —, ...427. var. H.197, 76
Blankets And next to these two blankets ore-....167. H.443, 94
So shall the Blankets which come over me,......392. N.230, 15
Blasphemies His mouth worse furr'd with oathes and blasphemies.......................................110. H.273, 4
Blast Blast these-like actions, or a thing that's worse;
79. H.197, 84
From the blast that burns by day;..............177. H.473, 4
To null his Numbers, and to blast his Crowne...188. H.506, 14
To blast the Aire, but Amber-greece and Gums...205. H.575, 6
Cloy'd they are up with Arse; but hope, one blast
226. H.650, 3
Blasting And (like a blasting Planet) found her out;
87. H.215, 4
Breath of a blasting wind;.....................104. H.257, 9
With blasting eye, the appetite,...............147. H.377, 48
Blaze Sometimes 'two'd blaze, and then abate,....67. H.175, 11
May blaze the vertue of their Sires...........116. H.283, 160
Blaze by this Sphere for ever: Or this doe,......264. H.789, 5
Blear Our eyes they'l blind, or if not blind, they'l bleer.
237. H.685, 12
Bleared Has blear'd his eyes: Besides, his head is bald.
33. H.99, 2
Bleat Then dream, ye heare the Lamb by many a bleat
36. H.106, 49
Bleating And with my sighs, call home my bleating sheep:
159. H.421, 38
Bleats Chor. Pan pipe to him, and bleats of lambs and sheep,
86. H.213, 17
Bled The finger bled, but burnt was all my heart...17. H.44, 8
Bleed Can make your's bleed a teare: 11. H.20, 5
That Heart to bleed, your's ne'r will ake..........11. H.20, 11
The fattest Oxe the first must bleed.............77. H.196, 2
Never see mine own heart bleed:................182. H.490, 2
To see me bleed, and not desire................272. H.828, 11
For, now unlesse ye see Him bleed,.............365. N.97, 17
Because the prettie Babe do's bleed............366. N.98, 21
Bleeding From this bleeding hand of mine,........88. H.217, 1
That little prettie bleeding part.................376. N.125, 1
And Ile returne a bleeding Heart,...............376. N.125, 3
Bleeding, that no Blood touch the ground:......377. N.129, 6
Love lyes a bleeding here, Evadne there..........415. A.7, 11
Bleer See Blear
Blend Where Anchus and rich Tullus blend......133. H.336, 26
or blend so as the sight.................431. ins. H.283, 50i
Blended Both to be blended in the Urn,.........233. H.670, 38
Bless I'm up, I'm up, and blesse that hand,.......72. H.185, 22
Did rather choose to blesse another clime?.......77. H.197, 22
We'll blesse the Babe, Then back to Countrie pleasures.
87. H.213, 48
Some blesse the Cart; some kisse the sheaves;..101. H.250, 19
Your praise, and bless you, sprinkling you with Wheat:
113. H.283, 46

And blesse his dainty Mistresse: see,...........114. H.283, 63
Blesse a Sack-posset; Luck go with it; take....115. H.283, 132
Weelcome! but yet no entrance, till we blesse..124. H.313, 1
Say, we must part (sweet mercy blesse........134. H.336, 65
Alas! we blesse, but see none here,............179. H.476, 25
Shall blesse thy Bed, and blesse thy Board.......192. H.521, 4
We blesse our Fortunes, when we see..........200. H.552, 17
Apollos Image side with Thee to blesse........254. H.756, 11
By all Aspects that blesse......................258. H.767, 11
Let's blesse the Babe: And, as we sing..........367. N.98, 25
His praise; so let us blesse the King:..........367. N.98, 26
God, and good Angells guide Thee; and so blesse.399. N.263, 32
And Hymen call'd to bless the Rites. Cha. Stop there.
416. A.8, 20
Blessed See Blest
As blessed soules cann't heare too much:..........22. H.68, 4
(More blessed in thy Brasse, then Land).........35. H.106, 24
A savour like unto a blessed field,..............112. H.283, 18
By, yet not blessed by his hands,...............119. H.293, 30
Hence a blessed soule is fled,..................211. H.593, 1
But yet those blessed gates I see...............277. H.854, 3
Whereon the blessed Babie lay.................355. N.60, 4
Would cry out, Thou are blessed...............375. N.123, 90
The blessed Image of a blushing rose...........405. A.1, 36
Whose blessèd Youth with endless flow'rs is crown'd.
417. A.8, 30
Blesses Seemes like Apollo's when the morne he blesses
404. A.1, 2
Blesseth So that, when she blesseth thee,.........236. H.684, 3
Blessing Drop the fat blessing of the spheares.....57. H.149, 152
Take thou my blessing, thus, and goe,...........98. H.238, 11
An easie blessing to your Bin,..................178. H.476, 2
Give them the blessing of encrease:.............221. H.633, 55
So a blessing light upon.......................224. H.638, 25
Half that blessing thou'lt give me..............236. H.684, 4
This Blessing I will leave thee, ere I go,........269. H.818, 3
The Blessing fall in mellow times on Thee.......269. H.818, 10
And this good blessing back them still,.........291. H.919, 11
Take wth my blessinge; and goe forth............409. A.2, 101
Blessings Blessings, in abundance come,..........124. H.314, 1
May a thousand blessings come!................220. H.633, 2
With thousand blessings by thy Fortune crown'd.
242. H.713, 6
To load with blessings, and unload from sins......341. N.14, 2
Among Gods Blessings, there is no one small.....353. N.55, 2
— — — — — — — — — —, ...427. var. H.197, 83
Blest See Blessed
Blest with perpetuall greene,......................30. H.89, 7
Thrice, and above, blest (my soules halfe) art thou,
34. H.106, 1
But thou at home, blest with securest ease,.......36. H.106, 69
Then to her Cabbin, blest she can escape.........37. H.106, 125
Live, and live blest; thrice happy Paire; Let Breath,
38. H.106, 141
And all in Your Blest Hand, which has the powers
62. H.161, 7
Blest in my love;..............................87. H.214, 10
Blest is the Bride, on whom the Sun doth shine;.113. H.283, 48
No, know (Blest Maide) when there's not one....146. H.376, 7
Have I not blest Thee? Then go forth; nor fear..155. H.405, 1
Of all those other Saints now blest;............169. H.449, 25
To thee, blest place of my Nativitie!...........242. H.713, 4
I be kist, or blest by thee.....................286. H.897, 12
No man is blest through ev'ry part..............351. N.50, 4
O virgin-martyr, ever blest....................359. N.83, 3
A quire of blest Soules circling in the Father.....383. N.177, 2
Blest with the Meditation of my end:............392. N.230, 2
And when He blest each sev'rall Day, whereon..396. N.249, 3
God blest His work done on the second day:.....396. H.249, 6
Of all that ever yet hath blest............435. ins. H. 293, ee
Blew See Blue
Blewer See Bluer
Blind When age or Chance has made me blind,.....32. H.98, 1
May blow my ashes up, and strike thee blind.....49. H.138, 8
Night now hath watch'd her self half blind;......54. H.149, 31
Though thou wert ne'r so blind.................80. H.201, 16
But home return'd, as he went forth, halfe blind...201. H.555, 4
Our eyes they'l blind, or if not blind, they'l bleer.
237. H.685, 12
Fortune's a blind profuser of her own,..........238. H.689, 1
Gifts blind the wise, and bribes do please,........357. N.72, 9
When drunck wth Rapture; Curse the blind & lame.
412. A.3, 89
— — — — — — — — — —, ...428. var. H.235, 6
— — — — — — — — — —, ...437. var. H.336, 108
Blindman's buff Of Blind-man-buffe, and of the care
126. H.319, 15
Blinks Tom Blinks his Nose is full of wheales, and these
273. H.834, 1
Bliss This is the portall to the bowre of blisse......406. A.1, 74
Blisse Blisse (last night drunk) did kisse his mothers knee:
295. H.943, 1
Blithe Drink frollick boyes, till all be blythe.....102. H.250, 43
Blitheful Drink Wine, and live here blithefull, while ye may:
228. H.655, 1
Come blithefull Neatherds, let us lay..........243. H.716, 1

Bloated A bloated Earewig, and a Flie;........119. H.293, 38
Bloater — — — — — — — —, ...434. ins. H.293, 41c
Block Light the new block, And...............263. H.784, 8
Blood See Frost-bound-blood, Royal-blood
And to all flowers ally'd in blood,................7. H.9, 7
To me, as blood to life and spirit; Neare,........45. H.128, 2
But their own flesh and blood,.................75. H.193, 31
Full goblets of thy gen'rous blood; his spright..78. H.197, 67
Swell up my nerves with spirit; let my blood....79. H.197, 77
When Youth and Blood are warmer;...........84. H.208, 10
Yet lost, ere that chast flesh and blood..........88. H.216, 8
We knew 'twas Flesh and Blood, that there sate mute.
95. H.228, 2
Fresh, as their blood; and ever grow,..........104. H.256, 19
There waves the Streamer of her blood.......107. H.263, 12
His blood to height; this done, commended....120. H.293, 53
Lately made of flesh and blood:...............123. H.310, 2
Which so betrayes her blood, as we discover....158. H.416, 3
If Accusation onely can draw blood,............194. H.528, 1
Drown'd in the bloud of Rubies there, not die...216. H.618, 16
Love must be fed by wealth: this blood of mine..258. H.768, 3
But must be niggards of the meanest bloud......260. H.775, 2
How cold it was, and how it child my blood;....262. H.783, 18
To stench the blood the while.................272. H.828, 12
But in their springing blood so play,............291. H.919, 19
But with this comfort, if my blood be shed,....335. H.1128, 5
Yet if Thy Bloud not wash me, there's no hope...357. N.73, 4
And from His sacred Bloud, here shed,..........366. N.97, 22
Bring'st in Thy Blood, a Balm, that shall........366. N.98, 23
Bleeding, that no Blood touch the ground:.......377. N.129, 6
Speak, did the Bloud of Abel cry...............387. N.203, 1
Ev'n as the sprinkled bloud cal'd on............387. N.203, 3
The bloud of Abel was a thing................388. N.204, 1
God bought man here wth his hearts blood expence;
389. N.213, 1
Pierc't through, and dropping bloud, for me,....400. N.267, 4
Bloud will be spilt;.........................401. N.268, 11
Or A colde Poyson, which his blood............409. A.2, 87
Skynne and colour, flesh and blood,..............418. A.9, 21
Fire unto all my functions, gives me blood,.426. ins. H.197, 48c
All mighty blood; and can doe more......437. var. H.336, 135
Blood-guiltiness And never shew blood-guiltinesse, or feare
64. H.168, 3
Bloodshot She now weares silk to hide her blood-shot eye.
207. H.578, 2
Bloom In bloome of Peach, and Roses bud,......107. H.263, 11
As is the childish Bloome of Beane,.............408. A.2, 56
Bloomed Bloom'd from the East, or faire Injewel'd May
112. H.283, 2
Blooming Get up, get up for shame, the Blooming Morne
67. H.178, 1
Unto our smiling, and our blooming King,......86. H.213, 34
So smels the flowre of blooming Clove;........145. H.375, 3
And their losse in blooming yeares;............152. H.391, 6
Who dying in her blooming yeares,..............257. H.764, 5
Blooms The Blooms that fell were white and red;
283. H.883, 3
Blossoms I sing of Brooks, of Blossomes, Birds, and Bowers:
5. H.1, 1
And Almond blossoms, that do mix............145. H.375, 13
Fresh blossoms from her cheekes did fall.........203. H.562, 2
As Blossomes of the Almond Tree..............203. H.562, 6
Sweet as the blossomes of the Vine...........230. H.662, 34
Wo'd ye oyle of Blossomes get?................244. H.719, 1
Love in a showre of Blossomes came...........283. H.883, 1
Blot Forgive me God, and blot each Line..........339. N.2, 5
Blouze And calls his Blouze, his Queene;.......259. H.772, 23
Blow See Fly-blow
Furze, three or foure times with his cheeks did blow
47. H.131, 3
May blow my ashes up, and strike thee blind.....49. H.138, 8
Cheeks like to Roses, when they blow...........120. H.295, 2
To blow, and seed, and so away;..............126. H.318, 2
You must blow;..............................137. H.340, 16
Looke red, and blow, and bluster, but not speake:.150. H.382, 8
Or any blow.................................161. H.426, 2
Trees never beare, unlesse they first do blow....180. H.477, 6
Ripe Cherries smiling, while that others blow.....193. H.523, 2
Will whirle about, and blow them thence at last..226. H.650, 4
Let her breath, or let her blow,................244. H.719, 5
Dead the Fire, though ye blow..................263. H.786, 4
Where the Northern Winds do blow.............266. H.803, 2
As aires doe breathe, or winds doe blow:........282. H.881, 8
And by that One blow set an end to all........310. H.1002, 4
As to withstand the blow....................335. H.1129, 4
And be the blow too what it will,................351. N.48, 3
The winds, to blow the tedious night away;.......358. N.77, 6
The blow of Ruine and of Chance.................407. A.2, 11
Blown See Full-blown
Now, now, blowne downe; needs must the old stock fall.
72. H.185, 14
Blowne out of April; or some New-.............112. H.283, 3
(Sweet as your selfe, and newly blown).........126. H.318, 8
Like to a field of beans, when newly blown;....159. H.421, 20
And tell Him, by that Bud now blown,...........354. N.59, 3
Blows Her blowes did make ye blew............105. H.260, 8
Though by well-warding many blowes w'ave past,.237. H.688, 1
Words beget Anger: Anger brings forth blowes:..287. H.901, 1
Blowes make of dearest friends immortall Foes...287. H.901, 2
As some plants prosper best by cuts and blowes;..292. H.929, 3
A crackt horne she blowes;...................334. H.1122, 14
First stripes, new blowes,......................363. N.92, 11
Whom ease makes his, without the help of blowes.372. N.116, 4
Blubbering He'll slit her nose; But blubb'ring, she replyes,
44. H.126, 2
Then blubbering, replyed he,...................50. H.139, 7
Now blubb'ring, cry,.........................296. H.946, 8
Blue See Stiff-blue-pig's-feet, Great-blue-ruler
His cheeks be-pimpled, red and blue;............38. H.108, 7
Her blowes did make ye blew.................105. H.260, 8
Brought and besweetned in a blew.............119. H.293, 22
The roome is hung with the blew skin.........166. H.443, 66
Nor shall the Tapers when I'm there, burn blew..222. H.634, 9
The flimsie Livers, and blew Gizzards are.......326. H.1079, 2
When the tapers now burne blew,...............348. N.41, 25
Blew pinnes, tagges, fescues, beades and thinges
440. ins. H.443, 45r
Bluer That shines upon the blewer Plum.........166. H.443, 58
Blunder And while we blunder in the dark,.......372. N.118, 7
Blush See Maiden's-blush, Soft-maiden's-blush
May blush, (while Brutus standeth by:)...........6. H.4, 2
Had not her Blush rebuked me.................14. H.33, 4
Faults done by night, will blush by day:..........20. H.56, 6
Ye may simper, blush, and smile,...............74. H.189, 1
Blush not at all for that; since we have set......76. H.194, 5
A blush their cheeks bespred;.................105. H.258, 6
And of her blush at such a feast...............135. H.336, 96
Cherrish the cheek, but make none blush at all...140. H.354, 12
The blush of cherries, when a Lawn's cast over..158. H.416, 4
To blush and gently smile;...................176. H.467, 5
So with a blush, beshrew'd the deed............187. H.504, 6
So Cherries blush, and Kathern Peares,..........268. H.811, 3
If blush thou must, then blush thou through....271. H.824, 9
And what we blush to speake, she bids us write...275. H.846, 2
Teach it to blush, to curtsie, lisp, and shew......290. H.914, 5
Ready to blush to death, sho'd he but chide.......301. H.963, 4
She with a dainty blush rebuk't her face;........311. H.1006, 3
Will blush to death, if ought be spi'd...........366. N.98, 13
— — — — — — — — — —, ...432. var. H.283, 97
Blushed They blush'd, and look'd more fresh then flowers
25. H.78, 5
Sweet Bridget blusht, & therewithall,............203. H.562, 1
She smiling blusht, and blushing smil'd,........251. H.740, 5
Blushes When Julia blushes, she do's show........120. H.295, 1
Forth into blushes, whensoere he speaks.........124. H.311, 2
T'ave your blushes seen by day.................276. H.850, 14
Blush-guiltiness If you say (I) Blush-guiltinesse will shew it.
274. H.837, 6
Blushing Name it I would; but being blushing red,.24. H.74, 13
Into the blushing Peare, or Plum:...............79. H.198, 4
Or seen rich Rubies blushing through..........164. H.440, 7
The blushing Apple, bashfull Peare,............192. H.521, 37
Of fragrant Apples, blushing Plums, or Peares:..205. H.575, 10
She smiling blusht, and blushing smil'd,..........251. H.740, 5
And sweetly blushing thus,.....................251. H.740, 6
Him in the Mornings blushing cheek,............367. N.102, 9
The blessed Image of a blushing rose............405. A.1, 36
Blushing-pretty-peeping A·blushing-pretty-peeping Rubelet:
227. H.652, 10
Bluster Looke red, and blow, and bluster, but not speake:
150. H.382, 8
Blythe See Blithe
Board To th' board, so hot, as none co'd touch the same:
47. H.131, 2
Which o're the board is smoothly spred,........91. H.223, 62
Upon this fetuous board doth stand............92. H.223, 68
The Bason stands the board upon...............92. H.223, 85
Where Trouble serves the board, we eate........124. H.312, 3
While Reverence, waiting at the bashfull board,..148. H.377, 75
Shall blesse thy Bed, and blesse thy Board.......192. H.521, 4
Here, here I live with what my Board,..........200. H.552, 1
Then for contriving so to loade thy Board,.....210. H.590, 5
To board the Magicke bowle, and spill....437. var. H. 336, 134
Boast Of Flanks and Chines of Beefe doth Gorrell boast
89. H.221, 1
Of antient honesty, may boast................147. H.377, 42
Pievish doth boast, that he's the very first......156. H.410, 1
These were those Three Horatii Rome did boast,.170. H.451, 13
Boasts Leech boasts, he has a Pill, that can alone,.125. H.315, 1
Spunge makes his boasts that he's the onely man.171. H.454, 1
Boat That made me thus hoist saile, and bring my Boat:
248. H.730, 12
For mending sails, for patching Boat and Oares?.248. H.730, 20
A little streame best fits a little Boat;.........249. H.733, 13
Euc. Charon, O Charon, draw thy Boat to th' Shore,
416, A.8, 1
A boat, A boat, hast to the ferry..........445. ins. H.730, 26a
Boats — — — — — — — —, ...445. var. H.730, 20
Bode Ill luck 'twill bode to th' Bridegroome and the Bride.
262. H.781, 12
Boded He Boded good-luck to thy Selfe and Spouse.
181. H.843, 12

Bodies Which **Bodies** do, when Souls from them depart. 42. H.122, 2
(**Bodies** and souls commingled)..................59. H.152, 10
And when all **Bodies** meet......................81. H.201, 49
Soules doe not with their **bodies** die:............89. H.219, 16
Of Planetary **bodies**; so commence............116. H.283, 156
Her silken **bodies**, but a breathing space:........157. H.414, 6
Great Spirits never with their **bodies** dye.........199. H.547, 2
Body Male to the female, soule to **body**: Life......45. H.128, 4
The **body** of the under-dead?....................103. H.256, 7
Has it a **body**? 2. I, and wings................130. H.329, 20
Prigg bears away the **body** and the sole.........143. H.368, 4
Whose pure-Immortall **body** doth transmit.......157. H.414, 9
The **body** sins not, 'tis the Will................175. H.465, 63
Leaving here the **body** dead:....................211. H.593, 2
Wisheth his **body**, not his soule, good speed......277. H.855, 2
The **Body** is the Soules poore house, or home,....279. H.865, 1
Salve for my **body**, and my mind................342. N.17, 4
For each one **Body**, that i'th earth is sowne,....388. N.208, 1
When sleep shall bath his **body** in mine eyes,....392. N.230, 19
I will believe, that then my **body** dies:..........392. N.230, 20
which sees the **body** fedd, yet pined........432. ins. H.283, 70j
Body's Life is the **Bodies** light; which once declining, 207. H.576, 1
The **body's** salt, the soule is; which when gon,...332. H.1111, 1
Boëtius Jehovah, as **Boëtius** saith,...............382. N.168, 1
Boil **See Overboil**
Ye **boil** with Love, as well as I.................157. H.413, 8
Add but a bit of flesh, to **boyle**:................377. N.130, 2
As my little Pot doth **boyle**,....................397. N.258, 1
Boiled **See Thrice-boiled-worts, Well-boiled**
To taste **boyl'd** Netties, Colworts, Beets, and eate 37. H.106, 113
He has at home; but who tasts **boil'd** or rost?....89. H.221, 2
Boils Wrath yf resisted ouer **boyles**,..............408. A.2, 71
Boisterous If after rude and **boystrous** seas,.......94. H.225, 1
No **boysterous** winds, or stormes, come hither,...361. N.83, 69
Bold Be so, **bold** spirit; Stand Center-like, unmov'd; 37. H.106, 101
Bold bolt of thunder he will make his way,....116. H.283, 148
Be **bold** my Booke, nor be abasht, or feare......212. H.603, 1
Of thy brave, **bold**, and sweet Maronian Muse...234. H.673, 12
I have been wanton, and too **bold** I feare,......329. H.1095, 1
So that with **bold** truth, thou canst now relate..330. H.1100, 7
Suffer me to be so **bold**,........................347. N.40, 3
To barr out **bolde** Adulteryes,...................408. A.2, 36
— — — — — — — — —, ...440. var. H.443, 76
Bold-faced No glaring light of **bold-fac't** Day,....167. H.443, 76
Boldly He ventures **boldly** on the pith..........119. H.293, 32
Immortall selfe, shall **boldly** trust.............278. H.859, 5
Then **boldly** give thine incense to the fire........299. H.957, 4
Boldly in sin, shall feel more punishment.........391. N.227, 4
— — — — — — — — — —, ...424. var. H.128, 49
Boldness And for their **boldness** stript them:........31. H.92, 6
With **boldness** that we feare......................259. H.772, 4
Bolt Barre close as you can, and **bolt** fast too your doore, 97. H.233, 1
Bold **bolt** of thunder he will make his way,....116. H.283, 148
The cleaving **Bolt** of Jove the Thunderer........181. H.483, 16
Bolts All **bolts**, all barres, all gates shall cleave; as when 52. H.46, 14
Bond To keep my **Bond** still free from forfeiture...136. H.338, 4
Or if thou tak'st that **bond** away,...............293. H.934, 5
His was the **Bond** and Cov'nant, yet............360. N.83, 21
By Law, the **Bond** once cancelled..............370. N.107, 15
Bondage In which **bondage** we will lie,.............235. H.678, 7
Bondage more Loued then Lybertye.............408. A.2, 64
Bondman A **bondman** unto thee..................293. H.934, 4
Bonds I brake my **bonds** of Love, and bad thee goe,..6. H.3, 5
He loves his **bonds**, who when the first are broke,..17. H.42, 5
Insteade of gould Pearle Rubies **Bonds**...........407. A.2, 7
Bondslave But thy **Bondslave** is my heart:.......128. H.322, 6
Bone **See Mutton-bone**
But of a little Transverce **bone**;................91. H.223, 57
The Cock and Hen he feeds; but not a **bone**....204. H.568, 5
To grace his own Gums, or of Box, or **bone**......211. H.595, 2
Poor relique of the beawty, **bone**,..................418. A.9, 24
Bones **See Nine-bones**
Whether thy **bones** had here their Rest, or no...27. H.82, 6
Amphion-like) men made of flesh and **bones**,....84. H.210, 6
Girt with small **bones**, instead of walls..........90. H.223, 10
Dry chips, old shooes, rags, grease, & **bones**;....93. H.223, 119
By the dead **bones** of our deare Ancestrie........278. H.860, 8
Boniface Elve **Boniface** shall next be Pope.......93. H.223, 112
Bonnet I'le seek him in your **Bonnet** brave;....156. H.412, 13
Bonny Once a brisk and **bonny** Lasse,..............14. H.36, 4
Book Well may my **Book** come forth like Publique Day 3. Ded.H., 1
Full is my **Book** of Glories; but all These........3. Ded.H, 9
The Seed; so sow'd these Tares throughout my **Book**. 4. Ap., 4
To read my **Booke** the Virgin shie..................6. H.4, 1
But if thou read'st my **Booke** unto the end,........7. H.6, 3
Better 'twere my **Book** were dead,................21. H.59, 5
Like to a Bride, come forth my **Book**, at last,....76. H.194, 1
I, and their **Book** of Canons too................92. H.223, 78
They have their **Book** of Articles:..............92. H.223, 80
They have their **Book** of Homilies:..............92. H.223, 82
And see your selfe to beautifie my **Book**;........94. H.226, 2
I see a Cloud of Glory fills my **Book**............99. H.245, 4
Permit my **Book** to have a free accesse........137. H.341, 11
Markt in thy **Book** for faithfull Witnesses.........188. H.507, 4
Be bold my **Booke**, nor be abasht, or feare......212. H.603, 1
Then but to read this in my **Booke**:............214. H.611, 2
That sho'd my **Booke** despised be,..............214. H.613, 3
Besides rare sweets, I had a **Book** which none..227. H.652, 5
About the Cover of this **Book** there went........227. H.652, 7
Who read'st this **Book** that I have writ,..........229. H.660, 1
Looke in my **Book**, and herein see,..............288. H.906, 1
The bound (almost) now of my **book** I see......313. H.1019, 1
And in my **Booke** now claim a two-fold right:..322. H.1062, 11
Nor thinke that Thou in this my **Booke** art worst, 329. H.1092, 1
Claspe thou his **Book**, then close thou up his Eyes. 329. H.1095, 8
Goe thou forth my **booke** though late;..........334. H.1125, 1
Out of my **Book**, that is not Thine..............339. N.2, 6
My **Book**, 'tis this; that Thou, my God, art in't...355. N.61, 2
But take no tincture from my sinfull **Book**:......371. N.113, 8
Reading Thy Bible, and my **Book**; so end......371. N.115, 12
Let them read this **booke** and learne..............418. A.9, 55
Book's Never my **Book's** perfection did appeare,...99. H.245, 1
Here, in my **Book's** Canonization:..............188. H.510, 2
To his **Book's** end this last line he'd have plac't,.335. H.1130, 1
Books Their Beads of Nits, Bels, **Books**, & Wax.93. H.223, 115
How dull and dead are **books**, that cannot show..141. H.359, 1
In **Bookes** of fame;..............................161. H.426, 13
Shall find much farcing Buckram in our **Books**...202. H.559, 2
When the Black Dooms-day **Bookes** (as yet unseal'd) 256. H.763, 15
Or reade in Volumes, and those **Bookes** (with all 330. H.1100, 3
The truth of Travails lesse in **bookes** then Thee..330. H.1100, 18
Boon With all her Owle-ey'd issue begs a **boon**..116. H.283, 152
Boot How co'd Luke Smeaton weare a shoe, or **boot**, 240. H.704, 1
Bo-peep As if they started at **Bo-peep**,...........194. H.525, 4
Bore **See Black-bore-cats**
Which **bore** my Love away......................156. H.412, 12
Then **bore** me through the eare;................293. H.934, 6
Boreman **Boreman** takes tole, cheats, flatters, lyes, yet **Boreman**, 315. H.1025, 1
Born **See Borne, First-born, Free-born, New-born, Sea-born, Stillborn**
Since I was **born**, then here;......................19. H.51, 2
So oft, we'll think, we see a King new **born**.......26. H.80, 2
But **borne**, and like a short Delight,..............69. H.180, 1
Thou mak'st me ayrie, active to be **born**,.........78. H.197, 49
To all our joy, a sweet-fac't child was **borne**,....86. H.213, 15
To Gods sweet Babe, when **borne** at Bethlehem;..86. H.213, 22
And Angels will be **borne**, while thou dost sing...102. H.252, 2
Who were but **borne**...........................104. H.257, 3
It is a creature **born** and bred..................130. H.329, 4
You, who are High **born**, and a Lord no lesse....141. H.359, 3
When it is **born**: (by some enstyl'd............167. H.443, 92
What, were yee **borne** to be....................176. H.467, 7
Borne I was to meet with Age,..................191. H.519, 1
Wo'd thou hast ne'r been **born**, or might'st not die. 193. H.522, 6
Born I was to be old,..........................197. H.540, 1
Men are not **born** Kings, but are men renown'd;..241. H.707, 1
To be, or not **borne** of the Royall-blood.........297. H.947, 8
Thou prettie Babie, **borne** here,..................345. N.33, 3
'Tis He is **borne**, whose quickning Birth........364. N.96, 19
Before Mans fall, the Rose was **born**............396. N.251, 1
Without the fragrant Rose-bud, **born**;..........396. N.251, 4
Borne **See Born, Home-Borne**
They must be **borne** with, and in rev'rence had.....32. H.97, 2
Be ye to the Barn then **born**,...................58. H.149, 169
His hungry belly **borne** by Legs Jaile-free.......332. H.1112, 4
Hence they have **born** my Lord: Behold! the Stone 403. N.271, 1
And vnder it two Chast **borne** spyes..............408. A.2, 35
Borrow And knowes not where i'th world to **borrow** more. 160. H.423, 4
Borrowing — — — — — — — — —, ...422. var. H.106, 81
Bosom A deale of courage in each **bosome** springs...25. H.77, 9
Within the **Bosome** of my Love your grave.......249. H.734, 2
Your Grave her **Bosome** is, the Lawne the Stone. 249. H.734, 4
To her warm **bosome**, then our Rites are ended...366. N.97, 29
— — — — — — — — — — —, ...426. var. H.197, 26
Botch A meere **Botch** of all and some............76. H.195, 4
Both But when that men have **both** well drunke, and fed, 7. H.8, 3
I dream'd we **both** were in a bed..................20. H.56, 1
The rest Ile speak, when we meet **both** in bed.....24. H.74, 14
Newly refresh't, **both** by the Sun, and showers.....25. H.77, 6
In thy **both** Last, and Better Vow:..............34. H.106, 2
And **both** are knowne to thee, who now can'st live.35. H.106, 11
Be so one Death, one Grave to **both**............38. H.106, 144
Horace, Anacreon **both** had lost their fame,......45. H.128, 31

Both bring one death; and I die here,..........50. H.140, 9
Any noise, they **both** will wake,..................52. H.145, 4
And now, **both** Love and Time................56. H.149, 123
And moisture, **both** compleat:..................57. H.149, 126
But when ye **both** can say,....................58. H.149, 167
Trees, at one time, shall be **both** sere and greene:..59. H.154, 2
See, **both** these Lady-flowers decay:.............61. H.159, 16
Both the cause, and make the heat.............62. H.162, 14
To shew at once, **both** night and day...........64. H.169, 8
He vow'd Destruction **both** to Birch, and Men:....65. H.171, 2
Many a kisse, **both** odde and even:.............69. H.178, 52
Thou hast **both** Wind and Tide with thee; Thy way.73. H.186, 3
How **both** his Meale and Oile will multiply.......73. H.188, 4
In a Cloud; while **both** did play,................74. H.190, 6
Both with her Husband's, and her own tough fleame.
98. H.237, 2
Who doth **both** love and feare you Honour'd Sir...99. H.245, 8
Both tormenting Lovers ever.................103. H.253, 10
Penance, and standing so, are **both** but one.......106. H.261, 4
And be **both** Princesse here, and Poetresse.......107. H.265, 10
A clammie Reume makes loathsome **both** his eyes:.110. H.273, 3
Both you two have...........................111. H.280, 1
Jealousie, and **both** will through:...............116. H.285, 4
First you, then you, and **both** for white successe...124. H.313, 2
That done; when **both** of you have seemly fed,..124. H.313, 9
We'll call on Night, to bring ye **both** to Bed:..124. H.313, 10
Which spent, one death, bring to ye **both** one Grave.
124. H.313, 14
On ye **both**; Goodnight to all.................125. H.314, 10
Both by a shining Salt-seller:..................133. H.336, 50
Us **both** i'th' Sea, Camp, Wildernesse).........134. H.336, 66
They are **both** hard, and marr'd,................138. H.344, 3
Give **both** the Gold and Garland unto it.........141. H.359, 16
Or **both** of them, that do agree.................142. H.362, 3
Fame, and his Name, **both** set, and sing his Lyricks.
143. H.366, 4
Where **both** may feed, and come againe:......146. H.377, 12
Safe stand thy Walls, and Thee, and so **both** will,
149. H.377, 115
Oft have I heard **both** Youths and Virgins say...149. H.378, 1
A scent, that fills **both** Heaven and Earth with it.
157. H.414, 10
Mon. Troth, bad are **both**; worse fruit, and ill the tree:
159. H.421, 2
Since Jack and Jill **both** wicked be;...........163. H.434, 1
We'l wish **both** Them and Thee, good night...165. H.443, 8
Covet not **both**; but if thou dost...............169. H.446, 9
Both, lest thou lose thy liberty:................174. H.465, 26
May **both** with manchet stand repleat;........178. H.476, 4
Both to the Cocks-tread say Amen;..........179. H.476, 20
Nor will they leave Thee, till they **both** have shown
181. H.483, 7
Where **both** seem'd proud; the Flie to have....185. H.497, 3
One Fate had **both**; **both** equall Grace;.......185. H.497, 7
Kissing and bussing differ **both** in this;.......189. H.512, 1
Both Bed, and Bride..........................190. H.515, 10
Of Lyrick Wine, **both** swell'd and crown'd,.....198. H.544, 16
To be my Counsell **both**, and Chanceller.........202. H.557, 30
Both for their comely need, and some to spare:..205. H.571, 2
Where **both** may rage, **both** drink and dance together.
206. H.575, 38
Pleasing alike; alike **both** singular:.............209. H.586, 4
Fall down together vanquisht **both**, and lye....216. H.618, 15
Both to be blended in the Urn,...............233. H.670, 38
Captive one, or **both**, to take:..................235. H.678, 6
But a just measure **both** of Heat and Cold.......236. H.683, 2
Since **both** have here deserved best............243. H.716, 36
But the Relation then of **both** growes poor,.....255. H.758, 3
Of **both** our Fortunes good and bad we find...257. H.765, 1
Pusse and her Prentice **both** at Draw-gloves play;
260. H.773, 1
They draw their clothes off **both**, so draw to bed.
260. H.773, 4
And Genius waits to have us **both** to bed.......261. H.781, 6
(Amongst the rest) **both** bright and singular;...267. H.804, 10
Is **both** unluckie; I, and foolish too...........268. H.813, 2
Hold but her hands; You hold **both** hands and wings.
271. H.823, 6
Who **both** your wooer, and your Poet is.......274. H.837, 2
Nature has pre-compos'd us **both** to Love;......274. H.837, 3
Wanting **both** Root, and Earth; but thy........278. H.859, 4
Of thy **both** Great, and everlasting fate.........280. H.869, 4
Both addresse to sacrifice:....................280. H.870, 2
One knell be rung for **both**; and let one grave...281. H.875, 5
Mistake the flesh, and flye-blow **both** his eyes;.282. H.879, 2
Both of a fresh, and fragrant kinne..........285. H.892, 15
Musique had **both** her birth, and death with Thee.
288. H.907, 10
Selecting here, **both** Herbs, and Flowers;......289. H.912, 2
Vertue and pleasure, **both** to dwell in one.......293. H.935, 2
And on a sudden **both** were drown'd...........294. H.937, 4
And bring t' th' heart destruction **both** alike...333. H.1120, 6
Bettering them **both**, but by a double straine,....343. N.24, 3
Adverse and prosperous Fortunes **both** work on..349. N.44, 1
Both soft, and drie;..........................349. N.47, 6
Both void of state;...........................350. N.47, 12
To a Love-Feast we **both** invited are:..........355. N.65, 1
Both hung upon the Willow-tree?..............361. N.84, 2
Devote to Thee, **both** incense, myrrhe, and gold,.369. N.105, 6
Both with the Rubie, Pearle, and Diamond.....369. N.105, 8
Which, rightly us'd, **both** in their time and place,
371. N.115, 7
And then to weep they **both** were licensed.....384. N.180, 12
We then **both** chew the Cud, and cleave the Hoof.
397. N.256, 4
The Lawes of Action, will **both** sigh, and weep;
399. N.263, 37
Both to the Judge, and Judgment-Hall:.........399. N.265, 6
A man **both** bruis'd, and broke, and one.......400. N.266, 4
For I have washt **both** hand and heart,.......402. N.269, 6
Which sweetly mixed **both** with white and redd...404. A.1, 17
That **both** her lipps doe part, doe meete, doe kisse;
405. A.1, 38
Resembling sheilds **both** smooth and christalline....406. A.1, 80
Both from the Morning to the Euening Chyme;..410. A.3, 16
We **both** were lost, if **both** of us not sunderd;....414. A.6, 6
With admiration **both** of them and thee,...........415. A.7, 4
— — — — — — — — — — — —, ...421. var. H.49, 3
— — — — — — — — — — — —, ...440. var. H.443, 56

Bottle A Bag and **Bottle** thou shalt have;......192. H.521, 21

Bottom Thy rockie **bottome**, that doth teare thy streams
29. H.86, 3
And well-laid **bottome**, on the iron and rock,...148. H.377, 109

Bottomless A depth in love, and that depth, **bottomlesse**.
15. H.38, 12
In our State-sanctions, deep, or **bottomlesse**.....187. H.506, 8

Bough To that soft Charm, that Spell, that Magick **Bough**,
62. H.161, 9
Devotion gives each House a **Bough**,............68. H.178, 32
Bear up the Magick **bough**, and spel:........136. H.336, 134
First dyes the Leafe, the **Bough** next, next the Tree.
203. H.565, 4
But, ah, alas! the Almond **Bough**,............375. N.123, 51

Boughs Upon your **Boughs**, and Requiems sung..169. H.449, 16
With cooler Oken **boughs**;....................285. H.892, 18
In Barge (with **boughes** and rushes beautifi'd).315. H.1028, 8

Bought His gifts go from him; if not **bought** with sweat.
177. H.469, 2
God **bought** man here wth his hearts blood expence;
389. N.213, 1
With mullet, Turbot, guilthead **bought**....436. ins. H.336, 48g

Bound See **Frost-bound-blood**
About thy neck a Carkanet is **bound**,.............30. H.88, 5
Gubbs call's his children Kitlings: and wo'd **bound**
80. H.200, 1
As lately I a Garland **bound**,.....................96. H.229, 1
The Harvest Swaines, and Wenches **bound**...101. H.250, 13
I am **bound**, and fast **bound** so,...............128. H.322, 10
Then, when I see thy Tresses **bound**..........202. H.560, 9
Time is the **Bound** of things, where e're we go..257. H.766, 1
The **bound** (almost) now of my book I see....313. H.1019, 1
The Haven reacht to which I first was **bound**...334. H.1127, 2
How am I **bound** to Two! God, who doth give...355. N.62, 1
And sullen clouds **bound** up his head...........393. N.232, 6

Bounding At which the hounds fall a **bounding**;..334. H.1122, 15

Boundless Into the **boundlesse** aire:............75. H.193, 21
But yet if **boundlesse** Lust must skaile........175. H.465, 53
Gods **boundlesse** mercy is (to sinfull man)......341. N.15, 1

Bounds Where the **bounds** of black Death be:....96. H.231, 4
But walk'st about thine own dear **bounds**,......230. H.662, 15
See this, View that, and all the other **bounds**:..259. H.771, 4
My kisse out-went the **bounds** of shamfastnesse:.294. H.936, 2
Men must have **Bounds** how farre to walke; for we
307. H.990, 1

Bounteous Let **bounteous** Fate your spindles full..58. H.149, 161

Bounty For love and **bountie**, to come neare, and see.
131. H.331, 3
First, may the hand of **bounty** bring..........291. H 919, 1
Had all been poore, who had His **Bounty** seen?...356. N.69, 4
Me thought, I did Thy **bounty** chide,..........358. N.75, 5
Gods **Bounty**, that ebbs lesse and lesse,..........358. N.76, 1
With that small stock, Thy **Bounty** gave or lent.
368. N.104, 12

Bourn See **Dean-Bourn**

Bousing See **Bouzing**

'Bout See **About**
'Bout a Virgin like a Vine:......................17. H.43, 4
So smiles that Riband **'bout** my Julia's waste:..40. H.114, 2
Then Willow-garlands, **'bout** the head,..........106. H.262, 7
And dancing **'bout** the Mystick Thyrse,........136. H.336, 135
Though while we living **'bout** the world do roame,
278. H.860, 5

Bouzing Still I be **Bousing**;....................197. H.540, 6

'Bove See **Above**
And having danc't (**'bove** all the best).........192. H.521, 33
'Bove all things lov'd it, for the puritie:........390. N.222, 2
Soaring them vpp, **boue** Ruyne, till the doome..410. A.3, 33

Bow See **Rainbow, Under-bow**
I saw he had a **Bow**,..........................27. H.81, 17
Let's try this **bow** of ours,.....................27. H.81, 26
Forthwith his **bow** he bent,.....................27. H.81, 29
A silver **bow** with green silk strung,...........51. H.142, 9

Sweet Bents wode **bow**, to give my Love the day:
159. H.421, 24
Oft bend the **Bow**, and thou with ease shalt do,.245. H.722, 1
And though I saw no **Bow**, I'm sure,.........295. H.942, 15
No Arrow nockt, onely a stringlesse **Bow**:......357. N.74, 2
— — — — — — — — — —, ...437. var. H.336, 134
Bowed Each Flower has wept, and **bow'd** toward the East,
68. H.178, 7
Bower Rosamond was in a **Bower**..............120. H.297, 3
This is the portall to the **bowre** of blisse.......406. A.1, 74
Bowers I sing of Brooks, of Blossomes, Birds, and **Bowers**:
5. H.1, 1
The Purling springs, groves, birds, and well-weav'd **Bowrs**,
36. H.106, 45
So smell those neat and woven **Bowers**,........145. H.375, 11
Thou leav'st our Hills, our Dales, our **Bowers**,..183. H.492, 13
Bowing **Bowing** my lips vnto y^t stately root.....406. A.1, 111
Bowl See **Wassail-bowl**
Fill me a mighty **Bowle**.....................227. H.653, 1
Thy Harvest home; thy Wassaile **bowle**,........231. H.662, 56
That while the Wassaile **Bowle** here............235. H.674, 9
Next crowne the **bowle** full...................317. H.1035, 19
And quaffe up a **Bowle**.......................320. H.1051, 4
A full brimm'd **bowle** of Furye and of rage....412. A.3, 87
To board the Magicke **bowle**, and spill....437. var. H.336, 134
Bowls But your **Boules** with Sack repleat.......217. H.620, 6
Quaffing his full-crown'd **bowles** of burning Wine,
206. H.575, 33
Yet send no **Boules** to him?...................290. H.918, 4
And giv'st me Wassaile **Bowles** to drink,.......350. N.47, 39
Bows He lowly to the Altar **bows**:.............93. H.223, 136
Box Clos'd in a **Box** of Yvorie:..................185. H.497, 2
To grace his own Gums, or of **Box**, or bone.....211. H.595, 2
The greener **Box** (for show.)..................285. H.892, 4
Let **Box** now domineere;.....................285. H.892, 6
Then youthfull **Box** which now hath grace,.....285. H.892, 9
Boxes In sev'rall tills, and **boxes** keepes 'em safe;.299. H.959, 2
Boy See **Schoolboy**
For I a **Boy** am, who..........................26. H.81, 9
There's not a budding **Boy**, or Girle, this day,..69. H.178, 43
And ere long, a **Boy** Love send ye.............125. H.314, 6
Boy's Help! O help! your **Boy's** a dying.........50. H.139, 5
Boys **Boyes** to the lash) that he do's whip with them.
39. H.110, 4
And the **boyes** with sweet tunes sing,..........54. H.149, 47
The eager **Boyes** to gather Nuts...............56. H.149, 122
Which **boyes**, and Bruckel'd children call.......91. H.223, 58
Well, on, brave **boyes**, to your Lords Hearth,...101. H.250, 26
Drink frollick **boyes**, till all be blythe...........102. H.250, 43
My merrie merrie **boyes**,......................263. H.784, 2
T'ave **Boyes**, and Gyrles too, as they will.......291. H.919, 12
Aha my **boyes**! heres wheat for Christmas Pies!.327. H.1086, 2
Brace She leads on a **brace**......................333. H.1122, 8
Bracelet A **Bracelet** richly Redolent:..............13. H.32, 2
I brake thy **Bracelet** 'gainst my will;..........240. H.705, 1
Bracelets So smell those **bracelets**, and those bands
145. H.375, 15
Brags Mease **brags** of Pullets which he eats: but Mease
142. H.361, 1
Brain 'Tis her erroneous self has made a **braine**..46. H.128, 43
Into the **Brain** by easie sleep:................79. H.198, 10
Brains Since when (me thinks) my **braines** about doe swim,
313. H.1017, 13
— — — — — — — — — —, ...427. var. H.197, 78
Brake I **brake** my bonds of Love, and bad thee goe,
6. H.3, 5
She **brake** in two the purer Glasse,............187. H.504, 4
I **brake** thy Bracelet 'gainst my will;..........240. H.705, 1
So the Divine Hand work't, and **brake** no thred,.385. N.184, 3
Brakes Through **Brakes** and through Bryars,.......225. H.643, 10
Bramble With a lash of a **Bramble** she rides now,
225. H.643, 9
Bran That **Bran** the Baker did his Breech bewray:
219. H.630, 2
So do the Skurfe and **Bran** too: Go Thy way,..398. N.263, 12
Branch See **Olive-branch**
And to that Hand, (the **Branch** of Heavens faire Tree)
62. H.161, 11
Or **Branch**: Each Porch, each doore, ere this,..68. H.178, 33
Bring in her Bill, once more, the **Branch** of Peace.
225. H.642, 22
No one least **Branch** there left behind:..........304. H.980, 6
The Olive **branch**, and Victors Song:..........360. N.83, 26
And Olive **Branch** is wither'd now..............375. N.123, 52
Branches One of the five straight **branches** of my hand
203. H.565, 1
From wch two armes like **branches** seem to spread
406. A.1, 97
rand See **Firebrand**
Shewing me there a fire **brand**;................153. H.399, 4
With the last yeeres **brand**.....................263. H.784, 7
Kindle the Christmas **Brand**, and then.........285. H.893, 1
rass (More blessed in thy **Brasse**, then Land)..35. H.106, 24
A heart thrice wall'd with Oke, and **Brasse**, that man
36. H.106, 75
It be with Rock, or walles of **Brasse**,.........116. H.283, 143

Remainder left of **Brasse** or stone,..............146. H.376, 8
With rock, and seven times circumflankt with **brasse**,
252. H.745, 12
Brasse, Leade, or Tinne, throw into th' mould;..297. H.948, 10
Out-during Marble, **Brasse**, or Jet,............335. H.1129, 2
Brave See **Three-brave-brothers**
Lovely in you, **brave** Prince of Cavaliers!........25. H.77, 8
Shor'd up by you, (**Brave** Earle of Westmerland.)
40. H.112, 4
Brave Porter! Poets ne'r will wanting be:........41. H.117, 2
Each way illustrious, **brave**; and like to those..45. H.128, 14
'Two'd make a **brave** expansion................67. H.175, 8
Had not *Joves son, that **brave** Tyrinthian Swain,.78. H.197, 65
To make a **brave**,...........................100. H.246, 6
Well, on, **brave** boyes, to your Lords Hearth,..101. H.250, 26
In thee **Brave** Man! Whose incorrupted fame,...131. H.331, 5
No roofs of Cedar, nor our **brave**.............133. H.336, 42
(Loving the **brave** Burgundian wine).........135. H.336, 130
Who was your **brave** exalted Uncle here,........137. H.341, 3
And these **brave** Measures go a stately trot;....141. H.359, 11
On, as thou hast begunne, **brave** youth, and get.150. H.384, 1
I'le seek him in your Bonnet **brave**;...........156. H.412, 13
Throughout that **Brave** Mosaick yard..........166. H.443, 47
Brave men can't die; whose Candid Actions are..168. H.444, 5
Such Three **brave** Brothers fell in Mars his Field.
170. H.451, 12
This, Three; which Three, you make up Foure **Brave** Prince.
170. H.451, 16
Their end, though ne'r so **brave**:..............176. H.467, 15
Stand with thy Graces forth, **Brave** man, and rise
181. H.483, 1
Come thou **Brave** man! And bring with Thee a Stone
185. H.496, 5
That richly wrought, and This as **brave**;......192. H.521, 22
The Calculation of thy Birth, **Brave** Mince.....194. H.526, 6
Come then, **brave** Knight, and see the Cell....198. H.544, 25
Brave Kinsman, markt out with the whiter stone:
199. H.545, 8
Eggs Ile not shave: But yet **brave** man, if I....202. H.557, 27
Or gallant Newark; which **brave** two.........218. H.626, 12
Of thy **brave**, bold, and sweet Maronian Muse...234. H.673, 12
For, if we gaze on These **brave** Lamps too neer,
237. H.685, 11
That **brave** Spirit comes agen..................242. H.714, 12
Stand forth **brave** man, since Fate has made thee here
251. H.745, 1
Besides too, in a **brave**,......................259. H.772, 16
That **brave** Vibration each way free;..........261. H.779, 5
One **Brave** Captain did command,..............276. H.850, 9
Thy loss **brave** man! whose Numbers have been hurl'd,
288. H.907, 5
For **brave** comportment, wit without offence,.....297. H.947, 1
Tell that **Brave** Man, fain thou wo'dst have access
301. H.963, 1
Go on **brave** Hopton, to effectuate that.........310. H.1002, 1
Stand forth **Brave** Man, here to the publique sight;
322. H.1062, 10
In the next sheet **Brave** Man to follow Thee....329. H.1092, 6
Confus'd, in this **brave** Extasie..............402. N.269, 21
T'was **braue**, t'was **braue** could we comand ye hand
413. A.4, 6
Swells with **brave** rage, yet comely every where,..415. A.7, 12
— — — — — — — — — —, ...422. var. H.106, 101
The **brave** cheape worke, and for to pave..440. ins. H.443, 45bb
— — — — — — — — — —, ...443. var. H.575, 54
But **brave** soules take illumination:.........443. var. H.575, 60
Bravely To make you **bravely** live;..............57. H.149, 154
Sing I co'd once; and **bravely** too enspire........84. H.210, 3
Fight **bravely** for the flame of mankinde, yeeld
433. ins. H.283, 140f
Bravery The Wante of Eare rings **brauerye**,.......409. A.2, 90
Bravest Verses out-live the **bravest** deeds of men?
264. H.791, 2
Who may do most, do's least: The **bravest** will
321. H.1057, 1
Brazen And sever'd, joyne in **brazen** yoke:......70. H.181, 18
Breach Ordaining that thy small stock find no **breach**,
38. H.106, 133
Thou for the **breach** shalt do;................240. H.705, 10
Bread See **Nobly-home-bred, Shew-bread**
Come thou not neere those men, who are like **Bread**
7. H.7, 1
To **Bread** and Water none is poore;............33. H.100, 1
Or with the first, or second **bread**.............37. H.106, 108
After short prayers, they set on **bread**;........119. H.293, 8
And with our Broth and **bread**, and bits; Sir, friend,
146. H.377, 23
No, no, thy **bread**, thy wine, thy jocund Beere..147. H.377, 57
The Paste of Filberts for thy **bread**..........192. H.521, 13
Grudgings turnes **bread** to stones, when to the Poore
220. H.632, 1
The Larder fills with meat; the Bin with **bread**..221. H.633, 45
Give for **bread**, a little bit....................223. H.638, 12
Fulfill the Larders, and with strengthning **bread**
245. H.723, 5

Pauls hands do give, what give they **bread** or meat, 248. H.731, 1
A little Bin best fits a little **Bread**,............249. H.733, 7
Must needs wax cold, if wanting **bread** and wine. 258. H.768, 4
And Bake the floure of Amber for thy **bread**....269. H.818, 6
Was cheese full ripe with Teares, with **Bread** as sad. 273. H.835, 4
Bring the holy crust of **Bread**,................284. H.888, 1
That surfeit tooke by **bread**, the worst of all...286. H.895, 2
For **Bread**, Drinke, Butter, Cheese; for every thing 287. H.903, 2
He askt an almes; I gave him **bread**,............295. H.942, 5
Brown **bread** Tom Pennie eates, and must of right, 309. H.997, 1
To soure the **Bread**, and turn the Beer.........321. H.1056, 9
For that holy piece of **Bread**,................323. H.1065, 5
Instead of **Bread**, Grubs gives them stones to eat. 325. H.1077, 4
That at the tide, he has not **bread** to eate.....327. H.1086, 4
As for to beg my **bread** from doore to doore;....347. N.39, 2
Which keeps my little loafe of **Bread**..........350. N.47, 21
Of **Bread**, and Wine with it:...................352. N.53, 8
Thou dost my **bread**...........................353. N.56, 7
With **Bread**, and Wine, and Vessells furnished;.355. N.65, 4
Who to that sweet **Bread** unprepar'd doth come..355. N.65, 9
Bread for our service, bread for shew;.........356. N.66, 3
That has not **bread**, and some to spare........358. N.75, 10
The Basket and the Bynn of **Bread**,..........374. N.123, 15
As Butter'd **bred**, the which the wild......439. ins. H.443, 45p

Break Ah my Anthea! Must my heart still **break**?....24. H.74, 1
Too strong for Fate to **break** us: Look upon....78. H.197, 71
And **break** thy self in shivers on her eye........87. H.215, 10
Fearing to **break** the Kings Commandement:....122. H.305, 4
Which **break** from the Injeweld tyres..........165. H.443, 30
I co'd never **breake** my sleepe,................182. H.490, 9
Breake, if thou lov'st us, this delay;..........184. H.492, 25
Of Day **break** from the pregnant East, 'tis time.207. H.575, 64
And bending, (yet it doth not **break**?)........208. H.580, 10
Is this a life, to **break** thy sleep?............233. H.670, 1
Break off Delay, since we but read of one......251. H.744, 1
When a cleare day, out of a Cloud do's **break**...324. H.1072, 2
Why do'st thou wound, & **break** my heart?...328. H.1090, 1
— — — — — — — — — — —, ...452. ins. H.443, 45u

Breakers See **Troch-breakers**

Breaking (As to the **breaking** of a Bride-Cake) home: 286. H.898, 10
— — — — — — — — — — —, ...439. var. H.443, 30

Breaks See **Barley-breaks**
Sneape has a face so brittle, that it **breaks**......124. H.311, 1
Of Patience wants. Grief **breaks** the stoutest Heart 169. H.447, 2
It is his own breech there that **breaks** the jest...265. H.795, 2

Breast See **Redbreast, Robin redbreast**
Of flowers, was thy spotlesse **breast**:.............8. H.11, 4
But of the heat of Julia's **breast**:...............25. H.78, 8
That's my Julia's **breast**; where dwels..........40. H.115, 13
Pants with a Downie **brest**,..................57. H.149, 135
If I kisse Anthea's **brest**,......................59. H.155, 1
To warme my **Breast**, when thou my Pulse art gone. 73. H.186, 16
The rubie niplet of her **breast**;................74. H.190, 8
False in **breast**, teeth, haire, and eyes:........77. H.195, 10
Hence then it is, that my poore **brest**..........96. H.229, 5
Whether my Sapho's **breast**,....................105. H.258, 3
Built up of odours, burneth in her **breast**.....113. H.283, 26
I made upon my Julia's **brest**;................135. H.336, 95
And by the Armes-full (with a **Brest** unhid).....147. H.377, 37
And thy **brest** the Altar, whence..............158. H.417, 3
Is each neate Niplet of her **breast**..............164. H.440, 10
Julia's **Breast** can give you them:.............183. H.491, 2
Still with a well-prepared **brest**:..............246. H.725, 2
I have in my poore **Brest**;....................272. H.828, 6
Naked I'le shew a sighing **brest**;................349. N.46, 6
A Princely Babe in's Mothers **Brest**.........367. N.102, 14
Her **brest** (a place for beawtyes throne most fitt) 405. A.1, 51
Nourish in's **breast**, a Tree of Life............409. A.2, 108

Breasts Between thy **Breasts** (then Doune of Swans more white)......................................30. H.88, 9
Display thy **breasts**, my Julia, there let me......96. H.230, 1
Soe Tullye look't, when from the **Brest's** of Rome 412. A.3, 75

Breath See **Sweet-breath**
With **breath** more sweet then Violet...............6. H.2, 14
But that I heard thy sweet **breath** say,..........20. H.56, 5
Live, and live blest; thrice happy Paire; Let **Breath**, 38. H.106, 141
Next, make his cheeks with **breath** to swell,...39. H.108, 11
Gryll either keeps his **breath** to coole his broth;..48. H.135, 2
Breath of a blasting wind;..................104. H.257, 9
Or else trans-fuse thy **breath** into the chest,.....129. H.327, 3
That **breath** the Balm, the myrrh, the Nard shal be, 129. H.327, 5
So smells the **Breath** about the hives,..........145. H.375, 7
The cooling **breath** of Respasses;.............145. H.375, 20
And sweetly sings, but yet his **breath** sayes no..149. H.381, 2
Ambo. Poor pittied youth! Mir. And here the **breth** of kine 159. H.421, 13
And sheep, grew more sweet, by that **breth** of Thine. 159. H.421, 14
Six dayes he hollows so much **breath** away,....163. H.435, 3
Made by the **breath** of great-ey'd kine,........166. H.443, 40
The **breath** of Munkies met to mix............166. H.443, 43
Is Fame, (the **breath** of popular applause.)......169. H.448, 2
And his last **breath**, let it be..................186. H.499, 3
But stinking **breath**, I do as hell abhorre it......210. H.588, 2
When 'twas her **breath** that was the Carrionere...212. H.598, 2
But that his **breath** do's Fly-blow all the meate...223. H.637, 2
Her **breath** do's stinke,........................229. H.659, 9
And smell'st the **breath** of great-ey'd Kine,.....230. H.662, 33
Spenke has a strong **breath**, yet short Prayers saith: 283. H.884, 1
Not out of want of **breath**, but want of faith...283. H.884, 2
Such let my life assure me, when my **breath**.....392. N.230, 33
Whose **breath** is rich perfume, that to the sence...404. A.1, 27
Or while that each from other's **breath** did drincke.410. A.3, 5
A **breath** of balm along the Elizean fields.........416. A.8, 8

Breathe Till you on it did **breathe**;..............51. H.144, 2
Breathe as the Damask Rose:.................57. H.149, 144
Breathe, Julia, **breathe**, and Ile protest,..........69. H.179, 1
The fat; **breathe** thou, and there's the rich perfume. 102. H.251, 4
Then but to **breath**, and every one gave way:...200. H.551, 4
Let her **breath**, or let her blow,................244. H.719, 5
As aires doe **breathe**, or winds doe blow:......282. H.881, 8

Breathed For as he **breath'd**, the People swore from thence 200. H.551, 5

Breathes **Breathes** Vine-yards and Pomgranats: O how sweet! 113. H.283, 22

Breathing Sho'd by his **breathing**, poyson thee.....39. H.108, 14
Her silken bodies, but a **breathing** space:......157. H.414, 6

Breaths And for your **breaths** too, let them smell...20. H.54, 3

Bred See **Bread, Nobly-home-bred**
It is a creature born and **bred**.................130. H.329, 4
To lard the shambles: Barbels **bred**...........133. H.336, 46
(**Bred** from the dung-hils, and adulterous rhimes,) 155. H.405, 13

Breech That Bran the Baker did his **Breech** bewray: 219. H.630, 2
It is his own **breech** there that breaks the jest...265. H.795, 2

Breeches Run after with their **breeches** rent......101. H.250, 25
Skoles stinks so deadly, that his **Breeches** loath..226. H.650, 1
But walks with dangling **breeches**,.............259. H.772, 18

Breed The place, where swelling Piles, do **breed**:......6. H.5, 2
(The skarcrow vnto Mankinde) that doth **breed**..411. A.3, 52
— — — — — — — — — —, ...436. var. H.336, 46

Breeds Adversity then **breeds** the discontent.....235. H.676, 2
The first event **breeds** confidence or feare.......292. H.924, 2

Breeze But lul'd to calmnesse, then succeeds a **breeze** 225. H.642, 15

Brew Prig mony wants, either to buy, or **brew**....71. H.183, 4

Briar Yet the fretfull **bryar** will tell,..............88. H.217, 4
Some brittle sticks of Thorne or **Briar**.........350. N.47, 23

Briars See **Sweetbriars**
Through Brakes and through **Bryars**,..........225. H.643, 10
A thousand thorns, and **Bryars** & Stings,.......272. H.828, 5

Bribe See **Postern-bribe**

Bribes Gifts blind the wise, and **bribes** do please,..357. N.72, 9

Bridal And makes more soft the **Bridall** Bed......130. H.329, 7
But in the **Bridall** Bed:......................160. H.422, 12
Be't for my **Bridall**, or my Buriall............232. H.667, 2
To the **Bridall** Bed,..........................239. H.695, 11

Bridal-bed But to dresse the **Bridall-Bed**,........141. H.360, 3

Bridal-cake That wedding smock, this **Bridal-Cake**; 215. H.616, 22

Bridal-cakes Of Bride-grooms, Brides, and of their **Bridall-cakes**. 5. H.1, 4

Bridal-rites **Bridall-Rites** goe on so slowly?......53. H.149, 12

Bride Looks like a **Bride** now, or a bed of flowers,..25. H.77, 5
To Christen thee, the **Bride**, the Bashfull Muse,..28. H.84, 2
The which was made a happy **Bride**,.............41. H.116, 5
Of the resigning, yet resisting **Bride**............45. H.128, 6
To the bed, the bashfull **Bride**.................53. H.149, 10
To the bed, the bashfull **Bride**.................53. H.149, 20
To the bed, the bashfull **Bride**.................54. H.149, 30
To the bed, the bashfull **Bride**.................54. H.149, 40
To the bed, the bashfull **Bride**.................54. H.149, 50
To the bed the bashfull **Bride**.................55. H.149, 70
With the Bride-groom, and the **Bride**...........57. H.149, 160
Like to a **Bride**, come forth my Book, at last,...76. H.194, 1
Like to a slumbring **Bride**, awake againe.......99. H.244, 8
That Morne which saw me made a **Bride**,.......109. H.271, 1
Unto the bed the bashfull **Bride**;..............109. H.271, 4
Blest is the **Bride**, on whom the Sun doth shine;.113. H.283, 48
And beautious **Bride** we do confess y'are wise,.113. H.283, 51
The youthfull Bride-groom, and the fragrant **Bride**: 114. H.283, 88
And soft-Maidens-blush, the **Bride**............114. H.283, 97
Up in a sheet your **Bride**, and what if so......116. H.283, 142
Of the most sweet and dainty **Bride**,..........120. H.293, 50

You, the brisk Bridegroome, you the dainty **Bride.** 124. H.313, 6
To the **Bride,** and to her Groome;............124. H.314, 2
And stils the **Bride** too, when she cries.......130. H.329, 11
Twice has Pudica been a **Bride,** and led........180. H.477, 1
Both Bed, and **Bride**......................190. H.515, 10
Spring with the Larke, most comely **Bride,** and meet 216. H.618, 1
To encourage on the **Bride;**..................221. H.633, 27
Lies softly panting like a **Bride**...............233. H.670, 14
Ill luck 'twill bode to th' Bridegroome and the **Bride.** 262. H.781, 12
For Mistresse **Bride,** the wedding Cake:.......267. H.805, 2
Is not for one, but every night his **Bride:**......286. H.898, 14
Then from the porch may many a **Bride**........291. H.919, 13
Last, may the **Bride** and Bridegroome be......291. H.919, 17
Or else because th' art like a modest **Bride,**....301. H.963, 3
The Bashfull **Bride,**..........................360. N.83, 46
For, here's a Babe, that (like a **Bride**).........366. N.98, 12
Some hours before I should have been his **Bride.** 416. A.8, 16
And ravish you his **Bride,** doe you........430. ins. H.283, 40c
Why then goe forward, sweet Auspicious **Bride** 431. ins. H.283, 50a
How long, soft **bride,** shall your deare C: make 431. ins. H.283, 60a

Bride-bed Prove in your **Bride-bed** numerous......208. H.581, 4

Bride-cake And for the **Bride Cake** ther'l be Spice..267. H.805, 6
(As to the breaking of a **Bride-Cake**) home:...286. H.898, 10

Bridegroom Now barre the doors, the **Bride-groom** puts 56. H.149, 121
With the **Bride-groom,** and the Bride.........57. H.149, 160
Display the **Bridegroom** in the porch,..........113. H.283, 34
The youthfull **Bride-groom,** and the fragrant Bride: 114. H.283, 88
You, the brisk **Bridegroome,** you the dainty Bride. 124. H.313, 6
If nine times you your **Bride-groome** kisse;....208. H.581, 1
Your eager **Bridegroome** with auspitious feet....216. H.618, 2
Ill luck 'twill bode to th' **Bridegroome** and the Bride. 262. H.781, 12
Last, may the Bride and **Bridegroome** be......291. H.919, 17
The time the **Bridegroom** stayes from hence,....380. N.153, 1
and come upon your **Bridegroome** like a Tyde 431. ins. H.283, 50b

Bridegroom's See, see the **Bride-grooms** Torch....54. H.149, 53
That ne'r knew Brides, or **Bride-grooms** touch,.57. H.149, 132
Encircle with the **Bride-grooms** Points.........114. H.283, 80

Bridegrooms **Of Bride-grooms,** Brides, and of their Bridall-cakes. 5. H.1, 4

Bride-maids And let the Young-men and the **Bride-maids** share 114. H.283, 78

Bride's By the Brides eyes, and by the teeming life 114. H.283, 81
To light their Tapers at the **Brides** bright eye..115. H.283, 108

Brides Of Bride-grooms, **Brides,** and of their Bridall-cakes. 5. H.1, 4
That ne'r knew **Brides,** or Bride-grooms touch,..57. H.149, 132
Of curious **Brides;** or like those mites..........165. H.443, 31
Or writhing **Brides;** when, (panting) they.....167. H.443, 110
And talke of **Brides;** & who shall make........215. H.616, 21
Shall we ere bring coy **Brides** to bed;.........360. N.83, 50

Bridgeman To paint a **Bridgeman** to the life:......38. H.108, 4

Bridget Of foure teeth onely **Bridget** was possest;.158. H.419, 1
Sweet **Bridget** blusht, & therewithall,..........203. H.562, 1

Brief Till you come forth. Wash, dresse, be **briefe** in praying 68. H.178, 27
But I'le be **brief,**...........................306. H.984, 37
a prayer must be said, be **briefe;**......431. ins. H.283, 60n

Briefly **Briefly** of my Julia?....................138. H.342, 2
Love as **briefly** did reply;......................219. H.628, 4

Briefs Those Sundayes onely, when as **Briefs** are read. 39. H.109, 2

Bright **Bright** as the Wise-men's Torch, which guided them 86. H.213, 21
To light their Tapers at the Brides **bright** eye...115. H.283, 108
Bright Tulips, we do know,....................184. H.493, 1
A Corps as **bright** as burnisht gold............185. H.497, 6
(Amongst the rest) both **bright** and singular;..267. H.804, 10
But yet how more admir'dly **bright**...........270. H.819, 6
Declare to us, **bright** Star, if we shall seek.....367. N.102, 8
Her forehead smooth full polisht **bright** and high..404. A.1, 5

Brighter Lyd. Though mine be **brighter** then the Star; 70. H.181, 21

Brim A Goblet, to the **brim,**...................198. H.544, 15
Up to the **brim:**.............................227. H.653, 2
In Goblets to the **brim,**.......................290. H.918, 2

Brimmed A full **brimm'd** bowle of Furye and of rage 412. A.3, 87

Brine Teares, though th'are here below the sinners **brine,** 226. H.645, 1
In stead of **Brine,**..........................401. N.268, 17

Brine-tub Look in his **Brine-tub,** and you shall find there 89. H.221, 3

Bring Dead when I am, first cast in salt, and **bring** 9. H.14, 7
Bring your Magicks, Spels, and Charmes,........10. H.19, 5
Come **bring** your sampler, and with Art,.........10. H.20, 1
Thus like a Bee, Love-gentle stil doth **bring**......16. H.40, 7
To **bring** him Lint, and Balsamum,...............18. H.46, 6
But now 'tis known, Behold; behold, I **bring**......27. H.82, 7
Youth, or sweet Nature, co'd **bring** forth,.........48. H.134, 2
Both **bring** one death; and I die here,............50. H.140, 9
Yet I **bring** Balme and Oile to heal your sore.....52. H.146, 22
Hymen, O Hymen **bring**.......................54. H.149, 48
Julia, I **bring**................................65. H.172, 1
But is got up, and gone to **bring** in May.........69. H.178, 44
Under the heavenly *Isis, that can **bring**........78. H.197, 54
You doe **bring**...............................83. H.205, 2
Mirt. 'Tis true indeed; and each of us will **bring**..86. H.213, 33
Pure hands **bring** hither, without staine.........91. H.223, 42
Bring me but one, Ile promise thee,............103. H.255, 5
Crosses doe still **bring** forth the best events.....110. H.275, 2
Æsculapius! come and **bring**..................122. H.302, 3
We'll call on Night, to **bring** ye both to Bed:..124. H.313, 10
Which spent, one death, **bring** to ye both one Grave. 124. H.313, 14
First wash thy heart in innocence, then **bring**....127. H.320, 3
Woman wo'd **bring** him more then co'd be told,..129. H.326, 4
No more shall I (I feare me) to thee **bring**......132. H.333, 5
Nere can repullulate, or **bring**.................133. H.336, 23
Who spurn'd at Envie; and co'd **bring,** with ease,.137. H.341, 5
And **bring** him home, but 'tis decreed,.........157. H.412, 27
Mont. Love for thy sake will **bring** her to these hills 159. H.421, 35
Or a sigh of such as **bring**......................170. H.450, 5
Come thou Brave man! And **bring** with Thee a Stone 185. H.496, 5
In Wicker-baskets Maids shal **bring**........192. H.521, 35
Of Hero, and Leander; then Ile **bring**..........206. H.575, 26
Ile **bring** thee Herrick to Anacreon,............206. H.575, 32
Bring me my Rose-buds, Drawer come;.........208. H.582, 1
Or **bring** some bane..........................210. H.591, 5
And **bring** those dew-drink-offerings to my Tomb..222. H.634, 2
Bring in her Bill, once more, the Branch of Peace. 225. H.642, 22
To seek, and **bring** rough Pepper home:........229. H.662, 6
To **bring** from thence the scorched Clove.........229. H.662, 8
I'le to thee a Simnell **bring,**...................236. H.684, 1
Some hung the head, while some did **bring**......237. H.686, 5
That made me thus hoist saile, and **bring** my Boat: 248. H.730, 12
And homeward she did **bring**...................250. H.740, 2
Holy Water come and **bring;**..................258. H.769, 1
Sacred Spittle **bring** ye hither;................258. H.769, 4
I'le **bring** a Fever; since thou keep'st no fire...262. H.783, 22
Come, **bring** with a noise,......................263. H.784, 1
For more or lesse fruits they will **bring,**.........264. H.787, 3
Imparitie doth ever discord **bring:**..............268. H.812, 1
Of the holy Beast we **bring**....................280. H.870, 11
Bring the holy crust of Bread,..................284. H.888, 1
And this rawly bak't will **bring**................284. H.890, 5
With reverend Curtsies come, and to him **bring**..286. H.898, 7
Since we fresh strewings will **bring** hither,......289. H.912, 7
First, may the hand of bounty **bring**............291. H.919, 1
Till that the Cooke cries, **Bring** no more.........291. H.919, 4
Tell me young man, or did the Muses **bring**....299. H.956, 1
Holy waters hither **bring**.......................303. H.974, 1
I **bring** ye Love, Quest. What will love do?.....309. H.1001, 1
I **bring** ye love: Quest. What will Love do?....309. H.1001, 3
I **bring** ye love: Quest. What will Love do?.....309. H.1001, 5
I **bring** ye love: Quest. What will love do?.....309. H.1001, 7
I **bring** ye love: Quest. What will love do?....310. H.1001, 9
I **bring** ye love: Quest. What will love do?....310. H.1001, 11
I **bring** ye love: Quest. What will love do?....310. H.1001, 13
I **bring** ye love: Quest. What will love do?....310. H.1001, 15
Bring in pailes of water then,.................315. H.1026, 9
Those ends in War the best contentment **bring,**..316. H.1029, 1
Bring the Holy-water hither;...................324. H.1069, 5
Wanton Wenches doe not **bring**................330. H.1098, 1
And **bring** t'th' heart destruction both alike.....333. H.1120, 6
Afflictions **bring** us joy in times to come,.........349. N.45, 1
And **bring** fresh strewings to thy Tombe..........359. N.83, 6
From teeming eyes; to these we **bring,**..........360. N.83, 41
Shall we ere **bring** coy Brides to bed;...........360. N.83, 50
What sweeter musick can we **bring,**..............364. N.96, 1
Bring Him along, most pious Priest,............365. N.97, 11
Come then, come then, and let us **bring**........368. N.102, 19
But therewithall I'le **bring** the Band,.............370. N.107, 7
God makes not good men wantons, but doth **bring**.370. N.108, 1
Come pitie us; and **bring** your eares,............373. N.123, 5
God did forbid the Israelites, to **bring**..........384. N.179, 1
That a Wave, and I will **bring**.................397. N.258, 3
And **bring** our Spices, to embalm Thee dead; ...399. N.263, 38
Bring Health to All..........................401. N.268, 13
Devotion bids me hither **bring**..................402. N.270, 3
Theis **bringe** thy husband, like to those..........407. A.2, 29
Bringe to hym next, and in it shew.............408. A.2, 49
White handes as smooth, as Mercies, **bring**........408. A.2, 59
And Lastly, see thou **bring** to hym..............408. A.2, 73
Bee sure thou **bringe** A Mayden head,..........409. A.2, 84
And when an other age shall **bring**.............418. A.9, 31

Bringest See Bring'st
Brings Next enters June, and brings us more......23. H.70, 5
More wealth brings in, then all those three.........23. H.70, 8
And, humbly, chives of Saffron brings,.........93. H.223, 133
He loves the gain that vanity brings in.........163. H.439, 4
That brings us either Ale or Beere;...........179. H.476, 26
Shee brings in much, by carnall usury:..........220. H.631, 2
He by extortion brings in three times more:.....220. H.631, 3
Among disasters that discention brings,..........260. H.774, 1
Yet ne'r can see that salve which brings......272. H.828, 7
Brings him not one, but many a Maiden-head...286. H.898, 16
Words beget Anger: Anger brings forth blowes:..287. H.901, 1
Know when to speake; for many times it brings..318. H.1037, 1
When Chub brings in his harvest, still he cries,..327. H.1086, 1
Wealth brings much woe:......................368. N.104, 4
Brings in Fabricius for a Combatant:.........370. N.108, 10
He never brings them once to th' push of Pikes...370. N.108, 12
Seldome brings order, but confusion............392. N.230, 8
But brings his stick of Cynamon,...............413. A.4, 26
Bring'st And say, thou bring'st this Hony-bag from me:
100. H.248, 2
Bring'st home the Ingot from the West.........229. H.662, 10
Bring'st, in Thy Blood, a Balm, that shall.......366. N.98, 23
Thou bring'st vnto his bedd A frost..............409. A.2, 86
Brink To the base from the brink..............317. H.1035, 17
Spic'd to the brink..........................350. N.47, 40
Brisk Once a brisk and bonny Lasse,..............14. H.36, 4
And the brisk Mouse may feast her selfe with crums,
37. H.106, 123
You, the brisk Bridegroome, you the dainty Bride.
124. H.313, 6
Brisk methinks I am, and fine,.................309. H.996, 1
Place then this mirror whose briske hue..........418. A.9, 51
To those virgins, whose briske heu..........450. ins. A.9, 52
Brisky — — — — — — — — — — —, ...450. ins. A.9, 52
Bristle — — — — — — — — — — — —, ...422. var. H.106, 123
Brittle Sneape has a face so brittle, that it breaks..124. H.311, 1
Some brittle sticks of Thorne or Briar..........350. N.47, 23
Broach See Turnbroach
Broad 'Tis then broad Day throughout the East...154. H.404, 4
Broad of fore-head, large of eye,...............305. H.984, 18
Broad-faced And a broad-fac't Owle shall be......195. H.530, 5
Brock To clense his eyes, Tom Brock makes much adoe,
110. H.273, 1
Broke He loves his bonds, who when the first are broke,
17. H.42, 5
You have broke promise twice..................32. H.94, 9
Broke at the Losse of Maiden-heads:..........167. H.443, 107
Love, I have broke............................172. H.458, 1
Neither broke i'th whole, or part...............183. H.490, 20
Broke is my Reed, hoarse is my singing too:.....205. H.573, 2
Where a Coxcomb will be broke,...............255. H.761, 17
When this or that Horne shall be broke, and when
256. H.763, 11
Had broke her wheele, or crackt her axeltree.......358. N.77, 4
A man both bruis'd, and broke, and one.........400. N.266, 4
— — — — — — — — — — — —, ...435. var. H.293, 46z
Broke-heart The broke-heart of a Nightingale....120. H.293, 46
Broken A weak, a soft, a broken beame;............75. H.193, 36
Be't to your praise, no peace was broken.........114. H.283, 90
Brook Close by a Silver-shedding Brook;..........51. H.142, 2
When peeping through a Brooke................271. H.824, 12
So purest pebbles in the brook:.................294. H.939, 4
Brooks I sing of Brooks, of Blossomes, Birds, and Bowers:
5. H.1, 1
Broom What here I promise, that no Broom......165. H.442, 13
Brooms They have their Ash-pans, & their Brooms
92. H.223, 101
Broomstead Broomsted a lamenesse got by cold and Beere;
201. H.555, 1
Broth See Beer-broth
Gryll either keeps his breath to coole his broth;....48. H.135, 2
And with our Broth and bread, and bits; Sir, friend,
146. H.377, 23
To make a lustie-gellie for his broth............299. H.959, 4
His hereby broth, and there close by......439. ins. H.443, 451
Brother Wert thou a Winckfield onely, not a Brother.
210. H.590, 10
Brothers See Three-brave-brothers
Such Essences as those Three Brothers; known..170. H.451, 7
Such Three brave Brothers fell in Mars his Field.
170. H.451, 12
Brought And brought a rod, so whipt me with the same:
16. H.40, 2
Brought him, (as Love professes)...............27. H.81, 22
Brought leaves and mosse to cover her:..........46. H.130, 6
Sweet Lady-Flower, I never brought............71. H.182, 13
What Love co'd ne'r be brought unto............74. H.191, 8
Those learned men brought Incense, Myrrhe, and Gold,
86. H.213, 30
Or brought a kisse............................104. H.257, 22
Conceiv'd with grief are, and with teares brought forth.
105. H.257, 28
Brought and besweetned in a blew............119. H.293, 22
Brought in a dainty daizie, which.............120. H.293, 51
Are to a wilde digestion brought,..............166. H.443, 35
Sell, and brought hither by the Elves...........166. H.443, 62
'Twas pitie Nature brought yee forth..........176. H.467, 10
But Age hath brought me right to Bed..........216. H.617, 6
Sho'd see safe brought to Bed..............220. H.633, 17
A Christall Violl Cupid brought,...............222. H.635, 1
But Ile returne; what mischief brought thee hither?
248. H.730, 13
He prayes his Harvest may be well brought home..270. H.822, 2
Love brought me to a silent Grove,............278. H.863, 1
And having once brought to and end...........289. H.911, 18
That thou has brought a Whistle new,............354. N.59, 8
Thy Father brought with him along............360. N.83, 25
Brought at the last to th' utmost bit,............376. N.124, 3
To[o] Calme A tempest, lett bee brought...........408. A.2, 66
At a high rate, and further brought.......436. ins. H.336, 48h
Brow Ne'r may Prophetique Daphne crown my Brow.
79. H.197, 92
My uncontrolled brow,..........................80. H.201, 11
Loathed Furrowes in your brow:.............97. H.232, 14
Can keepe the wrinkle from the brow:..........132. H.336, 4
And look with a contracted brow?.............188. H.508, 2
The cutting Thumb-naile, or the Brow severe.....212. H.603, 2
Brown See Nut-brown
Browne as his Tooth. A little Moth,............120. H.293, 41
Be my Girle, or faire or browne,................253. H.750, 4
Brown bread Tom Pennie eates, and must of right,
309. H.997, 1
Kisse my Brown wife, and black Posterity.......310. H.1003, 4
Dryed, hony-combs, Browne Achorne cupps.439. ins. H.443, 45j
— — — — — — — — —, ...440. var. H.443, 57
Browner Our browner Ale into the cruse:......135. H.336, 126
Brownest With brownest Toadstones, and the Gum
166. H.443, 57
Bruckeled Which boyes, and Bruckel'd children call
91. H.223, 58
Brugel Brugel and Coxu, and the workes out-doe,..150. H.384, 3
Bruise Beat me, bruise me, rack me, rend me,....351. N.48, 5
Bruised So she fell, and bruis'd, she dy'd..........15. H.36, 11
When I am bruised on the Shelfe..............134. H.336, 74
A man both bruis'd, and broke, and one........400. N.266, 4
They make it scent like bruized Cinnamon.......406. A.1, 94
Brush A little brush of Squirrils haires,..........91. H.223, 46
Set the Brush for sprinkling:..................258. H.769, 3
Brusle See Brustle
Brustle Yee see it brusle like a Swan,.........115. H.283, 114
Brutus May blush, (while Brutus standeth by:)......6. H.4, 2
No Brutus entring here;.......................259. H.772, 5
Bubble Flie thou made Bubble of my sighs, and tears.
87. H.215, 2
Bubbler — — — — — — — —, ...440. var. H.443, 88
Bubbles See Woolly-bubbles
Buck Who can with so small charges drive the buck.
178. H.474, 4
Buckingham It calls to mind, that mighty Buckingham,
137. H.341, 2
Buckittings And come all to Buckittings:..........21. H.61, 4
Buckram With inward Buckram, little else.)....118. H.291, 12
Shall find much farcing Buckram in our Books...202. H.559, 2
Bucksome See Buxom
Bucolics Some smooth, and harmlesse Beucolicks.....5. H.2, 10
Bud See Rose-bud
A bud in either cheek.........................18. H.45, 4
You are a sparkling Rose i'th'bud,..............88. H.216, 7
In bloome of Peach, and Roses bud,............107. H.263, 11
Here she lies, a pretty bud,.....................123. H.310, 1
And tell Him, by that Bud now blown,...........354. N.59, 3
At once, a Bud, and yet a Rose full-blowne.......384. N.183, 2
— — — — — — — — — — — —, ...424. var. H.164, 10
Budding There's not a budding Boy, or Girle, this day,
69. H.178, 43
Buds See Rose-buds
Like wanton rose buds growing out of snowe,....405. A.1, 54
Thus Crownd with Rose Budds, Sacke, thou mad'st mee flye
410. A.3, 27
— — — — — — — — — — — —, ...424. var. H.164, 9
— — — — — — — — — — — —, ...436. var. H.336, 33
Buff See Blindman's buff
Buggins Buggins is Drunke all night, all day he sleepes;
311. H.1011, 1
This is the Levell-coyle that Buggins keeps.....311. H.1011, 2
Build Or fret thy Seeling, or to build..........149. H.337, 120
Where build aloft; and being fixt by These,.....185. H.496, 9
— — — — — — — — — — — —, ...422. var. H.106, 128
Builds Whether high he builds or no:............84. H.209, 2
It is, which builds, 'gainst Fate to stand.......148. H.377, 102
Built Survey this Chappell, built, alone,..........90. H.223a, 3
Built up of odours, burneth in her breast.......113. H.283, 26
When what is strongly built, no chinke.......148. H.377, 106
The Jewes, when they built Houses (I have read).384. N.178, 1
— — — — — — — — — — — —, ...422. var. H.106, 95
Bulging Nor wrack, or Bulging thou hast cause to feare:
23. H.71, 2
Bull A Bull but then; and now a man.........215. H.616, 18
Bullace Are pucker'd Bullace, Canckers and dry
439. ins. H.443, 45m
Bullocks Nor Bullocks fed......................133. H.336, 45

Bullocks' 'Tis not a thousand **Bullocks** thies........22. H.63, 1
To eate thy **Bullocks** thighs, thy Veales, thy fat.147. H.377, 63
Where Rams are wanting, or large **Bullocks** thighs,
369. N.105, 3
Bulwark Or hell it selfe a powerfull **Bulwarke** is?
116. H.283, 146
Bundled The lictors **bundl'd** up their rods; beside,.291. H.920, 1
Bungie **Bungie** do's fast; looks pale; puts Sack-cloth on;
122. H.305, 1
Burden Create the **burden** light....................66. H.172, 24
Thanksgiving is a **burden**, and a paine;........292. H.923, 3
The **burden** of a Grashopper:...................303. H.973, 10
Burdensome Then to thy house be **Burdensome**;.321. H.1056, 14
Burglary Groynes, for his fleshly **Burglary** of late,.106. H.261, 1
Burgundian (Loving the brave **Burgundian** wine)
135. H.336, 130
Burial Tole forth my death; next, to my **buryall** come.
100. H.248, 6
His **buriall** in an yvory grave:..................185. H.497, 4
Serves but for place of **Buriall**................197. H.542, 4
Be't for my Bridall, or my **Buriall**.............232. H.667, 2
Give thou my sacred Reliques **Buriall**..........242. H.713, 20
Nature finds out some place for **buriall**..........267. H.807, 2
He that wants a **buriall** roome..................270. H.821, 7
And go with me to chuse my **Buriall** roome:....329. H.1095, 6
Buried Lastly, safely **buryed**.......................38. H.107, 6
The world with us is **buried**..................133. H.336, 36
The **Buried**, and the Burying-place.............185. H.497, 8
Of Amber quick was **buried**.....................186. H.497, 12
'Tis cowardice to bite the **buried**...............218. H.625, 2
Over my Turfe, when I am **buried**...............219. H.627, 4
Of Amber cleanly **buried**:.....................269. H.817, 2
When my Lot calls me to be **buried**,............277. H.853, 2
Do's but deride the Party **buried**...............319. H.1047, 2
Wo'd shrouded be, and therewith **buried**.........332. H.1114, 2
I'le thinke I'm going to be **buried**:.............392. N.230, 14
That done, wee'l see Thee sweetly **buried**.......399. N.263, 39
Burl He needs a Tucker for to **burle** his face....211. H.594, 2
Burling A **Burling** iron for his face:..............39. H.108, 10
Burn Thy sacred Corse with Odours I will **burne**;..11. H.22, 3
Or else because Grill's roste do's **burn** his Spit,..48. H.135, 3
I **burn**, I **burn**; and beg of you.................50. H.140, 1
And (like to mine) make your heart **burn**......61. H.159, 19
To Incense **burne**;............................87. H.214, 14
An **burn** thee 'up, as well as I...................98. H.238, 15
Serv'd, but as Tapers, for to **burne**,.............109. H.271, 5
And roule about, and in their motions **burne**....113. H.283, 38
This Mornings Incense to prepare, and **burne**.....196. H.539, 2
Nor shall the Tapers when I'm there, **burn** blew..222. H.634, 9
(Where I have cause to **burn** perfumes to it:)...234. H.673, 8
Burne, or drowne me, choose ye whether,......254. H.757, 1
Till Sunne-set, let it **burne**;....................285. H.893, 2
Burn first thine incense; next, when as thou see'st
286. H.898, 5
He toucht me so, as that I **burn**,.............295. H.942, 11
Burne the flax, and fire the tow:..............315. H.1026, 6
When the tapers now **burne** blew,...............348. N.41, 25
To **burn** the rod,...............................353. N.56, 23
Male-Incense **burn**..............................361. N.83, 76
To **burn**, not shine (as learned Basil saith.).....387. N.202, 2
Thy stripes I'le kisse, or **burn** the Rod.........399. N.265, 10
And see or Alter **burne**.........................413. A.4, 32
— — — — — — — — —, ...430. var. H.283, 30
Burned See **Burnt**
Burneth Built up of odours, **burneth** in her breast.
113. H.283, 26
Burning See **Lust-burning**
The **burning** of my heart:.......................28. H.85, 2
Or eare of **burning** jealousie...................49. H.136, 19
Quaffing his full-crown'd bowles of **burning** Wine,
206. H.575, 33
Wooers have Tongues of Ice, but **burning** hearts..274. H.837, 10
Burnished A Corps as bright as **burnisht** gold.....185. H.497, 6
With gilded hornes, and **burnisht** cleere.........243. H.716, 15
And in a **burnisht** Flagonet stood by.........262. H.783, 15
Burns **Burns** for the Altars ornament.............92. H.223, 96
He **burnes** to Embers on the Pile..............113. H.283, 30
From the blast that **burns** by day;..............177. H.473, 4
Burnt The finger bled, but **burnt** was all my heart...17. H.44, 8
That joynt to ashes sho'd be **burnt**,...............28. H.85, 7
Here **burnt**, whose smal return..................81. H.201, 42
No newes of Navies **burnt** at Seas;.............126. H.319, 1
Which will be **burnt** up by and by,............153. H.339, 9
That Satyre he but **burnt** his lips;.............203. H.563, 5
Which **burnt** me so, that I do thinke...........222. H.635, 7
Smells like the **burnt** Sabæan Frankinsense.......404. A.1, 28
Burr A Thorn or a **Burr**.......................225. H.643, 7
Burr is a smell-feast, and a man alone,..........296. H.944, 1
Burthens Riches to be but **burthens** to the mind..213. H.605, 2
Bury Who was thy servant. Dearest, **bury** me....20. H.55, 3
Burying All Flowers sent to'is **burying**..........186. H.497, 10
Burying-place The Buried, and the **Burying-place**..185. H.497, 8
Bush The dancing Frier. tatter'd in the **bush**;....155. H.405, 7
Bushel And giv'st me, for my **Bushell** sowne,.....350. N.47, 43
Business That fits the **businesse** of the Day.......243. H.716, 4
Where the **businesse** is the sport:...............255. H.761, 6
Buskin's The Sock grew loathsome, and the **Buskins** pride,
150. H.382, 2
Buskins With **Buskins** shortned to descrie........51. H.142, 15
Like thee; or dare the **Buskins** to unloose......234. H.673, 11
Buss We **busse** our Wantons, but our Wives we kisse.
189. H.512, 2
Bussing Kissing and **bussing** differ both in this;..189. H.512, 1
Busy And all the **busie** Factours come...........145. H.375, 9
This day is Loves day; and this **busie** night......216. H.618, 9
But (Partial List)
Were it **but** to pleasure you......................10. H.19, 14
Why wept it? **but** for shame,....................12. H.23, 2
Thou gav'st me life, (**but** Mortall;) For that one..27. H.82, 13
Wo'd **but** that heat recall:......................28. H.85, 6
To strike him dead, that **but** usurps a Throne...32. H.97, 6
The last is **but** the least; the first doth tell......35. H.106, 9
Nor are thine eares so deafe, **but** thou canst heare.36. H.106, 83
Wealth cannot make a life, **but** Love...........37. H.106, 128
Nor art thou so close-handed, **but** can't spend..38. H.106, 129
Never was Night so tedious, **but** it knew..........52. H.146, 3
And (oh!) had it **but** a tongue,.................57. H.149, 139
Love kill'd this man. No more **but** so.............61. H.159, 31
I shall be heal'd, if that my King **but** touch.....62. H.161, 14
Know, Lady, you have **but** your day:............63. H.164, 3
But is got up, and gone to bring in May.........69. H.178, 44
Now as I doe; and **but** for thee,...............72. H.185, 24
What was't that fell **but** now....................74. H.192, 1
You see how Creame **but** naked is;..............75. H.193, 9
Faire was the Dawne; and **but** e'ne now the Skies..81. H.202, 1
For having lost **but** once your prime,............84. H.208, 15
'Tis **but** a flying minute,.......................85. H.211, 5
Amint. O rare! **But** is't a trespasse if we three....86. H.213, 25
How high she's priz'd, and worth **but** small;....103. H.253, 17
If they **but** slip, and never fall.................118. H.291, 16
He keeps not one, **but** many Lents i' th'yeare.....122. H.305, 6
As Gilly flowers do **but** stay.....................126. H.318, 1
'Tis **but** silke that bindeth thee,................128. H.322, 7
When I of Villars doe **but** heare the name,......137. H.341, 1
'Tis **but** as day a kindling:.....................154. H.404, 2
And I **but** feasting with a Beane,..............173. H.461, 2
Believe, Love speaks it not, **but** Lust;.........175. H.465, 40
How can I choose **but** love, and follow her,......181. H.485, 1
How can I chuse **but** kisse her, whence do's come
181. H.485, 3
I askt my Lucia **but** a kisse;...................212. H.599, 1
But that his breath do's Fly-blow all the meate...223. H.637, 2
Twice fortie (bating **but** one year,.............226. H.644, 3
That man's not said to live, **but** last:...........233. H.670, 33
Their fashion is, **but** to say no, to take it.........235. H.675, 2
So I may **but** die together:.....................254. H.757, 2
'Tis never, or **but** seldome knowne,..............264. H.788, 1
Sweet Oenone, doe **but** say.....................264. H.790, 1
Kisses are **but** dry banquets to a Feast..........265. H.797, 2
Or kisse it thou, **but** once, or twice,............267. H.805, 5
These I **but** wish for; **but** thy selfe shall see,....269. H.818, 9
And leave their subjects **but** the starved ware.....272. H.826, 6
I co'd **but** see thee yesterday..................272. H.828, 1
All has been plundered from me, **but** my wit;....272. H.830, 1
Beauti's no other **but** a lovely Grace............274. H.840, 1
One short charme if you **but** say..............276. H.850, 11
Touch **but** thy Lire (my Harrie) and I heare....276. H.851, 1
Yet their Three praises, praise **but** One; that's Lawes.
276. H.851, 8
'Twas **but** a dream; **but** had I been..........279. H.863, 13
Truggin now lives **but** to belye his name..........283. H.882, 2
Serve **but** for matter to make Paper-kites.........286. H.896, 2
Numbers ne'r tickle, or **but** lightly please,........290. H.914, 7
'Tis **but** a fierce desire of hot and drie...........293. H.931, 2
Bind me **but** to thee with thine haire,..........293. H.934, 1
A Poet, or a Poet-like **but** Thee...............299. H.956, 4
If **but** lookt on; struck dead, if scan'd by Thee...301. H.962, 6
To kiss his hands, **but** that for fearfullness;......301. H.963, 2
Our Bastard-children are **but** like to Plate,.......312. H.1015, 1
Vice doth in some **but** lodge awhile, not dwell....314. H.1021, 2
Do's **but** deride the Party buried...............319. H.1047, 2
She can **but** spoile me of my Meanes, not Mind..322. H.1061, 2
But for to teach us, all the grace is there,........346. N.36, 2
Him **but** a while to stay;.......................346. N.38, 4
In which were sands **but** few,...................346. N.38, 14
Meet for nothing, **but** to kill;...................347. N.41, 19
Better he starv'd, then **but** to tast one crumme...355. N.65, 10
Can I not sin, **but** thou wilt be..................357. N.72, 1
Draw me, **but** first, and after Thee I'le run,......358. N.77, 14
Are **but** the handsells of our joyes hereafter.......362. N.90, 2
Where is the Babe **but** lately sprung?...........367. N.102, 2
And, if they do, they prove **but** cumbersome;....368. N.104, 3
Where round about Thou seest **but** all things vaine,
371. N.113, 3
Let **but** one beame of Glory on it shine,.........371. N.113, 9
Hell is no other, **but** a soundlesse pit,...........372. N.117, 1
Add **but** a bit of flesh, to boyle:................377. N.130, 2
Roaring is nothing **but** a weeping part,.........380. N.154, 1
In God there's nothing **but** 'tis known to be.....382. N.165, 1
God can do all things, save **but** what are known..382. N.166, 1
'Tis (as S. Bernard saith) **but** seemingly.........385. N.188, 4
'Tis **but** by Order, not by Entitie...............386. N.191, 6

No man is tempted so, but may o'recome,........389. N.211, 1
Or, ne're so meane a peece, but men might see...389. N.214, 3
May chance to be no other man, but Christ.....391. N.226, 2
Given by none, but by Thy selfe, to me:........398. N.262, 2
In which the tongue, though but a member small,.405. A.1, 29
Not soe, but that some Relique In my Harte.....412. A.3, 96
And not a man here but consumes..............413. A.4, 34
These Two asleep are: I'll but be Vndrest......419. A.10, 7
Butcher Who is his Butcher more then Guardian..201. H.557, 16
Butler And the smirk Butler thinks it...........114. H.283, 67
Butler's When checked by the Butlers look.......147. H.377, 56
Butter Butter of Amber, Cream, and Wine, and Oile 144. H.370, 5
Butter of Cowslips mixt with them;...........145. H.375, 22
For Bread, Drinke, Butter, Cheese; for everything 287. H.903, 2
Buttered With Cream of Cowslips buttered:......192. H.521, 14
As Butter'd bred, the which the wild......439. ins. H.443, 45p
Butterflies The hornes of paperie Butterflies,.......119. H.293, 26
Buttery A little Butterie, and therein...........350. N.47, 19
Buttocks Her Belly, Buttocks, and her Waste......16. H.41, 7
His dampish Buttocks furthermore to cloath:....226. H.650, 2
Button To loose the button, is no lesse,...........241. H.712, 1
Buttoned Fix here my Button'd Staffe and stay..216. H.617, 4
Buttoned-staff Beats with a button'd-staffe the poore: 146. H.377, 14
Buttresses Thy Genius with two strength'ning Buttresses, 252. H.745, 18
Buxom With bucksome meat and capring Wine:..127. H.319, 28
Her buxom smiles from me her worshipper..426. var. H.197, 26
Buy Full and faire ones; come and buy:..........19. H.53, 2
Prig mony wants, either to buy, or brew...........71. H.183, 4
Ile beg, and buy it too......................160. H.422, 4
This done, we'l draw lots, who shall buy......215. H.616, 25
So not one cross to buy thee..................321. H.1055, 3
Who cannot buie, or steale a second to't.........332. H.1110, 2
Too soon, too deere did Jephthah buy,..........360. N.83, 19
Buyest Buy'st Travell at the lowest price..........36. H.106, 82
Buys See O'erbuys
That Prickles buyes, puts Prickles out of frame;..287. H.903, 3
Buy'st See Buyest
By (Partial List)
May blush, (while Brutus standeth by:)...........6. H.4, 2
E'ne all the standers by........................9. H.15, 8
Because my Julia's lip was by,..................12. H.23, 3
Put on your silks; and piece by piece..........20. H.54, 1
Faults done by night, will blush by day:..........20. H.56, 6
Here we are all, by day; By night w'are hurl'd....21. H.57, 1
Then by one, to hazard all.......................21. H.61, 8
Whether by th' eye, or eare, or no:...............24. H.73, 2
Woe, woe to them, who (by a ball of strife).......26. H.79, 1
More then the stones i'th' street by farre:........32. H.98, 4
With those deeds done by day, which n'er affright.35. H.106, 37
To take her by the either hand:................37. H.106, 96
But on a Rock himselfe sate by,..............42. H.119, 3
Which, as they drop by drop doe passe..........44. H.127, 5
Comets we see by night; whose shagg'd portents..45. H.128, 15
It seem'd by this time to admit the touch;......47. H.131, 5
Whether by choice, or common flame:............50. H.140, 6
Close by a Silver-shedding Brook;..............51. H.142, 2
Well; though my griefe by you was gall'd, the more; 52. H.146, 21
Cynthius pluck ye by the eare,................52. H.147, 1
Thunder and Lightning Ile lay by,............58. H.152, 5
I glided by my Parents sight..................69. H.180, 2
Thou lighter then the Cork by far:.............70. H.181, 22
When I had Thee, my chiefe Preserver, by......72. H.185, 21
As soone dispatcht is by the Night, as Day.......73. H.186, 4
Thus Paines and Pleasures turne by turne succeed:.79. H.199, 3
Let them speak by gentle tones,................82. H.203, 9
How by Willowes we doe weep:..............82. H.203, 12
How by stealth we meet, and then..............82. H.203, 13
By and by...................................83. H.205, 14
Stoop, mount, passe by to take her eye, then glare 87. H.215, 5
Then in a Polisht Ovall by...................90. H.223, 13
Which one by one here set downe are...........91. H.223, 36
Stands in the Platter, or close by,.............91. H.223, 48
Of cleanest Cobweb, hanging by...............92. H.223, 99
Which, by the peepe of day, doe strew..........95. H.227, 25
Yet, quickly you'l see by the turne of a pin,....97. H.233, 3
Are, by the Sun-beams, tickel'd by degrees.....100. H.247, 4
With sev'rall dishes standing by,..............101. H.250, 32
In that ennamel'd Pansie by,..................107. H.263, 9
I went to pluck them one by one,.............107. H.263, 14
By, yet not blessed by his hands,..............119. H.293, 30
To read by th' Starres, the Kingdoms sick:......126. H.319, 6
Of what can hurt by day, or harme by night:....128. H.323, 10
While Baucis by,............................134. H.336, 83
W'are younger by a score of years............136. H.336, 144
By thy sonne thus grac't, and thee;............138. H.346, 2
A wafer Dol'd by thee, will swell................139. H.350, 3
Free by your fate, then Fortunes mightinesse,....141. H.359, 4
Skrew lives by shifts; yet sweares by no small oathes; 149. H.380, 1
By Dream I saw, one of the three.............153. H.399, 1
Which will be burnt up by and by,............153. H.399, 9
By sweet S. Phillis; pitie me:..................169. H.449, 23
By deare S. Iphis; and the rest,..............169. H.449, 24
Passe by,...................................178. H.475, 2
I vow by Pan, to come away..................184. H.492, 27
We shall discover, by and by,..................188. H.508, 3
As Robes laid by;..........................190. H.515, 40
Where thou shalt sit, and Red-brest by,.........192. H.521, 17
Venus standing Vulcan by......................194. H.527, 9
That we escape. Redemption comes by Thee.....197. H.539, 16
All things o'r-rul'd are here by Chance;.........197. H.542, 1
This I may do (perhaps) as I glide by,........222. H.634, 10
Tempting all the passers by:..................232. H.665, 10
Thousands each day passe by, which wee,........234. H.671, 1
An everlasting plenty, yeere by yeere...........242. H.713, 8
Chor. Lay by a while your Pipes, and rest,.....243. H.716, 35
Of living water by thy Benizon...............245. H.723, 4
I keep, which creeking day by day,............246. H.724, 10
Meane time thy Prophets Watch by Watch shall pray; 254. H.756, 13
By yea and by nay,...........................256. H.762, 17
Speak thou the word, they'l kindle by and by.....261. H.781, 4
And in a burnisht Flagonet stood by...........262. H.783, 15
And the Plums stand by.......................263. H.784, 17
Blaze by this Sphere for ever: Or this doe,......264. H.789, 5
Let Me and It shine evermore by you...........264. H.789, 6
Rich he will be by all unrighteousness:.........266. H.800, 6
The meane passe by, or over, none contemne;..322. H.1062, 7
Far away, if thou beest by....................324. H.1069, 4
See, the fier's by: Farewell..................334. H.1125, 8
Close by whose living coale I sit,..............350. N.47, 25
Are ready by, to make the Guest all pure:........355. N.65, 6
Can I not wooe thee to passe by................357. N.72, 3
A little piggin, and a pipkin by,................371. N.115, 5
Come pitie us, ye Passers by,..................373. N.123, 3
No, lay thy stately terrours by,...............393. N.232, 7
We merit all we suffer, and by far...............393. N.235, 1
Wo'd see Thy Face, and He not by..............395. N.245, 6
His hereby broth, and there close by......439. ins. H.443, 451
Byn See Bin
By'th'fire See Fire
Byways Next, to be rich by no by-wayes;.........42. H.121, 3

C Thus speaks the Oke, here; C. and M. shall meet, 26. H.79, 7
The words found true, C.M. remember me........26. H.79, 10
Not now perceive the soule of C:C:....430. ins. H.283, 40d
How long, soft bride, shall your deare C: make 431. ins. H.283, 60a
Cabbages Make him thus swell, or windy Cabbages. 327. H.1085, 2
Cabin Then to her Cabbin, blest she can escape.37. H.106, 125
Cabinet — — — — — — — —, ...447. var. A.1, 32
Cadmus As Cadmus once a new way found,....297. H.948, 5
Caesar Let but That Mighty Cesar speak, and then, 52. H.146, 13
Adored Cesar! and my Faith is such,........62. H.161, 13
If when these Lyricks (Cesar) You shall heare,.107. H.264, 1
Welcome, Great Cesar, welcome now you are,..300. H.961, 1
That done; O Cesar, live, and be to us,......300. H.961, 13
Caesar's 'Twas Cesars saying: Kings no lesse Conquerors are 271. H.825, 1
Cætera Cætera desunt——...................231. H.662, 76
Cake See Bridal-cake, Bride-cake, Holy-cake
Be thy hand the hallowed Cake:................158. H.417, 2
For me, and mine a Cake:....................173. H.460, 4
For Mistresse Bride, the wedding Cake:......267. H.805, 2
A little Wafer or a Cake;....................284. H.890, 4
With the cake full of plums,..................317. H.1035, 2
Joy-sops with the cake;.......................317. H.1035, 14
love to your welcome with the mistick Cake, 431. ins. H.283, 60b
Caker — — — — — — — —, ...452. ins. H.293, 31b
Cakes See Bridal-cakes, Sugar-cakes
Some have dispatcht their Cakes and Creame,..69. H.178, 47
To cakes of Ice, or flakes of Snow:...........79. H.198, 6
Of Twelf-tide Cakes, of Pease, and Beanes...127. H.319, 17
Tarts and Custards, Creams and Cakes,........255. H.761, 3
And Cakes Divine,.........................296. H.946, 20
Calais By Ornithes sonne, young Calais;........70. H.181, 14
Calamus The Saffron and the Calamus...........375. N.123, 54
Calcedon But by the Topaz, Opal, Calcedon........30. H.88, 12
Calculation The Calculation of thy Birth, Brave Mince. 194. H.526, 6
Calendar See Endless-calendar, Greeny-calendar
In this most curious Calendar..................91. H.223, 37
Thee here in my eternall Calender...........199. H.545, 10
— — — — — — — — —, ...437. var. H.336, 89
Calendars True Calenders, as Pusses eare......134. H.336, 89
Calenture My soules most desp'rate Calenture;..397. N.257, 2
Calf The calfe without meale n'ere was offered;..345. N.34, 2
Call Helpe me! helpe me! now I call............10. H.19, 1
Turn'd her to this Plant, we call..............15. H.36, 14
I kist thee (panting,) and I call.................20. H.56, 7
Nor can we that a ruine call,..................25. H.76, 3
Call on Bacchus; chaunt his praise;..........39. H.111, 7

Which Country people call a Bee............50. H.139, 9
Alas! I call; but ah! I see...................50. H.140, 11
Call forth fierce Lovers to their wisht Delights:.77. H.197, 6
Call me The sonne of Beere, and then confine..79. H.197, 87
Next, Virgil, Ile call forth,..................80. H.201, 17
And some have heard the Elves it call........91. H.223, 24
Which boyes, and Bruckel'd children call......91. H.223, 58
To call to Morn, and Even-Song..............93. H.223, 128
Charms, that call down the moon from out her sphere,
99. H.244, 1
I call, I call, who doe ye call?..............112. H.281, 1
Foule in these noble pastimes, lest ye call......114. H.283, 86
Which extract, all we can call pith..........116. H.283, 154
Of that we call the Cuckoes spittle...........119. H.293, 28
We'll call on Night, to bring ye both to Bed:..124. H.313, 10
Call not to mind those fled Decembers;........127. H.319, 38
What is the thing we call a kisse?...........130. H.329, 2
I can but name thee, and methinks I call.......131. H.331, 1
The Ages fled, Ile call agen:...............134. H.336, 80
I'le call my young...........................135. H.336, 93
Ile call to mind things half forgot:..........135. H.336, 114
Call me no more,............................144. H.371, 1
And with my sighs, call home my bleating sheep:
159. H.421, 38
I call all Maids to witnesse too..............165. H.442, 12
If full we charme; then call upon.............198. H.544, 7
(I dare not call ye Sweepers)................235. H.674, 14
For love he doth call........................247. H.727, 10
Discreet and prudent we that Discord call,...252. H.748, 1
Shall call to Judgment; tell us when the sound.257. H.763, 18
To call my Lord Maior knave;................259. H.772, 15
Lets call for Hymen if agreed thou art;.......261. H.781, 1
The loss of that we call a Maydenhead?.......262. H.781, 14
Give me a reason why men call...............273. H.832, 1
The factions of the great ones call,...........282. H.877, 1
Bad are all surfeits: but Physitians call......286. H.895, 1
But since th' art Printed, thou dost call........287. H.899, 3
Smooth was the Sea, and seem'd to call......294. H.937, 1
Hence I must, for time doth call.............306. H.984, 38
So much as to call.........................320. H.1051, 17
But when they call or cry on Grubs for meat;..325. H.1077, 3
God is not onely mercifull, to call............342. N.19, 1
Since rough the way is, help me when I call,..352. N.51, 7
Call, and I'le come; say Thou, the when, and where:
358. N.77, 13
Honour thy Parents; but good manners call....363. N.94, 1
Death and dreadfulnesse call on,..............373. N.121, 5
To make paiment, while I call.................373. N.121, 12
If I but call unto Thee.......................373. N.122, 4
Out of hell an horrour call,..................377. N.128, 14
God, in the holy Tongue, they call............385. N.185, 1
Christ did her Woman, not her Mary call:....386. N.192, 2
To change, or call back, His past Sentences.....389. N.216, 4
I'le call, and cry out, Thanks to Thee.........400. N.267, 5
— — — — — — — — — — —, ...424. var. H.164, 7
— — — — — — — — — — —, ...440. var. H.443, 107
— — — — — — — — — — —, ...441. var. H.465, 37
Listen, while they call backe the former yeare,
443. var. H.575, 52

Called Why this Flower is now call'd so,..........14. H.36, 1
He wept, he sobb'd, he call'd to some.........18. H.46, 5
Not so much call'd a tree,.....................30. H.89, 9
But alias call'd Fatuus ignis...................91. H.223, 31
Cal'd out by the clap of the Thunder..........225. H.643, 24
But since I'm cal'd (rare Denham) to be gone,.234. H.673, 13
Yet since cal'd back; henceforward let me be,...242. H.713, 15
Some have Thee call'd Amphion; some of us,...288. H.907, 7
And cal'd each line back to his rule and space..311. H.1006, 4
And I cal'd on................................346. N.38, 3
Implies His Power, when He's cal'd the LORD.379. N.141, 2
Angells are called Gods; yet of them, none.....379. N.143, 1
Moses, and Jesus, called Joshua:..............381. N.157, 2
God is Jehovah cal'd; which name of His....385. N.187, 1
But Mary cal'd then (as S. Ambrose saith)....386. N.192, 4
Ev'n as the sprinkled bloud cal'd on............387. N.203, 3
Call'd on the suddayne by the Jealouse Mother,..410. A.3, 7
And Hymen call'd to bless the Rites. Cha. Stop there.
416. A.8, 20
— — — — — — — — — —, ...426. var. H.197, 28

Callice — — — — — — — — — —, ...434. var. H.293, 51

Calls No sound calls back the yeere that once is past.
8. H.10, 4
Age cals me hence, and my gray haires bid come,..9. H.14, 3
Gubbs call's his children Kitlings: and wo'd bound
80. H.200, 1
His house of Rimmon, this he calls,..........90. H.223, 9
It calls to mind, that mighty Buckingham,......137. H.341, 2
If wounds in clothes, Cuts calls his rags, 'tis cleere,
144. H.373, 1
The Saints-bell calls; and, Julia, I must read....209. H.584, 1
Cock calls his Wife his Hen: when Cock goes too't,
213. H.610, 1
Snare, ten i' th' hundred calls his wife; and why?
220. H.631, 1
Calls forth the lilly-wristed Morne;..........230. H.662, 20
And calls his Blouze, his Queene;...........259. H.772, 23
Tom calls not pimples, but Pimpleides:.......273. H.834, 2
When my Lot calls me to be buried,...........277. H.853, 2
Cha. Who calls? who calls? Euc. One overwhelm'd with ruth;
416. A.8, 3
— — — — — — — — — —, ...425. var. H.197, 6

Calm What though the sea be calme? Trust to the shore:
85. H.212, 1
But turne soone after calme, as Balme, or Oile..105. H.259, 4
A gentle calme did follow.....................373. N.122, 8
There in calm and cooling sleep.............377. N.128, 17
To[o] Calme A tempest, lett bee brought........408. A.2, 66

Calmness But lul'd to calmnesse, then succeeds a breeze
225. H.642, 15

Calms And calmes succeeding, we perceive no more
254. H.756, 5

Calvary The Mount of Olives; Calverie, and where
330. H.1100, 13

Calves Her leggs with twoe cleire calves like siluer tride
406. A.1, 87

Came How Roses first came Red, and Lillies White.
5. H.1, 10
And ravish'd thus, It came to passe,............13. H.27, 5
Me thought, (last night) love in an anger came,..16. H.40, 1
How Love came in, I do not know,............24. H.73, 1
Or whether with the soule it came..............24. H.73, 3
Came one unto my gate,........................26. H.81, 3
Which Venus hearing; thither came,...........31. H.92, 5
For second course, last night, a Custard came....47. H.131, 1
Love, like a Gypsie, lately came;..............63. H.166, 1
When next he came a pilfring so,............71. H.182, 29
As Cleopatra came to Anthonie;.............79. H.197, 74
Till you (sweet Mistresse) came and enterwove..94. H.224, 7
But when your Playing, and your Voice came in,
95. H.228, 3
So Good-luck came, and on my roofe did light,..100. H.247, 1
The Roses first came red......................105. H.258, 8
Crept to that, and came to this..............120. H.297, 6
Of deep and arrant ignorance came in;........150. H.382, 14
I heard ye co'd coole heat; and came.........157. H.413, 1
Mirt. This way she came, and this way too she went;
159. H.421, 18
Mirt. In dewie-mornings when she came this way,
159. H.421, 23
Since to th' Country first I came,.............182. H.489, 1
But making haste, it came to passe,............187. H.504, 3
And forthwith came to me.....................188. H.509, 4
From whom we'l reckon. Wit came in, but since.194. H.526, 5
Streame to the Spring from whence it came....245. H.720, 10
I came; (tis true) and lookt for Fowle of price,
262. H.783, 7
Love in a showre of Blossomes came..........283. H.883, 1
Love, like a Beggar, came to me.............295. H.942, 1
Came a mad dog, and did bite,..............306. H.984, 34
Unto Pastillus ranke Gorgonius came,..........323. H.1066, 1

Camest See Cam'st

Camlets Cloath'd in her Chamlets of Delight.....47. H.133, 11

Camp Us both i'th' Sea, Camp, Wildernesse)..134. H.336, 66

Camphor This Camphire, Storax, Spiknard, Galbanum:
157. H.414, 2

Cam'st Thou cam'st to cure me (Doctor) of my cold,
97. H.236, 1

Can (Partial List)
Find that Medicine (if you can)..............10. H.19, 11
Tempting the two too modest; can...........115. H.283, 113
I am Sive-like, and can hold..................116. H.285, 1
By Time, and Counsell, doe the best we can,..120. H.294, 1
And as coy be, as you can,...................121. H.297, 13
Who writes sweet Numbers well as any can:.....172. H.459, 2
Tread, Sirs, as lightly as ye can...............226. H.644, 1
Serve or not serve, let Tom doe what he can,...265. H.796, 3
Can I not come to Thee, my God, for these....352. N.51, 1

Canary Grapes, before Herrick leaves Canarie Sack.
78. H.197, 48
As the Canary Isles were thine:............148. H.377, 84
For Canary...................................320. H.1051, 18

Cancelled By Law, the Bond once cancelled.....370. N.107, 15

Candid Brave men can't die; whose Candid Actions are
168. H.444, 5
The Candid Temples of her comely face:......197. H.543, 2
The candid Stole thrown ore the Pious Priest;..286. H.898, 6
To feed upon the Candid hares...........433. ins. H.293, 31a

Candi'd See Candied

Candidate Stood in the Holy-Forum Candidate:..106. H.261, 2
Part Ruby-like, part Candidate?................269. H.815, 2
Tha'st got a place here (standing candidate)....305. H.983, 2

Candied Of Candi'd dew in Moony nights......165. H.443, 32

Candle From that cheape Candle baudery:.......133. H.336, 54
Lighten my candle, so that I beneath..........358. N.77, 10
Thou art our candle there, or spark..........372. N.118, 8

Candle-light Soft Candle-light; the Kitling's eyne;
167. H.443, 74

Candlemas Candlemas to grace the Grave.........304. H.976, 6
— — — — — — — — — — —, ...440. var. H.443, 82

Candles Candles (forsooth) and other knacks:...93. H.223, 116
Candles Ile give to thee,.....................213. H.604, 9

Candlesticks Two pure, and holy Candlesticks:...92. H.223, 94

Candor While thou didst keep thy **Candor** undefil'd, 6. H.3, 1
Candor here, and lustre there..................377. N.128, 11
The Mayden **Candour** of thy Mynde:.............407. A.2, 34
Caned Being drunke, who 'twas that **Can'd** his Ribs last night. 186. H.501, 4
Canker See **Idol-canker**
The **Canker** of the heart:.......................170. H.452, 2
Of a dried **Canker**, with a sagge..........433. ins. H.293, 31b
Cankers Are pucker'd Bullace, **Canckers** and dry 439. ins. H.443, 45m
Cannot See **Can't**
Old I am, and **cannot** do.........................10. H.19, 3
What ye **cannot** quench, pull downe;............21. H.61, 5
So that the path I **cannot** find:..................32. H.98, 2
Wealth **cannot** make a life, but Love.........37. H.106, 128
Because he **cannot** sleep i' th' Church, free-cost...39. H.109, 4
Once gets a force, Floods **cannot** quench the flame. 40. H.113, 4
But if horrour **cannot** slake.................117. H.286, 9
That from thee I **cannot** go;..................128. H.322, 11
Though I **cannot** give thee fires..............129. H.324, 1
How dull and dead are books, that **cannot** show.141. H.359, 1
Save but his hat, and that he **cannot** mew.......144. H.372, 2
For all his shifts, he **cannot** shift his clothes.....149. H.380, 2
Since which I freeze, but **cannot** frie..........155. H.406, 4
I **cannot** suffer; And in this, my part............169. H.447, 1
First, for your shape, the curious **cannot** shew..189. H.511, 1
I **cannot** pipe as I was wont to do,...........205. H.573, 1
Who with a little **cannot** be content,............213. H.606, 1
How Herrick beggs, if that he **can-**
Not like the Muse; to love the man,...........214. H.611, 3-4
I **cannot** tell; unlesse there be..................218. H.626, 8
I **cannot** love, as I have lov'd before:..........258. H.768, 1
As whether (this) I **cannot** tell................283. H.883, 5
But for his heart, he **cannot** have it made:......302. H.969, 2
The reason is, his credit **cannot** get............302. H.969, 3
As my weake shoulders **cannot** beare............303. H.973, 9
Who **cannot** buie, or steale a second to't.......332. H.1110, 2
Thou bidst me come; I **cannot** come; for why,....352. N.52, 1
Although we **cannot** turne the fervent fit........356. N.67, 1
Night hath no wings, to him that **cannot** sleep;....358. N.77, 1
Alas! I **cannot** pay a jot; therefore..............368. N.103, 7
Which has no root, and **cannot** grow,............371. N.114, 2
But what God is, we **cannot** show...............394. N.238, 2
Wee **cannot** ease;.............................401. N.268, 30
Cannot deliuer vpp to'th rust,....................407. A.2, 17
Cha. I **cannot** stay; more souls for waftage wait,..416. A.8, 24
Canonical All that have been, or are **canonicall**..131. H.331, 2
Canonization Here, in my Book's **Canonization**:..188. H.510, 2
Canonized As to be **canoniz'd** 'mongst those,....169. H.449, 12
A stole of white, (and **Canonized** here)..........199. H.545, 6
Canons I, and their Book of **Canons** too..........92. H.223, 78
Their **Canons**, and their Chaunteries:..........93. H.223, 106
Canopies Are beawtifi'd with faire fring'd **canopies**.404. A.1, 10
Canopy Like a Celestiall **Canopie**................67. H.175, 10
That made that fairest **Canopie**.................382. N.164, 2
Canst And both are knowne to thee, who now **can'st** live 35. H.106, 11
And **can'st** instruct, that those who have the itch.35. H.106, 19
Thus thou **can'st** tearcely live to satisfie........35. H.106, 27
Canst in thy Map securely saile:.................36. H.106, 78
Nor are thine eares so deafe, but thou **canst** heare.36. H.106, 83
Can'st, and unurg'd, forsake that Larded fare,..37. H.106, 111
Nor art thou so close-handed, but **can'st** spend..38. H.106, 129
(Eternall in thy self) that **canst** controule.......45. H.128, 20
Thou Power that **canst** sever.....................95. H.227, 7
Thou sweetly **canst** convert the same...........95. H.227, 12
List of references: 108, H.267, 7; 148. H.377, 91; 157. H.414, 1; 174. H.465, 34; 181. H.483, 3; 200. H.554, 1; 203. H.564, 3; 206. H.575, 54; 229. H.660, 2; 246. H.725, 4; 271. H.824, 3; 272. H.828, 10; 276. H.851, 5; 297. H.947, 10; 298. H.955, 5; 330, H.1100, 7; 330, H.1100, 9; 339, N.3, 1; 340. N.3, 15; 354. N.59, 15; 356. N.71, 1; 365. N.97, 15; 367. N.102, 6; 389. N.216, 3; 412. A.3, 93; 421. var. H.106, 3; 422. ins. H.106, 116a; 437. var. H.336, 135.
Can't (Partial List) See **Cannot**
When I thy Parts runne o're, I **can't** espie........10. H.16, 1
You blame me too, because I **cann't** devise........15. H.38, 3
As blessed soules **cann't** heare too much:........22. H.68, 4
Goddesse Isis **cann't** transfer....................59. H.155, 7
Our comfort is, we **can't** be lost...............134. H.336, 58
Brave men **can't** die; whose Candid Actions are..168. H.444, 5
Tell I **can't** what's Resident......................191. H.519, 4
Which (since here they **can't** combine)..........211. H.593, 3
In our high art, although we **can't** excell,.......234. H.673, 10
What others **can't** with all their strength put to...245. H.722, 2
Can't send for a gift..........................256. H.762, 14
That will speake what this **can't** tell............289. H.910, 5
'Tis now his habit, which he **can't** give ore.....302. H.972, 2
Since longer I **can't** live,.......................328. H.1091, 5
Alas I **can't**, for tell me how..................329. H.1093, 1
Which if that **can't** Thy pittie wooe,...........349. N.46, 7
This **can't** endure;..............................353. N.56, 20
'Tis true, my God; but I **can't** pay one mite.....368. N.103, 10
God **can't** be wrathfull; but we may conclude,....397. N.259, 1

Cantharides His golden god, **Cantharides**..........90. H.223, 18
Cap See **Red-cap**
— — — — — — — —, ...435, var. H.293, 39m
Capacious And there Ile shew thee that **capacious** roome 207. H.575, 56
Capable So long are **capable** of cure,.............153. H.395, 2
And look as all were **capable** of Love:........326. H.1080, 12
Caper To dance and **caper** on the heads of flowers,.78. H.197, 52
Capering With bucksome meat and **capring** Wine: 127. H.319, 28
When I drinke my **capring** wine:.............309. H.996, 2
Capital No **Capitoll**, no Cornish free,............90. H.223, 20
Capitol Leaving no shew, where stood the **Capitoll**. 252. H.745, 16
Capring See **Capering**
Capt See **Red-capped**
Captain One Brave **Captain** did command,.......276. H.850, 9
Captive Thou my pretty **Captive** art?............128. H.322, 5
Captive one, or both, to take:...................235. H.678, 6
Fortune is now Your **Captive**; other Kings......271. H.823, 5
Captives All hearts your **captives**; yours, yet free:..61. H.160, 4
Captivity Such Freedome in **Captivity**;..........64. H.169, 10
Carbage The inward **carbage** for his cloathes as yet. 302. H.969, 4
Carbonadoed Nits **carbonado'd**, a device...435. ins. H.293, v
Carcanet I sent my Love a **Karkanet**:..............14. H.34, 2
About thy neck a **Carkanet** is bound,.............30. H.88, 5
Making a **Carkanet**..............................43. H.123, 8
In that rich **Carkanet**;.........................130. H.330, 2
Forth by a Ring, or some rich **Carkanet**?.........172. H.459, 6
Why then (forsooth) a **Carcanet** is shown........232. H.668, 5
Like pearle and gold make one rich **Carcanett**......405. A.1, 32
Carcanets Ile give thee Chaines and **Carkanets**..192. H.521, 19
Carcass Then the dead Corps, or **carkase** of the Wine. 301. H.964, 2
Card Those Picks or Diamonds in the **Card**:.....166. H.443, 48
Carded And then a Rug of **carded** wooll,........167. H.443, 96
Cardinal The Vertues Lesse, or **Cardinall**,........409. A.2, 100
Care I **care** not now how soone 'tis done,...........18. H.47, 11
When one is past, another **care** we hav...........18. H.48, 1
That, which subverts whole nature, grief and **care**; 45. H.128, 21
But **care** for crowns of flowers:.................65. H.170, 2
And sweet as Flora. Take no **care**..............68. H.178, 17
For my part, I never **care**.....................82. H.203, 1
Art quickens Nature; **Care** will make a face:......97. H.234, 1
There's that, which drowns all **care**, stout Beere; 101. H.250, 37
Of Blind-man-buffe, and of the **care**............126. H.319, 15
That Love last long; let it thy first **care** be.....185. H.494, 1
What need I **care**, though some dislike me sho'd,.187. H.506, 5
And since it was thy **care**......................220. H.633, 14
Whose life with **care** is overcast,................233. H.670, 32
It was, and still my **care** is,....................234. H.674, 1
The Masters charge and **care** to recompence.....245. H.723, 10
Where **care**....................................246. H.724, 31
Tread ore his gleab, but with such **care**, that where 259. H.771, 7
Go to Bed, and **care** not when..................276. H.850, 7
My **care** for thee is now the less;...............287. H.899, 5
Care keepes the Conquest; 'tis no lesse renowne,..307. H.989, 1
Next be sure ye have a **care**,....................322. H.1064, 3
And have a **care** no fire gos out,.................365. N.97, 5
Pale **care**, avant,...............................368. N.104, 10
Nor wo'd I **care** how short it were, if good:.....392. N.230, 10
Then vnto theis, bee itt thy **care**................408. A.2, 53
Fly hence Pale **Care**, noe more remember..........413. A.4, 1
— — — — — — — — — —, ...436. var. H.336, 14
Care-charming-spell Musick, thou Queen of Heaven, **Care-charming-spel**,.................................103. H.254, 1
Careful What store of Corn has **carefull** Nodes, thinke you, 270. H.822, 3
Careless Julia was **carelesse**, and withall,...........12. H.27, 1
A **carelesse** shooe-string, in whose tye...........28. H.83, 11
Cares Attended with those desp'rate **cares**,........36. H.106, 64
The yeare (your **cares**) that's fled and gon.......127. H.319, 44
As for my self, since time a thousand **cares**......140. H.355, 5
Howsoever, **cares**, adue;...........................191. H.519, 5
With feares, and **cares** uncumbered:.............233. H.670, 12
From **cares** and troubles free;...................259. H.772, 26
He that will live of all **cares** dispossest,...........305. H.981, 1
My many **cares** and much distress,...............312. H.1016, 1
Carest See **Car'st**
Carkanet See **Carcanet**
Carnal Shee brings in much, by **carnall** usury:....220. H.631, 2
Carnation Where such a rare **Carnation** grew.......63. H.164, 11
In yond' **Carnation** goe and seek,...............106. H.263, 7
Carnations How roses lillies and **carnations** grow,..404. A.1, 16
Carol Then a **Caroll**, for to sing...................364. N.96, 2
Chor. The **Caroll** of our gladnesse..............375. N.123, 57
And sing a **Caroll** here...........................413. A.4, 5
Carouse Sit crown'd with Rose-buds, and **carouse**,.127. H.319, 41
Which sweetly spic't, we'l first **carouse**........135. H.336, 127
Carousing There's no **Carousing**.....................197. H.540, 8
Carp And can'st not mend, but **carpe** at it:.......229. H.660, 2
Carpets To make these flowrie **Carpets** show....104. H.256, 18

Carriage With blamelesse **carriage**, I liv'd here,....41. H.116, 1
When her high **carriage** did at once present......79. H.197, 75
And for the comely **carriage** of it;..............194. H.526, 2
For Grace and **Carriage**, every one a Queene...326. H.1080, 24
Carriages Unlesse they have some wanton **carriages**.
290. H.914, 8
Carried Worship, and not to'th' Asse that **carried** her.
330. H.1099, 6
Carries And fretfull, **carries** Hay in's horne,......165. H.443, 14
Carrionere When 'twas her breath that was the **Carrionere**.
212. H.598, 2
Carry **Carry** the Garland from the rest.........192. H.521, 34
Carrie nothing but a Crust:.................323. H.1065, 4
Now singing, homeward let us **carrie**...........366. N.97, 26
Car'st Nor **car'st** which comes the first, the foule or faire;
37. H.106, 97
Cart **See Hock-cart**
Come forth, my Lord, and see the **Cart**..........101. H.250, 7
About the **Cart**, heare, how the Rout............101. H.250, 15
Some blesse the **Cart**; some kisse the sheaves;..101. H.250, 19
— — — — — — — — — — —, ...432. var. H.283, 96
Carted Letcher was **Carted** first about the streets,..195. H.532, 1
Carting His **Carting** was the Prologue to this Play.
195. H.532, 4
Carts **See Hock-carts**
Carve Ile **carve** thy name, and in that name kisse thee:
160. H.421, 40
But **carve** to him the fat flanks; and he shall....305. H.982, 3
Carved With Motto's **carv'd** on every tree,......169. H.449, 22
— — — — — — — — — — — —, ...450. var. A.9, 11
Case What's now the cause? we know the **case** is cleere:
71. H.183, 2
More faire in this transparent **case**,..............75. H.193, 6
And live, and in that **case**,.....................115. H.283, 139
Case is a Lawyer, that near pleads alone,........303. H.975, 1
Then **Case**, as loud as any Serjant there,.........303. H.975, 5
Cries out, (my lord, my Lord) the **Case** is clear:.303. H.975, 6
But when all's hush't, **Case** then a fish more mute,
303. H.975, 7
Cases In desp'rate **cases**, all, or most are known..272. H.827, 1
Casques Small griefs find tongues: Full **Casques** are ever found
15. H.38, 7
Cassia Roses and **Cassia** crown the untill'd soyle...205. H.575, 4
Let Balme, and **Cassia** send their scent.........361. N.83, 65
Cassiodore True rev'rence is (as **Cassiodore** doth prove)
380. N.147, 1
Then prayers repel'd, (sayes **Cassiodore**)........383. N.170, 2
Cassius Had **Cassius**, that weak Water-drinker, known
78. H.197, 61
Cast **See Downcast, Love-cast-off, O'ercast, Outcast, Overcast**
Dead when I am, first **cast** in salt, and bring........9. H.14, 7
She threw; I **cast**; and having thrown,............19. H.49, 3
Cast off (said he) all feare,.....................26. H.81, 7
Sighs numberlesse he **cast** about,.................42. H.119, 5
Over her fragrant cheek is **cast**..................55. H.149, 72
And (with your Mantle o're me **cast**)..........61. H.159, 24
And chose their Priest, ere we can **cast** off sloth:..69. H.178, 50
Without some Scean **cast** over,...................76. H.193, 39
Judith has **cast** her old-skin, and got new;......140. H.356, 1
Shift now has **cast** his clothes: got all things new;
144. H.372, 1
When others gain much by the present **cast**,....144. H.374, 1
The blush of cherries, when a Lawn's **cast** over...158. H.416, 4
If well the Dice runne, lets applaud the **cast**:....218. H.621, 1
The least grim looke, or **cast** a frown on you:....222. H.634, 8
Cast on my Girles a glance, and loving eye:....222. H.634, 11
Falls to a tempter, and doth mildly **cast**........225. H.642, 19
Then to **cast** off all bashfulnesse.................241. H.712, 2
Cast in Salt, for seasoning:...................258. H.769, 2
Next, when I **cast** mine eyes and see............261. H.779, 4
Be not dismaide, though crosses **cast** thee downe;
311. H.1007, 1
Where War and Peace the Dice by turns doe **cast**.
327. H.1083, 2
He lives, who lives to virtue: men who **cast**....328. H.1088, 9
And here my ship rides having Anchor **cast**.....334. H.1126, 2
I'le **cast** a mist and cloud, upon.................357. N.72, 5
Cast Holy Water all about,......................365. N.97, 4
Neglecting once to **cast** a frown on those........372. N.116, 3
That Manna, which God on His people **cast**,.....379. N.146, 1
Cast, leading his Euredice through hell,..........411. A.3, 68
But first **cast** off thy wonted Churlishness.........416. A.8, 6
Castalian **Castalian** sisters, sing, if wanting thee...45. H.128, 30
Casters' With **casters** duckets which poore they
440 ins. H.443, 56a
Castor's — — — — — — — —, ...440 ins. H.443, 56a
Casts **Casts** forth a light like to a Virgin flame:..131. H.331, 6
Cat A **Cat**...................................246. H.724, 21
Catch The Maids to **catch** this Cowslip-ball:....112. H.281, 2
Some gin, wherewith to **catch** your eyes.........114. H.283, 70
No ginne to **catch** the State, or wring..........126. H.319, 7
Lesse for to **catch** a sheep, then me..........193. H.521, 46
To **catch** the pilfring Birds, not Men...........231. H.662, 69
For to **catch** the Lookers on;................232. H.665, 13
To **catch** it..................................263. H.785, 4
Catching — — — — — — — — — —, ...432. var. H.283, 84

Cates Who keep'st no proud mouth for delicious **cates**:
37. H.106, 109
Which fain would waste upon thy **Cates**, but that
147. H.377, 49
Cato Let rigid **Cato** read these Lines of mine.........7. H.8, 10
Cato the Censor, sho'd he scan each here...........28. H.84, 6
As the wise **Cato** had approv'd of thee...........78. H.197, 64
Nor **Cato** the severe...........................259. H.772, 6
And as time past when **Cato** the Severe..........301. H.962, 1
Death for stout **Cato**; and besides all these,.....370. N.108, 7
Cats **See Black-bore-cats**
Catullus **Catullus**, I quaffe up....................80. H.201, 27
Then soft **Catullus**, sharp-fang'd Martial,........206. H.575, 43
Caught **Caught** my poore soule, as in a snare:....281. H.876, 8
Caught'st And **caught'st** thy selfe the more by twenty fold:
97. H.236, 2
Caul For either sheet, was spread the **Caule**......167. H.443, 90
Cauls To guild thy Tombe; besides, these **Caules**,.360. N.83, 43
Cause Ther's still more **cause**, why I the more should love.
10. H.16, 6
Nor wrack, or Bulging thou hast **cause** to feare:..23. H.71, 2
The **Cause**, th'effect wo'd die......................32. H.96, 4
Both the **cause**, and make the heat.............62. H.162, 14
What's now the **cause**? we know the case is cleere:.71. H.183, 2
Dead falls the **Cause**, if once the Hand be mute;..123. H.308, 1
Then next Ile **cause** my hopefull Lad..........135. H.336, 121
Drinks of distemper, or ha's **cause** to cry.......148. H.377, 87
To Print our Poems, the propulsive **cause**........169. H.448, 1
That art the **cause** Endimion;..................183. H.492, 7
Here, and his **Cause**.........................190. H.515, 24
Then **cause** we Horace to be read,.............198. H.544, 13
What is the **cause**? Why Gander will reply,......223. H.636, 3
(Where I have **cause** to burn perfumes to it:)..234. H.673, 8
What doth **cause** this pensiveness?..............305. H.984, 2
The **cause**, why things thus fragrant be:........364. N.96, 18
To create (or **cause** at all)...................377. N.128, 15
Predestination is the **Cause** alone..............389. N.215, 1
Sin is the **cause** of death; and sin's alone........390. N.219, 1
The **cause** of Gods Predestination:...............390. N.219, 2
Of man's the chief **cause** of Gods Prescience.....390. N.220, 2
Present, to plead my **cause** for me;.............395. N.245, 4
— — — — — — — — — —, ...439. var. H.443, 45
'Cause **See Because**
You say I love not, **'cause** I doe not play........15. H.38, 1
Who speak but little, **'cause** I love so much.......15. H.38, 14
But none co'd eate it, **'cause** it stunk so much.....47. H.131, 6
For the least trespasse; **'cause** the mind.........175. H.465, 61
'Cause my speech is now decaid;................348. N.41, 31
Causeless But **causelesse** whipping smarts the most of all.
319. H.1050, 2
Causeth Mou'd by the chinne whose motion **causeth** this
405. A.1, 37
Cavaliers Lovely in you, brave Prince of **Cavaliers**!.25. H.77, 8
Cave The excellency of this **Cave**,..............166. H.443, 54
My **Cave**......................................178. H.475, 12
— — — — — — — — — — — —, ...440. var. H.443, 78
Caverns By poares and **cavernes** back agen......245. H.720, 8
Cease That in short time my woes shall **cease**;....73. H.187, 10
Winds have their time to rage; but when they **cease**,
105. H.259, 5
And all Star-chamber-Bils doe **cease**,............190. H.515, 27
The Watch once downe, all motions then do **cease**;
202. H.558, 3
The gentle Dove may, when these turmoils **cease**,
225. H.642, 21
The lesse our sorrowes here and suffrings **cease**,..372. N.119, 1
Ceased In me, is dead or **ceast**..................144. H.371, 6
Cecubum Ile drink the aged **Cecubum**,..............208. H.582, 3
Cedar Which makes them worthy **Cedar**, and the Bayes.
45. H.128, 36
And **Cedar** wash thee, that no times consume thee.
89. H.219, 14
No roofs of **Cedar**, nor our brave..............133. H.336, 42
To be with juice of **Cedar** washt all over;........415. A.7, 6
Ceiling And **seeling** free,.......................133. H.336, 53
Or fret thy **Seeling**, or to build.............149. H.377, 120
Celerity **Celerity** even it self is slow..............378. N.133, 2
Celestial Like a **Celestiall** Canopie................67. H.175, 10
Chorus. Thus, thus the gods **celestial** still decree,..416. A.8, 17
Cell No Critick haunts the Poore mans **Cell**:........6. H.2, 22
Come then, brave Knight, and see the **Cell**......198. H.544. 25
Give me a **Cell**...............................258. H.770, 1
Lord, Thou hast given me a **cell**.................349. N.47, 1
Cement **See Sweet-cement**
Cense Which **cense** this Arch; and here and there,
166. H.443, 45
But **'cense** the porch, and place throughout.......365. N.97, 6
Censed The room is **cens'd**: help, help t'invoke....366. N.98, 15
Censer Take then thy **Censer**; Put in Fire, and thus,
197. H.539, 13
Censers Thy golden **Censors** fil'd with odours sweet,
128. H.320, 7
With golden **Censers**, and with Incense, here.....368. N.103, 1
Censor Cato the **Censor**, sho'd he scan each here...28. H.84, 6
Censure Prethee (lest Maids sho'd **censure** thee) but say
42. H.122, 9

Censured By no one tongue, there, **censured**.........6. H.2, 24
Censuring Your leane scalp to **sensuring**...........418. A.9, 32
Center And keep one **Centre**: This with that conspires,
35. H.106, 15
Center is known weak sighted, and he sells.......154. H.401, 1
Within a Lillie? **Center** plac't?................164. H.440, 4
To the **centre** of your love?...................276. H.850, 2
Nor stoope to'th **Center**, but suruiue as Longe....411. A.3, 45
Center-like Be so, bold spirit; Stand **Center-like**, unmov'd;
37. H.106, 101
Centinall See **Sentinel**
Cerecloth Wrapt up in **Seare-cloth** with thine Ancestrie:
231. H.664, 2
Cerecloths Our mortall parts may wrapt in **Seare-cloths** lye:
199. H.547, 1
And wth thayr **Ceareclothes** rotted, not to shew
411. A.3, 37
Ceremonies-sake See **Ceremony's-sake**
Ceremonious But spring from **ceremonious** feares...54. H.149, 22
Where **ceremonious** Hymen shall for thee......286. H.898, 11
Ceremony's-sake If needs we must for **Ceremonies-sake**,
115. H.283, 131
Certain 'Tis a **certain** Charm to keep...........284. H.888, 3
Lets drip a **certain** Gravie from her eyes.......331. H.1107, 2
Certainty This for **certainty** I know;...........277. H.852, 6
Cesar See **Caesar**
Cesar's See **Caesar's**
Cess Though much from out the **Cess** be spent,....33. H.100, 3
Ceston Or Citherea's **Ceston**, which...........166. H.443, 37
Chafe Seas **chafe** and fret, and beat, and over-boile;
105. H.259, 3
To **chafe** o're much the Virgins cheek or eare:...329. H.1095, 2
Chafed And **chaf'd** his hands with mine,..........27. H.81, 23
ing the **Chafte** Aire with fumes of Paradise....112. H.283, 16
Of Amber **chaf't** between the hands,..........145. H.375, 16
Chafes W[th] w[ch] Loue **Chafes** and warmes the soule
408. A.2, 48
Chain The Golden **chain** too, and the Civick Crown.
176. H.466, 8
A **chaine** of Cornes, pickt from her eares and toes:
232. H.668, 2
Chains May in like **Chains** of Darknesse lie.......64. H.169, 12
Ile give thee **Chaines** and Carkanets...........192. H.521, 19
Chains of sweet bents let us make,..............235. H.678, 5
Or **chaines** of Columbines shall make,...........361. N.83, 53
Chair Mine aged limbs above my **chaire**:........135. H.336, 108
Chalcedony See **Calcedon**
Chalice Small **Chalice** of thy frantick liquor; He..78. H.197, 63
From the plumpe **Challice**, and the Cup,........127. H.319, 35
— — — — — — — — — —, ...434. var. H.293, 51
Chalices They have their Cups and **Chalices**;.....93. H.223, 113
Challenged Is yours, in which you **challeng'd** are to fight
216. H.618, 10
Chamber See **Star-chamber, Star-chamber-bills**
But listen to thee, (walking in thy **chamber**)......22. H.67, 3
Within the **Chamber** here......................56. H.149, 108
Ah! then too late, close in your **chamber** keeping,.63. H.164, 12
Here I have found a **Chamber** fit,..............123. H.306, 7
Of clouts, wee'l make a **chamber**,..............345. N.33, 21
Where Thou my **chamber** for to ward..........349. N.47, 7
Chambers Charme then the **chambers**; make the beds for ease,
245. H.723, 11
Chamlets See **Camlets**
Chance Julia, if I **chance** to die...................21. H.59, 1
See, and not see; and if thou **chance** t'espie........32. H.95, 1
When age or **Chance** has made me blind,..........32. H.98, 1
To tell all prosp'rous **chance**...................55. H.149, 58
Let all chaste Matrons, when they **chance** to see..58. H.151, 1
And it may **chance** that Love may turn,..........61. H.159, 18
Mir. Not so, not so. Chor. But if it **chance** to prove
86. H.213, 27
Of **Chance**, (as made up all of rock, and oake:)..129. H.323, 12
Live here: But know 'twas vertue, & not **chance**,.152. H.392, 5
All things o'r-rul'd are here by **Chance**;..........197. H.542, 1
And working it, by **chance** from Umbers Erse....205. H.572, 2
Juno yet smiles; but if she **chance** to chide,.....262. H.781, 11
What I by **chance** did see;...................288. H.908, 6
Yet sho'd I **chance**, (my Wicks) to see.......321. H.1056, 7
When ye are (by **chance**) benighted:..........323. H.1065, 2
It may **chance** good-luck may send..............334. H.1125, 3
May **chance** to be no other man, but Christ.......391. N.226, 2
And if I **chance** to wake, and rise thereon,.......392. N.230, 21
That if the twig sho'd **chance** too much to smart,..394. N.241, 3
The blow of Ruine and of **Chance**................407. A.2, 11
— — — — — — — — — —, ...451. var. H.336, 90
Chanced The wanton Ambler **chanc'd** to see........12. H.27, 3
It **chanc't** a Bee did flie that way,...............71. H.182, 2
But so it **chanc't** to be;.......................188. H.509, 2
It **chanst** a ringlet of her haire,................281. H.876, 7
Chancellor To be my Counsell both, and **Chanceller**.
202. H.557, 30
Chancery Here those long suits of **Chancery** lie..190. H.515, 25
Change A **change**, when Fortune either comes, or goes:
128. H.323, 8
Washt o're, to tell[1] what **change** is neare......134. H.336, 90
T'ave found in me this sudden **change**;..........290. H.915, 4
Spend I my life (that's subject unto **change**:)..310. H.1003, 2
If thou canst **change** thy life, God then will please
389. N.216, 3
To **change**, or call back, His past Sentences.....389. N.216, 4
— — — — — — — — — —, ...452. var. H.197, 90
Changed See **Counter-changed**
But on a sudden, all was **chang'd** and gone........81. H.202, 3
In nothing **chang'd** but in their name...........180. H.478, 8
But **chang'd** above,..........................314. H.1024, 17
Changes You have **changes** in your life,..........96. H.232, 3
She shifts and **changes** like the Moone.........103. H.253, 14
Channel As in their **Channell** first they were.......339. N.3, 6
Chant Call on Bacchus; **chaunt** his praise;.........39. H.111, 7
Will **chant** new Hymnes to thee..............259. H.772, 28
If well, then **chant** Gods praise with cheerfulnesse.
395. N.243, 4
Chanters' Next, then, upon the **Chanters** side....93. H.223, 125
Chanticleer As not to rise when **Chanticlere**.......36. H.106, 56
Chantries Their Canons, and their **Chaunteries**:..93. H.223, 106
Chaos Shapelesse the world (as when all **Chaos** was)
59. H.154, 8
— — — — — — — — — — — —, ...437. var. H.336, 136
Chapel Survey this **Chappell**, built, alone, ...90. H.223a, 3
There is, that to the **Chappel** leads:.............90. H.223, 2
To purge the **Chappel** and the rooms:..........92. H.223, 102
A little **Chappell** fits a little Quire,.............249. H.733, 11
Chaplains Christ, I have read, did to his **Chaplains** say,
378. N.137, 1
Chaplet The **Chaplet**, and *Inarculum here be,....196. H.539, 3
I have my Laurel **Chaplet** on my head,........322. H.1062, 1
Chaplets And with **Chaplets** crown'd, we'l rost....280. H.870, 15
With Rosie **Chaplets**, Lillies, Pansies red,..442. ins. H.575, 20a
Chaps As to bind up her **chaps** when she is dead...205. H.571, 4
Nothing he loves on't but the **chaps** and ears:....305. H.982, 2
Charge And **charge**, he not forbears..............56. H.149, 97
Of her green hopes, we **charge** ye, that no strife,.114. H.283, 82
To thee, this my religious **charge**..............175. H.465, 68
The Masters **charge** and care to recompence....245. H.723, 10
W'ave more to beare our **charge**, then way to go?.308. H.995, 2
And I **charge** thee to bee knowne..............409. A.2, 75
I've more to beare my **Chardge**, then way to goe,..411. A.3, 54
— — — — — — — — — — —, ...449. var. A.3, 54
Charged **Charg'd** with tne Armes of all his Ancestors:
295. H.941, 2
Charges Who can with so small **charges** drive the buck.
178. H.474, 4
Chariot Make me a **Chariot**, and a Sun;..........47. H.133, 5
Slowly her **chariot** drives, as if that she..........358. N.77, 3
Charity Which **charity** they give to many........92. H.223, 89
When 'twas in's Feet, his **Charity** was small;....207. H.577, 3
Beere small as Comfort, dead as **Charity**.........262. H.783, 16
With **charity** throughout;......................352. N.53, 12
Charles **Charls** the best Husband, while Maria strives
26. H.79, 3
Go wooe young **Charles** no more to looke,........214. H.611, 1
The Starre-led-birth of **Charles** the Prince......214. H.611, 6
And **Charles** here Rule, as he before did Raign;..214. H.612, 8
Give way, give way, now, now my **Charles** shines here,
236. H.685, 1
While young **Charles** fights, and fighting wins the day.
254. H.756, 14
This Day is Yours, Great **CHARLES**! and in this War
271. H.823, 1
For which (my **Charles**) it is my pride to be,....297. H.947, 11
Charm See **Night-charm**
The sides: for 'tis a **charme**..................55. H.149, 87
To that soft **Charm**, that Spell, that Magick Bough,
62. H.161, 9
Begin to **charme**, and as thou stroak'st mine eares.67. H.176, 1
Charm me asleep, and melt me so................95. H.227, 1
To **charme** our soules, as thou enchant'st our eares.
103. H.254, 6
If full we **charme**; then call upon.............198. H.544, 7
Charme then the chambers; make the beds for ease,
245. H.723 11
One short **charme** if you but say...............276. H.850, 11
'Tis a certain **Charm** to keep...................284. H.888, 3
To **charme** his cries, (at time of need:)..........354. N.59, 10
And fowle thy Altar, **Charme** some Into froggs,..412. A.3, 91
Charmed **Charm'd** and enchanted so,............335. H.1129, 3
Charming See **Care-charming-spell**
Cooling sleep with **charming** wand..............56. H.149, 110
Ch. What voice so sweet and **charming** do I heare?
248. H.730, 3
Charms Bring your Magicks, Spels, and **Charmes**,..10. H.19, 5
Charms, that call down the moon from out her sphere,
99. H.244, 1
And **charmes** them there with lullabies;........130. H.329, 10
But Love by **charmes**,..........................213. H.609, 4
This 'mongst other mystick **charms**..............284. H.889, 5
Charmes the danger, and the dread............323. H.1065, 6
Charon Ph. **Charon**! O gentle **Charon**! let me wooe thee,
248. H.730, 1
Speak where thou art. Ph. O **Charon** pittie me!..248. H.730, 6
Euc. **Charon**, O **Charon**, draw thy Boat to th' Shore,
416. A.8, 1

That makes grim **Charon** thus to pity thee.......416. A.8, 22
Chaste And kisse, but yet be **chaste**...............13. H.31, 10
Which are so cleane, so **chast**, as none may feare..28. H.84, 5
Got, not so beautifull, as **chast**:...............35. H.106, 34
But still thy wife, by **chast** intentions led,.......35. H.106, 41
And as for me, my **chast** desire...................49. H.136, 33
Let all **chaste** Matrons, when they chance to see...58. H.151, 1
Yet lost, ere that **chast** flesh and blood........88. H.216, 8
Of which **chast** Order You are now the Queene:.107. H.265, 6
Of these **chaste** spirits, that are here possest......152. H.392, 2
Thou set'st their hearts, let **chaste** desire........174. H.465, 8
(As that **chaste** Queen of Ithaca..............174. H.465, 30
Chaste Syracusian Cyane.......................175. H.465, 58
And 'gainst your **chast** behaviour there's no Plea,.189. H.511, 3
Come then, and be to my **chast** side............190. H.515, 9
Chaste I liv'd, without a wife,................199. H.546, 3
Chaste Lucrece, or a wife as grave:............283. H.885, 8
With soft-smooth Virgins (for our **chast** disport)
315. H.1028, 9
Chaste words proceed still from a bashfull minde.
319. H.1043, 2
Jocond his Muse was; but his Life was **chast**...335. H.1130, 2
A new-borne Phoenix from His own **chast** fire.....367. N.98, 30
Where each **chast** Soule........................369. N.106, 7
And vnder it two **Chast** borne spyes...........408. A.2, 35
— — — — — — — — — — — —, ...423. var. H.128, 6
— — — — — — — — — — — —, ...430. var. H.283, 16
Chastely She who keeps **chastly** to her husbands side
286. H.898, 13
Chaster And In thy sence, her **Chaster** thoughtes Commend
421. ins. H.106, 42a
Chastity A mighty strife 'twixt Forme and **Chastitie**.
189. H.511, 6
Chattels God when He takes my goods and **chattels** hence
362. N.87, 1
Cheap To keep **cheap** Nature even, and upright;..35. H.106, 25
From that **cheape** Candle baudery:..............133. H.336, 54
The brave **cheape** worke, and for to pave..440. ins. H.443, 45bb
Cheapest With the **cheapest** Merriment:.........255. H.761, 22
Cheapness What others have with **cheapnesse** seene, and ease,
330. H.1100, 1
Cheapside **See Golden-Cheapside**
Once on a Lord-Mayors day, in **Cheapside**, when.200. H.551, 1
Cheat Sceanes to **cheat** us neatly drawne.........76. H.195, 8
Cheater's Without due reverence, playes the **cheaters** game.
347. N.39, 6
Cheats Eeles winds and turnes, and **cheats** and steales; yet Eeles
153. H.398, 1
Boreman takes tole, **cheats**, flatters, lyes, yet Boreman,
315. H.1025, 1
Checked When **checked** by the Butlers look......147. H.377, 56
Checks Shame **checks** our first attempts; but then 'tis prov'd
362. N.85, 1
Cheek And never staine a **cheeke** for it...............6. H.4, 4
For Health on Julia's **cheek** hath shed............7. H.9, 9
Claps my **cheek**, or kisseth me;.................17. H.43, 8
A bud in either **cheek**..........................18. H.45, 4
Love makes the **cheek**, and chin a sphere......49. H.136, 21
Cheek, and eye, and lip, and chin;..............52. H.147, 5
Over her fragrant **cheek** is cast.................55. H.149, 72
But find no Rose-bud in your **cheek**:............63. H.164, 9
Nor **cheek**, or tongue be dumbe:................80. H.201, 2
Within my Lucia's **cheek**,........................83. H.207, 5
Dry your sweet **cheek**, long drown'd with sorrows raine;
105. H.259, 1
Upon your **cheek** sate Ysicles awhile;..........105. H.259, 11
There thou shalt find her lip and **cheek**:......106. H.263, 8
And there to give the **cheek** a die..............118. H.291, 7
Then to the chin, the **cheek**, the eare,..........130. H.329, 12
Cherrish the **cheek**, but make none blush at all..140. H.354, 12
Corrols his **cheeke**, to see those Rites not done..216. H.618, 4
Her either **cheeke** with bashfullness............268. H.811, 10
For Roses, and in Julia's **cheeke**,...............281. H.876, 2
Upon thy **cheeke** that spangel'd Teare,.........328. H.1090, 8
To chafe o're much the Virgins **cheek** or eare:..329. H.1095, 2
Him in the Mornings blushing **cheek**,..........367. N.102, 9
Each **cheeke** resembling still a damaske rose,....404. A.1, 14
Then lett each **Cheeke** of thyne intice............408. A.2, 43
But let each p[r]sant **Cheeke** appear................413. A.4, 3
Cheeks Be her **cheeks** so shallow too,..............11. H.21, 9
His **cheeks** be-pimpled, red and blue;............38. H.108, 7
Next, make his **cheeks** with breath to swell,....39. H.108, 11
Furze, three or foure times with his **cheeks** did blow
47. H.131, 3
A blush their **cheeks** bespred;.................105. H.258, 6
Cheeks like to Roses, when they blow..........120. H.295, 2
Cheeks like Creame Enclarited:................138. H.342, 6
Rare are thy **cheeks** Susanna, which do show....193. H.523, 1
Fresh blossoms from her **cheekes** did fall........203. H.562, 2
Upon her **cheekes** she wept, and from those showers
204. H.567, 1
Those crimson clouds i'th'**cheeks** & lips leave shining
207. H.576, 2
Till that we see our **cheekes** Ale-dy'd..........219. H.629, 3
She wept upon her **cheeks**, and weeping so,....251. H.742, 1
Their **cheekes** unstain'd with shamefac'tnesse:..310. H.1004, 8
No question but Dols **cheeks** wo'd soon rost dry,
325. H.1078, 1
and cherries in her **cheekes**, there's Creame
430. ins. H.283, 20c
— — — — — — — — — — — —, ...437. var. H.336, 105
Cheer **See Good-cheer, Whipping-cheer**
And for to make the merry **cheere**,............101. H.250, 35
Ambo. Lets **cheer** him up. Sil. Behold him weeping ripe.
159. H.421, 7
Eaten I have; and though I had good **cheere**,..197. H.541, 1
Great be my fare, or small **cheere**,............235. H.674, 17
Drink rich wine; and make good **cheere**,......238. H.691, 3
— — — — — — — — — — — —, ...422. var. H.106, 111
Cheerful For his most **cheerfull** offerings........93. H.223, 134
Then will appeare a **cheerfull** Heaven..........188. H.508, 6
Cheerfull day shall spring agen................276. H.850, 8
That I might see the **cheerfull** peeping day.....358. N.77, 7
Cheerfulness In his Offering, **Cheerfulness**..........22. H.63, 4
With **Cheerfulnesse**,............................296. H.946, 2
If well, then chant Gods praise with **cheerfulnesse**.
395. N.243, 4
Cheer'st And **cheer'st** them up, by singing how..230. H.662, 27
Cheese O're-leven'd; or like **Cheese** o're-renetted......7. H.7, 2
Wo'd yee have fresh **Cheese** and Cream?........183. H.491, 1
Was **cheese** full ripe with Teares, with Bread as sad.
273. H.835, 4
For Bread, Drinke, Butter, **Cheese**; for every thing
287. H.903, 2
Chemist As when we sin; God, the great **Chymist**, thence
386. N.196, 3
Cherish **Cherrish** the cheek, but make none blush at all.
140. H.354, 12
Kings must not only **cherish** up the good,......260. H.775, 1
(Loue and Mercie, **cherrish** them),..............407. A.2, 22
Cherished But one by you be hug'd and **cherished**.
322. H.1062, 3
Cherishing He Acts the Crime, that gives it **Cherishing**.
10. H.17, 2
Hym for his better **Cherrishing**................408. A.2, 60
Cherries All the yeere, where **Cherries** grow......20. H.53, 8
Lips can make **Cherries** grow.................57. H.149, 148
When as **Cherries** come in place?................74. H.189, 6
Put Purple Grapes, or **Cherries** in-..............75. H.193, 25
With withered **cherries**; Mandrakes eares;....120. H.293, 43
The wine of **cherries**, and to these,............145. H.375, 19
The blush of **cherries**, when a Lawn's cast over...158. H.416, 4
Ripe **Cherries** smiling, while that others blow.....193. H.523, 2
So **Cherries** blush, and Kathern Peares,.........268. H.811, 3
Loues **Cherries** from such fyers growe..........408. A.2, 50
and **cherries** in her cheekes, there's Creame
430. ins. H.283, 20c
Cherrilets Twoe smelling swelling (bashful) **Cherriletts**,
404. A.1, 20
Cherry I saw a **Cherry** weep, and why?..........12. H.23, 1
Thus Lillie, Rose, Grape, **Cherry**, Creame,....75. H.193, 33
Plump as the **cherry**..........................136. H.336, 139
Another snapt the **Cherry**....................142. H.364, 8
Or else a **Cherrie** (double grac't)..............164. H.440, 3
As **Cherry** harvest, now high fed............165. H.443, 10
Cherry-isle There's the Land, or **Cherry-Ile**:......20. H.53, 6
Cherry-lipped Doe speake a virgin merry **cherry-lip't**.
404. A.1, 22
Cherry-pit Playing for sport, at **Cherry-pit**:......19. H.49, 2
Cherry-red Between the lips, (all **cherrie-red**,)..130. H.329, 5
Cherry-ripe **Cherrie-Ripe**, Ripe, Ripe, I cry,.......19. H.53, 1
Cherry-stone Know time past this **cherrystone**....417. A.9, 19
Cherubim Of many a warbling **Cherubim**:......115. H.283, 104
That rides the glorious **Cherubim**..............340. N.3, 16
Cherubin 'Twas no more you then, but a **Cherubin**.
95. H.228, 4
— — — — — — — — — — — —, ...432. var. H.283, 104
Chest Or else trans-fuse thy breath into the **chest**,.129. H.327, 3
And having washt thee, close thee in a **chest**....300. H.960, 5
Chestnuts Untill the fired **Chesnuts** leape........127. H.319, 33
Chests Into your **Chests**, drawn by your painfull Thumb.
221. H.633, 41
Cheveril Look in Prig's purse, the **chev'rell** there tells you
71. H.183, 3
Cheveron That Bar, this Bend; that Fess, this **Cheveron**;
295. H.941, 4
Chev'rell **See Cheveril**
Chew We not divide the Hoof, but **chew** the Cud:
397. N.256, 2
We then both **chew** the Cud, and cleave the Hoof.
397. N.256, 4
Chick As to be the **Chick** of Jove..............108. H.266, 8
And (Love knowes) tender as a **chick**.........167. H.443, 85
Chid When Julia **chid**, I stood as mute the while,.58. H.150, 1
Then smil'd, and sweetly **chid** her speed;.....187. H.504, 5
Chide Juno yet smiles; but if she chance to **chide**,.262. H.781, 11
Ready to blush to death, sho'd he but **chide**.....301. H.963, 4
Me thought, I did Thy bounty **chide**..........358. N.75, 5
Chides He gives an almes, and **chides** them from his doore.
220. H.632, 2
Chiding That **chiding** streams betray small depth below.
15. H.38, 10

Christ, when He hung the dreadfull Crosse upon,. 382. N.167, 1
The House of God, by **Christ** inhabited;.......385. N.190, 2
Christ did her Woman, not her Mary call:......386. N.192, 2
Christ never did so great a work, but there.....389. N.214, 1
Christ is the one sufficient Remedie............390. N.221, 2
Christ took our Nature on Him, not that He....390. N.222, 1
May chance to be no other man, but **Christ**.......391. N.226, 2
To come to Thee, if **Christ** not there!..........395. N.245, 2
If through my **Christ** I saw not Thee...........395. N.246, 6
That **Christ** did die, the Pagan saith;..........395. N.247, 1
We are Coheires with **Christ**; nor shall His own. 395. N.248, 1
For **Christ**, your loving Saviour, hath..........400. N.266, 10
And O! Deare **Christ**,........................401. N.268, 24
And live in Hell, if that my **Christ** stayes there. 403. N.271, 8

Christal'd See **Crystalled**
Christall See **Crystal**
Christalline See **Crystalline**
Christen To **Christen** thee, the Bride, the Bashfull Muse, 28. H.84, 2
Christening Enjoy a **Christning** yeare by yeare;. 291. H.919, 10
Christian Him to be here our **Christian** militant.. 129. H.323, 16
Christians' But that He rose, that's **Christians** Faith. 395. N.247, 2
Christmas Of **Christmas** sports, the Wassell-boule, 126. H.319, 13
And thus, throughout, with **Christmas** playes... 127. H.319, 49
And Queenes; thy **Christmas** revellings:.......231. H.662, 59
This **Christmas**, but his want wherwith, sayes Nay. 238. H.693, 2
The **Christmas** Log to the firing;..............263. H.784, 3
Kindle the **Christmas** Brand, and then..........285. H.893, 1
Till **Christmas** next returne....................285. H.893, 4
The **Christmas** Log next yeare;.................285. H.893, 6
And let all sports with **Christmas** dye.........285. H.894, 2
Wherewith ye drest the **Christmas** Hall:.......304. H.980, 4
Then bid **Christmas** sport good-night;.........315. H.1026, 12
Aha my boyes! heres wheat for **Christmas** Pies!. 327. H.1086, 2
But let no **Christmas** mirth begin............366. N.98, 7
Christmas-Pie Come guard this night the **Christmas-Pie**, 263. H.785, 1
Christ's Heaven, by **Christs** mercies, not my merit: 359. N.78, 12
No other, then **Christs** full Affection..........383. N.174, 2
Chronicle See **Love's-chronicle**
Worthy their everlasting **Chronicle**,............170. H.451, 10
Chronicles The best and truest **Chronicles** of me.. 304. H.978, 6
Chrysolite There playes the Saphire with the **Chrysolite**. 30. H.88, 10
And comely as the **Chrysolite**.................375. N.123, 76
Chub When **Chub** brings in his harvest, still he cries, 327. H.1086, 1
Church Cuffe comes to **Church** much; but he keeps his bed 39. H.109, 1
Because he cannot sleep i'th' **Church**, free-cost... 39. H.109, 4
God strikes His **Church**, but 'tis to this intent,... 344. N.31, 1
He His **Church** save, and the King,............363. N.93, 7
Churchyard I'th' **Church-yard**, made, one Tenement for me. 277. H.853, 4
Churlish A people currish; **churlish** as the seas;.. 29. H.86, 11
Churlishness But first cast off thy wonted **Churlishness**. 416. A.8, 6

Chuse See **Choose**
Chyme See **Chime**
Chymist See **Chemist**
Chyrurgions See **Chirurgeon's**
Cinders Their balls to **Cindars**: haste,..........113. H.283, 39
— — — — — — — — — — — —, ...437. var. H.336, 79
— — — — — — — — — — — —, ...453. var. H.283, 28
— — — — — — — — — — — —, ...453. var. H.283, 30
Cinnamon Perspiring pounded **Cynamon**........113. H.283, 24
The Storax and the **Cynamon**,................375. N.123, 56
They make it scent like bruized **Cinnamon**......406. A.1, 94
But brings his stick of **Cynamon**,...............413. A.4, 26
Cipresse See **Cypress**
Circle Love is a **circle** that doth restlesse move... 13. H.29, 1
Circle with a Diadem........................57. H.149, 130
A Spinners **circle** is bespread,................167. H.443, 101
Love is a **Circle**, and an Endlesse Sphere;....274. H.839, 1
Beyond its stinted **Circle**; giueing foode.........410. A.3, 31
— — — — — — — — — — — —, ...453. var. H.283, 80
Circles As the aire that **circles** me:............183. H.490, 18
(As is that ayre that **circles** thee)............233. H.670, 18
When on the Flood that nine times **circles** Hell.. 417. A.8, 36
Soft Saffron **Circles** to perfume the head.. 442. ins. H.575, 20b
Circlets But he will say, who e'r those **Circlets** seeth, 197. H.543, 3
Circling A quire of blest Soules **circling** in the Father. 383. N.177, 2
Circular Stray, to become lesse **circular**,........134. H.336, 68
Circumbinds The Fringe that **circumbinds** it too,.. 92. H.223, 64
Circumcise How canst thou this Babe **circumcise**?. 365. N.97, 15
Before ye purge, and **circumcise**................366. N.98, 8
To **circumcise** thy life........................391. N.228, 20
Circumcised For civill, cleane, and **circumcised** wit, 194. H.526, 1

Circumcision The signe of **Circumcision** in his eares. 232. H.666, 2
Circum-crossed **Circum-crost** by thy pure hand:. 227. H.651, 2
Circumference Keepes still within a just **circumference**: 210. H.590, 4
Circumflanked With rock, and seven times **circumflankt** with brasse,..................................252. H.745, 12
Circumfused Are **circumfused** there..............69. H.179, 4
Circumgyration And with **Circumgyration** every where; 301. H.966, 6
Circummortal Behold that **circummortall** purity:.. 96. H.230, 2
Circummortal-part (When hence thy **Circum-mortall-part** is gon) 168. H.444, 3
Circumspacious Entred the **circumspacious** Theater; 301. H.962, 2
Circumspangle To **circumspangle** this my spacious Sphere, 267. H.804, 7
Circumstances — — — — — — — —, ...428. var. H.197, 85
Circumstants When these **Circumstants** shall but live to see 79. H.197, 85
Circumvolve So that when 'ere we **circumvolve** our Eyes, 415. A.7, 15
Circumvolving Which, **circumvolving** gently, there 64. H.169, 3
Circumwalk Those Deities which **circum-walk** the Seas, 14. H.35, 5
Cirque The **Cirque** prophan'd was; and all postures rackt: 150. H.382, 5
Citherea's Or **Citherea's** Ceston, which.........166. H.443, 37
Cities Contempts in Courts and **Cities** dwell;......6. H.2, 21
Though Granges do not love thee, **Cities** shall.. 172. H.456, 10
But serving Courts, and **Cities**, be............229. H.662, 3
(As other Townes and **Cities** were) for gold,.. 251. H.745, 6
Great **Cities** seldome rest: If there be none.... 316. H.1030, 1
Citizen Grow up to be a Roman **Citizen**...........171. H.456, 2
That I amongst you live a **Citizen**...........242. H.713, 12
Cittern Tickling the **Citterne** with his quill......318. H.1036, 6
City Could'st leave the **City**, for exchange, to see. 35. H.106, 3
A **City** here of Heroes I have made,..........143. H.365, 9
(As many Conscripts of the **Citie** do)..........176. H.466, 6
Us i'th' **Citie**, and the Field:.................177. H.473, 2
True, if this **Citie** seven times rounded was... 252. H.745, 11
People a **City** or a Towne...................291. H.919, 22
To keepe a **Citie**, then to winne a Towne.......307. H.989, 2
A Free-born of our **Citie**......................345. N.33, 32
It, or to drawe the **Cittie** to his Eyes...........412. A.3, 78
City-health And let our **Citie-health** go round... 127. H.319, 30
City-Powers Next to which Two; among the **City-Powers**, 176. H.466, 3
City's **Cities** most sad and dire destruction......384. N.178, 4
Civet Either's welcome, Stinke or **Civt**............306. H.987, 3
Civic The Golden chain too, and the **Civick** Crown. 176. H.466, 8
Civil Lost in the **civill** Wildernesse of sleep:.....99. H.244, 6
Waste thou in that most **Civill** Government......171. H.456, 4
For **civill**, cleane, and circumcised wit,.........194. H.526, 1
Civil Behaviour, and Religion..................199. H.545, 4
Like a **civill** Wilderness;......................232. H.665, 6
Might stretch the cords of **civill** comelinesse:.... 311. H.1006, 2
Civility I see a wilde **civility**:..................28. H.83, 12
They wo'd have shew'd **civility**;..............89. H.219, 4
Play with a wild **civility**:....................202. H.560, 14
Unsmooth, or sowre, to all **civilitie**;..........378. N.137, 4
Civilly Each way smooth and **civilly**:............195. H.530, 4
Civt See **Civet**
Clad See **Thin-clad**
(**Clad**, all, in Linnen, white as Lillies.)........101. H.250, 12
Claim So sure he layes **claime** to the Evensong... 128. H.321, 6
If Wars goe well; each for a part layes **claime**:. 260. H.774, 3
Who **claim** the Fat, and Fleshie for their share,. 272. H.826, 5
Fortune her selfe can lay no **claim** to it.........272. H.830, 2
And in my Booke now **claim** a two-fold right:. 322. H.1062, 11
— — — — — — — — — — — —, ...449. var. A.5, 5
Clammy A **clammie** Reume makes loathsome both his eyes: 110. H.273, 3
Clamorous About their House, their **clamorous** I, or No: 303. H.975, 4
Clap Ye dance, and sing, and now **clap** hands... 94. H.225, 8
No **clap** of hands, or shout, or praises-proofe... 150. H.382, 11
Cal'd out by the **clap** of the Thunder.........225. H.643, 24
Claps See **Thunder-claps**
Claps my cheek, or kisseth me;................17. H.43, 8
Claret **Clarret**, and Creame commingled...........7. H.9, 10
Stain'd by the Beames of **Clarret** wine:..........268. H.811, 8
Soe full of **clarrett** that whoe soe pricks a vine.. 405. A.1, 49
Clark See **Clerk**
Clasp **Claspe** thou his Book, then close thou up his Eyes. 329. H.1095, 8
To Roughnes, **Claspe** hym lyke a Vine,..........408. A.2, 68
Clause For every sentence, **clause** and word,......339. N.2, 3
Claw To scratch or **claw**, so that thy tongue not railes: 66. H.173, 6
Cleane Which are so **cleane**, so chast, as none may feare 28. H.84, 5
Them, from that **cleane** and subtile skin,......75. H.193, 28
Thus faire and **cleane** you are, although there be. 189. H.511, 5

For civill, cleane, and circumcised wit,........194. H.526, 1
Clean my Roomes, as Temples be,............204. H.569, 5
A curious-comely clean Compartlement:........227. H.652, 8
Cleane in manners, cleere in voice:...........232. H.665, 2
Her decent legs, cleane, long and small........247. H.729, 4
To be accounted inside cleane:...............250. H.738, 2
Be she sluttish, be she cleane,................253. H.750, 17
Cleane was the herth, the mantle larded jet;...262. H.783, 11
Sweet are my Julia's lips and cleane,..........277. H.857, 1
Altar cleane, no fire prophane?...............280. H.870, 6
May all clean Nimphs and curious water Dames,
316. H.1028, 17
Tis much among the filthy to be clean;.......318. H.1042, 1
Wash clean the Vessell, lest ye soure..........320. H.1053, 1
Vertue's clean Conclave is sobriety............331. H.1109, 2
Made of a clean strait oaten reed,..............354. N.59, 9
That all things sweet, and clean may be:......366. N.98, 11
Clean washt, and laid out for the Beere;......374. N.123, 12
Cleane heap of wheat,........................375. N.123, 79
Plac't North and South, for these cleane purposes;
386. N.193, 2
And cleane..................................391. N.228, 3
That smooth as Oyle, sweet softe and Cleane...408. A.2, 55
Cleanest Of cleanest Cobweb, hanging by........92. H.223, 99
Cleanly Of Amber cleanly buried:..............269. H.817, 2
The feare of God, commixt with cleanly love...380. N.147, 2
Cleanly-wantonness By these, to sing of cleanly-Wantonnesse.
5. H.1, 6
Cleanse To clense his eyes, Tom Brock makes much adoe,
110. H.273, 1
Wash your Pailes, and clense your Dairies;...201. H.556, 5
Wash your hands, and cleanse your eyes.......322. H.1064, 2
Clear As beames of Corrall, but more cleare.......7. H.9, 12
Under a Lawne, then skyes more cleare,.........25. H.78, 1
Ile cleare the summe,........................29. H.87, 10
What's now the cause? we know the case is cleere:
71. H.183, 2
Her skins most smooth, and cleare expansion...82. H.204, 4
See'st, thou that Cloud as silver cleare,........139. H.348, 1
If wounds in clothes, Cuts calls his rags, 'tis cleere,
144. H.373, 1
Sing me to death; for till thy voice be cleare,....152. H.390, 1
Wo'd I see Lawn, clear as the Heaven, and thin?
158. H.416, 1
Cleere are her eyes,..........................193. H.524, 1
Like Tapers cleare without number............217. H.619, 15
Or how to pay thy Hinds, and cleere..........230. H.662, 13
Cleane in manners, cleere in voice:...........232. H.665, 2
With gilded hornes, and burnisht cleere.......243. H.716, 15
A sullen day will cleere againe...............247. H.725, 8
A cleare will come after a cloudy day..........293. H.930, 2
Cries out, (my lord, my Lord) the Case is clear:
303. H.975, 6
Clear of hoof, and clear of horn;.............306. H.984, 21
When a cleare day, out of a Cloud do's break...324. H.1072, 2
Cleere Thou my paths, or shorten Thou my miles,
352. N.51, 5
Cleer the walk, and then shall I...............355. N.64, 5
Tell us, thou cleere and heavenly Tongue,.......367. N.102, 1
Spangled with deaw-light; thou canst cleere....367. N.102, 6
All accompts must come to cleere:............373. N.121, 8
Her leggs with twoe cleire calves like siluer tride
406. A.1, 87
Round short and cleire, like pounded spices sweete
406. A.1, 92
Clearly But unamaz'd dares clearely sing,......318. H.1036, 3
Cleave All bolts, all barres, all gates shall cleave; as when
52. H.146, 14
Did crack the Play-house sides, or cleave her roofe.
150. H.382, 12
Cleave thou my heart in two.................240. H.705, 12
For if you cleave them, we shall see..........250. H.738, 3
We then both chew the Cud, and cleave the Hoof.
397. N.256, 4
Cleaver's Droops, dies, and falls without the cleavers stroke.
23. H.69, 6
Cleaving The cleaving Bolt of Jove the Thunderer.
181. H.483, 16
Cleft Two stiffe-blew-Pigs-feet, and a sow's cleft eare.
89. H.221, 4
Or the cleft eare of a Mouse..................223. H.638, 6
Cleopatra As Cleopatra came to Anthonie;........79. H.197, 74
Cleopatra's More rich then Cleopatra's Tombe...269. H.817, 4
Clerk Be thou the Clark,........................87. H.214, 6
Shall heare his Clarke say,....................256. H.762, 16
Night makes no difference 'twixt the Priest and Clark;
279. H.864, 1
Client But let that speak, the Client gets the suit..123. H.308, 2
The wronged Client ends his Lawes...........190. H.515, 23
Climb To their full height doe clime:..........56. H.149, 124
Clime See Climb
Did rather choose to blesse another clime?......77. H.197, 22
Cling Then to thy thighs so closely cling,........67. H.175, 14
They cling and close, some minutes of the night.
156. H.411, 4
Clings It clings about; so I by Thee............371. N.114, 4
Clipseby But love my Clipseby ever.............162. H.426, 25
Of Clipseby Crew..............................198. H.544, 36
Clock Telling the Clock strike, Ten, Eleven, Twelve, One.
114. H.283, 76
(The Bell-man of the night) proclaime the clock.207. H.575, 62
Though Clock,..................................246. H.724, 1
By the clock 'tis almost One...................373. N.121, 14
Cloe Nor Cloe was of more respect;..............70. H.181, 6
Hor. Now Thracian Cloe governs me,............70. H.181, 9
Admit I Cloe put away,.........................70. H.181, 19
Cloister-monks Of Cloyster-Monks they have enow,
93. H.223, 107
Close Kept as close as Danae was:................14. H.36, 5
But to live round, and close, and wisely true....38. H.106, 135
But bid Good-night, and close their lids for ever...41. H.118, 8
Had we kept close, or play'd within,.............48. H.136, 6
Close by a Silver-shedding Brook;..............51. H.142, 2
Close kisses, if she cry:......................56. H.149, 96
Let kisses, in their close,.....................57. H.149, 143
Ah! then too late, close in your chamber keeping,.63. H.164, 12
Close though it be,............................65. H.172, 7
Stands in the Platter, or close by,..............91. H.223, 48
Barre close as you can, and bolt fast too your doore,
97. H.233, 1
Close to my Beds side she did stand............153. H.399, 3
They cling and close, some minutes of the night...156. H.411, 4
Stay but till my Julia close....................164. H.441, 9
Close thou up thy Poets eyes:..................186. H.499, 2
And, hugging close, we will not feare..........190. H.515, 13
And as He shuts, close up to Maids again.......196. H.537, 4
Close keep your lips, if that you meane........250. H.738, 1
Where we may snug, and close together lye....278. H.860, 7
Close, but not too strictly lac't:..............282. H.878, 4
And having washt thee, close thee in a chest....300. H.960, 5
A young Enchantresse close by him did stand..313. H.1017, 7
Claspe thou his Book, then close thou up his Eyes.
329. H.1095, 8
Close by whose living coale I sit,..............350. N.47, 25
— — — — — — — — — — —, ...436. var. H.336, 50
His hereby broth, and there close by......439. ins. H.443, 451
Closed No Marigolds yet closed are;............164. H.441, 5
Clos'd in a Box of Yvorie:....................185. H.497, 2
Dead, and closed up in Yvorie................186. H.497, 18
But now 'tis clos'd; and being shut, & seal'd,..227. H.652, 11
And clos'd her up, as in a Tombe..............237. H.686, 16
Close-handed Nor art thou so close-handed, but can'st spend
38. H.106, 129
Closely (As they were closely set)................18. H.47, 2
Then to thy thighs so closely cling,..............67. H.175, 14
— — — — — — — — — — —, ...452. var. H.443, 71
Closes For if so be our closes......................74. H.192, 6
Close-stools Or spice, or fish, or fire, or close-stools here.
155. H.405, 2
Closet See Sweating-closet
No closset plot, or open vent,..................126. H.319, 3
Closet-gods Devoutly to thy Closet-gods then pray,..14. H.35, 3
When I goe Hence ye Closet-Gods, I feare......227. H.652, 1
Keep here still, Closet-Gods, 'fore whom I've set.227. H.652, 13
Closing Daysies wo'd shut, and closing, sigh and weep.
159. H.421, 26
Cloth See Hearse-cloth, Sackcloth, Cerecloth
Late fatned in a piece of cloth:...............120. H.293, 42
Of cloth;.....................................221. H.633, 34
From whence the house-wives cloth did come:..374. N.123, 36
Shall fray that silke, or fret this cloth..........393. N.231, 4
Clothe His dampish Buttocks furthermore to cloath:
226. H.650, 2
To feed and cloth the Needy...................374. N.123, 50
To cloath thy words in gentle Ayre.............408. A.2, 54
Clothed See Re-clothed
Cloath'd in her Chamlets of Delight.............47. H.133, 11
Cloth'd all with incorrupted light;.............270. H.819, 5
Clothes Kindles in cloathes a wantonnesse:..........28. H.83, 2
Still with my clothes, my Love:...............100. H.249, 4
Off then with grave clothes; put fresh colours on;
105. H.259, 9
Shift now has cast his clothes: got all things new;
144. H.372, 1
If wounds in clothes, Cuts calls his rags, 'tis cleere,
144. H.373, 1
For all his shifts, he cannot shift his clothes.....149. H.380, 2
Feacie (some say) doth wash her clothes i'th' Lie.178. H.474, 1
As in our clothes, so likewise he who lookes,....202. H.559, 1
Her cloaths held up, she shew'd withall..........247. H.729, 3
Base in action as in clothes:...................255. H.761, 12
They draw their clothes off both, so draw to bed..260. H.773, 4
That liquefaction of her clothes.................261. H.779, 3
We shall be wounded by the cloathes we weare...292. H.928, 2
The inward carbage for his cloathes as yet.......302. H.969, 4
So plaine and simple cloathes doe show........311. H.1010, 9
He's double honour'd, since h'as got gay cloathes:
330. H.1099, 2
Have soil'd my selfe, or cloaths,................351. N.49, 7
Clothes' For so decreeing, that thy clothes expence
210. H.590, 3
Clothing Thy clothing next, shall be a Gowne....192. H.521, 9

Immortall **clothing** I put on,....................270. H.819, 1
Is cut, that made us **clothing**...................374. N.123, 40
Cloths See **Cerecloths**
Laugh at my scraps of cloaths, and shun.........235. H.677, 5
Cloud Till, like Ixion's **Cloud** you be..............34. H.105, 9
That Leading **Cloud**, I follow'd still,...........67. H.175, 19
In a **Cloud**; while both did play,.................74. H.190, 6
And that white **cloud** divide.....................76. H.193, 53
Hid in a **cloud** of Frankincense:................93. H.223, 140
I see a **Cloud** of Glory fills my Book............99. H.245, 4
Some Goddesse, in a **cloud** of Tiffanie..........112. H.283, 8
The while the **cloud** of younglings sing,.........113. H.283, 43
Plumpe Bed beare up, and swelling like a **cloud**,
115. H.283, 112
And rend the **cloud**, and throw.................116. H.283, 149
See'st, thou that **Cloud** as silver cleare,..........139. H.348, 1
Seest thou that **Cloud** that rides in State........269. H.815, 1
When a cleare day, out of a **Cloud** do's break...324. H.1072, 2
Or fetch me back that **Cloud** againe,..............340. N.3, 9
I'le cast a mist and **cloud**, upon.................357. N.72, 5
The Temple, with a **cloud** of smoke..............366. N.98, 17
He that ascended in a **cloud**, shall come........382. N.162, 1
A while yo[r] forehead in a **Cloude**................413. A.4, 17
Cloud-like **Cloud-like**, the daintie Deitie..........167. H.443, 99
Clouds To these, make **Clouds** to poure downe raine;
47. H.133, 12
Since **Clouds** disperst, Suns guild the Aire again.
105. H.259, 2
Give up thy soule in **clouds** of frankinsence......128. H.320, 6
And when those **clouds** away are driven,.........188. H.508, 5
Those crimson **clouds** i'th'cheeks & lips leave shining.
207. H.576, 2
Mine eyes, like **clouds**, were drizling raine,.......237. H.687, 1
Clouds will not ever powre down raine;........247. H.725, 7
They tread on **clouds**, and though they sometimes fall,
250. H.737, 3
But, like full **clouds**, may they from thence....291. H.919, 7
In **clouds**, descending to the publike Doome.....382. N.162, 2
And sullen **clouds** bound up his head.............393. N.232, 6
Or e're dark **Clouds** do dull, or dead the Mid-dayes Sun.
401. N.268, 9
Its humble selfe twixt twoe aspiring **cloudes**,.....406. A.1, 84
— — — — — — — — —, ...453. var. H.283, 43
Cloudy A cleare will come after a **cloudy** day.....293. H.930, 2
— — — — — — — — —, ...451. var. H.197, 27
Clout See **Swaddling-clout**
Clouts Cob **clouts** his shooes, and as the story tells,
226. H.648, 1
Of **clouts**, wee'l make a chamber,..............345. N.33, 21
Clove So smels the flowre of blooming **Clove**;.....145. H.375, 3
To bring from thence the scorched **Clove**.........229. H.662, 8
Cloyed **Cloy'd** they are up with Arse; but hope, one blast
226. H.650, 3
You are **cloy'd** here,...........................307. H.988, 9
Club With peeps of Harts, of **Club** and Spade....166. H.443, 49
Clune And Nansagge, sonnes of **clune** and pith
437. var. H.336, 132
Clunn A rowle of Parchment **Clunn** about him beares,
295. H.941, 1
What joy can **Clun** have in that Coat, or this,....295. H.941, 7
Clusters And with rich **clusters** (hid among........16. H.41, 10
Crown'd with **clusters** of the Vine;..............39. H.111, 5
Where we such **clusters** had,....................289. H.911, 7
Their lustfull **Clusters** all the yeare,......436. ins. H.336, 48b
Clytemnestra For **Clytemnestra** most unkind,.....283. H.885, 3
Coach To kisse thy hand from out the **coach**;....239. H.696, 2
Coadjutor A **Coadjutor** in the Agonie............382. N.163, 2
Coal The **cole** once spent, we'l then to bed,..136. H.336, 151
Close by whose living **coale** I sit,...............350. N.47, 25
A Lipp Inkyndled wth that **Coale**...............408. A.2, 47
— — — — — — — — — —, ...437. var. H.336, 151
Coarse Hunger makes **coorse** meats, delicates.....37. H.106, 110
Herrick, thou art too **coorse** to love.............51. H.142, 22
That was too **coorse**; but then forthwith........119. H.293, 31
Coat What joy can Clun have in that **Coat**, or this,
295. H.941, 7
Coats Since **Coats**, and Hamlets, best agree..........5. H.2, 5
Farewell the **Coats**, the Garments, and........374. N.123, 43
These were the **Coats**, in these are read........375. N.123, 83
Cob **Cob** clouts his shooes, and as the story tells,..226, H.648, 1
Cobbler Each **Cobler** is a King;.................259. H.772, 11
Cobbler's The **coblers** getting time, is at the Last.
144. H.374, 2
Cobweb Of Tiffanie, or **Cob-web** Lawne;............8. H.11, 6
Of cleanest **Cobweb**, hanging by.................92. H.223, 99
Cob-web-curtains With **Cob-web-curtains**: from the roof
167. H.443, 102
Cobweb-lawn O'r it a **Cobweb-Lawne**:............75. H.193, 3
Cobwebs Where Rust and **Cobwebs** bind the gate;
179. H.476, 29
Cock And a gallant **Cock** shall be................122. H.302, 5
The **Cock**, the Curlew. and the quaile;........147. H.377, 66
The **Cock** and Hen he feeds; but not a bone....204. H.568, 5
And he one chiefe; But harke, I heare the **Cock**,
207. H.575, 61

Cock calls his Wife his Hen: when **Cock** goes too't,
213. H.610, 1
Cock treads his Hen, but treads her under-foot...213. H.610, 2
When now the **Cock** (the Plow-mans Horne)....230. H.662, 19
A **Cock**,..246. H.724, 3
Well, when sh'as kild, that Pig, Goose, **Cock** or Hen,
266. H.801, 3
Cockal (Playing for Points and Pins) **Cockall**.....91. H.223, 59
Cocker To coole, not **cocker** Appetite............35. H.106, 26
Cockering Paying before you praise; and **cokring** wit,
141. H.359, 15
Cockles For Sceva, darts; for **Cocles**, dangers; thus
370. N.108, 5
Cock-like And **Cock-like** Hens Ile tread:........160. H.422, 10
Cockring See **Cockering**
Cockrood Thou hast thy **Cockrood**, and thy Glade
231. H.662, 66
Cock's By the Time the **Cocks** first crow.........177. H.473, 8
Cocks She **cocks** out her Arse at the parting,....333. H.1122, 3
Cocks-tread Both to the **Cocks-tread** say Amen;..179. H.476, 20
Cocles See **Cockles**
Co'd (Partial List)
These and a thousand sweets, **co'd** never be......45. H.128, 9
To th'board, so hot, as none **co'd** touch the same:..47. H.131, 2
But none **co'd** eate it, 'cause it stunk so much....47. H.131, 6
Youth, or sweet Nature, **co'd** bring forth,........48. H.134, 2
In her wisdome **co'd** beget.....................57. H.149, 150
Aire coyn'd to words, my Julia **co'd** not heare;..58. H.150, 3
But she **co'd** see each eye to stamp a teare:......58. H.150, 4
That I **co'd** ne'r be Prince of Love,............64. H.166, 11
Drown'd in Delights; but **co'd** not die...........67. H.175, 18
But ah! I **co'd** not: sho'd it move..............67. H.175, 21
But to forsake thee ever, **co'd** there be..........78. H.197, 45
Illustrious Idoll! **co'd** th' Ægyptians seek........78. H.197, 57
Play I **co'd** once; but (gentle friend) you see....84. H.210, 1
Sing I **co'd** once; and bravely too enspire........84. H.210, 3
Draw I **co'd** once (although not stocks or stones,..84. H.210, 5
Long have I sought for: but **co'd** never see......121. H.301, 3
If I **co'd**, I wo'd not so........................128. H.322, 12
Woman wo'd bring him more then **co'd** be told,..129. H.326, 4
So old she was, that none **co'd** tell her yeares...129. H.326, 6
None, Posthumus, **co'd** ere decline.............132. H.336, 7
Such as **co'd** well..............................136. H.336, 133
I **co'd** rehearse...............................144. H.371, 10
I heard ye **co'd** coole heat; and came............157. H.413, 1
Co'd a noble Verse beget;.....................217. H.620, 5
Coddled And now y'are enter'd; see the **Codled** Cook
114. H.283, 61
Codlin's Subtile and ductile **Codlin's** skin;........91. H.223, 61
Codpiece To drive the Devill from the **Cod-piece**..93. H.223, 121
In his wide **Codpiece**, (dinner being done).......118. H.292, 5
Coffers Ha's none at home, in **Coffers**, Desks, or Trunks.
173. H.463, 4
Coheirs We are **Coheires** with Christ; nor shall His own
395. N.248, 1
Coil See **Level-coil**
Coincident (As Salust saith) **co-incident** to feare...162. H.430, 2
Coined Aire **coyn'd** to words, my Julia co'd not heare;
58. H.150, 3
Already **coin'd** to pay for it......................218. H.626, 7
Coiners Made by the **Coyners** illegitimate.......312. H.1015, 2
Coins To accept such **coynes** as these;............88. H.218, 8
Old **Coyne's** and Meddalls, wee expose............407. A.2, 30
Cold But I am not yet grown **cold**;...............17. H.43, 2
And while the Wood-nimphs my **cold** corps inter,..19. H.50, 3
And e'en with **cold** half starved...................26. H.81, 12
Let me be leane, and **cold**, and once grown poore,..31. H.93, 3
Where eternall **cold** does keep?..................40. H.115, 10
Continues **cold**, as is the night..................49. H.136, 31
Give my **cold** lips a kisse at last:.................61. H.159, 25
Have I been **cold** to hug thee, too remisse,......78. H.197, 34
Thou cam'st to cure me (Doctor) of my **cold**,.....97. H.236, 1
Freezing **cold**, and firie heats,..................102. H.253, 7
And you be **cold**...............................115. H.283, 115
Nothing hot, or nothing **cold**....................116. H.285, 2
Cold as Ice, or coole as I......................117. H.289, 10
By **cold** neglect, each one,......................131. H.330, 10
Nor suffer you the Poets to sit **cold**,.............141. H.359, 7
Expos'd to all the comming Winters **cold**.......151. H.387, 4
The **cold**, **cold** Earth doth shake him;..........156. H.412, 18
Thrice I have washt, but feel no **cold**,...........157. H.413, 3
Thy thoughts as **cold**, as is thy sleep:..........175. H.465, 48
Where all Desires are dead, or **cold**.............190. H.515, 15
Broomsted a lamenesse got by **cold** and Beere;...201. H.555, 1
Cold and hunger never yet....................217. H.620, 4
But a just measure both of Heat and **Cold**.......236. H.683, 2
Must needs wax **cold**, if wanting bread and wine..258. H.768, 4
How **cold** it was, and how it child my blood;..262. H.783, 18
I freeze as fast, and shake for **cold**.............290. H.915, 2
And starves with **cold** the self-same part.......290. H.915, 8
Untoucht by **cold** sterility;....................291. H.919, 18
Cold comfort still I'm sure lives there.........312. H.1014, 10
Ye quake for **cold** to looke on me................329. H.1093, 6
Thou kil'st with heate, and I strike dead with **cold**.
333. H.1120, 2
Either be hot, or **cold**: God doth despise,.........353. N.54, 3

Cold as Paddocks though they be,...............364. N.95, 3
Thy hands (though cold) yet spotlesse, white,..375. N.123, 75
Or a colde Poyson, which his blood.............409. A.2, 87
With as cold frost, as erst we mett with fire;....414. A.6, 10
Colde Hemlocke, or the Libbards bane..422. ins. H.106, 116b
— — — — — — — — — — — —, ...423. var. H.128, 18
— — — — — — — — — — — —; ....437. var. H.336, 82
Colder Colder yet then any one:.................40. H.115, 12
Colds — — — — — — — — — —, ...429. var. H.253, 7
Colewort — — — — — — — — —, ...422. var. H.106, 113
Coleworts To taste boyl'd Nettles, Colworts, Beets, and eate
37. H.106, 113
Collect One Holy Collect, said or sung for Thee...209. H.584, 4
College Welcome to this my Colledge, and though late
305. H.983, 1
Color And ask, Where's now the colour, forme and trust
49, H.138, 4
If you can see the colour come.................79. H.198, 3
(The Sun once set) all of one colour are......207. H.576, 4
Skynne and colour, flesh and blood,.............418. A.9, 21
— — — — — — — — — — — —, ...450. var. A.9, 53
Colored Party colour'd like a Pie;..............305. H.984, 19
With tender ryne and silver coloured,...........406. A.1, 98
Coloring For my haires black colouring:........330. H.1098, 2
Colorless Looke ye not wan, or colourlesse for feare.
222. H.634, 6
Colors Colours goe, and colours come..............15. H.37, 4
Fresh-quilted colours through the aire:..........67. H.178, 4
Those glaring colours laid......................76. H.193, 45
Off then with grave clothes; put fresh colours on;
105. H.259, 9
Of winning Colours, that shall move...........193. H.521, 53
Colours, let Art supply.........................224. H.641, 2
As colours steale into the Peare or Plum,......250. H.737, 6
Of lively colours, flowing from the face........274. H.840, 2
Of lines and colo^rs make them scorne...........418. A.9, 53
Their ayry coulors to discerne,.................418. A.9, 56
Columbine That smooth and silken Columbine...215. H.616, 24
Columbines Or chaines of Columbines shall make,..361. N.83, 53
Column Fix on That Columne then, and never fall;
329. H.1092, 7
Comb See Honeycomb
Combat Combate for men, by conquering the disease.
226. H.646, 2
Combatant Now I'm turn'd a combatant:........151. H.386, 2
Brings in Fabricius for a Combatant:..........370. N.108, 10
Combatants In Combatants to flye,........433. ins. H.283, 140i
Combine Have I divorc't thee onely to combine..78. H.197, 39
Which (since here they can't combine)..........211. H.593, 3
They were mine own. Lal. In love combine...244. H.716, 46
So that, in all He did, there did combine........389. N.214, 5
Combined Here was not with the act combin'd...175. H.465, 62
Combs See Honeycombs
Come See O'ercome, Overcome
Well may my Book come forth like Publique Day.3. Ded.H, 1
Come thou not neere those men, who are like Bread..7. H.7, 1
Age cals me hence, and my gray haires bid come,....9. H.14, 3
Come down, and dance ye in the toyle............9. H.15, 1
Come bring your sampler, and with Art,..........10. H.20, 1
Colours goe, and colours come....................15. H.37, 4
Full and faire ones; come and buy:..............19. H.53, 2
And come all to Buckittings:.....................21. H.61, 4
Like Streams, you are divorc'd; but't will come, when
26. H.79, 5
That for seven Lusters I did never come..........27. H.82, 1
I come to pay a Debt of Birth I owe...........27. H.82, 12
If it will come...................................29. H.87, 11
Woo'd to come such the milkie Teat:............36. H.106, 50
Come, skilfull Lupo, now, and take..............38. H.108, 1
Death will come and mar the song:.............39. H.111, 12
Duely, Morne and Ev'ning, come,................44. H.125, 3
Come, you are faire; and sho'd be seen........49. H.136, 24
Come in for Dowrie with a Wife.................49. H.137, 2
Come tel me then, how great's the smart.......50. H.139, 14
Promis'd sho'd come to crown your youth........53. H.149, 2
Then away; come, Hymen guide.................53. H.149, 9
Then away; come, Hymen guide.................53. H.149, 19
Then away; come, Hymen guide.................54. H.149, 29
Then away; come, Hymen guide.................54. H.149, 39
Then away; come Hymen, guide.................55. H.149, 69
Virgins, weep not; 'twill come, when,..........56. H.149, 111
Doth from Panchaia come.......................57. H.149, 146
May Death yet come at last;...................58. H.149, 165
Come, Let us now away........................58. H.149, 168
Ile come to thee in all those shapes..............58. H.152, 1
Stirring the waters, I am come; and here,........61. H.161, 4
Come, and coole ye; all who frie................62. H.162, 2
And time will come when you shall weare........63. H.164, 4
A fellon take it, or some Whit-flaw come........66. H.173, 3
To come forth, like the Spring-time, fresh and greene;
68. H.178, 16
Against you come, some Orient Pearls unwept:..68. H.178, 22
Come, and receive them while the light..........68. H.178, 23
Till you come forth. Wash, dresse, be briefe in praying:
68. H.178, 27
Come, my Corinna, come; and comming, marke..68. H.178, 29
Come, we'll abroad; and let's obay..............68. H.178, 39
But my Corinna, come, let's goe a Maying.......68. H.178, 42
A deale of Youth, ere this, is come............69. H.178, 45
Come, let us goe, while we are in our prime;....69. H.178, 57
Come, my Corinna, come, let's goe a Maying.....69. H.178, 70
When as Cherries come in place?................74. H.189, 6
Ile leave thee, and to Pansies come;..............74. H.191, 5
Like to a Bride, come forth my Book, at last,....76. H.194, 1
Come, come and kisse me; Love and lust commends
78. H.197, 69
As Queenes, meet Queenes; or come thou unto me,
79. H.197, 73
If you can see the colour come.................79. H.198, 3
The golden pomp is come.......................80. H.201, 4
The golden Pomp is come.......................80. H.201, 5
Come, I will drink a Tun.......................81. H.201, 35
Come thou not neere that Filmne so finely spred,..82. H.204, 7
Chor. Come let's away, and quickly let's be drest,.86. H.213, 45
This we will doe; we'll daily come...............89. H.219, 9
And times to come shall, weeping, read thy glory,
89. H.219, 21
Deare Perenna, prethee come,...................89. H.220, 1
Time, ere long, will come and plow..............97. H.232, 13
The Whore to come out, or the Letcher come in...97. H.233, 4
First cur'd thy selfe; then come and cure me.....97. H.236, 4
Of twenty shall come,..........................99. H.243, 5
Tole forth my death; next, to my buryall come...100. H.248, 6
Come Sons of Summer, by whose toile,.........101. H.250, 1
Crown'd with the eares of corne, now come,....101. H.250, 5
Come forth, my Lord, and see the Cart..........101. H.250, 7
And thousand Virgins come and weep,..........104. H.256, 17
Come to weep out the night....................106. H.262, 16
Witnesse their Homage, when they come and strew
107. H.265, 7
With Wicker Arks did come.....................110. H.274, 6
Pray come,......................................111. H.280, 7
Then come on, come on, and yeeld............112. H.283, 17
Now Autumne's come, when all those flowrie aids
114. H.283, 92
Let him come, who dares undo her..........114. H.283, 100
Æsculapius! come and bring....................122. H.302, 3
Good things, that come of course, far lesse doe please,
123. H.307, 1
Then those, which come by sweet contingences...123. H.307, 2
Blessings, in abundance come,..................124. H.314, 1
Crossing thy selfe; come thus to sacrifice:......127. H.320, 2
A man prepar'd against all ills to come,.........128. H.323, 1
For love and bountie, to come neare, and see,....131. H.331, 3
Come come away,..............................137. H.340, 1
Come with the Spring-time, forth Fair Maid, and be
140. H.354, 1
I who have favour'd many, come to be........142. H.365, 1
Come unto thee for Laurell, having spent,.......143. H.365, 5
And all the busie Factours come...............145. H.375, 9
Shall come to strew thy earth with flowers.......145. H.376, 6
Till I shall come again, let this suffice,..........146. H.377, 1
Where both may feed, and come againe:........146. H.377, 12
Tell, if thou canst, (and truly) whence doth come
157. H.414, 1
Come forth and sweetly dye....................161. H.425, 12
Shall now, or ever after come.................165. H.442, 14
Saints will come in to fill each Pew and Place....168. H.445, 6
Give way, give way to me, who come............169. H.449, 9
Come, leave this loathed Country-life, and then..171. H.456, 1
And if thy fall sho'd this way come,..........175. H.465, 65
Lean-horn'd, before I come again..............176. H.465, 78
Holy-Rood come forth and shield..............177. H.473, 1
The time will come, when you'l be sad,........179. H.476, 37
How can I chuse but kisse her, whence do's come
181. H.485, 3
Ah! Lycidas, come tell me why................183. H.492, 1
I vow by Pan, to come away..................184. H.492, 27
Come Virgins then, and see....................184. H.493, 9
Come thou Brave man! And bring with Thee a Stone
185. H.496, 5
Late you come in; but you a Saint shall be,....188. H.510, 3
Come thou, who art the Wine, and wit.......189. H.515, 1
Come then, and be to my chast side...........190. H.515, 9
O Flame of Beauty! come, appeare, appeare....191. H.516, 3
Thou shalt come forth, and then appeare........192. H.521, 31
Come thou in, with thy best part,............195. H.530, 2
Come then, brave Knight, and see the Cell......198. H.544, 25
Take Horse, and come; or be so kind,..........198. H.544, 31
For those good dayes that ne'r will come away...204. H.570, 2
Come then, and like two Doves with silv'rie wings
205. H.575, 1
By glim'ring of a fancie: Doe but come,........207. H.575, 55
Bring me my Rose-buds, Drawer come;..........208. H.582, 1
The Ev'ning's come; here now Ile stop,..........212. H.602, 3
But if that golden Age wo'd come again,........214. H.612, 7
Come sit we under yonder Tree,................215. H.616, 1
Thus, thus to come unto me:..................217. H.619, 17
Come sit we by the fires side;..................219. H.629, 1
May a thousand blessings come!................220. H.633, 2
And (Sweetling) marke you, what a Web will come
221. H.633, 40

Let wealth come in by comely thrift,..........221. H.633, 46
One night i'th' yeare, my dearest Beauties, come..222. H.634, 1
And thou O Cupid! come not to..............223. H.635, 13
Affrighted shall come,......................225. H.643, 23
Come then, and now enspire...................228. H.657, 5
Come Anthea, know thou this,.................235. H.678, 1
Into the which we come by warre................241. H.711, 2
Ravisht in spirit, I come, nay more, I flie......242. H.713, 3
Come blithefull Neatherds, let us lay...........243. H.716, 1
By tears and pitie now to come unto mee.........248. H.730, 2
So silently they one to th' other come,........250. H.737, 5
Come Anthea let us two.......................255. H.761, 1
Holy Water come and bring;..................258. H.769, 1
Come, Ile instruct thee. Know, the vestall fier...262. H.781, 15
Come, bring with a noise,.....................263. H.784, 1
Come while the Log is a teending...............263. H.784, 12
Come guard this night the Christmas-Pie,......263. H.785, 1
With his Flesh-hooks, don't come nie............263. H.785, 3
Here to be paid; Ile pay't i'th'world to come...267. H.804, 14
Will come on apace;..........................267. H.806, 5
Where ever Nodes do's in the Summer come,.....270. H.822, 1
Ile come and visit thee.........................271. H.824, 4
Virgins Come, and in a Ring...................274. H.838, 5
Back to come, (and make no stay.)............276. H.848, 3
When that Death bids come away...............277. H.852, 8
Come and let's in solemn wise.................280. H.870, 1
Unshorn Apollo, come, and re-inspire...........280. H.871, 2
(Not knowing what would come to passe)........281. H.876, 6
Come in for comely ornaments,................285. H.892, 19
With reverend Curtsies come, and to him bring..286. H.898, 7
All Rites well ended, with faire Auspice come....286. H.898, 9
Or come agen:..............................289. H.911, 12
Which got, the third, bids him a King come downe.
292. H.925, 2
A cleare will come after a cloudy day..........293. H.930, 2
Ile come before..............................296. H.946, 23
O Pompe of Glory! Welcome now, and come....300. H.961, 5
A mischance is come to pass,..................305. H.984, 11
That are most modest ere they come to warre.....308. H.994, 2
Which wee, and times to come, shall wonder at..310. H.1002, 2
When to a House I come, and see...........310. H.1004, 1
To come with their own bellies unto feasts:....310. H.1005, 2
Then come home and fother them...............315. H.1026, 4
In the hope of ease to come,..................315. H.1027, 1
No ruffling winds come hither to discease......316. H.1028, 21
Along, come along,............................320. H.1051, 1
I may a Poet come, though poor;..............321. H.1056, 4
I'de rather hungry go and come.............321. H.1056, 13
When to thy Porch I come, and (ravisht) see..324. H.1071, 1
I wo'd come back and live with thee?.........328. H.1090, 5
That done, my Julia, dearest Julia, come,......329. H.1095, 5
Shall by his hearing quickly come to see......330. H.1100, 17
Washt with sweet ointments; Thus at last I come
335. H.1128, 3
I come to Thee, in hope to find................342. N.17, 3
Come to fright a parting soule;...............348. N.41, 23
Afflictions bring us joy in times to come,.........349. N.45, 1
I'le come, I'le creep, (though Thou dost threat)..349. N.46, 1
Who thither come, and freely get..............350. N.47, 15
Can I not come to Thee, my God, for these......352. N.51, 1
Thou bidst me come; I cannot come, for why,....352. N.52, 1
Thou bidst me come away,......................352. N.53, 1
Stiles, and stops, and stayes, that come.........355. N.64, 3
Who to that sweet Bread unprepar'd doth come...355. N.65, 9
For times to come, I'le make this Vow,........357. N.72, 16
Call, and I'le come; say Thou, the when, and where:
358. N.77, 13
I do believe, that I must come,.................358. N.78, 5
Of all the Maiden-Traine! We come,............359. N.83, 5
No boysterous winds, or stormes, come hither,....361. N.83, 69
Come forth, to strew thy Tombe with flow'rs:....361. N.83, 74
May Virgins, when they come to mourn,........361. N.83, 75
Thus, on the sudden? 4. Come and see.........364. N.96, 17
We see Him come, and know him ours,.........364. N.96, 22
The Darling of the world is come,.............365. N.96, 25
Prepare for Songs; He's come, He's come;......365. N.97, 1
Heaven to come down, the while we choke......366. N.98, 16
Come then, and gently touch the Birth.........366. N.98, 18
But only come, and see Him rest.............367. N.102, 13
Come then, come then, and let us bring........368. N.102, 19
For things that will not come:.................368. N.104, 2
And might come in,............................370. N.111, 3
Come in, or force the gate....................370. N.111, 8
All accompts must come to cleere:............373. N.121, 8
Come pitie us, all ye, who see................373. N.123, 1
Come pitie us, ye Passers by,................373. N.123, 3
Come pitie us; and bring your eares,.........373. N.123, 5
Chor. And when you are come hither;..........373. N.123, 7
From whence the house-wives cloth did come:..374. N.123, 36
I crawle, I creep; my Christ, I come............377. N.129, 1
For All that now come, or hereafter may.......378. N.131, 2
He that ascended in a cloud, shall come.......382. N.162, 1
God's said to leave this place, and for to come..385. N.186, 1
But He hath made the world to come for few...387. N.198, 2
So shall the Blankets which come over me,....392. N.230, 15
To which the Pesant, so the Prince must come,..392. N.230, 24
Come to me God; but do not come..............393. N.232, 1
In power; or come Thou in that state,........393. N.232, 3
Then come my God, and hap what will........393. N.232, 16
The staffe might come to play the friendly part..394. N.241, 4
To come to Thee, if Christ not there!........395. N.245, 2
Thine houre is come; and the Tormentor stands.398. N.263 3
By no ill haunted; here I come,...............402. N.269, 2
Thus, thus I come to kisse Thy Stone.........402. N.269, 10
Wch sweeten Loue, yett ne're come nighe.........408. A.2, 41
(The generall Aprill of the worlde) dothe Come,
410. A.3, 34
Come then greate Lord.........................413. A.4, 31
For now behold the golden Pompe is come,....415. A.7, 2
Thy Pompe of Playes which thousands come to see,
415. A.7, 3
But now come in. Euc. More let me yet relate..416. A.8, 23
— — — — — — — — — — —, ...422. var. H.106, 104
— — — — — — — — — — — —, ...424. var. H.164, 6
and come upon your Bridegroome like a Tyde
431. ins. H.283, 50b
of the glad house? come come..........431. ins. H.283, 60i
aloft, and like two armies, come.........432. ins. H.283, 140d
Thy thoughts to say, I backe am come....441. ins. H.465, 14b

Comeliness What Gesture, Courtship; Comliness agrees,
148. H.377, 95
Of flowers set in comlinesse:.................202. H.560, 4
In that your owne prefixed comelinesse:......299. H.958, 4
Might stretch the cords of civill comelinesse:..311. H.1006, 2
Conformity gives comelinesse to things........318. H.1040, 1

Comely See Curious-comely
Then comely and most fragrant Maid,........49. H.136, 14
Down from her comely shoulders hung:........51. H.142, 10
Do all things sweetly, and in comely wise;....124. H.313, 7
Curld and comely, and so trimme,............125. H.314, 7
And in the Rind of every comely tree.........160. H.421, 39
And for the comely carriage of it;...........194. H.526, 2
The Candid Temples of her comely face:........197. H.543, 2
Both for their comely need, and some to spare:
205. H.571, 2
For being comely, consonant, and free........210. H.590, 1
Spring with the Larke, most comely Bride, and meet
216. H.618, 1
Let wealth come in by comely thrift,.........221. H.633, 46
Tripping the comely country round,...........230. H.662, 50
Comely Acts well; and when he speaks his part,
266. H.799, 1
Come in for comely ornaments,..............285. H.892, 19
To these a comely off-spring I desire,..........294. H.938, 3
As is your name, so is your comely face,......307. H.992 1
Out of my comely manners worne;............312. H.1016, 5
I'th' Court that's halfe so comly...............324. H.1068, 20
And comely as the Chrysolite..................375. N.123, 76
Her comly nose with vniformall grace.........404. A.1, 11
More Comely flowing: where les free..........407. A.2, 28
Swells with brave rage, yet comely every where,.415. A.7, 12
— — — — — — — — — —, ...448. var. A.1, 89

Comer No commer to thy Roofe his Guest-rite wants;
146. H.377, 19

Comers Who squeaks to all the commers there,...91. H.223, 40

Comes When that day comes, whose evening sayes I'm gone
14. H.35, 1
Then after her comes smiling May............23. H.70, 3
Then (lastly) July comes, and she..............23. H.70, 7
While Faunus in the Vision comes to keep,....36. H.106, 51
Fortune when she comes, or goes.............37. H.106, 94
Nor car'st which comes the first, the foule or faire;
37. H.106, 97
Thy selfe, if want comes to endure:.........37. H.106, 104
Till that the green-ey'd Kitling comes..........37. H.106, 124
Cuffe comes to Church much; but he keeps his bed
39. H.109, 1
Unbolts the doore, no shame comes in........48. H.136, 13
And when (though long it comes to passe)....63. H.164, 6
As your health or comes, or goes;............96. H.232, 6
Yet so it comes to passe,......................100. H.249, 7
See where she comes; and smell how all the street
113. H.283, 21
What comes in, runnes quickly out:...........116. H.285, 6
And with Tapers comes to fright.............117. H.289, 7
A change, when Fortune either comes, or goes:.128. H.323, 8
Prigg, when he comes to houses, oft doth use..143. H.368, 1
Youthfull Mirtillo, Here he comes, Griefdrownd..159. H.421, 6
Nothing comes Free-cost here; Jove will not let.177. H.469, 1
That we escape. Redemption comes by Thee....197. H.539, 16
But before that day comes,...................197. H.540, 5
Out of the world he must, who once comes in:.199. H.548, 1
What ever comes, content makes sweet:.......200. H.552, 6
Where no disease raignes, or infection comes....205. H.575, 5
So, when Death comes, Fresh tinctures lose their place,
207. H.576, 5
Give Want her welcome if she comes; we find,..213. H.605, 1
Seldome comes Glorie till a man be dead.......218. H.623, 2
No man comes late unto that place from whence.228. H.656, 1
That brave Spirit comes agen...............242. H.714, 12
When Yew is out, then Birch comes in,.......285. H.892, 13
Comes with his Cypresse, and devotes a teare?.288. H.907, 2

Mudge every morning to the Postern **comes**,..301. H.965, 1
Comes relieving..............................308. H.993, 18
Since after death **comes** glory, Ile not haste....314. H.1022, 2
Now, now the mirth **comes**...................317. H.1035, 1
Of life **comes** in, when he's Regenerate........326. H.1080, 28
He **comes** to play the part that is His own.....343. N.22, 4
Whatever **comes**, let's be content withall:......353. N.55, 1
Christ, He requires still, wheresoere He **comes**..356. N.68, 1
And when night **comes**, wee'l give Him wassailing:
368. N.102, 22
As when to man He **comes**, and there doth place
385. N.189, 3
Possesse my thoughts, next **comes** my dolefull knell
392. N.230, 12
Whom all the flux of Nations **comes** to see;....399. N.263, 22
And God, as Thou art, **comes** to suffering......399. N.263, 25
Then **comes** the belly seated next belowe......405. A.1, 59
Of yor beawty death **comes** soone..............418. A.9, 46
— — — — — — — — — — —, ...452. var. H.443, 79
Comet Like to a dreadfull **Comet** in the Aire:...87. H.215, 6
Comets **Comets** we see by night; whose shagg'd portents
45. H.128, 15
Comfort Or water; where's the **comfort** found?..50. H.140, 8
Ye coole, and **comfort** all, but me............50. H.140, 12
To conquer'd men, some **comfort** 'tis to fall....50. H.141, 1
To see what **comfort** it wo'd yeeld:............73. H.187, 2
Our **comfort** is, we can't be lost..............134. H.336, 58
And this for **comfort** thou must know,..........247. H.725, 5
Beere small as **Comfort**, dead as Charity.......262. H.783, 16
Cold **comfort** still I'm sure lives there.........312. H.1014, 10
The only **comfort** of my life...................320. H.1052, 1
This is my **comfort**, when she's most unkind,....322. H.1061, 1
But with this **comfort**, if my blood be shed,....335. H.1128, 5
Sweet Spirit **comfort** me!......................347. N.41, 4
Sweet Spirit **comfort** me!......................347. N.41, 8
Sweet Spirit **comfort** me!......................347. N.41, 12
Sweet Spirit **comfort** me!......................347. N.41, 16
Sweet Spirit **comfort** me!......................347. N.41, 20
Sweet Spirit **comfort** me!......................348. N.41, 24
Sweet Spirit **comfort** me!......................348. N.41, 28
Sweet Spirit **comfort** me!......................348. N.41, 32
Sweet Spirit **comfort** me!......................348. N.41, 36
Sweet Spirit **comfort** me!......................348. N.41, 40
Sweet Spirit **comfort** me!......................348. N.41, 44
Sweet Spirit **comfort** me!......................348. N.41, 48
Where no one beame of **comfort** peeps in it....372. N.117, 2
Which is the height of **comfort**, when I fall,...392. N.230, 35
Comforters And the **comforters** are few,........348. N.41, 26
Comforts **Comforts** you'l afford me some:.......74. H.191, 6
Though hourely **comforts** from the Gods we see,.111. H.276, 1
Comic Can'st write the **Comick**, Tragick straine, and fall
298. H.955, 5
Coming And **comming** downe, shall make no noise at all.
21. H.62, 6
Fore-tell the **comming** of some dire events:....45. H.128, 16
Yet **comming** home, but somewhat late, (last night)
65. H.171, 4
Come, my Corinna, come; and **comming**, marke.68. H.178, 29
Fruit, ye know, is **comming** on:...............74. H.189, 4
Pressing before, some **coming** after,...........101. H.250, 17
Expos'd to all the **comming** Winters cold.......151. H.387, 4
Stand for my **comming**, Sentinell.............174. H.465, 14
You had your **comming** hither;..................184. H.493, 2
But Ile spend my **comming** houres,...........191. H.519, 7
Because thy selfe art **comming** to the Presse:..298. H.955, 10
Coming from my Julia's eye:..................302. H.968, 2
The **coming** in of sorrow.......................353. N 56, 12
Expect the **coming** of it ev'ry day.............379. N.142, 4
Thy former **coming** was to cure................397. N.257, 1
Yawne for Thy **coming**; some e're this time crie,.398. N.263, 7
Command Open at your **command**;.............57. H.149, 158
And hast **command** of every part,..............109. H.267, 23
Two parts of us successively **command**;........137. H.339, 1
Let Kings **Command**, and doe the best they may,
138. H.345, 1
This is your houre; and best you may **command**,.140. H.354, 9
Command the Roofe great Genius, and from thence
245. H.723, 1
The first Commerce is, & the next **Command**....275. H.847, 2
One Brave Captain did **command**,..............276. H.850, 9
Who will have love comply with his **command**..323. H.1067, 2
T'was braue, t'was braue could we **command** ye hand
413. A.4, 6
I turne Apostate to the strict **Comande**...424. ins. H.128, 46c
Of fortune can have noe **command**,........436. ins. H.336, 48n
Commanded Nero **commanded**; but withdrew his eyes
236. H.679, 1
Commanders **Commanders**, few for execution.....272. H.827, 2
Commanding What thy **commanding** soule shall put it to.
79. H.197, 80
Commandment Fearing to break the Kings **Commandement**:
122. H.305, 4
Commands Playing at Questions and **Commands**:.215. H.616, 8
Old Religion first **commands**.................280. H.870, 3
Offer thy gift; but first the Law **commands**....299. H.957, 1
In Gods **commands**, ne're ask the reason why;..397. N.260, 1
Commence Of Planetary bodies; so **commence**..116. H.283, 156
And (ere we our rites **commence**)..............303. H.974, 5
Commend More beauty to **commend**............75. H.193, 27
And this their Flatt'rie do's **commend**..........175. H.465, 41
Thus, having talkt, we'l next **commend**.......216. H.616, 35
Or **commend** a Crickets-hip,...................223. H.638, 10
Most like his Suite, and all **commend** the Trim;.330. H.1099, 3
Yet, in torments, I'le **commend** Thee:.........351. N.48, 6
But yet this Gift Thou wilt **commend**,....... .376. N.125, 7
And In thy sence, her Chaster thoughtes **Commend**
421. ins. H.106, 42a
— — — — — — — — — — —, ...450. var. A.9, 14
Commendations Our Honours, and our **Commendations** be
120. H.296, 1
Commended His blood to height; this done, **commended**
120. H.293, 53
And that my dust was to the earth **commended**..334. H.1124, 4
And when we have the Child **commended**......366. N.97, 28
Commends For seldome use **commends** the pleasure.
38. H.106, 140
That my last Vow **commends** to you:.........61. H.159, 21
Come, come and kisse me; Love and lust **commends**
78. H.197, 69
It is the last **commends** the Play..............94. H.225, 10
He who **commends** the vanquisht, speaks the Power,
200. H.553, 1
These temp'rall goods God (the most Wise) **commends**
387. N.201, 1
Comends it to your eares soft tipp...........417. A.9, 14
Commerce The first **Commerce** is, & the next Command.
275. H.847, 2
Not by His Essence, but **commerce** of Grace..387. N.197, 2
Commingle Then if thy voice **commingle** with the String
276. H.851, 3
Commingled Clarret, and Creame **commingled**......7. H.9, 10
Of flowers a sweet **commingled** Coronet:........30. H.88, 4
(Bodies and souls **commingled**)................59. H.152, 10
When with white **commingled**..................194. H.527, 4
But with such sweets **commingled**,.............283. H.883, 4
Commit To **commit** it to the fire:................21. H.59, 4
There is no evill that we do **commit**,..........386. N.196, 1
Committed And was **committed**, not remitted there.
367. N.100, 2
Commix Commix with Meale a little **Pisse**......284. H.890, 2
Or rich Arabia did **commix**,...................402. N.269, 16
Commixed **Commixt** they meet, with endlesse Roses crown'd.
206. H.575, 20
Of Maydens-blush, **commixt** with Jessimine.....262. H.783, 10
The feare of God, **commixt** with cleanly love..380. N.147, 2
Common The **common** formes have no one eye,.49. H.136, 18
Whether by choice, or **common** flame:.........50. H.140, 6
Instead of **common** showers,..................103. H.255, 6
Paying but **common** thanks for it............321. H.1056, 6
To th' good and bad, in **common**, for two ends:..387. N.201, 2
Commonest In Man, Ambition is the **common'st** thing;
21. H.58, 1
Commons To side with them, the **Commons** all...282. H.877, 2
As when the disagreeing **Commons** throw.....303. H.975, 3
Common'st See **Commonest**
Commonwealth An Indian **Common-wealth**.......80. H.201, 20
Then to the Plough, (the **Common-wealth**)....102. H.250, 39
Not of one man, but all the **Common-wealth**...318. H.1041, 2
Commutual For whose **commutuall** flames here I..70. H.181, 15
Companion **Companion**,..........................161. H.426, 8
Starves, having no **companion**.................381. N.158, 2
Company One of the crowd, not of the **companie**..163. H.436, 2
As to accept my **companie**,...................399. N.265, 4
Compare And with a teare **compare** these last...134. H.336, 81
And title me without **compare**,................243. H.716, 34
With a teare yow may **compare**...............417. A.9, 17
Compared **Compar'd** (in this my ample Orbe) to Him.
236. H.685, 4
Compartlement A curious-comely clean **Compartlement**:
227. H.652, 8
Compass And from thy **Compasse** taking small advice,
36. H.106, 81
Then, in that **compass**, sayling here and there,.301. H.966, 5
Thus, thus, and thus we **compasse** round.........359. N.83, 7
Compasses In Varnisht maps; by'th' helpe of **Compasses**;
330. H.1100, 2
Compassion Dead to all **compassion**............62. H.162, 12
And in **compassion** of thy yeeres,...............89. H.219, 5
Complain Thou wilt **complaine**, False now's thy Looking-glasse
21. H.62, 2
Complains Yet Much-more still **complains** he is in want.
73. H.188, 2
When Jill **complaines** to Jack for want of meate;
186. H.498, 1
Complaints That di'd for love; and their **complaints**:
169. H.449, 6
What needs **complaints**,........................314. H.1024, 1
Complete And moisture, both **compleat**:.........57. H.149, 126
In every part alike **compleat**,................243. H.716, 9
Completely I'le leaue thee then **Compleatly** riche.407. A.2, 6
Complexion Me, with that full pride of **complexion**,
78. H.197, 72

That smil'd in that first-sweet complexion.......81. H.202, 4
One and the selfe-same priz'd complexion.......209. H.586, 6
Had a sweet complexion.......................417. A.9, 20
Comply Light of the Moon, seem'd to comply,...167. H.443, 98
Whom faire Corinna sits, and doth comply.....206. H.575, 40
Comply.......................................308. H.993, 10
Who will have love comply with his command...323. H.1067, 2
But with the wicked if He doth comply,........385. N.188, 3
Comportment Get their comportment, and the gliding tongue
172. H.456, 5
For brave comportment, wit without offence,..297. H.947, 1
Compose Whose hands did compose.............239. H.695, 5
Composed See Precomposed
(Compos'd of odde, not even paires)..........91. H.223, 47
Man is compos'd here of a two-fold part;.......153. H.394, 1
If thou compos'd of gentle mould..............272. H.828, 13
Composer Composer in your Quire..............228. H.657, 9
Compost That the best compost for the Lands...230. H.662, 23
He sets his foot, he leaves rich compost there...259. H.771, 8
Comprehend 'Tis hard to finde God, but to comprehend
340. N.8, 1
Compression Take this compression, so by this...175. H.465, 69
Compulsive (A happy Realme! When no compulsive Law,
326. H.1080, 19
Com'st And till thou com'st, thy Lycidas,......184. H.492, 37
Concave Within the concave of a Nut,..........120. H.293, 40
Concealed With some conceal'd delight;.........75. H.193, 19
Vertue conceal'd (with Horace you'l confesse)..173. H.459, 13
And for a while lye here conceal'd,............190. H.515, 45
Conceal'd in this most holy Ground:...........366. N.98, 4
Conceit That some conceit did melt me downe,..67. H.175, 15
High in your own conceipt, and some way teach
115. H.283, 128
Off craueing more: soe In Conceipt bee ritch..411. A.3, 56
Conceits — — — — — — — —, ...432. var. H.283, 128
Conceived Conceiv'd with grief are, and with teares brought forth.......................................105. H.257, 28
Concentered Them all concenter'd in one man, but Thee.
121. H.301, 4
Conception A King, before conception crown'd...368. N.102, 18
Conclave Vertue's clean Conclave is sobriety.....331. H.1109, 2
Conclude Daies may conclude in nights; and Suns may rest,
72. H.185, 5
God can't be wrathfull; but we may conclude,..397. N.259, 1
Conclusion Take from thy Herrick this conclusion:
234. H.673, 14
Conclusions Wiser Conclusions in mee, since I knowe
411. A.3, 53
Concupiscence Of fresh concupiscence, and cry,.135. H.336, 111
Concurrence Without the sweet concurrence of the Heart.
346. N.35, 2
Concurring (Counsell concurring with the end)..38. H.106, 130
And a sweet concurring stream..............220. H.633, 3
Concussions Despite of all concussions left the Stem
170. H.451, 3
Condemn Condemne the Printer, Reader, and not me;
4. Ap., 2
If so, we'll think too, (when he do's condemne.39. H.110, 3
Yet say; sho'd she condemne.................43. H.123, 25
The Gods are easie, and condemne............47. H.132, 13
Since none so good are, but you may condemne;.64. H.168, 5
The good applaud: the peccant lesse condemne,.322. H.1062, 8
Condemnation Luggs, by the Condemnation of the Bench,
79. H.199, 1
Condemned In dennes of Darkness, or condemn'd to die.
63. H.165, 4
Condition This short but strict condition:......265. H.798, 4
The fire of Hell this strange condition hath,....387. N.202, 1
Conditions All conditions I aime at............209. H.585, 3
Conduce What may conduce...................368. N.104, 13
Conduct When we conduct her to her Groome:...360. N.83, 47
Conduits The while the conduits of my Kine....350. N.47, 49
Confer Why frowns my Sweet? Why won't my Saint confer
77. H.197, 25
If we can meet, and so conferre,..............133. H.336, 49
For those gifts you do conferre...............182. H.489, 12
As to the Goddesse, people did conferre........330. H.1099, 5
To joyn with them, who here confer..........402. N.270, 1
Confess By Loves Religion, I must here confesse it,
15. H.38, 5
Yet justly too I must confesse;...............19. H.51, 5
True, I confesse; such Whites as these........34. H.105, 7
I must confesse, I co'd not be................72. H.185, 25
True, I confesse I left thee, and appeale......78. H.197, 41
He payes the halfe, who do's confesse the Debt...94. H.226, 10
And beautious Bride we do confess y'are wise,..113. H.283, 51
No fault in women, to confesse...............118. H.291, 3
Kisse the Altar, and confess..................138. H.346, 9
Onely Moons conscience, we confesse,.........143. H.369, 3
Vertue conceal'd (with Horace you'l confesse)..173. H.459, 13
I must confesse, mine eye and heart..........202. H.560, 17
Youth (I confess) hath me mis-led;...........216. H.617, 5
So, I confesse, 'tis somewhat to do well........234. H.673, 9
That's sweetly touch't, I must confesse:.......243. H.716, 25
But heard with anger, we confesse the crime....260. H.776, 2
Pardon my trespasse (Silvia) I confesse,......294. H.936, 1

I will confesse...............................296. H.946, 1
I must confess, distinction none I see.........301. H.966, 9
For a kiss or two, confesse,..................305. H.984, 1
I must confesse, I there descrie,..............310. H.1004, 11
In's Tusc'lanes, Tullie doth confesse,..........332. H.1115, 1
And when I my sins confesse,.................347. N.41, 3
Lord, I confesse too, when I dine,..............350. N.47, 27
Lord I confesse, that Thou alone art able.........357. N.73, 1
I'le kisse the Tally, and confesse the score.....368. N.103, 8
Then, with a wonder, I confesse,..............372. N.118, 5
If ill it goes with thee, thy faults confesse:....395. N.243, 3
Confessed And more had done (it is confest)....294. H.939, 9
Next, when I have my faults confest,..........349. N.46, 5
Confession Confession twofold is (as Austine sayes,)
395. N.243, 1
Confidence The first event breeds confidence or feare.
292. H.294, 2
Confine To teach Man to confine desires:........35. H.106, 16
Call me The sonne of Beere, and then confine..79. H.197, 87
Confined Confin'd to live with private Larr:......37. H.106, 106
Confines From the dull confines of the drooping West,
242. H.713, 1
For what life and death confines................417. A.9, 9
Confirm 'Twas done by me, more to confirme my zeale,
78. H.197, 42
Confirmed 'Tis Good Confirm'd; for you have Bishop't it.
64. H.168, 10
Chose first, confirm'd next, & at last are crown'd.
241. H.707, 2
Conformity Conformity was ever knowne.........25. H.76, 1
Conformity gives comelinesse to things...... ..318. H.1040, 1
Confounded Sinners confounded are a twofold way,.388. N.210, 1
Confounds God then confounds mans face, when He not hears
382. N.169, 1
Confused In wayes confus'd, nor slip or fall.....33. H.98, 10
And all confus'd, I there did lie..............67. H.175, 17
And all confused multitude:..................312. H.1016, 4
Confus'd in utter Admiration.................326. H.1080, 10
Confus'd, in this brave Extasie.................402. N.269, 21
Confusedly Entranc'd, and lost confusedly:......23. H.68, 6
Ribbands to flow confusedly:...................28. H.83, 8
Absyrtus-like all torne confusedly:............300. H.960, 2
Confusion Love the confusion of the place......115. H.283, 140
But when he hears the like confusion,.........303. H.975, 2
Seldome brings order, but confusion...........392. N.230, 8
Congealed Congeal'd to Pearle and stone;......131. H.330, 11
Congelation As that the Congelation will........40. H.115, 15
Congesting In that congesting element..........245. H.720, 6
Congregation To make up now a Congregation...168. H.445, 2
Conjecture Where he will kisse (next drunk) conjecture ye.
295. H.943, 2
Conjoined Power conjoyn'd with Natures Crueltie.211. H.597, 2
Conjure Which sho'd conjure up a line..........182. H.489, 8
Conjurement Conjurement of the rest:..........258. H.767, 18
Conning As well as spare: still conning o'r this Theame,
38. H.106, 131
Conquer Conquer we shall, but we must first contend:
293. H.933, 1
Conquered To conquer'd men, some comfort 'tis to fall
50. H.141, 1
The eies be first, that conquer'd are............118. H.290, 2
No part of pitie on a conquer'd foe...........199. H.550, 2
As will if you yeeld, lye down conquer'd too....216. H.618, 12
To vanquish Hell, as here He conquer'd Death?.403. N.271, 6
Conquering Combate for men, by conquering the disease.
226. H.646, 2
Conqueror And glorifies the worthy Conquerer.....200. H.553, 2
The same, who crownes the Conquerour, will be.382. N.163, 1
Conquerors 'Twas Cesars saying: Kings no lesse Conquerors are
271. H.825, 1
Conquest Your Standard's up, we fix a Conquest there.
25. H.77, 12
Care keepes the Conquest; 'tis no lesse renowne,
307. H.989, 1
And howsoe're we have the conquest mist;....356. N.67, 3
But for the conquest thou didst pay...........360. N.83, 24
Conscience Led by thy conscience; to give.....35. H.106, 12
Not out of Conscience, or Religion:............122. H.305, 2
Onely Moons conscience, we confesse,.........143. H.369, 3
What Conscience, say, is it in thee...........168. H.446, 1
The second is a Conscience trespasse-free;.....386. N.194, 3
When Hell and Horrour fright the Conscience...392. N.230, 28
And Conscience vnto Preist-hood, tis not Need.411. A.3, 51
Conscripts (As many Conscripts of the Citie do).176. H.466, 6
Consecrate Next, like a Bishop consecrate my ground,
245. H.723, 7
I consecrate this loving work of mine,.........406. A.1, 110
Consent While the milder Fates consent,........39. H.111, 1
Banish consent, and 'tis no sinne.............175. H.465, 56
Consent and play a friendly part.............177. H.471, 3
The Power of Princes rests in the Consent......325. H.1073, 1
Here's words with lines, and lines with Scenes consent,
415. A.7, 7
Consenting Whom (Stars consenting with thy Fate) thou hast
35. H.106, 33
Shewing a heart consenting;..................55. H.149, 75

Conserves Conserves of Atomes, and the mites, 435. ins. H.293, cc
Consider Ah then consider! What all this implies; 131. H.330, 14
When I consider (Dearest) thou dost stay.....193. H.522, 1
Consider sorrowes, how they are aright:........268. H.810, 1
Consonant For being comely, consonant, and free.210. H.590, 1
Consort (Most fit to be the Consort to a King)..107. H.265, 2
Conspicuous As In a more Conspicuous Text....407. A.2, 32
Conspire Then Thunder-claps and Lightning did conspire 81. H.202, 5
Conspired Thus, thou, that man art, whom the Fates conspir'd 121. H.301, 5
Conspires And keep one Centre: This with that conspires, 35. H.106, 15
Conspiring See One-self-sweet-conspiring
(Larr thus conspiring with our mirth)........135. H.336, 124
Constancy 'Tis constancy (my Wickes) which keepes 134. H.336, 62
Constancie, Bashfullnes, and all...............409. A.2, 99
Constellations All faire Constellations........116. H.283, 157
Constraint There's no constraint to do amisse,...390. N.225, 1
Consult Consult ere thou begin'st, that done, go on 252. H.749, 1
Consume I frie in fire, and so consume,.........50. H.140, 3
And Cedar wash thee, that no times consume thee. 89. H.219, 14
The Altar's ready; Fire to consume..........102. H.251, 3
Who therein wo'd not consume................113. H.283, 27
And consume, and grow again to die,.........115. H.283, 138
The cough, the ptisick, I consume............134. H.336, 78
But curse thy children, they consume thy wheat...141. H.358, 2
What needs she fire and ashes to consume,.....178. H.474, 5
Of such rare Saint-ships, who did here consume.185. H.496, 3
For which, her wrath is gone forth to consume..197. H.539, 11
Consumed Three quarters were consum'd of it;..153. H.399, 7
Consumes And not a man here but consumes......413. A.4, 34
Consuming From a consuming fire,..............95. H.227, 13
Love is then consuming fire...................273. H.836, 8
Contagion Where, with their own contagion they are fed; 417. A.8, 33
Contain Which, though enchas'd with Pearls, contain 222. H.635, 11
Canst drincke in Earthern Cupps, wch ne're Contayne 422. ins. H.106, 116a
Contemn The Christall I contemne;............222. H.635, 10
Contemne to recommend a Cruse,..............291. H.918, 7
The meane passe by, or over, none contemne;..322. H.1062, 7
Kings must be dauntlesse: Subjects will contemne 330. H.1097, 1
Contemns He's the Lord of thy life, who contemnes his own. 181. H.486, 2
He's the Lord of thy life, who contemnes his own. 240. H.702, 2
Contemplation Of contemplation, your,....432. ins. H.283, 70g
Contempts Contempts in Courts and Cities dwell;..6. H.2, 21
Contend Conquer we shall, but we must first contend; 293. H.933, 1
Content See Malcontent
To my content, I never sho'd behold,............29. H.86, 5
Nature with little is content...................33. H.100, 4
That plague; because thou art content.........35. H.106, 22
Content makes all Ambrosia..................37. H.106, 116
(So Fate spares her) am well content to die...70. H.181, 12
(To save his life) twice am content to die.....70. H.181, 16
'Tis not the food, but the content.............124. H.312, 1
Short lot, or not, to be content with all.......153. H.396, 2
Will be content with one?...................160. H.422, 20
But long or short, I'm well content with all.....163. H.437, 2
They well content my Prew and me..........200. H.552, 4
What ever comes, content makes sweet:.......200. H.552, 6
Who with a little cannot be content,..........213. H.606, 1
Well content a craving man...................223. H.638, 18
Of Land makes life, but sweet content........230. H.662, 18
Content, begin, and I will bet................243. H.716, 7
So my fancie be content,.....................253. H.750, 14
Happy Rusticks, best content 255. H.761, 21
False man would be content....................346. N.38, 10
And my content...............................350. N.47, 34
Whatever comes, let's be content withall:.......353. N.55, 1
I'le learn to be content.......................368. N.104, 11
Though they be few in number, I'm content;..392. N.230, 3
Contented In the contented mind, not mint.......35. H.106, 18
Contented with the bed of one..................41. H.116, 8
Shew they are well contented..................260. H.777, 7
How well contented in this private Grange.....310. H.1003, 1
Contenteth More then a Feast contenteth me....124. H.312, 8
Contentment Those ends in War the best contentment bring, 316. H.1029, 1
Contents Since love so much contents me.......296. H.946, 12
Continent Bearing a Christall continent:.........187. H.504, 2
Within her Lawnie Continent,................250. H.740, 3
Contingences Then those, which come by sweet contingences. 123. H.307, 2
Contingencies Dead all black contingencies:......286. H.897, 8
Contingent For Humane Joy, Contingent Misery...416. A.8, 18
Continual Continuall reaping makes a land wax old. 292. H.922, 4
To have continuall paine, or pleasure here:....394. N.236, 2
Continue Nor the Snow continue pure:...........60. H.159, 14
And will continue so?..........................137. H.340, 5
Continues Continues cold, as is the night..........49. H.136, 31
And, though it falls, continues still..........318. H.1036, 5
Contracted And look with a contracted brow?....188. H.508, 2
Contradiction For to imply a contradiction.......382. N.166, 2
Contrariety Thus every part in contrariety......406. A.1, 105
Contriving Then for contriving so to loade thy Board, 210. H.590, 5
Control (Eternall in thy self) that canst controule 45. H.128, 20
And may a while controule..................54. H.149, 25
Convenient — — — — — — — —, ...440. var. H.443, 88
Converse See Re-converse
Convert Thou sweetly canst convert the same....95. H.227, 12
Convex Upon this Convex, all the flowers.......166. H.443, 33
Convey — — — — — — — —, ...450. var. A.9, 14
Convince Thou didst convince....................363. N.92, 8
Nor Fate, nor Enuye, cann theyr Fames Conuince, 411. A.3, 40
Convinces So Kings & Queens meet, when Desire convinces 77. H.197, 7
Cook And now y'are enter'd; see the Codled Cook 114. H.283, 61
Till that the Cooke cries, Bring no more.......291. H.919, 4
Cool Still in the coole, and silent shades of sleep..9. H.14, 18
To coole, not cocker Appetite..................35. H.106, 26
These may coole; but there's a Zone..........40. H.115, 11
Gryll either keeps his breath to coole his broth;.48. H.135, 2
To quench, or coole me with your Dew........50. H.140, 2
Unlesse you coole me with a Teare:...........50. H.140, 10
Ye coole, and comfort all, but me..............50. H.140, 12
Come, and coole ye; all who frie...............62. H.162, 2
O Bacchus! coole thy Raies!..................81. H.201, 30
Cold as Ice, or coole as I.....................117. H.289, 10
I heard ye co'd coole heat; and came.........157. H.413, 1
Will coole his flames, or quench his fires with snow? 187. H.502, 6
That your teares may coole her fires..........269. H.814, 6
Ans. Heate ye to coole ye:....................309. H.1001, 8
One sighe of loue, and coole it with a teare;...414. A.6, 8
— — — — — — — — — —, ...433. var. H.293, 28
Cooled See Overcooled
Upon the Custard, and thus cooled so:........47. H.131, 4
Cooler As if here were those cooler shades of love. 68. H.178, 36
With cooler Oken boughs;.....................285. H.892, 18
Cooling Cooling sleep with charming wand.....56. H.149, 110
And underneath thy cooling shade,............106. H.262, 13
The cooling breath of Respasses;.............145. H.375, 20
There in calm and cooling sleep..............377. N.128, 17
Cools So the Fancie cooles, till when..........242. H.714, 11
Coone What is the reason Coone so dully smels?.210. H.589, 1
Coorse See Coarse
Cope — — — — — — — —, ...427. var. H.197, 54
Copes Their curious Copes and Surplices........92. H.223, 98
Coral As beames of Corrall, but more cleare........7. H.9, 12
Tell Him, for Corall, thou hast none;..........354. N.59, 11
Corals Which Rubies, Corralls, Scarlets, all......12. H.23, 7
Corrols his cheeke, to see those Rites not done..216. H.618, 4
So Corrolls looke more lovely Red,...........268. H.811, 5
Cord My Crosse; my Cord; and all farewell.......123. H.306, 4
Cordelion One Cordelion had that Age long since; 170. H.451, 15
Cords Might stretch the cords of civill comelinesse: 311. H.1006, 2
The Crosse, the Cords, the Nailes, the Speare, 400. N.266, 8
Core See Apple's-core
Coridon Of us, or Coridon.........................184. H.492, 24
Then Tityrus, and Coridon,...................184. H.492, 33
Corinna Next, Corinna, for her wit,............16. H.39, 9
Come, my Corinna, come; and comming, marke.68. H.178, 29
But my Corinna, come, let's goe a Maying......68. H.178, 42
Come, my Corinna, come, let's goe a Maying...69. H.178, 70
Whom faire Corinna sits, and doth comply....206. H.575, 40
Corinna's But onely my Corinna's eye?.........48. H.133, 17
Cork Thou lighter then the Cork by far:.......70. H.181, 22
Corn Two, like two ripe shocks of corn..........58. H.149, 170
Ripe eares of corne, and up to th'eares in snow:.59. H.154, 6
Like Iphyclus, upon the tops of Corn.........78. H.197, 50
Crown'd with the eares of corne, now come,....101. H.250, 5
As the Summers Corne has eares:............102. H.253, 4
Washes the golden eares of corne..............112. H.283, 20
Our salt, our Corn, our Honie, Wine, and Oile).225. H.642, 18
What store of Corn has carefull Nodes, thinke you, 270. H.822, 3
Of Corn, when Summer shakes his eares;.....340. N.3, 12
God gives not onely corne, for need,...........356. N.66, 1
Smile, like a field beset with corne?...........364. N.96, 15
For now the Corne and Wine must faile:......374. N.123, 14
— — — — — — — — — — —, ...433. var. H.293, 9
Cornfields Then to thy corn-fields thou dost goe,.230. H.662, 21

Cornish No Capitoll, no **Cornish** free,..........90. H.223, 20
Corns Of some rough Groom, who (yirkt with **Corns**) sayes, Sir
146. H.377, 21
A chaine of **Cornes**, pickt from her eares and toes:
232. H.668, 2
Who two and thirty **cornes** had on a foot.......240. H.704, 2
Ralph pares his nayles, his warts, his **cornes**, and Ralph
299. H.959, 1
Coronation Gave her a day of **Coronation**;......94. H.224, 6
For **Coronation**, then Your onely Praise........188. H.506, 12
Coronet Of flowers a sweet commingled **Coronet**:..30. H.88, 4
Within the Virgins **Coronet**..................88. H.216, 18
On many a head here, many a **Coronet**:........94. H.224, 4
Upon your Head this flowry **Coronet**:............140. H.354, 4
On many a head the Delphick **Coronet**,..........142. H.365, 4
The Muse give thee the Delphick **Coronet**.......194. H.529, 2
A Jem in this eternall **Coronet**:................264. H.789, 2
Upon my curles the Mirtle **Coronet**,...........335. H.1128, 2
Upon my head the golden **coronet**;..............343. N.25, 6
Coronets — — — — — — — —, ...447. var. A.1, 4
Corpse And while the Wood-nimphs my cold **corps** inter,
19. H.50, 3
A **Corps** as bright as burnisht gold............185. H.497, 6
Then the dead **Corps**, or carkase of the Wine...301. H.964, 2
Correct **Correct** my errors gently with Thy Rod...398. N.261, 4
Correction Of all His sonnes free from **correction**...378. N.134, 2
Corrupt What is **corrupt**, or sowr'd with sin,......366. N.98, 5
Corrupted **Corrupted** wood; serve here for shine..167. H.443, 75
Corruption Not subject to **corruption**.............334. H.1123, 6
Corse See **Corpse**
Thy sacred **Corse** with Odours I will burne;.....11. H.22, 3
And when I'm laid out for a **Corse**, then be;....111. H.279, 3
Cost See **Free-cost**
Is ne'r redeem'd by **cost**.........................53. H.149, 8
Can with the smallest **cost** afford................200. H.552, 2
For little **cost** he.............................320. H.1051, 14
for earth and sea; this **Cost**.............432. ins. H.283, 70c
Cotta Fabius, and **Cotta**, Lentulus, all live.........41. H.117, 3
Cottage Since shed or **Cottage** I have none,...321. H.1056, 1
Cottages The poore and private **Cottages**.............5. H.2, 4
When as the humble **Cottages** not feare........181. H.483, 15
Couch And now, Behold! the Bed or **Couch**....57. H.149, 131
Cough The **cough**, the ptisick, I consume........134. H.336, 78
Two she spat out, a **cough** forc't out the rest....158. H.419, 2
Could (Partial List) See **Co'd**
As, **could** they hear, the Damn'd would make no noise,
22. H.67, 2
For ought that I **could** say.....................346. N.38, 6
Could'st **Could'st** leave the City, for exchange, to see
35. H.106, 3
Counsel (**Counsell** concurring with the end)......38. H.106, 130
By time, and **Counsell**, doe the best we can,......120. H.294, 1
To be my **Counsell** both, and Chanceller.........202. H.557, 30
Will **counsell** be,............................210. H.591, 11
By their wise **Counsell**, then they be by Warre...271. H.825, 2
Counselest Yet ere thou **counsel'st** with thy Glasse,
271. H.824, 5
Counsels Still take advice; though **counsels** when they flye
318. H.1039, 1
Count Who **count** this night as long as three,....114. H.283, 74
Countenance Dash all bad Poems out of **countenance**.
187. H.506, 10
Of Thy most winning **countenance**;............395. N.246, 4
Counter Many a **Counter**, many a Die,.........166. H.443, 51
Counterchange This **counterchange** of Perle and Diamond.
295. H.941, 6
Counterchanged Those **counter-changed** Tabbies in the ayre,
207. H.576, 3
Counterfeit Some Pearls on Queens, that have been **counterfet**.
76. H.194, 6
Men in their substance, not in **counterfeit**.......170. H.451, 6
That shin'st thus in thy **counterfeit**?............270. H.819, 9
Countermand Say, do's she frown? still **countermand** her threats:......................................270. H.820, 3
Counter-proof That's **counter-proofe** against the Farms mishaps,
128. H.323, 5
Counter-stands Which tryes, and **counter-stands** the shock,
148. H.377, 110
Countries Seeing those painted **Countries**; and so guesse
36. H.106, 79
Fame tell of States, of **Countries**, Courts, and Kings;
36. H.106, 85
From **Countries** far, with Store of Spices, (sweet).86. H.213, 31
Thou hast beheld those seas, and **Countries** farre;
330. H.1100 5
Country But for the Court, the **Country** wit........6. H.2, 17
But that which most makes sweet thy **country** life,
35. H.106, 31
Which **Country** people call a Bee................50. H.139, 9
The **Country** has. Amint. From whence? Amar. From whence? Mir. The Court.................................86. H.213, 12
We'll blesse the Babe, Then back to **Countrie** pleasures.
87. H.213, 48
Drest up with all the **Country** Art.............101. H.250, 8
Of merry Crickets by my **Country** fire,..........132. H.333, 8
Since to th' **Country** first I came,...............182. H.489, 1
What sweets the **Country** can afford............192. H.521, 3
Sweet **Country** life, to such unknown,...........229. H.662, 1
Tripping the comely **country** round,.............230. H.662, 50
O native **countrey**, repossest by thee!..........242 H.713, 16
Our Sires betraid their **Countrey** and their King.
252. H.745, 10
Death to our **Countrey**, now hath lost his heat:..254. H.756, 4
In **country** Meadowes pearl'd with Dew,........323. H.1068, 5
Let **Country** wenches make 'em fine..........323. H.1068, 13
Froms Natiue **Cuntrye**, into Banishm^t,............411. A.3, 72
Country-life Come, leave this loathed **Country-life**, and then
171. H.456, 1
Country-round And He, who us'd to leade the **Country-round**,
159. H.421, 5
Country's The **Countries** sweet simplicity:..........35. H.106, 4
Country-seat At my homely **Country-seat**,........152. H.393, 1
Country-table To keep a **countrey-table**,..........235. H.674, 16
Couple Birds chuse their Mates, and **couple** too, this day:
149. H.378, 2
When I shall **couple** with my Valentine.........149. H.378, 4
Courage A deale of **courage** in each bosome springs
25. H.77, 9
Store of **courage** to me grant,...................151. H.386, 1
Yet he'l the **courage** have.....................259. H.772, 14
Course For second **course**, last night, a Custard came
47. H.131, 1
Good things, that come of **course**, far lesse doe please,
123. H.307, 1
A **course** in thy Fames-pledge, thy Sonne.......147. H.377, 44
This was the old way; and 'tis yet thy **course**,..201. H.557, 19
Courses E'ene all Religious **courses** to be rich.....266. H.800, 1
Court See **Fairy-court, Hampton Court**
The **Court** of Mab, and of the Fairie-King..........5. H.1, 12
But for the **Court**, the Country wit................6. H.2, 17
Vice rules the Most, or All at **Court**:...........37. H.106, 90
The Country has. Amint. From whence? Amar. From whence? Mir. The **Court**............................86. H.213, 12
The Fairie **Court** I give to thee:................165. H.443, 2
I meane the **Court**: Let Latmos be.............183. H.492, 17
My lov'd Endymions **Court**;.................183. H.492, 18
What ha's the **Court** to do with Swaines,.......184. H.492, 21
Here needs no **Court** for our Request,...........190. H.515, 29
Of **Court**, or Crown........................190. H.515, 34
Must revell, as Queene, in the **Court** here.........317. H.1035, 6
Live thou at **Court**, where thou mayst be......323. H.1068, 11
I'th' **Court** that's halfe so comly..............324. H.1068, 20
Out-stable for thy **Court** here....................345. N.33, 8
— — — — — — — — — —, ...441. var. H.446, 9
Courtesies For all thy many **courtesies** to me,....267. H.804, 1
Courtly Undreadfull too of **courtly** thunderclaps:..128. H.323, 6
Strik'st now a **Courtly** strain.................183. H.492, 12
But I the **Courtly** State wo'd see:..............183. H.492, 19
Courts Contempts in **Courts** and Cities dwell;........6. H.2, 21
Fame tell of States, of Countries, **Courts**, and Kings
36. H.106, 85
Nor **courts** thou Her because she's well attended..201. H.557, 7
But serving **Courts**, and Cities, be..............229. H.662, 3
— — — — — — — — — — —, ...422. var. H.106, 85
Courtship What Gesture, **Courtship**; Comliness agrees,
148. H.377, 95
Covenant Which was the **Covenant**, that she......237. H.687, 7
His was the Bond and **Cov'nant**, yet............360. N.83, 21
Covenant's That **Cov'nant's** here; The under-bow,..139. H.353, 5
Cover With leaves and mosse-work for to **cover** me:
19. H.50, 2
Loving, and gentle for to **cover** me:..............19. H.52, 2
Brought leaves and mosse to **cover** her:..........46. H.130, 6
Next, hollow out a Tombe to **cover**............61. H.159, 28
Thou Sexton (Red-brest) for to **cover** me.........111. H.279, 4
About the **Cover** of this Book there went........227. H.652, 7
Stones, or turfes to **cover** me....................270. H.821, 4
Present those Turfs, which once must **cover** me:..392. N.230, 16
O Volume worthy leafe, by leafe and **cover**........415. A.7, 5
Covered I shall, ere long, with green turfs **cover'd** be;
66. H.174, 3
Covering Cowslips for her **covering**...............170. H.450, 6
— — — — — — — — — — —, ...453. var. H.283, 46
Covers The earth, that lightly **covers** her.........123. H.310, 6
Th' easie earth that **covers** her...................224. H.640, 4
Covet Or Verse I **covet** none;......................30. H.89, 2
Covet not both; but if thou dost..............169. H.446, 9
Why sho'd we **covet** much, when as we know,....308. H.995, 1
Fain would I rest; yet **covet** not to die,..........352. N.51, 11
Coveting And, **coveting** no higher sphere,........402. N.269, 24
Covets Who **covets** more, is evermore a slave.....213. H.607, 2
Cow The Heifer, **Cow**, and Oxe draw neere......230. H.662, 38
Coward The **Coward** then takes Armes, and do's the deed.
309. H.999, 2
Cowardice 'Tis **cowardice** to bite the buried.......218. H.625, 2
Cowardly Next, that these ills none **cowardly** may shun;
387. N.201, 5
Cowards No **cowards** must his royall Ensignes beare.
280. H.872, 2
Cowl As big as a **Cowle**.......................320. H.1051, 5
Cow-like Chor. And Lallage (with **cow-like** eyes).243. H.716, 11

Cowslip — — — — — — — — —, ...438. var. H.412, 5
Cowslip-ball The Maids to catch this Cowslip-ball:.112. H.281, 2
Cowslip-balls We Cowslip balls,.................361. N.83, 52
Cowslips The richer Couslips home...........110. H.274, 8
But since these Cowslips fading be,..............112. H.281, 3
Butter of Cowslips mixt with them;............145. H.375, 22
With bands of Cow-slips bind him;............157. H.412, 26
This ball of Cow-slips, these she gave me here...159. H.421, 16
Cowslips for her covering.......................170. H.450, 6
Of sweetest Cow-slips filling Them............179. H.476, 15
With Cream of Cowslips buttered:..............192. H.521, 14
Balls of Cowslips, Daisie rings,................306. H.984, 25
There filling Maunds with Cowslips, you.......323. H.1068, 7
Coxcomb Where a Coxcomb will be broke,.....255. H.761, 17
Coxu Brugel and Coxu, and the workes out-doe,..150. H.384, 3
Coy To that coy Girle;..........................43. H.123, 3
Then be not coy, but use your time;..........84. H.208, 13
And as coy be, as you can,....................121. H.297, 13
Virgins coy, but not unkind....................138. H.346, 4
Shall we ere bring coy Brides to bed;.........360. N.83, 50
Coyest Rocks to relent, and coyest maids to love...287. H.900, 2
Coynes See Coins
Coyness This to your coynesse I will tell;......60. H.159, 11
Coynesse takes us to a measure;..............276. H.850, 5
Coy't Then feast, and coy't a little; then to bed...216. H.618, 8
Cozen Thou still wilt cozen me..................223. H.635, 16
Cozening Of Cupid, and his wittie coozning:......228. H.658, 6
Crab Crab faces gownes with sundry Furres: 'tis known,
232. H.669, 1
Crabbed No such crab'd vizard: Thou hast learnt thy Train,
147. H.377, 35
Crack Whose crack gives crushing unto all..........25. H.76, 4
Did crack the Play-house sides, or cleave her roofe.
150. H.382, 12
Flew out a crack, so mighty, that the Fart,.....205. H.572, 3
First, crack the strings, and after that,..........240. H.705, 11
When the great Crack not Crushes one, but all...319. H.1045, 2
No crack or Schisme leave i'th subtill skin:......385. N.184, 2
Cracked A crackt horne she blowes;............334. H.1122, 14
Had broke her wheele, or crackt her axeltree......358. N.77, 4
Crackling Of crackling Laurell, which fore-sounds,
127. H.319, 23
— — — — — — — — — —, ...422. var. H.106, 60
Cracks Craw cracks in sirrop; and do's stinking say,
162. H.428, 1
Let me (like him) first cracks of thunder heare;..343. N.25, 3
Cradle Thy cradle, Kingly Stranger,.............345. N.33, 13
Crammed Two Napkins cram'd up, and a silver Spoone.
118. H.292, 6
Craule See Crawl
Crave But onely crave...........................30. H.89, 3
And pardon crave,..............................100. H.246, 2
To those, who crave............................171. H.455, 4
Still shall I crave, and never get...............312. H.1014, 3
Craving Of craving more, are never rich.........35. H.106, 20
Demands no money by a craving way;..........142. H.363, 2
Well content a craving man....................223. H.638, 18
Off craueing more: soe In Conceipt bee ritch....411. A.3, 56
Craw Craw cracks in sirrop; and do's stinking say,.162. H.428, 1
Crawl My curles about her neck did craule,........16. H.41, 14
Whereon my Vine did crawle,..................72. H.185, 13
Meane time like Earth-wormes we will craule below,
257. H.763, 21
So long as I about Thee craule?...............371. N.114, 6
I crawle, I creep; my Christ, I come...........377. N.129, 1
Crawling Which crawling one and every way,.......16. H.41, 3
With crawling Woodbine over-spread:.........192. H.521, 6
A crawling Vine about Anacreon's head:.........313. H.1017, 2
Vnder the which twoe crawling eyebrowes twine..404. A.1, 7
— — — — — — — — — —, ...421. var. H.106, 43
Crazy Thus frantick crazie man (God wot)......135. H.336, 113
Creaking I keep, which creeking day by day,....246. H.724, 10
Cream Clarret, and Creame commingled...........7. H.9, 10
Part of the creame from that Religious Spring;..9. H.14, 8
Some have dispatcht their Cakes and Creame,....69. H.178, 47
Out of the which, the creame of light,..........74. H.190, 9
You see how Creame but naked is;..............75. H.193, 9
Thus Lillie, Rose, Grape, Cherry, Creame,....75. H.193, 33
Shew'd like to Creame, enspir'd with Strawberries:.81. H.202, 2
Cheeks like Creame Enclarited:................138. H.342, 6
Butter of Amber, Cream, and Wine, and Oile....144. H.370, 5
The smell of mornings milk, and cream;........145. H.375, 21
A Strawberry shewes halfe drown'd in Creame?...164. H.440, 6
Bankt all with Lillies, and the Cream..........179. H.476, 14
Wo'd yee have fresh Cheese and Cream?........183. H.491, 1
To your Cream, her's Strawberries..............183. H.491, 4
With Cream of Cowslips buttered:............192. H.521, 14
The Creame of meat;.........................198. H.544, 2
In Cream she bathes her thighs (more soft then silk)
203. H.561, 3
With superstition, (as the Cream of meates.)....204. H.568, 4
With Cream of Lillies (not of Kine)............216. H.616, 33
Run Creame, (for Wine.).......................350. N.47, 50
and cherries in her cheekes, there's Creame.430. ins. H.283, 20c
— — — — — — — — — —, ...445. var. H.761, 3
Creams More white then are the whitest Creames,..34. H.105, 3
Tarts and Custards, Creams and Cakes,..........255. H.761, 3
Create Create the burden light...................66. H.172, 24
To create in me a heate,.........................217. H.620, 2
To create (or cause at all).......................377. N.128, 15
That done, with Honour Thou dost me create...398. N.262, 3
— — — — — — — — — —, ...453. ins. H.283, 20f
Creates — — — — — — — — —, ...421. var. H.106, 31
— — — — — — — — — —, ...441. var. H.465, 64
Creator Who are my Works Creator, and alone....3. Ded.H, 3
Creature See Trencher-creature
When every creature rested,......................26. H.81, 2
It is a creature born and bred................130. H.329, 4
Like will to like, each Creature loves his kinde;..319. H.1043, 1
Onely, by this dull creature, to expresse........384. N.179, 3
Creatures Of creatures, woman is the best.........250. H.739, 4
Credit With Water fill'd, (Sirs, credit me)........44. H.127, 2
Heare all men speak; but credit few or none.....67. H.177, 4
Prethee goe home; and for thy credit be.........97. H.236, 3
And kept credit with my heart,.... ....183. H.490, 19
Or credit ye, when I am dead?..................218. H.626, 4
And next the Gospell wee will credit thee....257. H.763, 20
A Good and Bad. Sirs credit me...............283. H.885, 10
Falsehood winnes credit by uncertainties........287. H.902, 2
We credit most our sight; one eye doth please..287. H.904, 1
What credit can we give to seas,...............294. H.937, 5
The reason is, his credit cannot get...........302. H.969, 3
the creditt from the table of the Sunne....432. ins. H.283, 70b
Credits And credits Physick, yet not trusts his Pill:
125. H.315, 4
Creed Of Gift from God: And heres my Creed....359. N.78, 16
Creeking See Creaking
Creep If you can see, how Dreams do creep.......79. H.198, 9
Like snailes did creep...........................194. H.525, 2
I'le come, I'le creep, (though Thou dost threat)...349. N.46, 1
And Time seems then, not for to flie, but creep;..358. N.77, 2
I crawle, I creep; my Christ, I come............377. N.129, 1
Crept But when I crept with leaves to hide......17. H.41, 18
Crept to that, and came to this.................120. H.297, 6
Which crept into each aged Sire...............135. H.336, 104
Then crept into my heart;.....................295. H.942, 14
Cress See Water-cress
Crest Ensphere'd with Palm on Your Triumphant Crest.
271. H.823, 4
Crew (My dearest Crew,).........................161. H.426, 9
My Crew shall see,..............................162. H.426, 22
Of Clipseby Crew...............................198. H.544, 36
And rare, Ile say (my dearest Crew)............217. H.620, 11
Cricket See Idol-cricket
The merry Cricket, puling Flie,...............119. H.293, 17
As the crickit;..................................136. H.336, 141
Crickets Of singing Crickits by thy fire:........37. H.106, 122
Of merry Crickets by my Country fire,..........132. H.333, 8
Cricket's-hip Or commend a Crickets-hip,........223. H.638, 10
Crie See Cry
Cried He cry'd aloud, Help, help the wound:........18. H.44, 4
Cries Which done, to still their wanton cries,......31. H.92, 9
Scobble for Whoredome whips his wife; and cryes,.44. H.126, 1
And stils the Bride too, when she cries.........130. H.329, 11
For which their cryes might beate against thine eares,
149. H.377, 125
For Musick now; He has the cries...........167. H.443, 112
And if more; Each Nipple cries,................183. H.491, 3
Till that the Cooke cries, Bring no more.........291. H.919, 4
Cries out, (my lord, my Lord) the Case is clear:.303. H.975, 6
When Chub brings in his harvest, still he cries,..327. H.1086, 1
Old Widow Shopter, when so ere she cryes,....331. H.1107, 1
When the flames and hellish cries..............348. N.41, 41
To charme his cries, (at time of need:)..........354. N.59, 10
And hear'st His whimp'ring, and His cries;.......365. N.97, 14
Crime He Acts the Crime, that gives it Cherishing...10. H.17, 2
But heard with anger, we confesse the crime.....260. H.776, 2
Crimes And to repent some crimes,................352. N.53, 5
Crimson Enthralls the Crimson Stomacher:........28. H.83, 6
Those crimson clouds i'th'cheeks & lips leave shining.
207. H.576, 2
Crisped Unto the crisped Yew..................285. H.892, 12
Critic No Critick haunts the Poore mans Cell:........6. H.2, 22
Critics You Criticks means to live:..................32. H.96, 2
Crocodile As is the fish, or tonguelesse Crocadile...58. H.150, 2
True Love is tonguelesse as a Crocodile..........274. H.837, 8
Crofts Nothing I have (my Crofts) to send to Thee
267. H.804, 2
Crook Into the middle <most> sight pleasing crooke.
406. A.1, 82
Crooked Crooked you are, but that dislikes not me;
99. H.242, 1
To the rough Sickle, and crookt Sythe,........102. H.250, 42
Crookt See Crooked
Croot One silver spoon shines in the house of Croot;
332. H.1110, 1
Cross Some crosse the Fill-horse; some with great
101. H.250, 21
How crosse, how sullen, and how soone........103. H.253, 13
My Crosse; my Cord; and all farewell...........123. H.306, 4
Faire and foule dayes trip Crosse and Pile; The faire
189. H.513, 1

Who has not a Crosse,..........................256. H.762, 7
The sterner Fates, to cross his purposes;.......266. H.800, 4
A Primrose Banke did cross her way,............288. H.908, 3
So not one cross to buy thee..................321. H.1055, 3
Crosse your Dow, and your dispatch,..........322. H.1063, 3
Thy Crosse, my Christ, fixt 'fore mine eyes sho'd be,
371. N.115, 9
Christ, when He hung the dreadfull Crosse upon,.382. N.167, 1
From her Sonnes Crosse, not shedding once a teare:
384. N.180, 2
The Crosse shall be Thy Stage; and Thou shalt there
398. N.263, 17
The Crosse, the Cords, the Nailes, the Speare,..400. N.266, 8
Crossed See Circum-crossed
But (ah!) by starres malignant crost,........313. H.1020, 3
Crosses Crosses doe still bring forth the best events.
110. H.275, 2
Our Crosses are no other then the rods,..........278. H.862, 1
With my crosses..............................308. H.993, 12
Be not dismaide, though crosses cast thee downe;
311. H.1007, 1
Crosses we must have; or, hereafter woe.........359. N.81, 2
Crossing Crossing thy selfe; come thus to sacrifice:
127. H.320, 2
Cross-line And by some crosse-line show it;......64. H.166, 10
Cross-track Many a turn, and man a crosse-
Track they redeem a bank of mosse
165. H.443, 25-26
Cross-tree This Crosse-Tree here................401. N.268, 1
Crost See Circum-crossed, Crossed
Crow See Scarecrow-like
Flutter and crow, as in a fit..................135. H.336, 110
By the Time the Cocks first crow..............177. H.473, 8
For to denie my Master, do thou crow...........349. N.43, 2
Crowd One of the crowd, not of the companie.....163. H.436, 2
About whose Throne the crowd of Poets throng..206. H.575, 29
Crowing Stay me, by crowing, ere I do begin;....349. N.43, 4
Crown And with my Lawrell crown thy Golden Urne.
11. H.22, 4
Our Thyrse, for Scepter; and our Baies for Crown.
41. H.117, 8
Promis'd sho'd come to crown your youth.........53. H.149, 2
Still shall crown the happy life.................55. H.149, 59
And Love shall crown my End with Peace.......73. H.187, 11
Ne'r may Prophetique Daphne crown my Brow...79. H.197, 92
Render for that, a crowne of life to you.........94. H.224, 10
To honour thee, my little Parsly crown:........131. H.333, 4
Crown we our Heads with Roses then,..........133. H.336, 33
To crown the Hearth,........................135. H.336, 123
The Golden chain too, and the Civick Crown...176. H.466, 8
He rents his Crown, That feares the Peoples hate.
182. H.488, 2
To null his Numbers, and to blast his Crowne...188. H.506, 14
Of Court, or Crown...........................190. H.515, 34
Roses and Cassia crown the untill'd soyle.........205. H.575, 4
Crowne it agen agen;.........................227. H.653, 5
And crown thy temples too, and let............233. H.670, 19
My Priest-hood crown with bayes..............261. H.778, 11
It sparkles now like Ariadne's Crowne.......264. H.789, 4
And everlasting Harvest crown thy Soile!.......269. H.818, 8
Hard are the two first staires unto a Crowne;....292. H.925, 1
Thy fall is but the rising to a Crowne...........311. H.1007, 2
Snatcht off his Crown, and gave the wreath to me:
313. H.1017, 12
Next crowne the bowle full...................317. H.1035, 19
Rules but by leave, and takes his Crowne on trust.
331. H.1103, 2
Give thee the Laurell Crowne for lot;...........334. H.1123, 4
May Roses grow, to crown His own deare Head...366. N.97, 23
The Crowne of dutye is our dutye; well.........412. A.3, 103
— — — — — — — — — —, ...441. var. H.465, 38
Crowned See Full-crowned, Rose-crowned
Crown'd with clusters of the Vine;..............39. H.111, 5
With endless life are crown'd.................81. H.201, 52
(With whitest Wool be ever crown'd that day!)..86. H.213, 14
You first of all crown'd her; she must of due,....94. H.224, 9
Ye see the aged Vessell crown'd:................94. H.225, 6
Crown'd with the eares of corne, now come,.....101. H.250, 5
For joy, to see the Hock-cart crown'd...........101. H.250, 14
And left of love, are crown'd...................106. H.262, 4
With Hony-succles crown'd....................110. H.274, 12
Shew thy white feet, and head with Marjoram crown'd:
113. H.283, 32
Verse crown'd with Yvie, and with Holly:.......126. H.319, 10
Remember us in Cups full crown'd,.............127. H.319, 29
Sit crown'd with Rose-buds, and carouse,.......127. H.319, 41
Whom they neglected, thou hast crown'd a Poet...143. H.365, 8
That henceforth none be Laurel crown'd but Thee.
150. H.383, 2
But crown'd he is with store,..................160. H.422, 15
Drinking wine, & crown'd with flowres...........191. H.519, 8
Of Lyrick Wine, both swell'd and crown'd,.......198. H.544, 16
Commixt they meet, with endlesse Roses crown'd.
206. H.575, 20
Among which glories, (crown'd with sacred Bayes,
206. H.575, 49

To be in that Orbe crown'd (that doth include..207. H.575, 59
So, while I thus sit crown'd;..................208. H.582, 2
In Tyrian Dewes, and Head with Roses crown'd..214. H.612, 12
With Daffadils and Daisies crown'd.............230. H.662, 51
Crown'd Poets; yet live Princes under thee:....234. H.673, 16
The glory of flowers that crown'd it...........239. H.695, 6
Chose first, confirm'd next, & at last are crown'd..241. H.707, 2
With thousand blessings by thy Fortune crown'd.
242. H.713, 6
And with Chaplets crown'd, we'l rost..........280. H.870, 15
Wo'd I evermore be crown'd...................286. H.897, 3
My wearied Barke, O Let it now be Crown'd!..334. H.1127, 1
A King, before conception crown'd.............368. N.102, 18
Upon an Altar rear'd by Him, and crown'd....369. N.105, 7
Thus Crownd with Rose Budds, Sacke, thou mad'st mee flye
410. A.3, 27
Whose blessèd Youth with endless flow'rs is crown'd.
417. A.8, 30
Crownest See Crown'st
Crowns But care for crowns of flowers:...........65. H.170, 2
Your Walks with Flowers, and give their Crowns to you.
107. H.265, 8
It is the End that crownes us, not the Fight....123. H.309, 2
The feast of Shepheards fail. Sil. None crowns the cup
159. H.421, 3
With crowns of greenest Parsley,...............234. H.674, 3
'Tis not the Fight that crowns us, but the end...293. H.933, 2
The Person crowns the Place; your lot doth fall..304. H.977, 1
God crowns our goodnesse, where so ere He sees,
356. N.71, 3
The more our Crownes of Glory there increase...372. N.119, 2
The same, who crownes the Conquerour, will be..382. N.163, 1
Crown'st 'Tis Thou that crown'st my glittering Hearth
350. N.47, 37
O Thou, that crown'st the will, where wants the deed.
369. N.105, 2
Crows — — — — — — — — —, ...421. var. H.106, 57
Crucifixion Most dire and horrid crucifixion.......129. H.323, 14
Crucifixions What Crucifixions are in Love?......158. H.420, 8
Crucify To crucifie my life:.......................13. H.31, 4
Never crucifie my life;..........................182. H.490, 3
Delays in love but crucifie the heart.............261. H.781, 2
Cruel Ah cruell Sea! and looking on't,............42. H.119, 9
And Cruell Maid, because I see.................60. H.159, 1
Of those Girles, which cruell are................62. H.162, 18
Ah, cruell Love! must I endure................74. H.191, 1
The doome of cruell Proserpine.................132. H.336, 8
For cruell Love ha's me so whipt,..............164. H.442, 6
The cruell paine did his forsake,...............188. H.509, 3
No cruell truths of Philomell,.................215. H.616, 12
Of those that cruell be?........................272. N.828, 16
Ah cruell maides! Ile goe my way,............312. H.1014, 5
Cruels But we with Silks (not Cruells).........345. N.33, 17
Cruelties From the beholding Death, and cruelties..236. H.679, 2
Is the height of Cruelties.....................254. H.757, 4
Cruelty Love strikes, but 'tis with gentle crueltie...16. H.40, 4
'Tis cruelty in thee to'th'height,................34. H.103, 11
Tis worse then barbarous cruelty to show.........199. H.550, 1
Power conjoyn'd with Natures Crueltie.........211. H.597, 2
Crumb Or else a crum,........................171. H.455, 13
Better he starv'd, then but to tast one crumme...355. N.65, 10
Crumbled (Wert not for thee) haue Crumbled Into Mould,
411. A.3, 36
Crumbs And the brisk Mouse may feast her selfe with crums,
37. H.106, 123
Cruse Our browner Ale into the cruse:.........135. H.336, 126
By cruse and measure; thus devoting Wine,....148. H.377, 83
As my small Cruse best fits my little Wine.......249. H.733, 3
Contemne to recommend a Cruse,...............291. H.918, 7
Oyle from Thy Jarre, into my creuze;............357. N.75, 2
We bid the Creuse and Pannier too:..........374. N.123, 32
Crushes When the great Crack not Crushes one, but all.
319. H.1045, 2
Crushing Whose crack gives crushing unto all......25. H.76, 4
Crust Bring the holy crust of Bread,............284. H.888, 1
Carrie nothing but a Crust:...................323. H.1065, 4
Crutch His feet were helpt, and left his Crutch behind:
201. H.555, 3
Crutches Let Crutches then provided be..........303. H.973, 3
Cry Cherrie-Ripe, Ripe, Ripe, I cry,..............19. H.53, 1
Close kisses, if she cry:........................56. H.149, 96
But cry thee Mercy: Exercise thy nailes..........66. H.173, 5
And cry out, Hey, for our town green.........127. H.319, 20
Of fresh concupiscence, and cry,..............135. H.336, 111
Drinks of distemper, or ha's cause to cry........148. H.377, 87
Rook he sells feathers, yet he still doth crie......163. H.439, 1
But being so; then the beholders cry,............172. H.459, 7
With griefe of heart, methinks, I thus doe cry,..193. H.522, 5
Now blubb'ring, cry,...........................296. H.946, 8
Then while thou laugh'st; Ile, sighing, crie,...303. H.973, 5
But when they call or cry on Grubs for meat;..325. H.1077, 3
Since I do sob and crie,.......................351. N.49, 2
These done, I'le onely crie......................352. N.53, 15
Who see, or heare poor Widdowes crie:..........373. N.123, 4
Would cry out, Thou art blessed.............375. N.123, 90
Because the Law forbad to sit and crie..........384. N.180, 3

Speak, did the Bloud of Abel **cry**................387. N.203, 1
When as the poore **crie** out, to us..............394. N.239, 3
Yawne for Thy coming; some e're this time **crie**,.398. N.263, 7
I'le call, and **cry** out, Thanks to Thee...........400. N.267, 5
Cry'd See Cried
Cryes See Cries
Crying To his Mother, said thus **crying**;..........50. H.139, 4
Bird snatcht away from th' **cryinge** child,..439. ins. H.443, 45q
Crystal And in that sincere **Christall** seek,........63. H.164, 8
Tomb'd in a **Christal** stone,.....................75. H.193, 5
Their **Christal** natures to an union...............77. H.197, 4
And with the **Christal** humour of the spring,......78. H.197, 31
In Amber, or some **Chrystall** shell,............88. H.216, 14
In their **Christall** Nunneries;.................121. H.297, 10
Enclos'd within a **christall** shrine:............135. H.336, 98
Or **Christall** grow;..........................171. H.452, 10
Some **Christall** of the Spring;.................185. H.495, 2
Fill me my Wine in **Christall**; thus, and thus...187. H.502, 1
Bearing a **Christall** continent:..................187. H.504, 2
A **Christall** Violl Cupid brought,................222. H.635, 1
The **Christall** I contemne;....................222. H.635, 10
But weep not, **Christall**; for the shame was meant.249. H.732, 3
As Lillies shrin'd in **Christall**, so..............271. H.824, 13
So Lillies thorough **Christall** look:..............294. H.939, 3
No more shall I a long thy **christall** glide,......315. H.1028, 7
Receive these **Christall** Vialls fil'd..............360. N.83, 39
Through mid'st thereof a **christall** stream there flowes
406. A.1, 75
Swelling in likenes like twoe **christall** skyes......406. A.1, 78
Crystalled Thus let this **Christal'd** Lillie be......76. H.193, 41
Crystalline White, and Heaven-like **Chrystalline**:...16. H.39, 6
Resembling shields both smooth and **christalline**....406. A.1, 80
Cuckoes See Cuckoo's
Cuckoo's Of that we call the **Cuckoes** spittle.....119. H.293, 28
Cud We not divide the Hoof, but chew the **Cud**:..397. N.256, 2
We then both chew the **Cud**, and cleave the Hoof.
397. N.256, 4
Cudgel-play There will be a **Cudgell-Play**,......255. H.761, 16
Cuff A **Cuffe** neglectfull, and thereby............28. H.83, 7
Cuffe **Cuffe** comes to Church much; but he keeps his bed
39. H.109, 1
This makes **Cuffe** dull; and troubles him the most,
39. H.109, 3
Cuffed **Cuft** with those watrie savages,...........372. N.118, 2
Culled She smil'd; he kist; and kissing, **cull'd** her too;
313. H.1017, 9
Cumber Let not the darke thee **cumber**;.........217. H.619, 11
Cumbersome And, if they do, they prove but **cumbersome**;
368. N.104, 3
Cunctation That ever prosper'd by **Cunctation**....251. H.744, 2
Cup Then this immensive **cup**...................80. H.201, 25
I took him, put him in my **cup**,.............96. H.229, 3
Thee, that great **cup** Hercules:................122. H.304, 6
From the plumpe Challice, and the **Cup**,.......127. H.319, 35
Sphering about the wassail **cup**,..............136. H.336, 148
The feast of Shepheards fail. Sil. None crowns the **cup**
159. H.421, 3
In every Geniall **Cup**,........................184. H.492, 38
And I, about the **Cup** shall see...............185. H.495, 3
Now give me the **cup**;.........................239. H.695, 2
Your **Cup**,......................................307. H.988, 2
My **Cup** can say,..............................353. N.56, 5
Even Thou alone, the bitter **cup**...............400. N.267, 8
Cupid Saw **Cupid** bitten by a flea:..............18. H.46, 2
Cupid as he lay among.......................50. H.139, 1
Cupid and his Mother lay....................74. H.190, 5
'Mongst Roses, I there **Cupid** found:...........96. H.229, 2
Love's Chorus led by **Cupid**; and we'l be......206. H.575, 22
Not a kissing **Cupid** flyes....................221. H.633, 29
A Christall Violl **Cupid** brought,..............222. H.635, 1
And thou O **Cupid**! come not to...............223. H.635, 13
Of **Cupid**, and his wittie coozning:............228. H.658, 6
'Tis said, as **Cupid** danc't among..............241. H.706, 1
Sits **Cupid** kissing of his mother Queene,......405. A.1, 56
— — — — — — — — —, ...438. var. H.337, 1
Cupids Two **Cupids** fell at odds;.................31. H.92, 2
See, a thousand **Cupids** flye,.................115. H.283, 107
Cup's In Wine, whose each **cup's** worth........80. H.201, 19
Cups They have their **Cups** and Chalices;......93. H.223, 113
Remember us in **Cups** full crown'd,...........127. H.319, 29
Give me my earthen **Cups** again,.............222. H.635, 9
What bitter **cups** had been your due,..........400. N.266, 14
Canst drincke in Earthern **Cupps**, wch ne're Contayne
422. ins. H.106, 116a
Dryed, hony-combs, Browne Achorne **cupps**
439. ins. H.443, 45j
— — — — — — — — — — —, ...442. var. H.575, 33
Cup-shot And being **cup-shot**, more he co'd not doe.
313. H.1017, 10
Cure See Re-cure
A desp'rate grief, that finds no **cure**...........60. H.157, 2
No Herbs have power to **cure** Love...........60. H.157, 4
Mine is the Evill, but the **Cure**, the Kings.....62. H.161, 16
Of my **cure**, doe you beware.................62. H.162, 17
Thy many scorns, and find no **cure**?..........74. H.191, 2
Thou cam'st to **cure** me (Doctor) of my cold,..97. H.236, 1
First cur'd thy selfe; then come and **cure** me...97. H.236, 4
As to entrance his paine, or **cure** his woe.......99. H.244, 4
And why? he knowes he must of **Cure** despaire,
125. H.315, 5
So long are capable of **cure**,...................153. H.395, 2
Cure, **cure** your selves, for I discrie,..........157. H.413, 7
The wound I suffer, never find a **cure**.........159. H.421, 34
More dangerous faintings by her desp'rate **cure**.
214. H.612, 6
Not to cut off, but **cure** the vicious part.......268. H.808, 2
A soveraign balme found out to **cure** me........274. H.841, 4
Princes **cure** some faults by their patience.....309. H.998, 2
To an old soare a long **cure** must goe on;.....312. H.1012, 1
To ease this smart, or **cure** this wound;.......342. N.17, 6
The utmost smart, so Thou wilt **cure**..........342. N.17, 12
Speak but the word, and **cure** me quite........344. N.29, 10
The **Cure** was worse then the Disease..........360. N.83, 30
Thy former coming was to **cure**...............397. N.257, 1
To **cure** the Sore...........................401. N.268, 22
Cured First **cur'd** thy selfe; then come and cure me.
97. H.236, 4
And to the Bath went, to be **cured** there:......201. H.555, 2
Is halfe way **cured**, if the party will............319. H.1048, 2
Curing To Thee, for **curing**, Balsamum:.......377. N.129, 2
Curious A **curious** Armelet........................18. H.47, 4
Not **curious** whether Appetite be fed,..........37. H.106, 107
Ah! what is then this **curious** skie,............48. H.133, 16
Of blackest silk, a **curious** twist;..............64. H.169, 2
Is here the Halcion's **curious** nest:...........90. H.223, 4
In this most **curious** Calendar..................91. H.223, 37
Grac't with the Trout-flies **curious** wings,.......92. H.223, 72
Their **curious** Copes and Surplices.............92. H.223, 98
There thou shalt have her **curious** eye:.......107. H.263, 10
Curious, and un-familiar.......................119. H.293, 4
Of **curious** Brides; or like those mites.......165. H.443, 31
flies **curious** wings; and these among.........166. H.443, 69
First, for your shape, the **curious** cannot shew..189. H.511, 1
In the ascent of **curious** Lace,...............202. H.560, 6
That the **curious** may detect..................232. H.665, 7
Then, next, to match, Tradescant's **curious** shels,
232. H.668, 3
A **curious** Rainbow smiling there;...........237. H.687, 6
Or **curious** Wilson: Tell me, canst thou be...276. H.851, 5
And let such **curious** Net-works be.............282. H.881, 9
May all clean Nimphs and **curious** water Dames,
316. H.1028, 17
He did His **curious** operation;...................396. N.249, 4
Curious-comely A **curious-comely** clean Compartlement:
227. H.652, 8
Curled **Curld** and comely, and so trimme,.......125. H.314, 7
Curlew The Cock, the **Curlew**, and the quaile;...147. H.377, 66
Curls Still with your **curles**, and kisse the time away.
15. H.38, 2
My **curles** about her neck did craule,.........16. H.41, 14
I sho'd delight to have my **Curles** halfe drown'd.214. H.612, 11
Then maids shall strew Thee, and thy **Curles** from them
254. H.756, 17
Upon my **curles** the Mirtle Coronet,...........335. H.1128, 2
Currish A people **currish**; churlish as the seas;..29. H.86, 11
Keeping no **currish** Waiter to affright,.........147. H.377, 47
Curse Thy Fiers from me; but Apollo's **curse**...79. H.197, 83
Curse not the mice, no grist of thine they eat:.141. H.358, 1
But **curse** thy children, they consume thy wheat.
141. H.358, 2
A **curse** to Thee, or Thine; but all things even.149. H.377, 129
When drunck wth Rapture; **Curse** the blind & lame
412. A.3, 89
Cursed I **curst** the master; and I damn'd the souce;
262. H.783, 19
More **curst** for singing out of tune then he.....266. H.799, 4
— — — — — — — — — — —, ...436. var. H.336, 12
Cursed-cypress Save only the **Curst-Cipresse** tree:
132. H.336, 12
Curtains See Cob-web-curtains
Drawing thy **curtains** round: Good night.....146. H.376, 14
Ile have no Sceans, or **Curtains** drawn:........154. H.402, 2
Curtsey Teach it to blush, to **curtsie**, lisp, and shew
290. H.914, 5
Curtsies With reverend **Curtsies** come, and to him bring
286. H.898, 7
Custard For second course, last night, a **Custard** came
47. H.131, 1
Upon the **Custard**, and thus cooled so:........47. H.131, 4
As here a **Custard**, there a Pie,..............101. H.250, 33
Custards Tarts and **Custards**, Creams and Cakes,
255. H.761, 3
Customs All Nations, **Customes**, Kindreds, Languages!
242. H.713, 10
Who violates the **Customes**, hurts the Health,..318. H.1041, 1
Cut Or **cut**, if **cut** by you......................18. H.47, 12
That neither haire was **cut**, or true teares shed.27. H.82, 3
Let them not **cut** the thred..................58. H.149, 163
Those silver-pence, that **cut** the tongue........166. H.443, 70
Cut off thy haires; and let thy Teares be shed..219. H.627, 3
Cut the white loafe here,......................263. H.784, 14
Not to **cut** off, but cure the vicious part........268. H.808, 2

Is cut, that made us clothing.................374. N.123, 40
The poore to cut, and I to chuse,...........376. N.127, 8
Cuts Good Sir, make no more cuts i'th' outward skin, 44. H.126, 3
Guesse cuts his shooes, and limping, goes about..98. H.239, 1
If wounds in clothes, Cuts calls his rags, 'tis cleere, 144. H.373, 1
Best and more suppling piece he cuts, and by.147. H.377, 51
As some plants prosper best by cuts and blowes; 292. H.929, 3
— — — — — — — — — — —, ...440. var. H.443, 70
Cut'st O time that cut'st down all!.............85. H.211, 9
Cutting The cutting Thumb-naile, or the Brow severe. 212. H.603, 2
Cyane Chaste Syracusian Cyane...............175. H.465, 58
Cynamon See Cinnamon
Cynoe — — — — — — — — —, ...441. var. H.465, 58
Cynthius Cynthius pluck ye by the eare,........52. H.147, 1
Cyonë — — — — — — — —, ...441. var. H.465, 58
Cypress See Cursed-cypress
And look, what Smallage, Night-shade, Cypresse, Yew, 27. H.82, 9
Under that Cypresse tree:...................109. H.267, 18
Comes with his Cypresse, and devotes a teare?.288. H.907, 2
— — — — — — — — — — —, ...436. var. H.336, 12
Cypress-sprig Adde a Cypresse-sprig thereto,......89. H.220, 3

Dabbled — — — — — — — — —, ...438. var. H.412, 4
Dace The flying Pilcher, and the frisking Dace,...155. H.405, 11
Daff Daffe nuts, soft Jewes eares, and some thin 439. ins. H.443, 45f
Daffodil When a Daffadill I see,...............38. H.107, 1
Sickly the Prim-rose: Pale the Daffadill:.....41. H.118, 2
The Daffadill,..............................359. N.83, 10
Daffodils Daffadills g'en up to Thee...........122. H.304, 8
Faire Daffadills, we weep to see.............125. H.316, 1
With Daisies spread, and Daffadils;..........192. H.521, 16
With Daffadils and Daisies crown'd..........230. H.662, 51
The Tulips, Lillies, Daffadills do stoop;.......320. H.1054, 4
Of Daffadills, and Roses;...................345. N.33, 12
Dagger Give Thee a Dart, and Dagger too;......349. N.46, 4
Daily Nor are thy daily and devout affaires....36. H.106, 63
This we will doe; we'll daily come............89. H.219, 9
By daily Learning we wax old................187. H.505, 2
With daily Fyers: The last, neglect of Wine:..197. H.539, 10
Into the daily offering......................291. H.919, 2
Shall I a daily Begger be,...................312. H.1014, 1
Besides ye see me daily grow.................329. H.1093, 3
Gods Grace deserves here to be daily fed,....378. N.132, 1
Dainties My dearest daintyes, nay, 'tis the principall: 426. ins. H.197, 48b
Dainty Many dainty Mistresses:.................15. H.39, 2
Enthrall'd my dainty Lucia....................16. H.41, 4
Of soft and dainty Maiden-haire,...............18. H.47, 3
In each thy dainty, and peculiar part!..........30. H.88, 2
These, and sowre herbs, as dainty meat?.......37. H.106, 114
You are a dainty Violet,.....................88. H.216, 16
And blesse his dainty Mistresse: see,.........114. H.283, 63
Of the most sweet and dainty Bride,..........120. H.293, 50
Brought in a dainty daizie, which............120. H.293, 51
You, the brisk Bridegroome, you the dainty Bride. 124. H.313, 6
To kisse your hand, most Dainty Governesse....137. H.341, 12
Fain would I kiss my Julia's dainty Leg,......139. H 349, 1
Cloud-like, the daintie Deitie.................167. H.443, 99
And dainty Amarillis,........................184. H.492, 30
By dainty things undo me...................279. H.863, 8
She with a dainty blush rebuk't her face;.....311. H.1006, 3
Daintye tast for ladyes food..................418. A.9, 22
Dairies Next, may your Dairies Prosper so,......179. H.476, 10
Wash your Pailes, and clense your Dairies;...201. H.556, 5
Daisies If Sapho droop; Daisies will open never,...41. H.118, 7
Daysies wo'd shut, and closing, sigh and weep..159. H.421, 26
With Daisies spread, and Daffadils;..........192. H.521, 16
With Daffadils and Daisies crown'd...........230. H.662, 51
Daisy Brought in a dainty daizie, which........120. H.293, 51
Balls of Cowslips, Daisie rings,...............306. H.984, 25
Dales And dales again: Mir. No I will languish still; 159. H.421, 36
Thou leav'st our Hills, our Dales, our Bowers,..183. H.492, 13
Dam Whose Dam...........................246. H.724, 19
Damascene God (as the learned Damascen doth write) 381. N.161, 1
Damask Breathe as the Damask Rose:.........57. H.149, 144
'Fore Damask Roses..........................83. H.205, 12
Or Damask Roses, when they grow...........271. H.824, 15
The figur'd Damask, or pure Diaper,..........355. N.65, 2
Each cheeke resembling still a damaske rose,....404. A.1, 14
— — — — — — — — — — —, ...421. var. H.106, 43
Damasked The Damaskt medowes, and the peebly streames 35. H.106, 43
With little Seale-work Damasked.............91. H.223, 63
Dame While my good Dame, she...............263. H.784, 4
Dames May all clean Nimphs and curious water Dames, 316. H.1028, 17
Damnation — — — — — — — — —, ...432. var. H.283, 140
Damned As, could they hear, the Damn'd would make no noise, 22. H.67, 2
Vexation of the mind, and damn'd Despaire...45. H.128, 22
I curst the master; and I damn'd the souce;...262. H.783, 19
Damns And halfe damns me with untruth;......348. N.41, 39
D'Amour The youthfull Prince D'Amour here....63. H.166, 8
Damp Or in the dampe Jet read their Teares....149. H.377, 126
Dampish In the dead of dampish night...........177. H.473, 6
His dampish Buttocks furthermore to cloath:..226. H.650, 2
Damps Where all Damps, and Mists are found?.40. H.115, 6
Danae Kept as close as Danae was:.............14. H.36, 5
Ye Towre her up, as Danae was;.............116. H.283, 144
Kept, as Danae in a Tower:..................120. H.297, 4
Dance See House-dance, Morris-dance
Come down, and dance ye in the toyle..........9. H.15, 1
Drink, and dance, and pipe, and play;..........39. H.111, 3
To dance and play in: (Trust me) there........49. H.136, 22
To dance and caper on the heads of flowers,....78. H.197, 52
Ye dance, and sing, and now clap hands........94. H.225, 8
To dance the Heyes with nimble feet;.......192. H.521, 30
Where both may rage, both drink and dance together. 206. H.575, 38
That luckie Fairies here may dance their Round:.245. H.723, 8
— — — — — — — — — — —, ...433. var. H.293, 8
Danced Ships have been drown'd, where late they danc't before. 85. H.212, 2
Daunc't by the Streames.......................181. H.484, 8
And having danc't ('bove all the best).........192. H.521, 33
'Tis said, as Cupid danc't among............241. H.706, 1
Dancers See Morris-dancers
Dances Nor daunces in the eye...............75. H.193, 10
Dancing And dancing 'bout the Mystick Thyrse,.136. H.336, 135
The dancing Frier, tatter'd in the bush;.......155. H.405, 7
Then unto Dancing forth the learned Round...206. H.575, 19
To exercise their dancing feet:...............230. H.662, 49
Untill the dancing Easter-day,................285. H.892, 7
Dandelions Upon six plump Dandillions, high-..167. H.443, 86
Dandled Dandled the ringlets of her haire.......51. H.142, 12
Whom whitest Fortune dandled has too much..239. H.697, 2
Danger The sudden danger of a Rape............37. H.106, 126
Danger to give the best advice to Kings.......318. H.1037, 2
Charmes the danger, and the dread...........323. H.1065, 6
Dangerous More dangerous faintings by her desp'rate cure. 214. H.612, 6
Danger's Some private pinch tels danger's nie..147. H.377, 52
Her tongue, to tell what danger's neare.......246. H.724, 16
Dangers Will from all dangers, re-deliver me,.....14. H.35, 7
And watrie dangers; while thy whiter hap,....36. H.106, 71
For Sceva, darts; for Cocles, dangers; thus....370. N.108, 5
Dangling But walks with dangling breeches,.....259. H.772, 18
It ever dangling smil'd i' th' aire..............418. A.9, 26
— — — — — — — — — — —, ...442. var. H.575, 20
Daphe — — — — — — — —, ...428. var. H.197, 92
Daphne Ne'r may Prophetique Daphne crown my Brow. 79. H.197, 92
Give me the Daphne, that the world may know it, 143. H.365, 7
Dapper And many a dapper Chorister...........92. H.223, 104
Dardanium About thy wrist, the rich *Dardanium. 30. H.88, 8
Dare And I dare sweare, that I am gray?......63. H.164, 2
And beat ye so, (as some dare say)...........105. H.260, 7
Or bid me die, and I will dare...............109. H.267, 19
If I dare write to You, my Lord, who are,....187. H.506, 1
I dare not ask a kisse;......................231. H.663, 1
I dare not beg a smile;......................231. H.663, 2
Like thee; or dare the Buskins to unloose......234. H.673, 11
(I dare not call ye Sweepers)................235. H.674, 14
We know they dare not beate us;.............259. H.772, 8
But trust me now I dare not say,.............288. H.908, 5
Since mischiefs neither dare..................373. N.122, 11
So that I dare, with farre lesse feare,..........402. N.269, 8
— — — — — — — — — — —, ...433. var. H.293, 14
Dared Th'ast dar'd too farre; but Furie now forbeare 82. H.204, 1
Dares Give me that man, that dares bestride......30. H.90, 1
Let him come, who dares undo her...........114. H.283, 100
That dares to dead the fire of martirdome:.....128. H.323, 2
Dares now range the wood;..................225. H.643, 14
But unamaz'd dares clearely sing,............318. H.1036, 3
— — — — — — — — — — —, ...451. var. H.197, 47
Darest When thou thy selfe dar'st say, thy Iles shall lack 78. H.197, 47
Daring Which, in full force, did daring stand,.370. N.107, 8
Dark Dark was the Jayle; but as if light.......64. H.169, 5
And dark; let us meet;.......................195. H.534, 2
Let not the darke thee cumber;..............217. H.619, 11
(When drunke with Beere) to light him home, i'th' dark. 273. H.834, 4
Jone as my Lady is as good i'th' dark.........279. H.864, 2
So utter dark, as that no eye.................357. N.72, 7
Dark and dull night, flie hence away,...........364. N.96, 8
And while we blunder in the dark,.............372. N.118, 7
Along the dark, and silent night,.............372. N.121, 1
Or e're dark Clouds do dull, or dead the Mid-dayes Sun. 401. N.268, 9

But now my muse hath spi'de a darke descent..405. A.1, 65
Darken — — — — — — — — —, ...425. var. H.197, 12
Darkness Nor has the darknesse power to usher in
35. H.106, 39
In dennes of Darkness, or condemn'd to die....63. H.165, 4
Or so, as Darknesse made a stay............64. H.169, 7
May in like Chains of Darknesse lie..........64. H.169, 12
In utter darkenes did, and still will sit.......150. H.382, 18
And dismall Darknesse then doth smutch the face.
207. H.576, 6
And for my house I darknesse have?..........361. N.84, 4
Darling The Darling of the world is come,......365. N.96, 25
Dar'st See Darest
Dart Not that I thinke, that any Dart,..........10. H.20, 4
Of those, thou woundest with thy Dart!........50. H.139, 15
'Twas not Lov's Dart;.......................161. H.426, 1
Thou sayest Loves Dart......................273. H.833, 1
His finger was the dart.....................295. H.942, 16
Give Thee a Dart, and Dagger too;.............349. N.46, 4
— — — — — — — — — —, ...425. var. H.197, 12
Darts See Eye-darts, Out-darts
Then when he darts his radiant beams........75. H.193, 20
For Sceva, darts; for Cocles, dangers; thus...370. N.108, 5
Till they be hid o're with a wood of darts......370. N.109, 2
For through these Optickes, fly the dartes.....408. A.2, 37
Dash Dash all bad Poems out of countenance...187. H.506, 10
Is, when loves hony has a dash of gall........327. H.1084, 2
— — — — — — — — — — — —, ...425. var. H.197, 12
Dastards Necessity makes dastards valiant men...333. H.1118, 2
Date Me longer date, and more fresh springs to live:
140. H.355, 12
Your date is not so past;.....................176. H.467, 3
— — — — — — — — — — — —, ...422. var. H.106, 113
Date's When my date's done, and my gray age must die;
40. H.112, 1
Daughter One onely daughter lent to me:.......41. H.116, 4
The voices Daughter nea'r spake syllable......159. H.421, 28
Daughter's My daughters Dowrye; haueing which
407. A.2, 5
Daughters As Daughters to the instant yeare:....127. H.319, 40
The Daughters wild and loose in dresse;.......310. H.1004, 7
Of Daughters all, the Deerest Deere;..........360. N.83, 14
Ah! Sions Daughters, do not feare............400. N.266, 7
Daulian The while the Daulian Minstrell sweetly sings,
224. H.642, 7
Dauntless Kings must be dauntlesse: Subjects will contemne
330. H.1097, 1
Dawn Like to a Twi-light, or that simpring Dawn,
34. H.104, 3
Which done, that Dawne, turnes then to perfect day.
34. H.104, 6
Warnes the last Watch; but with the Dawne dost rise
36. H.106, 57
Faire was the Dawne; and but e'ne now the Skies
81. H.202, 1
Dawning The happy dawning of her thigh:......51. H.142, 16
The Last Watch out, and saw the Dawning too..52. H.146, 4
Till the Dawning of the day:.................199. H.549, 2
Day See Doomsday, Easter-day, Long-life's-day, Mid-day, Noon-day, Quarter-day, To-day, Twelfth-day, Welladay.
Well may my Book come forth like Publique Day
3. Ded.H, 1
O Primroses! let this day be...................7. H.9, 5
Me, day by day, to steale away from thee?.......9. H.14, 2
When that day comes, whose evening sayes I'm gone
14. H.35, 1
Love and my selfe (beleeve me) on a day.......17. H.44, 1
Faults done by night, will blush by day:......20. H.56, 6
Here we are all, by day; By night w'are hurl'd..21. H.57, 1
Which done, that Dawne, turnes then to perfect day.
34. H.104, 6
With those deeds done by day, which ne'r affright
35. H.106, 37
Nor feare, or wish your dying day............38. H.106, 146
Kisse our Dollies night and day:.............39. H.111, 4
What times of sweetnesse this faire day fore-shows,
44. H.124, 1
He weares all day, and drawes those teeth at night.
46. H.129, 6
The lid began to let out day;.................46. H.130, 9
And more then well becomes the day?..........48. H.136, 3
Never was Day so over-sick with showres,....52. H.146, 1
Wherein or Light, or Day, did never peep......52. H.146, 6
By day, and night on you.....................57. H.149, 156
The Rose, the Violet, one day.................61. H.159, 15
Know, Lady, you have but your day:..........63. H.164, 3
To shew at once, both night and day..........64. H.169, 8
This day Ile drowne all sorrow;..............65. H.170, 5
When as a thousand Virgins on this day,.....68. H.178, 13
Besides, the childhood of the Day has kept,....68. H.178, 21
There's not a budding Boy, or Girle, this day,.69. H.178, 43
As soone dispatcht is by the Night, as Day.....73. H.186, 4
Mony thou ow'st me; Prethee fix a day..........83. H.206, 1
And this same flower that smiles to day,.......84. H.208, 3
Amin. Good day, Mirtillo. Mirt. And to you no lesse:
85. H.213, 1
Or that this day Menalchas keeps a feast......86. H.213, 7
(With whitest Wool be ever crown'd that day!).86. H.213, 14
At Noone of Day, was seene a silver Star,...86. H.213, 20
Good speed, for I this day....................87. H.214, 1
You are a Tulip seen to day,.................87. H.216, 1
Gave her a day of Coronation;..................94. H.224, 6
Which, by the peepe of day, doe strew........95. H.227, 25
Love on a day (wise Poets tell)...............105. H.260, 1
But Venus having lost the day,...............105. H.260, 5
What's that we see from far? the spring of Day..112. H.283, 1
This the short'st day, and this the longest night;
114. H.283, 72
My Masters all, Good day to you..............121. H.299, 8
Untill the hasting day........................125. H.316, 6
Of what can hurt by day, or harme by night:..128. H.323, 10
Day with the white and Luckie stone..........133. H.336, 40
While sweet-breath Nimphs, attend on you this Day.
140. H.354, 8
Paske, though his debt be due upon the day......142. H.363, 1
Birds chuse their Mates, and couple too, this day:
149. H.378, 2
'Tis but as day a kindling:....................154. H.404, 2
'Tis then broad Day throughout the East.......154. H.404, 4
Skinns he din'd well to day; how do you think?
156. H.409, 1
Jolly and Jillie, bite and scratch all day,......156. H.411, 1
The reason is, though all the day they fight,...156. H.411, 3
Good morrow to the Day so fair;..............156. H.412, 1
Sweet Bents wode bow, to give my Love the day:
159. H.421, 24
Mont. Set with the Sunne, thy woes: Scil. The day grows old:
160. H.421, 41
Perfum'd (last day) to me:...................161. H.425, 2
No glaring light of bold-fac't Day,............167. H.443, 76
But ever doubtfull Day, or night..............167. H.443, 81
Co'd life return, 'twod never lose a day.........171. H.453, 2
With the Rotation of the Day.................172. H.457, 4
From the blast that burns by day;.............177. H.473, 4
For good luck in love (that day.)..............183. H.490, 16
To be another day re-worne,...................190. H.515, 41
This day, the Queen-Priest, thou art made t'appease
197. H.539, 5
But before that day comes,...................197. H.540, 5
The Month, the Week, the instant Day........198. H.544, 22
Till the Dawning of the day:..................199. H.549, 2
Once on a Lord-Mayors day, in Cheapside, when
200. H.551, 1
Purfling the Margents, while perpetuall Day....206. H.575, 14
Or Day break from the pregnant East, 'tis time.207. H.575, 64
So spend some minutes of the day:............215. H.616, 6
This day is Loves day; and this busie night..216. H.618, 9
Happy day....................................220. H.633, 5
All things have an ending day:...............224. H.639, 2
Who all the day themselves doe please,........231. H.662, 72
Let her Lucrece all day be,....................232. H.665, 15
To rise as soon as day doth peep?............233. H.670, 2
And thus lesse last, then live our Day........233. H.670, 31
Thousands each day passe by, which wee,......234. H.671, 1
But at push-pin (half the day:)...............235. H.678, 4
Thou'dst weep; but laugh, sho'd it not last a day.
241. H.709, 2
To see the day spring from the pregnant East,....242. H.713, 2
'Tis not ev'ry day, that I......................242. H.714, 1
That fits the businesse of the Day.............243. H.716, 4
Give me the prize: 2. The day is mine:.......244. H.716, 43
I have, to sing how day drawes on............246. H.724, 4
I keep, which creeking day by day,...........246. H.724, 10
A sullen day will cleere againe...............247. H.725, 8
While young Charles fights, and fighting wins the day.
254. H.756, 14
Neer the dying of the day,....................255. H.761, 15
To him, who is the triumph of the day,........256. H.763, 4
Of this or that great Aprill day shall be,........257. H.763, 19
That done, they kisse, and so draw out the day:.260. H.773, 2
This day my Julia thou must make............267. H.805, 1
This Day is Yours, Great CHARLES! and in this War
271. H.823, 1
By the next kindling of the day...............271. H.824, 1
But she has decreed a day....................276. H.848, 2
Cheerfull day shall spring agen................276. H.850, 8
T'ave your blushes seen by day...............276. H.850, 14
Then the last part of night, and first of day.....278. H.858, 2
This day I goe to wooe;......................281. H.874, 7
My soule would one day goe and seeke........281. H.876, 1
A cleare will come after a cloudy day..........293. H.930, 2
Peacefull by night; my day devoid of strife:....294. H.938, 2
On me all day,................................296. H.945, 5
Next day......................................308. H.993, 28
Buggins is Drunke all night, all day he sleepes;.311. H.1011, 1
Make her this day smile on me,...............313. H.1018, 3
Ye must on S. Distaffs day:..................315. H.1026, 2
Then Night now gone, and yet not sprung the Day.
319. H.1046, 2
And though we bid adieu to day,.............324. H.1068, 23
When a cleare day, out of a Cloud do's break...324. H.1072, 2

After a **day**, or two, or three,.................328. H.1090, 4
That I must go this **day**:.....................328. H.1091, 4
There give me **day**; but here my dreadfull night:
343. N.25, 7
What need there then be of a reckning **day**:.....343. N.27, 2
Her egg each **day**:............................350. N.47, 46
And **day**, by **day**,............................353. N.56, 4
Drown'd in one endlesse **Day**.................354. N.58, 12
That I might see the cheerfull peeping **day**.....358. N.77, 7
Lamented Maid! he won the **day**,.............360. N.83, 23
And give the honour to this **Day**,...............364. N.96, 9
Woe worth the Time, woe worth the **day**,.......374. N.123, 21
That ne're went out by **Day** or Night:........374. N.123, 46
By peep of **day**,..............................374. N.123, 49
Let not that **Day** Gods Friends and Servants scare:
376. N.126, 1
God hides from man the reck'ning **Day**, that He.379. N.142, 1
Expect the coming of it ev'ry **day**.............379. N.142, 4
God in His own **Day** will be then severe,.......381. N.156, 1
That in this world, one onely **day**..............388. N.206, 2
Teares, at that **day**, shall make but weake defence;
392. N.230, 27
But look how night succeeds the **day**, so He....394. N.236, 3
And when He blest each sev'rall **Day**, whereon..396. N.249, 3
God blest His work done on the second **day**:...396. N.249, 6
That must this **day** act the Tragedian,.........398. N.263, 20
For, long this work wil be, & very short this **Day**.
401. N.268, 6
As yow haue done yo[r] **day**,.......................413. A.4, 8
To vs the **day**...................................413. A.4, 22
But here's the Sun-set of a Tedious **day**:........419. A.10, 6
Daylight — — — — — — — —, ...437. var. H.336, 76
Day's **See Mid-day's**
So that an Angler, for a **daies** expence,........282. H.879, 3
Of thrice-boyl'd-worts, or third **dayes** fish;....321. H.1056, 12
Days **See Holy-days, Mid-days**
Lastly, with friends t'enjoy our **dayes**...........42. H.121, 4
And of those evill **dayes** that be...............47. H.132, 11
On your minutes, hours, **dayes**, months, years,..57. H.149, 151
Our life is short; and our **dayes** run..........69. H.178, 61
Daies may conclude in nights; and Suns may rest,
72. H.185, 5
Three **dayes** before the shutting in of May,.....86. H.213, 13
And offers Incense Nights and **dayes**,..........93. H.223, 130
His **dayes** to see a second Spring..............133. H.336, 24
Two **dayes** y'ave larded here; a third, yee know,
146. H.377, 25
Old Parson Beanes hunts six **dayes** of the week,.163. H.435, 1
Six **dayes** he hollows so much breath away,......163. H.435, 3
Faire and foule **dayes** trip Crosse and Pile; The faire
189. H.513, 1
Far lesse in number, then our foule **dayes** are...189. H.513, 2
For those good **dayes** that ne'r will come away...204. H.570, 2
By noone, and let thy good **dayes** passe,.......233. H.670, 4
Green, to the end of **dayes**.....................261. H.778, 12
For the evill evill **dayes**.......................267. H.806, 4
Unto the end of **daies**.........................281. H.874, 15
Look how our foule **Dayes** do exceed our faire;.339. N.1, 1
O thou, the wonder of all **dayes**!.............359. N.83, 1
What though my healthfull **dayes** are fled,......361. N.84, 5
So, here the remnant of my **dayes** I'd spend,....371. N.115, 11
The first of Time, or Sabbath here of **Dayes**;....386. N.194, 2
That did ordaine the Fast of forty **Dayes**........386. N.195, 2
A multitude of **dayes** still heaped on,...........392. N.230, 7
Dead **See Under-dead**
Dead when I am, first cast in salt, and bring.....9. H.14, 7
Down **dead** for grief, and end my woes withall:..11. H.22, 8
Give my **dead** picture one engendring kisse:....14. H.35, 12
Laid out for **dead**, let thy last kindnesse be.....19. H.50, 1
Better 'twere my Book were **dead**,.............21. H.59, 5
First, for Effusions due unto the **dead**,..........23. H.72, 1
By me, o'r thee, (as justments to the **dead**)......27. H.82, 4
To strike him **dead**, that but usurps a Thorne....32. H.97, 6
Secondly, I shall be **dead**;......................38. H.107, 5
Rouze Anacreon from the **dead**;..................39. H.111, 9
The gaines must **dead** the feare of detriment....42. H.120, 2
Do restless run when they are **dead**..............44. H.127, 10
And seeing her not **dead**, but all disleav'd;......46. H.130, 11
When you shall see that I am **dead**,...........61. H.159, 22
Dead to all compassion..........................62. H.162, 12
And lik'st the best? Still thou reply'st, The **dead**..66. H.174, 2
As **dead**, within the West;.......................72. H.185, 6
Dead thee to th' most, if not destroy thee all...82. H.204, 12
And since the last is **dead**, there's hope,........93. H.223, 111
Phill, the late **dead**, the late **dead** Deare,.......104. H.256, 8
And for this **dead** which under-lies,...........104. H.256, 13
When once the Lovers Rose is **dead**,...........106. H.262, 5
Dead falls the Cause, if once the Hand be mute;.123. H.308, 1
That dares to **dead** the fire of martirdome:....128. H.323, 2
We two are **dead**,.............................133. H.336, 35
How dull and **dead** are books, that cannot show.141. H.359, 1
In me, is **dead** or ceast......................144. H.371, 6
Pray hurt him not; though he be **dead**,......157. H.412, 21
As a Drink-offering, to the **dead**:..............169. H.449, 20
Thee live, as **dead** and in thy grave;..........174. H.465, 12
In the **dead** of dampish night..................177. H.473, 6

Dead, and closed up in Yvorie.................186. H.497, 18
Your Child lyes still, yet is not **dead**:.........189. H.514, 6
Where all Desires are **dead**, or cold............190. H.515, 15
As to bind up her chaps when she is **dead**......205. H.571, 4
The Proper Lessons for the Saints now **dead**:...209. H.584, 2
Dead when thou art, Deare Julia, thou shalt have
209. H.584, 5
Who **dead**, deserve our best remembrances......209. H.584, 8
Leaving here the body **dead**:..................211. H.593, 2
Dull to my selfe, and almost **dead** to these.....214. H.612, 1
And once more yet (ere I am laid out **dead**)...214. H.612, 13
Seldome comes Glorie till a man be **dead**......218. H.623, 2
Reproach we may the living; not the **dead**:....218. H.625, 1
Or credit ye, when I am **dead**?................218. H.626, 4
He'l never haunt ye now he's **dead**.............226. H.644, 10
At last, when prayers for the **dead**,..........237. H.686, 13
For, once **dead**, and laid i' th' grave,..........238. H.691, 5
An Orphan left him (lately **dead**.).............246. H.724, 20
Strikes me **dead** as any stone?.................254. H.757, 6
Who at a **dead** lift,............................256. H.762, 13
Beere small as Comfort, **dead** as Charity........262. H.783, 16
Dead the Fire, though ye blow.................263. H.786, 4
When all now **dead** shall re-appeare............265. H.794, 6
Lightly, lightly ore the **dead**.................274. H.838, 8
Thou hast made many Houses for the **Dead**;..277. H.853, 1
By the **dead** bones of our deare Ancestrie......278. H.860, 8
Where love begins, there **dead** thy first desire:..281. H.873, 1
Dead all black contingencies:..................286. H.897, 8
Weepe for the **dead**, for they have lost this light:
298. H.952, 1
If but lookt on; struck **dead**, if scan'd by Thee..301. H.962, 6
Then the **dead** Corps, or carkase of the Wine...301. H.964, 2
Now thou art **dead**, no eye shall ever see,.......302. H.967, 1
He who wears Blacks, and mournes not for the **Dead**,
319. H.1047, 1
In Den'-shire Kerzie Lusk (when he was **dead**).332. H.1114, 1
Thou kil'st with heate, and I strike **dead** with cold.
333. H.1120, 2
The Muses will weare blackes, when I am **dead**..335. H.1128, 6
When a mans Faith is frozen up, as **dead**;.....359. N.80, 1
No more, no more, since thou art **dead**,......360. N.83, 49
'Tis we are **dead**, though not i' th grave:......361. N.83, 57
And I lie numbred with the **dead**?.............361. N.84, 6
For, this is sure, the Debt is **dead**.............370. N.107, 14
For Tabitha, who **dead** lies here,..............374. N.123, 11
Thou being **dead**,.............................374. N.123, 38
And though thou here li'st **dead**, we see........375. N.123, 71
The monuments of Dorcas **dead**................375. N.123, 84
But 'twas not till their dearest Lord was **dead**;.384. N.180, 11
And bring our Spices, to embalm Thee **dead**;....399. N.263, 38
Or e're dark Clouds do dull, or **dead** the Mid-dayes Sun.
401. N.268, 9
Deadly Fainting swoones, and **deadly** sweats;....102. H.253, 8
A **deadly** draught in them.....................222. H.635, 12
Skoles stinks so **deadly**, that his Breeches loath.226. H.650, 1
Deads One drop now **deads** a spark; but if the same
40. H.113, 3
But o'racted **deads** the pleasure..............276. H.850, 6
Deaf Nor are thine eares so **deafe**, but thou canst heare
36. H.106, 83
Of teeth, as **deaf** as nuts, and all her own.......232. H.668, 6
— — — — — — — — —, ...439. ins. H.443, 45f
Deal A **deale** of courage in each bosome springs..25. H.77, 9
A **deale** of Youth, ere this, is come............69. H.178, 45
But if my **deal**.................................171. H.455, 7
Ph. A **deale** of Love, and much, much Griefe together.
248. H.730, 14
And a **deale** of nightly feare..................263. H.785, 7
Do with me, God! as Thou didst **deal** with John,
343. N.25, 1
The Bits, the Morsells, and the **deale**...........374. N.123, 24
A **deale** of beauty yet in thee..................375. N.123, 72
Dealing In **dealing** forth these bashfull jealousies:
113. H.283, 52
You shall; if righteous **dealing** I find there......136. H.338, 2
Dealt But temp'rate mirth **dealt** forth, and so discreet-
148. H.377, 79
Dean-Bourn **Dean-bourn**, farewell; I never look to see
29. H.86, 1
Deane **Deane**, or thy warty incivility.............29. H.86, 2
Dear If **deare** Anthea, my hard fate it be.........11. H.22, 1
Wherein thou liv'st for ever. **Deare** farewell......23. H.72, 4
(**Deare**) to undoe me;..........................32. H.94, 10
Deare, though to part it be a Hell,............33. H.103, 1
Farewell thou Thing, time-past so knowne, so **deare**
45. H.128, 1
So neare, or **deare**, as thou wast once to me.....45. H.128, 10
Deare, is it this you dread,...................53. H.149, 13
Before, my **deare** Perilla, I will be..............59. H.154, 9
And last, when thee (**deare** Spouse) I disavow,..79. H.197, 91
Griefe, (my **deare** friend) has first my Harp unstrung;
84. H.210, 9
But **dear** Amintas, and sweet Amarillis,.........86. H.213, 9
Amar. But **deare** Mirtillo, I have heard it told,.86. H.213, 29
Deare Perenna, prethee come,..................89. H.220, 1
Phill, the late dead, the late dead **Deare**,.......104. H.256, 8

But being poore, and knowing Flesh is **deare,**..122. H.305, 5
Dear, in thy bed of Roses, then,................146. H.376, 11
Dear Amarillis! Mon. Hark! Sil. mark: Mir. this earth grew sweet......................159. H.421, 11
By **deare** S. Iphis; and the rest,................169. H.449, 24
Dear Lycidas, e're long,.........................184. H.492, 26
If thou aske me (**Deare**) wherefore...........186. H.500, 1
Dead when thou art, **Deare** Julia, thou shalt have 209. H.584, 5
But walk'st about thine own **dear** bounds,......230. H.662, 15
And no man payes too **deare** for it............231. H.662, 61
If thou, my **Deere,** a winner be..............238. H.690, 5
Princes and Fav'rites are most **deere,** while they 255. H.758, 1
Deare, can you like, and liking love your Poet?.274. H.837, 5
By the dead bones of our **deare** Ancestrie......278. H.860, 8
That to me was far more **deer**..................305. H.984, 16
I, and kil'd my **dear** delight.................306. H.984, 35
Of my dearest **deare** last night;...............313. H.1018, 2
The while my **deer** Anthea do's but droop,.....320. H.1054, 3
By Thee, **Deare** God, God gives man seed....358. N.75, 7
Of Daughters all, the Deerest **Deere**;........360. N.83, 14
Too soon, too **deere** did Jephthah buy,........360. N.83, 19
Deer God,.......................................363. N.92, 1
May Roses grow, to crown His own **deare** Head..366. N.97, 23
God suffers not His Saints, and Servants **deere,**.394. N.236, 1
Fail'd in my part; O! Thou that art my **deare,**.398. N.261, 2
And O! **Deare** Christ,..........................401. N.268, 24
Of offending, Temperance, **Deare**.................409. A.2, 98
— — — — — — — — — —, ...422. var. H.106, 112
How long, soft bride, shall your **deare** C: make 431. ins. H.283, 60a
— — — — — — — — — —, ...449. var. A.3, 99
— — — — — — — — — —, ...451. ins. H.336, 48h
Dearer — — — — — — — —, ...427. ins. H.197, 48b
Dearest Who was thy servant. **Dearest,** bury me...20. H.55, 3
And Love will swear't, my **Dearest** did not so..42. H.122, 12
But (**Dearest**) of so short a stay;.............87. H.216, 2
Prue, my **dearest** Maid, is sick,...............122. H.302, 1
(My **dearest** Crew,)..............................161. H.426, 9
To thee, (my **dearest** Shepharling)..............192. H.521, 36
When I consider (**Dearest**) thou dost stay....193. H.522, 1
And rare, Ile say (my **dearest** Crew)...........217. H.620, 11
Dearest of thousands, now the time drawes neere, 219. H.627, 1
One night i' th' yeare, my **dearest** Beauties, come 222. H.634, 1
Then ever, **dearest** Silvia, yet..................240. H.705, 7
Now is your turne (my **Dearest**) to be set....264. H.789, 1
Blowes make of **dearest** friends immortall Foes..287. H.901, 2
As **dearest** Peace, after destructive Warre:....300. H.961, 2
Of my **dearest** deare last night;...............313. H.1018, 2
My **dearest** Love, since thou wilt go,...........323. H.1068, 1
Believe it (**dearest**) ther's not one............324. H.1068, 19
That done, my Julia, **dearest** Julia, come,......329. H.1095, 5
Of Daughters all, the **Deerest** Deere;.........360. N.83, 14
Thy **Deerest** Saviour renders thee but one......371. N.112, 3
But 'twas not till their **dearest** Lord was dead;..384. N.180, 11
Justly our **dearest** Saviour may abhorre us,......388. N.209, 1
My **dearest** daintyes, nay, 'tis the principall; 426. ins. H.197, 48b
Dearly **Deerely** I lov'd thee; as my first-borne child: 6. H.3, 2
Dearth To numb the sence of **Dearth,** which sho'd sinne haste it, 37. H.106, 119
Death Love to the **death** will pine,.............31. H.94, 3
By sudden **death** to give me ease:.............34. H.103, 14
But lost to one, be th' others **death**..........38. H.106, 142
Be so one **Death,** one Grave to both..........38. H.106, 144
Death will come and mar the song:............39. H.111, 12
Both bring one **death**; and I die here,..........50. H.140, 9
Trouble **Death** to lay agen......................52. H.145, 6
May **Death** yet come at last;....................58. H.149, 165
And that is **Death,** the end of Woe............60. H.157, 6
In **death** I thrive:..............................72. H.185, 16
Run to a sudden **Death,** and Funerall.........79. H.197, 90
Without a fame in **death**?......................85. H.211, 16
At my **death**; but thus much know,.............88. H.218, 3
Where the bounds of black **Death** be:.........96. H.231, 4
Tole forth my **death**; next, to my buryall come..100. H.248, 6
E'en **Death,** to die for thee....................109. H.267, 20
Which spent, one **death,** bring to ye both one Grave. 124. H.313, 14
That sighs at others **death**; smiles at his own..129. H.323, 13
Sing me to **death**; for till thy voice be cleare,.152. H.390, 1
Their lives in sweets, and left in **death** perfume..185. H.496, 4
For our neglect, Love did our **Death** decree,..197. H.539, 15
No man exempted is from **Death,** or sinne.....199. H.548, 2
So, when **Death** comes, Fresh tinctures lose their place, 207. H.576, 5
Ile sing no more of **death,** or shall the grave.228. H.658, 7
From the beholding **Death,** and cruelties.......236. H.679, 2
Who fed my life, I'le follow her in **death**.......248. H.730, 16
Death to our Countrey, now hath lost his heat:.254. H.756, 4
When that **Death** bids come away.............277. H.852, 8
His **Death** for Love that taketh................279. H.863, 12

Musique had both her birth, and **death** with Thee. 288. H.907, 10
Ready to blush to **death,** sho'd he but chide...301. H.963, 4
This shall my love doe, give thy sad **death** one.302. H.967, 3
His wife to **death** whipt with a Mirtle Rod.....306. H.986, 2
Drooping, I draw on to the vaults of **death,**...312. H.1013, 3
Since after **death** comes glory, Ile not haste.....314. H.1022, 2
His Wife and Children fast to **death** for fear..325. H.1077, 6
Sleep not for ever in the vaults of **death**:.......358. N.77, 11
Will blush to **death,** if ought be spi'd...........366. N.98, 13
Death for stout Cato; and besides all these,......370. N.108, 7
Death and dreadfulnesse call on,..................373. N.121, 5
Chor. All's gone, and **Death** hath taken..........374. N.123, 27
Sin is the cause of **death**; and sin's alone.........390. N.219, 1
Goes theeving from me, I am safe in **death**;....392. N.230, 34
The **Death** accurs't..................................401. N.268, 4
To vanquish Hell, as here He conquer'd **Death**?..403. N.271, 6
Vrging diuorcement (worse then **death** to theis)....410. A.3, 9
(Judgment and **Death,** denounc'd gainst Guilty men) 411. A.3, 62
For what life and **death** confines....................417. A.9, 9
Death with it still walkes along....................418. A.9, 41
Of yor beawty **death** comes soone...................418. A.9, 46
or Lar will freeze to **death** at home:.......431. ins. H.283, 60j
Death's Alas! the heat and **death's** the same;.......50. H.140, 5
Yet out alas! the **deaths** the same,...............155. H.406, 5
Fate gives a meeting. **Death's** the end of woe.....257. H.766, 2
But had it been of Birch, the **death's** the same...306. H.986, 4
Deaths Whose deeds, and **deaths** here written are.169. H.449, 13
Deb If seen, thou lik'st me, **Deb,** in none of these..331. H.1108, 2
Debate From old **debate,**..............................391. N.228, 18
Debility To shore up my **debilitie**.................303. H.973, 4
Debits And found my **Debits** to amount...........369. N.107, 2
Debt I come to pay a **Debt** of Birth I owe.........27. H.82, 12
Me pay the **debt**....................................29. H.87, 2
The **debt** is paid: for he who doth resigne........72. H.185, 26
He payes the halfe, who do's confesse the **Debt**..94. H.226, 10
Paske, though his **debt** be due upon the day....142. H.363, 1
Though long it be, yeeres may repay the **debt**;...228. H.654, 1
Thou paid'st the **debt,**...............................360. N.83, 22
For, this is sure, the **Debt** is dead...............370. N.107, 14
To pay the **debt,**......................................414. A.5, 2
Debtors Rise ye **Debters** then, and fall...........373. N.121, 11
Debts Having promis'd, pay your **debts,**...........44. H.125, 5
For why sayes he, all **debts** and their arreares,...142. H.363, 3
Decay All things **decay** with Time: The Forrest sees 23. H.69, 1
See, both these Lady-flowers **decay**:.............61. H.159, 16
As quick a growth to meet **Decay,**...............125. H.316, 13
But here awhile, to languish and **decay**;.......193. H.522, 2
Teares quickly drie: griefes will in time **decay**:..293. H.930, 1
Studies themselves will languish and **decay,**....316. H.1033, 1
And those great are, which ne're **decay**........381. N.158, 4
Then should we not **decay,**.......................413. A.4, 9
Decayed 'Cause my speech is now **decaid**;.........348. N.41, 31
Decaying Then while time serves, and we are but **decaying**; 69. H.178, 69
Decease So likewise after our **disseace,**...........139. H.353, 3
No ruffling winds come hither to **discease**......316. H.1028, 21
Deceits Tell me, what needs those rich **deceits,**.....282. H.881, 1
Deceived He chirpt for joy, to see himself **disceav'd.** 46. H.130, 12
Deceiv'd...308. H.993, 5
December That dyes with the next **December**....196. H.534, 18
That sees **December** turn'd to May...............364. N.96, 10
Past Sorrowes with the fled **December**..........413. A.4, 2
Decembers Call not to mind those fled **Decembers**; 127. H.319, 38
Decent Her **decent** legs, cleane, long and small...247. H.729, 4
Deck Of the shie Virgin, seems to **deck**...........166. H.443, 64
Declare Of any tackling can **declare**.............167. H.443, 104
Declare to us, bright Star, if we shall seek......367. N.102, 8
Decline First, I shall **decline** my head;...........38. H.107, 4
None, Posthumus, co'd ere **decline**...............132. H.336, 7
Decline or waste at all;............................335. H.1129, 12
Declines This way or that, it not **declines** at all...292. H.926, 2
Declining Each here **declining** Violet..............7. H.9, 4
Life is the Bodies light; which once **declining,**.....207. H.576, 1
Decree Or by thy love, **decree** me here to stay......60. H.156, 2
To honour thy **Decree**:.............................108. H.267, 10
Decree thy everlasting Topick there...............172. H.456, 8
For our neglect, Love did our Death **decree,**....197. H.539, 15
And smiling at our selves, **decree,**...............216. H.616, 29
Chorus. Thus, thus the gods celestial still **decree,**..416. A.8, 17
Decreed Thus has Infernall Jove **decreed**;........133. H.336, 28
And bring him home, but 'tis **decreed,**...........157. H.412, 27
What Fate **decreed,** Time now ha's made us see..254. H.756, 1
But she has **decreed** a day.........................276. H.848, 2
While others perish, here's thy life **decreed**.......280. H.869, 5
Which makes the Bapti'me; 'tis **decreed,**.........365. N.97, 18
Decreeing For so **decreeing,** that thy clothes expence 210. H.590, 3
Decrees With those thy primitive **decrees,**.........148. H.377, 96
Not knowing This, that Jove **decrees**............233. H.670, 5
Decrepit **See Dry-decrepit**
Decurted Thy free (and not **decurted**) offering.....286. H.898, 8

Dedicate I with discretion, dedicate...............119. H.293, 2
Deed Love, in pity of the deed,....................15. H.36, 12
So with a blush, beshrew'd the deed............187. H.504, 6
The Coward then takes Armes, and do's the deed..309. H.999, 2
Lastly, that JESUS is a Deed.................359. N.78, 15
O Thou, that crown'st the will, where wants the deed.
369. N.105, 2
Deeds With those deeds done by day, which n'er affright
35. H.106, 37
And the evil deads, the which................55. H.149, 89
Whose deeds, and deaths here written are.....169. H.449, 13
Verses out-live the bravest deeds of men?........264. H.791, 2
(Those wch must growe to Vertuous deeds)......407. A.2, 20
Deep Deep waters noyse-lesse are; And this we know,
15. H.38, 9
Or descend into the deep,.......................40. H.115, 9
Never was Dungeon so obscurely deep,.........52. H.146, 5
Tell me, said I, in deep distresse,................106. H.263, 3
Skin deepe into the Porke, or lights............147. H.377, 54
Of deep and arrant ignorance came in;.........150. H.382, 14
Glasse, out of deepe, and out of desp'rate want,..151. H.385, 1
In our State-sanctions, deep, or bottomlesse......187. H.506, 8
Discruciate a man in deep distresse.............239. H.699, 2
Tears will spring, where woes are deep..........306. H.984, 32
Of thy deep grone...........................314. H.1024, 11
Within the Kingdomes of the Deep;.............340. N.3, 8
Nor shalt thou give so deep a wound,............351. N.48, 9
And take me in, who am in Deep Distress;........416. A.8, 5
He was—Cha. Say what. Euc. Ay me, my woes are deep.
416. A.8, 11
But deepe mistery, not the stone..................417. A.9, 5
— — — — — — — — —, ...452. var. H.128, 22
Deeper She wept, and made it deeper by a teare...251. H.743, 2
Deeply And sobbing deeply, thus he said,..........42. H.119, 8
Nay more, Ile deeply sweare,...................69. H.179, 2
Deeps Amidst the deepes;......................134. H.336, 61
Defence Teares, at that day, shall make but weake defence;
392. N.230, 27
Defends 'Tis not the Walls, or purple, that defends.244. H.717, 1
Is the defensive vertue, Abstinence............333. H.1117, 2
Play their offensive and defensive parts,........370. N.109, 1
Defer Oh then no longer let my sweete deferre
426. var. H.197, 25
Deferred Desire deferr'd is, that it may encrease..264. H.793, 2
Defers God heares us when we pray, but yet defers
344. N.30, 1
How He deferres, how loath He is to die!......398. N.263, 8
Define Vineger is no other I define,............301. H.964, 1
Defining And is the best known, not defining Him..340. N.4, 2
Defy I did this God-head once defie;............155. H.406, 3
Degrees Are, by the Sun-beams, tickel'd by degrees.
100. H.247, 4
Thus to slay me by degrees,...................254. H.757, 3
Deign But if thou wilt not deigne so much,........344. N.29, 8
Deities Those Deities which circum-walk the Seas,..14. H.35, 5
Can please those Heav'nly Deities,................22. H.63, 2
Like those infernall Deities which eate..........272. H.826, 1
Though Frankinsense the Deities require,........295. H.940, 1
Deity This year again, the medows Deity.........140. H.354, 2
Cloud-like, the daintie Deitie.................167. H.443, 99
T'entertain that Deity........................204. H.569, 6
And give it to the Silvan Deitie................205. H.573, 4
As to a still protecting Deitie..................300. H.961, 16
Any part backward in the Deitie.................342. N.18, 2
Not an Affection, but a Deitie.................380. N.148, 2
— — — — — — — — —, ...452. var. H.443, 99
Dejected See dejected;.........................308. H.993, 27
Delay True love, we know, precipitates delay.......8. H.10, 6
Breake, if thou lov'st us, this delay;...........184. H.492, 25
Break off Delay, since we but read of one........251. H.744, 1
With Princely hand He'l recompence delay........344. N.30, 4
Delays Me with delayes;..........................43. H.123, 5
Of her Delayes must end; Dispose..............114. H.283, 93
Delays in love but crucifie the heart............261. H.781, 2
Delicate Vertuous instructions ne'r are delicate.....270. H.820, 2
My delicate transgression,.......................357. N.72, 6
Delicates Hunger makes coorse meats, delicates...37. H.106, 110
Delicious Who keep'st no proud mouth for delicious cates:
37. H.106, 109
With thy Delicious Numbers;....................95. H.227, 2
Delight May me delight, not fully please:..........34. H.105, 8
Cloath'd in her Chamlets of Delight............47. H.133, 11
All love, all liking, all delight...................69. H.178, 67
But borne, and like a short Delight,..............69. H.180, 1
With some conceal'd delight;....................75. H.193, 19
With full delight,...............................95. H.227, 30
Know the fulness of delight!...................124. H.314, 4
Have ye beheld (with much delight)...........164. H.440, 1
An houre or half's delight;....................176. H.467, 8
This begets the more delight,...................194. H.527, 6
I sho'd delight to have my Curles halfe drown'd.214. H.612, 11
Go to your banquet then, but use delight,.......220. H.633, 18
For to delight in wounds and murderings.........292. H.929, 2
I, and kil'd my dear delight....................306. H.984, 35
Who shall for the present delight here,.........317. H.1035, 9
If any thing delight me for to print.............355. N.61, 1

(Hatch't o're with Moone-shine, from their stolen delight)
410. A.3, 2
— — — — — — — — — — —, ...425. var. H.197, 6
Delighting Delighting:.........................377. N.128, 12
Delights Drown'd in Delights; but co'd not die...67. H.175, 18
Can such delights be in the street,..............68. H.178, 37
Call forth fierce Lovers to their wisht Delights:..77. H.197, 6
The silke wormes sperme, and the delights..435. ins. H.293, dd
Deliver See Re-deliver
Love to deliver me:.........................281. H.874, 12
Cannot deliuer vpp to'th rust,..................407. A.2, 17
Delivers See Re-delivers
Delphic On many a head the Delphick Coronet,..142. H.365, 4
The Muse give thee the Delphick Coronet.......194. H.529, 2
Deluge Yet the deluge here was known,.........302. H.968, 11
Demands Demands no money by a craving way;..142. H.363, 2
Demigod Live thou a Selden, that's a Demi-god...143. H.365, 12
Demophon To kill her selfe for Demophon.......215. H.616, 14
Demure Demure, but yet, full of temptation too...290. H.914, 6
Denham But since I'm cal'd (rare Denham) to be gone,
234. H.673, 13
Denied Who feares to aske, doth teach to be deny'd...8. H.12, 2
That done, the harder Fates deny'd..............69. H.180, 3
Being here their ends deny'd....................152. H.391, 3
But that deni'd; a griefe, though small,.........153. H.395, 4
And she with scorne deny'd me this:...........212. H.599, 2
Deni'd the Mask I wo'd have seen..............247. H.729, 8
Give unto all, lest he, whom thou deni'st,........391. N.226, 1
Denounced My vowes denounc'd in zeale, which thus much show three,....................................46. H.128, 47
(Judgment and Death, denounc'd gainst Guilty men)
411. A.3, 62
Dens In dennes of Darkness, or condemn'd to die...63. H.165, 4
Den'-shire See Devonshire
In Den-'shire Kerzie Lusk (when he was dead).332. H.1114, 1
Deny Do not deny...............................111. H.280, 9
Of white, where nature doth deny..............118. H.291, 8
And no again, and so deny,....................174. H.465, 35
Or let her Grant, or else Deny,.................207. H.579, 7
If Nature do deny.............................224. H.641, 1
But to desire what they denie.................249. H.735, 2
Ile give, if thou deny me.......................321. H.1055, 4
For to denie my Master, do thou crow............349. N.43, 2
Denie Thy suppliant.........................369. N.104, 18
Depart That when from hence she does depart,......24. H.73, 9
Which Bodies do, when Souls from them depart..42. H.122, 2
Loth to depart, but yet at last, each one........140. H.355, 1
Then depart, but see ye tread..................274. H.838, 7
Guesse, soe departe; yett stay A while to[o] see....411. A.3, 59
And now y' have wept enough, depart yon starres
432. ins. H.283, 140a
Departed When I departed am, ring thou my knell,
111. H.279, 1
For Saints and Soules departed hence,..........169. H.449, 17
That soules departed are not put out quite;......384. N.181, 3
Departeth And reverently departeth thence,....93. H.223, 139
Departing Departing hence, where Good and Bad souls go.
416. A.8, 26
Departures Their departures hence, and die........16. H.39, 14
Depth That chiding streams betray small depth below.
15. H.38, 10
A depth in love, and that depth, bottomlesse.......15. H.38, 12
Or depth, these last may yeeld, and yearly shrinke,
148. H.377, 105
In depth of silence, heard, and seene of none.....298. H.954, 3
Yet, in my depth of grief, I'de be.............321. H.1056, 15
Dereliction Had (as it were) a Dereliction;.......382. N.167, 2
Deride Do's but deride the Party buried.........319. H.1047, 2
Derision Neglecting thy derision..................235. H.677, 8
Derive He sho'd from her full lips derive,.........71. H.182, 30
Deriue their overwell grac'd motion..............406. A.1, 86
Thou didst deriue from that old stem............407. A.2, 21
Derogate Of His great Birth-right nothing derogate.
395. N.248, 4
Descend Or descend into the deep,................40. H.115, 9
Descend from heaven, to re-converse with men;..301. H.966, 12
God is then said for to descend, when He....395. N.244, 1
Descending In clouds, descending to the publike Doome.
382. N.162, 2
Descent But now my muse hath spi'de a darke descent
405. A.1, 65
Descried Luckie signes we have discri'd.........221. H.633, 26
Descry With Buskins shortned to descrie........51. H.142, 15
By which, mine angry Mistresse might descry,....58. H.150, 5
Say, or doe we not descrie.....................112. H.283, 7
When if the servants search, they may descry....118. H.292, 4
Cure, cure your selves, for I discrie,............157. H.413, 7
As in Pictures we descry,.......................194. H.527, 8
Nor did I know, or co'd descry..................203. H.563, 3
I follow'd after to descrie.....................247. H.729, 5
I must confesse, I there descrie,..............310. H.1004, 11
As flowrie vestures doe descrie.................311. H.1010, 7
Hee may (a prisoner) ther discrye...............408. A.2, 63
Whose incarvemts doe descrye...................417. A.9, 11
Desert One more by Thee, Love, and Desert have sent,
191. H.516, 1

God n'ere afflicts us more then our desert,.......341. N.10, 1
God still rewards us more then our desert:....394. N.242, 1
Spring hence thy faith, nor thinke it ill desert.......414. A.6, 3
Deserts Since for thy full deserts (with all the rest
152. H.392, 1
Deserve Who dead, deserve our best remembrances.
209. H.584, 8
Deserve these Mashes and those snares..........282. H.881, 6
Deserved And have deserv'd as much (Love knowes)
169. H.449, 11
Since both have here deserved best.............243. H.716, 36
Deserveless Deservelesse of the name of Paragon:..76. H.194, 4
Deserves Teare, that deserves of me a million...302. H.967, 4
Gods Grace deserves here to be daily fed,........378. N.132, 1
Deservest As thou deserv'st, be proud; then gladly let
194. H.529, 1
Deserving A winning wave (deserving Note)........28. H.83, 9
Design And other Scriptures, that designe..........92. H.223, 83
Here's a mad lover, there that high designe......415. A.7, 13
Designed These, or those ends, to which Thou wast design'd.
181. H.483, 4
Designments In all our high designments, 'twill appeare,
292. H.924, 1
Desire I most humbly thee desire..................21. H.59, 3
Water, water I desire,...........................21. H.61, 1
Let others drink thee freely; and desire........46. H.128, 49
And as for me, my chast desire...................49. H.136, 33
Slowly goes farre: The meane is best: Desire......51. H.143, 3
And tickled with Desire,.........................57. H.149, 134
So Kings & Queens meet, when Desire convinces..77. H.197, 7
By thy short absence, to desire and love thee?...77. H.197, 24
Too temp'rate in embracing? Tell me, ha's desire..78. H.197, 35
Then the next thing I desire,..................117. H.286, 11
How rich a man is, all desire to know;..........130. H.328, 1
If you desire..................................137. H.340, 13
Thou set'st their hearts, let chaste desire........174. H.465, 8
Thy sooty Godhead, I desire.....................214. H.613, 1
Of my desire, shall be.........................231. H.663, 6
Then I desire but this;........................238. H.690, 10
But to desire what they denie...................249. H.735, 2
Well, when to eat thou dost me next desire,....262. H.783, 21
Will not teend to your desire;..................263. H.786, 2
Desire deferr'd is, that it may encrease...........264. H.793, 2
To see me bleed, and not desire.................272. H.828, 11
Pardon my feares (sweet Sapho,) I desire.......279. H.866, 3
Where love begins, there dead thy first desire:....281. H.873, 1
'Tis but a fierce desire of hot and drie...........293. H.931, 2
To these a comely off-spring I desire,............294. H.938, 3
As much bewitching his desire..........434. ins. H.293, 41f
Desired That makes thee lov'd, and of the men desir'd,
299. H.956, 9
A hope of my desired bit?.....................312. H.1014, 4
A place desir'd of all but got by theis...........405. A.1, 69
Soe longe desir'd...............................413. A.4, 23
Desires To teach Man to confine desires:.......35. H.106, 16
And so thou dost: for thy desires are..........37. H.106, 105
In his desires..................................113. H.283, 35
Glit'ring to my free desires:.....................129. H.324, 2
By love and warme desires fed,..................130. H.329, 6
Where all Desires are dead, or cold............190. H.515, 15
In th' intrim she desires.........................269. H.814, 5
I, my desires screw from thee, and directe.......411. A.3, 49
Desirest Or else desir'st that Maids sho'd tell......34. H.103, 7
Desiring And drink to your hearts desiring.......263. H.784, 6
Desks Ha's none at home, in Coffers, Desks, or Trunks.
173. H.463, 4
Desolation Unto that watrie Desolation:...........14. H.35, 2
Despair Vexation of the mind, and damn'd Despaire.
45. H.128, 22
Gentle friends, though I despaire................62. H.162, 16
Bid me despaire, and Ile despaire,...............109. H.267, 17
And why? he knowes he must of Cure despaire,.125. H.315, 5
And shall dispaire, that any art.................164. H.442, 8
The Pearle of Princes, yet despaire............175. H.465, 38
Despaire takes heart, when ther's no hope to speed:
309. H.999, 1
Either with despaire, or doubt;.................348. N.41, 34
What need I then despaire,.....................373. N.122, 9
Oh then to lessen my dispaire..................414. A.5, 9
And that soe little we despaire..................418. A.9, 25
Despairs No man despaires to do what's done before.
236. H.680, 2
Desperate Attended with those desp'rate cares,..36. H.106, 64
And not with desp'rate hast:...................58. H.149, 166
A desp'rate grief, that finds no cure..............60. H.157, 2
To my revenge, and to her desp'rate feares,........87. H.215, 1
A hand too desp'rate, or a knife that bites....147. H.377, 53
Glasse, out of deepe, and out of desp'rate want,..151. H.385, 1
More dangerous faintings by her desp'rate cure..214. H.612, 6
In desp'rate cases, all, or most are known.......272. H.827, 1
My desp'rate feares, in love, had seen..........279. H.863, 15
No grief is grown so desperate, but the ill.......319. H.1048, 1
My soules most desp'rate Calenture;..........397. N.257, 2
Despicable Is despicable unto it.....................6. H.2, 18
Despight See Despite
Despise We blame, nay we despise her paines.....279. H.867, 1

Either be hot, or cold: God doth despise,..........353. N.54, 3
Despised Me; me, the most despised Lover:......61. H.159, 29
Am I despis'd, because you say,...................63. H.164, 1
That sho'd my Booke despised be,..............214. H.613, 3
Despite That keepes his own strong guard, in the despight
128. H.323, 9
Despite of all concussions left the Stem..........170. H.451, 3
Despight of all your infortunitie:...............299. H.958, 2
Destination Our Destination to eternall woe.......390. N.219, 4
Destined No, no, thy Stars have destin'd Thee to see
155. H.405, 15
Was destin'd forth to golden Soveraignty:......202. H.557, 28
Then reach those ends that thou wast destin'd to..254. H.756, 8
Art thou not destin'd? then, with hast, go on....389. N.216, 1
Destinies (Faire Destinies all three)................18. H.47, 6
High with thine own Auspitious Destinies:......181. H.483, 2
Destitute And when true love of words is destitute,.58. H.150, 7
Destroy Dead thee to th' most, if not destroy thee all.
82. H.204, 12
Destroyed Mens sins destroyed are, when they repent;
388. N.210, 3
Destruction He vow'd Destruction both to Birch, and Men:
65. H.171, 2
And bring t'th' heart destruction both alike.....333. H.1120, 6
Cities most sad and dire destruction..............384. N.178, 4
Destructive Such destructive Ysicles;............40. H.115, 14
As dearest Peace, after destructive Warre:......300. H.961, 2
Desunt Cætera desunt—........................231. H.662, 76
Detect That the curious may detect..............232. H.665, 7
Determines But Night determines here, Away....207. H.575, 66
Detestation His detestation to all slothfulnesse.....384. N.179, 4
Detriment The gaines must dead the feare of detriment.
42. H.120, 2
Device No new devise, or late found trick,.......126. H.319, 5
Nits carbonado'd, a device...............435. ins. H.293, v
Devil To drive the Devill from the Cod-piece....93. H.223, 121
To paint the Fiend, Pink would the Devill see;..110. H.272, 1
The Devill and shee together:...................225. H.643, 3
We'l love the Divell, so he lands the gold.......266. H.800, 8
Wo'd give (some say) her soule unto the Devill...266. H.801, 2
For all the Divell helps, will be a poore man.....315. H.1025, 2
The Devill tempts not least.......................344. N.28, 2
Devil's And Pink may paint the Devill's by his owne.
110. H.272, 4
Devise See Device
You blame me too, because I cann't devise......15. H.38, 3
But Ile devise,...................................43. H.123, 21
Each striving to devise.........................114. H.283, 69
Fortune no higher Project can devise,...........196. H.535, 1
And a Mimick to devise.........................255. H.761, 9
Into the Loathsoms<t> shapps, thou canst deuise
412. A.3, 93
Devised And thus devis'd, doe thou but this,......34. H.103, 15
Devoid Seas shall be sandlesse; Fields devoid of grasse;
59. H.154, 7
Peacefull by night; my day devoid of strife:......294. H.938, 2
Devonshire See Den'-shire
In this dull Devon-shire:.........................19. H.51, 4
Dwell, then in lothed Devonshire...............111. H.278, 8
Devote High-towring wil devote to them:..........22. H.66, 2
Here I devote; And something more then so;....27. H.82, 11
Devote to thee my graines of Frankinsence:......131. H.333, 2
Devote to Thee, both incense, myrrhe, and gold,..369. N.105, 6
Devoted And loving lie in one devoted bed...........8. H.10, 2
Devoted to the memory of me:.....................9. H.14, 16
Swans devoted unto thee........................122. H.303, 6
(Sometimes devoted unto Love)...............165. H.443, 20
Devotes Comes with his Cypresse, and devotes a teare?
288. H.907, 2
Devoting By cruse and measure; thus devoting Wine,
148. H.377, 83
Devotion Devotion gives each House a Bough,....68. H.178, 32
Devotion, stroak the home-borne wheat:........101. H.250, 22
Devotion bids me hither bring..................402. N.270, 3
Devour Or yawning rupture can the same devoure,
148. H.377, 107
He who with talking can devoure so much,.......191. H.518, 5
Then gives it to the children to devoure..........203. H.561, 2
Devoured — — — — — — — — —, ...426. var. H.197, 39
Devout Nor are thy daily and devout affaires......36. H.106, 63
Devoutly Devoutly to thy Closet-gods then pray,....14. H.35, 3
On, on devoutly, make no stay;..................54. H.149, 41
Dew To quench, or coole me with your Dew.......50. H.140, 2
Fall, like a spangling dew,.......................57. H.149, 155
(After a dew, or dew-like shower)..............71. H.182, 3
Like to a Dew,..................................74. H.190, 10
Th' Arabian Dew besmears......................80. H.201, 10
Leaves dropping downe the honyed dew,.........86. H.213, 40
Is Spangle-work of trembling dew,................92. H.223, 65
Fall on me like a silent dew,.....................95. H.227, 23
Like noyse-lesse Snow; or as the dew of night:..100. H.247, 2
When on her lip, thou hast thy sweet dew plac't,..100. H.248, 3
Teem'd her refreshing dew?......................104. H.257, 5
A pure seed-Pearle of Infant dew,...............119. H.293, 21
Thus a dew of Graces fall......................125. H.314, 9
Or as the pearles of Mornings dew..............125. H.316, 19

The spangling Dew dreg'd o're the grasse shall be
143. H.370, 3
Bedabled with the dew........................156. H.412, 4
Of Candi'd dew in Moony nights...............165. H.443, 32
Dew sate on Julia's haire,...................181. H.484, 1
With trembling Dew:..........................181. H.484, 4
The Dew of griefe upon this stone............203. H.564, 5
Like Morning-Sun-shine tinsilling the dew.......205. H.575, 12
His eye in dew of kisses, while he sleeps.......206. H.575, 42
This Primrose, thus bepearl'd with dew?.........208. H.580, 4
Like to a Deaw, or melted Frost...............233. H.670, 27
My Lucia in the deaw did go,..................247. H.729, 1
Or money? no, but onely deaw and sweat........248. H.731, 2
They fall like dew, but make no noise at all.....250. H.737, 4
In country Meadowes pearl'd with Dew,.........323. H.1068, 5
Which sits as Dew of Roses there:............328. H.1090, 9
Dew-bespangling The Dew-bespangling Herbe and Tree.
67. H.178, 6
Dew-drink-offerings And bring those dew-drink-offerings to my Tomb...222. H.634, 2
Dewlap See Dewlop
Dewlaps The unctuous dewlaps of a Snaile;......120. H.293, 45
Unto the Dew-laps up in meat:.................230. H.662, 36
Dew-light Spangled with deaw-light; thou canst cleere
367. N.102, 6
Dew-like (After a dew, or dew-like shower)........71. H.182, 3
Dew-locks Hangs on the Dew-locks of the night:..68. H.178, 24
Dewlop — — — — — — — —, ...434. var. H.293, 45
Dews I sing of Dewes, of Raines, and piece by piece...5. H.1, 7
In Tyrian Dewes, and Head with Roses crown'd..214. H.612, 12
Ile sing no more of Frosts, Snowes, Dews and Showers;
228. N.658, 3
By Dewes and drisling Raine,..................257. H.767, 5
Enspir'd by th' Sun-beams after dews & showers.
326. H.1080, 14
Dewy-mornings Mirt. In dewie-mornings when she came this way,..159. H.421, 23
Diadem Circle with a Diadem..................57. H.149, 130
Receive (with Songs) a flowrie Diadem.........254. H.756, 18
Those, who want Hearts, and weare a Diadem...330. H.1097, 2
Diamond Made of the Rubie, Pearle and Diamond:..30. H.88, 6
This counterchange of Perle and Diamond.......295. H.941, 6
Both with the Rubie, Pearle, and Diamond.......369. N.105, 8
Diamonds Seest thou those Diamonds which she weares
130. H.330, 1
Those Picks or Diamonds in the Card:........166. H.443, 48
Longe forfaite pawnèd diamonds..................407. A.2, 8
Diana Her legs were such Diana shows,...........51. H.142, 13
Dianeme Yet Dianeme now farewell:..............33. H.103, 2
O Dianeme, rather kill.........................34. H.103, 9
Diaper Re-cloth'd in fresh and verdant Diaper.....224. H.642, 2
So purest Diaper doth shine,....................268. H.811, 7
The figur'd Damask, or pure Diaper,.............355. N.65, 2
Dresse Thee with flowrie Diaper...............402. N.269, 13
Dice If well the Dice runne, lets applaud the cast:
218. H.621, 1
Where War and Peace the Dice by turns doe cast.
327. H.1083, 2
Dictator The proud Dictator of the State-like wood:..23. H.69, 4
Dictatorship To weaken this thy great Dictator-ship.
252. H.745, 20
Did (Partial List of Auxiliary) See Outdid
I did; and kist the Instep too:....................14. H.33, 2
I smiling, ask'd them what they did?............18. H.47, 5
Forgive, forgive me; since I did not know.........27. H.82, 5
With whom I did, and may re-sojourne when.....29. H.86, 13
And Love will swear't, my Dearest did not so...42. H.122, 12
As Jove did, when he made his rapes:............58. H.152, 2
As he did once to Semele.........................58. H.152, 4
Did rather choose to blesse another clime?.......77. H.197, 22
With Wicker Arks did come....................110. H.274, 6
But though it scar'd, it did not bite...........116. H.284, 6
As her little eyes did peep......................123. H.310, 4
As I did, not long ago,..........................131. H.332, 3
As the old Race of mankind did,..............147. H.377, 38
For men did strut, and stride, and stare, not act...150. H.382, 6
In utter darkenes did, and still will sit..........150. H.382, 18
Which did but only this portend,..................161. H.425, 3
Did to her suitors) this web done..............174. H.465, 31
As I did, my ravisht spirit......................182. H.489, 4
Did I or love, or could I others draw........201. H.557, 1
The wanton Satyre did;.........................203. H.563, 2
Or did I walk those Pean-Gardens through,......234. H.673, 3
My Lucia in the deaw did go,.................247. H.729, 1
Her Apron gave (as she did passe).............251. H.740, 9
Revolve he did his loving eye;..................265. H.798, 9
As in the River Julia did,....................294. H.939, 5
Tell me young man, or did the Muses bring.....299. H.956, 1
Then did I live when I did see................313. H.1020, 1
But why He did not, let me tell wherefore:....356. N.69, 2
Here did not make me sorrie,....................363. N.92, 3
He teares and tugs us, then he did before;......372. N.116, 2
Nor did the street...............................375. N.123, 68
Christ, I have read, did to His Chaplains say,....378. N.137, 1
For those, who did as malefactors die...........384. N.180, 4
Christ did her Woman, not her Mary call:......386. N.192, 2

Christ never did so great a work, but there......389. N.214, 1
So that, in all He did, there did combine.......389. N.214, 5
He did His curious operation;..................396. N.249, 4
I flie from Thee, as others did:................399. N.265, 2
— — — — — — — — — — —, ...427. var. H.197, 74
— — — — — — — — — — —, ...437. var. H.336, 136
Di'd See Died
Didst While thou didst keep thy Candor undefil'd,....6. H.3, 1
Which wrapt thy smooth limbs (when thou didst implore
9. H.14, 11
Thou did'st not mind it; though thou then might'st see
42. H.122, 3
Me turn'd to tears; yet did'st not weep for me.....42. H.122, 4
Lyd. While thou no other didst affect,..........70. H.181, 5
But thou kind Prew did'st with my Fates abide,..151. H.387, 5
Where, Amarillis, Thou didst set thy feet.......159. H.421, 12
Last night thou didst invite me home to eate;....161. H.424, 1
A willow Garland thou did'st send..............161. H.425, 1
Not unto thee, but That thou didst present....249. H.732, 4
To sup with thee thou didst me home invite;...262. H.783, 1
Do with me, God! as Thou didst deal with John,
343. N.25, 1
I dreamt, last night, Thou didst transfuse......357. N.75, 1
But for the conquest thou didst pay..........360. N.83, 24
Thou didst convince.............................363. N.92, 8
That Thou on Widdowes didst bestow.........374. N.123, 26
How Matron-like didst thou go drest!..........375. N.123, 63
Rich is the Jemme that thou did'st send,.......376. N.125, 5
When Thou Thy Lawes didst promulgate,......393. N.232, 4
Thou didst deriue from that old stem...........407. A.2, 21
Like fier-drakes, yett did'st mee no harme therby.
410. A.3, 28
O thou Allmightye Nature, who did'st giue....410. A.3, 29
Die Their departures hence, and die.............16. H.39, 14
Melting, and in fancie die:.....................17. H.43, 6
Julia, if I chance to die........................21. H.59, 1
Die, and be turn'd into a Lute..................23. H.68, 8
The Cause, th' effect wo'd die..................32. H.96, 4
When my date's done, and my gray age must die;
40. H.112, 1
Both bring one death; and I die here,..........50. H.140, 9
Grown violent, do's either die, or tire.........51. H.143, 4
Will find me out a path to die;..................60. H.159, 6
In dennes of Darkness, or condemn'd to die.....63. H.165, 4
Drown'd in Delights; but co'd not die........67. H.175, 18
We shall grow old apace, and die.............69. H.178, 59
(So Fate spares her) am well content to die.....70. H.181, 12
(To save his life) twice am content to die......70. H.181, 16
Will live with thee, or else for thee will die.....70. H.181, 24
But out of hope his wife might die to beare 'em..72. H.184, 2
Do mar'l how I co'd die,.........................72. H.185, 20
But die you must (faire Maid) ere long,........88. H.216, 20
Soules doe not with their bodies die:..........89. H.219, 16
I live and die...................................95. H.227, 21
But you must die.................................97. H.232, 17
For as these flowers, thy joyes must die,......107. H.263, 19
Or bid me die, and I will dare................109. H.267, 19
E'en Death, to die for thee..................109. H.267, 20
To live and die for thee........................109. H.267, 24
And consume, and grow again to die,..........115. H.283, 138
And there to give the cheek a die............118. H.291, 7
We die,..125. H.316, 15
If die I must, then my last vow shall be,....140. H.355, 9
And dye away upon thy Lute..................142. H.362, 6
Thou shalt not All die; for while Love's fire shines
143. H.366, 1
Then Juha weep, for I must dy.................153, H.399, 10
The whole world die, and turn to dust with thee.
155. H.405, 16
Under your shades, to sleep or die!..........158. H.420, 2
To dye upon the Tree...........................161. H.425, 8
Come forth and sweetly dye.................161. H.425, 12
May your fault dye,............................161. H.426, 11
It selfe to live or dye..........................164. H.441, 12
Many a Counter, many a Die,.................166. H.443, 51
Brave men can't die; whose Candid Actions are.168. H.444, 5
Will say our grace, and die...................173. H.460, 6
And die:.......................................178. H.475, 3
But dye ye must away:........................184. H.493, 7
Quiet, or die:................................190. H.515, 26
Wo'd thou hast ne'r been born, or might'st not die.
193. H.522, 6
And for to die here:..........................197. H.540, 2
Great Spirits never with their bodies dye........199. H.547, 2
Some parts may perish; dye thou canst not all:.200. H.554, 1
Live by thy Muse thou shalt; when others die..210. H.592, 1
Drown'd in the bloud of Rubies there, not die...216. H.618, 16
Soules transfusing thus, and die...............235. H.678, 8
Die when ye will, your sepulchre is knowne,....249. H.734, 3
Of woman-kind, first die I will;...............250. H.739, 2
So I may but die together:....................254. H.757, 2
Here I my selfe might likewise die,............265. H.794, 1
Who begs to die for feare of humane need,...277. H.855, 1
The bastard Slips may droop and die..........278. H.859, 3
And let all sports with Christmas dye..........285. H.894, 2
While other generations dye..................288. H.906, 4

Smooth in each limb as a die;................305. H.984, 20
Die ere long I'm sure, I shall;................321. H.1058, 1
Roses, you can never die,......................324. H.1070, 1
And swowne away to die,......................351. N.49, 3
Fain would I rest; yet covet not to die,......352. N.51, 11
God mercy; and so die........................352. N.53, 16
I do believe, that die I must,..................358. N.78, 1
But if that Tree sho'd fall, and die,............371. N.114, 7
For those, who did as malefactors die..........384. N.180, 4
I shall lesse swoone, then die for feare........393. N.232, 10
That Christ did die, the Pagan saith;.........395. N.247, 1
How He deferres, how loath He is to die!.......398. H.263, 8
With holye fier least that itt dye.............407. A.2, 24
Young men to swoone, and Maides to dye for love.
415. A.7, 10
A scripture how yow liue and dye.............417. A.9, 12
Died So she fell, and bruis'd, she dy'd...........15. H.36, 11
But thrice three Moones before she dy'd........41. H.116, 6
Virgins promis'd when I dy'd,.................44. H.125, 1
My longer stay, and so I dy'd................69. H.180, 4
To thee-ward dy'd i' th' embers, and no fire....78. H.197, 36
The Ev'ning witnest that I dy'd..............109. H.271, 2
After the rare Arch-Poet Johnson dy'd,........150. H.382, 1
Ran for Sweet-hearts mad, and dy'd...........152. H.391, 4
That di'd for love; and their complaints:.......169. H.449, 6
The Rose was sick, and smiling di'd;.........237. H.686, 1
He was my Life, my Love, my Joy; but di'd..416. A.8, 15
Dies Droops, dies, and falls without the cleavers stroke.
23. H.69, 6
If the chiefe author of the faction dyes;........132. H.335, 2
The stronger: Vertue dies when foes..........148. H.377, 112
Julia, when thy Herrick dies,..................186. H.499, 1
That dyes with the next December.............196. H.534, 18
If Men can say that beauty dyes;.............203. H.564, 1
First dyes the Leafe, the Bough next, next the Tree.
203. H.565, 4
No man dies ill, that liveth well.............321. H.1059, 2
My Fates are ended; when thy Herrick dyes,....329. H.1095, 7
I will believe, that then my body dies:........392. N.230, 20
Iff not, it dyes, or eles recoyles.............408. A.2, 72
Diest But let that instant when thou dy'st be known,
281. H.875, 3
E'en as Thou di'st,..........................401. N.268, 25
Diet Lesse with a neat, then needfull diet.......35. H.106, 30
If wholsome Diet can re-cure a man,...........319. H.1049, 1
Differ Kissing and bussing differ both in this;.189. H.512, 1
Our Lives do differ from our Lines by much...218. H.624, 2
Difference 'Twixt Kings & Tyrants there's this difference known;.......................................278. H.861, 1
Night makes no difference 'twixt the Priest and Clark;
279. H.864, 1
Twixt Truth and Errour, there's this difference known,
316. H.1031, 1
Encurlld together, and noe difference show
431. ins. H.283, 50f
Differing And you may find in Love these differing Parts;
274. H.837, 9
Differs Differs not much from drowzie slothfullnesse.
173. H.459, 14
Diffuse Diffuse their mighty influence..........291. H.919, 8
Diffused But every Line, and Limb diffused thence,
10. H.16, 3
Toucht every where with such diffused grace,..307. H.992, 2
Thy lips with all diffused grace!..............375. N.123, 74
Digestion Are to a wilde digestion brought,......166. H.443, 35
Dignify Here stand it stil to dignifie our Muse,..99. H.245, 5
Dignities State at a distance adds to dignities....236. H.682, 2
Dignity 'Tis dignity in others, if they be........234. H.673, 15
Dim Now is the time, when all the lights wax dim;
20. H.55, 1
Some starres were fixt before; but these are dim,
236. H.685, 3
Dimness And the dimnesse of your eye..........97. H.232, 15
Dimpled Next doth her chinne with dimpled beawty striue
405. A.1, 33
Din (As we think) singing to the dinne.........115. H.283, 103
Dinasty When this or that vast Dinastie must fall
256. H.763, 9
Dine Where Mirth and Friends are absent when we Dine
197. H.541, 3
Well I sup, and well I dine,..................309. H.996, 7
Lord, I confesse too, when I dine,.............350. N.47, 27
Dined Skinns he din'd well to day; how do you think?
156. H.409, 1
Dines Invites to supper him who dines,..........146. H.377, 8
Ding-thrift No, but because the Ding-thrift now is poore,
160. H.423, 3
Dinner In his wide Codpiece, (dinner being done).118. H.292, 5
But nothing so; The Dinner Adam had,.......273. H.835, 3
Diocesan Stand before you, my learn'd Diocesan?..64. H.168, 2
Dipped Y'ave dipt too long i' th' Vinegar;.......146. H.377, 22
Dire Fore-tell the comming of some dire events:.45. H.128, 16
Most dire and horrid crucifixion...............129. H.323, 14
Cities most sad and dire destruction...........384. N.178, 4
Direct I, my desires screw from thee, and directe.411. A.3, 49
Direction A milky high waye that direction yeilds.405. A.1, 67
Directions — — — — — — — —, ...448. var. A.1, 67
Directly Go on directly so, as just men may....149. H.377, 131
Directs And with the last he still directs the Just..340. N.6, 4
Direful With direful notes to fright your sleeps:.56. H.149, 102
Dirge Sing thou my Dirge, sweet-warbling Chorister!
19. H.50, 4
Meane time we two will sing the Dirge of these;.209. H.584, 7
The sacred Dirge and Trentall sung...........237. H.686, 10
I a Dirge will pen for thee;..................304. H.976, 1
And as we sing thy Dirge, we will............359. N.83, 9
Dirges No more my Dirges, and my Trentalls have.
228. H.658, 8
Dirty In a dirtie Haire-lace...................333. H.1122, 7
Disa — — — — — — — —, ...452. var. H.197, 91
Disacquainted Is disacquainted never............353. N.56, 18
Disadorned Disadorn'd, and scorn'd by thee?....273. H.836, 4
Disagree As divers strings do singly disagree.....406. A.1, 107
Disagreeing As when the disagreeing Commons throw
303. H.975, 3
Disallow — — — — — — — —, ...428. var. H.197, 91
Disallowed Two of a thousand things, are disallow'd,
10. H.18, 1
Disallows Loves doctrine disallowes...............32. H.94, 7
Disapprove What now we like, anon we disapprove:
191. H.517, 1
Disasters Many shrewd disasters met,...........209. H.585, 5
Among disasters that discention brings,........260. H.774, 1
In Battailes what disasters fall,...............290. H.913, 1
Disavow And last, when the (deare Spouse) I disavow,
79. H.197, 91
Discease See Decease
Discern Their ayry coulors to discerne,..........418. A.9, 56
Disciples All Thy Disciples Thee forsook, and fled.
399. N.264, 2
Discipline A short, but righteous discipline......92. H.223, 84
Your soft eare to Discipline...................96. H.232, 2
To noble Discipline!..........................228. H.657, 3
More then the teats of Discipline:.............310. H.1004, 6
Disclose And did my selfe disclose..............26. H.81, 15
Discloses Present their shapes; while fantasie discloses
36. H.106, 47
Discomfort Tis no discomfort in the world to fall,.319. H.1045, 1
Discomforted And with doubts discomforted,......347. N.41, 7
Discomposed Thee discomposed then, and still...240. H.705, 3
Let what is graceless, discompos'd, and rude,..290. H.914, 3
Or (discompos'd) I'm like a rude,.............312. H.1016, 3
Discontent Suspicion, Discontent, and Strife,....49. H.137, 1
That figure discontent;........................131. H.330, 8
Adversity then breeds the discontent............235. H.676, 2
Art discontent with me.........................240. H.705, 4
Men are suspicious; prone to discontent:.......291. H.921, 1
Discontented Flie discontented hence, and for a time
77. H.197, 21
Discontents More discontents I never had........19. H.51, 1
Discord Discord in, and so divide..............114. H.283, 87
Then to sow Discord 'mongst the Enemies.....196. H.535, 2
Discreet and prudent we that Discord call,....252. H.748, 1
Imparitie doth ever discord bring:............268. H.812, 1
Discover Rockie thou art; and rockie we discover.29. H.86, 7
Then if they sho'd discover...................76. H.193, 37
Which so betrayes her blood, as we discover...158. H.416, 3
We shall discover, by and by,..................188. H.508, 3
I will answer, These discover..................208. H.580, 11
Discovering Discovering from thence...........193. H.524, 3
Discreet Discreet and prudent we that Discord call,
252. H.748, 1
None is discreet at all times; no, not Jove.....294. H.936, 3
Discreetly But temp'rate mirth dealt forth, and so discreetly that it makes the meate more sweet;..148. H.377, 79-80
Go then discreetly to the Bed of pleasure;...220. H.633, 24
Thy Warre (discreetly made) with white successe.
254. H.756, 12
Discretion I with discretion, dedicate............119. H.293, 2
Discruciate Discruciate a man in deep distresse...239. H.699, 2
Discry See Descry
Disdain But no disdaine intended...............100. H.246, 7
The Jewes they did disdaine Thee,.............345. N.33, 25
Disease Where no disease raignes, or infection comes
205. H.575, 5
Combate for men, by conquering the disease....226. H.646, 2
The Cure was worse then the Disease.........360. N.83, 30
Diseases Store of diseases, where Physitians flow..244. H.718, 4
And our Diseases, Vultures of the Gods:......278. H.862, 2
Against diseases here the strongest fence........333. H.1117, 1
Disguise To make Fools hate them, onlye by disguise;
412. A.3, 94
Disgustful O Perverse man! If All disgustfull be....7. H.6, 5
Dish For Pollio's Lampries in our dish...........133. H.336, 48
Of thy glad table: not a dish more known.....147. H.377, 69
Or sho'dst thou prize me as a Dish........321. H.1056, 11
All are Fragments frim His dish...............363. N.93 6
Dol'd to us in That Lordly dish..............374. N.123, 34
Is it to quit the dish...........................391. N.228,5
Dishes With sev'rall dishes standing by.........101. H.250, 32
Take first the feat; these dishes gone;.........119. H. 293. 5
Disheveled And with dishevell'd Haire,..........110. H.274, 15

Or those on her **dishevel'd** haires,............130. H.330, 3
Her long **disheuel'd** rose-crown'd tramaletts:.....404. A.1, 4
Disleaved And seeing her not dead, but all **disleav'd**;
46. H.130, 11
Dislike No **Dislike** there is in love:.............11. H.21, 2
I shall **dislike**, what once I lov'd before........31. H.93, 4
I shall quite **dislike** agen.....................155. H.407, 6
What need I care, though some **dislike** me sho'd,
187. H.506, 5
To praise those Muses, and **dislike** our own?....234. H.673, 2
Ans. Like, and **dislike** ye:....................309. H.1001, 2
Disliked I **dislikt** but even now;.................155. H.407, 1
Sins first **dislik'd**, are after that belov'd........362. N.85, 2
Dislikes Crooked you are, but that **dislikes** not me;
99. H.242, 1
But, bastard-slips, and such as He **dislikes**,....370. N.108, 11
— — — — — — — — —, ...436. var. H.336, 14
Dislikest If thou **dislik'st** the Piece thou light'st on first;
7. H.6, 1
Dismal And **dismall** Darknesse then doth smutch the face.
207. H.576, 6
What **dismall** Stories will be told..............272. H.828, 15
With **dismall** smart............................353. N.56, 17
To whose **dismall** Barre, we there............373. N.121, 7
Dismayed Be not **dismaide**, though crosses cast thee downe;
311. H.1007, 1
Disorder A sweet **disorder** in the dresse...........28. H.83, 1
Disparkling More towring, more **disparkling** then thy fires:
113. H.283, 36
Mildly **disparkling**, like those fiers,. 165. H.443, 29
Dispatch But since It must be done, **dispatch**, and sowe
116. H.283, 141
For quick **dispatch**, Sculls made no longer stay,
200. H.551, 3
Dispatch your dressing then; and quickly wed:.216. H.618, 7
Crosse your Dow, and your **dispatch**,...........322. H.1063, 3
Dispatched Some have **dispatcht** their Cakes and Creame,
69. H.178, 47
As soone **dispatcht** is by the Night, as Day.....73. H.186, 4
Disperse To **disperse** the water farre...........322. H.1064, 4
Dispersed Since Clouds **disperst**, Suns guild the Aire again.
105. H.259, 2
Dispersion Passion, but for His sheeps **dispersion**..381. N.159, 2
Display **Display** thy breasts, my Julia, there let me.96. H.230, 1
Display the Bridegroom in the porch,..........113. H.283, 34
— — — — — — — — —, ...425. var. H.197, 17
Disport There to **disport** your selves with golden measure:
38. H.106, 139
With soft-smooth Virgins (for our chast **disport**).315. H.1028, 9
Dispose Of her Delayes must end; **Dispose**......114. H.283, 93
And let the whole world then **dispose**.........164. H.441, 11
Disposeress Shall be **Disposeresse** of the prize....243. H.716, 12
Disposition A gentle **disposition** then:..........42. H.121, 2
Mans **disposition** is for to requite...............292. H.923, 1
Dispossess And as we **dispossesse** thee..........345. N.33, 20
Dispossessed Quite **dispossest** of either fray, or fret.
82. H.204, 6
That done, then let him, **dispossest** of paine,...99. H.244, 7
I could wish you **dispossest**..................117. H.289, 5
He that will live of all cares **dispossest**,........305. H.981, 1
Dispute Then for to murder friendship, by **dispute**..287. H.901, 6
Dissembling For kissing Loves **dissembling** chips,.203. H.563, 7
Dissension Among disasters that **discention** brings,
260. H.774, 1
Dissever With such white vowes as fate can nere **dissever**
414. A.6, 11
Dissolution A foe to **Dissolution**:.................25. H.76, 2
Dissolve Till this world shall **dissolve** as men,...146. H.376, 12
Dissonant Any one part that's **dissonant** in you:.189. H.511, 2
Di'st See **Diest**
Distaff Give S. **Distaffe** all the right,............315. H.1026, 11
Distaff's Ye must on S. **Distaffs** day:..........315. H.1026, 2
Distance Manners knowes **distance**, and a man unrude
147. H.377, 31
State at a **distance** adds to dignities...........236. H.682, 2
The Virgin-Mother stood at **distance** (there)...384. N.180, 1
Leaving a **distance** for the beawtious small.....406. A.1, 89
Distance and sweet Vrbanitie,..................409. A.2, 96
Distances Must not be lookt on, but at **distances**:.237. H.685, 10
Distemper Drinks of **distemper**, or ha's cause to cry
148. H.377, 87
Nothing to **distemper** you;.....................177. H.472, 2
Argues a strong **distemper** of the mind.........356. N.70, 2
Distill Yet dry'd, ere you **distill** your Wine.......88. H.216, 12
O! may no eye **distill** a Teare.................104. H.256, 9
Thus let Thy lips but love **distill**,.............393. N.232, 15
Distilled With teares, **distil'd**.................360. N.83, 40
Distinction To make this neat **distinction** from the rest;
140. H.354, 5
I must confess, **distinction** none I see.........301. H.966, 9
Distinguish **Distinguish** all those Floods that are.339. N.3, 3
Distorted And **distorted** there-withall:.............11. H.21, 4
Distracted If Kings and kingdomes, once **distracted** be,
331. H.1102, 1
Distraction Into a fine **distraction**:...............28. H.83, 4
Distress Tell me, said I, in deep **distresse**,.......106. H.263, 3
To strip the Trees, and Fields, to their **distresse**,
224. H.642, 11
Discruciate a man in deep **distresse**.............239. H.699, 2
My many cares and much **distress**,.............312. H.1016, 1
In the houre of my **distresse**,...................347. N.41, 1
And take me in, who am in deep **Distress**;.......416. A.8, 5
Distressed Wherewith young men and maids **distrest**,
106. H.262, 3
Chor. And after us (**distressed**)................375. N.123, 87
Distrust See **Wise-distrust**
Be truer to him, then a wise **Distrust**..........67. H.177, 2
Take, if thou do'st **distrust**, that Vowe;........328. H.1090, 6
Disturbance To give the least **disturbance** to her haire:
82. H.204, 2
Ditches O're **Ditches**, and Mires,................225. H.643, 11
Divell See **Devil**
Divers As **divers** strings do singly disagree.......406. A.1, 107
Divide And that white cloud **divide**............76. H.193, 53
Discord in, and so **divide**......................114. H.283, 87
We not **divide** the Hoof, but chew the Cud:....397. N.256, 2
Divided Sorrowes **divided** amongst many, lesse...239. H.699, 1
Divination A **Divination** unto me:...............73. H.187, 9
Divine Or by Rose-buds **devine**,.................56. H.149, 115
'Tis she! 'tis she! or else some more **Divine**...112. H.283, 11
While that others doe **divine**;................113. H.283, 47
But by their flight I never can **divine**,.........149. H.378, 3
Sweet Aires move here; and more **divine**......166. H.443, 39
By which we sit, and doe **Divine**.............198. H.544, 4
There thou shalt hear **Divine** Musæus sing.....206. H.575, 25
An Odor more **divine**,.........................251. H.740, 10
And Cakes **Divine**,.............................296. H.946, 20
And that will make me, and my Work **divine**...371. N.113, 10
So the **Divine Hand** work't, and brake no thred,
385. N.184, 3
His Humane Nature, and His Part **Divine**.....389. N.214, 6
These be the Ruby portalls and **devine**...........404. A.1, 25
Vnto the Idoll of ye work **devine**.............406. A.1, 109
Divined — — — — — — — —, ...423. var. H.128, 19
Divinely How each thing smells **divinely** redolent!
159. H.421, 19
Diviner Knowe yet, (rare soule,) when my **diuiner** Muse
412. A.3, 99
— — — — — — — — — —, ...423. var. H.128, 19
Divinest 'Tis thou, above Nectar, O **Divinest** soule!
45. H.128, 19
Divinity Therein some beames of His **Divinitie**:...389. N.214, 4
Division Runs **division** with the Singer..........364. N.96, 7
The lucklesse number of **division**:..........396. N.249, 2
Divorced Like Streams, you are **divorc'd**; but 't will come, when
26. H.79, 5
Have I **divorc't** thee onely to combine.........78. H.197, 39
Divorcement Meet after long **divorcement** by the Iles:
77. H.197, 2
Vrging **diuorcement** (worse then death to theis)..410. A.3, 9
Do (Partial List of Auxiliary) See **Outdo**
Stay then at home, and **doe** not goe..............6. H.2, 19
Old I am, and cannot **do**........................10. H.19, 3
Yet **doe** it to this end: that I,..................11. H.20, 7
Long still **doe** tarry,..............................12. H.26, 3
What now I meane to **doe**;.......................13. H.31, 6
But yet for Loves-sake, let thy lips **doe** this,....14. H.35, 11
Doe, and have parted here a Man and Wife:....26. H.79, 2
To **doe** the Rites to thy Religious Tombe:......27. H.82, 2
This, this a virtuous man can **doe**,..............31. H.90, 7
I'le **doe** my best to win, when'ere I wooe:.......31. H.91, 1
Let's **doe** our best, our Watch and Ward to keep
32. H.95, 5
And thus devis'd, **doe** thou but this,...........34. H.103, 15
But **do** not so; for feare, lest he...............39. H.108, 13
Which Bodies **do**, when Souls from them depart..42. H.122, 2
Do in a trickling manner tell,...................44. H.127, 7
And **doe** an honour to thy teare;...............48. H.134, 6
Then Faire ones, **doe** not wrong................53. H.149, 3
And weep to see't; yet this thing **doe**,..........61. H.159, 20
At last, I find, (after my much to **doe**).......61. H.161, 5
Now as I **doe**; and but for thee,...............72. H.185, 24
You can ease my heart, and **doe**...............74. H.191, 7
Thou who wilt not love, **doe** this;............76. H.195, 1
And double my affection on thee; as **doe** those,..78. H.197, 43
Fill each part full of fire, active to **doe**.........79. H.197, 79
Which here I vow to serve, **doe** not remove....79. H.197, 82
Because I **doe**.....................................87. H.214, 3
This we will **doe**; we'll daily come............89. H.219, 9
They have their Text for what they **doe**;......92. H.223, 77
And tell her this, but **doe** not so,..............98. H.238, 12
And't shall **doe** so for thee...................108. H.267, 12
And **doe** some honour to my Tomb..............111. H.280, 8
I call, I call, who **doe** ye call?................112. H.281, 1
Yet, if that neither you will **doe**,..............112. H.281, 5
In Lov's name **do** so; and a price..............113. H.283, 53
And **do** it to the full; reach......................115. H.283, 127
By Time, and Counsell, **doe** the best we can,..120. H.294, 1
Do all things sweetly, and in comely wise;....124. H.313, 7
As your hours **doe**, and drie..................125. H.316, 16
For my embalming, Julia, **do** but this,........129. H.327, 1
How speaks it, say? 2. **Do** you but this,......130. H.329, 17

What can I do in Poetry,....................132. H.334, 1
To kisse our hands, nor do we wish...........133. H.336, 47
Do not you fall through frailty; Ile be sure...136. H.338, 3
Let Kings Command, and doe the best they may,.138. H.345, 1
See how the poore do waiting stand,..........139. H.350, 1
So draw, and paint, as none may do the like,..150. H.384, 5
Do but this; and there shall be..............151. H.386, 7
Skinns he din'd well to day; how do you think?.156. H.409, 1
Why do you sigh, and sob, and keep.........158. H.420, 5
I know ye do; and that's the why,............158. H.420, 9
Say, What sho'd Roots do with a Purse in print, 162. H.427, 3
That they no better do agree.................163. H.434, 3
Which mercy if you will but do,..............165. H.442, 11
He'll do no doubt; This flax is spun.........168. H.443, 121
(As many Conscripts of the Citie do)........176. H.466, 6
Trust me Ladies, I will do...................177. H.472, 1
But if they do, the more to flow.............179. H.476, 12
Where Chimneys do for ever weepe,..........179. H.476, 31
With oathes, and lyes, (as others do.)......182. H.490, 12
What ha's the Court to do with Swaines,........184. H.492, 21
Or else sweet Nimphs do you but this;.......185. H.495, 5
No more my Silvia, do I mean to pray.........204. H.570, 1
I cannot pipe as I was wont to do,............205. H.573, 1
This is the height of Justice, that to doe......214. H.614, 1
Or tell what strange Tricks Love can do,....215. H.616, 9
And sigh, and kiss, as Lovers do:.............215. H.616, 20
What will ye (my poor Orphans) do..........218. H.626, 1
This I may do (perhaps) as I glide by,......222. H.634, 10
For all I have, or else can do,...............223. H.635, 15
That doe our soules encline...................228. H.657, 2
And that wee'l do; as men, who know,........233. H.670, 36
So, I confesse, 'tis somwhat to do well.........234. H.673, 9
The while their wreaths and Purple Robes do shine, 234. H.673, 17
No man despaires to do what's done before....236. H.680, 2
That fleet of Lackeyes, which do run..........239. H.696, 3
Thou for the breach shalt do;................240. H.705, 10
Ev'n so, those streets and houses do but show.244. H.718, 3
This with a wonder when ye do,...............245. H.720, 11
Oft bend the Bow, and thou with ease shalt do,.245. H.722, 1
Something there yet remaines for Thee to do;.254. H.756, 7
Go to Feast, as others do....................255. H.761, 2
You'l do my Neice abundant honour...........257. H.764, 10
That doe in publike places,...................260. H.777, 2
Who doe with sweet embraces,................260. H.777, 6
Blaze by this Sphere for ever: Or this doe,.....264. H.789, 5
Serve or not serve, let Tom doe what he can...265. H.796, 3
Old Widdow Prouse to do her neighbours evill.266. H.801, 1
Haste is unhappy: What we Rashly do........268. H.813, 1
As purest Pearles, or Pebles do...............271. H.824, 11
Do thou to me appeare;.......................271. H.824, 14
Say, what wo'd many do?....................273. H.833, 6
To pray for me doe thou begin,..............277. H.854, 5
Instruct me how to doe......................281. H.874, 8
To house the Hag, you must doe this;.........284. H.890, 1
Can do not mischiefe (there.)................285. H.893, 8
This if ye do, each Piece will here be good,......290. H.914, 9
Man must do well out of a good intent,.......290. H.917, 1
To heare the worst from men, when they doe well. 293. H.932, 2
Doe that my Julia which the rites require,......299. H.957, 3
This shall my love doe, give thy sad death one.302. H.967, 3
Tell me, do thy kine now fail.................305. H.984, 7
Do,..307. H.988, 5
I bring ye Love, Quest. What will love do?....309. H.1001, 1
I bring ye love: Quest. What will Love do?...309. H.1001, 3
I bring ye love: Quest. What will Love do?...309. H.1001, 5
I bring ye love: Quest. What will love do?......309. H.1001, 7
I bring ye love: Quest. What will love do?....310. H.1001, 9
I bring ye love: Quest. What will love do?....310. H.1001, 11
I bring ye love: Quest. What will love do?....310. H.1001, 13
I bring ye love: Quest. What will love do?....310. H.1001, 15
You aske me what I doe, and how I live?......312. H.1013, 1
And being cup-shot, more he co'd not doe......313. H.1017, 10
Man may at first transgress, but next do well:.314. H.1021, 1
To bath in thee (as thousand others doe.)....315. H.1028, 6
And thus ye must doe.......................317. H.1035. 23
Who may do most, do's least: The bravest will.321. H.1057, 1
What have the Meades to do with thee,........323. H.1068, 9
Instruct me now, what love will do;...........325. H.1075, 1
Inform me next, what love will do;..........325. H.1075, 3
Teach me besides, what love will do;..........325. H.1075, 5
Tell me, now last, what love will do;..........325. H.1075, 7
That Prince, who may doe nothing but what's just, 331. H.1103, 1
To do ten Bad, for one Good Action.............339. N.1, 6
Do with me, God! as Thou didst deal with John, 343. N.25, 1
God pardons those, who do through frailty sin;....344. N.32, 1
When I am there, this then I'le do,.............349. N.46, 3
Then let Thy Justice do the rest,..............349. N.46, 8
Lord, do not scourge me,......................351. N.49, 5
Sick is my heart; O Saviour! do Thou please....358. N.77, 8
I do believe, I shall inherit....................359. N.78, 11
To do Him honour; who's our King,............365. N.96, 31
No, this ye need not do;........................367. N.102, 12
And, if they do, they prove but cumbersome;....368. N.104, 3
Do ravisht stand;..............................369. N.106, 10
Well, this I'le do; my mighty score............369. N107, 5
When Winds and Seas do rage,.................373. N.122, 1
God can do all things, save but what are known..382. N.166, 1
There's no constraint to do amisse,.............390. N.225, 1
God is all-present to what e're we do,..........394. N.237, 1
When well we speak, & nothing do that's good,..397. N.256, 1
God's wrathfull said to be, when He doth do....397. N.259, 3
So do the Skurfe and Bran too: Go Thy way,..398. N.263, 12
Ah! Sions Daughters, do not feare..............400. N.266, 7
Yet doe Thou please,..........................401. N.268, 31
Of all the good things whatsoe're we do,......403. N.272, 1
Doe speake a virgin merry cherry-lip't............404. A.1, 22
Euen such are wee; and in our parting, doe.......410. A.3, 13
Doe it like the Sun to write....................413. A.4, 18
— — — — — — — — —, ...429. var. H.263, 22
And ravish you his Bride, doe you........430. ins. H.283, 40c
— — — — — — — — —, ...431. var. H.283, 50
Not more, milde nymph, then they would have you doe; 431. ins. H.283, 60r
But dread that you doe more offend....431. ins. H.283, 60s
— — — — — — — — —, ...436. var. H.336, 6
All mighty blood; and can doe more......437. var. H.336, 135
Docility Prepares the way for mans docility......153. H.394, 4
Doctor Thou cam'st to cure me (Doctor) of my cold, 97. H.236, 1
The first as Doctor, and the last as Knight.....322. H.1062, 12
When the artlesse Doctor sees.................347. N.41, 13
Doctors The Doctors, in the Talmud, say,.........388. N.206, 1
Doctrine Loves doctrine disallowes.................32. H.94, 7
That ye may good doctrine heare...............52. H.147, 2
Doe See **Do**
Doer's No other, but the doers willingnesse.......275. H.845, 2
Does See **Overdoes**
That when from hence she does depart,............24. H.73, 9
Or Muse of Roses: since that name does fit........28. H.84, 3
But whither, onely Grief do's know...............33. H.103, 4
Fone sayes, those mighty whiskers he do's weare,..39. H.110, 1
If so, we'll think too, (when he do's condemne..39.H.110, 3
Boyes to the lash) that he do's whip with them...39. H.110, 4
Where eternall cold does keep?.................40. H.115, 10
Or else because Grill's roste do's burn his Spit,....48. H.135, 3
Grown violent, do's either die, or tire.............51. H.143, 4
As fast away as do's the Sunne:................69. H.178, 62
He smarts at last, who do's not first take heed...79. H.199, 4
For now each tree do's weare....................80. H.201, 6
Round, round, the roof do's run;.................81. H.201, 33
He who to the ground do's fall,.................84. H.209, 7
He payes the halfe, who do's confesse the Debt...94. H.226, 10
When Julia blushes, she do's show..............120. H.295, 1
Bungie do's fast; looks pale; puts Sack-cloth on;.122. H.305, 1
As sure a Mattins do's to him belong,...........128. H.321, 5
As Fate do's lead or draw us; none,.............132. H.336, 6
Goes with you mouth, or do's outrun your tongue; 141. H.359, 14
No Planke from Hallowed Altar, do's appeale..149. H.377, 127
To yond' Star-chamber, or do's seale...........149. H.377, 128
Hark, harke, the God do's play!...............151. H.388, 5
Craw cracks in sirrop; and do's stinking say,....162. H.428, 1
Thus, though the Rooke do's raile against the sin,.163. H.439, 3
Then publick praise do's runne upon the Stone,..172. H.459, 9
Huncks ha's no money (he do's sweare, or say)..173. H.463, 1
And this their Flatt'rie do's commend..........175. H.465, 41
He that doth suspect, do's haste..............175. H.465, 45
How can I chuse but kisse her, whence do's come.181. H.485, 3
Nor do's it mind the Rustick straines...........184. H.492, 23
And Fading-time do's show,....................184. H.493, 3
Nor that fine Worme that do's interre........186. H.497, 13
Spread as He spreads; wax lesse as He do's wane; 196. H.537, 3
The Quarter-day do's ne'r affright............200. H.552, 11
Ask me why this flower do's show..............208. H.580, 7
What though the Moon do's slumber?.........217. H.619, 12
But that his breath do's Fly-blow all the meate...223. H.637, 2
Her breath do's stinke,......................229. H.659, 9
That thou shalt swear, my Pipe do's raigne....244. H.716, 39
Do's she smile, or do's she frowne:..............253. H.750, 5
Be she bald, or do's she weare..................253. H.750, 10
Meane time that he from place to place do's rome. 253. H.753, 3
In whom the spirit of the Gods do's dwell,......256. H.763, 7
That Happines do's still the longest thrive,........264. H.792, 1
But now perceiving that it still do's please......266. H.800, 3
When a warm tongue do's with such Ambers meet. 269. H.816, 4
Do's Fortune rend thee? Beare with thy hard Fate: 270. H.820, 1
Say do's she frown? still countermand her threats: 270. H.820, 3
Where ever Nodes do's in the Summer come,....270. H.822, 1
In her white Stole; now Victory do's rest........271. H.823, 3
Peapes he do's strut, and pick his Teeth, as if....273. H.835, 1
Thus times do shift; each thing his turne do's hold; 285. H.892, 21

The Coward then takes Armes, and do's the deed.
309. H.999, 2
That do's infect, and make the rent...........311. H.1010, 5
Nor do's she minde,.........................314. H.1024, 13
Do's but deride the Party buried..............319. H.1047, 2
The while my deer Anthea do's but droop,......320. H.1054, 3
Who may do most, do's least: The bravest will..321. H.1057, 1
When a cleare day, out of a Cloud do's break...324. H.1072, 2
That love 'twixt men do's ever longest last......327. H.1083, 1
A mans transgression God do's then remit,........359. N.82, 1
Why do's the chilling Winters morne............364. N.96, 14
Because the prettie Babe do's bleed.............366. N.98, 21
O then, how restlesse do's she stray!............393. N.233, 2
How do's she erre in endlesse night!............393. N.233, 4
— — — — — — — — — —, ...426. var. H.197, 25
— — — — — — — — — —, ...443. var. H.580, 7
Doest See Dost
That when thou doest his necke Insnare,..........408. A.2, 61
— — — — — — — — —, ...449. var. A.3, 29
Dog The Dog, the triple Tunne?.................289. H.911, 6
Came a mad dog, and did bite,.................306. H.984, 34
Dog-like Tis but a dog-like madnesse in bad Kings,
292. H.929, 1
Dogs Instead of almes, sets dogs upon the poor...238. H.694, 2
Doing Pay then your Tythe; and doing thus,....208. H.581, 3
Let's be doing, though we play................235. H.678, 3
The readinesse of doing, doth expresse.........275. H.845, 1
In doing justice, God shall then be known,.......393. N.234, 1
Doing's, the Fruite of Doinge well, Farwell.....412. A.3, 104
Doing's Doing's, the Fruite of Doinge well, Farwell.
412. A.3, 104
Dole No: 'tis a Fast, to dole....................391. N.228, 13
Doled A wafer Dol'd by thee, will swell..........139. H.350, 3
Dol'd to us in That Lordly dish................374. N.123, 34
Doleful Possesse my thoughts, next comes my dolefull knell
392. N.230, 12
Doling — — — — — — — — —, ...431. var. H.283, 52
Doll Doll she so soone began the wanton trade;...149. H.379, 1
Dollies Kisse our Dollies night and day:..........39. H.111, 4
Dolour Forc'd from the mighty dolour of the heart.
380. N.154, 2
Dol's No question but Dols cheeks wo'd soon rost dry,
325. H.1078, 1
Domiduca While Domiduca leads the way:........54. H.149, 42
Domineer Let Box now domineere;..............285. H.892, 6
Dominion Here shall endure thy vast Dominion...210. H.592, 4
Domitian's Between Domitians Martiall then, and Thee.
301. H.966, 10
Don Do'n will I then my Beadsmans gown,......303. H.973, 7
To d'on my robes of love,.......................352. N.53, 9
Done That done, then wind me in that very sheet...9. H.14, 10
Which being done, the fretfull paine..............18. H.46, 9
I care not now how soone 'tis done,..............18. H.47, 11
Faults done by night, will blush by day:..........20. H.56, 6
Treble that million, and when that is done,.........24. H.74, 7
Which done, to still their wanton cries,............31. H.92, 9
Which done, that Dawne, turns then to perfect day.
34. H.104, 6
With those deeds done by day, which n'er affright
35. H.106, 37
Which done, thy painfull Thumb this sentence tells us,
36. H.106, 61
When my date's done, and my gray age must die;
40. H.112, 1
Her inadult'rate strength: what's done by me....46. H.128, 53
What now is done: since where no sin...........48. H.136, 12
A sleep, untill the act be done.................57. H.149, 142
Which done, then quickly we'll undresse..........58. H.152, 7
That done, sink down into a silv'rie straine;......67. H.176, 5
And sin no more, as we have done, by staying;..68. H.178, 41
That done, the harder Fates deny'd................69. H.180, 3
'Twas done by me, more to confirme my zeale,....78. H.197, 42
What's to be done? but on the Sands............94. H.225, 7
That done, then let him, dispossest of paine,......99. H.244, 7
But since It must be done, dispatch, and sowe..116. H.283, 141
In his wide Codpiece, (dinner being done)......118. H.292, 5
And pregnant violet; which done,..............119. H.293, 23
His blood to height; this done, commended....120. H.293, 53
For having now my journey done,..............123. H.306, 5
That done; when both of you have seemly fed,...124. H.313, 9
Beginne with Jove; then is the worke halfe done;
128. H.321, 1
Now Patrick with his footmanship has done,....158. H.418, 1
Which, done; and thence remov'd the light,....165. H.443, 7
We'll nobly think, what's to be done,..........168. H.443, 120
And say short Prayers; and when we have done so,
168. H.445, 4
Which may be done, if (Sir) you can beget......170. H.451, 5
Did to her suitors) this web done..............174. H.465, 31
(Undone as oft as done) I'm wonne;..........174. H.465, 32
(And hang the head when as the Act is done)...196. H.537, 2
Their Goales for Virgins kisses; which when done,
206. H.575, 18
To Linus, then to Pindar; and that done,......206. H.575, 31
This done, we'l draw lots, who shall buy........215. H.616, 25
Corrols his cheeke, to see those Rites not done...216. H.618, 4
And when once the Work is done;.............224. H.639, 3
This done, then to th' enameld Meads..........230. H.662, 29
No man despaires to do what's done before.......236. H.680, 2
To ask our wages, e're our work be done.........241. H.708, 2
Consult ere thou begin'st, that done, go on....252. H.749, 1
That done, our smooth-pac't Poems all shall be.254. H.756, 15
As these have done to Thee, who are the one,....256. H.763, 5
That done, they kisse, and so draw out the day:..260. H.773, 2
And more had done (it is confest).............294. H.939, 9
Which done; no more.........................296. H.946, 22
With spice; that done, Ile leave thee to thy rest.
300. H.960, 6
That done; O Cesar, live, and be to us,........300. H.961, 13
What's said or done..........................314. H.1024, 7
That done, my Julia, dearest Julia, come,.......329. H.1095, 5
The worke is done: young men, and maidens set
335. H.1128, 1
A sin, then fall to weeping when 'tis done.....349. N.43, 6
Done in the present times:......................352. N.53, 6
These done, I'le onely crie.......................352. N.53, 15
And make no one stop, till my race be done.....358. N.77, 15
Back, back again; each thing is done...........366. N.97, 24
And, when that's done, to re-aspire.............367. N.98, 29
Then ever, yet, like was done before............395. N.244, 4
God blest His work done on the second day:....396. N.249, 6
When I have done true Penance here for it.......397. N.255, 4
The work is done; now let my Lawrell be......398. N.262, 1
That done, with Honour Thou dost me create....398. N.262, 3
That done, wee'l see Thee sweetly buried.......399. N.263, 39
Which done, Lord say, The rest is mine.........400. N.267, 13
Why then, go on to act: Here's wonders to be done,
401. N.268, 7
And, when that's done,........................401. N.268, 20
As yow haue done yor day,......................413. A.4, 8
Since part we must Let's kisse, that done retire....414. A.6, 9
Prophan'd in Speech, or done an act that's fowle
426. ins. H.197, 29a
Dons And then he dons the Silk-worms shed,.....93. H.223, 137
Don't If the Vower don't express...................22. H.63, 3
With his Flesh-hooks, don't come nie............263. H.785, 3
Nor those false vows, which oft times don't prevaile.
331. H.1104, 2
Doom Till passengers shall spend their doome,..104. H.256, 20
The doome of cruell Proserpine.................132. H.336, 8
With others, to the dreadfull Doome:............358. N.78, 6
In clouds, descending to the publike Doome.....382. N.162, 2
Which must produce me to that Gen'rall Doome,
392. N.230, 23
To me, as to the gen'rall Doome,..............393. N.232, 2
Soaring them vpp, boue Ruyne, till the doome.....410. A.3, 33
The sad soule went, not with his Loue, but doome;
412. A.3, 76
And thinke each man thou seest doth doome
441. ins. H.465, 14a
Doomsday Let it be Doomes-day; nay, take longer scope;
83. H.206, 3
When the Black Dooms-day Bookes (as yet unseal'd)
256. H.763, 15
Door Unbolts the doore, no shame comes in.....48. H.136, 13
Or Branch: Each Porch, each doore, ere this,...68. H.178, 33
Barre close as you can, and bolt fast too your doore,
97. H.233, 1
For no black-bearded Vigil from thy doore......146. H.377, 13
He gives an almes, and chides them from his doore.
220. H.632, 2
Who, railing, drives the Lazar from his door,....238, H.694, 1
Finde out a Threshold or a doore,..............312. H.1014, 7
To whose glad threshold, and free door........321. H.1056, 3
Ile kisse the Threshold of thy dore............328. H.1090, 11
As for to beg my bread from doore to doore;......347. N.39, 2
And yet the threshold of my doore..............350. N.47, 13
At thy worne Doore,..........................374. N.123, 19
Into the which He enter'd: but, the Doore......385. N.190, 3
Thy Doore, as I do enter in:...................402. N.269, 5
Doors Now barre the doors, the Bride-groom puts
56. H.149, 121
Dorcas Ah Dorcas, Dorcas! now adieu...........374. N.123, 31
The monuments of Dorcas dead.................375. N.123, 84
Dorr The Humminge Dorre, the dyinge Swan
433. ins. H.293, 17a
Dorset If Dorset say, what Herrick writes, is good?
187. H.506, 6
Do's See Does
Dost For these Transgressions which thou here dost see,
4. Ap., 1
And still do'st this, and that verse reprehend:.......7. H.6, 4
Ah my Perilla! do'st thou grieve to see............9. H.14, 1
These things thou know'st to'th'height, and dost prevent
35. H.106, 21
By whose warme side thou dost securely sleep....35. H.106, 35
Warnes the last Watch; but with the Dawne dost rise
36. H.106, 57
But with thy equall thoughts, prepar'd dost stand,.37. H.106, 95
And so thou dost: for thy desires are..........37. H.106, 105
In thee, thou Man of Men! who here do'st give...41. H.117, 4
This if thou dost, woe to thee Furie, woe,........82. H.204, 9

Next, when thou **dost** perceive her fixed sight,....87. H.215, 7
Live, live thou **dost**, and shalt; for why?........89. H.219, 15
And Angels will be borne, while thou **dost** sing....102. H.252, 2
When with the Virgin morning thou **do'st** rise,..127. H.320, 1
When thou **do'st** play, and sweetly sing,.........142. H.362, 1
Thou **do'st** redeeme those times; and what was lost
147. H.377, 41
Do'st rather poure forth, then allow............148. H.377, 82
Whither **dost** thou whorry me,..................157. H.415, 1
Prithee, when next thou **do'st** invite, barre State,.161. H.424, 3
Covet not both; but if thou **dost**............169. H.446, 9
Where thou **do'st** dwell;......................170. H.452, 4
And think (as thou **do'st** walke the street)......174. H.465, 15
Me, or my shadow thou **do'st** meet............174. H.465, 16
In this regard, that thou **do'st** play.............183. H.492, 9
When I consider (Dearest) thou **dost** stay......193. H.522, 1
Who **dost** so fitly with the Lawes unite,..........201. H.557, 5
As Love shall helpe thee, when thou **do'st** go hence
219. H.627, 7
And thou Lucina, that **do'st** heare.............221. H.633, 56
Nor to the Eastern Ind **dost** rove..............229. H.662, 7
Then to thy corn-fields thou **dost** goe,..........230. H.662, 21
Which though well soyl'd, yet thou **dost** know,..230. H.662, 22
But thou art just and itchlesse, and **dost** please.252. H.745, 17
Firing thy soule, by which thou **dost** foretell....256. H.763, 8
And wonder at Those Things that thou **dost** know.
257. H.763, 22
Who with thy Thyrse **dost** thwack us:..........259. H.772, 2
And yet thou so **dost** back us..................259. H.772, 3
So long as thou **dost** heat us...................259. H.772, 9
Tell me Anthea, **dost** thou fondly dread........262. H.781, 13
Well, when to eat thou **dost** me next desire,......262. H.783, 21
Love thou **dost**, though Love sayes Nay.........264. H.790, 2
And thou **do'st** languish too:...................273. H.833, 3
But since th' art Printed, thou **dost** call........287. H.899, 3
When first I find those Numbers thou **do'st** write;
301. H.966, 1
Grow up in Beauty, as thou **do'st** begin,.........304. H.979, 1
Say, what is't that thou **do'st** aile?..............305. H.984, 9
Why **do'st** thou wound, & break my heart?....328. H.1090, 1
Take, if thou **do'st** distrust, that Vowe........328. H.1090, 6
If felt and heard, (unseen) thou **dost** me please;.331. H.1108, 1
For if thou **dost**, thou then shalt see............344. N.29, 3
I'le come, I'le creep, (though Thou **dost** threat)..349. N.46, 1
All these, and better Thou **dost** send............351. N.47, 51
Ere Thou **dost** threat me........................351. N.49, 4
Thou **dost** me fright,...........................353. N.56, 2
Thou **dost** my bread............................353. N.56, 7
Ten thousand Talents lent me, Thou **dost** write:..368. N.103, 9
Thou **dost** their wrath asswage................373. N.122, 3
Great things ask for, when thou **dost** pray,.......381. N.158, 3
That done, with Honour Thou **dost** me create....398. N.262, 3
His spunge, and stick, do ask why Thou **dost** stay?
398. N.263, 11
— — — — — — — — —, ...449. var. A.3, 29
Do't See **Much-good-do't**
Much good **do't** ye Gentlemen..................118. H.289, 12
— — — — — — — — —, ...430. var. H.267, 12
Dote If so, how much more shall I **dote** thereon,.139. H.347, 3
Doted That **doted** on a Maide of Gingerbred:....155. H.405, 10
As I've **doted** heretofore:.....................209. H.585, 8
Dotes **Dotes** less on Nature, then on Art.........202. H.560, 18
Doth Who feares to aske, **doth** teach to be deny'd...8. H.12, 2
The mellow touch of musick most **doth** wound.....12. H.24, 1
The soule, when it **doth** rather sigh, then sound...12. H.24, 2
Love is a circle that **doth** restlesse move..........13. H.29, 1
When what is lov'd, is Present, love **doth** spring;..13. H.30, 1
So when Love speechlesse is, she **doth** expresse....15. H.38, 11
Thus like a Bee, Love-gentle stil **doth** bring.......16. H.40, 7
But 'tis sweetness that **doth** please................22. H.65, 3
Thy rockie bottome, that **doth** teare thy streams....29. H.86, 3
The last is but the least; the first **doth** tell........35. H.106, 9
(While Love the Centinell **doth** keep)............35. H.106, 36
And back again, (tortur'd with fears) **doth** fly,..36. H.106, 67
And thus thy little-well-kept-stock **doth** prove,..37. H.106, 127
The lazie man the most **doth** love..............53. H.147, 14
Juno here, far off, **doth** stand..................56. H.149, 109
Doth from Panchaia come.......................57. H.149, 146
Nor **doth** this far-drawn Hemisphere.............72. H.185, 3
The debt is paid: for he who **doth** resigne........72. H.185, 26
Doth all at once impaire,.......................75. H.193, 23
Let them tell how she **doth** move.................82. H.203, 7
Of Flanks and Chines of Beefe **doth** Gorrell boast.89. H.221, 1
A little-Puppet-Priest **doth** wait,................91. H.223, 39
Upon this fetuous board **doth** stand.............92. H.223, 68
Whose foot-pace he **doth** stroak and kisse:.......93. H.223, 132
Me thinks that onely lustre **doth** appeare.......94. H.226, 3
Your sober Hand-maid; who **doth** wisely chuse,....99. H.245, 6
Who **doth** both love and feare you Honour'd Sir...99. H.245, 8
Blest is the Bride, on whom the Sun **doth** shine;.113. H.283, 48
You multiply, as **doth** a Fish..................113. H.283, 50
Of white, where nature **doth** deny...............118. H.291, 8
Look, how the Rainbow **doth** appeare..........139. H.353, 1
Prigg, when he comes to houses, oft **doth** use....143. H.368, 1
Learn this of me, where e'r thy Lot **doth** fall;....153. H.396, 1
Shew me that Hill (where smiling Love **doth** sit).154. H.403, 3
When out of bed my Love **doth** spring,..........154. H.404, 1
Pievish **doth** boast, that he's the very first......156. H.410, 1
The cold, cold Earth **doth** shake him;..........156. H.412, 18
Tell, if thou canst, (and truly) whence **doth** come
157. H.414, 1
Whose pure-Immortall body **doth** transmit......157. H.414, 9
That **doth** like me, this **doth** please;............157. H.415, 5
Who to the North, or South, **doth** set............162. H.429, 1
Of all that Nature **doth** entend.................163. H.432, 2
Rook he sells feathers, yet he still **doth** crie......163. H.439, 1
Nor **doth** the early Shepheards Starre............164. H.441, 7
Where Mab he finds; who there **doth** lie........165. H.443, 5
All with temptation **doth** bewitch...............166. H.443, 38
That **doth** the Infants face enthrall,............167. H.443, 91
Some Relique of a Saint **doth** weare:............169. H.449, 2
He that **doth** suspect, do's haste...............175. H.465, 45
Feacie (some say) **doth** wash her clothes i'th' Lie
178. H.474, 1
By thee **doth** so neglected lye;................183. H.492, 3
Where ere the luckie Lot **doth** fall,..............197. H.542, 3
A Stock of Saints; where ev'ry one **doth** weare..199. H.545, 5
Sweep your house: Who **doth** not so,............201. H.556, 7
Which like a Pinacle **doth** shew................202. H.560, 7
With paste of Almonds, Syb her hands **doth** scoure;
203. H.561, 1
This, that, and ev'ry Thicket **doth** transpire......205. H.575, 7
Whom faire Corinna sits, and **doth** comply.....206. H.575, 40
To be in that Orbe crown'd (that **doth** include..207. H.575, 59
And dismall Darknesse then **doth** smutch the face.
207. H.576, 6
And bending, (yet it **doth** not break?)..........208. H.580, 10
My head **doth** ake,..............................210. H.591, 1
Sick is the Land to'th' heart; and **doth** endure...214. H.612, 5
But what he **doth** at first entend,...............215. H.615, 5
Gander (they say) **doth** each night pisse a Bed:..223. H.636, 2
And look how when a frantick Storme **doth** tear.225. H.642, 13
So when this War (which tempest-like **doth** spoil
225. H.642, 17
Falls to a temper, and **doth** mildly cast.........225. H.642, 19
As so it **doth**? that's pittie...................229. H.659, 10
To rise as soon as day **doth** peep?...............233. H.670, 2
With North-down Ale **doth** troule here,.........235. H.674, 10
No sillable **doth** fall here,.....................235. H.674, 11
As the Godhead **doth** indite....................242. H.714, 6
Either slakes, or **doth** retire;...................242. H.714, 10
For love he **doth** call..........................247. H.727, 10
Bice laughs, when no man speaks; and **doth** protest
265. H.795, 1
He **doth** it with the sweetest tones of Art:.......266. H.799, 2
He tacks about, and now he **doth** profess.........266. H.800, 5
But ther's not one, **doth** praise the smell of thee..266. H.802, 2
Who after his transgression **doth** repent,..........268. H.809, 1
So purest Diaper **doth** shine,....................268. H.811, 7
As Julia looks when she **doth** dress.............268. H.811, 9
Imparitie **doth** ever discord bring:..............268. H.812, 1
The readinesse of doing, **doth** expresse..........275. H.845, 1
We credit most our sight; one eye **doth** please....287. H.904, 1
The Person crowns the Place; your lot **doth** fall.304. H.977, 1
What **doth** cause this pensiveness?..............305. H.984, 2
Hence I must, for time **doth** call...............306. H.984, 38
But yet a way there **doth** remaine,..............313. H.1020, 5
Vice **doth** in some but lodge awhile, not dwell...314. H.1021, 2
For as farre as that **doth** light,.................322. H.1064, 5
He raves, he rends, and while he thus **doth** tear,
325. H.1077, 5
Who by his gray Haires, **doth** his lusters tell,...328. H.1088, 5
Beg for my Pardon Julia; He **doth** winne.......329. H.1095, 3
In's Tusc'lanes, Tullie **doth** confesse,..........332. H.1115, 1
This is strong thrift that warie Rush **doth** use..332. H.1116, 3
God hath two wings, which He **doth** ever move,....340. N.6, 1
Gods Rod **doth** watch while men do sleep; & then
342. N.21, 1
The Rod **doth** sleep, while vigilant are men.......342. N.21, 2
When the house **doth** sigh and weep,.............347. N.41, 9
When the passing-bell **doth** tole,..............348. N.41, 21
Thanksgiving for a former, **doth** invite...........348. N.42, 1
Either be hot, or cold: God **doth** despise,........353. N.54, 3
How am I bound to Two! God, who **doth** give...355. N.62, 1
Who to that sweet Bread unprepar'd **doth** come....355. N.65, 9
God is all-sufferance here; here He **doth** show....357. N.74, 1
God makes not good men wantons, but **doth** bring.370. N.108, 1
True rev'rence is (as Cassiodore **doth** prove)....380. N.147, 1
God (as the learned Damascen **doth** write)......381. N.161, 1
But with the wicked if He **doth** comply,.........385. N.188, 3
As when to man He comes, and there **doth** place..385. N.189, 3
His holy Spirit, or **doth** plant His Grace..........385. N.189, 4
God **doth** embrace the good with love; & gaines..389. N.212, 1
And from Gods Prescience of mans sin **doth** flow.390. N.219, 3
Doth, here on earth, some thing of novitie;......395. N.244, 2
God **doth** not promise here to man, that He......396. N.252, 1
As my little Pot **doth** boyle,....................397. N.258, 1
God's wrathfull said to be, when He **doth** do....397. N.259, 3
That without wrath, which wrath **doth** force us to.
397. N.259, 4
Doth Jesus beare,.............................401. N.268, 2
Next **doth** her chinne with dimpled beawty striue..405. A.1, 33

In length each finger **doth** his next excell,........406. A.1, 101
True heate, whearw^th humanitie **doth** liue.........410. A.3, 30
(The generall Aprill of the worlde) **dothe** Come,..410. A.3, 34
(The skarcrow vnto Mankinde) that **doth** breed....411. A.3, 52
Shakeing the head, whilst each, to each **dothe** mourne,
411. A.3, 65
Doth not to the sight appeare...........418. A.9, 48
The first is Natures end: this **doth** imparte.421. ins. H.106, 26a
— — — — — — — — — — — —, ...421. var. H.106, 57
— — — — — — — — — — — —, ...426. var. H.197, 25
— — — — — — — — — — — —, ...436. var. H.336, 6
— — — — — — — — — — — —, ...438. var. H.412, 22
— — — — — — — — — — — —, ...438. var. H.412, 24
And thinke each man thou seest **doth** doome
441. ins. H.465, 14a
— — — — — — — — — — — —, ...441. var. H.465, 41
— — — — — — — — — — — —, ...441. var. H.465, 45
— — — — — — — — — — — —, ...443. var. H.580, 7
— — — — — — — — — — — —, ...443. var. H.637, 2
— — — — — — — — — — — —, ...445. var. H.772, 13
— — — — — — — — — — — —, ...448. var. A.1, 71
— — — — — — — — — — — —, ...453. var. H.283, 62
Doting Doting, Ile weep and say (In Truth)...135. H.336, 119
Double And **double** my affection on thee; as doe those,
78. H.197, 43
Double chinn'd, and forehead high:............138. H.342, 4
Or else a Cherrie (**double** grac't)...............164. H.440, 3
So **double** gilds the Aire, as that no night........206. H.575, 15
He's **double** honour'd, since h'as got gay cloathes:
330. H.1099, 2
Bettering them both, but by a **double** straine,....343. N.24, 3
Who by a **double** Proxie woes.................409. A.2, 82
This Janus looking **double** waye.................417. A.9, 16
Doublet With Hose and **Doublet** torne:..........295. H.942, 2
Doubt By lingring thus in **doubt**:................53. H.149, 6
Put in Feare, and hope, and **doubt**;.............116. H.285, 5
He'll do not **doubt**; This flax is spun.........168. H.443, 121
Their silv'rie Spheres, ther's none may **doubt**,....178. H.476, 8
Attempt the end, and never stand to **doubt**;....311. H.1008, 1
'Tis Wisdomes part to **doubt** a faithfull friend...333. H.1121, 2
Either with despaire, or **doubt**;..................348. N.41, 34
Doubted 'Tis to be **doubted** whether I next yeer,..140. H.355, 7
Doubtful Into a **doubtful** Twi-light; then,........76. H.193, 54
The first Act's **doubtfull**, (but we say)...........94. H.225, 9
But ever **doubtfull** Day, or night...............167. H.443, 81
Doubtless Who els with tears wo'd **doubtles** drown my ferry.
248. H.730, 26
Doubts Away with **doubts**, all scruples hence remove;
8. H.10, 7
You have hopes, and **doubts**, and feares...........96. H.232, 7
And with **doubts** discomforted,....................347. N.41, 7
All **doubts**, and manifest the where..............367. H.102, 7
— — — — — — — — — — — —, ...443. var. H.580, 12
Doucets — — — — — — — — —, ...440. ins. H.443, 56a
Dough Knead but the **Dow** and it will be........267. H.805, 3
Prosper thy Basket, and therein thy **Dow**.........269. H.818, 4
Crosse your **Dow**, and your dispatch,..........322. H.1063, 3
Of gentle Paste, and yeelding **Dow**,............374. N.123, 25
Dove The gentle **Dove** may, when these turmoils cease,
225. H.642, 21
Dove-like She kist, and wip'd thir **dove-like** eyes;..31. H.92, 11
His gently-gliding, **Dove-like** eyes,..............365. N.97, 13
Doves **Doves**, 'two'd say, yee bill too long.......57. H.149, 140
Come then, and like two **Doves** with silv'rie wings,
205. H.575, 1
Live in the Love of **Doves**, and having told....222. H.633, 32
Dow See Dough
Down See North-down
I'le drink **down** Flames, but if so be................8. H.13, 5
Come **down**, and dance ye in the toyle............9. H.15, 1
Down dead for grief, and end my woes withall:....11. H.22, 8
Tempting **down** to slide withall:...................15. H.36, 9
What ye cannot quench, pull **downe**;............21. H.61, 5
And comming **downe**, shall make no noise at all....21. H.62, 6
Then melted **down**, there let me lye..............23. H.68, 5
And looking **down** below,.........................27. H.81, 19
Between thy Breasts (then **Doune** of Swans more white)
30. H.88, 9
Hanging **down** his head t'wards me;............38. H.107, 2
For which, before thy Threshold, we'll lay **downe**..41. H.117, 7
That gallant Tulip will hang **down** his head,......41. H.118, 3
To these, make Clouds to poure **downe** raine;....47. H.133, 12
Down from her comely shoulders hung:..........51. H.142, 10
Made him take up his shirt, lay **down** his sword....65. H.171, 6
That some conceit did melt me **downe**,..........67. H.175, 15
That done, sink **down** into a silv'rie straine;....67. H.176, 5
Now, now, blowne **downe**; needs must the old stock fall.
72. H.185, 14
Fell **downe** on you,...........................74. H.190, 11
O time that cut'st **down** all!.....................85. H.211, 9
Downe, envious Time by thee...................85. H.211, 20
And laid them **downe** for Offrings at his feet.....86. H.213, 32
Leaves dropping **downe** the honyed dew,.......86. H.213, 40
Which one by one here set **downe** are...........91. H.223, 36
Charms, that call **down** the moon from out her sphere,
99. H.244, 1

Fall **down, down, down**, from those thy chiming spheres,
103. H.254, 5
And laugh no more; or laugh, and lie **down** next.
111. H.277, 2
The night, with you, in floods of **Downe**.......115. H.283, 120
Here **down** my wearyed limbs Ile lay;.........123. H.306, 1
No more shall I from mantle-trees hang **downe**,..131. H.333, 4
When as a publick ruine bears **down** All.......155. H.405, 18
Hir Mab-ship in obedient **Downe**............167. H.443, 89
Made of the Fleeces purest **Downe**...........192. H.521, 10
Wound up again: Once **down**, He's **down** for ever.
202. H.558, 2
The Watch once **downe**, all motions then do cease;
202. H.558, 3
Down fall,.....................................211. H.596, 15
As will if you yeeld, lye **down** conquer'd too.....216. H.618, 12
Fall **down** together vanquisht both, and lye....216. H.618, 15
Lungs (as some, say) ne'r sets him **down** to eate,
223. H.637, 1
And, lying **down**, have nought t' affright.......231. H.662, 74
Tumble me **down**, and I will sit.............235. H.677, 1
The Gods, he **down** the Nectar flung;..........241. H.706, 2
Chor. And lay we **down** our Pipes together,....244. H.716, 47
Into this house powre **downe** thy influence,....245. H.723, 2
And after that, lay **downe** some silver pence,....245. H.723, 9
Clouds will not ever powre **down** raine;.......247. H.725, 7
The Senators **down** tumbling with the Roofe,..252. H.745, 14
Still I write a Sweet-heart **downe**.............253. H.750, 6
Downe to a Fillit more Imperiall............256. H.763, 10
'Twas rich before; but since your Name is **downe**,
264. H.789, 3
Down, and halfe **drown'd** me with the same:....283. H.883, 2
Point be up, and Haft be **downe**;.............284. H.889, 3
Down with the Rosemary and Bayes,..........285. H.892, 1
Down with the Misleto;.......................285. H.892, 2
By laughing, too and lying **downe**,............291. H.919, 21
Which got, the third, bids him a King come **downe**.
292. H.925, 2
Thy faithfull friend, and to poure **downe**.......303. H.973, 17
Down with the Rosemary, and so.............304. H.980, 1
Down with the Baies, & misletoe:............304. H.980, 2
Down with the Holly, Ivie, all,................304. H.980, 3
Tell, and I'le lay **down** my Pipe...............305. H.984, 14
From the which hung **down** by strings,.......306. H.984, 24
Be not dismaide, though crosses cast thee **downe**;
311. H.1007, 1
With Swan-like-state, flote up & **down** thy streams:
316. H.1028, 18
Down before Baal, Bel, or Belial:............353. N.54, 2
Where God is merry, there write **down** thy fears:
355. N.63, 1
Fine flowre prest **down**, and running o're.......356. N.66, 8
Heaven to come **down**, the while we choke......366. N.98, 16
Tumble shall heav'n, and **down** will I...........371. N.114, 8
Puts **down** some prints of His high Majestie:..385. N.189, 2
Look **down**, and see.........................401. N.268, 26
Ravisht I am! and **down** I lie,...............402. N.269, 20
Thay may fall **downe** and stroake as the.......408. A.2, 57
— — — — — — — — — —, ...422. var. H.106, 61
bearing **downe** Time before you; hye....431. ins. H.283, 50c
Downcast A **down-cast** look, and sowre?........391. N.228, 12
Downfall The growth, and **down-fall** of her aged trees:
23. H.69, 2
Downy Pants with a **Downie** brest,..............57. H.149, 135
Dowry Come in for **Dowrie** with a Wife...........49. H.137, 2
My daughters **Dowrye**; haueing which...........407. A.2, 5
Doxology Sung in the high **Doxologie** of Thee...254. H.756, 16
Drakes See Fire-drakes
Drank He **drank** so much he scarce co'd stir;.....71. H.182, 9
Prig now drinks Water, who before **drank** Beere:
71. H.183, 1
And drunk with Wine, I **drank** him up..........96. H.229, 4
I have **drank** up for to please.................122. H.304, 5
Of which who **drank**, he said no thought......222. H.635, 3
Had He not **drank** them up for you...........400. N.266, 15
Drapery See Linen-drapery
Is wone with flesh, not **Drapery**.............154. H.402, 6
But such the **Drap'ry** did betray...............288. H.908, 7
Draught A deadly **draught** in them............222. H.635, 12
Draw **Draw** in't a wounded Heart:................10. H.20, 2
Draw him as like too, as you can,...............38. H.108, 5
If, Reader, then thou wilt **draw** neere,...........48. H.134, 5
Draw I co'd once (although not stocks or stones,
84. H.210, 5
As Fate do's lead or **draw** us; none,............132. H.336, 6
So **draw**, and paint, as none may do the like,....150. H.384, 5
And may'st **draw** thousands with a haire:........174. H.465, 4
Did soon **draw** in agen........................194. H.525, 5
If Accusation onely can **draw** blood,...........194. H.528, 1
Did I or love, or could I others **draw**.........201. H.557, 1
This done, we'l **draw** lots, who shall buy......215. H.616, 25
The Heifer, Cow, and Oxe **draw** neere.........230. H.662, 38
Thy witty wiles to **draw**, and get..............231. H.662, 64
Draw in your feeble fiers, while that He.......236. H.685, 5
Say what thou art. Ph. I prithee first **draw** neare.
248. H.730, 4

That done, they kisse, and so **draw** out the day:..260. H.773, 2
At night they **draw** to Supper; then well fed,..260. H.773, 3
They **draw** their clothes off both, so draw to bed. 260. H.773, 4
Drooping, I **draw** on to the vaults of death,...312. H.1013, 3
Put from, or **draw** unto the faithfull shore:....315. H.1028, 12
Draw me, but first, and after Thee I'le run,..358. N.77, 14
Draw out of bad a soveraigne good to man.....383. N.176, 2
It, or to **drawe** the Cittie to his Eyes..........412. A.3, 78
Euc. Charon, O Charon, **draw** thy Boat to th' Shore, 416. A.8, 1
— — — — — — — — — — —, ...423. var. H.128, 45
Your eyes are they, wherewith you **draw** the pure 432. ins. H.283, 70h

Drawer Bring me my Rose-buds, **Drawer** come; 208. H.582, 1

Drawers The **drawers** of the axeltree............239. H.696, 8
Draw-gloves At **Draw-Gloves** we'l play,...........99. H.243, 1
If not, at **Draw-gloves** we will play;..........215. H.616, 5
Pusse and her Prentice both at **Draw-gloves** play; 260. H.773, 1

Drawing **Drawing** thy curtains round: Good night. 146. H.376, 14
— — — — — — — — — — —, ...431. var. H.283, 52

Drawn See **Far-drawn**
Over the which a State was **drawne**...............8. H.11, 5
Who told me, they had **drawn** a thred..........18. H.47, 7
When Virgins hands have **drawn**..................75. H.193, 2
Sceanes to cheat us neatly **drawne**.............76. H.195, 8
Time-past so fragrant, sickly now **drawn** in....77. H.197, 28
Ile have no Sceans, or Curtains **drawn**:.........154. H.402, 2
Into your Chests, **drawn** by your painfull Thumb. 221. H.633, 41
The more th'are **drawn**, the lesse they wil grow dry. 273. H.831, 2
Drawn was his tooth; but stanke so, that some say, 323. H.1066, 3
Over the which a meet sweet skin is **drawne**.....404. A.1, 23
The Lines of Sorrowe, that lye **drawne** in mee....411. A.3, 60

Draws He weares all day, and **drawes** those teeth at night. 46. H.129, 6
Which **draws** the sight thereto,.................75. H.193, 13
Dearest of thousands, now the time **drawes** neere, 219. H.627, 1
When as her Aprill houre **drawes** neare,.......221. H.633, 58
To tell how night **drawes** hence, I've none,...246. H.724, 2
I have, to sing how day **drawes** on............246. H.724, 4
Drawes out th' Elixar of true penitence.........386. N.196, 4

Dread Deare, is it this you **dread**,..............53. H.149, 13
'Tis Omen full of **dread**:....................56. H.149, 106
That Towrs high rear'd **dread** most the lightnings threat: 181. H.483, 14
Tell me Anthea, dost thou fondly **dread**........262. H.781, 13
Dread not the shackles: on with thine intent;...317. H.1034, 1
Charmes the danger, and the **dread**...........323. H.1065, 6
When as the Mountains quak'd for **dread**,......393. N.232, 5
But **dread** that you doe more offend........431. ins. H.283, 60s
— — — — — — — — — — —, ...446. var. H.873, 1

Dreadful And look upon our **dreadfull** passages,....14. H.35, 6
Like to a **dreadfull** Comet in the Aire:........87. H.215, 6
His passage through that **dreadfull** shade:.....265. H.798, 8
There give me day; but here my **dreadfull** night:.343. N.25, 7
With others, to the **dreadfull** Doome:.........358. N.78, 6
Christ, when He hung the **dreadfull** Crosse upon, 382. N.167, 1
Thy **dreadfull** Woes.........................401. N.268, 29

Dreadfulness Death and **dreadfulnesse** call on,.....373. N.121, 5
Dreads Nor **dreads** he any thing:.............259. H.772, 12

Dream Then **dream**, ye heare the Lamb by many a bleat 36. H.106, 49
Before that we have left to **dreame**:..........69. H.178, 48
By **Dream** I saw, one of the three..............153. H.399, 1
I thought at first 'twas but a **dream**,..........203. H.562, 3
In a **Dreame**, Love bad me go..................219. H.628, 1
'Twas but a **dream**; but had I been...........279. H.863, 13
Me thought I saw (as I did **dreame** in bed)...313. H.1017, 1

Dreamed I **dream'd** this mortal part of mine......16. H.41, 1
I **dream'd** we both were in a bed..............20. H.56, 1

Dreams But ah! if empty **dreames** so please,.......20. H.56, 9
By **dreames**, each one, into a sev'rall world.......21. H.57, 2
Sweeten, and make soft your **dreames**:.........35. H.106, 44
With thousand such enchanting **dreams**, that meet 36. H.106, 53
If you can see, how **Dreams** do creep..........79. H.198, 9
And let thy **dreames** be only fed..............175. H.465, 49
Shall gently melt thee into **dreames**............192. H.521, 8
But that I understood by **dreames**,............290. H.915, 5
In this world (the Isle of **Dreames**)..........376. N.128, 1

Dreamt I **dreamt** the Roses one time went..........8. H.11, 1
I **dreamt**, last night, Thou didst transfuse.......357. N.75, 1

Dredged The spangling Dew **dreg'd** o're the grasse shall be 143. H.370, 3

Dregs But the base **dregs** and lees of vestiments?.302. H.970, 2
Drench To **drench**, but not to drown our seed...279. H.867, 6
Drenched **Drencht** in Ale, or drown'd in Beere...255. H.761, 20
Cha. Those souls which ne'er were **drencht** in pleasures stream, 417. A.8, 27

Dress A sweet disorder in the **dresse**..............28. H.83, 1
And with flowers **dresse** my Tomb.............44. H.125, 4
A Virgins face she had; her **dresse**..............51. H.142, 7
Till you come forth. Wash, **dresse**, be briefe in praying: 68. H.178, 27
And with Smallage **dresse** my Tomb:...........89. H.220, 2
And so **dresse** him up with Love,..............108. H.266, 7
How tedious they are in their **dresse**...........118. H.291, 4
But to **dresse** the Bridall-Bed,..................141. H.360, 3
And when I see that other **Dresse**..............202. H.560, 3
That **Dress**, this Sprig, that Leaf, this Vine;...215. H.616, 23
Be she shewing in her **dresse**,..................232. H.665, 5
As Julia looks when she doth **dress**............268. H.811, 9
To **dress** thy silent sepulchre...................289. H.912, 4
The Daughters wild and loose in **dresse**;......310. H.1004, 7
And Lilly-work will **dresse** Thee;...............345. N.33, 19
Dresse Thee with flowrie Diaper...............402. N.269, 13
To **dresse** my Maiden-Saviour...................402. N.270, 6
Some bitts of thimbles seeme to **dresse**.....440. ins. H.443, 45aa

Dressed Above an houre since; yet you not **drest**,.68. H.178, 8
Chor. Come let's away, and quickly let's be **drest**, 86. H.213, 45
Drest up with all the Country Art..............101. H.250, 8
Drest in her nak't simplicities:...............154. H.402, 4
But when She's up and fully **drest**,............154. H.404, 3
With Garlands **drest**, so I....................161. H.425, 10
Because with Flowers her Temple was not **drest**: 197. H.539, 8
Wherewith ye **drest** the Christmas Hall:........304. H.980, 4
How Matron-like didst thou go **drest**!.........375. N.123, 63
No, but He **drest** Him with our humane Trim,..390. N.222, 3
Where, **drest** with garlands, there they walk the ground, 417. A.8, 29

Dresses — — — — — — — —, ...447. var. A.1, 2
Dressing Dispatch your **dressing** then; and quickly wed: 216. H.618, 7

Drew So **drew** my life unto an end..........153. H.399, 6
Last night I **drew** up mine Account,...........369. N.107, 1

Dried And **dry'd** his dropping Tresses:..........27. H.81, 24
Yet **dry'd**, ere you distill your Wine...........88. H.216, 12
An Apples-core is hung up **dry'd**,.............93. H.223, 126
But when the drought has **dri'd** the knot;....279. H.867, 3
That Teare shall scarce be **dri'd** before........328. H.1090, 10
— — — — — — — — — — —, ...421. var. H.92, 11
Of a **dried** Canker, with a sagge........433. ins. H.293, 31b
Dryed, hony-combs, Browne Achorne cupps 439. ins. H.443, 45j

Drink See **Dew-drink-offerings**
I'le **drink** down Flames, but if so be.............8. H.13, 5
To **drink** in Notes, and Numbers; such.........22. H.68, 3
Drink, and dance, and pipe, and play;.........39. H.111, 3
O thou the **drink** of Gods, and Angels! Wine...45. H.128, 11
Of which, sweet Swans must **drink**, before they sing 45. H.128, 34
Let others **drink** thee freely; and desire.......46. H.128, 49
A Goblet next Ile **drink**......................80. H.201, 21
Come, I will **drink** a Tun.....................81. H.201, 35
This flood I **drink** to thee:....................81. H.201, 38
Which freely **drink** to your Lords health,......102. H.250, 38
Drink frollick boyes, till all be blythe.........102. H.250, 43
Bacchus, let me **drink** no more;................122. H.304, 1
We'l **drink**, my Wickes, untill we be.........136. H.336, 138
His Nails they were his meat, his Reume the **drink**. 156. H.409, 2
Their Milke thy **drinke**; and thou shalt eate..192. H.521, 12
Where both may rage, both **drink** and dance together. 206. H.575, 38
Ile **drink** the aged Cecubum,..................208. H.582, 3
And roundly **drinke** we here;..................219. H.629, 2
I greedy of the prize, did **drinke**,.............222. H.635, 5
Over-sowr'd in **drinke** of Souce:...............223. H.638, 7
That I may **drink**.........................227. H.653, 3
To **drink** to Thee my Ben....................227. H.653, 8
Drink Wine, and live here blithefull, while ye may: 228. H.655, 1
I'le eat and **drink** up all here.................235. H.674, 18
Drink rich wine; and make good cheere,......238. H.691, 3
I'le **drink** to the Garlands a-round it:..........239. H.695, 3
And **drink** your fill of it.....................261. H.778, 3
And **drink** to your hearts desiring............263. H.784, 6
Drink now the strong Beere,.................263. H.784, 13
For Bread, **Drinke**, Butter, Cheese; for every thing 287. H.903, 2
What can my Kellam **drink** his Sack.........290. H.918, 1
Thee lesse to taste, then to **drink** up their spring; 299. H.956, 2
Drinke up...................................307. H.988, 1
When I **drinke** my capring wine:..............309. H.996, 2
When I **drinke** my wanton wine:..............309. H.996, 4
When I **drinke** my sprightly wine:............309. H.996, 6
When I **drinke** my frolick wine:..............309. H.996, 8
Who unurg'd will not **drinke**.................317. H.1035, 16
So much as to **drink**........................320. H.1051, 11
And giv'st me Wassaile Bowles to **drink**.......350. N.47, 39

That for my sin, Thou, Thou must **drink**,......400. N.267, 7
Chor. Lord, I'le not see Thee to **drink** all.....400. N.267, 10
Or while that each from other's breath did **drincke** 410. A.3, 5
Canst **drincke** in Earthern Cupps, wch ne're Contayne 422. ins. H.106, 116a
To laugh and quaff and **drink** old sherry,.445. ins. H.730, 26c
Drinker **See Water-drinker**
Drinkers To Beer **Drinkers**....................320. H.1051, 6
Drinking When our **drinking** has no stint,.......122. H.304, 3
Which, Spunge-like **drinking** in the dull-......167. H.443, 97
Drinking wine, & crown'd with flowres.........191. H.519, 8
W^th Flame, and Rapture; **drincking** to the odd..410. A.3, 21
Drink-offering For one **drink-offering**, poured out by thee. 14. H.35, 8
As a **Drink-offering**, to the dead:.............169. H.449, 20
Drinks Prig now **drinks** Water, who before drank Beere: 71. H.183, 1
Drinks of distemper, or ha's cause to cry......148. H.377, 87
Drip Lets **drip** a certain Gravie from her eyes...331. H.1107, 2
Dripping Steale a swolne sop out of the **Dripping** pan. 331. H.1106, 2
Drive To **drive** the Devill from the Cod-piece..93. H.223, 121
Let the winds **drive**.........................134. H.336, 59
Drive all hurtfull Feinds us fro,...............177. H.473, 7
Who can with so small charges **drive** the buck..178. H.474, 4
Drive thence what ere encumbers,.............260. H.777, 3
Driven No more shall I, since I am **driven** hence,.131. H.333, 1
And when those clouds away are **driven**,.......188. H.508, 5
That thus from vices **driven**,..................363. N.92, 15
Drives The new successor **drives** away old Love.191. H.517, 2
Who, railing, **drives** the Lazar from his door,..238. H.694, 1
Slowly her chariot **drives**, as if that she........358. N.77, 3
Driving **Driving** these sharking trades, is out at heels. 153. H.398, 2
Drizzling Mine eyes, like clouds, were **drizling** raine, 237. H.687, 1
By Dewes and **drisling** Raine,..................257. H.767, 5
Droop **Droop**, **droop** no more, or hang the head......7. H.9, 1
If Sapho **droop**; Daisies will open never,.......41. H.118, 7
Ye **droop**, and weep;..........................104. H.257, 17
The bastard Slips may **droop** and die..........278. H.859, 3
Thou seest me Lucia this year **droope**,.........303. H.973, 1
The while my deer Anthea do's but **droop**,.....320. H.1054, 3
Drooping The **Drooping** West, which hitherto has stood 25. H.77, 3
The **drooping** Kingdome suffers all.............89. H.219, 8
From the dull confines of the **drooping** West,....242. H.713, 1
Drooping, I draw on to the vaults of death,....312. H.1013, 3
Droops **Droops**, dies, and falls without the cleavers stroke. 23. H.69, 6
Drop One **drop** now deads a spark; but if the same 40. H.113, 3
Which, as they **drop** by **drop** doe passe..........44. H.127, 5
Drop the fat blessing of the sphears............57. H.149, 152
Not one **drop** to light on me.....................62. H.162, 6
And as a vapour, or a **drop** of raine............69. H.178, 63
If you can see, that **drop** of raine............79. H.198, 7
Balm may thy Trees **drop**, and thy Springs runne oyle 269. H.818, 7
One that sho'd **drop** his Beads for thee.......321. H.1056, 16
How will it **drop** pure hony, speaking these?..328. H.1089, 4
For, rather then one **drop** shall fall............377. N.129, 7
Dropped **Dropt** from the eyes of ravisht Girles..167. H.443, 109
(**Dropt** for the jarres of heaven) fill'd t'engage.206. H.575, 46
Dropping **See Plenty-dropping**
And **dropping** here, and there:..................10. H.20, 3
And dry'd his **dropping** Tresses:..............27. H.81, 24
Leaves **dropping** downe the honyed dew,.......86. H.213, 40
Pierc't through, and **dropping** bloud, for me,....400. N.267, 4
Drops Beset with Mirtles; whose each leafe **drops** Love. 107. H.265, 4
Some **Drops** of Wine,.........................401. N.268, 16
Drosomell With handsome-handed **Drosomell**....184. H.492, 31
Drought But when the **drought** has dri'd the knot; 279. H.867, 3
A **drought** of wine, ale, beere (at all).........291. H.919, 6
No **drought** upon thy wanton waters fall.......316. H.1028, 19
Drown Wept as he'd **drowne** the Hellespont,.....42. H.119, 10
This day Ile **drowne** all sorrow;...............65. H.170, 5
Not sent ye for to **drowne** your paine,.......102. H.250, 54
And **drown** yee with a flowrie Spring:......113. H.283, 44
Of that white Pride, and **Drowne**.............115. H.283, 119
Whose woollie-bubbles seem'd to **drowne**........167. H.443, 88
No more wo'd **drown** mine eyes, or me..........237. H.687, 8
Who els with tears wo'd doubtles **drown** my ferry. 248. H.730, 26
Burne, or **drowne** me, choose ye whether,......254. H.757, 1
To drench, but not to **drown** our seed..........279. H.867, 6
Of a world to **drowne** but One................302. H.968, 12
Drowned **See Grief-drowned**
And thereupon, in tears half **drown'd**,............18. H.46, 3
When as Leander young was **drown'd**,..........42. H.119, 1
Like to a widdow **drown'd** in woe:...........47. H.132, 6
To be in Oyle of Roses **drown'd**,................50. H.140, 7
Drown'd in Delights; but co'd not die.........67. H.175, 18
Lies **drown'd** with us in endlesse night..........69. H.178, 68
(Some say) for joy, to see those Kitlings **drown'd**. 80. H.200, 2
In Lethe to be **drown'd**;.....................81. H.201, 50
Ships have been **drown'd**, where late they danc't before. 85. H.212, 2
Dry your sweet cheek, long **drown'd** with sorrows raine; 105. H.259, 1
A Strawberry shewes halfe **drown'd** in Creame? 164. H.440, 6
I sho'd delight to have my Curles halfe **drown'd** 214. H.612, 11
Drown'd in the bloud of Rubies there, not die...216. H.618, 16
Drencht in Ale, or **drown'd** in Beere...........255. H.761, 20
Drown'd in the Sea of wild Eternitie:.........256. H.763, 14
Down, and halfe **drown'd** me with the same:...263. H.883, 2
And on a sudden both were **drown'd**...........294. H.937, 4
And the world is **drown'd** in sleep,............347. N.41, 10
Drown'd in one endlesse Day..................354. N.58, 12
As to be **drown'd**,............................368. N.104, 8
But such as have been **drown'd** in this wilde sea, 417. A.8, 31
Drowning **Drowning**, **drowning**, I espie..........302. H.968, 1
It saves the soule, by **drowning** sin...........396. N.253, 2
Drowns There's that, which **drowns** all care, stout Beere; 101. H.250, 37
Drowsy Differs not much from **drowzie** slothfullnesse. 173. H.459, 14
Drum Know so long Treaties; beate the **drumme** 432. ins. H.283, 140c
Drunk But when that men have both well **drunke**, and fed, 7. H.8, 3
And return him **drunk** to bed:...............39. H.111, 10
And **drunk** with Wine, I drank him up.........96. H.229, 4
Being **drunke**, who 'twas that Can'd his Ribs last night. 186. H.501, 4
And having **drunk**, we raise a shout...........198. H.544, 10
Was **drunk** to Antonie.........................240. H.705, 8
(When **drunke** with Beere) to light him home, i'th' dark. 273. H.834, 4
Blisse (last night **drunk**) did kisse his mothers knee: 295. H.943, 1
Where he will kisse (next **drunk**) conjecture ye..295. H.943, 2
The Husband **drunke**, the Wife to be..........310. H.1004, 9
Buggins is **Drunke** all night, all day he sleepes; 311. H.1011, 1
Drunk up the wine of Gods fierce wrath;......400. N.266, 11
When **drunck** wth Rapture; Curse the blind & lame 412. A.3, 89
Dry Of them, the spring's once **drie**;............43. H.123, 20
Dry chips, old shooes, rags, grease, & bones;.93. H.223, 119
Dry your sweet cheek, long drown'd with sorrows raine; 105. H.259, 1
As your hours doe, and **drie**.................125. H.316, 16
My old leane wife, shall kisse it **dry**:.........134. H.336, 84
To **drye** the Widowes teares; and stop her Swoones, 201. H.557, 17
Who gripes too hard the **dry** and slip'rie sand..221. H.633, 52
No Goose layes good eggs that is trodden **drye**..223. H.636, 4
Kisses are but **dry** banquets to a Feast........265. H.797, 2
The more th'are drawn, the lesse they wil grow **dry**. 273. H.831, 2
Punchin a **dry** plant-animall...................273. H.832, 2
Teares quickly **drie**: griefes will in time decay:..293. H.930, 1
'Tis but a fierce desire of hot and **drie**..........293. H.931, 2
No question but Dols cheeks wo'd soon rost **dry**, 325. H.1078, 1
Both soft, and **drie**;...........................349. N.47, 6
— — — — — — — — — — —, ...434 var. H.293, 38
Are pucker'd Bullace, Canckers and **dry** 439. ins. H.443, 45m
Dry-decrepit For your **drie-decrepid** man:..........10. H.19, 12
Dry-house In a **drie-house** all things are neere...179. H.476, 27
Drying And kisses **drying** up his tears:.........50. H.139, 11
Dry-roasted **Dry-rosted** all, but raw yet in her eyes. 90. H.222, 2
Dual God hates the **Duall** Number; being known.396. N.249, 1
Ducats With casters **duckets** which poore they 440. ins. H.443, 56a
Duck Next may your **Duck** and teeming Hen...179. H.476, 19
Duckets **See Ducats**
Ducking **Ducking** in Mood, and perfect Tense,....91. H.223, 52
Ductile Subtile and **ductile** Codlin's skin;.......91. H.223, 61
Rich, by the **Ductile** Wool and Flax.........221. H.633, 43
Due First, for Effusions **due** unto the dead,........23. H.72, 1
Unto the shades have been, or now are **due**,....27. H.82, 10
For to say truth, all Garlands are thy **due**;....41. H.117, 9
You first of all crown'd her; she must of **due**,..94. H.224, 9
Due to the Merits, not Authoritie.............120. H.296, 2
Jove's is the first and last: The Morn's his **due**,.128. H.321, 3
Paske, though his debt be **due** upon the day......142. H.363, 1
Lambs, by the Law, which God requires as **due**..341. N.9, 2
Without **due** reverence, playes the cheaters game..347. N.39, 6
What bitter cups had been your **due**,...........400. N.266, 14
Which to thy Memorie stands as **due**..........414. A.5, 3
Dukeship May his pretty **Duke-ship** grow.......108. H.266, 1

Dull In this dull Devon-shire:....................19. H.51, 4
This makes Cuffe dull; and troubles him the most,
39. H.109, 3
Like a dull Twi-light? Tell me; and the fault...77. H.197, 29
How dull and dead are books, that cannot show
141. H.359, 1
Dull to my selfe, and almost dead to these.....214. H.612, 1
From the dull confines of the drooping West,...242. H.713, 1
Thou & I'le sing to make these dull Shades merry,
248. H.730, 25
Give me a man that is not dull,..............318. H.1036, 1
Thou say'st I'm dull; if edge-lesse so I be,....327. H.1081, 1
Dark and dull night, flie hence away,..........364. N.96, 8
Onely, by this dull creature, to expresse.......384. N.179, 3
Long before this, the base, the dull, the rude,..398. N.263, 5
Or e're dark Clouds do dull, or dead the Mid-dayes Sun.
401. N.268, 9
Dulled Nor dull'd wth Iron sleeps; but haue out-worne
410. A.3, 19
Dull-eyed Shut not so soon; the dull-ey'd night..164. H.441, 1
Dull-light Which, Spunge-like drinking in the dull-
Light of the Moon, seem'd to comply,
167. H.443, 97-98
Dully What is the reason Coone so dully smels?..210. H.589, 1
Duly Duely, Morne and Ev'ning, come,..........44. H.125, 3
Dumb Nor cheek, or tongue be dumbe:...........80. H.201, 2
And be it sin here to be dumb,................365. N.97, 2
Sho'd fame be dumb;.........................375. N.123, 88
Dundrige Dundrige his Issue hath; but is not styl'd
195. H.533, 1
Dungeon Never was Dungeon so obscurely deep,..52. H.146, 5
Dunghills (Bred from the dung-hils, and adulterous rhimes,)
155. H.405, 13
During See Out-during
Durst Had, first, durst plow the Ocean.........36. H.106, 76
Dust See Mill-dust, Pin-dust
When thou shalt laugh at my Religious dust;....49. H.138, 3
About this Urne, wherein thy Dust is laid,.....73. H.186, 18
Is more in thee, then in her dust,.............148. H.377, 104
And large she spreads by dust, and sweat....148. H.377, 114
The whole world die, and turn to dust with thee..155. H.405, 16
Alike i'th' dust..............................190. H.515, 32
And that my dust was to the earth commended..334. H.1124, 4
Tell me the motes, dust, sands, and speares.....340. N.3, 11
And be return'd from out my dust:..............358. N.78, 2
Yett I keepe peacefull in my dust...............407. A.2, 18
Duty The Crowne of dutye is our dutye; well....412. A.3, 103
Dwell Contempts in Courts and Cities dwell;........6. H.2, 21
Work that to life, and let me ever dwell........14. H.35, 13
First, let us dwell on rudest seas;.............111. H.278, 3
Dwell, then in lothed Devonshire..............111. H.278, 8
Besides (Ai me!) since she went hence to dwell,.159. H.421, 27
Where thou do'st dwell;.......................170. H.452, 4
I dwell,....................................178. H.475, 14
Wherein I dwell;............................198. H.544, 26
In whom the spirit of the Gods do's dwell,......256. H.763, 7
To dwell,...................................258. H.770, 2
Vertue and pleasure, both to dwell in one......293. H.935, 2
Vice doth in some but lodge awhile, not dwell...314. H.1021, 2
If thou know'st not where to dwell,...........334. H.1125, 7
Wherein to dwell.............................349. N.47, 2
Infinitie to dwell............................354. N.58, 4
Flie up, to dwell.............................363. N.92, 17
God's said to dwell there, wheresoever He......385. N.189, 1
Dwellest Thou dwel'st aloft, and I want wings to flie.
352. N.52, 2
Dwells I freeze, I freeze, and nothing dwels.........8. H.13, 1
That's my Julia's breast; where dwels.........40. H.115, 13
Dye See Die
Dyed See Ale-dyed, Died
Dyes See Dies
Dying Ile leave thy heart a dying................27. H.81, 36
Nor feare, or wish your dying day.............38. H.106, 146
Help! O help! your Boy's a dying..............50. H.139, 5
To morrow will be dying.......................84. H.208, 4
Neer the dying of the day,.....................255. H.761, 15
Who dying in her blooming yeares,............257. H.764, 5
What was't (ye Gods!) a dying man to save,..278. H.860, 3
The Humminge Dorre, the dyinge Swan..433. ins. H.293, 17a

Each Each here declining Violet.....................7. H.9, 4
By dreames, each one, into a sev'rall world......21. H.57, 2
Each one, by nature, loves to be a King..........21. H.58, 2
A deale of courage in each bosome springs........25. H.77, 9
Cato the Censor, sho'd he scan each here........28. H.84, 6
In each thy dainty, and peculiar part!...........30. H.88, 2
And taking thence from each his flame;.........31. H.92, 7
Gives thee each night a Maidenhead............35. H.106, 42
That they wo'd each Primrose-tide,.............44. H.125, 2
Each way illustrious, brave; and like to those....45. H.128, 14
For each Ringlet there's a snare...............52. H.147, 4
But she co'd see each eye to stamp a teare:....58. H.150, 4
Each Flower has wept, and bow'd toward the East,
68. H.178, 7
How each field turns a street; each street a Parke.68. H.178, 30
Devotion gives each House a Bough,...........68. H.178, 32
Or Branch: Each Porch, each doore, ere this,..68. H.178, 33
Fill each part full of fire, active to doe........79. H.197, 79
For now each tree do's weare..................80. H.201, 6
In Wine, whose each cup's worth..............80. H.201, 19
Mirt. 'Tis true indeed; and each of us will bring.86. H.213, 33
That each Lyrick here shall be.................88. H.218, 4
Beset with Mirtles; whose each leafe drops Love..107. H.265, 4
Each Virgin, like a Spring,....................110. H.274, 11
As a fir'd Altar, is each stone,.................113. H.283, 23
Each striving to devise.........................114. H.283, 69
And know each wile,..........................115. H.283, 125
Each hieroglyphick of a kisse or smile;........115. H.283, 126
Each must, in vertue, strive for to excell;......121. H.298, 1
Each way smoothly Musicall:.................122. H.303, 4
By cold neglect, each one,.....................131. H.330, 10
Our own fair wind, and mark each one.........133. H.336, 39
Which crept into each aged Sire...............135. H.336, 104
Loth to depart, but yet at last, each one......140. H.355, 1
But from thy warm-love-hatching gates each may
146. H.377, 15
Makes the smirk face of each to shine,........147. H.377, 72
Each like a poore and pitied widowhood.......150. H.382, 4
Good morrow to each maid;....................156. H.412, 6
How each thing smells divinely redolent!......159. H.421, 19
Is each neate Niplet of her breast.............164. H.440, 10
Unlesse you skin again each part..............164. H.442, 10
Saints will come in to fill each Pew and Place..168. H.445, 6
Yee silent shades, whose each tree here........169. H.449, 2
And if more; Each Nipple cries,...............183. H.491, 3
That turns each Sphere,......................193. H.524, 5
Each way smooth and civilly:..................195. H.530, 4
Set each Platter in his place:..................201. H.556, 2
Manners each way musicall:...................204. H.569, 10
My Love will fit each Historie................207. H.579, 8
A kiss to each; and so we'l end................216. H.616, 36
Gander (they say) doth each night pisse a Bed:..223. H.636, 2
Gives to each Mead a neat enameling...........224. H.642, 4
Imprinted in each Herbe and Flower:...........230. H.662, 32
And each Ringlet of her haire,.................232. H.665, 11
Thousands each day passe by, which wee,........234. H.671, 1
Each one to make his melody:..................243. H.716, 20
That through each room a golden pipe may run..245. H.723, 3
Each Cobler is a King;.......................259. H.772, 11
It Wars goe well; each for a part layes claime:..260. H.774, 3
That brave Vibration each way free;............261. H.779, 5
Seeal'd up with Night-gum, Loach each morning lyes,
269. H.816, 1
Sometimes (in mirth) he sayes each whelk's a sparke
273. H.834, 3
Each griefe we feele, that likewise is a Kite.....278. H.862, 3
Thus time do shift; each thing his turne do's hold;
285. H.892, 21
Sho'd I not put on Blacks, when each one here....288. H.907, 1
And yet each Verse of thine...................289. H.911, 9
This if ye do, each Piece will here be good,.....290. H.914, 9
Smooth in each limb as a die;.................305. H.984, 20
Kings must not use the Axe for each offence:....309. H.998, 1
And cal'd each line back to his rule and space...311. H.1006, 4
Like will to like, each Creature loves his kinde;..319. H.1043, 1
Each bending then, will rise a proper flower.....320. H.1054, 6
Forgive me God, and blot each Line.............339. N.2, 5
Three fatall Sisters wait upon each sin;..........341. N.11, 1
Her egg each day:............................350. N.47, 46
Me twins each yeare:.........................350. N.47, 48
Each evening and each morrow:.................353. N.56, 9
Each Maid, her silver Filleting,................360. N.83, 42
Back, back again; each thing is done............366. N.97, 24
Each one his severall offering;.................368. N.102, 21
Where each chast Soule........................369. N.106, 7
For each one Body, that i'th earth is sowne,...388. N.208, 1
But for each Graine, that in the ground is thrown,
388. N.208, 3
But look, how each transgressor onward went....391. N.227, 3
And when He blest each sev'rall Day, whereon....396. N.249, 3
By Thine approach, each their beholding eye.....398. N.263, 14
T'accept each Heart,.........................401. N.268. 33
Each cheeke resembling still a damaske rose,.......404. A.1, 14
In length each finger doth his next excell,........406. A.1, 101
Each richly headed with a pearly shell...........406. A.1, 102
Then lett each Cheeke of thyne intice............408. A.2, 43
Somewhat peculiar to each lymm,...............408. A.2, 74
Or while that each from other's breath did drincke
410. A.3, 5
Each takes A weeping farwell, rackt in mynde....411. A.3, 63
Shakeing the head, whilst each, to each dothe mourne,
411. A.3, 65
But let each p^rsant Cheeke appear...............413. A.4, 3
At each warning hees as much..................418. A.9, 49
Fill each part full of Fire, let all my good.427. ins. H.197, 77a
And each a choyse musitian...........433. ins. H.293, 17b
And thinke each man thou seest doth doome
441. ins. H.465, 14a
Eager The eager Boyes to gather Nuts...........56. H.149, 122
Your eager Bridegroome with auspitious feet.....216. H.618, 2
His eager Eye, or Smoother Smyle,..............413. A.4, 27
— — — — — — — — — — —, ...442. var. H.575, 20

— — — — — — — — — —, ...443. var. H.580, 10
Ear See **Earrings'**
My puling Pipe to beat against thine **eare**:......17. H.42, 2
Ile wish I might turne all to **eare**,................22. H.68, 2
Whether by th' eye, or **eare**, or no:..............24. H.73, 2
Or **eare** of burning jealousie....................49. H.136, 19
Cynthius pluck ye by the **eare**,..................52. H.147, 1
Sunk from the tip of your soft **eare**,..............61. H.160, 8
And lend a gentle **eare** to one report...........86. H.213, 11
Two stiffe-blew-Pigs-feet, and a sow's cleft **eare**...89. H.221, 4
Your soft **eare** to Discipline....................96. H.232, 2
And that Apollo shall so touch Your **eare**,......107. H.264, 2
We must not thinke his **eare** was sterv'd:......119. H.293, 14
Then to the chin, the cheek, the **eare**,...........130. H.329, 12
True Calenders, as Pusses **eare**................134. H.336, 89
'Twill never please the pallate of mine **eare**.....152. H.390, 2
Or the cleft **eare** of a Mouse....................223. H.638, 6
I have, which, with a jealous **eare**,...............246. H.724, 14
Then Lutes and Harpes shall stroke the **eare**.....247. H.725, 10
Having his eyes still in his **eare**,................263. H.785, 6
Then bore me through the **eare**;................293. H.934, 6
To chafe o're much the Virgins cheek or **eare**:..329. H.1095, 2
One **Eare** tingles; some there be,...............329. H.1096, 1
Then let the Harps inchantments strike mine **eare**;
343. N.25, 4
Why wore th' Egyptians Jewells in the **Eare**?....346. N.36, 1
Mine eye and **eare**.............................353. N.56, 10
Heart, **Eare**, and Eye, and every thing...........364. N.96, 5
But earth: such vowes nere reach Gods **eare**......381. N.158, 8
Frozen wth Griefe; and place it in thyne **eare**,....412. A.3, 82
Cha. Prethee relate, while I give **ear** and weep.....416. A.8, 12
This little pendant on your **eare**,..................417. A.9, 2
And though his visage hung i' th' **eare**............418. A.9, 47
— — — — — — — — — —, ...452. var. H.443, 13
Earl Shor'd up by you, (Brave **Earle** of Westmerland.)
40. H.112, 4
You are a Lord, an **Earle**, nay more, a Man,....172. H.459, 1
Earls Whose husbands may **Earles**...............239. H.695, 8
Early Opens the way for **early** flowers;............23. H.70, 2
Early setts ope to feast, and late:..............147. H.377, 46
Nor doth the **early** Shepheards Starre............164. H.441, 7
Early-rising As yet the **early-rising** Sun.........125. H.316, 3
Earrings' The Wante of **Eare rings** braueryе,.......409. A.2, 90
Ear's Commends it to your **eares** soft tipp.........417. A.9, 14
Ears Next, his wilde **eares**, like Lethern wings full spread,
33. H.99, 3
Nor are thine **eares** so deafe, but thou canst heare.36. H.106, 83
More in thine **eares**, then in thine eyes..........37. H.106, 88
Ripe **eares** of corne, and up to th'**eares** in snow:...59. H.154, 6
Begin to charme, and as thou stroak'st mine **eares**.67. H.176, 1
Crown'd with the **eares** of corne, now come,......101. H.250, 5
As the Summers Corne has **eares**:..............102. H.253, 4
To charme our soules, as thou enchant'st our **eares**.
103. H.254, 6
Washes the golden **eares** of corne..............112. H.283, 20
With withered cherries; Mandrakes **eares**;......120. H.293, 43
About your **eares**; and lay upon...............127. H.319, 43
Untill our tongues shall tell our **ears**,..........136. H.336, 143
Have reference to the shoulders, not the **eares**.....142. H.363, 4
For which their cryes might beate against thine **eares**,
149. H.377, 125
That sets all **eares** on fire.......................151. H.388, 4
As men, turne all to **eares**.......................151. H.388, 8
His eyes and **ears** strive which sho'd fastest run...158. H.418, 2
Lust ha's no **eares**; He's sharpe as thorn;......165. H.443, 13
Fashion'd like Thee; which though 'tave **eares**...174. H.465, 21
Beumont and Fletcher, Swans, to whom all **eares**
206. H.575, 51
I will whisper to your **eares**,...................208. H.580, 5
The signe of Circumcision in his **eares**.......232. H.666, 2
A chaine of Cornes, pickt from her **eares** and toes:
232. H.668, 2
Not for to hide his high and mighty **eares**;......275. H.843, 2
That Stubble stands, where once large **eares** have been.
275. H.843, 4
Nothing he loves on't but the chaps and **ears**:....305. H.982, 2
So that the man that will but lay his **eares**,....330. H.1100, 15
Of Corn, when Summer shakes his **eares**;.........340. N.3, 12
Fright mine **eares**, and fright mine eyes,......348. N.41, 42
Your hearts, and hands, lips, **eares**, and eyes.......366. N.98, 9
Come pitie us; and bring your **eares**,..........373. N.123, 5
Her **eares**, which like twoe Laborinth's are plac'd..405. A.1, 39
On eyther side of theis, quicke **Eares**............408. A.2, 39
— — — — — — — — —, ...433. var. H.293, 14
Daffe nuts, soft Jewes **eares**, and some thin.439. ins. H.443, 45f
Earth See **Under-earth**
O **Earth**! **Earth**! **Earth** heare thou my voice, and be
19. H.52, 1
For with the flowrie **earth**,.......................80. H.201, 3
The **earth**, that lightly covers her.................123. H.310, 6
As we were Lords of all the **earth**.............133. H.336, 56
Shall come to strew thy **earth** with flowers.......145. H.376, 6
The cold, cold **Earth** doth shake him;...........156. H.412, 18
A scent, that fills both Heaven and **Earth** with it.157. H.414, 10
Dear Amarillis! Mon. Hark! Sil. mark: Mir. this **earth** grew
sweet......................................159. H.421, 11
Th' easie **earth** that covers her...............224. H.640, 4
Wanting both Root, and **Earth**; but thy.........278. H.859, 4
Earth afford ye flowers to strew................306. H.984, 43
In **earth**:....................................314. H.1024, 8
Or to the Golden-cheap-side, where the **earth**...316. H.1028, 15
And that my dust was to the **earth** commended...334. H.1124, 4
For, 'tis no easie way from **Earth** to Heaven.......352. N.52, 4
Thy soft sweet **Earth**! but (like a spring).........361. N.83, 71
Of Him, who's Lord of Heav'n and **Earth**;......366. N.98, 19
But **earth**: such vowes nere reach Gods eare......381. N.158, 8
For each one Body, that i'th **earth** is sowne,.....388. N.208, 1
Doth, here on **earth**, some thing of novitie;......395. N.244, 2
As Hell, and **Earth**, and Heav'n may stand amaz'd.
399. N.263, 31
For **earth** and sea; this Cost..........432. ins. H.283, 70c
— — — — — — — — — — —, ...448. var. A.3, 5
Earthen Give me my **earthen** Cups again,.........222. H.635, 9
Canst drincke in **Earthern** Cupps, wch ne're Contayne
422. ins. H.106, 116a
Earthly I feare no **Earthly** Powers;...............65. H.170, 1
Earthquake That **Earth-quake** shook the house, and gave the stout...52. H.146, 15
Earth's To heale my **Earths** infirmitie............397. N.257, 4
Earthworms Meane time like **Earth-wormes** we will craule below,.......................................257. H.763, 21
Earwig A bloated **Earewig**, and a Flie;.........119. H.293, 38
Ear-witnesses Our trust farre more then ten **eare-witnesses.**
287. H.904, 2
Ease See **Heart's-ease**
By sudden death to give me **ease**....:...........34. H.103, 14
But thou at home, blest with securest **ease**,.......36. H.106, 69
Shall I seek (for speedy **ease**)...................40. H.115, 7
For to quench ye, or some **ease**...................62. H.162, 8
You can **ease** my heart, and doe..................74. H.191, 7
My wearyed Pinnace here finds **ease**:............94. H.225, 2
Ease my sick head,............................95. H.227, 5
That having **ease** me given,.....................95. H.227, 29
That sleeps at home; and sayling there at **ease**,..128. H.323, 3
Who spurn'd at Envie; and co'd bring, with **ease**,.137. H.341, 5
Can **ease** the rawnesse, or the smart;..........164. H.442, 9
Oft bend the Bow, and thou with **ease** shalt do,..245. H.722, 1
Charme then the chambers; make the beds for **ease**,
245. H.723, 11
But toyes, to give my heart some **ease**:........246. H.724, 30
Will, after **ease**, a richer harvest yield:........292. H.922, 2
Welcome as slumbers; or as beds of **ease**........300. H.961, 3
In the hope of **ease** to come,.................315. H.1027, 1
What others have with cheapnesse seene, and **ease**,
330. H.1100, 1
After thy labour take thine **ease**,..............334. H.1123, 1
To **ease** this smart, or cure this wound;............342. N.17, 6
I kenn my home; and it affords some **ease**,......352. N.51, 9
Or strike so as to **ease** me......................353. N.56, 24
Whom **ease** makes his, without the help of blowes.
372. N.116, 4
God on our Youth bestowes but little **ease**;......383. N.175, 1
The Jewes their beds, and offices of **ease**,........386. N.193, 1
God gives to none so absolute an **Ease**,..........387. N.199, 1
Wee cannot **ease**;.............................401. N.268, 30
Which gave his Elveships stomacke **ease**....435. ins. H.293, x
Easier As easie, and els **easier** too:..............245. H.720, 12
East Each Flower has wept, and bow'd toward the **East**,
68. H.178, 7
That all the Spices of the **East**.................69. H.179, 3
Yet the next Morne, re-guild the fragrant **East**...72. H.185, 7
Bloom'd from the **East**, or faire Injewel'd May...112. H.283, 2
'Tis then broad Day throughout the **East**........154. H.404, 4
Of Day break from the pregnant **East**, 'tis time.207. H.575, 64
To see the day spring from the pregnant **East**,....242. H.713, 2
With my face towards the **East**.................307. H.991, 8
Gods wayes and walks, which lie still **East** and West.
386. N.193, 4
Easter-day Untill the dancing **Easter-day**,........285. H.892, 7
Eastern And Titan on the **Eastern** hill...........68. H.178, 25
Nor to the **Eastern** Ind dost rove...............229. H.662, 7
Easter's Or **Easters** Eve appeare................285. H.892, 8
Easy Whose **easie** natures like it well,..............22. H.66, 3
Mak'st **easie** Feare unto thee say,..............36. H.106, 74
Then for an **easie** fansie; place..................39. H.108, 9
The Gods are **easie**, and condemne...............47. H.132, 13
Into the Brain by **easie** sleep:...................79. H.198, 10
Away in **easie** slumbers.........................95. H.227, 4
An **easie** blessing to your Bin,.................178. H.476, 2
With such an arm'd, but such an **easie** Foe,....216. H.618, 11
Th' **easie** earth that covers her...................224. H.640, 4
As **easie**, and els easier too:...................245. H.720, 12
For, 'tis no **easie** way from Earth to Heaven......352. N.52, 4
The **easy** Gods..........................431. ins. H. 283, 60o
— — — — — — — — — — —, ...440. var. H.443, 54
Eat To taste boyl'd Nettles, Colworts, Beets, and **eate**
37. H.106, 113
But none co'd **eate** it, 'cause it stunk so much.....47. H.131, 6
Or frantick I shall **eate**.........................81. H.201, 31
Feed, and grow fat; and as ye **eat**,.........102. H.250, 44
With some small glit'ring gritt, to **eate**........119. H.293, 10
Where Trouble serves the board, we **eate**........124. H.312, 3

We'le **eate** our Beane with that full mirth,.......133. H.336, 55
Curse not the mice, no grist of thine they **eat**:...141. H.358, 1
To **eate** thy Bullocks thighs, thy Veales, thy fat.147. H.377, 63
Last night thou didst invite me home to **eate**;....161. H.424, 1
That though a thousand, thousand **eat**;..........178. H.476, 6
All know a Fellon **eate** the Tenth away.........180. H.480, 2
Jack kisses Jill, and bids her freely **eate**:........186. H.498, 2
How wo'd he **eate**, were not his hindrance such?..191. H.518, 6
Their Milke thy drinke; and thou shalt **eate**....192. H.521, 12
Here we securely live, and **eate**...............198. H.544, 1
We **eate** our own, and batten more,...........200. H.552, 13
Lungs (as some, say) ne'r sets him down to **eate**,
223. H.637, 1
Give me then an Ant to **eate**;................223. H.638, 5
I'le **eat** and drink up all here................235. H.674, 18
Who though they do not **eat**,....................250. H.736, 5
The like not Heliogabalus did **eat**:..............262. H.783, 4
Well, when to **eat** thou dost me next desire,....262. H.783, 21
Like those infernall Deities which **eate**.........272. H.826, 1
Sent forth by them, our flesh to **eate**, or bite.....278. H.862, 4
Eate thou not all, but taste on some:............288. H.909, 2
Rid these, and those, and part by part **eat** all....305. H.982, 4
The servants thumblesse, yet to **eat**,..........310. H.1004, 3
Not to **eat** equall portions; but to rise..........310. H.1005, 3
And **eat** with thee a savory bit,................321. H.1056, 5
Who plants an Olive, but to **eate** the Oile?....322. H.1060, 1
Instead of Bread, Grubs gives them stones to **eat**.
325. H.1077, 4
That at the tide, he has not bread to **eate**........327. H.1086, 4
That which the Aunt did tast, not **eate**;..439. ins. H.443, 45e
Eaten Which **eaten**, they and I..................173. H.460, 5
Eaten I have; and though I had good cheere,....197. H.541, 1
Eatest For if thou **eat'st** it to excess;............288. H.909, 3
Eating With **eating** many a miching Mouse.......246. H.724, 24
Eats Gryll **eates**, but ne're sayes Grace; To speak the troth,
48. H.135, 1
Eates to ones thinking, of all there, the least.....118. H.292, 2
Of which he **eates**, and tastes a little............119. H.293, 27
Of sugred Rush, and **eates** the sagge...........119. H.293, 33
Mease brags of Pullets which he **eats**: but Mease..142. H.361, 1
Talkes most, **eates** most, of all the Feeders there..191. H.518, 2
Only, if one prove addled, that he **eates**........204. H.568, 3
Brown bread Tom Pennie **eates**, and must of right,
309. H.997, 1
Pray not for silver, rust **eats** this;..............381. N.158, 5
Ebb Never did Moone so **ebbe**, or seas so wane,...52. H.146, 7
Your Night, your Prison, and your **Ebbe**; you may
52. H.146, 10
As that your pans no **Ebbe** may know;.........179. H.476, 11
Ebbs You have **ebbes** of face and flowes,..........96. H.232, 5
But they fill up their **Ebbs** again:.............133. H.336, 20
That **ebs** from pittie lesse and lesse............143. H.369, 4
Gods Bounty, that **ebbs** lesse and lesse,.........358. N.76, 1
Eclogues And with thy **Eclogues** intermixe............5. H.2, 9
Economics All **Oeconomicks**, know'st to lead....148. H.377, 90
Ecstasy Confus'd, in this brave **Extasie**..........402. N.269, 21
Att that wch in her **extasie** had past;..........410. A.3, 26
Edgeless Thou say'st I'm dull; if **edge-lesse** so I be,
327. H.1081, 1
Edification Unto thine own **Edification**...........185. H.496, 6
Eels **Eeles** winds and turnes, and cheats and steales; yet **Eeles**
153. H.398, 1
E'en See **Even**
E'ne all the standers by.........................9. H.15, 8
And **e'en** with cold half starved...............26. H.81, 12
E'en all almost:...............................72. H.185, 9
Faire was the Dawne; and but **e'ne** now the Skies
81. H.202, 1
E'en Death, to die for thee..................109. H.267, 20
For as my Heart, **ene** so mine Eye..............154. H.402, 5
E'en but a bit,...............................171. H.455, 12
E'ene all Religious courses to be rich...........266. H.800, 1
Ther's loathsomnesse **e'en** in the sweets of love...297. H.949, 4
E'ene so my numbers will astonisht be.........301. H.962, 5
E'en as Thou di'st,..............................401. N.268, 25
E'er On with thy fortunes then, what **e're** they be;....6. H.3, 7
When **ere** my heart, Love's warmth, but entertaines,
40. H.113, 1
Goe, perjur'd man; and if thou **ere** return........49. H.138, 1
Tell me, has Strut got **ere** a title more?..........53. H.148, 3
And make, what **ere** they touch, turn sweet.....55. H.149, 62
So that where **ere** ye look, ye see,.............90. H.223, 19
What **ere** enters, out it shall:...................116. H.285, 8
None, Posthumus, co'd **ere** decline 132. H.336, 7
That when **ere** I wooe, I find..................138. H.346, 3
Learn this of me, where **e'r** thy Lot doth fall;...153. H.396, 1
Where **ere** the luckie Lot doth fall,.............197. H.542, 3
But he will say, who **e'r** those Circlets seeth,...197. H.543, 3
Where **e're** they met, or parting place has been..250. H.737, 8
As **ere** was wrapt in winding sheet..............257. H.764, 2
Time is the Bound of things, where **e're** we go,..257. H.766, 1
Drive thence what **ere** encumbers, ...260. H.777, 3
When **ere** I go, or what so **ere** befalls..........269. H.818, 1
Let not thy Tomb-stone **er'e** be laid by me:....281. H.875, 1
Love is a sirrup; and who **er'e** we see..........297. H.949, 1
How **ere** it fortuned; know for Truth, I meant..304. H.977, 3
Old Widow Shopter, when so **ere** she cryes,....331. H.1107, 1
God crowns our goodnesse, where so **ere** He sees,
356. N.71, 3
Shall we **ere** bring coy Brides to bed;..........360. N.83, 50
When **e're** thou speak'st, look with a lowly eye:..362. N.89, 3
God is all-present to what **e're** we do,..........394. N.237, 1
So that when **'ere** we circumvolve our Eyes,.....415. A.7, 15
— — — — — — — — — — —, ...450. var. A.9, 30
— — — — — — — — — — —, ...453. ins. H.283, 20j
Effect The Cause, **th'effect** wo'd die.............32. H.96, 4
But only by impression of **effect**...............385. N.186, 4
Which to **effect**, let ev'ry passing Bell..........392. N.230, 11
Effectuate Go on brave Hopton, to **effectuate** that.310. H.1002, 1
Effused Unto thy Ghost, th' **Effused** Offering:......27. H.82, 8
And there to lick th' **effused** sacrifice:..........222. H.634, 4
Effusions First, for **Effusions** due unto the dead,.....23. H.72, 1
Then for **effusions**, let none wanting be,.........219. H.627, 5
Some **effusions** let me have,.....................307. H.991, 5
Egg Which is as white and hair-less as an **egge**...139. H.349, 2
She goes her long white **egg** to lay.............246. H.724, 12
Her **egg** each day:..............................350. N.47, 46
Eggs Of Emits **eggs**; what wo'd he more?.......119. H.293, 36
And for their two **egs** render ten................179. H.476, 21
Eggs Ile not shave: But yet brave man, if I...202. H.557, 27
The **Eggs** of Pheasants wrie-nosed Tooly sells;..204. H.568, 1
No Goose layes good **eggs** that is trodden drye...223. H.636, 4
Eglantine Take this sprig of **Eglantine**..............88. H.217, 2
Egyptian — — — — — — — — —, ...427. var. H.197, 57
Egyptians Illustrious Idoll! co'd th' **Ægyptians** seek
78. H.197, 57
Why wore th' **Egyptians** Jewells in the Eare?....346. N.36, 1
Either A bud in **either** cheek.........................18. H.45, 4
To take her by the **either** hand:................37. H.106, 96
About the Arch of **either** eye;..................46. H.130, 8
Gryll **either** keeps his breath to coole his broth;....48. H.135, 2
Grown violent, do's **either** die, or tire............51. H.143, 4
Still **either** way;...............................65. H.172, 14
Of **either** may.................................66. H.172, 23
Prig mony wants, **either** to buy, or brew.........71. H.183, 4
Where **either** too much light his worth..........75. H.193, 22
Quite dispossest of **either** fray, or fret...........82. H.204, 6
In **either** which a small tall bent.................92. H.223, 95
A change, when Fortune **either** comes, or goes:..128. H.323, 8
Either is welcome; so I have...................158. H.420, 3
For **either** sheet, was spread the Caule..........167. H.443, 90
Either to send me kindly thine,..................168. H.446, 7
That sharply trickles from her **either** eye.........178. H.474, 2
That brings us **either** Ale or Beere;............179. H.476, 26
So that as **either** shall expresse................192. H.521, 23
Either slakes, or doth retire;....................242. H.714, 10
As wearie, not o'recome by **either**...............244. H.716, 48
That **either** profits, or not hurts at all...........252. H.748, 2
And a little Oyle to **either**:.......................258. H.769, 6
Either with old, or plant therein new thorne:....259. H.771, 6
Her **either** cheeke with bashfullness..............268. H.811, 10
Farre better 'twere for **either** to be mute,........287. H.901, 5
Here may sing the rest of **either**:.................304. H.976, 4
When **either** price, or praise is ta'ne away......316. H.1033, 2
Were they not basted by her **either** eye.......325. H.1078, 2
Science puffs up, sayes Gut, when **either** Pease..327. H.1085, 1
Either with despaire, or doubt;.................348. N.41, 34
Either be hot, or cold: God doth despise,.........353. N.54, 3
Heaving up my **either** hand;....................364. N.95, 2
Either as when (the learned Schoolemen say)...388. N.210, 2
On **either** side with rich rare Jewells grac'd,......405. A.1, 40
On **eyther** side of theis, quicke Eares...........408. A.2, 39
Have pity **either** on my tears or Youth,...........416. A.8, 4
Either's When **eithers** heart, and **eithers** hand did strive
147. H.377, 39
That gently purles from **eithers** Oat.............243. H.716, 18
Either's welcome, Stinke or Civt..............306. H.987, 3
Elbows When as his owne still out at **elboes** is?....295. H.941, 8
Electra Sweet **Electra**, and the choice............16. H.39, 7
O my **Electra**! be...............................258. H.767, 19
Element Were she an **Element** of fire...........115. H.283, 110
In that congesting **element**......................245. H.720, 6
Eleven Telling the Clock strike Ten, **Eleven**, Twelve, One.
114. H.283, 76
Elf See **Elve**
Elfish-majesty Rear'd, lyes her **Elvish-majestie**:..167. H.443, 87
Elfship's Which gave his **Elveships** stomacke ease.
435. ins. H.293, x
Elixir Drawes out th' **Elixar** of true penitence.....386. N.196, 4
Elixar to the minde,...........................432. ins. H.283, 70i
Elm The staffe, the **Elme**, the prop, the shelt'ring wall
72. H.185, 12
Else When no force **else** can get the masterdome...21. H.60, 2
Or **else** desir'st that Maids sho'd tell.............34. H.103, 7
Or **else** because Grill's roste do's burn his Spit,...48. H.135, 3
Armes, and hands, and all parts **else**,..............53. H.147, 7
To flaw, or **else** to sever:.......................66. H.172, 27
Retires himselfe, or **else** stands still..............68. H.178, 26
Will live with thee, or **else** for thee will die.......70. H.181, 24
'Tis she! 'tis she! or **else** some more Divine....112. H.283, 11
Or **else** to ashes he will waste...................113. H.283, 40
With inward Buckram, little **else**.)...............118. H.291, 12

Or else force a passage in:....................121. H.297, 12
Or else trans-fuse thy breath into the chest,....129. H.327, 3
And give me meate, or give me else thy Plate...161. H.424, 4
Or else a Cherrie (double grac't)...............164. H.440, 3
Or else a crum,................................171. H.455, 13
Or to Rewards, or else to Punishments.........182. H.487, 2
Or else sweet Nimphs do you but this;......185. H.495, 5
Or where else shall we find....................188. H.509, 6
To very few, or else to none....................200. H.552, 20
Or let her Grant, or else Deny,..................207. H.579, 7
Or else by Armes..............................:213. H.609, 5
Or else spin out the thread of sands,..........215. H.616, 7
For all I have, or else can do,................223. H.635, 15
Nailes from her fingers mew'd, she shewes: what els?
232. H.668, 4
As easie, and els easier too:..................245. H.720, 12
When all Birds els do of their musick faile,......247. H.726, 1
Who els with tears wo'd doubtles drown my ferry.
244. H.730, 26
Pauls hands do give, nought else for ought we know.
248. H.73¹, 4
Or els not one there must enter................256. H.762, 12
Wash your hands, or else the fire..............263. H.786, 1
Feed on the paste of Filberts, or else knead......269. H.818, 5
Truth, yet Teages truths are untruths, (nothing else.)
282. H.880, 2
Place my words, and all works else.............286. H.897, 9
Or else because th' art like a modest Bride,......301. H.963, 3
And as that part, so every portion else...........307. H.992, 5
Can live by love, or else grow fat by Play:.....325. H.1077, 2
Whether I was my selfe, or else did see........326. H.1080, 1
Known, or els seen to be the emptier:........341. N.15, 4
Was nothing els,..............................345. N.33, 15
And take me up; or els prevent the fall...........352. N.51, 8
God, He is there, where's nothing else (Schooles say)
388. N.207, 3
And nothing else is there, where He's away.....388. N.207, 4
I'le take my share; or els, my God,............399. N.265, 9
Or ells that she on that white waxen hill..........405. A.1, 63
Iff not, it dyes, or eles recoyles.................408. A.2, 72
— — — — — — — — —, ...426. ins. H.197, 48d
Elsewhere When the ruffe is set elsewhere?.......282. H.878, 8
Elve Elve Boniface shall next be Pope...........93. H.223, 112
Elves And some have heard the Elves it call......91. H.223, 24
Now, we must know, the Elves are led..........92. H.223, 74
The Elves, in formall manner, fix...............92. H.223, 93
The Elves present to quench his thirst.........119. H.293, 20
Among the Elves, (if mov'd) the stings.....165. H.443, 16
Sell, and brought hither by the Elves...........166. H.443, 62
The which the Elves make to excite............167. H.443, 114
The Gnats-watch-word the Elves are gone.....168. H.443, 117
And the Elves also,...........................217. H.619, 3
Any Orts the Elves refuse......................223. H.638, 19
Now they the Elves within a trice,......434. ins. H.293, a
Elveship's See Elfship's
Elvish-majesty See Elfish-majesty
Elysian Vnto the port mouth of th' Elisian feilds,..405. A.1, 68
A breath of balm along the Elizean fields..........416. A.8, 8
Elysium Elizium to thy wife and thee;..........38. H.106, 138
— — — — — — — — —, ...449. var. A.8, 8
'Em Thy long-black-Thumb-nail marks 'em out for ill:
66. H.173, 2
Batt he gets children, not for love to reare 'em;...72. H.184, 1
But out of hope his wife might die to beare 'em...72. H.184, 2
Of fie upon 'em! Lastly too, all witt..........150. H.382, 17
Let Country wenches make 'em fine...........323. H.1068, 13
For my Locks (Girles) let 'em be..........330. H.1098, 3
Embalm And bring our Spices, to embalm Thee dead:
399. N.263, 38
Embalmed Thy wings shall be embalm'd by me,..103. H.255, 7
For me embalm'd to live againe;...............313. H.1020, 6
Embalming For my Embalming (Sweetest) there will be
20. H.55, 9
For my embalming, Julia, do but this,..........129. H.327, 1
Embers To thee-ward dy'd i'th'embers, and no fire
78. H.197, 36
He burnes to Embers on the Pile...............113. H.283, 30
Then as ye sit about your embers,...........127. H.319, 37
From th' embers, then the kitlings eyne,........136. H.336, 146
Emblems — — — — — — — — —, ...441. var. H.465, 24
Embrace When I embrace thy knee;..............281. H.874, 4
God doth embrace the good with love; & gaines..389. N.212, 1
— — — — — — — — — —, ...425. var. H.197, 19
Embraced Which I will keep embrac'd,............13. H.31, 9
By my soft Nerv'lits were embrac'd:.............16. H.41, 8
And what though you had been embrac't........49. H.136, 26
Embraces Where hast thou been so long from my embraces,
77. H.197, 19
Who doe with sweet embraces,................260. H.777, 6
— — — — — — — — — —, ...426. var. H.197, 35
Embracing Too temp'rate in embracing? Tell me, ha's desire
78. H.197, 35
Embracings — — — — — — — — — — —, ...426. var. H.197, 35
Emergent Emergent Venus from the Sea?........112. H.283, 10
Emerging — — — — — — — —, ...430. var. H.283, 10
Emits See Emmets'

Emmets' Of Emits eggs; what wo'd he more?....119. H.293, 36
Empearl See Impearl
Empire's This Kingdomes fortune, and that Empires fate:
330. H.1100, 8
Empires Empires of Kings, are now, and ever were,
162. H.430, 1
Employed Live employ'd, and so live free........53. H.147, 11
Emptied And emptied soon the glasse;...........222. H.635, 6
Emptier Known, or els seen to be the emptier:....341. N.15, 4
Empty But ah! if empty dreames so please,........20. H.56, 9
Thee and thine Altars emptie..................296. H.946, 24
Chor. Stand empty here for ever:..............374. N.123, 17
Enamel Can ever rust th'Enamel of the light.....206. H.575, 16
Enameled With fields enameled with flowers,.....36. H.106, 46
In that ennamel'd Pansie by,..................107. H.263, 9
This done, then to th' enameld Meads..........230. H.662, 29
— — — — — — — — — —, ...430. var. H.283, 2
Enameling Gives to each Mead a neat enameling..224. H.642, 4
Encarved Encarv'd upon the Leaves and Rind.....169. H.449, 8
Enchant And to enchant yee more, see every where
115. H.283, 101
Enchanted Or some enchanted Place, I do not know
326. H.1080, 7
Charm'd and enchanted so,...................335. H.1129, 3
Enchantest To charme our soules, as thou enchant'st our eares.
103. H.254, 6
Enchanting With thousand such enchanting dreams, that meet
36. H.106, 53
Enchantment That high Enchantment I betake me now:
62. H.161, 10
With thy enchantment, melt me into tears.......67. H.176, 2
An Enchantment, or a Snare,.................232. H.665, 12
I shall find enchantment there.................253. H.750, 12
Enchantments Let my Enchantments then be sung, or read.
7. H.8, 4
On this sick youth work your enchantments here:
99. H.244, 2
And my Enchantments too;....................198. H.544, 27
Then let the Harps inchantments strike mine eare;
343. N.25, 4
Enchantress A young Enchantresse close by him did stand
313. H.1017, 7
Enchased A way enchac't with glasse & beads....90. H.223, 1
Which, though enchas'd with Pearls, contain....222. H.635, 11
Enchasing Wise hand enchasing here those warts,.166. H.443, 60
— — — — — — — — — —, ...452. var. H.443, 60
Enchequered Are neatly here enchequered.......166. H.443, 56
Encircle Encircle with the Bride-grooms Points...114. H.283, 80
Encircled But, amongst All encircled here, not one
94. H.224, 5
Enclarited Cheeks like Creame Enclarited:........138. H.342, 6
Encline See Incline
Enclosed You are like Balme inclosed (well)......88. H.216, 13
Enclos'd within a christall shrine:.............135. H.336, 98
Enclosures Instead of neat Inclosures.............345. N.33, 9
Encolorings With thousand rare encolourings:....130. H.329, 21
Encourage To encourage on the Bride;..........221. H.633, 27
Encouraged Parts be encouraged,......427. ins. H.197, 77b
Encrease See Increase
Encrystalled But Lovers tears inchristalled,.......44. H.127, 4
Encumbers Drive thence what ere encumbers,....260. H.777, 3
Encurled Locks incurl'd of other haire;........253. H.750, 11
Encurlld together, and noe difference show.431. ins. H.283, 50f
End But if thou read'st my Booke unto the end,.......7. H.6, 3
Yet doe it to this end: that I,...................11. H.20, 7
Down dead for grief, and end my woes withall:....11. H.22, 8
(Counsell concurring with the end)............38. H.106, 130
And that is Death, the end of Woe..............60. H.157, 6
And Love shall crown my End with Peace.......73. H.187, 11
By Arts wise hand, but to this end............76. H.193, 46
Or went'st thou to this end, the more to move me,
77. H.197, 23
Upon an end, the Fairie-Psalter,................92. H.223, 71
Of her Delayes must end; Dispose.............114. H.283, 93
And magicks for to end, and hells,............115. H.283, 134
Let my haire then stand an end:................117. H.286, 6
It is the End that crownes us, not the Fight.....123. H.309, 2
An end to all his stately purposes.............137. H.341, 6
Y'ave farced well, pray make an end;..........146. H.377, 24
Their taste unto the lower end.................147. H.377, 68
So drew my life unto an end...................153. H.399, 6
To give an end: Mir. To what? Scil. Such griefs as these.
159. H.421, 32
Putrefaction is the end.......................163. H.432, 1
Thee chiefly for their pleasures end............175. H.465, 42
Their end, though ne'r so brave:.............176. H.467, 15
The All, and End..............................189. H.515, 6
Be-pranckt with Ribbands, to this end,........193. H.521, 44
That he holds firmly to the end................215. H.615, 6
A kiss to each; and so we'l end...........216. H.616, 36
All scores; and so to end the yeere............230. H.662, 14
Fate gives a meeting. Death's the end of woe....257. H.766, 2
And end......................................258. H.770, 6
Green, to the end of dayes...................261. H.778, 12
A glorious end by such a Noose,..............279. H.863, 11
Unto the end of daies.........................281. H.874, 15

End now the White loafe, & the Pye,............285. H.894, 1
With the end that I propound?.................286. H.897, 4
And having once brought to an end..........289. H.911, 18
'Tis not the Fight that crowns us, but the end..293. H.933, 2
And by that One blow set an end to all........310. H.1002, 4
Attempt the end, and never stand to doubt;....311. H.1008, 1
But yet no end of those therein or me:.......313. H.1019, 2
Reward, we know, is the chiefe end of toile...322. H.1060, 2
To his Book's end this last line he'd have plac't,
335. H.1130, 1
Him, as He is, is labour without end..........340. N.8, 2
God has his whips here to a twofold end,......343. N.26, 1
Mine end near was,..........................346. N.38, 17
Me, to this end,.............................351. N.47, 52
Who slowly goes, rids (in the end) his way.....352. N.51, 4
Must last with Satan, to the end of life.........362. N.91, 2
Reading Thy Bible, and my Book; so end....371. N.115, 12
Blest with the Meditation of my end:..........392. N.230, 2
Then He will give a happy end to it...........396. N.252, 4
The first is Natures end: this doth imparte
421. ins. H.106, 26a
not halfe so much the Act, as end......421. ins. H.106, 42b
— — — — — — — — — — —, ...var. 425. H.197, 14
In that you doe beginne, then end:....431. ins. H.283, 60t
Endear Nor can these figures so thy rest endeare,.36. H.106, 55
This is to live, and to endeere.................233. H.670, 15
Ended Grace by his Priest; The feast is ended..120. H.293, 54
My wooing's ended: now my wedding's neere;..180. H.479, 1
All Rites well ended, with faire Auspice come...286. H.898, 9
My Fates are ended; when thy Herrick dyes,.329. H.1095, 7
Ile write no more of life; but wish twas ended,.334. H.1124, 3
To her warm bosome, then our Rites are ended...366. N.97, 29
Paul, he began ill, but he ended well;........387. N.200, 1
Ending And yet our way has no ending.........195. H.534, 12
All things have an ending day:................224. H.639, 2
Have ending.................................377. N.128, 24
Endite See Indite
Endless Here shall my endless Tabernacle be:....60. H.156, 4
As endless prove;...........................66. H.172, 29
Lies drown'd with us in endlesse night.........69. H.178, 68
What? shall we two our endlesse leaves take here
73. H.186, 9
With endless life are crown'd.................81. H.201, 52
But endlesse Peace, sit here, and keep.........104. H.256, 15
Who hold fast here an endlesse lively-hood......152. H.392, 8
Commixt they meet, with endlesse Roses crown'd.
206. H.575, 20
Endlesse Ice, and endlesse Snow:.............266. H.803, 3
Love is a Circle, and an Endlesse Sphere;......274. H.839, 1
To hold us two, an endlesse honour have......281. H.875, 6
Life endlesse sign'd to thee and me............288. H.906, 2
And weepe for me, lost in an endlesse night....298. H.952, 2
In endlesse mirth,...........................314. H.1024, 5
Of Roses have an endlesse flourishing..........330. H.1100, 10
Drown'd in one endlesse Day..................354. N.58, 12
How do's she erre in endlesse night!..........393. N.233, 4
Whose blessèd Youth with endless flow'rs is crown'd.
417. A.8, 30
Endless-calendar Writ in the Poets Endlesse-Kalendar:
168. H.444, 6
Ends To get thine ends, lay bashfulnesse aside;....8. H.12, 1
The bed for luckie ends:.......................54. H.149, 44
Welcome as are the ends unto my Vowes:.....77. H.197, 14
Upon the ends of these neat Railes...........92. H.223, 91
Shall make thy actions with their ends to meet...128. H.320, 8
Being here their ends deny'd..................152. H.391, 3
These, or those ends, to which Thou wast design'd.
181. H.483, 4
The wronged Client ends his Lawes...........190. H.515, 23
With wealth, but for those ends she was entended:
201. H.557, 8
Grow for two ends, it matters not at all,......232. H.667, 1
Then reach those ends that thou wast destin'd to.
254. H.756, 8
But the anger ends all here,...................255. H.761, 19
Those ends in War the best contentment bring,..316. H.1029, 1
Their ends for Pleasure, do not live, but last..328. H.1088, 10
Manners are good: but till his errand ends,....378. N.137, 7
Much as the ends are to be lookt unto..........387. N.200, 4
To th' good and bad, in common, for two ends:
387. N.201, 2
And shaps my Function, for more glorious ends:.411. A.3, 58
Fayrie land: so ends his feast............435. ins. H.293, ff
Endued With sweetness, smoothness, softness, be endu'd.
290. H.914, 4
Endure (Ulysses-like) all tempests to endure;.....23. H.71, 5
Thy selfe, if want comes to endure:...........37. H.106, 104
Love-sick I am, and must endure...............60. H.157, 1
The Lillie will not long endure;...............60. H.159, 13
Ah, cruell Love! must I endure................74. H.191, 1
Those ills that mortall men endure,............153. H.395, 1
Mirt. Never, O never! Still I may endure.....159. H.421, 33
Love in extreames, can never long endure......185. H.494, 4
Here shall endure thy vast Dominion...........210. H.592, 4
Sick is the Land to' th' heart; and doth endure.214. H.612, 5
The turmoiles they endure that love..........219. H.628, 6
Endure that luke-warme-name of Serving-man:.265. H.796, 2
'Tis sweet to thinke on what was hard t' endure.
276. H.849, 2
Th' inundation to endure......................302. H.968, 6
No Kingdomes got by Rapine long endure......314. H.1023, 2
Let's endure one Martyrdome.................315. H.1027, 2
And let it work, for I'le endure...............342. N.17, 11
This can't endure;..........................353. N.56, 20
Endured Long enough has endur'd,..............247. H.727, 8
Endures Endures an everlasting punishment.......213. H.606, 2
That as her selfe, or Heauen indures.....422. ins. H.106, 92d
Endymion That art the cause Endimion;.........183. H.492, 7
Shall write in Spice, Endimion 'twas..........184. H.492, 39
Endymion's My lov'd Endymions Court;.........183. H.492, 18
Endimions Moon to fill up full, remember me:..184. H.492, 42
Enemies Then to sow Discord 'mongst the Enemies.
196. H.535, 2
Enfeebles Enfeebles much the seeds of wickednesse.
109. H.270, 2
Enflamed See Inflamed
Enflesh To enflesh my thighs, and armes:.........10. H.19, 6
Enforce Will enforce the Moon to stay,.........276. H.850, 12
Enforced Since I must leave thee; and enforc'd, must say
46. H.128, 39
Enforcement Whereas but one enforcement is....390. N.225, 2
Enfreezed See Enfriezed
Enfriezed Of shifted Snake: enfreez'd throughout.166. H.443, 67
Engage (Dropt for the jarres of heaven) fill'd t'engage
206. H.575, 46
Engender Had met t'engender with the night;....64. H.169, 6
Let but thy voice engender with the string,...102. H.252, 1
Engendering Give my dead picture one engendring kisse:
14. H.35, 12
English The word is Roman; but in English knowne:
106. H.261, 3
Of English Poets, and 'tis thought the Worst...156. H.410, 2
Engrossed Or like old Testaments ingrost,......190. H.515, 43
Enjewelled Bloom'd from the East, or faire Injewel'd May
112. H.283, 2
Which break from the Injeweld tyres...........165. H.443, 30
Injewelld wth thy Natiue worthe,..............409. A.2, 102
Enjoy Let's enjoy our merryment:...............39. H.111, 2
Lastly, with friends t'enjoy our dayes...........42. H.121, 4
And here enjoy our Holiday....................132. H.336, 16
Having All, injoy not One.....................157. H.415, 8
We pray 'gainst Warre, yet we enjoy no Peace.264. H.793, 1
Enjoy a Christning yeare by yeare;............291. H.919, 10
Enjoying Wherein t'ave had an enjoying........195. H.534, 6
Less happy, less enjoying thee................229. H.662, 4
Enjoys Yet freedome, shee enjoyes withall......281. H.876, 10
Enkindled When thus enkindled they transpire...145. H.375, 17
A Lipp Inkyndled wth that Coale..............408. A.2, 47
Which thus enkindled we invoke...............413. A.4, 29
Enlarge I will not over-long enlarge............175. H.465, 67
Enlightened Enlightned substance; mark how from the Shrine
112. H.283, 12
Ennobled Ennobled numbers for the Presse,.......19. H.51, 7
Enough See Enow
One slit's enough to let Adultry in............44. H.126, 4
Hony enough to fill his hive..................71. H.182, 31
False in head, and false enough;..............77. H.195, 11
That Prince takes soone enough the Victors roome,
109. H.268, 1
Y'ave laught enough (sweet) vary now your Text;
111. H 277, 1
Now old enough to be our own.................134. H.336, 88
Pure enough, though not Precise:.............232. H.665, 4
Too much she gives to some, enough to none...238. H.689, 2
Long enough has endur'd,....................247. H.727, 8
And now y' have wept enough, depart yon starres
432. ins. H.283, 140a
Enow Of Cloyster-Monks they have enow,.......93. H.223, 107
Enquires See Inquires
Enrage — — — — — — — —, ...443. var. H.575, 46
Enraged Thus inrag'd, my lines are hurl'd,......242. H.714, 7
Enrich Jem to enrich her store;..................43. H.123, 14
To enrich you,...............................196. H.538, 5
Ens An Ens, but Supraentitie.....................340. N.5, 2
Ensigns No cowards must his royall Ensignes beare.
280. H.872, 2
Ensnare That when thou doest his necke Insnare,..408. A.2, 61
Enspangle T' enspangle this expansive Firmament.
191. H.516, 2
Ensphered Enspher'd with Palm on Your Triumphant Crest.
271. H.823, 4
Enspire See Inspire
Enspired See Inspired
Enstyle Let them enstile Thee Fairest faire,....175. H.465, 37
Enstyled When it is born: (by some enstyl'd....167. H.443, 92
And that is this, A verse Instylde...............407. A.2, 4
Ensures See Insures
Entend See Intend
Entended See Intended
Enter Since that Love and Night bid enter.......56. H.149, 100
O enter then! but see ye shun.................57. H.149, 141
Favour your tongues, who enter here...........91. H.223, 41

Yet ere ye enter, give us leave to set........140. H.354, 3
Or els not one there must enter..............256. H.762, 12
Enter and prosper; while our eyes doe waite....300. H.961, 9
Leave that without, then enter in;.............366. N.98, 6
Thy Doore, as I do enter in:.................402. N.269, 5
Then full affection, enter here................402. N.269, 9
All in, kisse and so enter, If............431. ins. H.283, 60m
Entered And now y'are enter'd; see the Codled Cook
114. H.283, 61
Entred the circumspacious Theater;...........301. H.962, 2
Into the which He enter'd: but, the Doore.....385. N.190, 3
Entering And Basket, by our entring in.........178. H.476, 3
Lust entring here:...........................190. H.515, 14
No Brutus entring here;......................259. H.772, 5
Enterplaced See Interplaced
Enters Next enters June, and brings us more....23. H.70, 5
What ere enters, out it shall:...............116. H.285, 8
Entertain With heart and hand to entertain:....147. H.377, 36
T' entertain that Deity.......................204. H.569, 6
And as they thus did entertaine...............237. H.687, 2
Ile entertaine................................296. H.946, 17
But we will entertaine Thee...................345. N.33, 26
Entertains When ere my heart, Love's warmth, but entertaines,
40. H.113, 1
Entertalk See Intertalk
Enterwove See Interwove
Enthrall My Jet t'enthrall such Ivorie.............14. 8.34, 6
And armes and hands they did enthrall:........16. H.41, 15
Set on purpose to enthrall....................53. H.147, 9
That doth the Infants face enthrall,...........167. H.443, 91
Then to enthrall,.............................172. H.458, 10
Enthralled Enthrall'd my dainty Lucia.............16. H.41, 4
Enthrall'd her Arme, as Prisoner...............64. H.169, 4
Enthralls Enthralls the Crimson Stomacher:........28. H.83, 6
Entice Then lett each Cheeke of thyne intice......408. A.2, 43
Entire And make me one entire.................228. H.657, 8
Entitle And entitle none to be..................108. H.266, 11
Entitled As just Men are intitled Gods, yet none.379. N.143, 3
Entitulated Entitulated the Greecian Prince of men.
442. ins. H.575, 28b
Entity Ev'n God Himself, in perfect Entitie.......382. N.165, 2
'Tis but by Order, not by Entitie............386. N.191, 6
Entombed — — — — — — — — —, ...437. var. H.336, 98
Entrance First, at the entrance of the gate,.......91. H.223, 38
As to entrance his paine, or cure his woe.........99. H.244, 4
Which you must grant; that's entrance; with..116. H.283, 153
Flames, which wo'd an entrance make;.........117. H.286, 10
Weelcome! but yet no entrance, till we blesse..124. H.313, 1
Thus to en-trance and ravish me:..............142. H.362, 4
The holy Entrance; where within.............166. H.443, 65
Withstanding entrance unto me................277. H.854, 4
Aboue the entrance there is written this.........406. A.1, 73
En-trance See Entrance
Entranced Entranc'd, and lost confusedly:.........23. H.68, 6
Ravish our spirits, that entranc't wee see........415. A.7, 17
Entreat Readers wee entreat ye pray..............269. H.814, 1
Pardon me God, (once more I Thee intreat)....371. N.113, 1
Lady I intreate yow weare.....................417. A.9, 1
Entwine And can with Tendrills love intwine,...88. H.216, 11
Envied See Unenvied
Envious Downe, envious Time by thee...........85. H.211, 20
But still the envious Scene between.............247. H.729, 7
Envy Then sure thou't like, or thou wilt envie me.
66. H.174, 4
Who spurn'd at Envie; and co'd bring, with ease,
137. H.341, 5
The Laundresses, They envie her good-luck,.....178. H.474, 3
Nor Fate, nor Enuye, cann theyr Fames Conuince,
411. A.3, 40
Envying Not envying others larger grounds:....230. H.662, 16
Epigram And then at last to truss the Epigram;.301. H.966, 8
Epitaph For Epitaph, in Foliage, next write this,..19. H.50, 5
This Epitaph, which here you see,............109. H.271, 7
Thy living Epitaph shall be,..................146. H.376, 9
Epithalamie See Epithalamion
Epithalamion Supply'd the Epithalamie...........109. H.271, 8
Provide a second Epithalamie..................286. H.898, 12
By way of Epithalamie,.......................393. N.232, 12
Epitome See th' Epitomè of yow,..................417. A.9, 8
— — — — — — — — — — —, ...450. var. A.9, 7
Equal But with thy equall thoughts, prepar'd dost stand,
37. H.106, 95
Find equall freedome, equall fare;............147. H.377, 60
One Fate had both; both equall Grace;........185. H.497, 7
All wise; all equall; and all just.............190. H.515, 31
Lal. The equall Umpire shall be I,...........243. H.716, 21
The Soldiers leave the Field with equall feare...268. H.813, 4
Not to eat equall portions; but to rise.........310. H.1005, 3
And equall shares exclude all murmerings.......318. H.1040, 2
An equall mind is the best sauce for griefe.....333. H.1119, 2
That makes all æquall. Manye thowsands should.411. A.3, 35
Ere Ere I print my Poetry;.....................21. H.59, 2
Nor wil't be long, ere this accomplish'd be;.....26. H.79, 9
Ere I wo'd love at all..........................28. H.85, 8
I doe beseech thee, ere we part,...............33. H.103, 5
Sing o're Horace; for ere long.................39. H.111, 11
And shame had follow'd long ere this,..........48. H.136, 8
Ere I go hence; know this from me,............60. H.159, 9
I shall, ere long, with green turfs cover'd be;...66. H.174, 3
Or Branch: Each Porch, each doore, ere this,..68. H.178, 33
A deale of Youth, ere this, is come..........69. H.178, 45
And chose their Priest, ere we can cast off sloth:
69. H.178, 50
Yet lost, ere that chast flesh and blood.........88. H.216, 8
Yet dry'd, ere you distill your Wine...........88. H.216, 12
Yet lost ere you transfuse your smell...........88. H.216, 15
Yet wither'd, ere you can be set...............88. H.216, 17
But die you must (faire Maid) ere long,........88. H.216, 20
Time, ere long, will come and plow............97. H.232, 13
Like those short sweets ere knit together......107. H.263, 22
Ere long a fleeting shade:....................111. H.280, 6
And ere long, a Boy Love send ye............125. H.314, 6
Ere long, a song, ere long, a shade.............133. H.336, 30
Yet ere ye enter, give us leave to set.........140. H.354, 3
Dear Lycidas, e're long,......................184. H.492, 26
Ile seek him there; I know, ere this,............156. H.412, 17
Yet, ere twelve Moones shall whirl about......178. H.476, 7
Water in, ere Sun be set......................201. H.556, 4
Hisped, and hairie, ere thy Palm shall know....202. H.557, 24
And once more yet (ere I am laid out dead)...214. H.612, 13
To ask our wages, e're our work be done......241. H.708, 2
Consult ere thou begin'st, that done, go on.....252. H.749, 1
Ere a good word can be spoke:................255. H.761, 18
This Blessing I will leave thee, ere I go,......269. H.818, 3
Ere Ave-Mary thou canst say...................271. H.824, 3
Yet ere thou counsel'st with thy Glasse,........271. H.824, 5
And (ere we our rites commence).............303. H.974, 5
That ere while was heard so shrill?............305. H.984, 6
That are most modest ere they come to warre...308. H.994, 2
Die ere long I'm sure, I shall;...............321. H.1058, 1
And I ere long, my Girles shall see,...........329. H.1093, 5
Stay me, by crowing, ere I do begin;..........349. N.43, 4
Ere Thou dost threat me......................351. N.49, 4
Let's go (my Alma) yet e're we receive,.......355. N.65, 7
Sorrowes our portion are: Ere hence we goe,...359. N.81, 1
Yawne for Thy coming; some e're this time crie,
398. N.263, 7
Or e're dark Clouds do dull, or dead the Mid-dayes Sun.
401. N.268, 9
Ere I goe hence and bee noe more.............407. A.2, 1
Hee may ere longe haue such a wyfe...........409. A.2, 107
— — — — — — — — — — —, ...442. var. H.465, 78
Erected See erected...........................308. H.993, 30
Err How do's she erre in endlesse night!.......393. N.233, 4
Errand Manners are good: but till his errand ends,
378. N.137, 7
Erring An erring Lace, which here and there.....28. H.83, 5
Which erring here, and wandring there,........66. H.175, 3
Erroneous 'Tis her erroneous self has made a braine
46. H.128, 43
Error Twixt Truth and Errour, there's this difference known,
316. H.1031, 1
Errour is fruitfull, Truth is onely one.........316. H.1031, 2
— — — — — — — — — — —, ...452. var. H.443, 83
Errors His Errours up; and now he finds......167. H.443, 83
Correct my errors gently with Thy Rod........398. N.261, 4
Errs The Pinnace up; which though she erres..134. H.336, 63
Erse See Arse
And working it, by chance from Umbers Erse...205. H.572, 2
Erst With as cold frost, as erst we mett with fire;
414. A.6, 10
Eruptions These my irruptions manifold;.......344. N.29, 6
Escape Then to her Cabbin, blest she can escape.37. H.106, 125
That we escape. Redemption comes by Thee....197. H.539, 16
They might escape the lash of punishment........291. H.920, 4
Not a straw co'd him escape;................306. H.984, 28
Escutcheon See 'Scutcheon
In this rag'd Escutcheon......................418. A.9, 35
Escutcheons When of thy ragg'd Escutcheons shall be seene
231. H.664, 3
Especially Especially to sweare by it.............388. N.204, 4
Espied And to these we have espi'd,...........221. H.633, 28
Espouse — — — — — — — — —, ...424. var. H.128, 50
Espoused Thee and their lips espous'd; while I admire,
46. H.128, 50
For one to whom espous'd are all the Arts;....121. H.301, 2
Espy When I thy Parts runne o're, I can't espie.....10. H.16, 1
See, and not see; and if thou chance t'espie........32. H.95, 1
Water, Water I espie:.........................62. H.162, 1
Such a fire I espie..........................204. H.566, 3
Drowning, drowning, I espie...................302. H.968, 1
Essay Essay of other giblets; make............146. H.377, 28
Essence Implies or Essence, or the He that Is...385. N.187, 2
Originall of Essence there is none............386. N.191, 3
Not by His Essence, but commerce of Grace...387. N.197, 2
Against thy purer Essence? For that fault . . .
426. ins. H.197, 29b
Essences Those Eternall Essences..................22. H.65, 4
Or Essences of Jessimine:....................145. H.375, 6
Such Essences as those Three Brothers; known..170. H.451, 7
Established What's got by Justice is establisht sure;
314. H.1023, 1

Estate Small shots paid often, waste a vast estate..13. H.28, 2
The Ev'ning sees in poore estate...............208. H.583, 3
Estates Your poore estates, alone...............110. H.274, 20
Esteem Esteeme it when 'tis lost:..............53. H.149, 16
God is above the sphere of our esteem,...........340. N.4, 1
First, that these goods none here may o're esteem, 387. N.201, 3
One man repentant is of more esteem.........388. N.205, 1
Esteemed Nor art thou lesse esteem'd, that I have plac'd 256. H.763, 1
Estimation Gives it estimation...................417. A.9, 6
Eternal And haste away to mine eternal home:....9. H.14, 4
Those Eternall Essences.......................22. H.65, 4
As the eternall monument of me...............30. H.89, 10
Or let me 'gender with eternall frost...........40. H.113, 6
Where eternall cold does keep?...............40. H.115, 10
(Eternall in thy self) that canst controule.....45. H.128, 20
To Life Eternal, I co'd love.................67. H.175, 22
Eternall Lamp of Love! whose radiant flame....77. H.197, 10
A Lamp Eternall to my Poetrie................94. H.226, 6
Of Life eternall) Time has made thee one,.....152. H.392, 3
With an eternall smart:......................161. H.426, 5
Eternall by their own production..............170. H.451, 8
Set up Thine own eternall Images..............185. H.496, 10
And keep eternal fires,........................198. H.544, 3
Thee here in my eternall Calender.............199. H.545, 10
Here in green Meddowes sits eternall May,......206. H.575, 13
With your eternall fire:........................228. H.657, 7
A Jem in this eternall Coronet:...............264. H.789, 2
But that eternall Poetrie.....................265. H.794, 3
To mine eternall Mansion......................270. H.819, 3
(Or Sharon, where eternall Roses grow.)........326. H.1080, 8
Held up by Fames eternall Pedestall............329. H.1092, 8
In Thy eternall Glorie........................363. N.92, 6
Sin once reacht up to Gods eternall Sphere,....367. N.100, 1
But eternall watch shall keep,.................377. N.128, 19
Our Destination to eternall woe...............390. N.219, 4
Holde their Eternall fiers; and ours of Late....411. A.3, 43
Like an Eternall Noone........................413. A.4, 14
But Vertue Rears the eternal Monument.......419. A.10, 4
— — — — — — — — — —, ...437. var. H.336, 76
Eternally Shall live with Him eternally:........359. N.78, 10
Eternity In the same sweet eternity of love......13. H.29, 2
Drown'd in the Sea of wild Eternitie:........256. H.763, 14
Of vast Eternitie.............................354. N.58, 8
Unto young Eternitie.........................377. N.128, 7
The last the Sabbath of Eternitie..............386. N.194, 4
More worth, then Heav'ns Eternitie...........388. N.206, 4
I'le my Eternitie spend here.................402. N.269, 25
Ethics No, thou know'st order, Ethicks, and ha's read 148. H.377, 89
Eucharist The salve for this i'th' Eucharist is found. 381. N.155, 2
Euphony And giv'st our Numbers Euphonie, and weight. 297. H.947, 6
Eure See Ewer
Euridice To fetch Euridice from Hell;..........265. H.798, 2
Him and Euridice for ever....................265. H.798, 12
Cast, leading his Euredice through hell,........411. A.3, 68
Evadne Sing their Evadne; and still more for thee 206. H.575, 53
Love lyes a bleeding here, Evadne there........415. A.7, 11
Eve Faire as Eve in Paradice:................274. H.838, 2
Or Easters Eve appeare.....................285. H.892, 8
Even See E'en
And makes them frantick, ev'n to all extreames;.29. H.86, 4
To keep cheap Nature even, and upright;......35. H.106, 25
Ev'n with the soule of love....................57. H.149, 138
Many a kisse, both odde and even:............69. H.178, 52
Then, even then, I will bequeath my heart......73. H.186, 14
(Compos'd of odde, not even paires)..........91. H.223, 47
A curse to Thee, or Thine; but all things even..149. H.377, 129
I dislikt but even now;.......................155. H.407, 1
Even as the meanest Flower..................184. H.493, 8
Ev'n so, those streets and houses do but show.244. H.718, 3
As stones and salt gloves use to give, even so..248. H.731, 3
Ev'n so those Lines, pen'd by my wanton Wit,..339. N.1, 3
Even as monilesse, as He....................354. N.59, 14
Celerity even it self is slow..................378. N.133, 2
Ev'n God Himself, in perfect Entitie...........382. N.165, 2
Ev'n as the sprinkled bloud cal'd on...........387. N.203, 3
Even Thou alone, the bitter cup..............400. N.267, 8
Euen such are wee; and in our parting, doe....410. A.3, 13
— — — — — — — — — — — —, ...427. var. H.197, 63
— — — — — — — — — — — —, ...429. var. H.263, 20
— — — — — — — — — — — —, ...432. var. H.283, 106
— — — — — — — — — — — —, ...448. var. A.3, 1
— — — — — — — — — — — —, ...452. var. H.443, 81
Evening So all my Morne, and Evening Stars from You 3. Ded.H, 7
When that day comes, whose evening sayes I'm gone 14. H.35, 1
Duely, Morne and Ev'ning, come,..............44. H.125, 3
The Ev'ning witnest that I dy'd..............109. H.271, 2
The midst is thine; but Joves the Evening too;..128. H.321, 4
'Tis Ev'ning, my Sweet,.......................195. H.534, 1
The Ev'ning sees in poore estate...............208. H.583, 3
To his Ev'ning Funerall.........................306. H.984, 40
Each evening and each morrow:...............353. N.56, 9
Both from the Morning to the Euening Chyme;.410. A.3, 16
Throaned in a saffron Evening, seemes to chyme 431. ins. H.283, 601
— — — — — — — — — — — , ...450. var. A.9, 42
Evening's The Ev'ning's come; here now Ile stop,.212. H.602, 3
Evenings Nor in the summers sweeter evenings go, 315. H.1028, 5
Evensong To call to Morn, and Even-Song.....93. H.223, 128
But to the Even-song;........................125. H.316, 8
So sure he layes claime to the Evensong.......128. H.321, 6
From Mattins to the Euensong,..................418. A.9, 42
Event Th'event is never in the power of man.....120. H.294, 2
The first event breeds confidence or feare.........292. H.924, 2
Events Fore-tell the comming of some dire events:.45. H.128, 16
Crosses doe still bring forth the best events.......110. H.275, 2
All things are open to these two events,..........182. H.487, 1
Ever See E'er
I write of Hell! I sing (and ever shall)...........5. H.1, 13
Work that to life, and let me ever dwell..........14. H.35, 13
Small griefs find tongues: Full Casques are ever found 15. H.38, 7
Wherein thou liv'st for ever. Deare farewell.........23. H.72, 4
Conformity was ever knowne......................25. H.76, 1
Gave them their ever flourishing..................25. H.78, 10
O men, O manners; Now, and ever knowne........29. H.86, 9
Troth-breakers ever.............................32. H.94, 8
Rather then love, let me be ever lost;.............40. H.113, 5
But bid Good-night, and close their lids for ever...41. H.118, 8
Sooner, then she, ever yet,.....................57. H.149, 149
There, where no language ever yet was known.....60. H.156, 6
You, and your name, for ever: yet...............60. H.159, 8
I live for ever; let the rest all lye............63. H.165, 3
I beg of Love, that ever I.......................64. H.169, 11
And pure as Gold for ever........................66. H.172, 30
But to forsake thee ever, co'd there be...........78. H.197, 45
You may for ever tarry...........................84. H.208, 16
(With whitest Wool be ever crown'd that day!)..86. H.213, 14
Fresh, and for ever flourishing..................89. H.219, 20
A Laurel for her, (ever young as love)...........94. H.224, 8
But like a Laurell, to grow green for ever.........98. H.240, 2
Both tormenting Lovers ever...................103. H.253, 10
Fresh, as their blood; and ever grow,...........104. H.256, 19
Sweeter far, then ever yet......................108. H.266, 3
Play then they ever knew before................115. H.283, 130
To live therein for ever: Frie..................115. H.283, 137
Ever full of pensive feare;......................117. H.286, 2
Where my small reliques must for ever rest:....129. H.327, 4
And for my sake, who ever did prefer.............137. H.341, 9
Whether or no, that we shall meet here ever......140. H.355, 4
To last, but not their ever: Vertues Hand.....148. H.377, 101
Keepe it for ever; grounded with the good,.......152. H.392, 7
But love my Clipseby ever......................162. H.426, 25
Empires of Kings, are now, and ever were,.......162. H.430, 1
Or ever mark't the pretty beam,.................164. H.440, 5
Shall now, or ever after come...................165. H.442, 14
But ever doubtfull Day, or night...............167. H.443, 81
Where Chimneys do for ever weepe,..............179. H.476, 31
A Virgin Taper, ever shining here...............191. H.516, 4
Be ever and ever a spending;....................195. H.534, 9
Among which Holies, be Thou ever known,.......199. H.545, 7
What ever comes, content makes sweet:........200. H.552, 6
Wound up again: Once down, He's down for ever. 202. H.558, 2
He ever pickt (as yet) of any one...............204. H.568, 6
Let our soules flie to' th' shades, where ever springs 205. H.575, 2
Can ever rust th'Enamel of the light...........206. H.575, 16
Him and his affections ever......................209. H.587, 4
What is beyond the mean is ever ill:............220. H.633, 22
Where I have had, what ever thing co'd be......227. H.652, 3
And ever live a true.............................228. H.657, 12
Then ever, dearest Silvia, yet...................240. H.705, 7
Made it for ever after red.......................241. H.706, 4
Clouds will not ever powre down raine;..........247. H.725, 7
More pleasing too, then ever was................251. H.740, 11
That ever prosper'd by Cunctation..............251. H.744, 2
Other mens sins wee ever beare in mind;.........253. H.751, 1
Blaze by this Sphere for ever: Or this doe,.......264. H.789, 5
Him and Euridice for ever.......................265. H.798, 12
Imparitie doth ever discord bring:...............268. H.812, 1
Where ever Nodes do's in the Summer come,....270. H.822, 1
To live for ever, with my Just...................278. H.859, 6
Which ever since has been in thrall,.............281. H.876, 9
For ever with thee here.........................293. H.934, 8
Now thou art dead, no eye shall ever see,.........302. H.967, 1
Ever gamesome as an ape:......................306. H.984, 29
That ever thou...................................314. H.1024, 15
Receive this vow, so fare-ye-well for ever.......316. H.1028, 26
If ever we think.................................320. H.1051, 10
What ever Liquor in ye powre..................320. H.1053, 2
Wee shall not part for ever......................324. H.1068, 24
As to make ye ever grow........................324. H.1070, 4
That love 'twixt men do's ever longest last....327. H.1083, 1

As if we sho'd for **ever** part?..................328. H.1090, 2
To this our poore, yet **ever** patient Flood........332. H.1112, 6
What **ever** men for Loyalty pretend,............333. H.1121, 1
But stand for **ever** by his owne................335. H.1129, 13
God hath two wings, which He doth **ever** move,....340. N.6, 1
Under the first the Sinners **ever** trust;............340. N.6, 3
Upon me beating **ever**:.........................353. N.56, 15
Sleep not for **ever** in the vaults of death:........358. N.77, 11
O Virgin-martyr, **ever** blest......................359. N.83, 3
Love keep it **ever** flourishing....................361. N.83, 72
Make it **ever** flourishing.........................363. N.93, 9
Chor. Stand empty here for **ever**:................374. N.123, 17
May feare it **ever** for uncertaintie:...............379. N.142, 2
The Bad among the Good are here mixt **ever**:....383. N.172, 1
Then **ever**, yet, the like was done before.........395. N.244, 4
Let me live **ever** here, and stir...................402. N.269, 18
Shall stand for **euer**, though I doe addresse........412. A.3, 97
To prompt mee, I shall **euer**.....................414. A.5, 7
But truth knitt fast; and so farewell for **euer**.......414. A.6, 12
In it all good, that is, and **ever** was...............416. A.8, 14
But there to live, where Love shall last for **ever**....417. A.8, 38
It **ever** dangling smil'd i' th' aire.................418. A.9, 26
There **ever** lived such a one......................418. A.9, 30
Of all that **ever** yet hath blest........435. ins. H.293, ee
— — — — — — — — — —, ...448. var. A.1, 86
Everlasting Worthy their **everlasting** Chronicle,..170. H.451, 10
Decree thy **everlasting** Topick there..............172. H.456, 8
Those Fields of **everlasting** happinesse...........177. H.470, 2
Endures an **everlasting** punishment..............213. H.606, 2
Unto thy **everlasting** residence...................219. H.627, 8
An **everlasting** plenty, yeere by yeere.............242. H.713, 8
(As Lamps for **everlasting** shining here:)........267. H.804, 8
And **everlasting** Harvest crown thy Soile!.......269. H.818, 8
Of thy both Great, and **everlasting** fate...........280. H.869, 4
In **everlasting** Properties.......................289. H.912, 6
Singing about my **everlasting** fire................294. H.938, 4
Are lost, and theirs, in **everlasting** night.........313. H.1019, 4
From thence, to **everlasting** woe:.................358. N.78, 8
So live in Heaven, in **everlasting** light............384. N.181, 5
Is spilt in **everlasting** night....................413, A.4, 11
Everlastingness Strong then the Heavens for **everlastingnesse**: 185. H.496, 8
Evermore Who covets more, is **evermore** a slave...213. H.607, 2
Be **evercome** these Bynns replenished............245. H.723, 6
Love and the Graces **evermore** do wait..........255. H.760, 1
For **evermore** protect me.........................260. H.777, 12
Let Me and It shine **evermore** by you............264. H.789, 6
Wo'd I **evermore** be crown'd....................286. H.897, 3
Those, that must live with Thee for **evermore**....329. H.1092, 4
Things are **evermore** sincere;...................377. N.128, 10
Those Garments lasting **evermore**,................393. N.231, 1
Ever-wealthy Like to the **ever-wealthy** Ocean:.....341. N.15, 2
Every May **every** Ill, that bites, or smarts,........6. H.5, 3
But **every** Line, and Limb diffused thence,.........10. H.16, 3
Which crawling one and **every** way,...............16. H.41, 3
Or, like the soule, whole **every** where:.............24. H.73, 6
When **every** creature rested,......................26. H.81, 2
Is too precise in **every** part.......................28. H.83, 14
Whose heart, whose hand, whose **ev'ry** part spake love. 42. H.122, 8
Suspicion questions **every** haire...................49. H.136, 23
Pleas'd with transgression **ev'ry** where:...........66. H.175, 4
Frown, and look sullen **ev'ry** where..............72. H.185, 4
In-laid Garbage **ev'ry** where......................76. H.195, 6
And hast command of **every** part,..............109. H.267, 23
And to enchant yee more, see **every** where......115. H.283, 101
Lookes for the treaders; **every** where is wove...115. H.283, 122
That takes and re-delivers **every** stroake........129. H.323, 11
And here, and there, and **every** where...........130. H.329, 15
Plump, soft & swelling **every** where?............139. H.348, 2
Those smooth-pac't Numbers, amble **every** where; 141. H.359, 10
And in the Rind of **every** comely tree..........160. H.421, 39
Every time seemes short to be,..................162. H.431, 1
And farther off, and **every** where,...............166. H.443, 46
With Motto's carv'd on **every** tree,..............169. H.449, 22
In **every** Geniall Cup,...........................184. H.492, 38
Beset with stately Figures (**every** where)........185. H.496, 2
Of **every** straight, and smooth-skin tree;........193. H.521, 41
A Stock of Saints; where **ev'ry** one doth weare..199. H.545, 5
Strewings need none, **every** flower...............199. H.546, 5
This, that, and **ev'ry** Thicket doth transpire......205. H.575, 7
Where **ev'ry** tree & wealthy issue beares..........205. H.575, 9
The Palms put forth their Gemmes, and **every** Tree 224. H.642, 5
But ah! what sweets smelt **every** where,........237. H.686, 11
'Tis not **ev'ry** day, that I........................242. H.714, 1
In **every** part alike compleat,....................243. H.716, 9
I'm a man for **ev'ry** Sceane.....................253. H.750, 18
Shut **every** gate; mend **every** hedge that's torne,..259. H.771, 5
Some salve to **every** sore, we may apply;........274. H.841, 1
Is not for one, but **every** night his Bride:....286. H.898, 14
This, that, and **every** base impression...........288. H.905, 2
Sho'd I not grieve (my Lawes) when **every** Lute, 288. H.907, 3
Mudge **every** morning to the Postern comes,......301. H.965, 1
And with Circumgyration **every** where;..........301. H.966, 6
Toucht **every** where with such diffused grace,....307. H.992, 2
And as that part, so **every** portion else,..........307. H.992, 5
For Grace and Carriage, **every** one a Queene....326. H.1080, 24
For **every** sentence, clause and word,.............339. N.2, 3
No man is blest through **ev'ry** part...............351. N.50, 4
Foure times bestrew thee **ev'ry** yeere............360. N.83, 36
Expect the coming of it **ev'ry** day................379. N.142, 4
Fitted it self to **ev'ry** Feeders tast...............379. N.146, 2
God's present **ev'ry** where; but most of all......388. N.207, 1
Which to effect, let **ev'ry** passing Bell..........392. N.230, 11
This, that, and **ev'ry** other part;................402. N.269, 7
Thus **every** part in contrariety................406. A.1, 105
Swells with brave rage, yet comely **every** where,...415. A.7, 12
— — — — — — — — — — —, ...429. var. H.253, 16
Everyone **See Every**
Then but to breath, and **every one** gave way:...200. H..551, 4
Law is to give to **ev'ry one** his owne...........201. H.557, 10
In reverence of his person, **every one**..........301. H.962, 3
And next morrow, **every one**................315. H.1026, 13
Everything And **every thing** assume............55. H.149, 65
In **every thing** that's sweet, she is..............106. H.263, 6
Pure hands, pure habits, pure, pure **every thing**..127. H.320, 4
Gracefull is **ev'ry thing** from her..............207. H.579, 6
Lost to all Musick now; since **every thing**......214. H.612, 3
The Mean the Musique makes in **every thing**...268. H.812, 2
For Bread, Drinke, Butter, Cheese; for **every thing** 287. H.903, 2
The Primrose sick, and sickly **every thing**:.....320. H.1054, 2
Heart, Eare, and Eye, and **every thing**..........364. N.96, 5
Everyway **See Every**
A wise man **ev'ry way** lies square..............37. H.106, 98
And Venus, **every way**:.........................281. H.874, 3
Faultless **every way** for shape;...............306. H.984, 27
Everywhere Or, like the soule, whole **every where**:.24. H.73, 6
Pleas'd with transgression **ev'ry where**:........66. H.175, 4
Frown, and look sullen **ev'ry where**...........72. H.185, 4
In-laid Garbage **ev'ry where**...................76. H.195, 6
And to enchant yee more, see **every where**....115. H.283, 101
Lookes for the treaders; **every where** is wove..115. H.283, 122
And here, and there, and **every where**......130. H.329, 15
Plump, soft, & swelling **every where**?........139. H.348, 2
Those smooth-pac't Numbers, amble **every where**; 141. H.359, 10
And farther off, and **every where**,.............166. H.443, 46
Beset with stately Figures (**every where**)....185. H.496, 2
But ah! what sweets smelt **every where**,......237. H.686, 11
And with Circumgyration **every where**;.......301. H.966, 6
Toucht **every where** with such diffused grace,....307. H.992, 2
God's present **ev'ry where**; but most of all......388. N.207, 1
Swells with brave rage, yet comely **every where**,.415. A.7, 12
Eves Thou hast thy **Eves**, and Holydayes:......230. H.662, 47
Evident God's **evident**, and may be said to be......385. N.188, 1
Evil And of those **evill** dayes that be.............47. H.132, 11
And the **evil** deads, the which..................55. H.149, 89
The **Evill** is not Yours: my sorrow sings,........62. H.161, 15
Mine is the **Evill**, but the Cure, the Kings.......62. H.161, 16
The fouler Fiend, and **evill** Spright,............123. H.306, 14
Or to the good, or **evill** action..................214. H.614, 4
Far from hence the **evill** Sp'rite...............258. H.769, 9
Old Widdow Prouse to do her neighbours **evill**..266. H.801, 1
For the **evill evill** dayes..........................267. H.806, 4
So farre keepes the **evill** Spright..............322. H.1064, 6
Evill no Nature hath; the losse of good..........367. N.101, 1
There is no **evill** that we do commit,............386. N.196, 1
Ewer The sacred Towell, and the holy **Eure**.......355. N.65, 5
Ewes Stirs in our Sheep-walk? Amin. None, save that my **Ewes**, 85. H.213, 4
Besides my healthfull **Ewes** to beare............350. N.47, 47
Exacted Since more and more is **exacted**;........247. H.727, 9
Exacter **See Exactor**
Exactor, Say, who's the worst, th' **exactor**, or the whore? 220. H.631, 4
Exalted Who was your brave **exalted** Uncle here,.137. H.341, 3
Knock at a Starre with my **exalted** Head.......214. H.612, 14
To an **exalted** vineger;.....................321. H.1056, 10
Examine **Examine** me with fire, and prove me......351. N.48, 7
Example What is't that wasts a Prince? **example** showes, 331. H.1105, 1
Let their **example** not a pattern be..............399. N.264, 3
Examples **Examples** lead us, and wee likely see,..255. H.759, 1
Excathedrated To see my Lines **Excathedrated** here. 64. H.168, 4
Exceed Or to **exceed** thy Tether's reach:........38. H.106, 134
Look how our foule Dayes do **exceed** our faire;.....339. N.1, 1
— — — — — — — — — — —, ...448. var. A.1, 71
Exceeds Here's golden fruit that farre **exceeds** all price 406. A.1, 71
Excel Whether the Violets sho'd **excell**,...........105. H.260, 3
Each must, in vertue, strive for to **excell**;........121. H.298, 1
In our high art, although we can't **excell**.......234. H.673, 10
In this misfortune Kings doe most **excell**,......293. H.932, 1
In length each finger doth his next **excell**,........406. A.1, 101
Excellence A faire, and unfamiliar **excellence**:......10. H.16, 4
At full their proper **excellence**;.................76. H.193, 38

And soule and spirit plot, and **excellence**.......399. N.263, 27
— — — — — — — — — — —, ...440. var. H.443, 54
Excellency The **excellency** of this Cave,........166. H.443, 54
Excellent She's to me most **excellent**.............253. H.750, 15
Exception Fully, without **exception**;..............191. H.520, 2
Excess For if thou eat'st it to **excess**;..........288. H.909, 3
Anthea laught, and fearing lest **excesse**.........311. H.1006, 1
Excesse is sluttish: keepe the meane; for why?..331. H.1109, 1
Exchange Could'st leave the City, for **exchange**, to see
35. H.106, 3
Excite The which the Elves make to **excite**......167. H.443, 114
Might me **excite** to fore, and after-grace.........371. N.115, 8
— — — — — — — — — — —, ...440 var. H.443, 114
Exclude And equall shares **exclude** all murmerings.
318. H.1040, 2
Excruciate Not after one sort, there **excruciate** all:
391. N.227, 2
Excuse He thus began himselfe t'**excuse**:........71. H.182, 12
Execution With all wise speed for **execution**.......252. H.749, 2
Commanders, few for **execution**..................272. H.827, 2
Mine **Execution**.....................................279. H.863, 16
To the sad place of **execution**:.....................398. N.263, 2
Executioner The **Executioner** of me...............34. H.103, 18
Exempt Is the beast **exempt** from staine,........280. H.870, 5
Exempted No man **exempted** is from Death, or sinne.
199. H.548, 2
Exercise So much for want, as **exercise**:..........37. H.106, 118
But cry thee Mercy: **Exercise** thy nailes.........66. H.173, 5
Are wanting to her **exercise**, but great........148. H.377, 113
To **exercise** their dancing feet:...................230. H.662, 49
His gifts, to **exercise** Petitioners:................344. N.30, 2
Exeter The Hector over Aged **Exeter**;..............251. H.745, 2
Exile Poore pittyed **Exile**? Tell me, did thy Graces.77. H.197, 20
Existence Have their **Existence**, and their Influence too.
3. Ded.H., 8
Sin no **Existence**; Nature none it hath,..........383. N.173, 1
Expansion The Flame of it, and the **Expansion**.....3. Ded.H., 4
'Two'd make a brave **expansion**....................67. H.175, 8
Her skins most smooth, and cleare **expansion**.....82. H.204, 4
For the **expansion** of thy hand..................139. H.350, 2
In an **expansion** no less large, then high;........301. H.966, 4
Expansive T' enspangle this **expansive** Firmament..191. H.516, 2
Expect If not; **expect** to be no less..............218. H.626, 14
Expect the coming of it ev'ry day...............379. N.142, 4
— — — — — — — — — — —, ...428. var. H.208, 11
Expecting **Expecting** when to fall: which soon will be;
203. H.565, 3
Expense Like to the Income must be our **expence**;.117. H.287, 1
For so decreeing, that thy clothes **expence**.......210. H.590, 3
So that an Angler, for a daies **expence**,..........282. H.879, 3
Such be our gifts, and such be our **expence**,.......295. H.940, 3
God bought man here wth his hearts blood **expence**;
389. N.213, 1
Experience The two last fayle, and by **experience** make
422. ins. H.106, 92e
Expiate Ile **expiate** with Sulphur, Haire, and Salt:.77. H.197, 30
Expiation God, for an **expiation**...................387. N.203, 4
Expiration The minute of mine **expiration**.........281. H.875, 4
Expire And make it thus **expire**...................95. H.227, 15
Let's trie of us who shall the first **expire**;....333. H.1120, 3
Expose **Expose** your jewels then unto the view,..173. H.459, 11
Old Coyne's and Meddalls, wee **expose**..........407. A.2, 30
Exposed **Expos'd** to all the comming Winters cold..151. H.387, 4
Since man **expos'd** is to a world of griefs.........153. H.397, 2
Exposeth Unto temptation God **exposeth** some;....380. N.150, 3
Express There with the Reed, thou mayst **expresse**...5. H.2, 7
The most I love, when I the least **expresse** it.......15. H.38, 6
So when Love speechlesse is, she doth **expresse**....15. H.38, 11
If the Vower don't **express**.........................22. H.63, 3
Now seems she to **expresse**.........................55. H.149, 73
Sin, in's Nap'rie, not to **express** his wit;........114. H.283, 68
Of all our parts, the eyes **expresse**..............121. H.300, 1
So that as either shall **expresse**.................192. H.521, 23
But hark how I can now **expresse**................243. H.716, 27
As many Lawes and Lawyers do **expresse**.......244. H.718, 1
The readinesse of doing, doth **expresse**..........275. H.845, 1
Onely, by this dull creature, to **expresse**..........384. N.179, 3
— — — — — — — — — — —, ...432. var. H.283, 68
— — — — — — — — — — —, ...441. var. H.465, 24
Expressed And sure his tongue had more **exprest**,..42. H.119, 11
Expressions Are the **expressions** of that itch,.....174. H.465, 24
Extend Lest they too far **extend**...................76. H.193, 48
These, and thy choicest viands do **extend**.......147. H.377, 67
Extent For well thou know'st, 'tis not th' **extent**..230. H.662, 17
Extinguished Then is the Lamp and oyle **extinguished**.
359. N.80, 2
Extol For which I might **extoll** thee, but speake lesse,
298. H.955, 9
Extortion He by **extortion** brings in three times more:
220. H.631, 3
Without **extortion**, from thy soyle:..............233. H.670, 8
Extract Which **extract**, all we can call pith......116. H.283, 154
Extraction But hath th' **extraction** of some good from it:
386. N.196, 2
Extreme The **Extreame** Scabbe take thee, and thine, for me.
7. H.6, 6

Flasht out between the Middle and **Extreame**.....33. H.102, 2
To shun the first, and last **extreame**............38. H.106, 132
Extremes And makes them frantick, ev'n to all **extreames**;
29. H.86, 4
Love in **extreames**, can never long endure.......185. H.494, 4
Extreames have still their fault;................221. H.633, 50
These only were but Loves **extreames**;..........290. H.915, 6
Extreames are fatall, where they once doe strike,.333. H.1120, 5
Eye Whether by th' **eye**, or eare, or no:............24. H.73, 2
The belly chiefly; not the **eye**:....................35. H.106, 28
Thee with the **eye** of admiration?...............45. H.128, 38
About the Arch of either **eye**;......................46. H.130, 8
But onely my Corinna's **eye**?.......................48. H.133, 17
The common formes have no one **eye**,............49. H.136, 18
Cheek, and **eye**, and lip, and chin;...............52. H.147, 5
But she co'd see each **eye** to stamp a teare:.......58. H.150, 4
Teares are the noble language of the **eye**..........58. H.150, 6
From out the **eye**, Loves Firmament:...........69. H.178, 54
Nor daunces in the **eye**..........................75. H.193, 10
Stoop, mount, passe by to take her **eye**, then glare
87. H.215, 5
And break thy self in shivers on her **eye**........87. H.215, 10
And the dimnesse of your **eye**..................97. H.232, 15
Like a Lightning, from her **eye**,...................98. H.238, 14
O! may no **eye** distill a Teare..................104. H.256, 9
There thou shalt have her curious **eye**:........107. H.263, 10
And in the turning of an **eye**;.................107. H.263, 20
To light their Tapers at the Brides bright **eye**....115. H.283, 108
But all this while his **eye** is serv'd,.............119. H.293, 13
Black and rowling is her **eye**,...................138. H.342, 3
With blasting **eye**, the appetite,.................147. H.377, 48
For as my Heart, ene so mine **Eye**.............154. H.402, 5
Her life-begetting **eye**;...........................164. H.441, 10
Half rotten, and without an **eye**,.................166. H.443, 52
See, see a Jemme (as rare as Bælus **eye**.)........172. H.459, 8
That sharply trickles from her either **eye**.........178. H.474, 2
I must confesse, mine **eye** and heart............202. H.560, 17
Walking in and out her **eye**,.....................204. H.566, 4
His **eye** in dew of kisses, while he sleeps.........206. H.575, 42
She now weares silk to hide her blood-shot **eye**...207. H.578, 2
Cast on my Girles a glance, and loving **eye**:....222. H.634, 11
Be she rowling in her **eye**,......................232. H.665, 9
A wanton and lascivious **eye**.....................254. H.755, 1
Revolve he did his loving **eye**;..................265. H.798, 9
We credit most our sight; one **eye** doth please....287. H.904, 1
Now thou art dead, no **eye** shall ever see,......302. H.967, 1
Coming from my Julia's **eye**:....................302. H.968, 2
Broad of fore-head, large of **eye**,...............305. H.984, 18
Were they not basted by her either **eye**.........325. H.1078, 2
My God! looke on me with thine **eye**...........344. N.29, 1
Mine **eye** and eare...............................353. N.56, 10
So utter dark, as that no **eye**...................357. N.72, 7
The **eye** of Virgins; nay, the Queen............360. N.83, 15
When e're thou speak'st, look with a lowly **eye**:.362. N.89, 3
Heart, Eare, and **Eye**, and every thing..........364. N.96, 5
But as Heavens publike and immortall **Eye**.....371. N.113, 5
By Thine approach, each their beholding **eye**...398. N.263, 14
The lovely shoulders now allure the **eye**..........406. A.1, 95
His eager **Eye**, or Smoother Smyle,..............413. A.4, 27
— — — — — — — — — — —, ...430. var. H.267, 22
— — — — — — — — — — —, ...452. var. H.443, 24
Eyeball — — — — — — — —, ...434. ins. H.293, 41b
Eyeballs Throwing his **eye** balls backward, to suruaye
411. A.3, 73
Eyebrows Vnder the which twoe crawling **eyebrowes** twine
404. A.1, 7
Eyed See Black-eyed, Dull-eyed, Great-eyed, Green-eyed, Mop-eyed, Owl-eyed, Squint-eyed
Eye-darts Shooting his **Eye-darts** 'gainst it, to surprise
412. A.3, 77
Eyen From th' embers, then the kitlings **eyne**,..136. H.336, 146
Soft Candle-light; the Kitling's **eyne**;.........167. H.443, 74
Eyes Be her forehead, and her **eyes**...............11. H.21, 7
Some sport, to please those Babies in your **eyes**:..15. H.38, 4
These **eyes** of mine shall see you mix agen.......26. H.79, 6
She kist, and wip'd thir dove-like **eyes**;..........31. H.92, 11
Has blear'd his **eyes**: Besides, his head is bald....33. H.99, 2
More in thine eares, then in thine **eyes**..........37. H.106, 88
How I may save mine **eyes**....................43. H.123, 24
The **Eyes** by tears speak, while the Tongue is mute.
58. H.150, 8
Sweet, be not proud of those two **eyes**,..........61. H.160, 1
False in breast, teeth, haire, and **eyes**:.........77. H.195, 10
Dry-rosted all, but raw yet in her **eyes**...........90. H.222, 2
Wept out our heart, as well as **eyes**............104. H.256, 14
While I have **eyes** to see:.....................109. H.267, 14
The very **eyes** of me:.........................109. H.267, 22
To clense his **eyes**, Tom Brock makes much adoe,
110. H.273, 1
A clammie Reume makes loathsome both his **eyes**:
110. H.273, 3
Shew her how his **eyes** do turne.............113. H.283, 37
Some gin, wherewith to catch your **eyes**.........114. H.283, 70
By the Brides **eyes**, and by the teeming life....114. H.283, 81

The eies be first, that conquer'd are...........118. H.290, 2
His kitling eyes begin to runne.................119. H.293, 24
Moles eyes; to these, the slain-Stags teares:.....120. H.293, 44
Or those Babies in your eyes,.................121. H.297, 9
Of all our parts, the eyes expresse.............121. H.300, 1
As her little eyes did peep......................123. H.310, 4
First, to the Babies of the eyes;...............130. H.329, 9
She that will weare thy teares, wo'd weare thine eyes.
131. H.330, 13
When the faire Hellen, from her eyes,.........135. H.336, 105
Ile seek him in your eyes;....................156. H.412, 14
His eyes and ears strive which sho'd fastest run..158. H.418, 2
Our eyes in sleepe;............................160. H.421, 45
And lightning in his eyes; and flings...........165. H.443, 15
With eyes of Peacocks Trains, & Trout-........166. H.443, 68
The glow-wormes eyes; the shining scales......166. H.443, 72
Dropt from the eyes of ravisht Girles..........167. H.443, 109
I know a thousand greedy eyes.................174. H.465, 17
And eyes, it neither sees or heares.............174. H.465, 22
With noise, the servants eyes from sleep.......179. H.476, 33
Close thou up thy Poets eyes:.................186. H.499, 2
Cleere are her eyes,...........................193. H.524, 1
Then at th' opening of mine eyes,...............199. H.549, 3
Her Eyes the Glow-worme lend thee,..........217. H.619, 1
Whose little eyes glow,.........................217. H.619, 4
Here about, but has his eyes,...................221. H.633, 30
Nero commanded; but withdrew his eyes.......236. H.679, 1
Kings must not oft be seen by publike eyes;....236. H.682, 1
Our eyes they'l blind, or if not blind, they'l bleer.
237. H.685, 12
Mine eyes, like clouds, were drizling raine,......237. H.687, 1
To mine eyes level'd opposite:..................237. H.687, 4
No more wo'd drown mine eyes, or me........237. H.687, 8
Chor. And Lallage (with cow-like eyes).......243. H.716, 11
Next, when I cast mine eyes and see..........261. H.779, 4
Having his eyes still in his eare,...............263. H.785, 6
Till his Wife licking, so unglews his eyes.......269. H.816, 2
Appeare thou to mine eyes.....................271. H.824, 6
He'l sell her Eyes, and Nose, for Beere and Ale..272. H.829, 4
Mine eyes must wooe you; (though I sigh the while)
274. H.837, 7
Reapes eyes so rawe are, that (it seemes) the flyes
282. H.879, 1
Mistake the flesh, and flye-blow both his eyes;.282. H.879, 2
Truth is best found out by the time, and eyes;..287. H.902, 1
Who with thine owne eyes read'st what we doe write,
297. H.945, 5
Enter and prosper; while our eyes doe waite...300. H.961, 9
See mine eyes are weeping ripe.................305. H.984, 13
Wash your hands, and cleanse your eyes........322. H.1064, 2
Claspe thou his Book, then close thou up his Eyes.
329. H.1095, 8
Lets drip a certain Gravie from her eyes.......331. H.1107, 2
Yet mine eyes the watch do keep;.............347. N.41, 11
Fright mine eares, and fright mine eyes,.......348. N.41, 42
And hold'st mine eyes from sleeping;...........353. N.56, 3
And these mine eyes shall see...................354. N.58, 5
Christ I shall see, with these same eyes:........358. N.78, 4
From teeming eyes; to these we bring,........360. N.83, 41
His gently-gliding, Dove-like eyes,..............365. N.97, 13
Your hearts, and hands, lips, eares, and eyes.....366. N.98, 9
Permit mine eyes to see........................369. N.106, 1
Thy Crosse, my Christ, fixt 'fore mine eyes sho'd be,
371. N.115, 9
And eyes, to pitie Widdowes teares...........373. N.123, 6
Our eyes out all together......................373. N.123, 10
We our eyes shall never steep;...............377. N.128, 18
God from our eyes all teares hereafter wipes,....379. N.139, 1
When sleep shall bath his body in mine eyes,...392. N.230, 19
Vnder whose shade twoe starry sparkling eyes.....404. A.1, 9
For puplike Eyes, take onlye theis..............409. A.2, 91
Thee, wth myne Eyes, or in, or out, of View.....411. A.3, 70
It, or to drawe the Cittie to his Eyes............412. A.3, 78
So that when 'ere we circumvolve our Eyes,......415. A.7, 15
— — — — — — — — — — —, ...423. var. H.128, 38
— — — — — — — — — — — —, ...424. ins. H.128, 46a
Lead on faire paranymphs, the while her eyes,
430. ins. H.283, 20a
See how he waves his hand, and through his eyes
430. ins. H.283, 40a
your eyes are they, wherewith you draw the pure
432. ins. H.283, 70h
— — — — — — — — — — — —, ...437. var. H.336, 108
— — — — — — — — — — — —, ...439. var. H.443, 38
— — — — — — — — — — — —, ...440. var. H.443, 57
— — — — — — — — — — — —, ...443. var. H.575, 42

Eye's-gleam Who with her eyes-gleam, or a glance of hand,
326. H.1080, 16

Fabius Fabius, and Cotta, Lentulus, all live.......41. H.117, 3

Fable A fable, song, or fleeting shade;...........69. H.178, 66

Fables We'll weary all the Fables there..........59. H.152, 12
But Fables we'l relate; how Jove...............215. H.616, 15

Fabricius Brings in Fabricius for a Combatant:..370. N.108, 10

Face But thou liv'st fearlesse; and thy face ne'r shewes
37. H.106, 93
A Burling iron for his face:...................39. H.108, 10
Your face no more: So live you free...........49. H.136, 35
A Virgins face she had; her dresse..............51. H.142, 7
You have ebbes of face and flowes,.............96. H.232, 5
Art quickens Nature; Care will make a face:...97. H.234, 1
Let but Pink's face i' th' Looking-glasse be showne,
110. H.272, 3
Of silke and silver at my face:..................116. H.284, 2
Sneape has a face so brittle, that it breaks.....124. H.311, 1
That weares one face (like heaven) and never showes
128. H.323, 7
And Proscenium of her face....................138. H.342, 8
Makes the smirk face of each to shine,.........147. H.377, 72
Here, for to make the face affraid;.............148. H.377, 78
That doth the Infants face enthrall,...........167. H.443, 91
'Tis Heresie in others: In your face............180. H.481, 1
The Candid Temples of her comely face:.......197. H.543, 2
And dismall Darknesse then doth smutch the face.
207. H.576, 6
He needs a Tucker for to burle his face........211. H.594, 2
He keeps the Fox-furre for to face his own......232. H.669, 2
Sibb when she saw her face how hard it was,...249. H.732, 1
But a Winters face in thee,.....................266. H.803, 5
Of lively colours, flowing from the face..........274. H.840, 2
From shame my face keepe free,...............281. H.874, 10
With my face towards the East................307. H.991, 8
As is your name, so is your comely face,.......307. H.992, 1
She with a dainty blush rebuk't her face;.....311. H.1006, 3
Flusht was his face; his haires with oyle did shine;
313. H.1017, 3
How sweetly shewes thy smiling face,.........375. N.123, 73
God then confounds mans face, when He not hears
382. N.169, 1
The shame of mans face is no more...........383. N.170, 1
Wo'd see Thy Face, and He not by............395. N.245, 6
By n' other Face, but by thyne owne,............409. A.2, 76
Soe must that faire face of yours................418. A.9, 27
— — — — — — — — — —, ...440. var. H.443, 76

Faced See Bold-faced, Broad-faced, Full-faced-moons, Shame-faced, Sweet-faced
— — — — — — — — — —, ...440. var. H.443, 76

Faces Read then, and when your faces shine....127. H.319, 27
Crab faces gownes with sundry Furres; 'tis known,
232. H.669, 1
Who do from sowre faces,....................260. H.777, 10
Those faces (sower as Vineger.).............279. H.868, 2

Faction If the chiefe author of the faction dyes;..132. H.335, 2

Factions The factions of the great ones call,.......282. H.877, 1

Factors And all the busie Factours come.........145. H.375, 9

Fade And you must fade, as well as they........61. H.159, 17
— — — — — — — — — —, ...450. var. A.9, 29

Fading But since these Cowslips fading be,.......112. H.281, 3

Fading-time And Fading-time do's show,..........184. H.493, 3

Fail Faile of thy former helps; and onely use.....46. H.128, 52
(Rather than fail) to steal from thence old shoes:
143. H.368, 2
The feast of Shepheards fail. Sil. None crowns the cup
159. H.421, 3
Thy Sheering-feast, which never faile.........231. H.662, 55
When all Birds els do of their musick faile,......247. H.726, 1
And not unlikely; rather too then fail,..........272. H.829, 3
Tell me, do thy kine now fail..................305. H.984, 7
If Tythe-pigs faile, then will he shift the scean,.325. H.1076, 3
All are not ill Plots, that doe sometimes faile;.331. H.1104, 1
For now the Corne and Wine must faile:......374. N.123, 14
Faile and scarce leaue to be showne............418. A.9, 29
The two last fayle, and by experience make
422. ins. H.106, 92e

Failed Fail'd in my part; O! Thou that art my deare,
398. N.261, 2

Fails Thus if our ship fails of her Anchor hold,..266. H.800, 7

Fain See Feign
Who would faine his strength renew,............10. H.19, 13
Fain would I kiss my Julia's dainty Leg,......139. H.349, 1
Which fain would waste upon thy Cates, but that
147. H.377, 49
Tell that Brave Man, fain thou wo'dst have access
301. H.963, 1
Fain would I rest; yet covet not to die,.......352. N.51, 11

Fained-lost-virginities See Feigned-lost-virginities L

Fainting Fainting swoones, and deadly sweats;...102. H.253, 8
What fainting hopes are in a Lover..........208. H.580, 12
More dangerous faintings by her desp'rate cure...214. H.612, 6

Fair A faire, and unfamiliar excellence:...........10. H.16, 4
(Faire Destinies all three)......................18. H.47, 6
Full and faire ones; come and buy:..............19. H.53, 2
When some shall say, Faire once my Silvia was;
21. H.62, 1
(If mercifull, as faire thou art;................33. H.103, 6
Nor car'st which comes the first, the foule or fair;
37. H.106, 97
What times of sweetnesse this faire day fore-shows,
44. H.124, 1
And all because, Faire Maid, thou art..........47. H.132, 9
With weather foule, then faire againe...........47. H.133, 13
Come, you are faire; and sho'd be seen........49. H.136, 24
Then Faire ones, doe not wrong.................53. H.149, 3

But all **faire** signs appeare....................56. H.149, 107
And to that Hand, (the Branch of Heavens **faire** Tree) 62. H.161, 11
See how Aurora throwes her **faire**.............67. H.178, 3
More **faire** in this transparent case,............75. H.193, 6
Faire was the Dawne; and but e'ne now the Skies 81. H.202, 1
Fresh and **faire**;...............................83. H.205, 6
And all **faire** Signs lead on our Shepardesse......85. H.213, 2
Smooth, **faire**, and fat; none better I can tell:....86. H.213, 6
But die you must (**faire** Maid) ere long,........88. H.216, 20
Ravisht, in that **faire** Via Lactea...............96. H.230, 4
Men say y'are **faire**; and **faire** ye are, 'tis true;.98. H.241, 1
Bloom'd from the East, or **faire** Injewel'd May..112. H.283, 2
All **faire** Constellations......................116. H.283, 157
Where being laid, all **Faire** signes looking on,....124. H.313, 11
Faire Daffadills, we weep to see...............125. H.316, 1
But when your own **faire** print was set........126. H.318, 6
Faire Pearles in order set?..................130. H.330, 4
Our own **fair** wind, and mark each one........133. H.336, 9
When the **faire** Hellen, from her eyes,..........135. H.336, 105
Come with the Spring-time, forth **Fair** Maid, and be 140. H.354, 1
For all this **fair** Transfiguration.............140. H.356, 4
But with thy **fair** Fates leading thee, Go on...155. H.405, 3
Good morrow to the Day so **fair**;.............156. H.412, 1
Though thou beest young, kind, soft, and **faire**,..174. H.465, 3
Let them enstile Thee Fairest **faire**,.............175. H.465, 37
Faire pledges of a fruitfull Tree,.............176. H.467, 1
Next is your lot (**Faire**) to be number'd one,..188. H.510, 1
Thus **faire** and cleane you are, although there be.189. H.511, 5
Faire and foule dayes trip Crosse and Pile; The **faire** 189. H.513, 1
Whom **faire** Corinna sits, and doth comply....206. H.575, 40
Let **faire** or foule my Mistresse be,............207. H.579, 1
All are alike **faire**, when no spots we see.......209. H.586, 2
Nor, **Faire**, must you be loth.................221. H.633, 35
Now for to win thy Heifer **faire**,...............243. H.716, 31
Be my Girle, or **faire** or browne,...............253. H.750, 4
Speak me **faire**; for Lovers be.................264. H.790, 3
Faire as Eve in Paradice:.....................274. H.838, 2
All Rites well ended, with **faire** Auspice come...286. H.898, 9
Look how our foule Dayes do exceed our **faire**;...339. N.1, 1
Heav'n is most **faire**; but fairer He...........382. N.164, 1
To make thy **faire** Predestination:...........389. N.216, 2
Are beawtifi'd with **faire** fring'd canopies.........404. A.1, 10
At whose **faire** topp to please the sight there growes 405. A.1, 35
Is the swan-stayning **faire** rare stately neck......405. A.1, 44
Like a **faire** mountaine in Riphean snowe,.....405. A.1, 60
Richer then that **faire** pretious virtuos horne......406. A.1, 103
Soe must that **faire** face of yours..............418. A.9, 27
And know (**faire** mistris) of yor youth.........418. A.9, 40
— — — — — — — — — — — —, ...424. var. H.164, 11
— — — — — — — — — — — —, ...425. var. H.197, 6
Lead on **faire** paranymphs, the while her eyes 430. ins. H.283, 20a
— — — — — — — — — — — —, ...437. var. H.336, 105
— — — — — — — — — — — —, ...450. var. A.9, 46
— — — — — — — — — — — —, ...453. ins. H.283, 50a
Fairer Heav'n is most faire; but **fairer** He......382. N.164, 1
Fairest The **fairest** most suspected be............49. H.136, 17
Let them enstile Thee **Fairest** faire,............175. H.465, 37
That made that **fairest** Canopie...............382. N.164, 2
The fresh and **fayrest** flourish of the Morne......410. A.3, 20
— — — — — — — — — — —, ...447. var. A.1, 36
Fairies Now this the **Fairies** wo'd have known,...91. H.223, 22
Sluts are loathsome to the **Fairies**:..............201. H.556, 6
That luckie **Fairies** here may dance their Round:.245. H.723, 8
Or whether **Fairies**, Syrens, Nymphes they were, 326. H.1080, 5
Fairies' Then this, the **Fairies** once, now Thine...90. H.223a, 6
Fairs Slouch he packs up, and goes to sev'rall **Faires**, 253. H.753, 1
Fair-set You are a full-spread **faire-set** Vine,.....88. H.216, 10
Fairy To purge the **Fairie** Family...............91. H.223, 49
And if that **Fairie** Knight not lies,.............92. H.223, 81
Shapcot! To thee the **Fairy** State............119. H.293, 1
Since you are Lady of this **Fairie** land........140. H.354, 10
The **Fairie** Court I give to thee:..............165. H.443, 2
Halfe tipsie to the **Fairie** Bed,................165. H.443, 4
Fayrie land: so ends his feast.............435. ins. H.293, ff
Fairy-Court Wee'l see the **Fairy-Court** anon......119. H.293, 6
Fairy-King The Court of Mab, and of the **Fairie-King**. 5. H.1, 12
Fairyland See **Fairy**
Fairy-Psalter Upon an end, the **Fairie-Psalter**,...92. H.223, 71
Faith And as there is one Love, one **Faith**, one Troth, 38. H.106, 143
Adored Cesar! and my **Faith** is such,..........62. H.161, 13
I am not jealous of thy **Faith**,................175. H.465, 43
In thee, all **faith** of Woman-kind..............176. H.465, 80
Faith, and Affection: which will never slip......252. H.745, 19
Not out of want of breath, but want of **faith**....283. H.884, 2
And in good **faith** I'd thought it strange........290. H.915, 3
Faith is a thing that's four-square; let it fall...292. H.926, 1
(In **faith** I know not how)....................295. H.942, 10
When a mans **Faith** is frozen up, as dead;......359. N.80, 1
By **Faith** we all walk here, not by the Spirit.....362. N.88, 2
For any ill; but, for the proof of **Faith**:........380. N.150, 2
So long (it seem'd) as Maries **Faith** was small,.386. N.192, 1
But no more Woman, being strong in **Faith**;....386. N.192, 3
But that He rose, that's Christians **Faith**.......395. N.247, 2
As **faith** can seale It you;......................414. A.5, 4
Spring hence thy **faith**, nor thinke it ill desert ...414. A.6, 3
Or their thought of **faith** may growe..............418. A.9, 37
— — — — — — — — — — —, ...422. var. H.106, 145
Of oyle, but onely rich in **faith**,........436. ins. H.336, 481
Faithful My **faithful** friend, if you can see........79. H.198, 1
With safety of a **faithful** Ore:..................94. H.225, 4
Markt in thy Book for **faithfull** Witnesses.....188. H.507, 4
Thy **faithfull** fields to yeeld thee Graine,........233. H.670, 9
Thy **faithfull** friend, and to poure downe........303. H.973, 17
Put from, or draw unto the **faithfull** shore:....315. H.1028, 12
'Tis Wisdomes part to doubt a **faithfull** friend..333. H.1121, 2
Faithless If you prove **faithlesse** thrice,............32. H.94, 11
Here **faithlesse** never;.......................162. H.426, 24
Fall See **Downfall**
Let **fall** a Primrose, and with it a teare:..........9. H.14, 14
Nere to thy Reverend Pitcher I will **fall**........11. H.22, 7
But pretty Fondling, let not **fall**..................12. H.23, 5
She rather took, then got a **fall**:...............12. H.27, 2
Better tis that one shu'd **fall**,.....................21. H.61, 7
Upon thy Forme more wrinkles yet will **fall**,.....21. H.62, 5
In wayes confus'd, nor slip or **fall**..............33. H.98, 10
For tears no more will **fall**.......................43. H.123, 18
To conquer'd men, some comfort 'tis to **fall**.....50. H.141, 1
Fall, like a spangling dew,....................57. H.149, 155
False to my vow, or **fall** away from thee........59. H.154, 10
As Lovers **fall** into a swoone:..................67. H.175, 16
And told her, (as some tears did **fall**).........71. H.182, 25
Now, now, blowne downe; needs must the old stock **fall**. 72. H.185, 14
He who to the ground do's **fall**,.................84. H.209, 7
But since th'art slaine; and in thy **fall**,........89. H.219, 7
Ignoble off-springs, they may **fall**..............89. H.219, 17
Fall on me like a silent dew,....................95. H.227, 23
Fall gently, gently, and a while him keep.........99. H.244, 5
Fall down, down, down, from those thy chiming spheres, 103. H.254, 5
O doe not **fall**...............................114. H.283, 85
Rather then to which I'le **fall**,.................117. H.286, 3
If they but slip, and never **fall**..................118. H.291, 16
Tune my words, that they may **fall**,...............122. H.303, 3
Thus a dew of Graces **fall**.....................125. H.314, 9
Where the fault springs, there let the judgement **fall**. 132. H.335, 4
Do not you **fall** through frailty; Ile be sure....136. H.338, 3
Learn this of me, where e'r thy Lot doth **fall**;..153. H.396, 1
He's greedie of his life, who will not **fall**,......155. H.405, 17
For that once lost, thou't **fall** to one,..........174. H.465, 27
And if thy **fall** sho'd this way come,............175. H.465, 65
Why do ye **fall** so fast?.......................176. H.467, 2
Fall thou must first, then rise to life with These,.188. H.507, 3
Where ere the luckie Lot doth **fall**,.............197. H.542, 3
Fresh blossoms from her cheekes did **fall**.......203. H.562, 2
Expecting when to **fall**: which soon will be;....203. H.565, 3
Down **fall**,.....................................211. H.596, 15
Fall down together vanquisht both, and lye.....216. H.618, 15
Then these, no feares more on your Fancies **fall**,.222. H.634, 14
No sillable doth **fall** here,......................235. H.674, 11
Weak I am grown, and must in short time **fall**; 242. H.713, 19
They tread on clouds, and though they sometimes **fall**, 250. H.737, 3
They **fall** like dew, but make no noise at all.....250. H.737, 4
Would into prais'd (but pitied) ruines **fall**,.....252. H.745, 15
When this or that vast Dinastie must **fall**........256. H.763, 9
The Blessing **fall** in mellow times on Thee......269. H.818, 10
And gave my Love a **fall**.......................288. H.908, 4
In Battailes what disasters **fall**,.................290. H.913, 1
Upon your hogsheads never **fall**................291. H.919, 5
Faith is a thing that's four-square; let it **fall**....292. H.926, 1
That I did **fall**..............................296. H.946, 10
Can'st write the Comick, Tragick straine, and **fall** 298. H.955, 5
Spend on that stock: and when your life must **fall**, 299. H.958, 5
When the waters by their **fall**..................302. H.968, 9
The Person crowns the Place; your lot doth **fall**.304. H.977, 1
Lift up thy Sword; next, suffer it to **fall**,........310. H.1002, 3
Thy **fall** is but the rising to a Crowne.........311. H.1007, 2
And lisping reeld, and reeling like to **fall**.......313. H.1017, 6
No drought upon thy wanton waters **fall**.......316. H.1028, 19
Tis no discomfort in the world to **fall**,..........319. H.1045, 1
Stripes justly given yerk us (with their **fall**)...319. H.1050, 1
After leaves, the tree must **fall**...............321. H.1058, 2
Fix on That Columne then, and never **fall**;......329. H.1092, 7
At which the hounds **fall** a bounding;........334. H.1122, 15
Tho Kingdoms **fal**,..............................335. H.1129, 10
A sin, then **fall** to weeping when 'tis done........349. N.43, 6
And take me up; or els prevent the **fall**...........352. N.51, 8

God will have all, or none; serve Him, or **fall**....353. N.54, 1
For a Benizon to **fall**..........................364. N.95, 5
But if that Tree sho'd **fall**, and die,...........371. N.114, 7
Rise ye Debters then, and **fall**.................373. N.121, 11
For rather then one drop shall **fall**............377. N.129, 7
Gods Hands are round, & smooth, that gifts may **fall**
380. N.151, 1
Of many standing, but of **fall** to none..........389. N.215, 2
Which is the height of comfort, when I **fall**,....392. N.230, 35
Before Mans **fall**, the Rose was born.............396. N.251, 1
Thay may **fall** downe and stroake as the..........408. A.2, 57
Fallen The nails **faln** off by Whit-flawes: Art's..166. H.443, 59
Of all those three-brave-brothers, **faln** i' th' Warre,
170. H.451, 1
— — — — — — — — — —, ...423. var. H.128, 23
Are trinkets **falne** from the Kites nest;....439. ins. H.443, 45o
Falling Still a **falling**, yet I see....................62. H.162, 5
Falls See **Pitfalls**
Droops, dies, and **falls** without the cleavers stroke..23. H.69, 6
And when my **falls** and stumblings are...........32. H.98, 3
Dead **falls** the Cause, if once the Hand be mute;
123. H.308, 1
Falls to a temper, and doth mildly cast........225. H.642, 19
And, though it **falls**, continues still...........318. H.1036, 5
False Thou wilt complaine, **False** now's thy Looking-glasse
21. H.62, 2
False to my vow, or fall away from thee.......59. H.154, 10
False in legs, and **false** in thighes;..............77. H.195, 9
False in breast, teeth, haire, and eyes:........77. H.195, 10
False in head, and **false** enough;................77. H.195, 11
How **false**, how hollow she's in heart;..........103. H.253, 15
For **false** Position in his neighbours sheets:......195. H.532, 2
Nor those **false** vows, which oft times don't prevaile.
331. H.1104, 2
False man would be content.................346. N.38, 10
Falsehood **Falsehood** winnes credit by uncertainties.
287. H.902, 2
Falsehood by Varnish and Vermillion...........329. H.1094, 2
Fame **Fame** tell of States, of Countries, Courts, and Kings;
36. H.106, 85
Horace, Anacreon both had lost their **fame**,.....45. H.128, 31
Rests here with him; who was the **Fame**,.......48. H.134, 3
As I meet thee. Soule of my life, and **fame**!...77. H.197, 9
Without a **fame** in death?....................85. H.211, 16
In thee Brave Man! Whose incorrupted **fame**,..131. H.331, 5
Fame, and his Name, both set, and sing his Lyricks.
143. H.366, 4
In Bookes of **fame**;.........................161. H.426, 13
Is **Fame**, (the breath of popular applause.)......169. H.448, 2
Leaving no **Fame** to long Posterity:...........210. H.592, 2
Then a mans frequent **Fame**, spoke out with praise.
241. H.710, 2
'Tis still observ'd, that **Fame** ne're sings........245. H.721, 1
Good wits get more **fame** by their punishment...317. H.1034, 2
Since **Fame** that sides with these, or goes before.329. H.1092, 3
That **Fame**, and Fames rear'd Pillar, thou shalt see
329. H.1092, 5
Sho'd **fame** be dumb;.......................375. N.123, 88
(White **Fame**) and Resurrection to the Good,....410. A.3, 32
As **Fame** or Rumour, hath or Trumpe or Tongue..411. A.3, 46
But voice of **fame**, and voice of heauen haue thunderd
414. A.6, 5
— — — — — — — — — — — —, ...423. var. H.128, 23
— — — — — — — — — — — —, ...449. var. A.3, 40
— — — — — — — — — — — —, ...453. var. H.283, 45
Famed See **Far-famed**
Fame's From **Fames** black lips, as you from me..49. H.136, 36
Of whom, from **Fam's** white Trumpet, This Ile Tell,
170. H.451, 9
His **Fame's** long life, who strives to set up Yours.
188. H.506, 16
Thou shalt thy Name have, and thy **Fames** best trust,
231. H.664, 5
That Fame, and **Fames** rear'd Pillar, thou shalt see
329. H.1092, 5
Held up by **Fames** eternall Pedestall...........329. H.1092, 8
Fames pillar here, at last, we set,............335. H.1129, 1
Fames Nor Fate, nor Enuye, cann theyr **Fames** Conuince,
411. A.3, 40
Fame's-pledge A course in thy **Fames-pledge**, thy Sonne.
147. H.377, 44
Familiar Made lovingly **familiar**:.................20. H.56, 4
The farting Tanner, and **familiar** King;........155. H.405, 6
Shall be **familiar**..........................162. H.426, 20
Familiarly To talk with thee **familiarly**...........58. H.152, 6
To talke with me **familiarly**;.................393. N.232, 8
Family To purge the Fairie **Family**...............91. H.223, 49
Famish **Famish** me, nor over-fill................232. H.665, 18
Fan 'Tis thou, alone, who with thy Mistick **Fan**,.45. H.128, 23
And **fan** her wanton haire....................103. H.255, 4
Fancies Among thy **Fancies**, tell me this,.......130. H.329, 1
Then these, no feares more on your **Fancies** fall,
222. H.634, 14
There no monstrous **fancies** shall...............377. N.128, 13
Fancy What I **fancy**, I approve,..................11. H.21, 1
That with the **fancie** I awook;..................17. H.41, 21

Melting, and in **fancie** die:.....................17. H.43, 6
Then for an easie **fansie**; place.................39. H.108, 9
One **fancie** more! but if there be................64. H.169, 9
By glim'ring of a **fancie**: Doe but come,......207. H.575, 55
So the **Fancie** cooles, till when.................242. H.714, 11
So my **fancie** be content,......................253. H.750, 14
— — — — — — — — — — —, ...429. var. H.263, 9
Fanes See **Fans**
Fanged See **Sharp-fanged**
Fans Next to your Flailes, your **Fanes**, your Fatts;
102. H.250, 40
Fantastic The **fantastick** Pannicles:..............242. H.714, 4
Fantasy Present their shapes; while **fantasie** discloses
36. H.106, 47
Far **Farre** safer 'twere to stay at home:.............5. H.2, 2
More then the stones i' th' street by **farre**:.......32. H.98, 4
More white .then whitest Lillies **far**,............34. H.105, 1
(**Far** more with wonder, then with feare)......36. H.106, 84
Slowly goes **farre**: The meane is best: Desire..51. H.143, 3
Juno here, **far** off, doth stand....................56. H.149, 109
Thou lighter then the Cork by **far**:...........70. H.181, 22
A Rule, how **far** to teach,......................76. H.193, 42
Lest they too **far** extend.......................76. H.193, 48
I! **far** more welcome then the happy soile,......77. H.197, 15
God, and **far** more transcendent then the rest?...78. H.197, 60
Th'ast dar'd too **farre**; but Furie now forbeare...82. H.204, 1
From Countries **far**, with Store of Spices, (sweet).86. H.213, 31
Sweeter **far**, then ever yet.....................108. H.266, 3
What's that we see from **far**? the spring of Day..112. H.283, 1
Good things, that come of course, **far** lesse doe please,
123. H.307, 1
'Tis now **farre** off, and then tis nere;..........130. H.329, 14
Can we so **farre**..............................134. H.336, 67
Farre more then night bewearied..............136. H.336, 152
To Thee, thy Lady, younglings, and as **farre**....146. H.377, 3
How **farre** a Figure ought to go,...............148. H.377, 92
Spungie and swelling, and **farre** more...........165. H.443, 27
Farre from me Ile remove.....................171. H.452, 7
Have made Thee prosperous in thy wayes, thus **farre**:
181. H.483, 6
Far lesse in number, then our foule dayes are.....189. H.513, 2
And knit in knots **far** more then I..............202. H.560, 11
The Morn's **farre** spent; and the immortall Sunne
216. H.618, 3
Farre hence be all speech, that may anger move:.222. H.633, 60
Far from hence the evill Sp'rite................258. H.769, 9
And old, old Age is a **farre** off:................267. H.806, 3
Farre better 'twere for either to be mute,........287. H.901, 5
Our trust **farre** more then ten eare-witnesses.....287. H.904, 2
Farre faster then the first can wither............289. H.912, 8
We'l from our owne, adde **far** more years to his..300. H.961, 20
That to me was **far** more deer.................305. H.984, 16
Men must have Bounds how **farre** to walke; for we
307. H.990, 1
Are made **farre** worse, by lawless liberty.........307. H.990, 2
That may **far** sooner speed the poore:..........312. H.1014, 8
T'invade from **far**: They'l finde worse foes at home.
316. H.1030, 2
To disperse the water **farre**...................322. H.1064, 4
For as **farre** as that doth light,................322. H.1064, 5
So **farre** keepes the evill Spright..............322. H.1064, 6
Far away, if thou beest by....................324. H.1069, 4
Thou hast beheld those seas, and Countries **farre**;
330. H.1100, 5
To see **far** off the smoaking Villages............352. N.51, 10
The teares of Saints more sweet by **farre**,........379. N.145, 1
Who hath more suffer'd by us **farre**, then for us...388. N.209, 2
We merit all we suffer, and by **far**..............393. N.235, 1
So that I dare, with **farre** lesse feare,..........402. N.269, 8
Here's golden fruit that **farre** exceeds all price....406. A.1, 71
To know his Queene, mixt with the **farre**..434. ins. H.293, 41g
Farced Y'ave **farced** well, pray make an end;....146. H.377, 24
Farc't with the food, that may themselves suffice.
310. H.1005, 4
Farcing Shall find much **farcing** Buckram in our Books.
202. H.559, 2
Fardel None sees the **fardell** of his faults behind...253. H.751, 2
Far-drawn Nor doth this **far-drawn** Hemisphere.....72. H.185, 3
Fare See **Welfare**
Can'st, and unurg'd, forsake that Larded **fare**,...37. H.106, 111
Find equall freedome, equall **fare**;..............147. H.377, 60
Great be my **fare**, or small cheere,..............235. H.674, 17
And **fare** it well: yet Herrick, if so be...........371. N.112, 2
— — — — — — — — — —, ...422. var. H.106, 106
Of nature: bidd mee nowe **fare** well, or smile
424. ins. H.128, 46d
Farewell See **Fare**
In thy remembrance (Julia.) So **farewell**..........14. H.35, 14
Farewell my shackles, (though of pearle they be)..17. H.42, 3
Wherein thou liv'st for ever. Deare **farewell**.........23. H.72, 4
Dean-bourn, **farewell**; I never look to see......29. H.86, 1
Yet Dianeme now **farewell**:.....................33. H.103, 2
Farewell thou Thing, time-past so knowne, so deare
45. H.128, 1
And having spoke it once, **Farewell**.............60. H.159, 12
When once true-lovers take their last **Fare-well**...73. H.186, 8

My Crosse; my Cord; and all **farewell**.......123. H.306, 4
Mirt. Ah! Amarillis, **farewell** mirth and pipe;...159. H.421, 8
Farewell....................................168. H.444, 9
Farewell....................................178. H.475, 15
Of his glory. So **farewell**.......................289. H.910, 6
Mournfull maid **farewell** to you;...............306. H.984, 42
See, the fier's by: **Farewell**....................334. H.1125, 8
O Yeares! and Age! **Farewell**:...................354. N.58, 1
Farewell the Flax and Reaming wooll,..........374. N.123, 41
Farewell the Coats, the Garments, and..........374. N.123, 43
Farewell thy Fier and thy Light,...............374. N.123, 45
Each takes A weeping **farwell**, rackt in mynde....411. A.3, 63
Doing's, the Fruite of Doinge well, **Farwell**......412. A.3, 104
But truth knitt fast; and so **farewell** for euer......414. A.6, 12

Fare-ye-well Receive this vow, so **fare-ye-well** for ever. 316. H.1028, 26

Far-famed Then Lydia, **far-fam'd** Lydia,..........70. H.181, 7

Far-fetch Beyound the **fare-fetch** Marchandize......409. A.2, 94

Farmer Of the gray **farmer**, and to these....439. ins. H.443, 45h

Farmhouse And to the **Farm-house** nere return at all; 172. H.456, 9

Farm's That's counter-proofe against the **Farms** mishaps, 128. H.323, 5

Fart Let me feed full, till that I **fart**, sayes Jill...186. H.498, 8
A **Fart** flew out, or a Sir-reverence..............200. H.551, 6
Flew out a crack, so mighty, that the **Fart**,....205. H.572, 3
May **fart** for joy, as well as shout:.............306. H.987, 2

Farther (**Farther** then Gentlenes tends) gets place 114. H.283, 83
And **farther** off, and every where,..............166. H.443, 46

Farthest — — — — — — — —, ...422. var. H.106, 66

Farting The **farting** Tanner, and familiar King;..155. H.405, 6
Halfe choakt with the stink of her **farting**....333. H.1122, 6

Fashion I'm sure they'l **fashion** Roses..........74. H.192, 8
Their **fashion** is, but to say no, to take it........235. H.675, 2

Fashioned **Fashion'd** like Thee; which though 'tave eares 174. H.465, 21

Fast And keep a **Fast**, and Funerall together,......41. H.118, 6
As **fast** away as do's the Sunne:.................69. H.178, 62
Barre close as you can, and bolt **fast** too your doore, 97. H.233, 1
Bungie do's **fast**; looks pale; puts Sack-cloth on;.122. H.305, 1
Who, as soone, fell **fast** asleep,..................123. H.310, 3
I am bound, and **fast** bound so,...................128. H.322, 10
My Organ **fast** asleep;...........................144. H.371, 15
Who hold **fast** here an endlesse lively-hood......152. H.392, 8
Here a solemne **Fast** we keepe,....................170. H.450, 1
Why do yee fall so **fast**?.........................176. H.467, 2
Never keep a **fast**, or pray......................183. H.490, 15
Time flyes away **fast**;...........................196. H.534, 13
But her self held **fast** by none..................232. H.665, 14
But all a solemne **Fast** there kept..............237. H.686, 8
Fix the foundation **fast**, and let the Roofe.......245. H.723, 13
His wife her owne ware sells as **fast** at home....253. H.753, 4
A **Fast**, while Jets and Marbles weep,..........257. H.764, 8
I freeze as **fast**, and shake for cold..............290. H.915, 2
Let others to the Printing Presse run **fast**,......314. H.1022, 1
His Wife and Children **fast** to death for fear.....325. H.1077, 6
A Lent for thee, to **fast** and weep..............361. N.83, 60
A **Fast**, and weep..............................373. N.123, 9
That did ordaine the **Fast** of forty Dayes.........386. N.195, 2
Is this a **Fast**, to keep........................391. N.228, 1
Is it to **fast** an houre,..........................391. N.228, 9
No: 'tis a **Fast**, to dole.......................391. N.228, 13
It is to **fast** from strife,......................391. N.228, 17
But truth knitt **fast**; and so **farewell** for euer.....414. A.6, 12

Fast-ball — — — — — — — — —, ...433. var. H.293, 29

Fastened Which to the knees by nature **fastned** on..406. A.1, 85

Faster Farre **faster** then the first can wither.......289. H.912, 8

Fastest His eyes and ears strive which sho'd **fastest** run. 158. H.418, 2

Fasting-Spittle Their Holy Oyle, their **Fasting-Spittle**; 93. H.223, 117

Fat Drop the **fat** blessing of the sphears.........57. H.149, 152
Smooth, faire, and **fat**; none better I can tell:....86. H.213, 6
Foundation of your Feast, **Fat** Beefe:.........101. H.250, 29
Feed, and grow **fat**; and as ye eat,............102. H.250, 44
The **fat**; breathe thou, and there's the rich perfume. 102. H.251, 4
To eate thy Bullocks thighs, thy Veales, thy **fat**.147. H.377, 63
Grow **fat** and smooth: The reason is,..........173. H.461, 3
He raves through leane, he rages through the **fat**; 191. H.518, 3
Grown **fat**,....................................246. H.724, 23
Be she **fat**, or be she leane,....................253. H.750, 16
Who claim the **Fat**, and Fleshie for their share,..272. H.826, 5
Fat be my Hinde; unlearned be my wife;.......294. H.938, 1
But carve to him the **fat** flanks; and he shall.....305. H.982, 3
Can live by love, or else grow **fat** by Play:......325. H.1077, 2
Fat Frankincense:............................361. N.83, 64
From **fat** of Veales, and Sheep?...............391. N.228, 4
and with the **fatt**.......................434. ins. H.293, 41a

Fatal No **Fatal** Owle the Bedsted keeps,.........56. H.149, 101
Fatall to me in my love.........................117. H.286, 8
Passe all we must the **fatall** Ferry:.............172. H.457, 2
Extreames are **fatall**, where they once doe strike, 333. H.1120, 5
Three **fatall** Sisters wait upon each sin;..........341. N.11, 1

Fate If deare Anthea, my hard **fate** it be...........11. H.22, 1
Live with a thrifty, not a needy **Fate**;............13. H.28, 1
Whom (Stars consenting with thy **Fate**) thou hast 35. H.106, 33
Let bounteous **Fate** your spindles full..........58. H.149, 161
(So **Fate** spares her) am well content to die....70. H.181, 12
Too strong for **Fate** to break us: Look upon......78. H.197, 71
Bestroaking **Fate** the while.....................113. H.283, 29
As **Fate** do's lead or draw us; none,..........132. H.336, 6
For needy **Fate**..................................137. H.340, 12
Free by your **fate**, then Fortunes mightinesse,....141. H.359, 4
It is, which builds, 'gainst **Fate** to stand...148. H.377, 102
Sisters of **Fate** appeare to me...................153. H.399, 2
And all live here with needy **Fate**..............179. H.476, 30
One **Fate** had both; both equall Grace;.........185. H.497, 7
All things subjected are to **Fate**;...............208. H.583, 1
Or Phyllis, whom hard **Fate** forc't on,..........215. H.616, 13
Whom gentle **fate** translated hence.............226. H.644, 5
London my home is: though by hard **fate** sent..242. H.713, 13
Stand forth brave man, since **Fate** has made thee here 251. H.745, 1
What **Fate** decreed, Time now ha's made us see..254. H.756, 1
Go on with Sylla's Fortune; let thy **Fate**........254. H.756, 9
Fate gives a meeting. Death's the end of woe....257. H.766, 2
Do's Fortune rend thee? Beare with thy hard **Fate**: 270. H.820, 1
Your **Fate**, and Ours, alike Victorious are......271. H.823, 2
If that my **Fate** has now fulfill'd my yeere,......278. H.860, 1
Of thy both Great, and everlasting **fate**...........280. H.869, 4
Our **Fate**, our Fortune, and our Genius;.......300. H.961, 14
This Kingdomes fortune, and that Empires **fate**: 330. H.1100, 8
Low is my porch, as is my **Fate**,................350. N.47, 11
Nor **Fate**, nor Enuye, cann theyr Fames Conuince, 411. A.3, 40
(Thy Mercie helping) shall resist stronge **fate**.....411. A.3, 44
With such white vowes as **fate** can nere dissever..414. A.6, 11
These have their **Fate**, and wear away as Men;...419. A.10, 2
Owes more to vertue then too **Fate**.......422. ins. H.106, 92b
— — — — — — — — — —, ...423. var. H.119, 9
— — — — — — — — — — —, ...428. var. H.197, 85

Fates While the milder **Fates** consent,.............39. H.111, 1
That done, the harder **Fates** deny'd.............69. H.180, 3
Thus, thou, that man art, whom the **Fates** conspir'd 121. H.301, 5
Your sometime Poet; but if **fates** do give......140. H.355, 11
But thou kind Prew did'st with my **Fates** abide,..151. H.387, 5
But with thy fair **Fates** leading thee, Go on......155. H.405, 3
While **Fates** permits us, let's be merry;..........172. H.457, 1
Fates revolve no Flax th'ave spun..............224. H.639, 4
Then, while **Fates** suffer, live thou free,........233. H.670, 17
That little, **Fates** me gave or lent..............246. H.724, 8
The sterner **Fates**, to cross his purposes;........266. H.800, 4
Go with thy Faults and **Fates**; yet stay..........287. H.899, 7
We o're the tombes, and **Fates** shall flye;......288. H.906, 3
My **Fates** are ended; when thy Herrick dyes,...329. H.1095, 7
With my **fates** neglected lye.....................334. H.1125, 6

Fat-fed The **fat-fed** smoking Temple, which in....146. H.377, 6

Father 'Tis strange, his **Father** long time has been ill, 125. H.315, 3
For all his Issue, **Father** of one Child..........195. H.533, 2
In which thy **Father** Johnson now is plac't,....207. H.575, 57
Thy **Father** brought with him along...............360. N.83, 25
A quire of blest Soules circling in the **Father**....383. N.177, 2
'Twixt God the **Father**, Holy Ghost, and Sonne: 386. N.191, 4
And though the **Father** be the first of Three,..386. N.191, 5

Fatherless Ill us'd, then Babes left **fatherless**.....218. H.626, 15

Father's Hide, and with them, their **Fathers** nakedness. 32. H.95, 4

Fathers May fost'ring **fathers** be to you.........218. H.626, 13
'Tis never read there (as the **Fathers** say).......396. N.249, 5

Fatted — — — — — — — — —, ...434. var. H.293, 42

Fattened Late **fatned** in a piece of cloth:........120. H.293, 42

Fattest The **fattest** Hogs we grease the more with Lard. 22. H.64, 2
The **fattest** Oxe the first must bleed..............77. H.196, 2

Fatts See **Vats**

Fatuus But alias call's here **Fatuus** ignis..........91. H.223, 31

Faules These Laces, Ribbands, and these **Faules**,..360. N.83, 44

Fault Making thy peace with heav'n, for some late **fault**, 36. H.106, 59
Is it (sweet maid) your **fault** these holy........53. H.149, 11
Like a dull Twi-light? Tell me; and the **fault**....77. H.197, 29
At most a **fault**, 'tis but a **fault** of love..........86. H.213, 28
For some small **fault**, to offer sacrifice:..........102. H.251, 2
No **fault** in women to refuse...................118. H.291, 1
No **fault** in women, to confesse................118. H.291, 3
No **fault** in women, to lay on..................118. H.291, 5
No **fault** in women, to make show..............118. H.291, 9
No **fault** in women, though they be............118. H.291, 13
No **fault** in womankind, at all,..................118. H.291, 15

Where the **fault** springs, there let the judgement fall. 132. H.335, 4
May your **fault** dye,..........................161. H.426, 11
Extreames have still their **fault**;..............221. H.633, 50
Prat He writes Satyres; but herein's the **fault**,..238. H.692, 1
Find'st here a **fault**, and mend'st the trespasse too: 298. H.955, 8
A **fault**, tis hid, if it be voic't by thee..........328. H.1089, 2
Not for the **fault** of Nature, but of will...........370. N.110, 2
But, for Mans **fault**, then was the Thorn,........396. N.251, 3
Against thy purer Essence? For that **fault**.426. ins. H.197, 29b
For that would prove more Heresy then **fault** 433. ins. H.283, 140h
Faultless As **faultlesse**; will not wish undone,....48. H.136, 11
Faultless every way for shape;................306. H.984, 27
Faults **Faults** done by night, will blush by day:....20. H.56, 6
Wink at small **faults**, the greater ne'rthelesse......32. H.95, 3
Night hides our thefts; all **faults** then pardon'd be: 209. H.586, 1
None sees the fardell of his **faults** behind........253. H.751, 2
Go with thy **Faults** and Fates; yet stay.........287. H.899, 7
Princes cure some **faults** by their patience.......309. H.998, 2
Great **faults** require great satisfaction..........312. H.1012, 2
Next, when I have my **faults** confest,............349. N.46, 5
For **faults** of former yeares;....................352. N.53, 4
To punish great sins, who small **faults** whipt here. 381. N.156, 2
If ill it goes with thee, thy **faults** confesse:.....395. N.243, 3
I know, that **faults** will many here be found,....398. N.261, 5
Faulty Mine's **faulty** too, and small:.............376. N.125, 6
Faunus While **Faunus** in the Vision comes to keep, 36. H.106, 51
We read how **Faunus**, he the shepheards God,....306. H.986, 1
Favonius By young **Favonius**....................251. H.740, 8
Favor **Favour**, Ile make full satisfaction;.........27. H.82, 14
Favour your tongues, who enter here............91. H.223, 41
That **favour** granted was;.....................100. H.249, 5
For which **favour**, there shall be................122. H.303, 5
Fortune did never **favour** one...................191. H.520, 1
If **favour** or occasion helpe not him.............298. H.953, 2
Favored I who have **favour'd** many, come to be...142. H.365, 1
Favorite Still wanting to her **Favourite**...........191. H.520, 4
Favorites Princes and **Fav'rites** are most deere, while they 255. H.758, 1
Favors **Favours** on me, her fierce Idolater?........77. H.197, 26
For **favours** here to warme me,.................234. H.674, 5
Kisses and **Favours** are sweet things;..........283. H.883, 13
Feacie **Feacie** (some say) doth wash her clothes i'th' Lie 178. H.474, 1
Fear Nor wrack, or Bulging thou hast cause to **feare**: 23. H.71, 2
Cast off (said he) all **feare**,......................26. H.81, 7
Which are so cleane, so chast, as none may **feare**...28. H.84, 5
We two are last in Hell: what may we **feare**......33. H.101, 1
Feare to those sheets, that know no sin.........35. H.106, 40
Mak'st easie **Feare** unto thee say,..............36. H.106, 74
(Far more with wonder, then with **feare**)........36. H.106, 84
Nor **feare**, or wish your dying day............38. H.106, 146
But do not so; for **feare**, lest he................39. H.108, 13
The gaines must dead the **feare** of detriment......42. H.120, 2
If twice you kisse, you need not **feare**,..........61. H.159, 26
Whom sho'd I **feare** to write to, if I can..........64. H.168, 1
And never shew blood-guiltinesse, or **feare**........64. H.168, 3
I **feare** no Earthly Powers;...................65. H.170, 1
Feare not; the leaves will strew................68. H.178, 19
Who doth both love and **feare** you Honour'd Sir. 99. H.245, 8
Put in **Feare**, and hope, and doubt;............116. H.285, 5
Ever full of pensive **feare**;.....................117. H.286, 2
Profane no Porch young man and maid, for **fear**.124. H.313, 3
No more shall I (I **feare** me) to thee bring..132. H.333, 5
Let but few smart, but strike a **feare** through all: 132. H.335, 3
Have I not blest Thee? Then go forth; nor **fear** 155. H.405, 1
(As Salust saith) co-incident to **feare**...........162. H.430, 2
When as the humble Cottages not **feare**........181. H.483, 15
And, hugging close, we will not **feare**.........190. H.515, 13
Nor need we here to **feare** the frowne.........190. H.515, 33
Wherein we rest, and never **feare**..............200. H.552, 9
Be bold my Booke, nor be abasht, or **feare**...212. H.603, 1
Looke ye not wan, or colourlesse for **feare**.....222. H.634, 6
When I goe Hence ye Closet-Gods, I **feare**.....227. H.652, 1
And possesse no other **feare**,.................255. H.761, 23
With boldness that we **feare**...................259. H.772, 4
And a deale of nightly **feare**..................263. H.785, 7
(For gentle **feare**, or jelousie)................265. H.798, 10
The Soldiers leave the Field with equall **feare**...268. H.813, 4
Who begs to die for **feare** of humane need......277. H.855, 1
Love is a kind of warre; Hence those who **feare**,.280. H.872, 1
Without a thought of hurt, or **feare**;...........283. H.883, 8
And stealing still with love, and **feare** to Bed,..286. H.898, 15
Nor do thou **feare** the want of these,..........289. H.912, 5
Not for the servile **feare** of punishment.........290. H.917, 2
The first event breeds confidence or **feare**......292. H.924, 2
Though from without no foes at all we **feare**;...292. H.928, 1
If ye **feare** to be affrighted..................323. H.1065, 1
His Wife and Children fast to death for **fear**...325. H.1077, 6
Or **feare** of it, but Love keeps all in awe.)....326. H.1080, 20
I have been wanton, and too bold I **feare**,......329. H.1095, 1
When **feare** admits no hope of safety, then....333. H.1118, 1
Peepes trembling for **feare**,....................334. H.1122, 17
First, **Fear** and Shame without, then Guilt within. 341. N.11, 2
For **feare** of future-biting penurie:............352. N.51, 12
So I'le not **feare** the Judge, or thee............357. N.72, 18
Feare me,......................................363. N.92, 13
What need I then to **feare** at all,..............371. N.114, 5
May **feare** it ever for uncertaintie:............379. N.142, 2
The **feare** of God, commixt with cleanly love....380. N.147, 2
I shall lesse swoone, then die for **feare**........393. N.232, 10
Good and great God! How sho'd I **feare**........395. N.245, 1
Ah! Sions Daughters, do not **feare**.............400. N.266, 7
So that I dare, with farre lesse **feare**,........402. N.269, 8
If so; I'le thither follow, without **feare**;.......403. N.271, 7
Safe Modestie, Lou'd Patience, **Feare**............409. A.2, 97
— — — — — — — — —, ...422. var. H.106, 67
to stroake not strike; **feare** you........431. ins. H.283, 60q
Feared Kings though th'are hated, will be **fear'd**...165. H.443, 18
Kings ought to be more lov'd, then **fear'd**.....234. H.672, 2
Me, as a **fear'd** infection:..................235. H.677, 6
That stroke most **fear'd** is, which is struck the last. 237. H.688, 2
Fearest — — — — — — — —, ...422. var. H.106, 93
Fearfulness To kiss his hands, but that for **fearfullness**; 301. H.963, 2
Fearing **Fearing** to break the Kings Commandement: 122. H.305, 4
Anthea laught, and **fearing** lest excesse.........311. H.1006, 1
Fearless But thou liv'st **fearlesse**; and thy face ne'r shewes 37. H.106, 93
But we as **fearlesse** of the Sunne,..............48. H.136, 0
Fears Who **feares** to aske, doth teach to be deny'd. 8. H.12, 2
And back again, (tortur'd with **fears**) doth fly,..36. H.106, 67
But spring from ceremonious **feares**............54. H.149, 22
Such Flesh-quakes, Palsies, and such **fears** as shall 82. H.204, 11
To my revenge, and to her desp'rate **feares**,....87. H.215, 1
You have hopes, and doubts, and **feares**..........96. H.232, 7
There be in Love as many **feares**,.............102. H.253, 3
Feares not the fierce sedition of the Seas:......128. H.323, 4
He rents his Crown, That **feares** the Peoples hate. 182. H.488, 2
He, who has suffer'd Ship-wrack, **feares** to saile..212. H.601, 1
Then these, no **feares** more on your Fancies fall,.222. H.634, 14
With **feares**, and cares uncumbered:............233. H.670, 12
But **feares** not now to see her safety sold......251. H.745, 5
My desp'rate **feares**, in love, had seen.........279. H.863, 15
Pardon my **feares** (sweet Sapho,) I desire......279. H.866, 3
And **feares** in summer to weare out the lether:.332. H.1116, 2
Where God is merry, there write down thy **fears**: 355. N.63, 1
Ther must bee plac'd, for season'd **feares**.......408. A.2, 40
So long as I haue **feares**.......................414. A.5, 6
— — — — — — — — —, ...443. var. H.580, 12
Feast See Love-feast, Shearing-feast, Smell-feast
And the brisk Mouse may **feast** her selfe with crums, 37. H.106, 123
Or that this day Menalchas keeps a **feast**......86. H.213, 7
Goes to the **Feast** that's now provided.........93. H.223, 142
Foundation of your **Feast**, Fat Beefe:..........101. H.250, 29
Shark, when he goes to any publick **feast**,.......118. H.292, 1
Take first the **feast**; these dishes gone;.......119. H.293, 5
They make a **feast** lesse great then nice.........119. H.293, 12
Grace by his Priest; The **feast** is ended.......120. H.293, 54
More then a **Feast** contenteth me..............124. H.312, 8
And of her blush at such a **feast**...............135. H.336, 96
You are the Prime, and Princesse of the **Feast**:..140. H.354, 6
The musick of a **Feast**;.......................144. H.371, 3
Early setts ope to **feast**, and late:..............147. H.377, 46
The **feast** of Shepheards fail. Sil. None crowns the cup 159. H.421, 3
After the **Feast** (my Shapcot) see,.............165. H.443, 1
Nay more, the **Feast**, and grace of it..........192. H.521, 28
Then **feast**, and coy't a little; then to bed.....216. H.618, 8
Let's **feast**, and frolick, sing, and play,.........233. H.670, 30
Go to **Feast**, as others do.......................255. H.761, 2
Then Roman Sylla powr'd out at his **feast**......262. H.783, 6
Kisses are but dry banquets to a **Feast**.........265. H.797, 2
Feasting And I but **feasting** with a Beane,........173. H.461, 2
Feasting-Tables Thy **Feasting-Tables** shall be Hills 192. H.521, 15
Feasts Meet at those Lyrick **Feasts**,.............289. H.911, 4
To come with their own bellies unto **feasts**:....310. H.1005, 2
Feat See Feet
Feathered And as I prune my **feather'd** youth, so I 72. H.185, 19
Feathers Rook he sells **feathers**, yet he still doth crie 163. H.439, 1
Feature Will on thy **Feature** tirannize,..........174. H.465, 18
Fed See Fat-fed, Full-fed

But when that men have both well drunke, and fed, 7. H.8, 3
Let me be warme; let me be fully fed:..........31. H.93, 1
Not curious whether Appetite be fed,........37. H.106, 107
That done; when both of you have seemly fed,.124. H.313, 9
By love and warme desires fed,..............130. H.329, 6
Nor Bullocks fed...........................133. H.336, 45
Thy house, well fed and taught, can show......147. H.377, 34
As Cherry harvest, now high fed..............165. H.443, 10
And let thy dreames be only fed.............175. H.465, 49
Love is a thing most nice; and must be fed....220. H.633, 20
I keep (tame) with my morsells fed,...........246. H.724, 18
Who fed my life, I'le follow her in death......248. H.730, 16
Love must be fed by wealth: this blood of mine 258. H.768, 3
At night they draw to Supper; then well fed,.260. H.773, 3
Of which, when he had fully fed,.............295. H.942, 7
Wherewith so many soules were fed............374. N.123, 16
Gods Grace deserves here to be daily fed,.....378. N.132, 1
Where, with their own contagion they are fed;..417. A.8, 33
which sees the body fedd, yet pined........432. ins. H.283, 70j
Fee See Forked-fee
Will paid have his fee,.......................256. H.762, 11
For 'tis Fee simple, and noe rent..............407. A.2, 13
Feeble To shore the Feeble up, against the strong; 201. H.557, 11
Draw in your feeble fiers, while that He......236. H.685, 5
And when so feeble I am grown,...............303. H.973, 8
— — — — — — — — — — — —, ...427. var. H.197, 77
Feed To find that Tree of Life, whose Fruits did feed, 61. H.161, 1
While leanest Beasts in Pastures feed,.........77. H.196, 1
Feed, and grow fat; and as ye eat,...........102. H.250, 44
Feed him ye must, whose food fils you..........102. H.250, 52
Thousands to feed by miracle..................139. H.350, 4
Where both may feed, and come againe:.......146. H.377, 12
Let Poets feed on aire, or what they will;.....186. H.498, 7
Let me feed full, till that I fart, sayes Jill......186. H.498, 8
Because we feed on no mans score:............200. H.552, 14
'Tis best to feed Love; but not over-fill:.......220. H.633, 23
And leav'st them (as they feed and fill)........230. H.662, 44
Feed on the paste of Filberts, or else knead....269. H.818, 5
To feed, or lodge, to have the best of Roomes:.356. N.68, 2
To feed and cloth the Needy..................374. N.123, 50
— — — — — — — — — — — —, ...422. var. H.106, 123
because you feede..........................432. ins. H.283, 70e
To feed upon the Candid hares..............433. ins. H.293, 31a
— — — — — — — — — — — —, ...436. var. H.336, 45
Feeder's Fitted it self to ev'ry Feeders tast......379. N.146, 2
Feeders Talkes most, eates most, of all the Feeders there. 191. H.518, 2
Feeds One feeds on Lard, and yet is leane;.......173. H.461, 1
The Cock and Hen he feeds; but not a bone..204. H.568, 5
Feel I feele in me, this transmutation now........84. H.210, 8
Thrice I have washt, but feel no cold,.........157. H.413, 3
Each griefe we feele, that likewise is a Kite....278. H.862, 3
(Ay me!) I feele,............................353. N.56, 14
As not to know, or feel some Grievances........387. N.199, 2
Boldly in sin, shall feel more punishment.......391. N.227, 4
<Fingring> the paps that feele like sleeded silke...405. A.1, 57
— — — — — — — — — — — —, ...437. var. H.336, 111
— — — — — — — — — — — —, ...443. var. H.575, 63
Feels Feels in it selfe a fire;..................57. H.149, 133
He feeles when Packs do pinch him; and the where. 60. H.158, 4
And (pretty Child) feeles now no more........189. H.514, 3
Sin leads the way, but as it goes, it feels.......362. N.86, 1
Fees No one hope, but of his Fees...............347. N.41, 14
Feet See Free-feet, Silver-feet, Stiff-blue-pigs-feet
With which (Perilla) wash my hands and feet;....9. H.14, 9
Move forward then your Rosie feet,..........55. H.149, 61
And laid them downe for Offrings at his feet....86. H.213, 32
Whose silv'rie feet did tread,.................110. H.274, 14
Shew thy white feet, and head with Marjoram crown'd: 113. H.283, 32
To which, with silver feet lead you the way,....140. H.354, 7
Shew me thy feet; shew me thy legs, thy thighes; 154. H.403, 1
Where, Amarillis, Thou didst set thy feet......159. H.421, 12
Beat with their num'rous feet, which by.......165. H.443, 23
The feet or hands;...........................172. H.458, 9
To dance the Heyes with nimble feet;.........192. H.521, 30
Her pretty feet.............................194. H.525, 1
His feet were helpt, and left his Crutch behind:.201. H.555, 3
Then from his Feet, it shifted to his Hand:...207. H.577, 2
When 'twas in's Feet, his Charity was small;....207. H.577, 3
Your eager Bridegroome with auspitious feet....216. H.618, 2
Thy silv'ry feet,..............................217. H.619, 19
Is the wise Masters Feet, and Hands..........230. H.662, 24
To exercise their dancing feet:.................230. H.662, 49
When Pimpes feat sweat (as they doe often use).332. H.1113, 1
With feet of innocence:.......................352. N.53, 14
Accuse thy feet..............................375. N.123, 69
Ready, to pierce Thy tender Feet, and Hands..398. N.263, 4
Then lowly yet most lovely stand the feete,.....406. A.1, 91
W^th Numerous feete to Hoofy Helicon,..........412. A.3, 84

— — — — — — — — — — — —, ...448. var. A.1, 90
Feign Æson had (as Poets faine)..................10. H.19, 9
Feigned-lost-virginities Of fained-lost-Virginities; 167. H.443, 113
Felicity That's measur'd by felicity:.............162. H.431, 2
Felicitie flies o're the Wall and Fence,..........257. H.765, 3
Fell So she fell, and bruis'd, she dy'd...........15. H.36, 11
Two Cupids fell at odds;.........................31. H.92, 2
Fell downe on you,............................74. H.190, 11
What was't that fell but now..................74. H.192, 1
Poore Girles, she fell on you;.................105. H.260, 6
Who, as soone, fell fast asleep,................123. H.310, 3
Such Three brave Brothers fell in Mars his Field. 170. H.451, 12
Of Thine; so Lucrece fell, and the............175. H.465, 57
So Medullina fell, yet none...................175. H.465, 59
Twice two fell out, all rotten at the root......247. H.728, 2
The Blooms that fell were white and red;......283. H.883, 3
Judas began well, but he foulely fell:...........387. N.200, 2
Fellow And that sowre Fellow, with his vineger,.398. N.263, 10
Felon A fellon take it, or some Whit-flaw come.....66. H.173, 3
All know a Fellon eate the Tenth away.........180. H.480, 2
Felt But when he felt him warm'd,..............27. H.81, 25
When I did goe from thee, I felt that smart,...42. H.122, 1
But when he felt he suckt from thence.........71. H.182, 7
Nor felt th'unkind...........................104. H.257, 8
Those paines it lately felt before..............189. H.514, 4
It felt and heard, (unseen) thou dost me please;.331. H.1108, 1
Female Male to the female, soule to body: Life..45. H.128, 4
Fie on this pride, this Female vanitie..........163. H.439, 2
Male perfumes, but Female fire................277. H.856, 4
I owe vnto A female Child,......................407. A.2, 3
Fence Because no fence,........................213. H.609, 2
Felicitie flies o're the Wall and Fence,.........257. H.765, 3
Against diseases here the strongest fence........333. H.1117, 1
Fend See Forefend
Ferrets' — — — — — — — — —, ...440. var. H.443, 57
Ferry Passe all we must the fatall Ferry:.......172. H.457, 2
Who els with tears wo'd doubtles drown my ferry. 248. H.730, 26
A boat, A boat, hast to the ferry..........445. ins. H.730, 26a
Fervent Although we cannot turne the fervent fit.356. N.67, 1
Fervently And fervently Ile love;...............160. H.422, 7
Fescas See Fescues
— — — — — — — — — — — —, ...440. ins. H.443, 45r
Fescues Blew pinnes, tagges, fescues, beades and thinges 440. ins. H.443, 45r
Fess That Bar, this Bend; that Fess, this Cheveron; 295. H.941, 4
Festers Since which, it festers so, that I can prove 17. H.44, 5
Festivals No more, at yeerly Festivalls..........361. N.83, 51
Fetch See Far-fetch
Spring, sooner then the Lark, to fetch in May..68. H.178, 14
To Fetch me Wine my Lucia went,..............187. H.504, 1
To fetch Euridice from Hell;...................265. H.798, 2
Or fetch me back that Cloud againe,............340. N.3, 9
— — — — — — — — — — — —, ...434. ins. H.293, 41h
Fetched Fetcht binding gellye of a starre...434. ins. H.293, 41h
Fetter Such precious thraldome ne'r shall fetter me. 17. H.42, 4
Shall fetter you.............................198. H.544, 30
To fetter Justice, when She might be free......202. H.557, 26
Made by that fetter or that snare..............293. H.934, 3
Fettered That so oft has fetter'd me...........98. H.238, 5
Fetters From these fetters; like to me...........53. H.147, 12
In fetters free;...............................296. H.946, 14
Fetuous Upon this fetuous board doth stand.....92. H.223, 68
Fever My Fever..................................95. H.227, 11
Now an Ague, then a Fever,...................103. H.253, 9
That Preternaturall Fever, which did threat....254. H.756, 3
I'le bring a Fever; since thou keep'st no fire...262. H.783, 22
Few To thine owne selfe; and knowne to few....38. H.106, 136
That thou, within few months, shalt be........63. H.166, 7
Heare all men speak; but credit few or none....67. H.177, 4
Few Beads are best, when once we goe a Maying. 68. H.178, 28
Let but few smart, but strike a feare through all: 132. H.335, 3
Save but some few Beanes left,.................173. H.460, 2
Many we are, and yet but few possesse.........177. H.470, 1
Few live the life immortall. He ensures........188. H.506, 15
(Though but in Numbers few)..................198. H.544, 33
To very few, or else to none...................200. H.552, 20
If here ye will some few teares shed,...........226. H.644, 9
Some few sands spent, we hence must go,.......233. H.670, 37
Ch. Talk not of love, all pray, but few soules pay me. 248. H.730, 18
To seeke, and find some few Immortals out.....267. H.804, 6
Commanders, few for execution................272. H.827, 2
As that in Lusters few they may,..............291. H.919, 20
But yet those yeers that I have liv'd, but few....328. H.1088, 4
In Numbers, and but these few,..................345. N.33, 1
In which were sands but few,...................346. N.38, 14
And the comforters are few,....................348. N.41, 26
Wip't out few, (God knowes) if any............373. N.121, 10

But He hath made the world to come for **few**...387. N.198, 2
Be those **few** hours, which I have yet to spend,..392. N.230, 1
Though they be **few** in number, I'm content;...392. N.230, 3
Who shewing mercy here, **few** priz'd, or none...393. N.234, 2
Few-sad-hours To live some **few-sad-howers** after thee:
11. H.22, 2
Fie Oh fie upon 'em! Lastly too, all witt........150. H.382, 17
Fie on this pride, this Female vanitie............163. H.439, 2
Fie, (quoth my Lady) what a stink is here?....212. H.598, 1
Fie, Lovely maid! Indeed you are too slow,....216. H.618, 5
Field Through that huge **field** of waters ride:......30. H.90, 3
How each **field** turns a street; each street a Parke
68. H.178, 30
Sadly I walk't within the **field,**..................73. H.187, 1
A savour like unto a blessed **field,**.............112. H.283, 18
Oft as your **field,** shall her old age renew,.....140. H.355, 13
First offer Incense, then thy **field** and meads..143. H.370, 1
(Fighting) lose not in the **field**.................151. H.386, 4
Like to a **field** of beans, when newly blown;....159. H.421, 20
Such Three brave Brothers fell in Mars his **Field.**
170. H.451, 12
Us i'th' Citie, and the **Field:**...................177. H.473, 2
The **Field** is pitcht; but such must be your warres,
216. H.618, 13
The Soldiers leave the **Field** with equall feare...268. H.813, 4
Whose **Field** his foot is, and whose Barn his shooe?
270. H.822, 4
Lay by the good a while; a resting **field**.......292. H.922, 1
Smile, like a **field** beset with corne?............364. N.96, 15
Them to the **field,** and, there, to skirmishing;...370. N.108, 2
The spacious **field** have for Thy Theater.......398. N.263, 18
and guild the **field**.......................432. ins. H.283, 140e
Fields See **Cornfields**
With **fields** enameled with flowers,.............36. H.106, 46
Seas shall be sandlesse; **Fields** devoid of grasse;.59. H.154, 7
And open **fields,** and we not see't?............68. H.178, 38
Those **Fields** of everlasting happinesse..........177. H.470, 2
Fled are the Frosts, and now the **Fields** appeare.224. H.642, 1
To strip the Trees, and **Fields,** to their distresse,.224. H.642, 11
Thy faithfull **fields** to yeeld thee Graine,........233. H.670, 9
Vnto the port mouth of th' Elisian **feilds**........405. A.1, 68
A breath of balm along the Elizean **fields**.......416. A.8, 8
The **Fields** of Pluto are reserv'd for them;......417. A.8, 28
Fiend To paint the **Fiend,** Pink would the Devill see;
110. H.272, 1
Of that **Fiend** that marres your rest;..........117. H.289, 6
The fouler **Fiend,** and evill Spright,.............123. H.306, 14
And where 'tis safely kept, the **Fiend,**..........285. H.893, 7
This I know, the **Fiend** will fly................324. H.1069, 3
Fiends Drive all hurtfull **Feinds** us fro,..........177. H.473, 7
Fierce Who wo'd not think this Yonker **fierce** to fight?
65. H.171, 3
Call forth **fierce** Lovers to their wisht Delights:.77. H.197, 6
Favours on me, her **fierce** Idolater?............77. H.197, 26
Thou that tam'st Tygers, and **fierce** storms (that rise)
103. H.254, 3
Feares not the **fierce** sedition of the Seas:.....128. H.323, 4
Umber was painting of a Lyon **fierce,**.........205. H.572, 1
'Tis but a **fierce** desire of hot and drie..........293. H.931, 2
How **fierce** was I, when I did see..............294. H.939, 1
Drunk up the wine of Gods **fierce** wrath;........400. N.266, 11
Of **fierce** Idolatrie shute into mee, and...424. ins. H.128, 46b
— — — — — — — — — —, ...452. var. H.128, 17
Fiery Freezing cold, and **firie** heats,.............102. H.253, 7
Fifty Ne'r had kept heat for **fifty** Maids that night.
78. H.197, 68
Fight **Fight** thou with shafts of silver, and o'rcome,
21. H.60, 1
Who wo'd not think this Yonker fierce to **fight?**.65. H.171, 3
It is the End that crownes us, not the **Fight**.....123. H.309, 2
The reason is, though all the day they **fight,**....156. H.411, 3
Is yours, in which you challeng'd are to **fight**..216. H.618, 10
Physitians **fight** not against men; but these....226. H.646, 1
'Tis not the **Fight** that crowns us, but the end..293. H.933, 2
When we 'gainst Satan stoutly **fight,** the more...372. N.116, 1
Fight bravely for the flame of mankinde, yeeld
433. ins. H.283, 140f
Fighting (**Fighting**) lose not in the field.........151. H.386, 4
While young Charles fights, and **fighting** wins the day.
254. H.756, 14
Rise up of men, a **fighting** race..................297. H.948, 12
Fights While young Charles **fights,** and fighting wins the day.
254. H.756, 14
Figure That **figure** discontent;.................131. H.330, 8
How farre a **Figure** ought to go,...............148. H.377, 92
To **figure** to us, nothing more then this,........345. N.34, 3
Figured The **figur'd** Damask, or pure Diaper,.....355. N.65, 2
Figures Nor can these **figures** so thy rest endeare,
36. H.106, 55
Beset with stately **Figures** (every where)......185. H.496, 2
Filberts The Paste of **Filberts** for thy bread....192. H.521, 13
Feed on the paste of **Filberts,** or else knead.....269. H.818, 5
Filched Chippinge, the mice **filcht** from the Binne,
439. ins. H.443, 45g
Filchers And thus surpriz'd (as **Filchers** use)....71. H.182, 11
Filed And griefs hath **fil'de** upon my silver hairs;.140. H.355, 6

Files — — — — — — — —, ...440. var. H.443, 107
Fill See **Overfill**
But they left Hope-seed to **fill** up againe.......52. H.146, 8
Fill, and winde up with whitest wooll.........58. H.149, 162
Hoping t'ave seene of it my **fill;**...............67. H.175, 20
Hony enough to **fill** his hive...................71. H.182, 31
Invites fresh Grapes to **fill** his Presse with Wine..72. H.185, 28
Fill each part full of fire, active to doe........79. H.197, 79
To **fill** a little Urne...........................81. H.201, 44
Saint Frip, Saint Trip, Saint **Fill,** S. Fillie,......91. H.223, 32
(As you) may have their **fill** of meat...........102. H.250, 46
But they **fill** up their Ebbs againe:...............133. H.336, 20
Saints will come in to **fill** each Pew and Place...168. H.445, 6
Endimions Moon to **fill** up full, remember me:..184. H.492, 42
Fill me my Wine in Christall; thus, and thus..187. H.502, 1
Fill me a mighty Bowle.......................227. H.653, 1
And leav'st them (as they feed and **fill**)......230. H.662, 44
And drink your **fill** of it......................261. H.778, 3
To **fill** the Paste that's a kneading..............263. H.784, 18
And not with Lutes to **fill** the roome...........365. N.97, 3
That **fill** the Throne;..........................369. N.106, 14
To **fill**.......................................391. N.228, 7
Amongest the thrice-three-sacred Virgins, **fill**.....412. A.3, 86
Fill each part full of Fire, let all my good
427. ins. H.197, 77a
Filled See **Fulfilled**
With Water **fill'd,** (Sirs, credit me).............44. H.127, 2
Hadst thou not **fill'd** them with thy fire and flame.
45. H.128, 32
Ye have been **fill'd** with flowers:................110. H.274, 2
Star **fill'd** with glory to our view,...............112. H.283, 4
Thy golden Censors **fil'd** with odours sweet,....128. H.320, 7
(Dropt for the jarres of heaven) **fill'd** t'engage..206. H.575, 46
Three Zodiaks **fill'd** more I shall stoope;........303. H.973, 2
Receive these Christall Vialls **fil'd**..............360. N.83, 39
Filled-full Full, and **fild-full,** then when full-fild before.
341. N.15, 6
Fillet Thy **fillit,**................................210. H.591, 3
Downe to a **Fillit** more Imperiall................256. H.763, 10
Filleth The Place that **filleth** All in all...........385. N.185, 2
Filleting Each Maid, her silver **Filleting,**.........360. N.83, 42
Filletings As were (time past) thy holy **Filitings**:.11. H.22, 6
Put on thy Holy **Fillitings,** and so.............286. H.898, 1
Fillets Let her, her **fillets** first.................55. H.149, 84
By all those Virgins **Fillets** hung...............169. H.449, 15
Fill-horse Some crosse the **Fill-horse;** some with great
101. H.250, 21
Fillie Saint Frip, Saint Trip, Saint Fill. S. **Fillie,**..91. H.223, 32
Fillies The Horses, Mares, and frisking **Fillies,**...101. H.250, 11
Filling See **All-filling, Fulfilling**
Of sweetest Cow-slips **filling** Them.............179. H.476, 15
There **filling** Maunds with Cowslips, you........323. H.1068, 7
Fillit See **Fillet**
Fills I see a Cloud of Glory **fills** my Book........99. H.245, 4
Feed him ye must, whose food **fils** you..........102. H.250, 52
A scent, that **fills** both Heaven and Earth with it.
157. H.414, 10
The Larder **fills** with meat; the Bin with bread...221. H.633, 45
No, but when the Spirit **fils**...................242. H.714, 3
Film Come thou not neere that **Filmne** so finely spred,
82. H.204, 7
Films Next, when those Lawnie **Filmes** I see....202. H.560, 13
Filth Looks on the **filth,** but is not soil'd thereby;.371. N.113, 6
Filthy Tis much among the **filthy** to be clean;...318. H.1042, 1
Find **Find** that Medicine (if you can)............10. H.19, 11
Small griefs **find** tongues: Full Casques are ever found
15. H.38, 7
So that the path I cannot **find:**.................32. H.98, 2
Th' industrious Merchant has; who for to **find**..36. H.106, 65
Ordaining that thy small stock **find** no breach,..38. H.106, 133
Let him the Land and Living **finde;**...........59. H.153, 3
Will **find** me out a path to die;...............60. H.159, 6
To **find** that Tree of Life, whose Fruits did feed,
61. H.161, 1
To **finde** Bethesda, and an Angel there,..........61. H.161, 3
At last, I **find,** (after my much to doe)........61. H.161, 5
But **find** no Rose-bud in your cheek:............63. H.164, 9
Thy many scorns, and **find** no cure?..............74. H.191, 2
The place, where I may **find** ye..................83. H.207, 4
I'm sure to **find** ye there.......................83. H.207, 8
Look in his Brine-tub, and you shall **find** there..89. H.221, 3
Co'd never since **find** any rest..................96. H.229, 6
To **find,**..100. H.246, 11
Where I may **find** my Shepardesse..............106. H.263, 4
There thou shalt **find** her lip and cheek:........106. H.263, 8
As in the whole world thou canst **find,**..........108. H.267, 7
You shall; if righteous dealing I **find** there.....136. H.338, 2
That when ere I wooe, I **find**...................138. H.346, 3
Find equall freedome, equall fare;..............147. H.377, 60
Good men, They **find** them all in Thee.........149. H.377, 136
For pitty, Sir, **find** out that Bee,..............156. H.412, 11
That I shall never **find** him..................157. H.412, 28
Nor **find** that true, which was foretold.........157. H.413, 4
The wound I suffer, never **find** a cure..........159. H.421, 34
Their wounded hearts; and names we **find**......169. H.449, 7
Waking shalt **find** me sleeping there...........175. H.465, 52

As one triumphant; when I find...............176. H.465, 79
Nor leave the search, and proofe, till Thou canst find
181. H.483, 3
To find a Wife, that is most fit for Thee.......185. H.494, 2
Or where else shall we find...................188. H.509, 6
Doe here find rest.............................190. H.515, 22
Walk in the Groves, and thou shalt find.......192. H.521, 39
If ye will with Mab find grace,.................201. H.556, 1
Shall find much farcing Buckram in our Books..202. H.559, 2
Give Want her welcome if she comes; we find,..213. H.605, 1
Acceptance it might find of thee...............214. H.613, 4
None are so harsh, but if they find............252. H.746, 5
I shall find enchantment there................253. H.750, 12
Of both our Fortunes good and bad we find....257. H.765, 1
To seeke, and find some few Immortals out....267. H.804, 6
And you may find in Love these differing Parts;.274. H.837, 9
Loving Alcestis there we find:.................283. H.885, 4
When first I find those Numbers thou do'st write;
301. H.966, 1
That so the superstitious find..................304. H.980, 5
Nothing's so hard, but search will find it out...311. H.1008, 2
Finde out a Threshold or a doore,.............312. H.1014, 7
T'invade from far: They'l finde worse foes at home.
316. H.1030, 2
The place where I may find thee...............323. H.1068, 4
May find your Amarillis........................323. H.1068, 8
Where Pleasures met: at last, doe find,.........327. H.1082, 3
Weigh me the Fire; or, canst thou find..........339. N.3, 1
'Tis hard to finde God, but to comprehend.......340. N.8, 1
I come to Thee, in hope to find.................342. N.17, 3
To seek of God more then we well can find,....356. N.70, 1
And fit it is, we finde a roome.................365. N.96, 26
To find him out?...............................367. N.102, 11
I finde in thee, that makes me thus to part,......414. A.6, 4
— — — — — — — — — — —, ...429. var. H.263, 10

Findest There at the Plough thou find'st thy Teame,
230. H.662, 25
And find'st their bellies there as full...........230. H.662, 42
Find'st here a fault, and mend'st the trespasse too:
298. H.955, 8
But if, 'mongst all, thou find'st here one...........339. N.2, 7
— — — — — — — — — — — —, ...441. var. H.465, 52

Finds A desp'rate grief, that finds no cure........60. H.157, 2
My wearyed Pinnace here finds ease:...........94. H.225, 2
Where Mab he finds; who there doth lie.......165. H.443, 5
His Errours up; and now he finds..............167. H.443, 83
Nature finds out some place for buriall.........267. H.807, 2
Your judgement finds a guilty Poem, there.....322. H.1062, 5
He finds a fire for mighty Mutius;..............370. N.108, 6

Fine They shew'd me then, how fine 'twas spun;...18. H.47, 9
Into a fine distraction:.........................28. H.83, 4
Or some fine tincture, like to this,..............75. H.193, 12
By those fine Shades, their Substances:.........36. H.106, 80
Then say, if one th'ast seene more fine..........90. H.223a, 5
Or Freeze, from this fine Fripperie............90. H.223, 21
A Lawn for me, so fine and thin,..............164. H.442, 4
Nor that fine Worme that do's interre..........186. H.497, 13
Thou shalt have Possets, Wassails fine,.........193. H.521, 47
Brisk methinks I am, and fine,..................309. H.996, 1
Let Country wenches make 'em fine...........323. H.1068, 13
Fine flowre prest down, and running o're.......356. N.66, 8
And to make fine,.............................360. N.83, 34
With plumpe soft flesh of mettle pure and fine.406. A.1, 79
— — — — — — — — — — —, ...437. var. H.336, 97

Finely Come thou not neere that Filmne so finely spred,
82. H.204, 7

Finer Our finer fleeced sheep:..................183. H.492, 14

Finest Soft then the finest Lemster Ore..........165. H.443, 28
Cast of the finest Gossamore....................167. H.443, 95

Finger Love prickt my finger with a golden pin:...17. H.44, 4
The finger bled, but burnt was all my heart......17. H.44, 8
But with my finger pointed to...................24. H.75, 3
Love scorch'd my finger, but did spare...........28. H.85, 1
Made for thy finger fit;..........................65. H.172, 3
He with his pretty finger prest..................74. H.190, 7
Your Finger to apply..........................221. H.633, 36
His finger was the dart........................295. H.942, 16
Between the finger, and the thumb;..............356. N.66, 6
Awake! the while the active Finger.............364. N.96, 6
In length each finger doth his next excell,......406. A.1, 101

Fingering <Fingring> the paps that feele like sleeded silke
405. A.1, 57

Fingers Nailes from her fingers mew'd, she shewes: what els?
232. H.668, 4
My fingers so, the Lyrick-strings to move,.......280. H.871, 3
With little hands and fingers long and small......406. A.1, 99

Finny-oar Never againe shall I with Finnie-Ore.315. H.1028, 11

Fire See Wildfire
Light from the Sun, that inexhausted Fire:....3. Ded.H., 6
When Laurell spirts 'ith fire, and when the Hearth
7. H.8, 5
By your owne jewels set on fire..................20. H.54, 6
To commit it to the fire:..........................21. H.59, 4
Here's a house of flesh on fire:..................21. H.61, 2
To be offer'd up by fire:........................22. H.65, 2
Of singing Crickits by thy fire:...............37. H.106, 122
Hadst thou not fill'd them with thy fire and flame.
45. H.128, 32
I frie in fire, and so consume,..................50. H.140, 3
Or let Love's fire goe out,.......................53. H.149, 5
But yet, Loves fire will wast....................54. H.149, 27
Feels in it selfe a fire;........................57. H.149, 133
Fire and water shall together lye..............59. H.154, 3
And make my spirits frantick with the fire.....67. H.176, 4
Lyd. My heart now set on fire is................70. H.181, 13
From out my Narde, and Fun'rall fire:..........72. H.185, 18
To thee-ward dy'd i'th'embers, and no fire........78. H.197, 36
Fill each part full of fire, active to doe..........79. H.197, 79
Are lost, i'th'funerall fire.......................81. H.201, 48
To teare the world, or set it all on fire............81. H.202, 6
From a consuming fire,..........................95. H.227, 13
Glitt'ring with fire; where, for your mirth,......101. H.250, 27
The Altar's ready; Fire to consume.............102. H.251, 3
Were she an Element of fire..................115. H.283, 110
Is to love, and live i'th fire....................117. H.286, 12
That dares to dead the fire of martirdome:......128. H.323, 2
Of merry Crickets by my Country fire,..........132. H.333, 8
By'th'fire, foretelling snow and slit,.............134. H.336, 86
Then that insinuating fire,.....................135. H.336, 103
Thus, till we see the fire lesse shine............136. H.336, 145
The peeping fire..............................137. H.340, 15
Thou shalt not All die; for while Love's fire shines
143. H.336, 1
A noble perfume from the fire..................145. H.375, 18
That sets all eares on fire.......................151. H.388, 4
Or spice, or fish, or fire, or close-stools here.....155. H.405, 2
The fire, and martyrdome of love................169. H.449, 4
Looke upon all; and though on fire.............174. H.465, 7
What needs she fire and ashes to consume,.......178. H.474, 5
Take then thy Censer; Put in Fire, and thus,....197. H.539, 13
Rake the Fier up, and get.......................201. H.556, 3
I plaid with Love, as with the fire..............203. H.563, 1
The fire scorctht my heart......................203. H.563, 8
Such a fire I espie............................204. H.566, 3
More sweet, then Storax from the hallowed fire:..205. H.575, 8
As in a Globe of Radiant fire, and grac't........207. H.575, 58
Still to be ready with thy fire:..................214. H.613, 2
Like the sparks of fire, befriend thee............217. H.619, 5
Who'l let ye by their fire sit?....................218. H.626, 5
The softest Fire makes the sweetest Mault.......221. H.633, 51
The fire of hell it was..........................222. H.635, 8
With your eternall fire:..........................228. H.657, 7
And not by fire to harme me....................234. H.674, 6
Full of fier; then I write.......................242. H.714, 5
Look how next the holy fier.....................242. H.714, 9
A little Hearth best fits a little Fire,............249. H.733, 10
Come, Ile instruct thee. Know, the vestall fier...262. H.781, 15
I'le bring a Fever; since thou keep'st no fire.....262. H.783, 22
Wash your hands, or else the fire..............263. H.786, 1
Dead the Fire, though ye blow..................263. H.786, 4
Love is then consuming fire.....................273. H.836, 8
Male perfumes, but Female fire..................277. H.856, 4
Altar cleane, no fire prophane?...................280. H.870, 6
A sparke neglected makes a mighty fire.........281. H.873, 2
Singing about my everlasting fire...............294. H.938, 4
We must not give all to the hallowed fire.........295. H.940, 2
Then boldly give thine incense to the fire........299. H.957, 4
Burne the flax, and fire the tow:................315. H.1026, 6
Or thou by frost, or I by quenchlesse fire:......333. H.1120, 4
Weigh me the Fire; or, canst thou find...........339. N.3, 1
Make me a fire,...............................350. N.47, 24
Examine me with fire, and prove me.............351. N.48, 7
And have a care no fire gos out,.................365. N.97, 5
The Altars all on fier be;........................365. N.97, 7
A new-borne Phoenix from His own chast fire.....367. N.98, 30
He finds a fire for mighty Mutius;..............370. N.108, 6
Farewell thy Fier and thy Light,................374. N.123, 45
The fire of Hell this strange condition hath,.......387. N.202, 1
One onely fire has Hell; but yet it shall,.........391. N.227, 1
With holye fier least that itt dye...............407. A.2, 24
Of Lust, which setts on fier our hartes............408. A.2, 38
With as cold frost, as erst we mett with fire;....414. A.6, 10
Fire unto all my functions, gives me blood,.426. ins. H.197, 48c
— — — — — — — — — — —, ...427. var. H.197, 54
Fill each part full of Fire, let all my good
427. ins. H.197, 77a
— — — — — — — — — — — —, ...433. var. H.293, 16
But most of all the glowwormes fire......434. ins. H.293, 41e
— — — — — — — — — — — —, ...451. var. H.336, 151

Firebrand Shewing me there a fire brand;.........153. H.399, 4
No Furie, or no Fire-brand to me..............170. H.452, 6
— — — — — — — — — — — —, ...430. var. H.283, 40

Fired As a fir'd Altar, is each stone,............113. H.283, 23
Untill the fired Chesnuts leape.................127. H.319, 33
Was I fier'd with a smile?......................155. H.407, 4
Which, fir'd with incense, I resigne,............351. N.47, 55
See we haue fyr'd...............................413. A.4, 24

Firedrakes Like fier-drakes, yett did'st mee no harme therby.
410. A.3, 28

Fire's Come sit we by the fires side;............219. H.629, 1
See, the fier's by: Farewell.......................334. H.1125, 8

Fires See Frantic-fires, Scare-fires

Throwing about his wild, and active fires.........45. H.128, 18
Raise greater fires in men......................76. H.193, 56
Salutes with tears of joy; when fires betray......77. H.197, 17
Thy Fiers from me; but Apollo's curse..........79. H.197, 83
More towring, more disparkling then thy fires:..113. H.283, 36
Springing from two such Fires,...............116. H.283, 159
Though I cannot give thee fires...............129. H.324, 1
Mildly disparkling, like those fiers,............165. H.443, 29
Will coole his flames, or quench his fires with snow?
187. H.502, 6
With daily Fyers: The last, neglect of Wine:....197. H.539, 10
And keep eternal fires,.........................198. H.544, 3
Draw in your feeble fiers, while that He........236. H.685, 5
She seem'd to quench loves fires that there did glow.
251. H.742, 2
That your teares may coole her fires............269. H.814, 6
Who fires with hope the Lovers heart,...........290. H.915, 7
Love's silent flames, and fires obscure..........295. H.942, 13
When I and they keep tearmly fires;..........303. H.973, 12
Loues Cherries from such fyers growe...........408. A.2, 50
Holde their Eternall fiers; and ours of Late......411. A.3, 43
Thy glaring fires, least in theire sight the sinne
424. ins. H.128, 46a
— — — — — — — — — — —, ...433. var. H.293, 16

Firing Firing thy soule, by which thou dost foretell
256. H.763, 8
The Christmas Log to the firing;...............263. H.784, 3

Firm Firm be my foundation.....................84. H.209, 4
Upon the rock, whose firm foundation laid,.......143. H.365, 10
Such is thy house, whose firme foundations trust
148. H.377, 103
Firme and well fixt foundation.................335. H.1129, 14
And with as firme behaviour I will meet........392. N.230, 17
— — — — — — — — — — —, ...422. var. H.106, 135

Firmament See Lawny-firmament
And Star-like, once more, guild our Firmament...52. H.146, 12
From out the eye, Loves Firmament:............69. H.178, 54
Guild still with flames this Firmament, and be....94. H.226, 5
T' enspangle this expansve Firmament...........191. H.516, 2

Firmly Good Precepts we must firmly hold,......187. H.505, 1
That he holds firmly to the end.................215. H.615, 6

First How Roses first came Red, and Lillies White...5. H.1, 10
If thou dislik'st the Piece thou light'st on first;......7. H.6, 1
Dead when I am, first cast in salt, and bring......9. H.14, 7
He loves his bonds, who when the first are broke,..17. H.42, 5
First, April, she with mellow showrs...............23. H.70, 1
First, for Effusions due unto the dead,............23. H.72, 1
(At first) infused with the same:.................24. H.73, 4
Let's kisse afresh, as when we first begun.........24. H.74, 8
First, for thy Queen-ship on thy head is set......30. H.88, 3
Doe they first pill thee, next, pluck off thy skin?..32. H.97, 3
We'll wish, in Hell we had been Last and First...33. H.101, 4
The last is but the least; the first doth tell........35. H.106, 9
To work, but first to sacrifice;..................36. H.106, 58
Had, first, durst plow the Ocean.................36. H.106, 76
Nor car'st which comes the first, the foule or faire;
37. H.106, 97
Or with the first, or second bread............37. H.106, 108
To shun the first, and last extreame............38. H.106, 132
First, I shall decline my head;..................38. H.107, 4
Health is the first good lent to men;............42. H.121, 1
Let her, her fillets first.........................55. H.149, 84
First, Jollies wife is lame; then next, loose-hipt:..62. H.163, 1
Hor. Say our first loves we sho'd revoke,........70. H.181, 17
From the first ye were not so:..................74. H.190, 2
The fattest Oxe the first must bleed............77. H.196, 2
He smarts at last, who do's not first take heed....79. H.199, 4
That Age is best, which is the first,..............84. H.208, 9
Griefe, (my deare friend) has first my Harp unstrung;
84. H.210, 9
First, in a Neech, more black than jet,..........90. H.223, 11
First, at the entrance of the gate,..............91. H.223, 38
You first of all crown'd her; she must of due,.....94. H.224, 9
The first Act's doubtfull, (but we say)............94. H.225, 9
First cur'd thy selfe; then come and cure me......97. H.236, 4
Who first to the Summe.........................99. H.243, 4
We rip up first, then reap our lands.............101. H.250, 4
Ye shall see first the large and cheefe..........101. H.250, 28
Roses at first were white,......................105. H.258, 1
The Roses first came red........................105. H.258, 8
Who first provides, not to be overcome...........109. H.268, 2
First, let us dwell on rudest seas;..............111. H.278, 3
The eies be first, that conquer'd are............118. H.290, 2
Take first the feast; these dishes gone;..........119. H.293, 5
And now, we must imagine first,................119. H.293, 19
That man lives twice, that lives the first life well.
121. H.298, 2
First you, then you, and both for white successe...124. H.313, 2
Put on your Garlands first, then Sacrifice:......124. H.313, 8
First wash thy heart in innocence, then bring....127. H.320, 3
Jove's is the first and last; The Morn's his due,..128. H.321, 3
First, to the Babies of the eyes;...............130. H.329, 9
Which sweetly spic't, we'l first carouse........135. H.336, 127
First offer Incense, then thy field and meads......143. H.370, 1
The first of Nature, and the next of Art:........153. H.394, 2
Pievish doth boast, that he's the very first........156. H.410, 1
Never since first Bellona us'd a Shield,..........170. H.451, 11
Man knowes where first he ships himselfe; but he.177. H.468, 1
By the Time the Cocks first crow..............177. H.473, 8
Trees never beare, unlesse they first do blow......180. H.477, 6
Since to th' Country first I came,...............182. H.489, 1
That Love last long; let it thy first care be......185. H.494, 1
Fall thou must first, then rise to life with These,
188. H.507, 3
First, for your shape, the curious cannot shew....189. H.511, 1
Letcher was Carted first about the streets,........195. H.532, 1
The first foundation of that zeale sho'd be........201. H.557, 3
Man is a Watch, wound up at first, but never...202. H.558, 1
I thought at first 'twas but a dream,............203. H.562, 3
First dyes the Leafe, the Bough next, next the Tree.
203. H.565, 4
But what he doth at first entend,...............215. H.615, 5
T'was to his Batch, but Leaven laid there first...219. H.630, 4
For ropes of pearle, first Madam Ursly showes....232. H.668, 1
But first unto those............................239. H.695, 4
First, crack the strings, and after that,..........240. H.705, 11
Chose first, confirm'd next, & at last are crown'd.
241. H.707, 2
I'le beg of thee first here to have mine Urne....242. H.713, 18
First, peales of Thunder we must heare,..........247. H.725, 9
Say what thou art. Ph. I prithee first draw neare.
248. H.730, 4
Of woman-kind, first die I will;................250. H.739, 2
Must be the first man up, and last in bed:........259. H.771, 2
The first Commerce is, & the next Command.....275. H.847, 2
Then the last part of night, and first of day.....278. H.858, 2
Old Religion first commands....................280. H.870, 3
Where love begins, there dead thy first desire:...281. H.873, 1
Burn first thine incense; next, when as thou see'st
286. H.898, 5
Farre faster then the first can wither............289. H.912, 8
First, may the hand of bounty bring............291. H.919, 1
The first event breeds confidence or feare.........292. H.924, 2
Hard are the two first staires unto a Crowne;....292. H.925, 1
Conquer we shall, but we must first contend;....293. H.933, 1
Offer thy gift; but first the Law commands....299. H.957, 1
Thee Julia, first, to sanctifie thy hands:.........299. H.957, 2
When first I find those Numbers thou do'st write;
301. H.966, 1
Man may at first transgress, but next do well:..314. H.1021, 1
The first as Doctor, and the last as Knight.....322. H.1062, 12
Lets kiss first, then we'l sever................324. H.1068, 22
Because not plac't here with the midst, or first...329. H.1092, 2
Let's trie of us who shall the first expire;......333. H.1120, 3
The Haven reacht to which I first was bound...334. H.1127, 2
As in their Channell first they were..............339. N.3, 6
Under the first the Sinners ever trust;...........340. N.6, 3
First, Fear and Shame without, then Guilt within.
341. N.11, 2
The first by patience, and the last by paine.......343. N.24, 4
Let me (like him) first cracks of thunder heare;...343. N.25, 3
To spoile the first impression...................354. N.59, 18
Draw me, but first, and after Thee I'le run,......358. N.77, 14
Shame checks our first attempts; but then 'tis prov'd
362. N.85, 1
Sins first dislik'd, are after that belov'd..........362. N.85, 2
First stripes, new blowes,.....................363. N.92, 11
Thee to adore thy God, the first of all............363. N.94, 2
And though the Father be the first of Three,....386. N.191, 5
The first of Time, or Sabbath here of Dayes;.....386. N.194, 2
Noah the first was (as Tradition sayes).........386. N.195, 1
First, that these goods none here may o're esteem,
387. N.201, 3
The first of Raine, the key of Hell next known:.390. N.224, 2
The first of sin is, and the next of praise:........395. N.243, 2
Who sweet'ned first,...........................401. N.268, 3
To powre first in..............................401. N.268, 15
But first cast off thy wonted Churlishness..........416. A.8, 6
The first is Natures end: this doth imparte..421. ins. H.106, 26a
Or Fortune too, for what the first secures..422. ins. H.106, 92c
— — — — — — — — — — —, ...423. var. H.128, 7

First-born Deerely I lov'd thee; as my first-borne child:
6.H.3, 2

First-fruits The kisse of Virgins; First-fruits of the bed;
45. H.128, 7
The first-Fruits give to them, who gave........226. H.647, 3

Firstling Understand, this First-ling was...........14. H.36, 3
— — — — — — — — — — —, ...443. var. H.580, 2

First-sweet That smil'd in that first-sweet complexion.
81. H.202, 4

Fish See Tunny-fish
As is the fish, or tonguelesse Crocadile...........58. H.150, 2
You multiply, as doth a Fish...................113. H.283, 50
Makes guests and fish smell strong; pray go....146. H.377, 26
Or spice, or fish, or fire, or close-stools here.....155. H.405, 2
Of silv'rie fish; wheat-strawes, the snailes......166. H.443, 73
Ch. What's that to me, I waft nor fish or fowles,
248. H.730, 9
But when all's hush't, Case then a fish more mute,
303. H.975, 7
Of thrice-boyl'd-worts, or third dayes fish;.....321. H.1056, 12
Have we flesh, or have we fish...................363. N.93, 5

The **flesh** soone sucks in putrifaction..........332. H.1111, 2
Sometimes He strikes us more then **flesh** can beare;
341. N.10, 3
Have we **flesh**, or have we fish..................363. N.93, 5
I and the **flesh**, for and the fish,...............374. N.123, 33
Add but a bit of **flesh**, to boyle:................377. N.130, 2
Because our **flesh** stood most in need of Him.....390. N.222, 4
Of **Flesh**, yet still..........................391. N.228, 6
With plumpe soft **flesh** of mettle pure and fine.....406. A.1, 79
Skynne and colour, **flesh** and blood,..............418. A.9, 21
not on the **flesh** of beasts, but on the seede
432. ins. H.283, 70f
Flesh-hooks With his **Flesh-hooks**, don't come nie..263. H.785, 3
Fleshly Groynes, for his **fleshly** Burglary of late,..106. H.261, 1
Flesh-quakes Such **Flesh-quakes**, Palsies, and such fears as shall
82. H.204, 11
Fleshy Shew me Those **Fleshie** Principalities;.....154. H.403, 2
Who claim the Fat, and **Fleshie** for their share,..272. H.826, 5
Fletcher Beumont and **Fletcher**, Swans, to whom all eares
206. H.575, 51
Flew Then laughing loud, he **flew**...............27. H.81, 33
Slept; and thus sleeping, thither **flew**............46. H.130, 3
At which poore Robin **flew** away:.............46. H.130, 10
Then temper **flew** from words; and men did squeake,
150. H.382, 7
The times of warmth; but then they **flew** away;
151. H.387, 2
A Fart **flew** out, or a Sir-reverence............200. H.551, 6
Flew out a crack, so mighty, that the Fart,......205. H.572, 3
And so away he **flew**..........................346. N.38, 18
Flies See **Butterflies**, **Musk-flies**
Of sacred * Orgies **flyes**, A round, A round.........7. H.8, 8
It is an active flame, that **flies**,................130. H.329, 8
It frisks, and **flyes**, now here, now there,........130. H.329, 13
And as it **flyes**, it gently sings,................130. H.329, 22
Time **flyes** away fast;.........................196. H.534, 13
Not a kissing Cupid **flyes**.....................221. H.633, 29
Flies no thought higher then a fleece:........229. H.662, 12
Felicitie **flies** o're the Wall and Fence,..........257. H.765, 3
Reapes eyes so rawe are, that (it seemes) the **flyes**
282. H.879, 1
Flies' See **Trout-flies'**
Fliest Who fli'st at all heights: Prose and Verse run'st through;
298. H.955, 7
Flight Life of my life, take not so soone thy **flight**,
73. H.186, 1
And take my **flight**........................95. H.227, 32
But by their **flight** I never can divine,...........149. H.378, 3
Flimsey Why walkes Nick **Flimsey** like a Male-content?
160. H.423, 1
Flimsy See **Flimsey**
The flimsie Livers, and blew Gizzards are........326. H.1079, 2
Fling Sometimes away 'two'd wildly **fling**;........67. H.175, 13
Flings And lightning in his eyes; and **flings**......165. H.443, 15
Flitches And shewes his naked **flitches**;.........259. H.772, 20
Float A little lead best fits a little **Float**;........249. H.733, 14
With Swan-like-state, flote up & down thy streams:
316. H.1028, 18
Flock Account of such a **flock** of sheep;..........133. H.336, 44
This **flock** of wooll, and this rich lock of hair..159. H.421, 15
Flocks And time it is our full-fed **flocks** to fold..160. H.421, 42
These seen, thou go'st to view thy **flocks**........230. H.662, 40
Flood Run through my veines, like to a hasty **flood**.
79. H.197, 78
This **flood** I drink to thee:.....................81. H.201, 38
Flood, if he has for him and his a bit,.........332. H.1112, 1
To this our poore, yet ever patient **Flood**.......332. H.1112, 6
Benummes like the forgettfull **floode**............409. A.2, 88
When on the **Flood** that nine times circles Hell....417. A.8, 36
Floods Once gets a force, **Floods** cannot quench the flame.
40. H.113, 4
All the **floods**, and frozen seas?..................40. H.115, 8
The night, with you, in **floods** of Downe........115. H.283, 120
Distinguish all those **Floods** that are..............339. N.3, 3
Flora And sweet as **Flora**. Take no care..........68. H.178, 17
Florabell Then Jessimine, with **Florabell**;........184. H.492, 29
Flosculet Once in a Virgin **Flosculet**,.............126. H.318, 7
Flour **Floure** of Fuz-balls, that's too good........223. H.638, 15
And Bake the **floure** of Amber for thy bread....269. H.818, 6
With lawlesse tooth the **floure** of wheate:......310. H.1004, 4
Fine **flowre** prest down, and running o're.......356. N.66, 8
Flourish Weeping, shall make ye **flourish** all the yeere.
138. H.343, 4
The fresh and fayrest **flourish** of the Morne.......410. A.3, 20
Flourished I **flourish't** more then Roman Ilia.......70. H.181, 8
Flourishing Gave them their ever **flourishing**......25. H.78, 10
Fresh, and for ever **flourishing**.................89. H.219, 20
Fresh Lillies **flourishing**.........................185. H.495, 4
Of Roses have an endlesse **flourishing**.........330. H.1100, 10
Love keep it ever **flourishing**....................361. N.83, 72
Make it ever **flourishing**........................363. N.93, 9
Flow See **Overflow**
Ribbands to **flow** confusedly:.....................28. H.83, 8
Yet, when your Lawns & Silks shal **flow**;.....76. H.193, 52
And **flow**, and flame, in your Vermillion.........105. H.259, 10
When my numbers full did **flow**?...............131. H.332, 4

But if they do, the more to **flow**................179. H.476, 12
And all those airie silks to **flow**,...............202. H.560, 15
That **flow** of Gallants which approach..........239. H.696, 1
Store of diseases, where Physitians **flow**.......244. H.718, 4
All rich spices thence will **flow**.................244. H.719, 6
Set free thy Tresses, let them **flow**..............282. H.881, 7
(That she may **flow** in Verse)....................291. H.918, 6
Where vertue walkes, not those that **flow**......311. H.1010, 10
And from Gods Prescience of mans sin doth **flow**
390. N.219, 3
like streames which **flow**...................431. ins. H.283, 50e
— — — — — — — — — — — —, ...432. var. H.283, 118
Flowed **Flow'd** all Panchaia's Frankincense;....402. N.269, 15
Flower See **Flour**, **July-flower**, **Lady-flower**, **Virgin-flower**
Why this **Flower** is now call'd so,................14. H.36, 1
Now, The **Flower** of the Wall...................15. H.36, 15
Each **Flower** has wept, and bow'd toward the East,
68. H.178, 7
To tipple freely in a **flower**.....................71. H.182, 4
For some rich **flower**, he took the lip...........71. H.182, 5
The **flower** that gives me nourishing:...........71. H.182, 20
And this same **flower** that smiles to day,......84. H.208, 3
That marres a **flower**;..........................104. H.257, 7
Then shall he read that **flowre** of mine........135. H.336, 97
So smels the **flowre** of blooming Clove;........145. H.375, 3
Even as the meanest **Flower**...................184. H.493, 8
But rather like a **flower** hid here.............189. H.514, 7
Strewings need none, every **flower**............199. H.546, 5
Ask me why this **flower** do's show............208. H.580, 7
Imprinted in each Herbe and **Flower**:........230. H.662, 32
Each bending then, will rise a proper **flower**...320. H.1054, 6
Go prettie child, and beare this **Flower**..........354. N.59, 1
To spring; though now a wither'd **flower**.......361. N.84, 8
Flowers See **Gillyflowers**, **July-flowers**, **Lady-flowers**, **Maiden-flowers**
And to all **flowers** ally'd in blood,..................7. H.9, 7
Of **flowers**, was thy spotlesse breast:...............8. H.11, 4
Voted the Rose; the Queen of **flowers**..............8. H.11, 8
Turn'd to **Flowers**. Still in some.................15. H.37, 3
Opens the way for early **flowers**;................23. H.70, 2
Looks like a Bride now, or a bed of **flowers**,......25. H.77, 5
They blush'd, and look'd more fresh then **flowers**
25. H.78, 5
Of **flowers** a sweet commingled Coronet:.........30. H.88, 4
With fields enameled with **flowers**,.............36. H.106, 46
And with **flowers** dresse my Tomb...............44. H.125, 4
Rifle the **Flowers** which the Virgins strew'd:....49. H.138, 6
And Graces strewing **flowers**...................54. H.149, 46
Of all those suppling-healing herbs and **flowers**...62. H.161, 8
Turn'd to **flowers**: Stil the hieu,..............64. H.167, 3
But care for crowns of **flowers**:...............65. H.170, 2
And with some **flowrs** my grave bestrew,.........70. H.180, 7
For some fresh, fragrant, luscious **flowers**:....71. H.182, 16
To dance and caper on the heads of **flowers**,....78. H.197, 52
Of **flowers**, ne'r suckt by th' theeving Bee:.....86. H.213, 37
You are the Queen all **flowers** among,.........88. H.216, 19
Sitting, and sorting severall sorts of **flowers**,......94. H.224, 2
A Baptime o're the **flowers**.....................95. H.227, 26
With other **Flowers**, bind my Love.............98. H.238, 2
And all beset with **flowers**.....................103. H.255, 8
Are not here Rose-buds, Pinks, all **flowers**,......103. H.256, 4
Such pretty **flowers**, (like to Orphans young)..104. H.257, 13
For as these **flowers**, thy joyes must die,.......107. H.263, 19
Your Walks with **Flowers**, and give their Crowns to you.
107. H.265, 8
Strew his hopes, and Him with **flowers**:........108. H.266, 6
Ye have been fill'd with **flowers**:...............110. H.274, 2
Troth, leave the **flowers**, and Maids, take me....112. H.281, 4
As Gilly **flowers** do but stay..................126. H.318, 1
All over-archt with Oringe **flowers**;............145. H.375, 12
Shall come to strew thy earth with **flowers**.....145. H.376, 6
Gave them Hearts-ease turn'd to **Flow'rs**........152. H.391, 8
That will with **flowers** the Tomb bestrew,......156. H.412, 7
Upon this Convex, all the **flowers**..............166. H.443, 33
All **Flowers** sent to'is burying.................186. H.497, 10
Turn'd to **Flowers**, still they be..............187. H.503, 3
Drinking wine, & crown'd with **flowres**........191. H.519, 8
Because with **Flowers** her Temple was not drest:.197. H.539, 8
In Wine and **Flowers**:......................198. H.544, 20
Of **flowers** set in comlinesse:...................202. H.560, 4
Sprang up a sweet Nativity of **Flowres**.........204. H.567, 2
No more of Groves, Meades, Springs, and wreaths of **Flowers**:
228. H.658, 4
To kick the **Flow'rs**, and scorn their odours too?.234. H.673, 4
The glory of **flowers** that crown'd it...........239. H.695, 6
To gather **Flowers** Sappha went,.................250. H.740, 1
And many **Flowers** beside;.....................285. H.892, 14
Selecting here, both Herbs, and **Flowers**;.......289. H.912, 2
With **Flowers** and Wine,.......................296. H.946, 19
Earth afford ye **flowers** to strew..................306. H.984, 43
The Queen of men, not **flowers**..............323. H.1068, 12
And in their motion smelt much like to **flowers**
326. H.1080, 13
And other **flowers**, lay upon....................359. N.83, 11
Come forth, to strew thy Tombe with **flow'rs**:..361. N.83, 74
Turnes all the patient ground to **flowers**.........364. N.96, 24

Sleeps, laid within some Ark of Flowers,.......367. N.102, 5
Whose blessèd Youth with endless flow'rs is crown'd. 417. A.8, 30
— — — — — — — — — — —, ...429. var. H.263, 22

Flowery As in a flowrie Nunnery:...............25. H.78, 4
May all, like flowrie Meads...................55. H.149, 63
For with the flowrie earth,...................80. H.201, 3
To make these flowrie Carpets show..........104. H.256, 18
And drown yee with a flowrie Spring:.......113. H.283, 44
Now Autumne's come, when all those flowrie aids 114. H.283, 92
Doe now your flowrie honours to my Herse....138. H.343, 2
Upon your Head this flowry Coronet:..........140. H.354, 4
The sweet, and flowrie Sisterhood...........237. H.686, 4
Receive (with Songs) a flowrie Diadem........254. H.756, 18
I' th flowrie Nunnerie:.........................257. H.767, 8
As flowrie vestures doe descrie...............311. H.1010, 7
Dresse Thee with flowrie Diaper..............402. N.269, 13

Flowery-sweet The Flowrie-sweet resemblances of Thee: 193. H.522, 4

Flowing Longer flowing, longer free,.............98. H.238, 4
Of lively colours, flowing from the face........274. H.840, 2
Words fully flowing, yet of influence:...........297. H.947, 2
When flowing garments I behold...............311. H.1010, 1
Chor. Thy vestures were not flowing:...........375. N.123, 67
More Comely flowing: where les free..........407. A.2, 28

Flown Or lookt I back unto the Times hence flown, 234. H.673, 1

Flows Led by some light that flows from thee......33. H.98, 8
You have ebbes of face and flowes,.............96. H.232, 5
Flowes from the Wine, and graces it:.........148. H.377, 74
Then, then (me thinks) how sweetly flowes....261. H.779, 2
Through mid'st thereof a christall stream there flowes 406. A.1, 75

Flung The Gods, he down the Nectar flung;......241. H.706, 2

Flushed Flusht was his face; his haires with oyle did shine; 313. H.1017, 3

Flushing Not all thy flushing Sunnes are set,.....72. H.185, 1

Flutter Flutter to flie, and beare away his head.....33. H.99, 4
Flutter and crow, as in a fit.................135. H.336, 110

Flux Whom all the flux of Nations comes to see;.399. N.263, 22

Fly See Idol-beetle-fly
Or flie abroad to seeke for woe..................6. H.2, 20
Thy Watch may stand, my minutes fly poste haste; 8. H.10, 3
These sweets, but let them fly;..................9. H.15, 6
Flutter to flie, and beare away his head..........33. H.99, 4
And back again, (tortur'd with fears) doth fly,..36. H.106, 67
Whither? Say, whither shall I fly,..............40. H.115, 1
'Tis strange, ye will not flie...................54. H.149, 33
It chanc't a Bee did flie that way,..............71. H.182, 2
Flie discontented hence, and for a time.........77. H.197, 21
Flie thou made Bubble of my sighs, and tears..87. H.215, 2
Then like a Globe, or Ball of Wild-fire, flie,....87. H.215, 9
Lest a handsome anger flye,.....................98. H.238, 13
Fly to my Mistresse, pretty pilfring Bee,........100. H.248, 1
See, a thousand Cupids flye,...................115. H.283, 107
The merry Cricket, puling Flie,.................119. H.293, 17
A bloated Earewig, and a Flie;..................119. H.293, 38
Ah Posthumus! Our yeares hence flye,..........132. H.336, 1
And salt, which frets thy Suters; fly..........174. H.465, 25
A golden Flie one shew'd to me...............185. H.497, 1
Where both seem'd proud; the Flie to have.....185. H.497, 3
More honour had, then this same Flie;.......186. H.497, 17
Fly me not, though I be gray,..................194. H.527, 1
Let our soules flie to' th' shades, where ever springs 205. H.575, 2
Ravisht in spirit, I come, nay more, I flie......242. H.713, 3
I saw a Flie within a Beade...................269. H.817, 1
We o're the tombes, and Fates shall flye;........288. H.906, 3
Still take advice; though counsels when they flye.318. H.1039, 1
This I know, the Fiend will fly................324. H.1069, 3
Then the Foe will fly affrighted................324. H.1069, 8
The wing, to flie away;........................346. N.38, 2
Thou dwel'st aloft, and I want wings to flie.....352. N.52, 2
To my heaven lesse run, then flie..............355. N.64, 6
His Arrowes flie; and all his stones are hurl'd..357. N.74, 3
And Time seems then, not for to flie, but creep;.358. N.77, 2
Flie up, to dwell...............................363. N.92, 17
Dark and dull night, flie hence away,............364. N.96, 8
But when once from hence we flie,.............377. N.128, 5
For me to flie, but now to follow Thee.........399. N.264, 4
I flie from Thee, as others did:.................399. N.265, 2
For through these Optickes, fly the dartes....408. A.2, 37
Thus Crownd with Rose Budds, Sacke, thou mad'st mee flye 410. A.3, 27
Fly hence Pale Care, noe more remember........413. A.4, 1
— — — — — — — — — —, ...422. var. H.106, 132
In Combatants to flye,.................433. ins. H.283, 140i

Fly-blow But that his breath do's Fly-blow all the meate. 223. H.637, 2
Mistake the flesh, and flye-blow both his eyes;.282. H.879, 2

Flying Away, and thus said flying,...............27. H.81, 34
Whereupon in anger flying.......................50. H.139, 3
Old Time is still a flying:.......................84. H.208, 2
'Tis but a flying minute,........................85. H.211, 5
The flying Pilcher, and the frisking Dace,......155. H.405, 11

Foam Thou never Plow'st the Oceans foame.....229. H.662, 5

Fodder Then come home and fother them........315. H.1026, 4

Foe A foe to Dissolution:.........................25. H.76, 2
Of want, or foe,................................161. H.426, 3
No part of pitie on a conquer'd foe...........199. H.550, 2
With such an arm'd, but such an easie Foe,.....216. H.618, 11
Then the Foe will fly affrighted...............324. H.1069, 8

Foes Whose love growes more enflam'd, by being Foes. 78. H.197, 44
The stronger: Vertue dies when foes..........148. H.377, 112
A Prince from Foes; but 'tis his Fort of Friends..244. H.717, 2
Blowes make of dearest friends immortall Foes...287. H.901, 2
Though from without no foes at all we feare;..292. H.928, 1
So Kings by killing doe encrease their foes.....292. H.929, 4
T' invade from far: They'l finde worse foes at home. 316. H.1030, 2
'Tis flatterie spends a King, more then his foes...331. H.1105, 2

Fold See Twofold
Fold now thine armes; and hang the head,......47. H.132, 1
And caught'st thy selfe the more by twenty fold:.97. H.236, 2
To meet it, when it woo's and seemes to fold...115. H.283, 116
And time it is our full-fed flocks to fold.......160. H.421, 42
Fold mine Armes, sob, sigh, or weep:..........182. H.490, 10
Or fold mine armes, and sigh, because I've lost.222. H.634, 12
Fould now thine armes, and in thy last looke reare 414. A.6, 7

Folded And when at night, she folded had her sheep, 159. H.421, 25

Foliage For Epitaph, in Foliage, next write this,...19. H.50, 5
Rise; and put on your Foliage, and be seene...68. H.178, 15

Follow Follow me weeping to my Turfe, and there 9. H.14, 13
Follow thy Perfumes by the smell:..............33. H.98, 6
To follow them: but chiefly, where.............49. H.136, 20
To follow thee,.................................132. H.336, 11
How can I choose but love, and follow her,.....181. H.485, 1
And Thyrsis, they shall follow.................184. H.492, 34
As great men lead; the meaner follow on,......214. H.614, 3
Follow to th' wilder Ocean:....................244. H.720, 4
Who fed my life, I'le follow her in death.......248. H.730, 16
In the next sheet Brave Man to follow Thee....329. H.1092, 6
A gentle calme did follow......................373. N.122, 8
For me to flie, but now to follow Thee..........399. N.264, 4
I'le follow Thee, hap, hap what shall,..........399. N.265, 5
If so; I'le thither follow, without feare;........403. N.271, 7

Followed And shame had follow'd long ere this,...48. H.136, 8
That Leading Cloud, I follow'd still,............67. H.175, 19
I follow'd after to descrie......................247. H.729, 5

Followers Two loving followers too unto the Grove, 206. H.575, 23

Following Following with love and active heate thy game, 301. H.966, 7
The following plague still treading on his heels..362. N.86, 2

Follows She followes the Spirit that guides now..225. H.643, 12

Folly And take the harmlesse follie of the time...69. H.178, 58

Fond Nor Beasts (fond thing) but only humane soules. 248. H.730, 10
— — — — — — — — — —, ...429. var. H.263, 18

Fondling But pretty Fondling, let not fall..........12. H.23, 5

Fondly Tell me Anthea, dost thou fondly dread..262. H.781, 13

Fone Fone sayes, those mighty whiskers he do's weare, 39. H.110, 1

Food Feed him ye must, whose food fils you.....102. H.250, 52
'Tis not the food, but the content..............124. H.312, 1
The food of Poets; so I thought sayes Jill,......186. H.498, 5
No Beast, for his food,........................225. H.643, 13
At which amaz'd, and pondring on the food,....262. H.783, 17
Give me the food that satisfies a Guest:........265. H.797, 1
Farc't with the food, that may themselves suffice. 310. H.1005, 4
Beyond its stinted Circle; giueing foode........410. A.3, 31
Daintye tast for ladyes food...................418. A.9, 22

Fool See Be-fool
Thou foole, said Love, know'st thou not this?..106. H.263, 5

Foolish Is both unluckie; I, and foolish too......268. H.813, 2

Foolishness No plague ther's like to foolishnesse..332. H.1115, 2

Fools These are traps to take fooles in...........52. H.147, 6
Fooles are they, who never know...............96. H.231, 1
To make Fools hate them, onlye by disguise;....412. A.3, 94

Foot See Ragged-soused-neat's-foot, Underfoot
Smell, where your soft foot treads;............55. H.149, 64
May his soft foot, where it treads,.............108. H.266, 13
Where humane foot, as yet, n'er trod:...........111. H.278, 6
Thou go'st; and as thy foot there treads,.......230. H.662, 30
Who two and thirty cornes had on a foot.......240. H.704, 2
Thus, thus with hallowed foot I touch the ground, 242. H.713, 5
Where no foot hath.........................258. H.770, 3
He sets his foot, he leaves rich compost there...259. H.771, 8
Whose Field his foot is, and whose Barn his shooe? 270. H.822, 4
To beawtify the legg and foote withall...........406. A.1, 90
Whence beawty springs, and thus I kisse thy foot. 406. A.1, 112

Footed See Silver-footed

Footman Truggin a Footman was; but now, growne lame, 283. H.882, 1

Footmanship Now Patrick with his footmanship has done, 158. H.418, 1

Foot-pace Whose foot-pace he doth stroak and kisse: 93. H.223, 132

For (Partial List) See Longed-for
Or flie abroad to seeke for woe..................6. H.2, 20
If good I'le smile, if bad I'le sigh for Thee.........6. H.3, 8
And never staine a cheeke for it....................6. H.4, 4
For Health on Julia's cheek hath shed..............7. H.9, 9
For pitties sake give your advice,..................8. H.13, 3
Down dead for grief, and end my woes withall:..11. H.22, 8
Why wept it? but for shame,.......................12. H.23, 2
But yet for Loves-sake, let thy lips doe this,...14. H.35, 11
Next, Corinna, for her wit,........................16. H.39, 9
For to number sorrow by...........................16. H.39, 13
At childish Push-pin (for our sport) did play:..17. H.44, 2
Laid out for dead, let thy last kindnesse be......19. H.50, 1
With leaves and mosse-work for to cover me:....19. H.50, 2
Loving, and gentle for to cover me:..............19. H.52, 2
Or for mine honour, lay me in that Tombe.......20. H.55, 7
Opens the way for early flowers;................23. H.70, 2
First, for Effusions due unto the dead,............23. H.72, 1
Wherein thou liv'st for ever. Deare farewell........23. H.72, 4
For I a Boy am, who...............................26. H.81, 9
For my life mortall, Rise from out thy Herse,....27. H.82, 15
I owe thee for a kisse............................29. H.87, 3
Make payment for his pleasure....................30. H.87, 18
And for their boldness stript them:................31. H.92, 6
Good princes must be pray'd for: for the bad......32. H.97, 1
Could'st leave the City, for exchange, to see......35. H.106, 3
Making thy peace with heav'n, for some late fault, 36. H.106, 59
Jove for our labour all things sells us...........36. H.106, 62
Th' industrious Merchant has; who for to find.36. H.106, 65
And so thou dost: for thy desires are.............37. H.106, 105
Who keep'st no proud mouth for delicious cates: 37. H.106, 109
So much for want, as exercise:....................37. H.106, 118
For seldome use commends the pleasure........38. H.106, 140
A Burling iron for his face:......................39. H.108, 10
And for to speak, if possible:....................39. H.108, 12
Sing o're Horace; for ere long....................39. H.111, 11
Shall I seek (for speedy ease)....................40. H.115, 7
For to say truth, all Garlands are thy due;....41. H.117, 9
But bid Good-night, and close their lids for ever..41. H.118, 8
Me turn'd to tears; yet did'st not weep for me...42. H.122, 4
For tears no more will fall........................43. H.123, 18
What next is lookt for? but we all sho'd see....44. H.124, 3
Scobble for Whoredome whips his wife; and cryes, 44. H.126, 1
He chirpt for joy, to see himself disceav'd......46. H.130, 12
Alas for pitty! and for us.........................48. H.136, 4
And as for me, my chast desire....................49. H.136, 33
This, as I wish for, so I hope to see;..........52. H.146, 17
For that, Matrons say, a measure.................55. H.149, 79
As she, so you'l be ripe for men.................56. H.149, 112
Praise me, for having such a fruitfull wombe;..58. H.151, 3
You, and your name, for ever: yet...............60. H.159, 8
I live for ever; let the rest all lye..............63. H.165, 3
'Tis Good Confirm'd; for you have Bishop't it..64. H.168, 10
But care for crowns of flowers:....................65. H.170, 2
Made for thy finger fit;............................65. H.172, 3
And pure as Gold for ever..........................66. H.172, 30
Thy long-black-Thumb-nail marks 'em out for ill: 66. H.173, 2
Get up, get up for shame, the Blooming Morne.67. H.178, 1
Alas for me! that I have lost......................72. H.185, 8
Blush not at all for that; since we have set....76. H.194, 5
Too strong for Fate to break us: Look upon..78. H.197, 71
Was lately whipt for lying with a Wench......79. H.199, 2
For my part, I never care.........................82. H.203, 1
For to tell, not publish it..........................82. H.203, 16
You may for ever tarry.............................84. H.208, 16
'Tis the lot ordain'd for me........................84. H.209, 6
I reare for me,.......................................85. H.211, 18
Amar. A Garland for my Gift shall be.............86. H.213, 36
Live, live thou dost, and shalt; for why?.......89. H.219, 15
Fresh, and for ever flourishing.....................89. H.219, 20
And rich for in and outward show:................90. H.223a, 2
Whose structure (for his holy rest)................90. H.223, 3
(Playing for Points and Pins) Cockall..........91. H.223, 59
Which serve for watched Ribbanings...........92. H.223, 73
The Oile was yours; and that I owe for yet:...94. H.226, 9
But like a Laurell, to grow green for ever......98. H.240, 2
Shall have for his winning a kisse...............99. H.243, 6
And for to make the merry cheere,............101. H.250, 35
Is it for want of sleep?..........................104. H.257, 18
For as these flowers, thy joyes must die,........107. H.263, 19
E'en Death, to die for thee......................109. H.267, 20
To live and die for thee..........................109. H.267, 24
And when I'm laid out for a Corse; then be...111. H.279, 3
Thou Sexton (Red-brest) for to cover me.......111. H.279, 4
If needs we must for Ceremonies-sake,........115. H.283, 131
And magicks for to end, and hells,..........115. H.283, 134
To live therein for ever: Frie...................115. H.283, 137
For sport my Julia threw a Lace...............116. H.284, 1
For mine own part I'de as lieve,..............117. H.285, 10
Long have I sought for: but co'd never see......121. H.301, 3
Of these, and such like things, for shift,.......127. H.319, 25
And for my sake, who ever did prefer.........137. H.341, 9
For why sayes he, all debts and their arreares, 142. H.363, 3
How for to make thee merry;...................142. H.364, 6
For no black-bearded Vigil from thy doore.....146. H.377, 13
Here, for to make the face affraid;.............148. H.377, 78
For all his shifts, he cannot shift his clothes...149. H.380, 2
Sing me to death; for till thy voice to cleare,...152. H.390, 1
Keepe it for ever; grounded with the good,....152. H.392, 7
Then Julia weep, for I must dy..................153. H.399, 10
For pitty, Sir, find out that Bee,...............156. H.412, 11
Cure, cure your selves, for I discrie,...........157. H.413, 7
You sigh for Love, as well as I...............158. H.420, 10
For why? that man is poore,......................160. H.422, 13
Corrupted wood; serve here for shine.........167. H.443, 75
That di'd for love; and their complaints:......169. H.449, 6
For that once lost, thou't fall to one,..........174. H.465, 27
I will not urge Thee, for I know,...............174. H.465, 33
Not wearing Purple only for the show;.........176. H.466, 5
And reckon this for fortune bad,...............179. H.476, 38
Nor will; for why, Pudica, this may know,...180. H.477, 5
For to thanke you (Noble Sir)...................182. H.489, 11
For lost like these, 'twill be,....................184. H.493, 11
Yellow, markt for Jealousie....................187. H.503, 4
The pleasures Ile prepare for thee:.............192. H.521, 2
And for to die here:..............................197. H.540, 2
Long for to lye here..............................197. H.540, 4
For I know, in the Tombs........................197. H.540, 7
Wound up again: Once down, He's down for ever. 202. H.558, 2
He needs a Tucker for to burle his face........211. H.594, 2
Looke ye not wan, or colourlesse for feare.......222. H.634, 6
Black I'm grown for want of meat;.............223. H.638, 4
This night for to ride;..........................225. H.643, 2
This night, and more for the wonder,............225. H.643, 21
Grow for two ends, it matters not at all,........232. H.667, 1
And have for all a kisse........................238. H.690, 12
Or, for revenge, I'le tell thee what............240. H.705, 9
For, rather then I'le to the West return,......242. H.713, 17
Now for to win thy Heifer faire,...............243. H.716, 31
Charme then the chambers; make the beds for ease, 245. H.723, 11
Our hope of one for the other..................247. H.727, 6
Ph. Alas for me! Ch. Shame on thy witching note, 248. H.730, 11
But weep not, Christall; for the shame was meant 249. H.732, 3
For if you cleave them, we shall see..........250. H.738, 3
With all wise speed for execution.............252. H.749, 2
For to let Affection in.........................253. H.750, 9
I'm a man for ev'ry Sceane....................253. H.750, 18
And weekly Markets for to sell his wares:....253. H.753, 2
If Wars goe well; each for a part layes claime:.260. H.774, 3
Behold, for us the Naked Graces stay..........261. H.781, 7
More curst for singing out of tune then he.......266. H.799, 4
These I but wish for; but thy selfe shall see,...269. H.818, 9
This for certainty I know;......................277. H.852, 6
For which I might extoll thee, but speake lesse,.298. H.955, 9
But stand for ever by his owne.................335. H.1129, 13
Thou bidst me come; I cannot come; for why,..352. N.52, 1
For why, my Saviour, with the sense.........354. N.57, 3
Let others look for Pearle and Gold,...........355. N.60, 1
If any thing delight me for to print............355. N.61, 1
What here we hope for, we shall once inherit:.362. N.88, 1
To such a height, as for to tell..................369. N.107, 3
I and the flesh, for and the fish,...............374. N.123, 33
shootes forth his jealous soule, for to surprize 430. ins. H.283, 40b
you, stand for to surrender up the keyes...431. ins. H.283, 60h
The brave cheape worke, and for to pave 440. ins. H.443, 45bb

Forbad But that his teares forbad the rest.......42. H.119, 12
But she forbad me, with a wand..............51. H.142, 19
Had not thy waves forbad the rest..............294. H.939, 10
Because the Law forbad to sit and crie..........384. N.180, 3

Forbear Mercie and Truth live with thee! and forbeare 14. H.35, 9
Th'ast dar'd too farre; but Furie now forbeare.82. H.204, 1
If Reader then thou canst forbeare,............203. H.564, 3
Forbeare therefore,...............................314. H.1024, 21
When times are troubled, then forbeare; but speake, 324. H.1072, 1

Forbears And charge, he not forbears..........56. H.149, 97

Forbid O Frost! O Snow! O Haile forbid the Banes. 40. H.113, 2
God did forbid the Israelites, to bring.........384. N.179, 1
If Thou beest taken, God forbid,................399. N.265, 1
— — — — — — — —, ...453. var. H.283, 89

Forbids (Love makes me write, what shame forbids to speak.) 24. H.74, 2

Force When no force else can get the masterdome..21. H.60, 2

Once gets a force, Floods cannot quench the flame. 40. H.113, 4
Now o're the threshold force her in...........55. H.149, 82
Will force you hence, (and in an houre.)......88. H.216, 6
Or else force a passage in:...................121. H.297, 12
And wildly force a passage in,................175. H.465, 55
To keep those pious Principles in force.........201. H.557, 20
Which, in full force, did daring stand,........370. N.107, 8
Come in, or force the gate....................370. N.111, 8
That without wrath, which wrath doth force us to. 397. N.259, 4

Forced Two she spat out, a cough forc't out the rest. 158. H.419, 2
Or Phyllis, whom hard Fate forc't on,.........215. H.616, 13
Forc'd from the mighty dolour of the heart.....380. N.154, 2
How stay thay would, yet forc't thay are to goe..410. A.3, 12
— — — — — — — — — — —, ...452. var. H.128, 39

'Fore See Before
Nor any was preferr'd 'fore me...............70. H.181, 2
Of hony, 'fore her Ladiship:.................71. H.182, 24
'Fore Damask Roses...........................83. H.205, 12
Keep here still, Closet-Gods, 'fore whom I've set 227. H.652, 13
Thy Crosse, my Christ, fixt 'fore mine eyes sho'd be, 371. N.115, 9
fore this or that hath gott the victory....433. ins. H.283, 140j

Fore Fore- or backward in her love:............82. H.203, 8
He sayes his fore and after Grace for it:.......332. H.1112, 2
Might me excite to fore, and after-grace.........371. N.115, 8

Forefend Which Love fore-fend; but spoken...114. H.283, 89
Mont. Fore-fend it Pan, and Pales do thou please 159. H.421, 31

Forehead Be her forehead, and her eyes.........11. H.21, 7
Double chinn'd, and forehead high:............138. H.342, 4
Broad of fore-head, large of eye,..............305. H.984, 18
Her forehead smooth full polisht bright and high 404. A.1, 5
That armes the forehead of the Vnicorne.......406. A.1, 104
(Thy fore-head) lett therin bee sign'd.........407. A.2, 33
A while yor forehead in a Cloude..............413. A.4, 17

Foreign Me in mine Age, or forraign Funerals,..269. H.818, 2
Fore-leader You a fore-leader in this Testament..304. H.977, 4
Foreman Strut, once a Fore-man of a Shop we knew; 53. H.148, 1
No; he's but Fore-man, as he was before........53. H.148, 4
Forepart God is all fore-part; for, we never see....342. N.18, 1
Foreright If well thou hast begun, goe on fore-right; 123. H.309, 1
Foresee Foresee,................................307. H.988, 8
Foreshow — — — — — — — — —, ...423. var. H.128, 16
Foreshows What times of sweetnesse this faire day foreshows, 44. H.124, 1
Foreskin Of Foreskin send to me:..............376. N.125, 2
Foresounds Of crackling Laurell, which fore-sounds, 127. H.319, 23
Forest All things decay with Time: The Forrest sees 23. H.69, 1
When I behold a Forrest spread................202. H.560, 1

Foretell Fore-tell the comming of some dire events: 45. H.128, 16
He might fore-tell my Fortune..................63. H.166, 4
Firing thy soule, by which thou dost foretell....256. H.763, 8
Foretelling By'th'fire, foretelling snow and slit,.134. H.336, 86
Foretold Nor find that true, which was foretold...157. H.413, 4
Remember that what thy Herrick Thee foretold..181. H.483, 10
Forever See Ever
Forfeit Longe forfaite pawnèd diamonds...........407. A.2, 8
Forfeiture To keep my Bond still free from forfeiture. 136. H.338, 4
Forged — — — — — — — — —, ...423. var. H.128, 43
Forget Or learne some way how to forget........60. H.159, 7
But I shall ne'r forget,.......................142. H.364, 5
But Least I should forgett his bedd............409. A.2, 83
You may vow Ile not forgett....................414. A.5, 1
Forgetful Benummes like the forgettfull floode.....409. A.2, 88
Forgive Forgive, forgive me; since I did not know..27. H.82, 5
Forgive me God, and blot each Line.............339. N.2, 5
Forgot How many lye forgot....................85. H.211, 13
Ile call to mind things half forgot:............135. H.336, 114
Believe him not; for he forgot it quite,.........186. H.501, 3
And all Affections are'forgot,.................190. H.515, 17
Forgotten Forgotten now, as I..................161. H.426, 15
And utterly forgotten lye,.......................265. H.794, 2
Forked And when thou art vppon that forked Hill..412. A.3, 85
Forked-fee A Postern-bribe tooke, or a Forked-Fee 202. H.557, 25
Forlorn Or laid aside forlorne;..................106. H.262, 6
Form Upon thy Forme more wrinkles yet will fall,..21. H.62, 5
And ask, Where's now the colour, forme and trust.49. H.138, 4
A glorious forme appeare to me:...................51. H.142, 6
Nor in a forme Triangular;........................91. H.223, 55
A mighty strife 'twixt Forme and Chastitie.....189. H.511, 6
Formal The Elves, in formall manner, fix........92. H.223, 93
Formed But form'd by number make sweet melody. 406. A.1, 108
A Nature, soe well form'd, soe wrought..........408. A.2, 65

— — — — — — — — — — —, ...423. var. H.128, 43

Former In my limbs their former heat?............10. H.19, 8
Faile of thy former helps; and onely use........46. H.128, 52
Times, still succeed the former.................84. H.208, 12
I have lost my former flame:....................182. H.489, 2
Those Prophets of the former Magnitude)......207. H.575, 60
New things succeed, as former things grow old...285. H.892, 22
Under which signe we may the former stone....300. H.961, 11
Mans former Birth is grace-lesse; but the state.326. H.1080 27
Thanksgiving for a former, doth invite..........348. N.42, 1
For faults of former yeares;....................352. N.53, 4
Thy former coming was to cure.................397. N.257, 1
Noe otherwise then as those former two..........410. A.3, 14
Listen, while they call backe the former yeare, 443. var. H.575, 52

Forms The common formes have no one eye,.....49. H.136, 18
Who formes a Godhead out of Gold or Stone,....117. H.288, 1
Three Formes of Heccate:........................258. H.767, 10

Forsake Can'st, and unurg'd, forsake that Larded fare, 37. H.106, 111
But to forsake thee ever, co'd there be..........78. H.197, 45
The cruell paine did his forsake,..............188. H.509, 3
Forsaken Me, me, forsaken, here admit.........170. H.449, 26
Thy Widdowes stand forsaken.....................374. N.123, 30
Forsook Sitting alone (as one forsook)............51. H.142, 1
I was forsooke by thee..........................161. H.425, 4
All Thy Disciples Thee forsook, and fled.........399. N.264, 2
Forsooth Candles (forsooth) and other knacks:..93. H.223, 116
Why then (forsooth) a Carcanet is shown.......232. H.668, 5
For't Love and they'l thank you for't. Adieu....70. H.180, 8
Fort Or Fort that I can make here;.............213. H.609, 3
A Prince from Foes; but 'tis his Fort of Friends. 244. H.717, 2

Forth Well may my Book come forth like Publique Day 3. Ded.H, 1
Who gave him forth good Grain, though he mistook.4. Ap. 3
Youth, or sweet Nature, co'd bring forth,........48. H.134, 2
To come forth, like the Spring-time, fresh and greene; 68. H.178, 16
Till you come forth. Wash, dresse, be briefe in praying: 68. H.178, 27
Or set it little forth...........................75. H.193, 24
Like to a Bride, come forth my Book, as last,....76. H.194, 1
Call forth fierce Lovers to their wisht Delights:...77. H.197, 6
Next, Virgil, Ile call forth,.....................80. H.201, 17
Tole forth my death; next, to my buryall come...100. H.248, 6
Come forth, my Lord, and see the Cart........101. H.250, 7
Conceiv'd with grief are, and with teares brought forth. 105. H.257, 28
Crosses doe still bring forth the best events.......110. H.275, 2
In dealing forth these bashfull jealousies:......113. H.283, 52
Forth into blushes, whensoere he speaks.........124. H.311, 2
Cast forth a light like to a Virgin flame:......131. H.331, 6
Shot forth her loving Sorceries:...............135. H.336, 106
Come with the Spring-time, forth Fair Maid, and be 140. H.354, 1
But temp'rate mirth dealt forth, and so discreet- 148. H.377, 79
Do'st rather poure forth, then allow............148. H.377, 82
Have I not blest Thee? Then go forth; nor fear..155. H.405, 1
Come forth and sweetly dye.......................161. H.425, 12
To shoot forth Generations like to them.........170. H.451, 4
Forth by a Ring, or some rich Carkanet?........172. H.459, 6
'Twas pitie Nature brought yee forth...........176. H.467, 10
Holy-Rood come forth and shield..............177. H.473, 1
Stand with thy Graces forth, Brave man, and rise 181. H.483, 1
Thou shalt come forth, and then appeare.......192. H.521, 31
For which, her wrath is gone forth to consume..197. H.539, 11
But home return'd, as he went forth, halfe blind..201. H.555, 4
Was destin'd forth to golden Soveraignty:......202. H.557, 28
Then unto Dancing forth the learned Round....206. H.575, 19
The Palms put forth their Gemmes, and every Tree 224. H.642, 5
Calls forth the lilly-wristed Morne;............230. H.662, 20
Some laid her forth, while other wept,..........237. H.686, 7
Stand forth brave man, since Fate has made thee here 251. H.745, 1
Sent forth by them, our flesh to eate, or bite.....278. H.862, 4
That he reacht forth unto me:..................279. H.863, 6
Words beget Anger: Anger brings forth blowes:..287. H.901, 1
Prickles is waspish, and puts forth his sting,.....287. H.903, 1
Stand forth Brave Man, here to the publique sight; 322. H.1062, 10
Goe thou forth my booke, though late;........334. H.1125, 1
Which though it sends forth thousand streams, 'tis ne're 341. N.15, 3
Then reach Thou forth that hand of Thine,......342. N.17, 9
Come forth, to strew thy Tombe with flow'rs:...361. N.83, 74
Sending them forth, Salute no man by th' way:..378. N.137, 2
May see it sprout forth streames of muscadine.....405. A.1, 50
Take wth thy blessinge; and goe forth..........409. A.2, 101
— — — — — — — — — — —, ...425. var. H.197, 12
— — — — — — — — — — —, ...430. var. H.283, 24
shootes forth his jealous soule, for to surprize 430. ins. H.283, 40b

Forthwith But **forthwith** bade my Julia shew......18. H.45, 3
Forthwith his bow he bent,......................27. H.81, 29
That was too coorse; but then **forthwith**.......119. H.293, 31
And **forthwith** came to me......................188. H.509, 4
Of him bewitcht: then **forthwith** make..........284. H.890, 3
Fortieth To' th' (almost) sev'n and **fortieth** yeare...41. H.116, 2
Fortress Thy **Fortress**, and will needs prevaile;..175. H.465, 54
Fortunate Whom this Morne sees most **fortunate**,..208. H.583, 2
Make Thee like Him, this, that way **fortunate**,..254. H.756, 10
Yet be timely **fortunate**.......................334. H.1125, 2
Fortune **Fortune** when she comes, or goes.........37. H.106, 94
What will, in time, your **Fortune** be:...........60. H.159, 10
He might fore-tell my **Fortune**..................63. H.166, 4
Mans **Fortune** must be had in reverence.........117. H.287, 2
A change, when **Fortune** either comes, or goes:..128. H.323, 8
(Binding the wheele of **Fortune** to his Sphere)..137. H.341, 4
And reckon this for **fortune** bad,...............179. H.476, 38
Where **Fortune** bears no sway o're things......190. H.515, 35
Fortune did never favour one..................191. H.520, 1
Fortune no higher Project can devise,..........196. H.535, 1
The happy **fortune** will not alwayes last.........218. H.621, 2
Whom whitest **Fortune** dandled has too much...239. H.697, 2
With thousand blessings by thy **Fortune** crown'd..242. H.713, 6
Go on with Sylla's **Fortune**; let thy Fate......254. H.756, 9
Do's **Fortune** rend thee? Beare with thy hard Fate: 270. H.820, 1
Fortune is now Your Captive; other Kings......271. H.823, 5
Fortune her selfe can lay no claim to it.........272. H.830, 2
Our Fate, our **Fortune**, and our Genius;......300. H.961, 14
This Kingdomes **fortune**, and that Empires fate:.330. H.1100, 8
Thou **Fortune** ow'st for tenement................407. A.2, 14
Or **Fortune** too, for what the first secures.422. ins. H.106, 92c
Of **fortune** can have noe command,.......436. ins. H.336, 48n
Fortuned How ere it **fortuned**; know for Truth, I meant 304. H.977, 3
Fortune's May **Fortunes** Lilly-hand............57. H.149, 157
Free by your fate, then **Fortunes** mightinesse,..141. H.359, 4
Fortune's blind profuser of her own,..........238. H.689, 1
Fortunes On with thy **fortunes** then, what e're they be; 6. H.3, 7
Whose **fortunes** I have frolickt with:..........136. H.336, 132
We blesse our **Fortunes**, when we see..........200. H.552, 17
Mans **fortunes** are according to his paines.......253. H.752, 2
Of both our **Fortunes** good and bad we find......257. H.765, 1
Whereas (perchance) my **fortunes** may........312. H.1014, 6
Adverse and prosperous **Fortunes** both work on...349. N.44, 1
And, since it **fortunes** so;......................368. N.104, 5
Forty Twice fortie (bating but one year,........226. H.644, 3
That did ordaine the Fast of **forty** Dayes........386. N.195, 2
Forum See **Holy-forum**
I'th **Forum** here, or Vineyard...................380. N.152, 2
Forward Move **forward** then your Rosie feet,.....55. H.149, 61
Looks **forward**, scornes what's left behind:.....132. H.336, 14
Forward, or backward, side-ward, and what pace 148. H.377, 93
Why then goe **forward**, sweet Auspicious Bride, 431. ins. H.283, 50a
Fostering May fost'ring fathers be to you........218. H.626, 13
Fother See **Fodder**
Foul Nor car'st which comes the first, the **foule** or faire; 37. H.106, 97
With weather **foule**, then faire againe...........47. H.133, 13
Foule in these noble pastimes, lest ye call......114. H.283, 86
Foule Judith was; and **foule** she will be known,..140. H.356, 3
Faire and **foule** dayes trip Crosse and Pile; The faire 189. H.513, 1
Far lesse in number, then our **foule** dayes are...189. H.513, 2
Let faire or **foule** my Mistresse be,.............207. H.579, 1
Though ne'r so **foule** be the weather...........225. H.643, 6
Look how our **foule** Dayes do exceed our faire;....339. N.1, 1
And **fowle** thy Altar, Charme some Into froggs,...412. A.3, 91
Prophan'd in Speech, or done an act that's **fowle** 426. ins. H.197, 29a
Fouler But not his mouth (the **fouler** of the two.) 110. H.273, 2
The **fouler** Fiend, and evill Spright,............123. H.306, 14
Foully Judas began well, but he **foulely** fell:.....387. N.200, 2
Found Small griefs find tongues: Full Casques are ever **found** 15. H.38, 7
And **found** (Ah me!) this flesh of mine...........17. H.41, 22
The words **found** true, C. M. remember me.......26. H.79, 10
Yet there's a way **found** (if thou please).........34. H.103, 13
Where all Damps, and Mists are **found**?.........40. H.115, 6
Or water; where's the comfort **found**?...........50. H.140, 8
Who have **found**, and still can prove,............53. H.147, 13
Pity me too, who **found** so soone a Tomb.........58. H.151, 4
Is no where **found**.............................66. H.172, 26
Once lost, can ne'r be **found** againe:............69. H.178, 64
And (like a blasting Planet) **found** her out;......87. H.215, 4
'Mongst Roses, I there Cupid **found**:............96. H.229, 2
The onely true plant **found**,....................106. H.262, 2
Here I have **found** a Chamber fit,............123. H.306, 7
Ne'r to be **found** againe......................125. H.316, 20
No new devise, or late **found** trick,............126. H.319, 5
Must all be left, no one plant **found**...........132. H.336, 10
Though lost in them, yet **found** in me.........146. H.376, 10
And when the Trumpet which thou late hast **found** 257. H.763, 17
A soveraign balme **found** out to cure me.......274. H.841, 4
That thou be righteous **found**; and I the Lyer....279. H.866, 4
A richess of those sweets she **found**,............281. H.876, 3
Truth is best **found** out by the time, and eyes;..287. H.902, 1
If thou hast **found** an honie-combe,............288. H.909, 1
T'ave **found** in me this sudden change;..........290. H.915, 4
As Cadmus once a new way **found**,...............297. H.948, 5
There is not one least solecisme **found**;.........307. H.992, 4
In Gilead though no Balme be **found**,............342. N.17, 5
But I as patient will be **found**..................351. N.48, 10
No jot of Leven must be **found**..................366. N.98, 3
And all rejoyce, that we have **found**............368. N.102, 17
And **found** my Debits to amount................369. N.107, 2
That **found** a way.............................374. N.123, 48
The salve for this i'th Eucharist is **found**.......381. N.155, 2
I know, that faults will many here be **found**,....398. N.261, 5
Yett to bee **found** when hee shall seeke..........409. A.2, 78
And now yf ther A man bee **founde**............409. A.2, 103
— — — — — — — — —, ...427. var. H.197, 65
Foundation Firm be my **foundation**...............84. H.209, 4
Foundation of your Feast, Fat Beefe:...........101. H.250, 29
Upon the rock, whose firm **foundation** laid,......143. H.365, 10
The first **foundation** of that zeale sho'd be.......201. H.557, 3
Fix the **foundation** fast, and let the Roofe......245. H.723, 13
Lay of our safeties new **foundation**:............300. H.961, 12
Here of my great and good **foundation**...........305. H.983, 4
Firme and well fixt **foundation**................335. H.1129, 14
But the **foundacōn** of this Architect.............405. A.1, 43
Foundation's Such is thy house, whose firme **foundations** trust 148. H.377, 103
Founders' This was the **Founders** grave and good intent, 201. H.557, 13
Fountain Having a living **Fountain** under it.......154. H.403, 4
Fountains Ope' the **fountains** and the springs,......21. H.61, 3
Milk stil your **Fountains**, and your Springs, for why? 273. H.831, 1
Four See **Lucky-four-leaved**
Furze, three or **foure** times with his cheeks did blow 47. H.131, 3
Of **foure** teeth onely Bridget was possest;......158. H.419, 1
This, Three; which Three, you make up **Foure** Brave Prince. 170. H.451, 16
Having but seven in all; three black, **foure** white..195. H.531, 2
Foure times bestrew thee ev'ry yeere............360. N.83, 36
God has **foure** keyes, which He reserves alone;...390. N.224, 1
Four-leaved The **four-leav'd** grasse, or mosse-like silk. 166. H.443, 42
Fourscore Threescore or **fourescore** spring up thence for one 388. N.208, 4
Foursquare The Altar is not here **foure-square**,....91. H.223, 54
Faith is a thing that's **four-square**, let it fall....292. H.926, 1
Fourth And with the **fourth** key He unlocks the tombe. 390. N.224, 4
Fowl I came; (tis true) and lookt for **Fowle** of price, 262. H.783, 7
— — — — — — — — —, ...445. var. H.730, 9
Fowls Ch. What's that to me, I waft nor fish or **fowles**, 248. H.730, 9
Fox See **Fox i'th' hole**
Of sheep, (safe from the Wolfe and **Fox**)......230. H.662, 41
That's tost up after **Fox** i' th' Hole............231. H.662, 57
Fox-fur He keeps the **Fox-furre** for to face his own. 232. H.669, 2
Fox i'th' hole That tost up, after **Fox-i'th' hole:** 126. H.319, 14
That's tost up after **Fox i' th' Hole**..............231. H.662, 57
Fragments Meat for our meales, and **fragments** too: 356. N.66, 4
All are **Fragments** from His dish..............363. N.93, 6
Fragrant Then comely and most **fragrant** Maid,...49. H.136, 14
Over her **fragrant** cheek is cast..................55. H.149, 72
For some fresh, **fragrant**, luscious flowers:......71. H.182, 16
Yet the next Morne, re-guild the **fragrant** East...72. H.185, 7
Time-past so **fragrant**, sickly now drawn in......77. H.197, 28
The youthfull Bride-groom, and the **fragrant** Bride: 114. H.283, 88
Of **fragrant** Apples, blushing Plums, or Peares:..205. H.575, 10
My many fresh and **fragrant** Mistresses:........214. H.612, 2
If **fragrant** Virgins you'l but keep..............257. H.764, 7
Both of a fresh, and **fragrant** kinne............285. H.892, 15
When I want my **fragrant** wine................309. H.996, 10
Instead of **fragrant** Posies......................345. N.33, 11
The cause, why things thus **fragrant** be:........364. N.96, 18
Without the **fragrant** Rose-bud, born;............396. N.251, 4
Fragrous — — — — — — — —, ...432. var. H.283, 88
Frailties Your **frailties**; and bemone ye;........184. H.493, 10
Frailty Do not you fall through **frailty**; Ile be sure 136. H.338, 3
God pardons those, who do through **frailty** sin;...344. N.32, 1
Frame That Prickles buyes, puts Prickles out of **frame;** 287. H.903, 3
To have a tooth twicht out of's native **frame**.....323. H.1066, 2
Framed O Place! O People! Manners! **fram'd** to please 242. H.713, 9

Franck **Franck** ne'r wore silk she sweares; but I reply, 207. H.578, 1
Franck wo'd go scoure her teeth; and setting to't, 247. H.728, 1
Frankincense Hid in a cloud of **Frankincense**:....93. H.223, 140
Give up thy soule in clouds of **frankinsence**.......128. H.320, 6
Devote to thee my graines of **Frankinsence**:......131. H.333, 2
Love may smell the **Frankincense**..............158. H.417, 4
(Here honour'd still with **Frankincense**)........169. H.449, 18
Though **Frankinsense** the Deities require,........295. H.940, 1
As for our selves to leave some **frankinsence**.....295. H.940, 4
Fat **Frankincense**:.............................361. N.83, 64
The **Frankincense** for Gods Offring...............396. N.254, 2
Flow'd all Panchaia's **Frankincense**;...........402. N.269, 15
Smells like the burnt Sabæan **Frankinsense**......404. A.1, 28
As in a bedd of **Frankensence**...................408. A.2, 46
Frantic And makes them **frantick**, ev'n to all extreames; 29. H.86, 4
Them **frantick** with thy raptures, flashing through.45. H.128, 27
And make my spirits **frantick** with the fire........67. H.176, 4
Small Chalice of thy **frantick** liquor; He........78. H.197, 63
Or **frantick** I shall eate.........................81. H.201, 31
Thus **frantick** crazie man (God wot).........135. H.336, 113
To grace the **frantick** Thyrse:..................198. H.544, 9
And look how when a **frantick** Storme doth tear.225. H.642, 13
Frantic-fires No Holy-Rage, or **frantick-fires** did stirre, 150. H.382, 9
Frantic-looks Like to His subject; and as his **Frantick-Looks**, shew him truly Bacchanalian like, 206. H.575, 35-36
Fray Quite dispossest of either **fray**, or fret.......82. H.204, 6
Shall **fray** that silke, or fret this cloth...........393. N.231, 4
Free See **Jail-free, Knot-free, Trespass-free, Trouble-free**
He could live **free** here?.......................12. H.26, 12
I'm **free** from thee; and thou no more shalt heare...17. H.42, 1
Your face no more: So live you **free**............49. H.136, 35
Live employ'd, and so live **free**..................53. H.147, 11
All hearts your captives; yours, yet **free**:.........61. H.160, 4
The joynt is **free**:.............................65. H.172, 8
No Capitoll, no Cornish **free**,...................90. H.223, 20
Longer flowing, longer **free**,.....................98. H.238, 4
A heart that's **free**,...........................100. H.246, 13
Number, Your owne, by **free** Adoption;..........107. H.264, 4
A heart as sound and **free**,.....................108. H.267, 6
From Powders and Perfumes keep **free**;........112. H.282, 3
But seldome from suspition **free**:...............118. H.291, 14
From noise of Scare-fires rest ye **free**,...........121. H.299, 1
A little while from Tramplers **free**;............123. H.306, 10
Knap the thread, and thou art **free**:............128. H.322, 8
Then live we **free**,.............................133. H.336, 37
And seeling **free**,..............................133. H.336, 53
Glit'ring to my **free** desires:....................129. H.324, 2
These accept, and Ile be **free**,..................129. H.324, 3
To keep my Bond still **free** from forfeiture.....136. H.338, 4
And since I'm **free**,............................137. H.340, 9
Permit my Book to have a **free** accesse..........137. H.341, 11
Free by your fate, then Fortunes mightinesse,..141. H.359, 4
To have my neck from Loves yoke-**free**...........155. H.408, 2
To keep still **free**.............................171. H.452, 11
The neck is **free**:..............................172. H.458, 3
But have hitherto liv'd **free**,...................183. H.490, 17
From Shackles **free**:............................190. H.515, 20
Though **free** she be, ther's something yet........191. H.520, 3
To make thy Maids and selfe **free** mirth,.........193. H.521, 49
To **free** the Orphan from that Wolfe-like-man,.201. H.557, 15
To fetter Justice, when She might be **free**.......202. H.557, 26
For being comely, consonant, and **free**..........210. H.590, 1
As from Love, from trouble **free**...............219. H.628, 10
Then, while Fates suffer, live thou **free**,........233. H.670, 17
From cares and troubles **free**;..................259. H.772, 26
That brave Vibration each way **free**;............261. H.779, 5
Bids ye all be **free**;...........................263. H.784, 5
From her Purgatory **free**:.......................269. H.814, 4
From shame my face keepe **free**.................281. H.874, 10
Set **free** thy Tresses, let them flow..............282. H.881, 7
Thy **free** (and not decurted) offering............286. H.898, 8
In fetters **free**;................................296. H.946, 14
To whose **free** knees we may our temples tye....300. H.961, 15
The Genius wastefull, more then **free**:...........310. H.1004, 2
From the Plough soone **free** your teame;........315. H.1026, 3
As **free** from offence,........................317. H.1035, 29
To whose glad threshold, and **free** door........321. H.1056, 3
His wrath is **free** from perturbation;..............340. N.7, 2
From aberrations to live **free**;....................357. N.72, 17
So kind, to set me **free**,........................370. N.111, 6
God had but one Son **free** from sin; but none....378. N.134, 1
Of all His sonnes **free** from correction...........378. N.134, 2
Sin is an act so **free**, that if we shall...........389. N.218, 1
Say, 'tis not **free**, 'tis then no sin at all.........389. N.218, 2
Will **free** him quickly from his miserie;..........396. N.252, 2
More Comely flowing: where les **free**.............407. A.2, 28
— — — — — — — — — —, ...438. var. H.408, 2
Free-born The **free-born** Nosthrills of the King,....126. H.319, 8
I am a **free-born** Roman; suffer then,..........242. H.713, 11
A **Free-born** of our Citie........................345. N.33, 32
Free-Cost Because he cannot sleep i'th' Church, **free-cost** 39. H.109, 4
Nothing comes **Free-cost** here; Jove will not let...177. H.469, 1
Freedom Such **Freedome** in Captivity;..........64. H.169, 10
Find equall **freedome**, equall fare;..............147. H.377, 60
As they of **freedome** may be sure:..............153. H.395, 3
(To **freedome** so unknown)....................160. H.422, 18
Which Love and noble **freedome** is;...........198. H.544, 28
Yet **freedome**, shee enjoyes withall..............281. H.876, 10
Free-feet Our **free-feet** here; but we'l away:.....179. H.476, 35
Freely So that she could not **freely** stir,...........16. H.41, 16
Let others drink thee **freely**; and desire.........46. H.128, 49
To tipple **freely** in a flower.....................71. H.182, 4
Which **freely** drink to your Lords health,.......102. H.250, 38
Jack kisses Jill, and bids her **freely** eate:........186. H.498, 2
Then to the poore she **freely** gives the milke.....203. H.561, 4
Who thither come, and **freely** get...............350. N.47, 15
Freely from them, and hold none back at all.....380. N.151, 2
Free-oblation To take the **Free-Oblation**:........92. H.223, 86
Freeze See **Frieze**
I **freeze**, I **freeze**, and nothing dwels..............8. H.13, 1
Sometimes **freeze**, and sometimes frie:............82. H.203, 6
Since which I **freeze**, but cannot frie............155. H.406, 4
As at once I **freeze**, and frie....................204. H.566, 5
I **freeze** as fast, and shake for cold.............290. H.915, 2
or Lar will **freeze** to death at home:......431. ins. H.283, 60j
Freezing **Freezing** cold, and firie heats,...........102. H.253, 7
Frenzies All times unto their **frenzies**; Thou shalt there 206. H.575, 47
Frenzy His inconsiderate **Frenzie** off (at last)...225. H.642, 20
In **frenzie** ne'r like thee.......................227. H.653, 12
And In that Misticke **frenzie**, wee haue hurl'de....410. A.3, 23
Frequent Then a mans **frequent** Fame, spoke out with praise. 241. H.710, 2
Frequents Magot **frequents** those houses of good-cheere, 191. H.518, 1
Fresh These **fresh** beauties (we can prove).........15. H.37, 1
They blush'd, and look'd more **fresh** then flowers..25. H.78, 5
To come forth, like the Spring-time, **fresh** and greene; 68. H.178, 16
For some **fresh**, fragrant, luscious flowers:......71. H.182, 16
Invites **fresh** Grapes to fill his Presse with Wine..72. H.185, 28
Fresh and faire;...............................83. H.205, 6
Fresh, and for ever flourishing..................89. H.219, 20
Why doe not all **fresh** maids appeare..........103. H.256, 1
Fresh, as their blood; and ever grow,..........104. H.256, 19
Off then with grave clothes; put **fresh** colours on; 105. H.259, 9
Ye have been **fresh** and green,..................110. H.274, 1
Of **fresh** concupiscence, and cry,..............135. H.336, 111
Though not so **fresh**, yet full as merry........136. H.336, 140
Me longer date, and more **fresh** springs to live:.140. H.355, 12
And walks **fresh** varnisht to the publick view.....140. H.356, 2
And spring **fresh** Rose-buds, while the salt, the wit 148. H.377, 73
Here, and there a **fresh** Love is................157. H.415, 4
Wo'd yee have **fresh** Cheese and Cream?........183. H.491, 1
Fresh Lillies flourishing.......................185. H.495, 4
Fresh blossoms from her cheekes did fall.........203. H.562, 2
So, when Death comes, **Fresh** tinctures lose their place, 207. H.576, 5
My many **fresh** and fragrant Mistresses:........214. H.612, 2
Re-cloth'd in **fresh** and verdant Diaper..........224. H.642, 2
Fresh strowings allow..........................256. H.762, 1
Paints them with **fresh** Vermilion:...............268. H.811, 2
Both of a **fresh**, and fragrant kinne............285. H.892, 15
Since we **fresh** strewings will bring hither,........289. H.912, 7
And bring **fresh** strewings to thy Tombe..........359. N.83, 6
And **fresh** thy Herse-cloth, we will, here,........360. N.83, 35
And **fresh** joyes, as never too.................377. N.128, 23
The **fresh** and fayrest flourish of the Morne......410. A.3, 20
Such rich, such **fresh**, such sweet varietyes,..... .415. A.7, 16
Fresh-quilted **Fresh-quilted** colours through the aire: 67. H.178, 4
Fret Or **fret** at all...............................65. H.172, 11
Quite dispossest of either fray, or **fret**..........82. H.204, 6
Seas chafe and **fret**, and beat, and over-boile;...105. H.259, 3
Or **fret** thy Seeling, or to build..............149. H.377, 120
To **fret**...172. H.458, 8
If I any **fret** or vex,...........................177. H.472, 3
Shall fray that silke, or **fret** this cloth...........393. N.231, 4
Fretful Which being done, the **fretfull** paine........18. H.46, 9
Yet the **fretfull** bryar will tell,...................88. H.217, 4
Say (if she's **fretfull**) I have bands..............98. H.238, 6
And **fretfull**, carries Hay in's horne,..........165. H.443, 14
Stung by a **fretfull** Bee;.......................272. H.828, 2
Frets And salt, which **frets** thy Suters; fly......174. H.465, 25
— — — — — — — — —, ...428. var. H.238, 6
Friar Of the **Fryar**, (of work an odde-piece.)....93. H.223, 122
The dancing **Frier**, tatter'd in the bush;........155. H.405, 7
Friars That the Monks and **Fryers** together,......304. H.976, 3
Fried I lately **fri'd**, but now behold.............290. H.915, 1
Friend Nay, thou more neare then kindred, **friend**, man, wife, 45. H.128, 3
My faithful **friend**, if you can see...............79. H.198, 1
Play I co'd once; but (gentle **friend**) you see....84. H.210, 1
Griefe, (my deare **friend**) has first my Harp unstrung; 84. H.210, 9

And with our Broth and bread, and bits; Sir, friend,
146. H.377, 23
Wilt thou my true Friend be?..................205. H.574, 1
Nor us (my Friend) when we are lost,.........233. H.670, 26
Thy faithfull friend, and to poure downe.......303. H.973, 17
And (Noble friend) this answer I must give:..312. H.1013, 2
'Tis Wisdomes part to doubt a faithfull friend...333. H.1121, 2
Thee a kinsman, or a friend,...................334. H.1125, 4
Friendly Take friendly morsels, and there stay..146. H.377, 16
Consent and play a friendly part..................177. H.471, 3
A friendly Patron unto thee:..................275. H.844, 2
The staffe might come to play the friendly part...394. N.241, 4
Friends Lastly, with friends t'enjoy our dayes.....42. H.121, 4
Gentle friends, though I despaire..............62. H.162, 16
Thee, and thy beauties; kisse, we will be friends,
78. H.197, 70
Gentle friends, then doe but please,............88. H.218, 7
Thankfull to you, or friends, for me............111. H.280, 12
(God and good friends be thankt for it).......123. H.306, 8
Then the next health to friends of mine........135. H.336, 129
Who can hold that (my friends) that will away?.162. H.428, 2
Furies to others, Friends to me.................174. H.465, 6
I did not sup, because no friends were there....197. H.541, 2
Where Mirth and Friends are absent when we Dine
197. H.541, 3
A Prince from Foes; but 'tis his Fort of Friends.
244. H.717, 2
Blowes make of dearest friends immortall Foes..287. H.901, 2
To have friends to beare a part:................302. H.968, 4
Let not that Day Gods Friends and Servants scare:
376. N.126, 1
Salute we must, nor Strangers, Kin, or Friends...378. N.137, 8
Friends' But for my friends transgression!........400. N.266, 6
Friendship Then for to murder friendship, by dispute.
287. H.901, 6
Fries The Storax fries; and ye may see,...........365. N.97, 8
Frieze Or Freeze, from this fine Fripperie........90. H.223, 21
Fright With direful notes to fright your sleeps:..56. H.149, 102
And with Tapers comes to fright...............117. H.289, 7
From all mischances, that may fright...........121. H.299, 3
Meane while, the Holy-Rood hence fright.......123. H.306, 13
Not wrathfull seem, or fright the Maide,........145. H.376, 4
Come to fright a parting soule;.................348. N.41, 23
Fright mine eares, and fright mine eyes,.......348. N.41, 42
Thou dost me fright,...........................353. N.56, 2
When Hell and Horrour fright the Conscience...392. N.230, 28
Frights That frights men with a Parliament:.....126. H.319, 4
Fringe The Fringe that circumbinds it too,.....92. H.223, 64
The Fringe about this, are those Threds.......167. H.443, 106
Fringed Are beawtifi'd with faire fring'd canopies...404. A.1, 10
Frip Saint Frip, Saint Trip, Saint Fill, S. Fillie,.91. H.223, 32
Frippery Or Freeze, from this fine Fripperie......90. H.223, 21
Frisking The Horses, Mares, and frisking Fillies,.101. H.250, 11
The flying Pilcher, and the frisking Dace,.....155. H.405, 11
Frisks It frisks, and flyes, now here, now there,..130. H.329, 13
Fro Drive all hurtfull Feinds us fro,...........177. H.473, 7
Frogs And fowle thy Altar, charme some Into froggs,
412. A.3, 91
Frolic Drink frollick boyes, till all be blythe.......102. H.250, 43
Frolick the full twelve Holy-dayes.............127. H.319, 50
Frollick Virgins once these were,..............152. H.391, 1
And make the frollick yeere,...................198. H.544, 21
Let's feast, and frolick, sing, and play,........233. H.670, 30
Out-did the meate, out-did the frolick wine......289. H.911, 10
When I drinke my frolick wine:...............309. H.996, 8
Who frolick will be,..........................320. H.1051, 13
My frolick Youths adieu;.......................328. H.1091, 6
Frolicked Whose fortunes I have frolickt with:..136. H.336, 132
From (Partial List)
Banish'd from thee I live; ne'r to return,.......19. H.52, 3
And thou (Anthea) must withdraw from him....20. H.55, 2
That when from hence she does depart,..........24. H.73, 9
For my life mortall, Rise from out thy Herse,..27. H.82, 15
Rouze Anacreon from the dead;................39. H.111, 9
Down from her comely shoulders hung:.........51. H.142, 10
Ere I go hence; know this from me,...........60. H.159, 9
From out the eye, Loves Firmament:..........69. H.178, 54
But when he felt he suckt from thence........71. H.182, 7
From out my Narde, and Fun'rall fire:........72. H.185, 18
Where hast thou been so long from my embraces,
77. H.197, 19
The time that I prevaricate from thee.........79. H.197, 86
The Country has. Amint. From whence? Amar. From whence?
Mir. The Court............................86. H.213, 12
Charms, that call down the moon from out her sphere.
99. H.244, 1
Though hourely comforts from the Gods we see,.111. H.276, 1
But seldome from suspition free:..............118. H.291, 14
Ne're ravisht from the flattering Vine,.........120. H.293, 48
No more shall I, from henceforth, heare a quire
132. H.333, 7
To make this neat distinction from the rest;...140. H.354, 5
(Rather than fail) to steal from thence old shoes:
143. H.368, 2
Then temper flew from words; and men did squeake,
150. H.382, 7
(Bred from the dung-hils, and adulterous rhimes,)
155. H.405, 13
To Take away that Heart from me,............168. H.446, 3
Differs not much from drowzie slothfullnesse....173. H.459, 14
Discovering from thence........................193. H.524, 3
One kisse from thee..........................210. H.591, 10
Our Lives do differ from our Lines by much.....218. H.624, 2
No man comes late unto that place from whence.228. H.656, 1
To bring from thence the scorched Clove........229. H.662, 8
From whence there's never a return............233. H.670, 39
To kisse thy hand from out the coach;.........239. H.696, 2
Streame to the Spring from whence it came.....245. H.720, 10
All has been plundered from me, but my wit;..272. H.830, 1
From good to good, revolving here, & there.....274. H.839, 2
Is the beast exempt from staine,...............280. H.870, 5
But, like full clouds, may they from thence.....291. H.919, 7
Though from without no foes at all we feare;..292. H.928, 1
Yet part ye from hence,......................317. H.1035, 28
His wrath is free from perturbation;............340. N.7, 2
To load with blessings, and unload from sins....341. N.14, 2
And hold'st mine eyes from sleeping;............353. N.56, 3
And be return'd from out my dust:..............358. N.78, 2
May Sweets grow here! & smoke from hence,..361. N.83, 63
From out thy Maiden-Monument...............361. N.83, 66
How sweet this place is! as from hence........402. N.269, 14
Is He, from hence, gone to the shades beneath,..403. N.271, 5
From's Froms Nature Cuntrye, into Banishm[t],......411. A.3, 72
Frost I'le rather keepe this frost, and snow,........8. H.13, 7
O Frost! O Snow! O Haile forbid the Banes...40. H.113, 2
Or let me 'gender with eternall frost..........40. H.113, 6
Of the Raine, Frost, Haile, and Snow?..........40. H.115, 4
Such frost and snow upon your haire:.........63. H.164, 5
Ile send such Frost, such Haile, such Sleet, and Snow,
82. H.204, 10
My locks behung with frost and snow:.........134. H.336, 76
To Frost or Snow............................137. H.340, 18
Kil'd by a frost or by a flame.................155. H.406, 6
Like to a Deaw, or melted Frost...............233. H.670, 27
Here Winter-like, to Frost and Snow..........329. H.1093, 4
Or thou by frost, or I by quenchlesse fire:.....333. H.1120, 4
Thou bring'st vnto his bedd A frost............409. A.2, 86
With as cold frost, as erst we mett with fire;...414. A.6, 10
Frost-bound-blood The frost-bound-blood, and spirits; and to make.......................................45. H.128, 26
Frosts Fled are the Frosts, and now the Fields appeare
224. H.642, 1
Ile sing no more of Frosts, Snowes, Dews and Showers;
228. H.658, 3
Frost-work Like Frost-work glitt'ring on the Snow.
92. H.223, 67
Froth Of all the raging Waves, into a froth......152. H.389, 2
That mars uncomely froth might not molest.....386. N.193, 3
Onely, there's left a little froth,...............400. N.266, 12
Frown Thy frown (last night) did bid me goe;...33. H.103, 3
Frown, and look sullen ev'ry where............72. H.185, 4
And no one mischief greater then your frown,..188. H.506, 13
Nor need we here to feare the frowne.........190. H.515, 33
The least grim looke, or cast a frown on you:..222. H.634, 8
Do's she smile, or do's she frowne:...........253. H.750, 5
Say, do's she frown? still countermand her threats:
270. H.820, 3
Neglecting once to cast a frown on those......372. N.116, 3
Frowned Who padling there, the Sea soone frown'd,
294. H.937, 3
Frowns Why frowns my Sweet? Why won't my Saint confer
77. H.197, 25
Froze — — — — — — — —, ...426. var. H 197, 44
Frozen All the floods, and frozen seas?...........40. H.115, 8
When a mans Faith is frozen up, as dead;.......359. N.80, 1
Frozen wth Greife; and place it in thyne eare,..412. A.3, 82
Fruit Fruit, ye know, is comming on:............74. H.189, 4
The Fruit to grow up, or the Tree:.............79. H.198, 2
Mon. Troth, bad are both; worse fruit, and ill the tree:
159. H.421, 2
Then, may your Plants be prest with Fruit,.....179. H.476, 16
Here's golden fruit that farre exceeds all price....406. A.1, 71
Doing's, the Fruite of Doinge well, Farwell....412. A.3, 104
— — — — — — — — — — —, ...423. var. H.128, 7
Fruitful Praise me, for having such a fruitfull wombe;
58. H.151, 3
Faire pledges of a fruitfull Tree,...............176. H.467, 1
O fruitfull Genius! that bestowest here.........242. H.713, 7
Errour is fruitfull, Truth is onely one..........316. H.1031, 2
— — — — — — — — — — —, ...442. var. H.575, 9
Fruition Is, the fruition of a wife:..............35. H.106, 32
Fruitless The Birth is fruitlesse: Chor. Then the work God speed...365. N.97, 19
Fruits See First-fruits
To find that Tree of Life, whose Fruits did feed,.61. H.161, 1
For joy, to see the fruits ye reape,..............127. H.319, 34
For more or lesse fruits they will bring,.......264. H.787, 3
Frumenty And here all tempting Frumentie.....101. H.250, 34
Frustrate Wo'd I frustrate, or prevent............286. H.897, 5
Fry To slack these flames wherein I frie?.........40. H.115, 2
I frie in fire, and so consume.................50. H.140, 3
Come, and coole ye; all who frie...............62. H.162, 2

And 'gainst your chast behaviour there's no Plea, 189. H.511, 3
'Gainst thou go'st a mothering,................236. H.684, 2
I brake thy Bracelet 'gainst my will;..........240. H.705, 1
We pray 'gainst Warre, yet we enjoy no Peace.264. H.793, 1
'Gainst all the indignation of the Times........280. H.869, 2
Of sin, we must strive 'gainst the streame of it:.356. N.67, 2
When we 'gainst Satan stoutly fight, the more.372. N.116, 1
With God, then one, that never sin'd 'gainst Him. 388. N.205, 2
(Judgment and Death, denounc'd gainst Guilty men) 411. A.3, 62
Shooting his Eye-darts 'gainst it, to surprise...412. A.3, 77
— — — — — — — — —, ...441. var. H.465, 14
— — — — — — — — — — —, ...441. var. H.465, 55
Galbanum This Camphire, Storax, Spiknard, Galbanum: 157. H.414, 2
Gale But thou at home without or tyde or gale,.36. H.106, 77
Upon the Seas, though with a gentle gale.......212. H.601, 2
Gall It must not gall,.........................65. H.172, 10
Or gall.......................................172. H.458, 11
Is, when loves hony has a dash of gall.........327. H.1084, 2
The Myrrhe, the Gall, the Vineger:............400. N.266, 9
The Vineger, the Myrrhe, the Gall:............400. N.267, 11
Nor gall the seas,.......................436. ins. H.336, 48e
Gallant See Topgallant
That gallant Tulip will hang down his head,....41. H.118, 3
And a gallant Cock shall be...................122. H.302, 5
Or gallant Newark; which brave two...........218. H.626, 12
Of that sweet Lady, or that gallant Knight:....228. H.658, 2
Gallantry Now swaggers in her Leavy gallantry...224. H.642, 6
Gallants That flow of Gallants which approach...239. H.696, 1
Galled Well; though my griefe by you was gall'd, the more; 52. H.146, 21
Galleys To the Gallies there to Rowe;..........219. H.628, 2
Game Many a Teaster by his game, and bets:....154. H.400, 2
Following with love and active heate thy game,..301. H.966, 7
Without due reverence, playes the cheaters game..347. N.39, 6
Gamesome Ever gamesome as an ape:..........306. H.984, 29
Can I be gamesome (aged now)..............329. H.1093, 2
Gander Since Gander did his prettie Youngling wed; 223. H.636, 1
Gander (they say) doth each night pisse a Bed:.223. H.636, 2
What is the cause? Why Gander will reply,.....223. H.636, 3
Garbage In-laid Garbage ev'ry where............76. H.195, 6
Garded See Guarded
Garden That wets her Garden when it raines:....279. H.867, 2
Christ was not sad, i'th garden, for His own....381. N.159, 1
Which like a garden manifestly show............404. A.1, 15
Garden-glories Like to these Garden-glories, which here be 193. H.522, 3
Gardens See Pean-gardens
Gardens thence produce and Meads:...........108. H.266, 14
Garden's-glory The gardens-glory liv'd a while,....126. H.318, 4
Garland See Willow garland
Amar. A Garland for my Gift shall be.........86. H.213, 36
As lately I a Garland bound,...................96. H.229, 1
Give both the Gold and Garland unto it.........141. H.359, 16
Carry the Garland from the rest...............192. H.521, 34
A little Garland fits a little Head:............249. H.733, 8
Garlands See Willow garlands
For to say truth, all Garlands are thy due;......41. H.117, 9
To make for others garlands; and to set.........94. H.224, 3
Put on your Garlands first, then Sacrifice:.....124. H.313, 8
With Garlands drest, so I.....................161. H.425, 10
Thy May-poles too with Garlands grac't:.......230. H.662, 53
I'le drink to the Garlands a-round it:.........239. H.695, 3
Are the Garlands, Is the Nard.................280. H.870, 7
Of which make Garlands here, and there,.......289. H.912, 3
And Garlands shar'd,.........................369. N.106, 5
Where, drest with garlands, there they walk the ground, 417. A.8, 29
Garlic Help from the Garlick, Onyon, and the Leek, 78. H.197, 58
My chives of Garlick for an offering:..........132. H.333, 6
And Garlick chives not scarcely:...............234. H.674, 4
Garments When flowing garments I behold......311. H.1010, 1
Farewell the Coats, the Garments, and........374. N.123, 43
Will shew these garments made by thee;.......375. N.123, 82
Those Garments lasting evermore,..............393. N.231, 1
Garters Your Garters; and their joynts..........114. H.283, 79
Gloves, Garters, Stockings, Shooes, and Strings.193. H.521, 52
Gate Came one unto my gate,.....................26. H.81, 3
First, at the entrance of the gate,...............91. H.223, 38
Thus, like a Roman Tribune, thou thy gate....147. H.377, 45
Where Rust and Cobwebs bind the gate;.........179. H.476, 29
Shut every gate; mend every hedge that's torne,.259. H.771, 5
High is the roof there; but the gate is low:......362. N.89, 2
Come in, or force the gate.....................370. N.111, 8
(Though ne're so rich) all beggars at His Gate..383. N.171, 2
Gates All bolts, all barres, all gates shall cleave; as when 52. H.146, 14
But from thy warm-love-hatching gates each may.146. H.377, 15
Give way, give way ye Gates, and win.........178. H.476, 1
But yet those blessed gates I see...............277. H.854, 3
Open thy gates...............................370. N.111, 1
Gather The eager Boyes to gather Nuts.........56. H.149, 122
Gather ye Rose-buds while ye may,.............84. H.208, 1
To gather Flowers Sappha went,...............250. H.740, 1
Paradise is (as from the Learn'd I gather).......383. N.177, 1
Gathering But gathering Roses as she was;.....281. H.876, 5
The Gathering of the Lipp: not hand...........408. A.2, 52
Gave Who gave him forth good Grain, though he mistook 4. Ap., 3
Gave them their ever flourishing.................25. H.78, 10
And gave the Bag between them................31. H.92, 12
With that Heav'n gave thee with a warie hand,..35. H.106, 23
That Earth-quake shook the house, and gave the stout 52. H.146, 15
Gave her a day of Coronation;.................94. H.224, 6
Which gave me honour for my Rhimes,........136. H.336, 150
My wreaths on those, who little gave or lent....143. H.365, 6
Gave them Hearts-ease turn'd to Flow'rs.........152. H.391, 8
That gave thee this so high inheritance.........152. H.392, 6
This ball of Cow-slips, these she gave me here...159. H.421, 16
Then but to breath, and every one gave way:..200. H.551, 4
The first-Fruits give to them, who gave.........226. H.647, 3
That little, Fates me gave or lent...............246. H.724, 8
Her Apron gave (as she did passe)..............251. H.740, 9
That gave Progermination unto them:...........251. H.745, 8
And gave a Twist to me.......................278. H.863, 4
And gave my Love a fall.......................288. H.908, 4
He askt an almes; I gave him bread,...........295. H.942, 5
Snatcht off his Crown, and gave the wreath to me: 313. H.1017, 12
Of Julia Herrick gave to me my Birth........316. H.1028, 16
One Birth their Parents gave them; but their new, 326. H.1080, 25
With that small stock, Thy Bounty gave or lent. 368. N.104, 12
Which gave his Elveships stomacke ease....435. ins. H.293, x
Gavest Thou gav'st me life, (but Mortall;) For that one 27. H.82, 13
Thou gav'st me leave to kisse;.................142. H.364, 1
Thou gav'st me leave to wooe;.................142. H.364, 2
Gav'st See Gavest
Gay He's double honour'd, since h'as got gay cloathes: 330. H.1099, 2
Gaze But why? why longer doe I gaze upon......45. H.128, 37
For, if we gaze on These brave Lamps too neer,.237. H.685, 11
Gazing Then no gazing more about,...............180. H.482, 3
— — — — — — — — —, ...424. ins. H.128, 46a
Gelli-flowers See Gillyflowers, July-flowers
Gellye See Jelly
Gem Jem to enrich her store;...................43. H.123, 14
See, see a Jemme (as rare as Bælus eye.)......172. H.459, 8
One jemme was lost; and I will get............240. H.705, 5
A Jem in this eternall Coronet:................264. H.789, 2
Rich is the Jemme that thou did'st send,.......376. N.125, 5
The gem is grac'd? or they grac'd by the Jemme? 405. A.1, 42
Gemmenayath's — — — — — — — —, ...450. var. A.9, 34
Gems Jems, then those two, that went before:......23. H.70, 6
Gemms in abundance upon you:.................68. H.178, 20
Say, if there be 'mongst many jems here; one....76. H.194, 3
Can make reflected from these jems,...........167. H.443, 79
The Palms put forth their Gemmes, and every Tree 224. H.642, 5
Lesse by their own jemms, then those beams of thine. 234. H.673, 18
For thee with richest Jemmes to shine,.........323. H.1068, 15
— — — — — — — — — — —, ...425. var. H.197, 11
G'en See Given
Daffadills g'en up to Thee.....................122. H.304, 8
'Gender See Engender
Or let me 'gender with eternall frost...........40. H.113, 6
General By th'hand of him who is the Generall.....50. H.141, 2
To the gen'rall Session;.......................373. N.121, 6
Which must produce me to that Gen'rall Doome,.392. N.230, 23
To me, as to the gen'rall Doome,...............393. N.232, 2
(The generall Aprill of the worlde) dothe Come, 410. A.3, 34
Generation To be A Rockie Generation!...........29. H.86, 10
Here with the Generation of my Just...........231. H.664, 6
Generations To shoot forth Generations like to them. 170. H.451, 4
While other generations dye....................288. H.906, 4
Generous Thanks to the gen'rous Vine;..........72. H.185, 27
Full goblets of thy gen'rous blood; his spright...78. H.197, 67
Genial In every Geniall Cup,....................184. H.492, 38
Genii What Genii support thy roofe,............148. H.377, 98
Genius Most great, and universall Genius!..........25. H.77, 2
While soft Opinion makes thy Genius say,......37. H.106, 115
And Genius who attends..........................54. H.149, 43
My Genius with a fuller blandishment?..........78. H.197, 56
Gratifie the Genius.............................96. H.231, 6
Unto the Genius of the house...................135. H.336, 128
As to thy Genius and thy Larre;...............146, H.377, 4
Thy lucky Genius, and thy guiding Starre,.......181. H.483, 5
O fruitfull Genius! that bestowest here.........242. H.713, 7
Command the Roofe great Genius, and from thence 245. H.723, 1

Thy Genius with two strength'ning Buttresses,..252. H.745, 18
And Genius waits to have us both to bed.......261. H.781, 6
Our Fate, our Fortune, and our Genius;........300. H.961, 14
The Genius wastefull, more then free:..........310. H.1004, 2
Gentle See Love-gentle
Love strikes, but 'tis with gentle crueltie..........16. H.40, 4
Loving, and gentle for to cover me:..............19. H.52, 2
A gentle disposition then:......................42. H.121, 2
Glide, gentle streams, and beare................43. H.123, 1
Gentle friends, though I despaire................62. H.162, 16
Let them speak by gentle tones,..................82. H.203, 9
Play I co'd once; but (gentle friend) you see....84. H.210, 1
And lend a gentle eare to one report............86. H.213, 11
Gentle friends, then doe but please,..............88. H.218, 7
A gentle mind to be unchaste.................175. H.465, 46
I want beliefe; O gentle Silvia, be............204. H.570, 3
Upon the Seas, though with a gentle gale.........212. H.601, 2
Sweet words must nourish soft and gentle Love..222. H.633, 61
What gentle Winds perspire? As if here.........224. H.642, 9
The gentle Dove may, when these turmoils cease.
225. H.642, 21
Whom gentle fate translated hence.............226. H.644, 5
The gentle Beams from Julia's sight............237. H.687, 3
You see this gentle streame, that glides,.........244. H.720, 1
Ph. Charon! O gentle Charon! let me wooe thee,
248. H.730, 1
(For gentle feare, or jelousie)................265. H.798, 10
If thou compos'd of gentle mould..............272. H.828, 13
With gentle lambs-wooll;......................317. H.1035, 20
That Prince must govern with a gentle hand,....323. H.1067, 1
My gentle God,...............................353. N.56, 22
Instead of that, a sweet and gentle word:........356. N.71, 2
A gentle calme did follow....................373. N.122, 8
Of gentle Paste, and yeelding Dow,............374. N.123, 25
When I Thy gentle Heart do see...............400. N.267, 3
To cloath thy words in gentle Ayre............408. A.2, 54
Cha. I will be gentle as that Air which yeelds......416. A.8, 7
— — — — — — — — — —, ...432. var. H.283, 88
— — — — — — — — — — —, ...432. var. H.283, 96
Gentle-heart But for Prick-madam, and for Gentle-heart;
114.H.283, 96
Gentle-licking Into a gentle-licking flame,.........95. H.227, 14
Gentlemen Much good do't ye Gentlemen.........118. H.289, 12
Gentleness (Farther then Gentlenes tends) gets place
114. H.283, 83
Gently Then gently lead her on.................55. H.149, 77
Which, circumvolving gently, there..............64. H.169, 3
More gently stroaks the sight,..................75. H.193, 18
Which, gently gleaming, makes a show,..........92. H.223, 66
Fall gently, gently, and a while him keep.........99. H.244, 5
Not all at once, but gently, as the trees..........100. H.247, 3
But gently prest from the soft side............120. H.293, 49
And as it flyes, it gently sings,................130. H.329, 22
To blush and gently smile;....................176. H.467, 5
Shall gently melt thee into dreames..............192. H.521, 8
That gently purles from eithers Oat............243. H.716, 18
Gently kill'd by Flatterie.......................264. H.790, 4
Me thought I saw them stir, and gently move,..326. H.1080, 11
My sinnes, by gently striking;..................363. N.92, 9
Touch gently, gently touch; and here............366. N.97, 20
Come then, and gently touch the Birth..........366. N.98, 18
Correct my errors gently with Thy Rod............398. N.261, 4
And lays it gently on ye Pyle,..................413. A.4, 28
gently thereon,..........................430. ins. H.283, 20e
Gently-gliding His gently-gliding, Dove-like eyes,..365. N.97, 13
George-a-Green So good as George-a-Green;......259. H.772, 22
Gesture What Gesture, Courtship; Comliness agrees,
148. H.377, 95
Get Now strength, and newer Purple get,............7. H.9, 3
To get thine ends, lay bashfulnesse aside;...........8. H.12, 1
When no force else can get the masterdome........21. H.60, 2
Get up, get up for shame, the Blooming Morne....67. H.178, 1
Get up, sweet-Slug-a-bed, and see................67. H.178, 5
Gifts will get ye, or the man...................121. H.297, 14
On, as thou hast begunne, brave youth, and get..150. H.384, 1
But yet get chilren (as the neighbours say.)......156. H.411, 2
Get their comportment, and the gliding tongue..172. H.456, 5
That season co'd get,.........................195. H.534, 5
Rake the Fier up, and get......................201. H.556, 3
To gaine her whom I wo'd get..................209. H.585, 6
Ile get me hence,.............................213. H.609, 1
Put on all shapes to get a Love:.............215. H.616, 16
Us hands to get what here we have.............226. H.647, 4
None loseth that, which he in time may get.......228. H.654, 2
Thy witty wiles to draw, and get..............231. H.662, 64
But if (my Sweetest) I shall get,..............238. H.690, 9
One jemme was lost; and I will get............240. H.705, 5
To get thy Steerling, once again,..............244. H.716, 37
Wo'd ye oyle of Blossomes get?................244. H.719, 1
What wo'd she give to get that soule agen?.....266. H.801, 4
The reason is, his credit cannot get............302. H.969, 3
Still shall I crave, and never get..............312. H.1014, 3
Things are uncertain, and the more we get,....316. H.1032, 1
Good wits get more fame by their punishment...317. H.1034, 2
Who thither come, and freely get................350. N.47, 15
And all sweet Meades; from whence we get......360. N.83, 17
— — — — — — — — — — —, ...440. var. H.443, 79

Gets Once gets a force, Floods cannot quench the flame.
40. H.113, 4
Batt he gets children, not for love to reare 'em;..72. H.184, 1
(Farther then Gentlenes tends) gets place......114. H.283, 83
But let that speak, the Client gets the suit.......123. H.308, 2
Raspe playes at Nine-holes; and 'tis known he gets
154. H.400, 1
When one hole wasts more then he gets by Nine.
154. H.400, 4
(What gets the master of the Meal by that?)....191. H.518, 4
Getting All thoughts, but such as aime at getting Princes,
77. H.197, 8
The higher he's a getting;......................84. H.208, 6
The coblers getting time, is at the Last..........144. H.374, 2
Gettings But of his gettings there's but little sign;
154. H.400, 3
Ghost Then shall my Ghost not walk about, but keep.9. H.14, 17
Unto thy Ghost, th' Effused Offering:.............27. H.82, 8
Since Ghost ther's none to affright thee.........217. H.619, 10
When thence ye see my reverend Ghost to rise,..222. H.634, 3
The ghost from the Tomb......................225. H.643, 22
(Which from his ghost a promise is)...........226. H.644, 8
'Twixt God the Father, Holy Ghost, and Sonne:.386. N.191, 4
Ghost-like That makes them looke so lanke, so Ghost-like still.
186. H.498, 6
Ghost-like, as in my meaner sepulcher;..........371. N.115, 4
Ghosts Whose restlesse Ghosts shall heare their children sing,
252. H.745, 9
Giblets Essay of other giblets; make...........146. H.377, 28
Gift Amar. A Garland for my Gift shall be.......86. H.213, 36
Love bade me aske a gift,.....................100. H.249, 1
We send in stead of New-yeares gift...........127. H.319, 26
Can't send for a gift.........................256. H.762, 14
Offer thy gift; but first the Law commands......299. H.957, 1
The richest New-yeeres Gift to me..............355. N.60, 6
Of Gift from God: And heres my Creed.........359. N.78, 16
'Tis a gift for Christ His sake:..................363. N.93, 2
Be the best New-yeares Gift to all.............366. N.98, 24
For New-yeers gift to thee....................376. N.125, 4
But yet this Gift Thou wilt commend,..........376. N.125, 7
Gifts Gifts will get ye, or the man...............121. H.297, 14
Gifts will be sent, and Letters, which...........174. H.465, 23
His gifts go from him; if not bought with sweat..177. H.469, 2
For those gifts you do conferre................182. H.489, 12
Such be our gifts, and such be our expence,......295. H.940, 3
Ans. Love gifts will send ye:................310. H.1001, 10
His gifts, to exercise Petitioners:................344. N.30, 2
Gifts blind the wise, and bribes do please,........357. N.72, 9
Gods Hands are round, & smooth, that gifts may fall
380. N.151, 1
Gifts to my Saviours Sepulcher;...............402. N.270, 2
Gild And Star-like, once more, guild our Firmament.
52. H.146, 12
Guild still with flames this Firmament, and be....94. H.226, 5
Since Clouds disperst, Suns guild the Aire again.
105. H.259, 2
The paper gild, and Laureat the pen...........141. H.359, 6
No Widowes Tenement was rackt to guild......149. H.377, 119
And guild the Baies and Rosemary:...........215. H.616, 26
To guild thy Tombe; besides, these Caules......360. N.83, 43
and guild the field......................432. ins. H.283, 140e
— — — — — — — — —, ...453. ins. H.283, 20b
Gilded When Gloves are giving, Guilded be you there.
180. H.479, 2
With gilded hornes, and burnisht cleere.........243. H.716, 15
Gilds Smiles to it selfe, and guilds the roofe with mirth;
7. H.8, 6
So double gilds the Aire, as that no night......206. H.575, 15
Gilead In Gilead though no Balme be found,......342. N.17, 5
Gillyflowers They were two Gelli-flowers..........74. H.192, 4
Make Gelli-flowers, then......................74. H.192, 7
As Gilly flowers do but stay....................126. H.318, 1
Gilthead With mullet, Turbot, guilthead bought
436. ins. H.336, 48g
Gimmals Return'd a Ring of Jimmals, to imply....173. H.464, 2
Gin Some gin, wherewith to catch your eyes.....114. H.283, 70
No ginne to catch the State, or wring..........126. H.319, 7
Ginger Adde sugar, nutmeg and ginger,..........317. H.1035, 21
Ginger-bread That doted on a Maide of Gingerbred:
155. H.405, 10
'Gins Of a Pease, that 'gins to chit,............223. H.638, 13
Gins — — — — — — — —, ...453. var. H.283, 70
Gird To gird my loynes about....................352. N.53, 11
Girdle — — — — — — — —, ...439. var. H.443, 37
Girl Or to a Girle (that keeps the Neat)...........6. H.2, 13
Then spoke I to my Girle,.........................24. H.75, 6
To that coy Girle;..............................43. H.123, 3
There's not a budding Boy, or Girle, this day,....69. H.178, 43
Goddesse, I do love a Girle.....................136. H.337, 1
Jone is a Girle that's tainted;..................229. H.659, 2
Jane is a Girle that's prittie;..................229. H.659, 6
Be my Girle, or faire or browne,...............253. H.750, 4
For (trust me Girle) shee ouer-does.............409. A.2, 81
— — — — — — — — — — —, ...429. var. H.260, 6
Girls Of those Girles, which cruell are...........62. H.162, 18
Sickly Girles, they beare of you.................64. H.167, 4

Poore Girles, neglected........................83. H.205, 16
Poore Girles, she fell on you;..................105. H.260, 6
Dropt from the eyes of ravisht Girles...........167. H.443, 109
Jealous Girles these sometimes were,...........187. H.503, 1
Cast on my Girles a glance, and loving eye:....222. H.634, 11
A health to my Girles,.........................239. H.695, 7
White as Zenobias teeth, the which the Girles...251. H.741, 1
T'ave Boyes, and Gyrles too, as they will.......291. H.919, 12
To prettie girles to play withall:...............294. H.937, 2
And I ere long, my Girles shall see,............329. H.1093, 5
For my Locks (Girles) let 'em be...............330. H.1098, 3
Girt Girt with small bones, instead of walls.....90. H.223, 10
Give For pitties sake give your advice,...............8. H.13, 3
That I must give thee the supremest kisse;........9. H.14, 6
Give my dead picture one engendring kisse:.......14. H.35, 12
To give (if any, yet) but little sound.............15. H.38, 8
Give them the scent of Amber-Greece:.............20. H.54, 2
Love give me more such nights as these...........20. H.56, 10
If meat the Gods give, I the steame...............22. H.66, 1
Give me a kisse, and to that kisse a score;.........24. H.74, 3
Were I to give thee Baptime, I wo'd chuse........28. H.84, 1
Give me that man, that dares bestride............30. H.90, 1
Ile write, because Ile give.......................32. H.96, 1
By sudden death to give me ease:..............34. H.103, 14
Twilight is yet, till that her Lawnes give way;....34. H.104, 5
Led by thy conscience; to give..................35. H.106, 12
In thee, thou Man of Men! who here do'st give...41. H.117, 4
O! give them active heat.......................57. H.149, 125
That good, which Heav'n can give...............57. H.149, 153
Give my cold lips a kisse at last:...............61. H.159, 25
Nor any bed to give the shew..................63. H.164, 10
To give the least disturbance to her haire:.......82. H.204, 2
Then Ile give o're,...........................85. H.211, 3
And quickly give, the swiftest Grace is best.......87. H.213, 46
Which charity they give to many...............92. H.223, 89
And give me such reposes,.....................95. H.227, 18
To give Perenn'as lip a kisse,..................103. H.255, 3
Your Walks with Flowers, and give their Crowns to you.
107. H.265, 8
Or bid me love, and I will give................108. H.267, 3
That heart Ile give to thee......................108. H.267, 8
The Gods to Kings the Judgement give to sway:..109. H.269, 1
And there to give the cheek a die...............118. H.291, 7
Give her strewings; but not stir................123. H.310, 5
With speed give sick men their salvation:......125. H.315, 2
To give that life, resign'd your own:............126. H.318, 9
Give up thy soule in clouds of frankinsence......128. H.320, 6
Though I cannot give thee fires................129. H.324, 1
Give thou my lips but their supreamest kiss:....129. H.327, 2
To give an incorruption unto me................129. H.327, 6
Give up the just applause to verse:...........136. H.336, 136
Yet ere ye enter, give us leave to set..........140. H.354, 3
Or no, shall give ye a re-meeting here...........140. H.355, 8
Your sometime Poet; but if fates do give......140. H.355, 11
Give both the Gold and Garland unto it.......141. H.359, 16
Give me the Daphne, that the world may know it,
143. H.365, 7
Not represent, but give reliefe.................146. H.377, 10
Can give, and what retract a grace;............148. H.377, 94
To give subsistance to thy house, and proofe,..148. H.377, 97
Part of which I give to Larr,..................152. H.393, 5
Give me my Mistresse, as she is,................154. H.402, 3
Sweet Bents wode bow, to give my Love the day:
159. H.421, 24
To give an end: Mir. To what? Scil. Such griefs as these.
159. H.421, 12
And give me meate, or give me else thy Plate....161. H.424, 4
The Fairie Court I give to thee:................165. H.443, 2
Give unto Love the straiter way...............167. H.443, 111
Besides I give Thee here a Verse that shall......168. H.444, 2
Or give me back my heart......................168. H.446, 8
Give way, give way to me, who come...........169. H.449, 9
And somewhat give,..........................171. H.455, 2
Give way, give way ye Gates, and win...........178. H.476, 1
Julia's Breast can give you them:...............183. H.491, 2
And give a righteous judgement upon it.........187. H.506, 4
For meat, shall give thee melody...............192. H.521, 18
Ile give thee Chaines and Carkanets............192. H.521, 19
The Muse give thee the Delphick Coronet........194. H.529, 2
Give way, and be ye ravisht by the Sun,........196. H.537, 1
Give me one kisse,..........................196. H.538, 1
Law is to give to ev'ry one his owne...........201. H.557, 10
Give me words wherewith to wooe,..............204. H.569, 7
And give it to the Silvan Deitie................205. H.573, 4
Candles Ile give to thee,......................213. H.604, 9
Give Want her welcome if she comes; we find,....213. H.605, 1
What Gloves we'l give, and Ribanings:........216. H.616, 28
Give me wine, and give me meate,..............217. H.620, 1
Give me these, (my Knight) and try............217. H.620, 7
Who'l give ye then a sheltring shed,...........218. H.626, 3
But give thy place to night,...................220. H.633, 9
Give them the blessing of encrease:............221. H.633, 55
Give me my earthen Cups again,...............222. H.635, 9
Give an Almes to one that's poore,..............223. H.638, 2
Give me then an Ant to eate;...................223. H.638, 5
Give for bread, a little bit.....................223. H.638, 12
For an Almes; then give me such.............223. H.638, 22
The first-Fruits give to them, who gave..........226. H.647, 3
Hast thou begun an act? ne're then give o're:....236. H.680, 1
Half that blessing thou'lt give me..............236. H.684, 4
Give way, give way, now, now my Charles shines here,
236. H.685, 1
Now give me the cup;........................239. H.695, 2
Give thou my sacred Reliques Buriall...........242. H.713, 20
To give the prize to thee, or me................243. H.716, 6
Give me the prize: The day is mine:...........244. H.716, 43
But toyes, to give my heart some ease:........246. H.724, 30
Ph. Ile give thee vows & tears. Ch. can tears pay skores
248. H.730, 19
Pauls hands do give, what give they bread or meat,
248. H.731, 1
As stones and salt gloves use to give, even so....248. H.731, 3
Pauls hands do give, nought else for ought we know.
248. H.731, 4
As sweetly Lady, give me leave to tell ye,......249. H.733, 17
When These can aske, and Kings can give no more.
255. H.758, 4
Give the Tapers here their light,................258. H.769, 7
Give me a Cell..............................258. H.770, 1
And richer Wine wo'dst give to me (thy guest)..262. H.783, 5
As you doe give them Wassailing...............264. H.787, 4
Give me the food that satisfies a Guest:........265. H.797, 1
Wo'd give (some say) her soule unto the Devill...266. H.801, 2
What wo'd she give to get that soule agen?......266. H.801, 4
Give me a reason why men call.................273. H.832, 1
Ai me! I love, give him your hand to kisse......274. H.837, 1
Three, unto whom the whole world give applause;
276. H.851, 7
Give house-roome to the best; 'Tis never known..293. H.935, 1
What credit can we give to seas,................294. H.937, 5
We must not give all to the hallowed fire........295. H.940, 2
Then boldly give thine incense to the fire........299. H.957, 4
This shall my love doe, give thy sad death one..302. H.967, 3
'Tis now his habit, which he can't give ore......302. H.972, 2
If we take it, as they give it...................306. H.987, 4
And (Noble friend) this answer I must give:...312. H.1013, 2
And Ile Roses give to thee.....................313. H.1018, 4
Give S. Distaffe all the right,..................315. H.1026, 11
Give then to the King.........................317. H.1035, 25
Give me a man that is not dull,.................318. H.1036, 1
Danger to give the best advice to Kings.........318. H.1037, 2
Ile give, if thou deny me......................321. H.1055, 4
Since Absolution you can give to them..........322. H.1062, 9
My Lamp to you Ile give,......................328. H.1091, 7
I will give them thanks for it..................329. H.1096, 4
Give thee the Laurell Crowne for lot;..........334. H.1123, 4
Here give me thornes; there, in thy Kingdome, set
343. N.25, 5
There give me day; but here my dreadfull night:.343. N.25, 7
Give Thee a Dart, and Dagger too;..............349. N.46, 4
Nor shalt thou give so deep a wound,............351. N.48, 9
How am I bound to Two! God, who doth give...355. N.62, 1
Give me Honours: what are these,..............355. N.64, 1
Give Him the choice; grant Him the nobler part....356. N.68, 3
Give, if thou canst, an Almes; if not, afford,......356. N.71, 1
And give the honour to this Day,..............364. N.96, 9
Which we will give Him; and bequeath..........365. N.96, 29
And when night comes, wee'l give Him wassailing:
368. N.102, 22
Give a wave-offring unto Thee..................377. N.130, 4
To give us more then Hope can fix upon........378. N.135, 2
Give unto all, lest he, whom thou deni'st,........391. N.226, 1
To heare the Judge give sentence on the Throne,.392. N.230, 25
Then He will give a happy end to it............396. N.252, 4
Loe! Thus I give a Virgin-Flower,..............402. N.270, 5
Seene to the world, Ile giue the skore..........407. A.2, 2
I give thee this that shall withstande............407. A.2, 10
Or lyke as woole meetes steele, giue way..........408. A.2, 69
Giue vpp his worth: to the painte;..............409. A.2, 80
O thou Allmightye Nature, who did'st giue......410. A.3, 29
Apollo sings, his harpe resounds; give roome,......415. A.7, 1
Cha. Prethee relate, while I give ear and weep.....416. A.8, 12
knowne, not thay giue againe, thay take....422. ins. H.106, 92f
Given See G'en
Many a green-gown has been given;............69. H.178, 51
That having ease me given,....................95. H.227, 29
Stripes justly given yerk us (with their fall)....319. H.1050, 1
Lord, Thou hast given me a cell................349. N.47, 1
To mount my Soule, she must have pineons given;
352. N.52, 3
Heaven is not given for our good works here:....390. N.223, 1
Yet it is given to the Labourer................390. N.223, 2
Given by none, but by Thy selfe, to me:........398. N.262, 2
When this to that, and that, to this, had giuen.....410. A.3, 3
Gives He Acts the Crime, that gives it Cherishing...10. H.17, 2
Whose crack gives crushing unto all.............25. H.76, 4
Gives thee each night a Maidenhead...........35. H.106, 42
To Jove who gives, and takes away:..............59. H.153, 2
Devotion gives each House a Bough,............68. H.178, 32
The flower that gives me nourishing:.............71. H.182, 20
When once he gives it incarnation?.............139. H.347, 4
What gives it hanging in the Aire............167. H.443, 105

Then **gives** it to the children to devoure...........203. H.561, 2
Then to the poore she freely **gives** the milke.....203. H.561, 4
Now tis in's Hand, he **gives** no Almes at all.......207. H.577, 4
He **gives** an almes, and chides them from his doore. 220. H.632, 2
Gives to each Mead a neat enameling...........224. H.642, 4
Too much she **gives** to some, enough to none.....238. H.689, 2
Fate **gives** a meeting. Death's the end of woe.....257. H.766, 2
Repullulation **gives** me here...................265. H.794, 4
Conformity **gives** comelinesse to things.........318. H.1040, 1
Instead of Bread, Grubs **gives** them stones to eat. 325. H.1077, 4
So where He **gives** the bitter Pills, be sure,.......344. N.31, 3
Happy's that man, to whom God **gives**..........351. N.50, 1
Of suffring **gives** me patience....................354. N.57, 4
God **gives** not onely corne, for need,.............356. N.66, 1
He **gives** not poorly, taking some...............356. N.66, 5
By Thee, Deare God, God **gives** man seed........358. N.75, 7
Gives me a portion, giving patience:............362. N.87, 2
He patience gives; He **gives** himselfe to me........362. N.87, 4
What God **gives**, and what we take,.............363. N.93, 1
Gives life and luster, publike mirth,............364. N.96, 20
Is that which **gives** to sin a livelihood.............367. N.101, 2
And **gives** His Children kisses then, not stripes...379. N.139, 2
Unlesse God **gives** the Benedicite...............379. N.140, 2
God **gives** to none so absolute an Ease,..........387. N.199, 1
Man to th' alluring object **gives** his will.........392. N.230, 32
Gives them by turnes their grief and jollitie.......394. N.236, 4
God, who me **gives** a will for to repent,..........397. N.255, 1
Gives it estimation.............................417. A.9, 6
Fire unto all my functions, **gives** me blood,.426. ins. H.197, 48c
— — — — — — — — — — — —, ...432. var. H.283, 106
But what she **gives** not, she not takes,.....436. ins. H.336, 48o
Givest Unlesse thou **giv'st** my small Remains an Urne. 19. H.52, 4
And **giv'st** our Numbers Euphonie, and weight...297. H.947, 6
And **giv'st** me Wassaile Bowles to drink,........350. N.47, 39
And **giv'st** me, for my Bushell sowne,...........350. N.47, 43
— — — — — — — — — — — —, ...426. ins. H.197, 48c
Giving When Gloves are **giving**, Guilded be you there. 180. H.479, 2
By **giving** and receiving hold the play:..........255. H.758, 2
Gives me a portion, **giving** patience:............362. N.87, 2
Beyond its stinted circle; **giueing** foode..........410. A.3, 31
Gizzards The flimsie Livers, and blew **Gizzards** are. 326. H.1079, 2
Glad Of thy **glad** table: not a dish more known..147. H.377, 69
To whose **glad** threshold, and free door.........321. H.1056, 3
His soule to **glad** you in perfumes...............413. A.4, 35
of the **glad** house? come come............431. ins. H.283 60i
Glade Thou hast thy Cockrood, and thy **Glade**..231. H.662, 66
Gladder So soft streams meet, so springs with **gladder** smiles 77. H.197, 1
Gladding **Gladding** his pallat with some store....119. H.293, 35
For **gladding** so my hearth here,...............234. H.674, 7
Gladly And thousands **gladly** wish.............113. H.283, 49
As thou deserv'st, be proud; then **gladly** let.....194. H.529, 1
That **gladly** would...........................401. N.268, 34
Gladness Chor. The Caroll of our **gladnesse**.......375. N.123, 57
Glads Of sugered rush a **glads** him with.....434. ins. H.293, 41d
Glance Many a **glance** too has been sent........69. H.178, 53
Whose smile can make a Poet; and your **glance**..187. H.506, 9
Cast on my Girles a **glance**, and loving eye:....222. H.634, 11
Who with her eyes-gleam, or a **glance** of hand,.326. H.1080, 16
And though all joyes spring from the **glance**....395. N.246, 3
Glancing Kissing and **glancing**, soothing, all make way 24. H.74, 11
Glare Stoop, mount, pass by to take her eye, then **glare** 87. H.215, 5
Glares See **Out-glares**
Glaring Those **glaring** colours laid..............76. H.193, 45
No **glaring** light of bold-fac't Day,.............167. H.443, 76
Thy **glaring** fires, least in theire sight the sinne 424. ins. H.128, 46a
Glasco **Glasco** had none, but now some teeth has got; 46. H.129, 1
Glass See **Hourglass, Looking-glass, Under-glass**
To **Glasse**, and thy will send...................75. H.193, 26
A way enchac't with **glasse** & beads.............90. H.223, 1
Nor made of **glasse**, or wood, or stone,..........91. H.223, 56
No One that's there his guilty **glasse**..........148. H.377, 86
Glasse, out of deepe, and out of desp'rate want,..151. H.385, 1
A Vicarige at last Tom **Glasse** got here,..........151. H.385, 3
To'th' **Glasse** your lips encline;................185. H.495, 6
With Lillies Tomb'd up in a **Glasse**;..........186. H.497, 16
She brake in two the purer **Glasse**,..............187. H.504, 4
And emptied soon the **glasse**;..................222. H.635, 6
Yet ere thou counsel'st with thy **Glasse**,..........271. H.824, 5
Let me in my **Glasse** behold....................277. H.852, 2
Yet before the **glasse** be out,....................348. N.41, 35
As Sun-beames pierce the **glasse**, and streaming in, 385. N.184, 1
— — — — — — — — — — — —, ...424. var. H.164, 7
— — — — — — — — — — — —, ...424. var. H.164, 8
Glassing — — — — — — — — — —, ...440. var. H.443, 76
Gleam See **Eye's-gleam**
allready spillt, her rayes must **gleame**.....430. ins. H.283, 20d
Gleaming Which, gently **gleaming**, makes a show, 92. H.223, 66
Gleams Out-glares the Heav'ns *Osiris; and thy **gleams** 77. H.197, 11
Glebe Tread ore his **gleab**, but with such care that where 259. H.771, 7
Glib Yet let these **glib** temptations be...........174. H.465, 5
Glide **Glide**, gentle streams, and beare...........43. H.125, 1
Glide by the banks of Virgins then, and passe..113. H.283, 41
Like you a while: They **glide**..................176. H.467, 17
This I may do (perhaps) as I **glide** by,.........222. H.634, 10
And we **glide** hence away with them............233. H.670, 23
No more shall I a long thy christall **glide**,......315. H.1028, 7
Glided Or **glided** through the street)...............9. H.15, 10
I **glided** by my Parents sight....................69. H.180, 2
Glides You see this gentle streame, that **glides**,....244. H.720, 1
Gliding See **Gently-gliding**
Get their comportment, and the **gliding** tongue....172. H.456, 5
— — — — — — — — — — — —, ...434. ins. H.293, 41h
Glimmering By **glim'ring** of a fancie: Doe but come, 207. H.575, 55
Glitter And like the Starres to **glitter**...........323. H.1068, 16
Glittered Or **glitter'd** to my sight,...............181. H.484, 5
Glittering Like Frost-work **glitt'ring** on the Snow..92. H.223, 67
Glitt'ring with fire; where, for your mirth,......101. H.250, 27
With some small **glit'ring** gritt, to eate..........119. H.293, 10
Glit'ring to my free desires:...................129. H.324, 2
Warme by a **glit'ring** chimnie all the yeare.......132. H.333, 10
All sitting neer the **glitt'ring** Hearth.............193. H.521, 50
O how that **glittering** taketh me!..............261. H.779, 6
'Tis Thou that crown'st my **glittering** Hearth....350. N.47, 37
Globe Then like a **Globe**, or Ball of Wild-fire, flie,..87. H.215, 9
As in a **Globe** of Radiant fire, and grac't......207. H.575, 58
Globes Beares vp twoe **globes** where loue and pleasure sitt, 405. A.1, 52
Glories See **Garden-glories**
Full is my Book of **Glories**; but all These........3. Ded.H, 9
Betweene whose **glories**, there my lips Ile lay,...96. H.230, 3
Among which **glories**, (crown'd with sacred Bayes, 206. H.575, 49
With **Glories** to await here......................345. N.33, 27
Glorified Grac't (now at last) or **glorifi'd** by thee..142. H.365, 2
Glorifies And **glorifies** the worthy Conquerer.....200. H.553, 2
Glorious In all that great and **glorious** light,......49. H.136, 30
A **glorious** forme appeare to me:.................51. H.142, 6
The **glorious** Lamp of Heaven, the Sun,..........84. H.208, 5
A **glorious** end by such a Noose,..............279. H.863, 11
In them a **glorious** leprosie.......................311. H.1010, 4
Out of my self that **Glorious** Hierarchie!......326. H.1080, 2
That rides the **glorious** Cherubim.................340. N. 3, 16
And shaps my Function, for more **glorious** ends:..411. A.3, 58
Glory See **Garden's-glory**
And times to come shall, weeping, read thy **glory**,.89. H.219, 21
I see a Cloud of **Glory** fills my Book:............99. H.245, 4
The Subjects onely **glory** to obay.................109. H.269, 2
Star fill'd with **glory** to our view,..............112. H.283, 4
Who for true **glory** suffers thus; we grant......129. H.323, 15
Together with the Stages **glory** stood..........150. H.382, 3
No, not the **glory** of the world, Vandike.........150. H.384, 6
That my poore name may have the **glory**......170. H.449, 28
(Not without **glory**) Noble Sir, you are,.......170. H.451, 2
Is this his **Glory**? then his Triumph's Poore;....171. H.454, 3
The Grace, the **Glorie**, and the best...........189. H.515, 3
Which seals Thy **Glorie**; since I doe prefer....199. H.545, 9
Seldome comes **Glorie** till a man be dead........218. H.623, 2
Where, if such **glory** flashes from His Name,...237. H.685, 7
The **glory** of flowers that crown'd it...........239. H.695, 6
Glory no other thing is (Tullie sayes)..........241. H.710, 1
One onely **glory** of a million,..................256. H.763, 6
Glory be to the Graces!.......................260. H.777, 1
Glory and worship be!.........................261. H.778, 4
Of his **glory**. So farewell.....................289. H.910, 6
O Pompe of **Glory**! Welcome now, and come....300. H.961, 5
Since after death comes **glory**, Ile not haste.....314. H.1022, 2
The **Glory** of my Work, and Me.................339. N.2, 10
'Tis for our **glory**, that we did resist............356. N.67, 4
In Thy eternall **Glorie**.........................363. N.92, 6
Let but one beame of **Glory** on it shine,........371. N.113, 9
The more our Crownes of **Glory** there increase....372. N.119, 2
Nor can wee **glory** of a great..............436. ins. H.336, 48i
— — — — — — — — — — — —, ...441. var. H.465, 66
Gloves See **Draw-gloves**
When **Gloves** are giving, Guilded be you there...180. H.479, 2
Gloves, Garters, Stockings, Shooes, and Strings.193. H.521, 52
What **Gloves** we'l give, and Ribanings:.........216. H.616, 28
As stones and salt **gloves** use to give, even so...248. H.731, 3
Glow My spark sho'd **glow**,.....................137. H.340, 14
Whose little eyes **glow**,.........................217. H.619, 4
She seem'd to quench loves fires that there did **glow**. 251. H.742, 2
And **glow** like it.............................350. N.47, 26
Glowing To testifie the **glowing** of a spark?......78. H.197, 38
Glowworm Her Eyes the **Glow-worme** lend thee,..217. H.619, 1
Glowworm's And by the **glow-worms** light wel guided, 93. H.223, 141

The **glow-wormes** eyes; the shining scales......166. H.443, 72
But most of all the **glowwormes** fire.......434. ins. H.293, 41e
Glue The sure sweet-Sement, **Glue**, and Lime of Love. 218. H.622, 2
Glut But, for our **glut**, and for our store,.........356. N.66, 7
Gnat Not Virgil's **Gnat** had such a Tomb.........104. H.256, 21
The piping **Gnat** for minstralcy................119. H.293, 18
Not Virgils **Gnat**, to whom the Spring..........186. H.497, 9
Gnat's — — — — — — — — —, ...434. var. H.293, 37
Gnat's-watchword The **Gnats-watch-word** the Elves are gone. 168. H.443, 117
Go Stay then at home, and doe not **goe**............6. H.2, 19
I brake my bonds of Love, and bad thee **goe**,....6. H.3, 5
Colours **goe**, and colours come...................15. H.37, 4
I bade him not **goe** seek;......................18. H.45, 2
Goes the world now, it will with thee **goe** hard:..22. H.64, 1
Goe thou afore; and I shall well...............33. H.98, 5
Thy frown (last night) did bid me **goe**;.........33. H.103, 3
Wisdome and she together **goe**,................35. H.106, 14
To the Treasures, shall I **goe**,.................40. H.115, 3
When I did **goe** from thee, I felt that smart,....42. H.122, 1
To all thy witching beauties, **Goe**, Away........46. H.128, 40
Then know, that Nature bids thee **goe**, not I.....46. H.128, 42
Then weep, and sigh, and softly **goe**,...........47. H.132, 5
Goe, perjur'd man; and if thou ere return........49. H.138, 1
Apostles, way (unshackled) to **goe** out.........52. H.146, 16
Or let Love's fire **goe** out,.....................53. H.149, 5
Bridall-Rites **goe** on so slowly?................53. H.149, 12
Permit me, Julia, now to **goe** away;............60. H.156, 1
Ile trouble you no more; but **goe**...............60. H.159, 3
Ere I **go** hence; know this from me,...........60. H.159, 9
Few Beads are best, when once we **goe** a Maying. 68. H.178, 28
But my Corinna, come let's **goe** a Maying.......68. H.178, 42
Come, let us **goe**, while we are in our prime;....69. H.178, 57
Come, my Corinna, come, let's **goe** a Maying......69. H.178, 70
At which she smil'd; and bade him **goe**..........71. H.182, 27
Let us not then so rudely henceforth **goe**.......73. H.186, 5
Pay we our Vowes, and **goe**; yet when we part,.73. H.186, 13
Stay while ye will, or **goe**;......................83. H.207, 1
And while ye may, **goe** marry:..................84. H.208, 14
Here **goe** about for to recite..................91. H.223, 34
That being ravisht, hence I **goe**................95. H.227, 3
How the times away doe **goe**:.................96. H.231, 2
Prethee **goe** home; and for thy credit be........97. H.236, 3
Goe happy Rose, and enterwove...............98. H.238, 1
Take thou my blessing, thus, and **goe**,..........98. H.238, 11
And all **goe** back unto the Plough..............102. H.250, 49
In yond' Carnation **goe** and seek,..............106. H.263, 7
Rise, Household-gods, and let us **goe**;..........111. H.278, 1
ly, **go**, yet, howsoever, **go**....................113. H.283, 60
Blesse a Sack-posset: Luck **go** with it; take....115. H.283, 132
If well thou hast begun, **goe** on fore-right;.....123. H.309, 1
Will **goe** with you along......................125. H.316, 10
And let our Citie-health **go** round,.............127. H.319, 30
That from thee I cannot **go**;...................128. H.322, 11
Go where I will, thou luckie Larr stay here,....132. H.333, 9
Or let me **go**;...............................137. H.340, 2
Back must now **go** to's habitation:.............140. H.355, 2
And these brave Measures **go** a stately trot;....141. H.359, 11
Makes guests and fish smell strong; pray **go**...146. H.377, 26
How farre a Figure ought to **go**,...............148. H.377, 92
Go on directly so, as just men may...........149. H.377, 131
Have I not blest Thee? Then **go** forth; nor fear.155. H.405, 1
But with thy fair Fates leading thee, **Go** on....155. H.405, 3
But I will **go**, or send a kisse.................156. H.412, 19
But lets **go** steepe............................160. H.421, 44
As Beasts unto the Altars **go**.................161. H.425, 9
For Lust and action; on he'l **go**,...............165. H.443, 11
Let's to the Altar of perfumes then **go**,........168. H.445, 3
Go hence, and with this parting kisse,..........174. H.465, 1
And **go** at last..............................176. H.467, 6
His gifts **go** from him; if not bought with sweat..177. H.469, 2
Jone wo'd **go** tel her haires; and well she might,.195. H.531, 1
Go I must; when I am gone,..................199. H.546, 1
Where shall I **goe**,...........................211. H.596, 5
Go wooe young Charles no more to looke,......214. H.611, 1
Of long'd-for lodging, **go** to rest:.............216. H.617, 2
When to the Temple Love sho'd runne, not **go**...216. H.618, 6
As Love shall helpe thee, when thou do'st **go** hence 219. H.627, 7
In a Dreame, Love bad me **go**................219. H.628, 1
Go to your banquet then, but use delight,......220. H.633, 18
Go then discreetly to the Bed of pleasure;.....220. H.633, 24
The Ravens yeares, **go** hence more Ripe then old..222. H.633, 63
When I **goe** Hence ye Closet-Gods, I feare.....227. H.652, 1
Then to thy corn-fields thou dost **goe**,..........230. H.662, 21
To these, thou hast thy times to **goe**..........231. H.662, 62
Some few sands spent, we hence must **go**,......233. H.670, 37
Go on too with this:.........................247. H.727, 2
Franck wo'd **go** scoure her teeth; and setting to't,.247. H.728, 1
My Lucia in the deaw did **go**,.................247. H.729, 1
Hast thou attempted greatnesse? then **go** on,...252. H.747, 1
Consult ere thou begin'st, that done, **go** on......252. H.749, 1
Go on with Sylla's Fortune; let thy Fate.......254. H.756, 9
Go to Feast, as others do....................255. H.761, 2
Time is the Bound of things, where e're we **go**,...257. H.766, 1
If Wars **goe** well; each for a part layes claime:.260. H.774, 3
Sapho, I will chuse to **go**.....................266. H.803, 1
When ere I **go**, or what so ere befalls...........269. H.818, 1
This Blessing I will leave thee, ere I **go**,.......269. H.818, 3
But it skills not; **go** your way;................270. H.821, 6
Shall I **go** to Love and tell,...................273. H.836, 1
Go to Bed, and care not when.................276. H.850, 7
Take mine advise, and **go** not neere...........279. H.868, 1
This day I **goe** to wooe;......................281. H.874, 7
My soule would one day **goe** and seeke.........281. H.876, 1
To th' Temple with the sober Midwife **go**......286. H.898, 2
Go with thy Faults and Fates; yet stay........287. H.899, 7
May (Great Augustus) **goe** along with You.....300. H.961, 18
Let us to the Altar **go**........................303. H.974, 4
W'ave more to beare our charge, then way to **go**? 308. H.995, 2
Go on brave Hopton, to effectuate that.........310. H.1002, 1
To an old soare a long cure must **goe** on;......312. H.1012, 1
Ah cruell maides! Ile **goe** my way,.............312. H.1014, 5
If the Maides a spinning **goe**,..................315. H.1026, 5
Nor in the summers sweeter evenings **go**,.......315. H.1028, 5
I'de rather hungry **go** and come,...............321. H.1056, 13
My dearest Love, since thou wilt **go**,...........323. H.1068, 1
I'm halfe return'd before I **go**.................328. H.1090, 13
That I must **go** this day:......................328. H.1091, 4
And **go** with me to chuse my Buriall roome:...329. H.1095, 6
Goe thou forth my booke, though late;.........334. H.1125, 1
Bell-man of Night, if I about shall **go**..........349. N.43, 1
Behold I **go**,....................................354. N.58, 2
Go prettie child, and beare this Flower.........354. N.59, 1
Let's **go** (my Alma) yet e're we receive,........355. N.65, 7
I do believe, the bad must **goe**.................358. N.78, 7
Sorrowes our portion are: Ere hence we **goe**,.....359. N.81, 1
Humble we must be, if to Heaven we **go**:.....362. N.89, 1
Then, if Thou bidst me pay, or **go**..............370. N.107, 11
How Matron-like didst thou **go** drest!...........375. N.123, 63
To him, who longs unto his CHRIST to **go**,....378. N.133, 1
Art thou not destin'd? then, with hast, **go** on...389. N.216, 1
Or rag'd to **go**,................................391. N.228, 10
Put off Thy Robe of Purple, then **go** on........398. N.263, 1
So do the Skurfe and Bran too: **Go** Thy way,...398. N.263, 12
Why then, **go** on to act: Here's wonders to be done, 401. N.268, 7
Ere I **goe** hence and bee noe more..............407. A.2, 1
Take wth my blessinge; and **goe** forth.........409. A.2, 101
How stay thay would, yet forc't thay are to **goe**..410. A.3, 12
I've more to beare my Chardge, then way to **goe**,.411. A.3, 54
Wth thought thay **goe**, whence thay must ner returne. 411. A.3, 66
Goe hence away, and in thy parting know........414. A.6, 1
Tis not my voice, but heauens, that bidds thee **goe**; 414. A.6, 2
Departing hence, where Good and Bad souls **go**...416. A.8, 26
Why then **goe** forward, sweet Auspicious Bride, 431. ins. H.283, 50a
— — — — — — — — — — —, ...432. var. H.283, 76
For we **goe** over to be merry,..............445. ins. H.730, 26b
Goals Their **Goales** for Virgins kisses; which when done, 206. H.575, 18
Goat To an old Ram **Goat**,.....................333. H.1122, 4
Goblet A **Goblet** next Ile drink..................80. H.201, 21
A **Goblet**, to the brim,........................198. H.544, 15
Goblets Full **goblets** of thy gen'rous blood; his spright 78. H.197, 67
In **Goblets** to the brim,.......................290. H.918, 2
Goblin The **Goblin** from ye, while ye sleep.........121. H.299, 6
Goblins So many **Goblins** you shall see..........304. H.980, 9
God—See Demigod, Threshold-god
Upon her wings presents the **god** unshorne.......67. H.178, 2
God, and far more transcendent then the rest?..78. H.197, 60
His golden **god**, Cantharides....................90. H.223, 18
Makes not a **God**; but he that prayes to one.......117. H.288, 2
(**God** and good friends be thankt for it).........123. H.306, 8
Thus frantick crazie man (**God** wot)...........135. H.336, 113
And Thou, like to that Hospitable **God**,..........147. H.377, 61
Teach man to keepe a **God** in man:............149. H.377, 134
Hark, harke, the **God** do's play!...............151. H.388, 5
Or let the Unshorne **God** lend thee his Lyre,..299. H.956, 13
We read how Faunus, he the shepheards **God**,..306. H.986, 1
Forgive me **God**, and blot each Line.............339. N.2, 5
God is above the sphere of our esteem,............340. N.4, 1
God is not onely said to be......................340. N.5, 1
God hath two wings, which He doth ever move,..340. N.6, 1
God when He's angry here with any one,..........340. N.7, 1
'Tis hard to finde **God**, but to comprehend.......340. N.8, 1
Lambs, by the Law, which **God** requires as due...341. N.9, 2
God n'ere afflicts us more then our desert,.......341. N.10, 1
God, the most Wise, is sparing of His talk......341. N.12, 2
God loads, and unloads, (thus His work begins)..341. N.14, 1
God He rejects all Prayers that are sleight,......342. N.16, 1
My **God**, I'm wounded by my sin, ...342. N.17, 1
God is all fore-part; for, we never see............342. N.18, 1
God is not onely mercifull, to call...............342. N.19, 1
God scourgeth some severely, some He spares; .342. N.20, 1
God when for sin He makes His Children smart,..343. N.22, 1
God, as He is most Holy knowne;................343. N.23, 1
Do with me, **God**! as Thou didst deal with John,.343. N.25, 1

God has his whips here to a twofold end,........343. N.26, 1
If **God** should punish no sin, here, of men,.......343. N.27, 3
Those Saints, which **God** loves best,...........344. N.28, 1
My **God**! looke on me with thine eye.............344. N.29, 1
God heares us when we pray, but yet defers......344. N.30, 1
God strikes His Church, but 'tis to this intent,...344. N.31, 1
God pardons those, who do through frailty sin;..344. N.32, 1
What **God** and Nature lent....................346. N.38, 12
When (**Gods** knowes) I'm tost about,...........348. N.41, 33
God to bestow a second benefit.................348. N.42, 2
Make, make me Thine, my gracious **God**,........351. N.48, 1
Happy's that man, to whom **God** gives..........351. N.50, 1
Can I not come to Thee, my **God**, for these......352. N.51, 1
No, no, (my **God**) Thou know'st my wishes be..352. N.51, 13
God mercy; and so die.........................352. N.53, 16
God will have all, or none; serve Him, or fall....353. N.54, 1
Either be hot, or cold: **God** doth despise,.......353. N.54, 3
My gentle **God**,...............................353. N.56, 22
My Book, 'tis this; that Thou, my **God**, art in't..355. N.61, 2
How am I bound to Two! **God**, who doth give..355. N.62, 1
Where **God** is merry, there write down thy fears:
355. N.63, 1
God gives not onely corne, for need,.............356. N.66, 1
God co'd have made all rich, or all men poore;..356. N.69, 1
To seek of **God** more then we well can find,.....356. N.70, 1
God crowns our goodnesse, where so ere He sees,.356. N.71, 3
God is all-sufferance here; here He doth show...357. N.74, 1
By Thee, Deare **God**, **God** gives man seed......358. N.75, 7
Of Gift from **God**: And heres my Creed........359. N.78, 16
A mans transgression **God** do's then remit,.....359. N.82, 1
God when He takes my goods and chattels hence.362. N.87, 1
What is in **God** is **God**; if so it be,.............362. N.87, 3
Deer **God**,......................................363. N.92, 1
What **God** gives, and what we take,..............363. N.93, 1
God be thank'd for those, and these:............363. N.93, 4
Thee to adore thy **God**, the first of all..........363. N.94, 2
The Birth is fruitlesse: Chor. Then the work **God** speed.
365. N.97, 19
'Tis true, my **God**; but I can't pay one mite.....368. N.103, 10
Almighty **God** me grant;.......................369. N.104, 15
God makes not good men wantons, but doth bring
370. N.108, 1
Pardon me **God**, (once more I Thee intreat)..371. N.113, 1
So Thou, my **God**, may'st on this impure look,...371. N.113, 7
I would to **God**, that mine old age might have..371. N.115, 1
Wip't out few, (**God** knowes) if any...........373. N.121, 10
But if it please my **God**, I be...................376. N.124, 2
God make me thankfull still for it.............376. N.124, 4
God! to my little meale and oyle,..............377. N.130, 1
God He refuseth no man; but makes way.......378. N.131, 1
God had but one Son free from sin; but none...378. N.134, 1
God, as He's potent, so He's likewise known,....378. N.135, 1
Science in **God**, is known to be.................378. N.136, 1
God from our eyes all teares hereafter wipes,....379. N.139, 1
Unlesse **God** gives the Benedicite..............379. N.140, 2
God, is His Name of Nature; but that word.....379. N.141, 1
God hides from man the reck'ning Day, that He.379. N.142, 1
That Manna, which **God** on His people cast,....379. N.146, 1
The feare of **God**, commixt with cleanly love....380. N.147, 2
God tempteth no one (as S. Aug'stine saith)....380. N.150, 1
Unto temptation **God** exposeth some;............380. N.150, 3
God in His own Day will be then severe,........381. N.156, 1
God, who's in Heav'n, will hear from thence;..381. N.160, 1
God (as the learned Damascen doth write).......381. N.161, 1
In **God** there's nothing, but 'tis known to be....382. N.165, 1
Ev'n **God** Himself, in perfect Entitie...........382. N.165, 2
God can do all things, save but what are known.382. N.166, 1
God then confounds mans face, when He not hears
382. N.169, 1
God on our Youth bestowes but little ease;.....383. N.175, 1
God is so potent, as His Power can............383. N.176, 1
God did forbid the Israelites, to bring.........384. N.179, 1
To work a wonder, **God** would have her shown,.384. N.183, 1
God, in the holy Tongue, they call.............385. N.185, 1
God is Jehovah cal'd; which name of His.......385. N.187, 1
The House of **God**, by Christ inhabited;.......385. N.190, 2
'Twixt **God** the Father, Holy Ghost, and Sonne:.386. N.191, 4
As when we sin; **God**, the great Chymist, thence
386. N.196, 3
God is more here, then in another place,.......387. N.197, 1
God hath this world for many made; 'tis true:..387. N.198, 1
God gives to none so absolute an Ease,........387. N.199, 1
These temp'rall goods **God** (the most Wise) commends
387. N.201, 1
To **God** for vengeance? yes say I;..............387. N.203, 2
God, for an expiation.........................387. N.203, 4
With **God**, then one, that never sin'd 'gainst Him.
388. N.205, 2
God, He is there, where's nothing else (Schooles say)
388. N.207, 3
God doth embrace the good with love; & gaines.389. N.212, 1
God bought man here wth his hearts blood expence;
389. N.213, 1
And man sold **God** here for base thirty pence.....339. N.213, 2
If thou canst change thy life, **God** then will please
389 N.216, 3
God has foure keyes, which He reserves alone;..390. N.224, 1

Come to me **God**; but do not come.............393. N.232, 1
Then come my **God**, and hap what will..........393. N.232, 16
And having not her **God** for light,.............393. N.233, 3
In doing justice, **God** shall then be known,......393. N.234, 1
More stripes, then **God** layes on the sufferer.....393. N.235, 2
God suffers not His Saints, and Servants deere,..394. N.236, 1
God is all-present to what e're we do,..........394. N.237, 1
That there's a **God**, we all do know,...........394. N.238, 1
But what **God** is, we cannot show..............394. N.238, 2
God has a Right Hand, but is quite bereft.......394. N.240, 1
Two instruments belong unto our **God**;..........394. N.241, 1
God still rewards us more then our desert:......394. N.242, 1
God is then said for to descend, when He.......395. N.244, 1
Good and great **God**! How sho'd I feare........395. N.245, 1
God hates the Duall Number; being known.....396. N.249, 1
God blest His work done on the second day:....396. N.249, 6
God doth not promise here to man, that He......396. N.252, 1
God, who me gives a will for to repent,.........397. N.255, 1
To my **God**, a Heave-offering..................397. N.258, 4
God can't be wrathfull; but we may conclude,..397. N.259, 1
My mild, my loving Tutor, Lord and **God**!......398. N.261, 3
And **God**, as Thou art, comes to suffering.......399. N.263, 25
God, and good Angells guide Thee; and so blesse
399. N.263, 32
If Thou beest taken, **God** forbid,...............399. N.265, 1
I'le take my share; or els, my **God**,.............399. N.265, 9
God is the ΑΡΧΗ, and the ΤΕΛΟΣ too...........403. N.272, 2
Number of Nyne, wch makes vs full wth **God**,...410. A.3, 22
But tis the **god** of Nature, who Intends..........411. A.3, 57
— — — — — — — — — — — —, ...422. var. H.106, 62
— — — — — — — — — — — —, ...432. var. H.283, 66
— — — — — — — — — — — —, ...432. var. H.283, 136

Godderick — — — — — — — —, ...437. var. H.336, 131

Goddess As **Goddesse** Isis (when she went,........9. H.15, 9
Goddesse Isis cann't transfer...................59. H.155, 7
Goddesse of Youth, and Lady of the Spring,.....107. H.265, 1
Some **Goddesse**, in a cloud of Tiffanie...........112. H.283, 8
Goddesse, I do love a Girle....................136. H.337, 1
Sea-born **Goddesse**, let me be,..................138. H.346, 1
Stately **Goddesse**, do thou please,................141. H.360, 1
Goddesse, I begin an Art;.....................195. H.530, 1
Goddesse of Pleasure, Youth and Peace,........221. H.633, 54
As to the **Goddesse**, people did conferre.........330. H.1099, 5

Goderiske Hind, **Goderiske**, Smith........437. var. H.336, 131

Godful Of those **god-full** prophetts longe before...411, A.3, 42

Godhead Who formes a **Godhead** out of Gold or Stone,
117. H.288, 1
I did this **God-head** once defie;.................155. H.406, 3
Thy sooty **Godhead**, I desire....................214. H.613, 1
As the **Godhead** doth indite....................242. H.714, 6

Godheads Where he of **God-heads** has such store,..90. H.223, 7

God-like Thou seest a present **God-like** Power...230. H.662, 31

Godliness In **godlinesse**, not the beginnings, so....387. N.200, 3

Godly — — — — — — — —, ...422. var. H.106, 91

God's To **Gods** sweet Babe, when borne at Bethlehem;
86. H.213, 22
Gods boundlesse mercy is (to sinfull man)......341. N.15, 1
Gods Rod doth watch while men do sleep; & then
342. N.21, 1
Among **Gods** Blessings, there is no one small....353. N.55, 2
Gods Bounty, that ebbs lesse and lesse,..........358. N.76, 1
Sin once reacht up to **Gods** eternall Sphere,.....367. N.100, 1
Let not that Day **Gods** Friends and Servants scare:
376. N.126, 1
Gods Grace deserves here to be daily fed,........378. N.132, 1
Gods Hands are round, & smooth, that gifts may fall
380. N.151, 1
But earth: such vowes nere reach **Gods** eare.....381. N.158, 8
Had no one Beame from **Gods** sweet Majestie...382. N.167, 4
Jacob **Gods** Beggar was; and so we wait.........383. N.171, 1
God's said to leave this place, and for to come..385. N.186, 1
God's evident, and may be said to be...........385. N.188, 1
God's said to dwell there, wheresoever He.......385. N.189, 1
God's undivided, One in Persons Three;........386. N.191, 1
Gods wayes and walks, which lie still East and West.
386. N.193, 4
God's present ev'ry where; but most of all......388. N.207, 1
The cause of **Gods** Predestination:.............390. N.219, 2
And from **Gods** Prescience of mans sin doth flow.390. N.219, 3
Gods Prescience makes none sinfull; but th' offence
390. N.220, 1
Of man's the chief cause of **Gods** Prescience.....390. N.220, 2
If well, then chant **Gods** praise with cheerfulnesse.
395. N.243, 4
God's said our hearts to harden then,...........396. N.250, 1
The Frankincense for **Gods** Offring.............396. N.254, 2
God's wrathfull said to be, when He doth do....397. N.259, 3
In **Gods** commands, ne're ask the reason why;..397. N.260, 1
Drunk up the wine of **Gods** fierce wrath;........400. N.266, 11

Gods See **Closet-gods, Household-gods**
Subjects are taught by Men; Kings by the **Gods**.
12. H.25, 2
If meat the **Gods** give, I the steame............22. H.66, 1
They vow'd to ask the **Gods**....................31. H.92, 4
Touch not the Tyrant; Let the **Gods** alone......32. H.97, 5
O thou the drink of **Gods**, and Angels! Wine...45. H.128, 11
The **Gods** are easie, and condemne............47. H.132, 13

The **Gods** to Kings the Judgement give to sway:.109. H.269, 1
Though hourely comforts from the **Gods** we see,.111. H.276, 1
The **Gods,** he down the Nectar flung;...........241. H.706, 2
The **Gods** require the thighes..................250. H.736, 1
In whom the spirit of the **Gods** do's dwell,.....256. H.763, 7
For I thinke the **gods** require..................277. H.856, 3
What was't (ye **Gods!**) a dying man to save,...278. H.860, 3
And our Diseases, Vultures of the **Gods**:........278. H.862, 2
And (while we the **gods** invoke)................280. H.870, 17
Let's strive to be the best; the **Gods,** we know it, 309. H.1000, 1
Grace with the **Gods,** who's sorry for his sinne..329. H.1095, 4
Angells are called **Gods**; yet of them, none......379. N.143, 1
Are **Gods,** but by participation:...............379. N.143, 2
As just Men are intitled **Gods,** yet none.........379. N.143, 3
Are **Gods,** of them, but by Adoption............379. N.143, 4
Chorus. Thus, thus the **gods** celestial still decree, 416. A.8, 17
The easy **Gods**..........................431. ins. H.283, 60o
— — — — — — — — — —, ...448. var. A.3, 22
Gods' The **Gods** protection, but the night before).9. H.14, 12
Goes **Goes** the world now, it will with thee goe hard: 22. H.64, 1
Fortune when she comes, or **goes**..............37. H.106, 94
None **goes** to warfare, but with this intent;......42. H.120, 1
When tuckt up she a hunting **goes**;............51. H.142, 14
Slowly **goes** farre: The meane is best: Desire...51. H.143, 3
With Juno **goes** the houres,....................54. H.149, 45
Goes to the Feast that's now provided..........93. H.223, 142
As your health or comes, or **goes**;..............96. H.232, 6
Guesse cuts his shooes, and limping, **goes** about..98. H.239, 1
Shark, when he **goes** to any publick feast,......118. H.292, 1
A change, when Fortune either comes, or **goes**:..128. H.323, 8
As when a Rain-bow in perfumes **goes** out......131. H.331, 8
Goes with your mouth, or do's outrun your tongue; 141. H.359, 14
As when to Jove Great Juno **goes** perfum'd......157. H.414, 8
Cock calls his Wife his Hen: when Cock **goes** too't, 213. H.610, 1
Yet Jone she **goes**............................229. H.659, 3
She **goes** her long white egg to lay.............246. H.724, 12
Slouch he packs up, and **goes** to sev'rall Faires,.253. H.753, 1
When as in silks my Julia **goes,**...............261. H.779, 1
Since Fame that sides with these, or **goes** before.329. H.1092, 3
A hunting she **goes**;.........................334. H.1122, 13
Who slowly **goes,** rids (in the end) his way......352. N.51, 4
Sin leads the way, but as it **goes,** it feels.......362. N.86, 1
And have a care no fire **gos** out,..............365. N.97, 5
Goes theeving from me, I am safe in death;...392. N.230, 34
If ill it **goes** with thee, thy faults confesse:....395. N.243, 3
Her heart's at home, howere she **goes**:...430. ins. H.283, 20j
— — — — — — — — — —, ...439. var. H.443, 11
Goest Me, when thou yeerly **go'st** Procession:....20. H.55, 6
Thou **go'st**; and as thy foot there treads,.......230. H.662, 30
These seen, thou **go'st** to view thy flocks.......230. H.662, 40
'Gainst thou **go'st** a mothering,...............236. H.684, 2
Going Anthea I am **going** hence...................277. H.854, 1
Of mincing in their **going**.....................375. N.123, 70
I'le thinke I'm **going** to be buried:..............392. N.230, 14
— — — — — — — — — —, ...431. var. H.283, 60
Gold Were thy streames silver, or thy rocks all **gold.** 29. H.86, 6
Gold, runneth to the Western Inde,............36. H.106, 66
And pure as **Gold** for ever......................66. H.172, 30
As ayrie as the leaves of **gold**;................66. H.175, 2
Those learned men brought Incense, Myrrhe, and **Gold,** 86. H.213, 30
Gold I've none, for use or show,..............88. H.218, 1
More precious, then we prize our **gold**:..........92. H.223, 88
Of Pearle, and **Gold,** to bind her hands:........98. H.238, 7
Through the world, but writ in **gold**............108. H.266, 20
Who formes a Godhead out of **Gold** or Stone,....117. H.288, 1
But warm their wits, and turn their lines to **gold.** 141. H.359, 8
Give both the **Gold** and Garland unto it.........141. H.359, 16
Pray once, twice pray; and turn thy ground to **gold.** 144. H.370, 8
That h'ad nor **Gold** or Silver to put in't?........162. H.427, 4
Then, when Thou see'st thine Age all turn'd to **gold,** 181. H.483, 9
A Corps as bright as burnish **gold**..............185. H.497, 7
And turn the iron Age to **Gold**.................233. H.670, 29
Rein'd in with Purple, Pearl, and **gold,**..........239. H.696, 6
(As other Townes and Cities were) for **gold,**.....251. H.745, 6
We'l love the Divell, so he lands the **gold**.......266. H.800, 8
The Halter was of silk, and **gold,**...............279. H.863, 5
So let us Yron, Silver, **Gold,**..................297. H.948, 9
Enspir'd with Purple, Pearle, and **Gold**;........311. H.1010, 2
I have a leaden, thou a shaft of **gold**;..........333. H.1120, 1
Let others look for Pearle and **Gold**............355. N.60, 1
And wilt not thou, with **gold,** be ti'd............357. N.72, 11
Gold I have none, but I present my need,.......369. N.105, 1
Devote to Thee, both incense, myrrhe, and **gold,**.369. N.105, 6
Ask not for **gold,** which metall is:..............381. N.158, 6
Thou load'st with **gold** thy vestiment?..........394. N.239, 2
Belongs all **gold** superfluous..................394. N.239, 4
Gold serves for Tribute to the King;...........396. N.254, 1
Like pearle and **gold** make one rich Carcanett....405. A.1, 32
Insteade of **gould** Pearle Rubies Bonds.........407. A.2, 7
— — — — — — — — — —, ...436. var. H.336, 52
Of **gold** and sylver there is spread,........440. ins. H.443, 45w
Golden And with my Lawrell crown thy **Golden** Urne. 11. H.22, 4
Love prickt my finger with a **golden** pin:.......17. H.44, 4
A **golden** ring, that shines upon thy thumb:.....30. H.88, 7
There to disport your selves with **golden** measure: 38. H.106, 139
The **golden** pomp is come.......................80. H.201, 4
The **golden** Pomp is come;......................80. H.201, 5
While **Golden** Angels (some have told to me)..86. H.213, 23
His **golden** god, Cantharides...................90. H.223, 18
Washes the **golden** eares of corne.............112. H.283, 20
Thy **golden** Censors fil'd with odours sweet,....128. H.320, 7
The **Golden** chain too, and the Civick Crown.....176. H.466, 8
A **golden** Flie one shew'd to me.................185. H.497, 1
Was destin'd forth to **golden** Soveraignty:......202. H.557, 28
But if that **golden** Age wo'd come again,......214. H.612, 7
That through each room a **golden** pipe may run.245. H.723, 3
That swell the **Golden** Graine:..................257. H.767, 6
These **golden** Toyles, and Trammel-nets,........282. H.881, 2
Upon my head the **golden** coronet;..............343. N.25, 6
Over the **golden** Altar now is spread,...........355. N.65, 3
With **golden** Censers, and with Incense, here,....368. N.103, 1
Here's **golden** fruit that farre exceeds all price..406. A.1, 71
For now behold the **golden** Pompe is come,.......415. A.7, 2
Golden-Cheapside Or to the **Golden-cheap-side,** where the earth 316. H.1028, 15
Gone But when He's **gone,** read through what's writ,..6. H.4, 3
When that day comes, whose evening sayes I'm **gone** 14. H.35, 1
With Perilla: All are **gone**;.....................16. H.39, 11
When all your world of Beautie's **gone**..........61. H.160, 10
But is got up, and **gone** to bring in May........69. H.178, 44
To warme my Breast, when thou my Pulse art **gone.** 73. H.186, 16
But (sweet things) ye must be **gone**;..........74. H.189, 3
But on a sudden, all was chang'd and **gone**....81. H.202, 3
But on a sudden all were **gone**................107. H.263, 16
Take first the feast; these dishes **gone**;........119. H.293, 5
The yeare (your cares) that's fled and **gon**.....127. H.319, 44
Now the good Spirit's **gone** from me?.........132. H.334, 2
Since thou art **gone,** no more I mean to play,..159. H.421, 9
But she is **gone.** Sil. Mirtillo, tell us whether,..159. H.421, 29
The Gnats-watch-word the Elves are **gone**......168. H.443, 117
(When hence thy Circum-mortall-part is **gon**)...168. H.444, 3
Steere Thee to me; and thinke (me **gone**).......174. H.465, 9
And **gon**:......................................178. H.475, 6
For which, her wrath is **gone** forth to consume.197. H.539, 11
Go I must; when I am **gone,**....................199. H.546, 1
When Monarchies trans-shifted are, and **gone**;..210. H.592, 3
But when that is **gone**; Again,.................227. H.651, 3
Once past and **gone,** no more shall see.........234. H.671, 2
But since I'm cal'd (rare Denham) to be **gone,**.234. H.673, 13
Ch. And is that all? I'm **gone.** Ph. By love I pray thee, 248. H.730, 17
So soone as Julia I am **gon**..................270. H.819, 2
Gone she is a long, long way,..................276. H.848, 1
Then Biancha, I am **gone**......................307. H.991, 4
Then Night now **gone,** and yet not sprung the Day. 319. H.1046, 2
The body's salt, the soule is; which when **gon,**.332. H.1111, 1
But he'd be **gone,**.............................346. N.38, 5
Ponder this, when I am **gone**;..................373. N.121, 13
Chor. All's **gone,** and Death hath taken.........374. N.123, 27
The Spice and Spiknard hence is **gone,**.........375. N.123, 55
Is rowl'd away; and my sweet Saviour's **gone!**..403. N.271, 2
Is He, from hence, **gone** to the shades beneath,.403. N.271, 5
— — — — — — — — — —, ...445. var. H.730, 13
— — — — — — — — — —, ...453. var. H.283, 75
Good See **Much-good-do't**
Who gave him forth **good** Grain, though he mistook 4. Ap., 3
If **good** I'le smile, if bad I'le sigh for Thee........6. H.3, 8
Good princes must be pray'd for: for the bad...32. H.97, 1
Good children kisse the rods, that punish sin.....32. H.97, 4
Health is the first **good** lent to men;...........42. H.121, 1
Good Sir, make no more cuts i'th' outward skin,.44. H.126, 3
That ye may **good** doctrine heare................52. H.147, 2
Of the **good** man and the wife..................55. H.149, 60
That **good,** which Heav'n can give...............57. H.149, 153
Since none so **good** are, but you may condemne;..64. H.168, 5
'Tis **Good** Confirm'd; for you have Bishop't it....64. H.168, 10
But stay the time till we have bade **Good** night..73. H.186, 2
Trust to **good** Verses then;....................81. H.201, 45
Amin. **Good** day, Mirtillo. Mirt. And to you no lesse: 85. H.213, 1
Good speed, for I this day....................87. H.214, 1
Though **good** things answer many good intents;..110. H.275, 1
Much **good** do't ye Gentlemen..................118. H.289, 12
My Masters all, **Good** day to you...............121. H.299, 8
(God and **good** friends be thankt for it).......123. H.306, 8
Good things, that come of course, far lesse doe please, 123. H.307, 1
But none enquires if **good** he be, or no.........130. H.328, 2

Now the good Spirit's gone from me?............132. H.334, 2
Reward it is, that makes us good or bad.........139. H.351, 2
Drawing thy curtains round: Good night.........146. H.376, 14
Good men, They find them all in Thee.........149. H.377, 136
Keepe it for ever; grounded with the good,........152. H.392, 7
Good morrow to the Day so fair;................156. H.412, 1
Good morning Sir to you:.......................156. H.412, 2
Good morrow to mine own torn hair..............156. H.412, 3
Good morning to this Prim-rose too;..............156. H.412, 5
Good morrow to each maid;.......................156. H.412, 6
We'l wish both Them and Thee, good night.......165. H.443, 8
That makes the Action, good, or ill.............175. H.465, 64
And in that Good, a great Patrician...............176. H.466, 2
T'ave lost the good ye might have had...........179. H.476, 39
For good luck in love (that day.)...............183. H.490, 16
Good Precepts we must firmly hold,.............187. H.505, 1
If Dorset say, what Herrick writes, is good?....187. H.506, 6
None shall be guiltlesse, be he n'er so good........194. H.528, 2
Eaten I have; and though I had good cheere,..197. H.541, 1
This was the Founders grave and good intent,..201. H.557, 13
For those good dayes that ne'r will come away..204. H.570, 2
But by the Muses sweare, all here is good,......212. H.603, 3
Or to the good, or evill action..................214. H.614, 4
No Goose layes good eggs that is trodden drye...223. H.636, 4
Floure of Fuz-balls, that's too good..........223. H.638, 15
And manners good requires, that we............226. H.647, 2
O happy life! if that their good................231. H.662, 70
By noone, and let thy good dayes passe,........233. H.670, 4
Drink rich wine; and make good cheere,........238. H.691, 3
A maid (my Prew) by good luck sent,..........246. H.724, 6
Ere a good word can be spoke:..............255. H.761, 18
Of both our Fortunes good and bad we find....257. H.765, 1
So good as George-a-Green;..................259. H.772, 22
Kings must not only cherish up the good,......260. H.775, 1
While my good Dame, she....................263. H.784, 4
For good successe in his spending,............263. H.784, 9
From good to good, revolving here, & there.....274. H.839, 2
Wisheth his body, not his soule, good speed.....277. H.855, 2
Kings seek their Subjects good: Tyrants their owne. 278. H.861, 2
Jone as my Lady is as good i'th' dark..........279. H.864, 2
Since for one Bad, one Good I know:..........283. H.885, 2
A good Penelope was had:...................283. H.885, 6
A Good and Bad. Sirs credit me..............283. H.885, 10
This if ye do, each Piece will here be good,....290. H.914, 9
And in good faith I'd thought it strange......290. H.915, 3
Man must do well out of a good intent,.........290. H.917, 1
And this good blessing back them still,.........291. H.919, 11
Lay by the good a while; a resting field........292. H.922, 1
We wished me all Good speed..................295. H.942, 8
Here of my great and good foundation..........305. H.983, 4
Good wits get more fame by their punishment...317. H.1034, 2
The good applaud: the peccant lesse condemne.332. H.1062, 8
Thus have, or have not, all alike is good,......332. H.1112, 5
And as our bad, more then our good Works are:..339. N.1, 2
Treble the number of these good I've writ.......339. N.1, 4
To do ten Bad, for one Good Action............339. N.1, 6
The bad to punish, and the good t'amend........343. N.26, 2
All serve to th' Augmentation of his good........349. N.44, 4
Good words, or meat:.......................350. N.47, 16
And tell Him, (for good handsell too)..........354. N.59, 7
I do believe, the good, and I,..................359. N.78, 9
Honour thy Parents; but good manners call......363. N.94, 1
Evill no Nature hath; the losse of good.........367. N.101, 1
God makes not good men wantons, but doth bring 370. N.108, 1
Manners are good: but till his errand ends,......378. N.137, 7
The Bad among the Good are here mixt ever:...383. N.172, 1
The Good without the Bad are here plac'd never. 383. N.172, 2
Or Good at all, (as learn'd Aquinas saith.)......383. N.173, 2
Draw out of bad a soveraigne good to man.......383. N.176, 2
But hath th' extraction of some good from it:....386. N.196, 2
To th' good and bad, in common, for two ends:..387. N.201, 2
God doth embrace the good with love; & gaines.389. N.212, 1
The good by mercy, as the bad by paines......389. N.212, 2
Heaven is not given for our good works here:..390. N.223, 1
Nor wo'd I care how short it were, if good:..392. N.230, 10
Good and great God! How sho'd I feare........395. N.245, 1
When well we speak, & nothing do that's good,..397. N.256, 1
But when good words, by good works, have their proof, 397. N.256, 3
God, and good Angells guide Thee; and so blesse 399. N.263, 32
Of all the good things whatsoe're we do,........403. N.272, 1
Soe good a soile bee-stocke and till,............409. A.2, 106
(White Fame) and Resurrection to the Good,....410. A.3, 32
In it all good, that is, and ever was............416. A.8, 14
Departing hence, where Good and Bad souls go...416. A.8, 26
And so to Bed: Pray wish us all Good Rest......419. A.10, 8
An active spiritt full marrow, and what's good; 426. ins. H.197, 48d
Fill each part full of Fire, let my good.427. ins. H.197, 77a
— — — — — — — — — — —, ...429. var. H.263, 6
Good-cheer Magot frequents those houses of good-cheere, 191. H.518, 1
Good-luck So Good-luck came, and on my roofe did light, 100. H.247, 1
Please him, and then all good-luck will betide..124. H.313, 5
The Laundresses, They envie her good-luck,.....178. H.474, 3
He Boded good-luck to thy Selfe and Spouse....181. H.483, 12
It may chance good-luck may send............334. H.1125, 3
Goodly Seeing thee Soame, I see a Goodly man,..176. H.466, 1
Women, although they ne're so goodly make it,..235. H.675, 1
Goodness Goodnes and Greatnes; not the oaken Piles; 148. H.377, 99
God crowns our goodnesse, where so ere He sees,.356. N.71, 3
Good-night See Night
But bid Good-night, and close their lids for ever..41. H.118, 8
And bid the world Good-night..................85. H.211, 4
On ye both; Goodnight to all.................125. H.314, 10
And so to bid goodnight?....................176. H.467, 9
Shortly I shall bid goodnight:................180. H.482, 2
Then bid Christmas sport good-night;........315. H.1026, 12
Goodrick — — — — — — — —, ...451. var. H.336, 132
Goods A stock of Goods, whereby he lives........351. N.50, 2
God when He takes my goods and chattels hence.362. N.87, 1
These temp'rall goods God (the most Wise) commends 387. N.201, 1
First, that these goods none here may o're esteem, 387. N.201, 3
Goose No Goose layes good eggs that is trodden drye. 223. H.636, 4
A Goose...................................246. H.724, 13
Well, when sh'as kild, that Pig, Goose, Cock or Hen, 266. H.801, 3
Gordian Hath in the middle ty'de a Gordian knott.405. A.1, 62
Gorgon Twixt this and them this Gorgon showne..418. A.9, 57
Gorgonius Unto Pastillus ranke Gorgonius came, 323. H.1066, 1
Gorrell Of Flanks and Chines of Beefe doth Gorrell boast 89. H.221, 1
Gospel And next the Gospell wee will credit thee. 257. H.763, 20
As Gospell tells,...........................345. N.33, 14
Gospel-tree Under that Holy-oke, or Gospel-tree:..20. H.55, 4
Gossamer Cast of the finest Gossamore.........167. H.443, 95
Gossamore See Gossamer
Gossips (While she gossips in the towne)........284. H.889, 4
Got She rather took, then got a fall:..............12. H.27, 2
Up she got upon a wall,........................15. H.36, 8
I got the Pit, and she the Stone................19. H.49, 4
Got, not so beautifull, as chast:................35. H.106, 34
Glasco had none, but now some teeth has got;....46. H.129, 1
Tell me, has Strut got ere a title more?.........53. H.148, 3
Pagget, a School-boy, got a Sword, and then....65. H.171, 1
But having got it; thereupon,..................67. H.175, 7
But is got up, and gone to bring in May.......69. H.178, 44
Til I had got the name of Villars here...........99. H.245, 2
Judith has cast her old-skin, and got new;......140. H.356, 1
Shift now has cast his clothes; got all things new; 144. H.372, 1
A Vicarige at last Tom Glasse got here,........151. H.385, 3
Broomsted a lamenesse got by cold and Beere;..201. H.555, 1
What off-spring other men have got,...........236. H.681, 1
Adopted some; none got by theft..............236. H.681, 4
She lookt as she'd been got with child..........251. H.740, 7
And swore I'de got the ague of the house.......262. H.783, 20
Which got, the third, bids him a King come downe. 292. H.925, 2
Tha'st got a place here (standing candidate)....305. H.983, 2
The life I got I quickly lost:.................313. H.1020, 4
What's got by Justice is establisht sure;.......314. H.1023, 1
No Kingdomes got by Rapine long endure.....314. H.1023, 2
But when again sh'as got her healthfull houre,..320. H.1054, 5
He's double honour'd, since h'as got gay cloathes: 330. H.1099, 2
He said, because he got his wealth thereby.....332. H.1114, 4
A place desir'd of all but got by theis............405. A.1, 69
fore this or that hath gott the victory....433, ins. H.283, 140j
Gotiere Then shall Wilson and Gotiere...........39. H.111, 13
Gotire From thee some raptures of the rare Gotire. 276. H.851, 2
Gotwit The Phesant, Partridge, Gotwit, Reeve, Ruffe, Raile, 147. H.377, 65
Gout To have men think he's troubled with the Gout: 98. H.239, 2
But 'tis no Gout (beleeve it) but hard Beere,....98. H.239, 3
Urles had the Gout so, that he co'd not stand;..207. H.577, 1
Govern That Prince must govern with a gentle hand, 323. H.1067, 1
Governess To kisse your hand, most Dainty Governesse. 137. H.341, 12
Government Waste thou in that most Civill Government. 171. H.456, 4
Preposterous is that Government, (and rude)....196. H.536, 1
Subjects still loath the present Government......291. H.921, 2
Governs Hor. Now Thracian Cloe governs me,....70. H.181, 9
Gown See Green-gown
For Jewels for your Gowne, or Haire:........68. H.178, 18
But for True Service, worthy of that Gowne,....176. H.466, 7
Thy clothing next, shall be a Gowne............192. H.521, 9
Do'n will I then my Beadsmans gown,..........303. H.973, 7
Gowns Crab faces gownes with sundry Furres; 'tis known, 232. H.669, 1

To make loose Gownes for Mackarell:..........275. H.844, 6

Grace See After-grace

Gryll eates, but ne're sayes Grace; To speak the troth, 48. H.135, 1
Gryll will not therefore say a Grace for it........48. H.135, 4
Then, Ah! Then, where is your grace,...........74. H.189, 5
And had but single grace......................75. H.193, 8
And quickly give, The swiftest Grace is best.....87. H.213, 46
Grace by his Priest; The feast is ended.........120. H.293, 54
And a nose that is the grace...................138. H.342, 7
Can give, and what retract a grace;...........148. H.377, 94
Will say our grace, and die....................173. H.460, 6
That Scarr's no Schisme, but the sign of grace...180. H.481, 2
One Fate had both; both equall Grace;.........185. H.497, 7
The Grace, the Glorie, and the best............189. H.515, 3
Nay more, the Feast, and grace of it...........192. H.521, 28
Ursley, she thinks those Velvet Patches grace...197. H.543, 1
To grace the frantick Thyrse:..................198. H.544, 9
If ye will with Mab find grace,................201. H.556, 1
When I behold another grace....................202. H.560, 5
To grace which Service, Julia, there shall be....209. H.584, 3
To grace his own Gums, or of Box, or bone....211. H.595, 2
Please your Grace, from out your Store,........223. H.638, 1
And, in the midst, to grace it more, was set.....227. H.652, 9
Beauti's no other but a lovely Grace...........274. H.840, 1
Then youthfull Box which now hath grace,.....285. H.892, 9
Candlemas to grace the Grave..................304. H.976, 6
Toucht every where with such diffused grace,...307. H.992, 2
For Grace and Carriage, every one a Queene..326. H.1080, 24
Grace with the Gods, who's sorry for his sinne..329. H.1095, 4
He sayes his fore and after Grace for it:......332. H.1112, 2
If meate he wants, then Grace he sayes to see..332. H.1112, 3
But yet still lesse then Grace can suffer here.....341. N.10, 4
But for to teach us, all the grace is there,......346. N.36, 2
Grace is increased by humility..................362. N.89, 4
Where all have Grace,.........................369. N.106, 4
Thy lips with all diffused grace!..............375. N.123, 74
Let me say grace when there's no more........376. N.124, 6
Gods Grace deserves here to be daily fed,.......378. N.132, 1
His holy Spirit, or doth plant His Grace.........385. N.189, 4
Not by His Essence, but commerce of Grace.....387. N.197, 2
When as His grace not supples men............396. N.250, 2
But where sin swells, there let Thy grace abound. 398. N.261, 6
Her comly nose with vniformall grace............404. A.1, 11
To grace a Lute, a vyall, Virginall.............406. A.1, 100

Graced As shews the Aire, when with a Rain-bow grac'd; 40. H.114, 1

With all that can be, this heaven grac't;........48. H.133, 15
And so grac't,..................................83. H.205, 10
Grac't with the Trout-flies curious wings,........92. H.223, 72
In time of life, I grac't ye with my Verse;......138. H.343, 1
By thy sonne thus grac't, and thee;...........138. H.346, 2
Grac't (now at last) or glorifi'd by thee........142. H.365, 2
Or else a Cherrie (double grac't)..............164. H.440, 3
As in a Globe of Radiant fire, and grac't......207. H.575, 58
Thy May-poles too with Garlands grac't:.......230. H.662, 53
Thrice happie Roses, so much grac't, to have....249. H.734, 1
On either side with rich rare Jewells grac'd,....405. A.1, 40
The gem is grac'd? or they grac'd by the Jemme?..405. A.1, 42
Deriue their overwell grac'd motion.............406. A.1, 86
— — — — — — — — —, ...434. var. H.293, 54

Graceful And for the graceful use of it:...........16. H.39, 10

Gracefull is ev'ry thing from her................207. H.579, 6
And gracefull made, by your neate Sisterhood...290. H.914, 10
Bares in it selfe a gracefull maiestye............404. A.1, 6

Graceless Let what is graceless, discompos'd, and rude, 290. H.914, 3

Mans former Birth is grace-lesse; but the state.326. H.1080, 27

Graces And Graces strewing flowers.............54. H.149, 46

Poore pittyed Exile? Tell me, did thy Graces...77. H.197, 20
May the Graces, and the Howers...............108. H.266, 5
Thus a dew of Graces fall......................125. H.314, 9
Flowes from the Wine, and graces it:..........148. H.377, 74
Stand with thy Graces forth, Brave man, and rise 181. H.483, 1
O ye Graces! Make me fit......................204. H.569, 3
Love and the Graces evermore do wait.........255. H.760, 1
Glory be to the Graces!.......................260. H.777, 1
Honour be to the Graces!......................260. H.777, 5
Worship be to the Graces!.....................260. H.777, 9
Behold, for us the Naked Graces stay..........261. H.781, 7

Gracious Make, make me Thine, my gracious God, 351. N.48, 1

Grain Who gave him forth good Grain, though he mistook 4. Ap. 3

A Moon-parcht grain of purest wheat,...........119. H.293, 9
Thy faithfull fields to yeeld thee Graine,........233. H.670, 9
That swell the Golden Graine:.................257. H.767, 6
But for each Graine, that in the ground is thrown, 388. N.208, 3

Grains Devote to thee my graines of Frankinsence: 131. H.333, 2

Then may ye recollect the graines............245. H.720, 13

Grange How well contented in this private Grange 310. H.1003, 1

Granges Though Granges do not love thee, Cities shall. 172. H.456, 10

Grant But grant that I sho'd wedded be,..........97. H.235, 3

Which you must grant; that's entrance; with..116. H.283, 153
Who for true glory suffers thus; we grant.....129. H.323, 15
Store of courage to me grant,..................151. H.386, 1
Or let her Grant, or else Deny,................207. H.579, 7
Your part's to grant; my Scean must be to move. 274. H.837, 4
Give Him the choice; grant Him the nobler part..356. N.68, 3
Almighty God me grant;.......................369. N.104, 15

Granted If unto me all Tongues were granted,....91. H.223, 26

That favour granted was;......................100. H.249, 5

Granting Or Lords be, (granting my wishes)....239. H.695, 9

Grape Thus Lillie, Rose, Grape, Cherry, Creame,.75. H.193, 33

Grapes Invites fresh Grapes to fill his Presse with Wine. 72. H.185, 28

Put Purple Grapes, or Cherries in-..............75. H.193, 25
Grapes, before Herrick leaves Canarie Sack.....78. H.197, 48
Besmear'd with Grapes; welcome he shall thee thither, 206. H.575, 37

Grass Seas shall be sandlesse; Fields devoid of grasse; 59. H.154, 7

The Shewers of Roses, lucky-foure-leav'd grasse: 113. H.283, 42
The spangling Dew dreg'd o're the grasse shall be 143. H.370, 3
The four-leav'd grasse, or mosse-like silk.......166. H.443, 42
Of short sweet grasse, as backs with wool......230. H.662, 43
— — — — — — — — — —, ...439. var. H.443, 28

Grasshopper His Spleen, the chirring Grasshopper; 119. H.293, 16

The burden of a Grashopper:..................303. H.973, 10

Grateful Be in Prose a gratefull man............182. H.489, 14

I have been gratefull for my store:............376. N.124, 5

Gratify Gratifie the Genius.......................96. H.231, 6

Grave A sacred Laurel springing from my grave:..30. H.89, 5

Be so one Death, one Grave to both...........38. H.106, 144
And with some flowrs my grave bestrew,..........70. H.180, 7
While we this Trentall sing about thy Grave.....89. H.219, 2
Off then with grave clothes; put fresh colours on; 105. H.259, 9
Relation to the grave:.........................111. H.280, 2
Which spent, one death, bring to ye both one Grave. 124. H.313, 14
Nay, now I think th'ave made his grave........156. H.412, 15
Or here my Bed, or here my Grave.............158. H.420, 4
Thee live, as dead and in thy grave;...........174. H.465, 12
Into the Grave.................................176. H.467, 18
I'th grave,....................................178. H.475, 10
His buriall in an yvory grave:.................185. H.497, 4
One Rest, one Grave..........................190. H.515, 12
This was the Founders grave and good intent,..201. H.557, 13
A Tentrall sung by Virgins o're thy Grave:....209. H.584, 6
Upon the grave of this old man................226. H.644, 2
Ile sing no more of death, or shall the grave....228. H.658, 7
For, once dead, and laid i'th grave,............238. H.691, 5
Within the Bosome of my Love your grave......249. H.734, 2
Your Grave her Bosome is, the Lawne the Stone. 249. H.734, 4
But while he met with his Paternall grave;....278. H.860, 4
One knell be rung for both; and let one grave..281. H.875, 5
Chaste Lucrece, or a wife as grave:...........283. H.885, 8
Candlemas to grace the Grave.................304. H.976, 6
Offer'd on my holy Grave;.....................307. H.991, 6
'Tis we are dead, though i' th grave:...........361. N.83, 57
What though my bed be now my grave,........361. N.84, 3
Before my last, but here a living grave,........371. N.115, 2
These hung, as honours o're thy Grave,........375. N.123, 86
Sate by the Grave; and sadly sitting there,......384. N.180, 9
Those Tapers, which we set upon the grave,....384. N.181, 1
To make my grave.............................401. N.268, 39
This for my Heaven, that was Thy Grave:.....402. N.269, 23

Gravy Lets drip a certain Gravie from her eyes..331. H.1107, 2

Gray Age cals me hence, and my gray haires bid come, 9. H.14, 3

When my date's done, and my gray age must die;.40. H.112, 1
And I dare sweare, that I am gray?.............63. H.164, 2
My Pilgrims staffe; my weed of grey:.........123. H.306, 2
Fly me not, though I be gray,.................194. H.527, 1
Who by his gray Haires, doth his lusters tell,..328. H.1088, 5
Gray or white, all's one to me...............330. H.1098, 4
Of the gray farmer, and to these.........439. ins. H.443, 45h

Grease The fattest Hogs we grease the more with Lard. 22. H.64, 2

Dry chips, old shooes, rags, grease, & bones;..93. H.223, 119

Greased The staffe is now greas'd,...............333. H.1122, 1

Great Most great, and universall Genius!..........25. H.77, 2

Nurse up, great Lord, this my posterity:........40. H.112, 2
In all that great and glorious light,............49. H.136, 30
More by Provocation great.....................62. H.162, 15
A neat, though not so great an Offering........86. H.213, 35
Saint Will o'th' Wispe (of no great bignes)....91. H.223, 30
Some crosse the Fill-horse; some with great....101. H.250, 21
The Heire to This great Realme of Poetry......107. H.264, 6
They make a feast lesse great then nice.......119. H.293, 12
Thee, that great cup Hercules:.................122. H.304, 6
Are wanting to her exercise, but great........148. H.377, 113
As when to Jove Great Juno goes perfum'd.....157. H.414, 8

Chor. The shades grow great; but greater growes our sorrow, 160. H.421, 43
'Tis fit they make no One with them too great..163. H.438, 2
No shadowes great appeare;..................164. H.441, 6
And in that Good, a great Patrician............176. H.466, 2
Lastly, be mindfull (when thou art grown great) 181. H.483, 13
Great men by small meanes oft are overthrown:..181. H.486, 1
Next, at that great Platonick yeere,...........190. H.515, 47
Great Spirits never with their bodies dye........199. H.547, 2
But pitie those whose flanks grow great,........200. H.552, 15
As great men lead; the meaner follow on,......214. H.614, 3
Great be my fare, or small cheere,............235. H.674, 17
To mortall men great loads allotted be,.........242. H.715, 1
Command the Roofe great Genius, and from thence 245. H.723, 1
To weaken this thy great Dictator-ship..........252. H.745, 20
In great Processions many lead the way........256. H.763, 3
Of this or that great Aprill day shall be,........257. H.763, 19
As for the rest, being too great a summe......267. H.804, 13
Griefe, if't be great, 'tis short; if long, 'tis light..268. H.810, 2
This Day is Yours, Great CHARLES! and in this War 271. H.823, 1
Of thy both Great, and everlasting fate.........280. H.869, 4
The factions of the great ones call,............282. H.877, 1
Thy wits great over-plus;....................289. H.911, 14
Welcome, Great Cesar, welcome now you are,...300. H.961, 1
May (Great Augustus) goe along with You.....300. H.961, 18
Here of my great and good foundation.........305. H.983, 4
Great faults require great satisfaction..........312. H.1012, 2
Great Cities seldome rest: If there be none....316. H.1030, 1
Among these Tempests great and manifold....319. H.1044, 1
When the great Crack not Crushes one, but all..319. H.1045, 2
Live you, great Mistresse of your Arts, and be.326. H.1080, 21
Yet I have hope, by Thy great power,..........361. N.84, 7
To punish great sins, who small faults whipt here. 381. N.156, 2
Great things ask for, when thou dost pray,......381. N.158, 3
And those great are, which ne're decay.........381. N.158, 4
In this regard, in those great terrors He.........382. N.167, 3
As when we sin; God, the great Chymist, thence 386. N.196, 3
So that the wonder is not halfe so great,........388. N.208, 5
Christ never did so great a work, but there......389. N.214, 1
Good and great God! How sho'd I feare........395. N.245, 1
Of His great Birth-right nothing derogate.......395. N.248, 4
Why then begin, great King! ascend Thy Throne, 399. N.263, 28
Come then greate Lord.........................413. A.4, 31
Euc. Great are my woes. Cha. And great must that Grief be, 416. A.8, 21
Tis not Jewell of great prize....................417. A.9, 3
— — — — — — — — —, ...427. var. H.197, 61
Nor can wee glory of a great...........436. ins. H.336, 48i
Great-blue-ruler The Great-blew-ruler of the seas; 175. H.465, 76
Greater Little the wound was; greater was the smart; 17. H.44, 7
Wink at small faults, the greater, ne'rthelesse......32. H.95, 3
Many a lesse and greater spheare...............47. H.133, 2
Raise greater fires in men.....................76. H.193, 56
Chor. The Shades grow great; but greater growes our sorrow, 160. H.421, 43
And no one mischief greater then your frown,..188. H.506, 13
(But min's the greater smart).................203. H.563, 6
But all in smart have lesse, or greater shares.....342. N.20, 2
I'th ayre, a greater Text of light................413. A.4, 19
— — — — — — — — — — —, ...452. ins. H.443, 45s
Greatest That things of greatest, so of meanest worth, 105. H.257, 27
That's the greatest shame of all,...............151. H.386, 5
The greatest mans Inheritance...............197. H.542, 2
Great-eyed Made by the breath of great-ey'd kine, 166. H.443, 40
And smell'st the breath of great-ey'd Kine,......230. H.662, 33
Great-little-kingly-guest Of this great-little-kingly-Guest. 168. H.443, 119
Greatness 'Tis not greatness they require,..........22. H.65, 1
Goodnes and Greatnes; not the oaken Piles;....148. H.377, 99
In wayes to greatnesse, think on this,.........229. H.661, 1
Hast thou attempted, greatnesse? then go on,....252. H.747, 1
Great's Come tel me then, how great's the smart..50. H.139, 14
Grecian Soe look't the Grecian Oratour when sent.411. A.3, 71
Entitulated the Greecian Prince of men....442. ins. H.575, 28b
Greece See Ambergris
'Greed See Agreed
— — — — — — — — — — —, ...448. var. A.1, 86
Greedily I stricke thy loues, and greedyly persue..411. A.3, 69
Greedy An old, old widow Greedy needs wo'd wed, 129. H.326, 1
He's greedie of his life, who will not fall,......155. H.405, 17
I know a thousand greedy eyes.................174. H.465, 17
I greedy of the prize, did drinke,..............222. H.635, 5
Greek This livery w[ch] the *greeke hath worne.....418. A.9, 54
Greeks — — — — — — — — —, ...437. var. H.336, 106
— — — — — — — — — —, ...450. var. A.9, 54
Green See George-a-Green, Yellow-green
Which renders that quite tarnisht, w[ch] was green; 21. H.62, 3
Blest with perpetuall greene,...................30. H.89, 7
While you are in your sprightfull green:........49. H.136, 25
A silver bow with green silk strung,............51. H.142, 9
Trees, at one time, shall be both sere and green:..59. H.154, 2
I shall, ere long, with green turfs cover'd be;....66. H.174, 3
To come forth, like the Spring-time, fresh and greene; 68. H.178, 16
Made green, and trimm'd with trees: see how....68. H.178, 31
But like a Laurell, to grow green for ever.........98. H.240, 2
Ye have been fresh and green,................110. H.274, 1
Of her green hopes, we charge ye, that no strife, 114. H.283, 82
And cry out, Hey, for our town green.........127. H.319, 20
Here in green Meddowes sits eternall May,....206. H.575, 13
Green, to the end of dayes..................261. H.778, 12
Green Rushes then, and sweetest Bents,........285. H.892, 17
Of this smooth Green,.........................360. N.83, 16
— — — — — — — — — —, ...443. var. H.580, 8
Greener The greener Box (for show.)...........285. H.892, 4
Greenest With crowns of greenest Parsley,.......234. H.674, 3
Green-eyed Till that the green-ey'd Kitling comes. 37. H.106, 124
Green-gown Many a green-gown has been given;..69. H.178, 51
Green-sicknesses Troubled with Green-sicknesses,..64. H.167, 2
Green-turfs And who with green-turfes reare his head, 157. H.412, 23
Greeny-calendar Within your Greenie-Kalendar:.169. H.449, 14
Greets — — — — — — — —, ...433. var. H.293, 10
Grew Patient I was: Love pitifull grew then,....16. H.40, 5
One ask'd me where the Roses grew?............18. H.45, 1
Some ask'd me where the Rubies grew?...........24. H.75, 1
Where such a rare Carnation grew..............63. H.164, 11
Then when it grew alone;.......................75. H.193, 7
That where you grew, scarce man can say.......87. H.216, 3
Can shew where you or grew, or stood...........88. H.216, 9
The Sock grew loathsome, and the Buskins pride, 150. H.382, 2
Dear Amarillis! Mon. Hark! Sil. mark: Mir. this earth grew sweet...................................159. H.421, 11
And sheep, grew more sweet, by that breth of Thine. 159. H.421, 14
Grief Down dead for grief, and end my woes withall: 11. H.22, 8
Next, how I love thee, that my griefe must tell,...23. H.72, 3
But whither, onely Grief do's know...............33. H.103, 4
That, which subverts whole nature, grief and care; 45. H.128, 21
Well; though my griefe by you was gall'd, the more; 52. H.146, 21
A desp'rate grief, that finds no cure............60. H.157, 2
Griefe, (my deare friend) has first my Harp unstrung; 84. H.210, 9
Speak griefe in you,..........................104. H.257, 2
Conceiv'd with grief are, and with teares brought forth. 105. H.257, 28
Griefe (ay me!) hath struck my Lute,..........131. H.332, 5
But that deni'd; a griefe, though small,.........153. H.395, 4
With griefe; seemes longer then a yeare.........162. H.431, 4
Of Patience wants. Grief breaks the stoutest Heart 169. H.447, 2
Ai me! How shal my griefe be stil'd?..........188. H.509, 5
With griefe of heart, methinks, I thus doe cry,..193. H.522, 5
The Dew of griefe upon this stone.............203. H.564, 5
Ph. A deale of Love, and much, much Griefe together. 248. H.730, 14
Griefe, if't be great, 'tis short; if long, 'tis light. 268. H.810, 2
Say, is't for reall griefe he mourns? not so;....275. H.842, 3
Each griefe we feele, that likewise is a Kite.....278. H.862, 3
With solemne tears, and with much grief of heart, 300. H.960, 3
Alack for grief!.............................306. H.984, 36
No grief is grown so desperate, but the ill......319. H.1048, 1
Yet, in my depth of grief, I'de be..........321. H.1056, 15
An equall mind is the best sauce for griefe.....333. H.1119, 2
Gives them by turnes their grief and jollitie.....394. N.236, 4
Frozen wth Greife; and place it in thyne eare,..412. A.3, 82
Euc. Great are my woes. Cha. And great must that Grief be, 416. A.8, 21
Grief-drowned Youthfull Mirtillo, Here he comes, Griefdrownd. 159. H.421, 6
Grief-rent To shew a heart grief-rent;..........391. N.228, 21
Griefs Small griefs find tongues: Full Casques are ever found 15. H.38, 7
And griefs hath fil'de upon my silver hairs;......140. H.355, 6
Since man expos'd is to a world of griefs.......153. H.397, 2
To give an end: Mir. to what? Scil. Such griefs as these. 159. H.421, 32
Where Joyes and Griefs have Turns Alternative..264. H.792, 2
Teares quickly drie: griefes will in time decay:..293. H.930, 1
Grievances As not to know, or feel some Grievances. 387. N.199, 2
Grieve Ah my Perilla! do'st thou grieve to see.....9. H.14, 1
Then grieve her not, with saying..............56. H.149, 113

Sho'd I not **grieve** (my Lawes) when every Lute,
288. H.907, 3
Grieving Not be **grieving**;....................308. H.993, 15
Grill's See **Gryll**
Or else because **Grill's** roste do's burn his Spit,..48. H.135, 3
Grim No threats of Tyrants, or the **Grim**........215. H.615, 3
The least **grim** looke, or cast a frown on you:....222. H.634, 8
And when we think His looks are sowre and **grim**,
340. N.7, 3
Yet sowre and **grim** Thou'dst seem to me;......395. N.246, 5
That makes **grim** Charon thus to pity thee.......416. A.8, 22
Grinders And her **grinders** black as jet;........11. H.21, 12
Grinning Many **grinning** properties............255. H.761, 10
Gripes Who **gripes** too hard the dry and slip'rie sand,
221. H.633, 52
Griping — — — — — — — —, ...437. var. H.336, 92
Gripings The **gripings** of the chine by age;.....134. H.336, 92
Grips See **Gripes**
Grist See **Holy-grist**
Curse not the mice, no **grist** of thine they eat:.141. H.358, 1
But he takes tole of? all the **Griest**...........376. N.127, 4
Grit With some small glit'ring **gritt**, to eate....119. H.293, 10
Groan Of thy deep **grone**....................314. H.1024, 11
Groans All now is silent; **groanes** are fled:......189. H.514, 5
Grocers Or see the **Grocers** in a trice,..........275. H.844, 7
Groom See **Bridegroom**
To the Bride, and to her **Groome**;...........124. H.314, 2
Of some rough **Groom**, who (yirkt with Corns) sayes. Sir
146. H.377, 21
When we conduct her to her **Groome**:........360. N.83, 47
Groom's See **Bridegroom's**
Grooms See **Bridegrooms**
Gross — — — — — — — — —, ...439. var. H.443, 28
Ground See **Underground**
So three in one small plat of **ground** shall ly,...11. H.22, 9
He who to the **ground** do's fall,...............84. H.209, 7
If having run my Barque on **ground**,..........94. H.225, 5
Himen, O Himen! Tread the sacred **ground**;..113. H 283, 31
The pleasing wife, the house, the **ground**......132. H.336, 9
Pray once, twice pray; and turn thy **ground** to gold.
144. H.370, 8
Thus, thus with hallowed foot I touch the **ground**,
242. H.713, 5
Next, like a Bishop consecrate my **ground**,.....245. H.723, 7
By throwing teeth into the **ground**:...........297. H.948, 6
Thy harmlesse and unhaunted **Ground**;........359. N.83, 8
Turnes all the patient **ground** to flowers.........364. N.96, 24
Conceal'd in this most holy **Ground**:..........366. N.98, 4
Let's kisse the sweet and holy **ground**;.......368. N.102, 16
Bleeding, that no Blood touch the **ground**:.....377. N.129, 6
But for each Graine, that in the **ground** is thrown.
388. N.208, 3
That Lookes for such prepared **grownd**,.......409. A.2, 104
Where, drest with garlands, there they walk the **ground**,
417. A.8, 29
Grounded Keepe it for ever; **grounded** with the good.
152. H.392, 7
Grounds A Plentious harvest to your **grounds**:..127. H.319, 24
Not envying others larger **grounds**:...........230. H.662, 16
With the Sun rising he must walk his **grounds**;.259. H.771, 3
Grove Be pleas'd to rest you in This Sacred **Grove**,
107. H.265, 3
Wine lead him on. Thus to a **Grove**..........165. H.443, 19
Two loving followers too unto the **Grove**,.....206. H.575, 23
Love brought me to a silent **Grove**,...........278. H.863, 1
Groves I write of **Groves**, of Twilights, and I sing
5. H.1, 11
The Purling springs, **groves**, birds, and well-weav'd Bowrs,
36. H.106, 45
Walk in the **Groves**, and thou shalt find.......192. H.521, 39
No more of **Groves**, Meades, Springs, and wreaths of Flowers:
228. H.658, 4
Grow They doe **grow**? I answer, There,..........19. H.53, 4
All the yeere, where Cherries **grow**............20. H.53, 8
Some ask'd how Pearls did **grow**, and where?...24. H.75, 5
May **grow** to be...............................30. H.89, 8
To **grow** the sooner innocent:................35. H.106, 6
Weak though it be; long may it **grow**, and stand,
40. H.112, 3
Lips can make Cherries **grow**...............57. H 149, 148
We shall **grow** old apace, and die............69. H.178, 59
The Fruit to **grow** up, or the Tree:...........79. H.198, 2
If you can see the water **grow**................79. H.198, 5
But like a Laurell, to **grow** green for ever......98. H.240, 2
Feed, and **grow** fat; and as ye eat,............102. H.250, 44
Fresh, as their blood; and ever **grow**,..........104. H.256, 19
May his pretty Duke-ship **grow**...............108. H 266, 1
And consume, and **grow** again to die,........115. H.283, 138
Or I shall quickly **grow**,......................137. H.340, 17
Chor. The shades **grow** great; but greater growes our sorrow,
160. H.421, 43
Or Christall **grow**;..........................171. H.452, 10
Shall fuller **grow**,............................171. H.455, 9
Grow up to be a Roman Citizen................171. H.456, 2
Grow fat and smooth: The reason is,.........173. H.461, 3
But pitie those, whose flanks **grow** great,......200. H.552, 15
Sooner the in-side of thy hand shall **grow**....202. H.557, 23
I might **grow** proud the while.................231. H.663, 4
Grow for two ends, it matters not at all,.......232. H.667, 1
Grow old with time, but yet keep weather-proofe. 245. H.723, 14
Or Damask Roses, when they **grow**..........271. H.824, 15
The more th'are drawn, the lesse they wil **grow** dry.
273. H.831, 2
Because as Plants by water **grow**,.............273. H.832, 3
New things succeed, as former things **grow** old.
285. H.892, 22
Live long and lovely, but yet **grow** no lesse...299. H.958, 3
Grow up in Beauty, as thou do'st begin,......304. H.979, 1
Grow young with Tydes, and though I see ye never,
316. H.1028, 25
As to make ye ever **grow**...................324. H.1070, 4
Can live by love, or else **grow** fat by Play:....325. H.1077, 2
(Or Sharon, where eternall Roses **grow**.).....326. H.1080, 8
Besides ye see me daily **grow**................329. H.1093, 3
If warre, or want shall make me **grow** so poore,.347. N.39, 1
When sins, by stripes, to us **grow** wearisome...349. N.45, 2
May Sweets **grow** here! & smoke from hence...361. N.83, 63
May Roses **grow**, to crown His own deare Head.
366. N.97, 23
Which has no root, and cannot **grow**,.........371. N.114, 2
How roses lillies and carnations **grow**,..........404. A.1, 16
(Those wch must **growe** to Vertuous deeds)....407. A.2, 20
Growe vpp wth Mylder Lawes to knowe.......407. A.2, 25
Loues Cherries from such fyers **growe**.........408. A.2, 50
Or their thought of faith may **growe**...........418. A.9, 37
— — — — — — — — — — —, ...426. var. H.197, 44
Growing Are twigs of Birch, and willow, **growing** there:
39. H.110, 2
A stubborn Oake, or Holme (long **growing** there)
225. H.642, 14
Like wanton rose buds **growing** out of snowe,..405. A.1, 54
Growing in this love garded paradice.........406. A.1, 72
Grown But I am not yet **grown** cold;............17. H.43, 2
When quiet **grown** sh'ad seen them,............31. H.92, 10
Let me be leane, and cold, and once **grown** poore,
31. H.93, 3
Grown violent, do's either die, or tire.........51. H.143, 4
Like to a flame **growne** moderate:..............67. H.175, 12
Your stock, and needy **grown**,................110. H.274, 18
And weather by our aches, **grown**.............134. H.336, 87
Leaving their Poet (being now **grown** old)....151. H.387, 3
Lastly, be mindfull (when thou art **grown** great)
181. H.483, 13
Black I'm **grown** for want of meat;...........223. H.638, 4
Weak I am **grown**, and must in short time fall;.242. H.713, 19
Grown fat,..................................246. H.724, 23
For, I'm **grown** old; &, with mine age, **grown** poore:
258. H.768, 2
Truggin a Footman was; but now, **growne** lame,
283. H.882, 1
Grown old, surrender must his place,.........285. H.892, 11
And when so feeble I am **grown**,............303. H.973, 8
No grief is **grown** so desperate, but the ill.....319. H.1048, 1
— — — — — — — — — — —, ...447. var. A.1, 16
Grows **Growes** still the stronger, strongly vext...37. H.106, 100
Whose love **growes** more enflam'd, by being Foes.
78. H.197, 44
And Ramme of time and by vexation **growes**..148. H.377, 111
Mont. Set with the Sunne, thy woes: Scil. The day **grows** old:
160. H.421, 41
Chor. The shades grow great; but greater **growes** our sorrow,
160. H.421, 43
Growes old with the yeere,...................196. H.534, 17
But the Relation then of both **growes** poor,....255. H.758, 3
At whose faire topp to please the sight there **growes**
405. A.1, 35
Growth The **growth**, and down-fall of her aged trees:
23. H.69, 2
As quick a **growth** to meet Decay,............125. H.316, 13
Their Resurrection, and their **growth** in you:..137. H.341, 8
It keeps a **growth** in thee; and so will runne..147. H.377, 43
For **growth** in this my rich Plantation:.......152. H.392, 4
Groynes **Groynes**, for his fleshly Burglary of late,.106. H.261, 1
Grubs **Grubs** loves his Wife and Children, while that they
325. H.1077, 1
But when they call or cry on **Grubs** for meat;.325. H.1077, 3
Instead of Bread, **Grubs** gives them stones to eat.
325. H.1077, 4
Grudge — — — — — — — — —, ...432. var. H.283, 136
Grudged Weathers, and never **grudged** at.......147. H.377, 64
Grudgings **Grudgings** turnes bread to stones, when to the Poore
220. H.632, 1
Grutch And of such Torture as no one would **grutch**
115. H.283, 136
Gryll See **Grill's**
Gryll eates, but ne're sayes Grace; To speak the troth,
48. H.135, 1
Gryll either keeps his breath to coole his broth;
48. H.135, 2
Gryll will not therefore say a Grace for it.....48. H.135, 4
Guard See **Safeguard**
To **guard** it so, as nothing here shall be......73. H.186, 19
That keepes his own strong **guard**, in the despight
128. H.323, 9

Of peltish wasps; we'l know his Guard.......165. H.443, 17
Safely guard us, now and aye,.................177. H.473, 3
Come guard this night the Christmas-Pie,....263. H.785, 1
Hast set a Guard...........................349. N.47, 8
Guarded Stands garded with a rosy hilly wall,...405. A.1, 30
Growing in this love garded paradice..........406. A.1, 72
Guardian Who is his Butcher more then Guardian.
201. H.557, 16
Gubbs Gubbs call's his children Kitlings: and wo'd bound
80. H.200, 1
Guess See Guesse
By this I guesse,...........................30. H.87, 13
Seeing those painted Countries; and so guesse.36. H.106, 79
Guesse I may, what I must be:..............38. H.107, 3
So that we may guesse by these,............138. H.342, 9
Guesse, soe departe; yett stay A while to[o] see
411. A.3, 59
Lyes here about, and as we guesse........440. ins. H.443, 45z
Guesse See Guess
Guesse cuts his shooes, and limping, goes about.98. H.239, 1
Guest See Great-little-kingly-guest
And richer Wine wo'dst give to me (thy guest).262. H.783, 5
Give me the food that satisfies a Guest:......265. H.797, 1
Guest-rite No commer to thy Roofe his Guest-rite wants;
146. H.377, 19
Guests Makes guests and fish smell strong; pray go
146. H.377, 26
Jove, joy'st when guests make their abode....147. H.377, 62
Shall we thy Guests.........................289. H.911, 3
This rule of manners I will teach my guests,..310. H.1005, 1
Are ready by, to make the Guests all pure:...355. N.65, 6
Guide Or be my guide; and I shall be............33. H.98, 7
Then away; come, Hymen guide..............53. H.149, 9
Then away; come, Hymen guide..............53. H.149, 19
Then away; come, Hymen guide..............54. H.149, 29
Then away; come, Hymen guide..............54. H.149, 39
Home the Turtles; Hymen guide.............54. H.149, 49
Then away; come Hymen, guide..............55. H.149, 69
Those holy lights, wherewith they guide.......109. H.271, 3
God, and good Angells guide Thee; and so blesse
399. N.263, 32
Guided Bright as the Wise-men's Torch, which guided them
86. H.213, 21
And by the glow-worms light wel guided,....93. H.223, 141
Guides She followes the Spirit that guides now..225. H.643, 12
Guiding Thy lucky Genius, and thy guiding Starre,
181. H.483, 5
Guild See Gild, Re-gild
Guilded See Gilded
Guilds See Gilds
Guilt Purge hence the guilt, and kill this quarrelling.
78. H.197, 32
First, Fear and Shame without, then Guilt within.
341. N.11, 2
— — — — — — — — — — —, ...436. ins. H.336, 48g
Guilthead See Gilthead
Guiltiness See Blood-guiltiness, Blush-guiltiness
Guiltless None shall be guiltlesse, be he n'er so good.
194. H.528, 2
With guiltlesse mirth;.......................350. N.47, 38
Thy way, Thou guiltlesse man, and satisfie....398. N.263, 13
Guilty No One that's there his guilty glasse.....148. H.377, 86
Known guilty here of incivility:................290. H.914, 2
Your judgement finds a guilty Poem, there...322. H.1062, 5
(Judgment and Death, denounc'd gainst Guilty men)
411. A.3, 62
guilty of somewhat, ripe the strawberries.430. ins. H.283, 20b
Gulf For those is kept the Gulf of Hecatè;......417. A.8, 32
Gulfs And 'midst a thousand gulfs to be secure....23. H.71, 6
Gull — — — — — — — — —, ...451. ins. H.336, 48e
Gum See Night-gum
Or sweet, as is that gumme...................57. H.149, 145
(Made of her Pap and Gum)..................80. H.201, 7
With brownest Toadstones, and the Gum......166. H.443, 57
Gums While other Gums their sweets perspire,....20. H.54, 5
To blast the Aire, but Amber-greece and Gums.
205. H.575, 6
To grace his own Gums, or of Box, or bone...211. H.595, 2
(His teeth all out) to rince and wash his gummes.
301. H.965, 2
And her white teeth which in the gums are sett
405. A.1, 31
Gut Science puffs up, sayes Gut, when either Pease
327. H.1085, 1
Gyges A Gyges Ring they beare about them still,
250. H.737, 1
Gypsy Love, like a Gypsie, lately came;.........63. H.166, 1
Habit 'Tis now his habit, which he can't give ore.
302. H.972, 2
Habitation Back must now go to's habitation:..140. H.355, 2
Habits Pure hands, pure habits, pure, pure every thing.
127. H.320, 4
Had (Partial List of Auxiliary) See Y'ad
Æson had (as Poets faine)....................10. H.19, 9
A telling what rare sights h'ad seen:..........13. H.27, 8
Had not her Blush rebuked me................14. H.33, 4
More discontents I never had..................19. H.51, 1
The warmth and sweetnes had me there........20. H.56, 3
I saw he had a Bow,...........................27. H.81, 17
I spy'd he had a Quiver......................27. H.81, 20
Whether thy bones had here their Rest, or no..27. H.82, 6
They must be borne with, and in rev'rence had..32. H.97, 2
Had, first, durst plow the Ocean..............36. H.106, 76
Vertue had, and mov'd her Sphere..............37. H.106, 92
Stout sons I had, and those twice three;.......41. H.116, 3
Glasco had none, but now some teeth has got;.46. H.129, 1
Had we kept close, or play'd within,..........48. H.136, 6
A Virgins face she had; her dresse...........51. H.142, 7
Of Mirtle she had in her hand:................51. H.142, 20
But that it had some intermitting houres.....52.. H.146, 2
(When you had power) the meanest remedy:..52. H.146, 20
Y'ave had at Barly-breaks.....................56. H.149, 118
And (oh!) had it but a tongue,...............57. H.149, 139
As if to stir it scarce had leave:.............66. H.175, 6
When I had Thee, my chiefe Preserver, by.....72. H.185, 21
And had but single grace......................75. H.193, 8
And had no other pride at all,.................75. H.193, 30
Had Cassius, that weak Water-drinker, known..78. H.197, 61
Thee in thy Vine, or had but tasted one......78. H.197, 62
The world had all one Nose..................80. H.201, 24
Had Wolves or Tigers seen but thee,..........89. H.219, 3
As Rome's Pantheon had not more.............90. H.223, 8
Had Lesbia (too-too-kind) but known.........104. H.256, 11
Not Virgil's Gnat had such a Tomb............104. H.256, 21
A shew, as if 't 'ad been a snake:.............116. H.284, 4
Mans Fortune must be had in reverence.......117. H.287, 2
(If a wild Apple can be had).................135. H.336, 122
Still to our gains our chief respect is had;....139. H.351, 1
And when at night, she folded had her sheep,.159. H.421, 25
Roots had no money; yet he went o'th score..162. H.427, 1
That h'ad nor Gold or Silver to put in't?......162. H.427, 4
When I a Heart had one,.....................168. H.446, 2
One Cordelion had that Age long since;......170. H.451, 15
Thy Love had one knot, mine a triple tye.......173. H.464, 3
Of these had imputation......................175. H.465, 60
T'ave lost the good ye might have had.........179. H.476, 39
You had your comming hither;................184. H.493, 2
One Fate had both; both equall Grace;.......185. H.497, 7
More honour had, then this same Flie;.......186. H.497, 17
Wherein t'ave had an enjoying.................195. H.534, 6
Eaten I have; and though I had good cheere,.197. H.541, 1
I vanish; more I had to say;.................207. H.575, 65
Urles had the Gout so, that he co'd not stand;.207. H.577, 1
Of better to be had!..........................211. H.596, 4
Had I then askt her Maidenhead?............212. H.599, 4
Which had a juice in it:......................222. H.635, 2
Where I have had, what ever thing co'd be...227. H.652, 3
Besides rare sweets, I had a Book which none..227. H.652, 5
Never man yet had a regredience..............228. H.656, 2
As Heaven had spent all perfumes there.......237. H.686, 12
Who two and thirty cornes had on a foot.......240. H.704, 2
Thou canst but have, what others had.........246. H.725, 4
And had her; but it was upon..................265. H.798, 3
One word more I had to say;..................270. H.821, 5
But nothing so; The Dinner Adam had,......273. H.835, 3
'Twas but a dream; but had I been..........279. H.863, 13
A good Penelope was had:....................283. H.885, 6
Musique had both her birth, and death with Thee.
288. H.907, 10
Where we such clusters had,..................289. H.911, 7
But had it been of Birch, the death's the same..306. H.986, 4
Happily I had a sight.........................313. H.1018, 1
Is, that I never yet had wife;................320. H.1052, 2
Abundant plagues I late have had,.............354. N.57, 1
Take then his Vowes, who, if he had it, would.369. N.105, 5
God had but one Son free from sin; but none..378. N.134, 1
Had (as it were) a Dereliction;...............382. N.167, 2
Had no one Beame from Gods sweet Majestie..382. N.167, 4
One Birth our Saviour had; the like none yet..384. N.182, 1
Had He not drank them up for you...........400. N.266, 15
Whether the world such Sperrits had or noe,..411. A.3, 38
Or had I not, I'de stopp the spreading itch...411. A.3, 55
Speak, what art thou? Euc. One, once that had a lover,
416. A.8, 9
Had a sweet complexion......................417. A.9, 20
— — — — — — — — — —, ...433. var. H.293, 15
Hadst Hadst thou not fill'd them with thy fire and flame.
45. H.128, 32
Thou had'st the wreath before, now take the Tree;
150. H.383, 1
Had'st power thy selfe to keep this vow;.....176. H.465, 82
And hadst thou wager'd twenty Kine,.......244. H.716, 45
Thou had'st, and hast thy mighty influence,....299. H.956, 8
Hadst for Thy place..........................345. N.33, 6
But if thou hadst, He sho'd have one;.......354. N.59, 12
Haft Made of a Haft, that was a Mutton-bone....46. H.129, 4
Point be up, and Haft be downe;............284. H.889, 3
Hag The Hag is astride,........................225. H.643, 1
To house the Hag, you must doe this;........284. H.890, 1
The old Hag in. No surer thing..............284. H.890, 6
Hence the Hag, that rides the Mare,.........284. H.891, 2
Hags Hags away, while Children sleep..........284. H.888, 4
Hail O Frost! O Snow! O Haile forbid the Banes.
40. H.113, 2

Of the Raine, Frost, Haile, and Snow?........40. H.115, 4
Ile send such Frost, such Haile, such Sleet, and Snow, 82. H.204, 10
Haile holy, and all-honour'd Tomb,...........402. N.269, 1

Hair See Maiden-hair
Ha's she thinne haire, hath she none,.........11. H.21, 13
That neither haire was cut, or true teares shed.27. H.82, 3
Suspicion questions every haire..............49. H.136, 23
Dandled the ringlets of her haire.............51. H.142, 12
Be you not proud of that rich haire,..........61. H.160, 5
Such frost and snow upon your haire:........63. H.164, 5
For Jewels for your Gowne, or Haire:.........68. H.178, 18
Pieces, patches, ropes of haire;.............76. H.195, 5
False in breast, teeth, haire, and eyes:.......77. H.195, 10
Ile expiate with Sulphur, Haire, and Salt:...77. H.197, 30
To give the least disturbance to her haire:...82. H.204, 2
And fan her wanton haire....................103. H.255, 4
And with dishevell'd Haire,..................110. H.274, 15
Let my haire then stand an end:..............117. H.286, 6
Good morrow to mine own torn hair..........156. H.412, 3
This flock of wooll, and this rich lock of hair,..159. H.421, 15
And may'st draw thousands with a haire:.....174. H.465, 4
Dew sate on Julia's haire,....................181. H.484, 1
I have seen many Maidens to have haire;.....205. H.571, 1
And each Ringlet of her haire,...............232. H.665, 11
Locks incurl'd of other haire;.................253. H.750, 11
Or if haire remaines to me...................277. H.852, 4
It chanst a ringlet of her haire,...............281. H.876, 7
Bind me but to thee with thine haire,.........293. H.934, 1
Or wth thy wrist or flattering Hayre,.........408. A.2, 62
— — — — — — — — — —, ...437. var. H.336, 118

Hair-lace In a dirtie Haire-lace...............333. H.1122, 7

Hairless Which is as white and hair-less as an egge. 139. H.349, 2

Hair's For my haires black colouring:..........330. H.1098, 2

Hairs Age cals me hence, and my gray haires bid come, 9. H.14, 3
At which she smil'd; then with her hairs......50. H.139, 10
And my retorted haires......................80. H.201, 12
A little brush of Squirrils haires,.............91. H.223, 46
Numberlesse, as are your haires...............96. H.232, 8
Or those on her dishevel'd haires,............130. H.330, 3
And twisting my Iülus hairs;...............135. H.336, 118
And griefs hath fil'de upon my silver hairs;...140. H.355, 6
Black your haires are; mine are white;........194. H.527, 5
Jone wo'd go tel her haires; and well she might, 195. H.531, 1
Cut off thy haires; and let thy Teares be shed.219. H.627, 3
To take thine haires when they are knowne....282. H.881, 3
'Tis I am wild, and more then haires..........282. H.881, 5
Flusht was his face; his haires with oyle did shine; 313. H.1017, 3
Who by his gray Haires, doth his lusters tell,.328. H.1088, 5
Receive this offering of our Haires:..........360. N.83, 38
To feed upon the Candid hares.........433. ins. H.293, 31a

Hairy Hisped, and hairie, ere thy Palm shall know 202. H.557, 24

Halcyon's Is here the Halcion's curious nest:....90. H.223, 4

Half And thereupon, in tears half drown'd,.......18. H.46, 3
And e'en with cold half starved...............26. H.81, 12
Orecome, or halfe betray'd by Tiffanies:......34. H.104, 2
Thrice, and above, blest (my soules halfe) art thou, 34. H.106, 1
Night now hath watch'd her self half blind;....54. H.149, 31
Halfe wasted in the porch.....................54. H.149, 54
Hard by, i' th' shell of halfe a nut,............91. H.223, 44
He payes the halfe, who do's confesse the Debt. 94. H.226, 10
Beginne with Jove; then is the worke halfe done; 128. H.321, 1
Ile call to mind things half forgot:...........135. H.336, 114
But one halfe houre, that's made up here.....162. H.431, 3
A Strawberry shewes halfe drown'd in Creame?.164. H.440, 6
Halfe tipsie to the Fairie Bed,.................165. H.443, 4
Half rotten, and without an eye,..............166. H.443, 52
But home return'd, as he went forth, halfe blind. 201. H.555, 4
I sho'd delight to have my Curles halfe drown'd 214. H.612, 11
But for to live that halfe seven well:.........233. H.670, 35
But at push-pin (half the day:)...............235. H.678, 4
Half that blessing thou'lt give me.:...........236. H.684, 4
Halfe of my just remuneration................267. H.804, 4
Is halfe, or altogether innocent...............268. H.809, 2
Where Venus sleeps (halfe smothered.)........269. H.815, 4
Down, and halfe drown'd me with the same:..283. H.883, 2
Halfe with a Lawne of water hid,.............294. H.939, 6
And seems halfe ravisht, when he looks upon..295. H.941, 3
Is halfe way cured, if the party will...........319. H.1048, 2
I'th' Court that's halfe so comly.............324. H.1068, 20
Of all those three-score, has not liv'd halfe three: 328. H.1088, 8
I'm halfe return'd before I go................328. H.1090, 13
Halfe choakt with the stink of her farting....333. H.1122, 6
And halfe damns me with untruth;...........348. N.41, 39
Least loane of Thine, half Restitution?........368. N.103, 6
So that the wonder is not halfe so great,......388. N.208, 5
not halfe so much the Act, as end......421. ins. H.106, 42b

Half-jet-rings Of higher price, as halfe-iet-ringes 440. ins. H.443, 45s

Half's An houre or half's delight;.............176. H.467, 8

Hall See Judgment-hall
To the worn Threshold, Porch, Hall, Parlour, Kitchin, 146. H.377, 5
Wherewith ye drest the Christmas Hall:......304. H.980, 4
Like as my Parlour, so my Hall.............350. N.47, 17

Hallowed No Planke from Hallowed Altar, do's appeale 149. H.377, 127
Be thy hand the hallowed Cake:.............158. H.417, 2
More sweet, then Storax from the hallowed fire: 205. H.575, 8
Thus, thus with hallowed foot I touch the ground, 242. H.713, 5
We must not give all to the hallowed fire.....295. H.940, 2
Euc. The hallowed Tapers all preparèd were,...416. A.8, 19

Hallowing — — — — — — — —, ...434. var. H.293, 48

Halter The Halter was of silk, and gold,..........279. H.863, 5

Ham A Spinners ham, the beards of mice,..435. ins. H.293, u

Hamlets Since Coats, and Hamlets, best agree.......5. H.2, 5

Hampton Court To Richmond, Kingstone, and to Hampton-Court:...................................315. H.1028, 10

Hanch Hanch, since he (lately) did interre his wife, 275. H.842, 1

Hand See Lily-hand
With that Heav'n gave thee with a warie hand,.35. H.106, 23
To take her by the either hand:..............37. H.106, 96
His head upon his hand he laid;...............42. H.119, 7
Whose heart, whose hand, whose ev'ry part spake love. 42. H.122, 8
Of Womans beauty? and with hand more rude.49. H.138, 5
By th' hand of him who is the Generall.......50. H.141, 2
Of Mirtle she had in her hand:...............51. H.142, 20
And all in Your Blest Hand, which has the powers 62. H.161, 7
And to that Hand, (the Branch of Heavens faire Tree) 62. H.161, 11
I kneele for help; O! lay that hand on me,...62. H.161, 12
To see my hand; that by the same...........63. H.166, 3
Then let thy active hand scu'd o're thy Lyre:.67. H.176, 3
I'm up, I'm up, and blesse that hand,..........72. H.185, 22
By Arts wise hand, but to this end..........76. H.193, 46
Wither'd my hand, and palsie-struck my tongue. 84. H.210, 10
From this bleeding hand of mine,.............88. H.217, 1
Something for Shew-bread, and at hand.......92. H.223, 69
Dead falls the Cause, if once the Hand be mute; 123. H.308, 1
The tongue in peace; but then in warre the hand. 137. H.339, 2
To kisse your hand, most Dainty Governesse...137. H.341, 12
For the expansion of thy hand...............139. H.350, 2
But you, my Lord, are One, whose hand along.141. H.359, 13
With heart and hand to entertain:............147. H.377, 36
When eithers heart, and eithers hand did strive 147. H.377, 39
A hand too desp'rate, or a knife that bites....147. H.377, 53
To last, but not their ever: Vertues Hand...148. H.377, 101
Be thy hand the hallowed Cake:.............158. H.417, 2
Wise hand enchasing here those warts,......166. H.443, 60
Sooner the in-side of thy hand shall grow....202. H.557, 23
One of the five straight branches of my hand..203. H.565, 1
Then from his Feet, it shifted to his Hand:...207. H.577, 2
Now tis in's Hand, he gives no Almes at all...207. H.577, 4
Left (of the large heart, and long hand).....218. H.626, 10
Holds none at all, or little in his hand........221. H.633, 53
Circum-crost by thy pure hand:..............227. H.651, 2
To kisse thy hand from out the coach;.......239. H.696, 2
Put then in my hand,.......................256. H.762, 5
Ai me! I love, give him your hand to kisse.....274. H.937, 1
First, may the hand of bounty bring..........291. H.919, 1
Ile kiss the hand that strikes me.............296. H.946, 6
Then will I heave my wither'd hand..........303. H.973, 15
Bestirs his Hand, but starves in hand the Suite. 303. H.975, 8
That Prince must govern with a gentle hand,.323. H.1067, 1
Who with her eyes-gleam, or a glance of hand, 326. H.1080, 16
Then reach Thou forth that hand of Thine,...342. N.17, 9
With Princely hand He'l recompence delay....344. N.30, 4
Lord, 'tis thy plenty-dropping hand,...........350. N.47, 41
Heaving up my either hand;...................364. N.95, 2
How heart and hand do all agree,............365. N.97, 9
And Palmes in hand,........................369. N.106, 9
The Sheets, the Rugs, made by thy hand.....374. N.123, 44
So the Divine Hand work't, and brake no thred, 385. N.184, 3
God has a Right Hand, but is quite bereft....394. N.240, 1
For I have washt both hand and heart,.......402. N.269, 6
The Gathering of the Lipp: not hand.........408. A.2, 52
T'was braue, t'was braue could we comand ye hand 413. A.4, 6
See how he waves his hand, and through his eyes 430. ins. H.283, 40a
Ore which the hand..................436. ins. H.336, 48m

— — — — — — — — — — — —, ...448. var. A.1, 99
Handed See **Close-handed, Handsome-handed**
Handle And softly **handle** Him: y'ad need,......366. N.98, 20
Handled Till after I had **handled** them;........203. H.562, 4
Handmaid Your sober **Hand-maid**; who doth wisely chuse,
99. H.245, 6
Shall want a **Hand-mayde**, (as she ofte will vse)
412. A.3, 100
— — — — — — — — — — — — —, ...449. var. A.3, 100
Handmaids and the smooth **Handmaides** pay their vowes
431. ins. H.283, 60d
Hands With which (Perilla) wash my **hands** and feet;
9. H.14, 9
And armes and **hands** they did enthrall:.......16. H.41, 15
And chaf'd his **hands** with mine,..............27. H.81, 23
With **hands** held up to Love, I wept;..........51. H.142, 3
Armes, and **hands**, and all parts else,..........53. H.147, 7
Hands, and thighs, and legs, are all..........59. H.155, 5
Till we have wept, kist, sigh't, shook **hands**, or so.
73. H.186, 6
Into thy loving **hands**: For Ile keep none.....73. H.186, 15
When Virgins **hands** have drawn..............75. H.193, 2
Pure **hands** bring hither without staine..........91. H.223, 42
Ye dance, and sing, and now clap **hands**.......94. H.225, 8
Of Pearle, and Gold to bind her **hands**:........98. H.238, 7
By whose tough labours, and rough **hands**,...101. H.250, 3
While you wring your **hands** and weep.........118. H.289, 14
By, yet not blessed by his **hands**,............119. H.293, 30
Pure **hands**, pure habits, pure, pure every thing.
127. H.320, 4
To kisse our **hands**, nor do we wish..........133. H.336, 47
Of Amber chaf't between the **hands**,..........145. H.375, 16
No clap of **hands**, or shout, or praises-proofe..150. H.382, 11
The feet or **hands**;..........................172. H.458, 9
Reach, with your whiter **hands**, to me,.......185. H.495, 1
With paste of Almonds, Syb her **hands** doth scoure;
203. H.561, 1
Us **hands** to get what here we have..........226. H.647, 4
Is the wise Masters Feet, and **Hands**.........230. H.662, 24
Whose **hands** did compose...................239. H.695, 5
Pauls **hands** do give, what give they bread or meat,
248. H.731, 1
Pauls **hands** do give, nought else for ought we know.
248. H.731, 4
Ready to joyne, as well our hearts as **hands**....262. H.781, 10
Wash your **hands**, or else the fire.............263. H.786, 1
Unwasht **hands**, ye Maidens, know,............263. H.786, 3
Hold but her hands; You hold both **hands** and wings.
271. H.823, 6
That we wash our hearts, and **hands**..........280. H.870, 4
Their **hands** for paine;.......................296. H.946, 16
Thee Julia, first, to sanctifie thy **hands**:.........299. H.957, 2
To kiss his **hands**, but that for fearfullness;.....301. H.963, 2
Wash our **hands** in innocence..................303. H.974, 6
Wash your **hands**, and cleanse your eyes.......322. H.1064, 2
Your hearts, and **hands**, lips, eares, and eyes.......366. N.98, 9
Thy **hands** (though cold) yet spotlesse, white,..375. N.123, 75
Gods **Hands** are round, & smooth, that gifts may fall
380. N.151, 1
Ready, to pierce Thy tender Feet, and **Hands**.....398. N.263, 4
With little **hands** and fingers long and small......406. A.1, 99
White **handes** as smooth, as Mercies, bring......408. A.2, 59
Handsel And tell Him, (for good **handsell** too)....354. N.59, 7
Handsels Are but the **handsells** of our joyes hereafter.
362. N.90, 2
Handsome Unto a **handsome** Shephardling;..........5. H.2, 12
Lest a **handsome** anger flye,..................98. H.238, 13
Here, naked Younglings, **handsome** Striplings run
206. H.575, 17
Hansome you are, and Proper you will be......299. H.958, 1
Handsome-handed With **handsome-handed** Drosomell
184. H.492, 31
Hang Droop, droop no more, or **hang** the head........7. H.9, 1
That gallant Tulip will **hang** down his head,.....41. H.118, 3
Fold now thine armes; and **hang** the head,........47, H.132, 1
And Harrow **hang** up resting now;............127. H.319, 46
No more shall I from mantle-trees **hang** downe,.131. H.333, 4
(And **hang** the head when as the Act is done)...196. H.537, 2
My wearied Oat Ile **hang** upon the Tree,........205. H.573, 3
Hang up Hooks, and Sheers to scare...........284. H.891, 1
— — — — — — — — — — —, ...450. var. A.9, 47
Hanged And Harrow, (though they'r **hang'd** up now.)
102. H.250, 50
Next, **hang'd** for Theeving: Now the people say,.195. H.532, 3
Where some had **hang'd** themselves for love,....278. H.863, 3
Hanger-on That (where meat is) will be a **hanger on**.
296. H.944, 2
Hanging **Hanging** down his head t'wards me;.....38. H.107, 2
Of cleanest Cobweb, **hanging** by...............92. H.223, 99
What gives it **hanging** in the Aire............167. H.443, 105
Hangs **Hangs** on the Dew-locks of the night:...68. H.178, 24
Hap And watrie dangers; while thy whiter **hap**,..36. H.106, 71
If **hap** it must, that I must see thee lye.........300. H.960, 1
Then come my God, and **hap** what will.........393. N.232, 16
I'le follow Thee, **hap**, **hap** what shall,.........399. N.265, 5
Happened But ah! it **hapned** as he made.........265. H.798, 7
Happier When of these truths, thy **happyer** knowledge lyes,
37. H.106, 87
Happily The Persian King liv'd not more **happily**...70. H.181, 4
Happily I had a sight........................313. H.1018, 1
At randome, sometimes hit most **happily**......318. H.1039, 2
Happiness The Shepherds Fleecie **happinesse**:........5. H.2, 8
Of **happinesse**...................................30. H.87, 14
Those Fields of everlasting **happinesse**...........177. H.470, 2
That **Happines** do's still the longest thrive,......264. H.792, 1
Happy Live, and live blest; thrice **happy** Paire; Let Breath,
38. H.106, 141
The which was made a **happy** Bride,............41. H.116, 5
The **happy** dawning of her thigh:..............51. H.142, 16
Still shall crown the **happy** life..................55. H.149, 59
Happy you, who can have seas..................62. H.162, 7
I! far more welcome then the **happy** soile,......77. H.197, 15
Goe **happy** Rose, and enterwove.................98. H.238, 1
The **happy** fortune will not alwayes last.........218. H.621, 2
Happy day......................................220. H.633, 5
To a more **happy** Residence....................226. H.644, 6
That **happy** heat;..............................227. H.653, 7
Less **happy**, less enjoying thee..................229. H.662, 4
O **happy** life! if that their good...............231. H.662, 70
Thrice **happie** Roses, so much grac't, to have....249. H.734, 1
Happy Rusticks, best content..................255. H.761, 21
From whose **happy** spark here let..............262. H.782, 3
In most **happy** Parallels?......................286. H.897, 10
(A **happy** Realme! When no compulsive Law,.326. H.1080, 19
O **happy** place!..................................369. N.106, 3
Then He will give a **happy** end to it...........396. N.252, 4
— — — — — — — — — — — —, ...421. var. H.106, 31
Nor knowe thy **happye**, and vn-enuey'de state
422. ins. H.106, 92a
— — — — — — — — — — —, ...426. var. H.197, 27
Happy's **Happy's** that man, to whom God gives....351. N.50, 1
Harbour That may **harbour** thee, when I,......334. H.1125, 5
Hard If deare Anthea, my **hard** fate it be........11. H.22, 1
Goes the world now, it will with thee goe **hard**:..22. H.64, 1
Me thought 'twas strange, that thou so hard sho'dst prove,
42. H.122, 7
With **hard** oppression.........................65. H.172, 12
Hard by, i'th'shell of halfe a nut,..............91. H.223, 44
But 'tis no Gout (beleeve it) but **hard** Beere,....98. H.239, 3
How **hard** a woman 'tis to please?..............103. H.253, 12
Thou say'st my lines are **hard**;.................138. H.344, 1
They are both **hard**, and marr'd,..............138. H.344, 3
Or Phyllis, whom **hard** Fate forc't on,..........215. H.616, 13
Who gripes too **hard** the dry and slip'rie sand,..221. H 633, 52
Nothing **hard**, or harsh can prove...............240. H.701, 1
London my home is: though by **hard** fate sent..242. H.713, 13
Sibb when she saw her face how hard it was,....249. H.732, 1
Do's Fortune rend thee? Beare with thy **hard** Fate:
270. H.820, 1
'Tis sweet to thinke on what was **hard** t' endure...276. H.849, 2
Hard are the two first staires unto a Crowne;..292. H.925, 1
(What's **hard** to others) nothing's troublesome...298. H 955, 4
Nothing's so **hard**, but search will find it out...311. H.1008, 2
'Tis **hard** to finde God, but to comprehend........340. N.8, 1
Labour we must, and labour **hard**...............380. N.152, 1
Harden God's said our hearts to **harden** then,....396. N.250, 1
Hardened Which, this night **hardned**, sodders up her nose.
296. H.945, 2
Harder That done, the **harder** Fates deny'd......69. H.180, 3
Hardly On with thy worke, though thou beest **hardly** prest;
311. H.1009, 1
Our heat of youth can **hardly** keep the mean...318. H.1042, 2
Hare And trace the **Hare** i' th' trecherous Snow:
231. H.662, 63
Hark But (**Hark**!) we praise the Painter now, not you.
98. H.241, 2
Hark, **harke**, the God do's play!................151. H.388, 5
Dear Amarillis! Mon. **Hark**! Sil. mark: Mir. this earth grew
sweet...159. H.421, 11
Sil. Words sweet as Love it self. Montano, **Hark**.
159. H.421, 17
And he one chiefe; But **harke**, I heare the Cock,
207. H.575, 61
But **hark** how I can now expresse..............243. H.716, 27
Harm Strong against future **harme**:...........55. H.149, 88
Of what can hurt by day, or **harme** by night:..128. H.323, 10
And not by fire to **harme** me..................234. H.674, 6
Like fier-drakes, yett did'st mee no **harme** therby..410. A.3, 28
Harmed And string if they be **harm'd**,..............27. H.81, 27
Harmless Some smooth, and **harmlesse** Beucolicks...5. H.2, 10
And take the **harmlesse** follie of the time.........69. H.178, 58
No, here Ile last, and walk (a **harmless** shade)..73. H.186, 17
Spend **Harmless** shade thy nightly Houres,......289. H.912, 1
But yet **harmless** as a sheep...................306. H.984, 30
Of **harmlesse** thoughts, to watch and keep........350. N.47, 9
Thy **harmlesse** and unhaunted Ground;..........359. N.83, 8
Harmony Meets in the whole and maks a **harmony**.406. A.1, 106
Harms Keeps the sleeping child from **harms**.......284. H.889, 6
Harp Skilfull i' th' **Harpe**, and Melodie:........70. H.181, 10
My **Harp** hung up, here on the Willow tree.......84. H.210, 2
Griefe, (my deare friend) has first my **Harp** unstrung;
84. H.210, 9
What though my **Harp**, and Violl be............361. N.84, 1

Apollo sings, his **harpe** resounds; give roome,....415. A.7, 1
Harp's Then let the **Harps** inchantments strike mine eare;
343. N.25, 4
Harps Then Lutes and **Harpes** shall stroke the eare.
247. H.725, 10
While **Harps**, and Violls then................369. N.106, 15
Our **Harps** hung on the Willow-tree:...........373. N.123, 2
Harrie See Harry
Harrow And **Harrow**, (though they'r hang'd up now.)
102. H.250, 50
And **Harrow** hang up resting now;............127. H.319, 46
Harrows Last, may your **Harrows**, Shares and Ploughes,
179. H.476, 22
Harry Touch but thy Lire (my **Harrie**) and I heare
276. H.851, 1
Harsh Nothing hard, or **harsh** can prove........240. H.701, 1
None are so **harsh**, but if they find..............252. H.746, 5
Hart See Heart
Harts See Hearts
Hartshorn Instead of **Harts-horne** (if he speakes the troth)
299. H.959, 3
Harvest And, to the Pipe, sing **Harvest** home...101. H.250, 6
The **Harvest** Swaines, and Wenches bound.....101. H.250, 13
A Plentious **harvest** to your grounds:..........127. H.319, 24
As Cherry **harvest**, now high fed..............165. H.443, 10
Thy **Harvest** home; thy Wassaile bowle,........231. H.662, 56
And everlasting **Harvest** crown thy Soile!......269. H.818, 8
He prayes his **Harvest** may be well brought home.
270. H.822, 2
Will, after ease, a richer **harvest** yeild:.........292. H.922, 2
When Chub brings in his **harvest**, still he cries,.327. H.1086, 1
And haue their **haruest**, wch must stand..........408. A.2, 51
Has (Partial List of Auxiliary)
Ha's she thinne haire, hath she none,............11. H.21, 13
To him that **has**, there shall be added more;......22. H.64, 3
Who **has** a little measure:.....................30. H.87, 15
Nor **has** the darknesse power to usher in.........35. H.106, 39
Th' industrious Merchant **has**; who for to find...36. H.106, 65
Six teeth he **has**, whereof twice two are known....46. H.129, 3
Large shoulders though he **has**, and well can beare,
60. H.158, 3
And all in Your Blest Hand, which **has** the powers
62. H.161, 7
Too temp'rate in embracing? Tell me, **ha's** desire.78. H.197, 35
She **has** Virgins many,........................83. H.205, 5
Has not whence to sink at all..................84. H.209, 8
The Country **has**. Amint. From whence? Amar. From whence?
Mir. The Court............................86. H.213, 12
He **has** at home; but who tasts boil'd or rost?....89. H.221, 2
Where he of God-heads **has** such store,..........90. H.223, 7
When, after these, **h'as** paid his vows,.........93. H.223, 135
As the Summers Corne **has** eares:..............102. H.253, 4
My Phill, the time he **has** to sleep,............104. H.256, 16
When our drinking **has** no stint,...............122. H.304, 3
Sneape **has** a face so brittle, that it breaks......124. H.311, 1
Leech boasts, he **has** a Pill, that can alone,....125. H.315, 1
Ha's it a speaking virtue? 2. Yes;...........130. H.329, 16
Has it a body? 2. I, and wings..............130. H.329, 20
Lips she **has**, all Rubie red,..................138. H.342, 5
Ther's no vice now, but **has** his president.......139. H.352, 2
Drinks of distemper, or **ha's** cause to cry......148. H.377, 87
No, thou know'st order, Ethicks, and **ha's** read..148. H.377, 89
Her Resurrection **ha's** again with Thee.........150. H.382, 20
And on the seaventh, he **has** his Notes to seek...163. H.435, 2
Ha's not as yet begunne......................164. H.441, 2
For cruell Love **ha's** me so whipt,............164. H.442, 6
Lust **ha's** no eares; He's sharpe as thorn;......165. H.443, 13
For Musick now; He **has** the cries...........167. H.443, 112
Huncks **ha's** no money (he do's sweare, or say)..173. H.463, 1
If he **ha's** none in's pockets, trust me, Huncks..173. H.463, 3
Ha's none at home, in Coffers, Desks, or Trunks.173. H.463, 4
What **ha's** the Court to do with Swaines,.......184. H.492, 21
And yet our way **has** no ending................195. H.534, 12
But Blanch **has** not so much upon her head,....205. H.571, 3
Of Pushes Spalt **has** such a knottie race,........211. H.594, 1
Horne sells to others teeth; but **has** not one....211. H.595, 1
Here about, but **has** his eyes,................221. H.633, 30
Sound Teeth **has** Lucie, pure as Pearl, and small,
226. H.649, 1
What Fate decreed, Time now **ha's** made us see..254. H.756, 1
Who **has** not a Crosse,........................256. H.762, 7
Although he **has** no riches,....................259. H.772, 17
For a Stone, **ha's** Heaven his Tombe,..........270. H.821, 8
What store of Corn **has** carefull Nodes, thinke you,
270. H.822, 3
Love **has** yet no wrathfull fit:.................273. H.836, 6
Spenke **has** a strong breath, yet short Prayers saith:
283. H.884, 1
Has with the race...........................314. H.1024, 3
My Ship **has** here one only Anchor-hold;.........319. H.1044, 2
Hog **has** a place i'th' Kitchen, and his share..326. H.1079, 1
Is, when loves hony **has** a dash of gall.........327. H.1084, 2
That at the tide, he **has** not bread to eate.......327. H.1086, 4
Flood, if he **has** for him and his a bit,........332. H.1112, 1
God **has** his whips here to a twofold end,.........343. N.26, 1
Has, or none, or little skill,.................347. N.41, 18
That **has** not bread, and some to spare..........358. N.75, 10
A poyson too He **has** for Socrates;..............370. N.108, 8
Which **has** no root, and cannot grow,............371. N.114, 2
If that he **has** a will to Masterdome............389. N.211, 2
God **has** foure keyes, which He reserves alone;...390. N.224, 1
One onely fire **has** Hell; but yet it shall,.......391. N.227, 1
God **has** a Right Hand, but is quite bereft......394. N.240, 1
Euc. He was an Hastings; and that one Name **has**
416. A.8, 13
Hast See Haste, Th'ast
Nor wrack, or Bulging thou **hast** cause to feare:.23. H.71, 2
Best with those Virgin-Verses thou **hast** writ:...28. H.84, 4
Whom (Stars consenting with thy Fate) thou **hast**
35. H.106, 33
And when, wise Artist, that thou **hast**,.........48. H.133, 14
I ask't thee oft, what Poets thou **hast** read,......66. H.174, 1
Thou **hast** both Wind and Tide with thee; Thy way
73. H.186, 3
Where **hast** thou been so long from my embraces,
77. H.197, 19
Rare Temples thou **hast** seen, I know,........90. H.223a, 1
Thou onely **hast** the power,....................100. H.246, 10
When on her lip, thou **hast** thy sweet dew plac't,
100. H.248, 3
List of References:......109. H.267, 23; 123. H.309, 1; 143. H 365, 8; 147. H.377, 35; 150. H.384, 1; 174. H.465, 10; 193. H.522, 6; 203. H.564, 6; 230. H.662, 47; 230. H.662, 52; 231. H.662, 62; 231. H.662, 66; 236. H.680, 1; 252. H.747, 1; 257. H.763, 17; 277. H.853, 1; 288. H.909, 1; 299. H.956, 8; 321. H.1056, 2; 328. H.1090, 3; 330. H.1100, 5; 330. H.1100, 14; 347. N.40, 1; 349. N.47, 1; 349. N.47, 8; 350. N.47, 33; 354. N.59, 5; 354. N.59, 8; 354. N.59, 11; 377. N.129, 3; 442. var. H.465, 82.
Haste Thy Watch may stand, my minutes fly poste **haste**;
8. H.10, 3
And **haste** away to mine eternal home;...........9. H.14, 4
To numb the sence of Dearth, which sho'd sinne **haste** it,
37. H.106, 119
And not with desp'rate **hast**:..................58. H.149, 166
Their balls to Cindars: **haste**,................113. H.283, 39
You **haste** away so soone:....................125. H.316, 2
Let's live in **hast**; use pleasures while we may:..171. H.453, 1
He that doth suspect, do's **haste**.............175. H.465, 45
But making **haste**, it came to passe,............187. H.504, 3
I make no **haste** to have my Numbers read.......218. H.623, 1
'Tis **haste**....................................221. H.633, 48
Haste is unhappy: What we Rashly do........268. H.813, 1
Make **haste** away, and let one be...............275. H.844, 1
Since after death comes glory, Ile not **haste**.....314. H.1022, 2
Art thou not destin'd? then, with **hast**, go on....389. N.216, 1
Here all things ready are, make **hast**, make **hast** away;
401. N.268, 5
— — — — — — — — — —, ...428. var. H.197, 90
A boat, A boat, **hast** to the ferry.........445. ins. H.730, 26a
Hastens By Time, that **hastens** on..............258. H.767, 15
Hasting Untill the **hasting** day.................125. H.316, 6
Hastings Euc. He was an **Hastings**; and that one Name has
416. A.8, 13
Hasty Run through my veines, like to a **hasty** flood.
79. H.197, 78
Parte wth a **hastye** kisse; and in that shew......410. A.3, 11
Hat My Palmers **hat**; my Scallops shell;...........123. H.306, 3
Save but his **hat**, and that he cannot mew......144. H.372, 2
With **Hat** and Shooes out-worne...............295. H.942, 4
Hatched (**Hatcht**, with the Silver-light of snails)..92. H.223, 92
(**Hatch't** o're with Moone-shine, from their stolen delight)
410. A.3, 2
Hatching See Warm-love-hatching
Hate He rents his Crown, That feares the Peoples **hate**.
182. H.488, 2
Pillars and men, **hate** an indifferent Poet.......309. H.1000, 2
Who loves too much, too much the lov'd will **hate**.
318. H.1038, 2
And **hate**;...................................391. N.228, 19
To make Fools **hate** them, onlye by disguise;...412. A.3, 94
— — — — — — — — — — —, ...427. var. H.197, 71
Hated Kings though th'are **hated**, will be fear'd..165. H.443, 18
Hates Her love me once, who now **hates** me.....79. H.198, 12
God **hates** the Duall Number; being known....396. H.249, 1
Hath (Partial List of Auxiliary)
For Health on Julia's cheek **hath** shed..............7. H.9, 9
That an Acre **hath** of Nose:......................11. H.21, 6
Ha's she thinne haire, **hath** she none,............11. H.21, 13
Night now **hath** watch'd her self half blind;...54. H.149, 31
Griefe (ay me!) **hath** struck my Lute,..........131. H.332, 5
And griefs **hath** fil'de upon my silver hairs;....140. H.355, 6
Who **hath** but one of many;...................160. H.422, 14
The scrip **hath** some........................171. H.455, 14
Dundrige his Issue **hath**; but is not styl'd......195. H.533, 1
Youth (I confess) **hath** me mis-led;............216. H.617, 5
But Age **hath** brought me right to Bed.........216. H.617, 6
Death to our Countrey, now **hath** lost his heat:..254. H.756, 4
Where no foot **hath**............................258. H.770, 3
Then youthfull Box which now **hath** grace,.....285. H.892, 9
No man such rare parts **hath**, that he can swim,..298. H.953, 1
God **hath** two wings, which He doth ever move,..340. N.6, 1
Who **hath** thee in his mouth, not in his heart.....347. N.39, 4
Night **hath** no wings, to him that cannot sleep;....358. N.77, 1

Evill no Nature hath; the losse of good........367. N.101, 1
And therewithall, behold, it hath...............372. N.118, 3
No number of the Plurall hath..................382. N.168, 2
Sin no Existence; Nature none it hath,.........383. N.173, 1
But hath th' extraction of some good from it:..386. N.196, 2
The fire of Hell this strange condition hath,......387. N.202, 1
Hath in the middle ty'de a Gordian knott........405. A.1, 62
Hath seal'd the promise of her vtmost skill.......405. A.1, 64
But now my muse hath spi'de a darke descent...405. A.1, 65
As Fame or Rumour, hath or Trumpe or Tongue...411. A.3, 46
— — — — — — — — — — — —, ...422. var. H.106, 65
— — — — — — — — — — — —, ...429. var. H.253, 4
— — — — — — — — — — — —, ...439. var. H.443, 13
— — — — — — — — — — — —, ...440. var. H.443, 112
Hats Then to the Maids with Wheaten Hats:...102. H.250, 41
Haunt He'l never haunt ye now he's dead.......226. H.644, 10
Haunted By no ill haunted; here I come,.......402. N.269, 2
Haunts No Critick haunts the Poore mans Cell:.....6. H.2, 22
Have (Partial List of Auxiliary) See Y'ave
Have their Existence, and their Influence too.....3. Ded. H, 8
I write of Youth, of Love, and have Accesse........5. H.1, 5
Of Heaven, and hope to have it after all...........5. H.1, 14
And to have it fully prov'd,.....................15. H.36, 7
When one is past, another care we hav........18. H.48, 1
In which thy sacred Reliques shall have roome:....20. H.55, 8
If we the roste have, they the smell..............22. H.66, 4
Of you, that I may have........................30. H.89, 4
And know, that Riches have their proper stint,..35. H.106, 17
And can'st instruct, that those who have the itch 35. H.106, 19
Say too, She wo'd have this;....................43. H.123, 31
And nothing have.............................43. H.123, 34
The common formes have no one eye,............49. H.136, 18
So you, my Lord though you have now your stay,.52. H.146, 9
Have, promis'd to your sheets;..................54. H.149, 36
No Herbs have power to cure Love..............60. H.157, 4
Happy you, who can have seas..................62. H.162, 7
I have one, and she alone,......................62. H.162, 10
Know, Lady, you have but your day:............63. H.164, 3
And have the power to move...................76. H.193, 50
As Men, the Heavens have their Hypocrisie?....81. H.202, 8
Tell-tales I wo'd have them be..................82. H.203, 3
Pay when th'art honest; let me have some hope...83. H.206, 4
I have to write,..................................85. H.211, 2
To have his little King-ship know,..............86. H.213, 43
Hence, hence, profane; soft silence let us have;...89. H.219, 1
Thou shalt have soules for sacrifice.............89. H.219, 12
They have their Text for what they doe;........92. H.223, 77
They have their Book of Articles:..............92. H.223, 80
They have their Book of Homilies:.............92. H.223, 82
For sanctity, they have, to these,..............92. H.223, 97
They have their Ash-pans, & their Brooms......92. H.223, 101
Of Cloyster-Monks they have enow,...........93. H.223, 107
They have their Cups and Chalices;............93. H.223, 113
You have changes in your life,...................96. H.232, 3
You have ebbes of face and flowes,..............96. H.232, 5
You have hopes, and doubts, and feares..........96. H.232, 7
You have Pulses that doe beat...................96. H.232, 9
Say (if she's fretfull) I have bands............98. H.238, 6
I have Mirtle rods, (at will)...................98. H.238, 9
Shall have for his winning a kisse..............99. H.243, 6
(As you) may have their fill of meat,..........102. H.250, 46
To speak by Teares, before ye have a Tongue...104. H.257, 14
Winds have their time to rage; but when they cease, 105. H.259, 5
There thou shalt have her curious eye:........107. H.263, 10
While I have eyes to see:.....................109. H.267, 14
Both you two have............................111. H.280, 1
The Night-Charme quickly; you have spells,...115. H.283, 133
And millions of spring-times may ye have,......124. H.313, 13
We have short time to stay, as you,..........125. H.316, 11
We have as short a Spring;...................125. H.316, 12
That young men have to shooe the Mare:......126. H.319, 16
We are not poore; although we have...........133. H.336, 41
And have our Roofe,..........................133. H.336, 51
Permit my Book to have a free accesse........137. H.341, 11
Have reference to the shoulders, not the eares...142. H.363, 4
For these, and marbles have their whiles......148. H.377, 100
I have there a little wheat;....................152. H.393, 2
Ile have no Sceans, or Curtains drawn:.........154. H.402, 2
To have my neck from Loves yoke-free..........155. H.408, 2
I have now; yet I alone,.......................157. H.415, 7
Either is welcome; so I have...................158. H.420, 3
Say, have ye sence, or do you prove............158. H.420, 7
That single may have any......................160. H.422, 16
And have no name.............................161. H.426, 12
That my poore name may have the glory......170. H.449, 28
Of what I have,...............................171. H.455, 3
May read how soon things have...............176. H.467, 14
There have....................................178. H.475, 11
Nor Bee, or Hive you have be mute;...........179. H.476, 17
Have their reflected light,.....................181. H.484, 7
I have still the manners left.................182. H.489, 10
Wo'd yee have fresh Cheese and Cream?........183. H.491, 1
Mean time, let Lycidas have leave to Pipe to thee. 184. H.492, 43
Where both seem'd proud; the Flie to have......185. H.497, 3
Unmixt. I love to have it smirke and shine,....187. H.502, 3
We two (as Reliques left) will have............190. H.515, 11
Ile have nought to say to you:.................191. H.519, 6
A Bag and Bottle thou shalt have;.............192. H.521, 21
Thou shalt have Possets, Wassails fine,........193. H.521, 47
Thou sha't have Ribbands, Roses, Rings,......193. H.521, 51
Eaten I have; and though I had good cheere,....197. H.541, 1
And I shall think I have the heart,............198. H.544, 34
For I know you have the skill.................204. H.569, 13
I have seen many Maidens to have haire;.......205. H.571, 1
If children you have ten, Sir John.............208. H.581, 5
Dead when thou art, Deare Julia, thou shalt have.209. H.584, 5
Jone, and my Lady have at that time one,......209. H.586, 5
Let's live with that smal pittance that we have;..213. H.607, 1
When Lawes full power have to sway, we see....213. H.608, 1
I make no haste to have my Numbers read......218. H.623, 1
Although ye have a stock of wit,..............218. H.626, 6
Extreames have still their fault;..............221. H.633, 50
For all I have, or else can do,................223. H.635, 15
That your mickle, may have more..............223. H.638, 3
All things have an ending day:................224. H.639, 2
Us hands to get what here we have............226. H.647, 4
Never againe to have ingression here:..........227. H.652, 2
No more my Dirges, and my Trentalls have.....228. H.658, 8
And, lying down, have nought t' affright......231. H.662, 74
Thou shalt thy Name have, and thy Fames best trust 231. H.664, 5
No; 'tis a life, to have thine oyle,............233. H.670, 7
To have thy mind, and nuptiall bed,...........233. H.670, 11
(Where I have cause to burn perfumes to it:)..234. H.673, 8
The wager thou shalt have, and me,...........238. H.690, 7
And have for all a kisse.......................238. H.690, 12
While we have our being here:.................238. H.691, 4
No return from thence we have...............238. H.691, 6
I'le beg of thee first here to have mine Urn.....242. H.713, 18
I have, to sing how day drawes on............246. H.724, 4
I have...246. H.724, 5
I have, which, with a jealous eare,............246. H.724, 14
Thou canst but have, what others had..........246. H.725, 4
Thrice happie Roses, so much grac't, to have...249. H.734, 1
Will paid have his fee,........................256. H.762, 11
Her name if next you wo'd have knowne,........257. H.764, 3
Yet he'l the courage have.....................259. H.772, 14
And Genius waits to have us both to bed.......261. H.781, 6
Where Joyes and Griefs have Turns Alternative..264. H.792, 2
Nothing I have (my Crofts) to send to Thee,....267. H.804, 2
I have in my poore Brest;.....................272. H.828, 6
Wooers have Tongues of Ice, but burning hearts. 274. H.837, 10
Teares have their springs from joy, as well as woe. 275. H.842, 4
No, but because he wo'd not have it seen,........275. H.843, 3
To hold us two, an endlesse honour have........281. H.875, 6
Yeilding I wo'd have them; yet...............282. H.878, 5
But Those have thorns, and These have stings...283. H.883, 14
For wanton Lais, then we have................283. H.885, 7
Of such a wit the world sho'd have no more...289. H.911, 20
Unlesse they have some wanton carriages.......290. H.914, 8
What joy can Clun have in that Coat, or this,..295. H.941, 7
Lines have, or sho'd have, thou the best canst show. 297. H.947, 10
Without their use we may have men?..........297. H.948, 2
Have we of Women or their seed?............297. H.948, 14
Tell that Brave Man, fain thou wo'dst have access 301. H.963, 1
To have friends to beare a part:..............302. H.968, 4
I have none; but must be sure................302. H.968, 5
But for his heart, he cannot have it made:.....302. H.969, 2
Next, I'm sure, the Nuns will have............304. H.976, 5
Men must have Bounds how farre to walke; for we 307. H.990, 1
Some effusions let me have,..................307. H.991, 5
Since shed or Cottage I have none,.............321. H.1056, 1
Shew mercy there, where they have power to kill. 321. H.1057, 2
I have my Laurel Chaplet on my head,.........322. H.1062, 1
Next be sure ye have a care,..................322. H.1064, 3
To have a tooth twitcht out of's native frame..323. H.1066, 2
Who will have love comply with his command..323. H.1067, 2
What have the Meades to do with thee,......323. H. 1068, 9
Thus have, or have not, all alike is good,......332. H.1112, 5
I have a leaden, thou a shaft of gold;.........333. H.1120, 1
Be yet assur'd, thou shalt have one............334. H.1123, 5
And want their Poise: words ought to have their weight. 342. N.16, 2
But all in smart have lesse, or greater shares.....342. N.20, 2
If all transgressions here should have their pay,..343. N.27, 1
To mount my Soule, she must have pineons given;.352. N.52, 3
God will have all, or none; serve Him, or fall...353. N.54, 1
But if thou hadst, He sho'd have one;..........354. N.59, 12
Fit, fit it is, we have our Parasceve..............355. N.65, 8
To feed, or lodge, to have the best of Roomes:...356. N.68, 2
Temptations hurt not, though they have accesse: 359. N.79, 1
Crosses we must have; or, hereafter woe.........359. N.81, 2

Or, if we have..............................361. N.83, 58
And for my house I darknesse have?..........361. N.84, 4
Yet I have hope, by Thy great power,............361. N.84, 7
Have we flesh, or have we fish...................363. N.93, 5
And have a care no fire gos out,...............365. N.97, 5
Gold I have none, but I present my need,........369. N.105, 1
Where all have Grace,.........................369. N.106, 4
I would to God, that mine old age might have....371. N.115, 1
Two raiments have I: Christ then makes........376. N.127, 5
Or have I two loaves; then I use..............376. N.127, 7
Have ending..................................377. N.128, 24
In fun'rall pomp, but this importance have;....384. N.181, 2
Be those few hours, which I have yet to spend,.392. N.230, 1
I'le have in mind my Resurrection,............392. N.230, 22
To have continuall paine, or pleasure here:...394. N.236, 2
But when good words, by good works, have their proof,
397. N.256, 3
The spacious field have for Thy Theater........398. N.263, 18
Have, have ye no regard, all ye..............400. N.266, 1
This Honour have,..........................401. N.268, 38
Here let me rest; and let me have............402. N.269, 22
And haue their haruest, wch must stand........408. A.2, 51
Theyre Nobly-home-bread, yett haue price.......409. A.2, 93
Hee may ere longe haue such a wyfe...........409. A.2, 107
(Wert not for thee) haue Crumbled Into Mould,
411. A.3, 36
As yow haue done yor day,.....................413. A.4, 8
So long as I haue feares......................414. A.5, 6
Have pity either on my tears or Youth,.........416. A.8, 4
These have their Fate, and wear away as Men;.419. A.10, 2
— — — — — — — — — — —, ...421. var. H.92, 1
— — — — — — — — — — —, ...428. var. H.197, 85
For such neglect, have only myrtle rodds..431. ins. H.283, 60p
Not more, milde nymph, then they would have you doe;
431, ins. H.283, 60r
Wee have noe vinyards which doe beare.436. ins. H.336, 48a
Wée have noe bath......................436. ins. H.336, 48k
Of fortune can have noe command,........436. ins. H.336, 48n
— — — — — — — — — — —, ...440. var. H.443, 60
— — — — — — — — — — —, ...443. var. H.575, 50
— — — — — — — — — — —, ...451. ins. H.197, 48d
Haven The Haven reacht to which I first was bound.
334. H.1127, 2
Having She threw; I cast; and having thrown,...19. H.49, 3
And having these, what need of more?..........33. H.100, 2
Having promis'd, pay your debts,..............44. H.125, 5
Praise me, for having such a fruitfull wombe;.58. H.151, 3
And having spoke it once, Farewell...........60. H.159, 12
But having got it; thereupon,..................67. H.175, 7
For having lost but once your prime,.........84. H.208, 15
If having run my Barque on ground,...........94. H.225, 5
That having ease me given,..................95. H.227, 29
But Venus having lost the day,...............105. H.260, 5
And having none, yet I will keep.............109. H.267, 15
Like Unthrifts, having spent,.................110. H.274, 17
For having now my journey done,............123. H.306, 5
And, having pray'd together, we.............125. H.316, 9
Come unto thee for Laurell, having spent,......143. H.365, 5
Having a living Fountain under it...........154. H.403, 4
Having All, injoy not One...................157. H.415, 8
Who having two or three,....................160. H.422, 19
In having all, that thou hast none............174. H.465, 10
But having scapt temptations shelfe,..........176. H.465, 83
And having danc't ('bove all the best)........192. H.521, 33
Having but seven in all; three black, foure white.
195. H.531, 2
And having drunk, we raise a shout...........198. H.544, 10
Thus, having talkt, we'l next commend........216. H.616, 35
So I, now having rid my way;.................216. H.617, 3
Live in the Love of Doves, and having told....222. H.633, 62
Lest having that, or this,....................231. H.663, 3
Trigg having turn'd his sute, he struts in state,.240. H.703, 1
Having his eyes still in his eare,............263. H.785, 6
And having fixt Thee in mine Orbe a Starre,....267. H.804, 9
(Having resign'd thy shamefac'tness:).........287. H.899, 6
And having once brought to an end............289. H.911, 18
I will be short, and having quickly hurl'd.....298. H.955, 1
And having washt thee, close thee in a chest..300. H.960, 5
And here my ship rides having Anchor cast...334. H.1126, 2
Christ having paid, I nothing owe:............370. N.107, 13
Starves, having no companion.................381. N.158, 2
And having not her God for light,.............393. N.233, 3
My daughters Dowrye; haueing which...........407. A.2, 5
Haws Kernells, and wither'd hawes: the rest
439. ins. H.443, 45n
Hay And fretfull, carries Hay in's horne,.......165. H.443, 14
One onely lock of that sweet Hay.............355. N.60, 3
Hazard Then by one, to hazard all................21. H.61, 8
Hazards And hazards those most, whom the most He loves;
370. N.108, 4
He (Partial List)
Batt he gets children, not for love to reare 'em;
72. H.184, 1
Rook he sells feathers, yet he still doth crie....163. H.439, 1
Slouch he packs up, and goes to sev'rall Faires,.253. H.753, 1
Orpheus he went (as Poets tell).............265. H.798, 1
Implies or Essence, or the He that Is..........385. N.187, 2
Head See Forehead, Godhead, Maidenhead, Overhead
Droop, droop no more, or hang the head..........7. H.9, 1
About her head I writhing hung,...............16. H.41, 9
First, for thy Queen-ship on thy head is set.....30. H.88, 3
Has blear'd his eyes: Besides, his head is bald...33. H.99, 2
Flutter to flie, and beare away his head..........33. H.99, 4
Hanging down his head t'wards me;............38. H.107, 2
First, I shall decline my head;................38. H.107, 4
That gallant Tulip will hang down his head,....41. H.118, 3
His head upon his hand he laid;..............42. H.119, 7
Fold now thine armes; and hang the head,....47. H.132, 1
False in head, and false enough;..............77. H.195, 11
(Like a Turks Turbant on his head)..........93. H.223, 138
On many a head here, many a Coronet:......94. H.224, 4
Ease my sick head,..........................95. H.227, 5
Then Willow-garlands, 'bout the head,.........106. H.262, 7
Shew thy white feet, and head with Marjoram crown'd:
113. H.283, 32
Upon your Head this flowry Coronet:.........140. H.354, 4
On many a head the Delphick Coronet,........142. H.365, 4
And who with green-turfes reare his head,.....157. H.412, 23
I held Love's head while it did ake;.........188. H.509, 1
(And hang the head when as the Act is done)..196. H.537, 2
With silken trees upon thy head;...........202. H.560, 2
But Blanch has not so much upon her head,....205. H.571, 3
With Yvorie wrists, his Laureat head, and steeps
206. H.575, 41
My head doth ake,..........................210. H.591, 1
In Tyrian Dewes, and Head with Roses crown'd.
214. H.612, 12
Knock at a Starre with my exalted Head.......214. H.612, 14
Some hung the head, while some did bring....237. H.686, 5
A little Garland fits a little Head:.............249. H.733, 8
(Twixt the hornes) upon the head.............280. H.870, 10
Lay it underneath the head;.................284. H.888, 2
A crawling Vine about Anacreon's head:.....313. H.1017, 2
I have my Laurel Chaplet on my head,.........322. H.1062, 1
Upon my head the golden coronet;..............343. N.25, 6
Sick in heart, and sick in head,................347. N.41, 6
May Roses grow, to crown His own deare Head.
366. N.97, 23
And sullen clouds bound up his head............393. N.232, 6
Whose head befringed with bescattered tresses...404. A.1, 1
Bee sure thou bringe A Mayden head,..........409. A.2, 84
Shakeing the head, whilst each, to each dothe mourne,
411. A.3, 65
— — — — — — — — — — — —, ...437. var. H.336, 76
— — — — — — — — — — — —, ...440. var. H.443, 91
Soft Saffron Circles to perfume the head...442. ins. H.575, 20b
Headed Which headed with twoe rich round rubies showe
405. A.1, 53
Each richly headed with a pearly shell.........406. A.1, 102
Heads See Godheads, Maidenheads
To dance and caper on the heads of flowers,....78. H.197, 52
Crown we our Heads with Roses then,........133. H.336, 33
— — — — — — — — — — — —, ...436. ins. H.336, 48g
— — — — — — — — — — — —, ...452. var. H.443, 106
Heal Yet I bring Balme and Oile to heal your sore.
52. H.146, 22
And Leaves did heale, all sick of humane seed:..61. H.161, 2
'Twill hurt and heal a heart pierc'd through...325. H.1075, 8
And heale me with thy looke, or touch:........344. N.29, 7
To heale my Earths infirmitie................397. N.257, 4
Healed I shall be heal'd, if that my King but touch.
62. H.161, 14
And heal'd the wound in thee................272. H.828, 4
Healing See Suppling-healing
Health See City-health
For Health on Julia's cheek hath shed............7. H.9, 9
Health is the first good lent to men;...........42. H.121, 1
Homer, this Health to thee,...................80. H.201, 13
To pledge this second Health................80. H.201, 18
As your health or comes, or goes;.............96. H.232, 6
Which freely drink to your Lords health,.....102. H.250, 38
Then the next health to friends of mine......135. H.336, 129
Health is no other (as the learned hold).......236. H.683, 1
A health to my Girles,......................239. H.695, 7
A health to the King and the Queene here.....317. H.1035, 18
Who violates the Customes, hurts the Health,..318. H.1041, 1
All saving health, and help for me............342. N.17, 8
Bring Health to All.........................401. N.268, 13
— — — — — — — — — — —, ...448. var. A.3, 6
Healthful But when again sh'as got her healthfull houre,
320. H.1054, 5
Besides my healthfull Ewes to beare..........350. N.47, 47
What though my healthfull dayes are fled,......361. N.84, 5
To my most healthfull use,...................368. N.104, 14
Healths Healthes to the Rose, the Violet, or Pinke,
410. A.3, 6
Heap See Ash-heap
Cleane heap of wheat,.........................375. N.123, 79
— — — — — — — — — — —, ...437. var. H.336, 79
Heaped A multitude of dayes still heaped on,....392. N.230 7
Heaps See Ash-heaps
Hear Where thou mayst hear thine own Lines read..6. H.2, 23

I'm free from thee; and thou no more shalt heare 17. H.42, 1
O Earth! Earth! Earth heare thou my voice, and be 19. H.52, 1
As, could they hear, the Damn'd would make no noise, 22. H.67, 2
When I thy singing next shall heare,.............22. H.68, 1
As blessed soules cann't heare too much:.........22. H.68, 4
Then dream, ye heare the Lamb by many a bleat 36. H.106, 49
Nor are thine eares so deafe, but thou canst heare 36. H.106, 83
'Tis true, I kist thee; but I co'd not heare.....42. H.122, 5
That ye may good doctrine heare................52. H.147, 2
Aire coyn'd to words, my Julia co'd not heare;..58. H.150, 3
And kissing, so as none may heare,............59. H.152, 11
Heare all men speak; but credit few or none.....67. H.177, 4
About the Cart, heare, how the Rout.........101. H.250, 15
If when these Lyricks (Cesar) You shall heare,.107. H.264, 1
Love's a thing, (as I do heare)..............117. H.286, 1
Heare ye Virgins, and Ile teach,...............120. H.297, 1
No more shall I, from henceforth, heare a quire 132. H.333, 7
When I of Villars doe but heare the name,....137. H.341, 1
Will ye heare, what I can say..................138. H.342, 1
There thou shalt hear Divine Musæus sing.....206. H.575, 25
To heare the incantation of his tongue:.......206. H.575, 30
And he one chiefe; But harke, I heare the Cock, 207. H.575, 61
And thou Lucina, that do'st heare...........221. H.633, 56
Chor. Why then begin, and let us heare......243. H.716, 16
Who'l hear, and so judge righteously..........243. H.716, 22
First, peales of Thunder we must heare,.......247. H.725, 9
Ch. What voice so sweet and charming do I heare? 248. H.730, 3
Ch. A sound I heare, but nothing yet can see,.248. H.730, 5
Whose restlesse Ghosts shall heare their children sing, 252. H.745, 9
Shall heare his Clarke say,...................256. H.762, 16
And thou shalt heare how we...................259. H.772, 27
Tap (better known then trusted) as we heare.272. H.829, 1
Touch but thy Lire (my Harrie) and I heare...276. H.851, 1
I heare in thee rare Laniere to sing;...........276. H.851, 4
To heare the worst from men, when they doe well. 293. H 932, 2
Where thrice we knock, and none will heare,...312. H.1014, 9
Let me (like him) first cracks of thunder heare;.343. N.25, 3
When we obey, by acting what we heare.......346. N.36, 3
Do see, and heare..........................353. N.56, 11
What He with laughter speaks, heare thou with tears. 355. N.63, 2
Let me Thy voice betimes i' th morning heare;.358. N.77, 12
Who see, or heare poor Widdowes crie:.......373. N.123, 4
God, who's in Heav'n, will hear from thence;..381. N.160, 1
To heare the Judge give sentence on the Throne, 392. N.230, 25
For if Thy thunder-claps I heare,..............393. N.232, 9

Heard But that I heard thy sweet breath say,.....20. H.56, 5
Amar. But deare Mirtillo, I have heard it told,.86. H.213, 29
And some have heard the Elves it call..........91. H.223, 24
Y'ave heard them sweetly sing,................110. H.274, 9
Oft have I heard both Youths and Virgins say,.149. H.378, 1
I heard ye co'd coole heat; and came..........157. H.413, 1
This Axiom I have often heard,...............234. H.672, 1
Tygers and Beares (I've heard some say)......252. H.746, 3
But heard with anger, we confesse the crime..260. H.776, 2
In depth of silence, heard, and seene of none...298. H.954, 3
That ere while was heard so shrill?.............305. H.984, 6
Hast thou not heard an Oath from me,.......328. H.1090, 3
If felt and heard, (unseen) thou dost me please; 331. H.1108, 1

Hearest And when thou hear'st by that too-true-Report, 37. H.106, 89
And hear'st His whimp'ring, and His cries;....365. N.97, 14

Hearing Which Venus hearing; thither came,....31. H.92, 5
And hearing it,...........................135. H.336, 109
Shall by his hearing quickly come to see......330. H.1100, 17
Know, to' th' hearing as the touch............418. A.9, 50
— — — — — — — — — — —, ...432. var. H.283, 76

Hears And eyes, it neither sees or heares.......174. H.465, 22
But when he hears the like confusion,..........303. H.975, 2
She heares:..................................314. H.1024, 12
As Inapostate, to the thing he heares,.........330. H.1100, 16
God heares us when we pray, but yet defers.....344. N.30, 1
God then confounds mans face, when He not hears 382. N.169, 1

Hearse For my life mortall, Rise from out thy Herse, 27. H.82, 15
Doe now your flowrie honours to my Herse....138. H.343, 2
Nor let my Herse, be wept upon by thee:......281. H.875, 2

Hearse-cloth Met in one Hearce-cloth, to ore-spred 103. H.256, 6
And fresh thy Herse-cloth, we will, here,........360. N.83, 35

Heart See Broke-heart, Gentle-heart, Sweetheart
Draw in't a wounded Heart:.................10. H.20, 2
That Heart to bleed, your's ne'r will ake.......11. H.20, 11
The finger bled, but burnt was all my heart.....17. H.44, 8
The out-let then is from the heart..............24. H.73, 10
Ah my Anthea! Must my heart still break?......24. H.74, 1
Quite through my heart and marrow...........27. H.81, 32
Ile leave thy heart a dying...................27. H.81, 36
The burning of my heart:.....................28. H.85, 2
A heart thrice wall'd with Oke, and Brasse, that man 36. H.106, 75
When ere my heart, Love's warmth, but entertaines, 40. H.113, 1
No heart by love receiv'd a wound;..........42. H.119, 2
Whose heart, whose hand, whose ev'ry part spake love. 42. H.122, 8
A poore, yet loving heart...................43. H.123, 30
To wound my heart, and never to apply,........52. H.146, 19
Shewing a heart consenting;....................55. H.149, 75
As with a heart possest:........................57. H.149, 136
And (like to mine) make your heart burn......61. H.159, 19
Lyd. My heart now set on fire is...............70. H.181, 13
Then, even then, I will bequeath my heart.....73. H.186, 14
You can ease my heart, and doe................74. H.191, 7
A heart that's free,.........................100. H.246, 13
How false, how hollow she's in heart;.........103. H.253, 15
Wept out our heart, as well as eyes............104. H.256, 14
A loving heart to thee........................108. H.267, 4
A heart as soft, a heart as kind,...............108. H.267, 5
A heart as sound and free,.....................108. H.267, 6
That heart Ile give to thee...................108. H.267, 8
Bid that heart stay, and it will stay,..........108. H.267, 9
A heart to weep for thee.....................109. H.267, 16
Thou art my life, my love, my heart,..........109. H.267, 21
I a merry heart will keep,......................118. H.289, 13
First wash thy heart in innocence, then bring..127. H.320, 3
But thy Bondslave is my heart:...............128. H.322, 6
No, no, that selfe same heart, that vow,.......134. H.336, 70
With heart and hand to entertain:.............147. H.377, 36
When eithers heart, and eithers hand did strive 147. H.377, 39
For as my Heart, ene so mine Eye............154. H.402, 5
Did wound my heart..........................161. H.426, 4
When I a Heart had one,......................168. H.446, 2
To Take away that Heart from me,............168. H.446, 3
Or give me back my heart.....................168. H.446, 8
Of Patience wants. Grief breaks the stoutest Heart 169. H.447, 2
The Canker of the heart:....................170. H.452, 2
To save; when thou may'st kill a heart........177. H.471, 4
Never see mine own heart bleed:...............182. H.490, 2
And kept credit with my heart,..................183. H.490, 19
Lesse is here, then in my heart...............186. H.500, 4
With griefe of heart, methinks, I thus doe cry,.193. H.522, 5
And I shall think I have the heart,............198. H.544, 34
I must confesse, mine eye and heart..........202. H.560, 17
The fire scorctht my heart....................203. H.563, 8
Then my poore heart,.........................210. H.591, 8
Sick is the Land to'th' heart; and doth endure.214. H.612, 5
Left (of the large heart, and long hand)......218. H.626, 10
Cleave thou my heart in two...................240. H.705, 12
But toyes, to give my heart some ease:........246. H.724, 30
Delays in love that but crucifie the heart.......261. H.781, 2
Hath prickt thy heart;.......................273. H.833, 2
Lulls swears he is all heart; but you'l suppose.284. H.886, 1
Neer the childs heart lay a knife:.............284. H.889, 2
Who fires with hope the Lovers heart,........290. H.915, 7
Then crept into my heart;....................295. H.942, 14
With solemne tears, and with much grief of heart, 300. H.960, 3
But for his heart, he cannot have it made:.....302. H.969, 2
Despaire takes heart, when ther's no hope to speed: 309. H.999, 1
'Twill hurt and heal a heart pierc'd through.....325. H.1075, 8
Why do'st thou wound, & break my heart?....328. H.1090, 1
And bring t'th' heart destruction both alike....333. H.1120, 6
Without the heart, lip-labour nothing is.........345. N.34, 4
Without the sweet concurrence of the Heart.....346. N.35, 2
Who hath thee in his mouth, not in his heart...347. N.39, 4
Sick in heart, and sick in head,...............347. N.41, 6
A thankfull heart;............................351. N.47, 54
Neer to the wishes of his heart:...............351. N.50, 3
While my sick heart.........................353. N.56, 16
Of all the House: the best of all's the Heart....356. N.68, 4
Sick is my heart; O Saviour! do Thou please....358. N.77, 8
Heart, Eare, and Eye, and every thing..........364. N.96, 5
Of all the house here, is the heart,.............365. N.96, 28
How heart and hand do all agree,...............365. N.97, 9
And Ile returne a bleeding Heart,.............376. N.125, 3
Forc'd from the mighty dolour of the heart....380. N.154, 2
To shew a heart grief-rent;.....................391. N.228, 21
When I Thy gentle Heart do see.............400. N.267, 3
T'accept each Heart,..........................401. N.268, 33
For I have washt both hand and heart,.........402. N.269, 6
Not soe, but that some Relique In my Harte..412. A.3, 96
— — — — — — — — — — —, ...435, var. H.293, 46z
— — — — — — — — — — —, ...453. ins. H.283, 20j

Hearth When Laurell spirts 'ith fire, and when the Hearth 7. H.8, 5
Well, on, brave boyes, to your Lords Hearth,..101. H.250, 26
That Milk-maids make about the hearth,......126. H.319, 12

To crown the **Hearth**,........................135. H.336, 123
Merry at anothers **hearth**; y'are here........146. H.377, 29
All sitting neer the glitt'ring **Hearth**........193. H.521, 50
For gladding so my **hearth** here,..............234. H.674, 7
A little **Hearth** best fits a little Fire,.........249. H.733, 10
Cleane was the **herth**, the mantle larded jet;..262. H.783, 11
'Tis Thou that crown'st my glittering **Hearth**..350. N.47, 37
Heart's Betrayes the **Hearts** Adulterie..........254. H.755, 2
And drink to your **hearts** desiring...........263. H.784, 6
God bought man here wth his **hearts** blood expence;
389. N.213, 1
Her **heart's** at home, howere she goes:...430. ins. H.283, 20j
Hearts See **Sweethearts**
All **hearts** your captives; yours, yet free:.....61. H.160, 4
With peeps of **Harts**, of Club and Spade......166. H.443, 49
Their wounded **hearts**; and names we find.....169. H.449, 7
Thou set'st their **hearts**, let chaste desire......174. H.465, 8
Ready to joyne, as well our **hearts** as hands....262. H.781, 10
Wooers have Tongues of Ice, but burning **hearts**.
274. H.837, 10
That we wash our **hearts**, and hands.........280. H.870, 4
Those, who want **Hearts**, and weare a Diadem.
330. H.1097, 2
Your **hearts**, and hands, lips, eares, and eyes...366. N.98, 9
God's said our **hearts** to harden then,.........396. N.250, 1
Of Lust, which setts on fier our **hartes**........408. A.2, 38
Heart's-ease Gave them **Hearts-ease** turn'd to Flow'rs.
152. H.391, 8
Heat Of pleasures, to a **Heate**;..................9. H.15, 2
In my limbs their former **heat**?................10. H.19, 8
But of the **heat** of Julia's breast:...............25. H.78, 8
Wo'd but that **heat** recall:....................28. H.85, 6
Alas! the **heat** and death's the same;..........50. H.140, 5
O! give them active **heat**.....................57. H.149, 125
Both the cause, and make the **heat**...........62. H.162, 14
Ne'r had kept **heat** for fifty Maids that night..78. H.197, 68
Wild I am now with **heat**;....................81. H.201, 29
High, and passions lesse of **heat**...............96. H.232, 10
In me a more transcendant **heate**,.............135. H.336, 102
I heard ye co'd coole **heat**; and came.........157. H.413, 1
And labour with unequall **heat**:................157. H.413, 6
To create in me a **heate**,.....................217. H.620, 2
That happy **heat**;............................227. H.653, 7
But a just measure both of **Heat** and Cold....236. H.683, 2
Death to our Countrey, now hath lost his **heat**:.254. H.756, 4
So long as thou dost **heat** us..................259. H.772, 9
Following with love and active **heate** thy game,.301. H.966, 7
Ans. **Heate** ye to coole ye:...................309. H.1001, 8
Our **heat** of youth can hardly keep the mean....318. H.1042, 2
Heat and moisture mixt are so,...............324. H.1070, 3
Thou kil'st with **heate**, and I strike dead with cold.
333. H.1120, 2
True **heate**, whearwth humanitie doth liue.......410. A.3, 30
— — — — — — — — — — —, ...427. var. H.197, 69
Heated Then to be thaw'd, or **heated** so............8. H.13, 8
Heats Freezing cold, and firie **heats**,............102. H.253, 7
Which **heats** those ravisht Soules above;.......395. N.246, 2
Heave Sometimes 'two'd pant, and sigh, and **heave**,
66. H.175, 5
Then will I **heave** my wither'd hand...........303. H.973, 15
Heaven Of **Heaven**, and hope to have it after all..5. H.1, 14
With that **Heav'n** gave thee with a warie hand,.35. H.106, 23
Making thy peace with **heav'n**, for some late fault,
36. H.106, 59
Make me a **heaven**; and make me there..........47. H.133, 1
With all that can be, this **heaven** grac't;.......48. H.133, 15
That good, which **Heav'n** can give.............57. H.149, 153
The glorious Lamp of **Heaven**, the Sun,.........84. H.208, 5
For **Heaven**...................................95. H.227, 33
Musick, thou Queen of **Heaven**, Care-charming-spel,
103. H.254, 1
Reaching at **heaven**,..........................112. H.283, 5
That weares one face (like **heaven**) and never showes
128. H.323, 7
Make for thy peace, and pace to **heaven**.......149. H.377, 130
Through **heaven**, the very Spheres,............151. H.388, 7
A scent, that fills both **Heaven** and Earth with it.
157. H.414, 10
Wo'd I see Lawn, clear as the **Heaven**, and thin?
158. H.416, 1
What though the **Heaven** be lowring now,.......188. H.508, 1
Then will appeare a cheerfull **Heaven**...........188. H.508, 6
(Dropt for the jarres of **heaven**) fill'd t'engage..206. H.575, 46
As **Heaven** had spent all perfumes there.......237. H.686, 12
For a Stone, ha's **Heaven** his Tombe,...........270. H.821, 8
Descend from **heaven**, to re-converse with men;.301. H.966, 12
Of night from **Heaven** for to rend her.........333. H.1122, 12
For, 'tis no easie way from Earth to **Heaven**....352. N.52, 4
To my **heaven** lesse run, then flie.............355. N.64, 6
Heaven, by Christs mercies, not my merit:....359. N.78, 12
Humble we must be, if to **Heaven** we go:.....362. N.89, 1
With Thee, and Thine in **Heaven**.............363. N.92, 18
To **Heaven**, and the under-Earth..............364. N.96, 21
Heaven to come down, the while we choke....366. N.98, 16
Of Him, who's Lord of **Heav'n** and Earth;...366. N.98, 19
Tumble shall **heav'n**, and down will I.........371. N.114, 8
God, who's in **Heav'n**, will hear from thence;....381. N.160, 1
Heav'n is most faire; but fairer He.........382. N.164, 1
So live in **Heaven**, in everlasting light........384. N.181, 5
Heaven is not given for our good works here:..390. N.223, 1
By houres we all live here, in **Heaven** is known.392. N.229, 1
As Hell, and Earth, and **Heav'n** may stand amaz'd.
399. N.263, 31
This for my **Heaven**, that was Thy Grave:......402. N.269, 23
A kisse to such a Jewell of the **heauen**:.......410. A.3, 4
(**Heauen** and my soule beare Record of my Vowe)
411. A.3, 48
But voice of fame, and voice of **heauen** haue thunderd
414. A.6, 5
That as her selfe, or **Heauen** indures......422. ins. H.106, 92d
— — — — — — — — — — —, ...427. var. H.197, 54
— — — — — — — — — — —, ...432. var. H.283, 106
Immediatly from **heaven**, but harke the Cocke
443. var. H.575, 61
Heaven-like White, and **Heaven-like** Chrystalline:..16. H.39, 6
Heavenly And look how all those **heavenly** Lamps acquire
3. Ded.H., 5
Can please those **Heav'nly** Deities,..............22. H.63, 2
Under the **heavenly** *Isis, that can bring........78. H.197, 54
Sung out his Birth with **Heav'nly** Minstralsie..86. H.213, 24
(Who writ that **heavenly** Revelation)............343. N.25, 2
The Birth of this our **heavenly** King?...........364. N.96, 3
Tell us, thou cleere and **heavenly** Tongue,......367. N.102, 1
Heaven's And to that Hand, (the Branch of **Heavens** faire Tree)........................62. H.161, 11
Out-glares the **Heav'ns** *Osiris; and thy gleams.77. H.197, 11
But as **Heavens** publike and immortall Eye....371. N.113, 5
More worth, then **Heav'ns** Eternitie...........388. N.206, 4
Tis not my voice, but **heauens**, that bidds thee goe;
414. A.6, 2
Heavens As Men, the **Heavens** have their Hypocrisie?
81. H.202, 8
Strong then the **Heavens** for everlastingnesse:...185. H.496, 8
Shewes like the **Heavens** aboue ye Moone,....413. A.4, 13
Heave-offering To my God, a **Heave-offering**.....397. N.258, 4
Heaving **Heaving** up my either hand;............364. N.95, 2
Heavy **Heavy**, to hurt those sacred seeds of thee..73. H.186, 20
Hecate Three Formes of **Heccate**:.............258. H.767, 10
For those is kept the Gulf of **Hecatè**;.........417. A.8, 32
Heccate See **Hecate**
Hector The **Hector** over Aged Exeter;.........251. H.745, 2
He'd Wept as **he'd** drowne the Hellespont,......42. H.119, 10
Made he the pledge, **he'd** think...............80. H.201, 23
To his Book's end this last **he'd** have plac't,....335. H.1130, 1
But **he'd** be gone,..........................346. N.38, 5
Hedge Shut every gate; mend every **hedge** that's torne,
259. H.771, 5
Heed He smarts at last, who do's not first take **heed**.
79. H.199, 4
But yet take **heed**;..........................113. H.283, 55
He's soft and tender (Pray take **heed**)........157. H.412, 25
Heedless I put, he pusht, and **heedless** of my skin,
17. H.44, 3
Heels Driving these sharking trades, is out at **heels**.
153. H.398, 2
The following plague still treading on his **heels**...362. N.86, 2
Heidelberg I know the Tunne of **Hidleberge** holds more.
171. H.454, 4
Heifer The untam'd **Heifer**, or the Pricket,.....136. H.336, 142
The **Heifer**, Cow, and Oxe draw neere........230. H.662, 38
A **Heifer** smooth, and black as jet,...........243. H.716, 8
Against thy **Heifer**, I will here...............243. H.716, 13
Now for to win thy **Heifer** faire,..............243. H.716, 31
Height See **Heighth**
'Tis cruelty in thee to'th'**height**,..............34. H.103, 11
These things thou know'st to'th'**height**, and dost prevent
35. H.106, 21
To their full **height** doe clime:...............56. H.149, 124
Our selves to such a **height**:..................66. H.172, 21
His blood to **height**; this done, commended...120. H.293, 53
Since neithers **height** was rais'd by th'ill......149. H.377, 116
This is the **height** of Justice, that to doe......214. H.614, 1
To such a **height**; but never surfeited..........220. H.633, 21
Is the **height** of Cruelties....................254. H.757, 4
'Tis the Chyrurgions praise, and **height** of Art...268. H.808, 1
To such a **height**, as for to tell...............369. N.107, 3
Which is the **height** of comfort, when I fall,...392. N.230, 35
To such an **height**, to such a period rais'd,...399. N.263, 30
— — — — — — — — — — —, ...442. var. H.465, 80
— — — — — — — — — — —, ...450. var. A.9, 37
Heighth See **Height**
— — — — — — — — — — —, ...442. var. H.465, 80
Heights Who fli'st at all **heights**: Prose and Verse run'st through;..................................298. H.955, 7
Heir The **Heire** to This great Realme of Poetry..107. H.264, 6
Who makes the slie Physitian his **Heire**........125. H.315, 6
Heirs The number here of **Heires**, shall from the state
395. N.248, 3
Heirship **Heire-ship** be lesse, by our adoption:...395. N.248, 2
Held Thus **held**, or led by thee, I shall...........33. H.98, 9
With hands **held** up to Love, I wept;..........51. H.142, 3
I **held** Love's head while it did ake;..........188. H.509, 1
But her self **held** fast by none...............232. H.665, 14
Her cloaths **held** up, she shew'd withall.......247. H.729, 3

Labour is held up, by the hope of rest.........311. H.1009, 2
Held up by Fames eternall Pedestall...........329. H.1092, 8
He held out then,...............................346. N.38, 7
But that held back by sin......................370. N.111, 4
Mercy, the wise Athenians held to be.........380. N.148, 1
Helen When the faire Hellen, from her eyes,...135. H.336, 105
Helicon Prince of Hellicon, but He.............108. H.266, 12
Wth Numerous feete to Hoofy Helicon,.........412. A.3, 84
Heliogabalus The like not Heliogabalus did eat:.262. H.783, 4
Hell I write of Hell; I sing (and ever shall).......5. H.1, 13
We two are last in Hell: what may we feare..33. H.101, 1
We'll wish, in Hell we had been Last and First..33. H.101, 4
Deare, though to part it be a Hell,............33. H.103, 1
There's paine in parting; and a kind of hell,......73. H.186, 7
That strik'st a stilnesse into hell:...............103. H.254, 2
Or hell it selfe a powerfull Bulwarke is?......116. H.283, 146
And mak'st all hell..............................170. H.452, 3
But stinking breath, I do as hell abhorre it...210. H.588, 2
The fire of hell it was..........................222. H.635, 8
To fetch Euridice from Hell;...................265. H.798, 2
I may from Hell.................................363. N.92, 16
For, once in hell, none knowes Remission there.
367. N.99, 2
Hell is no other, but a soundlesse pit,........372. N.117, 1
Hell is the place where whipping-cheer abounds,.372. N.120, 1
Out of hell an horrour call,....................377. N.128, 14
The fire of Hell this strange condition hath,...387. N.202, 1
The first of Raine, the key of Hell next known:
390. N.224, 2
One onely fire has Hell; but yet it shall,.......391. N.227, 1
When Hell and Horrour fright the Conscience..392. N.230, 28
To Hell I'd rather run, then I.................395. N.245, 5
As Hell, and Earth, and Heav'n may stand amaz'd.
399. N.263, 31
To vanquish Hell, as here He conquer'd Death?.403. N.271, 6
And live in Hell, if that my Christ stayes there..403. N.271, 8
Cast, leading his Euredice through hell,........411. A.3, 68
When on the Flood that nine times circles Hell..417. A.8, 36
He'l (Partial List)
He'll slit her nose; But blubb'ring, she replyes,.44. H.126, 2
And so he may, if he'll be rul'd by me:.......110. H.272, 2
He'l turn a Papist, rancker then before.........151. H.385, 6
For Lust and action; on he'l go,...............165. H.443, 11
He'll do no doubt; This flax is spun...........168. H.443, 121
He'l never haunt ye now he's dead.............226. H.644, 10
Yet he'l the courage have.......................259. H.772, 14
Yet he'le be thought or seen,...................259. H.772, 21
He'l sell her Eyes, and Nose, for Beere and Ale.
272. H.829, 4
With Princely hand He'l recompence delay.....344. N.30, 4
Hellespont Wept as he'd drowne the Hellespont,.42. H.119, 10
Hellish When the flames and hellish cries.......348. N.41, 1
— — — — — — — — —, ...452. var. H.443, 17
Hell's Led her through Hells obscuritie:.......265. H.798, 6
Hells And magicks for to end, and hells,.......115. H.283, 134
Help Helpe me! helpe me! now I call...........10. H.19, 1
He cry'd aloud, Help, help the wound:..........18. H.46, 4
Help! O help! your Boy's a dying...............50. H.139, 5
I kneele for help; O! lay that hand on me,....62. H.161, 12
Help from the Garlick, Onyon, and the Leek,.78. H.197, 58
Helpe me so, that I my shield,.................151. H.386, 3
As Love shall helpe thee, when thou do'st go hence
219. H.627, 7
As Love shall helpe me, I admire.............272. H.828, 9
If favour or occasion helpe not him..........298. H.953, 2
Help me, Julia, for to pray,...................324. H.1069, 1
In Varnisht maps; by'th' helpe of Compasses;.330. H.1100, 2
All saving health, and help for me.............342. N.17, 8
Since rough the way is, help me when I call,..352. N.51, 7
The room is cens'd: help, help t'invoke.........366. N.98, 15
Whom ease makes his, without the help of blowes.
372. N.116, 4
He that is hurt seeks help: sin is the wound;....381. N.155, 1
Helpe, if it could.................................401. N.268, 35
helpe on her pace; and though she lagg, yet stirre
430. ins. H.283, 20h
Helped His feet were helpt, and left his Crutch behind:
201. H.555, 3
Helpful To others store of helpfull spectacles.....154. H.401, 2
Helping (Thy Mercie helping) shall resist stronge fate
411. A.3, 44
Helps Faile of thy former helps; and onely use...46. H.128, 52
Helps to all others, but to me?.................74. H.191, 4
For all the Divell helps, will be a poore man...315. H.1025, 2
Hemisphere Nor doth this far-drawn Hemisphere..72. H.185, 3
But in one onely Hemisphere:...................139. H.353, 2
That paint the Hemisphere:......................257. H.767, 4
Hemlock Colde Hemlocke, or the Libbards bane
422. ins. H.106, 116b
Hen Next may your Duck and teeming Hen....179. H.476, 19
The Cock and Hen he feeds; but not a bone....204. H.568, 5
Cock calls his Wife his Hen: when Cock goes too't,
213. H.610, 1
Cock treads his Hen, but treads her under-foot...213. H.610, 2
A Hen...246. H.724, 9
Well, when sh'as kild, that Pig, Goose, Cock or Hen,
266. H.801, 3
Thou mak'st my teeming Hen to lay............350. N.47, 45
Hence Away with doubts, all scruples hence remove;.8. H.10, 7
Age cals me hence, and my gray haires bid come,..9. H.14, 3
Their departures hence, and die..................16. H.39, 14
That when from hence she does depart,............24. H.73, 9
And chiding me, said, Hence, Remove,...........51. H.142, 21
Ere I go hence; know this from me,............60. H.159, ?
Flie discontented hence, and for a time..........77. H.197, 21
Purge hence the guilt, and kill this quarrelling...78. H.197, 32
Will force you hence, (and in an houre.).........88. H.216, 6
Hence, hence, profane; soft silence let us have;..89. H.219, 1
A second pules, Hence, hence, profane...........91. H.223, 43
That being ravisht, hence I goe................95. H.227, 3
Hence then it is, that my poore brest...........96. H.229, 5
Meane while, the Holy-Rood hence fright......123. H.306, 13
So vanish hence, but leave a name, as sweet,....131. H.331, 9
No more shall I, since I am driven hence,......131. H.333, 1
Ah Posthumus! Our yeares hence flye,.........132. H.336, 1
Besides (Ai me!) since she went hence to dwell,
159. H.421, 27
(When hence thy Circum-mortall-part is gon)...168. H.444, 3
For Saints and Soules departed hence,.........169. H.449, 17
Go hence, and with this parting kisse,...........174. H.465, 1
Th'art hence removing, (like a Shepherds Tent)..188. H.507, 1
Hence a blessed soule is fled,...................211. H.593, 1
Ile get me hence,...............................213. H.609, 1
As Love shall helpe thee, when thou do'st go hence
219. H.627, 7
Farre hence be all speech, that may anger move:
222. H.633, 60
The Ravens yeares, go hence more Ripe then old.
222. H.633, 63
Whom gentle fate translated hence..............226. H.644, 5
When I goe Hence ye Closet-Gods, I feare......227. H.652, 1
And we glide hence away with them............233. H.670, 23
Some few sands spent, we hence must go,.......233. H.670, 37
Or lookt I back unto the Times hence flown,...234. H.673, 1
To tell how night drawes hence, I've none,....246. H.724, 2
Far from hence the evill Sp'rite................258. H.769, 9
Lest rapt from hence, I see thee lye...........275. H.844, 3
Till you warn her hence (away)..............276. H.850, 13
Anthea I am going hence......................277. H.854, 1
Love is a kind of warre; Hence those who feare,
280. H.872, 1
Hence the Hag, that rides the Mare,...........284. H.891, 2
Hence I must, for time doth call..............306. H.984, 38
And hence......................................308. H.993, 17
Yet part ye from hence,.......................317. H.1035, 28
And so to travaile hence......................352. N.53, 13
Sorrowes our portion are: Ere hence we goe,...359. N.81, 1
May Sweets grow here! & smoke from hence,..361. N.83, 63
God when He takes my goods and chattels hence..362. N.87, 1
Dark and dull night, flie hence away,...........364. N.96, 8
Hence, hence prophane, and none appeare........366. N.98, 1
The Spice and Spiknard hence is gone,.........375. N.123, 55
But when once from hence we flie,..............377. N.128, 5
The time the Bridegroom stayes from hence,....380. N.153, 1
How sweet this place is! as from hence........402. N.269, 14
Hence they have born my Lord: Behold! the Stone
403. N.271, 1
Is He, from hence, gone to the shades beneath...403. N.271, 5
Hence rise those twoe ambitious hills that looke..406. A.1, 81
Ere I goe hence and bee noe more..............407. A.2, 1
Fly hence Pale Care, noe more remember.........413. A.4, 1
Goe hence away, and in thy parting know........414. A.6, 1
Spring hence thy faith, nor thinke it ill desert......414. A.6, 3
And I must hence. Euc. Yet let me thus much know,
416. A.8, 25
Departing hence, where Good and Bad souls go..416. A.8, 26
— — — — — — — — — — — —, ...423. var. H.128, 42
— — — — — — — — — — — —, ...449. var. A.8, 37
Henceforth Let us not then so rudely henceforth goe
73. H.186, 5
No more shall I, from henceforth, heare a quire..132. H.333, 7
Henceforth at such a rate,.....................137. H.340, 11
That henceforth none be Laurel crown'd but Thee.
150. H.383, 2
Henceforth therefore I will be................219. H.628, 9
Henceforward Yet since cal'd back; henceforward let me be,
242. H.713, 15
Hens And Cock-like Hens Ile tread:...........160. H.422, 10
Her (Partial List)
Your Name to be a Laureat Wreathe to Hir,....99. H.245, 7
Hir Mab-ship in obedient Downe...............167. H.443, 89
Herb The Dew-bespangling Herbe and Tree.......67. H.178, 6
Imprinted in each Herbe and Flower:........230. H.662, 32
Herbs These, and sowre herbs, as dainty meat?..37. H.106, 11?
No Herbs have power to cure Love...........60. H.157, 4
Of all those suppling-healing herbs and flowers...62. H.161, 8
Selecting here, both Herbs, and Flowers;......289. H.912, 2
Herby His hereby broth, and there close by.439. ins. H.443, 451
Hercules Thee, that great cup Hercules:........122. H.304, 6
Herdess See Neatherdess
Herds See Neatherds
Here For these Transgressions which thou here dost see,
4. Ap., 1
Each here declining Violet.........................7. H.9, 4

And dropping **here**, and there:..................10. H.20, 3
Here that I...12. H.26, 5
What man would be **here**,........................12. H.26, 9
He could live free **here**?.......................12. H.26, 12
By Loves Religion, I must **here** confesse it,......15. H.38, 5
Here, here the Tomb of Robin Herrick is.........19. H.50, 6
Since I was born, then **here**;.....................19. H.51, 2
Here we are all, by day; By night w'are hurl'd....21. H.57, 1
Thou sail'st with others, in this Argus **here**;......23. H.71, 1
My solemne Vowes have **here** accomplished:.......23. H.72, 2
Whether in part 'tis **here** or there,...............24. H.73, 5
Doe, and have parted **here** a Man and Wife:....26. H.79, 2
Thus speaks the Oke, **here**; C. and M. shall meet,.26. H.79, 7
Whether thy bones had **here** their Rest, or no.....27. H.82, 6
Here I devote; And something more then so;....27. H.82, 11
An erring Lace, which **here** and there............28. H.83, 5
Cato the Censor, sho'd be scan each **here**..........28. H.84, 6
To be tormented, or kept Pris'ners **here**?........33. H.101, 2
Never sing, or play more **here**.....................39. H.111, 14
With blamelesse carriage, I liv'd **here**,..........41. H.116, 1
In thee, thou Man of Men! who **here** do'st give..41. H.117, 4
Maids, and **here** strew Violets.....................44. H.125, 6
Rests **here** with him; who was the Fame,......48. H.134, 3
Both bring one death; and I die **here**,..........50. H.140, 9
Here, with all her jealousies:.....................52. H.145, 2
No Furies, **here** about,...........................56. H.149, 103
Within the Chamber **here**..........................56. H.149, 108
Juno **here**, far off, doth stand.....................56. H.149, 109
Or by thy love, decree me **here** to stay...........60. H.156, 2
Here shall my endless Tabernacle be:..........60. H.156, 4
That I shall stir, or live more **here**.............61. H.159, 27
Stirring the waters, I am come; and **here**,........61. H.161, 4
I tell thee, by this score **here**;..................63. H.166, 6
The youthfull Prince D'Amour **here**...............63. H.166, 8
Though **here** the Princely Poet....................64. H.166, 12
To see my Lines Excathedrated **here**...............64. H.168, 4
Or **here** so bad, but you may pardon them.......64. H.168, 6
Which erring **here**, and wandring there,..........66. H.175, 3
As if **here** were those cooler shades of love......68. H.178, 36
For whose commutuall flames **here** I..........70. H.181, 15
What? shall we two our endlesse leaves take **here**
73. H.186, 9
No, **here** Ile last, and walk (a harmless shade)..73. H.186, 17
To guard it so, as nothing **here** shall be.........73. H.186, 19
And **here**, you see, this Lilly shows...............75. H.193, 4
Say, if there be 'mongst many jems **here**; one..76. H.194, 3
Which **here** I vow to serve, doe not remove....79. H 197, 82
Rich beads of Amber **here**.........................80. H.201, 8
Here burnt, whose smal return...................81. H.201, 42
My Harp hung up, **here** on the Willow tree.......84. H.210, 2
And scarce leav'st **here**............................85. H.211, 10
Here is my hope,...................................85. H.211, 23
Rest but a while **here**, by this bank of Lillies,..86. H.213, 10
That each Lyrick **here** shall be....................88. H.218, 4
Is **here** the Halcion's curious nest:................90. H.223, 4
I co'd not speak the Saints **here** painted.......91. H.223, 27
Who 'gainst Mabs-state plac't **here** right is.......91. H.223, 29
But alias call'd **here** Fatuus ignis..................91. H.223, 31
Here goe about for to recite.......................91. H.223, 34
Which one by one **here** set downe are.........91. H.223, 36
Favour your tongues, who enter **here**.............91. H.223, 41
The Altar is not **here** foure-square,.............91. H.223, 54
Their many mumbling Masse-priests **here**,.......92. H.223, 103
There ush'ring Vergers, **here** likewise,.........92. H.223, 105
Their sacred Salt **here**, (not a little.).........93. H.223, 118
On many a head **here**, many a Coronet:.........94. H.224, 4
But, amongst All encircled **here**, not one........94. H.224, 5
My wearyed Pinnace **here** finds ease:............94. H.225, 2
A Light ful-filling all the Region **here**...........94. H.226, 4
Whose acrimonious humour bites him **here**.......98. H.239, 4
On this sick youth work your enchantments **here**:
99. H.244, 2
Til I had got the name of Villars **here**...........99. H.245, 2
Here stand it stil to dignifie our Muse,..........99. H.245, 5
See, **here** a Maukin, there a sheet,.................101. H.250, 9
As **here** a Custard, there a Pie,..................101. H.250, 33
And **here** all tempting Frumentie.................101. H.250, 34
If smirking Wine be wanting **here**,...............101. H.250, 36
To work Love's Sampler onely **here**,.............103. H.256, 2
Are not **here** Rose-buds, Pinks, all flowers,.....103. H.256, 4
For you once lost, who weep not **here**!.........104. H.256, 10
But endlesse Peace, sit **here**, and keep.........104. H.256, 15
That Verse, of all the Verses, **here** shall be....107. H.264, 5
Many a sweet-fac't Wood-Nymph **here** is seene,..107. H.265, 5
And be both Princesse **here**, and Poetresse.....107. H.265, 10
This Epitaph, which **here** you see,..............109. H.271, 7
But now, we see, none **here**,................110. H.274, 13
Y'are left **here** to lament......................110. H.274, 19
Here down my wearyed limbs Ile lay;..........123. H.306, 1
Here I have found a Chamber fit,..............123. H.306, 7
Here she lies, a pretty bud,.....................123. H.310, 1
Ye wrong the Threshold-god, that keeps peace **here**:
124. H.313, 4
Pleasures, many **here** attend ye.................125. H.314, 5
We send to you; but **here** a jolly..............126. H.319, 9
Him to be **here** our Christian militant..........129. H.323, 16
It frisks, and flyes, now **here**, now there,......130. H.329, 13

And **here**, and there, and every where.........130. H.329, 15
Go where I will, thou luckie Larr stay **here**,....132. H.333, 9
And **here** enjoy our Holiday..................132. H.336, 16
Must I **here** stay,...................................137. H.340, 3
Who was your brave exalted Uncle **here**,........137. H.341, 3
You shall not languish, trust me: Virgins **here**..138. H.343, 3
That Cov'nant's **here**; The under-bow,...........139. H.353, 5
Whether or no, that we shall meet **here** ever.....140. H.355, 4
Or no, shall give ye a re-meeting **here**...........140. H.355, 8
A City **here** of Heroes I have made,...........143. H.365, 9
These are not to be reckon'd **here**;...............145. H.375, 24
Two dayes y'ave larded **here**; a third, yee know,
146. H.377, 25
Merry at anothers hearth; y'are **here**..........146. H.377, 29
Is not reserv'd for Trebius **here**,.................147. H.377, 58
Here, for to make the face affraid;.............148. H.377, 78
Turn'd, from a Papist **here**, a Predicant..........151. H.385, 2
A Vicarige at last Tom Glasse got **here**,.........151. H.385, 3
For which thy Love, live with thy Master **here**,..151. H.387, 7
Overloving, (living **here**:)........................152. H.391, 2
Being **here** their ends deny'd...................152. H.391, 3
Of these chaste spirits, that are **here** possest....152. H.392, 2
Live **here**: But know 'twas vertue, & not chance,.152. H.392, 5
Who hold fast **here** an endlesse lively-hood.....152. H.392, 8
Man is compos'd **here** of a two-fold part;........153. H.394, 1
Or spice, or fish, or fire, or close-stools **here**...155. H..405, 2
Here, and there a fresh Love is..................157. H.415, 4
Or **here** my Bed, or **here** my Grave...........158. H.420, 4
Youthfull Mirtillo, **Here** he comes, Griefdrownd...159. H.421, 6
Ambo. Poor pittied youth! Mir. And **here** the breth of kine
159. H.421, 13
This ball of Cow-slips, these she gave me **here**...159. H.421, 16
Here faithlesse never;..............................162. H.426, 24
But one halfe houre, that's made up **here**......162. H.431, 3
Shine like a spangle **here**.......................164. H.441, 8
What **here** I promise, that no Broom..........165. H.442, 13
As if Loves Sampler **here** was wrought:.........166. H.443, 36
Sweet Aires move **here**; and more divine......166. H.443, 39
Which cense this Arch; and **here** and there,.....166. H.443, 45
Are **here** most neatly inter-laid.................166. H.443, 50
Lies **here** abouts; and for to pave.............166. H.443, 53
Are neatly **here** enchequered...................166. H.443, 56
Wise hand enchasing **here** those warts,.........166. H.443, 60
Corrupted wood: serve **here** for shine...........167. H.443, 75
Besides I give Thee **here** a Verse that shall......168. H.444, 2
Yee silent shades, whose each tree **here**........169. H.449, 1
Here is the Legend of those Saints..............169. H.449, 5
Whose deeds, and deaths **here** written are......169. H.449, 13
(**Here** honour'd still with Frankincense).......169. H.449, 18
Me, me, forsaken, **here** admit...................170. H.449, 26
Here a solemne Fast we keepe,..................170. H.450, 1
Husht be all things; (no noyse **here**)..........170. H.450, 3
Here, here I live................................171. H.455, 1
Here was not with the act combin'd..........175. H.465, 62
But you may stay yet **here** a while,.............176. H.467, 4
Nothing comes Free-cost **here**; Jove will not let.177. H.469, 1
Alas! we blesse, but see none **here**,...........179. H.476, 25
And all live **here** with needy Fate............179. H.476, 30
Our free-feet **here**; but we'l away:............179. H.476, 35
Turn'd to these Springs, which wee see **here**:....180. H.478, 4
And smile **here** for your houre;..................184. H.493, 6
To this white Temple of my Heroes, **here**........185. H.496, 1
Of such rare Saint-ships, who did **here** consume..185. H.496, 3
High are These Statues **here**, besides no lesse..185. H.496, 7
Lesse is **here**, then in my heart.................186. H.500, 4
While they liv'd, or lasted **here**:...............187. H.503, 2
Here, in my Book's Canonization:..............188. H.510, 2
But rather like a flower hid **here**...............189. H.514, 7
Lust entring **here**:..............................190. H.515, 14
Here, **here** the Slaves and Pris'ners be........190. H.515, 19
Doe **here** find rest................................190. H.515, 22
Here, and his Cause...............................190. H.515, 24
Here those long suits of Chancery lie.........190. H.515, 25
Here needs no Court for our Request,...........190. H.515, 29
Nor need we **here** to feare the frowne.........190. H.515, 33
And for a while lye **here** conceal'd,...........190. H.515, 45
And then meet **here**................................190. H.515, 48
A Virgin Taper ever shining **here**...............191. H.516, 4
But **here** awhile, to languish and decay;.......193. H.522, 2
Like to these Garden-glories, which **here** be....193. H.522, 3
Long time w'ave **here** been a toying:..........195. H.534, 3
How soone our life, **here**,......................196. H.534, 16
The Chaplet, and * Inarculum **here** be,.........196. H.539, 3
And for to die **here**:.............................197. H.540, 2
Long for to lye **here**...............................197. H.540, 4
All things o'r-rul'd are **here** by Chance:........197. H.542, 1
Here we securely live, and eate...............198. H.544, 1
The longer **here**....................................198. H.544, 24
A stole of white, (and Canonized **here**).........199. H.545, 6
Thee **here** in my eternall Calender..............199. H.545, 10
Here, **here** I live with what my Board,.........200. H.552, 1
Here we reioyce, because no Rent..............200. H.552, 7
Marbles will sweare that **here** it lyes...........203. H.564, 2
Here in green Meddowes sits eternall May...206. H.575, 13
Here, naked Younglings, handsome Striplings run
206. H.575, 17
And **here** we'l sit on Primrose-banks, and see..206. H.575, 21

But Night determines here, Away..............207. H.575, 66
Aske me why I send you here..................208. H.580, 1
Here shall endure thy vast Dominion............210. H.592, 4
Leaving here the body dead:..................211. H.593, 2
Which (since here they can't combine).........211. H.593, 3
Fie, (quoth my Lady) what a stink is here?....212. H.598, 1
The Ev'ning's come; here now Ile stop,........212. H.602, 3
But by the Muses sweare, all here is good,......212. H.603, 3
Or Fort that I can make here;................213. H.609, 3
Will storme, or starving take here..............213. H.609, 6
Puts on the semblance here of sorrowing.........214. H.612, 4
And Charles here Rule, as he before did Raign;..214. H.612, 8
As when the Sweet Maria lived here:..........214. H.612, 10
Fix here my Button'd Staffe and stay...........216. H.617, 4
That with my Lines, my Life must full-stop here.
219. H.627, 2
And roundly drinke we here;..................219. H.629, 2
Here.......................................220. H.633, 7
Here about, but has his eyes,...............221. H.633, 30
Here we present a fleece.......................221. H.633, 32
Here a pretty Baby lies.......................224. H.640, 1
What gentle Winds perspire? As if here........224. H.642, 9
And thrice three weekes) he lived here.........226. H.644, 4
If here ye will some few teares shed,..........226. H.644, 9
Teares, though th'are here below the sinners brine,
226. H.645, 1
Us hands to get what here we have..............226. H.647, 4
Never againe to have ingression here:..........227. H.652, 2
Keep here still, Closet-Gods, 'fore whom I've set
227. H.652, 13
Drink Wine, and live here blithefull, while ye may:
228. H.655, 1
Here thou behold'st thy large sleek Neat......230. H.662, 35
Thy Wakes, thy Quintels, here thou hast,......230. H.662, 52
Here with the Generation of my Just...........231. H.664, 6
Those minutes, Time has lent us here.........233. H.670, 16
I might (and justly) be reputed (here)........234. H.673, 5
For favours here to warme me,................234. H.674, 5
For gladding so my hearth here,...............234. H.674, 7
With inoffensive mirth here;...................234. H.674, 8
That while the Wassaile Bowle here............235. H.674, 9
With North-down Ale doth troule here,.........235. H.674, 10
No sillable doth fall here,....................235. H.674, 11
To marre the mirth at all here.................235. H.674, 12
I'le eat and drink up all here..................235. H.674, 18
Give way, give way, now, now my Charles shines here,
236. H.685, 1
Love, and live here while we may;............238. H.691, 2
While we have our being here:.................238. H.691, 4
Need is no vice at all; though here it be,......239. H.698, 1
O fruitfull Genius! that bestowest here.........242. H.713, 7
Ile beg of thee first here to have mine Urn.....242. H.713, 18
Against thy Heifer, I will here.................243. H.716, 13
Since both have here deserved best............243. H.716, 36
That luckie Fairies here may dance their Round:.245. H.723, 8
Stand forth brave man, since Fate has made thee here
251. H.745, 1
But the anger ends all here,..................255. H.761, 19
Here lies a Virgin, and as sweet................257. H.764, 1
Give the Tapers here their light,...............258. H.769, 7
No Brutus entring here;......................259. H.772, 5
From whose happy spark here let...............262. H.782, 3
Cut the white loafe here,......................263. H.784, 14
Here I my selfe might likewise die,............265. H.794, 1
Repullulation gives me here....................265. H.794, 4
(As Lamps for everlasting shining here:)......267. H.804, 8
Here to be paid; Ile pay't i'th'world to come...267. H.804, 14
Thou, thou art here, to humane sight...........270. H.819, 4
Here she lyes (in Bed of Spice)...............274. H.838, 1
From good to good, revolving here, & there.....274. H.839, 2
Here, her ashes, or her Urne...................276. H.848, 5
Thee here among my righteous race:..........278. H.859, 2
And so soone stopt my longer living here;......278. H.860, 2
Ready here? Jul. All well prepar'd,............280. H.870, 8
Sho'd I not put on Blacks, when each one here..288. H.907, 1
Here lyes Johnson with the rest................289. H.910, 1
Selecting here, both Herbs, and Flowers;......289. H.912, 2
Of which make Garlands here, and there,........289. H.912, 3
Known guilty here of incivility:...............290. H.914, 2
This if ye do, each Piece will here be good,.....290. H.914, 9
Next, let the Lord, and Ladie here............291. H.919, 9
For ever with thee here........................293. H.934, 8
Here now I rest under this Marble stone:.......298. H.954, 2
Find'st here a fault, and mend'st the trespasse too:
298. H.955, 8
Of Beeves here ready stand for Sacrifice........300. H.961, 8
Then, in that compass, sayling here and there,..301. H.966, 5
Yet the deluge here was known,...............302. H.968, 11
Here may sing the rest of either:..............304. H.976, 4
Tha'st got a place here (standing candidate)...305. H.983, 2
Here of my great and good foundation..........305. H.983, 4
Then these kine, which I milke here.........305. H.984, 17
You are cloy'd here,..........................307. H.988, 9
But avoid here................................307. H.988, 12
Here to any;...............................308. H.993, 3
Here we begin new life; while thousands quite..313. H.1019, 3
As she did here,.............................314. H.1024, 19
I send, I send here my supremest kiss.........315. H.1028, 1
And Landing here, or safely Landing there,..316. H.1028, 13
Where Beane's the King of the sport here;....317. H.1035, 3
Must revell, as Queene, in the Court here......317. H.1035, 6
Who shall for the present delight here,.........317. H.1035, 9
Be Twelfe-day Queene for the night here......317. H.1035, 12
And let not a man then be seen here,..........317. H.1035, 15
A health to the King and the Queene here.....317. H.1035, 18
And though with ale ye be whet here;........317. H.1035, 27
As when ye innocent met here...............317. H.1035, 30
My Ship has here one only Anchor-hold;.......319. H.1044, 2
Here of Tinkers;..........................320. H.1051, 3
Stand forth Brave Man, here to the publique sight;
322. H.1062, 10
And leave me here behind thee;.............323. H.1068, 2
A wearied Pilgrim, I have wandred here......328. H.1088, 1
Because not plac't here with the midst, or first..329. H.1092, 2
Here Winter-like, to Frost and Snow.........329. H.1093, 4
Against diseases here the strongest fence......333. H.1117, 1
Here with the sweet Pierides..................334. H.1123, 2
And here my ship rides having Anchor cast.....334. H.1126, 2
Fames pillar here, at last, we set,............335. H.1129, 1
But if, 'mongst all, thou find'st here one..........339. N.2, 7
God when He's angry here with any one,..........340. N.7, 1
But yet still lesse then Grace can suffer here.....341. N.10, 4
Here give me thornes; there, in thy Kingdome, set
343. N.25, 5
There give me day; but here my dreadfull night:
343. N.25, 7
My sackcloth here; but there my Stole of white.
343. N.25, 8
God has his whips here to a twofold end,.......343. N.26, 1
If all transgressions here should have their pay,.343. N.27, 1
If God should punish no sin, here, of men,...343. N.27, 3
Thou prettie Babie, borne here,...............345. N.33, 3
With sup'rabundant scorn here:...............345. N.33, 4
Who for Thy Princely Port here,..............345. N.33, 5
Out-stable for thy Court here.................345. N.33, 8
But, here, a homely manger..................345. N.33, 16
With Glories to await here...................345. N.33, 27
Upon Thy Princely State here,................345. N.33, 28
Wee'l make Thee, here,......................345. N.33, 31
Here, for the righteous mans salvation:........349. N.44, 2
God is all-sufferance here; here He doth show.357. N.74, 1
Thou wonder of all Maids, li'st here,..........360. N.83, 13
We offer here, before thy Shrine,.............360. N.83, 32
And fresh thy Herse-cloth, we will, here,.....360. N.83, 35
May Sweets grow here! & smoke from hence,.361. N.83, 63
What here we hope for, we shall once inherit:..362. N.88, 1
By Faith we all walk here, not by the Spirit...362. N.88, 2
Our present Teares here (not our present laughter)
362. N.90, 1
Here did not make me sorrie,.................363. N.92, 3
And our Peace here, like a Spring,............363. N.93, 8
Here a little child I stand,..................364. N.95, 1
Here I lift them up to Thee,..................364. N.95, 4
The why, and wherefore all things here.......364. N.96, 12
Of all the house here, is the heart,............365. N.96, 28
And be it sin here to be dumb,...............365. N.97, 2
Touch gently, gently touch; and here.........366. N.97, 20
And from His sacred Bloud, here shed,........366. N.97, 22
With any thing unhallowed, here:.............366. N.98, 2
When I shall sin, pardon my trespasse here;..367. N.99, 1
With golden Censers, and with Incense, here,..368. N.103, 1
Before my last, but here a living grave,.......371. N.115, 2
So, here the remnant of my dayes I'd spend,..371. N.115, 11
The lesse our sorrowes here and suffrings cease,.372. N.119, 1
Scores of sins w'ave made here many,.........373. N.121, 9
For Tabitha, who dead lies here,.............374. N.123, 11
Chor. Stand empty here for ever:............374. N.123, 17
And though thou here li'st dead, we see......375. N.123, 71
Sleep with thy beauties here, while we.........375. N.123, 81
Candor here, and lustre there.................377. N.128, 11
Gods Grace deserves here to be daily fed,.....378. N.132, 1
I'th Forum here, or Vineyard.................380. N.152, 2
To punish great sins, who small faults whipt here.
381. N.156, 2
Nor yet for houses, which are here...........381. N.158, 7
The Bad among the Good are here mixt ever:.383. N.172, 1
The Good without the Bad are here plac'd never.
383. N.172, 2
But, as they walk't here in their vestures white,
384. N.181, 4
The first of Time, or Sabbath here of Dayes;..386. N.194, 2
God is more here, then in another place,......387. N.197, 1
First, that these goods none here may o're esteem,
387. N.201, 3
Being, oft here, the just mans portion.........387. N.201, 6
God bought man here wth his hearts blood expence;
389. N.213, 1
And man sold God here for base thirty pence..389. N.213, 2
To all our wounds, here, whatsoe're they be,....390. N.221, 1
Heaven is not given for our good works here:.390. N.223, 1
By houres we all live here, in Heaven is known.392. N.229, 1
Who shewing mercy here, few priz'd, or none...393. N.234, 2
To have continuall paine, or pleasure here:....394. N.236, 2
Doth, here on earth, some thing of novitie;...395. N.244, 2

The number **here** of Heires, shall from the state.395. N.248, 3
God doth not promise **here** to man, that He...396. N.252, 1
When I have done true Penance **here** for it....397. N.255, 4
If I have plaid the Truant, or have **here**....398. N.261, 1
I know, that faults will many **here** be found,.398. N.261, 5
Who suffers not **here** for mine own,..........400. N.266, 5
This Crosse-Tree **here**........................401. N.268, 1
Here all things ready are, make hast make hast away;
401. N.268, 5
By no ill haunted; **here** I come,...............402. N.269, 2
Then full affection, enter **here**................402. N.269, 9
And as I kisse, I'le **here** and there..........402. N.269, 12
Here, all her rare Aromaticks................402. N.269, 17
Let me live ever **here**, and stir..............402. N.269, 18
Here let me rest; and let me have............402. N.269, 22
I'le my Eternitie spend **here**..................402. N.269, 25
To joyn with them, who **here** confer..........402. N.270, 1
To vanquish Hell, as **here** He conquer'd Death?
403. N.271, 6
And sing a Caroll **here**.........................413. A.4, 5
And not a man **here** but consumes.............413. A.4, 34
Here melting numbers, words of power to move.415. A.7, 9
Love lyes a bleeding **here**, Evadne there......415. A.7, 11
Here Jemmonia's titles were...................418. A.9, 34
Lyes **here** about, and as we guesse......440. ins. H.443, 45z
— — — — — — — — — — —, ...449. var. A.8, 22
Hereabouts See Abouts
Hereafter **Hereafter**, shall smell of the Lamp, not thee.
46. H.128, 54
Which if it now, or shall **hereafter** shine,.......94. H.226, 7
That none **hereafter** sho'd be thought, or be....299. H.956, 3
Shall not times **hereafter** tell..................302. H.968, 7
Nor will **hereafter**; since I know..............320. H.1052, 3
Crosses we must have; or, **hereafter** woe.......359. N.81, 2
Are but the handsells of our joyes **hereafter**.....362. N.90, 2
For All that now come, or **hereafter** may......378. N.131, 2
God from our eyes all teares **hereafter** wipes,....379. N.139, 1
Herein Looke in my Book, and **herein** see,......288. H.906, 1
Herein's Prat He writes Satyres; but **herein's** the fault,
238. H.692, 1
Here's **Here's** a house of flesh on fire:...........21. H.61, 2
Besides us two, i'th' Temple **here's** not one.....168. H.445, 1
To your Cream, **her's** Strawberries...........183. H.491, 4
While others perish, **here's** thy life decreed...280. H.869, 5
Aha my boyes! **heres** wheat for Christmas Pies!
327. H.1086, 2
Of Gift from God: And **heres** my Creed.......359. N.78, 16
For, **here's** a Babe, that (like a Bride).......366. N.98, 12
Why then, go on to act: **Here's** wonders to be done,
401. N.268, 7
Here's golden fruit that farre exceeds all price..406. A.1, 71
Here's words with lines, and lines with Scenes consent,
415. A.7, 7
Here's a mad lover, there that high designe....415. A.7, 13
But **here's** the Sun-set of a Tedious day:.......419. A.10, 6
Here-spent-hours For their restlesse **here-spent-houres**,
152. H.391, 7
Heresy 'Tis **Heresie** in others: In your face.....180. H.481, 1
For that would prove more **Heresy** then fault
433. ins. H.283, 140h
Heretofore As **heretofore**,.......................144. H.371, 2
As **heretofore**,..............................162. H.426, 18
As I've doted **heretofore**:...................209. H.585, 8
Th' unequall Pulse to beat, as **heretofore**......254. H.756, 6
Hermaphrodite As if You Two, were one **Hermophrodite**:
201. H.557, 6
of two makes one **Hermaphrodite**.......431. ins. H.283, 50j
Hero Of **Hero**, and Leander; then Ile bring....206. H.575, 26
Heroes A City here of **Heroes** I have made,....143. H.365, 9
To this white Temple of my **Heroes**, here......185. H.496, 1
Herrick Anthea, **Herrick**, and his Poetry.........11. H.22, 10
Here, here the Tomb of Robin **Herrick** is.......19. H.50, 6
Herrick, thou art too coorse to love..........51. H.142, 22
Herrick, as yet:.............................72. H.185, 2
Grapes, before **Herrick** leaves Canarie Sack.....78. H.197, 48
Herrick keeps, as holds nothing...............117. H.285, 12
Herrick shall make the meddow-verse for you...140. H.355, 14
Remember what thy **Herrick** Thee foretold,..181. H.483, 10
Julia, when thy **Herrick** dies,................186. H.499, 1
If Dorset say, what **Herrick** writes, is good?..187. H.506, 6
Ile bring thee **Herrick** to Anacreon,..........206. H.575, 32
When I, thy **Herrick**,.........................213. H.604, 6
How **Herrick** beggs, if that he can-............214. H.611, 3
Take from thy **Herrick** this conclusion:........234. H.673, 14
And see his Robin **Herrick** lack,..............290. H.918, 3
Of Julia **Herrick** gave to me my Birth.........316. H.1028, 16
My Fates are ended; when thy **Herrick** dyes,..329. H.1095, 7
And fare it well: yet **Herrick**, if so be..........371. N.112, 2
Herrick's Onely **Herrick's** left alone,............16. H.39, 12
And learn'd Musicians shall to honour **Herricks**.143. H.366, 3
Herself See Self
He's (Partial List)
No; **he's** but Fore-man, as he was before......53. H.148, 4
The higher **he's** a getting;.....................84. H.208, 6
And neerer **he's** to Setting....................84. H.208, 8
As he is Prince, **he's** Shepherd too............86. H.213, 44
To have men think **he's** troubled with the Gout:.98. H.239, 2
He's greedie of his life, who will not fall,......155. H.405, 17
Pievish doth boast, that **he's** the very first......156. H.410, 1
He's soft and tender (Pray take heed).........157. H.412, 25
Lust ha's no eares; **He's** sharpe as thorn;.....165. H.443, 13
Spunge makes his boasts that **he's** the onely man
171. H.454, 1
Wound up again: Once down, **He's** down for ever.
202. H.558, 2
He's Lord of thy life, who contemnes his own..240. H.702, 2
At each warning **hees** as much.................418. A.9, 49
— — — — — — — — — — —, ...445. var. H.730, 15
Hesperides Or the rich **Hesperides**;.............120. H.297, 8
Whome love admitts to this **Hesperides**...........405. A.1, 70
Hey And cry out, **Hey**, for our town green......127. H.319, 20
Heyes To dance the **Heyes** with nimble feet;...192. H.521, 30
Hid And with rich clusters (**hid** among..........16. H.41, 10
Hid in a cloud of Frankincense:................93. H.223, 140
But rather like a flower **hid** here..............189. H.514, 7
What under there was **hid**.......................203. H.563, 4
Halfe with a Lawne of water **hid**,...............294. H.939, 6
A fault, tis **hid**, if it be voic't by thee..........328. H.1089, 2
Till they be **hid** o're with a wood of darts......370. N.109, 2
Like loving vines **hid** vnder Ivorye,............405. A.1, 48
Hidden There was **hidden** by the Witch.........55. H.149, 90
Then will your **hidden** Pride...................76. H.193, 55
Hide But when I crept with leaves to **hide**........17. H.41, 18
Hide, and with them, their Fathers nakedness...32. H.95, 4
Play ye at **Hide** or Seek,......................83. H.207, 7
Sleep, while we **hide** thee from the light,......146. H.376, 13
She now weares silk to **hide** her blood-shot eye.207. H.578, 2
Not for to **hide** his high and mighty eares;....275. H.843, 2
These Veiles, wherewith we use to **hide**.......360. N.83, 45
Hides That **hides** the loving flame:.............54. H.149, 24
Night **hides** our thefts; all faults then pardon'd be:
209. H.586, 1
God **hides** from man the reck'ning Day, that He.379. N.142, 1
Hidleberge See **Heidelberg**
Hie — — — — — — — —, ...422. var. H.106, 67
bearing downe Time before you; **hye**......431. ins. H.283, 50c
Hierarchy Out of my self that Glorious **Hierarchie**!
326. H.1080, 2
To be of that high **Hyrarchy**, where none.443. var. H.575, 59
Hieroglyphic Each **hieroglyphick** of a kisse or smile;
115. H.283, 126
High That **high** Enchantment I betake me now:..62. H.161, 10
When her **high** carriage did at once present...79. H.197, 75
Whether **high** he builds or no:................84. H.209, 2
High, and passions lesse of heat...............96. H.232, 10
How **high** she's priz'd, and worth but small;...103. H.253, 17
And his actions **high** be told.................108. H.266, 19
High in your own conceipt, and some way teach
115. H.283, 128
High sons of Pith,..........................136. H.336, 131
Double chinn'd, and forehead **high**:............138. H.342, 4
You, who are **High** born, and a Lord no lesse.141. H.359, 3
That gave thee this so **high** inheritance........152. H.392, 6
As Cherry harvest, now **high** fed.............165. H.443, 10
High with thine own Auspitious Destinies:.....181. H.483, 2
That Towrs **high** rear'd dread most the lightnings threat:
181. H.483, 14
High are These Statues here, besides no lesse...185. H.496, 7
His Odisees, and his **high** Iliads...............206. H.575, 28
That my pulses **high** may beate...............217. H.620, 3
In our **high** art, although we can't excell,......234. H.673, 10
Sung in the **high** Doxologie of Thee..........254. H.756, 16
Not for to hide his **high** and mighty eares;.....275. H.843, 2
In all our **high** designments, 'twill appeare,....292. H.924, 1
Tel'st when a Verse springs **high**, how understood
297. H.947, 7
In an expansion no lesse large, then **high**;......301. H.966, 4
You set too **high** a rate upon...............324. H.1068, 17
High is the roof there; but the gate is low:......362. N.89, 2
Torments for **high** Attilius; and, with want,....370. N.108, 9
Puts down some prints of His **high** Majestie:...385. N.189, 2
The platter **high** with Fish?..................391. N.228, 8
But like a Person of some **high** account:......398. N.263, 16
Her forehead smooth full polisht bright and **high**
404. A.1, 5
A milky **high** waye that direction yeilds.......405. A.1, 67
Here's a mad lover, there that **high** designe...415. A.7, 13
— — — — — — — — — — —, ...434. var. H.293, 53
At a **high** rate, and further brought......436. ins. H.336, 48h
— — — — — — — — — — —, ...437. var. H.336, 105
To be of that **high** Hyrarchy, where none..443. var. H.575, 59
Higher The **higher** he's a getting;.............84. H.208, 6
A piece, then of a **higher** text:.............135. H.336, 100
Fortune no **higher** Project can devise,..........196. H.535, 1
Flies no thought **higher** then a fleece:.........229. H.662, 12
Is not by mariage quencht, but flames the **higher**.
262. H.781, 16
And, coveting no **higher** sphere,..............402. N.269, 24
Of **higher** price, as halfe-iet-ringes.........440. ins. H.443, 45s
High-priest **High-Priest** to me,.................87. H.214, 12
High-reared Upon six plump Dandillions, **high-**
Rear'd, lyes her Elvish-majestie:
167. H.443, 86-87
Hight — — — — — — — — —, ...451. var. H.197, 75

High-towering High-towring wil devote to them: 22. H.66, 2
Highway A milky **high waye** that direction yeilds...405. A.1, 67
Hill And Titan on the Eastern **hill**............68. H.178, 25
Shew me that **Hill** (where smiling Love doth sit) 154. H.403, 3
A Shepherd piping on a **hill**................230. H.662, 45
Why so lonely on the **hill**?..................305. H.984, 4
Chor. Thy belly like a **hill** is,...............375. N.123, 77
Or ells that she on that white waxen **hill**......405. A.1, 63
And when thou art vppon that forked **Hill**.....412. A.3, 85
Hillock There on a **Hillock** thou mayst sing.....5. H.2, 11
Hills See **Dunghills**
Mont. Love for thy sake will bring her to these **hills** 159. H.421, 35
Thou leav'st our **Hills**, our Dales, our Bowers,.183. H.492, 13
Thy Feasting-Tables shall be **Hills**..........192. H.521, 15
Hence rise those twoe ambitious **hills** that looke.406. A.1, 81
Hilly Stands garded with a rosy **hilly** wall,......405. A.1, 30
Him (Partial List)
But when he felt **him** warm'd,...............27. H.81, 25
Lungs (as some, say) ne'r sets **him** down to eate, 223. H.637, 1
And thus they praise the Sumpter; but not **him**: 330. H.1099, 4
Himself Homer **himself**, in a long work, may sleep. 32. H.95, 6
But on a Rock **himselfe** sate by,............42. H.119, 3
He chirpt for joy, to see **himself** disceav'd......46. H.130, 12
The Volumne of **himselfe**, and Name..........48. H.134, 4
Retires **himselfe**, or else stands still...........68. H.178, 26
He thus began **himselfe** t'excuse:............71. H.182, 12
Man knowes where first he ships **himselfe**; but he 177. H.468, 1
Love turn'd **himselfe** into a Bee,..............283. H.883, 9
Himselfe, at one time, can be wise, and Love...294. H.936, 4
Who hath **himselfe** obaid the Soveraignty......325. H.1074, 2
He patience gives; He gives **himselfe** to me....362. N.87, 4
Ev'n God **Himself**, in perfect Entitie...........382. N.165, 2
Hind With a **Hind** whistling there to them:....230. H.662, 26
Fat be my **Hinde**; unlearned be my wife;......294. H.938, 1
Hind, Goderiske, Smith................437. var. H.336, 131
Hinder-parts Perplex him in his **hinder-parts**......6. H.5, 4
Hindrance How wo'd he eate, were not his **hindrance** such? 191. H.518, 6
Hindrances So very-many-meeting **hindrances**,.....352. N.51, 2
But the pleasing **hindrances**?..................355. N.64, 2
Hinds Or how to pay thy **Hinds**, and cleere....230. H.662, 13
Hip See **Cricket's-hip**
— — — — — — — — — — —, ...434. var. H.293, 39
Hipped See **Loose-hipped**
Hippocrene As if or'e washt in **Hippocrene**......277. H.857, 2
Hips — — — — — — — — —, ...434. var. H.293, 39
His (Partial List)
Such Three brave Brothers fell in Mars **his** Field. 170. H.451, 12
Tom Blinks **his** Nose is full of wheales, and these 273. H.834, 1
'Tis a gift for Christ **His** sake:...............363. N.93, 2
Hisped **Hisped**, and hairie, ere thy Pa'm shall know 202. H.557, 24
Hissed Such ignorance as theirs was, who once **hist** 150. H.382, 15
Hist See **Hissed**
History My Love will fit each **Historie**..........207. H.579, 8
Hit At randome, sometimes **hit** most happily.....318. H.1039, 2
Hither **Hither** the least one theeving thought:...71. H.182, 14
Pure hands bring **hither**, without staine........91. H.223, 42
Who **hither** at her wonted howers............145. H.376, 5
Sell, and brought **hither** by the Elves..........166. H.443, 62
You had your comming **hither**;...............184. H.493, 2
But Ile returne; what mischief brought thee **hither**? 248. H.730, 13
Sacred Spittle bring ye **hither**;...............258. H.769, 4
Since we fresh strewings will bring **hither**,......289. H.912, 7
Holy waters **hither** bring.....................303. H.974, 1
No ruffling winds come **hither** to discease....316. H.1028, 21
Bring the Holy-water **hither**;................324. H.1069, 5
No boysterous winds, or stormes, come **hither**,.361. N.83, 69
Chor. And when you are come **hither**;........373. N.123, 7
Devotion bids me **hither** bring...............402. N.270, 3
Shall **hither** waft it, and in leiu...............414. A.5, 15
Hitherto The Drooping West, which **hitherto** has stood 25. H.77, 3
But have **hitherto** liv'd free,.................183. H.490, 17
The Holly **hitherto** did sway;................285. H.892, 5
Hive Hony enough to fill his **hive**.............71. H.182, 31
Nor Bee, or **Hive** you have be mute;..........179. H.476, 17
Hives So smells the Breath about the **hives**,....145. H.375, 7
Hoards Much-more, provides, and **hoords** up like an Ant; 73. H.188, 1
Hoarse Broke is my Reed, **hoarse** is my singing too: 205. H.573, 2
But vnto mee, bee onlye **hoarse**, since now....411. A.3, 47
Hoarsely Nor thinke these Ages that do **hoarcely** sing 155. H.405, 5

Hock-cart For joy, to see the **Hock-cart** crown'd. 101. H.250, 14
Hock-carts I sing of May-poles, **Hock-carts**, Wassails, Wakes, 5. H.1, 3
Hoe **Hoe**,....................................307. H.988, 11
Hog **Hog** has a place i'th' Kitchen, and his share.326. H.1079, 1
Hogs The fattest **Hogs** we grease the more with Lard. 22. H.64, 2
Some to bee Ratts, and others to bee **hoggs**:...412. A.3, 92
Hogsheads Upon your **hogsheads** never fall.....291. H.919, 5
Hoise — — — — — — — —, ...445. var. H.730, 12
Hoist That made me **hoist** saile, and bring my Boat: 248. H.730, 12
Holbein Of **Holben**, and That mighty Ruben too..150. H.384, 4
Holben See **Holbein**
Hold See **Anchor-hold, Withhold**
A little Pin-dust; which they **hold**.............92. H.223, 87
I am Sive-like, and can **hold**..................116. H.285, 1
Who **hold** fast here an endlesse lively-hood......152. H.392, 8
Who can **hold** that (my friends) that will away?.162. H.428, 2
Arch-like, **hold** up, Thy Name's Inscription....168. H.444, 4
Can **hold** of Beere and Ale an Ocean;.........171. H.454, 2
The yvorie tooke State to **hold**................185. H.497, 5
Good Precepts we must firmly **hold**,...........187. H.505, 1
Or **hold** their peace..........................190. H.515, 28
Health is no other (as the learned **hold**)......236. H.683, 1
By giving and receiving **hold** the play:.........255. H.758, 2
Thus if our ship fails of her Anchor **hold**,.....266. H.800, 7
Hold but her hands; You **hold** both hands and wings. 271. H.823, 6
To **hold** us two, an endlesse honour have.....281. H.875, 6
Thus times do shift; each thing his turne do's **hold**; 285. H.892, 21
Because his stock will not **hold** out for white....309. H.997, 2
As to speak, Lord, say and **hold**...............347. N.40, 4
To **hold** things fitting my necessity;...........371. N.115, 6
Freely from them, and **hold** none back at all....380. N.151, 2
Holde their Eternall fiers; and ours of Late...411. A.3, 43
— — — — — — — — — — —, ...449. var. A.3, 43
Holdest And **hold'st** mine eyes from sleeping;...353. N.56, 3
Holding Then **holding** up (there) such religious Things, 11. H.22, 5
Holds Herrick keeps, as **holds** nothing..........117. H.285, 12
I know the Tunne of Hidleberge **holds** more.....171. H.454, 4
That he **holds** firmly to the end...............215. H.615, 6
Holds none at all, or little in his hand.........221. H.633, 53
Hole See **Fox i'th' Hole**
When one **hole** wasts more then he gets by Nine. 154. H.400, 4
That's tost up after Fox i'th' **Hole**............231. H.662, 57
Holes See **Nine-holes**
Holiday And here enjoy our **Holiday**..........132. H.336, 16
Holidays See **Holy-days**
Holies Among which **Holies**, be Thou ever known, 199. H.545, 7
Hollow Next, **hollow** out a Tombe to cover....61. H.159, 28
How false, how **hollow** she's in heart;.........103. H.253, 15
They be but signs of Ursleys **hollow** teeth.....197. H.543, 4
Hollows Six dayes he **hollows** so much breath away, 163. H.435, 3
Holly Verse crown'd with Yvie, and with **Holly**:.126. H.319, 10
In stead of **Holly**, now up-raise..............285. H.892, 3
The **Holly** hitherto did sway;..................285. H.892, 5
Down with the **Holly**, Ivie, all,................304. H.980, 3
This **Hollie**, and this Ivie Wreath,............365. N.96, 30
Holm A stubborn Oake, or **Holme** (long growing there) 225. H.642, 14
Holocaust With perfumes the **Holocaust**:......280. H.870, 16
Holy The **holy** incantation of a verse;...........7. H.8, 2
As were (time past) thy **holy** Filitings:........11. H.22, 6
Is it (sweet maid) your fault these **holy**........53. H.149, 11
Whose structure (for his **holy** rest)..........90. H.223, 3
Two pure, and **holy** Candlesticks:..............92. H.223, 94
Their **Holy** Oyle, their Fasting-Spittle;.......93. H.223, 117
Those **holy** lights, wherewith they guide.......109. H.271, 3
Of **holy** Saints she paces on,..................112. H.283, 13
Makes **holy** these, all others lay aside:.........114. H.283, 98
In **holy** meetings, there a man may be........163. H.436, 1
The **holy** Entrance; where within............166. H.443, 65
By **holy** Himen to the Nuptiall Bed...........180. H.477, 2
When at the **holy** Threshold of thine house,....181. H.483, 11
One **Holy** Collect, said or sung for Thee.......209. H.584, 4
I am **holy**, while I stand......................227. H.651, 1
The **holy** Sisters some among.................237. H.686, 9
Look how next the **holy** fier..................242. H.714, 9
Holy Water come and bring;...................258. H.769, 1
Of the **holy** Beast we bring....................280. H.870, 11
Bring the **holy** crust of Bread,................284. H.883, 1
Put on thy **Holy** Fillitings, and so...........286. H.898, 1
Unto the **Holy** Temple ride:..................291. H.919, 14
Holy waters hither bring....................303. H.974, 1
Offer'd on my **holy** Grave;...................307. H.991, 6
For that **holy** piece of Bread,................323. H.1065, 5
God, as He is most **Holy** knowne;..............343. N.23, 1
The sacred Towell, and the **holy** Eure..........355. N.65, 5
Cast **Holy** Water all about,..................365. N.97, 4
Conceal'd in this most **holy** Ground:...........366. N.98, 4

Let's kisse the sweet and **holy** ground;........368. N.102, 16
God, in the **holy** Tongue, they call.............385. N.185, 1
His **holy** Spirit, or doth plant His Grace......385. N.189, 4
'Twixt God the Father, **Holy** Ghost, and Sonne:
386. N.191, 4
Haile **holy**, and all-honour'd Tomb,...........402. N.269, 1
Which ope themselves to shewe an **holy** shrine..404. A.1, 26
With **holye** fier least that itt dye.............407. A.2, 24
Our **holy** Spicknard, & ther's none............413. A.4, 25
— — — — — — — — — —, ...423. var. H.128, 25
You with his just and **holy** Ire..........431. ins. H.283, 40g
Holy-cake Therewithall a **Holy-cake**:...........152. H.393, 4
Holy-days Frolick the full twelve **Holy-dayes**....127. H.319, 50
On **Holy-dayes**, when Virgins meet............192. H.521, 29
Thou hast thy Eves, and **Holydayes**:..........230. H.662, 47
Holy-forum Stood in the **Holy-Forum** Candidate:.106. H.261, 2
Holy-grist There off'ring up the **Holy-Grist**:.....91. H.223, 51
Holy-lays Their true-pac'd-Numbers, and their **Holy-Layes**,
45. H.128, 35
Holy-meal With **Holy-meale**, and spirting-salt...36. H.106, 60
Holy-oak Under that **Holy-oke**, or Gospel-tree:..20. H.55, 4
Holy-rage No **Holy-Rage**, or frantick-fires did stirre,
150. H.382, 9
Holy-rood Meane while, the **Holy-Rood** hence fright
123. H.306, 13
Holy-Rood come forth and shield.............177. H.473, 1
Holywater See **Holy**
The **Holy-water** there is put:.................91. H.223, 45
Bring the **Holy-water** hither;.................324. H.1069, 5
Holywaters See **Holy**
Homage Witnesse their **Homage**, when they come and strew
107. H.265, 7
Home See **Nobly-home-bred**
Farre safer 'twere to stay at **home**:............5. H.2, 2
Stay then at **home**, and doe not goe............6. H.2, 19
From house to house, and never stay at **home**;...6. H.3, 4
And haste away to mine eternal **home**;.........9. H.14, 4
But thou at **home**, blest with securest ease,....36. H.106, 69
But thou at **home** without or tyde or gale,......36. H.106, 77
Home the Turtles; Hymen guide.................54. H.149, 49
Yet comming **home**, but somewhat late, (last night)
65. H.171, 4
Back, and with White-thorn laden **home**.......69. H.178, 46
He has at **home**; but who tasts boil'd or rost?.89. H.221, 2
Prethee goe **home**; and for thy credit be......97. H.236, 3
And, to the Pipe, sing Harvest **home**..........101. H.250, 6
The richer Couslips **home**......................110. H.274, 8
That sleeps at **home**; and sayling there at ease,.128. H.323, 3
Laden with wax and hony **home**:..............145. H.375, 10
And bring him **home**, but 'tis decreed,.........157. H.412, 27
And with my sighs, call **home** my bleating sheep:
159. H.421, 38
Last night thou didst invite me **home** to eate;.161. H.424, 1
Ha's none at **home**, in Coffers, Desks, or Trunks.
173. H.463, 4
But **home** return'd, as he went forth, halfe blind.
201. H.555, 4
From the Temple to your **home**...............220. H.633, 1
To seek, and bring rough Pepper **home**:......229. H.662, 6
Bring'st **home** the Ingot from the West........229. H.662, 10
Thy Harvest **home**; thy Wassaile bowle,......231. H.662, 56
London my **home** is: though by hard fate sent.242. H.713, 13
His wife her owne ware sells as fast at **home**...253. H.753, 4
To sup with thee thou didst me **home** invite;.262. H.783, 1
He prayes his Harvest may be well brought **home**.
270. H.822, 2
(When drunke with Beere) to light him **home**, i'th' dark.
273. H.834, 4
We love to rest in peacefull Urnes at **home**,....278. H.860, 6
The Body is the Soules poore house, or **home**,..279. H.865, 1
(As to the breaking of a Bride-Cake) **home**:...286. H.898, 10
To re-possess once more your long'd-for **home**..300. H.961, 6
Then come **home** and fother them..............315. H.1026, 4
T'invade from far: They'l finde worse foes at **home**.
316. H.1030, 2
I kenn my **home**; and it affords some ease,......352. N.51, 9
In the way 'twixt me, and **home**:.............355. N.64, 4
And In a Whirl-wynd twirld her **home**, agast..410. A.3, 25
Her heart's at **home**, howere she goes:...430. ins. H.283, 20j
Or Lar will freeze to death at **home**:...431. ins. H.283, 60j
Home-borne Devotion, stroak the **home-borne** wheat:
101. H.250, 22
Homely At my **homely** Country-seat,...........152. H.393, 1
A Shepheardess so **homely**;.................324. H.1068, 18
But, here, a **homely** manger.................345. N.33, 16
Homer **Homer** himself, in a long work, may sleep.
32. H.95, 6
Homer, this Health to thee,.................80. H.201, 13
Thee to the Stand, where honour'd **Homer** reades
206. H.575, 27
Be they those that **Homer** bit,..............329. H.1096, 3
Homer, Musæus, Ouid, Maro, more............411. A.3, 41
Homeward And **homeward** she did bring........250. H.740, 2
Now singing, **homeward** let us carrie.........366. N.97, 26
— — — — — — — — —, ...453. ins. H.283, 20i
Homewards her **homewards**, well she knowes
430. ins. H.283, 20i

Homilies They have their Book of **Homilies**:....92. H.223, 82
Honest Pay when th'art **honest**; let me have some hope.
83. H.206, 4
Honesty Of antient **honesty**, may boast..........147. H.377, 42
Honey **Hony** to salve, where he before did sting...16. H.40, 8
Hony, and in the quintessence:..............71. H.182, 8
For **Honie**, that I beare away...............71. H.182, 22
Of **hony**, 'fore her Ladiship:..................71. H.182, 24
Hony enough to fill his hive..................71. H.182, 31
Love, **honie** yeelds; but never stings..........130. H.329, 23
When well the work of **hony** thrives;..........145. H.375, 8
Laden with wax and **hony** home:..............145. H.375, 10
Our salt, our Corn, our **Honie**, Wine, and Oile)
225. H.642, 18
Is, when loves **hony** has a dash of gall........327. H.1084, 2
How will it drop pure **hony**, speaking these?...328. H.1089, 4
Honey-bag And say, thou bring'st this **Hony-bag** from me:
100. H.248, 2
Honeycomb If thou hast found an **honie-combe**,.288. H.909, 1
Honeycombs Dryed, **hony-combs**, Browne Achorne cupps
439. ins. H.443, 45j
Honeyed Leaves dropping downe the **honyed** dew,.86. H.213, 40
Honey-suckles With **Hony-succles** crown'd.......110. H.274, 12
Honor The maide of **Honour** unto thee..........8. H.11, 10
The lace, to **honour** me, or it:................14. H.34, 4
Or for mine **honour**, lay me in that Tombe.....20. H.55, 7
And doe an **honour** to thy teare;.............48. H.134, 6
Welcome Maids of **Honour**,...................83. H.205, 1
To **honour** thy Decree:......................108. H.267, 10
And doe some **honour** to my Tomb..............111. H.280, 8
She weares as trophees of her **honour**..........131. H.330, 13
To **honour** thee, my little Parsly crown:......131. H.333, 4
Which gave me **honour** for my Rhimes,......136. H.336, 150
And learn'd Musicians shall to **honour** Herricks.143. H.366, 3
More **honour** had, then this same Flie;.........186. H.497, 17
You'l do my Neice abundant **honour**...........257. H.764, 10
Honour be to the Graces!....................260. H.777, 5
Honour to you who sit!......................261. H.778, 1
Who will not **honour** Noble Numbers, when.....264. H.791, 1
To hold us two, an endlesse **honour** have......281. H.875, 6
To **honour** Whitsontide......................285. H.892, 16
Honour thy Parents; but good manners call...363. N.94, 1
And give the **honour** to this Day,.............364. N.96, 9
To do Him **honour**; who's our King,..........365. N.96, 31
That done, with **Honour** Thou dost me create.398. N.262, 3
But if Thou wilt so **honour** me,...............399. N.265, 3
This **Honour** have,...........................401. N.268, 38
Thoughe as a seruant, yet a Mayde of **Honor**....412. A.3, 102
Honored See **All-honored**
That, which may the **honour'd** Stem..........57. H.149, 129
Who doth both love and feare you **Honour'd** Sir.
99. H.245, 8
Who hug our Poems (**Honourd** Sir) and then.141. H.359, 5
(Here **honour'd** still with Frankincense)......169. H.449, 18
Thee to the Stand, where **honour'd** Homer reades
206. H.575, 27
(Amongst mine **honour'd**) Thee (almost) the last:
256. H.763, 2
He's double **honour'd**, since h'as got gay cloathes:
330. H.1099, 2
Honoring **Honouring** thee, on my knee..........213. H.604, 7
Honors Our **Honours**, and our Commendations be.120. H.296, 1
Doe now your flowrie **honours** to my Herse.....138. H.343, 2
Honours my Lady and my Lord...............148. H.377, 76
Give me **Honours**: what are these,..............355. N.64, 1
And that His treble **Honours** may be seen,......368. N.102, 23
These hung, as **honours** o're thy Grave,......375. N.123, 86
Hood See **Livelihood, Long-lamented-widowhood, Needihood, Priesthood, Sisterhood**
Hoods See **Sisterhoods**
Make **hoods** of thee to serve out Spice...........275. H.844, 8
Hoof Clear of **hoof**, and clear of horn;........306. H.984, 21
We not divide the **Hoof**, but chew the Cud:....397. N.256, 2
We then both chew the Cud, and cleave the **Hoof**.
397. N.256, 4
Hoofed See **Strong-hoofed**
Hoofy W[th] Numerous feete to **Hoofy** Helicon,....412. A.3, 84
Hook See **Sheep-hook**
Shall pranke thy **Hooke** with Lillies............184. H.492, 32
This, this alluring **Hook** might be.............193. H.521, 45
May baite his **hooke**, with maggots taken thence..282. H.879, 4
Hook-nosed Squint-ey'd, **hook-nos'd**; and lastly, Kidney-lipt.
62. H.163, 2
Hooks See **Flesh-hooks**
Hang up **Hooks**, and Sheers to scare............284. H.891, 1
Hop The Pole of the **Hop**........................320. H.1051, 7
Hope Of Heaven, and **hope** to have it after all.......5. H.1, 14
She shall: Then my **hope** is,..................43. H.123, 32
This, as I wish for, so I **hope** to see;..........52. H.146, 17
But out of **hope** his wife might die to beare 'em...72. H.184, 2
Then there is **hope** that you may see..........79. H.198, 11
Pay when th'art honest; let me have some **hope**..83. H.206, 4
Here is my **hope**,..............................85. H.211, 23
And since the last is dead, there's **hope**,........93. H.223, 111
Put in Feare, and **hope**, and doubt;............116. H.285, 5
With **hope** you would allay the same:..........157. H.413, 2
Of **hope**..211. H.596, 3

Come tel me then, how great's the smart.......50. H.139, 14
Behold! how Hymens Taper-light..............54. H.149, 51
Shews you how much is spent of night..........54. H.149, 52
The best way how to loose the Zone............56. H.149, 92
Or learne some way how to forget..............60. H.159, 7
See how Aurora throwes her faire...............67. H.178, 3
How each field turns a street; each street a Parke
68. H.178, 30
Made green, and trimm'd with trees: see how....68. H.178, 31
Do mar'l how I co'd die,......................72. H.185, 20
How both his Meale and Oile will multiply.......73. H.188, 4
You see how Creame but naked is;..............75. H.193, 9
You see how Amber through the streams........75. H.193, 17
A Rule, how far to teach,......................76. H.193, 42
If you can see, how Dreams do creep...........79. H.198, 9
Let them prattle how that I....................82. H.203, 5
Let them tell how she doth move................82. H.203, 7
How we watch, and seldome sleep;.............82. H.203, 11
How by Willowes we doe weep:..................82. H.203, 12
How by stealth we meet, and then..............82. H.203, 13
Whether I wo'd; but (ah!) I know not how,......84. H.210, 7
How many lye forgot..........................85. H.211, 13
How the times away doe goe:...................96. H.231, 2
About the Cart, heare, how the Rout...........101. H.250, 15
How hard a woman 'tis to please?.............103. H.253, 12
How crosse, how sullen, and how soone........103. H.253, 13
How false, how hollow she's in heart;........103. H.253, 15
And how she is her owne least part:..........103. H.253, 16
How high she's priz'd, and worth but small;....103. H.253, 17
You have beheld, how they.....................110. H.274, 5
You say y'are sweet; how sho'd we know........112. H.282, 1
Then we shall smell how sweet you be.........112. H.282, 4
Enlightned substance; mark how from the Shrine
112. H.283, 12
See where she comes; and smell how all the street
113. H.283, 21
Breathes Vine-yards and Pomgranats: O how sweet!
113. H.283, 22
Shew her how his eyes do turne.............113. H.283, 37
O marke yee how...........................115. H.283, 105
How tedious they are in their dresse...........118. H.291, 4
But to shew thee how in part,..................128. H.322, 4
How rich a man is, all desire to know;........130. H.328, 1
How speaks it, say? 2. Do you but this,.......130. H.329, 17
How am I ravisht! When I do but see,..........139. H.347, 1
If so, how much more shall I dote thereon,......139. H.347, 3
See how the poore do waiting stand,............139. H.350, 1
Look, how the Rainbow doth appeare..........139. H.353, 1
How dull and dead are books, that cannot show..141. H.359, 1
How for to make thee merry;..................142. H.364, 6
How farre a Figure ought to go,..............148. H.377, 92
Now I love I know not how.................155. H.407, 2
Skinns he din'd well to day; how do you think?..156. H.409, 1
How each thing smells divinely redolent!......159. H.421, 19
Then we shall see, how in a little space,........168. H.445, 5
May read how soon things have...............176. H.467, 14
How long, Perenna, wilt thou see..............177. H.471, 1
How can I choose but love, and follow her,......181. H.485, 1
How can I chuse but kisse her, whence do's come
181. H.485, 3
For Loves-sake, tell me how....................183. H.492, 8
Ai me! How shal my griefe be stil'd?..........188. H.509, 5
How wo'd he eate, were not his hindrance such?.191. H.518, 6
How soone our life, here,.....................196. H.534, 16
Say then, how ill sho'd I have sped,...........212. H.599, 3
How Herrick beggs, if that he can-............214. H.611, 3
But Fables we'l relate; how Jove.............215. H.616, 15
Next we will act, how young men wooe;......215. H.616, 19
And how the Posset shall be made.............216. H.616, 32
In a Minutes space how I....................217. H.620, 8
And look how when a frantick Storme doth tear.225. H.642, 13
Or how to pay thy Hinds, and cleere..........230. H.662, 13
And cheer'st them up, by singing how.........230. H.662, 27
The how, where, when, I question not...........236. H.681, 2
How co'd Luke Smeaton weare a shoe, or boot,..240. H.704, 1
Look how next the holy fier....................242. H.714, 9
But hark how I can now expresse.............243. H.716, 27
To tell how night drawes hence, I've none,......246. H.724, 2
I have, to sing how day drawes on.............246. H.724, 4
Sibb when she saw her face how hard it was,....249. H.732, 1
By how much, neere to singlenesse..............254. H.754, 2
And thou shalt heare how we..................259. H.772, 27
And teach me how to sing.....................261. H.778, 7
Then, then (me thinks) how sweetly flowes......261. H.779, 2
O how that glittering taketh me!..............261. H.779, 6
How cold it was, and how it child my blood;..262 H.783, 13
Thou writes in Prose, how sweet all Virgins be;.266. H.802, 1
Consider sorrowes, how they are aright:........268. H.810, 1
But yet how more admir'dly bright............270. H.819, 6
How thou canst sit and smile,.................272. H.828, 10
Instruct me how to doe.........................281. H.874, 8
How well his nature's fitted to his name!........287. H.903, 4
Say how, or when.............................289. H.911, 2
How fierce was I, when I did see..............294. H.939, 1
(In faith I know not how)...................295. H.942, 10
Tel'st when a Verse springs high, how understood
297. H.947, 7

In teeming years, how soon my Sun was set,....304. H.978, 3
For look how many leaves there be.............304. H.980, 7
We read how Faunus, he the shepheards God,....306. H.986, 1
Men must have Bounds how farre to walke; for we
307. H.990, 1
How well contented in this private Grange.....310. H.1003, 1
You aske me what I doe, and how I live?......312. H.1013, 1
How will it drop pure hony, speaking these?...328. H.1089, 4
Alas I can't, for tell me how.................329. H.1093, 1
Look how our foule Dayes do exceed our faire;....339. N.1, 1
All times, how they..........................354. N.58, 6
How am I bound to Two! God, who doth give....355. N.62, 1
How heart and hand do all agree,.............365. N.97, 9
How I sho'd pay, 's impossible:................369. N.107, 4
How wise wast thou in all thy waies!..........375. N.123, 61
How worthy of respect and praise!..............375. N.123, 62
How Matron-like didst thou go drest!.........375. N.123, 63
How soberly above the rest....................375. N.123, 64
How sweetly shewes thy smiling face,..........375. N.123, 73
Observe we may, how Mary Joses then,........384. N.180, 7
But look, how each transgressor onward went..391. N.227, 3
Nor wo'd I care how short it were, if good:....392. N.230, 10
O then, how restlesse do's she stray!..........393. N.233, 2
How do's she erre in endlesse night!............393. N.233, 4
But look how night succeeds the day, so He....394. N.236, 3
Good and great God! How sho'd I feare........395. N.245, 1
How He deferres, how loath He is to die!......398. N.263, 8
How sweet this place is! as from hence........402. N.269, 14
How roses lillies and carnations grow,..........404. A.1, 16
How stay thay would, yet forc't thay are to goe...410. A.3, 12
A scripture how yow liue and dye...............417. A.9, 12
— — — — — — — — — —, ...421. var. H.106, 7
See how he waves his hand, and through his eyes
430. ins. H.283, 40a
How long, soft bride, shall your deare C: make
431. ins. H.283, 60a
how long, oh pardon, shall the house....431. ins. H.283, 60c
how long shall the page, to please........431. ins. H.283, 60g
— — — — — — — — — — —, ...431. var. H.283, 64
— — — — — — — — — — — —, ...432. var. H.283, 107
Howe'er How ere it fortuned; know for Truth, I meant
304. H.977, 3
Her heart's at home, howere she goes:....430. ins. H.283, 20j
Howers See Hours
However Howeuer after tymes will praise,........407. A.2, 15
— — — — — — — — — —, ...431. var. H.283, 60
Howl May no Wolfe howle, or Screech-Owle stir..361. N.83, 67
Howsoe'er And howsoe're we have the conquest mist;
356. N.67, 3
Howsoever ly go, yet, howsoever, go............113. H.283, 60
Howsoever, cares adue;......................191. H.519, 5
Hoyse See Hoise
Huckson Or his Huckson, to my Scrip..........223. H.638, 11
Hue His nose and lips of mulbrie hiew...........38. H.108, 8
Turn'd to flowers: Stil the hieu,................64. H.167, 3
Then when the paler hieu......................75. H.193, 35
Place then this mirror whose briske hue..........418. A.9, 51
To those virgins, whose briske heu...........450. ins. A.9, 52
Hug To hug thy whitest neck: Then I,..........70. H.181, 3
Have I been cold to hug thee, to remisse,......78. H.197, 34
The Armes to hugge it? throw, throw..........115. H.283, 117
Who hug our Poems (Honourd Sir) and then....141. H.359, 5
Ile hug, Ile kisse, Ile play,...................160. H.422, 9
Huge Through that huge field of waters ride:......30. H.90, 3
Hugged But one by you be hug'd and cherished..322. H.1062, 3
Shall see the hug'd impietie:..................357. N.72, 8
Hugging And, hugging close, we will not feare...190. H.515, 13
Hum If so, we live; if not, with mournfull humme,
100. H.248, 5
Human And Leaves did heale, all sick of humane seed:
61. H.161, 2
Where humane foot, as yet, n'er trod:..........111. H.278, 6
Nor Beasts (fond thing) but only humane soules.
248. H.730, 10
Thou, thou art here, to humane sight...........270. H.819, 4
Who begs to die for feare of humane need,......277. H.855, 1
His humane Nature did, in part, appeare:......389. N.214, 2
His humane Nature, and His Part Divine.......389. N.214, 6
No, but He drest Him with our humane Trim,..390. N.222, 3
As when, in humane nature He works more......395. N.244, 3
For Humane Joy, Contingent Misery............416. A.8, 18
Humanity Some Race of old humanitie..........218. H.626, 9
True heate, whearwth humanitie doth liue........410. A.3, 30
Humble Yet can thy humble roofe maintaine a Quire
37. H.106, 121
When as the humble Cottages not feare........181. H.483, 15
A little house, whose humble Roof..............349. N.47, 3
Humble we must be, if to Heaven we go:........362. N.89, 1
Its humble selfe twixt twoe aspiring cloudes,.....406. A.1, 84
Humbleness Which with ambitious humblenes stands vnder
405. A.1, 45
Humbly I most humbly thee desire..............21. H.59, 3
And, humbly, chives of Saffron brings,..........93. H.223, 133
Next to the Altar humbly kneele, and thence,...128. H.320, 5
Never beg, or humbly wooe....................182. H.490, 11
Humbly unto Thy Mercy-seat:..................349. N.46, 2
Humility Grace is increased by humility.........362. N.89, 4

Illustrous — — — — — — — — —, ...425. var. H.197, 13
I'm (Partial List)
When that day comes, whose evening sayes I'm gone 14. H.35, 1
I'm free from thee; and thou no more shalt heare 17. H.42, 1
No Spices wanting, when I'm laid by thee.......20. H.55, 10
That when I'm poore,........................43. H.123, 33
I'm sure she'll ask no more..................43. H.123, 36
I'm up, I'm up, and blesse that hand,.........72. H.185, 22
I'm sure they'l fashion Roses..................74. H.192, 8
I'm sure to find ye there......................83. H.207, 8
And when I'm laid out for a Corse; then be..111. H.279, 3
And since I'm free,..........................137. H.340, 9
This, this I know, I'm oft struck mute;.......142. H.362, 5
Because I'me odious in thy sight,.............344. N.29, 9
Image Apollos Image side with Thee to blesse...254. H.756, 11
The blessed Image of a blushing rose............405. A.1, 36
Images Set up Thine own eternall Images.......185. H.496, 10
Imagine And now, we must imagine first,.......119. H.293, 19
Immediately Immediatly from heaven, but harke the Cocke 443. var. H.575, 61
Immensive Then this immensive cup.............80. H.201, 25
A Publike Light (in this immensive Sphere.)...236. H.685, 2
Immodesty The wearers rich immodestie;.......311. H.1010, 8
Immortal See Pure-immortal
By You become Immortall Substances.........3. Ded.H., 10
And take a life immortall from my Verse........27. H.82, 16
But as thy meate, so thy immortall wine......147. H.377, 71
Few live the life immortall. He ensures.......188. H.506, 15
The Morn's farre spent; and the immortall Sunne 216. H.618, 3
Immortall clothing I put on,.................270. H.819, 1
Immortall selfe, shall boldly trust............278. H.859, 5
Because begot of my Immortall seed..........280. H.869, 6
Blowes make of dearest friends immortall Foes. 287. H.901, 2
But as Heavens publike and immortall Eye....371. N.113, 5
Immortalized Me immortaliz'd, and you;........377. N.128, 22
Immortals To seeke, and find some few Immortals out 267. H.804, 6
Immured Nor so immured wo'd I have..........174. H.465, 11
Impair Doth all at once impaire,...............75. H.193, 23
Imparity Imparitie doth ever discord bring:....268. H.812, 1
Impart The first is Natures end: this doth imparte 421. ins. H.106, 26a
Impearl Who as they lowe empearl with milk..166. H.443, 41
Imperial Downe to a Fillit more Imperiall......256. H.763, 10
Impiety Shall see the hug'd impietie:............357. N.72, 8
Implanted In w[ch] the veynes ymplanted seeme to lye 405. A.1, 47
Implies Ah then consider! What all this implies;.131. H.330, 14
Implies His Power, when He's cal'd the LORD.379. N.141, 2
Implies or Essence, or the He that Is..........385. N.187, 2
Implore Which wrapt thy smooth limbs (when thou didst implore...9. H.14, 11
Imply Mirtle the twigs were, meerly to imply;....16. H.40, 3
Will no other thing imply,....................97. H.232, 16
Return'd a Ring of Jimmals, to imply.........173. H.464, 2
To imply your Love is wise...................221. H.633, 31
For to imply a contradiction..................382. N.166, 2
swell, mixe, and loose your soules; implye 431. ins. H.283, 50d
— — — — — — — — — — —, ...440. var. H.443, 98
Importance In fun'rall pomp, but this importance have; 384. N.181, 2
Importune And did me much importune..........63. H.166, 2
Impossible How I sho'd pay, 's impossible:....369. N.107, 4
Impression This, that, and every base impression..288. H.905, 2
To spoile the first impression..................354. N.59, 18
But only by impression of effect..............385. N.186, 4
Imprinted Imprinted in each Herbe and Flower:.230. H.662, 32
Impure So Thou, my God, may'st on this impure look, 371. N.113, 7
Imputation Of these had imputation...........175. H.465, 60
In (Partial List)
Love, in pity of the deed,......................15. H.36, 12
To make a Tent, and put it in,.................18. H.46, 7
To drink in Notes, and Numbers; such..........22. H.68, 3
More wealth brings in, then all those three.......23. H.70, 8
How Love came in, I do not know,............24. H.73, 1
Whether in part 'tis here or there,............24. H.73, 5
Nor has the darknesse power to usher in......35. H.106, 39
One slit's enough to let Adultry in............44. H.126, 4
Unbolts the doore, no shame comes in.........48. H.136, 13
To dance and play in: (Trust me) there.......49. H.136, 22
Come in for Dowrie with a Wife...............49. H.137, 2
Whereupon in anger flying.....................50. H.139, 3
These are traps to take fooles in...............52. H.147, 6
Halfe wasted in the porch......................54. H.149, 54
Now o're the threshold force her in...........55. H.149, 82
Nay, profanation to keep in,...................68. H.178, 12
Spring, sooner then the Lark, to fetch in May...68. H.178, 14
Till you come forth. Wash, dresse, be briefe in praying: 68. H.178, 27
But is got up, and gone to bring in May......69. H.178, 44
Come, let us goe, while we are in our prime;..69. H.178, 57
Daies may conclude in nights; and Suns may rest, 72. H.185, 4
When as Cherries come in place?..............74. H.189, 6
False in legs, and false in thighes;..............77. H.195, 9
Onely true in shreds and stuffe.................77. H.195, 12
Time-past so fragrant, sickly now drawn in...77. H.197, 28
Three dayes before the shutting in of May,....86. H.213, 13
Blest in my love;............................87. H.214, 10
And rich for in and outward show:............90. H.223a, 2
But when your Playing, and your Voice came in, 95. H.228, 3
To keep out the Letcher, and keep in the whore: 97. H.233, 2
The Whore to come out, or the Letcher come in. 97. H.233, 4
(Clad, all, in Linnen, white as Lillies.)........101. H.250, 12
How false, how hollow she's in heart;.........103. H.253, 15
Speak griefe in you,..........................104. H.257, 2
Tell me, said I, in deep distresse,.............106. H.263, 3
And in the turning of an eye;.................107. H.263, 20
And seen them in a Round:....................110. H.274, 10
Display the Bridegroom in the porch,..........113. H.283, 34
And roule about, and in their motions burne..113. H.283, 38
In Lov's name do so; and a price.............113. H.283, 53
Discord in, and so divide......................114. H.283, 87
Put in practise, to understand................115. H.283, 124
Put in Love, and put in too...................116. H.285, 3
Put in Feare, and hope, and doubt;...........116. H.285, 5
What comes in, runnes quickly out:...........116. H.285, 6
Put in secrecies withall, ...116. H.285, 7
No fault in women to refuse..................118. H.291, 1
How tedious they are in their dresse...........118. H.291, 4
His choyce bitts with; then in a trice..........119. H.293, 11
Ore-come in musicke; with a wine,............120. H.293, 47
Or else force a passage in:....................121. H.297, 12
Them all concenter'd in one man, but Thee.....121. H.301, 4
Maides (in time) may ravish him..............125. H.314, 8
We send in stead of New-yeares gift..........127. H.319, 26
Remember us in Cups full crown'd,............127. H.319, 29
But to shew thee how in part,.................128. H.322, 4
That keepes his own strong guard, in the despight 128. H.323, 9
But in regard, 'twas often said, this old.......129. H.326, 3
Luckie in this Maide I love:...................136. H.337, 4
Of deep and arrant ignorance came in;.......150. H.382, 14
Love in pitie of their teares,..................152. H.391, 5
He loves the gain that vanity brings in.........163. H.439, 4
Then we shall see, how in a little space,........168. H.445, 5
Saints will come in to fill each Pew and Place..168. H.445, 6
And wildly force a passage in,.................175. H.465, 55
And Basket, by our entring in.................178. H.476, 3
But more's sent in, then was serv'd out.......178. H.476, 9
It is in vain to sing, or stay..................179. H.476, 34
'Tis Heresie in others: In your face.........180. H.481, 1
I beginne to waine in sight;...................180. H.482, 1
In regard I want that Wine,..................182. H.489, 7
In this regard, that thou do'st play............183. H.492, 9
Then see it in report..........................183. H.492, 20
Taken in by none but Thee...................186. H.499, 4
She brake in two the purer Glasse,...........187. H.504, 4
Late you come in; but you a Saint shall be,....188. H.510, 3
In Chiefe, in this Poetick Liturgie............188. H.510, 4
Any one part that's dissonant in you:.........189. H.511, 2
Far lesse in number, then our foule dayes are..189. H.513, 2
Did soon draw in agen.......................194. H.525, 5
From whom we'l reckon. Wit came in, but since 194. H.526, 5
Come thou in, with thy best part,.............195. H.530, 2
Out of the world he must, who once comes in:.199. H.548, 1
Water in, ere Sun be set......................201. H.556, 4
Walking in and out her eye,...................204. H.566, 4
Let wealth come in by comely thrift,..........221. H.633, 46
Now swaggers in her Leavy gallantry..........224. H.642, 6
Now out, and then in,..........................225. H.643, 5
Cleane in manners, cleere in voice:...........232. H.665, 2
Be she shewing in her dresse,..................232. H.665, 5
Be she rowling in her eye,.....................232. H.665, 9
Patient in my necessitie.......................235. H.677, 4
Draw in your feeble fiers, while that He........236. H.685, 5
Rein'd in with Purple, Pearl, and gold,.......239. H.696, 6
Trigg having turn'd his sute, he struts in state,..240. H.703, 1
Cleave thou my heart in two...................240. H.705, 12
For to let Affection in........................253. H.750, 9
Other mens sins wee ever beare in mind;.......253. H.751, 1
Sung in the high Doxologie of Thee...........254. H.756, 16
Base in action as in clothes:..................255. H.761, 12
While misery keeps in with patience..........257. H.765, 4
In love with none, but me....................258. H.767, 20
Thou writes in Prose, how sweet all Virgins be;.266. H.802, 1
If not to th' whole, yet satisfy'd in part.........267. H.804, 12
While w'are in our Prime;....................267. H.806, 2
Man may want Land to live in; but for all,....267. H.807, 1
In th' intrim she desires......................269. H.814, 5
The Blessing fall in mellow times on Thee......269. H.818, 10
Sometimes (in mirth) he sayes each whelk's a sparke 273. H.834, 3
O beware! in time submit;...................273. H.836, 5

The Porter then will let me **in**.................277. H.854, 6
The old Hag **in**. No surer thing...............284. H.890, 6
When Yew is out, then Birch comes **in**,........285. H.892, 13
Come **in** for comely ornaments,................285. H.892, 19
Bring **in** pailes of water then,.................315. H.1026, 9
Of life comes **in**, when he's Regenerate........326. H.1080, 28
When Chub brings **in** his harvest, still he cries, 327. H.1086, 1
And though it takes all **in**, 'tis yet no more.....341. N.15, 5
The coming **in** of sorrow......................353. N.56, 12
Leave that without, then enter **in**;.............366. N.98, 6
In, or without; all, all belongs to Thee:......368. N.103, 4
Brings **in** Fabricius for a Combatant:..........370. N.108, 10
And might come **in**,..........................370. N.111, 3
Come **in**, or force the gate....................370. N.111, 8
As Sun-beames pierce the glasse, and streaming **in**, 385. N.184, 1
The sheet I sleep **in**, as my Winding-sheet....392. N.230, 18
Thy Doore, as I do enter **in**:.................402. N.269, 5
And to thy many, take **in** one soul more.........416. A.8, 2
And take me **in**, who am in deep Distress;......416. A.8, 5
But now come **in**. Euc. More let me yet relate...416. A.8, 23
Or **in** respect of Merchandize,....................417. A.9, 4
Take it then and **in** a viewe......................417. A.9, 7
Inadulterate Her **inadult'rate** strength: what's done by me 46. H.128, 53
Induc't that **inadultrate** same...................245. H.720, 9
Inapostate As **Inapostate**, to the thing he heares, 330. H.1100, 16
Inarculum The Chaplet, and ***Inarculum** here be..196. H.539, 3
Incanonical Their large Narrations, **Incanonicall**) 330. H.1100, 4
Incantation The holy **incantation** of a verse;.........7. H.8, 2
To heare the **incantation** of his tongue:........206. H.575, 30
Incapable See **Uncapable**
Incarnation When once he gives it **incarnation**?..139. H.347, 4
Incarvements Whose **incarvem^ts** doe descrye.....417. A.9, 11
Incense See **Male-incense**
Altar of **Incense**, I smell there................59. H.155, 4
Those learned men brought **Incense**, Myrrhe, and Gold, 86. H.213, 30
To **Incense** burne;.............................87. H.214, 14
And offers **Incense** Nights and dayes,........93. H.223, 130
First offer **Incense**, then thy field and meads..143. H.370, 1
This Mornings **Incense** to prepare, and burne...196. H.539, 2
Or Sup, there wants the **Incense** and the Wine..197. H.541, 4
Burn first thine **incense**; next, when as thou see'st 286. H.898, 5
Then boldly give thine **incense** to the fire.......299. H.957, 4
Which, fir'd with **incense**, I resigne,..........351. N.47, 55
With golden Censers, and with **Incense**, here,..368. N.103, 1
Devote to Thee, both **incense**, myrrhe, and gold, 369. N.105, 6
Inchantments See **Enchantments**
Inchpin And wel-boyld **inkepin** of a batt...434. ins. H.293, 41b
Inchristalled See **Encrystalled**
Incident See **Coincident**
Incivility Deane, or thy warty **incivility**..........29. H.86, 2
Known guilty here of **incivility**:...............290. H.914, 2
A Baud to **incivility**:........................310. H.1004, 10
Incline Be not proud, but now **encline**............96. H.232, 1
For shame or pitty now **encline**...............168. H.446, 5
To'th' Glasse your lips **encline**;...............185. H.495, 6
That doe our soules **encline**...................228. H.657, 2
Then to love I do **encline**;.....................309. H.996, 3
W^th thee; that should hee but **Inclyne**..........408. A.2, 67
Inclosed See **Enclosed**
Inclosures See **Enclosures**
Include To be in that Orbe crown'd (that doth **include** 207. H.575, 59
Income Like to the **Income** must be our expence; 117. H.287, 1
Yarne is an **Income**; and the Huswives thread..221. H.633, 44
Inconfused And Three in **Inconfused** Unity:....386. N.191, 2
Incongruities Full of **incongruities**:................11. H.21, 8
Inconsiderate His **inconsiderate** Frenzie off (at last) 225. H.642, 20
Inconstant Th' **inconstant**, and unpurged Multitude 398. N.263, 6
Inconveniency With men, a loathed **inconveniencie**. 239. H.698, 2
Incorrupted In thee Brave Man! Whose **incorrupted** fame, 131. H.331, 5
Cloth'd all with **incorrupted** light;.............270. H.819, 5
Incorruption To give an **incorruption** unto me...129. H.327, 6
Increase Fit Organs for **encrease**,................57. H.149, 127
Fish-like, **encrease** then to a million:..........124. H.313, 12
Give them the blessing of **encrease**:..........221. H.633, 55
Desire deferr'd is, that it may **encrease**.........264. H.793, 2
So Kings by killing doe **encrease** their foes.....292. H.929, 4
The more our Crownes of Glory there **increase**..372. N.119, 2
— — — — — — — — — — —, ...426. var. H.197, 42
Increased Grace is **increased** by humility.........362. N.89, 4
That, thus **increast**, it might be perfected....378. N.132, 2
Incubi Those thy Lust-burning **Incubi**.........174. H.465, 36
Incurious The **incurious** Villages................255. H.761, 14
Incurled See **Encurled**
Ind Gold, runneth to the Western **Inde**,..........36. H.106, 66
Nor to the Eastern **Ind** dost rove..............229. H.662, 7
Indecency In any one, the least **indecencie**:........10. H.16, 2
Indeed Mirt. 'Tis true **indeed**; and each of us will bring 86. H.213, 33
What now you seem, be not the same **indeed**,..113. H.283, 56
I co'd never love **indeed**;.....................182. H.490, 1
Fie, Lovely maid! **Indeed** you are too slow,...216. H.618, 5
Indefinite A Sea of Substance is, **Indefinite**......381. N.161, 2
Indian An **Indian** Common-wealth...............80. H.201, 20
Indifferent Pillars and men, hate an **indifferent** Poet. 309. H.1000, 2
If otherwise, I stand **indifferent**:..............392. N.230, 4
Lett hym but w^th **indifferent** skill..............409. A.2, 105
Indignation 'Gainst all the **indignation** of the Times. 280. H.869, 2
Indite As the Godhead doth **indite**..............242. H.714, 6
When words we want, Love teacheth to **endite**;.275. H.846, 1
Induced **Induc't** that inadultrate same..........245. H.720, 9
Indulgence To the **indulgence** of the rugged Law: 201. H.557, 2
Indulgences Their Pardons and **Indulgences**:....93. H.223, 114
But on our Age most sweet **Indulgences**.......383. N.175, 2
Industrious Th' **industrious** Merchant has; who for to find 36. H.106, 65
Inexhausted Light from the Sun, that **inexhausted** Fire: 3. Ded.H., 6
Infant A pure seed-Pearle of **Infant** dew,........119. H.293, 21
Of the red **infant**, neatly hung.................166. H.443, 71
— — — — — — — — — —, ...443. var. H.580, 2
Infanta This sweet **Infanta** of the yeere?.......208. H.580, 2
Infant's That doth the **Infants** face enthrall,....167. H.443, 91
Infect And lungs that wo'd **infect** me,..........260. H.777, 11
That do's **infect**, and make the rent..........311. H.1010, 5
Infection Where no disease raignes, or **infection** comes 205. H.575, 5
Me, as a fear'd **infection**:.....................235. H.677, 6
Infernal Thus has **Infernall** Jove decreed;......133. H.336, 28
Like those **infernall** Deities which eate........272. H.826, 1
Infinite Their number (almost) **infinite**,..........91. H.223, 35
Infinity **Infinitie** to dwell.......................354. N.58, 4
Infirmity To heale my Earths **infirmitie**........397. N.257, 4
Inflamed Whose love growes more **enflam'd**, by being Foes. 78. H.197, 44
Influence Have their Existence, and their **Influence** too. 3. Ded.H., 8
Into this house powre downe thy **influence**,.....245. H.723, 2
Diffuse their mighty **influence**..................291. H.919, 8
Words fully flowing, yet of **influence**:..........297. H.947, 2
Thou had'st, and hast thy mighty **influence**,....299. H.956, 3
They noiselesse spill their **Influence**:..........340. N.3, 14
Inform **Inform** me next, what love will do;......325. H.1075, 3
Infortunity Despight of all your **infortunitie**:....299. H.958, 2
Infuse Then to **infuse**.........................135. H.336, 125
Infused (At first) **infused** with the same:........24. H.73, 4
Ingot Bring'st home the **Ingot** from the West...229. H.662, 10
Ingression Never againe to have **ingression** here:.227. H.652, 2
Ingrost See **Engrossed**
Inhabited The House of God, by Christ **inhabited**;.385. N.190, 2
Inherit And, methinks, I not **inherit**,............182. H.489, 3
I do believe, I shall **inherit**..................359. N.78, 11
What here we hope for, we shall once **inherit**:...362. N.88, 1
Inheritance That gave thee this so high **inheritance**. 152. H.392, 6
The greatest mans **Inheritance**................197. H.542, 2
Theis hurte not thyne **Inheritance**,............407. A.2, 12
Iniquity A short and sweet **iniquity**?.............357. N.72, 4
Iniured — — — — — — — — —, ...441. var. H.465, 11
Injewel'd See **Enjewelled**
Injured Most innocent, and **injur'd** thus..........48. H.136, 5
Or see thy **injur'd** Leaves serve well,..........275. H.844, 5
Injury An **injurie**, before a benefite:.............292. H.923, 2
Ink To lay thy pen and **ink** aside?..............357. N.72, 12
Inkepin See **Inchpin**
Inkyndled See **Enkindled**
Inlaid **In-laid** Garbage ev'ry where..............76. H.195, 6
That's not **inlaid** with Thee, (my Lord).........339. N.2, 4
Inly Or smile more **inly**; lest thy looks beguile.46. H.128, 46
— — — — — — — — — — —, ...424. ins. H.128, 46e
Innocence First wash thy heart in **innocence**, then bring 127. H.320, 3
With some small stock of **innocence**:..........277. H.854, 2
Wash our hands in **innocence**..................303. H.974, 6
With feet of **innocence**:.......................352. N.53, 14
Innocent To grow the sooner **innocent**:.........35. H.106, 6
Most **innocent**, and injur'd thus.................48. H.136, 5
Is halfe, or altogether **innocent**................268. H.809, 2
As when ye **innocent** met here...............317. H.1035, 30
Will add a power, to keep me **innocent**;........397. N.255, 2
Inoffensive With **inoffensive** mirth here:.........234. H.674, 8
Inquires But none **enquires** if good he be, or no..130. H.328, 2
Inrag'd See **Enraged**
In's Sin, **in's** Nap'rie, not to express his wit:...114. H.283, 68
And fretfull, carries Hay **in's** horne............165. H.443, 14
If he ha's none **in's** pockets, trust me, Huncks.173. H.463, 3
I see't **in's** puris naturalibus:.................187. H.502, 2
When 'twas **in's** Feet, his Charity was small;....207. H.577, 3

Now tis in's Hand, he gives no Almes at all...207. H.577, 4
In's Tusc'lanes, Tullie doth confesse,...........332. H.1115, 1
A Princely Babe in's Mothers Brest............367. N.102, 14
Nourish in's breast, a Tree of Life.............409. A.2, 108
Inscribe Nor is my Number full, till I inscribe..199. H.545, 1
Inscription Arch-like, hold up, Thy Name's Inscription.
168. H.444, 4
Insensible Insensible of all my smart;...........47. H.132, 10
Inside Sooner the in-side of thy hand shall grow.202. H.557, 23
To be accounted inside cleane:...............250. H.738, 2
Insinuating Then that insinuating fire,........135. H.336, 103
Insnare See Ensnare
Inspin See Inchpin
Inspire See Re-inspire
Sing I co'd once; and bravely too enspire......84. H.210, 3
Come then, and now enspire..................228. H.657, 5
Who still inspire me.........................261. H.778, 6
With Kisses to inspire..................431. ins. H.283, 40f
Inspired Shew'd like to Creame, enspir'd with Strawberries:
81. H.202, 2
It was full enspir'd by you...................217. H.620, 12
Enspir'd with Purple, Pearle, and Gold;.......311. H.1010, 2
Enspir'd by th' Sun-beams after dews & showers.
326. H.1080, 14
Inspires And Rage inspires....................198. H.544, 6
Instant As Daughters to the instant yeare:.....127. H.319, 40
The Month, the Week, the instant Day........198. H.544, 22
But let that instant when thou dy'st be known,..281. H.875, 3
— — — — — — — — — —, ...433. var. H.293, 21
Instead See Stead
Instead of Orient Pearls of Jet,..................14. H.34, 1
Girt with small bones, instead of walls.........90. H.223, 10
Instead of common showers,....................103. H.255, 6
Instead of almes, sets dogs upon the poor.....238. H.694, 2
Instead of Harts-horne (if he speakes the troth)
299. H.959, 3
Instead of Bread, Grubs gives them stones to eat.
325. H.1077, 4
Instead of neat Inclosures......................345. N.33, 9
Instead of fragrant Posies....................345. N.33, 11
Instead of that, a sweet and gentle word:......356. N.71, 2
Insteade of gould Pearle Rubies Bonds..........407. A.2, 7
It, and not Instead of Saint....................409. A.2, 79
Instep I did; and kist the Instep too:............14. H.33, 2
Instruct And can'st instruct, that those who have the itch
35. H.106, 19
Come, Ile instruct thee. Know, the vestall fier.262. H.781, 15
Instruct me how to doe......................281. H.874, 8
Instruct me now, what love will do;..........325. H.1075, 1
But to instruct them, to avoid all snares........378. N.137, 5
Instructions Vertuous instructions ne'r are delicate.
270. H.820, 2
Instruments Two instruments belong unto our God;
394. N.241, 1
Instylde See Enstyled
Insures Few live the life immortall. He ensures.188. H.506, 15
In't Draw in't a wounded Heart:................10. H.20, 2
There is no one pleasure in't..................122. H.304, 4
That h'ad nor Gold or Silver to put in't?.....162. H.427, 4
My Book, 'tis this; that Thou, my God, art in't..355. N.61, 2
Intelligence Like an Intelligence................193. H.524, 6
Intend If to love I should entend,...............117. H.286, 5
Of all that Nature doth entend................163. H.432, 2
Thou art of what I did intend.................189. H.515, 5
But what he doth at first entend,..............215. H.615, 5
Intended But no disdaine intended..............100. H.246, 7
With wealth, but for those ends she was entended:
201. H.557, 8
Intends But tis the god of Nature, who Intends..411. A.3, 57
Intent And it to know, and practice; with intent..35. H.106, 5
None goes to warfare, but with this intent;....42. H.120, 1
This was the Founders grave and good intent,..201. H.557, 13
Man must do well out of a good intent,........290. H.917, 1
Dread not the shackles: on with thine intent;.317. H.1034, 1
God strikes His Church, but 'tis to this intent,..344. N.31, 1
Tell me rich man, for what intent..............394. N.239, 1
Intentions But still thy wife, by chast intentions led,
35. H.106, 41
Intents Though good things answer many good intents;
110. H.275, 1
Inter And while the Wood-nimphs my cold corps inter,
19. H.50, 3
Nor that fine Worme that do's interre.........186. H.497, 13
These my Reliques, (pray) interre.............270. H.821, 2
Hanch, since he (lately) did interre his wife,....275. H.842, 1
Interim In th' intrim she desires...............269. H.814, 5
Interlaid Are here most neatly inter-laid.........166. H.443, 50
Intermitting But that it had some intermitting houres.
52. H.146, 2
Intermix And with thy Eclogues intermixe..........5. H.2, 9
Interplaced Enterplac't with ribbanings.........306. H.984, 26
Intertalk — — — — — — —, ...429, var. H.263, 2
Intertalked Love and my sighs thus intertalkt:..106. H.263, 2
Interwove Made up of white-thorn neatly enterwove;
68. H.178, 35
Till you (sweet Mistresse) came and enterwove.94. H.224, 7
Goe happy Rose, and enterwove................98. H.238, 1
Interwoven Of inter-woven Osiers;..............345. N.33, 10
Intext Co'd reade the Intext but my selfe alone..227. H.652, 6
Intitled See Entitled
Into (Partial List)
Die, and be turn'd into a Lute..................23. H.68, 8
Into an Ovall, square, or round;.............202. H.560, 10
Into the daily offering.........................291. H.919, 2
By throwing teeth into the ground:...........297. H.948, 6
And fowle thy Altar, Charme some Into froggs,.412. A.3, 91
Of fierce Idolatrie shute into mee, and....424. ins. H.128, 46b
Intreat See Entreat
Intrude Wo'd soon recoile, and not intrude......147. H.377, 32
Inundation Th' inundation to endure.............302. H.968, 6
Inure To be what I report thee; and inure.....37. H.106, 103
Invade T'invade from far: They'l finde worse foes at home.
316. H.1030, 2
Invented I ne'r invented such....................19. H.51, 6
With what I have invented...................260. H.777, 8
Invite Last night thou didst invite me home to eate;
161. H.424, 1
Prithee, when next thou do'st invite, barre State,
161. H.424, 3
To sup with thee thou didst me home invite;....262. H.783, 1
Thanksgiving for a former, doth invite...........348. N.42, 1
Invited (Invited to the Thesbian banquet) ta'ne..78. H.197, 66
To a Love-Feast we both invited are:............355. N.65, 1
Invites Invites fresh Grapes to fill his Presse with Wine.
72. H.185, 28
Invites to supper him who dines,..............146. H.377, 8
Now loue invites me to survey her thighes........406. A.1, 77
Invoke And (while we the gods invoke)........280, H.870, 17
The room is cens'd: help, help, t'invoke.........366. N.98, 15
Which thus enkindled we invoke.................413. A.4, 29
Inward With inward Buckram, little else.)......118. H.291, 12
The inward carbage for his cloathes as yet......302. H.969, 4
Iphis By deare S. Iphis; and the rest,..........169. H.449, 24
Iphyclus Like Iphyclus, upon the tops of Corn...78. H.197, 50
Iphycus — — — — — — — — —, ...427. var. H.197, 50
Ipitus — — — — — — —, ...427. var. H.197, 50
Ire If her patience turns to ire,..................273. H.836, 7
You with his just and holy Ire..........431. ins. H.283, 40g
Irene Angry if Irene be.........................204. H.566, 1
Irksome All thoughts of irksome Love:..........171. H.452, 8
Into a long and irksome banishment;...........242. H.713, 14
Iron A Burling iron for his face:.................39. H.108, 10
And well-laid bottome, on the iron and rock,..148. H.377, 109
And turn the iron Age to Gold.................233. H.670, 29
So let us Yron, Silver, Gold,..................297. H.948, 9
Nor dull'd wth Iron sleeps; but haue out-worne..410. A.3, 19
Is (Partial List) See Is't
There is an Act that will more fully please:......24. H.74, 10
Saint Tit, Saint Nit, Saint Is, Saint Itis,........91. H.223, 28
Hence then it is, that my poore brest............96. H.229, 5
Then is the Lamp and oyle extinguished..........359. N.80, 2
And Olive Branch is wither'd now..............375. N.123, 52
The Spice and Spiknard hence is gone,.........375. N.123, 55
Isis As Goddesse Isis (when she went,..............9. H.15, 9
Goddesse Isis cann't transfer....................59. H.155, 7
Under the heavenly *Isis, that can bring........78. H.197, 54
Island In that whiter Island, where..............377. N.128, 9
Isle See Cherry-isle
In this world (the Isle of Dreames)...........376. N.128, 1
— — — — — — — — — — —, ...425. var. H.197, 20
Isles Meet after long divorcement by the Iles:....77. H.197, 2
When thou thy selfe dar'st say, thy Iles shall lack
78. H.197, 47
As the Canary Isles were thine:.................148. H.377, 84
Israelites God did forbid the Israelites, to bring..384. N.179, 1
Issue Lest Issue lye asleep......................53. H.149, 18
My num'rous issue: Praise, and pitty me..........58. H.151, 2
With all her Owle-ey'd issue begs a boon......116. H.283, 152
Dundrige his Issue hath; but is not styl'd......195. H.533, 1
For all his Issue, Father of one Child...........195. H.533, 2
Where ev'ry tree & wealthy issue beares........205. H.575, 9
Is't Amint. O rare! But is't a trespasse if we three
86. H.213, 25
For what other reason is't,.....................128. H.322, 3
Nor is't a life, seven yeares to tell,............233. H.670, 34
Say, is't for reall griefe he mourns? not so;......275. H.842, 3
Say, what is't that thou do'st aile?............305. H.984, 9
What is't that wasts a Prince? example showes,.331. H.1105, 1
Wheat, Barley, Rie, or Oats; what is't..........376. H.127, 3
It (Partial List)
It chanc't a Bee did flie that way,................71. H.182, 2
Love he that will; it best likes me,..............155. H.408, 1
For her beauty it was such......................274. H.838, 3
Itch And can'st instruct, that those who have the itch
35. H.106, 19
Are wanton with their itch; scratch, and 'twill please.
66. H.173, 8
Are the expressions of that itch,..............174. H.465, 24
Or had I not, I'de stopp the spreading itch......411. A.3, 55
Itchless But thou art just and itchlesse, and dost please
252. H.745, 1
I'th' (Partial List) See I'
When Laurell spirts 'ith fire, and when the Hearth..7. H.8, 5

More then the stones i'th' street by farre:..........32. H.98, 4
Because he cannot sleep i'th' Church, free-cost.....39. H.109, 4
Good Sir, make no more cuts i'th' outward skin,..44. H.126, 3
Is to love, and live i'th fire..................117. H.286, 12
I'th' Seas, she saves her passengers...............134. H.336, 64
Us both i'th' Sea, Camp, Wildernesse)........134. H.336, 66
Y'ave dipt too long i'th' Vinegar;..............146. H.377, 22
And knowes not where i'th world to borrow more.
160. H.423, 4
Us i'th' Citie, and the Field:..................177. H.473, 2
Feacie (some say) doth wash her clothes i'th' Lie.178. H.474, 1
I'th grave,..................................178. H.475, 10
Neither broke i'th whole, or part.............183. H.490, 20
Her self i'th' silken Sepulchre.................186. H.497, 14
We know y'are learn'd i'th' Muses, and no lesse.187. H.506, 7
Alike i'th' dust..............................190. H.515, 32
For, once dead, and laid i'th grave,.............238. H.691, 5
(When drunke with Beere) to light him home, i'th' dark.
273. H.834, 4
I'th' Church-yard, made, one Tenement for me...277. H.853, 4
Jone as my Lady is as good i'th' dark............279. H.864, 2
— — — — — — — — — — —, ...450. var. A.9, 50
Ithaca The smoakie chimneys of his Ithaca.......77. H.197, 18
(As that chaste Queen of Ithaca.............174. H.465, 30
I'th'bed See Bed
I'th'bud See Bud
I'th'cheeks See Cheeks
I'th'embers See Embers
I'th'funeral. See Funeral
I'th'hole See Fox i'th' hole
I'th'shell See Shell
I'th'world See World
Itis Saint Tit, Saint Nit, Saint Is, Saint Itis.....91. H.223, 28
Its Its humble self twixt twoe aspiring cloudes,....406. A.1, 84
Beyond its stinted Circle; giueing foode..........410. A.3, 31
Itself See Self
Iülus Iülus to sing such a song................135. H.336, 94
And twisting my Iülus hairs;................135. H.336, 118
I've (Partial List)
Then say, I've sent one more..................43. H.123, 13
Gold I've none, for use or show,...............88. H.218, 1
If so it be I've gain'd the shore..............94. H.225, 3
Because I've liv'd so long a maid:..............97. H.235, 2
I've paid Thee, what I promis'd; that's not All;..168. H.444, 1
Of all I've writ:................................189. H.515, 2
As I've doted heretofore:......................209. H.585, 8
A long-lifes-day I've taken paines..............212. H.602, 1
Or fold mine armes, and sigh, because I've lost.222. H.634, 12
Keep here still, Closet-Gods, 'fore whom I've set
227. H.652, 13
To tell how night drawes hence, I've none,.....246. H.724, 2
Till thou shalt say, I've paid thee with a song...248. H.730, 22
Tygers and Beares (I've heard some say).......252. H.746, 3
For since I've travail'd all this Realm throughout.267. H.804, 5
Treble the number of these good I've writ.......339. N.1, 4
I've more to beare my Chardge, then way to goe,..411. A.3, 54
Ivory My Jet t'enthrall such Ivorie...............14. H.34, 6
Or Pelops Arme of Yvorie..................34. H.105, 6
Clos'd in a Box of Yvorie:...................185. H.497, 2
His buriall in an yvory grave:.................185. H.497, 4
The yvorie tooke State to hold................185. H.497, 5
Dead, and closed up in Yvorie.................186. H.497, 18
With Yvorie wrists, his Laureat head, and steeps.206. H.575, 41
Of Ivorie,....................................345. N.33, 23
Like loving vines hid vnder Ivorye,.............405. A.1, 48
To see two tablets of pure Ivory...............406. A.1, 96
Ivy The Laurell, Mirtle, Oke, and Ivie too.......41. H.117, 10
Verse crown'd with Yvie, and with Holly:........126. H.319, 10
And flatt'ring Ivie) Two recite their Plaies,....206. H.575, 50
Down with the Holly, Ivie all,.................304. H.980, 3
This Hollie, and this Ivie Wreath,.............365. N.96, 30
Ixion's Till, like Ixion's Cloud you be............34. H.105, 9
Jack Since Jack and Jill both wicked be;..........163. H.434, 1
When Jill complaines to Jack for want of meate;.186. H.498, 1
Jack kisses Jill, and bids her freely eate:........186. H.498, 2
Jill sayes, of what? sayes Jack, on that sweet kisse,
186. H.498, 3
Jacob Jacob Gods Beggar was; and so we wait....383. N.171, 1
Jail Dark was the Jayle; but as if light..........64. H.169, 5
Jailer But no one Jailor there to wash the wounds.
372. N.120, 2
Jail-free His hungry belly borne by Legs Jaile-free.
332. H.1112, 4
Jane Jane is a Girle that's prittie;..............229. H.659, 6
Jane is a wench that's wittie;..................229. H.659, 7
Janus This Janus looking double waye............417. A.9, 16
Jar As my small Jarre best fits my little Oyle.....249. H.733, 6
Oyle from Thy Jarre, into my creuze;............357. N.75, 2
— — — — — — — — —, ...443. var. H.575, 46
Jars (Dropt for the jarres of heaven) fill'd t'engage
206. H.575, 46
Javelin And I the Javelin suck't away,..........272. H.828, 3
And with his Javelin wounded me:............283. H.883, 10
Jaws His jawes had tir'd on some large Chine of Beefe.
273. H.835, 2
Jealous I am not jealous of thy Faith,..........175. H.465, 43
Jealous Girles these sometimes were,...........187. H.503, 1
I have, which, with a jealous eare,............246. H.724, 14
Call'd on the suddayne by the Jealouse Mother,....410. A.3, 7
shootes forth his jealous soule, for to surprize
430. ins. H.283, 40b
Jealousies Here, with all her jealousies:..........52. H.145, 2
In dealing forth these bashfull jealousies:......113. H.283, 52
Jealousy Or eare of burning jealousie...........49. H.136, 19
Jealousie, and both will through:..............116. H.285, 4
O Jealousie, that art..........................170. H.452, 1
(O! Soul-tormenting Jealousie,) from Thee.....171. H.452, 12
Yellow, markt for Jealousie....................187. H.503, 4
(For gentle feare, or jelousie)................265. H.798, 10
The Plague of wilder Jelousie...................408. A.2, 42
Jehovah Jehovah, as Boëtius saith,..............382. N.168, 1
God is Jehovah cal'd; which name of His........385. N.187, 1
Jelly See Lusty-jelly
This little Pipkin fits this little Jellie...........249. H.733, 18
Fetcht binding gellye of a starre.........434. ins. H.293, 41h
Jeminia's — — — — — — — —, ...450. var. A.9, 34
Jemmonia's Here Jemmonia's titles were...........418. A.9, 34
Jephthah Too soon, too deere did Jephthah buy,..360. N.83, 19
Jericho Like t' a Rose of Jericho:..............108. H.266, 2
Jerusalem Make knowne to us the now Jerusalem.
330. H.1100, 12
Jessamine Or Essences of Jessimine:............145. H.375, 6
Then Jessimine, with Florabell;..............184. H.492, 29
Of Maydens-blush, commixt with Jessimine.....262. H.783, 10
Jest Many a jest told of the Keyes betraying......69. H.178, 55
He tooke her; now the jest in this appeares,...129. H.326, 5
No scurrile jest; no open Sceane is laid........148. H.377, 77
It is his own breech there that breaks the jest...265. H.795, 2
Jesu I sing Thy Birth, Oh JESU!................345. N.33, 2
To wast, my JESU, I'le take all................377. N.129, 8
Jesus Lastly, that JESUS is a Deed............359. N.78, 15
Moses, and Jesus, called Joshua:...............381. N.157, 2
Doth Jesus beare,............................401. N.268, 2
Jet See Half-jet-rings
And her grinders black as jet;...................11. H.21, 12
Instead of Orient Pearls of Jet,..................14. H.34, 1
My Jet t'enthrall such Ivorie.....................14. H.34, 6
First, in a Neech, more black than jet,..........90. H.223, 11
The pillars up of weeping Jet,..................145. H.376, 2
The Pillars up of lasting Jet,................149. H.377, 124
Or in the dampe Jet read their Teares........149. H.377, 126
A Heifer smooth, and black as jet,.............243. H.716, 8
Cleane was the herth, the mantle larded jet;....262. H.783, 11
Where now I rest, these may be known by Jet...304. H.978, 4
Out-during Marble, Brasse, or Jet.............335. H.1129, 2
And jet it with their choice purfumes..........375. N.123, 66
Jets A Fast, while Jets and Marbles weep,......257. H.764, 8
Jewel What is a Jewell if it be not set...........172. H.459, 5
A kisse to such a Jewell of the heauen:..........410. A.3, 4
Tis not Jewell of great prize...................417. A.9, 3
Jewels By your owne jewels set on fire...........20. H.54, 6
For Jewels for your Gowne, or Haire:..........68. H.178, 18
With all thy richest jewels over-cast:............76. H.194, 2
Expose your jewels then unto the view,.........173. H.459, 11
With sundry precious Jewells,.................345. N.33, 18
Why wore th' Egyptians Jewells in the Eare?....346. N.36, 1
On either side with rich rare Jewells grac'd,......405. A.1, 40
Now for some Jewells to supplye................409. A.2, 89
Jews The Jewes they did disdaine Thee..........345. N.33, 25
The Jewes, when they built Houses (I have read).384. N.178, 1
The Jewes their beds, and offices of ease,.......386. N.193, 1
Jews' Daffe nuts, soft Jewes eares, and some thin
439. ins. H.443, 45t
Jill Since Jack and Jill both wicked be;..........163. H.434, 1
When Jill complaines to Jack for want of meate;
186. H.498, 1
Jack kisses Jill, and bids her freely eate:........186. H.498, 2
Jill sayes, of what? sayes Jack, on that sweet kisse,
186. H.498, 3
The food of Poets; so I thought sayes Jill,......186. H.498, 5
Let me feed full, till that I fart, sayes Jill.......186. H.498, 8
Jillie Jolly and Jillie, bite and scratch all day,....156. H.411, 1
Jimmals See Gimmals
Jingles Spur jingles now, and sweares by no meane oathes,
330. H.1099, 1
Jingling By the soone gingling of some sleepy keyes,
410. A.3, 10
Joan Jone wo'd go tel her haires; and well she might,
195. H.531, 1
Jone, and my Lady have at that time one,.......209. H.586, 5
Jone is a wench that's painted:.................229. H.659, 1
Jone is a Girle that's tainted;.................229. H.659, 2
Yet Jone she goes............................229. H.659, 3
Jone as my Lady is as good i'th' dark..........279. H.864, 2
Jocasta Or like Jocasta in a swoone..............47. H.132, 4
Jocund No, no, thy bread, thy wine, thy jocund Beere
147. H.377, 57
By jocund Larr,..............................162. H.426, 19
Let's be jocund while we may;..................224. H.639, 1
Jocond his Muse was; but his Life was chast...335. H.1130, 2
Joell Had been reherst, by Joell Michelditch:....266. H.800, 2
John If children you have ten, Sir John..........208. H.581, 5
Do with me, God! as Thou didst deal with John,.343. N.25, 1
Johnson See Jonson

Johnson's See **Jonson's**
Join And sever'd, **joyne** in brazen yoke:........70. H.181, 18
Of all joyes, to **joyn** with them................220. H.633, 4
Ready to **joyne**, as well our hearts as hands.....262. H.781, 10
To **joyn** with them, who here confer.............402. N.270, 1
Joined Part your **joyn'd** lips, then speaks your kisse;
130. H.329, 18
Joining Who then the **joyning** Priest shall be.....216. H.616, 30
Joins Which **joyns** two souls, remember this;....174. H.465, 2
Joint That **joynt** to ashes sho'd be burnt,...........28. H.85, 7
The **joynt** is free:..............................65. H.172, 8
Joints Your Garters; and their **joynts**...........114. H.283, 79
Jollies See **Jolly's**
Jollity Gives them by turnes their grief and **jollitie.**
394. N.236, 4
Jolly We send to you; but here a **jolly**..........126. H.319, 9
Jolly and Jillie, bite and scratch all day,.........156. H.411, 1
Jolly's First, **Jollies** wife is lame; then next, loose-hipt:
62. H.163, 1
Jone See **Joan**
Jonson After the rare Arch-Poet **Johnson** dy'd,......150. H.382, 1
In which thy Father **Johnson** now is plac't,....207. H.575, 57
Here lyes **Johnson** with the rest................289. H.910, 1
Jonson's Unto my **Johnsons** soule...............227. H.653, 4
Joses Observe we may, how Mary **Joses** then,.....384. N.180, 7
Joshua Moses, and Jesus, called **Joshua**:.........381. N.157, 2
Jot Sho'd I a **jot** the better see?..................97. H.235, 4
Age shall not wrong thee; or one **jot** abate......280. H.869, 3
No **jot** of Leven must be found..................366. N.98, 3
Alas! I cannot pay a **jot**; therefore............368. N.103, 7
Journey For having now my **journey** done,......123. H.306, 5
Jove **Jove** for our labour all things sells us.......36. H.106, 62
As **Jove** did, when he made his rapes:...........58. H.152, 2
To **Jove**, who gives, and takes away:............59. H.153, 2
When she lyes with **Jove**, then she..............59. H.155, 10
As to be the Chick of **Jove**.....................108. H.266, 8
Beginne with **Jove**; then is the worke halfe done;.128. H.321, 1
Thus has Infernall **Jove** decreed;..............133. H.336, 28
Jove, joy'st when guests make their abode......147. H.377, 62
Jove may afford us thousands of reliefs;........153. H.397, 1
As when to **Jove** Great Juno goes perfum'd.......157. H.414, 8
Jove prospers my meat, more then his...........173. H.461, 4
Nothing comes Free-cost here; **Jove** will not let..177. H.469, 1
The cleaving Bolt of **Jove** the Thunderer.......181. H.483, 16
But Fables we'l relate: how **Jove**............215. H.616, 15
Not knowing This, that **Jove** decrees...........233. H.670, 5
None is discreet at all times; no, not **Jove**......294. H.936, 3
If **Jove** wo'd speake, he wo'd accept of thine...301. H.966, 14
To **Jove** the Mighty for to stand.................303. H.973, 16
— — — — — — — — — — — —, ...427. var. H.197, 65
Then **Jove** and Chaos them before.......437. var. H.336, 136
— — — — — — — — — — — —, ...451. var. H.197, 10
Jove's Had not ***Joves** son, that brave Tyrinthian Swain,
78. H.197, 65
Jove's is the first and last; The Morn's his due,..128. H.321, 3
The midst is thine; but **Joves** the Evening too;
128. H.321, 4
Jovial — — — — — — — —, ...427, var. H.197, 67
Joy So sup'rabundant **joy** shall be..............34. H.103, 17
He chirpt for **joy**, to see himself disceav'd........46. H.130, 12
Salutes with tears of **joy**; when fires betray......77. H.197, 17
(Some say) for **joy**, to see those Kitlings drown'd.
80. H.200, 2
To all our **joy**, a sweet-fac't child was borne,....86. H.213, 15
For **joy**, to see the Hock-cart crown'd.........101. H.250, 14
For **joy**, to see the fruits ye reape,............127. H.319, 34
No **joy** to thee their sickly Lord................239. H.696, 12
Teares have their springs from **joy**, as well as woe.
275. H.842, 4
Praise they that will Times past, I **joy** to see...292. H.927, 1
What **joy** can Clun have in that Coat, or this,....295. H.941, 7
May fart for **joy**, as well as shout:..............306. H.987, 2
Afflictions bring us **joy** in times to come,........349. N.45, 1
He was my Life, my Love, my **Joy**; but di'd....416. A.8, 15
For Humane **Joy**, Contingent Misery.............416. A.8, 18
— — — — — — — — — — — —, ...427. var. H.197, 55
— — — — — — — — — — — —, ...429. var. H.263, 19
— — — — — — — — — — — —, ...443. var. H.575, 50
Joyest Jove, **joy'st** when guests make their abode.147. H.377, 62
Joys Your **joyes**, by staying long:................53. H.149, 4
For as these flowers, thy **joyes** must die,.......107. H.263, 19
Of all **joyes**, to joyn with them.................220. H.633, 4
Where **Joyes** and Griefs have Turns Alternative...264. H.792, 2
Are but the handsells of our **joyes** hereafter......362. N.90, 2
And fresh **joyes**, as never too..................377. N.128, 23
And though all **joyes** spring from the glance.....395. N.246, 3
W[th] **Joyes** before, and Pleasures left behind:.....411. A.3, 64
— — — — — — — — — — — —, ...449. var. A.8, 18
Joy-sops **Joy-sops** with the cake;..............317. H.1035, 14
Joy'st See **Joyest**
Judas **Judas** began well, but he foulely fell:......387. N.200, 2
Judge Chor. And Lallage the **Judge** shall be,......243. H.716, 5
Who'l hear, and so **judge** righteously...........243. H.716, 22
Be you a **Judge**; but not a **Judge** severe........322. H.1062, 6
So I'le not feare the **Judge**, or thee............357. N.72, 18
To heare the **Judge** give sentence on the Throne,
392. N.230, 25
Both to the **Judge**, and Judgment-Hall:........399. N.265, 6
Judgment The Gods to Kings the **Judgement** give to sway:
109. H.269, 1
Where the fault springs, there let the **judgement** fall.
132. H.335, 4
And give a righteous **judgement** upon it.........187. H.506, 4
Shall call to **Judgment**; tell us when the sound..257. H.763, 18
Your **judgement** finds a guilty Poem, there......322. H.1062, 5
When the **Judgment** is reveal'd.................348. N.41, 45
(**Judgment** and Death, denounc'd gainst Guilty men)
411. A.3, 62
Judgment-hall Both to the Judge, and **Judgment-Hall**:
399. N.265, 6
Judith **Judith** has cast her old-skin, and got new;..140. H.356, 1
Foule **Judith** was; and foule she will be known,..140. H.356, 3
Juggle To **juggle** with the sense..................76. H.193, 40
Juha Then **Juha** weep, for I must dy...........153. H.399, 10
Juice Which had a **juice** in it:...................222. H.635, 2
While **juice** she straines, and pith.............258. H.767, 13
To be with **juice** of Cedar washt all over;........415. A.7, 6
Julia **Julia** was carelesse, and withall,..............12. H.27, 1
To me my **Julia** lately sent......................13. H.32, 1
In thy remembrance (**Julia.**) So farewell..........14. H.35, 14
Stately **Julia**, prime of all;.......................15. H.39, 3
But forthwith bade my **Julia** shew.................18. H.45, 3
Julia and I did lately sit........................19. H.49, 1
Julia, if I chance to die.........................21. H.59, 1
The lips of **Julia**................................24. H.75, 4
How rich and pleasing thou my **Julia** art..........30. H.88, 1
When **Julia** chid, I stood as mute the while,......58. H.150, 1
Aire coyn'd to words, my **Julia** co'd not heare;....58. H.150, 3
Permit me, **Julia**, now to goe away;............60. H.156, 1
Julia, I bring...................................65. H.172, 1
Breathe, **Julia**, breathe, and Ile protest,..........69. H.179, 1
As **Julia** once a-slumb'ring lay,...................71. H.182, 1
Of **Julia**, and began to sip;......................71. H.182, 6
So **Julia** took the Pilferer......................71. H.182, 10
Display thy breasts, my **Julia**, there let me........96. H.230, 1
To-morrow, **Julia**, I betimes must rise,..........102. H.251, 1
For sport my **Julia** threw a Lace................116. H.284, 1
When **Julia** blushes, she do's show..............120. H.295, 1
Julia, this my silken twist;....................128. H.322, 2
For my embalming, **Julia**, do but this,.........129. H.327, 1
Briefly of my **Julia**?..........................138. H.342, 2
Ile tell thee; while my **Julia** did unlace..........157. H.414, 5
Stay but till my **Julia** close....................164. H.441, 9
Julia, when thy Herrick dies,...................186. H.499, 1
Thou know'st, my **Julia**, that it is thy turne....196. H.539, 1
The Saints-bell calls; and, **Julia**, I must read....209. H.584, 1
To grace which Service, **Julia**, there shall be....209. H.584, 3
Dead when thou art, Deare **Julia**, thou shalt have
209. H.584, 5
Then **Julia** let me wooe thee,..................217. H.619, 16
When as in silks my **Julia** goes,...............261. H.779, 1
This day my **Julia** thou must make.............267. H.805, 1
As **Julia** looks when she doth dress.............268. H.811, 9
So soone as **Julia** I am gon....................270. H.819, 2
My **Julia** thou shalt see,.......................271. H.824, 2
Yet if my **Julia** kisse me, there will be..........274. H.841, 3
For my well-fare (**Julia**).......................277. H.856, 2
My **Julia** wash her self in thee!.................294. H.939, 2
As in the River **Julia** did,......................294. H.939, 5
Thee **Julia**, first, to sanctifie thy hands:........299. H.957, 2
Doe that my **Julia** which the rites require,......299. H.957, 3
Of **Julia** Herrick gave to me my Birth.........316. H.1028, 16
Help me, **Julia**, for to pray,...................324. H.1069, 1
Beg for my Pardon **Julia**; He doth winne.......329. H.1095, 3
That done, my **Julia**, dearest **Julia**, come,.......329. H.1095, 5
Julia's For Health on **Julia's** cheek hath shed..........7. H.9, 9
Because my **Julia's** lip was by,...................12. H.23, 3
Where my **Julia's** lips doe smile;................20. H.53, 5
But of the heat of **Julia's** breast:..................25. H.78, 8
So smiles that Riband 'bout my **Julia's** waste:....40. H.114, 2
That's my **Julia's** breast; where dwels..........40. H.115, 13
I made upon my **Julia's** brest;................135. H.336, 95
Tis **Julia's** Bed, and she sleeps there.............139. H.348, 3
Fain would I kiss my **Julia's** dainty Leg,........139. H.349, 1
It sho'd be onely in my **Julia's** skin:..........158. H.416, 2
Dew sate on **Julia's** haire,.....................181. H.484, 1
Julia's Breast can give you them:.............183. H.491, 2
The gentle Beams from **Julia's** sight.............237. H.687, 3
I prest my **Julia's** lips, and in the kisse.........240. H.700, 1
Take it from my **Julia's** sweat:..................244. H.719, 2
Sweet are my **Julia's** lips and cleane,............277. H.857, 1
For Roses, and in **Julia's** cheeke,...............281. H.876, 2
Coming from my **Julia's** eye:.....................302. H.968, 2
Julus See **Iülus**
— — — — — — — — — — — —, ...451. var. H.336, 94
— — — — — — — — — — — —, ...451. var. H.336, 118
July Then (lastly) **July** comes, and she.............23. H.70, 7
July-flower You are a lovely **July-flower**,..........88. H.216, 4
July-flowers See **Gillyflowers**
Of April, May, of June, and **July-Flowers**...........5. H.1, 2
June Of April, May, of **June**, and July-Flowers.......5. H.1, 2
Next enters **June**, and brings us more............23. H.70, 5
Junkets Are the **Junketts** still at Wakes:........255. H.761, 4
Juno With **Juno** goes the houres,.................54. H.149, 45

Kerzie In Den'-shire **Kerzie** Lusk (when he was dead) 332. H.1114, 1
Key The first of Raine, the **key** of Hell next known: 390. N.224, 2
With the third **key** He opes and shuts the wombe; 390. N.224, 3
And with the fourth **key** He unlocks the tombe..390. N.224, 4
Keys God has foure **keyes**, which He reserves alone; 390. N.224, 1
By the soone gingling of some sleepy **keyes**,..410. A.3, 10
you, stand for to surrender up the **keyes** 431. ins. H.283, 60h
Keys' Many a jest told of the **Keyes** betraying....69. H.178, 55
Kick To **kick** the Flow'rs, and scorn their odours too? 234. H.673, 4
Kid Upon some part of **Kid**, as if mistooke,.....147. H.377, 55
And wanton as a **Kid** as yet..................243. H.716, 10
Kidney-lipped Squint-ey'd, hook-nos'd; and lastly, **Kidney-lipt** 62. H.163, 2
Kids My Weathers, Lambes, and wanton **Kids** are well, 86. H.213, 5
The tongues of **Kids** shall be thy meate;.......192. H.521, 11
Kill O Dianeme, rather **kill**....................34. H.103, 9
Thus, thus to wound, not **kill** out-right:.......34. H.103, 12
Me sooner starve, then those can **kill**...........40. H.115, 16
Purge hence the guilt, and **kill** this quarrelling..78. H.197, 32
Though thou not **kill**.......................95. H.227, 10
For to tame, though not to **kill**...............98. H.238, 10
To save; when thou may'st **kill** a heart........177. H.471, 4
Vines to prune, though not to **kill**,...........204. H.569, 14
To **kill** it...................................210. H.591, 6
To **kill** her selfe for Demophon...............215. H.616, 14
Who, kissing, **kill** such Saints as these?........294. H.937, 6
Ans. **Kisse** ye, to kill ye...................310. H.1001, 16
Shew mercy there, where they have power to **kill**. 321. H.1057, 2
Meet for nothing, but to **kill**;.................347. N.41, 19
Lord, I will kisse it, though it **kill**:...........351. N.48, 4
Killed Love **kill'd** this man. No more but so......61. H.159, 31
Kil'd by a frost or by a flame................155. H.406, 6
One like to me, who must be **kill'd**............188. H.509, 7
Gently **kill'd** by Flatterie....................264. H.790, 4
Well, when sh'as **kild**, that Pig, Goose, Cock or Hen, 266. H.801, 3
I, and **kil'd** my dear delight..................306. H.984, 35
Killest Thou **kil'st** with heate, and I strike dead with cold. 333. H.1120, 2
Killing So Kings by **killing** doe encrease their foes. 292. H.929, 4
— — — — — — — — — —, ...433. var. H.293, 24
Kin You, you that be of her neerest **kin**,.......55. H.149, 81
Both of a fresh, and fragrant **kinne**............285. H.892, 15
Salute we must, nor Strangers, **Kin**, or Friends..378. N.137, 8
Kind See **Too-too-kind, Womankind**
There's paine in parting; and a **kind** of hell,.....73. H.186, 7
In Sack of such a **kind**,.....................80. H.201, 14
A heart as soft, a heart as **kind**,..............108. H.267, 5
To bed, to bed, **kind** Turtles, now, and write..114. H.283, 71
The sweetest **kind** of bashfulnesse.............121. H.300, 2
But thou **kind** Prew did'st with my Fates abide,.151. H.387, 5
Though thou beest young, **kind**, soft, and faire,.174. H.465, 3
Take Horse, and come; or be so **kind**,.........198. H.544, 31
Softnesse in others, will be **kind**;.............252. H.746, 6
Kind at once to murder mee...................254. H.757, 8
Love is a **kind** of warre; Hence those who feare, 280. H.872, 1
Wast **kind**...................................314. H.1024, 16
Like will to like, each Creature loves his **kinde**; 319. H.1043, 1
So **kind**, to set me free,.....................370. N.111, 6
When as some **kinde**..........................414. A.5, 13
— — — — — — — — — —, ...442. var. H.465, 80
Kinder From your **kinder** Mistresses.............62. H.162, 9
Kindle Speak thou the word, they'l **kindle** by and by. 261. H.781, 4
Kindle the Christmas Brand, and then.........285. H.893, 1
Kindles **Kindles** in cloathes a wantonnesse:........28. H.83, 2
Kindling 'Tis but as day a **kindling**:............154. H.404, 2
By the next **kindling** of the day...............271. H.824, 1
Kindly Either to send me **kindly** thine,..........168. H.446, 7
Kindly swell vp with little pretty pride,.......406. A.1, 88
Kindness Laid out for dead, let thy last **kindnesse** be 19. H.50, 1
Which of Thy **kindnesse** Thou hast sent;......350. N.47, 33
Kindred Nay, thou more neare then **kindred**, friend, man, wife, 45. H.128, 3
Tell us thy Nation, **kindred**, or the whence....299. H.956, 7
Kindreds All Nations, Customes, **Kindreds**, Languages! 242. H.713, 10
Kine Ambo. Poor pittied youth! Mir. And here the breth of **kine**......................................159. H.421, 13
Made by the breath of great-ey'd **kine**,........166. H.443, 40
With Cream of Lillies (not of **Kine**)..........216. H.616, 33
And smell'st the breath of great-ey'd **Kine**,....230. H.662, 33
As **Kine**, when they at milking meet...........243. H.716, 30
And hadst thou wager'd twenty **Kine**,.........244. H.716, 45
Tell me, do thy **kine** now fail.................305. H.984, 7
Then these **kine**, which I milke here..........305. H.984, 17
The Sonnes to suck the milke of **Kine**,........310. H.1004, 5
The while the conduits of my **Kine**...........350. N.47, 49
King See **Fairy-king**
Each one, by nature, loves to be a **King**........21. H.58, 2
So oft, we'll think, we see a **King** new born...26. H.80, 2
I shall be heal'd, if that my **King** but touch....62. H.161, 14
The Persian **King** liv'd not more happily.......70. H.181, 4
Unto our smiling, and our blooming **King**,....86. H.213, 34
(Most fit to be the Consort to a **King**)........107. H.265, 2
The free-born Nosthrills of the **King**,.........126. H.319, 8
When as ye chuse your **King** and Queen,......127. H.319, 19
The farting Tanner, and familiar **King**;........155. H.405, 6
Our Sires betraid their Countrey and their **King** 252. H.745, 10
Each Cobler is a **King**;......................259. H.772, 11
The **King** he beares the blame of all.........290. H.913, 2
Which got, the third, bids him a **King** come downe. 292. H.925, 2
Chor. Long live the **King**; and to accomplish this, 300. H.961, 19
Where Beane's the **King** of the sport here;....317. H.1035, 3
Be a **King** by the lot,.......................317. H.1035, 10
A health to the **King** and the Queene here.....317. H.1035, 18
Give then to the **King**.......................317. H.1035, 25
We are Thy Prophets Porter; Thou our **King**..324. H.1071, 4
'Tis flatterie spends a **King**, more then his foes..331. H.1105, 2
The mind; the **King**, the meanes whereby I live..355. N.62, 2
He His Church save, and the **King**,...........363. N.93, 7
The Birth of this our heavenly **King**?.........364. N.96, 3
To do Him honour; who's our **King**,..........365. N.96, 31
His praise; so let us blesse the **King**:.........367. N.98, 26
A **King**, before conception crown'd...........368. N.102, 18
Unto our prettie Twelfth-Tide **King**...........368. N.102, 20
Wee'l chuse Him **King**, and make His Mother Queen. 368. N.102, 24
Gold serves for Tribute to the **King**;.........396. N.254, 1
Those act without regard, when once a **King**,..399. N.263, 24
Why then begin, great **King**! ascend Thy Throne, 399. N.263, 28
Of **King** and no **King** (and the rare Plott thine).415. A.7, 14
Kingdom The drooping **Kingdome** suffers all.....89. H.219, 8
No man so well a **Kingdome** Rules, as He,.....325. H.1074, 1
Where Pleasures rule a **Kingdome**, never there..327. H.1087, 1
Here give me thornes; there, in thy **Kingdome**, set 343. N.25, 5
Kingdom's To read by th' Starres, the **Kingdoms** sick: 126. H.319, 6
The **Kingdoms** portion is the Plow............230. H.662, 28
Nought but a **Kingdoms** ill-affectednesse:......244. H.718, 2
This **Kingdomes** fortune, and that Empires fate: 330. H.1100, 8
Kingdoms No **Kingdomes** got by Rapine long endure. 314. H.1023, 2
If Kings and **kingdomes**, once distracted be,...331. H.1102, 1
Tho **Kingdoms** fal,.........................335. H.1129, 10
Within the **Kingdomes** of the Deep;...........340. N.3, 8
Kingly See **Great-little-kingly-guest**
Thy cradle, **Kingly** Stranger,.................345. N.33, 13
King's Mine is the Evill, but the Cure, the **Kings**..62. H.161, 16
Fearing to break the **Kings** Commandement:...122. H.305, 4
The **Kings** undrest; and now upon............168. H.443, 116
Kings Twixt **Kings** and Subjects ther's this mighty odds, 12. H.25, 1
Subjects are taught by Men; **Kings** by the Gods. 12. H.25, 2
By your accesse; (O you the best of **Kings**!)..25. H.77, 10
Fame tell of States, of Countries, Courts, and **Kings**; 36. H.106, 85
So **Kings** & Queens meet, when Desire convinces 77. H.197, 7
The Gods to **Kings** the Judgement give to sway: 109. H.269, 1
Let **Kings** Command, and doe the best they may, 138. H.345, 1
Empires of **Kings**, are now, and ever were,.....162. H.430, 1
Kings though th'are hated, will be fear'd.......165. H.443, 18
There all are **Kings**.........................190. H.515, 36
When **Kings** obey the wilder Multitude.........196. H.536, 2
Thy Mummeries; thy Twelfe-tide **Kings**......231. H.662, 58
Kings ought to be more lov'd, then fear'd......234. H.672, 2
Kings must not oft be seen by publike eyes;...236. H.682, 1
Men are not born **Kings**, but are men renown'd; 241. H.707, 1
When These can aske, and **Kings** can give no more. 255. H.758, 4
This not the least is, which belongs to **Kings**...260. H.774, 2
If ill, then **Kings**, not Souldiers beare the blame. 260. H.774, 4
Kings must not only cherish up the good,......260. H.775, 1
Kings ought to sheare, not skin their sheepe...261. H.780, 2
Fortune is now Your Captive; other **Kings**....271. H.823, 5
'Twas Cesars saying: **Kings** no lesse Conquerors are 271. H.825, 1
So many **Kings**, and Primates too there are,...272. H.826, 4

'Twixt **Kings** & Tyrants there's this difference known;
278. H.861, 1
Kings seek their Subjects good: Tyrants their owne.
278. H.861, 2
Tis but a dog-like madnesse in bad **Kings**,.....292. H.929, 1
So **Kings** by killing doe encrease their foes.....292. H.929, 4
In this misfortune **Kings** doe most excell,......293. H.932, 1
Let **Kings** and Rulers, learne this line from me;
302. H.971, 1
Kings must not use the Axe for each offence:.309. H.998, 1
Danger to give the best advice to **Kings**.........318. H.1037, 2
Kings must be dauntlesse: Subjects will contemne
330. H.1097, 1
If **Kings** and kingdomes, once distracted be,....331. H.1102, 1
— — — — — — — — — — —, ...427. var. H.197, 73
Kingship To have his little **King-ship** know,....86. H.213, 43
Kingstone To Richmond, **Kingstone**, and to Hampton-Court:
315. H.1028, 10
Kinsman Brave **Kinsman**, markt out with the whiter stone:
199. H.545, 8
Thee a **kinsman**, or a friend,.................334. H.1125, 4
Kirnils See Kernels
Kiss That I must give thee the supremest **kisse**;...9. H.14, 6
And **kisse**, but yet be chaste..................13. H.31, 10
Give my dead picture one engendring **kisse**:....14. H.35, 12
Still with your curles, and **kisse** the time away..15. H.38, 2
Give me a **kisse**, and to that **kisse** a score;.....24. H.74, 3
A thousand to that hundred: so **kisse** on,......24. H.74, 5
Let's **kisse** afresh, as when we first begun......24. H.74, 8
I owe thee for a **kisse**.......................29. H.87, 3
Good children **kisse** the rods, that punish sin...32. H.97, 4
Bequeath to me one parting **kisse**:............34. H.103, 16
Kisse our Dollies night and day:..............39. H.111, 4
The **kisse** of Virgins; First-fruits of the bed;..45. H.128, 7
To **kisse** that tempting nakednesse:............51. H.142, 18
But now **kisse** her, and thus say,............56. H.149, 119
If I **kisse** Anthea's brest,....................59. H.155, 1
Give my cold lips a **kisse** at last:.............61. H.159, 25
If twice you **kisse**, you need not feare,........61. H.159, 26
Many a **kisse**, both odde and even:............69. H.178, 52
But with a **kisse**, or thanks, doe pay...........71. H.182, 21
From that warme **kisse** of ours?..............74. H.192, 2
Let's **kisse**, and **kisse** agen;..................74. H.192, 5
Come, come and **kisse** me; Love and lust commends
78. H.197, 69
Thee, and thy beauties; **kisse**, we will be friends,
78. H.197, 70
Kisse, and sigh, so part agen.................82. H.203, 14
Whose foot-pace he doth stroak and **kisse**:.....93. H.223, 132
Shall have for his winning a **kisse**............99. H.243, 6
Some blesse the Cart; some **kisse** the sheaves;.101. H.250, 19
To give Perenn'as lip a **kisse**,.................103. H.255, 3
Or brought a **kisse**..........................104. H.257, 22
To **kisse**, and beare away....................110. H.274, 7
Each hieroglyphick of a **kisse** or smile;.......115. H.283, 126
Give thou my lips but their supreamest **kiss**:..129. H.327, 2
What is the thing we call a **kisse**?...........130. H.329, 2
Part your joyn'd lips, then speaks your **kisse**;..130. H.329, 18
To **kisse** our hands, nor do we wish...........133. H.336, 47
My old leane wife, shall **kisse** it dry:........134. H.336, 84
To **kisse** your hand, most Dainty Governesse...137. H.341, 12
Let me when I **kisse** a maid,..................138. H.346, 5
Kisse the Altar, and confess..................138. H.346, 9
Fain would I **kiss** my Julia's dainty Leg.......139. H.349, 1
Thou gav'st me leave to **kisse**;................142. H.364, 1
But I will go, or send a **kisse**.................156. H.412, 19
Ile carve thy name, and in that name **kisse** thee:
160. H.421, 40
Ile hug, Ile **kisse**, Ile play,...................160. H.422, 9
Go hence, and with this parting **kisse**,.........174. H.465, 1
Means, I shall know what other **kisse**..........175. H.465, 70
How can I chuse but **kisse** her, whence do's come
181. H.485, 3
And I shall see by that one **kisse**,...........185. H.495, 7
Jill sayes, of what? sayes Jack, on that sweet **kisse**,
186. H.498, 3
We busse our Wantons, but our Wives we **kisse**.
189. H.512, 2
Where kissing that, Ile twice **kisse** thee.......193. H.521, 42
Give me one **kisse**,...........................196. H.538, 1
If nine times you your Bride-groome **kisse**;....208. H.581, 1
You say you'l **kiss** me, and I thanke you for it:
210. H.588, 1
One **kisse** from thee.........................210. H.591, 10
I askt my Lucia but a **kisse**;.................212. H.599, 1
And sigh, and **kiss**, as Lovers do:.............215. H.616, 20
A **kiss** to each; and so we'l end...............216. H.616, 36
What is a **Kisse**? Why this, as some approve;..218. H.622, 1
I dare not ask a **kisse**;.......................231. H.663, 1
Onely to **kisse** that Aire,.....................231. H.663, 7
And have for all a **kisse**.....................238. H.690, 12
To **kisse** thy hand from out the coach;........239. H.696, 2
I prest my Julia's lips, and in the **kisse**........240. H.700, 1
Begin with a **kisse**,...........................247. H.727, 1
That done, they **kisse**, and so draw out the day:
260. H.773, 2
Or **kisse** it thou, but once, or twice,...........267. H.805, 5
Ai me! I love, give him your hand to **kisse**......274. H.837, 1
Yet if my Julia **kisse** me, there will be..........274. H.841, 3
I abhor the slimie **kisse**,.......................282. H.878, 1
My **kisse** out-went the bounds of shamfastnesse:.294. H.936, 2
Blisse (last night drunk) did **kisse** his mothers knee:
295. H.943, 1
Where he will **kisse** (next drunk) conjecture ye.
295. H.943, 2
Ile **kiss** the hand that strikes me..............296. H.946, 6
Love is a Leven, and a loving **kisse**..........298. H.950, 1
To **kiss** his hands, but that for fearfullness;....301. H.963, 2
For a **kisse** or two, confesse,.................305. H.984, 1
Ans. **Kisse** ye, to kill ye...................310. H.1001, 16
Kisse my Brown wife, and black Posterity....310. H.1003, 4
I send, I send here my supremest **kiss**.........315. H.1028, 1
Lets **kiss** first, then we'l sever................324. H.1068, 22
Ile **kisse** the Threshold of thy dore..........328. H.1090, 11
I will no longer **kiss**,........................328. H.1091, 1
Lord, I will **kisse** it, though it kill:..........351. N.48, 4
Lastly, if thou canst win a **kisse**..............354. N.59, 15
Let's **kisse** the sweet and holy ground;.........368. N.102, 16
I'le **kisse** the Tally, and confesse the score.....368. N.103, 8
Thy stripes I'le **kisse**, or burn the Rod........399. N.265, 10
Thus, thus I come to **kisse** Thy Stone.........402. N.269, 10
And as I **kisse**, I'le here and there............402. N.269, 12
That both her lipps doe part, doe meete, doe **kisse**;
405. A.1, 38
Whence beawty springs, and thus I **kisse** thy foot.
406. A.1, 112
A **kisse** to such a jewell of the heauen:.........410. A.3, 4
Parte wth a hastye **kisse**; and in that shew....410. A.3, 11
Thus wth a **kisse** of warmth, and loue, I parte.412. A.3, 95
Meanes I may **kisse** thy **kisse**,...................414. A.5, 12
Since part we must Let's **kisse**, that done retire.414. A.6, 9
All in, **kisse** and so enter, If...........431. ins. H.283, 60m
— — — — — — — — — — —, ...449. var. A.3, 59
— — — — — — — — — — —, ...450. var. A.9, 13
Kissed The Beads I **kist**, but most lov'd her....13. H.32, 3
I did; and **kist** the Instep too...............14. H.33, 2
And would have **kist** unto her knee,...........14. H.33, 3
I **kist** thee (panting,) and I call..............20. H.56, 7
She **kist**, and wip'd thir dove-like eyes;..........31. H.92, 11
'Tis true, I **kist** thee; but I co'd not heare....42. H.122, 5
Till we have wept, **kist**, sigh't, shook hands, or so.
73. H.186, 6
That lately **kissed** thee......................231. H.663, 8
I be **kist**, or blest by thee....................286. H.897, 12
And strugling there, I **kist** thee too;...........294. H.939, 8
She smil'd; he **kist**; and kissing, cull'd her too;
313. H.1017, 9
Kisses And **kisses** drying up his tears:..........50. H.139, 11
Close **kisses**, if she cry:......................56. H.149, 96
Let **kisses**, in their close,.....................57. H.149, 143
So meet stolne **kisses**, when the Moonie nights.77. H.197, 5
Jack **kisses** Jill, and bids her freely eate:.......186. H.498, 2
Their Goales for Virgins **kisses**; which when done,
206. H.575, 18
His eye in dew of **kisses**, while he sleeps.......206. H.575, 42
As that your **kisses** must out-vie the Starres....216. H.618, 14
Kisses are but dry banquets to a Feast........265. H.797, 2
Kisses and Favours are sweet things;..........283. H.883, 13
And gives His Children **kisses** then, not stripes..379. N.139, 2
With **Kisses** to inspire...................431. ins. H.283, 40f
Kisseth Claps my cheek, or **kisseth** me;.........17. H.43, 8
Kissing Kissing and glancing, soothing, all make way
24. H.74, 11
Alas! If **kissing** be of plagues the worst,.......33. H.101, 3
And **kissing**, so as none may heare,...........59. H.152, 11
Kissing the Omen, said Amen:................73. H.187, 7
Kissing and bussing differ both in this;........189. H.512, 1
Where **kissing** that, Ile twice kisse thee........193. H.521, 42
For **kissing** Loves dissembling chips,..........203. H.563, 7
Not a **kissing** Cupid flyes....................221. H.633, 29
Who, **kissing**, kill such Saints as these?........294. H.937, 6
She smil'd; he kist; and **kissing**, cull'd her too;.313. H.1017, 9
Sits Cupid **kissing** of his mother Queene,.......405. A.1, 56
Kitchen To the worn Threshold, Porch, Hall, Parlour, **Kitchin**,
146. H.377, 5
Hog has a place i'th' **Kitchen**, and his share...326. H.1079, 1
Kitchen's And **Kitchin's** small:................350. N.47, 18
Kite Each griefe we feele, that likewise is a **Kite**.278. H.862, 3
Kite's Are trinkets falne from the **Kites** nest;
439. ins. H.443, 45o
Kites See Paper-kites
Kitling Till that the green-ey'd **Kitling** comes....37. H.106, 124
His **kitling** eyes begin to runne.............119. H.293, 24
— — — — — — — — — — —, ...440. var. H.443, 73
Kitling's From th' embers, then the **kitlings** eyne,
136. H.336, 146
Soft Candle-light; the **Kitling's** eyne;.........167. H.443, 74
Kitlings Gubbs call's his children **Kitlings**: and wo'd bound
80. H.200, 1
(Some say) for joy, to see those **Kitlings** drown'd.
80. H.200, 2
Knacks Candles (forsooth) and other **knacks**:...93. H.223, 116
Knap Knap the thread, and thou art free:........128. H.322, 8
Knave To call my Lord Maior **knave**;.........259. H.772, 15

Knead Knead but the Dow and it will be........267. H.805, 3
Feed on the paste of Filberts, or else knead....269. H.818, 5
With ashes knead,..........................353. N.56, 8
Kneading To fill the Paste that's a kneading.....263. H.784, 18
Knee And would have kist unto her knee,........14. H.33, 3
Honouring thee, on my knee.................213. H.604, 7
When I embrace thy knee;...................281. H.874, 4
His Shirt bedangling from his knee,...........295. H.942, 3
Blisse (last night drunk) did kisse his mothers knee: 295. H.943, 1
Kneel I kneele for help; O! lay that hand on me, 62. H.161, 12
Next to the Altar humbly kneele, and thence,..128. H.320, 5
Knees To whose free knees we may our temples tye 300. H.961, 15
Which to the knees by nature fastned on......406. A.1, 85
Knell When I departed am, ring thou my knell,...111. H.279, 1
One knell be rung for both; and let one grave.281. H.875, 5
Possesse my thoughts, next comes my dolefull knell 392. N.230, 12
Knew Never was Night so tedious, but it knew...52. H.146, 3
Strut, once a Fore-man of a Shop we knew,...53. H.148, 1
That ne'r knew Brides, or Bride-grooms touch,.57. H.149, 132
We knew 'twas Flesh and Blood, that there sate mute. 95. H.228, 2
Play then they ever knew before.............115. H.283, 130
I awoke, and then I knew....................219. H.628, 7
— — — — — — — — — —, ...441. var. H.465, 60
Knewest Knew'st thou, one moneth wo'd take thy life away, 241. H.709, 1
Knife A hand too desp'rate, or a knife that bites.147. H.377, 53
Neer the childs heart lay a knife:............284. H.889, 2
Knight And if that Fairie Knight not lies,......92. H.223, 81
Come then, brave Knight, and see the Cell......198. H.544, 25
Give me these (my Knight) and try............217. H.620, 7
Of that sweet Lady, or that gallant Knight:....228. H.658, 2
The first as Doctor, and the last as Knight.....322. H.1062, 12
Your mayden knight.....................430. ins. H.283, 40e
Knit About her spotlesse neck she knit.........14. H.34, 3
Knit to the posts: this point.................55. H.149, 85
Like those short sweets ere knit together......107. H.263, 22
And knit in knots far more then I...........202. H.560, 11
Knit them with knots (with much adoe unty'd).291. H.920, 2
But truth knitt fast; and so farewell for euer.....414. A.6, 12
Knock Knock at a Starre with my exalted Head..214. H.612, 14
Where thrice we knock, and none will heare,..312. H.1014, 9
Knocking And knocking, me molested...........26. H.81, 4
Knot See True-love-knot
Thy Love had one knot, mine a triple tye......173. H.464, 3
But when the drought has dri'd the knot;......279. H.867, 3
Hath in the middle ty'de a Gordian knott.....405. A.1, 62
Knot-free Of your horses, all knot-free..........284. H.891, 6
Knots See True-love-knots
And knit in knots far more then I...........202. H.560, 11
Knit them with knots (with much adoe unty'd).291. H.920, 2
Knotty Of Pushes Spalt has such a knottie race,.211. H.594, 1
Know True love, we know, precipitates delay.....8. H.10, 6
Some would know............................12. H.26, 1
List' sweet maids, and you shal know..........14. H.36, 2
Deep waters noyse-lesse are; And this we know, 15. H.38, 9
Now since my love is tongue-lesse, know me such, 15. H.38, 13
How Love came in, I do not know,..........24. H.73, 1
Forgive, forgive me; since I did not know....27. H.82, 5
But whither, onely Grief do's know...........33. H.103, 4
And it to know, and practice; with intent......35. H.106, 5
By studying to know vertue; and to aime.....35. H.106, 7
And know, that Riches have their proper stint,.35. H.106, 17
Feare to those sheets, that know no sin........35. H.106, 40
And that will please me somewhat: though I know, 42. H.122, 11
Then know, that Nature bids thee goe, not I...46. H.128, 42
That I have sworn, but by thy looks to know thee. 46. H.128, 48
Know, I have pray'd to Furie, that some wind.49. H.138, 7
Teach Nature now to know,..................57. H.149, 147
Only one Soveraign salve, I know,..............60. H.157, 5
My way, where you shall never know........60. H.159, 4
Ere I go hence; know this from me,..........60. H.159, 9
And write thereon, This, Reader, know,........61. H.159, 30
Know, Lady, you have but your day:..........63. H.164, 3
Before we know our liberty..................69. H.178, 60
Besides, know this, I never sting.............71. H.182, 19
And take his bag; but thus much know,......71. H.182, 28
What's now the cause? we know the case is cleere: 71. H.183, 2
Fruit, ye know, is comming on:...............74. H.189, 4
White though ye be; yet, Lillies, know,..........74. H.190, 1
Yet trust me, I shall know.....................83. H.207, 3
For my neighbour Ile not know,...............84. H.209, 1
Whether I wo'd; but (ah!) I know not how,....84. H.210, 7
To have his little King-ship know,.............86. H.213, 43
And know thy when..........................87. H.214, 7
At my death; but thus much know,.............88. H.218, 3
Rare Temples thou hast seen, I know,.........90. H.223a, 1
Now, we must know, the Elves are led.........92. H.223, 74
Fooles are they, who never know................96. H.231, 1
And know, besides, ye must revoke............102. H.250, 47
And, you must know, your Lords word's true,..102. H.250, 51
Wods't thou know, besides all these,...........103. H.253, 11
But whither, I my selfe not know..............111. H.278, 2
You say y'are sweet; how sho'd we know.......112. H.282, 1
And know each wile,........................115. H.283, 125
Know the fulness of delight!..................124. H.314, 4
How rich a man is, all desire to know;.........130. H.328, 1
This, this I know, I'm oft struck mute;........142. H.362, 5
Give me the Daphne, that the world may know it, 143. H.365, 7
No, know (Blest Maide) when there's not one..146. H.376, 7
Two dayes y'ave larded here; a third, yee know, 146. H.377, 25
Linnit playes rarely on the Lute, we know;....149. H.381, 1
Live here: But know 'twas vertue, & not chance,.152. H.392, 5
Now I love I know not how..................155. H.407, 2
Ile seek him there; I know, ere this,..........156. H.412, 17
I know ye do; and that's the why,.............158. H.420, 9
Yee pretty Huswives, wo'd ye know............164. H.442, 1
Of peltish wasps; we'l know his Guard........165. H.443, 17
I know the Tunne of Hidleberge holds more.....171. H.454, 4
I know a thousand greedy eyes...............174. H.465, 17
I will not urge Thee, for I know,...............174. H.465, 33
Means, I shall know what other kisse..........175. H.465, 70
Is mixt with mine; and truly know,...........175. H.465, 71
Know vertue taught thee, not thy selfe.........176. H.465, 84
As that your pans no Ebbe may know;........179. H.476, 11
Nor will; for why, Pudica, this may know,.....180. H.477, 5
All know a Fellon eate the Tenth away.........180. H.480, 2
Bright Tulips, we do know,...................184. H.493, 1
'Tis sin I know, 'tis sin to throtle Wine.........187. H.502, 4
We know y'are learn'd i'th' Muses, and no lesse.187. H.506, 7
Much I know of Time is spent,................191. H.519, 3
Lady, this I know you'l say;..................194. H.527, 2
For I know, in the Tombs....................197. H.540, 7
Hisped, and hairie, ere thy Palm shall know...202. H.557, 24
Nor did I know, or co'd descry...............203. H.563, 3
For I know you have the skill.................204. H.569, 13
There yet remaines to know, then thou can'st see 206. H.575, 54
The tenth you know the Parsons is............208. H.581, 2
I doe love I know not what;..................209. H.585, 1
Know I have praid thee,....................212. H.604, 2
Which though well soyl'd, yet thou dost know,..230. H.662, 22
And that wee'l do; as men, who know,.........233. H.670, 36
Come Anthea, know thou this,.................235. H.678, 1
And this for comfort thou must know,.........247. H.725, 5
Pauls hands do give, nought else for ought we know. 248. H.731, 4
Since that I know, 'mong all the rest.........250. H.739, 3
And wonder at Those Things that thou dost know. 257. H.763, 22
We know they dare not beate us;.............259. H.772, 8
Come, Ile instruct thee. Know, the vestall fier..262. H.781, 15
Unwasht hands, ye Maidens, know,.............263. H.786, 3
This for certainty I know;...................277. H.852, 6
Since for one Bad, one Good I know:.........283. H.885, 2
(In faith I know not how)....................295. H.942, 10
But this I know, should Jupiter agen..........301. H.966, 11
How ere it fortuned; know for Truth, I meant..304. H.977, 3
Why sho'd we covet much, when as we know,...308. H.995, 1
Let's strive to be the best; the Gods, we know it, 309. H.1000, 1
Beside we must know,........................317. H.1035, 4
Know when to speake; for many times it brings 318. H.1037, 1
Nor will hereafter; since I know.............320. H.1052, 3
Reward, we know, is the chiefe end of toile....322. H.1060, 2
For love or pitie let me know................323. H.1068, 3
This I know, the Fiend will fly...............324. H.1069, 3
Or some enchanted Place, I do not know.......326. H.1080, 7
Then weepe not sweet; but thus much know,..328. H.1090, 12
Yet, Lord, I know there is with Thee..........342. N.17, 7
Where I do know...........................354. N.58, 3
He slew the Ammonites, we know,.............360. N.83, 27
We see Him come, and know him ours,.........364. N.96, 22
As not to know, or feel some Grievances.........387. N.199, 2
That there's a God, we all do know,.............394. N.238, 1
I know, that faults will many here be found,....398. N.261, 5
Growe vpp wth Mylder Lawes to knowe.........407. A.2, 25
Wiser Conclusions in mee, since I knowe.........411. A.3, 53
Knowe yet, (rare soule,) when my diuiner Muse..412. A.3, 99
Goe hence away, and in thy parting know........414. A.6, 1
And I must hence. Euc. Yet let me thus much know, 416. A.8, 25
Know time past this cherrystone...............417. A.9, 19
And know (faire mistris) of yor youth.........418. A.9, 40
Know, to' th' hearing as the touch..............418. A.9, 50
Nor knowe thy happye, and vn-enuey'de state 422. ins. H.106, 92a
— — — — — — — — — — — —, ...422. var. H.106, 133
— — — — — — — — — — — —, ...426. var. H.197, 47
Know so long Treaties; beate the drumme 432. ins. H.283, 140c
To know his Queene, mixt with the farre.434. ins. H.293, 41g

— — — — — — — — — — —, ...437. var. H.336, 90
Such who **know** well....................437. var. H.336, 133
— — — — — — — — — — — —, ...449. var. A.8, 35

Knowest These things thou **know'st** to'th'height, and dost prevent.......................................35. H.106, 21
Thou foole, said Love, **know'st** thou not this?..106. H.263, 5
No, thou **know'st** order, Ethicks, and ha's read.148. H.377, 89
All Oeconomicks, **know'st** to lead..............148. H.377, 90
Thou **know'st**, my Julia, that it is thy turne....196. H.539, 1
For well thou **know'st**, 'tis not th' extent......230. H.662, 17
If thou **know'st** not where to dwell,............334. H.1125, 7
No, no, (my God) Thou **know'st** my wishes be..352. N.51, 13

Knowing But being poore, and **knowing** Flesh is deare, 122. H.305, 5
Not **knowing** thus much, when we once do sever, 140. H.355, 3
Not **knowing** This, that Jove decrees...........233. H.670, 5
(Not **knowing** what would come to passe)......281. H.876, 6

Knowledge When of these truths, thy happyer **knowledge** lyes, 37. H.106, 87

Known Conformity was ever **knowne**..............25. H.76, 1
But now 'tis **known**, Behold; behold, I bring......27. H.82, 7
O men, O manners; Now, and ever **knowne**......29. H.86, 9
No part besides must of thy selfe be **known**,......30. H.88, 11
And both are **knowne** to thee, who now can'st live 35. H.106, 11
To thine owne selfe; and **knowne** to few.......38. H.106, 136
My modest wedlock, that was **known**..........41. H.116, 7
Farewell thou Thing, time-past so **knowne**, so deare 45. H.128, 1
Six teeth he has, whereof twice two are **known**..46. H.129, 3
O Venus! thou, to whom is **known**............56. H.149, 91
There, where no language ever yet was **known**...60. H.156, 6
Of a thousand thousand **known**,...............62. H.162, 11
Virgins, time-past, **known** were these,..........64. H.167, 1
And to thy selfe be best this sentence **knowne**,....67. H.177, 3
Had Cassius, that weak Water-drinker, **known**...78. H.197, 61
Now this the Fairies wo'd have **known**,.......91. H.223, 22
Had Lesbia (too-too-kind) but **known**.........104. H.256, 11
Alas you have not **known** that shower,..........104. H.257, 6
Speak, whimp'ring Younglings, and make **known**.104. H.257, 15
The word is Roman; but in English **knowne**:...106. H.261, 3
May his ample Name be **knowne**..............108. H.266, 17
'Tis a **known** principle in War,...............118. H.290, 1
Foule Judith was; and foule she will be **known**,.140. H.356, 3
Of thy glad table: not a dish more **known**......147. H.377, 69
Raspe playes at Nine-holes; and 'tis **known** he gets 154. H.400, 1
Center is **known** weak sighted, and he sells......154. H.401, 1
My sometimes **known**........................161. H.426, 7
Were there not a Matter **known**,..............163. H.433, 1
Such Essences as those Three Brothers; **known**..170. H.451, 7
Two Youths sha's **known**, thrice two, and twice 3. yeares; 180. H.477, 3
Where Phillis is not **known**?.................184. H.492, 22
As Time had never **known** ye.................184. H.493, 12
Since you are **knowne** to be Penelope...........189. H.511, 4
Thou art The Man, the onely Man best **known**,.194. H.526, 3
Among which Holies, be Thou ever **known**,.....199. H.545, 7
And like our living, where we'are **known**......200. H.552, 19
Which were, (and still her offices are **known**).201. H.557, 9
Crab faces gownes with sundry Furres; 'tis **known**, 232. H.669, 1
Die when ye will, your sepulchre is **knowne**,..249. H.734, 3
Her name if next you wo'd have **knowne**,......257. H.764, 3
'Tis never, or but seldome **knowne**,...........264. H.788, 1
In desp'rate cases, all, or most are **known**......272. H.827, 1
Tap (better **known** then trusted) as we heare..272. H.829, 1
'Twixt Kings & Tyrants there's this difference **known**; 278. H.861, 1
But let that instant when thou dy'st be **known**,..281. H.875, 3
To take thine haires when they are **knowne**......282. H.881, 3
Reader, wo'dst thou more have **known**?.........289. H.910, 3
Known guilty here of incivility:...............290. H.914, 2
Give house-roome to the best; 'Tis never **known**..293. H.935, 1
Not so much **knowne**, as to be lov'd of thee.....297. H.947, 12
What was thy Birth, thy starre that makes thee **knowne**, 299. H.956, 5
Yet the deluge here was **known**,...............302. H.968, 11
Where now I rest, these may be **known** by Jet...304. H.978, 4
Twixt Truth and Errour, there's this difference **known**, 316. H.1031, 1
Which **knowne**, let us make..................317. H.1035, 13
Truth by her own simplicity is **known**,.........329. H.1094, 1
Make **knowne** to us the now Jerusalem.......330. H.1100, 12
And is the best **known**, not defining Him.........340. N.4, 2
Known, or els seen to be the emptier:...........341. N.15, 4
But when by stripes He saves them, then 'tis **known**, 343. N.22, 3
God, as He is most Holy **knowne**;..............343. N.23, 1
He is the Rose of Sharon **known**:..............354. N.59, 4
But poore thou art, and **knowne** to be..........354. N.59, 13
God, as He's potent, so He's likewise **known**,....378. N.135, 1
Science in God, is **known** to be................378. N.136, 1
Lasciviousnesse is **known** to be................378. N.138, 1
In God there's nothing, but 'tis **known** to be....382. N.165, 1
God can do all things, save but what are **known**..382. N.166, 1
The repetition of the name made **known**.........383. N.174, 1
The first of Raine, the key of Hell next **known**:.390. N.224, 2
By houres we all live here, in Heaven is **known**..392. N.229, 1
In doing justice, God shall then be **known**,....393. N.234, 1
God hates the Duall Number; being **known**....396. N.249, 1
And I charge thee to bee **knowne**...............409. A.2, 75
This **known**, the rest of thy sad story tell,........417. A.8, 35
knowne, not thay giue agaïne, thay take..422. ins. H.106, 92f
— — — — — — — — — — — —, ...439. var. H.443, 17
— — — — — — — — — — —, ...450. var. A.9, 50

Knows Who **knowes** to live to morrow?..........65. H.170, 6
He **knowes** not Love, that hath not this truth proved, 73. H.186, 11
And why? he **knowes** he must of Cure despaire,.125. H.315, 5
Seldome or never, **knows** a wain,................143. H.369, 2
Manners **knowes** distance, and a man unrude..147. H.377, 31
He **knowes** well who do love him,............157. H.412, 22
And **knowes** not where i'th world to borrow more. 160. H.423, 4
And (Love **knowes**) tender as a chick.........167. H.443, 85
And have deserv'd as much (Love **knowes**)....169. H.449, 11
Man **knowes** where first he ships himselfe; but he 177. H.468, 1
When (God **knowes**) I'm tost about,...........348. N.41, 33
For, once in hell, none **knowes** Remission there...367. N.99, 2
Wip't out few, (God **knowes**) if any...........373. N.121, 10
And tho (Love **knows**).......................401. N.268, 28
her homewards, well she **knowes**..........430. ins. H.283, 20i

Labor See **Lip-labor**
Jove for our **labour** all things sells us...........36. H.106, 62
And **labour** with unequall heat:.................157. H.413, 6
If little **labour**, little are our gaines:........253. H.752, 1
Labour we must, and **labour** hard............380. N.152, 1
After thy **labour** take thine ease,.............334. H.1123, 1
Him, as He is, is **labour** without end............340. N.8, 2
Labour we must, and **labour** hard.............380. N.152, 1

Laborer Yet it is given to the **Labourer**..........390. N.223, 2

Laboring Be mindfull, that the **lab'ring** Neat....102. H.250, 45

Labors By whose tough **labours**, and rough hands, 101. H.250, 3
In vain our **labours** are, whatsoe're they be,....379. N.140, 1

Labyrinths Her eares, which like twoe **Laborinths** are plac'd 405. A.1, 39

Lace See **Hair-lace, Necklace**
The **lace**, to honour me, or it:....................14. H.34, 4
An erring **Lace**, which here and there............28. H.83, 5
Among ye, striving for her **lace**:..............114. H.283, 84
For sport my Julia threw a **Lace**..............116. H.284, 1
In the ascent of curious **Lace**,................202. H.560, 6

Laced Close, but not too strictly **lac't**:..........282. H.878, 4

Laces These **Laces**, Ribbands, and these Faules,..360. N.83, 44

Lack When thou thy selfe dar'st say, thy Iles shall **lack** 78. H.197, 47
And see his Robin Herrick **lack**,................290. H.918, 3

Lackeys That fleet of **Lackeyes**, which do run....239. H.696, 3

Lacon (Pardon, **Lacon** if I weep).............306. H.984, 31
Live long, **Lacon**, so adew...................306. H.984, 41

Lactea Ravisht, in that faire Via **Lactea**..........96. H.230, 4

Lad Unto the **lad** benighted.....................26. H.81, 16
And why, my pretty **Lad**, said she?.............50. H.139, 6
Then next Ile cause my hopefull **Lad**.........135. H.336, 121

Ladanum The Storax, Spiknard, Myrrhe, and **Ladanum**. 181. H.485, 4

Laden Back, and with White-thorn **laden** home...69. H.178, 46
Laden with wax and hony home:..............145. H.375, 10
Where **laden** spits, warp't with large Ribbs of Beefe, 146. H.377, 9
Like Leaves that **laden** are...................181. H.484, 3
What though your **laden** Altar now has wonne 432. ins. H.283, 70a

Ladies Trust me **Ladies**, I will do.............177. H.472, 1
As those your **Ladies** may in time be seene,...326. H.1080, 23

Ladies' But turn'd a **Ladies** Usher now, ('tis true:) 53. H.148, 2
Daintye tast for **ladyes** food....................418. A.9, 22

Lady Take time **Lady** while ye may............56. H.149, 120
Know, **Lady**, you have but your day:...........63. H.164, 3
The **Lady** of the Lobster is,..................93. H.223, 131
'Twas by your splendour (**Lady**) not by mine.....94. H.226, 8
Your storme is over; **Lady**, now appeare.......105. H.259, 7
Goddesse of Youth, and **Lady** of the Spring,....107. H.265, 1
So you sweet **Lady** (sweet as May)............126. H.318, 3
Troth **Lady**, no..............................137. H.340, 6
Since you are **Lady** of this Fairie land..........140. H.354, 10
To Thee, thy **Lady**, younglings, and as farre....146. H.377, 3
Honours my **Lady** and my Lord..................148. H.377, 76
Lady, this I know you'l say;..................194. H.527, 2
Jone, and my **Lady** have at that time one,......209. H.586, 5
Fie, (quoth my **Lady**) what a stink is here?....212. H.598, 1
Or sweet **Lady** reach to me...................223. H.638, 8
Of that sweet **Lady**, or that gallant Knight:....228. H.658, 2
As sweetly **Lady**, give me leave to tell ye,......249. H.733, 17
Like a poore **Lady** lost in Widdowhood:........251. H.745, 4
Jone as my **Lady** is as good i'th' dark.........279. H.864, 2
Next, let the Lord, and **Ladie** here............291. H.919, 9
Lady I intreate yow weare.....................417. A.9, 1

Lady-Flower Sweet **Lady-Flower**, I never brought.71. H.182, 13

Lives in the pretty Lady-flower................126. H.318, 11
Lady-flowers See, both these Lady-flowers decay:.61. H.159, 16
Lady's This Lady's short, that Mistresse she is tall;
163. H.437, 1
Ladyship Of hony, 'fore her Ladiship:..........71. H.182, 24
Lady-smock That Lady-smock, that Pansie, and that Rose
114. H.283, 94
Lag helpe on her pace; and though she lagg, yet stirre
430. ins. H.283, 20h
— — — — — — — — — —, ...433. ins. H.293, 31b
Laid See Inlaid, Interlaid, O'erlaid, Overlaid, Well-laid
Laid out for dead, let thy last kindnesse be........19. H.50, 1
No Spices wanting, when I'm laid by thee........20. H.55, 10
His head upon his hand he laid;................42. H.119, 7
This said, he laid his little scrip................71. H.182, 23
About this Urne, wherein thy Dust is laid,......73. H.186, 18
Those glaring colours laid......................76. H.193, 45
And laid them downe for Offrings at his feet....86. H.213, 32
And when before him we have laid our treasures,.87. H.213, 47
Or laid aside forlorne;.........................106. H.262, 6
And when I'm laid out for a Corse; then be....111. H.279, 3
Where being laid, all Faire signes looking on,..124. H.313, 11
Upon the rock, whose firm foundation laid,....143. H.365, 10
Has laid, I see.............................144. H.371, 14
No scurrile jest; no open Sceane is laid.......148. H.377, 77
Wherein my Love is laid......................156. H.412, 8
And laid....................................178. H.475, 9
As Robes laid by;...........................190. H.515, 40
If so be a Toad be laid......................209. H.587, 1
And once more yet (ere I am laid out dead)....214. H.612, 13
'Twas to his Batch, but Leaven laid there first...219. H.630, 4
Some laid her forth, while other wept,..........237. H.686, 7
For, once dead, and laid i'th grave,............238. H.691, 5
The stakes are laid: let's now apply..........243. H.716, 19
In this little Urne is laid....................262. H.782, 1
Let not thy Tomb-stone er'e be laid by me:....281. H.875, 1
Or'e which you'l walk, when I am laid beneath.
312. H.1013, 4
(As with a Magick) laid them all agen:......326. H.1080, 18
Sleeps, laid within some Ark of Flowers,........367. N.102, 5
Clean washt, and laid out for the Beere;........374. N.123, 12
To the tombe wher't must be layd............418. A.9, 44
Apple or Plume is neately layd,..........439. ins. H.443, 45b
Lair But husht in his laire he lies lurking:......225. H.643, 15
Lais Lais and Lucrece, in the night time are.....209. H.586, 3
For wanton Lais, then we have................283. H.885, 7
Lake Thy Bice, thy Umber, Pink, and Lake;....38. H.108, 2
Our slothfull passage o're the Stygian Lake,....248. H.730, 24
Lallage Chor. And Lallage the Judge shall be,..243. H.716, 5
Chor. And Lallage (with cow-like eyes)........243. H.716, 11
Chor. And Lallage shall tell by this,............244. H.716, 41
Lamb Then dream, ye heare the Lamb by many a bleat
36. H.106, 49
A Lamb....................................246. H.724, 17
Lamb's There a poor Lamb's a plenteous sacrifice..369. N.105, 4
Lambs My Weathers, Lambes, and wanton Kids are well,
86. H.213, 5
Chor. Pan pipe to him, and bleats of lambs and sheep,
86. H.213, 17
Lambs, by the Law, which God requires as due...341. N.9, 2
Lamb's-Wool With gentle lambs-wooll;..........317. H.1035, 20
Lame First, Jollies wife is lame; then next, loose-hipt:
62. H.163, 1
Lame, and bad times, with those are past,....134. H.336, 82
Truggin a Footman was; but now, growne lame,.283. H.882, 1
When drunck wth Rapture; Curse the blind & lame
412. A.3, 89
Lameness Bromsted a lamenesse got by cold and Beere;
201. H.555, 1
Lament Y'are left here to lament..............110. H.274, 19
Lamented See Long-lamented-widowhood
Lamented Maid! he won the day,...............360. N.83, 23
Laments Weep then for him, for whom laments...48. H.134, 7
Lamp Hereafter, shall smell of the Lamp, not thee.
46. H.128, 54
Eternall Lamp of Love! whose radiant flame....77. H.197, 10
The glorious Lamp of Heaven, the Sun..........84. H.208, 5
A Lamp Eternall to my Poetrie.................94. H.226, 6
My Lamp to you Ile give,....................328. H.1091, 7
Then is the Lamp and oyle extinguished..........359. N.80, 2
Lampreys For Pollio's Lampries in our dish.....133. H.336, 48
Lamps And look how all those heavenly Lamps acquire
3. Ded.H, 5
For, if we gaze on These brave Lamps too neer,.237. H.685, 11
(As Lamps for everlasting shining here:)......267. H.804, 8
Land There's the Land, or Cherry-Ile:............20. H.53, 6
(More blessed in thy Brasse, then Land)........35. H.106, 24
Let him the Land and Living finde;..............59. H.153, 3
Since you are Lady of this Fairie land..........140. H.354, 10
Sick is the Land to'th' heart; and doth endure..214. H.612, 5
On Land and on Seas,.........................225. H.643, 17
Of Land makes life, but sweet content.........230. H.662, 18
Man may want Land to live in; but for all,....267. H.807, 1
Continuall reaping makes a land wax old........292. H.922, 4
That soiles my land;.........................350. N.47, 42
Be the Seas water, and the Land all Sope,.......357. N.73, 3
Or Antique pledges, House or lande,............407. A.2, 9

Fayrie land: so ends his feast...........435. ins. H.293, ff
Landing Never can tell, where shall his Landing be.
177. H.468, 2
And Landing here, or safely Landing there,..316. H.1028. 13
Landlord The Landlord, or the Usurer.........200. H.552, 10
Lands We rip up first, then reap our lands.......101. H.250, 4
That the best compost for the Lands...........230. H.662, 23
We'l love the Divell, so he lands the gold.......266. H.800, 8
Language Teares are the noble language of the eye.
58. H.150, 6
There, where no language ever yet was known...60. H.156, 6
And this loves sweetest language is...........130. H.329, 19
And speaks in language keene:................259. H.772, 24
The Romane Language full, and superfine,....301. H.966, 13
Languages All Nations, Customes, Kindreds, Languages!
242. H.713, 10
Languish Me, then to make me languish stil!....34. H.103, 10
Lillies will languish; Violets look ill;..........41. H.118, 1
Or bid it languish quite away,.................108. H.267, 11
You shall not languish, trust me: Virgins here..138. H.343, 3
And dales again: Mir. No I will languish still;.159. H.421, 36
Me languish for the love of Thee?............177. H.471, 2
But here awhile to languish and decay;........193. H.522, 2
And thou do'st languish too:..................273. H.833, 3
But I languish, lowre, and Pine,...............309. H.996, 9
Studies themselves will languish and decay,....316. H.1033, 1
Languish and looke but thy returne see neuer......414. A.5, 8
Languishing But being absent, Love lies languishing.
13. H.30, 2
To make them Leane, and languishing at all...316. H.1028, 20
Laniere I heare in thee rare Laniere to sing;....276. H.851, 4
Lank That makes them looke so lanke, so Ghost-like still.
186. H.498, 6
Lank-stranger To the lanke-Stranger, and the sowre Swain;
146. H.377, 11
Lantern With my Lantern, and my Light,.........372. N.121, 2
Lap In her lap too I can lye....................17. H.43, 5
The lap of Proserpine.........................251. H.740, 12
— — — — — — — — — — —, ...428. var. H.197, 88
Laps See Dewlaps
Lar See Lares
Confin'd to live with private Larr:............37. H.106, 106
Go where I will, thou luckie Larr stay here,.....132. H.333, 9
(Larr thus conspiring with our mirth)........135. H.336, 124
As to thy Genius and thy Larre;..............146. H.377, 4
Part of which I give to Larr,..................152. H.393, 5
By jocund Larr,............................162. H.426, 19
Which wanting Lar, and smoke, hung weeping wet;
262. H.783, 12
or Lar will freeze to death at home:......431. ins. H.283, 60j
Lard The fattest Hogs we grease the more with Lard.
22. H.64, 2
To lard the shambles: Barbels bred............133. H.336, 46
One feeds on Lard, and yet is leane;..........173. H.461, 1
Swel'd with the Lard of others meat..........200. H.552, 16
Larded Can'st, and unurg'd, forsake that Larded fare,
37. H.106, 111
Two dayes y'ave larded here; a third, yee know,
146. H.377, 25
Cleane was the herth, the mantle larded jet;....262. H.783, 11
Larder The Larder fills with meat; the Bin with bread.
221. H.633, 45
The Larder leane?............................391. N.228, 2
Larders Your Larders too so hung with meat,...178. H.476, 5
Fulfill the Larders, and with strengthning bread.245. H.723, 5
Lares See Lar
Yet to the Lares this we'l say,................179. H.476, 36
To worship ye, the Lares,.....................234. H.674, 2
Large Large shoulders though he has, and well can beare,
60. H.158, 3
Ye shall see first the large and cheefe..........101. H.250, 28
Where laden spits, warp't with large Ribbs of Beefe,
146. H.377, 9
And large she spreads by dust, and sweat....148. H.377, 114
Left (of the large heart, and long hand)........218. H.626, 10
Here thou behold'st thy large sleek Neat......230. H.662, 35
His jawes had tir'd on some large Chine of Beefe.
273. H.835, 2
That Stubble stands, where once large eares have been.
275. H.843, 4
In an expansion no less large, then high;........301. H.966, 4
Broad of fore-head, large of eye,............305. H.984, 18
Their large Narrations, Incanonicall)..........330. H.1100, 4
Where Rams are wanting, or large Bullocks thighs,
369. N.105, 3
Largeness Of largeness, when th'are nothing so:.118. H.291, 10
Larger Not envying others larger grounds:.....230. H.662, 16
Lark Spring, sooner then the Lark, to fetch in May.
68. H.178, 14
Sweet singing Lark,..........................87. H.214, 5
Spring with the Larke, most comely Bride, and meet
216. H.618, 1
The Larke into the Trammell net:............231. H.662, 65
Larr See Lar, Lares
Lascivious A wanton and lascivious eye..........254. H.755, 1
Lasciviousness Lasciviousnesse is known to be....378. N.138, 1

Lash Boyes to the **lash**) that he do's whip with them.
39. H.110, 4
With a **lash** of a Bramble she rides now,......225. H.643, 9
They might escape the **lash** of punishment......291. H.920, 4
Lasie See Lazy
Lass Once a brisk and bonny **Lasse**,..............14. H.36, 4
Last Let us (though late) at **last** (my Silvia) wed;..8. H.10, 1
Me thought, (**last** night) love in an anger came,..16. H.40, 1
Laid out for dead, let thy **last** kindnesse be........19. H.50, 1
We two are **last** in Hell: what may we feare......33. H.101, 1
We'll wish, in Hell we had been **Last** and First...33. H.101, 4
Thy frown (**last** night) did bid me goe;........33. H.103, 3
In thy both **Last**, and Better Vow:..............34. H.106, 2
The **last** is but the least; the first doth tell......35. H.106, 9
Warnes the **last** Watch; but with the Dawne dost rise
36. H.106, 57
To shun the first, and **last** extreame...........38. H.106, 132
For second course, **last** night, a Custard came..47. H.131, 1
The **Last** Watch out, and saw the Dawning too.
52. H.146, 4
Such bashfulnesse at **last**.....................54. H.149, 28
And now the yellow Vaile, at **last**,............55. H.149, 71
May Death yet come at **last**;................58. H.149, 165
That my **last** Vow commends to you:........61. H.159, 21
Give my cold lips a kisse at **last**:...........61. H.159, 25
Will **last** to be a precious Stone,..............61. H.160, 9
At **last**, I find, (after my much to doe)........61. H.161, 5
Yet comming home, but somewhat late, (**last** night)
65. H.171, 4
When once true-lovers take their **last** Fare-well..73. H.186, 8
No, here Ile **last**, and walk (a harmless shade).73. H.186, 17
Like to a Bride, come forth my Book, at **last**,.76. H.194, 1
And **last**, when thee (deare Spouse) I disavow,
79. H.197, 91
He smarts at **last**, who do's not first take heed..79. H.199, 4
As my **last** Remembrances.......................88. H.218, 9
And since the **last** is dead, there's hope,.......93. H.223, 111
It is the **last** commends the Play...............94. H.225, 10
To the **last** succession:........................108. H.266, 18
Last, let us make our best abode,.............111. H.278, 5
My **last** request; for I.........................111. H.280, 10
Jove's is the first and **last**: The Morn's his due,.128. H.321, 3
And with a teare compare these **last**..........134. H.336, 81
Loth to depart, but yet at **last**, each one.......140. H.355, 1
If die I must, then my **last** vow shall be,......140. H.355, 9
Grac't (now at **last**) or glorifi'd by thee.......142. H.365, 2
The coblers getting time, is at the **Last**.......144. H.374, 2
To **last**, but not their ever: Vertues Hand.....148. H.377, 101
Or depth, these **last** may yeeld, and yearly shrinke,
148. H.377, 105
A Vicarige at **last** Tom Glasse got here,......151. H.385, 3
Last night thou didst invite me home to eate;.161. H.424, 1
Perfum'd (**last** day) to me:...................161. H.425, 2
Whereof (at **last**) to make....................173. H.460, 3
And go at **last**...............................176. H.467, 6
Last, may your Harrows, Shares and Ploughes,.179. H.476, 22
That Love **last** long; let it thy first care be....185. H.494, 1
And his **last** breath, let it be..................186. H.499, 3
Being drunke, who 'twas that Can'd his Ribs **last** night.
186. H.501, 4
With daily Fyers: The **last**, neglect of Wine:..197. H.539, 10
And perish at the **last**.......................211. H.596, 16
The happy fortune will not alwayes **last**.......218. H.621, 2
What made that mirth **last** night? the neighbours say,
219. H.630, 1
That your plenty **last** till when,...............224. H.638, 27
His inconsiderate Frenzie off (at **last**).......225. H.642, 20
Will whirle about, and blow them thence at **last**.
226. H.650, 4
And thus lesse **last**, then live our Day.........233. H.670, 31
That man's not said to live, but **last**:..........233. H.670, 33
At **last**, when prayers for the dead,............237. H.686, 13
That stroke most fear'd is, which is struck the **last**.
237. H.688, 2
Chose first, confirm'd next, & at **last** are crown'd.
241. H.707, 2
Thou'dst weep; but laugh, sho'd it not **last** a day.
241. H.709, 2
(Amongst mine honour'd) Thee (almost) the **last**:
256. H.763, 2
Must be the first man up, and **last** in bed:......259. H.771, 2
At **last**, i' th' noone of winter, did appeare.....262. H.783, 13
With the **last** yeeres brand...................263. H.784, 7
Then the **last** part of night, and first of day..278. H.858, 2
Last, may the Bride and Bridegroome be......291. H.919, 17
Blisse (**last** night drunk) did kisse his mothers knee:
295. H.943, 1
And then at **last** to truss the Epigram;........301. H.966, 8
Last, yet to be with These a Principall..........304. H.977, 2
Now (ai me) (ai me.) **Last** night............306. H.984, 33
Of my dearest deare **last** night;..............313. H.1018, 2
The first as Doctor, and the **last** as Knight.....322. H.1062, 12
Tell me, now **last**, what love will do;..........325. H.1075, 7
Where Pleasures met: at **last**, doe find,.......327. H.1082, 3
That love 'twixt men do's ever longest **last**....327. H.1083, 1
Their ends for Pleasure, do not live, but **last**...328. H.1088, 10
Washt with sweet ointments; Thus at **last** I come
335. H.1128, 3
Fames pillar here, at **last**, we set,.............335. H.1129, 1
To his Book's end this **last** line he'd have plac't,
335. H.1130, 1
And with the **last** he still directs the Just.........340. N.6, 4
The first by patience, and the **last** by paine.....343. N.24, 4
When the Priest his **last** hath praid,............348. N.41, 29
I dreamt, **last** night, Thou didst transfuse.......357. N.75, 1
Must **last** with Satan, to the end of life........362. N.91, 2
Last night I drew up mine Account,...........369. N.107, 1
Before my **last**, but here a living grave,......371. N.115, 2
A mighty storm **last** night..................373. N.122, 5
Brought at the **last** to th' utmost bit,..........376. N.124, 3
The **last** the Sabbath of Eternitie..............386. N.194, 4
Let me, though late, yet at the **last**, begin....392. N.230, 29
Before the **last** least sand of Thy ninth houre be run;
401. N.268, 8
Fould now thine armes, and in thy **last** looke reare
414. A.6, 7
But there to live, where Love shall **last** for ever.
417. A.8, 38
The two **last** fayle, and by experience make
422. ins. H.106, 92e
— — — — — — — — — — —, ...423. var. H.128, 12
— — — — — — — — — — —, ...426. var. H.197, 40
— — — — — — — — — — —, ...428. var. H.208, 11
Welcome at **last** unto the Threshold, Time
431. ins. H.283, 60k
— — — — — — — — — — —, ...442. var. H.465, 69
Lasted While they liv'd, or **lasted** here:.........187. H.503, 2
Long I have **lasted** in this world; (tis true)....328. H.1088, 3
Last-full — — — — — — — — —, ...427, var. H.197, 67
Lasting The Pillars up of **lasting** Jet,..........149. H.377, 124
Those Garments **lasting** evermore,.............393. N.231, 1
Lastly Then **lastly**, let some weekly-strewings be...9. H.14, 15
Then (**lastly**) July comes, and she...............23. H.70, 7
Lastly, safely buryed.........................38. H.107, 6
Lastly, with friends t'enjoy our dayes..........42. H.121, 4
Squint-ey'd, hook-nos'd; and **lastly**, Kidney-lipt.
62. H.163, 2
Oh fie upon 'em! **Lastly** too, all witt..........150. H.382, 17
Lastly, be mindfull (when thou art grown great)
181. H.483, 13
Lastly, if thou canst win a kisse...............354. N.59, 15
Lastly, that JESUS is a Deed..................359. N.78, 15
And **Lastly**, see thou bring to hym..............408. A.2, 73
Lasts See Outlasts
Late Let us (though **late**) at last (my Silvia) wed;.8. H.10, 1
Quickned of **late** by Pearly showers;............25. H.78, 6
One silent night of **late**,........................26. H.81, 1
Said he, with these **late** showrs.................27. H.81, 28
Making thy peace with heav'n, for some **late** fault,
36. H.106, 59
Ah! then too **late**, close in your chamber keeping,
63. H.164, 12
Yet comming home, but somewhat **late**, (last night)
65. H.171, 4
Ships have been drown'd, where **late** they danc't before.
85. H.212, 2
Phill, the **late** dead, the **late** dead Deare,........104. H.256, 8
Groynes, for his fleshly Burglary of **late**,......106. H.261, 1
Late fatned in a piece of cloth:...............120. H.293, 42
No noise of **late** spawn'd Tittyries:............126. H.319, 2
No new devise, or **late** found trick,............126. H.319, 5
Early setts ope to feast, and **late**:..............147. H.377, 46
Squirrils and childrens teeth **late** shed,........166. H.443, 55
Late you come in; but you a Saint shall be,..188. H.510, 3
Of **late** struck one; and now I see the prime..207. H.575, 63
The morrowes life too **late** is, Live to-day.....228. H.655, 2
No man comes **late** unto that place from whence
228. H.656, 1
And when the Trumpet which thou **late** hast found
257. H.763, 17
Long Locks of **late** our Zelot Peason weares,..275. H.843, 1
Yet the houres say 'tis **late**:...................276. H.850, 4
It (Ah!) too **late** repents me..................296. H.946, 9
Welcome to this my Colledge, and though **late**..305. H.983, 1
Goe thou forth my booke, though **late**;........334. H.1125, 1
Abundant plagues I **late** have had,.............354. N.57, 1
And our **late** spring.............................375. N.123, 59
Let me, though **late**, yet at the last, begin....392. N.230, 29
Holde their Eternall fiers; and ours of **Late**....411. A.3, 43
Lately To me my Julia **lately** sent...............13. H.32, 1
I have lost, and **lately**, these...................15. H.39, 1
Julia and I did **lately** sit.......................19. H.49, 1
Love, like a Gypsie, **lately** came;..............63. H.166, 1
Was **lately** whipt for lying with a Wench.......79. H.199, 2
As **lately** I a Garland bound,...................96. H.229, 1
That **lately** I offended,.......................100. H.246, 3
Lately made of flesh and blood:...............123. H.310, 2
Or like a medow being **lately** mown..........159. H.421, 21
Nor my rare *Phil, that **lately** was............186. H.497, 15
Those paines it **lately** felt before.............189. H.514, 4
That **lately** kissed thee.........................231. H.663, 8
An Orphan left him (**lately** dead.).............246. H.724, 20
And Rubies **lately** polished:..................268. H.811, 6
Hanch, since he (**lately**) did interre his wife,..275. H.842, 1

I lately fri'd but now behold................290. H.915, 1
Where is the Babe but lately sprung?.........367. N.102, 2
Of Him, we lately seal'd up in this Tombe?...403. N.271, 4
— — — — — — — — — — —, ...434. var. H.293, 42
Lather See Soap-like-lather
Laths Whose Ribs the Laths are, & whose Flesh the Loame. 279. H.865, 2
Lations The Motions, Lations, and the Signes...47. H.133, 4
Latmos I meane the Court: Let Latmos be....183. H.492, 17
Laugh When thou shalt laugh at my Religious dust; 49. H.138, 3
And laugh no more; or laugh, and lie down next. 111. H.277, 2
Laugh at my scraps of cloaths, and shun......235. H.677, 5
Thou'dst weep; but laugh, sho'd it not last a day. 241. H.709, 2
— — — — — — — — — — —, ...442. var. H.575, 38
To laugh and quaff and drink old sherry...445. ins. H.730, 26c
Laughed Y'ave laught enough (sweet) vary now your Text; 111. H.277, 1
Anthea laught, and fearing lest excesse........311. H.1006, 1
Laughest Then while thou laugh'st; Ile, sighing, crie, 303. H.973, 5
Laughing Then laughing loud, he flew............27. H.81, 33
By laughing too, and lying downe,............291. H.919, 21
Laughs Bice laughs, when no man speaks; and doth protest 265. H.795, 1
Laughter Those with a shout, and these with laughter. 101. H.250, 18
What He with laughter speaks, heare thou with tears. 355. N.63, 2
Our present Teares here (not our present laughter) 362. N.90, 1
Launders Sudds Launders Bands in pisse; and starches them 98. H.237, 1
Laundresses The Laundresses, They envie her good-luck, 178. H.474, 3
Laureate Your Name to be a Laureat Wreathe to Hir, 99. H.245, 7
The paper gild, and Laureat the pen...........141. H.359, 6
With Yvorie wrists, his Laureat head, and steeps 206. H.575, 41
Thy Poet, and Thy Prophet Lawreat...........398. N.262, 4
Laurel When Laurell spirts 'ith fire, and when the Hearth 7. H.8, 5
And with my Lawrell crown thy Golden Urne....11. H.22, 4
A sacred Laurel springing from my grave:......30. H.89, 5
The Laurell, Mirtle, Oke, and Ivie too.........41. H.117, 10
A Laurel for her, (ever young as love).........94. H.224, 8
But like a Laurell, to grow green for ever.......98. H.240, 2
Of crackling Laurell, which fore-sounds,........127. H.319, 23
Come unto thee for Laurell, having spent,.....143. H.365, 5
That henceforth none be Laurel crown'd but Thee. 150. H.383, 2
Be lesse anothers Laurell, then thy praise......297. H.947, 14
Put on thy Laurell then; and in that trimme..299. H.956, 11
I have my Laurel Chaplet on my head,.......322. H.1062, 1
Give thee the Laurell Crowne for lot;.........334. H.1123, 4
The work is done; now let my Lawrell be.....398. N.262, 1
Lautitious Sho'd meet and tire, on such lautitious meat, 262. H.783, 3
Law To the indulgence of the rugged Law:.....201. H.557, 2
Law is to give to ev'ry one his owne...........201. H.557, 10
And by the Law I ought to stay..............293. H.934, 7
Offer thy gift; but first the Law commands....299. H.957, 1
(A happy Realme! When no compulsive Law,..326. H.1080, 19
Lambs, by the Law, which God requires as due...341. N.9, 2
By Law, the Bond once cancelled............370. N.107, 15
This Law; that He and I part stakes..........376. N.127, 6
Because the Law forbad to sit and crie........384. N.180, 3
Tortur'd her love, not to transgresse the Law...384. N.180, 6
Lawes See Laws
Yet their Three praises, praise but One; that's Lawes. 276. H.851, 8
Sho'd I not grieve (my Lawes) when every Lute, 288. H.907, 3
Lawful But all are toucht (like lawfull plate)....236. H.681, 5
Lawless Are made farre worse, by lawless liberty..307. H.990, 2
With lawlesse tooth the floure of wheate:......310. H.1004, 4
Lawn See Cobweb-lawn
Of Tiffanie, or Cob-web Lawne;.................8. H.11, 6
Under a Lawne, then skyes more cleare,.........25. H.78, 1
A Lawne about the shoulders thrown............28. H.83, 3
That Roses shew, when misted o're with Lawn..34. H.104, 4
Out-side silk, and out-side Lawne;.............76. H.195, 7
Away with silks, away with Lawn,.............154. H.402, 1
By the Assention of thy Lawn, see All.........154. H.403, 6
Wo'd I see Lawn, clear as the Heaven, and thin? 158. H.416, 1
A Lawn for me, so fine and thin,.............164. H.442, 4
Your Grave her Bosome is, the Lawne the Stone. 249. H.734, 4
A Lawn, that thou mayst looke................271. H.824, 10
Halfe with a Lawne of water hid,............294. H.939, 6
Which makes them shewe like roses vnder lawne. 404. A.1, 24
Lawn's The blush of cherries, when a Lawn's cast over. 158. H.416, 4
Lawns Twilight is yet, till that her Lawnes give way; 34. H.104, 5
Yet, when your Lawns & Silks shal flow;......76. H.193, 52
To these smooth Lawns, my mirthfull Roundelay. 159. H.421, 10
Lawny Next, when those Lawnie Filmes I see..202. H.560, 13
They, weeping, spread a Lawnie Loome,.......237. H.686, 15
Within her Lawnie Continent,...............250. H.740, 3
Lawny-firmament 'Tis like a Lawnie-Firmament as yet 82. H.204, 5
Laws See Lawes
The wronged Client ends his Lawes...........190. H.515, 23
Who dost so fitly with the Lawes unite,.......201. H.557, 5
When Lawes full power have to sway, we see...213. H.608, 1
As many Lawes and Lawyers do expresse......244. H.718, 1
When Thou Thy Lawes didst promulgate,......393. N.232, 4
The Lawes of Action, will both sigh, and weep;.399. N.263, 37
Growe vpp wth Mylder Lawes to knowe........407. A.2, 25
Lawyer Case is a Lawyer, that near pleads alone,.303. H.975, 1
Lawyers As many Lawes and Lawyers do expresse 244. H.718, 1
Lay To get thine ends, lay bashfulnesse aside;......8. H.12, 1
Or for mine honour, lay me in that Tombe......20. H.55, 7
For which, before thy Threshold,we'll lay downe 41. H.117, 7
Cupid as he lay among.......................50. H.139, 1
Trouble Death to lay agen....................52. H.145, 6
Thunder and Lightning Ile lay by, ...58. H.152, 5
I kneele for help; O! lay that hand on me,....62. H.161, 12
Made him take up his shirt, lay down his sword. 65. H.171, 6
As Julia once a-slumb'ring lay,................71. H.182, 1
An Olive-branch before me lay:................73. H.187, 4
Cupid and his Mother lay......................74. H.190, 5
But lesse presume to lay a Plait upon.........82. H.204, 3
Betweene whose glories, there my lips Ile lay,..96. H.230, 3
And prethee, let's lay..........................99. H.243, 2
Makes holy these, all others lay aside:........114. H.283, 98
No fault in women, to lay on.................118. H.291, 5
Here down my wearyed limbs Ile lay;.........123. H.306, 1
About your eares; and lay upon..............127. H.319, 43
Come blithefull Neatherds, let us lay..........243. H.716, 1
Lay to thy stake a lustie Steere,.............243. H.716, 14
Chor. Lay by a while your Pipes, and rest,....243. H.716, 35
Chor. And lay we down our Pipes together,....244. H.716, 47
And after that, lay downe some silver pence,....245. H.723, 9
She goes her long white egg to lay............246. H.724, 12
Fortune her selfe can lay no claim to it........272. H.830, 2
Lay it underneath the head;...................284. H.888, 2
Neer the childs heart lay a knife:............284. H.889, 2
Which quencht, then lay it up agen,..........285. H.893, 3
Lay by the good a while; a resting field.......292. H.922, 1
That let her lay..............................296. H.946, 4
Lay of our safeties new foundation:...........300. H.961, 12
Tell, and I'le lay down my Pipe..............305. H.984, 14
Maidens when ye Leavens lay,................322. H.1063, 2
So that the man that will but lay his eares,....330. H.1100, 15
Thou mak'st my teeming Hen to lay..........350. N.47, 45
Whereon the blessed Babie lay,...............355. N.60, 4
To lay thy pen and ink aside?................357. N.72, 12
And other flowers, lay upon.................359. N.83, 11
All, all we lay upon thy Tombe..............360. N.83, 48
Thy mercy-seat I'le lay before;...............369. N.107, 6
My mouth I'le lay unto Thy wound...........377. N.129, 5
No, lay thy stately terrours by,..............393. N.232, 7
Lays See Holy-lays
So sure he layes claime to the Evensong.......128. H.321, 6
No Goose layes good eggs that is trodden drye...223. H.636, 4
If Wars goe well; each for a part layes claime:..260. H.774, 3
More stripes, then God layes on the sufferer....393. N.235, 2
And lays it gently on ye Pyle,................413. A 4, 28
— — — — — — — — — —, ...423. var. H.128, 35
Lazar Who, railing, drives the Lazar from his door, 238. H.694, 1
Lazy The lazie man the most doth love...........53. H.147, 14
Lasie to others, but be long to me..............141. H.357, 2
Lead Of Wife) about I'le lead;...................13. H.31, 8
Then gently lead her on......................55. H.149, 77
And all faire Signs lead on our Shepardesse.....85. H.213, 2
As Fate do's lead or draw us; none,..........132. H.336, 6
To which, with silver feet lead you the way,..140. H.354, 7
All Oeconomicks, know'st to lead.............148. H.377, 90
And He, who us'd to leade the Country-round,.159. H.421, 5
Wine lead him on. Thus to a Grove...........165. H.443, 19
Lead by the shine of Snails; a way...........165. H.443, 22
Shalt lead, like young Apollo.................184. H.492, 36
As great men lead; the meaner follow on,......214. H.614, 3
A little lead best fits a little Float;...........249. H.733, 14
Examples lead us, and wee likely see,..........255. H.759, 1
In great Processions many lead the way......256. H.763, 3
Brasse, Leade, or Tinne, throw into th' mould;.297. H.948, 10
Lead on faire paranymphs, the while her eyes, 430. ins. H.283, 20a
Leaden I have a leaden, thou a shaft of gold;...333. H.1120, 1
Leader See Fore-leader

Leading That Leading Cloud, I follow'd still,....67. H.175, 19
But with thy fair Fates leading thee, Go on....155. H.405, 3
Cast, leading his Euredice through hell,..........411. A.3, 68
Leads When such a Light as You are leads the way:
3. Ded.H., 2
While Domiduca leads the way:...............54. H.149, 42
There is, that to the Chappel leads:.............90. H.223, 2
And as he leads the way.......................151. H.388, 6
She leads on a brace.........................333. H.1122, 8
Sin leads the way, but as it goes, it feels........362. N.86, 1
Leaf Beset with Mirtles; whose each leafe drops Love.
107. H.265, 4
First dyes the Leafe, the Bough next, next the Tree.
203. H.565, 4
That Dress, this Sprig, that Leaf, this Vine;..215. H.616, 23
O Volume worthy leafe, by leafe and cover.....415. A.7, 5
Leafy Now swaggers in her Leavy gallantry......224. H.642, 6
Leafy-throne Your Leavie-Throne (with Lilly-work) possesse;
107. H.265, 9
Leafy-trees The leavie-trees nod in a still-born peace.
105. H.259, 6
Lean Let me be leane, and cold, and once grown poore,
31. H.93, 3
My old leane wife, shall kisse it dry:.........134. H.336, 84
One feeds on Lard, and yet is leane;.........173. H.461, 1
He raves through leane, he rages through the fat;
191. H.518, 3
Be she fat, or be she leane,...................253. H.750, 16
To make them Leane, and languishing at all...316. H.1028, 20
The Larder leane?...........................391. N.228, 2
Your leane scalp to sensuring...................418. A.9, 32
Leander When as Leander young was drown'd,...42. H.119, 1
Of Hero, and Leander; then Ile bring.........206. H.575, 26
Leanest While leanest Beasts in Pastures feed,...77. H.196, 1
Lean-horned Lean-horn'd, before I come again..176. H.465, 78
Leap Untill the fired Chesnuts leape...........127. H.319, 33
Learn But learn, that Time once lost,............53. H.149, 7
Or learne some way how to forget............60. H.159, 7
Learne of me what Woman is..................76. H.195, 2
My Scholar, and learn this of me:..........102. H.253, 2
Learn this of me, where e'r thy Lot doth fall;..153. H.396, 1
Let Kings and Rulers, learne this line from me;.302. H.971, 1
I'le learn to be content.......................368. N.104, 11
Let them read this booke and learne............418. A.9, 55
Learned Stand before you, my learn'd Diocesan?..64. H.163, 2
Those learned men brought Incense, Myrrhe, and Gold,
86. H.213, 30
And learn'd Musicians shall to honour Herricks.143. H.366, 3
No such crab'd vizard: Thou hast learnt thy Train,
147. H.377, 35
We know y'are learn'd i'th' Muses, and no lesse
187. H.506, 7
Then unto Dancing forth the learned Round....206. H.575, 19
Health is no other (as the learned hold).......236. H.683, 1
God (as the learned Damascen doth write)....381. N.161, 1
Or Good at all, (as learn'd Aquinas saith.)....383. N.173, 2
Paradise is (as from the Learn'd I gather)....383. N.177, 1
To burn, not shine (as learned Basil saith.)....387. N.202, 2
Either as when (the learned Schoolemen say)..388. N.210, 2
Learning What Wisdome, Learning, Wit, or Worth,
48. H.134, 1
By daily Learning we wax old................187. H.505, 2
Least See Lest
In any one, the least indecencie:................10. H.16, 2
The most I love, when I the least expresse it.....15. H.38, 6
The last is but the least; the first doth tell....35. H.106, 9
Hither the least one theeving thought:..........71. H.182, 14
To give the least disturbance to her haire:......82. H.204, 2
For his Sheep-shearers. Mir. True, these are the least.
86. H.213, 8
And how she is her owne least part:..........103. H.253, 16
He that may sin, sins least; Leave to transgresse
109. H.270, 1
Eates to ones thinking, of all there, the least...118. H.292, 2
For the least trespasse; 'cause the mind........175. H.465, 61
The least grim looke, or cast a frown on you:..222. H.634, 8
This not the least is, which belongs to Kings...260. H.774, 2
No one least Branch there left behind:........304. H.980, 6
There is not one least solecisme found;........307. H.992, 4
Who may do most, do's least: The bravest will
321. H.1057, 1
Things precious are least num'rous: Men are prone
339. N.1, 5
The Devill tempts not least.....................344. N.28, 2
Least loane of Thine, half Restitution?........368. N.103, 6
Of locall motion, in no least respect,..........385. N.186, 3
Without the least hope of affection............392. N.230, 26
To shun the least Temptation to a sin;.......392. N.230, 30
Before the last least sand of Thy ninth houre be run;
401. N.268, 8
Least thankes to Nature, most to Art.....421. ins. H.106, 26b
Thy glaring fires, least in theire sight the sinne
424. ins. H.128, 46a
— — — — — — — — — — —, ...424. var. H.164, 10
Leather And feares in summer to weare out the lether:
332. H.1116, 2
Leathern Next, his wilde eares, like Lethern wings full spread,
33. H.99, 3
Leave Ile leave thy heart a dying................27. H.81, 36
Could'st leave the City, for exchange, to see....35. H.106, 3
Since I must leave thee; and enforc'd, must say.46. H.128, 39
She soon wo'd leave her spheare,...............54. H.149, 37
As if to stir it scarce had leave:..............66. H.175, 6
Love is most loth to leave the thing beloved.....73. H.186, 12
Ile leave thee, and to Pansies come;...........74. H.191, 5
And leave no scent behind ye:..................83. H.207, 2
I leave this light;..........................95. H.227, 31
He that may sin, sins least; Leave to transgresse
109. H.270, 1
Troth, leave the flowers, and Maids, take me...112. H.281, 4
So vanish hence, but leave a name, as sweet,..131. H.331, 9
And leave no sound; nor piety,..............132. H.336, 2
Yet ere ye enter, give us leave to set.........140. H.354, 3
Thou gav'st me leave to kisse;...............142. H.364, 1
Thou gav'st me leave to wooe;...............142. H.364, 2
Come, leave this loathed Country-life, and then..171. H.456, 1
Let's leave a longer time to wait,.............179. H.476, 28
When of the Banks their leave they take;......180. H.478, 6
Nor leave the search, and proofe, till Thou canst find
181. H.483, 3
Nor will they leave Thee, till they both have shown
181. H.483, 7
Mean time, let Lycidas have leave to Pipe to thee.
184. H.492, 43
Those crimson clouds i'th' cheeks & lips leave shining.
207. H.576, 2
When I must leave the World (and you)........218. H.626, 2
As sweetly Lady, give me leave to tell ye,.....249. H.733, 17
And Aire-like, leave no pression to be seen....250. H.737, 7
The Soldiers leave the Field with equall feare...268. H.813, 4
This Blessing I will leave thee, ere I go,......269. H.818, 3
And leave their servants, but the smoak & sweat:
272. H.826, 3
And leave their subjects but the starved ware..272. H.826, 6
As for our selves to leave some frankinsence....295. H.940, 4
Leave others Beauty, to set up withall..........299. H.958, 6
With spice; that done, Ile leave thee to thy rest.
300. H.960, 6
And leave me here behind thee;..............323. H.1068, 2
Rules but by leave, and takes his Crowne on trust.
331. H.1103, 2
To leave this life, not loving it, but Thee.......352. N.51, 14
And leave thee sleeping in thy Urn............361. N.83, 78
Leave that without, then enter in;.............366. N.98, 6
No crack or Schisme leave i'th subtill skin:....385. N.184, 2
God's said to leave this place, and for to come....385. N.186, 1
I'le leaue thee then Compleatly riche.............407. A.2, 6
Faile and scarce leaue to be showne............418. A.9, 29
— — — — — — — — —, ...426. var. H.197, 48
Leaved See Four-leaved, Lucky-four-leaved
Leaven See Love-like-leaven, Over-leaven-looks
Where Leaven wants, there Levill lies the nose..154. H.401, 4
A Tribe of one Lip; Leven, and of One........199. H.545, 3
'Twas to his Batch, but Leaven laid there first..219. H.630, 4
Love is a Leven, and a loving kisse...........298. H.950, 1
The Leven of a loving sweet-heart is...........298. H.950, 2
No jot of Leven must be found...............366. N.98, 3
Sacke is my life, my leaven, salt to all....426. ins. H.197, 48a
Leavened See O'er-leavened
Leavens Maidens when ye Leavens lay,.........322. H.1063, 2
Leaves Who with thy leaves shall wipe (at need)....6. H.5, 1
The leaves) her temples I behung:.............16. H.41, 11
But when I crept with leaves to hide..........17. H.41, 18
With leaves and mosse-work for to cover me:...19. H.50, 2
Brought leaves and mosse to cover her:.........46. H.130, 6
And Leaves did heale, all sick of humane seed:..61. H.161, 2
As ayrie as the leaves of gold;................66. H.175, 2
Feare not; the leaves will strew...............68. H.178, 19
What? shall we two our endlesse leaves take here
73. H.186, 9
Grapes, before Herrick leaves Canarie Sack.....78. H.197, 48
Leaves dropping downe the honyed dew,........86. H.213, 40
Some prank them up with Oaken leaves:......101. H.250, 20
Encarv'd upon the Leaves and Rind............169. H.449, 8
Like Sybels Leaves, throughout the ample world?
172. H.459, 4
But you are lovely Leaves, where we..........176. H.467, 13
Like Leaves that laden are...................181. H.484, 3
That scarcely stirs the nodding leaves of Trees:
225. H.642, 16
He sets his foot, he leaves rich compost there...259. H.771, 8
Or see thy injur'd Leaves serve well,...........275. H.844, 5
For look how many leaves there be............304. H.980, 7
After leaves, the tree must fall...............321. H.1058, 2
We take our leaves now of the Loome,.......374. N.123, 35
Like rose leaves, white and redd seeme mingled..404. A.1, 18
Leavest And scarce leav'st here.................85. H.211, 10
Thou leav'st our Hills, our Dales, our Bowers,.183. H.492, 13
And leav'st them (as they feed and fill).......230. H.662, 44
Leaving Leaving their Poet (being now grown old)
151. H.387, 3
Leaving no Fame to long Posterity:............210. H.592, 2
Leaving here the body dead:..................211. H.593, 2

Leaving them to a pittied nakednesse...........224. H.642, 12
Leaving no shew, where stood the Capitoll.....252. H.745, 16
Leaving a distance for the beawtious small......406. A.1, 89
Lecher See Letcher
To keep out the Letcher, and keep in the whore: 97. H.233, 2
The Whore to come out, or the Letcher come in. 97. H.233, 4
Lecture Wo'd have this Lecture read,...........105. H.257, 26
Led See Misled, Star-led-birth
Led by some light that flows from thee.........33. H.98, 8
Thus held, or led by thee, I shall..............33. H.98, 9
Led by thy conscience; to give.................35. H.106, 12
But still thy wife, by chast intentions led,......35. H.106, 41
Now, we must know, the Elves are led........92. H.223, 74
Where we'le present our Oberon led...........165. H.443, 3
Twice has Pudica been a Bride, and led.......180. H.477, 1
Love's Chorus led by Cupid; and we'l be......206. H.575, 22
Led her through Hells obscuritie:.............265. H.798, 6
Leech Leech boasts, he has a Pill, that can alone,.125. H.315, 1
Leek Help from the Garlick, Onyon, and the Leek, 78. H.197, 58
Lees But the base dregs and lees of vestiments?..302. H.970, 2
And his skill runs on the lees;.................347. N.41, 15
Left Onely Herrick's left alone,.................16. H.39, 12
But they left Hope-seed to fill up againe........52. H.146, 8
Before that we have left to dreame:...........69. H.178, 48
Left in this rak't-up Ash-heap, as a mark.......78. H.197, 37
True, I confesse I left thee, and appeale.......78. H.197, 41
Left to all posterity............................88. H.218, 6
And left of love, are crown'd..................106. H.262, 4
Y'are left here to lament......................110. H.274, 19
Must all be left, no one plant found............132. H.336, 10
Looks forward, scornes what's left behind:......132. H.336, 14
Remainder left of Brasse or stone,............146. H.376, 8
No Orphans pittance, left him, serv'd to set....149. H.377, 123
Despite of all concussions left the Stem........170. H.451, 3
Save but some few Beanes left,................173. H.460, 2
I have still the manners left...................182. H.489, 10
Their lives in sweets, and left in death perfume..185. H.496, 4
We two (as Reliques left) will have...........190. H.515, 11
His feet were helpt, and left his Crutch behind:.201. H.555, 3
Left (of the large heart, and long hand).......218. H.626, 10
Ill us'd, then Babes left fatherless.............218. H.626, 15
So little left, as if they ne'r had been:.........231. H.664, 4
These are the Children I have left;............236. H.681, 3
An Orphan left him (lately dead.).............246. H.724, 20
No one least Branch there left behind:.........304. H.980, 6
One seed of life left, 'tis to keep............361. N.83, 59
One part thereof left still unfinished:...........384. N.178, 2
Of that, which we do nominate the Left........394. N.240, 2
Onely, there's left a little froth,..............400. N.266, 12
Wth Joyes before, and Pleasures left behind:....411. A.3, 64
Leg Fain would I kiss my Julia's dainty Leg,...139. H.349, 1
To beawtify the legg and foote withall...........406. A.1, 90
Legacy Of my love a Legacie,..................88. H.218, 5
Legend And if their Legend doe not lye,........93. H.223, 109
Here is the Legend of those Saints.............169. H.449, 5
Legs Me thought, her long small legs & thighs....16. H.41, 5
Her legs were such Diana shows,..............51. H.142, 13
Hands, and thighs, and legs, are all...........59. H.155, 5
False in legs, and false in thighes;.............77. H.195, 9
Shew me thy feet; shew me thy legs, thy thighes; 154. H.403, 1
Her decent legs, cleane, long and small........247. H.729, 4
His hungry belly borne by Legs Jaile-free.....332. H.1112, 4
Suffer thy legs, but not thy tongue to walk:....341. N.12, 1
Her leggs with twoe cleire calves like siluer tride 406. A.1, 87
— — — — — — — — — — —, ...448. var. A.1, 90
Legs' Part of her leggs sinceritie:..................12. H.27, 4
Lemon — — — — — — — — —, ...427. var. H.197, 58
Lemster Soft then the finest Lemster Ore.......165. H.443, 28
Lend And lend a gentle eare to one report......86. H.213, 11
To lend the world your scent and smile........126. H.318, 5
Her Eyes the Glow-worme lend thee,...........217. H.619, 1
Will lend thee their light,.....................217. H.619, 14
Or let the Unshorne God lend thee his Lyre,..299. H.956, 13
Lendest Thou lend'st to me;.......................29. H.87, 4
Lends — — — — — — — — —, ...432. var. H.283, 83
Length In length each finger doth his next excell, 406. A.1, 101
Lent One onely daughter lent to me:............41. H.116, 4
Health is the first good lent to men;............42. H.121, 1
Or that this Yonker keeps so strict a Lent,....122. H.305, 3
My wreaths on those, who little gave or lent...143. H.365, 6
Those minutes, Time has lent us here..........233. H.670, 16
That little, Fates me gave or lent..............246. H.724, 8
What God and Nature lent....................346. N.38, 12
A Lent for thee, to fast and weep...........361. N.83, 60
Ten thousand Talents lent me, Thou dost write: 368. N.103, 9
With that small stock, Thy Bounty gave or lent..368. N.104, 12
And that's to keep thy Lent...................391. N.228, 24
Lentils The scraps of Lintells chitted, Pease 439. ins. H.443, 45i
Lents He keeps not one, but many Lents i' th'yeare. 122. H.305, 6
Lentulus Fabius, and Cotta, Lentulus, all live.....41. H.117, 3
Leopard's See Libbard's
Leopard's bane See Libbard's
Leprosy There in your teeth much Leprosie.......250. H.738, 4
A House spred through with Leprosie........310. H.1004, 12
In them a glorious leprosie...................311. H.1010, 4
Lesbia Had Lesbia (too-too-kind) but known...104. H.256, 11
Less See Edgeless, Graceless, Hairless, Noiseless, Tongueless
Wayes lesse to live, then to live well:.........35. H.106, 10
Lesse with a neat, then needfull diet...........35. H.106, 30
Many a lesse and greater spheare...............47. H.133, 2
But lesse presume to lay a Plait upon..........82. H.204, 3
Amin. Good day, Mirtillo. Mirt. And to you no lesse: 85. H.213, 1
And all most sweet; yet all lesse sweet then he. 86. H.213, 38
Lesse in these Marble stones, then in thy story...89. H.219, 22
High, and passions lesse of heat..............96. H.232, 10
While other Rusticks, lesse attent.............101. H.250, 23
They make a feast lesse great then nice.......119. H.293, 12
Good things, that come of course, far lesse doe please, 123. H.307, 1
Stray, to become lesse circular,..............134. H.336, 68
Thus, till we see the fire lesse shine...........136. H.336, 145
You, who are High born, and a Lord no lesse..141. H.359, 3
Wrinkles no more are, or no lesse,..............143. H.367, 1
That ebs from pittie lesse and lesse...........143. H.369, 4
High are These Statues here, besides no lesse..185. H.496, 7
Lesse is here, then in my heart................186. H.500, 4
We know y'are learn'd i'th' Muses, and no lesse 187. H.506, 7
Far lesse in number, then our foule dayes are...189. H.513, 2
Lesse for to catch a sheep, then me...........193. H.521, 46
Spread as He spreads; wax lesse as He do's wane; 196. H.537, 3
Dotes less on Nature, then on Art.............202. H.560, 18
But lesse that part,.........................210. H.591, 7
If not; expect to be no less...................218. H.626, 14
Less happy, less enjoying thee..............229. H.662, 4
And thus lesse last, then live our Day...........233. H.670, 31
Lesse by their own jemms, then those beams of thine. 234. H.673, 18
Sorrowes divided amongst many, lesse.........239. H.699, 1
To loose the button, is no lesse,................241. H.712, 1
By so much, vertue is the lesse,................254. H.754, 1
Nor art thou lesse esteem'd, that I have plac'd.256. H.763, 1
And for no less then Aromatick Wine..........262. H.783, 9
For more or lesse fruits they will bring,........264. H.787, 3
'Twas Cesars saying: Kings no lesse Conquerors are 271. H.825, 1
The more th'are drawn, the lesse they wil grow dry. 273. H.831, 2
Less then Apollo, that ursurp'st such Three?..276. H.851, 6
Lesse set for them, then spred for me.........282. H.881, 10
My care for thee is now the less;..............287. H.899, 5
And no less prais'd, then spread throughout the world. 288. H.907, 6
Be lesse anothers Laurell, then thy praise.....297. H.947, 14
For which I might extoll thee, but speake lesse, 298. H.955, 9
Thee lesse to taste, then to drink up their spring; 299. H.956, 2
And no lesse prais'd, then of the maides admir'd. 299. H.956, 10
Live long and lovely, but yet grow no lesse....299. H.958, 3
In an expansion no less large, then high;.....301. H.966, 4
Care keepes the Conquest; 'tis no lesse renowne, 307. H.989, 1
The good applaud: the peccant lesse condemne,.322. H.1062, 8
The truth of Travails lesse in bookes then Thee. 330. H.1100, 18
But yet still lesse then Grace can suffer here...341. N.10, 4
But all in smart have lesse, or greater shares...342. N.20, 2
To my heaven lesse run, then flie..............355. N.64, 6
Gods Bounty, that ebbs lesse and lesse,........358. N.76, 1
To make things sweet. Chor. Yet all less sweet then He. 365. N.97, 10
The lesse our sorrowes here and suffrings cease,.372. N.119, 1
I shall lesse swoone, then die for feare........393. N.232, 10
Heire-ship be lesse, by our adoption:...........395. N.248, 2
Lesse for to tast, then for to shew,...........400. N.266, 13
So that I dare, with farre lesse feare,...........402. N.269, 8
More Comely flowing: where les free..........407. A.2, 28
The Vertues Lesse, or Cardinall,..............409. A.2, 100
Lessen Oh then to lessen my dispaire.............414. A.5, 9
Lesson This lesson you must pearse to' th' truth.418. A.9, 39
Lessons The Proper Lessons for the Saints now dead: 209. H.584, 2
Lest But do not so; for feare, lest he..........39. H.108, 13
Prethee (lest Maids sho'd censure thee) but say.42. H.122, 9
Or smile more inly; lest thy looks beguile.....46. H.128, 46
Lest Issue lye asleep.........................53. H.149, 18
Lest they too far extend.......................76. H.193, 48
Lest a handsome anger flye,..................98. H.238, 13

Foule in these noble pastimes, **lest** ye call.....114. H.283, 86
Both, **lest** thou lose thy liberty:..............174. H.465, 26
Lest having that, or this,......................231. H.663, 3
Lest rapt from hence, I see thee lye..........275. H.844, 3
Lest we that Tallent spend:..................289. H.911, 17
Anthea laught, and fearing **lest** excesse........311. H.1006, 1
Wash clean the Vessell, **lest** ye soure.........320. H.1053, 1
Give unto all, **lest** he, whom thou deni'st,......391. N.226, 1
With holye fier **least** that itt dye................407. A.2, 24
But **Least** I should forgett his bedd..........409. A.2, 83
More mildlie **least** thy temptinge lookes beguile
424. ins. H.128, 46e

Let See Outlet
Let my Enchantments then be sung, or read........7. H.8, 4
Let rigid Cato read these Lines of mine..........7. H.8, 10
O Primroses! **let** this day be......................7. H.9, 5
Let us (though late) at last (my Silvia) wed;....8. H.10, 1
Let fall a Primrose, and with it a teare:........9. H.14, 14
Then lastly, **let** some weekly-strewings be.......9. H.14, 15
But if to moisture, **Let** the oyle..................9. H.15, 3
These sweets, but **let** them fly;..................9. H.15, 6
But pretty Fondling, **let** not fall................12. H.23, 5
But yet for Loves-sake, **let** thy lips doe this,.....14. H.35, 11
Work that to life, and **let** me ever dwell.......14. H.35, 13
Laid out for dead, **let** thy last kindnesse be......19. H.50, 1
And for your breaths too, **let** them smell.........20. H.54, 3
Then melted down, there **let** me lye.............23. H.68, 5
And **let** not Locks thus keep ye..................26. H.81, 8
Biancha, **Let**...................................29. H.87, 1
Let me be warme; **let** me be fully fed:...........31. H.93, 1
Let me be leane, and cold, and once grown poore,
31. H.93, 3
Next, **let** us marry:.............................31. H.94, 2
Touch not the Tyrant; **Let** the Gods alone.......32. H.97, 5
Thus **let** thy Rurall Sanctuary be............38. H.106, 137
Live, and live blest; thrice happy Paire; **Let** Breath,
38. H.106, 141
And **let** it be thy Pensils strife,...............38. H.108, 3
Let us sit, and quaffe our wine................39. H.111, 6
Rather then love, **let** me be ever lost;.........40. H.113, 5
Or **let** me 'gender with eternall frost..........40. H.113, 6
Let there be Patrons; Patrons like to thee,.....41. H.117, 1
One slit's enough to **let** Adultry in............44. H.126, 4
Let others drink thee freely; and desire.......46. H.128, 49
And love thee; but not taste thee. **Let** my Muse.46. H.128, 51
The lid began to **let** out day;..................46. H.130, 9
And **let** them through a Zodiac run:............47. H.133, 6
Let but That Mighty Cesar speak, and then,..52. H.146, 13
Or **let** Love's fire goe out,.....................53. H.149, 5
Let her, her fillets first......................55. H.149, 84
Let kisses, in their close,.....................57. H.149, 143
Let bounteous Fate your spindles full.........58. H.149, 161
Let them not cut the thred....................58. H.149, 163
Come, **Let** us now away......................58. H.149, 168
Let all chaste Matrons, when they chance to see
58. H.151, 1
Let him the Land and Living finde;...........59. H.153, 3
Let me alone to fit the mind..................59. H.153, 4
For pitty **let** a teare be shed;.................61. H.159, 23
I live for ever; **let** the rest all lye............63. H.165, 3
So **let** our love................................66. H.172, 28
Then **let** thy active hand scu'd o're thy Lyre:..67. H.176, 3
Come, **let** us goe, while we are in our prime;..69. H.178, 57
Let us not then so rudely henceforth goe......73. H.186, 5
Be, be it so, and **let** this be...................73. H.187, 8
Let Much-more justly pay his tythes; then try..73. H.188, 3
Thus **let** this Christal'd Lillie be............76. H.193, 41
Swell up my nerves with spirit; **let** my blood..79. H.197, 77
Me to the Tap, the Tost, the Turfe; **Let** Wine..79. H.197, 88
Let them prattle how that I....................82. H.203, 5
Let them tell how she doth move...............82. H.203, 7
Let them speak by gentle tones,................82. H.203, 9
Let it be Doomes-day; nay, take longer scope;...83. H.206, 3
Pay when th'art honest; **let** me have some hope..83. H.206, 4
Sound, or unsound, **let** it be;..................84. H.209, 5
Pillars **let** some set up,.......................85. H.211, 21
Let Lullaby the pretty Prince asleep!..........86. H.213, 18
Hence, hence, profane; soft silence **let** us have;..89. H.219, 1
Display thy breasts, my Julia, there **let** me.....96. H.230, 1
A wager, and **let** it be this;...................99. H.243, 3
That done, then **let** him, dispossest of paine,...99. H.244, 7
Let but thy voice engender with the string,...102. H.252, 1
Now **let** the Rose raigne like a Queene, and smile.
105. H.259, 12
Let but Pink's face i' th' Looking-glasse be showne,
110. H.272, 3
Rise, Houshold-gods, and **let** us goe;..........111. H.278, 1
First, **let** us dwell on rudest seas;.............111. H.278, 3
Last, **let** us make our best abode,...............111. H.278, 5
Mount up thy flames, and **let** thy Torch.......113. H.283, 33
And **let** the Young-men and the Bride-maids share
114. H.283, 78
Let him come, who dares undo her...........114. H.283, 100
Let my haire then stand an end:..............117. H.286, 6
Bacchus, **let** me drink no more;..............122. H.304, 1
But **let** that speak, the Client gets the suit.....123. H.308, 2
And **let** our Citie-health go round,.............127. H.319, 30

And **let** the russet Swaines the Plough.........127. H.319, 45
Let but few smart, but strike a feare through all:
132. H.335, 3
Where the fault springs, there **let** the judgement fall.
132. H.335, 4
As is the Air, and **let** us be..................133. H.336, 38
Let the winds drive..........................134. H.336, 59
Or **let** me go;...............................137. H.340, 2
Let Kings Command, and doe the best they may,
138. H.345, 1
Sea-born Goddesse, **let** me be,.................138. H.346, 1
Let me when I kisse a maid,..................138. H.346, 5
That was the Proverb. **Let** my mistresse be....141. H.357, 1
Or mournfull Marble; **let** thy shade...........145. H.376, 3
Till I shall come again, **let** this suffice,........146. H.377, 1
Shew me thy waste; Then **let** me there withall,.154. H.403, 5
I'm sick of Love; O **let** me lie...............158. H.420, 1
Or **let** it lye................................161. H.426, 14
And **let** the whole world then dispose..........164. H.441, 11
Yet **let** these glib temptations be.............174. H.465, 5
Thou set'st their hearts, **let** chaste desire......174. H.465, 8
Let them enstile Thee Fairest faire,..........175. H.465, 37
And **let** thy dreames be only fed..............175. H.465, 49
Nothing comes Free-cost here; Jove will not **let**
177. H.469, 1
I meane the Court: **Let** Latmos be...........183. H.492, 17
Mean time, **let** Lycidas have leave to Pipe to thee.
184. H.492, 43
That Love last long; **let** it thy first care be..185. H.494, 1
Let Poets feed on aire, or what they will;......186. H.498, 7
Let me feed full, till that I fart, sayes Jill......186. H.498, 8
And his last breath, **let** it be................186. H.499, 3
As thou deserv'st, be proud; then gladly **let**...194. H.529, 1
And dark; **let** us meet;........................195. H.534, 2
Then **let** not Love's flame,....................195. H.534, 8
Let me sleep this night away,.................199. H.549, 1
Let our soules flie to' th' shades, where ever springs
205. H.575, 2
Let faire or foule my Mistresse be,............207. H.579, 1
Or **let** her walk, or stand, or sit,...............207. H.579, 3
Or **let** her tongue be still, or stir,.............207. H.579, 5
Or **let** her Grant, or else Deny,................207. H.579, 7
Let not the darke thee cumber;................217. H.619, 11
Then Julia **let** me wooe thee,.................217. H.619, 16
Who'l **let** ye by their fire sit?.................218. H.626, 5
Cut off thy haires; and **let** thy Teares be shed..219. H.627, 3
Then for effusions, **let** none wanting be,.......219. H.627, 5
Let wealth come in by comely thrift,.........221. H.633, 46
Colours, **let** Art supply........................224. H.641, 2
Yet, Reader, **let** me tell thee this.............226. H.644, 7
Let her Lucrece all day be....................232. H.665, 15
By noone, and **let** thy good dayes passe,........233. H.670, 4
And crown thy temples too, and **let**.........233. H.670, 19
Chains of sweet bents **let** us make,............235. H.678, 5
At Stool-ball, Lucia, **let** us play,.............238. H.690, 1
Or for a Tansie **let** us pay,....................238. H.690, 3
Let us now take time, and play,...............238. H.691, 1
Yet since cal'd back; henceforward **let** me be,.242. H.713, 15
Come blithefull Neatherds, **let** us lay.........243. H.716, 1
Chor. Why then begin, and **let** us heare........243. H.716, 16
Let her breath, or **let** her blow,..............244. H.719, 5
Fix the foundation fast, and **let** the Roofe.....245. H.723, 13
Nor **let** the shackles make thee sad;............246. H.725, 3
And thus, thus, thus **let** us smother............247. H.727, 3
Ph. Charon! O gentle Charon! **let** me wooe thee,
248. H.730, 1
For to **let** Affection in.........................253. H.750, 9
Go on with Sylla's Fortune; **let** thy Fate......254. H.756, 9
Come Anthea **let** us two.......................255. H.761, 1
O Bacchus! **let** us be.........................259. H.772, 25
From whose happy spark here **let**............262. H.782, 3
Let Me and It shine evermore by you.........264. H.789, 6
Serve or not serve, **let** Tom doe what he can,...265. H.796, 3
Make haste away, and **let** one be.............275. H.844, 1
Let me in my Glasse behold.................277. H.852, 2
For Love or Pittie, prethee **let** there be.......277. H.853, 3
The Porter then will **let** me in................277. H.854, 6
Then **let** her use the watring pot.............279. H.867, 4
Let not thy Tomb-stone er'e be laid by me:.....281. H.875, 1
Nor **let** my Herse, be wept upon by thee:......281. H.875, 2
But **let** that instant when thou dy'st be known,
281. H.875, 3
One knell be rung for both; and **let** one grave.281. H.875, 5
Set free thy Tresses, **let** them flow..........282. H.881, 7
And **let** such curious Net-works be............282. H.881, 9
Let the superstitious wife.....................284. H.889, 1
Let Box now domineere;.......................285. H.892, 6
Till Sunne-set, **let** it burne;....................285. H.893, 2
And **let** all sports with Christmas dye..........285. H.894, 2
For which prevention (Sociate) **let** there be...287. H.901, 3
Let what is graceless, discompos'd, and rude,..290. H.914, 3
Next, **let** the Lord, and Ladie here............291. H.919, 9
Faith is a thing that's four-square; **let** it fall..292. H.926, 1
That **let** her lay............................296. H.946, 4
So **let** us Yron, Silver, Gold,..................297. H.948, 9
Or **let** the Unshorne God lend thee his Lyre,..299. H.956, 13

Let Kings and Rulers, learne this line from me;
302. H.971, 1
Let Crutches then provided be................303. H.973, 3
Let us to the Altar go........................303. H.974, 4
Some effusions **let** me have,..................307. H.991, 5
Then, Biancha, **let** me rest...................307. H.991, 7
Let others to the Printing Presse run fast,....314. H.1022, 1
Let the Maides bewash the men...............315. H.1026, 10
Which knowne, **let** us make..................317. H.1035, 13
And **let** not a man then be seen here,.........317. H.1035, 15
Let moderation on thy passions waite.........318. H.1038, 1
For love or pitie **let** me know.................323. H.1068, 3
Let Country wenches make 'em fine..........323. H.1068, 13
Let us wash, and pray together:...............324. H.1069, 6
Let me not live, if I not love,................327. H.1082, 1
For my Locks (Girles) **let** 'em be............330. H.1098, 3
My wearied Barke, O **Let** it now be Crown'd!..334. H.1127, 1
And **let** it work, for I'le endure..............342. N.17, 11
Let me (like him) first cracks of thunder heare;
343. N.25, 3
Then **let** the Harps inchantments strike mine eare;
343. N.25, 4
Lord! **let** me never act that beggars part,......347. N.39, 3
Then **let** Thy Justice do the rest,..............349. N.46, 8
Let others look for Pearle and Gold...........355. N.60, 1
But why He did not, **let** me tell wherefore:....356. N.69, 2
Let me Thy voice betimes i' th morning heare;.358. N.77, 12
Let Balme, and Cassia send their scent........361. N.83, 65
Now singing, homeward **let** us carrie..........366. N.97, 26
But **let** no Christmas mirth begin.............366. N.98, 7
His praise; so **let** us blesse the King:..........367. N.98, 26
Come then, come then, and **let** us bring........368. N.102, 19
Let mercy be..................................370. N.111, 5
Let but one beame of Glory on it shine,........371. N.113, 9
Let me say grace when there's no more.......376. N.124, 6
Let not that Day Gods Friends and Servants scare:
376. N.126, 1
Which to effect, **let** ev'ry passing Bell..........392. N.230, 11
Let me, though late, yet at the last, begin.....392. N.230, 29
Such **let** my life assure me, when my breath...392. N.230, 33
Thus **let** Thy lips but love distill,..............393. N.232, 15
Let thy obedience be the best Reply..........397. N.260, 2
But where sin swells, there **let** Thy grace abound.
398. N.261, 6
The work is done; now **let** my Lawrell be......398. N.262, 1
Let their example not a pattern be............399. N.264, 3
Let Oyle, next, run,..........................401. N.268, 21
Meane while, **let** mee,........................401. N.268, 36
Let me live ever here, and stir...............402. N.269, 18
Here **let** me rest; and **let** me have............402. N.269, 22
Lett Manners teach the <e>whear to bee.........407. A.2, 27
(Thy fore-head) **lett** therin bee sign'd..........407. A.2, 33
Then **lett** each Cheeke of thyne intice..........408. A.2, 43
To[o] Calme A tempest, **lett** bee brought.......408. A.2, 66
Lett itt (in Loues name) bee keept sleeke.....409. A.2, 77
Lett hym but w[th] indifferent skill.............409. A.2, 105
But **let** each p[r]sant Cheeke appear................413. A.4, 3
But now come in. Euc. More **let** me yet relate..416. A.8, 23
And I must hence. Euc. Yet **let** me thus much know,
416. A.8, 25
Let them read this booke and learne...........418. A.9, 55
— — — — — — — — — — — —, ...421. var. H.106, 12
— — — — — — — — — — — —, ...422. var. H.106, 145
Oh then no longer **let** my sweete deferre..426. var. H.197, 25
— — — — — — — — — — — —, ...427. var. H.197, 73
Fill each part full of Fire, **let** all my good
427. ins. H.197, 77a
— — — — — — — — — — — —, ...428. var. H.197, 83
— — — — — — — — — — — —, ...428. var. H.197, 89
— — — — — — — — — — — —, ...441. var. H.465, 29

Letcher See **Lecher**
Letcher was Carted first about the streets,....195. H.532, 1

Lethe In **Lethe** to be drown'd;....................81. H.201, 50

Let's Then sweetest Silvia, **let's** no longer stay;...8. H.10, 5
Let's kisse afresh, as when we first begun......24. H.74, 8
Let's try this bow of ours......................27. H.81, 26
Let's doe our best, our Watch and Ward to keep
32. H.95, 5
Let's enjoy our merryment:...................39. H.111, 2
Come, we'll abroad; and **let's** obay...........68. H.178, 39
But my Corinna, come, **let's** goe a Maying....68. H.178, 42
Come, my Corinna, come, **let's** goe a Maying...69. H.178, 70
Let's kisse, and kisse agen;...................74. H.192, 5
Chor. Come **let's** away, and quickly **let's** be drest,
86. H.213, 45
Let's live merrily, and thus..................96. H.231, 5
And prethee, **let's** lay.........................99. H.243, 2
Let's live, my Wickes, then, while we may,....132. H.336, 15
Lets make it full up, by our sport............133. H.336, 32
Ambo. **Lets** cheer him up. Sil. Behold him weeping ripe.
159. H.421, 7
But **lets** go steepe...........................160. H.421, 44
Let's to the Altar of perfumes then go,........168. H.445, 3
Let's live in hast; use pleasures while we may:.171. H.453, 1
While Fates permits us, **let's** be merry;........172. H.457, 1
Let's leave a longer time to wait,.............179. H.476, 28
Let's live with that smal pittance that we have;.213. H.607, 1
If well the Dice runne, **lets** applaud the cast:..218. H.621, 1
Let's be jocund while we may;................224. H.639, 1
Let's feast, and frolick, sing, and play,.........233. H.670, 30
Let's be doing, though we play...............235. H.678, 3
The stakes are laid: **let's** now apply...........243. H.716, 19
But **let's** not beguile..........................247. H.727, 5
Lets call for Hymen if agreed thou art;.......261. H.781, 1
Lets now take our time;.......................267. H.806, 1
Come and **let's** in solemn wise................280. H.870, 1
Let's strive to be the best; the Gods, we know it,
309. H.1000, 1
Let's endure one Martyrdome.................315. H.1027, 2
Let's meet in a throng......................320. H.1051, 2
Lets kiss first, then we'l sever................324. H.1068, 22
Let's trie of us who shall the first expire;...333. H.1120, 3
Whatever comes, **let's** be content withall:......353. N.55, 1
Let's go (my Alma) yet e're we receive,.........355. N.65, 7
Let's blesse the Babe: And, as we sing.......367. N.98, 25
Let's kisse the sweet and holy ground;.......368. N.102, 16
Since part we must **Let's** kisse, that done retire.414. A.6, 9

Lets See **Let's**
Lets loose....................................246. H.724, 15
Lets drip a certain Gravie from her eyes.........331. H.1107, 2

Letters Gifts will be sent, and **Letters**, which....174. H.465, 23

Level Where Leaven wants, there **Levill** lies the nose.
154. H.401, 4

Level-coil This is the **Levell-coyle** that Buggins keeps.
311. H.1011, 2
We will keep this **Levell-Coyle**;..............397. N.258, 2

Leveled To mine eyes **level'd** opposite:..........237. H.687, 4

Levill See **Level**

Liar That thou be righteous found; and I the **Lyer**.
279. H.866, 4

Libbard's Colde Hemlocke, or the **Libbards** bane
422. ins. H.106, 116b

Liber Till **Liber** Pater twirles the house........127. H.319, 42

Liberty Before we know our **liberty**.............69. H.178, 60
Repentance to his **liberty**......................148. H.377, 88
Both, lest thou lose thy **liberty**:...............174. H.465, 26
'Tis **liberty** to serve one Lord; but he........284. H.887, 1
Are made farre worse, by lawless **liberty**.........307. H.990, 2
By thy sad losse, our **liberty**:...................360. N.83, 20
Bondage more Loued then **Lybertye**............408. A.2, 64

Licensed And then to weep they both were **licensed**.
384. N.180, 12

Lick And there to **lick** th' effused sacrifice:.....222. H.634, 4
No question then, but such a **lick** is sweet,......269. H.816, 3

Licking See **Gentle-licking**
Till his Wife **licking**, so unglews his eyes......269. H.816, 2

Licks But ne'r so much as **licks** the speckled shells:
204. H.568, 2

Lictors What though the **Lictors** threat us,......259. H.772, 7
The **Lictors** bundl'd up their rods: beside,......291. H.920, 1

Lid The **lid** began to let out day;..............46. H.130, 9

Lids But bid Good-night, and close their **lids** for ever.
41. H.118, 8

Lie See **Lye**
And loving **lie** in one devoted bed...............8. H.10, 2
So three in one small plat of ground shall **ly**,....11. H.22, 9
In her lap too I can **lye**.........................17. H.43, 5
Then melted down, there let me **lye**.............23. H.68, 5
And snugging there, they seem'd to **lye**........25. H.78, 3
White, warme, and soft to **lye** with me........34. H.105, 10
Lest Issue **lye** asleep..........................53. H.149, 18
Fire and water shall together **lye**..............59. H.154, 3
I live for ever; let the rest all **lye**............63. H.165, 3
May in like Chains of Darknesse **lie**............64. H.169, 12
And all confus'd, I there did **lie**...............67. H.175, 17
Ye doe **lie**,.....................................83. H.205, 15
How many **lye** forgot...........................85. H.211, 13
And if their Legend doe not **lye**,..............93. H.223, 109
And laugh no more; or laugh, and **lie** down next.
111. H.277, 2
If that you **lye**, then I will sweare you love.....126. H.317, 2
I'm sick of Love; O let me **lie**................158. H.420, 1
Or let it **lye**....................................161. H.426, 14
Where Mab he finds; who there doth **lie**......165. H.443, 5
To **lye** with Mab, though all say no............165. H.443, 12
By thee doth so neglected **lye**;................183. H.492, 3
Here those long suits of Chancery **lie**..........190. H.515, 25
Or for a little time we'l **lye**,...................190. H.515, 39
And for a while **lye** here conceal'd,............190. H.515, 45
For to make the Texture **lye**...................195. H.530, 3
Long for to **lye** here...........................197. H.540, 4
Our mortall parts may wrapt in Seare-cloths **lye**:
199. H.547, 1
As will if you yeeld, **lye** down conquer'd too....216. H.618, 12
Fall down together vanquisht both, and **lye**....216. H.618, 15
In which bondage we will **lie**,..................235. H.678, 7
When times and seasons and all yeares must **lie**
256. H.763, 13
Loves thornie Tapers yet neglected **lye**:.......261. H.781, 3
And utterly forgotten **lye**,......................265. H.794, 2
If I **lye** unburied Sir,...........................270. H.821, 1
Lest rapt from hence, I see thee **lye**...........275. H.844, 3

Where we may snug, and close together lye...278. H.860, 7
If hap it must, that I must see thee lye........300. H.960, 1
Since the place wherein ye lye,................324. H.1070, 2
Which if away, proud Scepters then will lye....325. H.1073, 3
With my fates neglected lye..................334. H.1125, 6
When I lie within my bed,.....................347. N.41, 5
Under the sparres of which I lie...............349. N.47, 5
And I lie numbred with the dead?..............361. N.84, 6
Some one poore Almes-house; there to lie, or stir,
371. N.115, 3
Gods wayes and walks, which lie still East and West.
386. N.193, 4
Ravisht I am! and down I lie,.................402. N.269, 20
In wch the veynes ymplanted seeme to lye........405. A.1, 47
The Lines of Sorrowe, that lye drawne in mee....411. A.3, 60
— — — — — — — — —, ...447. var. A.1, 18

Lief For mine own part I'de as lieve,...........117. H.285, 10
Lies See Underlies
But being absent, Love lies languishing...........13. H.30, 2
So looks Anthea, when in bed she lyes,...........34. H.104, 1
When of these truths, thy happyer knowledge lyes,
37. H.106, 87
A wise man ev'ry way lies square..............37. H.106, 98
In this little Vault she lyes,...................52. H.145, 1
When she lyes with Jove, then she..............59. H.155, 10
Lies drown'd with us in endlesse night..........69. H.178, 68
Behold, Tibullus lies...........................81. H.201, 41
Wither'd with yeeres, and bed-rid Mumma lyes;
90. H.222, 1
And if that Fairie Knight not lies,...............92. H.223, 81
Here she lies, a pretty bud,....................123. H.310, 1
Where Leaven wants, there Levill lies the nose...154. H.401, 4
Those monstrous lies of little Robin Rush:......155. H.405, 8
Lies here abouts; and for to pave............166. H.443, 53
Rear'd, lyes her Elvish-majestie:...............167. H.443, 87
Thus soft she lies: and over-head.............167. H.443, 100
While all beauty lyes asleep....................170. H.450, 2
With oathes, and lyes, (as others do.).........182. H.490, 12
Your Child lyes still, yet is not dead:..........189. H.514, 6
Marbles will sweare that here it lyes............203. H.564, 2
Here a pretty Baby lies........................224. H.640, 1
But husht in his laire he lies lurking:.........225. H.643, 15
Lies softly panting like a Bride................233. H.670, 14
Here lies a Virgin, and as sweet..............257. H.764, 1
Seeal'd up with Night-gum, Loach each morning lyes,
269. H.816, 1
Here she lyes (in Bed of Spice)...............274. H.838, 1
Teage has told lyes so long, that when Teage tells
282. H.880, 1
Where most sweets are, there lyes a Snake.....283. H.883, 12
Here lyes Johnson with the rest................289. H.910, 1
Boreman takes tole, cheats, flatters, lyes, yet Boreman,
315. H.1025, 1
If I by lies and oaths.........................351. N.49, 6
Lies He the Lillie-banks among?...............367. N.102, 3
For Tabitha, who dead lies here,...............374. N.123, 11
Love lyes a bleeding here, Evadne there..........415. A.7, 11
Lyes here about and as we guesse........440. ins. H.443, 45z

Liest Thou wonder of all Maids, li'st here,........360. N.83, 13
And though thou here li'st dead, we see........375. N.123, 71

Lieu Shall hither waft it, and in leiu...........414. A.5, 15

Lieve See Lief

Life See Country-life
To crucifie my life:...............................13. H.31, 4
Work that to life, and let me ever dwell..........14. H.35, 13
And return to life, if she.......................17. H.43, 7
of Life, and 'twas for me........................18. H.47, 8
Thou gav'st me life, (but Mortall;) For that one
27. H.82, 13
For my life mortall, Rise from out thy Herse,....27. H.82, 15
And take a life immortall from my Verse.........27. H.82, 16
But that which most makes sweet thy country life,
35. H.106, 31
Wealth cannot make a life, but Love............37. H.106, 128
To paint a Bridgeman to the life:..............38. H.108, 4
To me, as blood to life and spirit: Neare,........45. H.128, 2
Male to the female, soule to body: Life..........45. H.128, 4
Still shall crown the happy life.................55. H.149, 59
Of life, untill ye bid.........................58. H.149, 164
To find that Tree of Life, whose Fruits did feed,
61. H.161, 1
To Life Eternal, I co'd love.....................67. H.175, 22
Our life is short; and our dayes run.............69. H.178, 61
(To save his life) twice am content to die.......70. H.181, 16
And all the loome of life undone:...............72. H.185, 11
Life of my life, take not so soone thy flight,......73. H.186, 1
As I meet thee. Soule of my life, and fame!......77. H.197, 9
More love unto my life, or can present...........78. H.197, 55
With endless life are crown'd...................81. H.201, 52
Render for that, a crowne of life to you.........94. H.224, 10
You have changes in your life,...................96. H.232, 3
Thou art my life, my love, my heart,..........109. H.267, 21
No life is yet life-proofe from miserie..........111. H.276, 2
By the Brides eyes, and by the teeming life....114. H.283, 81
That man lives twice, that lives the first life well.
121. H.298, 2
To give that life, resign'd your own:............126. H.318, 9

Why then, since life to us is short,.............133. H.336, 31
In time of life, I grac't ye with my Verse;......138. H.343, 1
Of Life eternall) Time has made thee one,....152. H.392, 3
So drew my life unto an end..................153. H.399, 6
He's greedie of his life, who will not fall,......155. H.405, 17
Co'd life return, 'twod never lose a day.........171. H.453, 2
And this our life too whirles away,.............172. H.457, 3
He's Lord of thy life, who contemnes his own.
181. H.486, 2
Never crucifie my life;.......................182. H.490, 3
Few live the life immortall. He ensures........188. H.506, 15
His Fame's long life, who strives to set up Yours.
188. H.506, 16
Fall thou must first, then rise to life with These,
188. H.507, 3
How soone our life, here,.....................196. H.534, 16
That's the Story of my life....................199. H.546, 4
But a Minutes life with me:..................204. H.566, 2
Life is the Bodies light; which once declining,...207. H.576, 1
That with my Lines, my Life must full-stop here.
219. H.627, 2
The morrowes life too late is, Live to-day......228. H.655, 2
Sweet Country life, to such unknown,..........229. H.662, 1
Of Land makes life, but sweet content.........230. H.662, 18
O happy life! if that their good..............231. H.662, 70
Is this a life, to break thy sleep?.............233. H.670, 1
No; 'tis a life, to have thine oyle,.............233. H.670, 7
Whose life with care is overcast,...............233. H.670, 32
Nor is't a life, seven yeares to tell,............233. H.670, 34
He's Lord of thy life, who contemnes his own,..240. H.702, 2
Knew'st thou, one moneth wo'd take thy life away,
241. H.709, 1
Who fed my life, I'le follow her in death.......248. H.730, 16
He weepes and sighs (as weary of his life.)....275. H.842, 2
While others perish, here's thy life decreed......280. H.869, 5
Life endlesse sign'd to thee and me............288. H.906, 2
Spend on that stock: and when your life must fall,
299. H.958, 5
This Stone can tell the storie of my life,........304. H.978, 1
Spend I my life (that's subject unto change:)..310. H.1003, 2
Here we begin new life; while thousands quite..313. H.1019, 3
The life I got I quickly lost:.................313. H.1020, 4
The only comfort of my life...................320. H.1052, 1
Of life comes in, when he's Regenerate.......326. H.1080, 28
Ile write no more of life; but wish twas ended,..334. H.1124, 3
Jocond his Muse was; but his Life was chast...335. H.1130, 2
To leave this life, not loving it, but Thee.......352. N.51, 14
One seed of life left, 'tis to keep...............361. N.83, 59
Must last with Satan, to the end of life.........362. N.91, 2
Gives life and luster, publike mirth,............364. N.96, 20
The longer thred of life we spin,...............379. N.144, 1
After this life, the wages shall.................380. N.149, 1
If thou canst change thy life, God then will please
389. N.216, 3
To circumcise thy life.........................391. N.228, 20
Might I make choice, long life sho'd be with-stood;
392. N.230, 9
Such let my life assure me, when my breath....392. N.230, 33
No, No, this Scene from Thee takes life and sense,
399. N.263, 26
Nourish in's breast, a Tree of Life.............409. A.2, 108
He was my Life, my Love, my Joy; but di'd.....416. A.8, 15
For what life and death confines.................417. A.9, 9
Sacke is my life, my leaven, salt to all..426. ins. H.197, 48a
— — — — — — — — — —, ...448. var. A.1, 110

Life-begetting Her life-begetting eye;..........164. H.441, 10
Life-proof No life is yet life-proofe from miserie..111. H.276, 2
Life's See Long-life's-day
And to walke Life's pilgrimage...............191. H.519, 2
Life-time That Lovers tears in life-time shed,......44. H.127, 9
Lift Who at a dead lift,.........................256. H.762, 13
Lift up thy Sword; next, suffer it to fall,......310. H.1002, 3
Remove the barrs, or lift me o're the stiles:......352. N.51, 6
Here I lift them up to Thee,...................364. N.95, 4

Light See Candle-light, Dew-light, Dull-light, Mis-light, Moon-light, Morning's-light, Silver-light, Taper-light, Twilight
When such a Light as You are leads the way:....3. Ded.H, 2
Light from the Sun, that inexhausted Fire:......3. Ded.H, 6
Led by some light that flows from thee...........33. H.98, 8
In all that great and glorious light,............49. H.136, 30
Wherein or Light, or Day, did never peep.........52. H.146, 6
Not one drop to light on me....................62. H.162, 6
Dark was the Jayle; but as if light.............64. H.169, 5
Create the burden light........................66. H.172, 24
Come, and receive them while the light........68. H.178, 23
Out of the which, the creame of light,.........74. H.190, 9
Where either too much light his worth........75. H.193, 22
And by the glow-worms light wel guided,......93. H.223, 141
A Light ful-filling all the Region here..........94. H.226, 4
I leave this light;.............................95. H.227, 31
Rather then mend, put out the light............97. H.235, 6
So Good-luck came, and on my roofe did light,..100. H.247, 1
(When weary of the light)....................106. H.262, 14
And light my Reliques to their Urne..........109. H.271, 6
To light their Tapers at the Brides bright eye...115. H.283, 108
Casts forth a light like to a Virgin flame:........131. H.331, 6

Sleep, while we hide thee from the light,........146. H.376, 13
To make a seisure on the light,...............164. H.441, 3
Which, done; and thence remov'd the light,......165. H.443, 7
No glaring light of bold-fac't Day,............167. H.443, 76
And multiply; Such is the light,..............167. H.443, 80
Have their reflected light,......................181. H.484, 7
Can ever rust th'Enamel of the light..........206. H.575, 16
Life is the Bodies light; which once declining,..207. H.576, 1
Will lend thee their light,.....................217. H.619, 14
So a blessing light upon.......................224. H.638, 25
A Publike Light (in this immensive Sphere.)...236. H.685, 2
Give the Tapers here their light,...............258. H.769, 7
Light the new block, And.......................263. H.784, 8
Griefe, if't be great, 'tis short; if long, 'tis light.
268. H.810, 2
Cloth'd all with incorrupted light;..............270. H.819, 5
(When drunke with Beere) to light him home, i'th' dark.
273. H.834, 4
Weepe for the dead, for they have lost this light:.298. H.952, 1
For as farre as that doth light,.................322. H.1064, 5
With my Lantern, and my Light,.............372. N.121, 2
But by the peep of light......................373. N.122, 7
Farewell thy Fier and thy Light,...............374. N.123, 45
So live in Heaven, in everlasting light............384. N.181, 5
And having not her God for light,.............393. N.233, 3
But all we wither and our Light.................413. A.4, 10
I'th ayre, a greater Text of light.................413. A.4, 19
— — — — — — — — — —, ...450. var. A.9, 37
Lighted And soon a Taper lighted;..............26. H.81, 14
Lighten Lighten my candle, so that I beneath....358. N.77, 10
Lighter Thou lighter then the Cork by far:......70. H.181, 22
Lightest If thou dislik'st the Piece thou light'st on first;
7. H.6, 1
Lightly The earth, that lightly covers her.........123. H.310, 6
Tread, Sirs, as lightly as ye can................226. H.644, 1
None is, slight things do lightly please..........246. H.724, 32
Lightly, lightly ore the dead....................274. H.838, 8
Numbers ne'r tickle, or but lightly please,.......290. H.914, 7
Lightning The soule, like lightning, and as active too.
45. H.128, 28
Thunder and Lightning Ile lay by,...............58. H.152, 5
Then Thunder-claps and Lightning did conspire...81. H.202, 5
Like a Lightning, from her eye,.................98. H.238, 14
And lightning in his eyes; and flings...........165. H.443, 15
Lightning's That Towrs high rear'd dread most the lightnings threat:......................................181. H.483, 14
Lights Now is the time, when all the lights wax dim;
20. H.55, 1
Those holy lights, wherewith they guide........109. H.271, 3
Skin deepe into the Porke, or lights............147. H.377, 54
Princes, and such like Publike Lights as these,...237. H.685, 9
Like See Absyrtus-like, Air-like, Ambrosia-like, Amphion-like, Arch-like, Center-like, Cloud-like, Cock-like, Cow-like, Dew-like, Dog-like, Dove-like, Fish-like, Ghost-like, God-like, Heaven-like, Love-like-leaven, Matron-like, Moss-like, Poet-like, Pup-like, Ruby-like, Scarecrow-like, Sieve-like, Soap-like-lather, Sponge-like, Star-like, State-like, Swan-like-state, Tempest-like, These-like, Ulysses-like, War-like, Winter-like, Wolf-like-man.
Well may my Book come forth like Publique Day.3. Ded.H, 1
Come thou not neere those men, who are like Bread..7. H.7, 1
O're-leven'd; or like Cheese o're-renetted..........7. H.7, 2
The Nagge (like to the Prophets Asse)............13. H.27, 6
Thus like a Bee, Love-gentle stil doth bring.......16. H.40, 7
More like a Stock, then like a Vine.............17. H.41, 23
'Bout a Virgin like a Vine:.....................17. H.43, 4
Whose easie natures like it well,.................22. H.66, 3
Or, like the soule, whole every where:............24. H.73, 6
Looks like a Bride now, or a bed of flowers,.......25. H.77, 5
Like Streams, you are divorc'd; but 't will come, when
26. H.79, 5
Next, his wilde eares, like Lethern wings full spread,
33. H.99, 3
Like to a Twi-light, or that simpring Dawn,......34. H.104, 3
Till, like Ixion's Cloud you be...................34. H.105, 9
And like a surly Oke with storms perplext;......37. H.106, 99
Draw him as like too, as you can,..............38. H.108, 5
Or like—Nay 'tis that Zonulet of love,...........40. H.114, 3
Let there be Patrons; Patrons like to thee,......41. H.117, 1
Like to a Virgin newly ravished.................41. H.118, 4
Each way illustrious, brave; and like to those....45. H.128, 14
The soule, like lightning, and as active too.......45. H.128, 28
Like to a Lillie withered:......................47. H.132, 2
Next, look thou like a sickly Moone;............47. H.132, 3
Or like Jocasta in a swoone.....................47. H.132, 4
Like to a widdow drown'd in woe:...........47. H.132, 6
Or like a Virgin full of ruth,...................47. H.132, 7
All such as are not soft like them..............47. H.132, 14
Was like a sprightly Spartanesse...............51. H.142, 8
From these fetters; like to me..................53. H.147, 12
May all, like flowrie Meads.....................55. H.149, 63
To it, the like perfume:........................55. H.149, 66
Fall, like a spangling dew,.....................57. H.149, 155
Two, like two ripe shocks of corn.............58. H.149, 170
And (like to mine) make your heart burn........61. H.159, 19
Love, like a Gypsie, lately came;...............63. H.166, 1
May in like Chains of Darknesse lie............64. H.169, 12
(Or sho'd be) like to it........................65. H.172, 6
Then sure thou't like, or thou wilt envie me.......66. H.174, 4
Like a Celestiall Canopie........................67. H.175, 10
Like to a flame growne moderate:..............67. H.175, 12
To come forth, like the Spring-time, fresh and greene;
68. H.178, 16
But borne, and like a short Delight,..............69. H.180, 1
And like a Phenix re-aspire......................72. H.185, 17
Much-more, provides, and hoords up like an Ant;..73. H.188, 1
Like to a Dew,.................................74. H.190, 10
Or some fine tincture, like to this,..............75. H.193, 12
Like to a Bride, come forth my Book, at last,....76. H.194, 1
Like a dull Twi-light? Tell me; and the fault....77. H.197, 29
A thought of such like possibilitie?............78. H.197, 46
Like Iphyclus, upon the tops of Corn...........78. H.197, 50
Run through my veines, like to a hasty flood....79. H.197, 78
Shew'd like to Creame, enspir'd with Strawberries:
81. H.202, 2
'Tis like a Lawnie-Firmament as yet............82. H.204, 5
And (like a blasting Planet) found her out;....87. H.215, 4
Like to a dreadfull Comet in the Aire:...........87. H.215, 6
Then like a Globe, or Ball of Wild-fire, flie,....87. H.215, 9
You are like Balme inclosed (well)..............88. H.216, 13
Like Frost-work glitt'ring on the Snow..........92. H.223, 67
(Like a Turks Turbant on his head)..........93. H.223, 138
Fall on me like a silent dew,....................95. H.227, 23
Or like those Maiden showrs,....................97. H.227, 24
Like a Lightning, from her eye,..................98. H.238, 14
But like a Laurell, to grow green for ever........98. H.240, 2
Like to a slumbring Bride, awake againe.........99. H.244, 8
Like noyse-lesse Snow; or as the dew of night:..100. H.247, 2
And that this pleasure is like raine,.............102. H.250, 53
She shifts and changes like the Moone.........103. H.253, 14
Such pretty flowers, (like to Orphans young)...104. H.257, 13
Like to the peeping spring-time of the yeare.....105. H.259, 8
Now let the Rose raigne like a Queene, and smile.
105. H.259, 12
Like those short sweets ere knit together.......107. H.263, 22
Like t' a Rose of Jericho:.......................108. H.266, 2
Each Virgin, like a Spring,......................110. H.274, 11
Like Unthrifts, having spent,.................110. H.274, 17
A savour like unto a blessed field,..............112. H.283, 18
Plumpe Bed beare up, and swelling like a cloud,.115. H.283, 112
Yee see it brusle like a Swan,.................115. H.283, 114
I tell yee no; but like a........................116. H.283, 147
The sheet about, like flakes of snow...........116. H.283, 150
Trust me, I'le not like at all;...................117. H.286, 4
Like to the Income must be our expence;........117. H.287, 1
Wisely wanton (like to me.)...................117. H.289, 4
But if flames best like ye, then.................118. H.289, 11
Cheeks like to Roses, when they blow...........120. H.295, 2
Be ye lockt up like to these,...................120. H.297, 7
Like to the Summers raine;......................125. H.316, 18
Of these, and such like things, for shift,........127. H.319, 25
That weares one face (like heaven) and never showes
128. H.323, 7
Casts forth a light like to a Virgin flame:......131. H.331, 6
Like to a Lilly-lost, nere can,..................133. H.336, 22
No lust theres like to Poetry.................135. H.336, 112
Cheeks like Creame Enclarited:.................138. H.342, 6
Love those, like these; regard, reward them not..141. H.359, 12
Smells like the maiden-Pomander...............145. H.375, 26
Thus, like a Roman Tribune, thou thy gate.....147. H.377, 45
And Thou, like to that Hospitable God,........147. H.377, 61
Each like a poore and pitied widowhood........150. H.382, 4
So draw, and paint, as none may do the like,......150. H.384, 5
A Just man's like a Rock that turnes the wroth..152. H.389, 1
Me thinks like mine, your pulses beat;........157. H.413, 5
That doth like me, this doth please;............157. H.415, 5
Like to a field of beans, when newly blown;....159. H.421, 20
Or like a medow being lately mown............159. H.421, 21
Though I do like to wooe;.......................160. H.422, 2
Why walkes Nick Flimsey like a Male-content?..160. H.423, 1
So like to this, nay all the rest,................164. H.440, 9
Shine like a spangle here.......................164. H.441, 8
Mildly disparkling, like those fiers,............165. H.443, 29
Of curious Brides; or like those mites.........165. H.443, 31
To shoot forth Generations like to them.........170. H.451, 4
Like Sybels Leaves, throughout the ample world?
172. H.459, 4
Them like some Picture, or some Mould......174. H.465, 20
Fashion'd like Thee; which though 'tave eares..174. H.465, 21
Like you a while: They glide...................176. H.467, 17
Like to a solemne sober Stream...............179. H.476, 13
But sweetly sounding like a Lute..............179. H.476, 18
Like Leaves that laden are.....................181. H.484, 3
Whose shadow smels like milder Pomander!.....181. H.485, 2
Never like their lips, to sweare................182. H.490, 7
Shalt lead, like young Apollo..................184. H.492, 36
For lost like these, 'twill be,..................184. H.493, 11
Th'art hence removing, (like a Shepherds Tent)..188. H.507, 1
One like to me, who must be kill'd..............188. H.509, 7
But rather like a flower hid here..............189. H.514, 7
Or like old Testaments ingrost,...............190. H.515, 43
What now we like, anon we disapprove:.........191. H.517, 1
Like to these Garden-glories, which here be......193. H.522, 3

Like purest Skies....193. H.524, 2
Like an Intelligence....193. H.524, 6
Like snailes did creep....194. H.525, 2
And like our living, where w'are known....200. H.552, 19
(Like to a sound that's vanishing away)....201. H.557, 22
Which like a Pinacle doth shew....202. H.560, 7
Come then, and like two Doves with silv'rie wings,
205. H.575, 1
Like Morning-Sun-shine tinsilling the dew....205. H.575, 12
Like to His subject; and as his Frantick-....206. H.575, 35
Looks, shew him truly Bacchanalian like,....206. H.575, 36
Listen, while they (like Syrens in their Spheres).206. H.575, 52
Not like the Muse; to love the man,....214. H.611, 4
Like the sparks of fire, befriend thee....217. H.619, 5
Like Tapers cleare without number....217. H.619, 15
In frenzie ne'r like thee....227. H.653, 12
Like one of those....229. H.659, 4
Like a civill Wilderness;....232. H.665, 6
Lies softly panting like a Bride....233. H.670, 14
Time steals away like to a stream,....233. H.670, 22
Like to a Deaw, or melted Frost....233. H.670, 27
Like thee; or dare the Buskins to unloose....234. H.673, 11
But all are toucht (like lawfull plate)....236. H.681, 5
Princes, and such like Publike Lights as these,..237. H.685, 9
Mine eyes, like clouds, were drizling raine,....237. H.687, 1
Then multiply all, like to Fishes....239. H.695, 12
Like the Sybells, through the world....242. H.714, 8
But of all packs, no pack like poverty....242. H.715, 2
From her moysture take the like:....244. H.719, 4
Next, like a Bishop consecrate my ground,....245. H.723, 7
They fall like dew, but make no noise at all....250. H.737, 4
Like a poore Lady lost in Widdowhood:....251. H.745, 4
Then you must like, because I love....252. H.746, 8
Make Thee like Him, this, that way fortunate,...254. H.756, 10
Meane time like Earth-wormes we will craule below,
257. H.763, 21
The like not Heliogabalus did eat:....262. H.783, 4
It sparkles now like Ariadne's Crowne....264. H.789, 4
Like those infernall Deities which eate....272. H.826, 1
Deare, can you like, and liking love your Poet?..274. H.837, 5
But, like full clouds, may they from thence....291. H.919, 7
Love, like a Beggar, came to me....295. H.942, 1
Or else because th' art like a modest Bride,....301. H.963, 3
For shape and service, Spaniell like to thee....302. H.967, 2
But when he hears the like confusion,....303. H.975, 2
Party colour'd like a Pie;....305. H.984, 19
Ans. Like, and dislike ye:....309. H.1001, 2
Our Bastard-children are but like to Plate,....312. H.1015, 1
Has made me like a wilderness:....312. H.1016, 2
Or (discompos'd) I'm like a rude,....312. H.1016, 3
And lisping reeld, and reeling like to fall....313. H.1017, 6
And I am wilde and wanton like to him....313. H.1017, 14
Like will to like, each Creature loves his kinde;
319. H.1043, 1
And like the Starres to glitter....323. H.1068, 16
And in their motion smelt much like to flowers.326. H.1080, 13
Those spirits rais'd; and with like precepts then
326. H.1080, 17
Most like his Suite, and all commend the Trim;.330. H.1099, 3
No plague ther's like to foolishnesse....332. H.1115, 2
Like to the ever-wealthy Ocean:....341. N.15, 2
Let me (like him) first cracks of thunder heare;..343. N.25, 3
Like as my Parlour, so my Hall....350. N.47, 17
And glow like it....350. N.47, 26
Thy soft sweet Earth! but (like a spring)....361. N.83, 71
And our Peace here, like a Spring,....363. N.93, 8
Seem like the Spring-time of the yeere?....364. N.96, 13
Smile, like a field beset with corne?....364. N.96, 15
Or smell, like to a Meade new-shorne,....364. N.96, 16
Then, like a perfum'd Altar, see....366. N.98, 10
For, here's a Babe, that (like a Bride)....366. N.98, 12
Lord, I am like to Misletoe,....371. N.114, 1
Chor. Thy belly like a hill is,....375. N.123, 77
One Birth our Saviour had; the like none yet....384. N.182, 1
Was, or will be a second like to it....384. N.182, 2
Then ever, yet, the like was done before....395. N.244, 4
But like a Person of some high account:....398. N.263, 16
Seemes like Apollo's when the morne he blesses....404. A.1, 2
Or like vnto Aurora when shee setts....404. A.1, 3
Like to the tendrells of a flattring vine,....404. A.1, 8
Like purest white stands in the middle place....404. A.1, 12
Which like a garden manifestly show....404. A.1, 15
Like rose leaves, white and redd seeme mingled....404. A.1, 18
Which makes them shewe like roses vnder lawne...404. A.1, 24
Smells like the burnt Sabæan Frankinsense....404. A.1, 28
Like pearle and gold make one rich Carcanett....405. A.1, 32
Her eares, which like twoe Laborinths are plac'd
405. A.1, 39
Like loving vines hid vnder Ivorye,....405. A.1, 48
Like wanton rose buds growing out of snowe,....405. A.1, 54
<Fingring> the paps that feele like sleeded silke...405. A.1, 57
Like a faire mountaine in Riphean snowe,....405. A.1, 60
Swelling in likenes like twoe christall skyes....406. A.1, 78
Her leggs with twoe cleire calves like siluer tride..406. A.1, 87
Round short and cleire, like pounded spices sweete
406. A.1, 92
They make it scent like bruized Cinnamon....406. A.1, 94
From wch two armes like branches seem to spread
406. A.1, 97
W^ch^ like a Vestall Vergine ply....407. A.2, 23
Theis bringe thy husband, like to those....407. A.2, 29
To Roughnes, Claspe hym lyke a Vine,....408. A.2, 68
Or lyke as woole meetes steele, giue way....408. A.2, 69
Benummes like the forgettful floode....409. A.2, 88
Natures, like ours, wee who haue spent our tyme
410. A.3, 15
Like fier-drakes, yett did'st mee no harme therby.410. A.3, 28
Soe wth like lookes, as once the Ministrell....411. A.3, 67
Shewes like the Heavens aboue ye Moone,....413. A.4, 13
Like an Eternall Noone....413. A.4, 14
Doe it like the Sun to write....413. A.4, 18
None writes lov's passion in the world, like Thee..415. A.7, 18
— — — — — — — — — — —, ...427. var. H.197, 51
— — — — — — — — — — —, ...430. var. H.283, 40
and come upon your Bridegroome like a Tyde
431. ins. H.283, 50b
like streames which flow....431. ins. H. 283, 50e
Into your selves like wooll together spunne,
431. ins. H.283, 50h
aloft, and like two armies, come....432. ins. H.283, 140d
Orchards like to Alcinous,....436. ins. H.336, 48d
— — — — — — — — — — —, ...438. var. H.337, 2
— — — — — — — — — — —, ...447. var. A.1, 50
Liked More lik'd by her, or lov'd by mee....145. H.375, 28
Likely Examples lead us, and wee likely see,....255. H.759, 1
Likeness When Love (the child of likenesse) urgeth on
77. H.197, 3
Swelling in likenes like twoe christall skyes....406. A.1, 78
Likes But yet, though Love likes well such Scenes as these,
24. H.74, 9
To Sun his thin-clad members, if he likes,....146. H.377, 17
Love he that will; it best likes me,....155. H.408, 1
Love is a thing so likes me,....296. H.946, 3
She likes not there,....314. H.1024, 18
Likest And lik'st the best? Still thou reply'st, The dead.
66. H.174, 2
If seen, thou lik'st me, Deb, in none of these...331. H.1108, 2
Likewise Be she likewise one of those,....11. H.21, 5
But likewise Oyle of Maintenance to it:....41. H.117, 6
There ush'ring Vergers, here likewise,....92. H.223, 105
And that terrour likewise prove,....117. H.286, 7
So likewise after our disseace,....139. H.353, 3
As in our clothes, so likewise he who lookes,....202. H.559, 1
That likewise I may pay the Bet,....238. H.690, 11
Here I my selfe might likewise die,....265. H.794, 1
Each griefe we feele, that likewise is a Kite....278. H.862, 3
But likewise sup'rabundant seed;....356. N.66, 2
God, as He's potent, so He's likewise known,....378. N.135, 1
Liking All love, all liking, all delight....69. H.178, 67
Deare, can you like, and liking love your Poet?.274. H.837, 5
According to Thy liking....363. N.92, 12
Lilies How Roses first came Red, and Lillies White.
5. H.1, 10
More white then whitest Lillies far,....34. H.105, 1
Millions of Lillies mixt with Roses....36. H.106, 48
Lillies will languish; Violets look ill;....41. H.118, 1
White though ye be; yet, Lillies, know....74. H.190, 1
Rest but a while here, by this bank of Lillies,..86. H.213, 10
(Clad, all, in Linnen, white as Lillies.)....101. H.250, 12
Bankt all with Lillies, and the Cream....179. H.476, 14
Shall pranke thy Hooke with Lillies....184. H.492, 32
Fresh Lillies flourishing....185. H.495, 4
With Lillies Tomb'd up in a Glasse;....186. H.497, 16
With Cream of Lillies (not of Kine)....216. H.616, 33
Oyl of Lillies, and of Spike,....244. H.719, 3
As Lillies shrin'd in Christall, so....271. H.824, 13
So Lillies thorough Christall look:....294. H.939, 3
The Tulips, Lillies, Daffadills do stoop;....320. H.1054, 4
And set about with Lillies;....323. H.1068, 6
All set about with Lillies....375. N.123, 80
How roses lillies and carnations grow,....404. A.1, 16
With Rosie Chaplets, Lillies, Pansies red,
442. ins. H.575, 20a
Lily When as the Lily marries with the Rose!..44. H.124, 2
Like to a Lillie withered:....47. H.132, 2
The Lillie will not long endure;....60. H.159, 13
And here, you see, this Lilly shows,....75. H.193, 4
Thus Lillie, Rose, Grape, Cherry, Creame,....75. H.193, 33
Thus let this Christal'd Lillie be....76. H.193, 41
Within a Lillie? Center plac't?....164. H.440, 4
Yet not a Lillie from the Bed appeares;....180. H.477, 4
— — — — — — — — — — —, ...437. var. H.336, 97
Lily-banks Lies He the Lillie-banks among?....367. N.102, 3
Lily-hand May Fortunes Lilly-hand....57. H.149, 157
Lily-lost Like to a Lilly-lost, nere can,....133. H.336, 22
Lily-work Your Leavie-Throne (with Lilly-work) possesse;
107. H.265, 9
And Lilly-work will dresse Thee;....345. N.35, 19
Lily-wristed Calls forth the lilly-wristed Morne:..230. H.662, 20
Limb But every Line, and Limb diffused thence,.10. H.16, 3
Smooth in each limb as a die;....305. H.984, 20
Somewhat peculiar to each lymm,....408. A.2, 74

Limbs Which wrapt thy smooth **limbs** (when thou didst implore 9. H.14, 11
In my **limbs** their former heat?..............10. H.19, 8
Here down my wearyed **limbs** Ile lay;.........123. H.306, 1
Mine aged **limbs** above my chaire:...........135. H.336, 108
— — — — — — — — —, ...450. var. A.9, 53
Lime Without or **Lime**, or Wood, or Stone:.....90. H.223a, 4
The sure sweet-Sement, Glue, and **Lime** of Love. 218. H.622, 2
Lime-twigs Thy **Lime-twigs**, Snares, and Pit-falls then 231. H.662, 68
Limon **See Lemon**
Limping Guesse cuts his shooes, and **limping**, goes about 98. H.239, 1
Linage **See Lineage**
Line **See Cross-line**
But every **Line**, and Limb diffused thence,.....10. H.16, 3
Which sho'd conjure up a **line**................182. H.489, 8
This **line** about, live Thou throughout the world; 298. H.955, 2
Let Kings and Rulers, learne this **line** from me; 302. H.971, 1
Keepes **line** for **line** with Beauties Parallels....307. H.992, 6
And cal'd each **line** back to his rule and space..311. H.1006, 4
To his Book's end this last **line** he'd have plac't, 335. H.1130, 1
Forgive me God, and blot each **Line**..........339. N.2, 5
Lineage — — — — — — — —, ...427. var. H.197, 75
Linen (Clad, all, in **Linnen**, white as Lillies.)...101. H.250, 12
Linen-drapery Whose **Linnen-Drapery** is a thin...91. H.223, 60
Linens Who can scoure **Linnens** with her own salt reeume? 178. H.474, 6
Lines There, there, (perhaps) such **Lines** as These 6. H.2, 15
Where thou mayst hear thine own **Lines** read....6. H.2, 23
Let rigid Cato read these **Lines** of mine.........7. H.8, 10
Make me the straight, and oblique **lines**;......47. H.133, 3
To see my **Lines** Excathedrated here...........64. H.168, 4
Thou say'st my **lines** are hard;...............138. H.344, 1
But warm their wits, and turn their **lines** to gold. 141. H.359, 8
Upon his Altar, men shall read thy **lines**;......143. H.366, 2
And in his Raptures speaking **Lines** of Thine,.206. H.575, 34
Our Lives do differ from our **Lines** by much...218. H.624, 2
That with my **Lines**, my Life must full-stop here. 219. H.627, 2
Thus inrag'd, my **lines** are hurl'd,............242. H.714, 7
Nis, he makes Verses; but the **Lines** he writes, 286. H.896, 1
Lines have, or sho'd have, thou the best canst show. 297. H.947, 10
Read thou my **Lines**, my Swetnaham, if there be 328. H.1089, 1
Ev'n so those **Lines**, pen'd by my wanton Wit,.339. N.1, 3
The **Lines** of Sorrowe, that lye drawne in mee..411. A.3, 60
Here's words with **lines**, and **lines** with Scenes consent, 415. A.7, 7
Looks through the passage of theis **lines**.......417. A.9, 10
Of **lines** and colors make them scorne.........418. A.9, 53
— — — — — — — — — — — —, ...449. var. A.3, 60
— — — — — — — — — — — —, ...451. var. H.336, 82
— — — — — — — — — — — —, ...451. var. H.336, 1:4
Ling **See Firstling**
Linger Or **linger** in it;........................85. H.211, 7
Lingering By **lingring** thus in doubt:............53. H.149, 6
Linings His **linings** are the matter running there. 144. H.373, 2
Linnit **Linnit** playes rarely on the Lute, we know; 149. H.381, 1
Lint To bring him **Lint**, and Balsamum,........18. H.46, 6
Lintells **See Lentils**
Linus To **Linus**, then to Pindar; and that done,.206. H.575, 31
Lion Umber was painting of a **Lyon** fierce,......205. H.572, 1
(As Umber sweares) did make his **Lyon** start..205. H.572, 4
Lip Because my Julia's **lip** was by,.............12. H.23, 3
Cheek, and eye, and **lip**, and chin;............52. H.147, 5
If her **lip**, the most sincere....................59. H.155, 3
For some rich flower, he took the **lip**..........71. H.182, 5
When on her **lip**, thou hast thy sweet dew plac't, 100. H.248, 3
To give Perenn'as **lip** a kisse,.................103. H.255, 3
There thou shalt find her **lip** and cheek:.......106. H.263, 8
A Tribe of one **Lip**; Leven, and of One.........199. H.545, 3
Look upon Sapho's **lip**, and you will swear,.....306. H.985, 1
With a warm **lip**, and solemne one:...........402. N.269, 11
A **Lipp** Inkyndled wth that Coale..............408. A.2, 47
The Gathering of the **Lipp**: not hand.........408. A.2, 52
Read it then before your **lipp**.................417. A.9, 13
Lip-labor Without the heart, **lip-labour** nothing is. 345. N.34, 4
Lipped **See Cherry-lipped, Kidney-lipped, Ruby-lipped**
Lips And those her **lips** doe now appeare.........7. H.9, 11
Be her **lips** ill hung, or set,....................11. H.21, 11
But yet for Loves-sake, let thy **lips** doe this,...14. H.35, 11
Where my Julia's **lips** do smile;..............20. H.53, 5
The **lips** of Julia..............................24. H.75, 4
To part her **lips**, and shew'd them there........24. H.75, 7
His nose and **lips** of mulbrie hiew.............38. H.108, 8
Soft speech, smooth touch, the **lips**, the Maiden-head: 45. H.128, 8
Thee and their **lips** espous'd; while I admire,...46. H.128, 50
From Fames black **lips**, as you from me.......49. H.136, 36
Lips can make Cherries grow....................57. H.149, 148
Give my cold **lips** a kisse at last:..............61. H.159, 25
But taking those rare **lips** of yours............71. H.182, 15
He sho'd from her full **lips** derive,.............71. H.182, 30
For those **lips**, that tongue-ty'd are:...........82. H.203, 2
This the **lips** we will permit...................82. H.203, 15
Betweene whose glories, there my **lips** Ile lay,.96. H.230, 3
Give thou my **lips** but their supreamest kiss:...129. H.327, 2
Between the **lips**, (all cherrie-red,)............130. H.329, 5
Part your joyn'd **lips**, then speaks your kisse;..130. H.329, 18
Lips she has, all Rubie red,..................138. H.342, 5
Taste her **lips**, so over-laid....................138. H.346, 6
Never like their **lips**, to sweare................182. H.490, 7
To'th' Glasse your **lips** encline;..............185. H.495, 6
That Satyre he but burnt his **lips**;.............203. H.563, 5
Those crimson clouds i'th'cheeks & **lips** leave shining. 207. H.576, 2
With mellow **Lips**, and luscious there withall....226. H.649, 2
I prest my Julia's **lips**, and in the kisse.......240. H.700, 1
Our **lips** for a while,.........................247. H.727, 4
Close keep your **lips**, if that you meane.......250. H.738, 1
Sweet are my Julia's **lips** and cleane,..........277. H.857, 1
Those **lips** please me which are plac't..........282. H.878, 3
Ile whet my **lips**, and sharpen Love on thee....327. H.1081, 2
In Prayer the **Lips** ne're act the winning part,..346. H.35, 1
From those mellifluous **lips** of his;............354. N.59, 16
Your hearts, and hands, **lips**, eares, and eyes....366. N.98, 9
Thy **lips** with all diffused grace!..............375. N.123, 74
Thus let Thy **lips** but love distill,.............393. N.232, 15
That both her **lipps** doe part, doe meete, doe kisse; 405. A.1, 38
Bowing my **lips** vnto yt stately root..........406. A.1, 111
Print thy **lips** into the ayre,...................414. A.5, 10
My **lipps** shall send a 1000 back to you........414. A.5, 16
— — — — — — — — — —, ...437. var. H.336, 84
Liquefaction That **liquefaction** of her clothes......261. H.779, 3
Liquor Small Chalice of thy frantick **liquor**; He..78. H.197, 63
What ever **Liquor** in ye powre.................320. H.1053, 2
Lisp Teach it to blush, to curtsie, **lisp**, and shew 290. H.914, 5
Lisped Tipled he was; and tipling **lispt** withall;..313. H.1017, 5
Lisping **See Pretty-lisping**
And **lisping** reeld, and reeling like to fall.......313. H.1017, 6
Li'st **See Liest**
List' **List'** sweet maids, and you shal know.......14. H.36, 2
— — — — — — — — — —, ...432. var. H.283, 105
Listen But **listen** to thee, (walking in thy chamber) 22. H.67, 3
Listen, while they (like Syrens in their Spheres) 206. H.575, 52
Listening By **listning** to thy Lire,..............151. H.388, 3
The **listning** to my numbers...................260. H.777, 4
Just so it is with me, who **list'ning**, pray......358. N.77, 5
Little **See Great-little-kingly-guest**
To give (if any, yet) but **little** sound...........15. H.38, 8
Who speak but **little**, 'cause I love so much.....15. H.38, 14
Little the wound was; greater was the smart;..17. H.44, 7
Sho'd be a **little** part...........................28. H.85, 4
Little I love; but if that he.................28. H.85, 5
Who has a **little** measure:.....................30. H.87, 15
Nature with **little** is content....................33. H.100, 4
Pray love me **little**, so you love me long.......51. H.143, 2
In this **little** Vault she lyes,...................52. H.145, 1
This said, he laid his **little** scrip..............71. H.182, 23
Or set it **little** forth............................75. H.193, 24
To fill a **little** Urne..............................81. H.201, 44
Onely a **little** more..............................85. H.211, 1
To have his **little** King-ship know,.............86. H.213, 43
A **little** brush of Squirrils haires,..............91. H.223, 46
But of a **little** Transverce bone;...............91. H.223, 57
With **little** Seale-work Damasked...............91. H.223, 63
A **little** Pin-dust; which they hold.............92. H.223, 87
Their sacred Salt here, (not a **little**.).........93. H.223, 118
Little thou't love, or not at all...............103. H.253, 18
With inward Buckram, **little** else.)............118. H.291, 12
A **little** mushroome table spred,................119. H.293, 7
Of which he eates, and tastes a **little**..........119. H.293, 27
A **little** Fuz-ball-pudding stands...............119. H.293, 29
Browne as his Tooth. A **little** Moth,...........120. H.293, 41
A **little** while from Tramplers free;...........123. H.306, 10
As her **little** eyes did peep.....................123. H.310, 4
A **little** Pipkin with a bit.....................124. H.312, 5
To honour thee, my **little** Parsly crown:.......131. H.333, 4
My wreaths on those, who **little** gave or lent...143. H.365, 6
I have there a **little** wheat;...................152. H.393, 2
Onely remaind a **little** bit,....................153. H.399, 8
But of his gettings there's but **little** sign;......154. H.400, 3
Those monstrous lies of **little** Robin Rush:....155. H.405, 8
And shew'st me there much Plate, but **little** meat; 161. H.424,

Then we shall see, how in a **little** space,.......168. H.445, 5
Little or much,...............................171. H.455, 5
Or for a **little** time we'l lye,...................190. H.515, 39
A **little** out, and then,.........................194. H.525, 3
Little you are; for Womans sake be proud;..212. H.600, 1
For my sake next, (though **little**) be not loud...212. H.600, 2
For very **little**, or no gaines:..................212. H.602, 2
Who with a **little** cannot be content,...........213. H.606, 1
Little or no part there of Tyrannie............213. H.608, 2
Then feast, and coy't a **little**; then to bed......216. H.618, 8
Whose **little** eyes glow,.........................217. H.619, 4
Holds none at all, or **little** in his hand.........221. H.633, 53
Give for bread, a **little** bit....................223. H.638, 12
Little bits, that nestle there..................224. H.638, 23
So **little** left, as if they ne'r had been:.........231. H.664, 4
Although with some, yet **little** paine:...........233. H.670, 10
That **little**, Fates me gave or lent..............246. H.724, 8
A **little** Saint best fits a **little** Shrine,.........249. H.733, 1
A **little** prop best fits a **little** Vine,............249. H.733, 2
As my small Cruse best fits my **little** Wine.....249. H.733, 3
A **little** Seed best fits a **little** Soyle,...........249. H.733, 4
A **little** Trade best fits a **little** Toyle:.........249. H.733, 5
As my small Jarre best fits my **little** Oyle.....249. H.733, 6
A **little** Bin best fits a **little** Bread,............249. H.733, 7
A **little** Garland fits a **little** Head:.............249. H.733, 8
As my small stuffe best fits my **little** Shed.....249. H.733, 9
A **little** Hearth best fits a **little** Fire,..........249. H.733, 10
A **little** Chappell fits a **little** Quire,.............249. H.733, 11
As my small Bell best fits my **little** Spire.......249. H.733, 12
A **little** streame best fits a **little** Boat;.........249. H.733, 13
A **little** lead best fits a **little** Float;...........249. H.733, 14
As my small Pipe best fits my **little** note.......249. H.733, 15
A **little** meat best fits a **little** bellie,..........249. H.733, 16
This **little** Pipkin fits this **little** Jellie..........249. H.733, 18
If **little** labour, **little** are our gaines:..........253. H.752, 1
And a **little** Oyle to either:.....................258. H.769, 6
In this **little** Urne is laid.......................262. H.782, 1
That in **little** time she be.......................269. H.814, 3
The Urne was **little**, but the room...............269. H.817, 3
Commix with Meale a **little** Pisse...............284. H.890, 2
A **little** Wafer or a Cake;.......................284. H.890, 4
And we shall see in **little** space.................297. H.948, 11
For **little** cost he...............................320. H.1051, 14
Has, or none, or **little** skill,....................347. N.41, 18
A **little** house, whose humble Roof..............349. N.47, 3
A **little** Butterie, and therein...................350. N.47, 19
A **little** Byn,......................................350. N.47, 20
Which keeps my **little** loafe of Bread..........350. N.47, 21
Unto thy **little** Saviour;..........................354. N.59, 2
Here a **little** child I stand,.....................364. N.95, 1
A **little** piggin, and a pipkin by,..................371. N.115, 5
That **little** prettie bleeding part................376. N.125, 1
God! to my **little** meale and oyle,...............377. N.130, 1
God on our Youth bestowes but **little** ease;....383. N.175, 1
As my **little** Pot doth boyle,.....................397. N.258, 1
Onely, there's left a **little** froth,................400. N.266, 12
Ver. Chor. But I will sip a **little** wine;.......400. N.267, 12
And prest a **little** they will weepe new milke....405. A.1, 58
Kindly swell vp with **little** pretty pride,.........406. A.1, 88
With **little** hands and fingers long and small...406. A.1, 99
This **little** pendant on your eare,................417. A.9, 2
And that soe **little** we despaire.................418. A.9, 25

Little-peeping-part A **little-peeping-part** of thee:.287. H.899, 2
Little-puppet-priest A **little-Puppet-Priest** doth wait,
91. H.223, 39
Little-well-kept-stock And thus thy **little-well-kept-stock** doth prove,.....................................37. H.106, 127
Liturgy In Chiefe, in this Poetick **Liturgie**.......188. H.510, 4
Live See **Outlive**
To **live** some few-sad-howers after thee:........11. H.22, 2
Live, and not marry?..........................12. H.26, 6
He could **live** free here?......................12. H.26, 12
Live with a thrifty, not a needy Fate;.........13. H.28, 1
Live as I have liv'd still,......................13. H.31, 2
Mercie and Truth **live** with thee! and forbeare..14. H.35, 9
Banish'd from thee I **live**; ne'r to return,......19. H.52, 3
Then to **live** not perfected......................21. H.59, 6
You Criticks meanes to **live**:....................32. H.96, 2
Wayes lesse to **live**, then to **live** well:..........35. H.106, 10
And both are knowne to thee, who now can'st **live**
35. H.106, 11
Thus thou can'st tearcely **live** to satisfie.......35. H.106, 27
Confin'd to **live** with private Larr:............37. H.106, 106
But to **live** round, and close, and wisely true...38. H.106, 135
Live, and **live** blest; thrice happy Paire; Let Breath,
38. H.106, 141
Till when, in such assurance **live**, ye may......38. H.106, 145
Fabius, and Cotta, Lentulus, all **live**..........41. H.117, 3
Your face no more: So **live** you free..........49. H.136, 35
Live employ'd, and so **live** free................53. H.147, 11
To make you bravely **live**;......................57. H.149, 154
If thou wilt say, that I shall **live** with thee;....60. H.156, 3
If not, (as banisht) I will **live** alone...........60. H.156, 5
That I shall stir, or **live** more here............61. H.159, 27
I **live** for ever; let the rest all lye.............63. H.165, 3
Who knowes to **live** to morrow?..................65. H.170, 6

Will **live** with thee, or else for thee will die...70. H.181, 24
When these Circumstants shall but **live** to see..79. H.197, 85
Live, **live** thou dost, and shalt; for why?....89. H.219, 15
I **live** and die..................................95. H.227, 21
Let's **live** merrily, and thus....................96. H.231, 5
If so, we **live**; if not, with mournfull humme,..100. H.248, 5
Bid me to **live**, and I will **live**..................108. H.267, 1
To **live** and die for thee......................109. H.267, 24
To **live** therein for ever: Frie..................115. H.283, 137
And **live**, and in that case,.....................115. H.283, 139
Is to love, and **live** i'th fire...................117. H.286, 12
Let's **live**, my Wickes, then, while we may,.....132. H.336, 15
Then **live** we free,...............................133. H.336, 37
Live in thy peace; as for my selfe,...........134. H.336, 73
Me longer date, and more fresh springs to **live**:.140. H.355, 12
Live thou a Selden, that's a Demi-god.........143. H.365, 12
For which thy Love, **live** with thy Master here,.151. H.387, 7
Live here: But know 'twas vertue, & not chance,
152. H.392, 5
Shall **live**, and thou not superlast all times?..155. H.405, 14
It selfe to **live** or dye.........................164. H.441, 12
To **live** remembred in your story...............170. H.449, 29
Let's **live** in hast; use pleasures while we may:.171. H.453, 1
Here, here I **live**,...............................171. H.455, 1
Of those mild Men, thou art to **live** among:....172. H.456, 6
Thee **live**, as dead and in thy grave;...........174. H.465, 12
No, **live** thee to thy selfe, and keep............175. H.465, 47
And all **live** here with needy Fate..............179. H.476, 30
And my most luckie Swain, when I shall **live** to see
184. H.492, 41
Few **live** the life immortall. He ensures......188. H.506, 15
Live, **live** with me, and thou shalt see......192. H.521, 1
If thou wilt love, and **live** with me............193. H.521, 56
Here we securely **live**, and eate................198. H.544, 1
Thus, thus, we **live**, and spend the houres.....198. H.544, 19
Here, here I **live** with what my Board,..........200. H.552, 1
Live by thy Muse thou shalt; when others die.210. H.592, 1
Let's **live** with that smal pittance that we have;
213. H.607, 1
Live in the Love of Doves, and having told....222. H.633, 62
Drink Wine, and **live** here blithefull, while ye may:
228. H.655, 1
The morrowes life too late is, **Live** to-day.......228. H.655, 2
And ever **live** a true............................228. H.657, 12
This is to **live**, and to endeere.................233. H.670, 15
Then, while Fates suffer, **live** thou free,.........233. H.670, 17
Then **live** we mirthfull, while we should,.....233. H.670, 28
And thus lesse last, then **live** our Day.........233. H.670, 31
That man's not said to **live**, but last:..........233. H.670, 33
But for to **live** that half seven well:............233. H.670, 35
Crown'd Poets; yet **live** Princes under thee:..234. H.673, 16
Love, and **live** here while we may;.............238. H.691, 2
That I amongst you **live** a Citizen.............242. H.713, 12
Man may want Land to **live** in; but for all,....267. H.807, 1
To **live** for ever, with my Just..................278. H.859, 6
My selfe now **live**: this age best pleaseth mee..292. H.927, 2
Long may I **live** so, and my wreath of Bayes,.297. H.947, 13
This line about, **live** Thou throughout the world;
298. H.955, 2
Live long and lovely, but yet grow no lesse....299. H.958, 3
That done; O Cesar, **live**, and be to us,.........300. H.961, 13
Chor. Long **live** the King; and to accomplish this,
300. H.961, 19
He that will **live** of all cares dispossest,.......305. H.981, 1
Live long, Lacon, so adew......................306. H.984, 41
You aske me what I doe, and how I **live**?.....312. H.1013, 1
Then did I **live** when I did see..................313. H.1020, 1
For me embalm'd to **live** againe;...............313. H.1020, 6
Ile **live** as one Regenerate......................313. H.1020, 8
Live thou at Court, where thou mayst be.....323. H.1068, 11
Can **live** by love, or else grow fat by Play:....325. H.1077, 2
Live you, great Mistresse of your Arts, and be
326. H.1080, 21
Let me not **live**, if I not love,.................327. H.1082, 1
Their ends for Pleasure, do not **live**, but last..328. H.1088, 10
I wo'd come back and **live** with thee?..........328. H.1090, 5
Since longer I can't **live**,.......................328. H.1091, 5
Those, that must **live** with Thee for evermore..329. H.1092, 4
The mind; the King, the meanes whereby I **live**.
355. N.62, 2
From aberrations to **live** free;..................357. N.72, 17
Shall **live** with Him eternally:..................359. N.78, 10
Long may He **live**, till He hath told..........367. N.98, 27
So **live** in Heaven, in everlasting light........384. N.181, 5
By houres we all **live** here, in Heaven is known..392. N.229, 1
If man **lives** long, and if he **live** not well...392. N.230, 6
Let me **live** ever here, and stir................402. N.269, 18
And **live** in Hell, if that my Christ stayes there.
403. N.271, 8
True heate, whearwth humanitie doth **liue**......410. A.3, 30
But there to **live**, where Love shall last for ever.
417. A.8, 38
A scripture how yow **liue** and dye..............417. A.9, 12

Lived See **Short-lived**
Live as I have **liv'd** still,......................13. H.31, 2
With blamelesse carriage, I **liv'd** here,........41. H.116, 1

The Persian King **liv'd** not more happily.......70. H.181, 4
Because I've **liv'd** so long a maid:............97. H.235, 2
The gardens-glory **liv'd** a while,..............126. H.318, 4
But have hitherto **liv'd** free,...................183. H.490, 17
While they **liv'd**, or lasted here:.............187. H.503, 2
Chaste I **liv'd**, without a wife,..................199. H.546, 3
As when the Sweet Maria **lived** here:..........214. H.612, 10
And thrice three weekes) he **lived** here.......226. H.644, 4
But yet those yeers that I have **liv'd**, but few...328. H.1088, 4
Of all those three-score, has not **liv'd** halfe three:
328. H.1088, 8
There ever **lived** such a one...................418. A.9, 30
Livelihood Who hold fast here an endlesse **lively-hood.**
152. H.392, 8
Is that which gives to sin a **livelihood**.........367. N.101, 2
Lively Of **lively** colours, flowing from the face....274. H.840, 2
Livers The flimsie **Livers**, and blew Gizzards are.
326. H.1079, 2
Livery (Whose **Livery** ye weare)..............83. H.207, 6
Though palenes be the **Livery** that I weare,..222. H.634, 5
This **livery** wch the *greeke hath worne.......418. A.9, 54
Lives That man **lives** twice, that **lives** the first life well.
121. H.298, 2
Lives in the pretty Lady-flower................126. H.318, 11
Skrew **lives** by shifts; yet sweares by no small oathes;
149. H.380, 1
Their **lives** in sweets, and left in death perfume.
185. H.496, 4
Our **Lives** do differ from our Lines by much..218. H.624, 2
Whose **lives** are others, not their own!........229. H.662, 2
Truggin now **lives** but to belye his name.......283. H.882, 2
Cold comfort still I'm sure **lives** there.........312. H.1014, 10
Lives not those yeers, but he that **lives** them well.
328. H.1088, 6
He **lives**, who **lives** to virtue: men who cast...328. H.1088, 9
A stock of Goods, whereby he **lives**...........351. N.50, 2
If man **lives** long, and if he live not well......392. N.230, 6
— — — — — — — — — —, ...422. var. H.106, 145
Livest Wherein thou **liv'st** for ever. Deare farewell.
23. H.72, 4
But thou **liv'st** fearlesse; and thy face ne'r shewes
37. H.106, 93
Liveth No man dies ill, that **liveth** well.........321. H.1059, 2
Living Let him the Land and **Living** finde;......59. H.153, 3
Behold this **living** stone,.......................85. H.211, 17
Thy **living** Epitaph shall be,....................146. H.376, 9
Overloving, (**living** here:)....................152. H.391, 2
Having a **living** Fountain under it............154. H.403, 4
And like our **living**, where w'are known......200. H.552, 19
Reproach we may the **living**; not the dead:...218. H.625, 1
Of **living** water by thy Benizon..............245. H.723, 4
And so soone stopt my longer **living** here;....278. H.860, 2
Though while we **living** 'bout the world do roame,
278. H.860, 5
Close by whose **living** coale I sit,.............350. N.47, 25
Before my last, but here a **living** grave,.......371. N.115, 2
Lo **Loe**, I, the Lyrick Prophet, who have set.....142. H.365, 3
Loe! Thus I give a Virgin-Flower,............402. N.270, 5
Loach Seeal'd up with Night-gum, **Loach** each morning lyes,
269. H.816, 1
Load Then for contriving so to **loade** thy Board,.210. H.590, 5
To **load** with blessings, and unload from sins...341. N.14, 2
Loadest Thou **load'st** with gold thy vestiment?...394. N.239, 2
Loads To mortall men great **loads** allotted be,...242. H.715, 1
God **loads**, and unloads, (thus His work begins)
341. N.14, 1
Loaf See **White-loaf**
Cut the white **loafe** here,.....................263. H.784, 14
Which keeps my little **loafe** of Bread.........350. N.47, 21
Loam Whose Ribs the Laths are, & whose Flesh the **Loame.**
279. H.865, 2
Loan Least **loane** of Thine, half Restitution?....368. N.103, 6
Loathe See **Loth**
Skoles stinks so deadly, that his Breeches **loath**
226. H.650, 1
Subjects still **loath** the present Government.....291. H.921, 2
Loathed Then where I **loath'd** so much.........19. H.51, 8
Loathed Furrowes in your brow:...............97. H.232, 14
Dwell, then in **lothed** Devonshire.............111. H.278, 8
Into the **loathed** West;.......................144. H.371, 9
Come, leave this **loathed** Country-life, and then.171. H.456, 1
With men, a **loathed** inconveniencie...........239. H.698, 2
Loathsome A clammie Reume makes **loathsome** both his eyes:
110. H.273, 3
The Sock grew **loathsome**, and the Buskins pride,
150. H.382, 2
Sluts are **loathsome** to the Fairies:...........201. H.556, 6
Nothing can be more **loathsome**, then to see...211. H.597, 1
(Which to me most **loathsome** is.)............282. H.878, 2
Nothing but **loathsome** sores in mee...........344. N.29, 4
Loathsomeness That sweetness turnes to **Loathsomness.**
288. H.909, 4
Ther's **loathsomnesse** e'en in the sweets of love.
297. H.949, 4
Loathsomest Into the **Loathsoms** <t> shapps, thou canst deuise
412. A.3, 93
Loaves Or have I two **loaves**; then I use......376. N.127, 7
Lobster The Lady of the **Lobster** is,............93. H.223, 131
Local Of **locall** motion, in no least respect,.....385. N.186, 3
Lock This flock of wooll, and this rich **lock** of hair,
159. H.421, 15
One onely **lock** of that sweet Hay.............355. N.60, 3
Locked Be ye **lockt** up like to these,...........120. H.297, 7
Lockt up, not lost:.........................190. H.515, 44
Locks See **Dew-locks**
When the Rose raignes, and **locks** with ointments shine,
7. H.8, 9
And let not **Locks** thus keep ye................26. H.81, 8
This night, and **Locks** pickt, yet w'are not a Maying.
69. H.178, 56
My **locks** behung with frost and snow:........134. H.336, 76
Locks incurl'd of other haire;...............253. H.750, 11
Long **Locks** of late our Zelot Peason weares,.275. H.843, 1
For my **Locks** (Girles) let 'em be.............330. H.1098, 3
— — — — — — — — — — — —, ...440. var. H.443, 96
— — — — — — — — — — — —, ...442. var. H.575, 20
Lodge Vice doth in some but **lodge** awhile, not dwell.
314. H.1021, 2
To feed, or **lodge**, to have the best of Roomes:.356. N.68, 2
Lodger Where if I can a **lodger** be.............123. H.306, 9
Lodging Of long'd-for **lodging**, go to rest:......216. H.617, 2
To make my **lodging** the sweeter;............256. H.762, 3
Log The Christmas **Log** to the firing;..........263. H.784, 3
Come while the **Log** is a teending.............263. H.784, 12
The Christmas **Log** next yeare;...............285. H.893, 6
Logomachy Betwixt us two no more **Logomachie.**
287. H.901, 4
Loins To gird my **loynes** about................352. N.53, 11
London **London** my home is: though by hard fate sent
242. H.713, 13
Lonely Why nothing now, but **lonely** sit,........132. H.334, 3
Why so **lonely** on the hill?..................305. H.984, 4
Long See **Overlong**
'Twill not be **long** (Perilla) after this,..........9. H.14, 5
Long still doe tarry,.........................12. H.26, 3
Me thought, her **long** small legs & thighs......16. H.41, 5
Nor wil't be **long**, ere this accomplish'd be;....26. H.79, 9
If we **long** tarry..............................31. H.94, 4
Homer himself, in a **long** work, may sleep......32. H.95, 6
Sing o're Horace; for ere **long**...............39. H.111, 11
Weak though it be; **long** may it grow, and stand,
40. H.112, 3
And shame had follow'd **long** ere this,........48. H.136, 8
Pray love me little, so you love me **long**......51. H.143, 2
Your joyes, by staying **long**:................53. H.149, 4
Doves, 'two'd say, yee bill too **long**............57. H.149, 140
The Lillie will not **long** endure;...............60. H.159, 13
And when (though **long** it comes to passe)....63. H.164, 6
I shall, ere **long**, with green turfs cover'd be;.66. H.174, 3
Meet after **long** divorcement by the Iles:......77. H.197, 2
Where hast thou been so **long** from my embraces,
77. H.197, 19
But die you must (faire Maid) ere **long**,.......88. H.216, 20
So **long** you did not sing, or touch your Lute,.95. H.228, 1
Time, ere **long**, will come and plow...........97. H.232, 13
Because I've liv'd so **long** a maid:..............97. H.235, 2
That **long** I love not any.....................100. H.249, 8
Dry your sweet cheek, **long** drown'd with sorrows raine;
105. H.259, 1
Ere **long** a fleeting shade:....................111. H.280, 6
Who count this night as **long** as three,........114. H.283, 74
Long have I sought for: but co'd never see...121. H.301, 3
And ere **long**, a Boy Love send ye............125. H.314, 6
'Tis strange, his Father **long** time has been ill,..125. H.315, 3
As I did, not **long** ago,......................131. H.332, 3
Ere **long**, a song, ere **long**, a shade.............133. H.336, 30
Lasie to others, but be **long** to me..............141. H.357, 2
Y'ave dipt too **long** i'th' Vinegar;.............146. H.377, 22
So **long** are capable of cure,....................153. H.395, 2
But **long** or short, I'm well content with all...163. H.437, 2
One Cordelion had that Age **long** since;......170. H.451, 15
How **long**, Perenna, wilt thou see............177. H.471, 1
Dear Lycidas, e're **long**,.....................184. H.492, 26
That Love last **long**; let it thy first care be..185. H.494, 1
Love in extreames, can never **long** endure.......185. H.494, 4
His Fame's **long** life, who strives to set up Yours.
188. H.506, 16
And weeping Widowes **long** opprest.........190. H.515, 21
Here those **long** suits of Chancery lie...........190. H.515, 25
Long time w'ave here been a toying:..........195. H.534, 3
Long for to lye here..........................197. H.540, 4
Leaving no Fame to **long** Posterity:............210. H.592, 2
Who by the Shepheards, sung (**long** since)......214. H.611, 5
Left (of the large heart, and **long** hand)........218. H.626, 10
Make no **long** stay...........................220. H.633, 6
A stubborn Oake, or Holme (**long** growing there)
225. H.642, 14
Though **long** it be, yeeres may repay the debt;..228. H.654, 1
So **long** as I am able..........................235. H.674, 15
Into a **long** and irksome banishment;...........242. H.713, 14
She goes her **long** white egg to lay.............246. H.724, 12
Long enough has endur'd,......................247. H.727, 8

Her decent legs, cleane, long and small.........247. H.729, 4
Ph. I'ie beg a penny, or Ile sing so long,.......248. H.730, 21
Who for a long sad time has weeping stood,.....251. H.745, 3
So long as thou dost heat us...................259. H.772, 9
Griefe, if't be great, 'tis short; if long, 'tis light.
268. H.810, 2
Long Locks of late our Zelot Peason weares,....275. H.843, 1
Gone she is a long, long way,..................276. H.848, 1
Teage has told lyes so long, that when Teage tells
282. H.880, 1
Long may I live so, and my wreath of Bayes,..297. H.947, 13
Live long and lovely, but yet grow no lesse....299. H.958, 3
After our long, and peevish sicknesses...........300. H.961, 4
Chor. Long live the King; and to accomplish this,
300. H.961, 19
Live long, Lacon, so adew.....................306. H.984, 41
To an old soare a long cure must goe on;......312. H.1012, 1
No Kingdomes got by Rapine long endure.....314. H.1023, 2
No more shall I a long thy christall glide,......315. H.1028, 7
Die ere long I'm sure, I shall;................321. H.1058, 1
Long I have lasted in this world; (tis true)....328. H.1088, 3
And I ere long, My Girles shall see,............329. .1093, 5
Long, long, I'm sure,...........................353. N.56, 19
Long may He live, till He hath told............367. N.98, 27
In long white stole,............................369. N.106, 8
So long as I about Thee craule?...............371. N.114, 6
So long (it seem'd) as Maries Faith was small,....386. N.192, 1
If man lives long, and if he live not well.........392. N.230, 6
Might I make choice, long life sho'd be with-stood;
392. N.230, 9
Long before this, the base, the dull, the rude,...398. N.263, 5
For, long this work wil be, & very short this Day.
401. N.268, 6
So long unsound:..............................401. N.268, 19
Her long disheuel'd rose-crown'd tramaletts:......404. A.1, 4
With little hands and fingers long and small......406. A.1, 99
Longe forfaite pawnèd diamonds..................407. A.2, 8
Hee may ere longe haue such a wyfe............409. A.2, 107
Of those god-full prophetts longe before..........411. A.3, 42
Nor stoope to'th Center, but suruiue as Longe....411. A.3, 45
Soe longe desir'd...............................413. A.4, 23
So long as I haue feares........................414. A.5, 6
— — — — — — — — — —, ...428. var. H.238, 5
How long, soft bride, shall your deare C: make
431. ins. H.283, 60a
how long, oh pardon, shall the house......431. ins. H.283, 60c
how long shall the page, to please.........431. ins. H.283, 60g
Know so long Treaties; beate the drumme.432. ins. H.283, 140c

Long-black-thumb-nail Thy long-black-Thumb-nail marks 'em out for ill:..............................66. H.173, 2

Longed-for Of long'd-for lodging, go to rest:....216. H.617, 2
To re-possess once more your long'd-for home...300. H.961, 6

Longer Then sweetest Silvia, let's no longer stay;..8. H.10, 5
But why? why longer doe I gaze upon..........45. H.128, 37
Then it no longer keep,.........................53. H.149, 17
My longer stay, and so I dy'd.................69. H.180, 4
Let it be Doomes-day; nay, take longer scope;.83. H.206, 3
Longer flowing, longer free,....................98. H.238, 4
Me longer date, and more fresh springs to live:.140. H.355, 12
With griefe; seemes longer then a yeare.......162. H.431, 4
Let's leave a longer time to wait,..............179. H.476, 28
Why, Madam, will ye longer weep,.............189. H.514, 1
The longer here...............................198. H.544, 24
For quick dispatch, Sculls made no longer stay,.200. H.551, 3
Ile sing no more, nor will I longer write......228. H.658, 1
And so soone stopt my longer living here;......278. H.860, 2
I will no longer kiss,...........................328. H.1091, 1
I can no longer stay;...........................328. H.1091, 2
Since longer I can't live,......................328. H.1091, 5
And I'le no longer stay,.........................352. N.53, 2
The longer thred of life we spin,...............379. N.144, 1

Longest This the short'st day, and this the longest night;
114. H.283, 72
That Happiness do's still the longest thrive,....264. H.792, 1
That love 'twixt men do's ever longest last.......327. H.1083, 1

Long-lamented-widowhood As one, in long-lamented-widowhood;....................................25. H.77, 4

Long-life's-day A long-lifes-day I've taken paines.212. H.602, 1

Longs To him, who longs unto his CHRIST to go,
378. N.133, 1

Look And look how all those heavenly Lamps acquire
3. Ded.H., 5
So, that the more I look, the more I prove,....10. H.16, 5
And look upon our dreadfull passages,...........14. H.35, 6
And look, what Smallage, Night-shade, Cypresse, Yew,
27. H.82, 9
Dean-bourn, farewell; I never look to see.......29. H.86, 1
Lillies will languish; Violets look ill;.........41. H.118, 1
Next, look thou like a sickly Moone;...........47. H.132, 3
Look in Prig's purse, the chev'rell there tells you
71. H.183, 3
Frown, and look sullen ev'ry where..........72. H.185, 4
Without a sad looke, or a solemne teare?.......73. H.186, 10
Look, look, by Love I vow....................74. H.192, 3
Too strong for Fate to break us: Look upon..78. H.197, 71
Onely this Ile look upon,......................84. H.209, 3
Look in his Brine-tub, and you shall find there.89. H.221, 3

So that where ere ye look, ye see,.............90. H.223, 19
When I through all my many Poems look,......94. H.226, 1
Now 'tis so full, that when therein I look,......99. H.245, 3
Runs from his Torrid Zone, to prie, and look,..114. H.283, 62
Look, how the Rainbow doth appeare..........139. H.353, 1
When checked by the Butlers look...........147. H.377, 56
Looke red, and blow, and bluster, but not speake:
150. H.382, 8
Looke upon all; and though on fire..........174. H.465, 7
That makes them looke so lanke, so Ghost-like still.
186. H.498, 6
And look with a contracted brow?............188. H.508, 2
Better look the Roses red,...................194. H.527, 3
Go wooe young Charles no more to looke,......214. H.611, 1
Looke ye not wan, or colourlesse for feare.....222. H.634, 6
The least grim looke, or cast a frown on you:..222. H.634, 8
And look how when a frantick Storme doth tear
225. H.642, 13
Look how next the holy fier...................242. H.714, 9
Backward he should not looke while he........265. H.798, 5
And looking back, that look did sever..........265. H.798, 11
So look the mornings when the Sun...........268. H.811, 1
So Corrolls looke more lovely Red,............268. H.811, 5
A Lawn, that thou mayst looke...............271. H.824, 10
Looke in my Book, and herein see,...........288. H.906, 1
So Lillies thorough Christall look:............294. H.939, 3
For look how many leaves there be...........304. H.980, 7
Look upon Sapho's lip, and you will swear,....306. H.985, 1
And look as all were capable of Love:.......326. H.1080, 12
Ye quake for cold to looke on me..............329. H.1093, 6
Look how our foule Dayes do exceed our faire;..339. N.1, 1
My God! looke on me with thine eye............344. N.29, 1
And heale me with thy looke, or touch:........344. N.29, 7
Let others look for Pearle and Gold,............355. N.60, 1
When e're thou speak'st, look with a lowly eye:.362. N.89, 3
So Thou, my God, may'st on this impure look,.371. N.113, 7
But look, how each transgressor onward went...391. N.227, 3
A down-cast look, and sowre?.................391. N.228, 12
But look how night succeeds the day, so He....394. N.236, 3
Look down, and see..........................401. N.268, 26
Hence rise those twoe ambitious hills that looke.406. A.1, 81
Languish and looke but thy returne see neuer.....414. A.5, 8
Fould now thine armes, and in thy last looke reare
414. A.6, 7

Looked They blush'd, and look'd more fresh then flowers
25. H.78, 5
What next is lookt for? but we all sho'd see....44. H.124, 3
Or lookt I back unto the Times hence flown,..234. H.673, 1
Must not be lookt on, but at distances:.......237. H.685, 10
She lookt as she'd been got with child.........251. H.740, 7
I came; (tis true) and lookt for Fowle of price,.262. H.783, 7
If but lookt on; struck dead, if scan'd by Thee.
301. H.962, 6
Much as the ends are to be lookt unto.........387. N.200, 4
Soe look't the Grecian Oratour when sent.........411. A.3, 71
Soe Tullye look't, when from the Brest's of Rome
412. A.3, 75

Lookers See Lookers-on

Lookers-on For to catch the Lookers on;........232. H.665, 13

Lookest And, as thou look'st, the wanton Steere,.230. H.662, 37

Looking And looking down below,...............27. H.81, 19
Ah cruell Sea! and looking on't,...............42. H.119, 9
Looking upon yee, That two Nations.........116. H.283, 158
Where being laid, all Faire signes looking on,..124. H.313, 11
And looking back, that look did sever..........265. H.798, 11
This Janus looking double waye................417. A.9, 16
— — — — — — — — —, ...424. var. H.164, 7

Looking-glass Thou wilt complaine, False now's thy Looking-glasse......................................21. H.62, 2
You question with your Looking-glasse;........63. H.164, 7
Let but Pink's face i' th' Looking-glasse be showne,
110. H.272, 3
For anger spat on thee her Looking-glasse:....249. H.732, 2
(As this looking-glasse assures)................418. A.9, 28

Looks See Frantic-looks, Over-leaven-looks
Looks like a Bride now, or a bed of flowers,....25. H.77, 5
Who, with his looks too, can appease...........31. H.90, 4
So looks Anthea, when in bed she lyes,.........34. H.104, 1
But if thy whimpring looks doe ask me why?...46. H.128, 41
Or smile more inly; lest thy looks beguile......46. H.128, 46
That I have sworn, but by thy looks to know thee.
46. H.128, 48
Why are Those Looks, Those Looks which have been
77. H.197, 27
Into the which who looks shall see............90. H.223, 5
Lookes for the treaders; every where is wove..115. H.283, 122
Bungie do's fast; looks pale; puts Sack-cloth on;
122. H.305, 1
Looks forward, scornes what's left behind:....132. H.336, 14
As in our clothes, so likewise he who lookes,...202. H.559, 1
As Julia looks when she doth dress............268. H.811, 9
And seems halfe ravisht, when he looks upon..295. H.941, 3
And when we think His looks are sowre and grim,
340. N.7, 3
Looks on the filth, but is not soil'd thereby;...371. N.113, 6
That Lookes for such prepared grownd,........409. A.2, 104

Soe w^t^h like **lookes**, as once the Ministrell......411. A.3, 67
Looks through the passage of theis lines........417. A.9, 10
More mildlie least thy temptinge **lookes** beguile
424. ins. H.128, 46e
Loom And all the **loome** of life undone:.........72. H.185, 11
To wrong a Spinner or her **Loome**............165. H.442, 15
They, weeping, spread a Lawnie **Loome**,........237. H.686, 15
We take our leaves now of the **Loome**,.........374. N.123, 35
Looms Of Persian **Loomes**, and antique Plate:...239. H.696, 10
Loose See **Lose**
Loud is our love, and **loose** our play,.............48. H.136, 2
The best way how to **loose** the Zone............56. H.149, 92
To **loose** the button, is no lesse,................241. H.712, 1
Lets **loose**.................................246. H.724, 15
To make **loose** Gownes for Mackarell:..........275. H.844, 6
The Daughters wild and **loose** in dresse;........310. H.1004, 7
swell, mixe, and **loose** your soules; implye
431. ins. H.283, 50d
Loose-hipped First, Jollies wife is lame; then next, **loose-hipt**:
62. H.163, 1
Lopped Is **lopt** already; and the rest but stand..203. H.565, 2
Lord See **Lord Mayor**
Nurse up, great **Lord**, this my posterity:........40. H.112, 2
So you, my **Lord**, though you have now your stay,
52. H.146, 9
Though you (my **Lord**) have been unkind to me:.52. H.146, 18
If then, (my **Lord**) to sanctifie my Muse..........64. H.168, 7
Come forth, my **Lord**, and see the Cart..........101. H.250, 7
You, who are High born, and a **Lord** no lesse...141. H.359, 3
But you, my **Lord**, are One, whose hand along..141. H.359, 13
Honours my Lady and my **Lord**...............148. H.377, 76
You are a **Lord**, an Earle, nay more, a Man,....172. H.459, 1
He's **Lord** of thy life, who contemnes his own...181. H.486, 2
If I dare write to You, my **Lord**, who are,.......187. H.506, 1
As that the Messes ne'r o'r-laid the **Lord**:.......210. H.590, 6
No joy to thee their sickly **Lord**...............239. H.696, 12
He's **Lord** of thy life, who contemnes his own....240. H.702, 2
Thou mighty **Lord** and master of the Lyre,......280. H.871, 1
'Tis liberty to serve one **Lord**; but he...........284. H.887, 1
Next, let the **Lord**, and Ladie here............291. H.919, 9
Cries out, (my **lord**, my **Lord**) the Case is clear:
303. H.975, 6
That's not inlaid with Thee, (my **Lord**)..........339. N.2, 4
Yet, **Lord**, I know there is with Thee...........342. N.17, 7
Lord! let me never act that beggars part,........347. N.39, 3
Thou hast promis'd, **Lord**, to be.................347. N.40, 1
As to speak, **Lord**, say and hold................347. N.40, 4
Lord, Thou hast given me a cell.................349. N.47, 1
Lord, I confesse too, when I dine,..............350. N.47, 27
Lord, 'tis thy plenty-dropping hand,.............350. N.47, 41
Lord, I will kisse it, though it kill:...........351. N.48, 4
Lord, do not beat me,.........................351. N.49, 1
Lord, do not scourge me,......................351. N.49, 5
Lord, I confesse, that Thou alone art able........357. N.73, 1
And **Lord** of all this Revelling..................365. N.96, 32
Of Him, who's **Lord** of Heav'n and Earth;......366. N.98, 19
Lord, I am like to Misletoe,....................371. N.114, 1
Implies His Power, when He's cal'd the **LORD**.
379. N.141, 2
But 'twas not till their dearest **Lord** was dead;..384. N.180, 11
My mild, my loving Tutor, **Lord** and God!.......398. N.261, 3
When Thou wast taken, **Lord**, I oft have read,...399. N.264, 1
Chor. **Lord**, I'le not see Thee to drink all.......400. N.267, 10
Which done, **Lord** say, The rest is mine.........400. N.267, 13
Hence they have born my **Lord**: Behold! the Stone
403. N.271, 1
Come then greate **Lord**.......................413. A.4, 31
Lordly Dol'd to us in That **Lord'y** dish..........374. N.123, 34
Lord Mayor To call my **Lord Maior** knave;....259. H.772, 15
Lord Mayor's Once on a **Lord-Mayors** day, in Cheapside, when
200. H.551, 1
Lord's Well, on, brave boyes, to your **Lords** Hearth,
101. H.250, 26
Which freely drink to your **Lords** health,......102. H.250, 38
And, you must know, your **Lords** word's true,..102. H.250, 51
Of tardidation in the **Lords** Affaires............378. N.137, 6
Lords We are the **Lords** of Wine and Oile:......101. H.250, 2
As we were **Lords** of all the earth.............133. H.336, 56
Or **Lords** be, (granting my wishes)............239. H.695, 9
Lose (Fighting) **lose** not in the field............151. H.386, 4
Co'd life return, 'twod never **lose** a day..........171. H.453, 2
Both, lest thou **lose** thy liberty:...............174. H.465, 26
And **lose** you quite..........................176. H.467, 12
So, when Death comes, Fresh tinctures **lose** their place.
207. H.576, 5
Wheare hee may roule, and **loose** his sence........408. A.2, 45
— — — — — — — — — — — —, ...424. var. H.164, 12
— — — — — — — — — — — —, ...431. ins. H.283, 50d
Loseth None **loseth** that, which he in time may get.
228. H.654, 2
Loss The **losse** of Maiden-head?................53. H.149, 14
And their **losse** in blooming yeares;.............152. H.391, 6
Broke at the **Losse** of Maiden-heads.........167. H.443, 107
In publique **loss** to shed a Teare...............203. H.564, 4
Nor, with the **losse** of thy lov'd rest,............229. H.662, 9
The **losse** or thine, or mine....................238. H.690, 4
Must sit with the **losse**,......................256. H.762, 8
The **loss** of that we call a Maydenhead?........262. H.781, 14
Violl, and Voice, is (by thy **losse**) struck mute?..288. H.907, 4
Thy **loss** brave man! whose Numbers have been hurl'd,
288. H.907, 5
By thy sad **losse**, our liberty:..................360. N.83, 20
Evill no Nature hath; the **losse** of good..........367. N.101, 1
Losses By my **losses**;..........................308. H.993, 9
Lost See **Feigned-lost-virginities, Lily-lost**
I have **lost**, and lately, these....................15. H.39, 1
Entranc'd, and **lost** confusedly:..................23. H.68, 6
But **lost** to one, be th' others death...........38. H.106, 142
Rather then love, let me be ever **lost**;...........40. H.113, 5
Horace, Anacreon both had **lost** their fame,......45. H.128, 31
For the **lost** sweet-heart of her **youth**:........47. H.132, 8
But learn, that Time once **lost**,..................53. H.149, 7
Esteeme it when 'tis **lost**:......................53. H.149, 16
Once **lost**, can ne'r be found againe:...........69. H.178, 64
Alas for me! that I have **lost**..................72. H.185, 8
Lost in the wild sea, once againe:..............79. H.198, 8
Are **lost**, i'th'funerall fire......................81. H.201, 48
For having **lost** but once your prime,...........84. H.208, 15
Yet **lost**, ere that chast flesh and blood..........88. H.216, 8
Yet **lost** ere you transfuse your smell...........88. H.216, 15
Lost in the civill Wildernesse of sleep:..........99. H.244, 6
For you once **lost**, who weep not here!......104. H.256, 10
But Venus having **lost** the day,...............105. H.260, 5
Thou art to all **lost** love the best,..............106. H.262, 1
For their love **lost**; their onely gaine..........106. H.262, 11
Our comfort is, we can't be **lost**...............134. H.336, 58
Though **lost** in them, yet found in me.........146. H.376, 10
Thou do'st redeeme those times; and what was **lost**
147. H.377, 41
Rom's were these Three Horatii we have **lost**...170. H.451, 14
For that once **lost**, thou't fall to one,.........174. H.465, 27
T'ave **lost** the good ye might have had.........179. H.476, 39
But **lost** to that they most approv'd:............180. H.478, 2
I have **lost** my former flame:..................182. H.489, 2
For **lost** like these, 'twill be,.................184. H.493, 11
Lockt up, not **lost**:.........................190. H.515, 44
Lost to all Musick now; since every thing.....214. H.612, 3
Or fold mine armes, and sigh, because I've **lost**.222. H.634, 12
Nor us (my Friend) when we are **lost**,.........233. H.670, 26
One jemme was **lost**; and I will get..........240. H.705, 5
Like a poore Lady **lost** in Widdowhood:.......251. H.745, 4
Death to our Countrey, now hath **lost** his heat:.254. H.756, 4
Weepe for the dead, for they have **lost** this light:
298. H.952, 1
And weepe for me, **lost** in an endless night.......298. H.952, 2
Lost to the world; **lost** to my selfe; alone....298. H.954, 1
I have **lost** my lovely steere,.................305. H.984, 15
Are **lost**, and theirs, in everlasting night.......313. H.1019, 4
The life I got I quickly **lost**:..................313. H.1020, 4
Are **lost** i' th' Sea..........................354. N.58, 7
All I have **lost**, that co'd be rapt from me;....371. N.112, 1
For we have **lost**, with thee, the Meale,.........374. N.123, 23
When once the Soule has **lost** her way,........393. N.233, 1
That is A Margarite, w^ch^ **Lost**................409. A.2, 85
We both were **lost**, if both of us not sunderd;..414. A.6, 6
Times, Titles, Trophies, may be **lost** and Spent;.419. A.10, 3
on you is altogether **lost**,..................432. ins. H.283, 70d
— — — — — — — — — —, ...436. var. H.336, 22
The Virgins **lost** at Barley-breakes,........440. ins. H.443, 45u
Lot 'Tis the **lot** ordain'd for me..................84. H.209, 6
Learn this of me, where e'r thy **Lot** doth fall;..153. H.396, 1
Short **lot**, or not, to be content with all........153. H.396, 2
Next is your **lot** (Faire) to be number'd one,....188. H.510, 1
Where ere the luckie **Lot** doth fall,............197. H.542, 3
When my **Lot** calls me to be buried,............277. H.853, 2
The Person crowns the Place; your **lot** doth fall
304. H.977, 1
Be a King by the **lot**,........................317. H.1035, 10
Give thee the Laurell Crowne for **lot**;.........334. H.1123, 4
Loth See **Loathe**
Love is most **loth** to leave the thing beloved....73. H.186, 12
Loth to depart, but yet at last, each one......140. H.355, 1
Nor, Faire, must you be **loth**..................221. H.633, 35
How He deferres, how **loath** He is to die!.....398. N.263, 8
Lots This done, we'l draw **lots**, who shall buy....215. H.616, 25
Loud Then laughing **loud**, he flew...............27. H.81, 33
Loud is our love, and loose our play,...........48. H.136, 2
For my sake next, (though little) be not **loud**..212. H.600, 2
Then Case, as **loud** as any Serjant there,......303. H.975, 5
Lov'dst And that, thou **lov'dst** me too..........142. H.364, 4
Love See **True-love, True-love-knot, True-love-knots, Warm-love-hatching**
I write of Youth, of **Love**, and have Accesse......5. H.1, 5
I brake my bonds of **Love**, and bad thee goe,.....6. H.3, 5
True **love**, we know, precipitates delay...........8. H.10, 6
No man at one time, can be wise, and **love**.......8. H.10, 8
Nothing but **love** can supple me;.................8. H.13, 6
No Dislike there is in **love**:.....................11. H.21, 2
Love is a circle that doth restlesse move.........13. H.29, 1
In the same sweet eternity of **love**...............13. H.29, 2
When what is lov'd, is Present, **love** doth spring;
13. H.30, 1
But being absent, **Love** lies languishing...........13. H.30, 2
I sent my **Love** a Karkanet:.....................14. H.34, 2

Love in extreames, can never long endure.....185. H.494, 4
Unmixt. I love to have it smirke and shine,...187. H.502, 3
One more by Thee, Love, and Desert have sent,.191. H.516, 1
The new successor drives away old Love........191. H.517, 2
Others to Lust, but me to Love................193. H.521, 54
If thou wilt love, and live with me..........193. H.521, 56
Love for our very-many Trespasses............197. H.539, 6
For our neglect, Love did our Death decree,...197. H.539, 15
Which Love and noble freedome is;...........198. H.544, 28
Did I or love, or could I others draw..........201. H.557, 1
I plaid with Love, as with the fire...............203. H.563, 1
When I love, (as some have told,..............204. H.569, 1
Love I shall when I am old)...................204. H.569, 2
Then love not mine, but me.....................205. H.574, 2
Where Poets sing the stories of our love.......206. H.575, 24
My Love will fit each Historie..................207. H.579, 8
The sweets of Love are mixt with tears.........208. H.580, 6
I doe love I know not what;....................209. H.585, 1
Therefore now Ile love no more,................209. H.585, 7
But Love by charmes,..........................213. H.609, 4
Not like the Muse; to love the man,..........214. H.611, 4
Or tell what strange Tricks Love can do,.......215. H.616, 9
Put on all shapes to get a Love:..............215. H.616, 16
When to the Temple Love sho'd runne, not go..216. H.618, 6
The sure sweet-Sement, Glue, and Lime of Love.
218. H.622, 2
As Love shall helpe thee, when thou do'st go hence
219. H.627, 7
In a Dreame, Love bad me go...............219. H.628, 1
Love as briefly did reply;....................219. H.628, 4
The turmoiles they endure that love............219. H.628, 6
What Love said was too too true:...............219. H.628, 8
As from Love, from trouble free...............219. H.628, 10
Love is a thing most nice; and must be fed....220. H.633, 20
'Tis best to feed Love; but not over-fill:.......220. H.633, 23
To imply your Love is wise....................221. H.633, 31
Sweet words must nourish soft and gentle Love.
222. H.633, 61
Live in the Love of Doves, and having told...222. H.633, 62
Of Love he sho'd admit.......................222. H.635, 4
Love is maintain'd by wealth; when all is spent,.235. H.676, 1
Love at no time idle is:......................235. H.678, 2
Love, and live here while we may;.............238. H.691, 2
Her Soule and Love were palpable in this......240. H.700, 2
Unto those that truly love....................240. H.701, 2
My love unto my Neatherdesse.................243. H.716, 28
They were mine own. Lal. In love combine......244. H.716, 46
For love he doth call.........................247. H.727, 10
Ph. A deale of Love, and much, much Griefe together.
248. H.730, 14
Ch. And is that all? I'm gone. Ph. By love I pray thee,
248. H.730, 17
Ch. Talk not of love, all pray, but few soules pay me.
248. H.730, 18
Within the Bosome of my Love your grave....249. H.734, 2
Yet love the smell of meat.....................250. H.736, 6
Love love begets, then never be...............252. H.746, 1
For profer'd love will love repay:..............252. H.746, 4
Then you must like, because I love............252. H.746, 8
Love and the Graces evermore do wait.........255. H.760, 1
In love with none, but me.....................258. H.767, 20
I cannot love, as I have lov'd before:.........258. H.768, 1
Love must be fed by wealth: this blood of mine..258. H.768, 3
Delays in love but crucifie the heart...........261. H.781, 2
Love thou dost, though Love sayes Nay......264. H.790, 2
We'l love the Divell, so he lands the gold......266. H.800, 8
As Love shall helpe me, I admire..............272. H.828, 9
Shall I go to Love and tell,..................273. H.836, 1
Love has yet no wrathfull fit:.................273. H.836, 6
Love is then consuming fire...................273. H.836, 8
Ai me! I love, give him your hand to kisse....274. H.837, 1
Nature has pre-compos'd us both to Love;.......274. H.837, 3
Deare, can you like, and liking love your Poet?.274. H.837, 5
True Love is tonguelesse as a Crocodile........274. H.837, 8
And you may find in Love these differing Parts;.274. H.837, 9
Love is a Circle, and an Endlesse Sphere;.....274. H.839, 1
When words we want, Love teacheth to endite;.275. H.846, 1
To the centre of your love?...................276. H.850, 2
For Love or Pittie, prethee let there be........277. H.853, 3
Love, love me now, because I place............278. H.859, 1
We love to rest in peacefull Urnes at home,.....278. H.860, 6
Love brought me to a silent Grove,...........278. H.863, 1
Where some had hang'd themselves for love,....278. H.863, 3
His Death for Love that taketh...............279. H.863, 12
My desp'rate feares, in love, had seen..........279. H.863, 15
But would to Love I could beleeve 'twas so!..279. H.866, 2
That I may play, and sing a Hymne to Love...280. H.871, 4
Love is a kind of warre; Hence those who feare,
280. H.872, 1
Where love begins, there dead thy first desire:.281. H.873, 1
In love, then prosper me......................281. H.874, 6
Love to deliver me:..........................281. H.874, 12
Love in a showre of Blossomes came..........283. H.883, 1
Love turn'd himselfe into a Bee,..............283. H.883, 9
And stealing still with love, and feare to Bed,..286. H.898, 15
Rocks to relent, and coyest maids to love.......287. H.900, 2
And gave my Love a fall.....................288. H.908, 4
For love or pitie to his Muse,.................291. H.918, 5
Himselfe, at one time, can be wise, and Love..294. H.936, 4
Love, like a Beggar, came to me................295. H.942, 1
Love is a thing so likes me,...................296. H.946, 3
To love at all,...............................296. H.946, 11
Since love so much contents me..............296. H.946, 12
The wounds of love with singing...............296. H.946, 18
Love is a sirrup; and who er'e we see..........297. H.949, 1
Ther's loathsomnesse e'en in the sweets of love..297. H.949, 4
Love is a Leven, and a loving kisse...........298. H.950, 1
Following with love and active heate thy game,.301. H.966, 7
This shall my love doe, give thy sad death one.302. H. 967, 3
Then to love I do encline;....................309. H.996, 3
I bring ye Love, Quest. What will love do?....309. H.1001, 1
I bring ye love: Quest. What will Love do?....309. H.1001, 3
I bring ye love: Quest. What will Love do?....309. H.1001, 5
Ans. Love will be-foole ye:...................309. H.1001, 6
I bring ye love: Quest. What will love do?....309. H.1001, 7
I bring ye love: Quest. What will love do?....310. H.1001, 9
Ans. Love gifts will send ye:.................310. H.1001, 10
I bring ye love: Quest. What will love do?....310. H.1001, 11
I bring ye love: Quest. What will love do?....310. H.1001, 13
Ans. Love will fulfill ye:.....................310. H.1001, 14
I bring ye love: Quest. What will love do?...310. H.1001, 15
And that's to love me; in which state.........313. H.1020, 7
Thy Love....................................314. H.1024, 20
Now, if you love me, tell me,...................321. H.1055, 1
Who will have love comply with his command..323. H.1067, 2
My dearest Love, since thou wilt go,..........323. H.1068, !
For love or pitie let me know.................323. H.1068, 3
Instruct me now, what love will do;...........325. H.1075, 1
Inform me next, what love will do;............325. H.1075, 3
Teach me besides, what love wil do;...........325. H.1075, 5
Tell me, now last, what love will do;..........325. H.1075, 7
Can live by love, or else grow fat by Play:....325. H.1077, 2
And look as all were capable of Love:.........326. H.1080, 12
Or fear of it, but Love keeps all in awe.)......326. H.1080, 20
Ile whet my lips, and sharpen Love on thee....327. H.1081, 2
Let me not live, if I not love,.................327. H.1082, 1
That love 'twixt men do's ever longest last.....327. H.1083, 1
Il'e write no more of Love; but now repent...334. H.1124, 1
The one is Mercy, and the next is Love:........340. N.6, 2
And more for love, then pittie................345. N.33, 29
To the full, yet I will love Thee:...............351. N.48, 8
To d'on my robes of love,......................352. N.53, 9
(The Altar of our love) thy Stone............359. N.83, 12
Love keep it ever flourishing..................361. N.83, 72
The feare of God, commixt with cleanly love..380. N.147, 2
Tortur'd her love, not to transgresse the Law..384. N.180, 6
God doth embrace the good with love; & gaines.389. N.212, 1
Speake thou of love and I'le reply.............393. N.232, 11
Thus let Thy lips but love distill,.............393. N.232, 15
Though Thou beest all that Active Love,......395. N.246, 1
And tho (Love knows).......................401. N.268, 28
Beares vp twoe globes where loue and pleasure sitt,
405. A.1, 52
Whome love admitts to this Hesperides.........405. A.1, 70
Growing in this love garded paradice...........406. A.1, 72
Now loue invites me to survey her thighes......406. A.1, 77
(Loue and Mercie, cherrish them),.............407. A.2, 22
W^{ch} sweeten Loue, yett ne're come nighe......408. A.2, 41
Wth wch Loue Chafes and warmes the soule....408. A.2, 48
The sad soule went, not with his Loue, but doome;
412. A.3, 76
Ther was not Varnish (only) in my loue.......412. A.3, 80
Thus wth a kisse of warmth, and loue, I parte.412. A.3, 95
With loue of yor Returne......................413. A.4, 33
One sighe of loue, and coole it with a teare;...414. A.6, 8
Young men to swoone, and Maides to dye for love.
415. A.7, 10
Love lyes a bleeding here, Evadne there........415. A.7, 11
He was my Life, my Love, my Joy; but di'd....416. A.8, 15
But there to live, where Love shall last for ever..417. A.8, 38
— — — — — — — — — —, ...421. var. H.92, 9
love to your welcome with the mistick Cake,
431. ins. H.283, 60b
— — — — — — — — — —, ...449. var. A.3, 69

Love-cast-off And love againe love-cast-off Lydia?
70. H.181, 20

Loved Deerely I lov'd thee; as my first-borne child:.6. H.3, 2
When what is lov'd, is Present, love doth spring;
13. H.30, 1
The Beads I kist, but most lov'd her...........13. H.32, 3
Who a sprightly Springall lov'd,................15. H.36, 6
I shall dislike, what once I lov'd before.........31. H.93, 4
Hor. While, Lydia, I was lov'd of thee,........70. H.181, 1
More lik'd by her, or lov'd by mee............145. H.375, 28
These Springs were Maidens once that lov'd,...180. H.478, 1
My lov'd Endymions Court;...................183. H.492, 18
Nor, with the losse of thy lov'd rest,..........229. H.662, 9
Kings ought to be more lov'd, then fear'd.......234. H.672, 2
I cannot love, as I have lov'd before:..........258. H.768, 1
Not so much knowne, as to be lov'd of thee....297. H.947, 12
That makes thee lov'd, and of the men desir'd,.299. H.956, 9
Who loves too much, too much the lov'd will hate.
318. H.1038, 2
'Bove all things lov'd it, for the puritie:.......390. N.222, 2

Lucky-four-leaved The Shewers of Roses, **lucky-foure-leav'd** grasse:....................................113. H.283, 42
Lucrece Of Thine; so **Lucrece** fell, and the......175. H.465, 57
Lais and **Lucrece**, in the night time are.......209. H.586, 3
Let her **Lucrece** all day be,....................232. H.665, 15
Chaste **Lucrece**, or a wife as grave:.........283. H.885, 8
Lucy Sound Teeth has **Lucie**, pure as Pearl, and small, 226. H.649, 1
Luggs **Luggs**, by the Condemnation of the Bench, 79. H.199, 1
Luke How co'd **Luke** Smeaton weare a shoe, or boot, 240. H.704, 1
Lukewarm Endure that **luke-warme** name of Serving-man: 265. H.796, 2
Lull And **Lull** asleepe...........................314. H.1024, 22
Lullabies With thy soule-melting **Lullabies**:......103. H.254, 4
And charmes them there with **lullabies**;........130. H.329, 10
Sung asleep with **Lullabies**:...................224. H.640, 2
Lullaby Let **Lullaby** the pretty Prince asleep!....86. H.213, 18
Or childish **Lullabie**?.........................104. H.257, 19
Lulled When as your Baby's **lull'd** asleep?......189. H.514, 2
As **lull'd** asleep;..............................190. H.515, 38
Bul **lul'd** to calmnesse, then succeeds a breeze..225. H.642, 15
Lulls **Lulls** swears he is all heart; but you'l suppose 284. H.886, 1
Lunatic Almost to be **Lunatick**:................122. H.302, 2
Lungs **Lungs** (as some, say) ne'r sets him down to eate, 223. H.637, 1
And **lungs** that wo'd infect me,...............260. H.777, 11
Lupes **Lupes** for the outside of his suite has paide; 302. H.969, 1
Lupo Come, skilfull **Lupo**, now, and take.........38. H.108, 1
Lurking But husht in his laire he lies **lurking**:.225. H.643, 15
Luscious For some fresh, fragrant, **luscious** flowers: 71. H.182, 16
(With **luscious** Numbers) my melodious Lyre....84. H.210, 4
With mellow Lips, and **luscious** there withall...226. H.649, 2
Lusk In Den'-shire Kerzie **Lusk** (when he was dead) 332. H.1114, 1
Lust That scatter'st Spirit and **Lust**; whose purest shine, 45. H.128, 12
Come, come and kisse me; Love and **lust** commends 78. H.197, 69
No **lust** theres like to Poetry..................135. H.336, 112
For **Lust** and action; on he'l go,..............165. H.443, 11
Lust ha's no eares; He's sharpe as thorn;....165. H.443, 13
Believe, Love speaks it not, but **Lust**:..........175. H.465, 40
But yet if boundlesse **Lust** must skaile..........175. H.465, 53
Lust entring here:..........................190. H.515, 14
Others to **Lust**, but me to Love..............193. H.521, 54
Of **Lust**, which setts on fier our hartes........408. A.2, 38
— — — — — — — — — —, ...426. var. H.197, 40
And soe begett **lust** and temptation........430. ins. H.283, 20f
Lust-burning Those thy **Lust-burning** Incubi.....174. H.465, 36
Luster Me thinks that onely **lustre** doth appeare..94. H.226, 3
Gives life and **luster**, publike mirth,............364. N.96, 20
Candor here, and **lustre** there.................377. N.128, 11
Lusters That Timber tall, which three-score **lusters** stood 23. H.69, 3
That for seven **Lusters** I did never come........27. H.82, 1
When after many **Lusters** thou shalt be........231. H.664, 1
After a thousand **Lusters** hurld,................245. H.720, 15
As that in **Lusters** few they may,..............291. H.919, 20
Who by his gray Haires, doth his **lusters** tell,..328. H.1088, 5
Lustful — — — — — — — — —, ...427. var. H.197, 67
Their **lustfull** Clusters all the yeare,......436. ins. H.336, 48b
Lust-sop — — — — — — — — —, ...426. var. H.197, 40
Lusty Thaw'd are the snowes, and now the **lusty** Spring 224. H.642, 3
Lay to thy stake a **lustie** Steere,..............243. H.716, 14
— — — — — — — — — — — —, ...427. var. H.197, 78
— — — — — — — — — — — —, ...453. var. H.283, 114
Lusty-jelly To make a **lustie-gellie** for his broth..299. H.959, 4
Lute Myrha, for the **Lute**, and Voice.............16. H.39, 8
Die, and be turn'd into a **Lute**..................23. H.68, 8
So long you did not sing, or touch your **Lute**,.95. H.228, 1
Griefe (ay me!) hath struck my **Lute**,..........131. H.332, 5
And dye away upon thy **Lute**...................142. H.362, 6
Linnit playes rarely on the **Lute**, we know;....149. H.381, 1
Play Phoebus on thy **Lute**;....................151. H.388, 1
But sweetly sounding like a **Lute**..............179. H.476, 18
Sho'd I not grieve (my Lawes) when every **Lute**, 288. H.907, 3
To'th **Lute** or Violl, then 'tis ravishing.........331. H.1101, 2
To it my Violl and my **Lute**:..................393. N.232, 14
To grace a **Lute**, a vyall, Virginall............406. A.1, 100
Lutes Melting melodious words, to **Lutes** of Amber. 22. H.67, 4
Then **Lutes** and Harpes shall stroke the eare...247. H.725, 10
And not with **Lutes** to fill the roome..........365. N.97, 3
Luxurious **Luxurious** Love by Wealth is nourished. 31. H.93, 2
Lycidas Ah! **Lycidas**, come tell me why.........183. H.492, 1
Dear **Lycidas**, e're long,........................184. H.492, 26
And till thou com'st, thy **Lycidas**,.............184. H.492, 37
Mean time, let **Lycidas** have leave to Pipe to thee. 184. H.492, 43
Lydia Hor. While, **Lydia**, I was lov'd of thee,....70. H.181, 1
Then Lydia, far-fam'd **Lydia**,....................70. H.181, 7
For whose affection, **Lydia**, I..................70. H.181, 11
And love againe love-cast-off **Lydia**?............70. H.181, 20
Lye See **Lie**
Feacie (some say) doth wash her clothes i'th' **Lie** 178. H.474, 1
Lying A **lying** Rich man, and a Poore man proud. 10. H.18, 2
An old, poore, **lying**, flatt'ring man:............38. H.108, 6
Was lately whipt for **lying** with a Wench.......79. H.199, 2
Lying alone,..................................114. H.283, 75
And, **lying** down, have nought t' affright......231. H.662, 74
By laughing too, and **lying** downe,.............291. H.919, 21
Lyre Then let thy active hand scu'd o're thy **Lyre**: 67. H.176, 3
(With luscious Numbers) my melodious **Lyre**...84. H.210, 4
By listning to thy **Lire**,.......................151. H.388, 3
My violl and my **lyre**..........................228. H.657, 6
Touch but thy **Lire** (my Harrie) and I heare..276. H.851, 1
Thou mighty Lord and master of the **Lyre**,....280. H.871, 1
Or let the Unshorne God lend thee his **Lyre**,....299. H.956, 13
Lyric That each **Lyrick** here shall be............88. H.218, 4
Loe, I, the **Lyrick** Prophet, who have set......142. H.365, 3
A **Lyrick** verse,................................144. H.371, 11
Of **Lyrick** Wine, both swell'd and crown'd,.....198. H.544, 16
Offer my **Lyrick**...............................213. H.604, 8
Unto the **Lyrick** string........................261. H.778, 8
Meet at those **Lyrick** Feasts,..................289. H.911, 4
Lyrics If when these **Lyricks** (Cesar) You shall heare, 107. H.264, 1
Fame, and his Name, both set, and sing his **Lyricks**. 143. H.366, 4
Lyric-strings My fingers so, the **Lyrick-strings** to move, 280. H.871, 3
M Thus speaks the Oke, here; C. and **M.** shall meet, 26. H.79, 7
The words found true, C. **M.** remember me.....26. H.79, 10
Mab The Court of **Mab**, and of the Fairie-King....5. H.1, 12
Where **Mab** he finds; who there doth lie......165. H.443, 5
To lye with **Mab**, though all say no............165. H.443, 12
His Moon-tann'd **Mab**, as somewhat sick,....167. H.443, 84
And now the bed, and **Mab** possest..........168. H.443, 118
If ye will with **Mab** find grace,................201. H.556, 1
Mab will pinch her by the toe.................201. H.556, 8
Mab's — — — — — — — —, ...452. var. H.443, 118
Mabship Hir **Mab-ship** in obedient Downe.......167. H.443, 89
Mab's-state Who 'gainst **Mabs-state** plac't here right is. 91. H.223, 29
Mackarell See **Maquerel**
Mad Whither, **Mad** maiden wilt thou roame?.......5. H.2, 1
Ran for Sweet-hearts **mad**, and dy'd...........152. H.391, 4
Can runne **mad**, and Prophesie.................217. H.620, 9
One nicely **mad**, or peevishly severe............234. H.673, 6
As made us nobly wild, not **mad**;...............289. H.911, 8
Came a **mad** dog, and did bite,................306. H.984, 34
Here's a **mad** lover, there that high designe......415. A.7, 13
Madam See **Prick-madam**
Why, **Madam**, will ye longer weep,............189. H.514, 1
For ropes of pearle, first **Madam** Ursly showes.232. H.668, 1
Made **Made** all that touch't her with her scent,.9. H.15, 11
Baths that **made** him young againe:..............10. H.19, 10
(All parts there **made** one prisoner.)...........16. H.41, 17
Made lovingly familiar:.........................20. H.56, 4
Made of the Rubie, Pearle and Diamond:......30. H.88, 6
When age or Chance has **made** me blind,..........32. H.98, 1
The which was **made** a happy Bride,.............41. H.116, 5
'Tis her erroneous self has **made** a braine.......46. H.128, 43
Made of a Haft, that was a Mutton-bone.......46. H.129, 4
Which when I saw, I **made** accesse...........51. H.142, 17
As Jove did, when he **made** his rapes:...........58. H.152, 2
Or so, as Darknesse **made** a stay..............64. H.169, 7
Made him take up his shirt, lay down his sword. 65. H.171, 6
Made for thy finger fit;.......................65. H.172, 3
Made green, and trimm'd with trees: see how.68. H.178, 31
Made up of white-thorn neatly enterwove:.........68. H.178, 35
The Proclamation **made** for May:..................68. H.178, 40
So when or you or I are **made**....................69. H.178, 65
And seeing it, I **made** a stay......................73. H.187, 5
And **made** ye white...............................74. H.190, 12
Say, are thy medicines **made** to be................74. H.191, 3
Something **made** of thred and thrumme;.........76. H.195, 3
(**Made** of her Pap and Gum).....................80. H.201, 7
Made he the pledge, he'd think.................80. H.201, 23
Amphion-like) men **made** of flesh and bones,..84. H.210, 6
Flie thou **made** Bubble of my sighs, and tears..87. H.215, 2
Nor **made** of glasse, or wood, or stone,.........91. H.223, 56
(**Made** rivall with the aire).....................103. H.255, 2
That Morne which saw me **made** a Bride,......109. H.271, 1
I shall be **made**................................111. H.28?, 5
Lately **made** of flesh and blood:................123. H.310, 2
Of Chance, (as **made** up all of rock, and oake:).129. H.323, 12
We must be **made**,..............................133. H.336, 29
Which **made** us one, shall ne'r undoe;..........134. H.336, 71
I **made** upon my Julia's brest;..................135. H.336, 95
A City here of Heroes I have **made**,..........143. H.365, 9

Of Life eternall) Time has **made** thee one,.....152. H.392, 3
Nay, now I think th'ave **made** his grave........156. H.412, 15
But one halfe houre, that's **made** up here.......162. H.431, 3
Made by the breath of great-ey'd kine,........166. H.443, 40
I'm **made**......................................178. H.475, 7
Have **made** Thee prosperous in thy wayes, thus farre:
181. H.483, 6
And what was **made**, was **made** to meet.......190. H.515, 7
Made of the Fleeces purest Downe............192. H.521, 10
Not **made** of Ale, but spiced Wine;..........193. H.521, 48
This day, the Queen-Priest, thou art **made** t'appease
197. H.539, 3
For quick dispatch, Sculls **made** no longer stay,
200. H.551, 3
And how the Posset shall be **made**...........216. H.616, 32
What **made** that mirth last night? the neighbours say,
219. H.630, 1
To take the precious Phesant **made**:...........231. H.662, 67
Made it for ever after red.....................241. H.706, 4
That **made** me thus hoist saile, and bring my Boat:
248. H.730, 12
She wept, and **made** it deeper by a teare.......251. H.743, 2
Stand forth brave man, since Fate has **made** thee here
251. H.745, 1
What Fate decreed, Time now ha's **made** us see.254. H.756, 1
Thy Warre (discreetly **made**) with white successe.
254. H.756, 12
But ah! it hapned as he **made**................265. H.798, 7
Thou hast **made** many Houses for the Dead;..277. H.853, 1
I'th' Church-yard, **made**, one Tenement for me..277. H.853, 4
Made at the Sun,..............................289. H.911, 5
As **made** us nobly wild, not mad;.............289. H.911, 8
And gracefull **made**, by your neate Sisterhood..290. H.914, 10
Made by that fetter or that snare.............293. H.934, 3
But for his heart, he cannot have it **made**:....302. H.969, 2
Some Odes I **made** of Lucia:..................303. H.973, 14
Are **made** farre worse, by lawless liberty.......307. H.990, 2
Made by the Coyners illegitimate..............312. H.1015, 2
Has **made** me like a wilderness:...............312. H.1016, 2
Whose Peace is **made** up with a Pardoning....316. H.1029, 2
Made up One State of Sixtie Venuses;........326. H.1080, 4
Yet none of these have **made** me sad:.........354. N.57, 2
Made of a clean strait oaten reed,.............354. N.59, 9
God co'd have **made** all rich, or all men poore;.356. N.69, 1
Made void for millions, as for me...............370. N.107, 10
Scores of sins w'ave **made** here many,.........373. N.121, 9
Is cut, that **made** us clothing...................374. N.123, 40
The Sheets, the Rugs, **made** by thy hand.......374. N.123, 44
Will shew these garments **made** by thee;.......375. N.123, 82
That **made** that fairest Canopie................382. N.164, 2
The repetition of the name **made** known........383. N.174, 1
God hath this world for many **made**; 'tis true:.387. N.198, 1
But He hath **made** the world to come for few..387. N.198, 2
Sinne **made** before.............................401. N.268, 23
— — — — — — — — — — — — —, ...425. var. H.197, 2
— — — — — — — — — — — — —, ...448. var. A.3, 22

Madest Thou **mad'st** me thinke by this,..........142. H.364, 3
Thou **mad'st** me chop, but yet,................142. H.364, 7
And **mad'st** a promise that mine appetite.......262. H.783, 2
Thus Crownd with Rose Budds, Sacke, thou **mad'st** mee flye
410. A.3, 27

Madman's What **Mad-man's** he, that when it sparkles so,
187. H.502, 5

Madness To rouze the sacred **madnesse**; and awake
45. H.128, 25
Tis but a dog-like **madnesse** in bad Kings,.....292. H.929, 1

Magazine And stuffed **Magazine** of wheat;..436. ins. H.336, 48j

Magdalen And th' other Mary (Mary **Magdalen**).384. N.180, 8

Maggot — — — — — — — — —, ...434. var. H.293, 38

Maggots May baite his hooke, with **maggots** taken thence.
282. H.879, 4

Magic To that soft Charm, that Spell, that **Magick** Bough,
62. H.161, 9
Bear up the **Magick** bough, and spel:.......136. H.336, 134
Stand by the **Magick** of my powerfull Rhymes..280. H.869, 1
(As with a **Magick**) laid them all agen:......326. H.1080, 18
— — — — — — — — — —, ...432. var. H.283, 134

Magics Bring your **Magicks**, Spels, and Charmes,
10. H.19, 5
And **magicks** for to end, and hells,............115. H.283, 134

Magnitude Those Prophets of the former **Magnitude**)
207. H.575, 60

Magot **Magot** frequents those houses of good-cheere,
191. H.518, 1

Maid See Handmaid
The **maide** of Honour unto thee...............8. H.11, 10
And all because, Faire **Maid**, thou art..........47. H.132, 9
Then comely and most fragrant **Maid**,.........49. H.136, 14
Then, beauteous **Maid**, you may retire;.........49. H.136, 32
Is it (sweet **maid**) your fault these holy.......53. H.149, 11
Of Virgins! Tell the **Maid**,....................56. H.149, 93
And Cruell **Maid**, because I see................60. H.159, 1
But die you must (faire **Maid**) ere long,........88. H.216, 20
Because I've liv'd so long a **maid**:............97. H.235, 2
The love-spent Youth, and love-sick **Maid**,.....106. H.262, 15
Prue, my dearest **Maid**, is sick,...............122. H.302, 1
Profane no Porch young man and **maid**, for fear.124. H.313, 3

Luckie in this **Maide** I love:.................136. H.337, 4
Let me when I kisse a **maid**,..................138. H.346, 5
Come with the Spring-time, forth Fair **Maid**, and be
140. H.354, 1
Not wrathfull seem, or fright the **Maide**,.......145. H.376, 4
No, know (Blest **Maide**) when there's not one.146. H.376, 7
She ne'r remembers that she was a **maide**.....149. H.379, 2
That doted on a **Maide** of Gingerbred:........155. H.405, 10
Good morrow to each **maid**;..................156. H.412, 6
Or for Widow, **Maid**, or Wife..................182. H.490, 4
Fie, Lovely **maid**! Indeed you are too slow,...216. H.618, 5
A **maid** (my Prew) by good luck sent,........246. H.724, 6
Prewdence Baldwin (once my **maid**)...........262. H.782, 2
Mournfull **maid** farewell to you;...............306. H.984, 42
Lamented **Maid**! he won the day,..............360. N.83, 23
Each **Maid**, her silver Filleting,...............360. N.83, 42
Thoughe as a seruant, yet a **Mayde** of Honor...412. A.3, 102
— — — — — — — — — — — —, ...432. var. H.283, 81
— — — — — — — — — — — —, ...449. var. A.8, 9
— — — — — — — — — — — —, ...453. var. H.283, 97

Maiden Whither, Mad **maiden** wilt thou roame?....5. H.2, 1
Y'are the **Maiden** Posies,......................83. H.205, 9
Or like those **Maiden** showrs,.................95. H.227, 24
The **Mayden** Candour of thy Mynde:...........407. A.2, 34
Your **mayden** knight...................430. ins. H.283, 40e
— — — — — — — — — — — —, ...432. var. H.283, 97
— — — — — — — — — — — —, ...440. var. H.443, 64

Maiden-flowers Of **Maiden-flowers**!...............43. H.123, 9

Maiden-hair Of soft and dainty **Maiden-haire**,.....18. H.47, 3
Play not with the **maiden-haire**;...............52. H.147, 3
That ye singe no **maiden-haire**.................315. H.1026, 8

Maidenhead Give thee each night a **Maidenhead**..35. H.106, 42
Soft speech, smooth touch, the lips, the **Maiden-head**:
45. H.128, 8
The losse of **Maiden-head**?...................53. H.149, 14
Yet not a **Maiden-head** resign'd!..............54. H.149, 32
And for a **maidenhead**.........................160. H.422, 3
Had I then askt her **Maidenhead**?..............212. H.599, 4
The loss of that we call a **Maydenhead**?.......262. H.781, 14
Brings him not one, but many a **Maiden-head**...286. H.898, 16
But, in a Mother, kept a **maiden-head**..........385. N.184, 4
Bee sure thou bringe A **Mayden head**,...........409. A.2, 84
— — — — — — — — — — — —, ...436. var. H.336, 22

Maidenheads Broke at the Losse of **Maiden-heads**:
167. H.443, 107

Maiden-monument From out thy **Maiden-Monument**.
361. N.83, 66

Maiden-pleasures No, no; our **Maiden-pleasures** be.361. N.83, 55

Maiden-pomander Smells like the **maiden-Pomander**.
145. H.375, 26

Maiden's See Soft-maiden's-blush

Maidens These Springs were **Maidens** once that lov'd,
180. H.478, 1
I have seen many **Maidens** to have haire;......205. H.571, 1
Unwasht hands, ye **Maidens**, know,............263. H.786, 3
Maidens tell me I am old;.....................277. H.852, 1
And I wish all **maidens** mine,..................309. H.996, 5
Maidens when ye Leavens lay,.................322. H.1063, 2
The worke is done: young men, and **maidens** set
335. H.1128, 1

Maiden-saviour To dresse my **Maiden-Saviour**.....402. N.270, 6

Maiden's-blush And **Maiden's-blush**, for spiced wine.
216. H.616, 34
Of **Maydens-blush**, commixt with Jessimine.....262. H.783, 10

Maiden-train Of all the **Maiden-Traine**! We come,
359. N.83, 5

Maids See Bride-maids, Milk-maids, Tender-whimpering-maids
List' sweet **maids**, and you shal know..........14. H.36, 2
Those parts, which **maids** keep unespy'd,........17. H.41, 19
Or else desir'st that **Maids** sho'd tell...........34. H.103, 7
Prethee (lest **Maids** sho'd censure thee) but say.42. H.122, 9
Maids, and here strew Violets..................44. H.125, 6
Ne'r had kept heat for fifty **Maids** that night...78. H.197, 68
Welcome **Maids** of Honour,....................83. H.205, 1
Then to the **Maids** with Wheaten Hats:........102. H.250, 41
Why doe not all fresh **maids** appeare..........103. H.256, 1
Wherewith young men and **maids** distrest,......106. H.262, 3
Poore **Maids** rewarded be,.....................106. H.262, 10
Where **Maids** have spent their houres..........110. H.274, 4
The **Maids** to catch this Cowslip-ball:..........112. H.281, 2
Troth, leave the flowers, and **Maids**, take me...112. H.281, 4
Maides sho'd say, or Virgins sing,.............117. H.285, 11
Maides (in time) may ravish him..............125. H.314, 8
Quite through the young **maids** and the men,..127. H.319, 31
Those **maids** that never vary;..................160. H.422, 6
I call all **Maids** to witnesse too...............165. H.442, 12
In Wicker-baskets **Maids** shal bring............192. H.521, 35
To make thy **Maids** and selfe free mirth.......193. H.521, 49
And as He shuts, close up to **Maids** again.....196. H.537, 4
Where merry as the **Maids** we'l be.............215. H.616, 2
On which the young men and **maids** meet......230. H.662, 48
Then **maids** shall strew Thee, and thy Curles from them
254. H.756, 17
To you sweet **Maids** (thrice three)............261. H.778, 5
Rocks to relent, and coyest **maids** to love......287. H.900, 2

And no lesse prais'd, then of the maides admir'd.
299. H.956, 10

Neglected there (maids trust to me)...........304. H.980, 8
Ah cruell maides! Ile goe my way,............312. H.1014, 5
If the Maides a spinning goe,..................315. H.1026, 5
Let the Maides bewash the men...............315. H.1026, 10
Thou wonder of all Maids, li'st here,.........360. N.83, 13
May all shie Maids, at wonted hours,.........361. N.83, 73
Young men to swoone, and Maides to dye for love.
415. A.7, 10
— — — — — — — — — — —, ...432. ins. H.283, 140a

Maids' Maids nay's are nothing, they are shie...249. H.735, 1

Main — — — — — — — — — —, ...424. var. H.128, 49
— — — — — — — — — — —, ...432. var. H.283, 118

Maintain Yet can thy humble roofe maintaine a Quire
37. H.106, 121

Maintained Love is maintain'd by wealth; when all is spent,
235. H.676, 1

Maintenance But likewise Oyle of Maintenance to it:
41. H.117, 6

Majesty See Elfish-majesty
Not without mickle majesty...................165. H.443, 6
Appeares but in His Meaner Majestie..........236. H.685, 6
Where power is weake, unsafe is Majestie......302. H.971, 2
Low, and of Thrones the Ancient Majesty.....325. H.1073, 4
A nursing Mother so to Majesty;..............326. H.1080, 22
Had no one Beame from Gods sweet Majestie..382. N.167, 4
Puts down some prints of His high Majestie:..385. N.189, 2
Bares in it selfe a gracefull maiestye..........404. A.1, 6

Make Can make your's bleed a teare:...........11. H.20, 5
Though you can make..........................11. H.20, 10
To make a Tent, and put it in,.................18. H.46, 7
And comming downe, shall make no noise at all..21. H.62, 6
As, could they hear, the Damn'd would make no noise,
22. H.67, 2
To make that thousand up a million...........24. H.74, 6
Kissing and glancing, soothing, all make way...24. H.74, 11
Favour, Ile make full satisfaction;.............27. H.82, 14
Make payment for his pleasure..................30. H.87, 18
Me, then to make me languish stil!...........34. H.103, 10
Sweeten, and make soft your dreames:..........35. H.106, 44
To make sleep not so sound, as sweet:.......36. H.106, 54
Wealth cannot make a life, but Love..........37. H.106, 128
Next, make his cheeks with breath to swell,....39. H.108, 11
Good Sir, make no more cuts i'th' outward skin,
44. H.126, 3
The frost-bound-blood, and spirits; and to make
45. H.128, 26
Make me a heaven; and make me there........47. H.133, 1
Make me the straight, and oblique lines;......47. H.133, 3
Make me a Chariot, and a Sun;................47. H.133, 5
Make me a Sun-set; and a Night:.............47. H.133, 9
To these, make Clouds to poure downe raine;..47. H.133, 12
Quiet yet; but if ye make.....................52. H.145, 3
On, on devoutly, make no stay;...............54. H.149, 41
And make, what ere they touch, turn sweet....55. H.149, 62
Watch, or did make the bed:.................56. H.149, 105
Lips can make Cherries grow..................57. H.149, 148
To make you bravely live;.....................57. H.149, 154
And (like to mine) make your heart burn.....61. H.159, 19
Both the cause, and make the heat............62. H.162, 14
'Two'd make a brave expansion...............67. H.175, 8
And make my spirits frantick with the fire...67. H.176, 4
And make me smooth as Balme, and Oile againe.
67. H.176, 6
Make Gelli-flowers, then.....................74. H.192, 7
That it wo'd make thee see,..................80. H.201, 15
To make for others garlands; and to set......94. H.224, 3
And make my bed,............................95. H.227, 6
And make it thus expire.......................95. H.227, 15
Then make me weep...........................95. H.227, 16
Art quickens Nature; Care will make a face:..97. H.234, 1
To make a brave,............................100. H.246, 6
And for to make the merry cheere,............101. H.250, 35
But for to make it spring againe...............102. H.250, 55
To make these flowrie Carpets show..........104. H.256, 18
Speak, whimp'ring Younglings, and make known
104. H.257, 15
Her blowes did make ye blew...................105. H.260, 8
To make of parts an union;...................107. H.263, 15
As for to make this, that, or any one..........107. H.264, 3
Last, let us make our best abode,..............111. H.278, 5
Bold bolt of thunder he will make his way,...116. H.283, 148
Watchet the silke was; and did make.........116. H.284, 3
Flames, which wo'd an entrance make;........117. H.286, 10
No fault in women, to make show............118. H.291, 9
They make a feast lesse great then nice.......119. H.293, 12
To make but One (and that's thy selfe) admir'd.
121. H.301, 6
That Milk-maids make about the hearth,.......126. H.319, 12
Wherewith ye make those merry Sceanes,.....127. H.319, 18
Shall make thy actions with their ends to meet.
128. H.320, 8
Lets make it full up, by our sport............133. H.336, 32
Or ravell so, to make us two.................134. H.336, 72
Weeping, shall make ye flourish all the yeere..138. H.343, 4
To make this neat distinction from the rest;..140. H.354, 5

Cherrish the cheek, but make none blush at all..140. H.354, 12
Herrick shall make the meddow-verse for you...140. H.355, 14
How for to make thee merry;...................142. H.364, 6
To make rich these Aromatikes:...............145. H.375, 14
Y'ave farced well, pray make an end;........146. H.377, 24
Essay of other giblets; make....................146. H.377, 28
Jove, joy'st when guests make their abode....147. H.377, 62
Here, for to make the face affraid;............148. H.377, 78
Make for thy peace, and pace to heaven........149. H.377, 130
Which I worke to Meale, and make............152. H.393, 3
When my off'ring next I make,................158. H.417, 1
'Tis fit they make no One with them too great...163. H.438, 2
To make a seisure on the light,................164. H.441, 3
Can make reflected from these jems,...........167. H.443, 79
The which the Elves make to excite..........167. H.443, 114
To make up now a Congregation...............168. H.445, 2
This, Three; which Three, you make up Foure Brave Prince.
170. H.451, 16
Whereof (at last) to make....................173. H.460, 3
The pretty whimpering that they make,........180. H.478, 5
Whose smile can make a Poet; and your glance.187. H.506, 9
To make thy Maids and selfe free mirth,......193. H.521, 49
For to make the Texture lye....................195. H.530, 3
O Pious-Priestresse! make a Peace for us......197. H.539, 14
And make the frollick yeere,..................198. H.544, 21
O ye Graces! Make me fit.....................204. H.569, 3
You can make a Mercury........................204. H.569, 16
(As Umber sweares) did make his Lyon start..205. H.572, 4
When I a Verse shall make,....................212. H.604, 1
Make the way smooth for me,..................213. H.604, 5
Or Fort that I can make here;.................213. H.609, 3
And talke of Brides; & who shall make......215. H.616, 21
I make no haste to have my Numbers read.....218. H.623, 1
Make no long stay..............................220. H.633, 6
To make a peece...............................221. H.633, 33
And make me one entire........................228. H.657, 8
To make a pleasing pastime there.............230. H.662, 39
Women, although they ne're so goodly make it,.235. H.675, 1
Chains of sweet bents let us make,...........235. H.678, 5
Drink rich wine; and make good cheere,.......238. H.691, 3
Each one to make his melody:................243. H.716, 20
Charme then the chambers; make the beds for ease,
245. H.723, 11
Nor let the shackles make thee sad;...........246. H.725, 3
Ch. Why then begin, and all the while we make
248. H.730, 23
Thou & I'le sing to make these dull Shades merry,
248. H.730, 25
They fall like dew, but make no noise at all...250. H.737, 4
Make Thee like Him, this, that way fortunate,.254. H.756, 10
To make my lodging the sweeter;.............256. H.762, 3
To make her Philters with:...................258. H.767, 14
This day my Julia thou must make...........267. H.805, 1
Can make thee sick,............................273. H.833, 5
Make haste away, and let one be.............275. H.844, 1
To make loose Gownes for Mackarell:......275. H.844, 6
Make hoods of thee to serve out Spice........275. H.844, 8
Two things do make society to stand;..........275. H.847, 1
Back to come, (and make no stay.)...........276. H.848, 3
And make short pray'rs to thee:...............281. H.874, 5
What sho'd poking-sticks make there,.........282. H.878, 7
From which mishap this use I make,...........283. H.883, 11
Of him bewitcht: then forthwith make..........284. H.890, 3
Serve but for matter to make Paper-kites......286. H.896, 2
Blowes make of dearest friends immortall Foes..287. H.901, 2
Of which make Garlands here, and there,......289. H.912, 3
Or mourne, or make a Marble Verse for me,..298. H.952, 3
To make a lustie-gellie for his broth..........299. H.959, 4
Thou a Trentall make for me:..................304. H.976, 2
That do's infect, and make the rent...........311. H.1010, 5
Make her this day smile on me,..............313. H.1018, 3
Make way to my Beloved Westminster:......316. H.1028, 14
To make them Leane, and languishing at all...316. H.1028, 20
Never make sick your Banks by surfeiting......316. H.1028, 24
Which knowne, let us make...................317. H.1035, 13
To make the wassaile a swinger...............317. H.1035, 24
Let Country wenches make 'em fine..........323. H.1068, 13
As to make ye ever grow........................324. H.1070, 4
'Twill make a tongless man to wooe..........325. H.1075, 2
'Twill strangely make a one of too............325. H.1075, 4
'Twill quickly mar, & make ye too............325. H.1075, 6
Make him thus swell, or windy Cabbages.....327. H.1085, 2
Thy mouth will make the sourest numbers please;
328. H.1089, 3
Make knowne to us the now Jerusalem........330. H.1100, 12
To make, not marre her, by this punishment;..344. N.31, 2
'Tis not to poyson, but to make thee pure......344. N.31, 4
Of clouts, wee'l make a chamber,.............345. N.33, 21
Wee'l make Thee, here,........................345. N.33, 31
If warre, or want shall make me grow so poore,.347. N.39, 1
Make me a fire,................................350. N.47, 24
Make, make me Thine, my gracious God........351. N.48, 1
That slack my pace; but yet not make me stay?
352. N.51, 3
Are ready by, to make the Guests all pure:...355. N.65, 6
For times to come, I'le make this Vow,........357. N.72, 16
To make my bed soft in my sicknesses:.......358. N.77, 9

And make no one stop, till my race be done...358. N.77, 15
And to make fine,..............................360. N.83, 34
Or chaines of Columbines shall make,.........361. N.83, 53
And make this place all Paradise:............361. N.83, 62
Here did not make me sorrie,.................363. N.92, 3
Make it ever flourishing......................363. N.93, 9
To make things sweet. Chor. Yet all less sweet then He.
365. N.97, 10
Wee'l chuse Him King, and make His Mother Queen.
368. N.102, 24
Where shall I now begin to make, for one....368. N.103, 5
And that will make me, and my Work divine..371. N.113, 10
To make paiment, while I call.................373. N.121, 12
God make me thankfull still for it............376. N.124, 4
To make them, thereby, mindfull of their own..384. N.178, 3
To make thy faire Predestination:.............389. N.216, 2
Might I make choice, long life sho'd be with-stood;
392. N.230, 9
Teares, at that day, shall make but weake defence;
392. N.230, 27
Here all things ready are, make hast, make hast away;
401. N.268, 5
To make my grave..............................401. N.268, 39
Like pearle and gold make one rich Carcanett..405. A.1, 32
They make it scent like bruized Cinnamon......406. A.1, 94
But form'd by number make sweet melody.....406. A.1, 108
To make Fools hate them, onlye by disguise;..412. A.3, 94
Of lines and colo^rs make them scorne.........418. A.9, 53
The two last fayle, and by experience make
422. ins. H.106, 92e
— — — — — — — — — — —, ...423. var. H.128, 36
How long, soft bride, shall your deare C: make
431. ins. H.283, 60a
— — — — — — — — — — —, ...448, var. A.1, 106
Maker As He, the maker of this Song..........88. H.216, 21
Makes (Love makes me write, what shame forbids to speak.)
24. H.74, 2
And makes them frantick, ev'n to all extreames;
29. H.86, 4
But that which most makes sweet thy country life.
35. H.106, 31
Hunger makes coorse meats, delicates..........37. H.106, 110
Which Art, not Nature, makes so rare;.......37. H.106, 112
While soft Opinion makes thy Genius say,....37. H.106, 115
Content makes all Ambrosia...................37. H.106, 116
This makes Cuffe dull; and troubles him the most,
39. H.109, 3
Which makes them worthy Cedar, and the Bayes.
45. H.128, 36
Love makes the cheek, and chin a sphere.....49. H.136, 21
Which makes me stand.........................72. H.185, 23
Which, gently gleaming, makes a show,.......92. H.223, 66
And Bacon, (which makes full the meale).....101. H.250, 31
Then the sand, that makes the shore:..........102. H.253, 6
To clense his eyes, Tom Brock makes much adoe,
110. H.273, 1
A clammie Reume makes loathsome both his eyes:
110. H.273, 3
Makes holy these, all others lay aside:........114. H.283, 98
Makes not a God; but he that prayes to one...117. H.288, 2
That makes the Tables merriment.............124. H.312, 2
Who makes the slie Physitian his Heire........125. H.315, 6
And makes more soft the Bridall Bed..........130. H.329, 7
Reward it is, that makes us good or bad......139. H.351, 2
Makes guests and fish smell strong; pray go..146. H.377, 26
Makes the smirk face of each to shine,.......147. H.377, 72
ly that it makes the meate more sweet;.......148. H.377, 80
And mak'st all hell...........................170. H.452, 3
Spunge makes his boasts that he's the onely man
171. H.454, 1
That makes the Action, good, or ill...........175. H.465, 64
That makes them looke so lanke, so Ghost-like still.
186. H.498, 6
When Themilis his pastime makes,............192. H.521, 26
Makes you poore;..............................196. H.538, 4
What ever comes, content makes sweet:.......200. H.552, 6
Makes waste;...................................221. H.633, 49
The softest Fire makes the sweetest Mault......221. H.633, 51
Of Land makes life, but sweet content.........230. H.662, 18
Sweet sleep, that makes more short the night..231. H.662, 75
The Mean the Musique makes in every thing...268. H.812, 2
Night makes no difference 'twixt the Priest and Clark;
279. H.864, 1
A sparke neglected makes a mighty fire.......281. H.873, 2
Nis, he makes Verses; but the Lines he writes,.286. H.896, 1
Continuall reaping makes a land wax old.......292. H.922, 4
What was thy Birth, thy starre that makes thee knowne,
299. H.956, 5
That makes thee lov'd, and of the men desir'd,.299. H.956, 9
Necessity makes dastards valiant men.........333. N.1118, 2
God when for sin He makes His Children smart,
343. N.22, 1
And though a while He makes Requesters stay,.344. N.30, 3
Makes those, and my beloved Beet, ...350. N.47, 35
When man he makes a Penitent for it.........359. N.82, 2
Which makes the Bapti'me; 'tis decreed,.......365. N.97, 18

God makes not good men wantons, but doth bring
370. N.108, 1
Whom ease makes his, without the help of blowes.
372. N.116, 4
Two raiments have I: Christ then makes......376. N.127, 5
God He refuseth no man; but makes way......378. N.131, 1
Gods Prescience makes none sinfull; but th' offence
390 N.220, 1
Nor makes it matter, Nestors yeers to tell,....392. N.230, 5
Which makes them shewe like roses vnder lawne.
404. A.1, 24
Meets in the whole and maks a harmony......406. A.1, 106
Number of Nyne, wch makes vs full wth God,..410. A.3, 22
That makes all æquall. Manye thowsands should.411. A.3, 35
I finde in thee, that makes me thus to part,....414. A.6, 4
That makes grim Charon thus to pity thee.......416. A.8, 22
— — — — — — — — — — —, ...427. var. H.197, 49
— — — — — — — — — — —, ...427. var. H.197, 51
of two makes one Hermaphrodite.........431. ins. H.283, 50j
But of her owne a spoile shee makes.....436. ins. H.336, 48p
Makest Mak'st easie Feare unto thee say,......36. H.106, 74
Thou mak'st me ayrie, active to be born,......78. H.197, 49
Thou mak'st me nimble, as the winged howers,.78. H.197, 51
Thou mak'st my teeming Hen to lay..........350. N.47, 45
Maketh And told me too, he maketh...........279. H.863, 10
Making Making thy peace with heav'n, for some late fault,
36. H.106, 59
Making a Carkanet...........................43. H.123, 8
Shall never shrink, where making thine abode,.143. H.365, 11
But making haste, it came to passe,...........187. H.504, 3
By quickly making one of two.................215. H.616, 10
Not making a stay,............................217. H.619, 9
Malcontent Why walkes Nick Flimsey like a Male-content?
160. H.423, 1
Male Male to the female, soule to body: Life....45. H.128, 4
His Bed, Male children shall beget............162. H.429, 2
Male perfumes, but Female fire...............277. H.856, 4
Malefactors For those, who did as malefactors die.
384. N.180, 4
Male-incense Male-Incense burn.................361. N.83, 76
Malevolent All Aspects malevolent?.............286. H.897, 6
Malignant But (ah!) by starres malignant crost,.313. H.1020, 3
Malt The softest Fire makes the sweetest Mault..221. H.633, 51
Man See Bellman, Foreman, Serving-man, Trencher-man, Wolf-like-man
O Perverse man! If All disgustfull be,.............7. H.6, 5
No man at one time, can be wise, and love......8. H.10, 8
A lying Rich man, and a Poore man proud....10. H.18, 2
For your drie-decrepid man:..................10. H.19, 12
What man would be here,......................12. H.26, 9
In Man, Ambition is the common'st thing;....21. H.58, 1
Doe, and have parted here a Man and Wife:..26. H.79, 2
Give me that man, that dares bestride.........30. H.90, 1
This, this a virtuous man can doe,.............31. H.90, 7
That man loves not, who is not zealous too....31. H.91, 2
To teach Man to confine desires:..............35. H.106, 16
A heart thrice wall'd with Oke, and Brasse, that man
36. H.106, 75
A wise man ev'ry way lies square.............37. H.106, 98
An old, poore, lying, flatt'ring man:...........38. H.108, 6
In thee, thou Man of Men! who here do'st give
41. H.117, 4
Nay, thou more neare then kindred, friend, man, wife,
45. H.128, 3
Goe, perjur'd man; and if thou ere return......49. H.138, 1
The lazie man the most doth love...............53. H.147, 14
Of the good man and the wife..................55. H.149, 60
Though a wise man all pressures can sustaine;.60. H.158, 1
Love kill'd this man. No more but so.........61. H.159, 31
To safe-guard Man from wrongs, there nothing must
67. H.177, 1
That where you grew, scarce man can say.....87. H.216, 3
And for what use, scarce man wo'd think it...93. H.223, 124
Th'event is never in the power of man.........120. H.294, 2
Gifts will get ye, or the man..................121. H.297, 14
That man lives twice, that lives the first life well.
121. H.298, 2
Them all concenter'd in one man, but Thee.....121. H.301, 4
Thus, thou, that man art, whom the Fates conspir'd
121. H.301, 5
Profane no Porch young man and maid, for fear.124. H.313, 3
A man prepar'd against all ills to come,........128. H.323, 1
How rich a man is, all desire to know;........130. H.328, 1
Beleeve young man all those were teares......131. H.330, 5
In thee Brave Man! Whose incorrupted fame,..131. H.331, 5
But vanisht man,..............................133. H.336, 21
Thus frantick crazie man (God wot)...........135. H.336, 113
Manners knowes distance, and a man unrude..147. H.377, 31
Teach man to keepe a God in man:........149. H.377, 134
Man is compos'd here of a two-fold part;......153. H.394, 1
Since man expos'd is to a world of griefs......153. H.397, 2
For why? that man is poore,.................160. H.422, 13
In holy meetings, there a man may be........163. H.436, 1
Spunge makes his boasts that he's the onely man
171. H.454, 1
You are a Lord, an Earle, nay more, a Man,....172. H.459, 1

Seeing thee Soame, I see a Goodly **man**,........176. H.466, 1
Man knowes where first he ships himselfe; but he
177. H.468, 1
Stand with thy Graces forth, Brave **man**, and rise
181. H.483, 1
Be in Prose a gratefull **man**..................182. H.489, 14
Come thou Brave **man**! And bring with Thee a Stone
185. H.496, 5
Can teach a **man** the Art of memory:........186. H.501, 2
Thou art The **Man**, the onely **Man** best known,.194. H.526, 3
No **man** exempted is from Death, or sinne.......199. H.548, 2
Eggs Ile not shave: But yet brave **man**, if I....202. H.557, 27
Man is a Watch, wound up at first, but never.202. H.558, 1
And that ty'd to **man** 'twil sever..............209. H.587, 3
Not like the Muse; to love the **man**,........214. H.611, 4
A Bull but then; and now a **man**............215. H.616, 18
Seldome comes Glorie till a **man** be dead......218. H.623, 2
For a **man** in needy-hood:...................223. H.638, 16
Well content a craving **man**..................223. H.638, 18
Upon the grave of this old **man**..............226. H.644, 2
No **man** comes late unto that place from whence
228. H.656, 1
Never **man** yet had a regredience...............228. H.656, 2
And no **man** payes too deare for it.............231. H.662, 61
No **man** despaires to do what's done before.....236. H.680, 2
Discruciate a **man** in deep distresse............239. H.699, 2
Thou art a **man** of worthinesse:...............243. H.716, 26
Stand forth brave **man**, since Fate has made thee here
251. H.745, 1
I'm a **man** for ev'ry Sceane...................253. H.750, 18
Upon the **man** that is a Potentate..............255. H.760, 2
Must be the first **man** up, and last in bed:....259. H.771, 2
Bice laughs, when no **man** speaks; and doth protest
265. H.795, 1
Man may want Land to live in; but for all,..267. H.807, 1
What was't (ye Gods!) a dying **man** to save,..278. H.860, 3
Ne'r please the supercillious **man**.............279. H.868, 4
Thy loss brave **man**! whose Numbers have been hurl'd,
288. H.907, 5
Man must do well out of a good intent,.......290. H.917, 1
Burr is a smell-feast, and a **man** alone,........296. H.944, 1
Thou art that **man** of men, the **man** alone,..297. H.947, 3
No **man** such rare parts hath, that he can swim,
298. H.953, 1
Who art a **man** for all Sceanes; unto whom....298. H.955, 3
Tell me young **man**, or did the Muses bring....299. H.956, 1
Tell that Brave **Man**, fain thou wo'dst have access
301. H.963, 1
Man may at first transgress, but next do well:.314. H.1021, 1
For all the Divell helps, will be a poore **man**...315. H.1025, 2
And let not a **man** then be seen here,..........317. H.1035, 15
Give me a **man** that is not dull,...............318. H.1036, 1
Not of one **man**, but all the Common-wealth...318. H.1041, 2
If wholsome Diet can re-cure a **man**,..........319. H.1049, 1
No **man** dies ill, that liveth well..............321. H.1059, 2
Stand forth Brave **Man**, here to the publique sight:
322. H.1062, 10
No **man** so well a Kingdome Rules, as He,....325. H.1074, 1
'Twill make a tongless **man** to wooe..........325. H.1075, 2
One **man** has reatch't his sixty yeers, but he..328. H.1088, 7
In the next sheet Brave **Man** to follow Thee....329. H.1092, 6
So that the **man** that will but lay his eares,...330. H.1100, 15
Gods boundlesse mercy is (to sinfull **man**).....341. N.15, 1
False **man** would be content..................346. N.38, 10
Happy's that **man**, to whom God gives........351. N.50, 1
No **man** is blest through ev'ry part...........351. N.50, 4
By Thee, Deare God, God gives **man** seed....358. N.75, 7
When **man** he makes a Penitent for it........359. N.82, 2
When **man** is punisht, he is plagued still,......370. N.110, 1
God He refuseth no **man**; but makes way.....378. N.131, 1
Sending them forth, Salute no **man** by th' way:
378. N.137, 2
God hides from **man** the reck'ning Day, that He.379. N.142, 1
Draw out of bad a soveraigne good to **man**....383. N.176, 2
As when to **man** He comes, and there doth place
385. N.189, 3
One **man** repentant is of more esteem..........388. N.205, 1
No **man** is tempted so, but may o'recome,.....389. N.211, 1
God bought **man** here wth his hearts blood expence;
389. N.213, 1
And **man** sold God here for base thirty pence..389. N.213, 2
May chance to be no other **man**, but Christ...391. N.226, 2
If **man** lives long, and if he live not well.......392. N.230, 6
Man to th' alluring object gives his will.......392. N.230, 32
Tell me rich **man**, for what intent............394. N.239, 1
God doth not promise here to **man**, that He....396. N.252, 1
Thy way, Thou guiltlesse **man**, and satisfie....398. N.263, 13
Thou art that Roscius, and that markt-out **man**,
398. N.263, 19
Who am a **man** of miserie!..................400. N.266, 3
A **man** both bruis'd, and broke, and one......400. N.266, 4
And now yf ther A **man** bee founde..........409. A.2, 103
And not a **man** here but consumes............413. A.4, 34
— — — — — — —, ...429. var. H.263, 18
And thinke each **man** thou seest doth doome
441. ins. H.465, 14a

Man' See Many

Many a turn, and **man'** a crosse-............165. H.443, 25
Manacles Are but Toiles, or **Manicles**............53. H.147, 8
Manche This **Manch**, that Moone; this Martlet, and that Mound;..................................295. H.941, 5
Manchet May both with **manchet** stand repleat;.178. H.476, 4
Mandrake's With withered cherries; **Mandrakes** eares;
120. H.293, 43
Manes This observ'd, the **Manes** shall be........284. H.891, 5
Mange — — — — — — — —, ...421. var. H.106, 22
Manger But, here, a homely **manger**...........345. N.33, 16
Manifest All doubts, and **manifest** the where......367. N.102, 7
Manifestly Which like a garden **manifestly** show...404. A.1, 15
Manifold Among these Tempests great and **manifold**
319. H.1044, 1
These my irruptions **manifold**;...............344. N.29, 6
Tissues, or Tabbies **manifold**:................355. N.60, 2
Mankind As the old Race of **mankind** did,.......147. H.377, 38
(The skarcrow vnto **Mankinde**) that doth breed.411. A.3, 52
Fight bravely for the flame of **mankinde**, yeeld
433. ins. H.283, 140f
Manna Turn'd all to Mell, and **Manna** there for thee.
143. H.370, 4
Marrow, and **Manna** unto thee................288. H.909, 6
That **Manna**, which God on His people cast,....379. N.146, 1
Manner Do in a trickling **manner** tell,..........44. H.127, 7
The Elves, in formall **manner**, fix............92. H.223, 93
Manners O men, O **manners**; Now, and ever knowne
29. H.86, 9
Manners knowes distance, and a man unrude...147. H.377, 31
I have still the **manners** left.................182. H.489, 10
Manners each way musicall:...................204. H.569, 10
And **manners** good requ'res, that we...........226. H.647, 2
Cleane in **manners**, cleere in voice:.............232. H.665, 2
O Place! O People! **Manners**! fram'd to please.242. H.713, 9
This rule of **manners** I will teach my guests,..310. H.1005, 1
Out of my comely **manners** worne;............312. H.1016, 5
Honour thy Parents; but good **manners** call....363. N.94, 1
Manners are good: but till his errand ends,...378. N.137, 7
Lett **Manners** teach the <e> whear to bee.....407. A.2, 27
Man's **See Blindman's buff, Madman's, Plowman's, Poorman's**
No Critick haunts the Poore **mans** Cell:........6. H.2, 22
That **man's** unwise will search for Ill,............6. H.2, 25
Mans Fortune must be had in reverence........117. H.287, 2
A Just **man's** like a Rock that turnes the wroth.152. H.389, 1
Prepares the way for **mans** docility.............153. H.394, 4
The greatest **mans** Inheritance.................197. H.542, 2
Because we feed on no **mans** score:..........200. H.552, 14
And **Mans** Pulse stopt, All Passions sleep in Peace.
202. H.558, 4
Can shake a just **mans** purposes:..............215. H.615, 2
Some mirth, t'adulce **mans** miseries?..........233. H.670, 6
That **man's** not said to live, but last:.........233. H.670, 33
Then a **mans** frequent Fame, spoke out with praise.
241. H.710, 2
Mans fortunes are according to his paines......253. H.752, 2
Mans disposition is for to requite..............292. H.923, 1
Mans former Birth is grace-lesse; but the state.326. H.1080, 27
Here, for the righteous **mans** salvation:........349. N.44, 2
When a **mans** Faith is frozen up, as dead;......359. N.80, 1
A **mans** transgression God do's then remit,....359. N.82, 1
God then confounds **mans** face, when He not hears
382. N.169, 1
The shame of **mans** face is no more............383. N.170, 1
That **mans** uncomely froth might not molest....386. N.193, 3
Being, oft here, the just **mans** portion..........387. N.201, 6
And from Gods Prescience of **mans** sin doth flow
390. N.219, 3
Of **man's** the chief cause of Gods Prescience...390. N.220, 2
Before **Mans** fall, the Rose was born...........396. N.251, 1
But, for **Mans** fault, then was the Thorn,.....396. N.251, 3
Mansion To mine eternall **Mansion**.............270. H.819, 3
Mantel Cleane was the herth, the **mantle** larded jet;
262. H.783, 11
Mantel-trees No more shall I from **mantle-trees** hang downe,
131. H.333, 3
Mantle And (with your **Mantle** o're me cast)....61. H.159, 24
Many **See Man', Very-many, Very-many-meeting**
Many dainty Mistresses:......................15. H.39, 2
Then dream, ye heare the Lamb by **many** a bleat
36. H.106, 49
(By **many** a watrie syllable)..................44. H.127, 8
Many a lesse and greater spheare..............47. H.133, 2
Not one, but **many** Monuments...............48. H.134, 8
If 'mongst my **many** Poems, I can see........63. H.165, 1
Many a green-gown has been given;...........69. H.178, 51
Many a kisse, both odde and even:............69. H.178, 52
Many a glance too has been sent.............69. H.178, 53
Many a jest told of the Keyes betraying.......69. H.178, 55
Thy **many** scorns, and find no cure?..........74. H.191, 2
Say, if there be 'mongst **many** jems here; one..76. H.194, 3
She has Virgins **many**,......................83. H.205, 5
How **many** lye forgot.......................85. H.211, 13
Many thorns to be in Love..................88. H.217, 6
Which charity they give to **many**...............92. H.223, 89
Their **many** mumbling Masse-priests here,.....92. H.223, 103
And **many** a dapper Chorister.................92. H.223, 104
Many a trifle too, and trinket,...............93. H.223, 123

My Muse in Meads has spent her **many** houres,.94. H.224, 1
On **many** a head here, **many** a Coronet:.......94. H.224, 4
When I through all my **many** Poems look,......94. H.226, 1
Since which, though I love **many**,.............100. H.249, 6
There be in Love as **many** feares,............102. H.253, 3
Many a sweet-fac't Wood-Nymph here is seene,.107. H.265, 5
Though good things answer **many** good intents;.110. H.275, 1
Of **many** a warbling Cherubim:..............115. H.283, 104
He keeps not one, but **many** Lents i' th'yeare..122. H.305, 6
Pleasures, **many** here attend ye,.............125. H.314, 5
Their **many** vertues volum'd up in thee;.........131. H.331, 4
I who have favour'd **many**, come to be........142. H.365, 1
On **many** a head the Delphick Coronet,........142. H.365, 4
Many a Teaster by his game, and bets:.......154. H.400, 2
Who hath but one of **many**;...................160. H.422, 14
Many a neat perplexity,......................165. H.443, 24
Many a turn, and man' a crosse-............165. H.443, 25
Many a Counter, **many** a Die,................166. H.443, 51
Not **many** full-fac't-moons shall waine,........176. H.465, 77
(As **many** Conscripts of the Citie do)........176. H.466, 6
Many we are, and yet but few possesse.......177. H.470, 1
One, or **many** Mistresses:.....................182. H.490, 6
I have seen **many** Maidens to have haire;......205. H.571, 1
Many shrewd disasters met,....................209. H.585, 5
My **many** fresh and fragrant Mistresses:.......214. H.612, 2
When after **many** Lusters thou shalt be.......231. H.664, 1
Though by well-warding **many** blowes w'ave past,
237. H.688, 1
Sorrowes divided amongst **many**, lesse........239. H.699, 1
As **many** Lawes and Lawyers do expresse.....244. H.718, 1
With eating **many** a miching Mouse...........246. H.724, 24
Many grinning properties.....................255. H.761, 10
In great Processions **many** lead the way......256. H.763, 3
You **many** a Plum, and **many** a Peare:.........264. H.787, 2
For all thy **many** courtesies to me,............267. H.804, 1
So **many** Kings, and Primates too there are,..272. H.826, 4
Say, what wo'd **many** do?......................273. H.833, 6
Thou hast made **many** Houses for the Dead;..277. H.853, 1
Who **many** serves, serves base servility.........284. H.887, 2
And **many** Flowers beside;......................285. H.892, 14
Brings him not one, but **many** a Maiden-head...286. H.898, 16
Then from the porch may **many** a Bride.......291. H.919, 13
Who writ for **many**. Benedicite...............298. H.952, 4
Upon thee **many** a Benizon....................303. H.973, 18
For other things, my **many** Children be.......304. H.978, 5
For look how **many** leaves there be............304. H.980, 7
So **many** Goblins you shall see.................304. H.980, 9
By so **many**:...................................308. H.993, 6
My **many** cares and much distress.............312. H.1016, 1
Whereon so **many** Stately Structures stand:..315. H.1028, 4
Know when to speake; for **many** times it brings
318. H.1037, 1
If 'mongst these **many** Numbers to be read,...322. H.1062, 2
Scores of sins w'ave made here **many**,........373. N.121, 9
Wherewith so **many** soules were fed..........374. N.123, 16
Shed for their Master **many** a bitter teare:....384. N.180, 10
God hath this world for **many** made; 'tis true:.387. N.198, 1
Of **many** standing, but of fall to none.........389. N.215, 2
I know, that faults will **many** here be found,..398. N.261, 5
That makes all æquall. **Manye** thowsands should
411. A.3, 35
And to thy **many**, take in one soul more........416. A.8, 2
— — — — — — — — — — —, ...424. var. H.128, 49
— — — — — — — — — — —, ...439. var. H.443, 25
Many a Purse-stringe, **many** a thred,......440. ins. H.443, 45v

Map But sees these things within thy **Map**.....36. H.106, 72
Canst in thy **Map** securely saile:..............36. H.106, 78
Maps In Varnisht **maps**; by'th' helpe of Compasses;
330. H.1100, 2
Maquerel To make loose Gownes for **Mackarell**:.275. H.844, 6
Mar Death will come and **mar** the song:........39. H.111, 12
To **marre** the mirth at all here...............235. H.674, 12
'Twill quickly **mar**, & make ye too............325. H.1075, 6
To make, not **marre** her, by this punishment:..344. N.31, 2
Marble Lesse in these **Marble** stones, then in thy story.
89. H.219, 22
Or mournfull **Marble**; let thy shade..........145. H.376, 3
The **Marble** speaks it Mary Stone:............257. H.764, 4
Or mourne, or make a **Marble** Verse for me,..298. H.952, 3
Here now I rest under this **Marble** stone:......298. H.954, 2
Out-during **Marble**, Brasse, or Jet,............335. H.1129, 2
Marbles For these, and **marbles** have their whiles
148. H.377, 100
Marbles will sweare that here it lyes..........203. H.564, 2
A Fast, while Jets and **Marbles** weep,..........257. H.764, 8
No trust to Metals nor to **Marbles**, when......419. A.10, 1
Marchandize See **Merchandise**
Mare That young men have to shooe the **Mare**:.126. H.319, 16
Hence the Hag, that rides the **Mare**,...........284. H.891, 2
Mares The Horses, **Mares**, and frisking Fillies,..101. H.250, 11
Margarite That is A **Margarite**, wch Lost.......409. A.2, 85
Margents Purfling the **Margents**, while perpetual! Day
206. H.575, 14
Maria Charls the best Husband, while **Maria** strives
26. H.79, 3
As when the Sweet **Maria** lived here:..........214. H.612, 10
Marian **Marian** too in Pagentrie:................255. H.761, 8

Marie The Babe unto His Mother **Marie**;.......366. N.97, 27
The Virgin **Marie** was (as I have read).......385. N.190, 1
Marie's So long (it seem'd) as **Maries** Faith was small,
386. N.192, 1
Marigolds Pansies will weep; and **Marygolds** will wither;
41. H.118, 5
No **Marigolds** yet closed are;..................164. H.441, 5
Marjoram Shew thy white feet, and head with **Marjoram** crown'd:..................................113. H.283, 32
Mark And **mark** it for a Rapture nobly writ,....64. H.168, 9
Come, my Corinna, come; and comming, **marke**.68. H.178, 29
Left in this rak't-up Ash-heap, as a **mark**.......78. H.197, 37
Mark, if her tongue, but slily, steale a taste....100. H.248, 4
Enlightned substance; **mark** how from the Shrine
112. H.283, 12
O **marke** yee how.............................115. H.283, 105
Our own fair wind, and **mark** each one........133. H.336, 39
Dear Amarillis! Mon. Hark! Sil **mark**: Mir. this earth grew sweet....................................159. H.421, 11
And (Sweetling) **marke** you, what a Web will come
221. H.633, 40
— — — — — — — — — — —, ...427. var. H.197, 74
— — — — — — — — — — —, ...432. var. H.283, 107
Marked Or ever **mark't** the pretty beam,........164. H.440, 5
Yellow, **markt** for Jealousie..................187. H.503, 4
Markt in thy Book for faithfull Witnesses.....188. H.507, 4
Markt for the True-wit of a Million:.........194. H.526, 4
Brave Kinsman, **markt** out with the whiter stone:
199. H.545, 8
Marked-out Thou art that Roscius, and that **markt-out** man,
398. N.263, 19
Marketh The Trencher-creature **marketh** what...147. H.377, 50
Markets And weekly **Markets** for to sell his wares:
253. H.753, 2
Marks Thy long-black-Thumb-nail **marks** 'em out for ill:
66. H.173, 2
Mar'l See **Marvel**
Marmalet Oblations oft, of sweetest **Marmelet**....227. H.652, 14
Marning See **Morning**
— — — — — — — — —, ...450. var. A.9, 49
Maro Homer, Musæus, Ouid, **Maro**, more.......411. A.3, 41
Maronian Of thy brave, bold, and sweet **Maronian** Muse.
234. H.673, 12
Marred They are both hard, and **marr'd**,........138. H.344, 3
Marriage No, I sho'd think, that **Marriage** might,
97. H.235, 5
Is not by **mariage** quencht, but flames the higher.
262. H.781, 16
Marriages Who art chief at **marriages**,.........141. H.360, 2
Married A wife most richly **married**.............291. H.919, 16
— — — — — — — — — —, ...428. var. H.235, 3
Marries When as the Lilly **marries** with the Rose!.44. H.124, 2
Marrow Quite through my heart and **marrow**....27. H.81, 32
Marrow, and Manna unto thee................288. H.909, 6
An active spiritt full **marrow**, and what's good;
426. ins. H.197, 48d
Marry Live, and not **marry**?..................12. H.26, 6
Next, let us **marry**:..........................31. H.94, 2
And while ye may, goe **marry**:.................84. H.208, 14
But yet I would not **marry**..................160. H.422, 8
What need we **marry** Women, when..........297. H.948, 1
Mars That **marres** a flower;...................104. H.257, 7
Of that Fiend that **marres** your rest;..........117. H.289, 6
Such Three brave Brothers fell in **Mars** his Field.
170. H.451, 12
Marshal's See **Martial's**
Martial Then soft Catullus, sharp-fang'd **Martial**,
206. H.575, 43
Between Domitians **Martiall** then, and Thee.....301. H.966, 10
Martial's Not **Marshals** Bee, which in a Bead....186. H.497, 11
Martlet This Manch, that Moone; this **Martlet**, and that Mound;.................................295. H.941, 5
Martyr See **Virgin-martyr**
Martyrdom That dares to dead the fire of **martirdome**:
128. H.323, 2
The fire, and **martyrdome** of love..............169. H.449, 4
Scorch't with the selfe-same **martyrdome**:......169. H.449, 10
Triumph in such a **Martirdome**................175. H.465, 66
Let's endure one **Martyrdome**..................315. H.1027, 2
To suffer in the Muses **Martyrdome**:..........335. H.1128, 4
Marvel Do **mar'l** how I co'd die,....... ....72. H.185, 20
Mary See **Ave-Mary**
The Marble speaks it **Mary** Stone:..............257. H.764, 4
Observe we may, how **Mary** Joses then,.........384. N.180, 7
And th' other **Mary** (**Mary** Magdalen).........384. N.180, 8
Christ did her Woman, not her **Mary** call:.......386. N.192, 2
But **Mary** cal'd then (as S. Ambrose saith).....386. N.192, 4
Mashes Deserve these **Mashes** and those snares...282. H.881, 6
Mask Deni'd the **Mask** I wo'd have seen.........247. H.729, 8
Mass-priests Their many mumbling **Masse-priests** here.
92. H.223, 103
Master Untrusse, his **Master** bade him; and that word
65. H.171, 5
What saves the **master** of the House thereby?..118. H.292, 3
These Summer-Birds did with thy **Master** stay..151. H.387, 1
For which thy Love, live with thy **Master** here,
151. H.387, 7

(What gets the master of the Meal by that?)....191. H.518, 4
A master of a house (as I have read)..........259. H.771, 1
I curst the master; and I damn'd the souce;....262. H.783, 19
Thou mighty Lord and master of the Lyre,......280. H.871, 1
And next to him, be Master of the Quire......299. H.956, 14
For to denie my Master, do thou crow............349. N.43, 2
Shed for their Master many a bitter teare:......384. N.180, 10
Masterdom When no force else can get the masterdome.
21. H.60, 2
If that he has a will to Masterdome.............389. N.211, 2
Masterpiece No, thy Ambition's Master-piece....229. H.662, 11
Master's Is the wise Masters Feet, and Hands...230. H.662, 24
The Masters charge and care to recompence.....245. H.723, 10
Masters My Masters all, Good day to you........121. H.299, 8
Match Then, next, to match Tradescant's curious shels,
232. H.668, 3
Mates See Playmates
Birds chuse their Mates, and couple too, this day:
149. H.378, 2
Matins When all the Birds have Mattens seyd,....68. H.178, 10
Betimes my Mattens say:.......................87. H.214, 2
As sure a Mattins do's to him belong,..........128. H.321, 5
Mattens sing, or Mattens say:................324. H.1069, 2
From Mattins to the Euensong,..................418. A.9, 42
Matron-like How Matron-like didst thou go drest!
375. N.123, 63
Matrons For that, Matrons say, a measure.......55. H.149, 79
Let all chaste Matrons, when they chance to see..58. H.151, 1
O modest Matrons, weep and waile!...........374. N.123, 13
Matter See Subject-matter
His linings are the matter running there.......144. H.373, 2
Were there not a Matter known,................163. H.433, 1
Serve but for matter to make Paper-kites.........286. H.896, 2
Nor makes it matter, Nestors yeers to tell,......392. N.230, 5
Matters Grow for two ends, it matters not at all,
232. H.667, 1
It matters not, since thou art chosen one.......305. H.983, 3
Maukin See, here a Maukin, there a sheet,.......101. H.250, 9
Maundie Our Maundie; thus,...................374. N.123, 29
Maunds See Mounds
Maundy See Maundie
May (Partial List for Auxiliary)
Of April, May, of June, and July-Flowers...........5. H.1, 2
Then after her comes smiling May...............23. H.70, 3
Which are so cleane, so chast, as none may feare..28. H.84, 5
Till when, in such assurance live, ye may.......38. H.106, 145
Guesse I may, what I must be:...............38. H.107, 3
Take time Lady while ye may..................56. H.149, 120
Spring, sooner then the Lark, to fetch in May...68. H.178, 14
The Proclamation made for May:..............68. H.178, 40
But is got up, and gone to bring in May.........69. H.178, 44
Gather ye Rose-buds while ye may,.............84. H.208, 1
And while ye may, goe marry:................84. H.208, 14
Three dayes before the shutting in of May,.......86. H.213, 13
Bloom'd from the East, or faire Injewel'd May..112. H.283, 2
So you sweet Lady (sweet as May)............126. H.318, 3
Let's live, my Wickes, then, while we may,....132. H.336, 15
Let Kings Command, and doe the best they may,
138. H.345, 1
Let's live in hast; use pleasures while we may:..171. H.453, 1
May both with manchet stand repleat;..........178. H.476, 4
Next, may your Dairies Prosper so,............179. H.476, 10
Then, may your Plants be prest with Fruit,....179. H.476, 16
Next may your Duck and teeming Hen..........179. H.476, 19
Last, may your Harrows, Shares and Ploughes,.179. H.476, 22
Skurffe by his Nine-bones sweares, and well he may,
180. H.480, 1
Here in green Meddowes sits eternall May,.....206. H.575, 13
May a thousand blessings come!................220. H.633, 2
Let's be jocund while we may;...............224. H.639, 1
Drink Wine, and live here blithefull, while ye may:
228. H.655, 1
Love, and live here while we may;.............238. H.691, 2
It may chance good-luck may send............334. H.1125, 3
That sees December turn'd to May.............364. N.96, 10
Mayest Where thou mayst sit, and piping please......5. H.2, 3
There with the Reed, thou mayst expresse..........5. H.2, 7
There on a Hillock thou mayst sing............5. H.2, 11
Where thou mayst hear thine own Lines read......6. H.2, 23
Where (though thou see'st not) thou may'st think upon
20. H.55, 5
And may'st draw thousands with a haire:......174. H.465, 4
To save; when thou may'st kill a heart.........177. H.471, 4
A Lawn, that thou mayst looke................271. H.824, 10
Teares most prevaile; with teares too thou mayst move
287. H.900, 1
Live thou at Court, where thou mayst be......323. H.1068, 11
So Thou, my God, may'st on this impure look,...371. N.113, 7
— — — — — — — — — — — —, ...429. var. H.263, 8
Maying She must no more a Maying:..........56. H.149, 114
Few Beads are best, when once we goe a Maying..68. H.178, 28
But my Corinna, come, let's goe a Maying.......68. H.178, 42
This night, and Locks pickt, yet w'are not a Maying.
69. H.178, 56
Come, my Corinna, come, let's goe a Maying.....69. H.178, 70
Mayor See Lord Mayor
Mayor's See Lord Mayor's
Maypole The May-pole is up,....................239. H.695, 1
Maypoles I sing of May-poles, Hock-carts, Wassails, Wakes,
5. H.1, 3
Thy May-poles too with Garlands grac't:.......230. H.662, 53
Maze The bed is ready, and the maze of Love..115. H.283, 121
Me (Partial List)
Me thought, (last night) love in an anger came,...16. H.40, 1
Me thought, her long small legs & thighs..........16. H.41, 5
And found (Ah me!) this flesh of mine...........17. H.41, 22
Me thought t'was strange, that thou so hard sho'dst prove,
42. H.122, 7
Make me a heaven; and make me there..........47. H.133, 1
Make me a Chariot, and a Sun;.................47. H.133, 5
Next, place me Zones, and Tropicks there;.......47. H.133, 7
But since (me thinks) it shows..................51. H.144, 3
Ah me! I try; and trying, prove,................60. H.157, 3
Me thinks that onely lustre doth appeare......94. H.226, 3
Griefe (ay me!) hath struck my Lute,..........131. H.332, 5
No more shall I (I feare me) to thee bring......132. H.333, 5
But time (Ai me)...........................144. H.371, 13
Love he that will; it best likes me,.............155. H.408, 1
Ah woe is me, woe, woe is me,..................156. H.412, 9
Me thinks like mine, your pulses beat;..........157. H.413, 5
Besides (Ai me!) since she went hence to dwell,.159. H.421, 27
Steere Thee to me; and thinke (me gone)......174. H.465, 9
Ai me! How shal my griefe be stil'd?...........188. H.509, 5
Ile get me hence,.............................213. H.609, 1
Then, then (me thinks) how sweetly flowes.....261. H.779, 2
Ai me! I love, give him your hand to kisse......274. H.837, 1
Me thought I saw (as I did dreame in bed)....313. H.1017, 1
For which (me thought) in prittie anger she..313. H.1017, 11
Since when (me thinks) my braines about doe swim,
313. H.1017, 13
Me thought I saw them stir, and gently move,.326. H.1080, 11
(Ay me!) I feele,...............................353. N.56, 14
Me thought, I did Thy bounty chide,............358. N.75, 5
Let me live ever here, and stir................402. N.269, 18
Mead Adorn'd this smoother Mead...............110. H.274, 16
Gives to each Mead a neat enameling............224. H.642, 4
Or smell, like to a Meade new-shorne,..........364. N.96, 16
Meadow Or like a medow being lately mown....159. H.421, 21
Meadow's This year again, the medows Deity.....140. H.354, 2
Meadows The Damaskt medowes, and the peebly streames
35. H.106, 43
And those Meddowes full be set...............108. H.266, 15
Here in green Meddowes sits eternall May,.......206. H.575, 13
In country Meadowes pearl'd with Dew,........323. H.1068, 5
Meadow-verse Herrick shall make the meddow-verse for you.
140. H.355, 14
Meads May all, like flowrie Meads...............55. H.149, 63
My Muse in Meads has spent her many houres,...94. H.224, 1
Gardens thence produce and Meads:............108. H.266, 14
First offer Incense, then thy field and meads.....143. H.370, 1
Sit smiling in the Meads; where Balme and Oile,.205. H.575, 3
No more of Groves, Meades, Springs, and wreaths of Flowers:
228. H.658, 4
This done, then to th' enameld Meads..........230. H.662, 29
What have the Meades to do with thee,........323. H.1068, 9
And all sweet Meades; from whence we get......360. N.83, 17
Meal See Holy-meal, Piecemeal
How both his Meale and Oile will multiply.......73. H.188, 4
And Bacon, (which makes full the meale)......101. H.250, 31
His Stomach to a second Meale. No, no,........147. H.377, 33
Which I worke to Meale, and make............152. H.393, 3
Of Oyl and Meal..............................171. H.455, 8
(What gets the master of the Meal by that?)...191. H.518, 4
But the Meal of Mill-dust can..................223. H.638, 17
Meale and it now mix together;................258. H.769, 5
Commix with Meale a little Pisse...............284. H.890, 2
The calfe without meale n'ere was offered;......345. N.34, 2
Be the meale of Beanes and Pease,..............363. N.93, 3
For we have lost, with thee, the Meale,.........374. N.123, 23
God! to my little meale and oyle,...............377. N.130, 1
Meals Meat for our meales, and fragments too:....356. N.66, 4
Mean What now I meane to doe;..................13. H.31, 6
I meane (the Soveraigne of all Plants) the Oke....23. H.69, 5
Slowly goes farre: The meane is best: Desire....51. H.143, 3
Since thou art gone, no more I mean to play,....159. H.421, 9
I meane the Court: Let Latmos be............183. H.492, 17
The Wearer's no meane Shepheardesse..........192. H.521, 24
Though ne'r so mean the Viands be,............200. H.552, 3
No more my Silvia, do I mean to pray..........204. H.570, 1
What is beyond the mean is ever ill:............220. H.633, 22
Close keep your lips, if that you meane.........250. H.738, 1
The Mean the Musique makes in every thing....268. H.812, 2
This for no meane miracle;.....................302. H.968, 8
Our heat of youth can hardly keep the mean.....318. H.1042, 2
The meane passe by, or over, none contemne;..322. H.1062, 7
Spur jingles now, and sweares by no meane oathes,
330. H.1099, 1
Excesse is sluttish: keepe the meane; for why?..331. H.1109, 1
That I have plac'd Thee in so meane a seat,...371. N.113, 2
Or, ne're so meane a peece, but men might see..389. N.214, 3
Meaner With this thy meaner Minstralsie............5. H.2, 6
As great men lead; the meaner follow on,.......214. H.614, 3

Appeares but in His **Meaner** Majestie...........236. H.685, 6
Ghost-like, as in my **meaner** sepulcher;..........371. N.115, 4
Meanest (When you had power) the **meanest** remedy: 52. H.146, 20
That things of greatest, so of **meanest** worth,...105. H.257, 27
When as the **meanest** part of her,..............145. H.375, 25
Even as the **meanest** Flower....................184. H.493, 8
But must be niggards of the **meanest** bloud.......260. H.775, 2
— — — — — — — — — —, ...425. var. H.197, 23
Means You Criticks **means** to live:...............32. H.96, 2
Means for her recovering;.....................122. H.302, 4
Means, I shall know what other kisse..........175. H.465, 70
Great men by small **meanes** oft are overthrown:..181. H.486, 1
By the weak'st **means** things mighty are o'rethrown, 240. H.702, 1
And as in **meanes**, in minde all torne.........312. H.1016, 6
She can but spoile me of my **Meanes**, not Mind. 322. H.1061, 2
The mind; the King, the **meanes** whereby I live..355. N.62, 2
Meanes I may kisse thy kisse,..................414. A.5, 12
Meant But weep not, Christall; for the shame was **meant** 249. H.732, 3
How ere it fortuned; know for Truth, I **meant**..304. H.977, 3
The Prophets Mountains of the Old are **meant**;..381. N.157, 3
Meantime **Mean time** be it......................171. H.455, 11
Mean time, let Lycidas have leave to Pipe to thee. 184. H.492, 43
Meane time we two will sing the Dirge of these;..209. H.584, 7
Meane time that he from place to place do's rome, 253. H.753, 3
Meane time thy Prophets Watch by Watch shall pray; 254. H.756, 13
Meane time like Earth-wormes we will craule below, 257. H.763, 21
Meanwhile **Meane while**, the Holy-Rood hence fright 123. H.306, 13
Meane while, let mee,.........................401. N.268, 36
Mease **Mease** brags of Pullets which he eats: but **Mease** 142. H.361, 1
Measure Who has a little **measure**:................30. H.87, 15
There to disport your selves with golden **measure**; 38. H.106, 139
For that, Matrons say, a **measure**..............55. H.149, 79
By cruse and **measure**; thus devoting Wine,....148. H.377, 83
And this remember, Vertue keepes the **measure**..220. H.633, 25
But a just **measure** both of Heat and Cold.......236. H.683, 2
Coynesse takes us to a **measure**;...............276. H.850, 5
A way to **measure** out the Wind;...............339. N.3, 2
Measured That's **measur'd** by felicity:...........162. H.431, 2
Measures And these brave **Measures** go a stately trot; 141. H.359, 11
My **measures** ravishing.......................261. H.778, 9
Peruse my **Measures** thoroughly, and where....322. H.1062, 4
— — — — — — — — —, ...450. var. A.9, 11
Meat If **meat** the Gods give, I the steame........22. H.66, 1
These, and sowre herbs, as dainty **meat**?.......37. H.106, 114
(As you) may have their fill of **meat**...........102. H.250, 46
The Platters there, as soone as **meat**...........124. H.312, 4
With bucksome **meat** and capring Wine:.......127. H.319, 28
But as thy **meate**, so thy immortall wine.......147. H.377, 71
ly that it makes the **meate** more sweet;........148. H.377, 80
His Nails they were his **meat**, his Reume the drink. 156. H.409, 2
And shew'st me there much Plate, but little **meat**; 161. H.424, 2
And give me **meate**, or give me else thy Plate...161. H.424, 4
Jove prospers my **meat**, more then his...........173. H.461, 4
Your Larders too so hung with **meat**,...........178. H.476, 5
When Jill complaines to Jack for want of **meate**; 186. H.498, 1
The tongues of Kids shall be thy **meate**;......192. H.521, 11
For **meat**, shall give thee melody.............192. H.521, 18
The Creame of **meat**;..........................198. H.544, 2
Swel'd with the Lard of others **meat**............200. H.552, 16
Give me wine, and give me **meate**,..............217. H.620, 1
The Larder fills with **meat**; the Bin with bread..221. H.633, 45
But that his breath do's Fly-blow all the **meate**...223. H.637, 2
Black I'm grown for want of **meat**;............223. H.638, 4
Unto the Dew-laps up in **meat**:...............230. H.662, 36
Pauls hands do give, what give they bread or **meat**, 248. H.731, 1
A little **meat** best fits a little bellie,...........249. H.733, 16
Yet love the smell of **meat**......................250. H.736, 6
Sho'd meet and tire, on such lautitious **meat**,....262. H.783, 3
The while the **meat** is a shredding;............263. H.784, 15
The best of all the sacrificed **meate**;...........272. H.826, 2
Out-did the **meate**, out-did the frolick wine.....289. H.911, 10
And **meat** too, for his need:..................295. H.942, 6
That (where **meat** is) will be a hanger on........296. H.944, 2
But when they call or cry on Grubs for **meat**;..325. H.1077, 3
If **meate** he wants, then Grace he sayes to see..332. H.1112, 3
Good words, or **meat**:........................350. N.47, 16
Meat for our meales, and fragments too:........356. N.66, 4
On our **meat**, and on us all. Amen...............364. N.95, 6
And **meat**,.....................................391. N.228, 15
Meats Hunger makes coorse **meats**, delicates.....37. H.106, 110
With superstition, (as the Cream of **meates**.)....204. H.568, 4
Medals Old Coyne's and **Meddalls**, wee expose.....407. A.2, 30
Medea For one **Medea** that was bad,............283. H.885, 5
Medicine Find that **Medicine** (if you can).........10. H.19, 11
Medicines Say, are thy **medicines** made to be......74. H.191, 3
Meditation Blest with the **Meditation** of my end:.392. N.230, 2
Medullina So **Medullina** fell, yet none..........175. H.465, 59
Medullino — — — — — — — — —, ...441. var. H.465, 59
Meet To **meet** and sit in Parliament:...............8. H.11, 2
That my wing'd ship may **meet** no Remora.........14. H.35, 4
The rest Ile speak, when we **meet** both in bed.....24. H.74, 14
Thus speaks the Oke, here; C. and M. shall **meet**, 26. H.79, 7
With thousand such enchanting dreams, that **meet** 36. H.106, 53
So soft streams **meet**, so springs with gladder smiles 77. H.197, 1
Meet after long divorcement by the Iles:........77. H.197, 2
So **meet** stolne kisses, when the Moonie nights...77. H.197, 5
So Kings & Queens **meet**, when Desire convinces.77. H.197, 7
As I **meet** thee. Soule of my life, and fame!....77. H.197, 9
As Queenes, **meet** Queenes; or come thou unto me, 79. H.197, 73
And when all Bodies **meet**.....................81. H.201, 49
How by stealth we **meet**, and then............82. H.203, 13
To **meet** it, when it woo's and seemes to fold..115. H.283, 116
As quick a growth to **meet** Decay,............125. H.316, 13
Shall make thy actions with their ends to **meet**..128. H.320, 8
As Benjamin, and Storax, when they **meet**.......131. H.331, 10
If we can **meet**, and so conferre,.............133. H.336, 49
Whether or no, that we shall **meet** here ever.....140. H.355, 4
Mirt. Where she and I shall never **meet** together. 159. H.421, 30
And **meet** to weepe..........................160. H.421, 46
Me, or my shadow thou do'st **meet**.............174. H.465, 16
And what was made, was made to **meet**.........190. H.515, 7
And then **meet** here..........................190. H.515, 48
Borne I was to **meet** with Age,................191. H.519, 1
On Holy-dayes, when Virgins **meet**............192. H.521, 29
When things **meet** most opposite:.............194. H.527, 7
And dark; let us **meet**;......................195. H.534, 2
Con.mixt they **meet**, with endlesse Roses crown'd. 206. H.575, 20
Spring with the Larke, most comely Bride, and **meet** 216. H.618, 1
And when I shall **meet**......................217. H.619, 18
On which the young men and maids **meet**,......230. H.662, 48
As Kine, when they at milking **meet**...........243. H.716, 30
Sho'd **meet** and tire, on such lautitious meat,....262. H.783, 3
When a warm tongue do's with such Ambers **meet**. 269. H.816, 4
Meet at those Lyrick Feasts,...................289. H.911, 4
Let's **meet** in a throng.......................320. H.1051, 2
All Pleasures **meet** in Woman-kind.............327. H.1082, 4
Although our suffering **meet** with no reliefe,.....333. H.1119, 1
Meet for nothing, but to kill;.................347. N.41, 19
And with as firme behaviour I will **meet**......392. N.230, 17
Over the which a **meet** sweet skin is drawne......404. A.1, 23
That both her lipps doe part, doe **meete**, doe kisse; 405. A.1, 38
— — — — — — — — — — —, ...448. var. A.1, 106
Meeting See **Re-meeting**, **Very-many-meeting**
Fate gives a **meeting**. Death's the end of woe....257. H.766, 2
Meetings In holy **meetings**, there a man may be..163. H.436, 1
Meets **Meets** in the whole and maks a harmony...406. A.1, 106
Or lyke as woole **meetes** steele, giue way.........408. A.2, 69
Megg **Megg** yesterday was troubled with a Pose,..296. H.945, 1
Mell Turn'd all to **Mell**, and Manna there for thee. 143. H.370, 4
Mellifluous From those **mellifluous** lips of his:..354. N.59, 16
Mellow The **mellow** touch of musick most doth wound 12. H.24, 1
First, April, she with **mellow** showrs.............23. H.70, 1
With **mellow** Lips, and luscious there withall...226. H.649, 2
The soft, the sweet, the **mellow** note..........243. H.716, 17
The Blessing fall in **mellow** times on Thee......269. H.818, 10
— — — — — — — — — — —, ...442. var. H.575, 10
Melodious Melting **melodious** words, to Lutes of Amber. 22. H.67, 4
(With luscious Numbers) my **melodious** Lyre.....84. H.210, 4
Melody Skilfull i' th' Harpe, and **Melodie**:......70. H.181, 10
For meat, shall give thee **melody**..............192. H.521, 18
Each one to make his **melody**:...............243. H.716, 20
But form'd by number make sweet **melody**.......406. A.1, 108
Melt To **melt** this snow, and thaw this ice;.........8. H.13, 4
That some conceit did **melt** me downe,..........67. H.175, 15
With thy enchantment, **melt** me into tears.........67. H.176, 2
Charm me asleep, and **melt** me so.............95. H.227, 1
Melt, **melt** my paines,.......................95. H.227, 27
Shall gently **melt** thee into dreames...........192. H.521, 8
Melted Then **melted** down, there let me lye........23. H.68, 5
Like to a Deaw, or **melted** Frost.............233. H.670, 27
Melting See **Soul-melting**
Melting, and in fancie die:.....................17. H.43, 6
Melting melodious words, to Lutes of Amber......22. H.67, 4
Here **melting** numbers, words of power to move....415. A.7, 9
Melts The soule of Nature **melts** in numbers: now 115. H.283, 106
This Stone, for names sake, **melts** to teares......257. H.764, 6

Member In which the tongue, though but a member small, 405. A.1, 29
Members To Sun his thin-clad members, if he likes, 146. H.377, 17
Memorial Memoriall............................85. H.211, 11
Memory Devoted to the memory of me:...........9. H.14, 16
Can teach a man the Art of memory:..........186. H.501, 2
Which to thy Memorie stands as due...........414. A.5, 3
Men See Young-men
Come thou not neere those men, who are like Bread.7. H.7, 1
But when that men have both well drunke, and fed,.7. H.8, 3
Subjects are taught by Men; Kings by the Gods..12. H.25, 2
Thy men; and rockie are thy wayes all over.......29. H.86, 8
O men, O manners; Now, and ever knowne......29. H.86, 9
Rockes turn to Rivers, Rivers turn to Men.......29. H.86, 14
In thee, thou Man of Men! who here do'st give..41. H.117, 4
Health is the first good lent to men;............42. H.121, 1
To conquer'd men, some comfort 'tis to fall......50. H.141, 1
Men, but Slothfulls most of all...................53. H.147, 10
As she, so you'l be ripe for men...............56. H.149, 112
He vow'd Destruction both to Birch, and Men:..65. H.171, 2
Heare all men speak; but credit few or none.....67. H.177, 4
A world of men to love:.......................76. H.193, 51
Raise greater fires in men.....................76. H.193, 56
When Pyramids, as men,.....................81. H.201, 47
As Men, the Heavens have their Hypocrisie?....81. H.202, 8
Amphion-like) men made of flesh and bones,......84. H.210, 6
Of any men that were.......................85. H.211, 12
Those learned men brought Incense, Myrrhe, and Gold, 86. H.213, 30
To have men think he's troubled with the Gout:..98. H.239, 2
Men say y'are faire; and faire ye are, 'tis true;..98. H.241, 1
Wherewith young men and maids distrest,......106. H.262, 3
With speed give sick men their salvation:......125. H.315, 2
That frights men with a Parliament:...........126. H.319, 4
That young men have to shooe the Mare:......126. H.319, 16
Quite through the young maids and the men,..127. H.319, 31
Upon his Altar, men shall read thy lines;......143. H.366, 2
Till this world shall dissolve as men,..........146. H.376, 12
Go on directly so, as just men may............149. H.377, 131
Good men, They find them all in Thee.........149. H.377, 136
For men did strut, and stride, and stare, not act..150. H.382, 6
Then temper flew from words; and men did squeake, 150. H.382, 7
As men, turne all to eares.....................151. H.388, 8
Those ills that mortall men endure,............153. H.395, 1
Brave men can't die; whose Candid Actions are..168. H.444, 5
Men in their substance, not in counterfeit.......170. H.451, 6
Of those mild Men, thou art to live among:.....172. H.456, 6
Men they shall be, not your sex.................177. H.472, 4
Great men by small meanes oft are overthrown:..181. H.486, 1
Skulls co'd not well passe through that scum of men. 200. H.551, 2
If Men can say that beauty dyes;..............203. H.564, 1
To most of men, but most of all to me:.........210. H.590, 2
Thy selfe, which thou put'st other men unto.....214. H.614, 2
As great men lead; the meaner follow on,......214. H.614, 3
No wrath of Men, or rage of Seas.............215. H.615, 1
Next we will act, how young men wooe;......215. H.616, 19
Physitians fight not against men; but these....226. H.646, 1
Combate for men, by conquering the disease....226. H.646, 2
On which the young men and maids meet,......230. H.662, 48
To catch the pilfring Birds, not Men...........231. H.662, 69
And that wee'l do; as men, who know,.........233. H.670, 36
What off-spring other men have got,..........236. H.681, 1
With men, a loathed inconveniencie............239. H.698, 2
Men are not born Kings, but are men renown'd;.241. H.707, 1
To mortall men great loads allotted be,........242. H.715, 1
Verses out-live the bravest deeds of men?........264. H.791, 2
Give me a reason why men call.................273. H.832, 1
Ill it fits old men to play,....................277. H.852, 7
That if (unknitting) men wo'd yet repent,......291. H.920, 3
Men are suspicious; prone to discontent:........291. H.921, 1
To heare the worst from men, when they doe well. 293. H.932, 2
Thou art that man of men, the man alone,......297. H.947, 3
Without their use we may have men?..........297. H.948, 2
Rise up of men, a fighting race..............297. H.948, 12
That makes thee lov'd, and of the men desir'd,..299. H.956, 9
Descend from heaven, to re-converse with men;.301. H.966, 12
Men must have Bounds how farre to walke; for we 307. H.990, 1
'Tis still observ'd, those men most valiant are,..308. H.994, 1
Pillars and men, hate an indifferent Poet.......309. H.1000, 2
Let the Maides bewash the men................315. H.1026, 10
The Queen of men, not flowers................323. H.1068, 12
That love 'twixt men do's ever longest last....327. H.1083, 1
He lives, who lives to virtue: men who cast....328. H.1089, 9
Necessity makes dastards valiant men.........333. H.1118, 2
What ever men for Loyalty pretend,............333. H.1121, 1
But if so be that men will not...............334. H.1123, 3
The worke is done: young men, and maidens set 335. H.1128, 1
Things precious are least num'rous: Men are prone 339. N.1, 5
Men to repent, but when He strikes withall.......342. N.19, 2
Gods Rod doth watch while men do sleep; & then 342. N.21, 1
The Rod doth sleep, while viligant are men.....342. N.21, 2
If God should punish no sin, here, of men,......343. N.27, 3
God co'd have made all rich, or all men poore;....356. N.69, 1
As men do wane in thankfulnesse.................358. N.76, 2
God makes not good men wantons, but doth bring 370. N.108, 1
As just Men are intitled Gods, yet none........379. N.143, 3
Present with just men, to the veritie:..........385. N.188, 2
Or when, for sins, men suffer punishment.......388. N.210, 4
Or, ne're so meane a peece, but men might see..389. N.214, 3
When as His grace not supples men............396. N.250, 2
(Judgment and Death, denounc'd gainst Guilty men) 411. A.3, 62
Young men to swoone, and Maides to dye for love. 415. A.7, 10
These have their Fate, and wear away as Men;..419. A.10, 2
Entitulated the Greecian Prince of men...442. ins. H.575, 28b
Menalchas Or that this day Menalchas keeps a feast 86. H.213, 7
Mend Rather then mend, put out the light.........97. H.235, 6
And can'st not mend, but carpe at it:...........229. H.660, 2
Shut every gate; mend every hedge that's torne,..259. H.771, 5
Mendest Find'st here a fault, and mend'st the trespasse too: 298. H.955, 8
Mending For mending sails, for patching Boat and Oares? 248. H.730, 20
Men's See Wise-men's
Other mens sins wee ever beare in mind;......253. H.751, 1
Mens sins destroyed are, when they repent;.....388. N.210, 3
— — — — — — — — — — —, ...424. var. H.164, 4
Merchandise Beyound the fare-fetch Marchandize...409. A.2, 94
Or in respect of Merchandize,...................417. A.9, 4
Merchant Th' industrious Merchant has; who for to find 36. H.106, 65
The Sea-scourg'd Merchant, after all his toile,....77. H.197, 16
Mercies Heaven, by Christs mercies, not my merit: 359. N.78, 12
White handes as smooth, as Mercies, bring......408. A.2, 59
Merciful (If mercifull, as faire thou art;..........33. H.103, 6
God is not onely mercifull, to call...............342. N.19, 1
Mercury You can make a Mercury.............204. H.569, 16
Mercy Mercie and Truth live with thee! and forbeare 14. H.35, 9
But cry thee Mercy: Exercise thy nailes........66. H.173, 5
Mercie secure ye all, and keep.................121. H.299, 5
Say, we must part (sweet mercy blesse.........134. H.336, 65
Which mercy if you will but do,..............165. H.442, 11
O shew mercy then, and be.....................254. H.757, 7
Shew mercy there, where they have power to kill. 321. H.1057, 2
The one is Mercy, and the next is Love:........340. N.6, 2
Gods boundlesse mercy is (to sinfull man)......341. N.15, 1
God mercy; and so die.........................352. N.53, 16
Let mercy be..................................370. N.111, 5
Mercy, the wise Athenians held to be...........380. N.148, 1
The good by mercy, as the bad by paines.......389. N.212, 2
Are works of mercy to the poore,..............393. N.231, 2
Or sing of mercy, and I'le suit...............393. N.232, 13
Who shewing mercy here, few priz'd, or none....393. N.234, 2
Who Mercie art,...............................401. N.268, 32
(Loue and Mercie, cherrish them),.............407. A.2, 22
(Thy Mercie helping) shall resist stronge fate....411. A.3, 44
Mercy's See Mercies
O then! for mercies sake, behold................344. N.29, 5
Mercy-seat Humbly unto Thy Mercy-seat:........349. N.46, 2
Thy mercy-seat I'le lay before;................369. N.107, 6
Mere A meere Botch of all and some............76. H.195, 4
Merely Mirtle the twigs were, meerly to imply;...16. H.40, 3
Which not for use, but meerly for the sight,...46. H.129, 5
Meerly to shew your worth,..................176. H.467, 11
Merit Heaven, by Christs mercies, not my merit:.359. N.78, 12
We merit all we suffer, and by far............393. N.235, 1
Merits Due to the Merits, not Authoritie.......120. H.296, 2
Merrily Let's live merrily, and thus............96. H.231, 5
Merriment Let's enjoy our merryment:.........39. H.111, 2
To Prayers, then to Merryment,...............101. H.250, 24
That makes the Tables merriment..............124. H.312, 2
With the cheapest Merriment:.................255. H.761, 22
Merry And for to make the merry cheere,........101. H.250, 35
I a merry heart will keep,...................118. H.289, 13
The merry Cricket, puling Flie,...............119. H.293, 17
Wherewith ye make those merry Sceanes,......127. H.319, 18
Of merry Crickets by my Country fire,........132. H.333, 8
A merry mind..................................132. H.336, 13
Though not so fresh, yet full as merry........136. H.336, 140
How for to make thee merry;..................142. H.364, 6
Merry at anothers hearth; y'are here..........146. H.377, 29
While Fates permits us, let's be merry;.......172. H.457, 1
Thy whilome merry Oate.......................183. H.492, 2
Where merry as the Maids we'l be............215. H.616, 2
Thou & I'le sing to make these dull Shades merry, 248. H.730, 25
My merrie merrie boyes,.......................263. H.784, 2
Where God is merry, there write down thy fears: 355. N.63, 1

Doe speake a virgin **merry** cherry-lip't..........404. A.1, 22
For we goe over to be **merry**,..........445. ins. H.730, 26b
Meshes See Mashes
Mess The Worts, the Purslain, and the **Messe**..350. N.47, 31
Messes As that the **Messes** ne'r o'r-laid the Lord:.210. H.590, 6
Met Had **met** t'engender with the night;.........64. H.169, 6
Met in one Hearce-cloth, to ore-spred..........103. H.256, 6
Part of the way be **met**; or sit stone-still.......113. H.283, 58
The breath of Munkies **met** to mix...........166. H.443, 43
Many shrewd disasters **met**,...................209. H.585, 5
Where e're they **met**, or parting place has been..250. H.737, 8
But while he **met** with his Paternall grave;....278. H.860, 4
As when ye innocent **met** here................317. H.1035, 30
Where Pleasures **met**: at last, doe find,........327. H.1082, 3
With as cold frost, as erst we **mett** with fire;....414. A.6, 10
— — — — — — — — — —, ...425. var. H.197, 9
Metal Ask not for gold, which **metall** is:........381. N.158, 6
Metals No trust to **Metals** nor to Marbles, when.419. A.10, 1
Metamorphosed Was **Metamorphoz'd** to a Vine;.16. H.41, 2
Metamorphosis Behold a suddaine **Metamorphosis**.
325. H.1076, 2
Methinks See Thinks
I can but name thee, and **methinks** I call.....131. H.331, 1
And, **methinks**, I not inherit,..................182. H.489, 3
With griefe of heart, **methinks**, I thus doe cry,.193. H.522, 5
Brisk **methinks** I am, and fine,...............309. H.996, 1
Method But with that wisdome, and that **method**, as
148. H.377, 85
Mettle With plumpe soft flesh of **mettle** pure and fine
406. A.1, 79
Mew Save but his hat, and that he cannot **mew**..144. H.372, 2
Me-wards You say, to **me-wards** your affection's strong;
51. H.143, 1
Mewed Nailes from her fingers **mew'd**, she shewes: what els?
232. H.668, 4
Mice But Beards of **Mice**, a Newt's stew'd thigh,
119. H.293, 37
Curse not the **mice**, no grist of thine they eat:.141. H.358, 1
— — — — — — — — — —, ...433. var. H.293, 12
Chippinge, the **mice** filcht from the Binne,.439. ins. H.443, 45g
Micheldитch Had been reherst, by Joell **Micheldитch**:
266. H.800, 2
Miching With eating many a **miching** Mouse....246. H.724, 24
Mickle Not without **mickle** majesty...............165. H.443, 6
That your **mickle**, may have more..............223. H.638, 3
Midday Out-shine the splendour of his **mid-day** beams.
77. H.197, 12
Midday's Or e're dark Clouds do dull, or dead the **Mid-dayes** Sun.......................................401. N.268, 9
— — — — — — — — — —, ...451. var. H.197, 12
Middle I lasht out between the **Middle** and Extreame.
33. H.102, 2
(Just in the **middle** of the Altar).............92. H.223, 70
Like purest white stands in the **middle** place...404. A.1, 12
Hath in the **middle** ty'de a Gordian knott.....405. A.1, 62
Middlemost Into the **middle** <**most**> sight pleasing crooke
406. A.1, 82
Midnignt Noone-day and **Midnight** shall at once be seene:
59. H.154, 1
— — — — — — — — — —, ...437. var. H.336, 108
Midst And '**midst** a thousand gulfs to be secure..23. H.71, 6
In **mid'st** of all their outrages...................31. H.90, 6
The **midst** is thine; but Joves the Evening too;.128. H.321, 4
And, in the **midst**, to grace it more, was set...227. H.652, 9
Because not plac't here with the **midst**, or first..329. H.1092, 2
Thou stop'st S. Peter in the **midst** of sin;......349. N.43 3
Through **mid'st** thereof a christall stream there flowes
406. A.1, 75
— — — — — — — — — —, ...436. var. H.336, 61
Midwife To th' Temple with the sober **Midwife** go.
286. H.898, 2
Midwife-moon All now is husht in silence; **Midwife-moone**,
116. H.283, 151
Might (Partial List of Auxiliary)
I thought I **might** there take a taste,..........71. H.182, 17
But out of hope his wife **might** die to beare 'em.
72. H.184, 2
Jone wo'd go tel her haires; and well she **might**,.195. H.531, 1
The staffe **might** come to play the friendly part..394. N.241, 4
Mightiness Free by your fate, then Fortunes **mightinesse**,
141. H.359, 4
Might'st Thou **might'st** but onely see't, not taste it.
37.H.106,120
Thou did'st not mind it; though thou then **might'st** see
42. H.122, 3
Wo'd thou hast ne'r been born, or **might'st** not die.
193. H.522, 6
Mighty Twixt Kings and Subjects ther's this **mighty** odds,
12. H.25, 2
Fone sayes, those **mighty** whiskers he do's weare,
39. H.110, 1
Let but That **Mighty** Cesar speak, and then,...52. H.146, 13
Your selves into the **mighty** over-flow........115. H.283, 118
Mighty Neptune, may it please 129. H.325, 1
It calls to mind, that **mighty** Buckingham,.....137. H.341, 2
The wholesome savour of thy **mighty** Chines...146. H.377, 7
Of Holben, and That **mighty** Ruben too........150. H.384, 4
A **mighty** strife 'twixt Forme and Chastitie......189. H.511, 6
Flew out a crack, so **mighty**, that the Fart,....205. H.572, 3
You, and **mighty** Oberon:......................224. H.638, 26
Fill me a **mighty** Bowle......................227. H.653, 1
By the weak'st means things **mighty** are o'rethrown,
240. H.702, 1
Shall by the **mighty** Angell be reveal'd:........256. H.763, 16
Not for to hide his high and **mighty** eares;....275. H.843, 2
Thou **mighty** Lord and master of the Lyre,....280. H.871, 1
A sparke neglected makes a **mighty** fire.........281. H.873, 2
Diffuse their **mighty** influence................291. H.919, 8
Thou had'st, and hast thy **mighty** influence,...299. H.956, 8
To Jove the **Mighty** for to stand.............303. H.973, 16
Well, this I'le do; my **mighty** score...........369. N.107, 5
He finds a fire for **mighty** Mutius;............370. N.108, 6
A **mighty** storm last night.....................373. N.122, 5
Forc'd from the **mighty** dolour of the heart.....380. N.154, 2
So she, to keep her **mighty** woes in awe,........384. N.180, 5
All **mighty** blood; and can doe more.....437. var. H.336, 135
— — — — — — — — — —, ...452. var. H.128, 32
Mild Of those **mild** Men, thou art to live among:.172. H.456, 6
My **mild**, my loving Tutor, Lord and God!......398. N.261, 3
Not more, **milde** nymph, then they would have you doe;
431. ins. H.283, 60r
Milder While the **milder** Fates consent,..........39. H.111, 1
Whose shadow smels like **milder** Pomander!....181. H. 485, 2
Growe vpp wth **Mylder** Lawes to knowe.......407. A.2, 25
Mildly **Mildly** disparkling, like those fiers,.......165. H.443, 29
Falls to a temper, and doth **mildly** cast........225. H.642, 19
More **mildlie** least thy temptinge lookes beguile
424. ins. H.128, 46e
Miles Cleere Thou my paths, or shorten Thou my **miles**,
352. N.51, 5
Militant Him to be here our Christian **militant**...129. H.323, 16
Milk The smell of mornings **milk**, and cream;...145. H.375, 21
soft-skin, or bath in Asses **milke**:.............149. H.377, 122
Who as they lowe empearl with **milk**..........166. H.443, 41
Their **Milke** thy drinke; and thou shalt eate...192. H.521, 12
Then to the poore she freely gives the **milke**....203. H.561, 4
Milk stil your Fountains, and your Springs, for why?
273. H.831, 1
Then these kine, which I **milke** here..........305. H.984, 17
The Sonnes to suck the **milke** of Kine,.........310. H.1004, 5
And prest a little they will weepe new **milke**....405. A.1, 58
Milking As Kine, when they at **milking** meet....243. H.716, 30
Milking-pail To fulfill the **milkin-paile**?..........305. H.984, 8
Milkmaids That **Milk-maids** make about the hearth,
126. H.319, 12
Milky Woo'd to come suck the **milkie** Teat:......36. H.106, 50
And in the **milky** vally that's betweene.........405. A.1, 55
A **milky** high waye that direction yeilds.......405. A.1, 67
Mill-dust But the Meal of **Mill-dust** can.........223. H.638, 17
Million To make that thousand up a **million**.....24. H.74, 6
Treble that **million**, and when that is done,....24. H.74, 7
Unto a **Million**...............................29. H.87, 12
Fish-like, encrease then to a **million**:..........124. H.313, 12
Then prostrate to a **million**....................174. H.465, 28
Markt for the True-wit of a **Million**:..........194. H.526, 4
One onely glory of a **million**,..................256. H.763, 6
Teare, that deserves of me a **million**...........302. H.967, 4
Whearas by thee, those, and A **Million** since...411. A.3, 39
Millions **Millions** of Lillies mixt with Roses......36. H.106, 48
And **millions** of spring-times may ye have,......124. H.313, 13
Made void for **millions**, as for me..............370. N.107, 10
Mimic And a **Mimick** to devise.....................255. H.761, 9
Mince The Calculation of thy Birth, Brave **Mince**..194. H.526, 6
Mince pie For the rare **Mince-Pie**...............263. H.784, 16
Mincing Of **mincing** in their going.................375. N.123, 70
Mind In the contented **mind**, not mint............35. H.106, 18
Thou did'st not **mind** it; though thou then might'st see
42. H.122, 3
Vexation of the **mind**, and damn'd Despaire.....45. H.128, 22
Let me alone to fit the **mind**..................59. H.153, 4
Call not to **mind** those fled Decembers;........127. H.319, 38
A merry **mind**..................................132. H.336, 13
Ile call to **mind** things half forgot:............135. H.336, 114
It calls to **mind**, that mighty Buckingham,.....137. H.341, 2
A gentle **mind** to be unchaste.................175. H.465, 46
For the least trespasse: 'cause the **mind**......175. H.465, 61
Nor do's it **mind** the Rustick straines..........184. H.492, 23
To send your **mind**...........................198. H.544, 32
Riches to be but burthens to the **mind**.:.........213. H.605, 2
To have thy **mind**, and nuptiall bed............233. H.670, 11
Other mens sins wee ever beare in **mind**;......253. H.751, 1
Prosperitie more searching of the **mind**:........257. H.765, 2
And as in meanes, in **minde** all torne..........312. H.1016, 6
Nor do's she **minde**,..........................314. H.1024, 13
Chaste words proceed still from a bashfull **minde**.
319. H.1043, 2
She can but spoile me of my Meanes, not **Mind**.
322. H.1061, 2
An equall **mind** is the best sauce for griefe.....333. H.1119, 2
Salve for my body, and my **mind**..............342. N.17, 4
The **mind**; the King, the meanes whereby I live..355. N.62, 2
Argues a strong distemper of the **mind**.........356. N.70, 2
I'le have in **mind** my Resurrection,............392. N.230, 22
The Mayden Candour of thy **Mynde**:..........407. A.2, 34

Each takes A weeping farwell, rackt in mynde..411. A.3, 63
Elixar to the minde,....................432. ins. H.283, 70i
Mindful Be mindfull, that the lab'ring Neat....102. H.250, 45
Lastly, be mindfull (when thou art grown great)
181. H.483, 13
To make them, thereby, mindfull of their own..384. N.178, 3
Mine (Partial List)
To see the small remainders in mine Urne:.....49. H.138, 2
By which, mine angry Mistresse might descry,.58. H.150, 5
Begin to charme, and as thou stroak'st mine eares
67. H.176, 1
Then at th' opening of mine eyes,.............199. H.549, 3
Give me the prize: 2. The day is mine:........244. H.716, 43
(Amongst mine honour'd) Thee (almost) the last:
256. H.763, 2
Mine end near was,..........................346. N.38, 17
Mine's (But min's the greater smart)...........203. H.563, 6
Mine's faulty too, and small:..................376. N.125, 6
Mingled Like rose leaves, white and redd seeme mingled.
404. A.1, 18
Ministers Not, that He taught His Ministers to be
378. N.137, 3
Minstrel The while the Daulian Minstrell sweetly sings,
224. H.642, 7
Soe wth like lookes, as once the Ministrell.....411. A.3, 67
Minstrelsy With this thy meaner Minstralsie.......5. H.2, 6
Sung out his Birth with Heav'nly Minstralsie...86. H.213, 24
The piping Gnat for minstralcy..............119. H.293, 18
Mint In the contented mind, not mint............35. H.106, 18
— — — — — — — — — — —, ...422. var. H.106, 113
Minute 'Tis but a flying minute,.................85. H.211, 5
The minute of mine expiration.................281. H.875, 4
Minute's But a Minutes life with me:..........204. H.566, 2
In a Minutes space how I....................217. H.620, 8
Minutes Thy Watch may stand, my minutes fly poste haste;
8. H.10, 3
On your minutes, hours, dayes, months, years,.57. H.149, 151
They cling and close, some minutes of the night.
156. H.411, 4
So spend some minutes of the day:............215. H.616, 6
Those minutes, Time has lent us here..........233. H.670, 16
Miracle Thousands to feed by miracle...........139. H.350, 4
This for no meane miracle;....................302. H.968, 8
Mire With the mire, and the sweat:............284. H.891, 4
Mires O're Ditches, and Mires,................225. H.643, 11
Mirk That in the mirk and tonguelesse night,....357. N.72, 13
Mirror Place then this mirror whose briske hue...418. A.9, 51
Mirth Smiles to it selfe, and guilds the roofe with mirth;
7. H.8, 6
Now is the time for mirth,....................80. H.201, 1
Glitt'ring with fire; where, for your mirth,.....101. H.250, 27
That tels of Winters Tales and Mirth,.........126. H.319, 11
We'le eate our Beane with that full mirth,.....133. H.336, 55
(Larr thus conspiring with our mirth).........135. H.336, 124
Full mirth wait on you; and such mirth as shall
140. H.354, 11
The mirth, that was.........................144. H.371, 5
But temp'rate mirth dealt forth, and so discreet-
148. H.377, 79
Mirt. Ah! Amarillis, farewell mirth and pipe;..159. H.421, 8
To make thy Maids and selfe free mirth,......193. H.521, 49
Where Mirth and Friends are absent when we Dine
197. H.541, 3
What made that mirth last night? the neighbours say,
219. H.630, 1
Thy Nut-browne mirth; thy Russet wit;......231. H.662, 60
Some mirth, t'adulce mans miseries?..........233. H.670, 6
With inoffensive mirth here;..................234. H.674, 8
To marre the mirth at all here................235. H.674, 12
Sometimes (in mirth) he sayes each whelk's a sparke
273. H.834, 3
In endlesse mirth,............................314. H.1024, 5
Now, now the mirth comes....................317. H.1035, 1
True mirth resides not in the smiling skin:....341. N.13, 1
With guiltlesse mirth;........................350. N.47, 38
Gives life and luster, publike mirth,...........364. N.96, 20
But let no Christmas mirth begin.............366. N.98, 7
Of mirth is turn'd to sadnesse................375. N.123, 60
Mirthful To these smooth Lawns, my mirthfull Roundelay.
159. H.421, 10
Then live we mirthfull, while we should,......233. H.670, 28
Mirtillo Amin. Good day, Mirtillo. Mirt. And to you no lesse:
85. H.213, 1
Amar. But deare Mirtillo, I have heard it told,.86. H.213, 29
Youthfull Mirtillo, Here he comes, Griefdrownd.
159. H.421, 6
But she is gone. Sil. Mirtillo, tell us whether,..159. H.421, 29
Mischance A mischance is come to pass,.........305. H.984, 11
Mischances From all mischances, that may fright
121. H.299, 3
Mischief And no one mischief greater then your frown,
188. H.506, 13
But Ile returne; what mischief brought thee hither?
248. H.730, 13
Can do no mischiefe (there.).................285. H.893, 8
Mischiefs While mischeifs, by these,............225. H.643, 16
Since mischiefs neither dare..................373. N.122, 11

Miseries Some mirth, t'adulce mans miseries?....233. H.670, 6
Misery No life is yet life-proofe from miserie.....111. H.276, 2
While misery keeps in with patience............257. H.765, 4
With me in my miserie;........................347. N.40, 2
Will free him quickly from his miserie;........396. N.252, 2
Who am a man of miserie!....................400. N.266, 3
For Humane Joy, Contingent Misery...........416. A.8, 18
Misfortune In this misfortune Kings doe most excell,
293. H.932, 1
Misfortunes And my misfortunes all............238. H.690, 8
Mishap From which mishap this use I make,....283. H.883, 11
Mishaps That's counter-proofe against the Farms mishaps,
128. H.323, 5
Misled Youth (I confess) hath me mis-led;.....216. H.617, 5
Mislight No Will-o-th'-Wispe mis-light thee;....217. H.619, 6
Missed And howsoe're we have the conquest mist;
356. N.67, 3
Mist See Missed
I'le cast a mist and cloud, upon..............357. N.72, 5
Mistake Mistake the flesh, and flye-blow both his eyes;
282. H.879, 2
Misted That Roses shew, when misted o're with Lawn.
34. H.104, 4
Mistletoe Down with the Misleto;...............285. H.892, 2
Down with the Baies, & misletoe:.............304. H.980, 2
Lord, I am like to Misletoe,..................371. N.114, 1
Mistook Who gave him forth good Grain, though he mistook
4. Ap., 3
Upon some part of Kid, as if mistooke,........147. H.377, 55
Mistress Be my Mistresse short or tall,..........11. H.21, 3
By which, mine angry Mistresse might descry,..58. H.150, 5
Of my Mistresse, and of me....................82. H.203, 4
Till you (sweet Mistresse) came and enterwove.94. H.224, 7
Fly to my Mistresse, pretty pilfring Bee,......100. H.248, 1
And blesse his dainty Mistresse: see,..........114. H.283, 63
That was the Proverb. Let my mistresse be....141. H.357, 1
Give me my Mistresse, as she is,..............154. H.402, 3
This Lady's short, that Mistresse she is tall;..163. H.437, 1
Let faire or foule my Mistresse be,...........207. H.579, 1
Be the Mistresse of my choice,................232. H.665, 1
'Tis a Mistresse unto mee.....................253. H.750, 3
For Mistresse Bride, the wedding Cake:.......267. H.805, 2
Live you, great Mistresse of your Arts, and be..326. H.1080, 21
Some strickter M$^{ris.}$ or suspitious other.......410. A.3, 8
And know (faire mistris) of yor youth.........418. A.9, 40
— — — — — — — — — — —, ...450. var. A.9, 40
Mistress' — — — — — — — —, ...437. var. H.336, 95
Mistresses Many dainty Mistresses:..............15. H.39, 2
From your kinder Mistresses....................62. H.162, 9
From your Mistresses, and be,.................117. H.289, 3
Thus a thousand Mistresses,...................157. H.415, 6
One, or many Mistresses:......................182. H.490, 6
My many fresh and fragrant Mistresses:.......214. H.612, 2
Mists Where all Damps, and Mists are found?...40. H.115, 6
Spring up afresh; when all these mists are spent,
52. H.146, 11
Mite To th'utmost mite,.........................30. H.87, 17
In no one Satyre there's a mite of salt.........238. H.692, 2
'Tis true, my God; but I can't pay one mite....368. N.103, 10
Mites Of curious Brides; or like those mites....165. H.443, 31
Those mites of Time, which yet remain unspent,
171. H.456, 3
Conserves of Atomes, and the mites,.......435. ins. H.293, cc
Mix See Intermix
These eyes of mine shall see you mix agen......26. H.79, 6
And Almond blossoms, that do mix............145. H.375, 13
The breath of Munkies met to mix............166. H.443, 43
Meale and it now mix together;................258. H.769, 5
swell, mixe, and loose your soules; implye.431. ins. H.283, 50d
Mixed Millions of Lillies mixt with Roses.........36. H.106, 48
Theirs is a mixt Religion......................91. H.223, 23
Butter of Cowslips mixt with them;...........145. H.375, 22
Is mixt with mine; and truly know,............175. H.465, 71
The sweets of Love are mixt with tears.........208. H.580, 6
Heat and moisture mixt are so,...............324. H.1070, 3
Mixt in that watrie Theater;..................339. N.3, 4
My wine is mixt with weeping................353. N.56, 6
The Bad among the Good are here mixt ever:..383. N.172, 1
Which sweetly mixed both with white and redd.404. A.1, 17
To know his Queene, mixt with the farre.434. ins. H.293, 41g
By the round Urchin, some mixt wheate.439. ins. H.443, 45d
Mixeth, — — — — — — — —, ...447. var. A.1, 17
Mixture No mixture did admit.................75. H.193, 16
Moderate Like to a flame growne moderate:...67. H.175, 12
Moderation In things a moderation keepe,.......261. H.780, 1
Let moderation on thy passions waite..........318. H.1038, 1
Modest My modest wedlock, that was known....41. H.116, 7
Just as the modest Morne....................104. H.257, 4
Tempting the two too modest; can............115. H.283, 113
Modest I will be; but one word Ile say.......201. H.557, 21
Or else because th' art like a modest Bride,...301. H.963, 3
That are most modest ere they come to warre..308. H.994, 2
O modest Matrons, weep and waile!...........374. N.123, 13
Modesty Safe Modestie, Lou'd Patience, Feare...409. A.2, 97
Moistened Which as a warme, and moistned spring,
25. H.78, 9
Moisture But if to moisture, Let the oyle..........9. H.15, 3

And moisture, both compleat:................57. H.149, 126
From her moysture take the like:..............244. H.719, 4
Heat and moisture mixt are so,...............324. H.1070, 3
Mold See Mould
Wod'st thou to sincere-silver turn thy mold?...144. H.370, 7
Them like some Picture, or some Mould.......174. H.465, 20
If thou compos'd of gentle mould..............272. H.828, 13
Brasse, Leade, or Tinne, throw into th' mould;.297. H.948, 10
Mole The tempting Mole, stoln from the neck....166. H.443, 63
Moles' Moles eyes; to these, the slain-Stags teares: 120. H.293, 44
Molest That mans uncomely froth might not molest 386. N.193, 3
Molested And knocking, me molested............26. H.81, 4
Molt' — — — — — — — —, ...453. ins. H.283, 50g
Monarchies When Monarchies trans-shifted are, and gone; 210. H.592, 3
Money Prig mony wants, either to buy, or brew..71. H.183, 4
Mony thou ow'st me; Prethee fix a day.......83. H.206, 1
Demands no money by a craving way;..........142. H.363, 2
Is it because his money all is spent?...........160. H.423, 2
Roots had no money; yet he went o'th score..162. H.427, 1
Hunck ha's no money (he do's sweare, or say).173. H.463, 1
Or money? no, but onely deaw and sweat.......248. H.731, 2
Moneyless Even as monilesse, as He...........354. N.59, 14
Money's Money's the still-sweet-singing Nightingale. 247. H.726, 2
'Mong Since that I know, 'mong all the rest......250. H.739, 3
Mongers See Ballad-mongers
'Mongst If 'mongst my many Poems, I can see..63. H.165, 1
Say, if there be 'mongst many jems here; one..76. H.194, 3
'Mongst Roses...............................95. H.227, 22
'Mongst Roses, I there Cupid found:..........96. H.229, 2
As to be canoniz'd 'mongst those,.............169. H.449, 12
Then to sow Discord 'mongst the Enemies....196. H.535, 2
This 'mongst other mystick charms............284. H.889, 5
If 'mongst these many Numbers to be read,...322. H.1062, 2
But if, 'mongst all, thou find'st here one........339. N.2, 7
Monkeys The breath of Munkies met to mix....166. H.443, 43
Monks See Cloister-monks
That the Monks and Fryers together,..........304. H.976, 3
Monstrous Artlesse the Sceane was; and that monstrous sin 150. H.382, 13
Those monstrous lies of little Robin Rush:.....155. H.405, 8
There no monstrous fancies shall..............377. N.128, 13
Montano Sil. Words sweet as Love it self. Montano, Hark. 159. H.421, 17
Month The Month, the Week, the instant Day..198. H.544, 22
Knew'st thou, one moneth wo'd take thy life away, 241. H.709, 1
Months On your minutes, hours, dayes, months, years, 57. H.149, 151
That thou, within few months, shalt be........63. H.166, 7
Monument See Maiden-monument
As the eternall monument of me...............30. H.89, 10
But Vertue Rears the eternal Monument.......419. A.10, 4
Monuments Not one, but many Monuments.......48. H.134, 8
The monuments of Dorcas dead..............375. N.123, 84
Mood Ducking in Mood, and perfect Tense,....91. H.223, 52
Moon See Full-moon, Midwife-moon
Next, look thou like a sickly Moone;..........47. H.132, 3
No, no, no more then is yond' Moone,..........49. H.136, 28
Never did Moone so ebbe, or seas so wane,.....52. H.146, 7
Charms, that call down the moon from out her sphere, 99. H.244, 1
She shifts and changes like the Moone.........103. H.253, 14
Moon is an Usurer, whose gain,................143. H.369, 1
Light of the Moon, seem'd to comply,..........167. H.443, 98
Endimions Moon to fill up full, remember me:.184. H.492, 42
What though the Moon do's slumber?..........217. H.619, 12
Will enforce the Moon to stay,................276. H.850, 12
This Manch, that Moone; this Martlet, and that Mound; 295. H.941, 5
Who scratch at the Moone,..................333. H.1122, 10
While th' Moone in her sphere...............334. H.1122, 16
Where never Moone shall sway................354. N.58, 9
Shewes like the Heavens aboue ye Moone,.....413. A.4, 13
Moonless By Moonlesse nights have swerved;...26. H.81, 10
Moonlight Or Moone-light tinselling the streames:.34. H.105, 4
Moon-parched A Moon-parcht grain of purest wheat, 119. H.293, 9
Moon's Onely Moons conscience, we confesse,...143. H.369, 3
Moons See Full-faced-moons
But thrice three Moones before she dy'd......41. H.116, 6
And Moons to wain;.........................133. H.336, 19
Yet, ere twelve Moones shall whirl about......178. H.476, 7
Moonshine (Hatch't o're with Moone-shine, from their stolen delight).....................................410. A.3, 2
— — — — — — — — — — — —, ...425. var. H.197, 5
Moon-tan — — — — — — — —, ...440. var. H.443, 84
Moon-tanned His Moon-tann'd Mab, as somewhat sick, 167. H.443, 84
Moony So meet stolne kisses, when the Moonie nights 77. H.197, 5
Of Candi'd dew in Moony nights.............165. H.443, 32
Mop-eyed Mop-ey'd I am, as some have said,...97. H.235, 1
Moral — — — — — — — —, ...450. var. A.9, 5

More See Much-more
With breath more sweet then Violet..............6. H.2, 14
Droop, droop no more, or hang the head..........7. H.9, 1
As beames of Corrall, but more cleare..........7. H.9, 12
So, that the more I look, the more I prove,.....10. H.16, 5
Ther's still more cause, why I the more should love. 10. H.16, 6
More like a Stock, then like a Vine...........17. H.41, 23
I'm free from thee; and thou no more shalt heare 17. H.42, 1
More discontents I never had.................19. H.51, 1
Love give me more such nights as these.......20. H.56, 10
Upon thy Forme more wrinkles yet will fall,..21. H.62, 5
The fattest Hogs we grease the more with Lard. 22. H.64, 2
To him that has, there shall be added more;...22. H.64, 3
In a more rich and sweet aray:..............23. H.70, 4
Next enters June, and brings us more..........23. H.70, 5
More wealth brings in, then all those three....23. H.70, 8
Then to that twenty, adde an hundred more:...24. H.74, 4
There is an Act that will more fully please:...24. H.74, 10
Under a Lawne, then skyes more cleare,.......25. H.78, 1
They blush'd, and look'd more fresh then flowers 25. H.78, 5
Here I devote; And something more then so;.27. H.82, 11
Doe more bewitch me, then when Art.........28. H.83, 13
Between thy Breasts (then Doune of Swans more white) 30. H.88, 9
More then the stones i'th' street by farre:......32. H.98, 4
And having these, what need of more?........33. H.100, 2
More white then whitest Lillies far,............34. H.105, 1
More white then are the whitest Creames,......34. H.105, 3
More white then Pearls, or Juno's thigh;......34. H.105, 5
More at her nature, then her name:............35. H.106, 8
Of craving more, are never rich...............35. H.106, 20
(More blessed in thy Brasse, then Land).......35. H.106, 24
And viewing them with a more safe survey,....36. H.106, 73
(Far more with wonder, then with feare).....36. H.106, 84
More in thine eares, then in thine eyes........37. H.106, 88
Never sing, or play more here.................39. H.111, 14
And sure his tongue had more exprest,........42. H.119, 11
Then say, I've sent one more.................43. H.123, 13
For tears no more will fall...................43. H.123, 18
I'm sure she'll ask no more..................43. H.123, 36
Good Sir, make no more cuts i'th' outward skin,.44. H.126, 3
Nay, thou more neare then kindred, friend, man, wife, 45. H.128, 3
More radiant then the Summers Sun-beams shows; 45. H.128, 13
Work'st more then Wisdome, Art, or Nature can, 45. H.128, 24
Or smile more inly; lest thy looks beguile.....46. H.128, 46
And more then well becomes the day?.........48. H.136, 3
Be you more warie, then afraid...............49. H.136, 15
No, no, no more then is yond' Moone,........49. H.136, 28
Your face no more: So live you free.........49. H.136, 35
Of Womans beauty? and with hand more rude..49. H.138, 5
And Star-like, once more, guild our Firmament..52. H.146, 12
Well; though my griefe by you was gall'd, the more; 52. H.146, 21
Tell me, has Strut got ere a title more?......53. H.148, 3
She must no more a Maying:.................56. H.149, 114
Musks and Ambers more from her:...........59. H.155, 8
Ile trouble you no more; but goe.............60. H.159, 3
That I shall stir, or live more here.............61. H.159, 27
Love kill'd this man, No more but so..........61. H.159, 31
More by Provocation great....................62. H.162, 15
I smil'd; and bade him once more prove,........64. H.166, 9
One[1] fancie more! but if there be..............64. H.169, 9
And sin no more, as we have done, by staying;..68. H.178, 41
Nay more, Ile deeply sweare,.................69. H.179, 2
The Persian King liv'd not more happily.......70. H.181, 4
Nor Cloe was of more respect;................70. H.181, 6
I flourish't more then Roman Ilia.............70. H.181, 8
More faire in this transparent case,............75. H.193, 6
More by that wantoning with it;..............75. H.193, 14
More gently stroaks the sight,................75. H.193, 18
More beauty to commend......................75. H.193, 27
More love, when they transfer.................75. H.193, 35
I! far more welcome then the happy soile,.....77. H.197, 15
Or went'st thou to this end, the more to move me, 77. H.197, 23
'Twas done by me, more to confirme my zeale,.78. H.197, 42
Whose love growes more enflam'd, by being Foes. 78. H.197, 44
More love unto my life, or can present.........78. H.197, 55
God, and far more transcendent then the rest?.78. H.197, 60
More shak't thy selfe, then she is scorch't by thee. 82. H.204, 14
More sweet then any.........................83. H.205, 8
Onely a little more..........................85. H.211, 1
More tender then the childhood of the Morne...86. H.213, 16
Mirt. And that his birth sho'd be more singular,.86. H.213, 19
Then say, if one th'ast seene more fine........90. H.223a, 5
As Rome's Pantheon had not more...........90. H.223, 8
First, in a Neech, more black than jet,..........90. H.223, 11
More precious, then we prize our gold:........92. H.223, 88

'Twas no more you then, but a Cherubin.......95. H.228, 4
And caught'st thy selfe the more by twenty fold:
97. H.236, 2
No more Ile vaunt,............................100. H.246, 8
And I no more did move,.......................100. H.249, 2
Sighs, and sobs, and sorrowes more...........102. H.253, 5
Or they more white sho'd be..................105. H.258, 4
And laugh no more; or laugh, and lie down next.
111. H.277, 2
'Tis she! 'tis she! or else some more Divine..112. H.283, 11
More towring, more disparkling then thy fires:..113. H.283, 36
And to enchant yee more, see every where.....115. H.283, 101
And to your more bewitching, see, the proud..115. H.283, 111
Nature and Art, one more....................115. H.283, 129
Of Emits eggs; what wo'd he more?...........119. H.293, 36
Or some numbers more rehearse;..............122. H.303, 2
Bacchus, let me drink no more;..............122. H.304, 1
Urge no more; and there shall be............122. H.304, 7
More then a Feast contenteth me.............124. H.312, 8
Woman wo'd bring him more then co'd be told,..129. H.326, 4
And makes more soft the Bridall Bed..........130. H.329, 7
No more shall I, since I am driven hence,....131. H.333, 1
No more shall I from mantle-trees hang downe,.131. H.333, 3
No more shall I (I feare me) to thee bring....132. H.333, 5
No more shall I, from henceforth, heare a quire.132. H.333, 7
In me a more transcendant heate,.............135. H.336, 102
Farre more then night bewearied..............136. H.336, 152
If so, how much more shall I dote thereon,....139. H.347, 3
No more is seen the Arch of Peace............139. H.353, 4
Me longer date, and more fresh springs to live:.140. H.355, 12
Wrinkles no more are, or no lesse,............143. H.367, 1
Call me no more,.............................144. H.371, 1
More lik'd by her, or lov'd by mee............145. H.375, 28
Best and more suppling piece he cuts, and by.147. H.377, 51
Of thy glad table: not a dish more known.....147. H.377, 69
ly that it makes the meate more sweet;........148. H.377, 80
Is more in thee, then in her dust,............148. H.377, 104
A thousand times, more sweare, then say,......149. H.377, 132
Adde to that thirty five, but five pounds more,..151. H.385, 5
When one hole wasts more then he gets by Nine.
154. H.400, 4
Since thou art gone, no more I mean to play,..159. H.421, 9
And sheep, grew more sweet, by that breth of Thine.
159. H.421, 14
And knowes not where i'th world to borrow more.
160. H.423, 4
And now no more,.............................162. H.426, 17
Spungie and swelling, and farre more..........165. H.443, 27
Sweet Aires move here; and more divine......166. H.443, 39
A more unconquer'd appetite..................167. H.443, 115
I know the Tunne of Hidleberge holds more...171. H.454, 4
More Ile bestow:............................171. H.455, 10
You are a Lord, an Earle, nay more, a Man,..172. H.459, 1
Jove prospers my meat, more then his..........173. H.461, 4
But if they do, the more to flow..............179. H.476, 12
Then no gazing more about,...................180. H.482, 3
And if more; Each Nipple cries,..............183. H.491, 3
More honour had, then this same Flie;.........186. H.497, 17
I do write of thee no more:..................186. H.500, 2
And (pretty Child) feeles now no more........189. H.514, 3
One more by Thee, Love, and Desert have sent,.191. H.516, 1
Nay more, the Feast, and grace of it..........192. H.521, 28
These (nay) and more, thine own shal be,.....193. H.521, 55
This begets the more delight,.................194. H.527, 6
And no more;.................................196. H.538, 2
We eate our own, and batten more,.............200. H.552, 13
Who is his Butcher more then Guardian.......201. H.557, 16
And knit in knots far more then I............202. H.560, 11
In Cream she bathes her thighs (more soft then silk)
203. H.561, 3
No more my Silvia, do I mean to pray.........204. H.570, 1
More sweet, then Storax from the hallowed fire:
205. H.575, 8
Sing their Evadne; and still more for thee....206. H.575, 53
I vanish; more I had to say;.................207. H.575, 65
Therefore now Ile love no more,..............209. H.585, 7
Nothing can be more loathsome, then to see...211. H.597, 1
And work no more; but shut up Shop..........212. H.602, 4
Who covets more, is evermore a slave.........213. H.607, 2
Go wooe young Charles no more to looke,......214. H.611, 1
More dangerous faintings by her desp'rate cure..214. H.612, 6
And once more yet (ere I am laid out dead)..214. H.612, 13
He by extortion brings in three times more:...220. H.631, 3
The Ravens yeares, go hence more Ripe then old.
222. H.633, 63
Then these, no feares more on your Fancies fall,.222. H.634, 14
That your mickle, may have more.............223. H.638, 3
Bring in her Bill, once more, the Branch of Peace.
225. H.642, 22
This night, and more for the wonder,..........225. H.643, 21
To a more happy Residence...................226. H.644, 6
And, in the midst, to grace it more, was set...227. H.652, 9
Be it, O be it, never more reveal'd!..........227. H.652, 12
Ile sing no more, nor will I longer write......228. H.658, 1
Ile sing no more of Frosts, Snowes, Dews and Showers;
228. H.658, 3
No more of Groves, Meades, Springs, and wreaths of Flowers:
228. H.658, 4
Ile write no more, nor will I tell or sing......228. H.658, 5
Ile sing no more of death, or shall the grave...228. H.658, 7
No more my Dirges, and my Trentalls have....228. H.658, 8
Sweet sleep, that makes more short the night...231. H.662, 75
Be she witty, more then wise;...............232. H.665, 3
Once past and gone, no more shall see.........234. H.671, 2
Kings ought to be more lov'd, then fear'd......234. H.672, 2
No more wo'd drown mine eyes, or me.........237. H.687, 8
All these, and more, shall then afford..........239. H.696, 11
Ravisht in spirit, I come, nay more, I flie......242. H.713, 3
More then for peevish pining sicknesses........245. H.723, 12
The more my rurall privacie:...................246. H.724, 28
Since more and more is exacted;..............247. H.727, 9
An Odor more divine,..........................251. H.740, 10
More pleasing too, then ever was..............251. H.740, 11
And calmes succeeding, we perceive no more...254. H.756, 5
When These can aske, and Kings can give no more.
255. H.758, 4
Downe to a Fillit more Imperiall..............256. H.763, 10
Prosperitie more searching of the mind:........257. H.765, 2
For more or lesse fruits they will bring,.......264. H.787, 3
More curst for singing out of tune then he......266. H.799, 4
So Corrolls looke more lovely Red,............268. H.811, 5
More rich then Cleopatra's Tombe.............269. H.817, 4
But yet how more admir'dly bright............270. H.819, 6
One word more I had to say;..................270. H.821, 5
The more th'are drawn, the lesse they wil grow dry.
273. H.831, 2
'Tis I am wild, and more then haires..........282. H.881, 5
My sight was pleas'd more, or my smell:......283. H.883, 6
Betwixt us two no more Logomachie...........287. H.901, 4
Our trust farre more then ten eare-witnesses....287. H.904, 2
Reader, wo'dst thou more have known?.........289. H.910, 3
Of such a wit the world sho'd have no more.....289. H.911, 20
Till that the Cooke cries, Bring no more........291. H.919, 4
And more had done (it is confest).............294. H.939, 9
Which done; no more.........................296. H.946, 22
More from the sweet then sower things........298. H.951, 2
To re-possess once more your long'd-for home...300. H.961, 6
We'l from our owne, adde far more years to his.
300. H.961, 20
Three Zodiaks fill'd more I shall stoope;.......303. H.973, 2
But when all's hush't, Case then a fish more mute,
303. H.975, 7
That to me was far more deer.................305. H.984, 16
W'ave more to beare our charge, then way to go?
308. H.995, 2
The Genius wastefull, more then free:........310. H.1004, 2
More then the teats of Discipline:...........310. H.1004, 6
More mortall in the vestiment................311. H.1010, 6
And being cup-shot, more he co'd not doe......313. H.1017, 10
No more......................................314. H.1024, 24
No more shall I reiterate thy Strand,..........315. H.1028, 3
No more shall I a long thy christall glide,....315. H.1028, 7
Things are uncertain, and the more we get,....316. H.1032, 1
The more on ycie pavements we are set.......316. H.1032, 2
Good wits get more fame by their punishment..317. H.1034, 2
I sing the more, that thou hast one;..........321. H.1056, 2
'Tis flatterie spends a King, more then his foes..331. H.1105, 2
Il'e write no more of Love; but now repent....334. H.1124, 1
Ile write no more of life; but wish twas ended,.334. H.1124, 3
And as our bad, more then our good Works are:
339. N.1, 2
God n'ere afflicts us more then our desert,......341. N.10, 1
Sometimes He strikes us more then flesh can beare;
341. N.10, 3
And though it takes all in, 'tis yet no more....341. N.15, 5
And more for love, then pittie.................345. N.33, 29
To figure to us, nothing more then this,.......345. N.34, 3
And that number more then true;.............348. N.41, 27
To be more sweet...........................350. N.47, 36
To seek of God more then we well can find,....356. N.70, 1
No more, no more, since thou art dead,........360. N.83, 49
No more, at yeerly Festivalls..................361. N.83, 51
Ye must not be more pitifull then wise;........365. N.97, 16
I'le hope no more,...........................368. N.104, 1
Pardon me God, (once more I Thee intreat)...371. N.113, 1
When we 'gainst Satan stoutly fight, the more..372. N.116, 1
The more our Crownes of Glory there increase..372. N.119, 2
Let me say grace when there's no more.......376. N.124, 6
More and more approaching nigh.............377. N.128, 6
Thou hast, nay more, Thou art the Tree,.......377. N.129, 3
To give us more then Hope can fix upon.......378. N.135, 2
The more occasion still to sin.................379. N.144, 2
The teares of Saints more sweet by farre,......379. N.145, 1
The shame of mans face is no more............383. N.170, 1
Once shut, was never to be open'd more........385. N.190, 4
But no more Woman, being strong in Faith;...386. N.192, 3
God is more here, then in another place,.......387. N.197, 1
One man repentant is of more esteem..........388. N.205, 1
More worth, then Heav'ns Eternitie...........388. N.206, 4
Who hath more suffer'd by us farre, then for us..388. N.209, 2
Boldly in sin, shall feel more punishment.......391. N.227, 4
More stripes, then God layes on the sufferer....393. N.235, 2

God still rewards us more then our desert:....394. N.242, 1
As when, in humane nature He works more....395. N.244, 3
Ere I goe hence and bee noe more............407. A.2, 1
More Comely flowing: where les free..........407. A.2, 28
As In a more Conspicuous Text..........407. A.2, 32
Bondage more Loued then Lybertye...........408. A.2, 64
Homer, Musæus, Ouid, Maro, more...........411. A.3, 41
I've more to beare my Chardge, then way to goe,
411. A.3, 54
Off craueing more: soe In Conceipt bee ritch...411. A.3, 56
And shaps my Function, for more glorious ends:
411. A.3, 58
Fly hence Pale Care, noe more remember.......413. A.4, 1
And to thy many, take in one soul more.......416. A.8, 2
But now come in. Euc. More let me yet relate...416. A.8, 23
Cha. I cannot stay; more souls for waftage wait,
416. A.8, 24
What more than these can Tombs or Tomb-stones Pay?
419. A.10, 5
Owes more to vertue then too Fate......422. ins. H.106, 92b
— — — — — — — — — — —, ...423. var. H.128, 9
— — — — — — — — — — —, ...423. var. H.128, 10
More mildlie least thy temptinge lookes beguile
424. ins. H.128, 46e
— — — — — — — — — — —, ...425. var. H.197, 24
— — — — — — — — — — —, ...426. ins. H.197, 29a
Not more, milde nymph, then they would have you doe;
431. ins. H.283, 60r
But dread that you doe more offend......431. ins. H.283, 60s
For that would prove more Heresy then fault
433. ins. H.283, 140h
All mighty blood; and can doe more......437. var. H.336, 135
To teach the truth of Scenes, and more for thee,
443. var. H.575, 53
— — — — — — — — — — —, ...451. var. H.336, 113
More's But more's sent in, then was serv'd out..178. H.476, 9
Morn So all my Morne, and Evening Stars from You
3. Ded.H., 7
As oft as Night is banish'd by the Morne,.....26. H.80, 1
Duely, Morne and Ev'ning, come,.............44. H.125, 3
Get up, get up for shame, the Blooming Morne.67. H.178, 1
Yet the next Morne, re-guild the fragrant East..72. H.185, 7
More tender then the childhood of the Morne...86. H.213, 16
To call to Morn, and Even-Song..............93. H.223, 128
Just as the modest Morne...................104. H.257, 4
That Morne which saw me made a Bride,.......109. H.271, 1
When the bedabled Morne....................112. H.283, 19
Whom this Morne sees most fortunate,.........208. H.583, 2
Calls forth the lilly-wristed Morne;...........230. H.662, 20
Why do's the chilling Winters morne...........364. N.96, 14
Seemes like Apollo's when the morne he blesses.404. A.1, 2
The fresh and fayrest flourish of the Morne....410. A.3, 20
Whether in the morne or noone...............418. A.9, 45
Morning When with the Virgin morning thou do'st rise,
127. H.320, 1
Good morning Sir to you:....................156. H.412, 2
Good morning to this Prim-rose too;...........156. H.412, 5
Seeal'd up with Night-gum, Loach each morning lyes,
269. H.816, 1
Mudge every morning to the Postern comes,....301. H.965, 1
In the morning when ye rise..................322. H.1064, 1
Let me Thy voice betimes i' th morning heare;.358. N.77, 12
Both from the Morning to the Euening Chyme;
410. A.3, 16
Morning's Or as the pearles of Mornings dew...125. H.316, 19
The smell of mornings milk, and cream;.......145. H.375, 21
This Mornings Incense to prepare, and burne...196. H.539, 2
Him in the Mornings blushing cheek,..........367. N.102, 9
Mornings See Dewy-mornings
In sober mornings, doe not thou reherse...........7. H.8, 1
So look the mornings when the Sun...........268. H.811, 1
Morning's-light And then present the Mornings-light
47. H.133, 10
Morning-sunshine Like Morning-Sun-shine tinsilling the dew.
205. H.575, 12
Morn's Jove's is the first and last: The Morn's his due,
128. H.321, 3
The Morn's farre spent; and the immortall Sunne
216. H.618, 3
Morris-dance Thy Morris-dance; thy Whitsun-ale;
230. H.662, 54
Morris-dancers Morris-dancers thou shalt see,....255. H.761, 7
Morrow See Tomorrow
Who knowes to live to morrow?..............65. H.170, 6
To morrow will be dying....................84. H.208, 4
Good morrow to the Day so fair;...............156. H.412, 1
Good morrow to mine own torn hair..........156. H.412, 3
Good morrow to each maid;...................156. H.412, 6
To morrow...............................160. H.421, 47
To morrow thou shalt see...................161. H.425, 6
And next morrow, every one.................315. H.1026, 13
Each evening and each morrow:..............353. N.56, 9
— — — — — — — — — — —, ...438. var. H.412, 2
— — — — — — — — — — —, ...438. var. H.412, 5
Morrow's The morrowes life too late is, Live to-day.
228. H.655, 2
Morsels Take friendly morsels, and there stay....146. H.377, 16
I keep (tame) with my morsells fed,...........246. H.724, 18
The Bits, the Morsells, and the deale...........374. N.123, 24
Mortal See Circum-mortal-part
I dream'd this mortal part of mine.............16. H.41, 1
Thou gav'st me life, (but Mortall;) For that one.27. H.82, 13
For my life mortall, Rise from out thy Herse,...27. H.82, 15
Those ills that mortall men endure,............153. H.395, 1
Our mortall parts may wrapt in Seare-cloths lye:
199. H.547, 1
To mortall men great loads allotted be,........242. H.715, 1
More mortall in the vestiment.................311. H.1010, 6
Mortals Chorus. We sail along, to visit mortals never;
417. A.8, 37
Mosaic Throughout that Brave Mosaick yard....166. H.443, 47
Moses Moses, and Jesus, called Joshua:..........381. N.157, 2
Moss Brought leaves and mosse to cover her:...46. H.130, 6
Track they redeem a bank of mosse............165. H.443, 26
The soft sweet Mosse shall be thy bed,.........192. H.521, 5
Moss-like The four-leav'd grasse, or mosse-like silk.
166. H.443, 42
Moss-work With leaves and mosse-work for to cover me:
19. H.50, 2
Under whose Roofe with Mosse-worke wrought, there I
310. H.1003, 3
Most The mellow touch of musick most doth wound
12. H.24, 1
The Beads I kist, but most lov'd her..........13. H.32, 3
The most I love, when I the least expresse it...15. H.38, 6
I most humbly thee desire...................21. H.59, 3
Welcome, most welcome to our Vowes and us,..25. H.77, 1
Most great, and universall Genius!.............25. H.77, 2
But that which most makes sweet thy country life,
35. H.106, 31
Vice rules the Most, or All at Court:.........37. H.106, 90
This makes Cuffe dull; and troubles him the most,
39. H.109, 3
Most innocent, and injur'd thus................48. H.136, 5
Then comely and most fragrant Maid,..........49. H.136, 14
The fairest most suspected be.................49. H.136, 17
Men, but Slothfulls most of all................53. H.147, 10
The lazie man the most doth love..............53. H.147, 14
Beleeve me; you will most.....................53. H.149, 15
If her lip, the most sincere....................59. H.155, 3
Me; me, the most despised Lover:............61. H.159, 29
Love is most loth to leave the thing beloved....73. H.186, 12
Her skins most smooth, and cleare expansion....82. H.204, 4
Dead thee to th' most, if not destroy thee all...82. H.204, 12
At most a fault, 'tis but a fault of love.........86. H.213, 28
And all most sweet; yet all lesse sweet then he..86. H.213, 38
For thy revenge to be most opposite;..........87. H.215, 8
In this most curious Calendar.................91. H.223, 37
The Saint, to which the most he prayes.......93. H.223, 129
For his most cheerfull offerings...............93. H.223, 134
(Most fit to be the Consort to a King).........107. H.265, 2
The offer, which they most wo'd chuse.........118. H.291, 2
Of the most sweet and dainty Bride,..........120. H.293, 50
And runnes most smoothly, when tis well begunne.
128. H.321, 2
Most dire and horrid crucifixion................129. H.323, 14
To kisse your hand, most Dainty Governesse...137. H.341, 12
With thy most white Predestination............155. H.405, 4
Are here most neatly inter-laid.................166. H.443, 50
Waste thou in that most Civill Government.....171. H.456, 4
For a most rich, a rare, a precious One........172. H.459, 10
But lost to that they most approv'd:..........180. H.478, 2
That Towrs high rear'd dread most the lightnings threat:
181. H.483, 14
And my most luckie Swain, when I shall live to see
184. H.492, 41
To find a Wife, that is most fit for Thee.......185. H.494, 2
Talkes most, eates most, of all the Feeders there.
191. H.518, 2
When things meet most opposite:.............194. H.527, 7
The most of Thee shall scape the funerall.......200. H.554, 2
Whom this Morne sees most fortunate,..........208. H.583, 2
To most of men, but most of all to me:.......210. H.590, 2
O! Times most bad,..........................211. H.596, 1
Spring with the Larke, most comely Bride, and meet
216. H.618, 1
Love is a thing most nice; and must be fed....220. H.633, 20
The world so soon, and in it, you the most.....222. H.634, 13
That stroke most fear'd is, which is struck the last.
237. H.688, 2
Of Rome did weare for their most precious Pearles.
251. H.741, 2
She's to me most excellent....................253. H.750, 15
Princes and Fav'rites are most deere, while they..255. H.758, 1
Besides, the most religious Prophet stands......262. H.781, 9
In desp'rate cases, all, or most are known......272. H.827, 1
(Which to me most loathsome is.)............282. H.878, 2
Where most sweets are, there lyes a Snake.....283. H.883, 12
For Clytemnestra most unkind,................283. H.885, 3
In most happy Parallels?......................286. H.897, 10
Attended thus (in a most solemn wise)........286. H.898, 3

Teares most prevaile; with teares too thou mayst move 287. H.900, 1
We credit most our sight; one eye doth please.287. H.904, 1
A wife most richly married....................291. H.919, 16
In this misfortune Kings doe most excell,.......293. H.932, 1
To be most soft, terce, sweet, and perpolite:...301. H.966, 2
Thou most lovely Neat-heardesse:..............305. H.984, 3
'Tis still observ'd, those men most valiant are,..308. H.994, 1
That are most modest ere they come to warre..308. H.994, 2
At randome, sometimes hit most happily........318. H.1039, 2
But causelesse whipping smarts the most of all..319. H.1050, 2
Who may do most, do's least: The bravest will.321. H.1057, 1
This is my comfort, when she's most unkind,...322. H.1061, 1
Most like his Suite, and all commend the Trim;.330. H.1099, 3
God, the most Wise, is sparing of His talk.......341. N.12, 2
God, as He is most Holy knowne;............343. N.23, 1
So He is said to be most One...............343. N.23, 2
Afflictions they most profitable are............343. N.24, 1
Bring Him along, most pious Priest,........365. N.97, 11
Conceal'd in this most holy Ground:..........366. N.98, 4
To my most healthfull use,...................368. N.104, 14
And hazards those most, whom the most He loves; 370. N.108, 4
Heav'n is most faire; but fairer He...........382. N.164, 1
But on our Age most sweet Indulgences.......383. N.175, 2
Cities most sad and dire destruction...........384. N.178, 4
These temp'rall goods God (the most Wise) commends 387. N.201, 1
God's present ev'ry where; but most of all.....388. N.207, 1
Because our flesh stood most in need of Him...390. N.222, 4
Of Thy most winning countenance;...........395. N.246, 4
My soules most desp'rate Calenture;..........397. N.257, 2
Her brest (a place for beawtyes throne most fitt) 405. A.1, 51
Into the middle <most> sight pleasing crooke...406. A.1, 82
Then lowly yet most lovely stand the feete,....406. A.1, 91
Most maye smile, beleiue will none,............418. A.9, 36
Least thankes to Nature, most to Art...421. ins. H.106, 26b
— — — — — — — — — — — —, ...431. ins. H.283, 50g
But most of all the glowwormes fire.......434. ins. H.293, 41e
Motes Tell me the motes, dust, sands, and speares.340. N.3, 11
Moth Browne as his Tooth. A little Moth,.......120. H.293, 41
Which neither Tettar, Time, or Moth..........393. N.231, 3
Mother See Virgin-mother
To his Mother, said thus crying;...............50. H.139, 4
Cupid and his Mother lay.......................74. H.190, 5
A nursing Mother so to Majesty;..............326. H.1080, 22
The Babe unto His Mother Marie;.............366. N.97, 27
Wee'l chuse Him King, and make His Mother Queen. 368. N.102, 24
But, in a Mother, kept a maiden-head...........385. N.184, 4
Sits Cupid kissing of his mother Queene,.......405. A.1, 56
Call'd on the suddayne by the Jealouse Mother,.410. A.3, 7
Mothering 'Gainst thou go'st a mothering,.......236. H.684, 2
Mother's But so, as still the mothers power......126. H.318, 10
Sold his old Mothers Spectacles for Beere:....272. H.829, 2
Blisse (last night drunk) did kisse his mothers knee: 295. H.943, 1
A Princely Babe in's Mothers Brest...........367. N.102, 14
— — — — — — — — — — —, ...447. var. A.1, 56
Motion And in their motion smelt much like to flowers 326. H.1080, 13
Of locall motion, in no least respect,............385. N.186, 3
Mou'd by the chinne whose motion causeth this.405. A.1, 37
Deriue their overwell grac'd motion............406. A.1, 86
Motions The Motions, Lations, and the Signes....47. H.133, 4
And roule about, and in their motions burne...113. H.283, 38
The Watch once downe, all motions then do cease; 202. H.558, 3
Mottoes With Motto's carv'd on every tree,......169. H.449, 22
Mould See Mold
As is the mould:..........................190. H.515, 16
After that, in the mould......................197. H.540, 3
(Wert not for thee) haue Crumbled Into Mould,.411. A.3, 36
Mound This Manch, that Moone; this Martlet, and that Mound;......................................295. H.941, 5
Mounds With maunds of roses for to strew the way: 261. H.781, 8
There filling Maunds with Cowslips, you.........323. H.1068, 7
Mount Stoop, mount, passe by to take her eye, then glare 87. H.215, 5
Mount up thy flames, and let thy Torch.......113. H.283, 33
The Mount of Olives; Calverie, and where....330. H.1100, 13
To mount my Soule, she must have pineons given; 352. N.52, 3
Not as a thief, shalt Thou ascend the mount,...398. N.263, 15
Mountain Or Muses, on their mountaine sitting there; 326. H.1080, 6
Like a faire mountaine in Riphean snowe,.....405. A.1, 60
Mountains The Mountains of the Scriptures are (some say) 381. N.157, 1
The Prophets Mountains of the Old are meant;.381. N.157, 3
When as the Mountains quak'd for dread,......393. N.232, 5
Mounts Th' Apostles Mounts of the New Testament. 381. N.157, 4

Mourn Or mourne, or make a Marble Verse for me, 298. H.952, 3
May Virgins, when they come to mourn,........361. N.83, 75
Shakeing the head, whilst each, to each dothe mourne, 411. A.3, 65
Mournful If so, we live; if not, with mournfull humme, 100. H.248, 5
In mournfull Hyacinths and Rue,.............131. H.330, 7
Or mournfull Marble; let thy shade...........145. H.376, 3
Mournfull maid farewell to you;..............306. H.984, 42
— — — — — — — — —, ...445. var. H.730, 8
Mourning In our mourning;...................308. H.993, 21
Mourns Say, is 't for reall griefe he mourns? not so; 275. H.842, 3
He who wears Blacks, and mournes not for the Dead, 319. H.1047, 1
Mouse And the brisk Mouse may feast her selfe with crums, 37. H.106, 123
Or the cleft eare of a Mouse.................223. H.638, 6
With eating many a miching Mouse............246. H.724, 24
Mouth Who keep'st no proud mouth for delicious cates: 37. H.106, 109
But not his mouth (the fouler of the two.)....110. H.273, 2
His mouth worse furr'd with oathes and blasphemies. 110. H.273, 4
Goes with your mouth, or do's outrun your tongue; 141. H.359, 14
And as he spake, his mouth ranne ore with wine. 313. H.1017, 4
Thy mouth will make the sourest numbers please; 328. H.1089, 3
Who hath thee in his mouth, not in his heart.....347. N.39, 4
My mouth I'le lay unto Thy wound............377. N.129, 5
Vnto the port mouth of th' Elisian feilds,......405. A.1, 68
Move Love is a circle that doth restlesse move..13. H.29, 1
Shall move t'wards you; although I see........49. H.136, 34
Move forward then your Rosie feet,...........55. H.149, 61
Shrugging as it did move,....................57. H.149, 137
But ah! I co'd not: sho'd it move.............67. H.175, 21
And have the power to move.................76. H.193, 50
Or went'st thou to this end, the more to move me, 77. H.197, 23
Let them tell how she doth move..............82. H.203, 7
And I no more did move,.....................100. H.249, 2
To move, or rather the........................112. H.283, 9
And who do rudely move him..................157. H.412, 24
Sweet Aires move here; and more divine......166. H.443, 39
Of winning Colours, that shall move...........193. H.521, 53
Farre hence be all speech, that may anger move: 222. H.633, 60
Affection will affection move,.................252. H.746, 7
Your part's to grant; my Scean must be to move. 274. H.837, 4
Why so slowly do you move.................276. H.850, 1
My fingers so, the Lyrick-strings to move,.....280. H.871, 3
Teares most prevaile; with teares too thou mayst move 287. H.900, 1
Me thought I saw them stir, and gently move,..326. H.1080, 11
Is sober virtue, seen to move her sphere.......327. H.1087, 2
God hath two wings, which He doth ever move,..340. N.6, 1
Here melting numbers, words of power to move.415. A.7, 9
Moved Vertue had, and mov'd her Sphere.........37. H.106, 92
Among the Elves, (if mov'd) the stings........165. H.443, 16
Mou'd by the chinne whose motion causeth this.405. A.1, 37
Moves — — — — — — — — —, ...439. var. H.443, 39
Moving Mooving a question whether that by them 405. A.1, 41
Mown Or like a medow being lately mown.......159. H.421, 21
Mows Your Stacks, your Stocks, your sweetest Mowes, 179. H.476, 23
Mris. See Mistress
Mrs. See Mistress
Much Who speak but little, 'cause I love so much..15. H.38, 14
Then where I loath'd so much..................19. H.51, 8
As blessed soules cann't heare too much:.......22. H.68, 4
Not so much call'd a tree,....................30. H.89, 9
Though much from out the Cess be spent,.....33. H.100, 3
So much for want, as exercise:.................37. H.106, 118
Cuffe comes to Church much; but he keeps his bed 39. H.109, 1
My vowes denounc'd in zeale, which thus much show thee, 46. H.128, 47
But none co'd eate it, 'cause it stunk so much..47. H.131, 6
Not so much Rose, as Wreathe................51. H.144, 4
Shews you how much is spent of night........54. H.149, 52
At last, I find, (after my much to doe)........61. H.161, 5
And did me much importune..................63. H.166, 2
Nay! not so much as out of bed?............68. H.178, 9
He drank so much he scarce co'd stir;..........71. H.182, 9
Where so much sirrop ran at waste............71. H.182, 18
And take his bag; but thus much know,.......71. H.182, 28
Where either too much light his worth.........75. H.193, 22
At my death; but thus much know,...........88. H.218, 3
They much affect the Papacie:...............93. H.223, 110
Enfeebles much the seeds of wickednesse.......109. H.270, 2
To clense his eyes, Tom Brock makes much adoe, 110. H.273, 1

Much good do't ye Gentlemen..................118. H.289, 12
If so, how much more shall I dote thereon,....139. H.347, 3
Not knowing thus much, when we once do sever,.140. H.355, 3
When others gain much by the present cast,....144. H.374, 1
And shew'st me there much Plate, but litte meat;
161. H.424, 2
Six dayes he hollows so much breath away,......163. H.435, 3
Have ye beheld (with much delight)............164. H.440, 1
And have deserv'd as much (Love knowes)....169. H.449, 11
Little or much,.................................171. H.455, 5
Differs not much from drowzie slothfullnesse....173. H.459, 14
'Tis with very much ado;......................182. H.489, 6
He who with talking can devoure so much,......191. H.518, 5
Much I know of Time is spent,................191. H.519, 3
Shall find much farcing Buckram in our Books...202. H.559, 2
But ne'r so much as licks the speckled shells:...204. H.568, 2
But Blanch has not so much upon her head,....205. H.571, 3
Our Lives do differ from our Lines by much.....218. H.624, 2
Shee brings in much, by carnall usury:..........220. H.631, 2
But if this may seem too much................223. H.638, 21
Too much she gives to some, enough to none.....238. H.689, 2
Whom whitest Fortune dandled has too much.....239. H.697, 2
Chor. Much time is spent in prate; begin,......243. H.716, 23
Ph. A deale of Love, and much, much Griefe together.
248. H.730, 14
Thrice happie Roses, so much grac't, to have....249. H.734, 1
There in your teeth much Leprosie.............250. H.738, 4
By so much, vertue is the lesse,................254. H.754, 1
By how much, neere to singlenesse..............254. H.754, 2
Poets co'd not praise too much.................274. H.838, 4
Knit them with knots (with much adoe unty'd)..291. H.920, 2
Since love so much contents me................296. H.946, 12
Not so much knowne, as to be lov'd of thee.....297. H.947, 12
With solemne tears, and with much grief of heart,
300. H.960, 3
Why sho'd we covet much, when as we know,..308. H.995, 1
My many cares and much distress,.............312. H.1016, 1
Who loves too much, too much the lov'd will hate,
318. H.1038, 2
Tis much among the filthy to be clean;........318. H.1042, 1
So much as to drink..........................320. H.1051, 11
So much as to call...........................320. H.1051, 17
And in their motion smelt much like to flowers.326. H.1080, 13
Then weepe not sweet; but thus much know,..328. H.1090, 12
To chafe o're much the Virgins cheek or eare:..329. H.1095, 2
But if thou wilt not deigne so much,............344. N.29, 8
Wealth brings much woe:.....................368. N.104, 4
Much as the ends are to be lookt unto...........387. N.200, 4
That if the twig sho'd chance too much to smart,
394. N.241, 3
And I must hence. Euc. Yet let me thus much know,
416. A.8, 25
At each warning hees as much..................418. A.9, 49
not halfe so much the Act, as end........421. ins. H.106, 42b
As much bewitching his desire.........434. ins. H.293, 41f
— — — — — — — — — — — —, ...437. var. H.336, 151
— — — — — — — — — — — —, .437. var. H.336, 152
Much-good-do't With (much-good-do't him) reverence.
91. H.223, 53
Much-more Much-more, provides, and hoords up like an Ant;
73. H.188, 1
Yet Much-more still complains he is in want.....73. H.188, 2
Let Much-more justly pay his tythes; then try....73. H.188, 3
Mudge Mudge every morning to the Postern comes,
301. H.965, 1
Mulberry His nose and lips of mulbrie hiew.......38. H.108, 8
Mules Those strong-hoof'd Mules, which we behold,
239. H.696, 5
Mullet With mullet, Turbot, guilthead bought
436. ins. H.336, 48g
Multiplies — — — — — — — — —, ...452. var. H.443, 80
Multiply How both his Meale and Oile will multiply.
73. H.188, 4
You multiply, as doth a Fish.................113. H.283, 50
And multiply; Such is the light,...............167. H.443, 80
Then multiply all, like to Fishes...............239. H.695, 12
Multitude When Kings obey the wilder Multitude.
196. H.536, 2
We Trust not to the multitude in Warre,........290. H.916, 1
And all confused multitude:..................312. H.1016, 4
A multitude of dayes still heaped on,..........392. N.230, 7
Th' inconstant, and unpurged Multitude.........398. N.263, 6
Mumbling Their many mumbling Masse-priests here,
92. H.223, 103
Mumma Wither'd with yeeres, and bed-rid Mumma lyes:
90. H.222, 1
Mummeries Thy Mummeries; thy Twelfe-tide Kings
231. H.662, 58
Murder Kind at once to murder mee.............254. H.757, 8
Then for to murder friendship, by dispute.......287. H.901, 6
For murder fit, or mutinie;...................297. H.948, 4
Murderings For to delight in wounds and murderings.
292. H.929, 2
Murder's From Murders Benedicitie............121. H.299, 2
Murmurings Soft and soule-melting murmurings,..46. H.130, 2
And equall shares exclude all murmerings.......318. H.1040, 2

Musæus There thou shalt hear Divine Musæus sing
206. H.575, 25
Homer, Musæus, Ouid, Maro, more.............411. A.3, 41
Muscadine May see it sprout forth streames of muscadine.
405. A.1, 50
Muse To Christen thee, the Bride, the Bashfull Muse,
28. H.84, 2
Or Muse of Roses: since that name does fit......28. H.84, 3
And love thee; but not taste thee. Let my Muse..46. H.128, 51
If then, (my Lord) to sanctifie my Muse........64. H.168, 7
To that Terce Muse of thine...................80. H.201, 28
My Muse in Meads has spent her many houres,....94. H.224, 1
Here stand it stil to dignifie our Muse,..........99. H.245, 5
Yet, though now of Muse bereft,...............182. H.489, 9
The Muse give thee the Delphick Coronet.......194. H.529, 2
Live by thy Muse thou shalt; when others die....210. H.592, 1
Not like the Muse; to love the man,............214. H.611, 4
Pleasant, and precious to my Muse and me.......227. H.652, 4
Of thy brave, bold, and sweet Maronian Muse...234. H.673, 12
For love or pitie to his Muse,..................291. H.918, 5
Jocond his Muse was; but his Life was chast...335. H.1130, 2
But now my muse hath spi'de a darke descent.....405. A.1, 65
Knowe yet, (rare soule,) when my diuiner Muse.412. A.3, 99
Muses We know y'are learn'd i'th' Muses, and no lesse
187. H.506, 7
But by the Muses sweare, all here is good,......212. H.603, 3
By all the muses! thou shalt be................229. H.660, 3
To praise those Muses, and dislike our own?....234. H.673, 2
Tell me young man, or did the Muses bring....299. H.956, 1
Or Muses, on their mountaine sitting there;....326. H.1080, 6
The Muses will weare blackes, when I am dead..335. H.1128, 6
Muses' To suffer in the Muses Martyrdome:....335. H.1128, 4
Mushroom A little mushroome table spred,.......119. H.293, 7
Mushrumpe — — — — — — — —, ...433. var. H.293, 7
Music The mellow touch of musick most doth wound
12. H.24, 1
And by thy Musique strucken mute,..............23. H.68, 7
Musick, thou Queen of Heaven, Care-charming-spel,
103. H.254, 1
Ore-come in musicke; with a wine,............120. H.293, 47
The musick of a Feast;......................144. H.371, 3
For Musick now; He has the cries..........167. H.443, 112
Lost to all Musick now; since every thing......214. H.612, 3
When all Birds els do of their musick faile,......247. H.726, 1
The Mean the Musique makes in every thing....268. H.812, 2
Musique had both her birth, and death with Thee.
288. H.907, 10
What sweeter musick can we bring,..............364. N.96, 1
— — — — — — — — — —, ...435. var. H.293, 33aa
Musical Each way smoothly Musicall:...........122. H.303, 4
Manners each way musicall:...................204. H.569, 10
Musician And each a choyse musitian.....433. ins. H.293, 17b
Musicians And learn'd Musicians shall to honour Herricks
143. H.366, 3
Musk-flies With Musk-flies, are th' Aromaticks,..166. H.443, 44
Musks Musks and Ambers more from her:........59. H.155, 8
These Musks, these Ambers, and those other smells
157. H.414, 3
Musky Passing the sweet sweet of a musky rose...406. A.1, 76
Must (Partial List)
And then I must away.......................85. H.211, 8
But die you must (faire Maid) ere long.........88. H.216, 20
Who now must sway.........................114. H.283, 65
Of her Delayes must end: Dispose............114. H.283, 93
But we must on,..............................132. H.336, 5
But one we must, and thither tend,............133. H.336, 25
Go I must; when I am gone....................199. H.546, 1
Out of the world he must, who once comes in:..199. H.548, 1
Yet we must all.............................211. H.596, 14
Hence I must, for time doth call..............306. H.984, 38
I prithee stay. (Am.) I must away,..........324. H.1068, 21
And I must hence. Euc. Yet let me thus much know,
416. A.8, 25
— — — — — — — — — — — —, ...424. var. H.128, 47
— — — — — — — — — — — —, ...426. var. H.197, 41
Mute And by thy Musique strucken mute.......... 23. H.68, 7
When Julia chid, I stood as mute the while.......58. H.150, 1
The Eyes by tears speak, while the Tongue is mute.
58. H.150, 8
We knew 'twas Flesh and Blood, that there sate mute.
95. H.228, 2
Dead falls the Cause, if once the Hand be mute;..123. H.308, 1
And my tongue at one time mute...............131. H.332, 6
This, this I know, I'm oft struck mute;........142. H.362, 5
And we will, all site mute:....................151. H.388, 2
Nor Bee, or Hive you have be mute;..........179. H.476, 17
Farre better 'twere for either to be mute,........287. H.901, 5
Violl, and Voice, is (by thy losse) struck mute?..288. H.907, 4
But when all's hush't, Case then a fish more mute,
303. H.975, 7
Mutiny For murder fit, or mutinie;...............297. H.948, 4
Mutius He finds a fire for might Mutius;........370. N.108, 6
Mutton With Upper Stories, Mutton, Veale......101. H.250, 30
Of Mutton, or of Veale in it,..................124. H.312, 6
Mutton-bone Made of a Haft, that was a Mutton-bone.
46. H.129, 4

Of nature: bidd·mee nowe fare well, or smile 424. ins. H.128, 46d
— — — — — — — — — — —, ...426. ins. H.197, 29b
Nature's Power conjoyn'd with Natures Crueltie...211. H.597, 2
How well his nature's fitted to his name!.......287. H.903, 4
The first is Natures end: this doth imparte.421. ins. H.106, 26a
Natures Whose easie natures like it well,..........22. H.66, 3
Their Christal natures to an union............77. H.197, 4
Natures, like ours, wee who haue spent our tyme..410. A.3, 15
Naught See Nought
Naught are all Women: I say no,................283. H.885, 1
Navel — — — — — — — — —, ...426. ins. H.197, 48b
Navies No newes of Navies burnt at Seas;.........126. H.319, 1
Nay Or like—Nay 'tis that Zonulet of love,........40. H.114, 3
Nay, thou more neare then kindred, friend, man, wife, 45. H.128, 3
Nay! not so much as out of bed?................68. H.178, 9
Nay, profanation to keep in,..................68. H.178, 12
Nay more, Ile deeply sweare,....................69. H.179, 2
Let it be Doomes-day; nay, take longer scope;...83. H.206, 3
The House (Love shield her) with her Yea and Nay: 114. H.283, 66
Nay, now I think th'ave made his grave......156. H.412, 15
So like to this, nay all the rest,................164. H.440, 9
You are a Lord, an Earle, nay more, a Man,....172. H.459, 1
Nay more, the Feast, and grace of it..........192. H.521, 28
These (nay) and more, thine own shal be,.......193. H.521, 55
This Christmas, but his want wherwith, sayes Nay. 238. H.693, 2
Ravisht in spirit, I come, nay more, I flie......242. H.713, 3
By yea and by nay,.........................256. H.762, 17
Love thou dost, though Love sayes Nay.........264. H.790, 2
We blame, nay we despise her paines...........279. H.867, 1
The eye of Virgins; nay, the Queen..........360. N.83, 15
Thou hast, nay more, Thou art the Tree,........377. N.129, 3
Nay tell the Bell-man of the Night had tould......410. A.3, 17
— — — — — — — — — — —, ...425. var. H.197, 15
My dearest daintyes, nay, 'tis the principall: 426. ins. H.197, 48b
Nays Maids nay's are nothing, they are shie......249. H.735, 1
Near Come thou not neere those men, who are like Bread 7. H.7, 1
Nere to thy Reverend Pitcher I will fall..........11. H.22, 7
To me, as blood to life and spirit: Neare,........45. H.128, 2
Nay, thou more neare then kindred, friend, man, wife, 45. H.128, 3
So neare, or deare, as thou wast once to me.....45. H.128, 10
If, Reader, then thou wilt draw neere,............48. H.134, 5
Come thou not neere that Filmne so finely spred, 82. H.204, 7
Neere to the Altar stands the Priest,...........91. H.223, 50
'Tis now farre off, and then tis nere;..........130. H.329, 14
For love and bountie, to come neare, and see,....131. H.331, 3
Washt o're, to tell[1] what change is neare........134. H.336, 90
In a drie-house all things are neere............179. H.476, 27
My wooing's ended: now my wedding's neere;..180. H.479, 1
All sitting neer the glitt'ring Hearth............193. H.521, 50
Dearest of thousands, now the time drawes neere,.219. H.627, 1
When as her Aprill houre drawes neare,.........221. H.633, 58
The Heifer, Cow, and Oxe draw neere..........230. H.662, 38
For, if we gaze on These brave Lamps too neer,.237. H.685, 11
Her tongue, to tell what danger's neare.........246. H.724, 16
Say what thou art. Ph. I prithee first draw neare. 248. H.730, 4
By how much, neere to singlenesse............254. H.754, 2
Neer the dying of the day,..................255. H.761, 15
Neere to the well of wit;......................261. H.778, 2
Take mine advise, and go not neere...........279. H.868, 1
Neer the childs heart lay a knife:..............284. H.889, 2
Mine end near was,...........................346. N.38, 17
Neer to the wishes of his heart:.................351. N.50, 3
Nearer And neerer he's to Setting.................84. H.208, 8
To be the nearer Relative:....................147. H.377, 40
Nearer to that place, then to other some:........385. N. 186, 2
Nearest You, you that be of her neerest kin,......55. H.149, 81
Neat Or to a Girle (that keeps the Neat)..........6. H.2, 13
Lesse with a neat, then needfull diet............35. H.106, 30
A neat, though not so great an Offering.........86. H.213, 35
Upon the ends of these neat Railes..............92. H.223, 91
Be mindfull, that the lab'ring Neat............102. H.250, 45
To make this neat distinction from the rest;.....140. H.354, 5
So smell those neat and woven Bowers,........145. H.375, 11
Is each neate Niplet of her breast...............164. H.440, 10
Many a neat perplexity,.......................165. H.443, 24
Gives to each Mead a neat enameling...........224. H.642, 4
Here thou behold'st thy large sleek Neat........230. H.662, 35
And gracefull made, by your neate Sisterhood...290. H.914, 10
Instead of neat Inclosures......................345. N.33, 9
Or as a neat..................................375. N.123, 78
— — — — — — — — — — —, ...422. var. H.106, 135
— — — — — — — — — — —, ...433. var. H.293, 28
— — — — — — — — — — —, ...447. var. A.1, 23
Neatherdess My love unto my Neatherdesse......243. H.716, 28
Thou most lovely Neat-heardesse:..............305. H.984, 3
Neatherds Come blithefull Neatherds, let us lay..243. H.716, 1
Neatly Made up of white-thorn neatly enterwove;.68. H.178, 35
Sceanes to cheat us neatly drawne................76. H.195, 8
Neatly apart;.............................114. H.283, 95
A House-dance neatly, and can'st truly show,....148. H.377, 91
Are here most neatly inter-laid................166. H.443, 50
Are neatly here enchequered...................166. H.443, 56
Of the red infant, neatly hung.................166. H.443, 71
So neatly sunck, as that no proof............167. H.443, 103
— — — — — — — — — — —, ...437. var. H.336, 127
Apple or Plume is neately layd,..........439. ins. H.443, 45b
Neat's See Ragged-soused-neat's-foot
Nebo Of Sion, Sinai, Nebo, and with them,.....330. H.1100, 11
Necessity Patient in my necessitie...............235. H.677, 4
Necessity makes dastards valiant men...........333. H.1118, 2
To hold things fitting my necessity;............371. N.115, 6
Neck About her spotlesse neck she knit............14. H.34, 3
My curles about her neck did craule,.............16. H.41, 14
Submits his neck unto a second yoke..............17. H.42, 6
About thy neck a Carkanet is bound,.............30. H.88, 5
To hug thy whitest neck: Then I,...............70. H.181, 3
To have my neck from Loves yoke-free..........155. H.408, 2
The tempting Mole, stoln from the neck.......166. H.443, 63
The neck is free:...........................172. H.458, 3
The neck with bands........................172. H.458, 12
With a neck by yoke unworn.................306. H.984, 23
Is the swan-stayning faire rare stately neck.......405. A.1, 44
That when thou doest his necke Insnare..........408. A.2, 61
Necklace He bade me then that Neck-lace use;...279. H.863, 9
Nectar 'Tis thou, above Nectar, O Divinest soule!.45. H.128, 19
Which full of Nectar and Ambrosia is,..........186. H.498, 4
The Gods, he down the Nectar flung;...........241. H.706, 2
— — — — — — — — — — —, ...427. var. H.197, 63
Nectarell Ambrosia-like, or Nectarell:...............20. H.54, 4
Ned Tom Chipperfeild, and pritty-lisping Ned,....155. H.405, 9
Neech First, in a Neech, more black than jet,....90. H.223, 11
Need Who with thy leaves shall wipe (at need)......6. H.5, 1
And having these, what need of more?............33. H.100, 2
She need not be afraid:........................56. H.149, 94
If twice you kisse, you need not feare,..........61. H.159, 26
What need I care, though some dislike me sho'd, 187. H.506, 5
Nor need we here to feare the frowne..........190. H.515, 33
Strewings need none, every flower............199. H.546, 5
Both for their comely need, and some to spare:..205. H.571, 2
Need is no vice at all; though here it be,........239. H.698, 1
In all thy need, be thou possest.................246. H.725, 1
Who begs to die for feare of humane need,......277. H.855, 1
We pray for showers (at our need)............279. H.867, 5
And meat too, for his need:...................295. H.942, 6
What need we marry Women, when............297. H.948, 1
If this can be, say then, what need............297. H.948, 13
What need of Physick, or Physitian?............319. H.1049, 2
What need there then be of a reckning day:......343. N.27, 2
To charme his cries, (at time of need:).........354. N.59, 10
Oft-times for wast, as for his need...............358. N.75, 8
God gives not onely corne, for need,.............356. N.66, 1
And softly handle Him: y'ad need,..............366. N.98, 20
No, this ye need not do;......................367. N.102, 12
Gold I have none, but I present my need,.......369. N.105, 1
What need I then to feare at all,...............371. N.114, 5
What need I then despaire,....................373. N.122, 9
Because our flesh stood most in need of Him.....390. N.222, 4
And Conscience vnto Preist-hood, tis not Need...411. A.3, 51
Needest — — — — — — — —, ...441. var. H.465, 27
Needful Lesse with a neat, then needfull diet......35. H.106, 30
Needihood For a man in needy-hood:...........223. H.638, 16
Needs Now, now, blowne downe; needs must the old stock fall. 72. H.185, 14
If needs we must for Ceremonies-sake,........115. H.283, 131
An old, old widow Greedy needs wo'd wed,......129. H.326, 1
Thy Fortress, and will needs prevaile;..........175. H.465, 54
What needs she fire and ashes to consume,......178. H.474, 5
So, that an Author needs no other Bayes........188. H.506, 11
Here needs no Court for our Request,..........190. H.515, 29
He needs a Tucker for to burle his face.........211. H.594, 2
What needs twenty stabs, when one.............254. H.757, 5
Must needs wax cold, if wanting bread and wine..258. H.768, 4
Tell me, what needs those rich deceits,..........282. H.881, 1
What needs complaints,.......................314. H.1024, 1
— — — — — — — — — — —, ...441. var. H.465, 27
Needy Live with a thrifty, not a needy Fate;......13. H.28, 1
Your stock, and needy grown,.................110. H.274, 18
For needy Fate.............................137. H.340, 12
And all live here with needy Fate...............179. H.476, 30
To feed and cloth the Needy...................374. N.123, 50
Ne'er That Heart to bleed, your's ne'r will ake....11. H.20, 11
Such precious thraldome ne'r shall fetter me.......17. H.42, 4
I ne'r invented such..........................19. H.51, 6
Banish'd from thee I live; ne'r to return,.........19. H.52, 3
With those deeds done by day, which n'er affright 35. H.106, 37
But thou liv'st fearlesse; and thy face ne'r shewes 37. H.106, 93
Brave Porter! Poets ne'r will wanting be:........41. H.117, 2
Gryll eates, but ne're sayes Grace; To speak the troth, 48. H.135, 1
Is ne'r redeem'd by cost.........................53. H.149, 8

Never beg, or humbly wooe....................182. H.490, 11
I co'd never walke alone;....................183. H.490, 13
Never keep a fast, or pray....................183. H.490, 15
And never purls a Note?....................183. H.492, 4
As Time had never known ye....................184. H.493, 12
Love in extreames, can never long endure......185. H.494, 4
Fortune did never favour one....................191. H.520, 1
And never, as yet,....................195. H.534, 4
The while we never remember,....................196. H.534, 15
Great Spirits never with their bodies dye......199. H.547, 2
Wherein we rest, and never feare..............200. H.552, 9
Man is a Watch, wound up at first, but never..202. H.558, 1
Cold and hunger never yet....................217. H.620, 4
To such a height; but never surfeited..........220. H.633, 21
Never had been the Northern Plunderer........224. H.642, 10
He'l never haunt ye now he's dead............226. H.644, 10
Never againe to have ingression here:.........227. H.652, 2
Be it, O be it, never more reveal'd!............227. H.652, 12
Never man yet had a regredience..............228. H.656, 2
Thou never Plow'st the Oceans foame.........229. H.662, 5
Thy Sheering-feast, which never faile..........231. H.662, 55
From whence there's never a return...........233. H.670, 39
Faith, and Affection: which will never slip....252. H.745, 19
Love love begets, then never be..............252. H.746, 1
'Tis never, or but seldome knowne,............264. H.788, 1
Tom shifts the Trenchers; yet he never can....265. H.796, 1
Upon your hogsheads never fall...............291. H.919, 5
Give house-roome to the best; 'Tis never known.293. H.935, 1
Attempt the end, and never stand to doubt;....311. H.1008, 1
Still shall I crave, and never get.............312. H.1014, 3
Never againe shall I with Finnie-Ore..........315. H.1028, 11
Never make sick your Banks by surfeiting.....316. H.1028, 24
Grow young with Tydes, and though I see ye never,
316. H.1028, 25
Is, that I never yet had wife;................320. H.1052, 2
Roses, you can never die,....................324. H.1070, 1
Since I as yet did never prove,................327. H.1082, 2
Where Pleasures rule a Kingdome, never there..327. H.1087, 1
Fix on That Columne then, and never fall;....329. H.1092, 7
This pillar never shall.......................335. H.1129, 11
God is all fore-part; for, we never see.........342. N.18, 1
But never those that persevere therein.........344. N.32, 2
Lord! let me never act that beggars part,......347. N.39, 3
Is disacquainted never.......................353. N.56, 18
Where never Moone shall sway................354. N.58, 9
Then never take a second on,.................354. N.59, 17
He never brings them once to th' push of Pikes..370. N.108, 12
Shall be releeved never......................374. N.123, 20
We our eyes shall never steep;................377. N.128, 18
And fresh joyes, as never too..................377. N.128, 23
The Good without the Bad are here plac'd never.
383. N.172, 2
Once shut, was never to be open'd more.......385. N.190, 4
With God, then one, that never sin'd 'gainst Him.
388. N.205, 2
Christ never did so great a work, but there....389. N.214, 1
Sin never slew a soule, unlesse there went....389. N.217, 1
'Tis never read there (as the Fathers say)......396. N.249, 5
To'th shew, but Neuer part wth; next..........407. A.2, 31
Languish and looke but thy returne see neuer...414. A.5, 8
Chorus. We sail along, to visit mortals never;..417. A.8, 37
— — — — — — — — — —, ...427. var. H.197, 82
New So oft, we'll think, we see a King new born...26. H.80, 2
With oaten pipes, as sweet, as new.............86, H.213, 41
Wit and new misterie; read, and...............115. H.283, 123
No new devise, or late found trick,............126. H.319 5
Nothing is New: we walk where others went...139. H.352 1
Judith has cast her old-skin, and got new;......140. H.356, 1
Shift now has cast his clothes: got all things new;
144. H.372, 1
The new successor drives away old Love.......191. H.517, 2
And a new Altar;............................213. H.604, 10
Then if any Peece proves new,................217. H.620, 10
With Roses sweet and new;....................228. H.657, 11
Either with old, or plant therein new thorne:..259. H.771, 6
Will chant new Hymnes to thee...............259. H.772, 28
Light the new block, And.....................263. H.784, 8
New things succeed, as former things grow old..285. H.892, 22
As Cadmus once a new way found,............297. H.948, 5
Lay of our safeties new foundation:..........300. H.961, 12
Here we begin new life; while thousands quite..313. H.1019, 3
One Birth their Parents gave them; but their new,
326. H.1080, 25
That thou hast brought a Whistle new,.........354. N.59, 8
First stripes, new blowes,......................363. N.92, 11
Or say, if this new Birth of ours..............367. N.102, 4
Th' Apostles Mounts of the New Testament.....381. N.157, 4
And prest a little they will weepe new milke.....405. A.1, 58
— — — — — — — — — —, ...437. var. H.336, 112
Newark Or gallant Newark; which brave two....218. H.626, 12
New-born A new-borne Phoenix from His own chast fire.
367. N.98, 30
Newer Now strength, and newer Purple get,........7. H.9, 3
Newly Newly refresh't, both by the Sun, and showers.
25. H.77, 6
Like to a Virgin newly ravished...............41. H.118, 4
(Sweet as your selfe, and newly blown)........126. H.318, 8
Like to a field of beans, when newly blown;...159. H.421, 20
In a Sheeps-skin newly flaid,..................209. H.587, 2
News Amar. With all white luck to you. Mirt. But say, What
news.:.......................................85. H.213, 3
No newes of Navies burnt at Seas;..........126. H.319, 1
New-shorn Or smell, like to a Meade new-shorne,.364. N.96, 16
New-star Blowne out of April; or some New-
Star fill'd with glory to our view,....112. H.283, 3-4
Newt's But Beards of Mice, a Newt's stew'd thigh,
119. H.293, 37
New Year's We send in stead of New-yeares gift.
127. H.319, 26
The richest New-yeeres Gift to me..............355. N.60, 6
Be the best New-yeares Gift to all............366. N.98, 24
For New-yeers gift to thee...................376. N.125, 4
New Years His New-yeeres trebled to His old:..367. N.98, 28
Next Sapho next, a principall:....................15. H.39, 4
Next, Corinna, for her wit,.....................16. H.39, 9
For Epitaph, in Foliage, next write this,........19. H.50, 5
When I thy singing next shall heare,............22. H.68, 1
Next enters June, and brings us more...........23. H.70, 5
Next, how I love thee, that my griefe must tell,..23. H.72, 3
Next, let us marry:.............................31. H.94, 2
Doe they first pill thee, next, pluck off thy skin?.32. H.97, 3
Next, his wilde eares, like Lethern wings full spread,
33. H.99, 3
Next, make his cheeks with breath to swell,....39, H.108, 11
Next, to be rich by no by-wayes;..............42. H.121, 3
What next is lockt for? but we all sho'd see...44. H.124, 3
Next, look thou like a sickly Moone;..........47. H.132, 3
Next, place me Zones, and Tropicks there;.....47. H.133, 7
Next, hollow out a Tombe to cover...........61. H.159, 28
First, Jollies wife is lame; then next, loose-hipt:.62. H.163, 1
When next he came a pilfring so,.............71. H.182, 29
Yet the next Morne, re-guild the fragrant East..72. H.185, 7
Next, Virgil, Ile call forth,....................80. H.201, 17
A Goblet next Ile drink........................80. H.201, 21
Now, to Tibullus next,........................81. H.201, 37
Next, when thou dost perceive her fixed sight,..87. H.215, 7
Next in an Arch, akin to this,..................90. H.223, 15
Elve Boniface shall next be Pope..............93. H.223, 112
Next, then, upon the Chanters side.............93. H.223, 125
Tole forth my death; next, to my buryall come..100. H.248, 6
Next to your Flailes, your Fanes, your Fatts;.102. H.250, 40
And laugh no more; or laugh, and lie down next..111. H.277, 2
Next, with severest Salvages;.................111. H.278, 4
Then the next thing I desire,..................117. H.286, 11
At my up-rising next, I shall,..................123. H.306, 11
Next to the Altar humbly kneele, and thence,..128. H.320, 5
A Primrose next;..............................135. H.336, 99
Then next Ile cause my hopefull Lad..........135. H.336, 121
Then the next health to friends of mine........135. H.336, 129
'Tis to be doubted whether I next yeer,.........140. H.355, 7
The first of Nature, and the next of Art:.......153. H.394, 2
When my off'ring next I make,................158. H.417, 1
Prithee, when next thou do'st invite, barre State,
161. H.424, 3
And next to these two blankets ore-...........167. H.443, 94
But when I'm next...........................172. H.458, 4
Next to which Two; among the City-Powers,...176. H.466, 3
Next, may your Dairies Prosper so............179. H.476, 10
Next may your Duck and teeming Hen........179. H.476, 19
Next is your lot (Faire) to be number'd one,....188. H.510, 1
Next, at that great Platonick yeere,............190. H.515, 47
Thy clothing next, shall be a Gowne...........192. H.521, 9
Next, hang'd for Theeving: Now the people say,.195. H.532, 3
That dyes with the next December............196. H.534, 18
The next, because her Altars did not shine.....197. H.539, 9
Next, when those Lawnie Filmes I see.........202. H.560, 13
First dyes the Leafe, the Bough next, next the Tree.
203. H.565, 4
Next for Ordaining, that thy words not swell....210. H.590, 7
For my sake next, (though little) be not loud..212. H.600, 2
Next we will act, how young men wooe;......215. H.616, 19
Thus, having talkt, we'l next commend.........216. H.616, 35
Then, next, to match Tradescant's curious shels,
232. H.668, 3
Chose first, confirm'd next, & at last are crown'd.
241. H.707, 2
Look how next the holy fier.................242. H.714, 9
Next, from that world of waters, then..........245. H.720, 7
Next, like a Bishop consecrate my ground,.......245. H.723, 7
Then to want the Wake next Yeare.............255. H.761, 24
And next the Gospell wee will credit thee......257. H.763, 20
Her name if next you wo'd have knowne,.......257. H.764, 3
Next, when I cast mine eyes and see............261. H.779, 4
Well, when to eat thou dost me next desire,....262. H.783, 21
By the next kindling of the day................271. H.824, 1
The first Commerce is, & the next Command...275. H.847, 2
All is well; now next to these................280. H.870, 13
Till Christmas next returne...................285. H.893, 4
The Christmas Log next yeare;................285. H.983, 6
Burn first thine incense; next, when as thou see'st
286. H.898, 5

Next, let the Lord, and Ladie here............291. H.919, 9
Trees this year beare; **next**, they their wealth with-hold:
292. H.922, 3
Where he will kisse (**next** drunk) conjecture ye...295. H.943, 2
And **next** to him, be Master of the Quire......299. H.956, 14
Next, when I see Thee towring in the skie,....301. H.966, 3
Next, I'm sure, the Nuns will have...........304. H.976, 5
Next day..................................308. H.993, 28
Lift up thy Sword; **next**, suffer it to fall,......310. H.1002, 3
Man may at first transgress, but **next** do well:.314. H.1021, 1
And **next** morrow, every one................315. H.1026, 13
Next crowne the bowle full...................317. H.1035, 19
Next be sure ye have a care,.................322. H.1064, 3
Inform me **next**, what love will do;............325. H.1075, 3
In the **next** sheet Brave Man to follow Thee...329. H.1092, 6
The one is Mercy, and the **next** is Love:........340. N.6, 2
Next, when I have my faults confest,..........349. N.46, 5
And **next**, to take a bit.......................352. N.53, 7
Next, that these ills none cowardly may shun;..387. N.201, 5
The first of Raine, the key of Hell **next** known:.390. N.224, 2
Possesse my thoughts, **next** comes my dolefull knell
392. N.230, 12
The one a Staffe is, and the **next** a Rod:.......394. N.241, 2
The first of sin is, and the **next** of praise:.....395. N.243, 2
Let Oyle, **next**, run,.........................401. N.268, 21
Next doth her chinne with dimpled beawty striue
405. A.1, 33
Then comes the belly seated **next** belowe.......405. A.1, 59
In length each finger doth his **next** excell,.....406. A.1, 101
To'th shew, but Neuer part w^th; **next**..........407. A.2, 31
Bringe to hym **next**, and in it shew...........408. A.2, 49
— — — — — — — — — — — —, ...421. var. H.106, 31
— — — — — — — — — — — —, ...435. var. H.293, 39m
— — — — — — — — — — — —, ...437. var. H.336, 125

Nice Set on your selfe, by being **nice**:..........113. H.283, 54
They make a feast lesse great then **nice**.......119. H.293, 12
Love is a thing most **nice**; and must be fed...220. H.633, 20
Nicely One **nicely** mad, or peevishly severe.......234. H.673, 6
Niceness On your **niceness** though we wait,......276. H.850, 3
Nicholas — — — — — — — — —, ...421. var. H.49, 1
Nick Why walkes **Nick** Flimsey like a Male-content?
160. H.423, 1
Niece You'l do my **Neice** abundant honour......257. H.764, 10
Niggards But must be **niggards** of the meanest bloud.
260. H.775, 2
Nigh Some private pinch tels danger's **nie**........147. H.377, 52
With his Flesh-hooks, don't come **nie**.........263. H.785, 3
More and more approaching **nigh**...............377. N.128, 6
W^ch sweeten Loue, yett ne're come **nighe**.........408. A.2, 41

Night See Good-night
The Gods protection, but the **night** before).....9. H.14, 12
Me thought, (last **night**) love in an anger came,.16. H.40, 1
Faults done by **night**, will blush by day:........20. H.56, 6
Night to the Record! that was all...............20. H.56, 8
Here we are all, by day; By **night** w'are hurl'd.21. H.57, 1
As oft as **Night** is banish'd by the Morne,.......26. H.80, 1
One silent **night** of late,.........................26. H.81, 1
Thy frown (last **night**) did bid me goe;........33. H.103, 3
Thy silken slumbers in the **night**...............35. H.106, 38
Gives thee each **night** a Maidenhead...........35. H.106, 42
Kisse our Dollies **night** and day:................39. H.111, 4
Comets we see by **night**; whose shagg'd portents.45. H.128, 15
He weares all day, and drawes those teeth at **night**.
46. H.129, 6
For second course, last **night**, a Custard came..47. H.131, 1
Make me a Sun-set; and a **Night**:..............47. H.133, 9
Continues cold, as is the **night**................49. H.136, 31
Never was **Night** so tedious, but it knew........52. H.146, 3
Your **Night**, your Prison, and your Ebbe; you may
52. H.146, 10
Night now hath watch'd her self half blind;...54. H.149, 31
Shews you how much is spent of **night**.........54. H.149, 52
Since that Love and **Night** bid enter..........56. H.149, 100
By day, and **night** on you....................57. H.149, 156
Had met t'engender with the **night**;............64. H.169, 6
To shew at once, both **night** and day...........64. H.169, 8
Yet comming home, but somewhat late, (last **night**)
65. H.171, 4
Hangs on the Dew-locks of the **night**:..........68. H.178, 24
This **night**, and Locks pickt, yet w'are not a Maying.
69. H.178, 56
Lies drown'd with us in endlesse **night**.........69. H.178, 68
But stay the time till we have bade Good **night**..73. H.186, 2
As soone dispatcht is by the **Night**, as Day.....73. H.186, 4
Ne'r had kept heat for fifty Maids that **night**.....78. H.197, 68
Like noyse-lesse Snow; or as the dew of **night**:..100. H.247, 2
Come to weep out the **night**...................106. H.262, 16
This the short'st day, and this the longest **night**;
114. H.283, 72
Who count this **night** as long as three,........114. H.283, 74
The **night**, with you, in floods of Downe........115. H.283, 120
Your weake senses in the **night**...............117. H.289, 8
Your pleasing slumbers in the **night**:...........121. H.299, 4
From scaring you or yours this **night**..........123. H.306, 15
We'll call on **Night**, to bring ye both to Bed:..124. H.313, 10
May the Bed, and this short **night**,...........124. H.314, 3
Of what can hurt by day, or harme by **night**:..128. H.323, 10
Farre more then **night** bewearied.............136. H.336, 152
Drawing thy curtains round: Good **night**.......146. H.376, 14
They cling and close, some minutes of the **night**..156. H.411, 4
And when at **night**, she folded had her sheep,..159. H.421, 25
Last **night** thou didst invite me home to eate;.161. H.424, 1
Shut not so soon; the dull-ey'd **night**..........164. H.441, 1
We'l wish both Them and Thee, good **night**....165. H.443, 8
But ever doubtfull Day, or **night**...............167. H.443, 81
In the dead of dampish **night**.................177. H.473, 6
Being drunke, who 'twas that Can'd his Ribs last **night**.
186. H.501, 4
Let me sleep this **night** away,.................199. H.549, 1
Our Peacefull slumbers in the **night**...........200. H.552, 12
So double gilds the Aire, as that no **night**......206. H.575, 15
(The Bell-man of the **night**) proclaime the clock
207. H.575, 62
But **Night** determines here, Away.............207. H.575, 66
Night hides our thefts; all faults then pardon'd be:
209. H.586, 1
Lais and Lucrece, in the **night** time are.......209. H.586, 3
This day is Loves day; and this busie **night**...216. H.618, 9
The Starres of the **night**.....................217. H.619, 13
What made that mirth last **night**? the neighbours say,
219. H.630, 1
But give thy place to **night**,..................220. H.633, 9
'Tis fit that **Night**, the Paire,................220. H.633, 16
One **night** i' th' yeare, my dearest Beauties, come
222. H.634, 1
Gander (they say) doth each **night** pisse a Bed:
223. H.636, 2
This **night** for to ride;.......................225. H.643, 2
At noone of **Night** are a working...............225. H.643, 18
This **night**, and more for the wonder,.........225. H.643, 21
Sweet sleep, that makes more short the **night**..231. H.662, 75
Thais in the **night**, to me....................232. H.665, 16
To tell how **night** drawes hence, I've none,....246. H.724, 2
At **night** they draw to Supper; then well fed,..260. H.773, 3
Come guard this **night** the Christmas-Pie,.....263. H.785, 1
Then the last part of **night**, and first of day....278. H.858, 2
Night makes no difference 'twixt the Priest and Clark;
279. H.864, 1
Is not for one, but every **night** his Bride:.....286. H.898, 14
Peacefull by **night**; my day devoid of strife:...294. H.938, 2
Blisse (last **night** drunk) did kisse his mothers knee:
295. H.943, 1
Which, this **night** hardned, sodders up her nose..296. H.945, 2
And weepe for me, lost in an endlesse **night**.....298. H.952, 2
Now (ai me) (ai me.) Last **night**.............306. H.984, 33
Buggins is Drunke all **night**, all day he sleepes;..311. H.1011, 1
Of my dearest deare last **night**;...............313. H.1018, 2
Are lost, and theirs, in everlasting **night**.......313. H.1019, 4
(This **night** as ye use).......................317. H.1035, 8
Be Twelfe-day Queene for the **night** here.......317. H.1035, 12
Then **Night** now gone, and yet not sprung the Day.
319. H.1046, 2
Of **night** from Heaven for to rend her.........333. H.1122, 12
There give me day; but here my dreadfull **night**:
343. N.25, 7
Bell-man of **Night**, if I about shall go.........349. N.43, 1
Through all the **night**.......................353. N.56, 1
And **Night**, shall be..........................354. N.58, 11
That in the mirk and tonguelesse **night**,........357. N.72, 13
I dreamt, last **night**, Thou didst transfuse.........357. N.75, 1
Night hath no wings, to him that cannot sleep;.358. N.77, 1
The winds, to blow the tedious **night** away;......358. N.77, 6
Dark and dull **night**, flie hence away,..........364. N.96, 8
And when **night** comes, wee'l give Him wassailing:
368. N.102, 22
Last **night** I drew up mine Account,..........369. N.107, 1
Along the dark, and silent **night**,..............372. N.121, 1
A mighty storm last **night**....................373. N.122, 5
That ne're went out by Day or **Night**:........374. N.123, 46
And when the **night** perswades me to my bed,..392. N.230, 13
How do's she erre in endlesse **night**!..........393. N.233, 4
But look how **night** succeeds the day, so He...394. N.236, 3
I haue beheld two louers in a **night**...........410. A.3, 1
Nay tell the Bell-man of the **Night** had tould...410. A.3, 17
Past Noone of **night**, yett weare the howers not old
410. A.3, 18
Is spilt in everlasting **night**....................413. A.4, 11
— — — — — — — — — — — —, ...424. var. H.164, 4
— — — — — — — — — — — —, ...425. var. H.197, 5

Night-bewearied — — — — — — — — —, ...451. var. H.336, 152
Night-charm The **Night-Charme** quickly; you have spells,
115. H.283, 133
Night-gum Seeal'd up with **Night-gum**, Loach each morning lyes,.....................................269. H.816, 1
Nightingale The broke-heart of a **Nightingale**...120. H.293, 46
Money's the still-sweet-singing **Nightingale**......247. H.726, 2
Nightly And a deale of **nightly** feare...........263. H.785, 7
Spend Harmless shade thy **nightly** Houres,......289. H.912, 1
Night's And **night's** afraid of the sounding......334. H.1122, 18
Nights Love give me more such **nights** as these..20. H.56, 10
By Moonlesse **nights** have swerved;............26. H.81, 10

Daies may conclude in **nights**; and Suns may rest, 72. H.185, 5
So meet stolne kisses, when the Moonie **nights**...77. H.197, 5
And offers Incense **Nights** and dayes,..........93. H.223, 130
Of Candi'd dew in Moony **nights**.............165. H.443, 32
By silent **Nights**, and the.....................258. H.767, 9
Nightshade And look, what Smallage, **Night-shade**, Cypresse, Yew,.......................................27. H.82, 9
Night-time See Night
Nimble Thou mak'st me **nimble**, as the winged howers, 78. H.197, 51
To dance the Heyes with **nimble** feet;..........192. H.521, 30
I'le strike thee such a **nimble** Ayre,............243. H.716, 32
The **nimble** howers wooe us on to wed,........261. H.781, 5
Nine When one hole wasts more then he gets by **Nine**. 154. H.400, 4
If **nine** times you your Bride-groome kisse;....208. H.581, 1
Or **nine**; but thrive...........................227. H.653, 11
O! you the Virgins **nine**!.......................228. H.657, 1
Number of **Nyne**, wch makes vs full wth God,..410. A.3, 22
When on the Flood that **nine** times circles Hell...417. A.8, 36
Nine-bones Skurffe by his **Nine-bones** sweares, and well he may, 180. H.480, 1
Nine-holes Raspe playes at **Nine-holes**; and 'tis known he gets 154. H.400, 1
Ninth To the **ninth** number, if not tenne;........127. H.319, 32
Before the last least sand of Thy **ninth** houre be run; 401. N.268, 8
Niplet The rubie **niplet** of her breast;...........74. H.190, 8
Is each neate **Niplet** of her breast.............164. H.440, 10
Nipped — — — — — — — —, ...439. ins. H.443, 45d
Nipple And if more; Each **Nipple** cries,.........183. H.491, 3
— — — — — — — — — — —, ...425. var. H.190, 8
Nis **Nis**, he makes Verses; but the Lines he writes, 286. H.896, 1
Nit Saint Tit, Saint **Nit**, Saint Is, Saint Itis,....91. H.223, 28
Nits Their Beads of **Nits**, Bels, Books, & Wax...93. H.223, 115
Nits carbonado'd, a device...............435. ins. H.293, v
No (Partial List of Adverb)
No Critick haunts the Poore mans Cell:.........6. H.2, 22
By **no** one tongue, there, censured.............6. H.2, 24
Regardlesse whether well thou sped'st, or **no**.....6. H.3, 6
No sound calls back the yeere that once is past...8. H.10, 4
Then sweetest Silvia, let's **no** longer stay;......8. H.10, 5
No man at one time, can be wise, and love......8. H.10, 8
Is there **no** way to beget......................10. H.19, 7
No Dislike there is in love:..................11. H.21, 2
That my wing'd ship may meet **no** Remora.....14. H.35, 4
No Spices wanting, when I'm laid by thee....20. H.55, 10
When **no** force else can get the masterdome....21. H.60, 2
And comming downe, shall make **no** noise at all....21. H.62, 6
As, could they hear, the Damn'd would make **no** noise, 22. H.67, 2
Whether by th' eye, or eare, or **no**:............24. H.73, 2
Whether thy bones had here their Rest, or **no**..27. H.82, 6
No part besides must of thy selfe be known,.....30. H.88, 11
Beauty, **no** other thing is, then a Beame......33. H.102, 1
Feare to those sheets, that know **no** sin.......35. H.106, 40
Who keep'st **no** proud mouth for delicious cates: 37. H.106, 109
Ordaining that thy small stock find **no** breach,..38. H.106, 133
No heart by love receiv'd a wound;...........42. H.119, 2
Next, to be rich by **no** by-wayes;.............42. H.121, 3
I'm sure she'll ask **no** more..................43. H.123, 36
What now is done: since where **no** sin..........48. H.136, 12
Unbolts the doore, **no** shame comes in..........48. H.136, 13
The common formes have **no** one eye,...........49. H.136, 18
No, **no**, **no** more then is yond' Moone,..........49. H.136, 28
No; he's but Fore-man, as he was before.........53. H.148, 4
On, on devoutly, make **no** stay;................54. H.149, 41
No Fatal Owle the Bedsted keeps,..............56. H.149, 101
No Furies, here about,........................56. H.149, 103
She must **no** more a Maying:....................56. H.149, 114
There, where **no** language ever yet was known...60. H.156, 6
A desp'rate grief, that finds **no** cure.............60. H.157, 2
No Herbs have power to cure Love..............60. H.157, 4
Love kill'd this man. **No** more but so...........61, H.159, 31
But find **no** Rose-bud in your cheek:............63. H.164, 9
I feare **no** Earthly Powers;.....................65. H.170, 1
Is **no** where found.............................66. H.172, 26
And sweet as Flora. Take **no** care..............68. H.178, 17
And sin **no** more, as we have done, by staying;..68. H.178, 41
Lyd. While thou **no** other didst affect,..........70. H.181, 5
No, here Ile last, and walk (a harmlesse shade)...73. H.186, 17
Thy many scorns, and find **no** cure?.............74. H.191, 2
No mixture did admit...........................75. H.193, 16
And had **no** other pride at all,..................75. H.193, 30
And that, **no** further, then we see..............76. H.193, 44
To thee-ward dy'd i'th' embers, and **no** fire.......78. H.197 36
And pay **no** vowes to thee? who wast their best..78. H.197, 59
Where **no** one piece is yet unlevelled.............82. H.204, 8
And leave **no** scent behind ye:.................83. H.207, 2
Whether high he builds or **no**:.................84. H.209, 2
Amin. Good day, Mirtillo. Mirt. And to you **no** lesse: 85. H.213, 1
And Cedar wash thee, that **no** times consume thee. 89. H.219, 14
No Capitoll, **no** Cornish free,..................90. H.223, 20
Saint Will o'th' Wispe (of **no** great bignes)......91. H.223, 30
'Twas **no** more you then, but a Cherubin.........95. H.228, 4
Will **no** other thing imply,....................97. H.232, 16
No, I sho'd think, that Marriage might,..........97. H.235, 5
But 'tis **no** Gout (beleeve it) but hard Beere,....98. H.239, 3
But **no** disdaine intended........................100. H.246, 7
O! may **no** eye distill a Teare..................104. H.256, 9
No, **no**, this sorrow shown....................104. H.257, 24
No life is yet life-proofe miserie...............111. H.276, 2
Whether that you be sweet or **no**?..............112. H.282, 2
Of her green hopes, we charge ye, that **no** strife, 114. H.283, 82
Be't to your praise, **no** peace was broken.......114. H.283, 90
And of such Torture as **no** one would grutch..115. H.283, 136
I tell yee **no**; but like a......................116. H.283, 147
No fault in women to refuse..................118. H.291, 1
No fault in women, to confesse.................118. H.291, 3
No fault in women, to lay on..................118. H.291, 5
No fault in women, to make show..............118. H.291, 9
No fault in women, though they be.............118. H.291, 13
No fault in womankind, at all,..................118. H.291, 15
When our drinking has **no** stint,...............122. H.304, 3
There is **no** one pleasure in't...................122. H.304, 4
Weelcome! but yet **no** entrance, till we blesse..124. H.313, 1
Profane **no** Porch young man and maid, for fear..124. H.313, 3
No newes of Navies burnt at Seas;.............126. H.319, 1
No noise of late spawn'd Tittyries:............126. H.319, 2
No closset plot, or open vent,..................126. H.319, 3
No new devise, or late found trick,............126. H.319, 5
No ginne to catch the State, or wring.........126. H.319, 7
But none enquires if good he be, or **no**..........130. H.328, 2
And leave **no** sound; nor piety,..................132. H.336, 2
Must all be left, **no** one plant found...........132. H.336, 10
No roofs of Cedar, nor our brave..............133. H.336, 42
No, **no**, that selfe same heart, that vow,........134. H.336, 70
No lust theres like to Poetry.................135. H.336, 112
Troth Lady, **no**...............................137. H.340, 6
Ther's in love, **no** bitternesse..................138. H.346, 10
Ther's **no** vice now, but has his president.......139. H.352, 2
Whether or **no**, that we shall meet here ever.....140. H.355, 4
Or **no**, shall give ye a re-meeting here...........140. H.355, 8
Curse not the mice, **no** grist of thine they eat:....141. H.358, 1
Demands **no** money by a craving way;..........142. H.363, 2
No, know (Blest Maide) when there's not one...146. H.376, 7
For **no** black-bearded Vigil from thy doore......146. H.377, 13
For thou **no** Porter keep'st who strikes.........146. H.377, 18
No commer to thy Roofe his Guest-rite wants;..146. H.377, 19
His Stomach to a second Meale. **No**, **no**,......147. H.377, 33
No such crab'd vizard: Thou hast learnt thy Train, 147. H.377, 35
Keeping **no** currish Waiter to affright,........147. H.377, 47
No, **no**, thy bread, thy wine, thy jocund Beere..147. H.377, 57
No scurrile jest; **no** open Sceane is laid.......148. H.377, 77
No One that's there his guilty glasse..........148. H.377, 86
No, thou know'st order, Ethicks, and ha's read..148. H.377, 89
When what is strongly built, **no** chinke........148. H.377, 106
Of others; since **no** Stud, **no** Stone, **no** Piece,..149. H.377, 117
No Widowes Tenement was rackt to guild....149. H.377, 119
No Orphans pittance, left him, serv'd to set....149. H.377, 123
No Planke from Hallowed Altar, do's appeale..149. H.377, 127
Skrew lives by shifts; yet sweares by **no** small oathes; 149. H.380, 1
And sweetly sings, but yet his breath sayes **no**...149. H.381, 2
No Holy-Rage, or frantick-fires did stirre,......150. H.382, 9
No clap of hands, or shout, or praises-proofe...150. H.382, 11
No, not the glory of the World, Vandike.......150. H.384, 6
Ile have **no** Sceans, or Curtains drawn:.........154. H.402, 2
No, **no**, thy Stars have destin'd Thee to see..155. H.405, 15
Thrice I have washt, but feel **no** cold,.........157. H.413, 3
Since thou art gone, **no** more I mean to play,..159. H.421, 9
And dales again: Mir. **No** I will languish still;..159. H.421, 36
No, but because the Ding-thrift now is poore,....160. H.423, 3
And have **no** name..........................161. H.426, 12
Roots had **no** money; yet he went o'th score....162. H.427, 1
There wo'd be **no** Passion.....................163. H.433, 2
That they **no** better do agree..................163. H.434, 3
'Tis fit they make **no** One with them too great..163. H.438, 2
No Marigolds yet closed are;..................164. H.441, 5
No shadowes great appeare;...................164. H.441, 6
What here I promise, that **no** Broom.........165. H.442, 13
To lye with Mab, though all say **no**............165. H.443, 12
Lust ha's **no** eares; He's sharpe as thorn;......165. H.443, 13
No glaring light of bold-fac't Day,.............167. H.443, 76
So neatly sunck, as that **no** proof...........167. H.443, 103
He'll do **no** doubt; This flax is spun..........168. H.443, 121
Husht be all things; (**no** noyse here)...........170. H.450, 3
No Furie, or **no** Fire-brand to me...............170. H.452, 6
Huncks ha's **no** money (he do's sweare, or say)..173. H.463, 1
Though thou art young, thou canst say **no**,....174. H.465, 34
And **no** again, and so deny,....................174. H.465, 35
No, live thee to thy selfe, and keep...........175. H.465, 47
Banish consent, and 'tis **no** sinne.............175. H.465, 56
Returning, if 't be mine or **no**:................175. H.465, 72

As that your pans no Ebbe may know;........179. H.476, 11
That Scarr's no Schisme, but the sign of grace. 180. H.481, 2
Then no gazing more about,..................180. H.482, 3
So, that an Author needs no other Bayes.......188. H.506, 11
And no one mischief greater then your frown,..188. H.506, 13
And 'gainst your chast behaviour there's no Plea, 189. H.511, 3
Here needs no Court for our Request,..........190. H.515, 29
Where Fortune bears no sway o're things......190. H.515, 35
The Wearer's no meane Shepheardesse.........192. H.521, 24
And yet our way has no ending..............195. H.534, 12
Fortune no higher Project can devise,..........196, H.535, 1
And no more;..............................196. H.538, 2
There's no Carousing........................197. H.540, 8
I did not sup, because no friends were there......197. H.541, 2
No man exempted is from Death, or sinne.......199. H.548, 2
No part of pitie on a conquer'd foe...........199. H.550, 2
For quick dispatch, Sculls made no longer stay,.200. H.551, 3
Here we rejoyce, because no Rent.............200. H.552, 7
Because we feed on no mans score:............200. H.552, 14
Where no disease raignes, or infection comes....205. H.575, 5
So double gilds the Aire, as that no night......206. H.575, 15
Now tis in's Hand, he gives no Almes at all.....207. H.577, 4
All are alike faire, when no spots we see.......209. H.586, 2
Leaving no Fame to long Posterity:............210. H.592, 2
No places are.............................211. H.596, 9
For very little, or no gaines:..................212. H.602, 2
Little or no part there of Tyrannie.............213. H.608, 2
Because no fence,..........................213. H.609, 2
No wrath of Men, or rage of Seas............215. H.615, 1
No threats of Tyrants, or the Grim...........215. H.615, 3
No cruell truths of Philomell,................215. H.616, 12
No Will-o'th'-Wispe mis-light thee;...........217. H.619, 6
I make no haste to have my Numbers read......218. H.623, 1
Make no long stay..........................220. H.633, 6
Then these, no feares more on your Fancies fall,.222. H.634, 14
Though then I smile, and speake no words at all. 222. H.634, 15
Of which who drank, he said no thought........222. H.635, 3
No Goose layes good eggs that is trodden drye...223. H.636, 4
Fates revolve no Flax th'ave spun.............224. H.639, 4
No Beast, for his food,......................225. H.643, 13
No man comes late unto that place from whence.228. H.656, 1
No, thy Ambition's Master-piece...............229. H.662, 11
Flies no thought higher then a fleece:..........229. H.662, 12
And no man payes too deare for it.............231. H.662, 61
No, no, the utmost share....................231. H.663, 5
No; 'tis a life, to have thine oyle,.............233. H.670, 7
No sound recalls the houres once fled,.........233. H.670, 24
No sillable doth fall here,....................235. H.674, 11
Their fashion is, but to say no, to take it.......235. H.675, 2
Love at no time idle is:.....................235. H.678, 2
No man despaires to do what's done before.....236. H.680, 2
And no Verse illegitimate....................236. H.681, 6
Health is no other (as the learned hold).........236. H.683, 1
No return from thence we have...............238. H.691, 6
In no one Satyre there's a mite of salt..........238. H.692, 2
No joy to thee their sickly Lord..............239. H.696, 12
Need is no vice at all; though here it be,........239. H.698, 1
Glory no other thing is (Tullie sayes)..........241. H.710, 1
No, but when the Spirit fils..................242. H.714, 3
But of all packs, no pack like poverty..........242. H.715, 2
I am a bird, and though no name I tell,........248. H.730, 7
Or money? no, but onely deaw and sweat.......248. H.731, 2
They fall like dew, but make no noise at all.....250. H.737, 4
And Aire-like, leave no pression to be seen.....250. H.737, 7
Leaving no shew, where stood the Capitoll.....252. H.745, 16
And possesse no other feare,..................255. H.761, 23
And no whit further must venture;............256. H.762, 9
No pennie, no Pater Noster..................256. H.762, 18
Where no foot hath.........................258. H.770, 3
No Brutus entring here;....................259. H.772, 5
Although he has no riches,...................259. H.772, 17
And for no less then Aromatick Wine..........262. H.783, 9
I'le bring a Fever; since thou keep'st no fire...262. H.783, 22
We pray 'gainst Warre, yet we enjoy no Peace..264. H.793, 1
Bice laughs, when no man speaks; and doth protest 265. H.795, 1
It is no other then the Bed...................269. H.815, 3
No question then, but such a lick is sweet,......269. H.816, 3
'Twas Cesars saying: Kings no lesse Conquerors are 271. H.825, 1
Fortune her selfe can lay no claim to it.........272. H.830, 2
Love has yet no wrathfull fit:................273. H.836, 6
Beauti's no other but a lovely Grace..........274. H.840, 1
Only for my wound there's no remedy..........274. H.841, 2
No, but because he wo'd not have it seen,......275. H.843, 3
No other, but the doers willingnesse...........275. H.845, 2
Back to come, (and make no stay.)............276. H.848, 3
Twilight, no other thing is, Poets say,..........278. H.858, 1
Our Crosses are no other then the rods,........278. H.862, 1
No otherwise, then if he would................279. H.863, 7
Night makes no difference 'twixt the Priest and Clark; 279. H.864, 1
Thou saist thou lov'st me Sapho; I say no;.....279. H.866, 1
Altar cleane, no fire prophane?................280. H.870, 6
No cowards must his royall Ensignes beare......280. H.872, 2
Naught are all Women: I say no,.............283. H.885, 1
The old Hag in. No surer thing...............284. H.890, 6
Can do no mischiefe (there.)................285. H.893, 8
Betwixt us two no more Logomachie..........287. H.901, 4
And no less prais'd, then spread throughout the world. 288. H.907, 6
Of such a wit the world sho'd have no more.....289. H.911, 20
Yet send no Boules to him?...................290. H.918, 4
Till that the Cooke cries, Bring no more........291. H.919, 4
Though from without no foes at all we feare;....292. H.928, 1
None is discreet at all times; no, not Jove.....294. H.936, 3
And though I saw no Bow, I'm sure,..........295. H.942, 15
No, no, Ile be..............................296. H.946, 13
No man such rare parts hath, that he can swim,.298. H.953, 1
And no lesse prais'd, then of the maides admir'd..299. H.956, 10
Vineger is no other I define,..................301. H.964, 1
Now thou art dead, no eye shall ever see,.......302. H.967, 1
This for no meane miracle;....................302. H.968, 8
About their House, their clamorous I, or No:...303. H.975, 4
No one least Branch there left behind:.........304. H.980, 6
If so, no...................................307. H.988, 10
Care keepes the Conquest; 'tis no lesse renowne,.307. H.989, 1
Despaire takes heart, when ther's no hope to speed: 309. H.999, 1
I think no other but I see....................311. H.1010, 3
But yet no end of those therein or me:.........313. H.1019, 2
No Kingdomes got by Rapine long endure......314. H.1023, 2
She sees no teares,..........................314. H.1024, 9
That ye singe no maiden-haire................315. H.1026, 8
No drought upon thy wanton waters fall......316. H.1028, 19
No ruffling winds come hither to discease......316. H.1028, 21
Tis no discomfort in the world to fall,.........319. H.1045, 1
The Twi-light is no other thing (we say).......319. H.1046, 1
No grief is grown so desperate, but the ill......319. H.1048, 1
No man dies ill, that liveth well..............321. H.1059, 2
No man so well a Kingdome Rules, as He,....325. H.1074, 1
No question but Dols cheeks wo'd soon rost dry, 325. H.1078, 1
(A happy Realme! When no compulsive Law,..326. H.1080, 19
I will no longer kiss,........................328. H.1091, 1
Spur jingles now, and sweares by no meane oathes, 330. H.1099, 1
No plague ther's like to foolishnesse..........332. H.1115, 2
When feare admits no hope of safety, then....333. H.1118, 1
Although our suffering meet with no reliefe,....333. H.1119, 1
The sweetest solace is to act no sin.............341. N.13, 2
And though it takes all in, 'tis yet no more......341. N.15, 5
In Gilead though no Balme be found,...........342. N.17, 5
If God should punish no sin, here, of men,.......343. N.27, 3
No one hope, but of his Fees..................347. N.41, 14
No man is blest through ev'ry part.............351. N.50, 4
No, no, (my God) Thou know'st my wishes be..352. N.51, 13
For, 'tis no easie way from Earth to Heaven.....352. N.52, 4
Among Gods Blessings, there is no one small.....353. N.55, 2
So utter dark, as that no eye..................357. N.72, 7
Yet if Thy Bloud not wash me, there's no hope...357. N.73, 4
No Arrow nockt, onely a stringlesse Bow:.......357. N.74, 2
Night hath no wings, to him that cannot sleep;...358. N.77, 1
And make no one stop, till my race be done.....358. N.77, 15
No, no; our Maiden-pleasures be..............361. N.83, 55
May no Wolfe howle, or Screech-Owle stir......361. N.83, 67
No boysterous winds, or stormes, come hither,..361. N.83, 69
And have a care no fire gos out,...............365. N.97, 5
No jot of Leven must be found................366. N.98, 3
But let no Christmas mirth begin..............366. N.98, 7
Evill no Nature hath; the losse of good........367. N.101, 1
No, this ye need not do;.....................367. N.102, 12
Unto the prison, I'le say, no;.................370. N.107, 12
But take no tincture from my sinfull Book;......371. N.113, 8
Which has no root, and cannot grow,..........371. N.114, 2
Hell is no other, but a soundlesse pit,..........372. N.117, 1
Where no one beame of comfort peeps in it.......372. N.117, 2
In all that way no beaten path;................372. N.118, 4
But no one Jailer there to wash the wounds......372. N.120, 2
Chor. No, or thy zeale so speedy,.............374. N.123, 47
Let me say grace when there's no more........376. N.124, 6
There no monstrous fancies shall..............377. N.128, 13
Bleeding, that no Blood touch the ground:......377. N.129, 6
God He refuseth no man; but makes way........378. N.131, 1
Sending them forth, Salute no man by th' way:..378. N.137, 2
God tempteth no one (as S. Aug'stine saith)....380. N.150, 1
Starves, having no companion.................381. N.158, 2
Had no one Beame from Gods sweet Majestie....382. N.167, 4
No number of the Plurall hath................382. N.168, 2
Sin no Existence; Nature none it hath,.........383. N.173, 1
No other, then Christs full Affection............383. N.174, 2
No crack or Schisme leave i'th subtill skin:.....385. N.184, 2
So the Divine Hand work't, and brake no thred,..385. N.184, 3
Of locall motion, in no least respect,...........385. N.186, 3
But no more Woman, being strong in Faith;....386. N.192, 3
There is no evill that we do commit,............386. N.196, 1
No man is tempted so, but may o'recome,........389. N.211, 1
Say, 'tis not free, 'tis then no sin at all........389. N.218, 2
No, but He drest Him with our humane Trim,...390. N.222, 3

There's **no** constraint to do amisse,..............390. N.225, 1
May chance to be **no** other man, but Christ......391. N.226, 2
No: 'tis a Fast, to dole......................391. N.228, 13
No spring of Time, or Times succession.........392. N.229, 2
Though to be tempted be **no** sin, untill.........392. N.230, 31
No, lay thy stately terrours by,................393. N.232, 7
No, **No**, this Scene from Thee takes life and sense, 399. N.263, 26
Have, have ye **no** regard, all ye................400. N.266, 1
By **no** ill haunted; here I come,................402. N.269, 2
No one step from this Sepulcher...............402. N.269, 19
And, coveting **no** higher sphere,...............402. N.269, 24
For 'tis Fee simple, and **noe** rent.................407. A.2, 13
Att what tyme to say I, or **noe**,................407. A.2, 26
Noe otherwise then as those former two..........410. A.3, 14
Like fier-drakes, yett did'st mee **no** harme therby..410. A.3, 28
Whether the world such Sperritts had or **noe**......411. A.3, 38
In speach, in Picture; **noe** otherwise then when..411. A.3, 61
That sees **noe** setting Sunn.....................413. A.4, 15
Of King and **no** King (and the rare Plott thine)..415. A.7, 14
No trust to Metals nor to Marbles, when.........419. A.10, 1
Encurlld together, and **noe** difference show.431. ins. H.283, 50f
Wee have **noe** vinyards which doe beare...436. ins. H.336, 48a
Wee have **noe** bath....................436. ins. H.336, 48k
Of fortune can have **noe** command,......436. ins. H.336, 48n
List of references:............17. H.42, 1; 43. H.123, 18; 44. H.126, 3; 49. H.136, 35; 53. H.149, 17; 60. H.159, 3; 100. H.246, 8; 100. H.249, 2; 111. H.277, 2; 122. H.304, 1; 122. H.304, 7; 131. H.333, 1; 131. H.333, 3; 132. H.333, 5; 132. H.333, 7; 139. H.353, 4; 141. H.359, 3; 143. H.367, 1; 144. H.371, 1; 162. H.426, 17; 185. H.496, 7; 186. H.500, 2; 187. H.506, 7; 189. H.514, 3; 204. H.570, 1; 209. H.585, 7; 212. H.602, 4; 214. H.611, 1; 218. H.626, 14; 228, H.658, 1; 228. H.658, 3; 228. H.658, 4; 228. H.658, 5; 228. H.658, 7; 228. H.658, 8; 234. H.671, 2; 237. H.687, 8; 241. H.712, 1; 254. H.756, 5; 255. H.758, 4; 296. H.946, 22; 299. H.958, 3; 301. H.966, 4; 314. H.1024, 24; 315. H.1028, 3; 315. H.1028, 7; 328. H.1091, 2; 334. H.1124, 1; 334. H.1124, 3; 352. N.53, 2; 360. N.83, 49; 361. N.83, 51; 368. N.104, 1; 383. N.170, 1; 407. A.2, 1; 413. A.4, 1; 424 var. H.164, 10; 436. var. H.336, 3; 440. var. H.443, 77; 445. var. H.730, 18; 450. var. A.9, 3; 451. ins. H.336, 48c.

Noah **Noah** the first was (as Tradition sayes)....386. N.195, 1

Noble But trust to this, my **noble** passenger;......23. N.71, 3
Teares are the **noble** language of the eye.........58. H.150, 6
Foule in these **noble** pastimes, lest ye call......114. H.283, 86
A **noble** perfume from the fire.................145. H.375, 18
(Not without glory) **Noble** Sir, you are,........170. H.451, 2
For to thanke you (**Noble** Sir)..................182. H.489, 11
Which Love and **noble** freedome is;............198. H.544, 28
Co'd a **noble** Verse beget;....................217. H.620, 5
Alive, as **Noble** Westmorland;.................218. H.626, 11
To **noble** Discipline!..........................228. H.657, 3
Who will not honour **Noble** Numbers, when.....264. H.791, 1
And (**Noble** friend) this answer I must give:..312. H.1013, 2
— — — — — — — — —, ...430. var. H.283, 6

Nobler To adde a **nobler** Planet to the seven?....112. H.283, 6
For these, and **Nobler** numbers can.............279. H.868, 3
Give Him the choice; grant Him the **nobler** part..356. N.68, 3
To welcome Him. 2. The **nobler** part...........365. N.96, 27

Nobly And mark it for a Rapture **nobly** writ,.....64. H.168, 9
We'll **nobly** think, what's to be done,..........168. H.443, 120
As made us **nobly** wild, not mad;...............289. H.911, 8

Nobly-home-bred Theyre **Nobly-home-bread**, yett haue price 409. A.2, 93

Nocked No Arrow **nockt**, onely a stringlesse Bow: 357. N.74, 2

Nod The leavie-trees **nod** in a still-born peace...105. H.259, 6
Nod to this vow of mine:.......................228. H.657, 4
And I **nod** to what is said,....................348. N.41, 30

Nodding That scarcely stirs the **nodding** leaves of Trees: 225. H.642, 16

Nodes Where ever **Nodes** do's in the Summer come, 270. H.822, 1
What store of Corn has carefull **Nodes**, thinke you, 270. H.822, 3

'Noint See Annoint
And **'noint** with Tirian Balme; for when........133. H.336, 34

Noise And comming downe, shall make no **noise** at all. 21. H.62, 6
As, could they hear, the Damn'd would make no **noise**, 22. H.67, 2
Any **noise**, they both will wake,.................52. H.145, 4
From **noise** of Scare-fires rest ye free,...........121. H.299, 1
No **noise** of late spawn'd Tittyries:............126. H.319, 2
Into the **noise**................................144. H.371, 17
Husht be all things; (no **noyse** here)..........170. H.450, 3
With **noise**, the servants eyes from sleep........179. H.476, 33
They fall like dew, but make no **noise** at all.....250. H.737, 4
Come, bring with a **noise**,.....................263. H.784, 1

Noiseless Deep waters **noyse-lesse** are; And this we know, 15. H.38, 9
Like **noyse-lesse** Snow; or as the dew of night:..100. H.247, 2
They **noiselesse** spill their Influence:...........340. N.3, 14

Nominate Of that, which we do **nominate** the Left. 394. N.240, 2

None Ha's she thinne haire, hath she **none**,........11. H.21, 13
Which are so cleane, so chast, as **none** may feare..28. H.84, 5
Or Verse I covet **none**;.........................30. H.89, 2
None then will wooe you.........................32. H.94, 12
To Bread and Water **none** is poore;.............33. H.100, 1
None goes to warfare, but with this intent;.......42. H.120, 1
Glasco had **none**, but now some teeth has got;...46. H.129, 1
To th'board, so hot, as **none** co'd touch the same:.47. H.131, 2
But **none** co'd eate it, 'cause it stunk so much....47. H.131, 6
And kissing, so as **none** may heare,..............59. H.152, 11
In your loves; but **none** as I....................62. H.162, 3
Since **none** so good are, but you may condemne;..64. H.168, 5
Heare all men speak; but credit few or **none**......67. H.177, 4
Into thy loving hands: For Ile keep **none**.......73. H.186, 15
Stirs in our Sheep-walk? Amin. **None**, save that my Ewes, 85. H.213, 4
Smooth, faire, and fat; **none** better I can tell:...86. H.213, 6
Gold I've **none**, for use or show,................88. H.218, 1
And entitle **none** to be........................108. H.266, 11
And having **none**, yet I will keep.............109. H.267, 15
But now, we see, **none** here,........... ....110. H.274, 13
So old she was, that **none** co'd tell her yeares....129. H.326, 6
But **none** enquires if good he be, or no..........130. H.328, 2
As Fate do's lead or draw us; **none**,............132. H.336, 6
None, Posthumus, co'd ere decline..............132. H.336, 7
Cherrish the cheek, but make **none** blush at all..140. H.354, 12
That henceforth **none** be Laurel crown'd but Thee. 150. H.383, 2
So draw, and paint, as **none** may do the like,....150. H.384, 5
Why weres he **none**? Because we may suppose,..154. H.401, 3
The feast of Shepheards fail. Sil. **None** crowns the cup 159. H.421, 3
If he ha's **none** in's pockets, trust me, Hunncks...173. H.463, 3
Ha's **none** at home, in Coffers, Desks, or Trunks..173. H.463, 4
In having all, that thou hast **none**.............174. H.465, 10
So Medullina fell, yet **none**...................175. H.465, 59
Their silv'rie Spheres, ther's **none** may doubt,....178. H.476, 8
Alas! we blesse, but see **none** here,............179. H.476, 25
Taken in by **none** but Thee.....................186. H.499, 4
None shall be guiltlesse, be he n'er so good.....194. H.528, 2
Strewings need **none**, every flower.............199. H.546, 5
To very few, or else to **none**...................200. H.552, 20
Will tell thee Pitie thou hast **none**.............203. H.564, 6
Since Ghost ther's **none** to affright thee.........217. H.619, 10
Then for effusions, let **none** wanting be,.........219. H.627, 5
None pities him that's in the snare,............219. H.628, 11
Holds **none** at all, or little in his hand..........221. H.633, 53
Besides rare sweets, I had a Book which **none**..227. H.652, 5
None loseth that, which he in time may get.......228. H.654, 2
But her self held fast by **none**.................232. H.665, 14
Adopted some; **none** got by theft..............236. H.681, 4
Too much she gives to some, enough to **none**.....238. H.689, 2
Adversity hurts **none**, but onely such...........239. H.697, 1
To tell how night drawes hence, I've **none**,......246. H.724, 2
None is, slight things do lightly please.........246. H.724, 32
None are so harsh, but if they find.............252. H.746, 5
None sees the fardell of his faults behind.........253. H.751, 2
In love with **none**, but me...................258. H.767, 20
But when he sings a Psalme, ther's **none** can be..266. H.799, 3
None is discreet at all times; no, not Jove.......294. H.936, 3
In depth of silence, heard, and seene of **none**...298. H.954, 3
That **none** hereafter sho'd be thought, or be......299. H.956, 3
I must confess, distinction **none** I see..........301. H.966, 9
I have **none**; but must be sure................302. H.968, 5
None of these; but out, alas!................305. H.984, 10
Where thrice we knock, and **none** will heare,..312. H.1014, 9
Perilla smile on **none** but me.................313. H.1020, 2
Great Cities seldome rest: If there be **none**....316. H.1030, 1
Since shed or Cottage I have **none**,.............321. H.1056, 1
The meane passe by, or over, **none** contemne;..322. H.1062, 7
If seen, thou lik'st me, Deb, in **none** of these..331. H.1108, 2
Has, or **none**, or little skill,.....................347. N.41, 18
God will have all, or **none**; serve Him, or fall....353. N.54, 1
Yet **none** of these have made me sad:............354. N.57, 2
Tell Him, for Corall, thou hast **none**;...........354. N.59, 11
Satan o'recomes **none**, but by willingnesse........359. N.79, 2
Hence, hence prophane, and **none** appeare........366. N.98, 1
For, once in hell, **none** knowes Remission there...367. N.99, 2
Gold I have **none**, but I present my need,.......369. N.105, 1
God had but one Son free from sin; but **none**....378. N.134, 1
Angells are called Gods; yet of them, **none**......379. N.143, 1
As just Men are intitled Gods, yet **none**........379. N.143, 3
But **none**, of purpose, to be overcome............380. N.150, 4
Freely from them, and hold **none** back at all.....380. N.151, 2
Sin no Existence; Nature **none** it hath...........383. N.173, 1
One Birth our Saviour had; the like **none** yet....384. N.182, 1
Originall of Essence there is **none**..............386. N.191, 3
God gives to **none** so absolute an Ease..........387. N.199, 1
First, that these goods **none** here may o're esteem, 387. N.201, 3
Next, that these ills **none** cowardly may shun;...387. N.201, 5
Of many standing, but of fall to **none**...........389. N.215, 2
Gods Prescience makes **none** sinfull; but th' offence 390. N.225, 1
Who shewing mercy here, few priz'd, or **none**.....393. N.234, 2
Given by **none**, but by Thy selfe, to me:.......398. N.262, 2

Our holy Spicknard, & ther's none..............413. A.4, 25
None writes lov's passion in the world, like Thee...415. A.7, 18
Most maye smile, beleiue will none,..............418. A.9, 36
To be of that high Hyrarchy, where none..443. var. H.575, 59
Noon Which shining in her perfect Noone;.......49. H.136, 29
At Noone of Day, was seene a silver Star,....86. H.213, 20
Has not attain'd his Noone..................125. H.316, 4
At noone of Night are a working...............225. H.643, 18
By noone, and let thy good dayes passe,........233. H.670, 4
At last, i' th' noone of winter, did appeare......262. H.783, 13
It is Noone and past with me:..................307. H.991, 2
And threaten at noone.......................333. H.1122, 11
Past Noone of night, yett weare the howers not old
410. A.3, 18
Like an Eternall Noone.........................413. A.4, 14
Whether in the morne or noone..................418. A.9, 45
Noonday Noone-day and Midnight shall at once be seene:
59. H.154, 1
Noose A glorious end by such a Noose,.........279. H.863, 11
Nor (Partial List)
Nor wrack, or Bulging thou hast cause to feare:.23. H.71, 2
Nor can we that a ruine call,.....................25. H.76, 3
Nor wil't be long, ere this accomplish'd be;......26. H.79, 9
In wayes confus'd, nor slip or fall..............33. H.98, 10
Nor has the darknesse power to usher in........35. H.106, 39
Nor can these figures so thy rest endeare,......36. H.106, 55
Nor are thy daily and devout affaires...........36. H.106, 63
Nor are thine eares so deafe, but thou canst heare
36. H.106, 83
Nor car'st which comes the first, the foule or faire;
37. H.106, 97
Nor is it, that thou keep'st this stricter size....37. H.106, 117
Nor feare, or wish your dying day..............38. H.106, 146
Nor will I seek supply..........................43. H.123, 19
Nor name those wanton reaks..................56. H.149, 117
Nor can Juno sweeter be,........................59. H.155, 9
Nor the Snow continue pure:...................60. H.159, 14
Nor be you proud, that you can see..........61. H.160, 3
Nor any bed to give the shew.................63. H.164, 10
Nor any was preferr'd 'fore me...............70. H.181, 2
Nor Cloe was of more respect;................70. H.181, 6
Nor doth this far-drawn Hemisphere...........72. H.185, 3
Nor daunces in the eye.........................75. H.193, 10
Nor cheek, or tongue be dumbe:...............80. H.201, 2
Nor in a forme Triangular;....................91. H.223, 55
Nor made of glasse, or wood, or stone,..........91. H.223, 56
Nor felt th'unkind............................104. H.257, 8
Nor are ye worne with yeares;..................104. H.257, 10
And leave no sound; nor piety,..................132. H.336, 2
No roofs of Cedar, nor our brave...............133. H.336, 42
Baiæ, nor keep.................................133. H.336, 43
Nor Bullocks fed...............................133. H.336, 45
To kisse our hands, nor do we wish.........133. H.336, 47
Nor suffer you the Poets to sit cold,............141. H.359, 7
Have I not blest Thee? Then go forth; nor fear.155. H.405, 1
Nor thinke these Ages that do hoarcely sing....155. H.405, 5
I do not love, nor can it be...................155. H.406, 1
Nor find that true, which was foretold.........157. H.413, 4
That h'ad nor Gold or Silver to put in't?.......162. H.427, 4
That on the seaventh, he can nor preach, or pray.
163. H.435, 4
Nor doth the early Shepheards Starre...........164. H.441, 7
Nor so immured wo'd I have....................174. H.465, 11
Nor wo'd I have thee thinke, that Thou......176. H.465, 81
Nor Bee, or Hive you have be mute;..........179. H.476, 17
Nor will; for why, Pudica, this may know,.......180. H.477, 5
Nor leave the search, and proofe, till Thou canst find
181. H.483, 3
Nor will they leave Thee, till they both have shown
181. H.483, 7
Nor do's it mind the Rustick straines..........184. H.492, 23
Nor that fine Worme that do's interre..........186. H.497, 13
Nor my rare *Phil, that lately was............186. H.497, 15
Nor need we here to feare the frowne..........190. H.515, 33
Nor is my Number full, till I inscribe...........199. H.545, 1
Nor courts thou Her because she's well attended..201. H.557, 7
Nor did I know, or co'd descry..................203. H.563, 3
Be bold my Booke, nor be abasht, or feare......212. H.603, 1
Nor Snake, or Slow-worme bite thee:..........217. H.619, 7
Nor, Faire, must you be loth...................221. H.633, 35
Nor shall the Tapers when I'm there, burn blew..222. H.634, 9
Ile sing no more, nor will I longer write........228. H.658, 1
Ile write no more, nor will I tell or sing........228. H.658, 5
Nor to the Eastern Ind dost rove...............229. H.662, 7
Nor, with the losse of thy lov'd rest,..........229. H.662, 9
Famish me, nor over-fill.......................232. H.665, 18
Nor us (my Friend) when we are lost,........233. H.670, 26
Nor is't a life, seven yeares to tell,............233. H.670, 34
Nor let the shackles make thee sad;..........246. H.725, 3
Ch. What's that to me, I waft nor fish or fowles,.248. H.730, 9
Nor Beasts (fond thing) but only humane soules.
248. H.730, 10
Nor art thou lesse esteem'd, that I have plac'd..256. H.763, 1
Nor Cato the severe............................259. H.772, 6
Nor dreads he any thing:.....................259. H.772, 12
Nor let my Herse, be wept upon by thee:........281. H.875, 2
Nor do's she minde,..........................314. H.1024, 13
Nor in the summers sweeter evenings go,......315. H.1028, 5
Nor will hereafter; since I know.............320. H.1052, 3
Nor thinke that Thou in this my Booke art worst,
329. H.1092, 1
Nor shall the seas,...........................335. H.1129, 6
Nor shalt thou give so deep a wound,..........351. N.48, 9
Salute we must, nor Strangers, Kin, or Friends.
378. H.137, 8
Nor yet for houses, which are here............381. N.158, 7
Nor makes it matter, Nestors yeers to tell,......392. N.230, 5
Nor wo'd I care how short it were, if good:....392. N.230, 10
We are Coheires with Christ; nor shall His own.395. N.248, 1
Nor dull'd wth Iron sleeps; but haue out-worne..410. A.3, 19
Nor Fate, nor Enuye, cann theyr Fames Conuince,
411. A.3, 40
Nor stoope to'th Center, but suruiue as Longe....411. A.3, 45
Spring hence thy faith, nor thinke it ill desert....414. A.6, 3
No trust to Metals nor to Marbles, when........419. A.10, 1
Nor knowe thy happye, and vn-enuey'de state
422. ins. H.106, 92a
— — — — — — — — — — — —, ...422. var. H.106, 117
— — — — — — — — — — — —, ...423. var. H.128, 29
— — — — — — — — — — — —, ...426. var. H.197, 33
— — — — — — — — — — — —, ...434. var. H.293, 36
— — — — — — — — — — — —,.............436. var. H.336, 3
Nor odoriferous...........................436. ins. H.336, 48c
Nor gall the seas,.......................436. ins. H.336, 48e
Nor can wee glory of a great............436. ins. H.336, 48i
— — — — — — — — — — — —, ...438. var. H.367, 1
— — — — — — — — — — — —, ...440. var. H.443, 77
— — — — — — — — — — — —, ...441. var. H.465, 22
— — — — — — — — — — — —, ...441. var. H.465, 44
— — — — — — — — — — — —, ...451. var. H.336, 10
North Who to the North, or South, doth set....162. H.429, 1
Plac't North and South, for these cleane purposes;
386. N.193, 2
North-down With North-down Ale doth troule here,
235. H.674, 10
Northern Never had been the Northern Plunderer
224. H.642, 10
Where the Northern Winds do blow..........266. H.803, 2
Nose That an Acre hath of Nose:................11. H.21, 6
His nose and lips of mulbrie hiew.............38. H.108, 8
He'll slit her nose; But blubb'ring, she replyes,..44. H.126, 2
The world had all one Nose...................80. H.201, 24
And a nose that is the grace.................138. H.342, 7
Where Leaven wants, there Levill lies the nose..154. H.401, 4
His Nose is over-cool'd with Isicles..........210. H.589, 2
He'l sell her Eyes, and Nose, for Beere and Ale..272. H.829, 4
Tom Blinks his Nose is full of wheales, and these
273. H.834, 1
By his Probossis that he is all nose...........284. H.886, 2
Which, this night hardned, sodders up her nose..296. H.945, 2
The Barber stopt his Nose, and ranne away....323. H.1066, 4
Her comly nose with vniformall grace..........404. A.1, 11
Nosed See Hook-nosed, Wry-nosed
Noses And noses tann'd with Beere............219. H.629, 4
Noster No pennie, no Pater Noster............256. H.762, 18
Nostrils The free-born Nosthrills of the King,....126. H.319, 8
Not (Partial List) See Cannot
Mir. Not so, not so. Chor. But if it chance to prove
86. H.213, 27
Note A winning wave (deserving Note)...........28. H.83, 9
And never purls a Note?.......................183. H.492, 4
The soft, the sweet, the mellow note..........243. H.716, 17
Chor. A suger'd note! and sound as sweet....243. H.716, 29
My warbling note will say I'm Phylomel.......248. H.730, 8
Ph. Alas for me! Ch. Shame on thy witching note,
248. H.730, 11
As my small Pipe best fits my little note.......249. H.733, 15
Notes To drink in Notes, and Numbers; such.....22. H.68, 3
With direful notes to fright your sleeps:......56. H.149, 102
And on the seaventh, he has his Notes to seek...163. H.435, 2
With warbling Notes, her Tyrrean sufferings....224. H.642, 8
Nothing I freeze, I freeze, and nothing dwels......8. H.13, 1
Nothing but love can supple me;...............8. H.13, 6
And nothing I did say:........................24. H.75, 2
And nothing have...............................43. H.123, 34
To safe-guard Man from wrongs, there nothing must
67. H.177, 1
To guard it so, as nothing here shall be........73. H.186, 19
Nothing hot, or nothing cold...................116. H.285, 2
Herrick keeps, as holds nothing................117. H.285, 12
Of largeness, when th'are nothing so:...........118. H.291, 10
Why nothing now, but lonely sit,..............132. H.334, 3
Unto an almost nothing; then,.................134. H.336, 79
Nothing is New: we walk where others went...139. H.352, 1
That nothing shoots, but war and woe..........139. H.353, 6
Nothing comes Free-cost here; Jove will not let.177. H.469, 1
Nothing to distemper you;....................177. H.472, 2
In nothing chang'd but in their name...........180. H.478, 8
Nothing can be more loathsome, then to see....211. H.597, 1
Nothing hard, or harsh can prove..............240. H.701, 1
Ch. A sound I heare, but nothing yet can see,..248. H.730, 5
Maids nay's are nothing, they are shie.........249. H.735, 1

All now is silent; groanes are fled:............189. H.514, 5
What now we like, anon we disapprove:.......191. H.517, 1
Next, hang'd for Theeving: Now the people say,.195. H.532, 3
Since now to the Port......................195. H.534, 10
In which thy Father Johnson now is plac't,....207. H.575, 57
Of late struck one; and now I see the prime...207. H.575, 63
Now tis in's Hand, he gives no Almes at all....207. H.577, 4
She now weares silk to hide her blood-shot eye..207. H.578, 2
The Proper Lessons for the Saints now dead:..209. H.584, 2
Therefore now Ile love no more,..............209. H.585, 7
Now is sick:.................................210. H.591, 9
The Ev'ning's come; here now Ile stop,.......212. H.602, 3
Lost to all Musick now; since every thing......214. H.612, 3
As now a Satyr, then a Swan;.................215. H.616, 17
A Bull but then; and now a man...............215. H.616, 18
So I, now having rid my way;.................216. H.617, 3
Dearest of thousands, now the time drawes neere,
219. H.627, 1
Fled are the Frosts, and now the Fields appeare.224. H.642, 1
Thaw'd are the snowes, and now the lusty Spring
224. H.642, 3
Now swaggers in her Leavy gallantry...........224. H.642, 6
Now out, and then in,........................225. H.643, 5
With a lash of a Bramble she rides now,.......225. H.643, 9
She followes the Spirit that guides now..........225. H.643, 12
Dares now range the wood;...................225. H.643, 14
He'l never haunt ye now he's dead.............226. H.644, 10
But now 'tis clos'd; and being shut, & seal'd,..227. H.652, 11
Come then, and now enspire..................228. H.657, 5
When now the Cock (the Plow-mans Horne)...230. H.662, 19
Give way, give way, now, now my Charles shines here,
236. H.685, 1
Let us now take time, and play,..............238. H.691, 1
Now give me the cup;........................239. H.695, 2
And tells the world, he's now regenerate........240. H.703, 2
The stakes are laid: let's now apply............243. H.716, 19
But hark how I can now expresse.............243. H.716, 27
Now for to win thy Heifer faire,..............243. H.716, 31
Whose now the prize and wager is............244. H.716, 42
By tears and pitie now to come unto mee.......248. H.730, 2
Ch. What's thy request? Ph. That since she's now beneath
248. H.730, 15
But feares not now to see her safety sold.....251. H.745, 5
What Fate decreed, Time now ha's made us see.254. H.756, 1
Death to our Countrey, now hath lost his heat:.254. H.756, 4
To my Sepulcher now,.......................256. H.762, 2
Meale and it now mix together;...............258. H.769, 5
Drink now the strong Beere...................263. H.784, 13
Now is your turne (my Dearest) to be set......264. H.789, 1
It sparkles now like Ariadne's Crowne.........264. H.789, 4
When all now dead shall re-appeare............265. H.794, 6
But now perceiving that it still do's please.....266. H.800, 3
He tacks about, and now he doth profess......266. H.800, 5
Lets now take our time;......................267. H.806, 1
In her white Stole; now Victory do's rest......271. H.823, 3
Fortune is now Your Captive; other Kings....271. H.823, 5
Love, love me now, because I place............278. H.859, 1
If that my Fate has now fulfill'd my yeere,....278. H.860, 1
All is well; now next to these.................280. H.870, 13
Truggin a Footman was; but now, growne lame,
283. H.882, 1
Truggin now lives but to belye his name.......283. H.882, 2
In stead of Holly, now up-raise...............285. H.892, 3
Let Box now domineere;.....................285. H.892, 6
Then youthfull Box which now hath grace,....285. H.892, 9
End now the White-loafe, & the Pye,..........285. H.894, 1
My care for thee is now the less;.............287. H.899, 5
But trust me now I dare not say,.............288. H.908, 5
I lately fri'd, but now behold................290. H.915, 1
My selfe now live: this age best pleaseth mee..292. H.927, 2
And am tormented now.......................295. H.942, 12
Now blubb'ring, cry,........................296. H.946, 8
Here now I rest under this Marble stone:......298. H.954, 2
Welcome, Great Cesar, welcome now you are,...300. H.961, 1
O Pompe of Glory! Welcome now, and come...300. H.961, 5
Now thou art dead, no eye shall ever see,......302. H.967, 1
'Tis now his habit, which he can't give ore......302. H.972, 2
Where now I rest, these may be known by Jet..304. H.978, 4
Tell me, do thy kine now fail.................305. H.984, 7
Now (ai me) (ai me.) Last night..............306. H.984, 33
Ah Biancha! now I see,......................307. H.991, 1
The bound (almost) now of my book I see....313. H.1019, 1
Or think on't now..........................314. H.1024, 14
Now, now the mirth comes..................317. H.1035, 1
Then Night now gone, and yet not sprung the Day.
319. H.1046, 2
Now, if you love me, tell me,.................321. H.1055, 1
And in my Booke now claim a two-fold right:.322. H.1062, 11
Instruct me now, what love will do;..........325. H.1075, 1
Tell me, now last, what love will do;.........325. H.1075, 7
Trap, of a Player turn'd a Priest now is;......325. H.1076, 1
This second Protestation now.................328. H.1090, 7
Can I be gamesome (aged now)...............329. H.1093, 2
That are snarling now at me:................329. H.1096, 2
Spur jingles now, and sweares by no meane oathes,
330. H.1099, 1
So that with bold truth, thou canst now relate..330. H.1100, 7
Make knowne to us the now Jerusalem.........330. H.1100, 12
The staffe is now greas'd,....................333. H.1122, 1
Il'e write no more of Love; but now repent...334. H.1124, 1
My wearied Barke, O Let it now be Crown'd!..334. H.1127, 1
When the tapers now burne blew,.............348. N.41, 25
'Cause my speech is now decaid;...............348. N.41, 31
And tell Him, by that Bud now blown,.........354. N.59, 3
Over the golden Altar now is spread,..........355. N.65, 3
It will not be: And, therefore, now,...........357. N.72, 15
What though my bed be now my grave,.........361. N.84, 3
To spring; though now a wither'd flower.........361. N.84, 8
For, now unlesse ye see Him bleed,...........365. N.97, 17
Now singing, homeward let us carrie...........366. N.97, 26
Where shall I now begin to make, for one.....368. N.103, 5
For now the Corne and Wine must faile:......374. N.123, 14
Ah Dorcas, Dorcas! now adieu................374. N.123, 31
We take our leaves now of the Loome,........374. N.123, 35
The web affords now nothing;...............374. N.123, 37
And Olive Branch is wither'd now.............375. N.123, 52
The Wine Presse now is ta'ne from us,........375. N.123, 53
For All that now come, or hereafter may.......378. N.131, 2
The work is done; now let my Lawrell be......398. N.262, 1
For me to flie, but now to follow Thee.........399. N.264, 4
Tell me, white Angell; what is now become...403. N.271, 3
But now my muse hath spi'de a darke descent..405. A.1, 65
Now loue invites me to survey her thighes.......406. A.1, 77
The lovely shoulders now allure the eye........406. A.1, 95
Now for some Jewells to supplye...............409. A.2, 89
And now yf ther A man bee founde............409. A.2, 103
But vnto mee, bee onlye hoarse, since now......411. A.3, 47
Fould now thine armes, and in thy last looke reare
414. A.6, 7
For now behold the golden Pompe is come,......415. A.7, 2
But now come in. Euc. More let me yet relate....416. A.8, 23
All's now fledd saue this alone................418. A.9, 23
— — — — — — — — —, ...422. var. H.106, 105
Of nature: bidd mee nowe fare well, or smile
424. ins. H.128, 46d
— — — — — — — — — —, ...428. var. H.238, 11
Not now perceive the soule of C: C:.....430. ins. H.283, 40d
What though your laden Altar now has wonne
432. ins. H.283, 70a
And now y' have wept enough, depart yon starres
432. ins. H.283, 140a
Now they the Elves within a trice,.........434. ins. H.293, a
— — — — — — — — — — —, ...437. var. H.336, 113
— — — — — — — — — — —, ...452. var. H.128, 39
— — — — — — — — — — —, ...453. var. H.283, 131

Nowhere Is no where found....................66. H.172, 26

Now's Thou wilt complaine, False now's thy Looking-glasse
21. H.62, 2
Now, now's the time; so oft by truth...........53. H.149, 1

Null To null his Numbers, and to blast his Crowne.
188. H.506, 14

Numb To numb the sence of Dearth, which sho'd sinne haste it,
37. H.106, 119

Number For to number sorrow by..............16. H.39, 13
Their number (almost) infinite,...............91. H.223, 35
Number, Your owne, by free Adoption;........107. H.264, 4
To the ninth number, if not tenne;...........127. H.319, 32
Far lesse in number, then our foule dayes are...189. H.513, 2
Nor is my Number full, till I inscribe..........199. H.545, 1
Like Tapers cleare without number............217. H.619, 15
To th' number five,..........................227. H.653, 10
Treble the number of these good I've writ........339. N.1, 4
And that number more then true;.............348. N.41, 27
No number of the Plurall hath................382. N.168, 2
Though they be few in number, I'm content;..392. N.230, 3
The number here of Heires, shall from the state.395. N.248, 3
God hates the Duall Number; being known....396. N.249, 1
The lucklesse number of division:.............396. N.249, 2
But form'd by number make sweet melody......406. A.1, 108
Number of Nyne, wch makes vs full wth God,..410. A.3, 22

Numbered Next is your lot (Faire) to be number'd one,
188. H.510, 1
And I lie numbred with the dead?.............361. N.84, 6

Numbering — — — — — — — — —, ...453. var. H.283, 76

Numberless Sighs numberlesse he cast about,......42. H.119, 5
Numberlesse, as are your haires.................96. H.232, 8

Numbers See True-paced-numbers
Ennobled numbers for the Presse,................19. H.51, 7
To drink in Notes, and Numbers; such..........22. H.68, 3
Some numbers prurient are, and some of these...66. H.173, 7
Ne'r shine upon me; May my Numbers all.....79. H.197, 89
Then onely Numbers sweet,...................81. H.201, 51
(With luscious Numbers) my melodious Lyre...84. H.210, 4
With thy Delicious Numbers;..................95. H.227, 2
Bind up his senses with your numbers, so,......99. H.244, 3
The soule of Nature melts in numbers: now....115. H.283, 106
Or some numbers more rehearse;..............122. H.303, 2
When my numbers full did flow?..............131. H.332, 4
Those smooth-pac't Numbers, amble every where;
141. H.359, 10
Who writes sweet Numbers well as any can:...172. H.459, 2
To null his Numbers, and to blast his Crowne..188. H.506, 14

'Tis still observ'd, those men most valiant are,..308. H.994, 1
Occasion If favour or occasion helpe not him...298. H.953, 2
The more occasion still to sin..................379. N.144, 2
Occasion's For this, or that occasions sake......361. N.83, 54
Ocean Had, first, durst plow the Ocean.........36. H.106, 76
Can hold of Beere and Ale an Ocean;.........171. H.454, 2
Follow to th' wilder Ocean:...................244. H.720, 4
Like to the ever-wealthy Ocean:..................341. N.15, 2
Ocean's Thou never Plow'st the Oceans foame...229. H.662, 5
O'clock Past one aclock, and almost two,.......121. H.299, 7
Odd Many a kisse, both odde and even:........69. H.178, 52
(Compos'd of odde, not even paires)............91. H.223, 47
W'th Flame, and Rapture; drincking to the odd..410. A.3, 21
Odd-piece Of the Fryar, (of work an odde-piece.).93. H.223, 122
Odds Twixt Kings and Subjects ther's this mighty odds,
12. H.25, 2
Two Cupids fell at odds;........................31. H.92, 2
Ode — — — — — — — —, ...448. var. A.3, 21
Odes Some Odes I made of Lucia:..............303. H.973, 14
Odious Because I'me odious in thy sight,.......344. N.29, 9
Odor The passive Aire such odour then assum'd,.157. H.414, 7
An Odor more divine,.......................251. H.740, 10
Odoriferous Nor odoriferous...............436. ins. H.336, 48c
Odors Thy sacred Corse with Odours I will burne;
11. H.22, 3
Built up of odours, burneth in her breast.......113. H.283, 26
Thy golden Censors fil'd with odours sweet,....128. H.320, 7
So smell those odours that do rise.............145. H.375, 1
To kick the Flow'rs, and scorn their odours too?.234. H.673, 4
Odysseys His Odisees, and his high Iliads.......206. H.575, 28
Oenone Sweet Oenone, doe but say............264. H.790, 1
O'er See Over
When I thy Parts runne o're, I can't espie........10. H.16, 1
By me, o'r thee, (as justments to the dead)........27. H.82, 4
That Roses shew, when misted o're with Lawn...34. H.104, 4
As well as spare: still conning o'r this Theame,.38. H.106, 131
Sing o're Horace; for ere long..................39. H.111, 11
Now o're the threshold force her in...............55. H.149, 82
And (with your Mantle o're me cast)..........61. H.159, 24
Then let thy active hand scu'd o're thy Lyre:....67. H.176, 3
O'r it a Cobweb-Lawne:.........................75. H.193, 3
Then Ile give o're,...............................85. H.211, 3
Which o're the board is smoothly spred,........91. H.223, 62
A Baptime o're the flowers.....................95. H.227, 26
Washt o're, to tell[1] what change is neare......134. H.336, 90
The spangling Dew dreg'd o're the grasse shall be
143. H.370, 3
Where Fortune bears no sway o're things......190. H.515, 35
A Tentrall sung by Virgins o're thy Grave:....209. H.584, 6
O're Ditches, and Mires,......................225. H.643, 11
Hast thou begun an act? ne're then give o're:..236. H.680, 1
Our slothfull passage o're the Stygian Lake,....248. H.730, 24
Felicitie flies o're the Wall and Fence,..........257. H.765, 3
Tread ore his gleab, but with such care, that where
259. H.771, 7
Lightly, lightly ore the dead.................274. H.838, 8
As if or'e washt in Hippocrene.................277. H.857, 2
The candid Stole thrown ore the Pious Priest;..286. H.898, 6
We o're the tombes, and Fates shall flye;........288. H.906, 3
'Tis now his habit, which he can't give ore.......302. H.972, 2
Or'e which you'l walk, when I am laid beneath..312. H.1013, 4
And as he spake, his mouth ranne ore with wine.
313. H.1017, 4
To chafe o're much the Virgins cheek or eare:..329. H.1095, 2
Remove the barrs, or lift me o're the stiles:......352. N.51, 6
Fine flowre prest down, and running o're.........356. N.66, 8
The vessell full, did then run ore:...............357. N.75, 4
Till they be hid o're with a wood of darts.......370. N.109, 2
These hung, as honours o're thy Grave,........375. N.123, 86
First, that these goods none here may o're esteem.
387. N.201, 3
(Hatch't o're with Moone-shine, from their stolen delight)
410. A.3, 2
— — — — — — — — — — — —, ...427. var. H.197, 52
— — — — — — — — — — — —, ...435. var. H.293, 25i
Ore which the hand....................436. ins. H.336, 48m
— — — — — — — — — — — —, ...437. var. H.336, 76
— — — — — — — — — — — —, ...449. var. A.8, 3
O'eracted But o'racted deads the pleasure.......276. H.850, 6
O'erbear Of storms orebear........................335. H.1129, 8
O'erbuys Who Weds, ore-buyes his weal with woe.
320. H.1052, 4
O'ercast And next to these two blankets ore-
Cast of the finest Gossamore.......167. H.443, 94-95
O'ercome Fight thou with shafts of silver, and o'rcome,
21. H.60, 1
Orecome, or halfe betray'd by Tiffanies:..........34. H.104, 2
Ore-come in musicke; with a wine,............120. H.293, 47
As wearie, not o'recome by either..............244. H.716, 48
No man is tempted so, but may o'recome,........389. N.211, 1
— — — — — — — — — — — —, ...435. var. H.293, 33aa
O'ercomes Satan o'recomes none, but by willingnesse.
359. N.79, 2
O'erlaid As that the Messes ne'r o'r-laid the Lord:
210. H.590, 6
O'er-leavened O're-leven'd; or like Cheese o're-renetted.
7. H.7, 2
O'er-renneted O're-leven'd; or like Cheese o're-renetted.
7. H.7, 2
O'erruled All things o'r-rul'd are here by Chance;.197. H.542, 1
O'erspread Met in one Hearce-cloth, to ore-spred.103. H.256, 6
O'erthrown By the weak'st means things mighty are o're-thrown,..240. H.702, 1
Of (Partial List)
I sing of Brooks, of Blossomes, Birds, and Bowers:..5. H.1, 1
I write of Youth, of Love, and have Accesse........5. H.1, 5
Thinke that of All, that I have writ, the worst:......7. H.6, 2
Two of a thousand things, are disallow'd,........10. H.18, 1
Instead of Orient Pearls of Jet,..................14. H.34, 1
Love, in pity of the deed,.......................15. H.36, 12
Stately Julia, prime of all;.......................15. H.39, 3
I put, he pusht, and heedless of my skin,......17. H.44, 3
Quickned of late by Pearly showers;...........25. H.78, 6
But of the heat of Julia's breast:................25. H.78, 8
To be, and is, the very best of Wives:...........26. H.79, 4
One silent night of late,........................26. H.81, 1
He must of right,...............................30. H.87, 16
Alas! If kissing be of plagues the worst,..........33. H.101, 3
Fame tell of States, of Countries, Courts, and Kings;
36. H.106, 85
In thee, thou Man of Men! who here do'st give..41. H.117, 4
And Pendant Pearle of ours......................43. H.123, 12
Of which, sweet Swans must drink, before they sing
45. H.128, 34
Uncapable of such a Soveraigne,..............46. H.128, 44
Faile of thy former helps; and onely use........46. H.128, 52
Hereafter, shall smell of the Lamp, not thee.....46. H.128, 54
Or like a Virgin full of ruth,.....................47. H.132, 7
Insensible of all my smart;......................47. H.132, 10
But we as fearlesse of the Sunne,...............48. H.136, 10
I burn, I burn; and beg of you...................50. H.140, 1
You, you that be of her neerest kin,............55. H.149, 81
Seas shall be sandlesse; Fields devoid of grasse;..59. H.154, 7
His vertue still is sensible of paine:.............60. H.158, 2
You scornfull of my love, and me:................60. H.159, 2
What is become of me: there I....................60. H.159, 5
Sweet, be not proud of those two eyes,............61. H.160, 1
And Leaves did heale, all sick of humane seed:...61. H.161, 2
Of my cure, doe you beware.......................62. H.162, 17
Sickly Girles, they beare of you.................64. H.167, 4
One onely Poem out of all you'l chuse;........64, H.168, 8
I beg of Love, that ever I.......................64. H.169, 11
Nay; not so much as out of bed?.................68. H.178, 9
Made up of white-thorn neatly enterwove;......68. H.178, 35
Hor. While, Lydia, I was lov'd of thee,..........70. H.181, 1
Nor Cloe was of more respect;...................70. H.181, 6
But taking those rare lips of yours..............71. H.182, 15
But out of hope his wife might die to beare 'em...72. H.184, 2
Life of my life, take not so soone thy flight,......73. H.186, 1
Out of the which, the creame of light,............74. H.190, 9
Deservelesse of the name of Paragon:............76. H.194, 4
Learne of me what Woman is.....................76. H.195, 2
As the wise Cato had approv'd of thee...........78. H.197, 64
Fill each part full of fire, active to doe..........79. H.197, 79
Quite dispossest of either fray, or fret...........82. H.204, 6
At Noone of Day, was seene a silver Star,......86. H.213, 20
But (Dearest) of so short a stay;................87. H.216, 2
Of Flanks and Chines of Beefe doth Gorrell boast..89. H.221, 1
Girt with small bones, instead of walls..........90. H.223, 10
Saint Will o'th' Wispe (of no great bignes)......91. H.223, 30
(Compos'd of odde, not even paires)............91. H.223, 47
You first of all crown'd her; she must of due,...94. H.224, 9
Thou cam'st to cure me (Doctor) of my cold,....97. H.236, 1
That done, then let him, dispossest of paine,......99. H.244, 7
Instead of common showers,....................103. H.255, 6
Is it for want of sleep?.......................104. H.257, 18
Groynes, for his fleshly Burglary of late,.........106. H.261, 1
(When weary of the light)......................106. H.262, 14
To make of parts an union;......................107. H.263, 15
The true resemblances of thee;..................107. H.263, 18
And in the turning of an eye;...................107. H.263, 20
That Verse, of all the Verses here, shall be......107. H.264, 5
The very eyes of me:...........................109. H.267, 22
Blowne out of April; or some New-..........112. H.283, 3
Built up of odours, burneth in her breast.........113. H.283, 26
Strip her of Spring-time, tender-whimpring-maids,
114. H.283, 91
Each hieroglyphick of a kisse or smile;........115. H.283, 126
Who formes a Godhead out of Gold or Stone,....117. H.288, 1
Eates to ones thinking, of all there, the least.....118. H.292, 2
What the times of old did preach.................120. H.297, 2
Not out of Conscience, or Religion:.............122. H.305, 2
Good things, that come of course, far lesse doe please,
123. H.307, 1
And why? he knowes he must of Cure despaire,..125. H.315, 5
No newes of Navies burnt at Seas;...............126. H.319, 1
No noise of late spawn'd Tittyries:...............126. H.319, 2
We send in stead of New-yeares gift............127. H.319, 26
Till sleep takes place of wearinesse..............127. H.319, 48
Undreadfull too of courtly thunderclaps:.........128. H.323, 6
When I of Villars doe but heare the name,......137. H.341, 1

Mease brags of Pullets which he eats: but Mease.142. H.361, 1
Essay of other giblets; make....................146. H.377, 28
Glasse out of deepe, and out of desp'rate want,...151. H.385, 1
Love in pitie of their teares,..................152. H.391, 5
So long are capable of cure,....................153. H.395, 2
When out of bed my Love doth spring..........154. H.404, 1
He's greedie of his life, who will not fall,......155. H.405, 17
I'm sick of Love; O let me lie.................158. H.420, 1
One of the crowd, not of the companie.........163. H.436, 2
That of my skin, I all am stript;..............164. H.442, 7
Of any tackling can declare...................167. H.443, 104
Some Relique of a Saint doth weare:...........169. H.449, 2
Despite of all concussions left the Stem........170. H.451, 3
I am of all bereft;............................173. H.460, 1
I am not jealous of thy Faith,.................175. H.465, 43
But for True Service, worthy of that Gowne,....176. H.466, 7
Me languish for the love of Thee?...............177. H.471, 2
In the dead of dampish night...................177. H.473, 6
For want of warmth, and Stomachs keepe......179. H.476, 32
When of the Banks their leave they take;......180. H.478, 6
He's Lord of thy life, who contemnes his own...181. H.486, 2
Jill sayes, of what? sayes Jack, on that sweet kisse,
186. H.498, 3
Dash all bad Poems out of countenance.........187. H.506, 10
Here those long suits of Chancery lie..........190. H.515, 25
They be but signs of Ursleys hollow teeth.......197. H.543, 4
He ever pickt (as yet) of any one.............204. H.568, 6
Umber was painting of a Lyon fierce,..........205. H.572, 1
Acceptance it might find of thee..............214. H.613, 4
By quickly making one of two.................215. H.616, 10
Of long'd-for lodging, go to rest:.............216. H.617, 2
Left (of the large heart, and long hand)......218. H.626, 10
Partaker of this sight.........................220. H.633, 13
I greedy of the prize, did drinke,.............222. H.635, 5
Black I'm grown for want of meat;............223. H.638, 4
At noone of Night are a working..............225. H.643, 18
Acknowledger of you..........................228. H.657, 13
Ile sing no more of Frosts, Snowes, Dews and Showers;
228. H.658, 3
Be the Mistresse of my choice,................232. H.665, 1
At trundling of the Ball,......................238. H.690, 6
In no one Satyre there's a mite of salt.........238. H.692, 2
Shall be Disposeresse of the prize..............243. H.716, 12
Thou art a man of worthinesse:...............243. H.716, 26
When all Birds els do of their musick faile,....247. H.726, 1
Ph. A deale of Love, and much, much Griefe together.
248. H.730, 14
Ch. Talk not of love, all pray, but few soules pay me.
248. H.730, 18
Break off Delay, since we but read of one......251. H.744, 1
Locks incurl'd of other haire;.................253. H.750, 11
Green, to the end of dayes.....................261. H.778, 12
I came; (tis true) and lookt for Fowle of price,..262. H.783, 7
At last, i' th' noone of winter, did appeare......262. H.783, 13
And swore I'de got the ague of the house.......262. H.783, 20
Thus if our ship fails of her Anchor hold,......266. H.800, 7
But ther's not one, doth praise the smell of thee...266. H.802, 2
Before we can be aware of.....................267. H.806, 6
He weepes and sighs (as weary of his life.)....275. H.842, 2
Make hoods of thee to serve out Spice...........275. H.844, 8
Because begot of my Immortall seed............280. H.869, 6
Not so much knowne, as to be lov'd of thee.....297. H.947, 12
In depth of silence, heard, and seene of none.....298. H.954, 3
And no lesse prais'd, then of the maides admir'd..299. H.956, 10
If Jove wo'd speake, he wo'd accept of thine...301. H.966, 14
And be of all admired, Tomasin................304. H.979, 2
'Twill strangely make a one of too.............325. H.1075, 4
Trap, of a Player turn'd a Priest now is;......325. H.1076, 1
God, the most Wise, is sparing of His talk......341. N.12, 2
Sits Cupid kissing of his mother Queene,........405. A.1, 56
A place desir'd of all but got by theis...........405. A.1, 69
guilty of somewhat, ripe the strawberries..430. ins. H.283, 20b
Nor can wee glory of a great.............436. ins. H.336, 48i
Bite of themselves to scape away.........440. ins. H.443, 56b

Off See Love-cast-off
Cast off (said he) all feare,......................26. H.81, 7
Doe they first pill thee, next, pluck off thy skin?
32. H.97, 3
Juno here, far off, doth stand..................56. H.149, 109
And chose their Priest, ere we can cast off sloth:.69. H.178, 50
Off then with grave clothes; put fresh colours on;
105. H.259, 9
'Tis now farre off, and then tis nere;..........130. H.329, 14
And farther off, and every where,..............166. H.443, 46
The nails faln off by Whit-flawes: Art's........166. H.443, 59
Cut off thy haires; and let thy Teares be shed..219. H.627, 3
His inconsiderate Frenzie off (at last)..........225. H.642, 20
Then to cast off all bashfulnesse...............241. H.712, 2
Break off Delay, since we but read of one......251. H.744, 1
They draw their clothes off both, so draw to bed..260. H.773, 4
And old old Age is a farre off:.................267. H.806, 3
Not to cut off, but cure the vicious part........268. H.808, 2
Snatcht off his Crown, and gave the wreath to me:
313. H.1017, 12
To see far off the smoaking Villages...........352. N.51, 10
Put off thy Robe of Purple, then go on........398. N.263, 1
With shoes put off, to tread thy Roome.........402. N.269, 3
But first cast off thy wonted Churlishness.........416. A.8, 6

Offence For brave comportment, wit without offence,
297. H.947, 1
Kings must not use the Axe for each offence:..309. H.998, 1
As free from offence,........................317. H.1035, 29
Gods Prescience makes none sinfull; but th' offence
390. N.220, 1

Offend But dread that you doe more offend.431. ins. H.283, 60s

Offended That lately I offended................100. H.246, 3

Offending Of offending, Temperance, Deare........409. A.2, 98

Offensive Play their offensive and defensive parts,.370. N.109, 1

Offer And offer Tears upon thy Tomb:..........89. H.219, 10
For some small fault, to offer sacrifice:........102. H.251, 2
The offer, which they most wo'd chuse...........118. H.291, 2
First offer Incense, then thy field and meads....143. H.370, 1
Offer my Lyrick..............................213. H.604, 8
Offer thy gift; but first the Law commands......299. H.957, 1
We offer here, before thy Shrine,...............360. N.83, 32

Offered To be offer'd up by fire:..................22. H.65, 2
Offer'd up by Her, to Thee...................122. H.302, 6
Offer'd up, with thanks to thee................129. H.325, 6
Mirtles offer'd up to Thee.....................136. H.337, 6
Offerd up by us, to thee.......................141. H.360, 5
Offer'd up a Wolfe to thee.....................151. H.386, 8
Offer'd up with Vows to Thee.................195. H.530, 6
Offer'd on my holy Grave;....................307. H.991, 6
The calfe without meale n'ere was offered;........345. N.34, 2

Offering See Drink-offering, Heave-offering, Thank-offering, Trespass-offering, Wave-offering
In his Offering, Cheerfulness.....................22. H.63, 4
Unto thy Ghost, th' Effused Offering:.............27. H.82, 8
A neat, though not so great an Offering..........86. H.213, 35
There off'ring up the Holy-Grist:...............91. H.223, 51
Offering Poppy unto thee.....................129. H.324, 4
My chives of Garlick for an offering:..........132. H.333, 6
When my off'ring next I make,.................158. H.417, 1
Thy free (and not decurted) offering............286. H.898, 8
Into the daily offering.........................291. H.919, 2
Receive this offering of our Haires:............360. N.83, 38
Each one his severall offering;.................368. N.102, 21
An Asse unto Him, for an offering:............384. N.179, 2
The Frankincense for Gods Offring.............396. N.254, 2

Offerings See Dew-drink-offerings
And laid them downe for Offrings at his feet.....86. H.213, 32
For his most cheerful offerings................93. H.223, 134

Offers And offers Incense Nights and dayes,....93. H.223, 130

Offices Which were, (and still her offices are known)
201. H.557, 9
The Jewes their beds, and offices of ease,........386. N.193, 1

Offspring What off-spring other men have got,....236. H.681, 1
To these a comely off-spring I desire,..........294. H.938, 3

Offsprings Ignoble off-springs, they may fall.....89. H.219, 17

Of's To have a tooth twitcht out of's native frame.
323. H.1066, 2

Oft As oft as Night is banish'd by the Morne,......26. H.80, 1
So oft, we'll think, we see a King new born.......26. H.80, 2
Now, now's the time; so oft by truth.............53. H.149, 1
I ask't thee oft, what Poets thou hast read,......66. H.174, 1
That so oft has fetter'd me......................98. H.238, 5
And oft betweeen,...........................135. H.336, 115
Oft as your field, shall her old age renew,.......140. H.355, 13
This, this I know, I'm oft struck mute;..........142. H.362, 5
Prigg, when he comes to houses, oft doth use....143. H.368, 1
Oft have I heard both Youths and Virgins say,..149. H.378, 1
(Undone as oft as done) I'm wonne;..........174. H.465, 32
Great men by small meanes oft are overthrown:..181. H.486, 1
Oblations oft, of sweetest Marmelet............227. H.652, 14
Kings must not oft be seen by publike eyes;..236. H.682, 1
Oft bend the Bow, and thou with ease shalt do,..245. H.722, 1
Nor those false vows, which oft times don't prevaile.
331. H.1104, 2
Being, oft here, the just mans portion...........387. N.201, 6
When Thou wast taken, Lord, I oft have read,..399. N.264, 1
Shall want a Hand-mayde, (as she ofte will vse)..412. A.3, 100

Often Small shots paid often, waste a vast estate...13. H.28, 2
Old wives have often told, how they..............18. H.46, 1
But in regard, 'twas often said, this old........129. H.326, 3
This Axiom I have often heard,..............234. H.672, 1
When Pimpes feat sweat (as they doe often use).332. H.1113, 1
In the old Scripture I have often read,..........345. N.34, 1

Oft-times See Times
Oft-times for wast, as for his need.............358. N.75, 8

Oh See O
And (oh!) had it but a tongue,.................57. H.149, 139
Oh fie upon 'em! Lastly too, all witt..........150. H.382, 17
I sing Thy Birth, Oh JESU!....................345. N.33, 2
Oh then to lessen my dispaire..................414. A.5, 9
Oh then no longer let my sweete deferre....426. var. H.197, 25
how long, oh pardon, shall the house....431. ins. H.283, 60c
— — — — — — — — — — — —, ...432. var. H.283, 105
— — — — — — — — — — — —, ...436. var. H.336, 70

Oil Of Balme, of Oyle, of Spice, and Amber-Greece...5. H.1, 8
But if to moisture, Let the oyle...................9. H.15, 3
But likewise Oyle of Maintenance to it:.........41. H.117, 6
To be in Oyle of Roses drown'd,................50. H.140, 7

Yet I bring Balme and **Oile** to heal your sore...52. H.146, 22
With Wine and **Oile** besmear'd..................65. H.170, 4
And make me smooth as Balme, and **Oile** againe...67. H.176, 6
How both his Meale and **Oile** will multiply.......73. H.188, 4
Their Holy **Oyle,** their Fasting-Spittle;.........93. H.223, 117
The **Oile** was yours; and that I owe for yet:......94. H.226, 9
We are the Lords of Wine and **Oile**:.........101. H.250, 2
But turne soone after calme, as Balme, or **Oile**..105. H.259, 4
Butter of Amber, Cream, and Wine, and **Oile**..144. H.370, 5
Of **Oyl** and Meal..........................171. H.455, 8
Oyle of Roses still smelt there................182. H.490, 8
By pouring Balme and **Oyle** into her wounds...201. H.557, 18
Sit smiling in the Meads; where Balme and **Oile,** 205. H.575, 3
Our salt, our Corn, our Honie, Wine, and **Oile**).225. H.642, 18
No; 'tis a life, to have thine **oyle**.............233. H.670, 7
Wo'd ye **oyle** of Blossomes get?..............244. H.719, 1
Oyl of Lillies, and of Spike,.................244. H.719, 3
As my small Jarre best fits my little **Oyle**.......249. H.733, 6
And a little **Oyle** to either:...................258. H.769, 6
Balm may thy Trees drop, and thy Springs runne **oyle** 269. H.818, 7
Flusht was his face; his haires with **oyle** did shine; 313. H.1017, 3
Who plants an Olive, but to eate the **Oile**?..322. H.1060, 1
That powres in **oyle,** as well as wine..........342. N.17, 10
Oyle from Thy Jarre, into my creuze;...........357. N.75, 2
Then is the Lamp and **oyle** extinguished.........359. N.80, 2
God! to my little meale and **oyle,**...............377. N.130, 1
Let **Oyle,** next, run,.........................401. N.268, 21
That smooth as **Oyle,** sweet softe and Cleane....408. A.2, 55
with **oyle** and wine,.....................431. ins. H.283, 60e
Of **oyle,** but onely rich in faith,...........436. ins. H.336, 481

Ointments When the Rose raignes, and locks with **ointments** shine,.......................................7. H.8, 9
Washt with sweet **ointments**; Thus at last I come 335. H.1128, 3

Old **Old** I am, and cannot do...................10. H.19, 3
Young I was, but now am **old,**....................17. H.43, 1
Old wives have often told, how they..............18. H.46, 1
An **old,** poore, lying, flatt'ring man:............38. H.108, 6
That you are **old**;............................63. H.164, 14
We shall grow **old** apace, and die..............69. H.178, 59
Now, now, blowne downe; needs must the **old** stock fall. 72. H.185, 14
Old Time is still a flying:......................84. H.208, 2
Dry chips, **old** shooes, rags, grease, & bones;..93. H.223, 119
You are young, but must be **old,**................97. H.232, 11
What the times of **old** did preach...............120. H.297, 2
And **old, old** widow Greedy needs wo'd wed,...129. H.326, 1
But in regard, 'twas often said, this **old**........129. H.326, 3
So **old** she was, that none co'd tell her yeares...129. H.326, 6
My **old** leane wife, shall kisse it dry:..........134. H.336, 84
Now **old** enough to be our own..................134. H.336, 88
Oft as your field, shall her **old** age renew,......140. H.355, 13
(Rather than fail) to steal from thence **old** shoes:.143. H.368, 2
As the **old** Race of mankind did,..............147. H.377, 38
Leaving their Poet (being now grown **old**)......151. H.387, 3
Mont. Set with the Sunne, thy woes: Scil. The day grows **old**: 160. H.421, 41
Old Parson Beanes hunts six dayes of the week,..163. H.435, 1
To be but three, Black-ey'd, wee'l thinke y'are **old.** 173. H.462, 2
By daily Learning we wax **old**.................187. H.505, 2
Or like **old** Testaments ingrost,................190. H.515, 43
The new successor drives away **old** Love.........191. H.517, 2
Growes **old** with the yeere,....................196. H.534, 17
Born I was to be **old,**........................197. H.540, 1
This was the **old** way; and 'tis yet thy course,..201. H.557, 19
Love I shall when I am **old**)....................204. H.569, 2
For **old** Religions sake,........................212. H.604, 3
Some Race of **old** humanitie...................218. H.626, 9
The Ravens yeares, go hence more Ripe then **old**..222. H.633, 63
Upon the grave of this **old** man................226. H.644, 2
Grow **old** with time, but yet keep weather-proofe. 245. H.723, 14
For, I'm grown **old**; &, with mine age, grown poore: 258. H.768, 2
Either with **old,** or plant therein new thorne:....259. H.771, 6
Old Widdow Prouse to do her neighbours evill..266. H.801, 1
And **old, old** Age is a farre off:..............267. H.806, 3
Sold his **old** Mothers Spectacles for Beere:....272. H.829, 2
Maidens tell me I am **old**;....................277. H.852, 1
Ill it fits **old** men to play,.....................277. H.852, 7
Old Religion first commands..................280. H.870, 3
The **old** Hag in. No surer thing...............284. H.890, 6
Grown **old,** surrender must his place,..........285. H.892, 11
New things succeed, as former things grow **old**..285. H.892, 22
Continuall reaping makes a land wax **old**.......292. H.922, 4
To an **old** soare a long cure must goe on;......312. H.1012, 1
Old Widow Shopter, when so ere she cryes,...331. H.1107, 1
To an **old** Ram Goat,.........................335. H.1122, 4
In the **old** Scripture I have often read,.........345. N.34, 1
His New-yeeres trebled to His **old**:.............367. N.98, 28
I would to God, that mine **old** age might have..371. N.115, 1
The Prophets Mountains of the **Old** are meant;.381. N.157, 3
As that the **old** World thought it fit,...........388. N.204, 3
From **old** debate,............................391. N.228, 18
Thou didst deriue from that **old** stem............407. A.2, 21
Old Coyne's and Meddalls, wee expose..........407. A.2, 30
Past Noone of night, yett weare the howers not **old** 410. A.3, 18
To laugh and quaff and drink **old** sherry...445. ins. H.730, 26c

Old-skin Judith has cast her **old-skin,** and got new; 140. H.356, 1

Olive Who plants an **Olive,** but to eate the Oile?.322. H.1060, 1
The **Olive** branch, and Victors Song:..........360. N.83, 26
And **Olive** Branch is wither'd now..............375. N.123, 52

Olive-branch An **Olive-branch** before me lay:......73. H.187, 4

Olives The Mount of **Olives**; Calverie, and where 330. H.1100, 13

Omen 'Tis **Omen** full of dread:.................56. H.149, 106
Kissing the **Omen,** said Amen:.................73. H.187, 7
The luckie **Omen** of the child)..............167. H.443, 93

Omens Ride on with all white **Omens**; so, that where 25. H.77, 11

On (Partial List) **See Hanger-on**
On with thy fortunes then, what e're they be;......6. H.3, 7
If thou dislik'st the Piece thou light'st **on** first;.....7. H.6, 1
Love and my selfe (beleeve me) **on** a day..........17. H.44, 1
Put **on** your silks; and piece by piece............20. H.54, 1
By your owne jewels set **on** fire..................20. H.54, 6
Here's a house of flesh **on** fire:..................21. H.61, 2
A thousand to that hundred: so kisse **on,**..........24. H.74, 5
Ride **on** with all white Omens; so, that where....25. H.77, 11
Call **on** Bacchus; chaunt his praise;.............39. H.111, 7
Now posting **on** to punish thee..................47. H.132, 12
Till you **on** it did breathe;.....................51. H.144, 2
Set **on** purpose to enthrall......................53. H.147, 9
Bridall-Rites goe **on** so slowly?.................53. H.149, 12
On, on devoutly, make no stay;................54. H.149, 41
Then gently lead her **on**.......................55. H.149, 77
So when Love's yoke is **on,**....................65. H.172, 9
Rise; and put **on** your Foliage, and be seene....68. H.178, 15
Hangs **on** the Dew-locks of the night:...........68. H.178, 24
Lyd. My heart now set **on** fire is..............70. H.181, 13
Fruit, ye know, is comming **on**:.................74. H.189, 4
When Love (the child of likenesse) urgeth **on**....77. H.197, 3
And double my affection **on** thee; as doe those,..78. H.197, 43
But **on** a sudden, all was chang'd and gone......81. H.202, 3
To teare the world, or set it all **on** fire..........81. H.202, 6
And all faire Signs lead **on** our Shepardesse.......85. H.213, 2
Well, **on,** brave boyes, to your Lords Hearth,..101. H.250, 26
Off then with grave clothes; put fresh colours **on**; 105. H.259, 9
Love **on** a day (wise Poets tell).............105. H.260, 1
But **on** a sudden all were gone...............107. H.263, 16
Of holy Saints she paces **on,**..................112. H.283, 13
Then come **on,** come **on,** and yeeld...........112. H.283, 17
Blest is the Bride, **on** whom the Sun doth shine; 113. H.283, 48
On then, and though you slow-...............113. H.283, 59
No fault in women, to lay **on**...................118. H.291, 5
After short prayers, they set **on** bread;........119. H.293, 8
Bungie do's fast; looks pale; puts Sack-cloth **on**; 122. H.305, 1
If well thou hast begun, goe **on** fore-right;....123. H.309, 1
Put **on** your Garlands first, then Sacrifice:......124. H.313, 8
We'll call **on** Night, to bring ye both to Bed:....124. H.313, 10
Where being laid, all Faire signes looking **on,**..124. H.313, 11
But think **on** these, that are t'appeare,..........127. H.319, 39
But we must **on,**..............................132. H.336, 5
But **on** we must, and thither tend,..............133. H.336, 25
While sweet-breath Nimphs, attend **on** you this Day. 140. H.354, 8
Full mirth wait **on** you; and such mirth as shall.140. H.354, 11
Go **on** directly so, as just men may..........149. H.377, 131
Linnit playes rarely **on** the Lute, we know;......149. H.381, 1
On, as thou hast begunne, brave youth, and get..150. H.384, 1
Play Phœbus **on** thy Lute;....................151. H.388, 1
That sets all eares **on** fire....................151. H.388, 4
But with thy fair Fates leading thee, Go **on**....155. H.405, 3
That doted **on** a Maide of Gingerbred:..........155. H.405, 10
Love will in vain spend shafts **on** me:..........155. H.406, 2
Fie **on** this pride, this Female vanitie..........163. H.439, 2
For Lust and action; **on** he'l go,...............165. H.443, 11
Wine lead him **on.** Thus to a Grove...........165. H.443, 19
One feeds **on** Lard, and yet is leane;...........173. H.461, 1
Looke upon all; and though **on** fire............174. H.465, 7
Will **on** thy Feature tirannize,.................174. H.465, 18
Put a shirt of sackcloth **on**:...................183. H.490, 14
I prithee speake: Lyc. I will. End. Say **on**:....183. H.492, 5
Jill sayes, of what? sayes Jack, **on** that sweet kisse, 186. H.498, 3
Let Poets feed **on** aire, or what they will;......186. H.498, 7
Because we feed **on** no mans score:...........200. H.552, 14
Dotes less **on** Nature, then on Art............202. H.560, 18
Honouring thee, **on** my knee..................213. H.604, 7
As great men lead; the meaner follow **on,**.......214. H.614, 3
Or Phyllis, whom hard Fate forc't **on,**........215. H.616, 13
Put **on** all shapes to get a Love:..............215. H.616, 16
But **on, on** thy way..........................217. H.619, 8

To encourage on the Bride;....................221. H.633, 27
The least grim looke, or cast a frown on you:..222. H.634, 8
On Land and on Seas,......................225. H.643, 17
In wayes to greatnesse, think on this,...........229. H.661, 1
For to catch the Lookers on;................232. H.665, 13
Must not be lookt on, but at distances:........237. H.685, 10
For, if we gaze on These brave Lamps too neer,.237. H.685, 11
Shov'd on, by quick succeeding Tides:..........244. H.720, 2
I have, to sing how day drawes on.............246. H.724, 4
Go on too with this:......................247. H.727, 2
Ph. Alas for me! Ch. Shame on thy witching note, 248. H.730, 11
For anger spat on thee her Looking-glasse:....249. H.732, 2
They tread on clouds, and though they sometimes fall, 250. H.737, 3
Hast thou attempted greatnesse? then go on,....252. H.747, 1
Consult ere thou begin'st, that done, go on......252. H.749, 1
Go on with Sylla's Fortune; let thy Fate.....254. H.756, 9
By Time, that hastens on....................258. H.767, 15
The nimble howers wooe us on to wed,..........261. H.781, 5
Sho'd meet and tire, on such lautitious meat,....262. H.783, 3
At which amaz'd, and pondring on the food,....262. H.783, 17
On your Psaltries play,.......................263. H.784, 10
Will come on apace;.........................267. H.806, 5
The Blessing fall in mellow times on Thee......269. H.818, 10
Immortall clothing I put on,...................270. H.819, 1
His jawes had tir'd on some large Chine of Beefe. 273. H.835, 2
'Tis sweet to thinke on what was hard t' endure...276. H.849, 2
Put we on pure Surplices;....................280. H.870, 14
Put on thy Holy Fillitings, and so..............286. H.898, 1
Sho'd I not put on Blacks, when each one here..288. H.907, 1
Eate thou not all, but taste on some:...........288. H.909, 2
And on a sudden both were drown'd............294. H.937, 4
That (where meat is) will be a hanger on.......296. H.944, 2
Put on thy Laurell then; and in that trimme..299. H.956, 11
If but lookt on; struck dead, if scan'd by Thee...301. H.962, 6
Offer'd on my holy Grave;....................307. H.991, 6
On with thy worke, though thou beest hardly prest; 311. H.1009, 1
To an old soare a long cure must goe on;......312. H.1012, 1
Drooping, I draw on to the vaults of death,....312. H.1013, 3
Perilla smile on none but me..................313. H.1020, 2
She thinks not on...........................314. H.1024, 6
Dread not the shackles: on with thine intent;..317. H.1034, 1
But when they call or cry on Grubs for meat;..325. H.1077, 3
Ye quake for cold to looke on me..............329. H.1093, 6
She leads on a brace.........................333. H.1122, 8
My God! looke on me with thine eye............344. N.29, 1
And I cal'd on..............................346. N.38, 3
Adverse and prosperous Fortunes both work on....349. N.44, 1
Then never take a second on,..................354. N.59, 17
On our part, wanting all abilities...............356. N.71, 4
Thus, on the sudden? 4. Come and see..........364. N.96, 17
The Altars all on fier be;......................365. N.97, 7
Death and dreadfulnesse call on,................373. N.121, 5
Art thou not destin'd? then, with hast, go on....389. N.216, 1
A multitude of dayes still heaped on,............392. N.230, 7
Put off Thy Robe of Purple, then go on..........398. N.263, 1
Why then, go on to act: Here's wonders to be done, 401. N.268, 7
Which to the knees by nature fastned on........406. A.1, 85
Of Lust, which setts on fier our hartes...........408. A.2, 38
Then Parte in name of peace; & softely on........412. A.3, 83
Lead on faire paranymphs, the while her eyes, 430. ins. H.283, 20a
helpe on her pace; and though she lagg, yet stirre 430. ins. H.283, 20h
on you is altogether lost,.................432. ins. H.283, 70d

Once No sound calls back the yeer that once is past...8. H.10, 4
Once a brisk and bonny Lasse,................14. H.36, 4
Once were Virgins sick of love,..................15. H.37, 2
When some shall say, Faire once my Silvia was;..21. H.62, 1
And Priceless now, what Peerless once had been:.21. H.62, 4
Let me be leane, and cold, and once grown poore,..31. H.93, 3
I shall dislike, what once I lov'd before...........31. H.93, 4
Once gets a force, Floods cannot quench the flame..40. H.113, 4
Of them, the spring's once drie;.................43. H.123, 20
So neare, or deare, as thou wast once to me.....45. H.128, 10
And Star-like, once more, guild our Firmament...52. H.146, 12
Strut, once a Fore-man of a Shop we knew;......53. H.148, 1
But learn, that Time once lost,.................53. H.149, 7
As he did once to Semele.......................58. H.152, 4
Noone-day and Midnight shall at once be seene:..59. H.154, 1
And having spoke it once, Farewell..............60. H.159, 12
I smil'd; and bade him once more prove,........64. H.166, 9
To shew at once, both night and day............64. H.169, 8
Few Beads are best, when once we goe a Maying. 68. H.178, 28
Once lost, can ne'r be found againe:...........69. H.178, 64
As Julia once a-slumb'ring lay,..................71. H.182, 1
When once true-lovers take their last Fare-well...73. H.186, 8
Doth all at once impaire,......................75. H.193, 23
When her high carriage did at once present....79. H.197, 75
Lost in the wild sea, once againe:..............79. H.198, 8
Her love me once, who now hates me............79. H.198, 12

For having lost but once your prime,............84. H.208, 15
Play I co'd once; but (gentle friend) you see....84. H.210, 1
Sing I co'd once; and bravely too enspire........84. H.210, 3
Draw I co'd once (although not stocks or stones,..84. H.210, 5
Then this, the Fairies once, now Thine..........90. H.223a, 6
Not all at once, but gently, as the trees.........100. H.247, 3
For you once lost, who weep not here!........104. H.256, 10
When once the Lovers Rose is dead,...........106. H.262, 5
Dead falls the Cause, if once the Hand be mute;..123. H.308, 1
Once in a Virgin Flosculet,....................126. H.318, 7
The cole once spent, we'l then to bed,.......136. H.336, 151
When once he gives it incarnation?............139. H.347, 4
Not knowing thus much, when we once do sever,.140. H.355, 3
Pray once, twice pray; and turn thy ground to gold. 144. H.370, 8
Such ignorance as theirs was, who once hist....150. H.382, 15
Frollick Virgins once these were,...............152. H.391, 1
I did this God-head once defie;.................155. H.406, 3
For that once lost, thou't fall to one,..........174. H.465, 27
These Springs were Maidens once that lov'd....180. H.478, 1
When the Tapers once are out..................180. H.482, 4
Out of the world he must, who once comes in:..199. H.548, 1
Once on a Lord-Mayors day, in Cheapside, when.200. H.551, 1
Wound up again: Once down, He's down for ever. 202. H.558, 2
The Watch once downe, all motions then do cease; 202. H.558, 3
As at once I freeze, and frie...................204. H.566, 5
Life is the Bodies light; which once declining,..207. H.576, 1
(The Sun once set) all of one colour are.........207. H.576, 4
And once more yet (ere I am laid out dead)....214. H.612, 13
As wearied Pilgrims, once possest..............216. H.617, 1
Trust me I will not hurt ye; or once shew......222. H.634, 7
And when once the Work is done;.............224. H.639, 3
Bring in her Bill, once more, the Branch of Peace. 225. H.642, 22
No sound recalls the houres once fled,........233. H.670, 24
Once past and gone, no more shall see.........234. H.671, 2
For, once dead, and laid i'th grave,...........238. H.691, 5
To get thy Steerling, once again,..............244. H.716, 37
Kind at once to murder mee....................254. H.757, 8
Prewdence Baldwin (once my maid)..........262. H.782, 2
Rather then I once wo'd see,.................266. H.803, 4
Or kisse it thou, but once, or twice,...........267. H.805, 5
That Stubble stands, where once large eares have been. 275. H.843, 4
And having once brought to an end...........289. H.911, 18
As Cadmus once a new way found,.............297. H.948, 5
To re-possess once more your long'd-for home...300. H.961, 6
And, from a Priest, turne Player once again...325. H.1076, 4
And tel'st to us, what once they were, and are..330. H.1100, 6
If Kings and kingdomes, once distracted be,....331. H.1102, 1
Extreames are fatall, where they once doe strike, 333. H.1120, 5
When once the sin has fully acted been,.........346. N.37, 1
What here we hope for, we shall once inherit:..362. N.88, 1
For, once in hell, none knowes Remission there..367. N.99, 2
Sin once reacht up to Gods eternall Sphere,....367. N.100, 1
By Law, the Bond once cancelled...............370. N.107, 15
He never brings them once to th' push of Pikes..370. N.108, 12
Pardon me God, (once more I Thee intreat)....371. N.113, 1
Neglecting once to cast a frown on those......372. N.116, 3
But when once from hence we flie,.............377. N.128, 5
From her Sonnes Crosse, not shedding once a teare: 384. N.180, 2
At once, a Bud, and yet a Rose full-blowne.....384. N.183, 2
Once shut, was never to be open'd more........385. N.190, 4
Present those Turfs, which once must cover me: 392. N.230, 16
When once the Soule has lost her way,........393. N.233, 1
Those act without regard, when once a King,..399. N.263, 24
Soe wth like lookes, as once the Ministrell....411. A.3, 67
Speak, what art thou? Euc. One, once that had a lover, 416. A.8, 9
Vnto the Prince of Shades, whom once his Pen 442. ins. H.575, 28a

One By no one tongue, there, censured............6. H.2, 24
And loving lie in one devoted bed................8. H.10, 2
No man at one time, can be wise, and love.......8. H.10, 8
I dreamt the Roses one time went..............8. H.11, 1
In any one, the least indecencie:................10. H.16, 2
Be she likewise one of those,..................11. H.21, 5
So three in one small plat of ground shall ly,....11. H.22, 9
For one drink-offering, poured out by thee........14. H.35, 8
Give my dead picture one engendring kisse:....14. H.35, 12
Which crawling one and every way,............16. H.41, 5
(All parts there made one prisoner.)...........16. H.41, 17
One ask'd me where the Roses grew?..........18. H.45, 1
When one is past, another care we hav..........18. H.48, 1
By dreames, each one, into a sev'rall world......21. H.57, 2
Each one, by nature, loves to be a King........21. H.58, 2
Better tis that one shu'd fall,....................21. H.61, 7
Then by one, to hazard all......................21. H.61, 8
As one, in long-lamented-widow-hood;...........25. H.77, 4
One silent night of late,........................26. H.81, 1
Came one unto my gate,........................26. H.81, 3

Thou gav'st me life, (but Mortall;) For that one 27. H.82, 13
For that so rich a one;..........................29. H.87, 9
Bequeath to me one parting kisse:.............34. H.103, 16
And keep one Centre: This with that conspires,.35. H.106, 15
But lost to one, be th' others death............38. H.106, 142
And as there is one Love, one Faith, one Troth,.38. H.106, 143
Be so one Death, one Grave to both...........38. H.106, 144
One drop now deads a spark; but if the same..40. H.113, 3
Colder yet then any one:...................40. H.115, 12
One onely daughter lent to me:...............41. H.116, 4
Contented with the bed of one................41. H.116, 8
Thou shed'st one teare, when as I went away;.42. H.122, 10
Then say, I've sent one more..................43. H.123, 13
One slit's enough to let Adultry in.............44. H.126, 4
Not one, but many Monuments..................48. H.134, 8
The common formes have no one eye,..........49. H.136, 18
Both bring one death; and I die here,.........50. H.140, 9
Sitting alone (as one forsook)................51. H.142, 1
To one and th'others nakednesse..............58. H.152, 8
Trees, at one time, shall be both sere and greene: 59. H.154, 2
Summer and Winter shall at one time show....59. H.154, 5
Only one Soveraign salve, I know,............60. H.157, 5
The Rose, the Violet, one day.................61. H.159, 15
Not one drop to light on me...................62. H.162, 6
I have one, and she alone,.....................62. H.162, 10
Such an one, as will repeat....................62. H.162, 13
One, onely, worthy to be washt by thee:......63. H.165, 2
One onely Poem out of all you'l chuse;........64. H.168, 8
One fancie more! but if there be...............64. H.169, 9
Hither the least one theeving thought:........71. H.182, 14
Say, if there be 'mongst many jems here; one.76. H.194, 3
Thee in thy Vine, or had but tasted one.......78. H.197, 62
The world had all one Nose...................80. H.201, 24
One and th'others passions:...................82. H.203, 10
Where no one piece is yet unlevelled..........82. H.204, 8
And lend a gentle eare to one report...........86. H.213, 11
Yet one rude wind, or ruffling shower,.........88. H.216, 5
Then say, if one th'ast seene more fine.........90. H.223a, 5
Which one by one here set downe are..........91. H.223, 36
But, amongst All encircled here, not one.......94. H.224, 5
Bring me but one, Ile promise thee,...........103. H.255, 5
Met in one Hearce-cloth, to ore-spred..........103. H.256, 6
Penance, and standing so, are both but one.....106. H.261, 4
I went to pluck them one by one,.............107. H.263, 14
As for to make this, that, or any one.........107. H.264, 3
Telling the Clock strike Ten, Eleven, Twelve, One. 114. H.283, 76
Nature and Art, one more....................115. H.283, 129
And of such Torture as no one would grutch..115. H.283, 136
Makes not a God; but he that prayes to one...117. H.288, 2
Past one aclock, and almost two,..............121. H.299, 7
For one so rarely tun'd to fit all parts;........121. H.301, 1
For one to whom espous'd are all the Arts;...121. H.301, 2
Them all concenter'd in one man, but Thee....121. H.301, 4
To make but One (and that's thy selfe) admir'd. 121. H.301, 6
There is no one pleasure in't.................122. H.304, 4
He keeps not one, but many Lents i' th'yeare..122. H.305, 6
Which spent, one death, bring to ye both one Grave. 124. H.313, 14
That weares one face (like heaven) and never showes 128. H.323, 7
By cold neglect, each one,....................131. H.330, 10
And my tongue at one time mute..............131. H.332, 6
Must all be left, no one plant found...........132. H.336, 10
Our own fair wind, and mark each one........133. H.336, 39
Which made us one, shall ne'r undoe;..........134. H.336, 71
But in one onely Hemisphere:................139. H.353, 2
Loth to depart, but yet at last, each one......140. H.355, 1
But you, my Lord, are One, whose hand along.141. H.359, 13
No, know (Blest Maide) when there's not one.146. H.376, 7
To thee, then unto any one:.................147. H.377, 70
No One that's there his guilty glasse..........148. H.377, 86
Of Life eternall) Time has made thee one,....152. H.392, 3
By Dream I saw, one of the three............153. H.399, 1
When one hole wasts more then he gets by Nine. 154. H.400, 4
Having All, injoy not One....................157. H.415, 8
Who hath but one of many;..................160. H.422, 14
Will be content with one?....................160. H.422, 20
But one halfe houre, that's made up here.......162. H.431, 3
One of the crowd, not of the companie.........163. H.436, 2
'Tis fit they make no One with them too great..163. H.438, 2
Besides us two, i'th' Temple here's not one....168. H.445, 1
When I a Heart had one,.....................168. H.446, 2
One Cordelion had that Age long since;........170. H.451, 15
For a most rich, a rare, a precious One........172. H.459, 10
One feeds on Lard, and yet is leane;..........173. H.461, 1
Thy Love had one knot, mine a triple tye.....173. H.464, 3
For that once lost, thou't fall to one,..........174. H.465, 27
As one triumphant; when I find.............176. H.465, 79
And Thrones, thy selfe one of Those Senatours: 176. H.466, 4
As One,......................................178. H.475, 4
Thee to the World a Prime and Publique One..181. H.483, 8
One, or many Mistresses:....................182. H.490, 6
And I shall see by that one kisse,.............185. H.495, 7
A golden Flie one shew'd to me...............185. H.497, 1
One Fate had both; both equall Grace;.........185. H.497, 7
And no one mischief greater then your frown,..188. H.506, 13
One like to me, who must be kill'd...........188. H.509, 7
Next is your lot (Faire) to be number'd one,..188. H.510, 1
Any one part that's dissonant in you:..........189. H.511, 2
One Rest, one Grave.........................190. H.515, 12
One more by Thee, Love, and Desert have sent, 191. H.516, 1
Fortune did never favour one.................191. H.520, 1
For all his Issue, Father of one Child.........195. H.533, 2
Give me one kisse,...........................196. H.538, 1
For that one, two............................196. H.538, 7
One chiefe transgression is among the rest,.....197. H.539, 7
Thee sprightly Soame, one of my righteous Tribe: 199. H.545, 2
A Tribe of one Lip; Leven, and of One........199. H.545, 3
A Stock of Saints; where ev'ry one doth weare 199. H.545, 5
Then but to breath, and every one gave way:..200. H.551, 4
As if You Two, were one Hermophrodite:.....201. H.557, 6
Law is to give to ev'ry one his owne..........201. H.557, 10
Modest I will be: but one word Ile say.........201. H.557, 21
One of the five straight branches of my hand..203. H.565, 1
Only, if one prove addled, that he eates........204. H.568, 3
He ever pickt (as yet) of any one.............204. H.568, 6
And he one chiefe; But harke, I heare the Cock, 207. H.575, 61
Of late struck one; and now I see the prime...207. H.575, 63
(The Sun once set) all of one colour are.......207. H.576, 4
Won't for his tenth part ask you one..........208. H.581, 6
One Holy Collect, said or sung for Thee.......209. H.584, 4
Jone, and my Lady have at that time one,....209. H.586, 5
One and the selfe-same priz'd complexion.......209. H.586, 6
To any one unsober syllable...................210. H.590, 8
One kisse from thee.........................210. H.591, 10
Horne sells to others teeth; but has not one...211. H.595, 1
By quickly making one of two................215. H.616, 10
One night i'th' yeare, my dearest Beauties, come.222. H.634, 1
Give an Almes to one that's poore,............223. H.638, 2
Twice fortie (bating but one year,.............226. H.644, 3
Cloy'd they are up with Arse; but hope, one blast 226. H.650, 3
And make me one entire......................228. H.657, 8
Like one of those.............................229. H.659, 4
One nicely mad, or peevishly severe...........234. H.673, 6
Yet scarre-crow-like I'le walk, as one,.........235. H.677, 7
Captive one, or both, to take:.................235. H.678, 6
In no one Satyre there's a mite of salt.........238. H.692, 2
One jemme was lost; and I will get............240. H.705, 5
Knew'st thou, one moneth wo'd take thy life away, 241. H.709, 1
Each one to make his melody:................243. H.716, 20
Our hope of one for the other................247. H.727, 6
So silently they one to th' other come,.........250. H.737, 5
Break off Delay, since we but read of one......251. H.744, 1
What needs twenty stabs, when one...........254. H.757, 5
Or els not one there must enter..............256. H.762, 12
As these have done to Thee, who art the one,..256. H.763, 5
One onely glory of a million,.................256. H.763, 6
Power and Peace to keep one Throne...........264. H.788, 2
But ther's not one, doth praise the smell of thee..266. H.802, 2
For the requitall; save this only one.........267. H.804, 3
One word more I had to say;.................270. H.821, 5
If one poore prick,.........................273. H.833, 4
Make haste away, and let one be..............275. H.844, 1
One Brave Captain did command,..............276. H.850, 9
One short charme if you but say..............276. H.850, 11
Yet their Three praises, praise but One; that's Lawes. 276. H.851, 8
I'th' Church-yard, made, one Tenement for me.277. H.853, 4
Age shall not wrong thee; or one jot abate.....280. H.869, 3
One knell be rung for both; and let one grave.281. H.875, 5
My soule would one day goe and seeke.........281. H.876, 1
Since for one Bad, one Good I know:.........283. H.885, 2
For one Medea that was bad,..................283. H.885, 5
'Tis liberty to serve one Lord; but he.........284. H.887, 1
Is not for one, but every night his Bride:.....286. H.898, 14
Brings him not one, but many a Maiden-head...286. H.898, 16
Before the Press scarce one co'd see..........287. H.899, 1
Whom one belov'd will not suffice,...........287. H.899, 9
We credit most our sight; one eye doth please..287. H.904, 1
Sho'd I not put on Blacks, when each one here.288. H.907, 1
Vertue and pleasure, both to dwell in one.....293. H.935, 2
Himselfe, at one time, can be wise, and Love...294. H.936, 4
At twice ten yeares, a prime and publike one?..299. H.956, 6
In reverence of his person, every one..........301. H.962, 3
This shall my love doe, give thy sad death one.302. H.967, 3
Of a world to drowne but One...............302. H.968, 12
No one least Branch there left behind:........304. H.980, 6
It matters not, since thou art chosen one.....305. H.983, 3
In a while it will strike one;..................307. H.991, 3
There is not one least solecisme found;........307. H.992, 4

As one.......................................308. H.993, 7
And by that One blow set an end to all.........310. H.1002, 4
Ile live as one Regenerate.....................313. H.1020, 8
And next morrow, every one.....................315. H.1026, 13
Let's endure one Martyrdome....................315. H.1027, 2
Errour is fruitfull, Truth is onely one..........316. H.1031, 2
Not of one man, but all the Common-wealth...318. H.1041, 2
My Ship has here one only Anchor-hold;......319. H.1044, 2
That is my hope; which if that slip, I'm one....319. H.1044, 3
When the great Crack not Crushes one, but all..319. H.1045, 2
So not one cross to buy thee...................321. H.1055, 3
I sing the more, that thou hast one;............321. H.1056, 2
One that sho'd drop his Beads for thee.........321. H.1056, 16
But one by you be hug'd and cherished........322. H.1062, 3
Believe it (dearest) ther's not one...........324. H.1068, 19
'Twill strangely make a one of too............325. H.1075, 4
Made up One State of Sixtie Venuses;.........326. H.1080, 4
This I am sure; I Ravisht stood, as one.......326. H.1080, 9
For Grace and Carriage, every one a Queene...326. H.1080, 24
One Birth their Parents gave them; but their new,
326. H.1080, 25
Twice five and twenty (bate me but one yeer)..328. H.1088, 2
One man has reatch't his sixty yeers, but he..328. H.1088, 7
One Eare tingles; some there be,..............329. H.1096, 1
Gray or white, all's one to me.................330. H.1098, 4
One silver spoon shines in the house of Croot;.332. H.1110, 1
Be yet assur'd, thou shalt have one...........334. H.1123, 5
Part of the worke remaines; one part is past:..334. H.1126, 1
To do ten Bad, for one Good Action..............339. N.1, 6
But if, 'mongst all, thou find'st here one........339. N.2, 7
That One of all the rest, shall be..............339. N.2, 9
The one is Mercy, and the next is Love:.........340. N.6, 2
God when He's angry here with any one,.......340. N.7, 1
So He is said to be most One...................343. N.23, 2
No one hope, but of his Fees,..................347. N.41, 14
Twice ten for one:.............................350. N.47, 44
Among Gods Blessings, there is no one small....353. N.55, 2
Drown'd in one endlesse Day....................354. N.58, 12
But if thou hadst, He sho'd have one;..........354. N.59, 12
One onely lock of that sweet Hay...............355. N.60, 3
Or one poore Swadling-clout, shall be.........355. N.60, 5
Better he starv'd, then but to tast one crumme..355. N.65, 10
And make no one stop, till my race be done...358. N.77, 15
I do believe, the One in Three,................359. N.78, 13
One seed of life left, 'tis to keep.............361. N.83, 59
Each one his severall offering;................368. N.102, 21
Where shall I now begin to make, for one......368. N.103, 5
'Tis true, my God; but I can't pay one mite...368. N.103, 10
Of Three in One,...............................369. N.106, 13
Thy Deerest Saviour renders thee but one.....371. N.112, 3
Smile, that one smile's full restitution..........371. N.112, 4
Let but one beame of Glory on it shine,.......371. N.113, 9
Some one poore Almes-house; there to lie, or stir,
371. N.115, 3
Where no one beame of comfort peeps in it.....372. N.117, 2
But no one Jailor there to wash the wounds...372. N.120, 2
By the clock 'tis almost One....................373. N.121, 14
For, rather then one drop shall fall...........377. N.129, 7
God had but one Son free from sin; but none..378. N.134, 1
That being ignorant of that one, he may.......379. N.142, 3
God tempteth no one (as S. Aug'stine saith)..380. N.150, 1
Had no one Beame from Gods sweet Majestie...382. N.167, 4
One part thereof left still unfinished:..........384. N.178, 2
One Birth our Saviour had; the like none yet..384. N.182, 1
God's undivided, One in Persons Three;.......386. N.191, 1
One man repentant is of more esteem.........388. N.205, 1
With God, then one, that never sin'd 'gainst Him.
388. N.205, 2
That in this world, one onely day.............388. N.206, 2
For each one Body, that i'th earth is sowne,...388. N.208, 1
There's an up-rising but of one for one:......388. N.208, 2
Threescore or fourescore spring up thence for one.388. N.208, 4
Christ is the one sufficient Remedie...........390. N.221, 2
Whereas but one enforcement is................390. N.225, 2
One onely fire has Hell; but yet it shall,......391. N.227, 1
Not after one sort, there excruciate all:.......391. N.227, 2
The one a Staffe is, and the next a Rod:......394. N.241, 2
A man both bruis'd, and broke, and one........400. N.266, 4
With one, and all parts, full of pain:..........400. N.267, 2
With a warm lip, and solemne one:...........402. N.269, 11
No one step from this Sepulcher...............402. N.269, 19
Like pearle and gold make one rich Carcanett...405. A.1, 32
One sighe of loue, and coole it with a teare;...414. A.6, 8
And to thy many, take in one soul more.......416. A.8, 2
Cha. Who calls? who calls? Euc. One overwhelm'd with ruth;
416. A.8, 3
Speak, what art thou? Euc. One, once that had a lover,
416. A.8, 9
Euc. He was an Hastings; and that one Name has
416. A.8, 13
There ever lived such a one...................418. A.9, 30
— — — — — — — — —, ...428. var. H.235, 4
of two makes one Hermaphrodite.........431. ins. H.283, 50j
— — — — — — — — — —, ...439. var. H.443, 19
One's Eates to ones thinking, of all there, the least.
118. H.292, 2

Ones Full and faire ones; come and buy:........19. H.53, 2
Then Faire ones, doe not wrong................53. H.149, 3
The factions of the great ones call,..........282. H.877, 1
One-self-sweet-conspiring In one-self-sweet-conspiring sympathie:..59. H.154, 4
Onion Help from the Garlick, Onyon, and the Leek,
78. H.197, 58
Only Not only to your selves assume.............9. H.15, 5
Onely Herrick's left alone,.....................16. H.39, 12
But onely crave................................30. H.89, 3
But whither, onely Grief do's know.............33. H.103, 4
And be not onely thought, but prov'd.........37. H.106, 102
Thou might'st but onely see't, not taste it......37. H.106, 120
Those Sundayes onely, when as Briefs are read..39. H.109, 2
One onely daughter lent to me:................41. H.116, 4
Not onely subject-matter for our wit,.........41. H.117, 5
Faile of thy former helps; and onely use.......46. H.128, 52
But onely my Corinna's eye?...................48. H.133, 17
Onely, Ile not appeare to thee,..................58. H.152, 3
Only one Soveraign salve, I know,.............60. H.157, 5
One, onely, worthy to be washt by thee:......63. H.165, 2
One onely Poem out of all you'l chuse;.......64. H.168, 8
Onely true in shreds and stuffe...............77. H.195, 12
Have I divorc't thee onely to combine.........78. H.197, 39
They onely will aspire,.........................81. H.201, 46
Then onely Numbers sweet,.....................81. H.201, 51
Onely this Ile look upon,.......................84. H.209, 3
Onely a little more.............................85. H.211, 1
Me thinks that onely lustre doth appeare......94. H.226, 3
Thou onely hast the power,....................100. H.246, 10
To work Love's Sampler onely here,...........103. H.256, 2
The onely true plant found,.....................106. H.262, 2
For their love lost; their onely gaine..........106. H.262, 11
The Subjects onely glory to obay...............109. H.269, 2
Save only the Curst-Cipresse tree:.............132. H.336, 12
But in one onely Hemisphere:..................139. H.353, 2
Onely Moons conscience, we confesse,..........143. H.369, 3
Onely remaind a little bit,......................153. H.399, 8
It sho'd be onely in my Julia's skin:...........158. H.416, 2
Of foure teeth onely Bridget was possest;......158. H.419, 1
Which did but only this portend,...............161. H.425, 3
But only you,....................................161. H.426, 6
Spunge makes his boasts that he's the onely man
171. H.454, 1
And let thy dreames be only fed...............175. H.465, 49
Not wearing Purple only for the show;........176. H.466, 5
Upon him, who only can.........................182. H.489, 13
'Tis thou, and only thou,.......................183. H.492, 6
Parrat protests 't's he, and only he...........186. H.501, 1
For Coronation, then Your onely Praise.........188. H.506, 12
Thou art The Man, the onely Man best known,.194. H.526, 3
If Accusation onely can draw blood,...........194. H.528, 1
Only, if one prove addled, that he eates........204. H.568, 3
Wert thou a Winckfield onely, not a Brother...210. H.590, 10
Onely to kisse that Aire,.......................231. H.663, 7
Adversity hurts none, but onely such..........239. H.697, 1
Nor Beasts (fond thing) but only humane soules.
248. H.730, 10
Or money? no, but onely deaw and sweat.....248. H.731, 2
One onely glory of a million,..................256. H.763, 6
Kings must not only cherish up the good,.......260. H.775, 1
For the requitall; save this only one...........267. H.804, 3
Only for my wound there's no remedy.........274. H.841, 2
These only were but Loves extreames;..........290. H.915, 6
Errour is fruitfull, Truth is onely one...........316. H.1031, 2
My Ship has here one only Anchor-hold;.......319. H.1044, 2
The only comfort of my life....................320. H.1052, 1
Of onely those, who are obedient:............325. H.1073, 2
God is not onely said to be...................340. N.5, 1
God is not onely mercifull, to call.............342. N.19, 1
These done, I'le onely crie....................352. N.53, 15
One onely lock of that sweet Hay.............355. N.60, 3
God gives not onely corne, for need,..........356. N.66, 1
No Arrow nockt, onely a stringlesse Bow:.....357. N.74, 2
But only come, and see Him rest..............367. N.102, 13
Onely, by this dull creature, to expresse.......384. N.179, 3
But only by impression of effect...............385. N.186, 4
That in this world, one onely day..............388. N.206, 2
One onely fire has Hell; but yet it shall,......391. N.227, 1
Onely, there's left a little froth,..............400. N.266, 12
For puplike Eyes, take onlye theis.............409. A.2, 91
But vnto mee, bee onlye hoarse, since now....411. A.3, 47
Ther was not Varnish (only) in my loue.......412. A.3, 80
To make Fools hate them, onlye by disguise:..412. A.3, 94
For such neglect, have only myrtle rodds.431. ins. H.283, 60p
Of oyle, but onely rich in faith,...........436. ins. H.336, 481
On't Ah cruell Sea! and looking on't,.........42. H.119, 9
Nothing he loves on't but the chaps and ears:.305. H.982, 2
Or think on't now,..............................314. H.1024, 14
— — — — — — — — — —, ...450. var. A.9, 5
Onward But look, how each transgressor onward went
391. N.227, 3
Opal But by the Topaz, Opal, Calcedon..........30. H.88, 12
Ope See Open
Ope' the fountains and the springs,..............21. H.61, 3

Early setts ope to feast, and late:..............147. H.377, 46
Which ope themselves to shewe an holy shrine..404. A.1, 26
Open If Sapho droop; Daisies will open never,...41. H.118, 7
Open at your command;......................57. H.149, 158
And open fields, and we not see't?...........68. H.178, 38
No closset plot, or open vent,..................126. H.319, 3
No scurrile jest; no open Sceane is laid.......148. H.377, 77
All things are open to these two events,.......182. H.487, 1
Open thy gates..............................370. N.111, 1
— — — — — — — — — — —, ...436. var. H.336, 54
Opened And that open'd which was seal'd,.......348. N.41, 46
Once shut, was never to be open'd more........385. N.190, 4
Opening Then at th' opening of mine eyes,......199. H.549, 3
Opens Opens the way for early flowers;..........23. H.70, 2
Operation He did His curious operation;........396. N.249, 4
Opes See Opens
With the third key He opes and shuts the wombe; 390. N.224, 3
Opinion While soft Opinion makes thy Genius say, 37. H.106, 115
Oppose Doe oppose;..............................12. H.26, 8
Opposed Be he oppos'd, or be he not withstood,..349. N.44, 3
Opposite For thy revenge to be most opposite;...87. H.215, 8
When things meet most opposite:...............194. H.527, 7
To mine eyes level'd opposite:.................237. H.687, 4
Oppress When temptations me oppresse,........347. N.41, 2
Oppressed And weeping Widowes long opprest..190. H.515, 21
Oppression With hard oppression...............65. H.172, 12
Optics For through these Optickes, fly the dartes.408. A.2, 37
Or (Partial List)
Nor wrack, or Bulging thou hast cause to feare:..23. H.71, 2
In wayes confus'd, nor slip or fall..............33. H.98, 10
But thou at home without or tyde or gale,....36. H.106, 77
Wherein or Light, or Day, did never peep....52. H.146, 6
So when or you or I are made..................69. H.178, 65
Till we have wept, kist, sigh't, shook hands, or so. 73. H.186, 6
Nor cheek, or tongue be dumbe:...............80. H.201, 2
Can shew where you or grew, or stood........88. H.216, 9
As your health or comes, or goes;.............96. H.232, 6
Whether that you be sweet or no?.............112. H.282, 2
'Tis she! 'tis she! or else some more Divine..112. H.283, 11
Whether or no, that we shall meet here ever.....140. H.355, 4
Or spice, or fish, or fire, or close-stools here....155. H.405, 2
Or here my Bed, or here my Grave..............158. H.420, 4
That h'ad nor Gold or Silver to put in't?......162. H.427, 4
That on the seaventh, he can nor preach, or pray. 163. H.435, 4
Nor Bee, or Hive you have be mute;...........179. H.476, 17
Or to Rewards, or else to Punishments........182. H.487, 2
Or Pea, or Bean, or Wort, or Beet,...........200. H.552, 5
Did I or love, or could I others draw..........201. H.557, 1
Or low, or tall, she pleaseth me:..............207. H.579, 2
Or let her walk, or stand, or sit,..............207. H.579, 3
Or let her tongue be still, or stir,............207. H.579, 5
Or let her Grant, or else Deny,................207. H.579, 7
To grace his own Gums, or of Box, or bone....211. H.595, 2
Nor Snake, or Slow-worme bite thee:..........217. H.619, 7
Or lookt I back unto the Times hence flown,...234. H.673, 1
The losse or thine, or mine....................238. H.690, 4
Ch. What's that to me, I waft nor fish or fowles, 248. H.730, 9
Be my Girle, or faire or browne,...............253. H.750, 4
Tell me young man, or did the Muses bring...299. H.956, 1
Has, or none, or little skill,...................347. N.41, 18
Or by our selves, or from the Pulpit read......396. N.249, 8
Oracles (Sweet as the Vestrie of the Oracles.)..157. H.414, 4
Orange All over-archt with Oringe flowers;......145. H.375, 12
Orator Soe look't the Grecian Oratour when sent.411. A.3, 71
Orb To be in that Orbe crown'd (that doth include 207. H.575, 59
Compar'd (in this my ample Orbe) to Him....236. H.685, 4
And having fixt Thee in mine Orbe a Starre,...267. H.804, 9
Orchards Orchards like to Alcinous,......436. ins. H.336, 48d
Ordain That did ordaine the Fast of forty Dayes...386. N.195, 2
Ordained 'Tis the lot ordain'd for me...........84. H.209, 6
Ordaining Ordaining that thy small stock find no breach, 38. H.106, 133
Next for Ordaining, that thy words not swell..210. H.590, 7
Order Of which chast Order You are now the Queene: 107. H.265, 6
Faire Pearles in order set?....................130. H.330, 4
No, thou know'st order, Ethicks, and ha's read.148. H.377, 89
Order in a sweet neglect:......................232. H.665, 8
Prepost'rous is that order, when we run.......241. H.708, 1
The order, but the Sum of things..............245. H.721, 2
'Tis but by Order, not by Entitie.............386. N.191, 6
Seldome brings order, but confusion...........392. N.230, 8
Orders Or whether those (in orders rare) or these 326. H.1080, 3
Ore See Finny-oar
Soft then the finest Lemster Ore..............165. H.443, 28
Organ My Organ fast asleep;....................144. H.371, 15
Organs Fit Organs for encrease,..................57. H.149, 127
Orgies Of sacred *Orgies flyes, A round, A round. 7. H.8, 8
When we thy Orgies sing,......................259. H.772, 10
Orient Instead of Orient Pearls of Jet,..........14. H.34, 1
This Orient,..................................43. H.123, 11
Against you come, some Orient Pearls unwept:..68. H.178, 22
A pure smooth Pearle, and Orient too?......164. H.440, 8
Original Originall of Essence there is none.......386. N.191, 3
Ornament Burns for the Altars ornament..........92. H.223, 96
Ornaments Come in for comely ornaments,.......285. H.892, 19
Ornith's By Ornithes sonne, young Calais;.....70. H.181, 14
Orphan To free the Orphan from that Wolfe-like-man, 201. H.557, 15
An Orphan left him (lately dead.)............246. H.724, 20
Orphan's No Orphans pittance, left him, serv'd to set 149. H.377, 123
Orphans Such pretty flowers, (like to Orphans young) 104. H.257, 13
What will ye (my poor Orphans) do..........218. H.626, 1
Orpheus Orpheus he went (as Poets tell).......265. H.798, 1
Nam'd thee Terpander, or sweet Orpheus:......288. H.907, 8
Ort And further of some ort of Peare.....439. ins. H.443, 45a
Orts Any Orts the Elves refuse................223. H.638, 19
Osiers Of inter-woven Osiers;...................345. N.33, 10
Osiris Out-glares the Heav'ns *Osiris; and thy gleams 77. H.197, 11
O'th' (Partial List)
Saint Will o'th' Wispe (of no great bignes)...91. H.223, 30
Roots had no money; yet he went o'th score....162. H.427, 1
Other While other Gums their sweets perspire,....20. H.54, 5
As any other, this can tell;....................24. H.73, 8
Beauty, no other thing is, then a Beame.......33. H.102, 1
Lyd. While thou no other didst affect,..........70. H.181, 5
And had no other pride at all,..................75. H.193, 30
And other Scriptures, that designe............92. H.223, 83
Candles (forsooth) and other knacks:..........93. H.223, 116
Will no other thing imply,.......................97. H.232, 16
With other Flowers, bind my Love.............98. H.238, 2
While other Rusticks, lesse attent.............101. H.250, 23
For what other reason is't,.....................128. H.322, 3
The other parts will richly please.............138. H.342, 10
You to some other chimney, and there take....146. H.377, 27
Essay of other giblets; make...................146. H.377, 28
These Musks, these Ambers, and those other smells 157. H.414, 3
Or other over radiant Ray......................167. H.443, 77
Of all those other Saints now blest;...........169. H.449, 25
Means, I shall know what other kisse..........175. H.465, 70
Upon an other Plain:............................183. H.492, 10
So, that an Author needs no other Bayes......188. H.506, 11
And when I see that other Dresse..............202. H.560, 3
Thy selfe, which thou put'st other men unto....214. H.614, 2
Or other Rites that doe belong to me;..........219. H.627, 6
What off-spring other men have got,..........236. H.681, 1
Health is no other (as the learned hold)......236. H.683, 1
Some laid her forth, while other wept,..........237. H.686, 7
Glory no other thing is (Tullie sayes)..........241. H.710, 1
Our hope of one for the other..................247. H.727, 6
So silently they one to th' other come,.........250. H.737, 5
(As other Townes and Cities were) for gold,...251. H.745, 6
Locks incurl'd of other haire;..................253. H.750, 11
Other mens sins wee ever beare in mind;.....253. H.751, 1
And possesse no other feare,...................255. H.761, 23
See this, View that, and all the other bounds:..259. H.771, 4
It is no other then the Bed....................269. H.815, 3
Fortune is now Your Captive; other Kings.....271. H.823, 5
Beauti's no other but a lovely Grace...........274. H.840, 1
No other, but the doers willingnesse...........275. H.845, 2
Twilight, no other thing is, Poets say,.........278. H.858, 1
Our Crosses are no other then the rods,........278. H.862, 1
(As in an other Rosamond.)....................281. H.876, 4
This 'mongst other mystick charms.............284. H.889, 5
While other generations dye...................288. H.906, 4
Vineger is no other I define,...................301. H.964, 1
For other things, my many Children be.........304. H.978, 5
I think no other but I see......................311. H.1010, 3
The Twi-light is no other thing (we say)......319. H.1046, 1
And all those other Bits, that bee.............350. N.47, 29
And winde all other witnesses:.................357. N.72, 10
And other flowers, lay upon....................359. N.83, 11
Hell is no other, but a soundlesse pit,.........372. N.117, 1
No other, then Christs full Affection...........383. N.174, 2
And th' other Mary (Mary Magdalen).........384. N.180, 8
Nearer to that place, then to other some:.....385. N.186, 2
May chance to be no other man, but Christ.....391. N.226, 2
This, that, and ev'ry other part;...............402. N.269, 7
By n' other Face, but by thyne owne,.........409. A.2, 76
Some strickter Mrls. or suspitious other.......410. A.3, 8
And when an other age shall bring.............418. A.9, 31
— — — — — — — — — — —, ...425. var. H.197, 22
— — — — — — — — — — —, ...426. var. H.197, 40
— — — — — — — — — — —, ...438. var. H.374, 1
— — — — — — — — — — —, ...453. var. H.283, 98
Other's But lost to one, be th' others death......38. H.106, 142
To one and th'others nakednesse...............58. H.152, 8
One and th'others passions:.....................82. H.203, 10

Or while that each from **other's** breath did drincke 410. A.3, 5
Others Thou sail'st with **others,** in this Argus here;.23. H.71, 1
Let **others** drink thee freely; and desire........46. H.128, 49
Where **others** love, and praise my Verses; still..66. H.173, 1
Helps to all **others,** but to me?...............74. H.191, 4
To make for **others** garlands; and to set........94. H.224, 3
While that **others** doe divine;.................113. H.283, 47
Makes holy these, all **others** lay aside:.........114. H.283, 98
Nothing is New: we walk where **others** went...139. H.352, 1
Lasie to **others,** but be long to me.............141. H.357, 2
Others there be, who righteously will swear...141. H.359, 9
When **others** gain much by the present cast,....144. H.374, 1
Of **others;** since no Stud, no Stone, no Piece,..149. H.377, 117
To **others** store of helpfull spectacles...........154. H.401, 2
Which we to **others** (from our selves).........166. H.443, 61
Furies to **others,** Friends to me.................174. H.465, 6
'Tis Heresie in **others:** In your face.............180. H.481, 1
With oathes, and lyes, (as **others** do.)..........182. H.490, 12
And walk thou must the way that **others** went:.188. H.507, 2
Others to Lust, but me to Love...............193. H.521, 54
Ripe Cherries smiling, while that **others** blow...193. H.523, 2
Did I or love, or could I **others** draw........201. H.557, 1
Live by thy Muse thou shalt; when **others** die.210. H.592, 1
Horne sells to **others** teeth; but has not one..211. H.595, 1
I, as **others,** am Prophane.....................227. H.651, 4
Not envying **others** larger grounds:...........230. H.662, 16
'Tis dignity in **others,** if they be...............234. H.673, 15
What **others** can't with all their strength put to..245. H.722, 2
Thou canst but have, what **others** had.........246. H.725, 4
Softnesse in **others,** will be kind;.............252. H.746, 6
Go to Feast, as **others** do.....................255. H.761, 2
Others shall spring up in their place agen:....256. H.763, 12
While **others** perish, here's thy life decreed....280. H.869, 5
While **others** they sit wringing...............296. H.946, 15
(What's hard to **others**) nothing's troublesome..298. H.955, 4
Leave **others** Beauty, to set up withall.........299. H.958, 6
Let **others** to the Printing Presse run fast,.....314. H.1022, 1
To bath in thee (as thousand **others** doe.)......315. H.1028, 6
What **others** have with cheapnesse seene, and ease, 330. H.1100, 1
Let **others** look for Pearle and Gold,.............355. N.60, 1
With **others,** to the dreadfull Doome:..........358. N.78, 6
I flie from Thee, as **others** did:...............399. N.265, 2
Some to bee Ratts, and **others** to bee hoggs:...412. A.3, 92
Others' That sighs at **others** death; smiles at his own 129. H.323, 13
Swel'd with the Lard of **others** meat...........200. H.552, 16
Whose lives are **others,** not their own!.........229. H.662, 2
Other-saintships Neither those **other-Saint-ships** will I 91. H.223, 33
Otherwise But 'tis **otherwise** with me;..........128. H.322, 9
No **otherwise,** then if he would...............279. H.863, 7
If **otherwise,** I stand indifferent:...............392. N.230, 4
Noe **otherwise** then as those former two.........410. A.3, 14
In speach, in Picture; noe **otherwise** then when.411. A.3, 61
Ought See **Aught**
How farre a Figure **ought** to go,..............148. H.377, 92
Kings **ought** to be more lov'd, then fear'd......234. H.672, 2
Kings **ought** to sheare, not skin their sheepe....261. H.780, 2
And by the Law I **ought** to stay...............293. H.934, 7
And want their Poise: words **ought** to have their weight. 342. N.16, 2
Wherefore two prayers **ought** not to be said,....396. N.249, 7
Our (Partial List)
Loud is **our** love, and loose **our** play,..........48. H.136, 2
Out (Partial List) See **Marked-out**
For one drink-offering, poured **out** by thee.....14. H.35, 8
Laid **out** for dead, let thy last kindnesse be....19. H.50, 1
For my life mortall, Rise from **out** thy Herse,..27. H.82, 15
Though much from **out** the Cess be spent,......33. H.100, 3
Flasht **out** between the Middle and Extreame...33. H.102, 2
And all his Tapers thus put **out**:...............42. H.119, 6
Out them, to keep..........................43. H.123, 29
The lid began to let **out** day;.................46. H.130, 9
The Last Watch **out,** and saw the Dawning too..52. H.146, 4
Apostles, way (unshackled) to goe **out**.........52. H.146, 16
Or let Love's fire goe **out,**...................53. H.149, 5
To put the Tapers **out,**.......................56. H.149, 104
Will find me **out** a path to die;:..............60. H.159, 6
Next, hollow **out** a Tombe to cover............61. H.159, 28
One onely Poem **out** of all you'l chuse;.......64. H.168, 8
Thy long-black-Thumb-nail marks 'em **out** for ill: 66. H.173, 2
Nay! not so much as **out** of bed?..............68. H.178, 9
From **out** the eye, Loves Firmament:..........69. H.178, 54
But **out** of hope his wife might die to beare 'em. 72. H.184, 2
From **out** my Narde, and Fun'rall fire:........72. H.185, 18
Out of the which, the creame of light,..........74. H.190, 9
And (like a blasting Planet) found her **out;**....87. H.215, 4
To keep **out** the Letcher, and keep in the whore: 97. H.233, 2
The Whore to come **out,** or the Letcher come in..97. H.233, 4
Rather then mend, put **out** the light...........97. H.235, 6
Charms, that call down the moon from **out** her sphere, 99. H.244, 1
Wept **out** our heart, as well as eyes..........104. H.256, 14
Come to weep **out** the night..................106. H.262, 16
And when I'm laid **out** for a Corse; then be....111. H.279, 3
Blowne **out** of April; or some New-............112. H.283, 3
The Aged point **out,** This is she,.............114. H.283, 64
What comes in, runnes quickly **out**:...........116. H.285, 6
What ere enters, **out** it shall:.................116. H.285, 8
Who formes a Godhead **out** of Gold or Stone,..117. H.288, 1
Not **out** of Conscience, or Religion:............122. H.305, 2
And cry **out,** Hey, for our town green.........127. H.319, 20
As when a Rain-bow in perfumes goes **out**.....131. H.331, 8
From **out** the wealthy spiceries:...............145. H.375, 2
And when wise Poets shall search **out** to see...149. H.377, 135
Sleeping the lucklesse Age **out,** till that she...150. H.382, 19
Glasse, **out** of deepe, and **out** of desp'rate want,..151. H.385, 1
Driving these sharking trades, is **out** at heels...153. H.398, 2
When **out** of bed my Love doth spring,........154. H.404, 1
Yet **out** alas! the deaths the same,............155. H.406, 5
For pitty, Sir, find **out** that Bee,..............156. H.412, 11
Two she spat **out,** a cough forc't **out** the rest..158. H.419, 2
But more's sent in, then was serv'd **out**.........178. H.476, 9
When the Tapers once are **out**................180. H.482, 4
Dash all bad Poems **out** of countenance........187. H.506, 10
A little **out,** and then,.........................194. H.525, 3
Brave Kinsman, markt **out** with the whiter stone: 199. H.545, 8
Out of the world he must, who once comes in:.199. H.548, 1
A Fart flew **out,** or a Sir-reverence............200. H.551, 6
Walking in and **out** her eye,..................204. H.566, 4
Flew **out** a crack, so mighty, that the Fart,....205. H.572, 3
And once more yet (ere I am laid **out** dead)...214. H.612, 13
Or else spin **out** the thread of sands,..........215. H.616, 7
Please your Grace, from **out** your Store,......223. H.638, 1
Now **out,** and then in,........................225. H.643, 5
Cal'd **out** by the clap of the Thunder..........225. H.643, 24
To kisse thy hand from **out** the coach;........239. H.696, 2
Then a mans frequent Fame, spoke **out** with praise. 241. H.710, 2
Twice two fell **out,** all rotten at the root.......247. H.728, 2
That done, they kisse, and so draw **out** the day:.260. H.773, 2
Then Roman Sylla powr'd **out** at his feast.....262. H.783, 6
More curst for singing **out** of tune then he.....266. H.799, 4
To seeke, and find some few Immortals **out**....267. H.804, 6
Nature finds **out** some place for buriall.........267. H.807, 2
A soveraign balme found **out** to cure me.......274. H.841, 4
Make hoods of thee to serve **out** Spice.........275. H.844, 8
Not **out** of want of breath, but want of faith..283. H.884, 2
When Yew is **out,** then Birch comes in,........285. H.892, 13
Truth is best found **out** by the time, and eyes;.287. H.902, 1
That Prickles buyes, puts Prickles **out** of frame;.287. H.903, 3
Man must do well **out** of a good intent,........290. H.917, 1
When as his owne still **out** at elboes is?........295. H.941, 8
(His teeth all **out**) to rince and wash his gummes. 301. H.965, 2
Cries **out,** (my lord, my Lord) the Case is clear: 303. H.975, 6
None of these; but **out,** alas!.................305. H.984, 10
Because his stock will not hold **out** for white...309. H.997, 2
Nothing's so hard, but search will find it **out**....311. H.1008, 2
Finde **out** a Threshold or a doore,............312. H.1014, 7
Out of my comely manners worne;.............312. H.1016, 5
To have a tooth twitcht **out** of's native frame...323. H.1066, 2
Out of my self that Glorious Hierarchie!.......326. H.1080, 2
And feares in summer to weare **out** the lether:.332. H.1116, 2
She cocks **out** her Arse at the parting,........333. H.1122, 3
A way to measure **out** the Wind;...............339. N.3, 2
He held **out** then,.............................346. N.38, 7
Yet before the glasse be **out,**.................348. N.41, 35
Abhorre, and spew **out** all Neutralities...........353. N.54, 4
And be return'd from **out** my dust:...........358. N.78, 2
From **out** thy Maiden-Monument..............361. N.83, 66
And have a care no fire gos **out,**.............365. N.97, 5
To find him **out**?............................367. N.102, 11
Wip't **out** few, (God knowes) if any............373. N.121, 10
Our eyes **out** all together.....................373. N.123, 10
Clean washt, and laid **out** for the Beere;......374. N.123, 12
That ne're went **out** by Day or Night:........374. N.123, 46
Would cry **out,** Thou art blessed..............375. N.123, 90
Out of hell an horrour call,....................377. N.128, 14
Draw **out** of bad a soveraigne good to man.....383. N.176, 2
That soules departed are not put **out** quite;....384. N.181, 3
Drawes **out** th' Elixar of true penitence........386. N.196, 4
When as the poore crie **out,** to us.............394. N.239, 3
I'le call, and cry **out,** Thanks to Thee........400. N.267, 5
Like wanton rose buds growing **out** of snowe,..405. A.1, 54
To barr **out** bolde Adulteryes,.................408. A.2, 36
Thee, wth myne Eyes, or in, or **out,** of View..411. A.3, 70
Outcast To keepe the **out-cast** in his Tenement:.201. H.557, 14
Out-darts — — — — — — — —, ...425. var. H.197, 11
Outdid **Out-did** the meate, **out-did** the frolick wine. 289. H.911, 10
Outdo Brugel and Coxu, and the workes **out-doe,**.150. H.384, 3
Out-during **Out-during** Marble, Brasse, or Jet,..335. H.1129, 2

Out-glares **Out-glares** the Heav'ns *Osiris; and thy gleams 77. H.197, 11
Outlasts That our love **out-lasts** our yeeres........17. H.43, 10
Outlet The **out-let** then is from the heart.........24. H.73, 10
Outlive Verses **out-live** the bravest deeds of men?.264. H.791, 2
Outrages In mid'st of all their **outrages**.........31. H.90, 6
Or **Outrages**..................................335. H.1129, 7
Out-red And did **out-red** the same................12. H.23, 4
Outright Thus, thus to wound, not kill **out-right**:.34. H.103, 12
Outrun Goes with your mouth, or do's **outrun** your tongue; 141. H.359, 14
Outshine **Out-shine** the splendour of his mid-day beams. 77. H.197, 12
Outside **Out-side** silk, and **out-side** Lawne;......76. H.195, 7
(When true it is, the **out-side** swels..........118. H.291, 11
Lupes for the **outside** of his suite has paide;....302. H.969, 1
Outstable **Out-stable** for thy Court here..........345. N.33, 8
Out-stares — — — — — — — — —, ...425. var. H.197, 11
Out-stars — — — — — — — — —, ...425. var. H.197, 11
Out-vie As that your kisses must **out-vie** the Starres. 216. H.618, 14
Outward Good Sir, make no more cuts i'th' **outward** skin, 44. H.126, 3
And rich for in and **outward** show:...........90. H.223a, 2
Outwent My kisse **out-went** the bounds of shamfastnesse: 294. H.936, 2
Outworn With Hat and Shooes **out-worne**......295. H.942, 4
Nor dull'd wth Iron sleeps; but haue **out-worne**.410. A.3, 19
Oval Then in a Polisht **Ovall** by................90. H.223, 13
Into an **Ovall**, square, or round;...............202. H.560, 10
Over See **O'er**
Over the which a State was drawne............8. H.11, 5
Thy men; and rockie are thy wayes all **over**....29. H.86, 8
Over her fragrant cheek is cast................55. H.149, 72
Without some Scean cast **over**,................76. H.193, 39
Your storme is **over**; Lady, now appeare.......105. H.259, 7
The blush of cherries, when a Lawn's cast **over**..158. H.416, 4
Or other **over** radiant Ray.....................167. H.443, 77
Over my Turfe, when I am buried.............219. H.627, 4
Over thine Oat, as Soveraigne................244. H.716, 40
The Hector **over** Aged Exeter;................251. H.745, 2
Till they be all **over** wet,......................284. H.891, 3
The meane passe by, or **over**, none contemne;...322. H.1062, 7
Over the golden Altar now is spread,..........355. N.65, 3
So shall the Blankets which come **over** me,.....392. N.230, 15
Over the which a meet sweet skin is drawne...404. A.1, 23
Wrath yf resisted **ouer** boyles,................408. A.2, 71
To be with juice of Cedar washt all **over**;......415. A.7, 6
Then which, thy self ne'er wafted sweeter **over**..416. A.8, 10
For we goe **over** to be merry,.............445. ins. H.730, 26b
Overact Though He may seem to **over-act** His part: 341. N.10, 2
Overarched All **over-archt** with Oringe flowers;.145. H.375, 12
Overboil Seas chafe and fret, and beat, and **over-boile**; 105. H.259, 3
Overboils Wrath yf resisted **ouer boyles**,..........408. A.2, 71
Overcast With all thy richest jewels **over-cast**:..76. H.194, 2
Whose life with care is **overcast**,.............233. H.670, 32
Overcome Who first provides, not to be **overcome**. 109. H.268, 2
But none, of purpose, to be **overcome**...........380. N.150, 4
Overcooled His Nose is **over-cool'd** with Isicles..210. H.589, 2
Overdoes For (trust me Girle) shee **ouer-does**....409. A.2, 81
Overfill 'Tis best to feed Love; but not **over-fill**:..220. H.633, 23
Famish me, nor **over-fill**.......................232. H.665, 18
Overflow Your selves into the mighty **over-flow**.115. H.283, 118
Overhead Thus soft she lies: and **over-head**....167. H.443, 100
Overlaid Taste her lips, so **over-laid**............138. H.346, 6
Over-leaven-looks An **over-leven-looks** in thee,..321. H.1056, 8
Overlong I will not **over-long** enlarge..........175. H.465, 67
Overloving **Overloving**, (living here:)..........152. H.391, 2
Overplus Thy wits great **over-plus**;............289. H.911, 14
Over-read And **over-read** what I have writ 132. H.334, 4
Over-sick Never was Day so **over-sick** with showres, 52. H.146, 1
Overslide To **over-slide**;.......................65. H.172, 17
Oversoured **Over-sowr'd** in drinke of Souce:....223. H.638, 7
Overspread With crawling Woodbine **over-spread**:.192. H.521, 6
Overthrow This publique **overthrow**?...........211. H.596, 8
Of **overthrow**:..............................335. H.1129, 5
Overthrown Great men by small meanes oft are **overthrown**: 181. H.486, 1
Over-well Deriue their **overwell** grac'd motion.....406. A.1, 86
Overwhelmed Or **overwhelm'd** with store........368. N.104, 9
Cha. Who calls? who calls? Euc. One **overwhelm'd** with ruth; 416. A.8, 3
Ovid To **Ovid**; and suppose,...................80. H.201, 22
Then stately Virgil, witty **Ovid**, by...........206. H.575, 39
Homer, Musæus, **Ouid**, Maro, more.............411. A.3, 41
Owe I come to pay a Debt of Birth I **owe**.......27. H.82, 12
I **owe** thee for a kisse.........................29. H.87, 3
The Oile was yours; and that I **owe** for yet:...94. H.226, 9
Posterity will pay thee what I **owe**............298. H.955, 12
To pay Thee that I **owe**, since what I see......368. N.103, 3
Christ having paid, I nothing **owe**:............370. N.107, 13
I **owe** vnto A female Child,....................407. A.2, 3
Owes **Owes** more to vertue then too Fate 422. ins. H.106, 92b
Owest Mony thou **ow'st** me; Prethee fix a day....83. H.206, 1
Thou Fortune **ow'st** for tenement..............407. A.2, 14
Owl See **Screech-owl**
No Fatal **Owle** the Bedsted keeps,.............56. H.149, 101
And a broad-fac't **Owle** shall be...............195. H.530, 5
Owl-eyed With all her **Owle-ey'd** issue begs a boon 116. H.283, 152
Own (Partial List)
Where thou mayst hear thine **own** Lines read....6. H.2, 23
By your **owne** jewels set on fire...............20. H.54, 6
To thine **owne** selfe; and knowne to few.......38. H.106, 136
But their **own** flesh and blood,................75. H.193, 31
Both with her Husband's, and her **own** tough fleame. 98. H.237, 2
And how she is her **owne** least part:..........103. H.253, 16
This Sparrow, she had scorn'd her **own**:.......104. H.256, 12
Number, Your **owne**, by free Adoption;.......107. H.264, 4
And Pink may paint the Devill's by his **owne**...110. H.272, 4
High in your **own** conceipt, and some way teach 115. H.283, 128
For mine **own** part I'de as lieve,..............117. H.285, 10
But when your **own** faire print was set........126. H.318, 6
To give that life, resign'd your **own**:..........126. H.318, 9
That keepes his **own** strong guard, in the despight 128. H.323, 9
That sighs at others death; smiles at his **own**..129. H.323, 13
Our **own** fair wind, and mark each one.......133. H.336, 39
Now old enough to be our **own**................134. H.336, 88
But fixt it stands, by her **own** power,.........148. H.377, 108
Good morrow to mine **own** torn hair.........156. H.412, 3
And to retain thy **own**?........................168. H.446, 4
Eternall by their **own** production..............170. H.451, 8
Who can scoure Linnens with her **own** salt reeume? 178. H.474, 6
High with thine **own** Auspitious Destinies:....181. H.483, 2
He's Lord of thy life, who contemnes his **own**..181. H.486, 2
Never see mine **own** heart bleed:..............182. H.490, 2
These (nay) and more, thine **own** shal be,.....193. H.521, 55
We eate our **own**, and batten more,...........200. H.552, 13
Our **own** beloved privacie:.....................200. H.552, 18
Law is to give to ev'ry one his **owne**..........201. H.557, 10
They were mine **own**. Lal. In love combine...244. H.716, 46
His wife her **owne** ware sells as fast at home..253. H.753, 4
Kings seek their Subjects good: Tyrants their **owne**. 278. H.861, 2
In that your **owne** prefixed comelinesse:.......299. H.958, 4
Truth by her **own** simplicity is known,........329. H.1094, 1
But stand for ever by his **owne**..............335. H.1129, 13
By n' other Face, but by thyne **owne**,........409. A.2, 76
Where, with their **own** contagion they are fed;.417. A.8, 33
But of her **owne** a spoile shee makes.....436. ins. H.336, 48p
Ox The fattest **Oxe** the first must bleed.........77. H.196, 2
The patient **Oxe** unto the Yoke,................102. H.250, 48
The Heifer, Cow, and **Oxe** draw neere........230. H.662, 38
To tire thy patient **Oxe** or Asse...............233. H.670, 3
Oysters In **oysters** and Burgundian wine,...437. var. H.336, 130
Pace See **Foot-pace**
Forward, or backward, side-ward, and what **pace**.148. H.377, 93
Make for thy peace, and **pace** to heaven.......149. H.377, 130
That slack my **pace**; but yet not make me stay?.352. N.51, 3
helpe on her **pace**; and though she lagg, yet stirre 430. ins. H.283, 20h
Paced See **Smooth-paced**, **True-paced-numbers**
Paces Of holy Saints she **paces** on,............112. H.283, 13
Pack But of all packs, no **pack** like poverty......242. H.715, 2
Packs He feeles when **Packs** do pinch him; and the where. 60. H.158, 4
But of all **packs**, no pack like poverty..........242. H.715, 2
Slouch he **packs** up, and goes to sev'rall Faires,.253. H.753, 1
Paddling Who **padling** there, the Sea soone frown'd, 294. H.937, 3
Paddocks Cold as **Paddocks** though they be,......364. N.95, 3
Pagan Part **Pagan**, part Papisticall..............91. H.223, 25
That Christ did die, the **Pagan** saith;.........395. N.247, 1
Page how long shall the **page**, to please..431. ins. H.283, 60g
Pageantry For Sports, for **Pagentrie**, and Playes,.230. H.662, 46
Marian too in **Pagentrie**:.....................255. H.761, 8
Pagget **Pagget**, a School-boy, got a Sword, and then 65. H.171, 1
Paid Small shots **paid** often, waste a vast estate..13. H.28, 2
The debt is **paid**: for he who doth resigne.....72. H.185, 26
When, after these, h'as **paid** his vows,..........93. H.223, 135
I've **paid** Thee, what I promis'd; that's not All; 168. H.444, 1
Till thou shalt say, I've **paid** thee with a song..248. H.730, 22
Will **paid** have his fee,........................256. H.762, 11
Here to be **paid**; Ile pay't i'th'world to come...267. H.804, 14
Lupes for the outside of his suite has **paide**;...302. H.969, 1
Christ having **paid**, I nothing owe:...........370. N.107, 13
(As if it was a tribute **paid**)...........439. ins. H.443, 45c
Paid'st Thou **paid'st** the debt,....................360. N.83, 22
Pail See **Milking-pail**
Pails Wash your **Pailes**, and clense your Dairies;.201. H.556, 5
Bring in **pailes** of water then,................315. H.1026, 9

Pain Which being done, the fretfull paine........18. H.46, 9
His vertue still is sensible of paine:...........60. H.158, 2
There's paine in parting; and a kind of hell,...73. H.186, 7
As to entrance his paine, or cure his woe.......99. H.244, 4
That done, then let him, dispossest of paine,...99. H.244, 7
Not sent ye for to drowne your paine,.........102. H.250, 54
The cruell paine did his forsake,..............188. H.509, 3
And bind the paine;...........................210. H.591, 4
Although with some, yet little paine:..........233. H.670, 10
Thanksgiving is a burden, and a paine;.........292. H.923, 3
Their hands for paine;........................296. H.946, 16
The first by patience, and the last by paine......343. N.24, 4
To have continuall paine, or pleasure here:...394. N.236, 2
With one, and all parts, full of pain:..........400. N.267, 2
Painful Which done, thy painfull Thumb this sentence tells us,
36. H.106, 61
Into your Chests, drawn by your painfull Thumb.
221. H.633, 41
Pains Thus Paines and Pleasures turne by turne succeed:
79. H.199, 3
My paines asleep;.............................95. H.227, 17
Melt, melt my paines,..........................95. H.227, 27
Those paines it lately felt before..............189. H.514, 4
A long-lifes-day I've taken paines..............212. H.602, 1
Mans fortunes are according to his paines.......253. H.752, 2
We blame, nay we despise her paines............279. H.867, 1
The good by mercy, as the bad by paines.......389. N.212, 2
Paint To paint a Bridgeman to the life:.........38. H.108, 4
To paint the Fiend, Pink would the Devill see;110. H.272, 1
And Pink may paint the Devill's by his owne..110. H.272, 4
So draw, and paint, as none may do the like,..150. H.384, 5
That paint the Hemisphere:...................257. H.767, 4
Giue vpp his worth: to the painte;............409. A.2, 80
Painted Seeing those painted Countries; and so guesse
36. H.106, 79
I co'd not speak the Saints here painted.......91. H.223, 27
Jone is a wench that's painted;..............229. H.659, 1
Painter But (Hark!) we praise the Painter now, not you.
98. H.241, 2
Painter's The Painters art in thy Sciography?...139. H.347, 2
Painting Umber was painting of a Lyon fierce,....205. H.572, 1
Paints Paints them with fresh Vermilion:........268. H.811, 2
Pair Live, and live blest; thrice happy Paire; Let Breath,
38. H.106, 141
'Tis fit that Night, the Paire,................220. H.633, 16
At Post and Paire, or Slam, Tom Tuck would play
238. H.693, 1
— — — — — — — — — —, ...453. ins. H.283, 20a
Pairs (Compos'd of odde, not even paires)......91. H.223, 47
Palate Gladding his pallat with some store......119. H.293, 35
'Twill never please the pallate of mine eare.....152. H.390, 2
Pale Sickly the Prim-rose: Pale the Daffadill:.41. H.118, 2
Bungie do's fast; looks pale; puts Sack-cloth on;
122. H.305, 1
Pale care, avant,.............................368. N.104, 10
Parting the paire, as wee may well suppose.....404. A.1, 13
Fly hence Pale Care, noe more remember.......413. A.4, 1
Paleness Though palenes be the Livery that I weare,
222. H.634, 5
Paler Then when the paler hieu................75. H.193, 15
Pales Mont. Fore-fend it Pan, and Pales do thou please
159. H.421, 31
Palm He saw my Palme; and then, said he,......63. H.166, 5
The Palme from Urbin, Titian, Tintarret,.......150. H.384, 2
Hisped, and hairie, ere thy Palm shall know....202. H.557, 24
Enspher'd with Palm on Your Triumphant Crest..271. H.823, 4
Palmers' My Palmers hat; my Scallops shell;....123. H.306, 3
Palms The Palms put forth their Gemmes, and every Tree
224. H.642, 5
And Palmes in hand,.........................369. N.106, 9
Palpable Her Soule and Love were palpable in this.
240. H.700, 2
Palsies Such Flesh-quakes, Palsies, and such fears as shall
82. H.204, 11
Palsy-struck Wither'd my hand, and palsie-struck my tongue.
84. H.210, 10
Pan Chor. Pan pipe to him, and bleats of lambs and sheep,
86. H.213, 17
Mont. Fore-fend it Pan, and Pales do thou please
159. H.421, 31
I vow by Pan, to come away....................184. H.492, 27
Steale a swolne sop out of the Dripping pan...331. H.1106, 2
Panchaia Doth from Panchaia come..............57. H.149, 146
Panchaia's Flow'd all Panchaia's Frankincense;..402. N.269, 15
Panicles The fantastick Pannicles:..............242. H.714, 4
Pannier In the Pris'ners Panier.................224. H.638, 24
We bid the Creuse and Pannier too:...........374. N.123, 32
Pans See Ash-pans
As that your pans no Ebbe may know;........179. H.476, 11
Pansies Pansies will weep; and Marygolds will wither;
41. H.118, 5
Ile leave thee, and to Pansies come:...........74. H.191, 5
With Rosie Chaplets, Lillies, Pansies red,
442. ins. H.575, 20a
Pansy In that ennamel'd Pansie by,.............107. H.263, 9
That Lady-smock, that Pansie, and that Rose...114. H.283, 94

Pant Sometimes 'two'd pant, and sigh, and heave,.66. H.175, 5
Pantheon As Rome's Pantheon had not more.....90. H.223, 8
Panting I kist thee (panting,) and I call.........20. H.56, 7
Or writhing Brides; when, (panting) they....167. H.443, 110
Lies softly panting like a Bride..............233. H.670, 14
Pants Pants with a Downie brest,...............57. H.149, 135
Pap (Made of her Pap and Gum)...............80. H.201, 7
Papacy They much affect the Papacie:..........93. H.223, 110
Paper The paper gild, and Laureat the pen.......141. H.359, 6
Paper-kites Serve but for matter to make Paper-kites.
286. H.896, 2
Papery The hornes of paperie Butterflies,.........119. H.293, 26
Papist Turn'd, from a Papist here, a Predicant...151. H.385, 2
He'l turn a Papist, rancker then before........151. H.385, 6
Papistical Part Pagan, part Papisticall............91. H.223, 25
Paps <Fingring> the paps that feele like sleeded silke
405. A.1, 57
Paradise ing the Chafte Aire with fumes of Paradise.
112. H.283, 16
The bastard Phenix; bird of Paradice;........262. H.783, 8
The prime of Paradice........................271. H.824, 8
Faire as Eve in Paradice:.....................274. H.838, 2
And make this place all Paradise:.............361. N.83, 62
Paradise is (as from the Learn'd I gather)....383. N.177, 1
Growing in this love garded paradice............406. A.1, 72
Paragon She's to me a Paragon..................11. H.21, 14
Deservelesse of the name of Paragon:...........76. H.194, 4
O Paragon, and Pearle of praise!..............359. N.83, 2
Paragraphs By Reading all her Paragraphs in Thee.
201. H.557, 4
Parallels In most happy Parallels?..............286. H.897, 10
Keepes line for line with Beauties Parallels.....307. H.992, 6
Paranymphs Lead on faire paranymphs, the while her eyes,
430. ins. H.283, 20a
Parasceve Fit, fit it is, we have our Parasceve...355. N.65, 8
Parched See Moon-parched
Parchment A rowle of Parchment Clunn about him beares,
295. H.941, 1
Pardon Or here so bad, but you may pardon them.
64. H.168, 6
And pardon crave,.............................100. H.246, 2
Pardon my feares (sweet Sapho,) I desire.....279. H.866, 3
Pardon my trespasse (Silvia) I confesse,.........294. H.936, 1
(Pardon, Lacon if I weep)...................306. H.984, 31
Beg for my Pardon Julia; He doth winne......329. H.1095, 3
When I shall sin, pardon my trespasse here;....367. N.99, 1
Pardon me God, (once more I Thee intreat)....371. N.113, 1
how long, oh pardon, shall the house......431. ins. H.283, 60c
Pardoned Night hides our thefts; all faults then pardon'd be:
209. H.586, 1
Pardoning Whose Peace is made up with a Pardoning.
316. H.1029, 2
Pardons Their Pardons and Indulgences:........93. H.223, 114
God pardons those, who do through frailty sin;.. 344. N. 32, 1
Pared See Thumb-nails-pared
Parents Our Houshold-gods our Parents be;......226. H.647, 1
One Birth their Parents gave them; but their new.
326. H.1080, 25
Honour thy Parents; but good manners call....363. N.94, 1
Parents' I glided by my Parents sight...........69. H.180, 2
If pittying my sad Parents Teares,............70. H.180, 5
Pares Ralph pares his nayles, his warts, his cornes, and Ralph
299. H.959, 1
Parish Poore of the Parish, (if there's any)......92. H.223, 90
Park How each field turns a street; each street a Parke
68. H.178, 30
Parley Then in that Parly, all those powers.......8. H.11, 7
Parliament To meet and sit in Parliament:........8. H.11, 2
That frights men with a Parliament:...........126. H.319, 4
Parlor To the worn Threshold, Porch, Hall, Parlour, Kitchin,
146. H.377, 5
Like as my Parlour, so my Hall..............350. N.47, 17
Parrat Parrat protests 'tis he, and only he......186. H.501, 1
Parrot See Parrat
Parsley To honour thee, my little Parsly crown:.131. H.333, 4
With crowns of greenest Parsley,..............234. H.674, 3
Parson And, as Sir Thomas Parson tells,........92. H.223, 79
Old Parson Beanes hunts six dayes of the week,
163. H.435, 1
Parson's The tenth you know the Parsons is......208. H.581, 2
Part See Circum-mortal-part, Fore-part, Little-peeping-part
Part of the creame from that Religious Spring;....9. H.14, 8
Part of her leggs sinceritie:....................12. H.27, 4
I dream'd this mortal part of mine..............16. H.41, 1
Whether in part 'tis here or there,..............24. H.73, 5
To part her lips, and shew'd them there.......24. H.75, 7
Is too precise in every part....................28. H.83, 14
Sho'd be a little part..........................28. H.85, 4
In each thy dainty, and peculiar part!.........30. H.88, 2
No part besides must of thy selfe be known,....30. H.88, 11
Deare, though to part it be a Hell,............33. H.103, 1
I doe beseech thee, ere we part,...............33. H.103, 5
Whose heart, whose hand, whose ev'ry part spake love.
42. H.122, 8
Then say; my part..........................43. H.123, 27
And must we part, because some say,.........48. H.136, 1

Pay we our Vowes, and goe; yet when we part,.73. H.186, 13
Fill each part full of fire, active to doe........79. H.197, 79
For my part, I never care.....................82. H.203, 1
Kisse, and sigh, so part agen....................82. H.203, 14
Part Pagan, part Papisticall.....................91. H.223, 25
And how she is her owne least part:..........103. H.253, 16
And hast command of every part,.............109. H.267, 23
Part of the way be met; or sit stone-still.......113. H.283, 58
For mine own part I'de as lieve,...............117. H.285, 10
But to shew thee how in part,..................128. H.322, 4
Part your joyn'd lips, then speaks your kisse;.130. H.329, 18
Say, we must part (sweet mercy blesse........134. H.336, 65
When as the meanest part of her,.............145. H.375, 25
Upon some part of Kid, as if mistooke,........147. H.377, 55
Part of which I give to Larr,..................152. H.393, 5
Part is my peculiar.............................152. H.393, 6
Man is compos'd here of a two-fold part;.......153. H.394, 1
And all the while my part shall be to weepe;...159. H.421, 37
Unlesse you skin again each part..............164. H.442, 10
To play a loving part;.........................168. H.446, 6
Resolve to part with neither;...................169. H.446, 10
I cannot suffer; And in this, my part.........169. H.447, 1
Consent and play a friendly part..............177. H.471, 3
Neither broke i'th whole, or part..............183. H.490, 20
I must answer (Sweet) thy part..............186. H.500, 3
Any one part that's dissonant in you:.........189. H.511, 2
Come thou in, with thy best part,.............195. H.530, 2
Or part...198. H.544, 35
No part of pitie on a conquer'd foe...........199. H.550, 2
Won't for his tenth part ask you one...........208. H.581, 6
But lesse that part,............................210. H.591, 7
Little or no part there of Tyrannie...........213. H.608, 2
In every part alike compleat,..................243. H.716, 9
And that's the part to be acted................247. H.727, 12
Part of the nak't sincerity;....................247. H.729, 6
If Wars goe well; each for a part layes claime:.260. H.774, 3
Comely Acts well; and when he speaks his part,..266. H.799, 1
If not to th' whole, yet satisfy'd in part.......267. H.804, 12
Not to cut off, but cure the vicious part.........268. H.808, 2
Part Ruby-like, part Candidate?...............269. H.815, 2
'Tis religious part to see......................270. H.821, 3
Then the last part of night, and first of day.....278. H.858, 2
Part must be kept wherewith to teend........285. H.893, 5
And starves with cold the self-same part.......290. H.915, 8
Ile recollect thee (weeping) part by part;......300. H.960, 4
To have friends to beare a part:..............302. H.968, 4
Rid these, and those, and part by part eat all..305. H.982, 4
And as that part, so every portion else,.......307. H 992, 5
Yet part ye from hence,......................317. H.1035, 28
Wee shall not part for ever..................324. H.1068, 24
As if we sho'd for ever part?................328. H.1090, 2
'Tis Wisdomes part to doubt a faithfull friend..333. H.1121, 2
Part of the worke remaines; one part is past:.334. H.1126, 1
Though He may seem to over-act His part:...341. N.10, 2
Any part backward in the Deitie...............342. N.18, 2
His own He acts not, but anothers part:.....343. N.22, 2
He comes to play the part that is His own.....343. N.22, 4
In Prayer the Lips ne're act the winning part,..346. N.35, 1
Lord! let me never act that beggars part,.......347. N.39, 3
That I should render, for my part,...........351. N.47, 53
No man is blest through ev'ry part..........351. N.50, 4
Give Him the choice; grant Him the nobler part
356. N.68, 3
On our part, wanting all abilities..............356. N.71, 4
To welcome Him. 2. The nobler part..........365. N.96, 27
Part, or the whole of Thee,..................369. N.106, 2
That little prettie bleeding part..............376. N.125, 1
This Law; that He and I part stakes..........376. N.127, 6
Roaring is nothing but a weeping part,.........380. N.154, 1
One part thereof left still unfinished:.........384. N.178, 2
His humane Nature did, in part, appeare:......389. N.214, 2
His Humane Nature, and His Part Divine.....389. N.214, 6
The staffe might come to play the friendly part.
394. N.241, 4
But when He strikes, He quarter-acts His part..394. N.242, 2
Fail'd in my part; O! Thou that art my deare,.398. N 261, 2
This, that, and ev'ry other part;..............402. N.269, 7
That both her lipps doe part, doe meete, doe kisse;
405. A.1, 38
Thus every part in contrariety...............406. A.1, 105
To'th shew, but Neuer part wth; next..........407. A.2, 31
Parte wth a hastye kisse; and in that shew....410. A.3, 11
Then Parte in name of peace; & softely on.....412. A.3, 83
Thus with a kisse of warmth, and loue, I parte.412. A.3, 95
I finde in thee, that makes me thus to part,....414. A.6, 4
Since part we must Let's kisse, that done retire
414. A.6, 9
Fill each part full of Fire, let all my good
427. ins. H.197, 77a
— — — — — — — — — — —, ...429. var. H.263, 15
Partake Because the wicked do partake of them:.387. N.201, 4
Partaker Partaker of this sight..................220. H.633, 13
Parted Doe, and have parted here a Man and Wife:
26. H.79, 2
We parted are,............................162. H.426, 16
Participation Are Gods, but by participation:....379. N.143, 2
Particular Of my particular Remaines;..........245. H.720, 14
Parting Bequeath to me one parting kisse:......34. H.103, 16
There's paine in parting; and a kind of hell,....73. H.186, 7
Go hence, and with this parting kisse,.........174. H.465, 1
Where e're they met, or parting place has been..250. H.737, 8
She cocks out her Arse at the parting,........333. H.1122, 3
Come to fright a parting soule; 348. N.41, 23
Parting the paire, as wee may well suppose.....404. A.1, 13
Euen such are wee; and in our parting, doe......410. A.3, 13
Such is my parting wth thee; and to proue.....412. A.3, 79
Goe hence away, and in thy parting know.......414. A.6, 1
— — — — — — — — — — —, ...448. var. A.3, 10
Partly Partly worke and partly play............315. H.1026, 1
Partridge The Phesant, Partridge, Gotwit, Reeve, Ruffe, Raile,
147. H.377, 65
Part's Your part's to grant; my Scean must be to move.
274. H.837, 4
— — — — — — — — — — —, ...451. var. H.197, 79
Parts See Hinder-parts
When I thy Parts runne o'er, I can't espie........10. H.16, 1
(All parts there made one prisoner.)...........16. H.41, 17
Those parts, which maids keep unespy'd,........17. H.41, 19
Armes, and hands, and all parts else,..........53. H.147, 7
To make of parts an union;..................107. H.263, 15
Of all our parts, the eyes expresse.............121. H.300, 1
For one so rarely tun'd to fit all parts;........121. H.301, 1
Two parts of us successively command;........137. H.339, 1
The other parts will richly please..............138. H.342, 10
Our mortall parts may wrapt in Seare-cloths lye:
199. H.547, 1
Some parts may perish; dye thou canst not all:..200. H.554, 1
And you may find in Love these differing Parts;
274. H.837, 9
No man such rare parts hath, that he can swim,
298. H.953, 1
Play their offensive and defensive parts,......370. N.109, 1
Not those poor Theeves that act their parts with Thee:
399. N.263, 23
Thee in Thy severall parts of bitternesse;......399. N.263, 33
With one, and all parts, full of pain:..........400. N.267, 2
Parts be encouraged,.....................427. ins. H.197, 77b
Party See Party-colored
Do's but deride the Party buried..............319. H.1047, 2
Is halfe way cured, if the party will:...........319. H.1048, 2
Party-colored Party colour'd like a Pie;........305. H.984, 19
Paske Paske, though his debt be due upon the day
142. H.363, 1
Pass And ravish'd thus, It came to passe,.......13. H.27, 5
I! and a world of Pikes passe through.........31. H.90, 9
Which, as they drop by drop doe passe.........44. H.127, 5
And when (though long it comes to passe)....63. H.164, 6
Stoop, mount, passe by to take her eye, then glare
87. H.215, 5
Yet so it comes to passe,....................100. H.249, 7
Glide by the banks of Virgins then, and passe..113. H.283, 41
To passe; but such..........................115. H.283, 135
Passe all we must the fatall Ferry:............172. H.457, 2
Passe by,......................................178. H.475, 2
But making haste, it came to passe,...........187. H.504, 3
Skulls co'd not well passe through that scum of men.
200. H.551, 2
By noone, and let thy good dayes passe,.......233. H.670, 4
Thousands each day passe by, which wee,......234. H.671, 1
Her Apron gave (as she did passe)............251. H.740, 9
(Not knowing what would come to passe)......281. H.876, 6
A mischance is come to pass,.................305. H.984, 11
The meane passe by, or over, none contemne;..322. H.1062, 7
As he did passe,..............................346. N.38, 15
Can I not wooe thee to passe by..............357. N.72, 3
Who passe this way, to pitie me,..............400. N.266, 2
Passage Or else force a passage in:............121. H.297, 12
And wildly force a passage in,...............175. H.465, 55
Our slothful passage o're the Stygian Lake,...248. H.730, 24
His passage through that dreadfull shade:......265. H.798, 8
Looks through the passage of theis lines...........417.A.9, 10
Passages And look upon our dreadfull passages,...14. H.35, 6
Passed See Past
Some storms w'ave past;..................211. H.596, 13
Though by well-warding many blowes w'ave past, 237. H.688, 1
Att that wch in her extasie had past;............410. A.3, 26
Passenger But trust to this, my noble passenger;....23. H.71, 3
Passengers Till passengers shall spend their doome,
104. H.256, 20
I'th' Seas, she saves her passengers.............134. H.336, 64
Passers See Passersby
Passersby Tempting all the passers by:........232. H.665, 10
Come pitie us, ye Passers by,...............373. N.123, 3
Passes — — — — — — — — —, ...453. var. H.283, 13
Passing Which to effect, let ev'ry passing Bell....392. N.230, 11
Passing the sweet sweet of a musky rose.........406. A.1, 76
— — — — — — — — — — —,..............433. var. H.293, 17
— — — — — — — — — — —,..............441. var. H.465, 55
Passing-bell When the passing-bell doth tole,.....348. N.41, 21
Passion Of that Passion sweetens Pleasure........55. H.149, 80
Mont. A sweet-sad passion.—................159. H.421, 22
There wo'd be no Passion.....................163. H.433, 2

Passion, but for His Sheeps dispersion.........381. N.159, 2
And thence proceed, to act Thy Passion........399. N.263, 29
Vnto the passion, not to stay;..................408. A.2, 70
None writes lov's passion in the world, like Thee. 415. A.7, 18
Passions One and th'others passions:............82. H.203, 10
High and passions lesse of heat...............96. H.232, 10
And Mans Pulse stopt, All Passions sleep in Peace. 202. H.558, 4
My Passions any rest.......................272. H.828, 8
Let moderation on thy passions waite..........318. H.1038, 1
Passive The passive Aire such odour then assum'd, 157. H.414, 7
Past See Passed, Time-past
No sound calls back the yeere that once is past...8. H.10, 4
As were (time past) thy holy Filitings:..........11. H.22, 6
When one is past, another care we hav............18. H.48, 1
Past one aclock, and almost two,...............121. H.299, 7
Lame, and bad times, with those are past,......134. H.336, 82
Your date is not so past;......................176. H.467, 3
Once past and gone, no more shall see...........234. H.671, 2
Praise they that will Times past, I joy to see....292. H.927, 1
And as time past when Cato the Severe........301. H.962, 1
It is Noone and past with me:................307. H.991, 2
Part of the worke remaines; one part is past:..334. H.1126, 1
To change, or call back, His past Sentences.....389. N.216, 4
Past Noone of night, yett weare the howers not old 410. A.3, 18
Past Sorrowes with the fled December..........413. A.4, 2
Know time past this cherrystone................417. A.9, 19
— — — — — — — — — —,................436. var. H.336, 17
Past-best W'ave seen the past-best Times, and these 133. H.336, 17
Paste The Paste of Filberts for thy bread.....192. H.521, 13
With paste of Almonds, Syb her hands doth scoure; 203. H.561, 1
To fill the Paste that's a kneading.............263. H.784, 18
To paste of Almonds turn'd by thee:..........267. H.805, 4
Feed on the paste of Filberts, or else knead.....269. H.818, 5
Of gentle Paste, and yeelding Dow,...........374. N.123, 25
Pasterie See Pastry
Pastillus Unto Pastillus ranke Gorgonius came,.323. H.1066, 1
Pastime When Themilis his pastime makes,......192. H.521, 26
To make a pleasing pastime there...........230. H.662, 39
Pastimes Foule in these noble pastimes, lest ye call 114. H.283, 86
Pastoral From these to penne the pleasing Pastorall: 298. H.955, 6
Pastry Torn for the use of Pasterie:...........275. H.844, 4
Past-times — — — — — — — — —, ...451. var. H.336, 17
Pastures While leanest Beasts in Pastures feed,...77. H.196, 1
Patches Pieces, patches, ropes of haire;..........76. H.195, 5
Ursley, she thinks those Velvet Patches grace..197. H.543, 1
What are our patches, tatters, raggs, and rents,..302. H.970, 1
Patching For mending sails, for patching Boat and Oares? 248. H 730, 20
Pater Till Liber Pater twirles the house.........127. H.319, 42
No pennie, no Pater Noster..................256. H.762, 18
Paternal But while he met with his Paternall grave; 278. H.860, 4
Path So that the path I cannot find:..............32. H.98, 2
Will find me out a path to die;..................60. H.159, 6
The path is but short;........................195. H.534, 11
A path:......................................258. H.770, 4
In all that way no beaten path;.................372. N.118, 4
Paths Cleere Thou my paths, or shorten Thou my miles, 352. N.51, 5
Patience Of Patience wants. Grief breaks the stoutest Heart 169. H.447, 2
While misery keeps in with patience...........257. H.765, 4
If her patience turns to ire,....................273. H.836, 7
Princes cure some faults by their patience......309. H.998, 2
The first by patience, and the last by paine.....343. N.24, 4
Of suffring gives me patience..................354 N.57, 4
Had all been rich, where then had Patience been?..356. N.69, 3
Gives me a portion, giving patience:............362. N.87, 2
He patience gives; He gives himselfe to me......362. N.87, 4
Safe Modestie, Lou'd Patience, Feare...........409. A.2, 97
Patient Patient I was: Love pitifull grew then,....16. H.40, 5
The patient Oxe unto the Yoke,...............102. H.250, 48
The patient Saint, and send up vowes for me.....204. H.570, 4
To tire thy patient Oxe or Asse...............233. H.670, 3
Patient in my necessitie.......................235. H.677, 4
To this our poore, yet ever patient Flood.....332. H 1112, 6
But I as patient will be found.................351. N.48, 10
Turnes all the patient ground to flowers.........364. N.96, 24
Patrician And in that Good, a great Patrician....176. H.466, 2
Patrick Now Patrick with his footmanship has done. 158. H.418, 1
Patron A friendly Patron unto thee:..........275. H.844, 2
Patrons Let there be Patrons; Patrons like to thee, 41. H.117, 1
Pattern Let their example not a pattern be........399. N.264, 3
Paul Paul, he began ill, but he ended well;.......387. N.200, 1
Paul's Pauls hands do give, what give they bread or meat, 248. H.731, 1
Pauls hands do give, nought else for ought we know 248. H.731, 4
Pave Lies here abouts; and for to pave.........166. H.443, 53
The brave cheape worke, and for to pave 440. ins. H.443, 45b
Pavements The more on ycie pavements we are set. 316. H.1032, 2
Pawncy — — — — — — — — —, ...453. var. H.283, 94
Pawned Longe forfaite pawnèd diamonds..........407. A.2, 8
Pay See Pay't
I come to pay a Debt of Birth I owe...........27. H.82, 12
Me pay the debt..............................29. H.87, 2
Ten will not pay..............................29. H.87, 8
Having promis'd, pay your debts,..............44. H.125, 5
But with a kisse, or thanks, doe pay............71. H.182, 21
Pay we our Vowes, and goe; yet when we part,..73. H.186, 13
Let Much-more justly pay his tythes; then try...73. H.188, 3
And pay no vowes to thee? who wast their best..78. H.197, 59
For payment promis'd, though thou never pay:..83. H.206, 2
Pay when th'art honest; let me have some hope...83. H.206, 4
About him, when the Taverns shot's to pay......173. H.463, 2
For my wisht safety pay thy vowes,...........175. H.465, 74
We pay for our poore Tenement:...............200. H.552, 8
Pay then your Tythe; and doing thus,..........208. H.581, 3
Already coin'd to pay for it...................218. H.626, 7
Or how to pay thy Hinds, and cleere........230. H.662, 13
Or for a Tansie let us pay,...................238. H.690, 3
That likewise I may pay the Bet,...........238. H.690, 11
Ch. Talk not of love, all pray, but few soules pay me. 248. H.730, 18
Ph. Ile give thee vows & tears. Ch. can tears pay skores 248. H.730, 19
With a pennie to pay S. Peter.................256. H.762, 6
Posterity will pay thee what I owe............298. H.955, 12
If all transgressions here should have their pay,..343. N.27, 1
To pay agen,................................346. N.38, 11
But for the conquest thou didst pay............360. N.83, 24
To pay Thee that I owe, since what I see......368. N.103, 3
Alas! I cannot pay a jot; therefore............368. N 103, 7
'Tis true, my God; but I can't pay one mite.....368. N.103, 10
How I sho'd pay, 's impossible:..............369. N.107, 4
Then, if Thou bidst me pay, or go.............370. N.107, 11
And since you pay...............................413. A.4, 21
To pay the debt,...............................414. A.5, 2
What more than these can Tombs or Tomb-stones Pay? 419. A.10, 5
and the smooth Handmaides pay their vowes 431. ins. H.283, 60d
Paying Paying before you praise; and cockring wit. 141. H.359, 15
Paying but common thanks for it...........321. H.1056, 6
Payment Make payment for his pleasure..........30. H.87, 18
For payment promis'd, though thou never pay:..83. H.206, 2
To make paiment, while I call...............373. N.121, 12
Pays He payes the halfe, who do's confesse the Debt. 94. H.226 10
And no man payes too deare for it...........231. H.662, 61
— — — — — — — — — —,...............445. var. H.730, 18
Pay't Here to be paid; Ile pay't i'th'world to come. 267. H.804, 14
Pea Or Pea, or Bean, or Wort, or Beet,........200. H.552, 5
The Pea also...................................317. H.1035, 5
Peace Making thy peace with heav'n, for some late fault, 36. H.106, 59
And love shall crown my End with Peace......73. H.187, 11
Sleepe in thy peace, while we with spice perfume thee. 89. H.219, 13
Sometimes peace, and sometimes strife:.........96. H.232, 4
But endlesse Peace, sit here, and keep........104. H.256, 15
The leavie-trees nod in a still-born peace.........105. H.259, 6
Be't to your praise, no peace was broken.......114. H.283, 90
Ye wrong the Threshold-god, that keeps peace here: 124. H.313, 4
Live in thy peace; as for my selfe,...........134. H.336, 73
The tongue in peace; but then in warre the hand. 137. H.339, 2
No more is seen the Arch of Peace............139. H 353, 4
Make for thy peace, and pace to heaven.......149. H.377, 130
Or hold their peace.........................190. H.515, 28
O Pious-Priestresse! make a Peace for us.......197. H.539, 14
And Mans Pulse stopt, All Passions sleep in Peace. 202. H.558, 4
Goddesse of Pleasure, Youth and Peace,.......221. H.633, 54
Bring in her Bill, once more, the Branch of Peace. 225. H.642, 22
Power and Peace to keep one Throne.........264. H.788, 2
We pray 'gainst Warre, yet we enjoy no Peace...264. H.793, 1
As dearest Peace, after destructive Warre:......300. H.961, 2
Thou the Queen of Peace and Quorum.........303. H.974, 8
Whose Peace is made up with a Pardoning.....316. H.1029, 2
Where War and Peace the Dice by turns doe cast. 327. H.1083, 2
And in the purchase of our Peace,.............360. N.83, 29
Sleep in thy peace, thy bed of Spice;...........361. N.83, 61
And our Peace here, like a Spring,..............363. N.93, 8
Obedience, Wise-Distrust, Peace, shy..........409. A.2, 95
Then Parte in name of peace; & softely on.......412. A.3, 83
— — — — — — — — — —,.............453. var. H.283, 66
Peaceful Our Peacefull slumbers in the night....200. H.552, 12
We love to rest in peaceful Urnes at home......278. H.860, 6
Peacefull by night; my day devoid of strife:....294. H.938, 2

Yett I keepe peacefull in my dust..............407. A.2, 18
Beames of the sunn, the peacefull sea..........408. A.2, 58
Peach In bloome of Peach, and Roses bud,.......107. H.263, 11
Peacock And a Peacock proud shall be.........141. H.360, 5
Peacocks' With eyes of Peacocks Trains, & Trout-
166. H.443, 68.
Peals First, peales of Thunder we must heare,....247. H.725, 9
Pean-gardens Or did I walk those Pean-Gardens through,
234. H.673, 3
Peapes Peapes he do's strut, and pick his Teeth, as if
273. H.835, 1
Pear Into the blushing Peare, or Plum:........79. H.198, 4
Of rosted warden, or bak'd peare,..............145. H.375, 23
The blushing Apple, bashfull Peare,............192. H.521, 37
As colours steale into the Peare or Plum,......250. H.737, 6
You many a Plum, and many a Peare:............264 H.787, 2
And further of some ort of Peare.........439. ins. H.443, 45a
Pearl See Seed-pearl
Farewell my shackles, (though of pearle they be) 17. H.42, 3
The Quarelets of Pearl.........................24. H.75, 8
Made of the Rubie, Pearle and Diamond:........30. H.88, 6
And strings my tears as Pearle..................43. H.123, 6
And Pendant Pearle of ours.....................43. H.123, 12
Of Pearle, and Gold, to bind her hands:........98. H.238, 7
Congeal'd to Pearle and stone;.................131. H.330, 11
Rubie-lipt, and tooth'd with Pearl:............136. H.337, 2
A pure smooth Pearle, and Orient too?........164. H.440, 8
The Pearle of Princes, yet despaire...........175. H.465, 38
Sound Teeth has Lucie, pure as Pearl, and small,
226. H.649, 1
For ropes of pearle, first Madam Ursly showes..232. H.668, 1
Rein'd in with Purple, Pearl, and gold,........239. H.695, 6
A richer pearle for thee,......................240. H.705, 6
This counterchange of Perle and Diamond.......295. H.941, 6
Enspir'd with Purple, Pearle, and Gold;.......311. H.1010, 2
Let others look for Pearle and Gold............355. N.60, 1
O Paragon, and Pearle of praise!...............359. N.83, 2
Both with the Rubie, Pearle, and Diamond.......369. N.105, 8
Like pearle and gold make one rich Carcanett...405. A.1, 32
Insteade of gould Pearle Rubies Bonds...........407. A 2, 7
— — — — — — — — — — — —,..............435. var. H.293, 21e
— — — — — — — — — — — —,..............439. var. H.443, 41
— — — — — — — — — — — —,..............447. var. A.1, 3
Pearled
In country Meadowes pearl'd with Dew.......323. H.1068, 5
Pearls Instead of Orient Pearls of Jet,..............14. H.34, 1
Some ask'd how Pearls did grow, and where?....24. H.75, 5
More white then Pearls, or Juno's thigh;.......34. H.105, 5
Against you come, some Orient Pearls unwept:..68. H.178, 22
Some Pearls on Queens, that have been counterfet.
76. H.194, 6
Or as the pearles of Mornings dew............12 . H.316, 19
Faire Pearles in order set?....................130. H.330, 4
And all behung with these pure Pearls, ...167. H.443, 108
Which, though enchas'd with Pearls, contain....222. H.635, 11
Of Rome did weare for their most precious Pearles.
251. H.741, 2
As purest Pearles, or Pebles do...............271. H.824, 11
— — — — — — — — — — —,..............447. var. A.1, 32
Pearly See Precious-pearly-purling
Quicknd of late by Pearly showers;............25. H.78, 6
Each richly headed with a pearly shell.........406. A.1, 102
But substance, to! receaue this Pearlye Teare....412. A.3, 81
— — — — — — — — — — —,..................448. var. A.1, 66
Pears Of fragrant Apples, blushing Plums, or Peares:
205. H 575. 10
So Cherries blush, and Kathern Peares,.........268. H.811, 3
Peas See Pease
Peasant To which the Pesant, so the Prince must come,
392. N.230, 24
Pease Of Twelf-tide Cakes, of Pease, and Beanes 127. H.319, 17
Of a Pease, that 'gins to chit,................223. H.638, 13
Science puffs up, sayes Gut, when either Pease..327. H.1085, 1
Be the meale of Beanes and Pease,..............363. N.93, 3
The scraps of Lintells chitted Pease......439. ins. H.443, 45i
Peason Long Locks of late our Zelot Peason weares,
275. H.843. 1
Pebbles As purest Pearles, or Pebles do........271. H.824. 11
So purest pebbles in the brook:...............294. H.939, 4
Pebbly The Damaskt medowes, and the peebly streames
35. H.106, 43
Peccant The good applaud: the peccant lesse condemne
322. H.1062. 8
Peculiar In each thy dainty and peculiar part!....30. H.88, 2
Part is my peculiar...........................152. H 393, 6
Somewhat peculiar to each hymn,..............408. A.2, 74
Pedestal Held up by Fames eternall Pedestall....329. H.1092, 8
Peep See Bo-peep
Wherein or Light, or Day, did never peep........52. H.146, 6
Which, by the peepe of day, doe strew.......95. H 227, 25
As her little eyes did peep...................123. H.310, 4
To rise as soon as day doth peep?...........233. H 670, 2
But by the peep of light......................373. N.122, 7
By peep of day,...............................374. N.123, 49
Peeping See Blushing-pretty-peeping, Little-peeping-part
Like to the peeping spring time of the yeare....105. H.259, 8
The peeping fire..............................137. H.340, 15
A red-Rose peeping through a white?...........164. H.440, 2
When peeping through a Brooke...............271. H.824, 12
That I might see the cheerfull peeping day.......358. No.77, 7
Peeps With peeps of Harts, of Club and Spade..166. H.443, 49
Peepes trembling for feare,...................334. H.1122, 17
Where no one beame of comfort peeps in it.......372. N.117, 2
Peerless And Priceless now, what Peerless once had been:
21. H.62, 4
From this soe peereles pretious permanent,.......405. A.1, 66
Peevish See Pievish
More then for peevish pining sicknesses.........245. H.723, 12
After our long, and peevish sicknesses...........300. H.961, 4
— — — — — — — — — —,..................428. var. H.238, 4
Peevishly One nicely mad, or peevishly severe....234. H.673, 6
Pelops' Or Pelops Arme of Yvorie................34. H.105, 6
Peltish Of peltish wasps; we'l know his Guard..165. H. 443, 17
Pemberton This is that Princely Pemberton, who can
149. H.377, 133
Pembroke A Prince of Pembroke, and that Pembroke, you!
141. H.359, 2
Pen The paper gild, and Laureat the pen.........141. H.359, 6
From these to penne the pleasing Pastoral:......298. H.955, 6
I a Dirge will pen for thee;...................304. H. 976, 1
To lay thy pen and ink aside?..................357. N.72, 12
Vnto the Prince of Shades, whom once his Pen
442. ins. H.575, 28a
Penance Penance, and standing so, are both but one.
106. H.261, 4
When I have done true Penance here for it.......397. N.255, 4
Pence See Silver-pence
And after that, lay downe some silver pence,....245, H. 723, 9
And man sold God here for base thirty pence...389. N.213, 2
Pencil's And let it be thy Pensils strife,...........38. H.108, 3
Pendant And Pendant Pearle of ours...........43. H.123, 12
This little pendant on your eare,..................417. A.9, 2
Penelope Since you are knowne to be Penelope....189. H.511, 4
A good Penelope was had:.......................283. H.885, 6
Penitence Is but the time of penitence............380, N.153, 2
Drawes out th' Elixar of true penitence.........386. N.196, 4
Penitent When man he makes a Penitent for it....359. N.82, 2
Penned Ev'n so those Lines, pen'd by my wanton Wit,
339, N.1, 3
Pennie See Penny
Brown bread Tom Pennie eates, and must of right,
309. H.997, 1
Pennies — — — — — — — — —, ...440. var. H.443, 70
Penny See Pennie
Ph. I'le beg a penny, or Ile sing so long,.......248. H.730, 21
With a pennie to pay S. Peter.................256. H.762, 6
No pennie, no Pater Noster...................256. H.762, 18
Pensive Ever full of pensive feare;...............117. H.286, 2
Pensiveness What doth cause this pensiveness?....305. H.984, 2
Penurious Who is penurious, he shall still be poore. 22. H.64, 4
Penury For feare of future-biting penurie:........352. N.51, 12
People A people currish; churlish as the seas;....29. H.86, 11
Which Country people call a Bee...............50. H.139, 9
Next, hang'd for Theeving: Now the people say,
195. H.532, 3
For as he breath'd, the People swore from thence 200. H.551, 5
O place! O People! Manners! fram'd to please..242. H.713, 9
Such as the Prince is, will his People be.........255. H.759, 2
People a City or a Towne......................291. H 919, 22
As to the Goddesse, people did conferre.........330. H.1099, 5
Tell me the People that do keep.................340. N.3, 7
That Manna, which God on His people cast,....379. N.146, 1
People's He rents his Crown, That feares the Peoples hate.
182. H.488, 2
Pepper To seek, and bring rough Pepper home:..229. H.662, 6
Perceive Next, when thou dost perceive her fixed sight.
87. H 215, 7
And calmes succeeding, we perceive no more....254. H.756, 5
Not now perceive the soule of C:C:......430. ins. H.283, 40
Perceiving But now perceiving that it still do's please
266. H.800, 3
Perchance Whereas (perchance) my fortunes may 312. H.1014, 6
Perenna Deare Perenna, prethee come,............89. H.220, 1
How long, Perenna, wilt thou see..............177. H.471.
Perenna's To give Perenn'as lip a kisse,..........103. H.255, 3
Perfect Which done, that Dawne, turnes then to perfect day.
34. H.104, 6
Which shining in her perfect Noone;...........49. H.136, 29
Ducking in Mood, and perfect Tense,............91. H 223, 52
And Three in perfect Unitie:..................359. N.78, 14
Ev'n God Himself, in perfect Entitie............382. N.165, 2
Perfected Then to live not perfected...............21. H.59, 6
That, thus increast, it might be perfected.......378. N.132, 2
Perfection Never my Book's perfection did appeare. 99. H.245, 1
Things to perfection:...........................258. H.767, 16
Perfume From this, to that, and so Perfume.........9. H.15, 7
That did perfume the Pomander................13. H.32, 4
Although the Pile be all perfume...............50. H.140, 4
To it, the like perfume:.........................55. H.149, 66
And perfume the aire a while:....................74, H.189, 2
Sleepe in thy peace, while we will spice perfume thee
89. H 219, 13

The fat: breathe thou and there's the rich perfume.
102. H.251, 4
His soule to Ash-heaps in that rich perfume?....113. H.283, 28
A noble perfume from the fire..................145. H.375, 18
Their lives in sweets, and left in death perfume...185. H.496, 4
Us all, unlesse preserv'd by thy Perfume.........197. H.539, 12
Whose breath is rich perfume, that to the sence....404. A.1, 27
Soft Saffron Circles to perfume the head...442. ins. H.575, 200
Perfumed As when to Jove Great Juno goes perfum'd.
157. H.414, 8
Perfum'd (last day) to me:.....................161. H.425, 2
Then, like a perfum'd Altar, see................366. N.98, 10
Perfumes Follow thy Perfumes by the smell:........33. H.98, 6
From Powders and Perfumes keep free;........112. H.282, 3
As when a Rain-bow in perfumes goes out.........131. H.331, 8
And adds perfumes unto the Wine, which thou..148. H.377, 81
Let's to the Altar of perfumes then go,..........168. H.445, 3
(Where I have cause to burn perfumes to it:)..234. H.673, 8
As Heaven had spent all perfumes there.........237. H.685, 12
Male perfumes, but Female fire.................277. H.850, 4
With perfumes the Holocaust:...................280. H.870, 16
And yet it with their choice purfumes...........375. N.123, 66
His soule to glad you in perfumes...............413. A.4, 35
Perhaps There, there, (perhaps) such Lines as These
6. H.2, 15
This I may do (perhaps) as I glide by,..........222. H.634, 10
The Rod (perhaps) was better'd by the name;..306. H.986, 3
Perilla Ah my Perilla! do'st thou grieve to see.......9. H.14, 1
'Twill not be long (Perilla) after this,..............9. H.14, 5
With which (Perilla) wash my hands and feet;....9. H.14, 9
With Perilla: All are gone;......................16. H.39, 11
Before, my deare Perilla, I will be................59. H.154, 9
Perilla smile on none but me.....................313. H.1020, 2
Period To such an height, to such a period rais'd,..399. N.263, 30
Perish Some parts may perish; dye thou canst not all:
200. H.554, 1
And perish at the last..........................211. H.595, 16
While others perish, here's thy life decreed......280. H.869, 5
Perished — — — — — — — — —, ...451. var. H.336, 36
Perisheth Neglected beauty perisheth apace........97. H.234, 2
Perjured Goe, perjur'd man; and if thou ere return
49. H.138, 1
Perking But while he, perking, there did prie....46. H.130, 7
Perky — — — — — — — — —, ...433. var. H.293, 9
Permanent From this soe peereles pretious permanent,
405. A.1, 66
Permit Permit me, Julia, now to goe away;......60. H.156, 1
This the lips we will permit....................82. H.203, 15
Permit my Book to have a free accesse........137. H.341, 11
Permit mine eyes to see.........................369. N.106, 1
Permits While Fates permits us, let's be merry;..172. H.457, 1
Pernicious Such a pernicious torment is:........50. H.139, 13
Perpetual Blest with perpetuall greene,............30. H.89, 7
Purfling the Margents, while perpetuall Day....206. H.575, 14
Perplex Perplex him in his hinder-parts..............6. H.5, 4
Perplexed And like a surly Oke with storms perplext;
37. H.106, 99
— — — — — — — — —, ...452. var. H.443, 24
Perplexity Many a neat perplexity,.............165. H.443, 24
Perpolite To be most soft, terce, sweet, and perpolite:
301. H.966, 2
Perseus And Snakie Perseus, these, and those, whom Rage
206. H.575, 45
Persevere But never those that persevere therein...344. N.32, 2
Persian The Persian King liv'd not more happily..70. H.181, 4
Of Persian Loomes, and antique Plate:........239. H.696, 10
Person In reverence of his person, every one.....301. H.962, 3
The Person crowns the Place; your lot doth fall 304. H.977, 1
But like a Person of some high account:......398. N.263, 16
Persons God's undivided, One in Persons Three;..386. N.191, 1
Perspire While other Gums their sweets perspire,..20. H.54, 5
What gentle Winds perspire? As if here........224. H.642, 9
Perspiring Perspiring pounded Cynamon.........113. H.283, 24
Persuades And when the night perswades me to my bed,
392. N.230, 13
Perturbation His wrath is free from perturbation;..340. N.7, 2
Peruse Peruse my Measures thoroughly, and where
322. H.1062, 4
Perverse O Perverse man! If All disgustfull be,.....7. H.6, 5
Peter With a pennie to pay S. Peter...........256. H.762, 6
Thou stop'st S. Peter in the midst of sin;........349. N.43, 3
Petitioners His gifts, to exercise Petitioners: 344. N.30, 2
The Vowes of those, who are Petitioners.........382. N.169, 2
Petticoat In the tempestuous petticote:...........28. H.83, 10
Pettish — — — — — — — — —, ...439. var. H.443, 17
Pew Saints will come in to fill each Pew and Place.
168. H.445, 6
Pewter Then please alike the Pewter and the Plate:
209. H.586, 7
Pheasant The Phesant, Partridge, Gotwit, Reeve, Ruffe, Raile,
147. H.377, 65
To take the precious Phesant made:...........231. H.662, 67
Pheasants The Eggs of Pheasants wrie-nosed Tooly sells;
204. H.568, 1
Pheban See Phoebean
Phil Phill, the late dead, the late dead Deare,....104. H.256, 8

My Phill, the time he has to sleep,............104. H.256, 16
Nor my rare *Phil, that lately was...........186. H.497, 15
Phill See Phil
Philomel Thou pittifull, and pretty Philomel:....111. H.279, 2
No cruell truths of Philomell,.................215. H.616, 12
My warbling note will say I'm Phylomel........248. H.730, 8
Philters To make her Philters with:.............258. H.767, 14
Phlegm Both with her Husband's, and her own tough fleame.
98. H.237, 2
Phoebean Phoebean splendour! and thou Thespian spring!
45. H.128, 33
— — — — — — — — —, ...423. var. H.128, 33
Phoebus Phoebus! when that I a Verse,........122. H.303, 1
Play Phoebus on thy Lute;......................151. H.388, 1
Phoenix There I smell the Phenix nest:............59. H.155, 2
And like a Phenix re-aspire....................72. H.185, 17
The Phenix nest,..............................113. H.283, 25
The bastard Phenix; bird of Paradice;.........262. H.783, 8
A new-borne Phoenix from His own chast fire.....367. N.98, 30
Phthisic The cough, the ptisick, I consume......134. H.336, 78
Phyllis By sweet S. Phillis; pitie me:...........169. H.449, 23
Where Phillis is not known?...................184. H.492, 22
The name of Phillis in the Rind................192. H.521, 40
Or Phyllis, whom hard Fate forc't on,.........215. H.616, 13
Physic And credits Physick, yet not trusts his Pill:
125. H.315, 4
And Physick...................................210. H.591, 12
What need of Physick, or Physitian?...........319. H.1049, 2
Physician Who makes the slie Physitian his Heire. 125. H.315, 6
What need of Physick, or Physitian? 319. H.1049, 2
Physicians Physitians fight not against men; but these
226. H.646, 1
Store of diseases, where Physitians flow..........244. H.718, 4
Bad are all surfeits: but Physitians call........286. H.895, 1
Physitians say Repletion springs...............298. H.951, 1
Pick Peapes he do's strut, and pick his Teeth, as if
273. H.835, 1
Pickaxe From the Pickaxe to the spade,...........418. A.9, 43
Picked This night, and Locks pickt, yet w'are not a Maying.
69. H.178, 56
He ever pickt (as yet) of any one.............204. H.568, 6
A chaine of Cornes, pickt from her eares and toes:
232. H.668, 2
Pickled — — — — — — — — —, ...434. var. H.293, 38
Picks Those Picks or Diamonds in the Card:.....166. H.443, 48
Picture Give my dead picture one engendring kisse:
14. H.35, 12
Them like some Picture, or some Mould........174. H.465, 20
In speach, in Picture; noe otherwise then when...411. A.3, 61
Pictures As in Pictures we descry,...............194. H.527, 8
Pie See Christmas-pie, Mince pie
As here a Custard, there a Pie,...............101. H.250, 33
End now the White-loafe, & the Pye..........285. H.894, 1
Party colour'd like a Pie;....................305. H.984, 19
Piece See Codpiece, Masterpiece, Odd-piece
I sing of Dewes, of Raines, and piece by piece......5. H.1, 7
If thou dislik'st the Piece thou light'st on first;.....7. H.6, 1
Put on your silks; and piece by piece............20. H.54, 1
Where no one piece is yet unlevelled............82. H.204, 8
Late fatned in a piece of cloth:...............120. H.293, 42
A piece, then of a higher text:..............135. H.336, 100
Best and more suppling piece he cuts, and by..147. H.377, 51
Of others; since no Stud, no Stone, no Piece,..149. H.377, 117
Piece of the rest.............................189. H.515, 4
Then if any Peece proves new,................217. H.620, 10
To make a peece.............................221. H.633, 33
This if ye do, each Piece will here be good,......290. H.914, 9
For that holy piece of Bread,..................323. H.1065, 5
Or, ne're so meane a peece, but men might see...389. N.214, 3
Piecemeal And piece-meale rot...................85. H.211, 15
Pieces Pieces, patches, ropes of haire;............76. H.195, 5
Pierce Or peirce it any where:....................11. H.20, 6
As Sun-beames pierce the glasse, and streaming in,
385. N.184, 1
Ready, to pierce Thy tender Feet, and Hands....398. N.263, 4
This lesson you must pearse to' th' truth.........418. A.9, 39
Pierced Where the Steletto pierc'd the skin:.......18. H.46, 8
'Twill hurt and heal a heart pierc'd through.....325. H.1075, 8
Pierc't through, and dropping bloud, for me,....400. N.267, 4
Piercing — — — — — — — — —, ...423. var. H.128, 18
Pierides Here with the sweet Pierides..............334. H.1123, 2
Pies Aha my boyes! heres wheat for Christmas Pies!
327. H.1086, 2
Piety And leave no sound; nor piety,............132. H.336, 2
Pievish See Peevish
Pievish doth boast, that he's the very first......156. H.410, 1
Pig A Pig to the Priest for a Roster,..........256. H.762, 15
Well, when sh'as kild, that Pig, Goose, Cock or Hen,
266. H.801, 3
Spokes when he sees a rosted Pig, he swears.....305. H.982, 1
Piggin A little piggin, and a pipkin by,..........371. N.115, 5
Pigs See Tithe-pigs
Pigs' See Stiff-blue-pigs'-feet
Pike — — — — — — — — —, ...450. var. A.9, 43
Pikes I! and a world of Pikes passe through.......31. H.90, 9
He never brings them once to th' push of Pikes. 370. N.108, 12

Pilcher The flying Pilcher, and the frisking Dace, 155. H.405, 11
Pile Although the Pile be all perfume............50. H.140, 4
He burnes to Embers on the Pile..............113. H.283, 30
Faire and foule dayes trip Crosse and Pile; The faire 189. H.513, 1
And lays it gently on ye Pyle,..................413. A.4, 28
Piles The place, where swelling Piles do breed:......6. H.5, 2
Goodnes and Greatnes; not the oaken Piles;....148. H.377, 99
Pilferer So Julia took the Pilferer..............71. H.182, 10
Pilfering When next he came a pilfring so,.......71. H.182, 29
Fly to my Mistresse, pretty pilfring Bee,.......100. H.248, 1
To catch the pilfring Birds, not Men..........231. H.662, 69
Pilgrim A wearied Pilgrim, I have wandred here 328. H.1088, 1
Pilgrimage And to walke Life's pilgrimage.......191. H.519, 2
Pilgrims As wearied Pilgrims, once possest.......216. H.617, 1
Pilgrims' My Pilgrims staffe; my weed of grey:..123. H.306, 2
Pill Doe they first pill thee, next pluck off thy skin? 32. H.97, 3
Leech boasts, he has a Pill, that can alone,.....125. H.315, 1
And credits Physick, yet not trusts his Pill:....125. H.315, 4
When his Potion and his Pill,..................347. N.41, 17
Pillar That Fame, and Fames rear'd Pillar, thou shalt see 329. H.1092, 5
Fames pillar here, at last, we set,............335. H.1129, 1
This pillar never shall.......................335. H.1129, 11
Pillars Pillars let some set up,..................85. H.211, 21
The pillars up of weeping Jet,..................145. H.376, 2
The Pillars up of lasting Jet,.................149. H.377, 124
Pillars and men, hate an indifferent Poet.......309. H.1000, 2
Pills So where He gives the bitter Pills, be sure,...344. N.31, 3
Pimpled See Be-pimpled
Pimpleides Tom calls not pimples, but Pimpleides: 273. H.834, 2
Pimples Tom calls not pimples, but Pimpleides:..273. H.834, 2
Pimp's When Pimpes feat sweat (as they doe often use) 332. H.1113, 1
Pin See Push-pin
Love prickt my finger with a golden pin:.........17. H.44, 4
Yet, quickly you'l see by the turne of a pin,......97. H.233, 3
Pinch He feeles when Packs do pinch him; and the where. 60. H.158. 4
Some private pinch tels danger's nie..........147. H.377, 52
Mab will pinch her by the toe..................201. H.556, 8
Pindar To Linus, then to Pindar; and that done,.206. H.575, 31
Pin-dust A little Pin-dust; which they hold......92. H.223, 87
Pine Love to the death will pine,..................31. H.94, 3
But I languish, lowre, and Pine,..............309. H.996, 9
for your approach, yet see their Altars pine? 431. ins. H.283, 60f
Pined which sees the body fedd, yet pined. 432. ins. H.283, 70j
Pining More then for peevish pining sicknesses..245. H.723, 12
Pinions To mount my Soule, she must have pineons given: 352. N.52, 3
Pink Thy Bice, thy Umber, Pink, and Lake;.....38. H.108, 2
To paint the Fiend, Pink would the Devill see;..110. H.272, 1
And Pink may paint the Devill's by his owne...110. H.272, 4
Healthes to the Rose, the Violet, or Pinke,........410. A.3, 6
begin to pinke as weary that the warres..432. ins. H.283, 140b
Pink's Let but Pink's face i' th' Looking-glasse be showne, 110. H.272, 3
Pinks Are not here Rose-buds, Pinks, all flowers, 103. H.256, 4
Pinnace My wearyed Pinnace here finds ease:....94. H.225, 2
The Pinnace up; which though she erres.......134 H.336, 63
Pinnacle Which like a Pinacle doth shew........202. H.560, 7
Pins (Playing for Points and Pins) Cockall......91. H.223, 59
Blew pinnes, tagges, fescues, beades and thinges 440. ins. H.443, 45r
Pious Thy pious wishes are, (though thou not there) 37. H.106, 91
To keep those pious Principles in force........201. H.557, 20
The candid Stole thrown ore the Pious Priest;..286. H.898, 6
Bring Him along, most pious Priest,...........365. N.97, 11
Pious-priestess O Pious-Priestresse! make a Peace for us. 197. H.539, 14
Pipe See Bagpipe
My puling Pipe to beat against thine eare:.......17. H.42, 2
Drink, and dance, and pipe, and play;..........39. H.111, 3
Chor. Pan pipe to him, and bleats of lambs and sheep, 86. H.213, 17
And, to the Pipe, sing Harvest home...........101. H.250, 6
Mirt. Ah! Amarillis, farewell mirth and pipe;...159. H.421, 8
And Pipe unto thy Song.......................184. H.492, 28
Mean time, let Lycidas have leave to Pipe to thee. 184. H.492, 43
I cannot pipe as I was wont to do,...........205. H.573, 1
That thou shalt swear, my Pipe do's raigne....244. H.716, 39
Not so; my Pipe has silenc't thine:...........244. H.716, 44
That through each room a golden pipe may run 245. H.723, 3
As my small Pipe best fits my little note.......249. H.733, 15
Why thy pipe by thee so still,..................305. H.984, 5
Tell, and I'le lay down my Pipe................305. H.984, 14
Pipes With oaten pipes, as sweet, as new.........86. H.213, 41
Chor. Lay by a while your Pipes, and rest,....243. H.716, 35
Chor. And lay we down our Pipes together,....244. H.716, 47
Piping Where thou mayst sit, and piping please.....5. H.2, 3
The piping Gnat for minstralcy...............119. H.293, 18
That kept his Piping up......................184. H.492, 40
A Shepherd piping on a hill....................230. H.662, 45
Pipkin A little Pipkin with a bit................124. H.312, 5
This little Pipkin fits this little Jellie..........249. H.733, 18
A little piggin, and a pipkin by,..............371. N.115, 5
Pipkinet And Thou my Pipkinnet shalt see,.........377. N.130, 3
Piss Sudds Launders Bands in pisse; and starches them 98. H.237, 1
Gander (they say) doth each night pisse a Bed:..223. H.636, 2
Commix with Meale a little Pisse...............284. H.890, 2
Pit See Cherry-pit
I got the Pit, and she the Stone..................19. H.49, 4
Hell is no other, but a soundlesse pit,..........372. N.117, 1
Pitched The Field is pitcht; but such must be your warres, 216. H.618, 13
Pitcher Nere to thy Reverend Pitcher I will fall....11. H.22, 7
Pitfalls Thy Lime-twigs, Snares, and Pit-falls then 231. H.662 68
Pith Which extract, all we can call pith........116. H.283, 154
He ventures boldly on the pith................119. H.293, 32
High sons of Pith,..........................136. H.336, 131
While juice she straines, and pith..............258. H.767, 13
Pitied See Poor-pitied
Poore pittyed Exile? Tell me, did thy Graces....77. H.197, 20
Each like a poore and pitied widowhood........150. H.382, 4
Ambo. Poor pittied youth! Mir. And here the breth of kine 159. H.421, 13
Leaving them to a pittied nakednesse...........224. H.642, 12
Would into prais'd (but pitied) ruines fall,....252. H.745, 15
Pities None pities him that's in the snare,.......219. H.628, 11
Pitiful Patient I was: Love pitifull grew then,....16. H.40, 5
I pittifull arose,..............................26. H.81, 13
Thou pittifull, and pretty Philomel:.............111. H.279, 2
Ye must not be more pitifull then wise;.........365. N.97, 16
Pittance No Orphans pittance, left him, serv'd to set 149. H.377, 123
Let's live with that smal pittance that we have; 213. H. 607, 1
Pittering — — — — — — — —, ...433. var. H.293, 16
Pity Love, in pity of the deed,...................15. H.36, 12
Thy pitty by Loves-Chronicle)...................34. H.103, 8
Alas for pitty! and for us.......................48. H.136, 4
My num'rous issue: Praise, and pitty me........58. H.151, 2
Pity me too, who found so soone a Tomb.........58. H.151, 4
For pitty let a teare be shed;.................61. H.159, 23
That ebs from pittie lesse and lesse............143. H.369, 4
Love in pitie of their teares,..................152. H.391, 5
For pitty, Sir, find out that Bee,...............156. H.412, 11
For shame or pitty now encline...............168. H.446, 5
By sweet S. Phillis; pitie me:.................169. H.449, 23
For pitie be....................................170. H.452, 5
'Twas pitie Nature brought yee forth..........176. H.467, 10
For pitty or shame,...........................195. H.534, 7
No part of pitie on a conquer'd foe............199. H.550, 2
But pitie those, whose flanks grow great,......200. H.552, 15
Will tell thee Pitie thou hast none.............203. H.564, 6
As so it doth? that's pittie...................229. H.659, 10
By tears and pitie now to come unto mee.......248. H.730, 2
Speak where thou art. Ph. O Charon pittie me! 248. H.730, 6
For Love or Pittie, prethee let there be........277. H.853, 3
For love or pitie to his Muse,..................291. H.918, 5
For love or pitie let me know...................323. H.1068, 3
Of pittie, not of scrutinie;......................344. N.29, 2
And more for love, then pittie...................345. N.33, 29
Which if that can't Thy pittie wooe,............349. N.46, 7
Come pitie us, all ye, who see..................373. N.123, 1
Come pitie us, ye Passers by,...................373. N.123, 3
Come pitie us; and bring your eares,............373. N.123, 5
And eyes, to pitie Widdowes teares..............373. N.123, 6
May (though they scorn Thee) praise and pitie Thee. 399. N.263, 35
Who passe this way, to pitie me,...............400. N.266, 2
Have pity either on my tears or Youth,.... ......416. A.8, 4
That makes grim Charon thus to pity thee.......416. A.8, 22
Pitying If pittying my sad Parents Teares,........70. H.180, 5
— — — — — — — — — —...............433. var. H.293, 16
Pity's For pitties sake give your advice,............8. H.13, 3
Place See Burying-place
The place, where swelling Piles do breed:...........6. H.5, 2
The place for these, and for the rest..............8. H.11, 3
Then for an easie fansie; place...................39. H.108, 9
Next, place me Zones, and Tropicks there;......47. H.133, 7
When as Cherries come in place?..................74. H.189, 6
The place, where I may find ye...................83. H.207, 4
(Farther then Gentlenes tends) gets place......114. H.283, 83
Love the confusion of the place...............115. H.283, 140
But that there was in place to stir..............119. H.293, 15
Till sleep takes place of wearinesse............127. H.319, 48
Saints will come in to fill each Pew and Place...168. H.445, 6
In this securer place we'l keep,................190. H.515, 37
Serves but for place of Buriall..................197. H.542, 4

Raspe playes at Nine-holes; and 'tis known he gets
154. H.400, 1
And flatt'ring Ivie) Two recite their Plaies,....206. H.575, 50
For Sports, for Pagentrie, and Playes,.........230. H.662, 46
I keep, that playes about my House,...........246. H.724, 22
Without due reverence, playes the cheaters game...347. N.39, 6
Thy Pompe of Playes which thousands come to see,
415. A.7, 3
Plea And 'gainst your chast behaviour there's no Plea,
189. H.511, 3
Plead Present, to plead my cause for me;........395. N.245, 4
Pleads Case is a Lawyer, that near pleads alone,..303. N.975, 1
Pleasant Pleasant, and precious to my Muse and me.
227. H.652, 4
— — — — — — — — — —, ...451. ins. H.336, 48b
Please Where thou mayst sit, and piping please......5. H.2, 3
Some sport, to please those Babies in your eyes:..15. H 38, 4
But ah! if empty dreames so please,..............20. H 56, 9
Can please those Heav'nly Deities,................22. H.63, 2
But 'tis sweetness that doth please...............22. H.65, 3
There is an Act that will more fully please:......24. H.74, 10
Yet there's a way found (if thou please)........34. H.103, 13
May me delight, not fully please:................34. H.105, 8
And that will please me somewhat: though I know,
42. H.122, 11
Are wanton with their itch; scratch, and 'twill please.
66. H.173, 8
(If so they please)..........................85. H.211, 22
Gentle friends, then doe but please,.............88. H.218, 7
How hard a woman 'tis to please?.............103. H.253, 12
I have drank up for to please...................122. H.304, 5
Good things, that come of course, far lesse doe please,
123. H.307, 1
Please him, and then all good-luck will betide...124. H.313, 5
Mighty Neptune, may it please...................129. H.325, 1
The other parts will richly please..............138. H 342, 10
Stately Goddesse, do thou please,...............141. H.360, 1
'Twill never please the pallate of mine eare......152. H.390, 2
That doth like me, this doth please;............157. H.415, 5
Mont. Fore-fend it Pan, and Pales do thou please
159. H 421, 31
And prayers to Venus; if it please..............175. H.465, 75
I co'd never seeke to please...................182. H.490, 5
Then please alike the Pewter and the Plate;....209. H.586, 7
Please your Grace, from out your Store,........223. H.638, 1
Who all the day themselves doe please,.........231. H.662, 72
O Place! O People! Manners! fram'd to please..242. H.713, 9
I please.......................................246. H 724, 27
None is, slight things do lightly please.........246. H 724, 32
But thou art just and itchlesse, and dost please..252. H.745, 17
Yet with strutting they will please............255. H.761, 13
But now perceiving that it still do's please......266. H.800, 3
Ne'r please the supercillious man...............279. H.868, 4
Those lips please me which are plac't...........282. H 878, 3
We credit most our sight; one eye doth please..287. H 904, 1
Numbers ne'r tickle, or but lightly please,......290. H.914, 7
Thy mouth will make the sourest numbers please;
328. H.1089, 3
If felt and heard, (unseen) thou dost me please;
331. H.1108, 1
But in short time 'twill please Thee,............353. N.56, 21
Gifts blind the wise, and bribes do please,.......357. N.72, 9
Sick is my heart; O Saviour! do Thou please.....358. N.77, 8
But if it please my God, I be.................376. N.124, 2
If thou canst change thy life, God then will please
389. N.216, 3
Yet doe Thou please,........................401. N.268, 31
At whose faire topp to please the sight there growes
405. A.1, 35
how long shall the page, to please........431. ins. H.283, 60g
Our witty appetites to please,............436. ins. H.336, 48f
Pleased See Soon-pleased
Pleas'd with transgression ev'ry where:..........66. H.175, 4
Be pleas'd to rest you in This Sacred Grove,....107. H.265, 3
The posture hers, I'm pleas'd with it...........207. H.579, 4
My sight was pleas'd more, or my smell:.........283. H.883, 6
And very well pleas'd,.........................333. H.1122, 2
Pleaseth Or low, or tall, she pleaseth me:........207. H.579, 2
My selfe now live: this age best pleaseth mee...292. H 927, 2
Pleasing How rich and pleasing thou my Julia art..30. H.88, 1
Your pleasing slumbers in the night:...........121. H.299, 4
The pleasing wife, the house, the ground........132. H.336, 9
Pleasing alike; alike both singular:............209. H.586, 4
To make a pleasing pastime there.............230. H 662, 39
A Pleasing Wife, that by thy side............233. H.670, 13
More pleasing too, then ever was..............251. H.740, 11
Revenge is pleasing to us, as our gaine.........292. H.923, 4
Shall by this pleasing trespasse quickly prove,...297. H.949, 3
From these to penne the pleasing Pastorall:....298. H.955, 6
But the pleasing hindrances?..................355. N.64, 2
Into the middle <most> sight pleasing crooke..406. A.1, 82
Pleasure Were it but to pleasure you.............10. H.19, 14
Make payment for his pleasure.................30. H 87, 18
For seldome use commends the pleasure........38. H.106, 140
Of that Passion sweetens Pleasure.............55. H.149, 80
And that this pleasure is like raine,............102. H.250, 53
There is no one pleasure in't.....................122. H.304, 4
Go then discreetly to the Bed of pleasure;....220. H.633, 24
Goddesse of Pleasure, Youth and Peace,........221. H.633, 54
But o'racted deads the pleasure................276. H.850, 6
Vertue and pleasure, both to dwell in one.......293. H.935, 2
Their ends for Pleasure, do not live, but last...328. H.1088, 10
To have continuall paine, or pleasure here:.....394. N.236, 2
Beares vp twoe globes where loue and pleasure sitt.
405. A.1, 52
Pleasured — — — — — — — — —, ...441. var. H.465, 42
Pleasure's Thee chiefly for their pleasures end...175. H.465, 42
Cha. Those souls which ne'er were drencht in pleasures stream,
417. A.8, 27
Pleasures See Maiden-pleasures
Of pleasures, to a Heate;........................9. H.15, 2
Such fleeting pleasures there I took............17. H.41, 20
Wherein all pleasures of the world are wove.......40. H.114, 4
Thus Paines and Pleasures turne by turne succeed:
79. H.199, 3
We'll blesse the Babe, Then back to Countrie pleasures.
87. H.213, 48
Pleasures, many here attend ye,...............125. H.314, 5
Let's live in hast; use pleasures while we may:..171. H.453, 1
The pleasures Ile prepare for thee:.............192. H.521, 2
Where Pleasures met: at last, doe find,........327. H.1082, 3
All Pleasures meet in Woman-kind.............327. H.1082, 4
Where Pleasures rule a Kingdome, never there..327. H.1087, 1
Pleasures, such as shall pursue..............377. N.128, 21
Wth Joyes before, and Pleasures left behind:....411. A.3, 64
Pledge See Fame's-pledge
To pledge this second Health..................80. H.201, 18
Made he the pledge, he'd think..................80. H.201, 23
Pledges Faire pledges of a fruitfull Tree,........176. H.467, 1
Or Antique pledges, House or lande.............407. A.2, 9
Plenteous A Plentious harvest to your grounds:..127. H.319, 24
There a poor Lamb's a plenteous sacrifice.......369. N.105, 4
Plentiful With which thy house was plentifull.....374. N.123, 42
Plenty That your plenty last till when,.........224. H.638, 27
An everlasting plenty, yeere by yeere..........242. H.713, 8
Plenty-dropping Lord, 'tis thy plenty-dropping hand,
350. N.47, 41
Plighted And some have wept, and woo'd, and plighted Troth,
69. H.178, 49
Plot No closset plot, or open vent,............126. H.319, 3
And soule and spirit plot, and excellence.......399. N.263, 27
Of King and no King (and the rare Plott thine)
415. A.7, 14
Plots All are not ill Plots, that doe sometimes faile;
331. H.1104, 1
Plow Had, first, durst plow the Ocean...........36. H.106, 76
Time, ere long, will come and plow............97. H.232, 13
Then to the Plough, (the Common-wealth)....102. H.250, 39
And all goe back unto the Plough.............102. H.250, 49
And let the russet Swaines the Plough.........127. H.319, 45
There at the Plough thou find'st thy Teame,...230. H.662, 25
The Kingdoms portion is the Plow.............230. H.662, 28
From the Plough soone free your teame;........315. H.1026, 3
— — — — — — — — — — —, ...439. var. H.443, 41
Plowest Thou never Plow'st the Oceans foame..229. H.662, 5
Plowman's When now the Cock (the Plow-mans Horne)
230. H.662, 19
Plows Last, may your Harrows, Shares and Ploughes.
179. H.476, 22
Pluck Doe they first pill thee, next, pluck off thy skin?
32. H.97, 3
Cynthius pluck ye by the eare,...................52. H.147, 1
I went to pluck them one by one,............107. H.263, 14
Plucked — — — — — — — —, ...429. var. H.263, 14
Plucks He who plucks the sweets shall prove......88. H.217, 5
Plum Into the blushing Peare, or Plum:.........79. H.198, 4
That shines upon the blewer Plum.............166. H.443, 58
And shame-fac't Plum, (all simp'ring there)....192. H 521, 38
As colours steale into the Peare or Plum,.......250. H.737, 6
You many a Plum, and many a Peare:..........264. H.787, 2
Apple or Plume is neately layd,...........439. ins. H.443, 45b
Plumes Of those that prank it with their Plumes;
375. N.123, 65
Plump Plumpe Bed beare up, and swelling like a cloud,
115. H.283, 112
From the plumpe Challice, and the Cup,......127. H.319, 35
Plump as the cherry,.........................136. H.336, 139
Plump, soft, & swelling every where?..........139. H.348, 2
Upon six plump Dandillions, high-............167. H.443, 86
Tapping his plump thighes with a mirtle wand:
313. H.1017, 8
For his plumpe white and smooth prerogatiue,....405. A.1, 34
With plumpe soft flesh of mettle pure and fine....406. A.1, 79
Plums Of fragrant Apples, blushing Plums, or Peares:
205. H.575, 10
And the Plums stand by......................263. H.784, 17
With the cake full of plums,..................317. H.1035, 2
Plundered All has been plundered from me, but my wit;
272. H.830, 1
Plunderer Never had been the Northern Plunderer
224. H.642, 10
Plunge And ravisht, plunge into the bed,.........59. H.152, 9

Plural No number of the Plurall hath..........382. N.168, 2
Plus See Overplus
Pluto The Fields of Pluto are reserv'd for them; 417. A.8, 28
Ply Wch like a Vestall Vergine ply.............407. A.2, 23
Poares See Pores
Pocket In your Pocket for a trust,............323. H.1065, 3
Pockets If he ha's none in's pockets, trust me, Huncks 173. H.463, 3
Poem One onely Poem out of all you'l chuse;....64. H.168, 8
Your judgement finds a guilty Poem, there....322. H.1062, 5
Poems If 'mongst my many Poems, I can see.....63. H.165, 1
When I through all my many Poems look,......94. H.226, 1
Who hug our Poems (Honourd Sir) and then....141. H.359, 5
To Print our Poems, the propulsive cause........169. H.448, 1
Dash all bad Poems out of countenance........187. H.506, 10
That done, our smooth-pac't Poems all shall be 254. H.756, 15
Poesies See Posies
Poet See Arch-poet
Though here the Princely Poet................64. H.166, 12
Your sometime Poet; but if fates do give......140. H.355, 11
Whom they neglected, thou hast crown'd a Poet. 143. H 365, 8
Leaving their Poet (being now grown old).....151. H.387, 3
Whose smile can make a Poet; and your glance 187. H.506, 9
Who both your wooer, and your Poet is.........274. H.837, 2
Deare, can you like, and liking love your Poet?..274. H.837, 5
A Poet, or a Poet-like but Thee..............299. H.956, 4
Pillars and men, hate an indifferent Poet.......309. H.1010, 2
I may a Poet come, though poor;..............321. H.1056, 4
Thy Poet, and Thy Prophet Lawreat...........398. N.262, 4
Poetess And be both Princesse here, and Poetresse. 107. H.265, 10
Poetic In Chiefe, in this Poetick Liturgie.........188. H.510, 4
Poet-like A Poet, or a Poet-like but Thee.........299. H.956, 4
Poetress See Poetess
Poetry Anthea, Herrick, and his Poetry...........11. H.22, 10
Ere I print my Poetry;..........................21. H.59, 2
Some Aberrations in my Poetry;..................32. H.95, 2
A Lamp Eternall to my Poetrie.................94. H.226, 6
The Heire to This great Realme of Poetry......107. H.264, 6
What can I do in Poetry,......................132. H.334, 1
No lust theres like to Poetry................135. H 336, 112
And the pure Starres the praising Poetrie.......168. H.444, 8
But that eternall Poetrie.......................265. H.794, 3
Poet's Writ in the Poets Endlesse-Kalendar:....168. H.444, 6
Close thou up thy Poets eyes:.................186. H.499, 2
Poets Æson had (as Poets faine)..................10. H.19, 9
Brave Porter! Poets ne'r will wanting be:.......41. H.117, 2
I ask't thee oft, what Poets thou hast read,......66. H.174, 1
Love on a day (wise Poets tell).............105. H.260, 1
Nor suffer you the Poets to sit cold,.............141. H.359, 7
And when wise Poets shall search out to see..149. H.377, 135
Of English Poets, and 'tis thought the Worst...156. H.410, 2
The food of Poets; so I thought sayes Jill,......186. H.498, 5
Let Poets feed on aire, or what they will;........186. H.498, 7
Where Poets sing the stories of our love.........206. H.575, 24
About whose Throne the crowd of Poets throng. 206. H.575, 29
Crown'd Poets; yet live Princes under thee:...234. H.673, 16
Orpheus he went (as Poets tell)...............265. H.798, 1
Poets co'd not praise too much.................274. H.838, 4
Twilight, no other thing is, Poets say,.........278. H 858, 1
Of the Poets; but the Best......................289. H.910, 2
The State of Poets there attending Thee:......324. H.1071, 2
Point Knit to the Posts: this point............55. H.149, 85
The Aged point out, This is she,.............114. H.283, 64
Point be up, and Haft be downe;..............284. H.889, 3
Pointed But with my finger pointed to............24 H.75, 3
Sharply pointed as a thorn:..................306. H.984, 22
Points (Playing for Points and Pins) Cockall.....91. H.223, 59
Encircle with the Bride-grooms Points.........114. H.283, 80
Poise And want their Poise: words ought to have their weight. 342. N.16, 2
Poison 'Twas but a trick to poyson me with love:..17 H 44, 6
Sho'd by his breathing, poyson thee............39. H.108, 14
'Tis not to poyson, but to make thee pure.......344. N.31, 4
A poyson too He has for Socrates:............370. N.108, 8
Or A colde Poyson, which his blood.............409. A.2, 87
Poking-sticks What sho'd poking-sticks make there, 282. H.878, 7
Pole See Maypole
The Pole of the Hop.........................320. H.1051, 7
Poles See Maypoles
Polished Then in a Polisht Ovall by............90. H 223, 13
And Rubies lately polished:...................268. H.811, 6
Her forehead smooth full polish bright and high..404. A.1, 5
Pollio's For Pollio's Lampries in our dish......133. H.336, 48
Pomander See Maiden-pomander
That did perfume the Pomander..................13. H.32, 4
Whose shadow smels like milder Pomander!....181. H.485, 2
Pomegranates Breathes Vine-yards and Pomgranats: O how sweet!...................................113. H.283, 22
Pomp The golden pomp is come..................80. H.201, 4
The golden Pomp is come;......................80. H.201, 5
O Pompe of Glory! Welcome now, and come....300. H.961, 5
In fun'rall pomp, but this importance have;......384. N.181, 2
For now behold the golden Pompe is come,.......415. A.7, 2
Thy Pompe of Playes which thousands come to see, 415. A.7, 3
Ponder Ponder my words, if so that any be......290. H.9.4, 1
Ponder this, when I am gone;...............373. N.121, 13
Pondering At which amaz'd, and Pondring on the food. 262. H.783. 17
Poor The poore and private Cottages.................5. H.2, 4
No Critick haunts the Poore mans Cell:............6. H.2, 22
A lying Rich man, and a Poore man proud.......10. H.18, 2
Who is penurious, he shall still be poore...........22. H.64, 4
Let me be leane, and cold, and once grown poore,.31. H.93, 3
To Bread and Water none is poore;............33. H.100, 1
An old, poore, lying, flatt'ring man:............38. H.108, 6
A poore, yet loving heart......................43. H.123, 30
That when I'm poore,.........................43. H.123, 33
At which poore Robin flew away:............46. H.130, 10
Poore pittyed Exile? Tell me, did thy Graces....77. H.197, 20
Poore Girles, neglected.........................83. H.205, 16
Poore of the Parish, (if there's any)...........92. H.223, 90
That I, poore I,........... ....95. H.227, 19
Hence then it is, that my poore brest...........96. H.229, 5
Poore Girles, she fell on you;..................105. H.260, 6
Poore Maids rewarded be,.....................106. H.262, 10
Your poore estates, alone.....................110. H.274, 20
But being poore, and knowing Flesh is deare,....122. H.305, 5
We are not poore; although we have..........133. H.336, 41
See how the poore do waiting stand,............139. H.350, 1
Beats with a button'd-staffe the poore:........146. H 377, 14
Each like a poore and pitied widowhood.........150. H.382. 4
Ambo. Poor pittied youth! Mir. And here the breth of kine 159. H.421, 13
For why? that man is poore,...............160. H.422, 13
No, but because the Ding-thrift now is poore,....160. H.423, 3
That my poore name may have the glory,......170. H.449, 28
Is this his Glory? then his Triumph's Poore;...171. H.454, 3
Be She too wealthy, or too poore; be sure,......185. H.494, 3
Makes you poore;.............................196. H.538, 4
We pay for our poore Tenement:..............200. H.552, 8
To shield the Stranger, and the Poore from wrong: 201. H.557, 12
Then to the poore she freely gives the milke.....203. H.561, 4
The Ev'ning sees in poore estate...............208. H.583, 3
He who must be, shall be poore..............209. H.585, 9
Then my poore heart,.........................210. H.591, 8
What will ye (my poor Orphans) do...........218. H.626, 1
Grudgings turnes bread to stones, when to the Poore 220. H.632, 1
Give an Almes to one that's poore,.............223. H.638, 2
Instead of almes, sets dogs upon the poor.........238. H.694, 2
Like a poore Lady lost in Widdowhood:.......251. H.745, 4
Rich or poore although it be;..................253. H.750, 2
But the Relation then of both growes poor,.....255. H.758, 3
For, I'm grown old; &, with mine age, grown poore: 258. H 768, 2
I have in my poore Brest;....................272. H.828, 6
If one poore prick,...........................273. H.833, 4
The Body is the Soules poore house, or home,....279. H.865, 1
Caught my poore soule, as in a snare:.........281. H.876, 8
(From which poore seed, and rudely sown)......297. H.948, 7
For thirty yeares, Tubbs has been proud and poor; 302. H.972, 1
That may far sooner speed the poore:..........312. H.1014, 8
For all the Divel helps, will be a poore man....315. H.1025, 2
I may a Poet come, though poor;..............321. H.1056, 4
To this our poore, yet ever patient Flood.......332. H.1112, 6
If warre, or want shall make me grow so poore,...347. N.39, 1
Is worn by'th poore,.........................350. N.47, 14
But poore thou art, and knowne to be..........354. N.59, 13
Or one poore Swadling-clout, shall be............355. N.60, 5
God co'd have made all rich, or all men poore;....356. N.69, 1
Had all been poore, who had His Bounty seen?...356. N.69, 4
'Tis better to be poore,........................368. N.104, 6
There a poor Lamb's a plenteous sacrifice.........369. N.105, 4
Some one poore Almes-house; there to lie, or stir, 371. N.115, 3
Who see, or heare poor Widdowes crie:.........373. N.123, 4
And ah! the Poore,...........................374. N.123, 18
That is the portion of the poore:.............376. N.127, 2
The poore to cut, and I to chuse..............376. N.127, 8
Are works of mercy to the poore,..............393. N.231, 2
When as the poore crie out, to us..............394. N.239, 3
Not those poor Theeves that act their parts with Thee: 399. N.263, 23
Poor relique of the beawty, bone,................418. A.9, 24
With casters duckets which poore they.....430. ins. H.443, 56a
Poorly He gives not poorly, taking some..........356. N.66, 5
Poor-man's Was rear'd up by the Poore-mans fleece: 149. H.377, 118
Poor-pitied Poore-pittied Child! Who from Thy Stall 366. N.98, 22
Pope Elve Boniface shall next be Pope..........93. H.223, 112
Poppy Offering Poppy unto thee................129. H.324, 4

Popular Is Fame, (the breath of popular applause.) 169. H.448, 2
Porch Halfe wasted in the porch...............54. H.149, 54
O · Branch: Each Porch, each doore, ere this,..68. H.178, 33
Display the Bridegroom in the porch,..........113. H.283, 34
Profane no Porch young man and maid, for fear..124. H.313, 3
To the worn Threshold, Porch, Hall, Parlour, Kitchin, 146. H.377, 5
Then from the porch may many a Bride........291. H.919, 13
When to thy Porch I come, and (ravisht) see ..324. H.1071, 1
Low is my porch, as is my Fate,...............350. N.47, 11
But 'cense the porch, and place throughout.......365. N.97, 6
Pores By poares and cavernes back agen........245. H.720, 8
Pork Skin deepe into the Porke, or lights.......147. H.377, 54
Port Since now to the Port...................195. H.534, 1)
Who for Thy Princely Port here,...............345. N.33, 5
Vnto the port mouth of th' Elisian feilds,.........405. A.1, 68
Portal This is the portall to the bowre of blisse....406. A.1, 74
Portals These be the Ruby portalls and devine....404. A.1, 25
Portend Which did but only this portend,.........161. H.425, 3
Portents Comets we see by night; whose shagg'd portents 45. H.128, 15
Porter Brave Porter! Poets ne'r will wanting be:..41. H.117, 2
Yet, Porter, while thou keep'st alive,............72. H.185, 15
For thou no Porter keep'st who strikes.........146. H.377, 18
Since the Porter he..........................256. H.762, 10
The Porter then will let me in.................277. H.854, 6
We are Thy Prophets Porter; Thou our King...324. H.1071, 4
Portion The Kingdoms portion is the Plow.....230. H.662, 28
And as that part, so every portion else,..........307. H.992, 5
Sorrowes our portion are: Ere hence we goe,......359. N.81, 1
Gives me a portion, giving patience:............362. N.87, 2
That is the portion of the poore:.............376. N.127, 2
Being, oft here, the just mans portion............387. N.201, 6
This Portion my Prophetique Bayes............407. A.2, 16
Portions Not to eat equall portions; but to rise..310. H.1005, 3
Pose Megg yesterday was troubled with a Pose,...296. H.945, 1
Posies Y'are the Maiden Posies,.................83. H.205, 9
What Posies for our Wedding Rings;..........216. H.616, 27
With Poesies, since 'tis fitter................323. H.1068, 14
Instead of fragrant Posies....................345. N.33, 11
Position For false Position in his neighbours sheets: 195. H.532, 2
Possess See Re-possess
Your Leavie-Throne (with Lilly-work) possesse;.107. H 265, 9
That Princes may possesse a surer seat,........163. H.438, 1
Many we are, and yet but few possesse........177. H.470, 1
And possesse no other feare,...................255. H.761, 23
Possesse my thoughts, next comes my dolefull knell 392. N.230, 12
Possessed And all, because they were possest......25. H.78, 7
As with a heart possest:......................57. H.149, 136
Of these chaste spirits, that are here possest.......152. H.392, 2
Of foure teeth onely Bridget was possest;......158. H.419, 1
And now the bed, and Mab possest...............168. H.443, 118
As wearied Pilgrims, once possest.............216. H.617, 1
In all thy need, be thou possest..............246. H.725, 1
Possessions Those possessions short-liv'd are,......241. H.711, 1
Posset See Sack-posset
And how the Posset shall be made.............216. H.616, 32
Possets Thou shalt have Possets, Wassails fine,..193. H.521, 47
Possible And for to speak, if possible:..........39. H.108, 12
Possibility A thought of such like possibilitie?....78. H.197, 46
Post Thy Watch may stand, my minutes fly poste haste: 8. H.10, 3
At Post and Paire, or Slam, Tom Tuck would play 238. H.693, 1
Posted And, if I see Thee posted there,..........399. N.265, 7
Posterity Nurse up, great Lord, this my posterity:..40. H.112, 2
To spring from these a sweet Posterity.........44. H.124, 4
Left to all posterity.........................88. H.218, 6
Leaving no Fame to long Posterity:.............210. H.592, 2
Posterity will pay thee what I owe..............298. H.955, 12
Kisse my Brown wife, and black Posterity.......310. H.1003, 4
Postern Mudge every morning to the Postern comes, 301. H.965, 1
Postern-bribe A Postern-bribe tooke, or a Forked-Fee 202 H.557, 25
Posthumus Ah Posthumus! Our yeares hence flye,.132. H.336, 1
None, Posthumus, co'd ere decline............132. H.336, 7
Postilion Before thy swift Postilion;...........239. H.696, 4
Posting Now posting on to punish thee...........47. H.132, 12
Posts Knit to the posts: this point.............55. H.149, 85
Posture The posture hers, I'm pleas'd with it....207. H.579, 4
Postures The Cirque prophan'd was; and all postures rack't 150. H.382, 5
Winning postures; and withall,................204. H.569, 9
Pot Then let her use the watring pot...........279. H.867, 4
As my little Pot doth boyle,..................397. N.258, 1
Potent God, as He's potent, so He's likewise known, 378. N.135, 1
God is so potent, as His Power can............383. N.176, 1
Potentate Upon the man that is a Potentate.......255. H.760, 2
Potion When his Potion and his Pill,.............347. N.41, 17
Pounced And pounc't with Stars, it shew'd to me..67. H.175, 9
Pounded Perspiring pounded Cynamon...........113. H.283, 24
Round short and cleire, like pounded spices sweete 406. A.1, 92
Pounds Just upon five and thirty pounds a yeare...151. H.385, 4
Adde to that thirty five, but five pounds more,..151. H.385, 5
Pour To these, make Clouds to poure downe raine; 47. H.133, 12
Do'st rather poure forth, then allow..........148. H.377, 82
My soule Ile poure into thee..................217. H.619, 20
Into this house powre downe thy influence,....245. H.723, 2
Clouds will not ever powre down raine;........247. H.725, 7
Thy faithfull friend, and to poure downe........303. H.973, 17
What ever Liquor in ye powre................320. H.1053, 2
To powre first in..........................401. N.268, 15
Poured For one drink-offering, poured out by thee...14. H.35, 8
Then Roman Sylla powr'd out at his feast.......262. H.783, 6
Pouring By pouring Balme and Oyle into her wounds. 201. H.557, 18
And powring still, Thy wealthy store,..........357. N.75, 3
Pours That powres in oyle, as well as wine.......342. N.17, 10
Poverty Untaught, to suffer Poverty.............36. H.106, 68
But of all packs, no pack like poverty...........242. H.715, 2
Powdered — — — — — — — —, ...453. var. H 283. 24
Powders From Powders and Perfumes keep free;..112. H.282, 3
Power Nor has the darknesse power to usher in..35. H.106, 39
(When you had power) the meanest remedy:....52. H.146, 20
No Herbs have power to cure Love.............60. H.157, 4
And have the power to move..................76. H.193, 50
Thou Power that canst sever.................95. H.227, 7
Thou onely hast the power,..................100. H.246, 10
Th'event is never in the power of man.........120. H.294, 2
But so, as still the mothers power............126. H.318, 10
But fixt it stands, by her own power,..........148. H 377, 108
Had'st power thy selfe to keep this vow;......176. H.465, 82
He who commends the vanquisht, speaks the Power, 200. H.553, 1
Power conjoyn'd with Natures Crueltie.........211. H.597, 2
When Lawes full power have to sway, we see....213. H.608, 1
Thou seest a present God-like Power..........230. H.662, 31
Power and Peace to keep one Throne...........264. H.788, 2
Where power is weake, unsafe is Majestie.....302. H.971, 2
Shew mercy there, where they have power to kill. 321. H.1057, 2
The Power of Princes rests in the Consent......325. H.1073, 1
Yet I have hope, by Thy great power,............361. N.84, 7
Implies His Power, when He's cal'd the LORD...379. N.141, 2
God is so potent, as His Power can............383. N.176, 1
In power; or come Thou in that state,..........393. N 232, 3
Will add a power, to keep me innocent;........397. N.255, 2
Here melting numbers, words of power to move..415. A.7, 9
— — — — — — — — — — —, ...428. var. H.197, 85
Powered — — — — — — — — —, ...448. var. A.1, 92
Powerful As is thy powerful selfe. Prethee not smile; 46. H.128, 45
Or hell it selfe a powerfull Bulwarke is?......116. H.283, 146
Stand by the Magick of my powerfull Rhymes..280. H.869, 1
Powers See City-powers
Then in that Parly, all those powers............8. H.11, 7
And all in Your Blest Hand, which has the powers 62. H.161, 7
I feare no Earthly Powers;....................65. H.170, 1
Powred See Powered
Practice And it to know, and practice; with intent.35. H.106, 5
Put in practise, to understand.................115. H.283, 124
Praise Call on Bacchus; chaunt his praise;........39. H.111, 7
My num'rous issue: Praise, and pitty me.......58. H.151, 2
Praise me, for having such a fruitfull wombe;....58. H.151, 3
Where others love, and praise my Verses; still....66. H.173, 1
But (Hark!) we praise the Painter now, not you..98. H.241, 2
Your praise, and bless you, sprinkling you with Wheat: 113. H 283, 46
Be't to your praise, no peace was broken.......114. H.283, 90
Paying before you praise; and cockring wit,....141. H.359, 15
Ile praise, and Ile approve....................160. H.422, 5
Then publick praise do's runne upon the Stone,..172. H.459, 9
That we may praise Them, or themselves prize You. 173. H.459, 12
For Coronation, then Your onely Praise.........188. H.506, 12
To praise his Verse..........................198. H.544, 12
These I co'd praise thee for beyond another,....210. H 590, 9
To praise those Muses, and dislike our own?....234. H.673, 2
Then a mans frequent Fame, spoke out with praise. 241. H.710, 2
I sing thy praise Iacchus,......................259. H.772, 1
Then while I sing your praise,................261. H.778, 10
But ther's not one, doth praise the smell of thee..266. H.802, 2
'Tis the Chyrurgions praise, and height of Art,...268. H.808, 1
Poets co'd not praise too much...............274. H.838, 4
Yet their Three praises, praise but One; that's Lawes. 276. H 851, 8
So shall I sing thy praise;....................281. H 874, 13
Praise they that will Times past, I joy to see....292. H.927, 1
Be lesse anothers Laurell, then thy praise.......297. H.947, 14
When either price, or praise is ta'ne away......316. H.1033, 2
And thus they praise the Sumpter; but not him:.330. H.1099, 4
O Paragon, and Pearle of praise!..............359. N.83, 2
Receive, for this thy praise, our teares:.........360. N.83, 37

His praise; so let us blesse the King:........367. N.98, 26
How worthy of respect and praise!............375. N.123, 62
The first of sin is, and the next of praise:........395. N.243, 2
If well, then chant Gods praise with cheerfulnesse.
395. N.243, 4
May (though they scorn Thee) praise and pitie Thee.
399. N.263, 35
Howeuer after tymes will praise,................407. A.2, 15
— — — — — — — — —, ...445. var. H.730, 18
Praised Would into prais'd (but pitied) ruines fall,
252. H.745, 15
And no less prais'd, then spread throughout the world.
288. H.907, 6
And no lesse prais'd, then of the maides admir'd.
299. H.956, 10
Praises Yet their Three praises, praise but One; that's Lawes.
276. H.851, 8
Prayers and Praises are those spotlesse two......341. N.9, 1
The praises sing..........................369. N.106, 12
Praises-proof No clap of hands, or shout, or praises-proofe
150. H.382, 11
Praising And the pure Starres the praising Poetrie.
168. H.444, 8
And then sho'd I in praising thee be slow,......298. H.955, 11
Prank Some prank them up with Oaken leaves:..101. H.250, 20
Shall pranke thy Hooke with Lillies...........184. H 492, 32
Of those that prank it with their Plumes;......375. N.123, 65
Pranked See Be-pranked
Prat Prat He writes Satyres; but herein's the fault,
238. H.692, 1
Prate Chor. Much time is spent in prate; begin,..243. H.716, 23
Prattle Let them prattle how that I..............82. H.203, 5
Pray Devoutly to thy Closet-gods then pray,........14. H.35, 3
Pray love me little, so you love me long...........51. H.143, 2
It is sufficient if we pray.......................59. H.153, 1
Pray come,....................................111. H.280, 7
In your Temple, when I pray,................138. H.346, 8
Pray once, twice pray; and turn thy ground to gold.
144. H.370, 8
Y'ave farced well, pray make an end;..........146. H.377, 24
Makes guests and fish smell strong; pray go.....146. H.377, 26
Ile too work, or pray; and then...............155. H.407, 5
Pray hurt him not; though he be dead,........157. H.412, 21
He's soft and tender (Pray take heed).........157. H.412, 25
That on the seaventh, he can nor preach, or pray.
163. H.435, 4
Never keep a fast, or pray....................183. H.490, 15
No more my Silvia, do I mean to pray..........204. H.570, 1
Pray be silent, and not stirre.................224. H.640, 3
Ch. And is that all? I'm gone. Ph. By love I pray thee,
248. H.730, 17
Ch. Talk not of love, all pray, but few soules pay me.
248. H.730, 18
Meane time thy Prophets Watch by Watch shall pray:
254. H.756, 13
We pray 'gainst Warre, yet we enjoy no Peace..264. H.793, 1
Readers wee entreat ye pray...................269. H.814, 1
These my Reliques, (pray) interre.............270. H.821, 2
To pray for me doe thou begin,................277. H.854, 5
I am zeallesse, prethee pray...................277. H.856, 1
We pray for showers (at our need)............279. H.867, 5
Help me, Julia for to pray,...................324. H.1069, 1
Let us wash, and pray together:...............324. H.1069, 6
God heares us when we pray, but yet defers......344. N.30, 1
Just so it is with me, who list'ning, pray........358. N.77, 5
Great things ask for, when thou dost pray,.......381. N 158, 3
Pray not for silver, rust eats this;.............381. N.158, 5
And so to Bed: Pray wish us all Good Rest.......419. A.10, 8
— — — — — — — — — —, ...453. var. H.283, 62
Prayed Good princes must be pray'd for: for the bad
32. H.97, 1
Know, I have pray'd to Furie, that some wind....49. H.138, 7
And, having pray'd together, we................125. H.316, 9
Know I have praid thee,......................212. H.604, 2
When the Priest his last hath praid,...........348. N.41, 29
Prayer In Prayer the Lips ne're act the winning part,
346. N.35, 1
A prayer, that is said alone,..................381. N.158, 1
a prayer must be said, be briefe;........431. ins. H.283, 60n
— — — — — — — — — —, ...436. var. H.336, 3
Prayers To Prayers, then to Merryment,........101. H.250, 24
After short prayers, they set on bread;..........119. H.293, 8
Or prayers, or vow............................132. H.336, 3
And say short Prayers; and when we have done so,
168. H.445, 4
And prayers to Venus; if it please..........175. H.465, 75
What short sweet Prayers shall be said;.........216. H.616, 31
At last, when prayers for the dead,...........237. H.686, 13
And make short pray'rs to thee:..............281. H.874, 5
Spenke has a strong breath, yet short Prayers saith:
283. H.884, 1
And thence return, (short prayers seyd)......291. H.919, 15
Prayers and Praises are those spotlesse two........341. N.9, 1
God He rejects all Prayers that are sleight,......342. N.16, 1
Then prayers repel'd, (sayes Cassiodore).........383. N.170, 2
Wherefore two prayers ought not to be said,....396. N.249, 7
Praying Till you come forth. Wash, dresse, be briefe in praying:
68. H.178, 27
And praying, strew some Roses on her,........257. H.764, 9
Prays The Saint, to which the most he prayes....93. H.223, 129
Makes not a God; but he that prayes to one.....117. H.288, 2
He prayes his Harvest may be well brought home.
270. H.822, 2
Preach What the times of old did preach.........120. H.297, 2
That on the seaventh, he can nor preach, or pray..163. H.435, 4
Precedent Ther's no vice now, but has his president. 139. H.352, 2
Precepts Good Precepts we must firmly hold,......187. H.505, 1
Those spirits rais'd; and with like precepts then
326. H.1080, 17
Precious Such precious thraldome ne'r shall fetter me.
17. H.42, 4
Will last to be a precious Stone,................61. H.160, 9
More precious, then we prize our gold:........92. H.223, 88
Which precious spoiles upon her,...............131. H.330, 12
For a most rich, a rare, a precious One.......172. H.459, 10
Pleasant, and precious to my Muse and me.......227. H.652, 4
To take the precious Phesant made:...........231. H.662, 67
Of Rome did weare for their most precious Pearles.
251. H.741, 2
That precious stock; the store.................289. H.911, 19
Things precious are least num'rous: Men are prone.339. N.1, 5
With sundry precious Jewells,...................345. N.33, 18
From this soe peereles pretious permanent,........405. A.1, 66
Richer then that faire pretious virtuos horne....406. A.1, 103
Precious-pearly-purling These Precious-Pearly-Purling teares,
54. H.149, 21
Precipitates True love, we know, precipitates delay...8. H.10, 6
Precise Is too precise in every part...............28. H.83, 14
Pure enough, though not Precise:..............232. H.665, 4
Precomposed Nature has pre-compos'd us both to Love;
274. H.837, 3
Predestination With thy most white Predestination.
155. H.405, 4
Predestination is the Cause alone..............389. N.215, 1
To make thy faire Predestination:...............389. N.216, 2
The cause of Gods Predestination:...............390. N.219, 2
Predicant Turn'd, from a Papist here, a Predicant.
151. H.385, 2
Prefer And for my sake, who ever did prefer......137. H.341, 9
Which seals Thy Glorie; since I doe prefer....199. H.545, 9
A Prince I'de be, that I might Thee preferre....202. H 557, 29
Preferred Nor any was preferr'd 'fore me..........70. H.181, 2
Prefixed In that your owne prefixed comelinesse:.299. H.958, 4
Pregnant And pregnant violet; which done......119. H.293, 23
Of Day break from the pregnant East, 'tis time..207. H.575, 64
To see the day spring from the pregnant East,...242. H.713, 2
Premonished Better it is, premonish'd, for to shun
349. N.43, 5
Prentice Pusse and her Prentice both at Draw-gloves play;
260. H.773, 1
Prepare Quickly, quickly then prepare;..........114. H.283, 77
The pleasures Ile prepare for thee:.............192. H.521, 2
This Mornings Incense to prepare, and burne.....196. H.539, 2
Prepare for Songs; He's come, He's come;......365. N.97, 1
— — — — — — — — — —, ...434. var. H.293, 20d
Prepared See Well-prepared
But with thy equall thoughts, prepar'd dost stand,
37. H.106, 95
A man prepar'd against all ills to come,........128. H.323, 1
Ready here? Jul. All well prepar'd,..............280. H.870, 8
That Lookes for such prepared grownd,........409. A.2, 104
Euc. The hallowed Tapers all preparèd were,......416. A.8, 19
— — — — — — — — — —, ...434. var H.293, 12b
Prepares Prepares the way for mans docility.......153. H.394, 4
Preposterous Preposterous is that Government, (and rude)
196. H.536, 1
Prepost'rous is that order, when we run........241. H.708, 1
Prerogative For his plumpe white and smooth prrogatiue.
405. A.1, 34
Prescience And from Gods Prescience of mans sin doth flow
390. N.219, 3
Gods Prescience makes none sinfull; but th' offence
390. N.220, 1
Of man's the chief cause of Gods Prescience.....390. N.220, 2
Present See All-present
When what is lov'd, is Present, love doth spring;...13. H.30, 1
Present their shapes; while fantasie discloses....36. H.106, 47
There, there present...........................43. H.123, 10
And then present the Mornings-light...........47. H.133, 10
More love unto my life, or can present..........78. H.197, 55
When her high carriage did at once present......79. H.197, 75
The Elves present to quench his thirst..........119. H.293, 20
When others gain much by the present cast,....144. H.374, 1
Where we present our Oberon led...........165. H.443, 3
Here we present a fleece......................221. H.633, 32
Thou seest a present God-like Power..........230. H.662, 31
Not unto thee, but That thou didst present.....249. H.732, 4
The present Age will tell the world thou art....267. H 804, 11
Subjects still loath the present Government.......291. H.921, 2
Who shall for the present delight here,........317. H.1035, 9
Done in the present times:......................352. N.53, 6

Our present Teares here (not our present laughter)
362. N.90, 1
Gold I have none, but I present my need,........369. N.105, 1
Present with just men, to the veritie:..........385. N.188, 2
God's present ev'ry where; but most of all......388. N.207, 1
Present by Union Hypostaticall:..............388. N.207, 2
Present those Turfs, which once must cover me:
392. N.230, 16
Present, to plead my cause for me;............395. N.245, 4
But let each p^r^sant Cheeke appear................413. A.4, 3
Presents Upon her wings presents the god unshorne.
67. H.178, 2
That this presents to me......................81. H.201, 40
Preserved Us all, unlesse preserv'd by thy Perfume.
197. H.539, 12
Preserver When I had Thee, my chiefe Preserver, by.
72. H.185, 21
President See Precedent
Press Ennobled numbers for the Presse,...........19. H.51, 7
Invites fresh Grapes to fill his Presse with Wine..72. H.185, 28
Before the Press scarce one co'd see............287. H.899, 1
Because thy selfe art comming to the Presse:..298. H.955, 10
Let others to the Printing Presse run fast,......314. H.1022, 1
The Wine Presse now is ta'ne from us,..........375. N.123, 53
Pressed He with his pretty finger prest..........74. H.190, 7
But gently prest from the soft side..........120. H.293, 49
Then, may your Plants be prest with Fruit,....179. H.476, 16
I prest my Julia's lips, and in the kisse........240. H.700, 1
On with thy worke, though thou beest hardly prest;
311. H.1009, 1
Fine flowre prest down, and running o're.........356. N.66, 8
And prest a little they will weepe new milke.....405. A.1, 58
Pressing Pressing before, some coming after,....101. H.250, 17
Pression And Aire-like, leave no pression to be seen
250. H.737, 7
Pressures Though a wise man all pressures can sustaine;
60. H.158, 1
Presume But lesse presume to lay a Plait upon....82. H.204, 3
Presupposes Art presupposes Nature; Nature shee.153. H.394, 3
Pretend What ever men for Loyalty pretend,.....333. H.1121, 1
Preternatural That Preternaturall Fever, which did threat
254. H.756, 3
Prethee See Prithee
Prettily And prettily bedabled so,...............247. H.729, 2
Pretty See Blushing-pretty-peeping
To my pretty Witchcrafts all:...................10. H.19, 2
But pretty Fondling, let not fall..................12. H.23, 5
And whose the pretty prize shu'd be,............31. H.92, 3
And why, my pretty Lad, said she?..............50. H.139, 6
He with his pretty finger prest..................74. H.190, 7
Let Lullaby the pretty Prince asleep!..........86. H.213, 18
Fly to my Mistresse, pretty pilfring Bee,........100. H.248, 1
Such pretty flowers, (like to Orphans young)...104. H.257, 13
May his pretty Duke-ship grow..................108. H.266, 1
Thou pittifull, and pretty Philomel:..............111. H.279, 2
Here she lies, a pretty bud,.....................123. H.310, 1
Lives in the pretty Lady-flower................126. H.318, 11
Thou my pretty Captive art?.....................128. H.322, 5
Or ever mark't the pretty beam,................164. H.440, 5
Yee pretty Huswives, wo'd ye know............164. H.442, 1
The pretty whimpering that they make,..........180. H.478, 5
And (pretty Child) feeles now no more..........189. H.514, 3
Her pretty feet....................................194. H.525, 1
Since Gander did his prettie Youngling wed:....223. H.636, 1
Here a pretty Baby lies..........................224. H.640, 1
Jane is a Girle that's prittie;....................229. H.659, 6
To prettie girles to play withall:..................294. H.937, 2
For which (me thought) in prittie anger she...313. H.1017, 11
Thou prettie Babie, borne here,..................345. N.33, 3
Go prettie child, and beare this Flower..........354. N.59, 1
Because the prettie Babe do's bleed............366. N.98, 21
Unto our prettie Twelfth-Tide King,..........368. N.102, 20
That little prettie bleeding part................376. N.125, 1
Kindly swell vp with little pretty pride,..........406. A.1, 88
Pretty-lisping Tom Chipperfeild, and pritty-lisping Ned,
155. H.405, 9
Prew See Prue
Prewdence See Prudence
Prevail Thy Fortress, and will needs prevaile;...175. H.465, 54
Teares most prevaile; with teares too thou mayst move
287. H.900, 1
Nor those false vows, which oft times don't prevaile.
331. H.1104, 2
Prevaricate The time that I prevaricate from thee..79. H.197, 86
Prevent And may prevent it, sitting still............6. H.2, 26
These things thou know'st to'th'height, and dost prevent
35. H.106, 21
Wo'd I frustrate, or prevent.....................286. H.897, 5
And take me up; or els prevent the fall..........352. N.51, 8
Prevention For which prevention (Sociate) let there be
287. H.901, 3
Price Buy'st Travell at the lowest price.........36. H.106, 82
In Lov's name do so; and a price...........113. H.283, 53
I came; (tis true) and lookt for Fowle of price,..262. H.783, 7
When either price, or praise is ta'ne away.......316. H.1033, 2
Here's golden fruit that farre exceeds all price....406. A.1, 71
Theyre Nobly-home-bread, yett haue price........409. A.2, 93
Of higher price, as halfe-iet-ringes........440. ins. H.443, 45s
— — — — — — — — — — —, ...450. var. A.9, 3
Priceless And Priceless now, what Peerless once had been:
21. H.62, 4
Prick If one poore prick,...... ....273. H.833, 4
Pricked Love prickt my finger with a golden pin:..17. H.44, 4
Hath prickt thy heart;..........................273. H.833, 2
Pricket The untam'd Heifer, or the Pricket,....136. H.336, 142
Prickles Prickles is waspish, and puts forth his sting,
287. H.903, 1
That Prickles buyes, puts Prickles out of frame;..287. H.903, 3
Prick-madam But for Prick-madam, and for Gentle-heart;
114. H.283, 96
Pricks Soe full of clarrett that whoe soe pricks a vine
405. A.1, 49
Pride The active Sea-horse, & with pride,..........30. H.90, 2
Or some full flame, which with a pride aspires,..45. H.128, 17
And had no other pride at all,....................75. H.193, 30
Then will your hidden Pride......................76. H.193, 55
Me, with that full pride of complexion,..........78. H.197, 72
Of that white Pride, and Drowne.............115. H.283, 119
The Sock grew loathsome, and the Buskins pride,.150. H.382, 2
Fie on this pride, this Female vanitie...........163. H.439, 2
And after they have shown their pride,.........176. H.467, 16
For which (my Charles) it is my pride to be,..297. H.947, 11
Kindly swell vp with little pretty pride,..........406. A.1, 88
Priest See High-priest, Little-puppet-priest, Queen-priest
And chose their Priest, ere we can cast off sloth:.69. H.178, 50
Neere to the Altar stands the Priest,...........91. H.223, 50
Grace by his Priest; The feast is ended.........120. H.293, 54
Who then the joyning Priest shall be.........216. H.616, 30
A Pig to the Priest for a Roster,.............256. H.762, 15
Night makes no difference 'twixt the Priest and Clark;
279. H.864, 1
The candid Stole thrown ore the Pious Priest;..286. H.898, 6
Trap, of a Player turn'd a Priest now is;......325. H.1076, 1
And, from a Priest, turne Player once again....325. H.1076, 4
When the Priest his last hath praid,............348. N.41, 29
Bring Him along, most pious Priest,............365. N.97, 11
Priestess See Pious-priestess
Priesthood My Priest-hood crown with bayes....261. H.778, 11
And Conscience vnto Preist-hood, tis not Need....411. A.3, 51
Priestresse See Pious-priestess
Priests See Mass-priests
Prig Prig now drinks Water, who before drank Beere:
71. H.183, 1
Prig mony wants, either to buy, or brew.........71. H.183, 4
Prigg, when he comes to houses, oft doth use....143. H.368, 1
Prigg bears away the body and the sole.........143. H.368, 4
Prig's Look in Prig's purse, the chev'rell there tells you
71. H.183, 3
Primates So many Kings, and Primates too there are,
272. H.826, 4
Prime Stately Julia, prime of all;..................15. H.39, 3
Come, let us goe, while we are in our prime;....69. H.178, 57
For having lost but once your prime,..........84. H.208, 15
You are the Prime, and Princesse of the Feast:..140. H.354, 6
Thee to the World a Prime and Publique One...181. H.483, 8
Of late struck one; and now I see the prime..207. H.575, 63
While w'are in our Prime;......................267. H.806, 2
The prime of Paradice..........................271. H.824, 8
At twice ten yeares, a prime and publike one?....299. H.956, 6
Primitive With those thy primitive decrees,......148. H.377, 96
Primrose Let fall a Primrose, and with it a teare:..9. H.14, 14
Sickly the Prim-rose: Pale the Daffadill:........41. H.118, 2
A Primrose next;..............................135. H.336, 99
Good morning to this Prim-rose too;............156. H.412, 5
This Primrose, thus bepearl'd with dew?........208. H.580, 4
A Primrose Banke did cross her way,...........288. H.908, 3
The Primrose sick, and sickly every thing:....320. H.1054, 2
The Primrose, and the Violet..................360. N.83, 18
— — — — — — — — — — —, ...448. var. A.1, 64
Primrose-banks And here we'l sit on Primrose-banks, and see
206. H.575, 21
Primroses O Primroses! let this day be..............7. H.9, 5
Of Primroses and Violets......................192. H.521, 20
And as on Primroses we sit,.....................215. H.616, 3
Primrose-tide That they wo'd each Primrose-tide,..44. H.125, 2
Prince Lovely in you, brave Prince of Cavaliers!....25. H.77, 8
The youthfull Prince D'Amour here...............63. H.166, 8
That I co'd ne'r be Prince of Love,..............64. H.166, 11
Let Lullaby the pretty Prince asleep!..........86. H.213, 18
As he is Prince, he's Shepherd too..............86. H.213, 44
Prince of Hellicon, but He.....................108. H.266, 12
That Prince takes soone enough the Victors roome,
109. H.268, 1
A Prince or Pembroke, and that Pembroke, you!.141. H.359, 2
This, Three; which Three, you make up Foure Brave Prince.
170. H.451, 16
A Prince I'de be, that I might Thee preferre..202. H.557, 29
The Starre-led-birth of Charles the Prince.......214. H.611, 6
A Prince from Foes; but 'tis his Fort of Friends.
244. H.717, 2
Such as the Prince is, will his People be.......255. H.759, 2
That Prince must govern with a gentle hand,....323. H.1067, 1

That Prince, who may doe nothing but what's just, 331. H.1103, 1
What is't that wasts a Prince? example showes,..331. H.1105, 1
To which the Pesant, so the Prince must come,..392. N.230, 24
Vnto the Prince of Shades, whom once his Pen 442. ins. H.575, 28a
Entitulated the Greecian Prince of men....442. ins. H.575, 28b
Princely Though here the Princely Poet.........64. H.166, 12
This is that Princely Pemberton, who can....149. H.377, 133
With Princely hand He'l recompence delay.......344. N.30, 4
Who for Thy Princely Port here,................345. N.33, 5
Upon Thy Princely State here,..................345. N.33, 28
A Princely Babe in's Mothers Brest..........367. N.102, 14
Princes Good princes must be pray'd for: for the bad 32. H.97, 1
All thoughts, but such as aime at getting Princes,..77. H.197, 8
That Princes may possesse a surer seat,........163. H.438, 1
The Pearle of Princes, yet despaire............175. H.465, 38
Crown'd Poets; yet live Princes under thee:....234. H.673, 16
Princes, and such like Publike Lights as These,..237. H.685, 9
Princes and Fav'rites are most deere, while they..255. H.758, 1
Princes cure some faults by their patience.......309. H.998, 2
The Power of Princes rests in the Consent....325. H.1073, 1
Princess And be both Princesse here, and Poetresse. 107. H.265, 10
You are the Prime, and Princesse of the Feast:..140. H.354, 6
Principal Sapho next, a principall:................15. H.39, 4
Last, yet to be with These a Principall.........304. H.977, 2
My dearest daintyes, nay, 'tis the principall: 426. ins. H.197, 48b
Principalities Shew me Those Fleshie Principalities; 154. H.403, 2
Principle 'Tis a known principle in War,........118. H.290, 1
Principles To keep those pious Principles in force. 201. H.557, 20
Print Ere I print my Poetry;....................21. H.59, 2
But when your own faire print was set........126. H.318, 6
Say, What sho'd Roots do with a Purse in print, 162. H.427, 3
To Print our Poems, the propulsive cause........169. H.448, 1
If any thing delight me for to print.............355. N.61, 1
Print thy lips into the ayre,....................414. A.5, 10
Printed But since th' art Printed, thou dost call..287. H.899, 3
Printer Condemne the Printer, Reader, and not me; 4. Ap., 2
Printing Let others to the Printing Presse run fast, 314. H.1022, 1
Prints Puts down some prints of His high Majestie: 385. N.189, 2
Prison Your Night, your Prison, and your Ebbe; you may 52. H.146, 10
Unto the prison, I'le say, no;.................370. N.107, 12
Prisoner (All parts there made one prisoner.)......16. H.41, 17
Enthrall'd her Arme, as Prisoner...............64. H.169, 4
Hee may (a prisoner) ther discrye.............408. A.2, 63
Prisoner's In the Pris'ners Panier...............224. H.638, 24
Prisoners To be tormented, or kept Pris'ners here? 33. H.101, 2
Here, here the Slaves and Pris'ners be........190. H.515, 19
Prithee Prethee (lest Maids sho'd censure thee) but say 42. H.122, 9
As is thy powerful selfe. Prethee not smile;.....46. H.128, 45
Mony thou ow'st me; Prethee fix a day..........83. H.206, 1
Deare Perenna, prethee come,....................89. H.220, 1
Prethee goe home; and for thy credit be.........97. H.236, 3
And prethee, let's lay...........................99. H.243, 2
Prithee, when next thou do'st invite, barre State, 161. H.424, 3
I prithee speake: Lyc. I will. End. Say on:......183. H.492, 5
Say what thou art. Ph. I prithee first draw neare.248. H.730, 4
For Love or Pittie, prethee let there be......277. H.853, 3
I am zeallesse, prethee pray...................277. H.856, 1
I prithee stay. (Am.) I must away,............324. H.1068, 21
Cha. Prethee relate, while I give ear and weep....416. A.8, 12
Privacy Our own beloved privacie:............200. H.552, 18
The more my rurall privacie:...................246. H.724, 28
Private The poore and private Cottages.............5. H.2, 4
But to the acting of this private Play:..........24. H.74, 12
Confin'd to live with private Larr:............37. H.106, 106
And as I went my private way,.................73. H.187, 3
Some private pinch tels danger's nie............147. H.377, 52
How well contented in this private Grange......310. H.1003, 1
My private Protonotarie?.......................357. N.72, 2
Prize And whose the pretty prize shu'd be,........31. H.92, 3
More precious, then we prize our gold:..........92. H.223, 88
That we may praise Them, or themselves prize You. 173. H.459, 12
I greedy of the prize, did drinke,...............222. H.635, 5
To give the prize to thee, or me................243. H.716, 6
Shall be Disposeresse of the prize..............243. H.716, 12
Whose now the prize and wager is..............244. H.716, 42
Give me the prize: 2. The day is mine:........244. H.716, 43
Or sho'dst thou prize me as a Dish............321. H.1056, 11
Tis not Jewell of great prize....................417. A.9, 3
Prized How high she's priz'd, and worth but small; 103. H.253, 17
One and the selfe-same priz'd complexion........209. H.586, 6
Who shewing mercy here, few priz'd, or none....393. N.234, 2
Prizest Because thou prizest things that are......119. H.293, 3
Probability — — — — — — — —, ...426. var. H.197, 46
Proboscis By his Probossis that he is all nose......284. H.886, 2
Proceed Chaste words proceed still from a bashfull minde. 319. H.1043, 2
And thence proceed, to act Thy Passion........399. N.263, 29
Procession Me, when thou yeerly go'st Procession: 20. H.55, 6
Processions In great Processions many lead the way 256. H.763, 3
Proclaim (The Bell-man of the night) proclaime the clock 207. H.575, 62
Proclaims — — — — — — — —, ...443. var. H.575, 62
Proclamation The Proclamation made for May:...68. H.178, 40
Produce Gardens thence produce and Meads:....108. H.266, 14
Which must produce me to that Gen'rall Doome, 392. N.230, 23
Production Eternall by their own production......170. H.451, 8
Profanation Nay, profanation to keep in,........68. H.178, 12
Profane Hence, hence, profane; soft silence let us have; 89. H.219, 1
A second pules, Hence, hence, profane.........91. H.223, 43
Profane no Porch young man and maid, for fear..124. H.313, 3
I, as others, am Prophane......................227. H.651, 4
Altar cleane, no fire prophane?................280. H.870, 6
Hence, hence prophane, and none appeare........366. N.98, 1
Uncircumcis'd, unseason'd, and prophane........371. N.113, 4
I'le not prophane, by soile of sin,.............402. N.269, 4
Profaned The Cirque prophan'd was; and all postures rackt: 150. H.382, 5
Prophan'd in Speech, or done an act that's fowle 426. ins. H.197, 29a
Profess He tacks about, and now he doth profess 266. H.800, 5
Chiefelye my selfe to what I must proffess:......412. A.3, 98
Professes Brought him, (as Love professes).......27. H.81, 22
Proffered For profer'd love will repay:...........252. H.746, 4
Profitable Afflictions they most profitable are......343. N.24, 1
Profits That either profits, or not hurts at all.....252. H.748, 2
Profuser Fortune's a blind profuser of her own,..238. H.689, 1
Progermination That gave Progermination unto them: 251. H.745, 8
Project Fortune no higher Project can devise,....196. H.535, 1
Prologue His Carting was the Prologue to this Play. 195. H.532, 4
Promise Promise, and keep your vowes,...........32. H.94, 5
You have broke promise twice...................32. H.94, 9
Bring me but one, Ile promise thee,............103. H.255, 5
I will promise there shall be...................136. H.337, 5
What here I promise, that no Broom.........165. H.442, 13
(Which from his ghost a promise is)...........226. H.644, 8
And mad'st a promise that mine appetite.......262. H.783, 2
God doth not promise here to man, that He......396. N.252, 1
Hath seal'd the promise of her vtmost skill.......405. A.1, 64
Promised Virgins promis'd when I dy'd,.........44. H.125, 1
Having promis'd, pay your debts,...............44. H.125, 5
Promis'd sho'd come to crown your youth........53. H.149, 2
Have, promis'd to your sheets;.................54. H.149, 36
For payment promis'd, though thou never pay:..83. H.206, 2
I've paid Thee, what I promis'd; that's not All; 168. H.444, 1
Thou hast promis'd, Lord, to be.................347. N.40, 1
Prompt To prompt mee, I shall euer..............414. A.5, 7
— — — — — — — — —, ...422. var. H.106, 145
Promulgate When Thou Thy Lawes didst promulgate 393. N.232, 4
Prone Men are suspicious; prone to discontent:..291. H.921, 1
Things precious are least num'rous: Men are prone 339. N.1, 5
Pronounced — — — — — — — — —, ...424. var. H.128, 47
Proof See Counter-proof, Life-proof, Praises-proof, Weather-proof
Although not archt, yet weather proofe,........133. H.336, 52
To give subsistance to thy house, and proofe,..148. H.377, 97
So neatly sunck, as that no proof............167. H.443, 103
Nor leave the search, and proofe, till Thou canst find 181. H.483, 3
Yet if thou wert not, Berkley, loyall proofe,....252. H.745, 13
For any ill; but, for the proof of Faith:........380. N.150, 2
But when good words, by good works, have their proof, 397. N.256, 3
Prop The staffe, the Elme, the prop, the shelt'ring wall 72. H.185, 12
A little prop best fits a little Vine,............249. H.733, 2
Proper And know, that Riches have their proper stint. 35. H.106, 17
At full their proper excellence;..................76. H.193, 38
The Proper Lessons for the Saints now dead:....209. H.584, 2
Hansome you are, and Proper you will be......299. H.958, 1
Each bending then, will rise a proper flower.....320. H.1054, 6
Properties Many grinning properties...............255. H.761, 10
In everlasting Properties......................289. H.912, 6
Propertius To my Propertius.....................81. H.201, 36
Prophesy Can runne mad, and Prophesie.........217. H.620, 9
Fitted am to prophesie:..........................242. H.714, 2
Prophet Loe, I, the Lyrick Prophet, who have set 142. H.365, 3
Besides, the most religious Prophet stands......262. H.781, 9
Thy Poet, and Thy Prophet Lawreat............398. N.262, 4

Prophetic Ne'r may **Prophetique** Daphne crown my Brow. 79. H.197, 92
This Portion my **Prophetique** Bayes............407. A.2, 16
Prophet's The Nagge (like to the **Prophets** Asse)..13. H.27, 6
We are Thy **Prophets** Porter; Thou our King...324. H.1071, 4
Prophets Those **Prophets** of the former Magnitude) 207. H.575, 60
Meane time thy **Prophets** Watch by Watch shall pray; 254. H.756, 13
Of those god-full **prophetts** longe before..........411. A.3, 42
And quafe it to the **Prophets** of our Age;........412. A.3, 88
Prophets' The **Prophets** Mountains of the Old are meant; 381. N.157, 3
Propitious Be thou then **propitious** there.........221. H.633, 59
Propound With the end that I **propound?**.......286. H.897, 4
Propulsive To Print our Poems, the **propulsive** cause 169. H.448, 1
Proscenium And **Proscenium** of her face.........138. H.342, 8
Prose Be in **Prose** a gratefull man..............182. H.489, 14
Thou writes in **Prose**, how sweet all Virgins be; 266. H.802, 1
Who fli'st at all heights: **Prose** and Verse run'st through; 298. H.955, 7
Proserpine The doome of cruell **Proserpine**.......132. H.336, 8
The lap of **Proserpine**..........................251. H.740, 12
Prosper Next, may your Dairies **Prosper** so,......179. H.476, 10
All **prosper** by your Virgin-vowes...............179. H.476, 24
Prosper thy Basket, and therein thy Dow.......269. H.818, 4
In love, then **prosper** me.......................281. H.874, 6
All will **prosper**, if so be......................286. H.897, 11
As some plants **prosper** best by cuts and blowes; 292. H.929, 3
Enter and **prosper**; while our eyes doe waite.....300. H.961, 9
Or **prosper**, but by that same tree..............371. N.114, 3
Prospered That ever **prosper'd** by Cunctation......251. H.744, 2
Prosperity **Prosperitie** more searching of the mind: 257. H.765, 2
Prosperous To tell all **prosp'rous** chance..........55. H.149, 58
Have made Thee **prosperous** in thy wayes, thus farre: 181. H.483, 6
Adverse and **prosperous** Fortunes both work on..349. N.44, 1
Prospers Jove **prospers** by meat, more then his...173. H.461, 4
Prostitute — — — — — — — —, ...441. var. H.465, 28
Prostrate Then **prostrate** to a million...........174. H.465, 28
Protect For evermore **protect** me................260. H.777, 12
Protecting As to a still **protecting** Deitie.........300. H.961, 16
Protection The Gods **protection**, but the night before) 9. H.14, 12
Protest Breathe, Julia, breathe, and Ile **protest**,...69. H.179, 1
Bice laughs, when no man speaks; and doth **protest** 265. H.795, 1
Protestant Thy **Protestant** to be:...............108. H.267, 2
Protestation This second **Protestation** now......328. H.1090, 7
Protests Parrat **protests** 'tis he, and only he.......186. H.501, 1
Protonotary My private **Protonotarie?**...........357. N. 72, 2
Proud A lying Rich man, and a Poore man **proud**...10. H.18, 2
The **proud** Dictator of the State-like wood:......23. H.69, 4
Who keep'st no **proud** mouth for delicious cates:.37. H.106, 109
Sweet, be not **proud** of those two eyes,..........61. H.160, 1
Nor be you **proud**, that you can see.............61. H.160, 3
Be you not **proud** of that rich haire,.............61. H.160, 5
Be not **proud**, but now encline...................96. H.232, 1
And to your more bewitching, see, the **proud**..115. H.283, 111
And a Peacock **proud** shall be..................141. H.360, 5
Where both seem'd **proud**; the Flie to have......185. H.497, 3
As thou deserv'st, be **proud**; then gladly let....194. H.529, 1
Little you are; for Womans sake be **proud**;.....212. H.600, 1
I might grow **proud** the while..................231. H.663, 4
For thirty yeares, Tubbs has been **proud** and poor; 302. H.972, 1
Which if away, **proud** Scepters then will lye....325. H.1073, 3
Prouse Old Widdow **Prouse** to do her neighbours evill 266. H.801, 1
Prove So, that the more I look, the more I **prove**,..10. H.16, 5
These fresh beauties (we can **prove**)............15. H.37, 1
Since which, it festers so, that I can **prove**......17. H.44, 5
If you **prove** faithlesse thrice,..................32. H.94, 11
And thus thy little-well-kept-stock doth **prove**,..37. H.106, 127
Me thought 'twas strange, that thou so hard sho'dst **prove**, 42. H.122, 7
Who have found, and still can **prove**,........53. H. 147, 13
Ah me! I try; and trying, **prove**,................60. H.157, 3
I smil'd; and bade him once more **prove**,........64. H. 166, 9
As endless **prove**;..............................66. H.172, 29
Mir. Not so, not so. Chor. But if it chance to **prove** 86. H.213, 27
And if I **prove**...................................87. H.214. 9
He who plucks the sweets shall **prove**...........88. H.217, 5
And that terrour likewise **prove**,................117. H.286, 7
You say, you love me; that I thus must **prove**;..126. H.317, 1
If so be, I may but **prove**......................136. H.337, 3
Say, have ye sence, or do you **prove**...........158. H.420, 7
Who for some sweet-hearts sake, did **prove**.......169. H.449, 3
Only, if one **prove** addled, that he eates.......204. H.568, 3
Prove in your Bride-bed numerous.............208. H.581, 4
'Twas better there to toyle, then **prove**.........219. H.628, 5
And shod with silver, **prove** to be..............239. H.696, 7
Nothing hard, or harsh can **prove**............240. H.701, 1
Examine me with fire, and **prove** me............351. N.48, 7
Shall by this pleasing trespasse quickly **prove**,....297. H.949, 3
Since I as yet did never **prove**,..............327. H.1082, 2
And, if they do, they **prove** but cumbersome;....368. N.104, 3
True rev'rence is (as Cassiodore doth **prove**)....380. N.147, 1
Such is my parting wth thee; and to **proue**.....412. A.3, 79
For that would **prove** more Heresy then fault 433. ins. H.283, 140h
Proved And to have it fully **prov'd**,...............15. H.36, 7
And be not onely thought, but **prov'd**...........37. H.106, 102
He knowes not Love, that hath not this truth **proved**, 73. H.186, 11
Shame checks our first attempts; but then 'tis **prov'd** 362. N.85, 1
Proverb That was the **Proverb**. Let my mistresse be 141. H.357, 1
Proves Then if any Peece **proves** new,........217. H.620, 10
With trialls those, with terrors these He **proves**,..370. N.108, 3
Provide **Provide** a second Epithalamie..........286. H.898, 12
Provided Goes to the Feast that's now **provided**...93. H.223, 142
Let Crutches then **provided** be................303. H.973, 3
Providence His **Providence** who would not question then? 343. N.27, 4
Provides Much-more, **provides**, and hoords up like an Ant; 73. H.188, 1
Who first **provides**, not to be overcome.........109. H.268, 2
Provision Of full **provision**; such a store,........291. H.919, 3
Provocation More by **Provocation** great..........62. H.162, 15
Proxy Who by a double **Proxie** woes............409. A.2, 82
Prudence **Prewdence** Baldwin (once my maid)....262. H.782, 2
Prudent Discreet and **prudent** we that Discord call, 252. H.748, 1
Prue **Prue**, my dearest Maid, is sick,............122. H.302, 1
But thou kind **Prew** did'st with my Fates abide,..151. H.387, 5
They well content my **Prew** and me.............200. H.552, 4
A maid (my **Prew**) by good luck sent,.........246. H.724, 6
Prune And as I **prune** my feather'd youth, so I....72. H.185, 19
Vines to **prune**, though not to kill,............204. H.569, 14
Prurient Some numbers **prurient** are, and some of these 66. H.173, 7
Pry But while he, perking, there did **prie**........46. H.130, 7
Runs from his Torrid Zone, to **prie**, and look,..114. H.283, 62
Psalm But when he sings a **Psalme**, ther's none can be 266. H.799, 3
Psalter See **Fairy-psalter**
Writ in my **Psalter**...........................213. H.604, 12
Psalteries On your **Psaltries** play,..............263. H.784, 10
Ptisick See **Phthisic**
Public Well may my Book come forth like **Publique** Day 3. Ded.H, 1
Shark, when he goes to any **publick** feast,........118. H.292, 1
And walks fresh varnisht to the **publick** view.....140. H.356, 2
When as a **publick** ruine bears down All.........155. H.405, 18
Then **publick** praise do's runne upon the Stone,..172. H.459, 9
Thee to the World a Prime and **Publique** One...181. H.483, 8
Of your own selfe, a **Publick** Theater..........187. H.506, 2
In **publique** loss to shed a Teare:.............203. H.564, 4
This **publique** overthrow?......................211. H.596, 8
Kings must not oft be seen by **publike** eyes;....236. H.682, 1
A **Publike** Light (in this immensive Sphere.)..236. H.685, 2
Princes, and such like **Publike** Lights as these,..237. H.685, 9
That doe in **publike** places,.....................260. H.777, 2
Worthy the **Publique** Admiration:............297. H.947, 4
At twice ten yeares, a prime and **publike** one?....299. H.956, 6
Stand forth Brave Man, here to the **publique** sight; 322. H.1062, 10
Gives life and luster, **publike** mirth,.............364. N.96, 20
But as Heavens **publike** and immortall Eye.......371. N.113, 5
In clouds, descending to the **publike** Doome......382. N.162, 2
Publish For to tell, not **publish** it..............82. H.203, 16
Puckered Are **pucker'd** Bullace, Canckers and dry 439. ins. H.443, 45m
Pudding See **Fuz-ball-pudding**
Pudica Twice has **Pudica** been a Bride, and led..180. H.477, 1
Nor will; for why, **Pudica**, this may know,......180. H.477, 5
Puffs Science **puffs** up, sayes Gut, when either Pease 327. H.1085, 1
Puisneirs — — — — — — — — —, ...440. var. H.443, 70
Puisneis — — — — — — — — —, ...440. var. H.443, 70
Puisnes See **Puneys**
Pules A second **pules**, Hence, hence, profane.....91. H. 223, 43
Puling My **puling** Pipe to beat against thine eare:..17. H.42, 2
The merry Cricket, **puling** Flie,..............119. H.293, 17
Pull What ye cannot quench, **pull** downe;..........21. H.61, 5
Pullets Mease brags of **Pullets** which he eats: but Mease 142. H.361, 1
Pulpit Or by our selves, or from the **Pulpit** read...396. N.249, 8
Pulse To warme my Breast, when thou my **Pulse** art gone. 73. H.186, 16
And Mans **Pulse** stopt, All Passions sleep in Peace. 202. H.558, 4
Th' unequall **Pulse** to beat, as heretofore.......254. H.756, 6
The **Pulse** is Thine,...........................350. N.47, 28
Pulses You have **Pulses** that doe beat............96. H.232, 9
Me thinks like mine, your **pulses** beat;..........157. H.413, 5
That my **pulses** high may beate.............217. H.620, 3
Punchin **Punchin** a dry plant-animall............273. H.832. 2

Punchin by Beere and Ale, spreads so.........273. H.832, 4
Puneys — — — — — — — —, ...440. var. H.443, 70
Punish Good children kisse the rods, that **punish** sin. 32. H.97, 4
Now posting on to **punish** thee.................47. H.132, 12
The bad to **punish**, and the good t'amend.........343. N.26, 2
If God should **punish** no sin, here, of men,.......343. N.27, 3
To **punish** great sins, who small faults whipt here. 381. N.156, 2
And there do **punish**, and are punishèd...........417. A.8, 34
Punished When man is **punisht**, he is plagued still, 370. N.110, 1
And there do punish,, and are **punishèd**...........417. A.8, 34
Punishment For **punishment** in warre, it will suffice, 132. H.335, 1
Endures an everlasting **punishment**.............213. H.606, 2
Not for the servile feare of **punishment**...........290. H.917, 2
They might escape the lash of **punishment**.........291. H.920, 4
Good wits get more fame by their **punishment**...317. H.1034, 2
To make, not marre her, by this **punishment**:....344. N.31, 2
Or when, for sins, men suffer **punishment**.......388. N.210, 4
Boldly in sin, shall feel more **punishment**.........391. N.227, 4
Punishments Or to Rewards, or else to **Punishments**. 182. H.487, 2
Pup-like For puplike Eyes, take onlye theis......409. A.2, 91
Puppet See **Little-puppet-priest**
Purchase And in the **purchase** of our Peace,......360. N.83, 29
Pure Nor the Snow continue **pure**:..............60. H.159, 14
And **pure** as Gold for ever......................66. H.172, 30
Pure hands bring hither, without staine.......91. H.223, 42
Two **pure**, and holy Candlesticks:..............92. H.223, 94
As spotlesse **pure**, as it is sweet:..............101. H.250, 10
A **pure** seed-Pearle of Infant dew,............119. H.293, 21
Pure hands, **pure** habits, **pure**, **pure** every thing..127. H.320, 4
A **pure** smooth Pearle, and Orient too?..........164. H.440, 8
And all behung with these **pure** Pearls,........167. H.443, 108
And the **pure** Starres the praising Poetrie.........168. H.444, 8
Sound Teeth has Lucie, **pure** as Pearl, and small, 226. H.649, 1
Circum-crost by thy **pure** hand:................227. H.651, 2
Pure enough, though not Precise:..............232. H.665, 4
Is Zelot **pure**? he is: ye see he weares..........232. H.666, 1
Put we on **pure** Surplices;.....................280. H.870, 14
Thy **pure**, and Silver-wristed Naides..........316. H.1028, 22
How will it drop **pure** hony, speaking these?....328. H.1089, 4
'Tis not to poyson, but to make thee **pure**.........344. N.31, 4
The figur'd Damask, or **pure** Diaper,............355. N.65, 2
Are ready by, to make the Guests all **pure**:......355. N.65, 6
Pure Balm, that shall......................401. N.268, 12
With plumpe soft flesh of mettle **pure** and fine....406. A.1, 79
To see two tablets of **pure** Ivory................406. A.1, 96
your eyes are they, wherewith you draw the **pure** 432. ins. H.283. 70h
— — — — — — — — — —,.................448. var. A.1, 80
Pure-immortal Whose **pure-Immortal** body doth transmit 157. H.414, 9
Purer She brake in two the **purer** Glasse,........187. H.504, 4
— — — — — — — — — — —,...............423. var. H.128, 12
Against thy **purer** Essence? For that fault.426. ins. H.197, 29b
— — — — — — — — — —,...............427. var. H.197, 63
Purest That scatter'st Spirit and Lust; whose **purest** shine, 45. H.128, 12
A Moon-parcht grain of **purest** wheat,..........119. H.293, 9
Made of the Fleeces **purest** Downe.............192. H.521, 10
Like **purest** Skies.............................193. H.524, 2
So **purest** Diaper doth shine,...................268. H.811. 7
As **purest** Pearles, or Pebles do...............271. H.824, 11
So **purest** pebbles in the brook:...............294. H.939 4
Like **purest** white stands in the middle place.....404. A.1, 12
Purfling **Purfling** the Margents, while perpetuall Day 206. H.575, 14
Purgatory From her **Purgatory** free:.............269. H.814, 4
Purge **Purge** hence the guilt, and kill this quarrelling. 78. H.197, 32
To **purge** the Fairie Family....................91. H.223, 49
To **purge** the Chappel and the rooms:..........92. H.223, 102
But rather **purge** me...........................351. N.49, 8
Before ye **purge**, and circumcise...............366. N.98, 8
— — — — — — — — — —,..............426. var. H.197, 32
Purify To **purifie** this my Augean stable:.........357. N.73, 2
Puris I see't in's **puris** naturalibus:.............187. H.502, 2
Purity Behold that circummortall **purity**: 96. H.230, 2
Whom **purity** had Sainted.....................229. H.659, 5
'Bove all things lov'd it, for the **puritie**:........390. N.222, 2
Purling See **Precious-pearly-purling**
The **Purling** springs, groves, birds, and well-weav'd Bowrs, 36. H.106, 45
Purls And never **purls** a Note?..................183. H.492, 4
That gently **purles** from eithers Oat.............243. H.716, 18
Purple Now strength, and newer **Purple** get,........7. H.9, 3
Put **Purple** Grapes, or Cherries in-............75. H.193, 25
Washt those thy **purple** wounds with tears.......89. H.219, 6
Not wearing **Purple** only for the show;.........176. H.466, 5
The while their wreaths and **Purple** Robes do shine, 234. H.673, 17
Rein'd in with **Purple**, Pearl, and gold,.........239. H.696, 6
'Tis not the Walls, or **purple** that defends........244. H.717, 1
Spring the **purple** Violet.......................262. H.782, 4
Enspir'd with **Purple**, Pearle, and Gold;........311. H.1010, 2
Put off Thy Robe of **Purple**, then go on........398. N.263, 1
Purpose Set on **purpose** to enthrall..............53. H.147, 9
But none, of **purpose**, to be overcome..........380. N.150, 4
Purposes An end to all his stately **purposes**.......137. H.341, 6
Can shake a just mans **purposes**:...............215. H.615, 2
The sterner Fates, to cross his **purposes**;........266. H.800, 4
Plac't North and South, for these cleane **purposes**; 386. N.193, 2
Purse Look in Prig's **purse**, the chev'rell there tells you 71. H.183, 3
For a wrought **Purse**; can any tell wherefore?..162. H.427, 2
Say, What sho'd Roots do with a **Purse** in print, 162. H.427, 3
Purse-string Many a **Purse-string**, many a thred, 440. ins. H.443, 45v
Purslane The Worts, the **Purslain**, and the Messe..350. N.47, 31
Pursue Pleasures, such as shall **pursue**.........377. N.128, 21
I stricke thy loues, and greedyly **persue**..........411. A.3, 69
Pursueth When the Tempter me **pursu'th**.........348. N.41, 37
Push He never brings them once to th' **push** of Pikes. 370. N.108, 12
Pushed I put, he **pusht**, and heedless of my skin,...17. H.44, 3
Pushes Of **Pushes** Spalt has such a knottie race,..211. H.594, 1
Push-pin At childish **Push-pin** (for our sport) did play: 17. H.44, 2
But at **push-pin** (half the day:)...............235. H.678, 4
Pusse **Pusse** and her Prentice both at Draw-gloves play; 260. H.773, 1
Puss's True Calenders, as **Pusses** eare...........134. H.336, 89
Put I **put**, he pusht, and heedless of my skin,......17. H.44, 3
To make a Tent, and **put** it in,..................18. H.46, 7
Put on your silks; and piece by piece...........20. H.54, 1
And all his Tapers thus **put** out:................42. H.119, 6
To **put** the Tapers out,.........................56. H.149, 104
Rise; and **put** on your Foliage, and be seene....68. H.178, 15
Admit I Cloe **put** away,.......................70. H.181, 19
Put Purple Grapes, or Cherries in-.............75. H.193, 25
What thy commanding soule shall **put** it to......79. H.197, 80
The Holy-water there is **put**:...................91. H.223, 45
I took him, **put** him in my cup,.................96. H.229, 3
Rather then mend, **put** out the light.............97. H.235, 6
Off then with grave clothes; **put** fresh colours on; 105. H.259, 9
Put in practise, to understand................115. H.283, 124
Put in Love, and **put** in too....................116. H.285, 3
Put in Feare, and hope, and doubt;..............116. H.285, 5
Put in secrecies withall,......................116. H.285, 7
Put on your Garlands first, then Sacrifice:......124. H.313, 8
That h'ad nor Gold or Silver to **put** in't?........162. H.427, 4
The worke that I wo'd **put** ye to?..............164. H.442, 2
Put a shirt of sackcloth on:...................183. H.490, 14
Take then thy Censer; **Put** in Fire, and thus...197. H.539, 13
Put on all shapes to get a Love:...............215. H.616, 16
The Palms **put** forth their Gemmes, and every Tree 224. H.642, 5
What others can't with all their strength **put** to..245. H.722, 2
Put then in my hand,.........................256. H.762, 5
Immortall clothing I **put** on,...................270. H.819, 1
Put we on pure Surplices;....................280. H.870, 14
Put on thy Holy Fillitings, and so..............286. H.898, 1
Sho'd I not **put** on Blacks, when each one here..288. H.907, 1
Put on thy Laurell then; and in that trimme....299. H.956, 11
Put from, or draw unto the faithfull shore:.....315. H.1028, 12
That soules departed are not **put** out quite;....384. N.181, 3
Put off Thy Robe of Purple, then go on..........398. N.263, 1
With shoes **put** off, to tread thy Roome.........402. N.269, 3
Putest See **Put'st**
Putrefaction **Putrefaction** is the end..............163. H.432, 1
The flesh soone sucks in **putrifaction**............332. H.1111, 2
Puts Now barre the doors, the Bride-groom **puts**.56. H.149, 121
Bungie do's fast; looks pale; **puts** Sack-cloth on;.122. H.305, 1
Puts on the semblance here of sorrowing.........214. H.612, 4
Prickles is waspish, and **puts** forth his sting,....287. H.903, 1
That Prickles buyes, **puts** Prickles out of frame;..287. H.903, 3
Puts down some prints of His high Majestie:....385. N.189, 2
Put'st Thy selfe, which thou **put'st** other men unto. 214. H.614, 2
This worke thou **put'st** me too.................281. H.874, 9
Pyramids When **Pyramids**, as men,.............81. H.201, 47
And my **Pyramides**...........................85. H.211, 24
Quaff Let us sit, and **quaffe** our wine.............39. H.111, 6
Catullus, I **quaffe** up........................80. H.201, 27
We **quaffe** to him.............................198. H.544, 18
Well I can **quaffe**, I see,......................227. H.653, 9
And **quaffe** up a Bowle.......................320. H.1051, 4
And **quafe** it to the Prophets of our Age;..........412. A.3, 88
To laugh and **quaff** and drink old sherry...445. ins. H.730, 26c
Quaffing **Quaffing** his full-crown'd bowles of burning Wine, 206. H.575, 33
Quaffs He fully **quaffs** up to bewitch...........120. H.293, 52
Quail The Sock, the Curlew, and the **quaile**;.....147. H.377, 66
Quaint By this **quaint** Taper-light he winds......167. H.443, 82
Quake See **Earthquake**
Ye **quake** for cold to looke on me............329. H.1093, 6
Quaked When as the Mountains **quak'd** for dread,.393. N.232, 5

Quakes See **Flesh-quakes**
Quality A Substance, not a **Qualitie**.............378. N.136, 2
Quarelets The **Quarelets** of Pearl..................24. H.75, 8
Quarreling Purge hence the guilt, and kill this **quarrelling.** 78. H.197, 32
Quarter-acts But when He strikes, He **quarter-acts** His part. 394. N.242, 2
Quarter-day The **Quarter-day** do's ne'r affright..200. H.552, 11
Quarters Three **quarters** were consum'd of it;....153. H.399, 7
Queen Voted the Rose; the **Queen** of flowers.........8. H.11, 8
You are the **Queen** all flowers among,..........88. H.216, 19
Musick, thou **Queen** of Heaven, Care-charming-spel, 103. H.254, 1
Now let the Rose raigne like a **Queene**, and smile. 105. H.259, 12
Of which chast Order You are now the **Queene**: 107. H.265, 6
When as ye chuse your King and **Queen**,......127. H.319, 19
(As that chaste **Queen** of Ithaca..............174. H.465, 30
The **Queen** of Roses for that yeere............192. H.521, 32
And calls his Blouze, his **Queene**;.............259. H.772, 23
Thou the **Queen** of Peace and Quorum.........303. H.974, 8
Must revell, as **Queene**, in the Court here.......317. H.1035, 6
Be Twelfe-day **Queen** for the night here......317. H.1035, 12
A health to the King and the **Queene** here.....317. H.1035, 18
And **Queene** wassailing;......................317. H.1035, 26
The **Queen** of men, not flowers..................323. H.1068, 12
For Grace and Carriage, every one a **Queene**...326. H.1080, 24
The eye of Virgins; nay, the **Queen**............360. N.83, 15
Wee'l chuse Him King, and make His Mother **Queen**. 368. N.102, 24
Sits Cupid kissing of his mother **Queene**,........405. A.1, 56
To know his **Queene**, mixt with the farre..434. ins. H.293, 41g
Queen-priest This day, the **Queen-Priest**, thou art made t'appease 197. H.539, 5
Queens Some Pearls on **Queens**, that have been counterfet. 76. H. 194, 6
So Kings & **Queens** meet, when Desire convinces..77. H.197, 7
As **Queenes**, meet **Queenes**; or come thou unto me, 79. H.197, 73
And **Queenes**; thy Christmas revellings:.......231. H.662, 59
Queen-ship First, for thy **Queen-ship** on thy head is set 30. H.88, 3
Quench What ye cannot **quench**, pull downe;......21. H.61, 5
Once gets a force, Floods cannot **quench** the flame. 40. H.113, 4
To **quench**, or coole me with your Dew...........50. H.140, 2
For to **quench** ye, or some ease.................62. H.162, 8
The Elves present to **quench** his thirst.........119. H.293, 20
Will coole his flames, or **quench** his fires with snow? 187. H.502, 6
She seem'd to **quench** loves fires that there did glow. 251. H.742, 2
— — — — — — — — — — —,...............421. var. H.106, 26
— — — — — — — — — — —,...............426. var. H.197, 40
Quenched Is not by mariage **quencht**, but flames the higher. 262. H.781, 16
Which **quencht**, then lay it up agen,...........285. H.893, 3
— — — — — — — — — — —,...... ....426. var. H.197, 40
Quenchless Or thou by frost, or I by **quenchlesse** fire: 333. H.1120, 4
Question You **question** with your Looking-glasse;..63. H.164, 7
The how, where, when, I **question** not..........236. H.681, 2
No **question** then, but such a lick is sweet,......269. H.816, 3
No **question** but Dols cheeks wo'd soon rost dry, 325. H.1078, 1
His Providence who would not **question** then?....343. N.27, 4
Mooving a **question** whether that by them.......405. A.1, 41
Questions Suspicion **questions** every haire.........49. H.136, 23
Playing at **Questions** and Commands:..........215. H.616, 8
Quick To **quick** action, or the warme soft side....45. H.128, 5
As **quick** a growth to meet Decay,............125. H.316, 13
Of Amber **quick** was buried..................186. H.497, 12
For **quick** dispatch, Sculls made no longer stay,..200. H.551, 3
Shov'd on, by **quick** succeeding Tides:...........244. H.720, 2
On eyther side of theis, **quicke** Eares............408. A.2, 39
Quickened **Quickned** of late by Pearly showers;....25. H.78, 6
Quickening 'Tis He is borne, whose **quickning** Birth 364. N.96, 19
Quickens Art **quickens** Nature; Care will make a face: 97. H.234, 1
Quickly Which done, then **quickly** we'l undresse...58. H.152, 7
Chor. Come let's away, and **quickly** let's be drest, 86. H.213, 45
And **quickly** give, The swiftest Grace is best.....87. H.213, 46
And **quickly** still:...........................95. H.227, 9
Yet, **quickly** you'l see by the turne of a pin,....97. H.233, 3
Quickly, quickly then prepare;................114. H.283, 77
The Night-Charme **quickly**; you have spells,...115. H.283, 133
What comes in, runnes **quickly** out:..........116. H.285, 6
Or I shall **quickly** grow,.....................137. H.340, 17
That Ye must **quickly** wither..................184. H.493, 4
By **quickly** making one of two...............215. H.616, 10
Dispatch your dressing then; and **quickly** wed:..216. H.618, 7
Teares **quickly** drie: griefes will in time decay:..293. H.930, 1
And **quickly** I shall be........................293. H.934, 2
Shall by this pleasing trespasse **quickly** prove,....297. H.949, 3
I will be short, and having **quickly** hurl'd......298. H.955, 1
The life I got I **quickly** lost:..................313. H.1020, 4
'Twill **quickly** mar, & make ye too............325. H.1075, 6
Shall by his hearing **quickly** come to see......330. H.1100, 17
Will free him **quickly** from his miserie;........396. N.252, 2
Quiet When **quiet** grown sh'ad seen them,.........31. H.92, 10
Keeping the barking stomach wisely **quiet**,......35. H.106, 29
Quiet yet; but if ye make.......................52. H.145, 3
Quiet, or die:.................................190. H.515, 26
Quill Tickling the Citterne with his **quill**........318. H.1036, 6
Quilted See **Fresh-quilted**
Quintal Of Wassaile now, or sets the **quintell** up: 159. H.421, 4
Up with the **Quintill**, that the Rout,............306. H.987, 1
Quintals Thy Wakes, thy **Quintels**, here thou hast, 230. H.662, 52
Quintessence Hony, and in the **quintessence**:......71. H.182, 8
And **quintiscence**...........................116. H.283, 155
Quire See **Choir**
Quit Is it to **quit** the dish.......................391. N.228, 5
Quite Which renders that **quite** tarnisht, wch was green; 21. H.62, 3
Quite through my heart and marrow..............27. H.81, 32
Quite dispossest of either fray, or fret............82. H.204, 6
But being vanquisht **quite**,.....................105. H.258, 5
Or bid it languish **quite** away,.................108. H.267, 11
Quite through the table, where he spies..........119. H.293, 25
Quite through the young maids and the men,...127. H.319, 31
I shall **quite** dislike agen.......................155. H.407, 6
And lose you **quite**.............................176. H.467, 12
Believe him not; for he forgot it **quite**,..........186. H.501, 3
Here we begin new life; while thousands **quite**..313. H.1019, 3
Speak but the word, and cure me **quite**..........344. N.29, 10
That soules departed are not put out **quite**;.....384. N.181, 3
God has a Right Hand, but is **quite** bereft.........394. N.240, 1
— — — — — — — — — — —..............428. var. H.235, 6
Quiver I spy'd he had a **Quiver**...................27. H.81, 20
Quorum Thou the Queen of Peace and **Quorum**...303. H.974, 8
Quoth Fie, (**quoth** my Lady) what a stink is here? 212. H.598, 1
Rabble With all the **rabble** of Tim-Trundells race, 155. H.405, 12
Race The sooner will his **Race** be run,............84. H.208, 7
As the old **Race** of mankind did,..............147. H.377, 38
With all the rabble of Tim-Trundells **race**,.....155. H.405, 12
Of Pushes Spalt has such a knottie **race**,........211. H.594, 1
Some **Race** of old humanitie...................218. H.626, 9
Thee here among my righteous **race**:.............278. H.859, 2
Rise up of men, a fighting **race**.................297. H.948, 12
Has with the **race**..............................314. H.1024, 3
And make no one stop, till my **race** be done......358. N.77, 15
Rack Beat me, bruise me, **rack** me, rend me,......351. N.48, 5
Racked No Widowes Tenement was **rackt** to guild 149. H.377, 119
The Cirque prophan'd was; and all postures **rackt**: 150. H.382, 5
Each takes A weeping farewell, **rackt** in mynde...411. A.3, 63
Radiant More **radiant** then the Summers Sun-beams shows; 45. H.128, 13
Then when he darts his **radiant** beams.........75. H.193, 20
Eternall Lamp of Love! whose **radiant** flame.....77. H.197, 10
Or other over **radiant** Ray.....................167. H.443, 77
As in a Globe of **Radiant** fire, and grac't......207. H.575, 58
Rag'd See **Ragged**
Rage See **Holy-rage**
Winds have their time to **rage**; but when they cease, 105. H.259, 5
And **Rage** inspires............................198. H.544, 6
Where both may **rage**, both drink and dance together. 206. H.575, 38
And Snakie Perseus, these, and those, whom **Rage** 206. H.575, 45
No wrath of Men, or **rage** of Seas.............215. H.615, 1
When Winds and Seas do **rage**,................373. H.122, 1
A full brimm'd bowle of Furye and of **rage**......412. A.3, 87
Swells with brave **rage**, yet comely every where,..415. A.7, 12
Rages He raves through leane, he **rages** through the fat; 191. H.518, 3
Ragged When of thy **ragg'd** Escutcheons shall be seene 231. H.664, 3
Or **rag'd** to go,...............................391. H.228, 10
In this **rag'd** Escutcheon......................418. A.9, 35
— — — — — — — — — — —, ...450. var. A.9, 35
Ragged-soused-neat's-foot A **ragd-soust-neats-foot** with sick vinegar:..............................262. H.783, 14
Raging The ruffling winds and **raging** Seas,........31. H.90, 5
Of all the **raging** Waves, into a froth.........152. H.389, 2
Rags Dry chips, old shoes, **rags**, grease, & bones; 93. H.223, 119
If wounds in clothes, Cuts calls his **rags**, 'tis cleere, 144. H.373, 1
What are our patches, tatters, **raggs**, and rents,..302. H.970, 1
Rail The Phesant, Partridge, Gotwit, Reeve, Ruffe, **Raile**, 147. H.377, 65
Thus, though the Rooke do's **raile** against the sin, 163. H.439, 3

Railing Who, railing, drives the Lazar from his door, 238. H.694, 1
Rails To scratch or claw, so that thy tongue not railes: 66. H.173,6
Upon the ends of these neat Railes............92. H.223, 91
Raiments Two raiments have I: Christ then makes 376. N.127, 5
Rain Of the Raine, Frost, Haile, and Snow?......40. H.115, 4
To these, make Clouds to poure downe raine;...47. H.133, 12
And as a vapour, or a drop of raine............69. H.178, 63
If you can see, that drop of raine.................79. H.198, 7
And that this pleasure is like raine,............102. H.250, 53
Dry your sweet cheek, long drown'd with sorrows raine; 105. H.259, 1
Like to the Summers raine;..................125. H.316, 18
Mine eyes, like clouds, were drizling raine,.....237. H.687, 1
Clouds will not ever powre down raine;........247. H.725, 7
By Dewes and drisling Raine,..................257. H.767, 5
Beshiver'd into seeds of Raine;................340. N.3, 10
The first of Raine, the key of Hell next known: 390. N.224, 2
Rainbow As shews the Aire, when with a Rain-bow grac'd; 40. H.114, 1
As when a Rain-bow in perfumes goes out.......131. H.331, 8
Look, how the Rainbow doth appeare..........139. H.353, 1
A curious Rainbow smiling there;.............237. H.687, 6
Rains I sing of Dewes, of Raines, and piece by piece 5. H.1, 7
That wets her Garden when it raines:.........279. H.867, 2
Raise See Up-raise
And such spirits raise, 'twill then................52. H.145, 5
Raise greater fires in men.....................76. H.193, 56
Of Rurall Younglings raise the shout;..........101. H.250, 16
And having drunk, we raise a shout...........198. H.544, 10
And to thee Altars raise,......................281. H.874, 14
To raise an Act to full astonishment;............415. A.7, 8
— — — — — — — — — —,..............423. var. H.128, 25
Raised When up the * Thyrse is rais'd, and when the sound 7. H.8, 7
Since neithers height was rais'd by th'ill......149. H.377, 116
Those spirits rais'd; and with like precepts then 326. H.1080, 17
To such an height, to such a period rais'd,....399. N.263, 30
— — — — — — — — — —,..............440. var. H.443, 87
Rake Rake the Fier up, and get................201. H.556, 3
Raked — — — — — — — —, ...426. var. H.197, 37
Raked-up Left in this rak't-up Ash-heap, as a mark 78. H.197, 37
Ralph Ralph pares his nayles, his warts, his cornes, and Ralph 299. H.959, 1
Ram And Ramme of time and by vexation growes 148. H.377, 111
To an old Ram Goat,........................333. H.1122, 4
Rams Where Rams are wanting, or large Bullocks thighs, 369. N.105, 3
Ran Where so much sirrop ran at waste.........71. H.182, 18
Ran for Sweet-hearts mad, and dy'd............152. H.391, 4
From me my Silvia ranne away,...............288. H.908, 1
And as he spake, his mouth ranne ore with wine. 313. H.1017, 4
The Barber stopt his Nose, and ranne away. ..323. H.1066, 4
Random At randome, sometimes hit most happily. 318. H.1039, 2
Range Dares now range the wood;.............225. H.643, 14
Rank Unto Pastillus ranke Gorgonius came,....323. H.1066, 1
Ranker He'l turn a Papist, rancker then before...151. H.385, 6
Ranks — — — — — — — — —, ...431. var. H.283, 41
Ransacks Ransacks this roome; but what weak beams 167. H.443, 78
Rape The sudden danger of a Rape...........37. H.106, 126
Raped Lest rapt from hence, I see thee lye........275. H.844, 3
All I have lost, that co'd be rapt from me:......371. N.112, 1
Rapes As Jove did, when he made his rapes:.........58. H.152, 2
Rapine No Kingdomes got by Rapine long endure. 314. H.1023, 2
Rapine has yet tooke nought from me;.........376. N.124, 1
Rapt Then think how wrapt was I to see..........14. H.34, 5
Rapture And mark it for a Rapture nobly writ,....64. H.168, 9
W^th Flame, and Rapture; drincking to the odd..410. A.3, 21
When drunck wth Rapture; Curse the blind & lame 412. A.3, 89
Raptures Them frantick with thy raptures, flashing through 45. H.128, 27
And in his Raptures speaking Lines of Thine,..206. H.575, 34
From thee some raptures of the rare Gotire......276. H.851, 2
Rare A telling what rare sights h'ad seen:........13. H.27, 8
Which Art, not Nature, makes so rare;........37. H.106, 112
Where such a rare Carnation grew...............63. H.164, 11
But taking those rare lips of yours..............71. H.182, 15
Amint. O rare! But is't a trespasse if we three..86. H.213, 25
Rare Temples thou hast seen, I know,..........90. H.223a, 1
With thousand rare encourings:..............130. H.329, 21
After the rare Arch-Poet Johnson dy'd,..........150. H.382, 1
See, see a Jemme (as rare as Bœlus eye.)......172. H.459, 8
For a most rich, a rare, a precious One.........172. H.459, 10
Of such rare Saint-ships, who did here consume 185. H.496, 3
Nor my rare *Phil, that lately was............186. H.497, 15
Rare are thy cheeks Susanna, which do show....193. H.523, 1
And rare, Ile say (my dearest Crew)..........217. H.620, 11
Besides rare sweets, I had a Book which none..227. H.652, 5
But since I'm cal'd (rare Denham) to be gone,..234. H.673, 13
That thou shalt say (thy selfe) 'tis rare;......243. H.716, 33
For the rare Mince-Pie.......................263. H.784, 16
From thee some raptures of the rare Gotire.....276. H.851, 2
I heare in thee rare Laniere to sing;...........276. H.851, 4
No man such rare parts hath, that he can swim,..298. H.953, 1
Or whether those (in orders rare) or these....326. H.1080, 3
Rare is the voice it selfe; but when we sing....331. H.1101, 1
Here, all her rare Aromaticks.................402. N.269, 17
On either side with rich rare Jewells grac'd,......405. A.1, 40
Is the swan-stayning faire rare stately neck......405. A.1, 44
Knowe yet, (rare soule), when my diuiner Muse..412. A.3, 99
Of King and no King (and the rare Plott thine)..415. A.7, 14
Rarely For one so rarely tun'd to fit all parts;...121. H.301, 1
Linnit playes rarely on the Lute, we know;....149. H.381, 1
Rashly Haste is unhappy: What we rashly do....268. H.813, 1
Rashness Where War with rashnesse is attempted, there 268. H.813, 3
Raspe Raspe playes at Nine-holes; and 'tis known he gets 154. H.400, 1
Rate Henceforth at such a rate,................137. H.340, 11
You set too high a rate upon..................324. H.1068, 17
At a high rate, and further brought......436. ins. H.336, 48h
Rated See Well-rated
Rather I'le rather keepe this frost, and snow,.........8. H.13, 7
The soule, when it doth rather sigh, then sound...12. H.24, 2
She rather took, then got a fall:..................12. H.27, 2
O Dianeme, rather kill..........................34. H.103, 9
Rather then love, let me be ever lost;............40. H.113, 5
Did rather choose to blesse another clime?.....77. H.197, 22
Rather then mend, put out the light.............97. H.235, 6
Search worlds of Ice; and rather there.........111. H.278, 7
To move, or rather the.........................112, H.283, 9
Rather then to which I'le fall,................117. H.286, 3
(Rather than fail) to steal from thence old shoes: 143. H.368, 2
Do'st rather poure forth, then allow..........148. H.377, 82
But rather like a flower hid here..............189. H.514, 7
I rather thinke (though they may speake the worst) 219. H.630, 3
For, rather then I'le to the West return,......242. H.713, 17
Rather then I once wo'd see,..................266. H.803, 4
And not unlikely; rather too then fail,.........272. H.829, 3
I'de rather hungry go and come,............321. H.1056, 13
But rather purge me..........................351. N.49, 8
For, rather then one drop shall fall............377. N.129, 7
To Hell I'd rather run, then I................395. N.245, 5
— — — — — — — — — — —,.............432. var. H.283, 128
— — — — — — — — — — —,.............453. var. H.283, 11
Rats Some to bee Ratts, and others to bee hoggs:.412. A.3, 92
Rattles That rattles i'th' throat,...............333. H.1122, 5
Rattling With ratling Kirnils, which is rung....93. H.223, 127
Rave And though he doe not rave,..............259. H.772, 13
Ravel Or ravell so, to make us two...........134. H.336, 72
Ravening From rav'ning wolves, the fleecie sheep. 36. H.106, 52
Ravenous — — — — — — — —, ...421. var. H.106, 52
Raven's The Ravens yeares, go hence more Ripe then old. 222. H.633, 63
Raves He raves through leane, he rages through the fat; 191. H.518, 3
He raves, he rends, and while he thus doth tear, 325. H.1077, 5
Ravish Maides (in time) may ravish him........125. H.314, 8
Thus to en-trance and ravish me:.............142. H.362, 4
Ravish our spirits, that entranc't wee see........415. A.7, 17
And ravish you his Bride, doe you........430. ins. H.283, 40c
Ravished And ravish'd thus, It came to passe,......13. H.27, 5
Young Bacchus ravisht by his tree...............16. H.41, 13
Like to a Virgin newly ravished..................41. H.118, 4
And ravisht, plunge into the bed,...............59. H.152, 9
And being ravisht thus,.......................81. H.201, 34
That being ravisht, hence I goe..................95. H.227, 3
Ravisht, in that faire Via Lactea..................96. H.230, 4
Ne're ravisht from the flattering Vine,........120. H.293, 48
How am I ravisht! When I do but see,...........139. H.347, 1
Dropt from the eyes of ravisht Girles..........167. H.443, 109
As I did, my ravisht spirit....................182. H.489, 4
Give way, and be ye ravisht by the Sun,.......196. H.537, 1
Ravisht in spirit, I come, nay more, I flie......242. H.713, 3
That fully ravisht me.........................288. H.908, 8
And seems halfe ravisht, when he looks upon....295. H.941, 3
When to thy Porch I come, and (ravisht) see..324. H.1071, 1
This I am sure; I Ravisht stood, as one.......326. H.1080, 9
Do ravisht stand;.........................369. N.106, 10
Which heats those ravisht Soules above;.......395. N.246, 2
Ravisht I am! and down I lie,................402. N.269, 20
Ravishing My measures ravishing................261. H.778, 9
To'th Lute or Violl, then 'tis ravishing........331. H.1101, 2
Raw Dry-rosted all, but raw yet in her eyes.........90. H.222, 2
Reapes eyes to rawe are, that (it seemes) the flyes 282. H.879, 1
Rawly And this rawly bak't will bring..........284. H.890, 5
Rawness Can ease the rawnesse, or the smart;....164. H.442, 9

Ray Or other over radiant Ray................167. H.443, 77
Rays O Bacchus! coole thy Raies!..............81. H.201, 30
allready spillt, her rayes must gleame.....430. ins. H.283, 20d
Reach Or to exceed thy Tether's reach:.........38. H.106, 134
Your nakednesse much reach:................76. H.193, 43
And do it to the full; reach..................115. H.283, 127
Reach, with your whiter hands, to me,..........185. H.495, 1
Or sweet Lady reach to me..................223. H.638, 8
Then reach those ends that thou wast destin'd to.254. H.756, 8
Then reach Thou forth that hand of Thine,......342. N.17, 9
But earth: such vowes nere reach Gods eare....381. N.158, 8
Reached That he reacht forth unto me:..........279. H.863, 6
One man has reatch't his sixty yeers, but he....328. H.1088, 7
The Haven reacht to which I first was bound...334. H.1127, 2
Sin once reacht up to Gods eternall Sphere,......367. N.100, 1
Reaching Reaching at heaven,..................112. H.283, 5
Read See Over-read
Where thou mayst hear thine own Lines read......6. H.2, 23
To read my Booke the Virgin shie..............6. H.4, 1
But when He's gone, read through what's writ,.....6. H.4, 3
Let my Enchantments then be sung, or read.........7. H.8, 4
Let rigid Cato read these Lines of mine..........7. H.8, 10
Those Sundayes onely, when as Briefs are read....39. H.109, 2
The humour was, (as I have read)............44. H.127, 3
I ask't thee oft, what Poets thou hast read,....66. H.174, 1
And times to come shall, weeping, read thy glory,
89. H.219, 21
Right by the Rubrick, which they read..........92. H.223, 75
Wo'd have this Lecture read,.................105. H.257, 26
Wit and new misterie; read, and.............115. H.283, 123
To read by th' Starres, the Kingdoms sick:....126. H.319, 6
Read then, and when your faces shine..........127. H.319, 27
Then shall he read that flowre of mine........135. H.336, 97
Upon his Altar, men shall read thy lines;.......143. H.366, 2
No, thou know'st order, Ethicks, and ha's read..148. H.377, 89
Or in the dampe Jet read their Teares.........149. H.377, 126
May read how soon things have..............176. H.467, 14
Then cause we Horace to be read,............198. H.544, 13
The Saints-bell calls; and, Julia, I must read...209. H.584, 1
If but well read; or ill read, understood........212. H.603, 4
Then but to read this in my Booke:............214. H.611, 2
I make no haste to have my Numbers read.....218. H.623, 1
Co'd reade the Intext but my selfe alone.........227. H.652, 6
Break off Delay, since we but read of one......251. H.744, 1
A master of a house (as I have read).........259. H.771, 1
Reade acceptance by the smoake..............280. H.870, 18
We read how Faunus, he the shepheards God,..306. H.986, 1
If 'mongst these many Numbers to be read,...322. H.1062, 2
Read thou my Lines, my Swetnaham, if there be 328. H.1089, 1
Or reade in Volumes, and those Bookes (with all
330. H.1100, 3
In the old Scripture I have often read,..........345. N.34, 1
These were the Coats, in these are read......375. N.123, 83
Christ, I have read, did to His Chaplains say,..378. N.137, 1
The Jewes, when they built Houses (I have read) 384. N.178, 1
The Virgin Marie was (as I have read).......385. N.190, 1
'Tis never read there (as the Fathers say).....396. N.249, 5
Or by our selves, or from the Pulpit read.....396. N.249, 8
When Thou wast taken, Lord, I oft have read,..399. N.264, 1
Read it then before your lipp..................417. A.9, 13
Let them read this booke and learne...........418. A.9, 55
— — — — — — — — — — —,.............437. var. H.336, 75
— — — — — — — — — — —,..............450. var. A.9, 7
Reader Condemne the Printer, Reader, and not me;..4. Ap., 2
If, Reader, then thou wilt draw neere,..........48. H.134, 5
And write thereon, This, Reader, know,.........61. H.159, 30
If Reader then thou canst forbeare,............203. H.564, 3
Yet, Reader, let me tell thee, this 226. H.644, 7
Reader, wo'dst thou more have known?........289. H.910, 3
Readers Readers wee entreat ye pray..........269. H.814, 1
Readest But if thou read'st my Booke unto the end,.7. H.6, 3
If thou not read'st them well..................138. H.344, 4
Who read'st this Book that I have writ,.......229. H.660, 1
Who with thine owne eyes read'st what we doe write,
297. H.947, 5
Readiness The readinesse of doing, doth expresse..275. H.845, 1
Reading By Reading all her Paragraphs in Thee..201. H.557, 4
Reading Thy Bible, and my Book; so end.......371. N.115, 12
Re-adorn To re-adorn the house..............285. H.892, 20
Reads Thee to the Stand, where honour'd Homer reades
206. H.575, 27
Ready The Altar's ready; Fire to consume......102. H.251, 3
The bed is ready, and the maze of Love......115. H.283, 121
Still to be ready with thy fire:.................214. H.613, 2
Ready to joyne, as well our hearts as hands......262. H.781, 10
Ready here? Jul. All well prepar'd,............280. H.870, 8
Of Beeves here ready stand for Sacrifice.......300. H.961, 8
Ready to blush to death, sho'd he but chide......301. H.963, 4
Are ready by, to make the Guests all pure:......355. N.65, 6
Ready, to pierce Thy tender Feet, and Hands...398. N.263, 4
Here all things ready are, make hast, make hast away;
401. N.268, 5
Bee readye, thou In mee, to wayte vppon her....412. A.3, 101
Real Say, is't for reall griefe he mourns? not so;.275. H.842, 3
Really There really alone;....................279. H.863, 14
Realm The Heire to This great Realme of Poetry.
107. H.264, 6
For since I've travail'd all this Realm throughout
267. H.804, 5
(A happy Realme! When no compulsive Law,..326. H.1080, 19
Reaming Farewell the Flax and Reaming wooll,..374. N.123, 41
Reap We rip up first, then reap our lands.......101. H.250, 4
For joy, to see the fruits ye reape,..........127. H.319, 34
Reape's Reapes eyes so rawe are, that (it seemes) the flyes
282. H.879, 1
Reaping Continuall reaping makes a land wax old.
292. H.922, 4
Reappear When all now dead shall re-appeare.....265. H.794, 6
Rear See Up-rear
This beame, must reare........................66. H.172, 20
Batt he gets children, not for love to reare 'em;.72. H.184, 1
I reare for me,...............................85. H.211, 18
At which I'le reare..........................135. H.336, 107
And who with green-turfes reare his head,......157. H.412, 23
Fould now thine armes, and in thy last looke reare
414. A.6, 7
Reared See High-reared
Was rear'd up by the Poore-mans fleece:......149. H.377, 118
That Towrs high rear'd dread most the lightnings threat:
181. H.483, 14
That Fame, and Fames rear'd Pillar, thou shalt see
329. H.1092, 5
Upon an Altar rear'd by Him, and crown'd......369. N.105, 7
Rears But Vertue Rears the eternal Monument...419. A.10, 4
— — — — — — — — —, ...438. var. H.412, 23
Reason The reason, why.....................104. H.257, 16
For what other reason is't,....................128. H.322, 3
The reason is, though all the day they fight,.....156. H.411, 3
Grow fat and smooth: The reason is,............173. H.461, 3
What is the reason Coone so dully smels?......210. H.589, 1
Give me a reason why men call................273. H.832, 1
The reason is, his credit cannot get............302. H.969, 3
When his Assignes askt him the reason why?..332. H.1114, 3
If we may ask the reason, say;.................364. N.96, 11
In Gods commands, ne're ask the reason why;..397. N.260, 1
Re-aspire And like a Phenix re-aspire..........72. H.185, 17
And, when that's done, to re-aspire............367. N.98, 29
Reaved That reav'd us of thee Tabitha!........374. N.123, 22
Rebuked Had not her Blush rebuked me..........14. H.33, 4
She with a dainty blush rebuk't her face;......311. H.1006, 3
Recall Wo'd but that heat recall:...............28. H.85, 6
Recalls No sound recalls the houres once fled,..233. H.670, 24
Recant Love, I recant,.......................100. H.246, 1
Receive Come, and receive them while the light..68. H.178, 23
Receive (with Songs) a flowrie Diadem.........254. H.756, 18
Receive this vow, so fare-ye-well for ever.....316. H.1028, 26
And better Being, they receive from You.....326. H.1080, 26
Let's go (my Alma) yet e're we receive,........355. N.65, 7
Receive, for this thy praise, our teares:........360. N.83, 37
Receive this offering of our Haires:............360. N.83, 38
Receive these Christall Vialls fil'd............360. N.83, 39
But substance, to! receaue this Pearlye Teare....412. A.3, 81
Received No heart by love receiv'd a wound;....42. H.119, 2
Receiving By giving and receiving hold the play:..255. H.758, 2
Recite Here goe about for to recite............91. H.223, 34
And flatt'ring Ivie) Two recite their Plaies,....206. H.575, 50
Reciting Reciting:..........................376. N.128, 4
Reckon And reckon this for fortune bad,........179. H.476, 38
From whom we'l reckon. Wit came in, but since.194. H.526, 5
Reckoned These are not to be reckon'd here;....145. H.375, 24
Reckoning What need there then be of a reckning day:
343. N.27, 2
God hides from man the reck'ning Day, that He.379. N.142, 1
Of such a rev'rend reckoning,..................388. N.204, 2
Re-clothed Re-cloth'd in fresh and verdant Diaper.
224. H.642, 2
Recoil Wo'd soon recoile, and not intrude......147. H.377, 32
Recoils Iff not, it dyes, or eles recoyles...........408. A.2, 72
Recollect Then may ye recollect the graines.....245. H.720, 13
Ile recollect thee (weeping) part by part;......300. H.960, 4
Recommend Contemne to recommend a Cruse,....291. H.918, 7
Recommit That I shall ne're that trespasse recommit,
397. N.255, 3
Recompense The Masters charge and care to recompence.
245. H.723, 10
For all our workes, a recompence is sure:......276. H.849, 1
With Princely hand He'l recompence delay.......344. N.30, 4
Re-converse Descend from heaven, to re-converse with men;
301. H.966, 12
Record Night to the Record! that was all.........20. H.56, 8
(Heauen and my soule beare Record of my Vowe)
411. A.3, 48
Recovering Means for her recovering;..........122. H.302, 4
Rector Thee, the Rector of the Seas,..........129. H.325, 2
Rectoress There did I see the Reverend Rectresse stand,
326. H.1080, 15
Rectresse See Rectoress
Re-cure If wholsome Diet can re-cure a man,...319. H.1049, 1
Red See Cherry-red, Out-red, Robin Redbreast
How Roses first came Red, and Lillies White......5. H.1, 10
Name it I would; but being blushing red,........24. H.74, 13

His cheeks be-pimpled, red and blue;...........38. H.108, 7
The Roses first came red....................105. H.258, 8
Lips she has, all Rubie red,...................138. H.342, 5
Looke red, and blow, and bluster, but not speake:
150. H.382, 8
Full as a Bee with Thyme, and Red,..........165. H.443, 9
Of the red infant, neatly hung................166. H.443, 71
Better look the Roses red,......................194. H.527, 3
Made it for ever after red......................241. H.706, 4
So Corrolls looke more lovely Red,...........268. H.811, 5
The Blooms that fell were white and red;......283. H.883, 3
Which sweetly mixed both with white and redd...404. A.1, 17
Like rose leaves, white and redd seeme mingled..404. A.1, 18
— — — — — — — — — —, ...435. var. H.293, 39m
With Rosie Chaplets, Lillies, Pansies red,..442. ins. H.575, 20a
Redbreast Thou Sexton (Red-brest) for to cover me.
111. H.279, 4
Where thou shalt sit, and Red-brest by,........192. H.521, 17
Red-cap — — — — — — — —, ...434. var. H.293, 39
Red-capped With the Red-capt worme, that's shut
120. H.293, 39
Redeem Thou do'st redeeme those times; and what was lost
147. H.377, 41
Track they redeem a bank of mosse...........165. H.443, 26
Redeemed Is ne'r redeem'd by cost..............53. H.149, 8
Redeemer Till my Redeemer (on the Tree)......370. N.107, 9
Re-deliver Will from all dangers, re-deliver me,.....14. H.35, 7
Re-delivers That takes and re-delivers every stroake
129. H.323, 11
Redemption That we escape. Redemption comes by Thee.
197. H.539, 16
Redness The which with ruby rednes being tipt....404. A.1, 21
Redolent A Bracelet richly Redolent:..............13. H.32, 2
How each thing smells divinely redolent!.......159. H.421, 19
Red-rose A red-Rose peeping through a white?..164. H.440, 2
Reed There with the Reed, thou mayst expresse......5. H.2, 7
Broke is my Reed, hoarse is my singing too:....205. H.573, 2
Made of a clean strait oaten reed,..............354. N.59, 9
Reeks Nor name those wanton reaks............56. H.149, 117
Reeled And lisping reeld, and reeling like to fall..313. H.1017, 6
Reeling And lisping reeld, and reeling like to fall.
313. H.1017, 6
Reeve The Phesant, Partridge, Gotwit, Reeve, Ruffe, Raile,
147. H.377, 65
Reference Have reference to the shoulders, not the eares.
142. H.363, 4
Reflected Can make reflected from these jems,..167. H.443, 79
Have their reflected light,......................181. H.484, 7
Reflection — — — — — — — — —, ...440. var. H.443, 79
Refrain And had told all; but did refraine,.........13. H.27, 9
Refreshed Newly refresh't, both by the Sun, and showers.
25. H.77, 6
Refreshing Teem'd her refreshing dew?..........104. H.257, 5
Refulgent In thy refulgent Thronelet,............270. H.819, 8
Refuse No fault in women to refuse...........118. H.291, 1
Any Orts the Elves refuse...................223. H.638, 19
Refuseth God He refuseth no man; but makes way
378. N.131, 1
Regard But in regard, 'twas often said, this old..129. H.326, 3
Love those, like these; regard, reward them not..141. H.359, 12
In regard I want that Wine,.....................182. H.489, 7
In this regard, that thou do'st play............183. H.492, 9
In this regard, in those great terrors He........382. N.167, 3
Those act without regard, when once a King,....399. N.263, 24
Have, have ye no regard, all ye...............400. N.266, 1
— — — — — — — — — — —, ...450. var. A.9, 4
Regardless Regardlesse whether well thou sped'st, or no.
6. H.3, 6
Regenerate And tells the world, he's now regenerate.
240. H.703, 2
Ile live as one Regenerate......................313. H.1020, 8
Of life comes in, when he's Regenerate.......326. H.1080, 28
Re-gild Yet the next Morne, re-guild the fragrant East.
72. H.185, 7
Region See Watery-region
A Light ful-filling all the Region here...........94. H.226, 4
Wildred in this vast watry Region.............319. H.1044, 4
Regredience Never man yet had a regredience.....228. H.656, 2
Regret — — — — — — — —, ...442. var. H.465, 69
Rehearse In sober mornings, doe not thou reherse....7. H.8, 1
Or some numbers more rehearse;...............122. H.303, 2
I co'd rehearse...............................144. H.371, 10
Rehearsed Had been reherst, by Joell Michelditch:.266. H.800, 2
Reign Now let the Rose raigne like a Queene, and smile.
105. H.259, 12
And Charles here Rule, as he before did Raign;.214. H.612, 8
That thou shalt swear, my Pipe do's raigne....244. H.716, 39
Reined Rein'd in with Purple, Pearl, and gold,..239. H.696, 6
Reigns When the Rose raignes, and locks with ointments shine,
7. H.8, 9
Now raignes the Rose, and now................80. H.201, 9
Where no disease raignes, or infection comes....205. H.575, 5
Re-inspire Unshorn Apollo, come, and re-inspire..280. H.871, 2
Reiterate No more shall I reiterate thy Strand,..315. H.1028, 3
Rejects God He rejects all Prayers that are sleight.
342. N.16, 1
Rejoice Here we rejoyce, because no Rent.......200. H.552, 7
And all rejoyce, that we have found..........368. N.102, 17
Relate But Fables we'l relate; how Jove........215. H.616, 15
So that with bold truth, thou canst now relate..330. H.1100, 7
Cha. Prethee relate, while I give ear and weep....416. A.8, 12
But now come in. Euc. More let me yet relate.....416. A.8, 23
Relation Relation to the grave:...................111. H.280, 2
But the Relation then of both growes poor,......255. H.758, 3
Relative To be the nearer Relative:............147. H.377, 40
Release To keep, and to release.................57. H.149, 128
Relent Rocks to relent, and coyest maids to love...287. H.900, 2
Relic Some Relique of a Saint doth weare:......169. H.449, 2
Not soe, but that some Relique In my Harte....412. A.3, 96
Poor relique of the beawty, bone,................418. A.9, 24
Relics In which thy sacred Reliques shall have roome:
20. H.55, 8
And light my Reliques to their Urne...........109. H.271, 6
Where my small reliques must for ever rest:....129. H.327, 4
For his love then, whose sacred Reliques show..137. H.341, 7
We two (as Reliques left) will have...........190. H.515, 11
Give thou my sacred Reliques Buriall.........242. H.713, 20
These my Reliques, (pray) interre...............270. H.821, 2
Relief Not represent, but give reliefe..........146. H.377, 10
Although our suffering meet with no reliefe,....333. H.1119, 1
Reliefs Jove may afford us thousands of reliefs;..153. H.397, 1
Relieved Shall be releeved never...............374. N.123, 20
Relieving Comes relieving.....................308. H.993, 18
Religion By Loves Religion, I must here confesse it,
15. H.38, 5
Theirs is a mixt Religion......................91. H.223, 23
Not out of Conscience, or Religion:............122. H.305, 2
Civil Behaviour, and Religion.................199. H.545, 4
Old Religion first commands...................280. H.870, 3
Religion's For old Religions sake,..............212. H.604, 3
Religious Part of the creame from that Religious Spring;
9. H.14, 8
Then holding up (there) such religious Things,....11. H.22, 5
To doe the Rites to thy Religious Tombe:........27. H.82, 2
When thou shalt laugh at my Religious dust;....49. H.138, 3
In their Religious Vesterie....................92. H.223, 100
To thee, this my religious charge...............175. H.465, 68
Besides, the most religious Prophet stands......262. H.781, 9
E'ene all Religious courses to be rich............266. H.800, 1
'Tis religious part to see......................270. H.821, 3
Remain Those mites of Time, which yet remain unspent,
171. H.456, 3
But yet a way there doth remaine,............313. H.1020, 5
Remainder Remainder left of Brasse or stone,....146. H.376, 8
Remainders To see the small remainders in mine Urne:
49. H.138, 2
Remained Onely remaind a little bit,............153. H.399, 8
Remains Unlesse thou giv'st my small Remains an Urne.
19. H.52, 4
There yet remaines to know, then thou can'st see
206. H.575, 54
Of my particular Remaines;.................245. H.720, 14
Something there yet remaines for Thee to do;....254. H.756, 7
Of if haire remaines to me.....................277. H.852, 4
Part of the worke remaines; one part is past:..334. H.1126, 1
Remedy (When you had power) the meanest remedy:
52. H.146, 20
Only for my wound there's no remedy.........274. H.841, 2
Christ is the one sufficient Remedie............390. N.221, 2
Re-meeting Or no, shall give ye a re-meeting here..140. H.355, 8
Remember The words found true, C. M. remember me.
26. H.79, 10
Remember us in Cups full crown'd,............127. H.319, 29
You'l with a tear or two, remember me,.........140. H.355, 10
Which joyns two souls, remember this;........174. H.465, 2
Remember what thy Herrick Thee foretold,....181. H.483, 10
Endimions Moon to fill up full, remember me:..184. H.492, 42
The while we never remember,................196. H.534, 15
And this remember, Vertue keepes the measure..220. H.633, 25
Fly hence Pale Care, noe more remember.........413. A.4, 1
Remembered To live remembred in your story....170. H.449, 29
Remembering Remembring, to anoint.............55. H.149, 86
Remembers She ne'r remembers that she was a maide.
149. H.379, 2
Remembrance In thy remembrance (Julia.) So farewell.
14. H.35, 14
Remembrances As my last Remembrances.........88. H.218, 9
Who dead, deserve our best remembrances.......209. H.584, 8
Remiss Have I been cold to hug thee, too remisse,
78. H.197, 34
Remission For, once in hell, none knowes Remission there.
367. N.99, 2
Remit A mans transgression God do's then remit,.359. N.82, 1
Remitted And was committed, not remitted there..367. N.100, 2
Remnant So, here the remnant of my dayes I'd spend,
371. N.115, 11
Remora That my wing'd ship may meet no Remora...14. H.35, 4
Remove Away with doubts, all scruples hence remove;
8. H.10, 7
And chiding me, said, Hence, Remove,.........51. H.142, 21
Which here I vow to serve, doe not remove.....79. H.197, 82
That ye could your thoughts remove...........117. H.289, 2
Farre from me Ile remove....................171. H.452, 7
Remove the barrs, or lift me o're the stiles:......352. N.51, 6

Removed Which, done; and thence **remov'd** the light, 165. H.443, 7
Removing Th'art hence **removing**, (like a Shepherds Tent) 188. H.507, 1
Remuneration Halfe of my just **remuneration**.....267. H.804, 4
Rend And **rend** the cloud, and throw..........116. H.283, 149
Do's Fortune **rend** thee? Beare with thy hard Fate: 270. H.820, 1
Of night from Heaven for to **rend** her.........333. H.1122, 12
Beat me, bruise me, rack me, **rend** me,..........351. N.48, 5
Render Will **render** ten for this:..................29. H.87, 6
Render for that, a crowne of life to you.........94. H.224, 10
And for their two egs **render** ten................179. H.476, 21
That I should **render**, for my part,............351. N.47, 53
— — — — — — — — — —, ...442. var. H.575, 36
Renders Which **renders** that quite tarnisht, wch was green; 21. H.62, 3
Thy Deerest Saviour **renders** thee but one......371. N.112, 3
Rends He raves, he **rends**, and while he thus doth tear, 325. H.1077, 5
Renew Who would faine his strength **renew**,......10. H.19, 13
Oft as your field, shall her old age **renew**,......140. H.355, 13
Your houses to **renew**;.....................285. H.892, 10
Renneted See **O'er-renneted**
Renovation A **Renovation** of the West by Thee...254. H.756, 2
Renown Care keepes the Conquest; 'tis no lesse **renowne**, 307. H.989, 1
Renowned Men are not born Kings, but are men **renown'd**; 241. H.707, 1
Rent See **Grief-rent**
Run after with their breeches **rent**.............101. H.250, 25
Sound or unsound, be they **rent** or whole,......143. H.368, 3
Here we rejoyce, because no **Rent**...............200. H.552, 7
Be she whole, or be she **rent**,................253. H.750, 13
That do's infect, and make the **rent**...........311. H.1010, 5
For 'tis Fee simple, and noe **rent**..............407. A.2, 13
Rents He **rents** his Crown, That feares the Peoples hate. 182. H.488, 2
What are our patches, tatters, raggs, and **rents**,.302. H.970, 1
Repay Though long it be, yeeres may **repay** the debt; 228. H.654, 1
For profer'd love will love **repay**:..............252. H.746, 4
Repeat Such an one, as will **repeat**...............62. H.162, 13
While some **repeat**...........................113. H.283, 45
Repeat the Times that I have seen!..........135. H.336, 116
And thrice **repeat**...........................227. H.653, 6
Repel'd See **Repelled**
Repelled Then prayers **repel'd**, (sayes Cassiodore).383. N.170, 2
Repent Who after his transgression doth **repent**,..268. H.809, 1
That if (unknitting) men wo'd yet **repent**,.......291. H.920, 3
Il'e write no more of Love; but now **repent**....334. H.1124, 1
Men to **repent**, but when He strikes withall.....342. N.19, 2
And to **repent** some crimes,.....................352. N.53, 5
Mens sins destroyed are, when they **repent**;....388. N.210, 3
God, who me gives a will for to **repent**,........397. N.255, 1
Repentance **Repentance** to his liberty...........148. H.377, 88
In true **repentance** spent, will be................388. N.206, 3
Repentant One man **repentant** is of more esteem..388. N.205, 1
Repenting As with a will **repenting**.............55. H.149, 76
Repents It (Ah!) too late **repents** me............296. H.946, 9
Repetition The **repetition** of the name made known 383. N.174, 1
Replenished Be evermore these Bynns **replenished**. 245. H.723, 6
Replete May both with manchet stand **repleat**;....178. H.476, 4
But your Boules with Sack **repleat**.............217. H.620, 6
Repletion Physitians say **Repletion** springs......298. H.951, 1
Replied And I **reply'd** thereto,...................18. H.47, 10
Then blubbering, **replyed** he,.....................50. H.139, 7
To see the waste; but 'twas **repli'd**.............358. N.75, 6
Replies He'll slit her nose; But blubb'ring, she **replyes**, 44. H.126, 2
Repliest And lik'st the best? Still thou **reply'st**, The dead. 66. H.174, 2
Reply Franck ne'r wore silk she sweares; but I **reply**, 207. H.578, 1
Love as briefly did **reply**;.....................219. H.628, 4
What is the cause? Why Gander will **reply**,....223. H.636, 3
Aske me what hunger is, and Ile **reply**,........293. H.931, 1
Speake thou of love and I'le **reply**............393. N.232, 11
Let thy obedience be the best **Reply**...........397. N.260, 2
Report See **Too-true-report**
To be what I **report** thee; and inure..........37. H.106, 103
And lend a gentle eare to one **report**............86. H.213, 11
And if **Report** of them be true,..................92. H.223, 76
Then see it in **report**,........................183. H.492, 20
Reports Of these **Reports**; because you see......49. H.136, 16
Reposes And give me such **reposes**,.............95. H.227, 18
Repossess To **re-possess** once more your long'd-for home. 300. H.961, 6
Repossessed O native countrey, **repossest** by thee! 242. H.713, 16
Reprehend And still do'st this, and that verse, **reprehend**: 7. H.6, 4
Represent Not **represent**, but give reliefe........146. H.377, 10
Reproach **Reproach** we may the living; not the dead: 218. H.625, 1
Reprobate The chosen Rubie, and the **Reprobate**...209. H.586, 8
Repullulate Nere can **repullulate**, or bring.......133. H.336, 23
Repullulation **Repullulation** gives me here........265. H.794, 4
Repurgation A **Repurgation** of the Skie:.........188. H.508, 4
Reputed I might (and justly) be **reputed** (here).234. H.673, 5
Request My last **request**; for I.................111. H.280, 10
Here needs no Court for our **Request**,........190. H.515, 29
Ch. What's thy **request**? Ph. That since she's now beneath 248. H.730, 15
Requesters And though a while He makes **Requesters** stay, 344. N.30, 3
Requiem Her supreamest **Requiem** sing;........274. H.838, 6
Requiems Upon your Boughs, and **Requiems** sung 169. H.449, 16
Require 'Tis not greatness they **require**,..........22. H.65, 1
The Gods **require** the thighes..................250. H.736, 1
For I thinke the gods **require**.................277. H.856, 3
Though Frankinsense the Deities **require**,......295. H.940, 1
Doe that my Julia which the rites **require**,......299. H.957, 3
Great faults **require** great satisfaction.........312. H.1012, 2
Requires And manners good **requires**, that we....226. H.647, 2
Lambs, by the Law, which God **requires** as due......341. N.9, 2
Christ, He **requires** still, wheresoere He comes,...356. N.68, 1
Requital For the **requitall**; save this only one..267. H.804, 3
Requite If not **requite**, yet thank ye all.........123. H.306, 12
Mans disposition is for to **requite**.............292. H.923, 1
Resemblances The true **resemblances** of thee;....107. H.263, 18
The Flowrie-sweet **resemblances** of Thee:........193. H.522, 4
Resembling Each cheeke **resembling** still a damaske rose, 404. A.1, 14
Resembling sheilds both smooth and christalline..406. A.1, 80
Reserved Is not **reserv'd** for Trebius here,......147. H.377, 58
The Fields of Pluto are **reserv'd** for them;......417. A.8, 28
Reserves God has foure keyes, which He **reserves** alone; 390. N.224, 1
Residence Unto thy everlasting **residence**.........219. H.627, 8
To a more happy **Residence**.....................226. H.644, 6
Resident Tell I can't, what's **Resident**...........191. H.519, 4
Resides True mirth **resides** not in the smiling skin: 341. N.13, 1
Resign The debt is paid: for he who doth **resigne**..72. H.185, 26
Which, fir'd with incense, I **resigne**,..........351. N.47, 55
Resigned Yet not a Maiden-head **resign'd**!......54. H.149, 32
To give that life, **resign'd** your own:..........126. H.318, 9
(Having **resign'd** thy shamefac'tness:).........287. H.899, 6
Resigning Of the **resigning**, yet resisting Bride...45. H.128, 6
Resist 'Tis for our glory, that we did **resist**.......356. N.67, 4
(Thy Mercie helping) shall **resist** stronge fate....411. A.3, 44
Resisted Wrath yf **resisted** ouer boyles,...........408. A.2, 71
Resisting Of the resigning, yet **resisting** Bride.....45. H.128, 6
Re-sojourn With whom I did, and may **re-sojourne** when 29. H.86, 13
Resolution Back-turning slackens **Resolution**......252. H.747, 2
Resolve I shall **resolve** ye, what it is.............130. H.329, 3
Resolve to part with neither;..................169. H.446, 10
Resort Unto which the Tribes **resort**,.............255. H.761, 5
Resounds Apollo sings, his harpe **resounds**; give roome, 415. A.7, 1
Respasses The cooling breath of **Respasses**;......145. H.375, 20
Respect Nor Cloe was of more **respect**;...........70. H.181, 6
Still to our gains our chief **respect** is had;......139. H.351, 1
How worthy of **respect** and praise!.............375. N.123, 62
Of locall motion, in no least **respect**,..........385. N.186, 3
Them and my thoughts to that sublim'd **respecte**..411. A.3, 50
Or in **respect** of Merchandize,....................417. A.9, 4
Respected Yet though thus **respected**,............83. H.205, 13
Rest The place for these, and for the **rest**..........8. H.11, 3
The **rest** Ile speak, when we meet both in bed...24. H.74, 14
Whether thy bones had here their **Rest**, or no.....27. H.82, 6
Nor can these figures so thy **rest** endeare,.......36. H.106, 55
But that his teares forbad the **rest**..............42. H.119, 12
(Among the **rest**)..............................43. H.123, 22
I live for ever; let the **rest** all lye..............63. H.165, 3
Daies may conclude in nights; and Suns may **rest**, 72. H.185, 5
God, and far more transcendent then the **rest**?..78. H.197, 60
Rest but a while here, by this bank of Lillies,..86. H.213, 10
Whose structure (for his holy **rest**)..............90. H.223, 3
Co'd never since find any **rest**....................96. H.229, 6
Since which (beleeve the **rest**)..................105. H.258, 7
Be pleas'd to **rest** you in This Sacred Grove,....107. H.265, 3
Of that Fiend that marres your **rest**;............117. H.289, 6
From noise of Scare-fires **rest** ye free,..........121. H.299, 1
Where my small reliques must for ever **rest**:....129. H.327, 4
To make this neat distinction from the **rest**;....140. H.354, 5
Since for thy full deserts (with all the **rest**.....152. H.392, 1
Two she spat out, a cough forc't out the **rest**...158. H.419, 2
So like to this, nay all the **rest**,...............164. H.440, 9
By deare S. Iphis; and the **rest**,................169. H.449, 24
With all the **rest**; while thou alone............184. H.492, 35
Piece of the **rest**..............................189. H.515, 4
One **Rest**, one Grave..........................190. H.515, 12
Doe here find **rest**............................190. H.515, 22
Carry the Garland from the **rest**.................192. H.521, 34
One chiefe transgression is among the **rest**,......197. H.539, 7

'Twas rich before; but since your Name is downe, 264. H.789, 3
E'ene all Religious courses to be rich..........266. H.800, 1
Rich he will be by all unrighteousness:..........266. H.800, 6
More rich then Cleopatra's Tombe..............269. H.817, 4
Tell me, what needs those rich deceits,........282. H.881, 1
The wearers rich immodestie;..................311. H.1010, 8
God co'd have made all rich, or all men poore;..356. N.69, 1
Had all been rich, where then had Patience been? 356. N.69, 3
Rich is the Jemme that thou did'st send,........376. N.125, 5
(Though ne're so rich) all beggars at His Gate...383. N.171, 2
Tell me rich man, for what intent.............394. N.239, 1
Or rich Arabia did commix,..................402. N.269, 16
Whose breath is rich perfume, that to the sence..404. A.1, 27
Like pearle and gold make one rich Carcanett.....405. A.1, 32
On either side with rich rare Jewells grac'd,......405. A.1, 40
Bearing aloft this rich round world of wonder....405. A.1, 46
Which headed with twoe rich round rubies showe 405. A.1, 53
I'le leaue thee then Compleatly riche............407. A.2, 6
Off craueing more: soe In Conceipt bee ritch...411. A.3, 56
Such rich, such fresh, such sweet varietyes,......415. A.7, 16
Of oyle, but onely rich in faith,..........436. ins. H.336, 481
Richer The richer Couslips home................110. H.274, 8
A richer pearle for thee,......................240. H.705, 6
And richer Wine wo'dst give to me (thy guest)..262. H.783, 5
Will, after ease, a richer harvest yeild:..........292. H.922, 2
Richer then that faire pretious virtuos horne....406. A.1, 103
Riches And know, that Riches have their proper stint, 35. H.106, 17
Riches to be but burthens to the mind..........213. H.605, 2
Although he has no riches,.....................259. H.772, 17
Richesse A richess of those sweets she found,.....281. H.876, 3
Richest With all thy richest jewels over-cast:.....76. H.194, 2
For thee with richest Jemmes to shine,........323. H.1068, 15
The richest New-yeeres Gift to me..............355. N.60, 6
Richly A Bracelet richly Redolent:................13. H.32, 2
Richly Aromaticall...........................59. H.155, 6
The other parts will richly please.............138. H.342, 10
That richly wrought, and This as brave;........192. H.521, 22
A wife most richly married...................291. H.919, 16
Each richly headed with a pearly shell..........406. A.1, 102
— — — — — — — — — —, ...440. var. H.443, 71
Richmond To Richmond, Kingstone, and to Hampton-Court: 315. H.1028, 10
Rid See Bed-rid
So I, now having rid my way;..................216. H.617, 3
Rid these, and those, and part by part eat all...305. H.982, 4
Ride Ride on with all white Omens; so, that where 25. H.77, 11
Through that huge field of waters ride:..........30. H.90, 3
And ride the Sun-beams. Can there be a thing..78. H.197, 53
This night for to ride;.........................225. H.643, 2
Unto the Holy Temple ride:..................291. H.919, 14
Rides With a lash of a Bramble she rides now,..225. H.643, 9
Seest thou that Cloud that rides in State......269. H.815, 1
Hence the Hag, that rides the Mare,...........284. H.891, 2
And here my ship rides having Anchor cast.....334. H.1126, 2
That rides the glorious Cherubim...............340. N.3, 16
Rids Who slowly goes, rids (in the end) his way...352. N.51, 4
Rifle Rifle the Flowers which the Virgins strew'd:.49. H.138, 6
Rifts When all the world with rifts is full:......318. H.1036, 2
Right See Birthright, Foreright, Outright
He must of right,............................30. H.87, 16
Who 'gainst Mabs-state plac't here right is.......91. H.223, 29
Right by the Rubrick, which they read.........92. H.223, 75
But Age hath brought me right to Bed.........216. H.617, 6
Brown bread Tom Pennie eates, and must of right, 309. H.997, 1
Give S. Distaffe all the right,................315. H.1026, 11
And in my Booke now claim a two-fold right:.322. H.1062, 11
God has a Right Hand, but is quite bereft......394. N.240, 1
Righteous A short, but righteous discipline........92. H.223, 84
You shall; if righteous dealing I find there.......136. H.338, 2
And give a righteous judgement upon it.........187. H.506, 4
Thee sprightly Soame, one of my righteous Tribe: 199. H.545, 2
Thee here among my righteous race:...........278. H.859, 2
That thou be righteous found; and I the Lyer...279. H.866, 4
Here, for the righteous mans salvation:..........349. N.44, 2
Righteously Others there be, who righteously will swear 141. H.359, 9
Who'l hear, and so judge righteously...........243. H.716, 22
Rightly Which, rightly us'd, both in their time and place, 371. N.115, 7
Rigid Let rigid Cato read these Lines of mine.......7. H.8, 10
Rimes Which gave me honour for my Rhimes,..136. H.336, 150
(Bred from the dung-hils, and adulterous rhimes,) 155. H.405, 13
Stand by the Magick of my powerfull Rhymes..280. H.869, 1
For Those my unbaptized Rhimes,...............339. N.2, 1
Rimmon His house of Rimmon, this he calls,......90. H.223, 9
Rind And in the Rind of every comely tree......160. H.421, 39
Encarv'd upon the Leaves and Rind...........169. H.449, 8
The name of Phillis in the Rind..............192. H.521, 40
With tender ryne and silver coloured,............406. A.1, 98
— — — — — — — — —, ...448. var. A.1, 98
Ring A golden ring, that shines upon thy thumb:...30. H.88, 7
To thee this Ring...............................65. H.172, 2
When I departed am, ring thou my knell,.......111. H.279, 1
No ginne to catch the State, or wring.........126. H.319, 7
Forth by a Ring, or some rich Carkanet?........172. H.459, 6
Return'd a Ring of Jimmals, to imply...........173. H.464, 2
A Gyges Ring they beare about them still,......250. H.737, 1
Ring the Saints-Bell, to affright...............258. H.769, 8
Virgins Come, and in a Ring.................274. H.838, 5
So in a ring,................................369. N.106, 11
Ringlet For each Ringlet there's a snare...........52. H.147, 4
And each Ringlet of her haire..................232. H.665, 11
It chanst a ringlet of her haire,................281. H.876, 7
Ringlets Dandled the ringlets of her haire........51. H.142, 12
Rings See Half-jet-rings
Thou sha't have Ribbands, Roses, Rings,......193. H.521, 51
What Posies for our Wedding Rings;...........216. H.616, 27
Balls of Cowslips, Daisie rings,...............306. H.984, 25
Rings' The Wante of Eare rings brauerye,........409. A.2, 90
Rinse (His teeth all out) to rince and wash his gummes. 301. H.965, 2
Rip We rip up first, then reap our lands.........101. H.250, 4
Ripe See Cherry-ripe
Cherrie-Ripe, Ripe, Ripe, I cry,..................19. H.53, 1
As she, so you'l be ripe for men..............56. H.149, 112
Two, like two ripe shocks of corn..............58. H.149, 170
Ripe eares of corne, and up to th'eares in snow:..59. H.154, 6
Thus ripe with tears,..........................135. H.336, 117
Ambo. Lets cheer him up. Sil. Behold him weeping ripe. 159. H.421, 7
Ripe Cherries smiling, while that others blow...193. H.523, 2
The Ravens yeares, go hence more Ripe then old. 222. H.633, 63
Was cheese full ripe with Teares, with Bread as sad. 273. H.835, 4
See mine eyes are weeping ripe................305. H.984, 13
guilty of somewhat, ripe the strawberries..430. ins. H.283, 20b
Ripened — — — — — — — — —, ...442. var. H.575, 10
Riphdan — — — — — — — — —, ...447. var. A.1, 60
Riphean Like a faire mountaine in Riphean snowe,.405. A.1, 60
Rise For my life mortall, Rise from out thy Herse,.27. H.82, 15
As not to rise when Chanticlere................36. H.106, 56
Warnes the last Watch; but with the Dawne dost rise 36. H.106, 57
Rise; and put on your Foliage, and be seene....68. H.178, 15
To-morrow, Julia, I betimes must rise,.........102. H.251, 1
Thou that tam'st Tygers, and fierce storms (that rise) 103. H.254, 3
Rise, Houshold-gods, and let us goe;............111. H.278, 1
When with the Virgin morning thou do'st rise,..127. H.320, 1
So smell those odours that do rise.............145. H.375, 1
Stand with thy Graces forth, Brave man, and rise.181. H.483, 1
Fall thou must first, then rise to life with These,.188. H.507, 3
I, and all the world shall rise.,................199. H.549, 4
So as to rise still with an appetite.............220. H.633, 19
When thence ye see my reverend Ghost to rise,..222. H.634, 3
To rise as soon as day doth peep?..............233. H.670, 2
Rise up of men, a fighting race................297. H.948, 12
Not to eat equall portions; but to rise.........310. H.1005, 3
Each bending then, will rise a proper flower.....320. H.1054, 6
In the morning when ye rise...................322. H.1064, 1
I do believe, that when I rise,..................358. N.78, 3
Rise ye Debters then, and fall................373. N.121, 11
And if I chance to wake, and rise thereon,.......392. N.230, 21
I rise triumphant in my Funerall...............392. N.230, 36
Hence rise those twoe ambitious hills that looke..406. A.1, 81
— — — — — — — — — —, ...437. var. H.336, 107
Rises — — — — — — — — —, ...453. var. H.283, 112
Rising See Early-rising, Uprising
With the Sun rising he must walk his grounds;..259. H.771, 3
There is a love-like-leven rising there...........306. H.985, 2
Thy fall is but the rising to a Crowne.........311. H.1007, 2
Of ours, as is the rising of the wheat...........388. N.208, 6
— — — — — — — — — — —, ...432. var. H.283, 112
Rite See Guest-rite
Rites See Bridal-rites
To doe the Rites to thy Religious Tombe:........27. H.82, 2
Corrols his cheeke, to see those Rites not done...216. H.618, 4
Or other Rites that doe belong to me;..........219. H.627, 6
And Rites were all accomplished;...........237. H.686, 14
All Rites well ended, with faire Auspice come...286. H.898, 9
Doe that my Julia which the rites require 299. H.957, 3
And (ere we our rites commence)..............303. H.974, 5
To her warm bosome, then our Rites are ended...366. N.97, 29
And Hymen call'd to blcss the Rites. Cha. Stop there. 416. A.8, 20
Rival (Made rivall with the aire)...............103. H.255, 2
River She by the River sate, and sitting there,....251. H.743, 1
As in the River Julia did,......................294. H.939, 5
Rivers Rockes turn to Rivers, Rivers turn to Men..29. H.86, 14
Shall run, as rivers, all throughout thy soyl.....144. H.370, 6
Roach — — — — — — — — —, ...440. var. H.443, 73
Roam Whither, Mad maiden wilt thou roame?......5. H.2, 1
But when I saw thee wantonly to roame...........6. H.3, 3

And spring fresh Rose-buds, while the salt, the wit 148. H.377, 73
Bring me my Rose-buds, Drawer come;........208. H.582, 1
Like wanton rose buds growing out of snowe,....405. A.1, 54
Thus Crownd with Rose Budds, Sacke, thou mad'st mee flye 410. A.3, 27
Rose-crowned Her long disheuel'd rose-crown'd tramaletts: 404. A.1, 4
Rosemary And guild the Baies and Rosemary:...215. H.616, 26
Down with the Rosemary and Bayes,............285. H.892, 1
Down with the Rosemary, and so.............304. H.980, 1
Rose's In bloome of Peach, and Roses bud,....107. H.263, 11
Roses How Roses first came Red, and Lillies White..5. H.1, 10
Ye Roses almost withered;........................7. H.9, 2
I dreamt the Roses one time went................8. H.11, 1
Of Roses be your sweat...........................9. H.15, 4
One ask'd me where the Roses grew?............18. H.45, 1
Of Roses, almost smothered:.....................20. H.56, 2
Some ruffled Roses nestling were:.................25. H.78, 2
Or Muse of Roses: since that name does fit......28. H.84, 3
That Roses shew, when misted o're with Lawn...34. H.104, 4
Millions of Lillies mixt with Roses.............36. H.106, 48
Roses, by a Bee was stung.........................50. H.139, 2
To be in Oyle of Roses drown'd,..................50. H.140, 7
I'm sure they'l fashion Roses.....................74. H.192, 8
'Fore Damask Roses.................................83. H.205, 12
'Mongst Roses.......................................95. H.227, 22
'Mongst Roses, I there Cupid found:............96. H.229, 2
Roses at first were white,.......................105. H.258, 1
The Roses first came red.........................105. H.258, 8
The Shewers of Roses, lucky-foure-leav'd grasse: 113. H.283, 42
Cheeks like to Roses, when they blow...........120. H.295, 2
Crown we our Heads with Roses then,........133. H.336, 33
Or Roses smother'd in the stove:...............145. H.375, 4
Dear, in thy bed of Roses, then,..............146. H.376, 11
Oyle of Roses still smelt there..................182. H.490, 8
The Queen of Roses for that yeere.............192. H.521, 32
Thou sha't have Ribbands, Roses, Rings,......193. H.521, 51
Better look the Roses red,.......................194. H.527, 3
Roses and Cassia crown the untill'd soyle.......205. H.575, 4
Commixt they meet, with endlesse Roses crown'd. 206. H.575, 20
In Tyrian Dewes, and Head with Roses crown'd..214. H.612, 12
With Roses sweet and new;.........................228. H.657, 11
Or Roses, being withered:.........................233. H.670, 25
Thrice happie Roses, so much grac't, to have....249. H.734, 1
And praying, strew some Roses on her,..........257. H.764, 9
With maunds of roses for to strew the way:....261. H.781, 8
Or Damask Roses, when they grow............271. H.824, 15
For Roses, and in Julia's cheeke,................281. H.876, 2
But gathering Roses as she was;...............281. H.876, 5
And Ile Roses give to thee.......................313. H.1018, 4
Roses, you can never die,.........................324. H.1070, 1
(Or Sharon, where eternall Roses grow.)......326. H.1080, 8
Which sits as Dew of Roses there:..............328. H.1090, 9
Of Roses have an endlesse flourishing.........330. H.1100, 10
Of Daffadills, and Roses;..........................345. N.33, 12
May Roses grow, to crown His own deare Head..366. N.97, 23
How roses lillies and carnations grow,............404. A.1, 16
Which makes them shewe like roses vnder lawne...404. A.1, 24
— — — — — — — — — — —, ...424. var. H.164, 9
Roster See Roaster
Rosy Move forward then your Rosie feet,........55. H.149, 61
Stands garded with a rosy hilly wall,............405. A.1, 30
— — — — — — — — — —, ...429. var. H.263, 11
With Rosie Chaplets, Lillies, Pansies red,..442. ins. H.575, 20a
Rot Which though they furre, will neither ake, or rot. 46. H.129, 2
And piece-meale rot...........................85. H.211, 15
Rotation With the Rotation of the Day.........172. H.457, 4
Rotted And wth thayr Ceareclothes rotted, not to shew 411. A.3, 37
Rotten Half rotten, and without an eye,........166. H.443, 52
Twice two fell out, all rotten at the root.......247. H.728, 2
Rough Rough as th' Adratick sea, yet I...........70. H.181, 23
By whose tough labours, and rough hands,......101. H.250, 3
To the rough Sickle, and crookt Sythe,........102. H.250, 42
Of some rough Groom, who (yirkt with Corns) sayes, Sir 146. H.377, 21
To seek, and bring rough Pepper home:........229. H.662, 6
Be she rough, or smooth of skin;..............253. H.750, 7
Since rough the way is, help me when I call,....352. N.51, 7
Roughness To Roughnes, Claspe hym lyke a Vine,..408. A.2, 68
Round See Around, Country-round
Of sacred *Orgies flyes, A round, A round...........7. H.8, 8
But to live round, and close, and wisely true..38. H.106, 135
And as this round...................................66. H.172, 25
Round, round, the roof do's run;..............81. H.201, 33
Then in a Round, is plac't by these,............90. H.223, 17
And seen them in a Round:.....................110. H.274, 10
And let our Citie-health go round,.............127. H.319, 30
Drawing thy curtains round: Good night.......146. H.376, 14
A Round...198. H.544, 17
Into an Ovall, square, or round;..............202. H.560, 10
Then unto Dancing forth the learned Round....206. H.575, 19
Untill the roofe turne round.................208. H.582, 4
Tripping the comely country round,..........230. H.662, 50
That luckie Fairies here may dance their Round: 245. H.723, 8
As that in all that admirable round,............307. H.992, 3
And plaister'd round with Amber..............345. N.33, 24
Thus, thus, and thus we compasse round........359. N.83, 7
He's seen, He's seen, why then a Round,......368. N.102, 15
Where round about Thou seest but all things vaine, 371. N.113, 3
Though ills stand round about me;...........373. N.122, 10
Gods Hands are round, & smooth, that gifts may fall 380. N.151, 1
Bearing aloft this rich round world of wonder...405. A.1, 46
Which headed with twoe rich round rubies showe 405. A.1, 53
Round short and cleire, like pounded spices sweete 406. A.1, 92
— — — — — — — — — —, ...430. var. H.283, 31
By the round Urchin, some mixt wheate..439. ins. H.443, 45d
Rounded True, if this Citie seven times rounded was 252. H.745, 11
Roundelay To these smooth Lawns, my mirthfull Roundelay. 159. H.421, 10
And for a Rurall Roundelay,...................183. H.492, 11
Of thee, or I, the Roundelay,...................243. H.716, 3
Roundly And roundly drinke we here;..........219. H.629, 2
Rouse Rouze Anacreon from the dead;............39.H.111, 9
To rouze the sacred madnesse; and awake......45. H.128, 25
Rout About the Cart, heare, how the Rout....101. H.250, 15
Up with the Quintill, that the Rout,............306. H.987, 1
Rove Nor to the Eastern Ind dost rove..........229. H.662, 7
Row To the Gallies there to Rowe;............219. H.628, 2
Rowled See Rolled
Rowling See Rolling
Royal No cowards must his royall Ensignes beare. 280. H.872, 2
Royal-blood To be, or not borne of the Royall-blood. 297. H.947, 8
Rubelet A blushing-pretty-peeping Rubelet:.....227. H.652, 10
Ruben Of Holben, and That mighty Ruben too...150. H.384, 4
Rubens See Ruben
Rubies Which Rubies, Corralls, Scarlets, all........12. H.23, 7
Some ask'd me where the Rubies grew?..........24. H.75, 1
Or seen rich Rubies blushing through..........164. H.440, 7
Drown'd in the bloud of Rubies there, not die...216. H.618, 16
And Rubies lately polished:.....................268. H.811, 6
Which headed with twoe rich round rubies showe.405. A.1, 53
Insteade of gould Pearle Rubies Bonds..........407. A.2, 7
Rubric Right by the Rubrick, which they read.....92. H.223, 75
Ruby Made of the Rubie, Pearle and Diamond:....30. H.88, 6
When as that Rubie, which you weare,..........61. H.160, 7
The rubie niplet of her breast;....................74. H.190, 8
Lips she has, all Rubie red,.....................138. H.342, 5
The chosen Rubie, and the Reprobate..........209. H.586, 8
Both with the Rubie, Pearle, and Diamond.....369. N.105, 8
The which with ruby rednes being tipt............404. A.1, 21
These be the Ruby portalls and devine..........404. A.1, 25
Ruby-like Part Ruby-like, part Candidate?.........269. H.815, 2
Ruby-lipped Rubie-lipt, and tooth'd with Pearl:..136. H.337, 2
Rude And rude (almost) as rudest Salvages.......29. H.86, 12
Of Womans beauty? and with hand more rude..49. H.138, 5
Yet one rude wind, or ruffling shower,...........88. H.216, 5
If after rude and boystrous seas,................94. H.225, 1
Preposterous is that Government, (and rude)....196. H.536, 1
Let what is graceless, discompos'd, and rude,..290. H.914, 3
Or (discompos'd) I'm like a rude,............312. H.1016, 3
Long before this, the base, the dull, the rude,..398. N.263, 5
Rudely Let us not then so rudely henceforth goe..73. H.186, 5
And who do rudely move him.................157. H.412, 24
(From which poore seed, and rudely sown)......297. H.948, 7
Rudest And rude (almost) as rudest Salvages.....29. H.86, 12
First, let us dwell on rudest seas;..............111. H.278, 3
Rue In mournfull Hyacinths and Rue,..........131. H.330, 7
Ruff The Phesant, Partridge, Gotwit, Reeve, Ruffe, Raile, 147. H.377, 65
When the ruffe is set elsewhere?................282. H.878, 8
Ruffled Some ruffled Roses nestling were:.........25. H.78, 2
Ruffling The ruffling winds and raging Seas,.......31. H.90, 5
Yet one rude wind, or ruffling shower,..........88. H.216, 5
By ruffling winds, about the world..............245. H.720, 16
No ruffling winds come hither to discease....316. H.1028, 21
Rug And then a Rug of carded wooll,...........167. H.443, 96
Rugged To the indulgence of the rugged Law:...201. H.557, 2
Rugs The Sheets, the Rugs, made by thy hand...374. N.123, 44
Ruin Nor can we that a ruine call,..............25. H.76, 3
When as a publick ruine bears down All.......155. H.405, 18
Threatn'd ruine unto all?.......................302. H.968, 10
A Ruine underpropt am I:........................303. H.973, 6
The blow of Ruine and of Chance................407. A.2, 11
Soaring them vpp, boue Ruyne, till the doome.....410. A.3, 33
Ruins Shakes the whole Roofe, or ruines all.......153. H.395, 5
Upon my ruines (smiling yet:)..................235. H.677, 2
Would into prais'd (but pitied) ruines fall,......252. H.745, 15
Rule A Rule, how far to teach,....................76. H.193, 42
And Charles here Rule, as he before did Raign;.214. H.612, 8
This rule of manners I will teach my guests,....310. H.1005, 1
And cal'd each line back to his rule and space...311. H.1006, 4

Where Pleasures **rule** a Kingdome, never there..327. H.1087, 1
Ruled See **O'erruled**
And so he may, if he'll be **rul'd** by me:........110. H.272, 2
Ruler See **Great-blue-ruler**
Rulers Let Kings and **Rulers**, learne this line from me; 302. H.971, 1
Rules Vice **rules** the Most, or All at Court:....37. H.106, 90
No man so well a Kingdome **Rules**, as He,....325. H.1074, 1
Rules but by leave, and takes his Crowne on trust. 331. H.1103, 2
Rumor As Fame or **Rumour**, hath or Trumpe or Tongue. 411. A.3, 46
Rump Ne'r yet set tooth in stump, or **rump** of these. 142. H.361, 2
Rumpe is a Turne-broach, yet he seldome can..331. H.1106, 1
Run When I thy Parts **runne** o're, I can't espie....10. H.16, 1
Do restless **run** when they are dead.............44. H.127, 10
And let them through a Zodiac **run**:.............47. H.133, 6
Our life is short; and our dayes **run**............69. H.178, 61
Run through my veines, like to a hasty flood.....79. H.197, 78
Run to a sudden Death, and Funerall...........79. H.197, 90
Round, round, the roof do's **run**;..............81. H.201, 33
The sooner will his Race be **run**,..............84. H.208, 7
If having **run** my Barque on ground,............94. H.225, 5
Run after with their breeches rent.............101. H.250, 25
His kitling eyes begin to **runne**................119. H.293, 24
Has **run**.....................................125. H.316, 7
That my Barque may safely **runne**.............129. H.325, 3
Shall **run**, as rivers, all throughout thy soyl.....144. H.370, 6
It keeps a growth in thee; and so will **runne**..147. H.377, 43
His eyes and ears strive which sho'd fastest **run**..158. H.418, 2
Then publick praise do's **runne** upon the Stone,..172. H.459, 9
Here, naked Younglings, handsome Striplings **run** 206. H.575, 17
Or whither **run**..............................211. H.596, 6
When to the Temple Love sho'd **runne**, not go...216. H.618, 6
Can **runne** mad, and Prophesie.................217. H.620, 9
If well the Dice **runne**, lets applaud the cast:....218. H.621, 1
That fleet of Lackeyes, which do **run**..........239. H.696, 3
Prepost'rous is that order, when we **run**........241. H.708, 1
That through each room a golden pipe may **run**..245. H.723, 3
Balm may thy Trees drop, and thy Springs **runne** oyle 269. H.818, 7
She'l **runne** to all adulteries..................287. H.899, 10
Let others to the Printing Presse **run** fast,....314. H.1022, 1
Run Creame, (for Wine.).....................350. N.47, 50
To my heaven lesse **run**, then flie...............355. N.64, 6
The vessell full, did then **run** ore:.............357. N.75, 4
Draw me, but first, and after Thee I'le **run**,....358. N.77, 14
To Hell I'd rather **run**, then I.................395. N.245, 5
Before the last least sand of Thy ninth houre be **run**; 401. N.268, 8
Let Oyle, next, **run**,.........................401. N.268, 21
In their silver waters; **runne**...........431. ins. H.283, 50g
Rung With ratling Kirnils, which is **rung**.....93. H.223, 127
One knell be **rung** for both; and let one grave..281. H.875, 5
Runnest Who fli'st at all heights: Prose and Verse **run'st** through;....................................298. H.955, 7
Runneth Gold, **runneth** to the Western Inde,......36. H.106, 66
Running His linings are the matter **running** there..144. H.373, 2
And **running** therewithall;.....................288. H.908, 2
Fine flowre prest down, and **running** o're........356. N.66, 8
Runs **Runs** from his Torrid Zone, to prie, and look, 114. H.283, 62
What comes in, **runnes** quickly out:.........116. H 285, 6
And **runnes** most smoothly, when tis well begunne. 128. H.321, 2
And his skill **runs** on the lees;................347. N.41, 15
Runs division with the Singer..................364. N.96, 7
Rupture Or yawning **rupture** can the same devoure, 148. H.377, 107
Rural Thus let thy **Rurall** Sanctuary be........38. H.106, 137
Of **Rurall** Younglings raise the shout;........101. H.250, 16
And for a **Rurall** Roundelay,.................183. H.492, 11
The more my **rurall** privacie:................246. H.724, 28
Rush Of sugred **Rush**, and eates the sagge.......119. H.293, 33
Those monstrous lies of little Robin **Rush**:......155. H.405, 8
Rush saves his shooes, in wet and snowie wether; 332. H.1116, 1
This is strong thrift that warie **Rush** doth use..332. H.1116, 3
Rushes Green **Rushes** then, and sweetest Bents,..285. H.892, 17
In Barge (with boughes and **rushes** beautifi'd)..315. H.1028, 8
Russet And let the **russet** Swaines the Plough..127. H.319, 45
Thy Nut-browne mirth; thy **Russet** wit;......231. H.662, 60
Rust Where **Rust** and Cobwebs bind the gate;..179. H.476, 29
Can ever **rust** th'Enamel of the light..........206. H.575, 16
Pray not for silver, **rust** eats this;.............381. N.158, 5
Cannot deliuer vpp to'th **rust**,..................407. A.2, 17
Rustic Nor do's it mind the **Rustick** straines....184. H.492, 23
Rustics While other **Rusticks**, lesse attent......101. H.250, 23
Happy **Rusticks**, best content.................255. H.761, 21
Ruth Or like a Virgin full of **ruth**,..............47. H.132, 7
Cha. Who calls? who calls? Euc. One overwhelm'd with **ruth**; 416. A.8, 3
Rye Wheat, Barley, **Rie**, or Oats; what is't......376. N.127, 3
Ryne See **Rind**
S Saint Frip, Saint Trip, Saint Fill, **S.** Fillie,....91. H.223, 32
By sweet **S.** Phillis; pitie me:................169. H.449, 23
By deare **S.** Iphis; and the rest,.............169. H.449, 24
With a pennie to pay **S.** Peter..................256. H.762, 6
Ye must on **S.** Distaffs day:..................315. H.1026, 2
Give **S.** Distaffe all the right,.................315. H.1026, 11
Thou stop'st **S.** Peter in the midst of sin;........349. N.43, 3
God tempteth no one (as **S.** Aug'stine saith)....380. N.150, 1
'Tis (as **S.** Bernard saith) but seemingly.......385. N.188, 4
But Mary cal'd then (as **S.** Ambrose saith).....386. N.192, 4
Sabbaths are threefold, (as **S.** Austine sayes:)..386. N.194, 1
(**S.** Ambrose sayes) without the Thorn:........396. N.251, 2
'S (Partial List)
How I sho'd pay, **'s** impossible:................369. N.107, 4
Sabæan Smells like the burnt **Sabæan** Frankinsense 404. A.1, 28
Sabbath The first of Time, or **Sabbath** here of Dayes; 386. N.194, 2
The last the **Sabbath** of Eternitie..............386. N.194, 4
Sabbaths **Sabbaths** are threefold, (as S. Austine sayes:) 386. N.194, 1
Sacietie See **Satiety**
Sack Grapes, before Herrick leaves Canarie **Sack**..78. H.197, 48
In **Sack** of such a kind,......................80. H.201, 14
But your Boules with **Sack** repleat............217. H.620, 6
What can my Kellam drink his **Sack**...........290. H.918, 1
Thus Crownd with Rose Budds, **Sacke**, thou mad'st mee flye 410. A.3, 27
Sacke is my life, my leaven, salt to all....426. ins. H.197, 48a
— — — — — — — — — — —, ...427. var. H.197, 49
— — — — — — — — — — —, ...427. var. H.197, 51
— — — — — — — — — — —, ...427. var. H.197, 73
Sackcloth Bungie do's fast; looks pale; puts **Sack-cloth** on; 122. H.305, 1
Put a shirt of **sackcloth** on:................183. H.490, 14
My **sackcloth** here; but there my Stole of white...343, N.25, 8
Sack-posset Blesse a **Sack-posset**; Luck go with it; take 115. H.283, 132
Sacred See **Thrice-three-sacred**
Of **sacred** *Orgies flyes, A round, A round...........7. H.8, 8
Thy **sacred** Corse with Odours I will burne;......11. H.22, 3
In which thy **sacred** Reliques shall have roome:....20. H.55, 8
A **sacred** Laurel springing from my grave:........30. H.89, 5
To rouze the **sacred** madnesse; and awake......45. H.128, 25
Heavy, to hurt those **sacred** seeds of thee.....73. H.186, 20
Their **sacred** Salt here, (not a little.)..........93. H.223, 118
Be pleas'd to rest you in This **Sacred** Grove,....107. H.265, 3
Himen, O Himen! Tread the **sacred** ground;..113. H.283, 31
Their **sacred** seed:...........................133. H.336, 27
For his love then, whose **sacred** Reliques show..137. H.341, 7
Among which glories, (crown'd with **sacred** Bayes, 206. H.575, 49
The **sacred** Dirge and Trentall sung...........237. H.686, 10
Give thou my **sacred** Reliques Buriall.........242. H.713, 20
Sacred Spittle bring ye hither;..................258. H.769, 4
For the **sacred** sprinkling:....................303. H.974, 2
He who asks almes in that so **sacred** Name,....347. N.39, 5
The **sacred** Towell, and the holy Eure...........355. N.65, 5
And from His **sacred** Bloud, here shed,..........366. N.97, 22
Yor name amidst the **sacred** smoke...............413. A.4, 30
— — — — — — — — — — —, ...423. var. H.128, 35
Sacrifice To work, but first to **sacrifice**;..........36. H.106, 58
Love's, and my **Sacrifice**.......................87. H.214, 16
Thou shalt have soules for **sacrifice**.............89. H.219, 12
For some small fault, to offer **sacrifice**:.........102, H.251, 2
Put on your Garlands first, then **Sacrifice**:.......124. H.313, 8
Crossing thy selfe; come thus to **sacrifice**:......127. H.320, 2
I send my salt, my **sacrifice**....................146. H.377, 2
And there to lick th' effused **sacrifice**:..........222. H.634, 4
Of Beeves for **sacrifice**;.......................250. H.736, 2
Must **sacrifice** to them:........................250. H.736, 4
Both addresse to **sacrifice**:.....................280. H.870, 2
Of Beeves here ready stand for **Sacrifice**.........300. H.961, 8
There a poor Lamb's a plenteous **sacrifice**........369. N.105, 4
Sacrificed The best of all the **sacrificed** meate;....272. H.826, 2
Sacrorum Then I'le be the Rex **Sacrorum**,........303. H.974, 7
Sad See **Few-sad-hours, Sweet-sad**
Where I have been, and still am **sad**,............19. H.51, 3
If pittying my **sad** Parents Teares,...............70. H.180, 5
Without a **sad** looke, or a solemne teare?........73. H.186, 10
The time will come, when you'l be **sad**,........179. H 476, 37
Nor let the shackles make thee **sad**;............246. H.725, 3
Who for a long **sad** time has weeping stood,.......251. H.745, 3
Was cheese full ripe with Teares, with Bread as **sad**. 273. H.835, 4
This shall my love doe, give thy **sad** death one..302. H.967, 3
Me, and my **sad** Play-mates all,................306. H.984, 39
And **sad**....................................308. H.993, 23
Yet none of these have made me **sad**:...........354. N.57, 2
By thy **sad** losse, our liberty:..................360. N.83, 20
Christ was not **sad**, i'th garden, for His own.....381. N.159, 1
Cities most **sad** and dire destruction............384. N.178, 4
To the **sad** place of execution:.................398. N.263, 2
The **sad** soule went, not with his Loue, but doome; 412. A.3, 76
This known, the rest of thy **sad** story tell,......417. A.8, 35
Sadly **Sadly** I walk't within the field,............73. H.187, 1
Sate by the Grave; and **sadly** sitting there,......384. N.180, 9

Sadness Of mirth is turn'd to **sadnesse**.........375. N.123, 60
Safe And viewing them with a more **safe** survey,..36. H.106, 73
Safe stand thy Walls, and Thee, and so both will, 149. H.377, 115
Sho'd see **safe** brought to Bed...............220. H.633, 17
Of sheep, (**safe** from the Wolfe and Fox)......230. H.662, 41
In sev'rall tills, and boxes keepes 'em **safe**;......299. H.959, 2
Goes theeving from me, I am **safe** in death;....392. N.230, 34
Safe Modestie, Lou'd Patience, Feare...........409. A.2, 97
Safeguard To **safe-guard** Man from wrongs, there nothing must 67. H.177, 1
Safely Lastly, **safely** buryed.....................38. H.107, 6
That my Barque may **safely** runne............129. H.325, 3
Safely guard us, now and aye,...............177. H.473, 3
And where 'tis **safely** kept, the Fiend,..........285. H.893, 7
And Landing here, or **safely** Landing there,....316. H.1028, 13
Safer Farre **safer** 'twere to stay at home:............5. H.2, 2
Safeties Lay of our **safeties** new foundation:....300. H.961, 12
Safety With **safety** of a faithful Ore:...............94. H.225, 4
For my wisht **safety** pay thy vowes,............175. H.465, 74
But feares not now to see her **safety** sold........251. H.745, 5
When feare admits no hope of **safety**, then......333. H.1118, 1
Saffron And, humbly, chives of **Saffron** brings,..93. H.223, 133
The **Saffron** and the Calamus..................375. N.123, 54
throaned in a **saffron** Evening, seemes to chyme 431. ins. H.283, 601
Soft **Saffron** Circles to perfume the head...442. ins. H.575, 20b
Sagge Of sugred Rush, and eates the **sagge**.....119. H.293, 33
Of a dried Canker, with a **sagge**.........433. ins. H.293, 31b
Said Who's that (**said** I) beats there,.............26. H.81, 5
Cast off (**said** he) all feare,.......................26. H.81, 7
Said he, with these late showrs.................27. H.81, 28
Away, and thus **said** flying,......................27. H.81, 34
And sobbing deeply, thus he **said**,................42. H.119, 8
To his Mother, **said** thus crying;..................50. H.139, 4
And why, my pretty Lad, **said** she?.............50. H.139, 6
Alas! **said** she, my Wag! if this.................50. H.139, 12
And chiding me, **said**, Hence, Remove,..........51. H.142, 21
He saw my Palme; and then, **said** he,...........63. H.166, 5
When all the Birds have Mattens **seyd**,.........68. H.178, 10
This **said**, he laid his little scrip.................71. H.182, 23
Kissing the Omen, **said** Amen:...................73. H.187, 7
Mop-ey'd I am, as some have **said**,..............97. H.235, 1
Tell me, **said** I, in deep distresse,..............106. H.263, 3
Thou foole, **said** Love, know'st thou not this?..106. H 263, 5
'Tis true, **said** I, and thereupon..............107. H.263, 13
At which I stopt; **Said** Love, these be.........107. H.263, 17
But in regard, 'twas often **said**, this old........129. H.326, 3
Which sung, or **seyd**,..........................198. H.544, 14
One Holy Collect, **said** or sung for Thee.........209. H.584, 4
What short sweet Prayers shall be **said**;........216. H.616, 31
What Love **said** was too too true:..............219. H.628, 8
Of which who drank, he **said** no thought.......222. H.635, 3
That man's not **said** to live, but last:..........233. H.670, 33
'Tis **said**, as Cupid danc't among...............241. H.706, 1
And thence return, (short prayers **seyd**)......291. H.919, 15
What's **said** or done...........................314. H.1024, 7
He **said**, because he got his wealth thereby.....332. H.1114, 4
God is not onely **said** to be.......................340. N.5, 1
So He is **said** to be most One.................343. N.23, 2
And I nod to what is **said**,.....................348. N.41, 30
When thou hast **said** so, stick it there...........354. N.59, 5
A prayer, that is **said** alone,...................381. N.158, 1
God's **said** to leave this place, and for to come....385. N.186, 1
God's evident, and may be **said** to be..........385. N.188, 1
God's **said** to dwell there, wheresoever He......385. N 189, 1
God is then **said** for to descend, when He......395. N.244, 1
Wherefore two prayers ought not to be **said**,....396. N.249, 7
God's **said** our hearts to harden then,..........396. N.250, 1
God's wrathfull **said** to be, when He doth do...397. N.259, 3
a prayer must be **said**, be briefe;........431. ins. H.283, 60n
Sail **Saile** against Rocks, and split them too;......31. H.90, 8
Canst in thy Map securely **saile**:..................36. H.106, 78
He, who has suffer'd Ship-wrack, feares to **saile**..212. H.601, 1
That made me thus hoist **saile**, and bring my Boat: 248. H.730, 12
Chorus. We **sail** along, to visit mortals never;....417. A.8, 37
— — — — — — — — — —,..............445. var. H.730. 20
Sailest Thou **sail'st** with others, in this Argus here;..23. H.71, 1
Sailing That sleeps at home; and **sayling** there at ease, 128. H.323, 3
Then, in that compass **sayling** here and there,....301. H.966, 5
Sails For mending **sails**, for patching Boat and Oares? 248. H.730, 20
Saint See S. Other-saintships
Why frowns my Sweet? Why won't my **Saint** confer 77. H.197, 25
Saint Tit, **Saint** Nit, **Saint** Is, **Saint** Itis,.......91. H.223, 28
Saint Will o'th' Wispe (of no great bignes)......91. H.223, 30
Saint Frip, **Saint** Trip, **Saint** Fill, S. Fillie,.....91. H.223, 32
The **Saint**, to which the most he prayes........93. H.223, 129
Some Relique of a **Saint** doth weare..........169. H.449, 2
Late you come in; but you a **Saint** shall be,....188. H.510, 3
The patient **Saint**, and send up vowes for me...204. H.570, 4
For the **Saint**, we'l keep the Shrine............211. H.593, 4
Saint Ben to aide me...........................212. H.604, 4
And thou **Saint** Ben, shalt be.................213. H.604, 11
A little **Saint** best fits a little Shrine,..........249. H.733, 1
It, and not Instead of **Saint**....................409. A.2, 79
Sainted Whom purity had **Sainted**..............229. H.659, 5
Saints I co'd not speak the **Saints** here painted...91. H.223, 27
Of holy **Saints** she paces on,...................112. H.283, 13
Saints will come in to fill each Pew and Place...168. H.445, 6
Here is the Legend of those **Saints**............169. H.449, 5
For **Saints** and Soules departed hence,..........169. H.449, 17
Of all those other **Saints** now blest;...........169. H.449, 25
A Stock of **Saints**; where ev'ry one doth weare..199. H.545, 5
The Proper Lessons for the **Saints** now dead:....209. H.584, 2
Who, kissing, kill such **Saints** as these?........294. H.937, 6
Of **Saints**?..314. H.1024, 4
Those **Saints**, which God loves best,.............344. N.28, 1
The teares of **Saints** more sweet by farre,........379. N.145, 1
God suffers not His **Saints**, and Servants deere,..394. N.236, 1
Saints'-bell The **Saints-bell** calls; and, Julia, I must read 209. H.584, 1
Ring the **Saints-Bell**, to affright...............258. H.769, 8
Saintships Of such rare **Saint-ships**, who did here consume 185. H.496, 3
Saith (As Salust **saith**) co-incident to feare.......162. H.430, 2
Or will be; for the Axiome **saith**,..............175. H.465, 44
Spenke has a strong breath, yet short Prayers **saith**: 283. H.884, 1
God tempteth no one (as S. Aug'stine **saith**)....380. N.150, 1
Jehovah, as Boëtius **saith**,......................382. N.168, 1
Or Good at all, (as learn'd Aquinas **saith**.).....383. N.173, 2
'Tis (as S. Bernard **saith**) but seemingly.........385. N.188, 4
But Mary cal'd then (as S. Ambrose **saith**).....386. N.192, 4
To burn, not shine (as learned Basil **saith**.)....387. N. 202, 2
That Christ did die, the Pagan **saith**;..........395. N.247, 1
Sake See Ceremony's-sake, Love's-sake
For pitties **sake** give your advice,...................8. H.13, 3
And for my **sake**, who ever did prefer..........137. H.341, 9
Mont. Love for thy **sake** will bring her to these hills 159. H.421, 35
Who for some sweet-hearts **sake**, did prove......169. H.449, 3
Little you are; for Womans **sake** be proud;.....212. H.600, 1
For my **sake** next, (though little) be not loud...212. H.600, 2
For old Religions **sake**,.........................212. H.604, 3
This Stone, for names **sake**, melts to teares.....257. H.764, 6
For loves **sake** asking almes of thee?...........312. H.1014, 2
O then! for mercies **sake**, behold.................344. N.29, 5
For this, or that occasions **sake**................361. N.83, 54
'Tis a gift for Christ His **sake**:..................363. N.93, 2
Salt See Spurting-salt
Dead when I am, first cast in **salt**, and bring......9. H.14, 7
Ile expiate with Sulphur, Haire, and **Salt**:.......77. H.197, 30
Their sacred **Salt** here, (not a little.)..........93. H.223, 118
I send my **salt**, my sacrifice...................146. H.377, 2
And spring fresh Rose-buds, while the **salt**, the wit 148. H.377, 73
And **salt**, which frets thy Suters; fly...........174. H.465, 25
Who can scoure Linnens with her own **salt** reeume? 178. H.474, 6
Our **salt**, our Corn, our Honie, Wine, and Oile) 225. H.642, 18
In no one Satyre there's a mite of **salt**..........238. H.692, 2
As stones and **salt** gloves use to give, even so...248. H.731, 3
Cast in **Salt**, for seasoning....................258. H.769, 2
The body's **salt**, the soule is; which when gon...332. H.1111, 1
— — — — — — — —,...........422. var. H.106, 60
Sacke is my life, my leaven, **salt** to all....426. ins. H.197, 48a
Saltcellar Both by a shining **Salt-seller**;..........133. H.336, 50
Saltless And tast thou them as **saltlesse** there,.....339. N.3, 5
Salust (As **Salust** saith) co-incident to feare.......162. H.430, 2
Salute Sending them forth, **Salute** no man by th' way: 378. N.137, 2
Salute me must, nor Strangers, Kin, or Friends...378. N.137, 8
— — — — — — — — —,..............422. var. H.106, 96
Salutes **Salutes** with tears of joy; when fires betray 77. H.197, 17
Salvages See Savages
Salvation With speed give sick men their **salvation**: 125. H.315, 2
Here, for the righteous mans **salvation**:...........349. N.44, 2
Salve Honey to **salve**, where he before did sting.....16. H.40, 8
Only one Soveraign **salve**, I know,..............60. H.157, 5
Yet ne'r can see that **salve** which brings........272. H.828, 7
Some **salve** to every sore, we may apply;.......274. H.841, 1
Salve for my body, and my mind...............342. N.17, 4
Affording **salve** of Soveraigntie................377. N.129, 4
The **salve** for this i'th Eucharist is found.......381. N.155, 2
Same See Selfsame
And did out-red the **same**.......................12. H.23, 4
In the **same** sweet eternity of love...............13. H.29, 2
And brought a rod, so whipt me with the **same**:....16. H.40, 2
(At first) infused with the **same**:.................24. H.73, 4
One drop now deads a spark; but if the **same**....40. H.113, 3
To th' board, so hot, as none co'd touch the **same**: 47. H.131, 2
Alas! the heat and death's the **same**;............50. H.140, 5
To see my hand; that by the **same**..............63. H.166, 3
And this **same** flower that smiles to day,.........84. H.208, 3
Thou sweetly canst convert the **same**............95. H.227, 12
What now you seem, be not the **same** indeed,..113. H.283, 56

No, no, that selfe **same** heart, that vow,.......134. H.336, 70
Or yawning rupture can the **same** devoure,....148. H.377, 107
Yet out alas! the deaths the **same**,..............155. H.406, 5
With hope you would allay the **same**:...........157. H.413, 2
Tels ye but this, they are the **same**,............180. H.478, 7
More honour had, then this **same** Flie;........186. H.497, 17
Induc't that inadultrate **same**.................245. H.720, 9
Down, and halfe drown'd me with the **same**:....283. H.883, 2
But had it been of Birch, the death's the **same**...306. H.986, 4
Christ I shall see, with these **same** eyes:........358. N.78, 4
Or prosper, but by that **same** tree.............371. N.114, 3
The **same**, who crownes the Conquerour, will be..382. N.163, 1
— — — — — — — — — — —,............436. var. H.336, 55
Sampler Come bring your **sampler**, and with Art,...10. H.20, 1
To work Love's **Sampler** onely here,............103. H.256, 2
As if Loves **Sampler** here was wrought:.......166. H.443, 36
Sanctified And (being to be **sanctifi'd**).........237. H.686, 2
Sanctify If then, (my Lord) to **sanctifie** my Muse..64. H.168, 7
Thee Julia, first, to **sanctifie** thy hands:..........299. H.957, 2
Sanctions See **State-sanctions**
Sanctity For **sanctity**, they have, to these,........92. H.223, 97
Sanctuary Thus let thy Rurall **Sanctuary** be....38. H.106, 137
Sand Then the **sand**, that makes the shore:.....102. H.253, 6
Who gripes too hard the dry and slip'rie **sand**,..221. H.633, 52
Before the last least **sand** of Thy ninth houre be run;
401. N.268, 8
— — — — — — — — — — —,..............421. var. H.106, 24
Sandless Seas shall be **sandlesse**; Fields devoid of grasse;
59. H.154, 7
Sands What's to be done? but on the **Sands**......94. H.225, 7
Or else spin out the thread of **sands**,............215. H.616, 7
Some few **sands** spent, we hence must go,.......233. H.670, 37
Tell me the motes, dust, **sands**, and speares......340. N.3, 11
In which were **sands** but few,..................346. N.38, 14
Sandy — — — — — — — — — — — —,........433. var. H.293, 10
Saphire There playes the **Saphire** with the Chrysolite.
30. H.88, 10
Sappha To gather Flowers **Sappha** went,........250. H.740, 1
Sappho **Sapho** next, a principall:..................15. H.39, 4
If **Sapho** droop; Daisies will open never,........41. H.118, 7
O **Sappho**! take..............................210. H.591, 2
Sapho, I will chuse to go.....................266. H.803, 1
Thou saist thou lov'st me **Sapho**; I say no;.....279. H.866, 1
Pardon my feares (sweet **Sapho**,) I desire......279. H.866, 3
Sappho's Whether my **Sapho's** breast,..........105. H.258, 3
Look upon **Sapho's** lip, and you will swear,......306. H.985, 1
Sat But on a Rock himselfe **sate** by,.............42. H.119, 3
We knew 'twas Flesh and Blood, that there **sate** mute.
95. H.228, 2
Upon your cheek **sate** Ysicles awhile:..........105. H.259, 11
Dew **sate** on Julia's haire,......................181. H.484, 1
She by the River **sate**, and sitting there,........251. H.743, 1
Sate by the Grave; and sadly sitting there,.......384. N.180, 9
Satan **Satan** o'recomes none, but by willingnesse....359. N.79, 2
Must last with **Satan**, to the end of life........362. N.91, 2
When we 'gainst **Satan** stoutly fight, the more....372. N.116, 1
Sate See **Sat**
Satiety Sick and surcharg'd with this **sacietie**:....297. H.949, 2
Satire In no one **Satyre** there's a mite of salt.....238. H.692, 2
Satires Prat He writes **Satyres**; but herein's the fault,
238. H.692, 1
Satisfaction Favour, Ile make full **satisfaction**;....27. H.82, 14
Great faults require great **satisfaction**...........312. H.1012, 2
Satisfied If not to th' whole, yet **satisfy'd** in part. 267. H.804, 12
Satisfies Give me the food that **satisfies** a Guest:..265. H.797, 1
Satisfy Thus thou can'st tearcely live to **satisfie**..35. H.106, 27
Thy way, Thou guiltlesse man, and **satisfie**.....398. N.263, 13
Saturity The sister to **saturitie**.................378. N.138, 2
Satyr The wanton **Satyre** did;..................203. H.563, 2
That **Satyre** he but burnt his lips;...............203. H.563, 5
As now a **Satyr**, then a Swan;...................215. H.616, 17
Satyre See **Satire**
Satyres See **Satires**
Sauce An equall mind is the best **sauce** for griefe. 333. H.1119, 2
To these for **sauce** the slaine stagges teares..435. ins. H.293, p
Saucy The **saucie** Subjects still will beare the sway.
138. H.345, 2
Savages And rude (almost) as rudest **Salvages**,....29. H.86, 12
Next, with severest **Salvages**;..................111. H.278, 4
Cuft with those watrie **savages**, ...372. N.118, 2
Save Spoile a house, to **save** a towne:..............21. H.61, 6
How I may **save** mine eyes.....................43. H.123, 24
To send, or **save**;..............................43. H.123, 35
(To **save** his life) twice am content to die.......70. H.181, 16
Stirs in our Sheep-walk? Amin. None **save** that my Ewes,
85. H.213, 4
Save only the Curst-Cipresse tree:...........132. H.336, 12
Save but his hat, and that he cannot mew.......144. H.372, 2
Save but some few Beanes left,.................173. H.460, 2
To **save**; when thou may'st kill a heart.........177. H.471, 4
To **save**.......................................246. H.724, 7
For the requitall; **save** this only one..........267. H.804, 3
What was't (ye Gods!) a dying man to **save**,...278. H.860, 3
Summer and Winter still to **save** his shoes,.....332. H.1116, 4
He His Church **save**, and the King,.............363. N.93, 7
God can do all things, **save** but what are known 382. N.166, 1
All's now fledd **saue** this alone.................418. A.9, 23

— — — — — — — — — — —,..............425. var. H.197, 8
Saves What **saves** the master of the House thereby?
118. H.292, 3
I'th' Seas, she **saves** her passengers..........134. H.336, 64
Rush **saves** his shooes, in wet and snowie wether;
332. H.1116, 1
But when by stripes He **saves** them, then 'tis known,
343. N.22, 3
It **saves** the soule, by drowning sin.............396. N.253, 2
Saving All **saving** health, and help for me.........342. N.17, 8
Saviour See **Maiden-saviour**
For why, my **Saviour**, with the sense............354. N.57, 3
Unto thy little **Saviour**;........................354. N.59, 2
Sick is my heart; O **Saviour**! do Thou please....358. N.77, 8
Thy Deerest **Saviour** renders thee but one.......371. N.112, 3
One Birth our **Saviour** had; the like none yet...384. N.182, 1
Justly our dearest **Saviour** may abhorre us,......388. N.209, 1
For Christ, your loving **Saviour**, hath..........400. N.266, 10
Saviour's Is (and hast seene) thy **Saviours** Sepulcher.
330. H.1100, 14
Gifts to my **Saviours** Sepulcher:...............402. N.270, 2
Is rowl'd away; and my sweet **Saviour's** gone!...403. N.271, 2
Savor A **savour** like unto a blessed field........112. H.283, 18
The wholesome **savour** of thy mighty Chines....146. H.377, 7
Savory And eat with thee a **savory** bit,..........321. H.1056, 5
Saw But when I **saw** thee wantonly to roame........6. H.3, 3
I **saw** a Cherry weep, and why?.................12. H.23, 1
Saw Cupid bitten by a flea:....................18. H.46, 2
I **saw** he had a Bow,...........................27. H.81, 17
Which when I **saw**, I made accesse.............51. H.142, 17
The Last Watch out, and **saw** the Dawning too...52. H.146, 4
He **saw** my Palme; and then, said he,..........63. H.166, 5
I **saw** about her spotlesse wrist,................64. H.169, 1
That Morne which **saw** me made a Bride,.......109. H.271, 1
By Dream I **saw**, one of the three.............153. H.399, 1
Sibb when she **saw** her face how hard it was,....249. H.732, 1
I **saw** a Flie within a Beade....................269. H.817, 1
And though I **saw** no Bow, I'm sure,..........295. H.942, 15
Me thought I **saw** (as I did dreame in bed)....313. H.1017, 1
Me thought I **saw** them stir, and gently move,..326. H.1080, 11
If through my Christ I **saw** not Thee..........395. N.246, 6

Say You **say** I love not, 'cause I doe not play......15. H.38, 1
But that I heard thy sweet breath **say**,............20. H.56, 5
When some shall **say**, Faire once my Silvia was;..21. H.62, 1
And nothing I did **say**:..........................24. H.75, 2
If thou wilt **say**,...............................29. H.87, 7
Mak'st easie Feare unto thee **say**,..............36. H.106, 74
While soft Opinion makes thy Genius **say**,......37. H.106, 115
Whither? **Say**, whither shall I fly,...............40. H.115, 1
For to **say** truth, all Garlands are thy due;......41. H.117, 9
Prethee (lest Maids sho'd censure thee) but **say**..42. H.122, 9
Then **say**, I've sent one more..................43. H.123, 13
Yet **say**; sho'd she condemne..................43. H.123, 25
Then **say**; my part.............................43. H.123, 27
Say too, She wo'd have this;...................43. H.123, 31
Since I must leave thee; and enforc'd, must **say**..46. H.128, 39
Gryll will not therefore **say** a Grace for it.........48. H.135, 4
And must we part, because some **say**,...........48. H.136, 1
You **say**, to me-wards your affection's strong;....51. H.143, 1
For that, Matrons **say**, a measure.............55. H.149, 79
But now kisse her, and thus **say**, ...56. H.149, 119
Doves, two'd **say**, yee bill too long..............57. H.149, 140
But when ye both can **say**,.....................58. H.149, 167
If thou wilt **say**, that I shall live with thee;......60. H.156, 3
Am I despis'd, because you **say**,.................63. H.164, 1
Hor. **Say** our first loves we sho'd revoke,........70. H.181, 17
Say, are thy medicines made to be...............74. H.191, 3
Say, if there be 'mongst many jems here; one....76. H.194, 3
When thou thy selfe dar'st **say**, thy Iles shall lack
78. H.197, 47
(Some **say**) for joy, to see those Kitlings drown'd 80. H.200, 2
Amar. With all white luck to you. Mirt. But **say**, What news
85. H.213, 3
Betimes my Mattens **say**:.......................87. H.214, 2
To **say**, Amen.................................87. H.214, 8
That where you grew, scarce man can **say**........87. H.216, 3
Then **say**, if one th'ast seene more fine.........90. H.223a, 5
The first Act's doubtfull, (but we **say**)..........94. H.225, 9
Say (if she's fretfull) I have bands 98 H.238, 6
Men **say** y'are faire; and faire ye are, 'tis true;..98. H.241, 1
And **say**, thou bring'st this Hony-bag from me:..100. H.248, 2
And beat ye so, (as some dare **say**)............105. H.260, 7
You **say** y'are sweet; how sho'd we know.......112. H.282, 1
Say, or doe we not descrie...................112. H.283, 7
Maides sho'd **say**, or Virgins sing,............117. H.285, 11
You **say**, you love me; that I thus must prove;..126. H.317, 1
How speaks it, **say**? 2. Do you but this,........130. H.329, 17
Say, we must part (sweet mercy blesse........134. H.336, 65
Doting, Ile weep and **say** (In Truth).........135. H.336, 119
Will ye heare, what I can **say**................138. H.342, 1
A thousand times, more sweare, then **say**,.....149. H.377, 132
Oft have I heard both Youths and Virgins **say**,..149. H.378, 1
But yet get children (as the neighbours **say**.)....156. H.411, 2
Say, have ye sence, or do you prove............158. H.420, 7
Why then, **say**, what is he...................160. H.422, 17
Say, What sho'd Roots do with a purse in print,..162. H.427, 3

Craw cracks in sirrop; and do's stinking say,...162. H.428, 1
To lye with Mab, though all say no............165. H.443, 12
And say short Prayers; and when we have done so,
168. H.445, 4
What Conscience, say, is it in thee............168. H.446, 1
Will say our grace, and die...................173. H.460, 6
You say y'are young; but when your Teeth are told
173. H.462, 1
Huncks ha's no money (he do's sweare, or say)..173. H.463, 1
But if they wooe thee, do thou say,............174. H.465, 29
Though thou art young, thou canst say no,......174. H.465, 34
Feacie (some say) doth wash her clothes i'th' Lie
178. H.474, 1
Both to the Cocks-tread say Amen;...........179. H.476, 20
Yet to the Lares this we'l say,...............179. H.476, 36
I prithee speake: Lyc. I will. End. Say on:....183. H.492, 5
If Dorset say, what Herrick writes, is good?....187. H.506, 6
Ile have nought to say to you:.................191. H.519, 6
Lady, this I know you'l say;...................194. H.527, 2
Next, hang'd for Theeving: Now the people say, 195. H.532, 3
But he will say, who e'r those Circlets seeth,....197. H.543, 3
Modest I will be; but one word Ile say.......201. H.557, 21
If Men can say that beauty dyes;.............203. H.564, 1
I vanish; more I had to say:..................207. H.575, 65
You say you'l kiss me, and I thanke you for it: 210. H.588, 1
Say then, how ill sho'd I have sped............212. H.599, 3
And rare, Ile say (my dearest Crew)..........217. H.620, 11
What made that mirth last night? the neighbours say,
219. H.630, 1
Say, who's the worst, th' exactor, or the whore? 220. H.631, 4
Gander (they say) doth each night pisse a Bed: 223. H.636, 2
Lungs (as some, say) ne'r sets him down to eate, 223. H.637, 1
Their fashion is, but to say no, to take it.......235. H.675, 2
That thou shalt say (thy selfe) 'tis rare;......243. H.716, 33
Say what thou art. Ph. I prithee first draw neare. 248. H.730, 4
My warbling note will say I'm Phylomel.........248. H.730, 8
Till thou shalt say, I ve paid thee with a song...248. H.730, 22
Tygers and Beares (I've heard some say)......252. H.746, 3
Shall heare his Clarke say,....................256. H.762, 16
Sweet Oenone, doe but say....................264. H.790, 1
Wo'd give (some say) her soule unto the Devill...266. H.801, 2
Say, do's she frown? still countermand her threats:
270. H.820, 3
One word more I had to say;..................270. H.821, 5
Ere Ave-Mary thou canst say..................271. H.824, 3
Say, what wo'd many do?......................273. H.833, 6
Shall I say her Altars be......................273. H.836, 3
If you say (I) Blush-guiltinesse will shew it....274. H.837, 6
Say, is 't for reall griefe he mourns? not so;...275. H.842, 3
Yet the houres say 'tis late:..................276. H.850, 4
One short charme if you but say..............276. H.850, 11
Twilight, no other thing is, Poets say,..........278. H.858, 1
Thou saist thou lov'st me Sapho; I say no;......279. H.866, 1
Naught are all Women: I say no,..............283. H.885, 1
But trust me now I dare not say,..............288. H.908, 5
Say how, or when.............................289. H.911, 2
If this can be, say then, what need............297. H.948, 13
Physitians say Repletion springs...............298. H.951, 1
With my weake voice Ile sing, or say..........303. H.973, 13
Say, what is't that thou do'st aile?............305. H.984, 9
The Twi-light is no other thing (we say).......319. H.1046, 1
Drawn was his tooth; but stanke so, that some say,
323. H.1066, 3
Mattens sing, or Mattens say:................324. H.1069, 2
For ought that I could say....................346. N.38, 6
As to speak, Lord, say and hold................347. N.40, 4
My Cup can say,...............................353. N.56, 5
Then I co'd say, that house is bare,............358. N.75, 9
Call, and I'le come; say Thou, the when, and where:
358. N.77, 13
If we may ask the reason, say;.................364. N.96, 11
Or say, if this new Birth of ours..............367. N.102, 4
To Voices, say, Amen.........................369. N.106, 16
Unto the prison, I'le say, no;.................370. N.107, 12
Let me say grace when there's no more.........376. N.124, 6
Christ, I have read, did to His Chaplains say,...378. N.137, 1
The Mountains of the Scriptures are (some say) 381. N.157, 1
To God for vengeance? yes say I;..............387. N.203, 2
The Doctors, in the Talmud, say,...............388. N.206, 1
God, He is there, where's nothing else (Schooles say)
388. N.207, 3
Either as when (the learned Schoolemen say)..388. N.210, 2
Say, 'tis not free, 'tis then no sin at all........389. N.218, 2
'Tis never read there (as the Fathers say).......396. N.249, 5
Which done, Lord say, The rest is mine.......400. N.267, 13
Att what tyme to say I, or noe,...............407. A.2, 26
He was—Cha. Say what. Euc. Ay me, my woes are deep.
416. A.8, 11
Thy thoughts to say, I backe am come...441. ins. H.465, 14b
Sayest Thou say'st my lines are hard;...........138. H.344, 1
Thou sayest Loves Dart.......................273. H.833, 1
Thou saist thou lov'st me Sapho; I say no;......279. H.866, 1
Thou say'st I'm dull; if edge-lesse so I be,....327. H.1081, 1
Saying Then grieve her not, with saying........56. H.149, 113
'Twas Cesars saying: Kings no lesse Conquerors are
271. H.825, 1

Says When that day comes, whose evening sayes I'm gone
14. H.35, 1
Fone sayes, those mighty whiskers he do's weare, 39. H.110, 1
Gryll eates, but ne're sayes Grace; To speak the troth,
48. H.135, 1
For why sayes he, all debts and their arreares,...142. H.363, 3
Of some rough Groom, who (yirkt with Corns) sayes, Sir
146. H.377, 21
And sweetly sings, but yet his breath sayes no...149. H.381, 2
Jill sayes, of what? sayes Jack, on that sweet kisse,
186. H.498, 3
The food of Poets; so I thought sayes Jill,......186. H.498, 5
Let me feed full, till that I fart, sayes Jill......186. H.498, 8
This Christmas, but his want wherwith, sayes Nay.
238. H.693, 2
Glory no other thing is (Tullie sayes)..........241. H.710, 1
Love thou dost, though Love sayes Nay........264. H.790, 2
Sometimes (in mirth) he sayes each whelk's a sparke
273. H.834, 3
Science puffs up, sayes Gut, when either Pease..327. H.1085, 1
He sayes his fore and after Grace for it:.......332. H.1112, 2
If meate he wants, then Grace he sayes to see..332. H.1112, 3
Then prayers repel'd, (sayes Cassiodore)........383. N.170, 2
Sabbaths are threefold, (as S. Austine sayes.)...386. N.194, 1
Noah the first was (as Tradition sayes)..........386. N.195, 1
Confession twofold is (as Austine sayes,)........395. N.243, 1
(S. Ambrose sayes) without the Thorn:........396. N.251, 2
Scab The Extreame Scabbe take thee, and thine, for me.
7. H.6, 6
Scald See Scall
Scale But yet if boundlesse Lust must skaile...175. H.465, 53
Scales The glow-wormes eyes; the shining scales 166. H.443, 72
Scall Blanch swears her Husband's lovely; when a scald
33. H.99, 1
Scallop's My Palmers hat; my Scallops shell;...123. H.306, 3
Scalp Your leane scalp to sensuring..............418. A.9, 32
Scan Cato the Censor, sho'd he scan each here.....28. H.84, 6
Scanned If but lookt on; struck dead, if scan'd by Thee.
301. H.962, 6
'Scape The most of Thee shall scape the funerall..200. H.554, 2
Bite of themselves to scape away.........440. ins. H.443, 56b
'Scaped But having scapt temptations shelfe,....176. H.465, 83
Scarce As if to stir it scarce had leave:..........66. H.175, 6
He drank so much he scarce co'd stir;..........71. H.182, 9
Of ashes, scarce suffice.........................81. H.201, 43
And scarce leav'st here........................85. H.211, 10
That where you grew, scarce man can say..........87. H.216, 3
And for what use, scarce man wo'd think it....93. H.223, 124
Before the Press scarce one co'd see...........287. H.899, 1
That Teare shall scarce be dri'd before.........328. H.1090, 10
Faile and scarce leaue to be showne............418. A.9, 29
Scarcely That scarcely stirs the nodding leaves of Trees:
225. H.642. 16
And Garlick chives not scarcely:..............234. H.674, 4
Scare Hang up Hooks, and Sheers to scare......284. H.891, 1
Let not that Day Gods Friends and Servants scare:
376. N.126, 1
Scarecrow (The skarcrow vnto Mankinde) that doth breed
411. A.3, 52
Scarecrow-like Yet scarre-crow-like I'le walk, as one,
235. H.677, 7
Scared But though it scar'd, it did not bite......116. H.284, 6
Scare-fires From noise of Scare-fires rest ye free, 121. H.299, 1
Scaring From scaring you or yours this night...123. H.306, 15
Scarlet — — — — — — — —, ...435. var. H.293, 42t
Scarlets Which Rubies, Corralls, Scarlets, all......12. H.23, 7
Scar's That Scarr's no Schisme, but the sign of grace.
180. H.481, 2
Scatterest That scatter'st Spirit and Lust; whose purest shine,
45. H.128, 12
Scean See Scene
Sceans See Scenes
Scene Without some Scean cast over,............76. H.193, 39
No scurrile jest; no open Sceane is laid........148. H.377, 77
Artlesse the Sceane was; and that monstrous sin 150. H.382, 13
But still the envious Scene between............247. H.729, 7
I'm a man for ev'ry Sceane...................253. H.750, 18
Your part's to grant; my Scean must be to move.
274. H.837, 4
If Tythe-pigs faile, then will he shift the scean, 325. H.1076, 3
No, No, this Scene from Thee takes life and sense,
399. N.263, 26
Scenes But yet, though Love likes well such Scenes as these,
24. H.74, 9
Sceanes to cheat us neatly drawne...............76. H.195, 8
Wherewith ye make those merry Sceanes,.......127. H.319, 18
Ile have no Sceans, or Curtains drawn:..........154. H.402, 2
Who art a man for all Sceanes; unto whom....298. H.955, 3
Here's words with lines, and lines with Scenes consent,
415, A.7, 7
To teach the truth of Scenes, and more for thee,
443. var. H.575, 53
Scent Made all that touch't her with her scent,......9. H.15, 11
Give them the scent of Amber-Greece:...........20. H.54, 2
And leave no scent behind ye:...................83. H.207, 2
Or she, in sweetest scent......................105. H.260, 4
To lend the world your scent and smile.........126. H.318, 5

Well I can quaffe, I **see**,....................227. H.653, 9
Is Zelot pure? he is: ye **see** he weares.........232. H.666, 1
Once past and gone, no more shall **see**.........234. H.671, 2
And, wretched, I did **see**,...................240. H.705, 2
To **see** the day spring from the pregnant East,..242. H.713, 2
You **see** this gentle streame, that glides,........244. H.720, 1
And **see**, if there it keeps unspent.............245. H.720, 5
Ch. A sound I heare, but nothing yet can **see**,..248. H.730, 5
For if you cleave them, we shall **see**...........250. H.738, 3
But feares not now to **see** her safety sold........251. H.745, 5
Whatsoever thing I **see**,........................253. H.750, 1
What Fate decreed, Time now ha's made us **see**..254. H.756, 1
Examples lead us, and wee likely **see**,..........255. H.759, 1
Morris-dancers thou shalt **see**,.................255. H.761, 7
See this, View that, and all the other bounds:..259. H.771, 4
Next, when I cast mine eyes and **see**..........261. H.779, 4
Rather then I once wo'd **see**,.................266. H.803, 4
These I but wish for; but thy selfe shall **see**,....269. H.818, 9
'Tis religious part to **see**......................270. H.821, 3
My Julia thou shalt **see**,......................271. H.824, 2
I co'd but **see** thee yesterday..................272. H.828, 1
Yet ne'r can **see** that salve which brings........272. H.828, 7
To **see** me bleed, and not desire...............272, H.828, 11
Then depart, but **see** ye tread..................274. H.838, 7
Lest rapt from hence, I **see** thee lye..........275. H.844, 3
Or **see** thy injur'd Leaves serve well,..........275. H.844, 5
Or **see** the Grocers in a trice,..................275. H.844, 7
But yet those blessed gates I **see**..............277. H.854, 3
And thus through Woman-kind we **see**..........283. H.885, 9
Before the Press scarce one co'd **see**............287. H.899, 1
Looke in my Book, and herein **see**,............288. H.906, 1
What I by chance did **see**;.....................288. H.908, 6
And **see** his Robin Herrick lack,................290. H.918, 3
Praise they that will Times past, I joy to **see**....292. H.927, 1
How fierce was I, when I did **see**..............294. H.939, 1
And we shall **see** in little space...............297. H.948, 11
Love is a sirrup; and who er'e we **see**..........297. H.949, 1
If hap it must, that I must **see** thee lye......300. H.960, 1
Next, when I **see** Thee towring in the skie,......301. H.966, 3
I must confess, distinction none I **see**..........301. H.966, 9
Now thou art dead, no eye shall ever **see**,......302. H.967, 1
So many Goblins you shall **see**..................304. H.980, 9
See mine eyes are weeping ripe................305. H.984, 13
Ah Biancha! now I **see**,.......................307. H.991, 1
See dejected;..................................308. H.993, 27
See erected....................................308. H.993, 30
When to a House I come, and **see**.............310. H.1004, 1
I think no other but I **see**.....................311. H.1010, 3
The bound (almost) now of my book I **see**....313. H.1019, 1
Then did I live when I did **see**..............313. H.1020, 1
Grow young with Tydes, and though I **see** ye never,
316. H.1028, 25
Yet sho'd I chance, (my Wicks) to **see**........321. H.1056, 7
When to thy Porch I come, and (ravisht) **see**..324. H.1071, 1
Whether I was my selfe, or else did **see**.......326. H.1080, 1
There did I **see** the Reverend Rectresse stand,..326. H.1080, 15
That Fame, and Fames rear'd Pillar, thou shalt **see**
329. H.1092, 5
Besides ye **see** me daily grow..................329. H.1093, 3
And I ere long, my Girles shall **see**,............329. H.1093, 5
Shall by his hearing quickly come to **see**......330. H.1100, 17
If meate he wants, then Grace he sayes to **see**..332. H.1112, 3
See, the fier's by: Farewell...................334. H.1125, 8
God is all fore-part; for, we never **see**..........342. N.18, 1
For if thou dost, thou then shalt **see**............344. N.29, 3
To **see** far off the smoaking Villages............352. N.51, 10
Do **see**, and heare.............................353. N.56, 11
And these mine eyes shall **see**..................354. N.58, 5
Shall **see** the hug'd impietie:....................357. N.72, 8
To **see** the waste; but 'twas repli'd..............358. N.75, 6
That I might **see** the cheerfull peeping day.......358. N.77, 7
Christ I shall **see**, with these same eyes:........358. N.78, 4
Thus, on the sudden? 4. Come and **see**..........364. N.96, 17
We **see** Him come, and know him ours,..........364. N.96, 22
The Storax fries; and ye may **see**,...............365. N.97, 8
For, now unlesse ye **see** Him bleed,..............365. N.97, 17
Then, like a perfum'd Altar, **see**................366. N.98, 10
But only come, and **see** Him rest..............367. N.102, 13
To pay Thee that I owe, since what I **see**.......368. N.103, 3
Permit mine eyes to **see**........................369. N.106, 1
When I a ship **see** on the Seas,..................372. N.118, 1
Come pitie us, all ye, who **see**..................373. N.123, 1
Who **see**, or heare poor Widdowes crie:.......373. N. 123, 4
And though thou here li'st dead, we **see**........375. N.123, 71
And Thou my Pipkinnet shalt **see**,..............377. N.130, 3
Or, ne're so meane a peece, but men might **see**..389. N.214, 3
Wo'd **see** Thy Face, and He not by..............395. N.245, 6
Whom all the flux of Nations comes to **see**;.....399. N.263, 22
That those, who **see** Thee nail'd unto the Tree,..399. N.263, 34
And we (Thy Lovers) while we **see** Thee keep..399. N.263, 36
That done, wee'l **see** Thee sweetly buried.......399. N.263, 39
And, if I **see** Thee posted there,................399. N.265, 7
When I Thy gentle Heart do **see**...............400. N.267, 3
Chor. Lord, I'le not **see** Thee to drink all.....400. N.267, 10
Look down, and **see**.........................401. N.268, 26
May **see** it sprout forth streames of muscadine.....405. A.1, 50
To **see** two tablets of pure Ivory.................406. A.1, 96
And Lastly, **see** thou bring to hym...............408. A.2, 73
Guesse, soe departe; yett stay A while to[o] **see** 411. A.3, 59
See we haue fyr'd..............................413. A.4, 24
And see o[r] Alter burne........................413. A.4, 32
Languish and looke but thy returne **see** neuer.....414, A.5, 8
Thy Pompe of Playes which thousands come to **see**, 415. A.7, 3
Ravish our spirits, that entranc't wee **see**........415. A.7, 17
See th' Epitomè of yow,........................417. A.9, 8
— — — — — — — — — — —,.............422. var. H.106, 120
— — — — — — — — — — —,.............427. var. H.197, 73
See how he waves his hand, and through his eyes
430. ins. H.283, 40a
for your approach, yet **see** their Altars pine?
431. ins. H.283, 60f
— — — — — — — — — — — —,.............432. var. H.283, 121
— — — — — — — — — — — —,.............436. var. H.336, 51
— — — — — — — — — — —,.................448. var. A.3, 1
— — — — — — — — — — — —,..............453. var. H.283, 12

Seed See Hope-seed
The **Seed**; so sow'd these Tares throughout my Book.
4. Ap., 4
And Leaves did heale, all sick of humane **seed**:..61. H.161, 2
When as the chosen **seed** shall spring.........89. H.219, 19
To blow, and **seed**, and so away;.............126. H.318, 2
Their sacred **seed**:...........................133. H.336, 27
A little **Seed** best fits a little Soyle,............249. H.733, 4
To drench, but not to drown our **seed**...........279. H.867, 6
Because begot of my Immortall **seed**.............280. H.869, 6
(From which poore **seed**, and rudely sown)......297. H.948, 7
Have we of Women or their **seed**?.............297. H.948, 14
But likewise sup'rabundant **seed**;.................356. N.66, 2
By Thee, Deare God, God gives man **seed**........358. N.75, 7
One **seed** of life left, 'tis to keep................361. N.83, 59
not on the flesh of beasts, but on the **seede**
432. ins. H.283, 70f
The silkwormes **seed**, a little moth........434. ins. H.293, 41i
— — — — — — — — — — — —,.............435. var. H.293, 21e

Seed-pearl A pure **seed-Pearle** of Infant dew,..119. H.293, 21

Seeds The **seeds** of Treason choake up as they spring,
10. H.17, 1
Heavy, to hurt those sacred **seeds** of thee......73. H.186, 20
Enfeebles much the **seeds** of wickednesse.........109. H.270, 2
Beshiver'd into **seeds** of Raine;.................340. N.3, 10
As for thy birth, and better **seeds**..............407. A.2, 19

Seeing **Seeing** those painted Countries; and so guesse
36. H.106, 79
Not **seeing** her at all to stir,....................46. H.130, 5
And **seeing** her not dead, but all disleav'd;.......46. H.130, 11
And **seeing** it, I made a stay....................73. H.187, 5
Seeing thee Soame, I see a Goodly man,.........176. H.466, 1

Seek Or flie abroad to **seeke** for woe..............6. H.2, 20
I bade him not goe **seek**;.........................18. H.45, 2
Shall I **seek** (for speedy ease)...................40. H.115, 7
Nor will I **seek** supply..........................43. H.123, 19
And in that sincere Christall **seek**, ...63. H.164, 8
Illustrious Idoll! co'd th' Ægyptians **seek**.......78. H.197, 57
Play ye at Hide or **Seek**,.........................83. H.207, 7
In yond' Carnation goe and **seek**, ...106. H.263, 7
I'le **seek** him in your Bonnet brave;............156. H.412, 13
Ile **seek** him in your eyes;.....................156. H.412, 14
Ile **seek** him there; I know, ere this,.........156. H.412, 17
And on the seaventh, he has his Notes to **seek**...163. H.435, 2
I co'd never **seeke** to please....................182. H.490, 5
To **seek**, and bring rough Pepper home:......229. H.662, 6
To **seeke**, and find some few Immortals out.....267. H.804, 6
Kings **seek** their Subjects good: Tyrants their owne.
278. H.861, 2
My soule would one day goe and **seeke**.......281. H.876, 1
To **seek** of God more then we well can find,......356, N.70, 1
Declare to us, bright Star, if we shall **seek**......367. N.102, 8
Did **seek** my soule to swallow,..................373. N.122, 6
Yett to bee found when hee shall **seeke**..........409. A.2, 78

Seeks He that is hurt **seeks** help: sin is the wound;
381. N.155, 1

Seem What now you **seem**, be not the same indeed,
113. H.283, 56
Not wrathfull **seem**, or fright the Maide,......145. H.376, 4
But if this may **seem** too much...............223. H.638, 21
Though He may **seem** to over-act His part:....341. N.10, 2
Seem like the Spring-time of the yeere?........364. N.96, 13
Yet sowre and grim Thou'dst **seem** to me;......395. N.246, 5
Like rose leaves, white and redd **seeme** mingled...404. A.1, 18
In w[ch] the veynes ymplanted **seeme** to lye........405. A.1, 47
From w[ch] two armes like branches **seem** to spread..406. A.1, 97
Some bitts of thimbles **seeme** to dresse...440. ins. H.443, 45aa
— — — — — — — — — — — —,.............440. var. H.443, 88

Seemed So that my Lucia **seem'd** to me.........16. H.41, 12
And snugging there, they **seem'd** to lye.........25. H.78, 3
It **seem'd** by this time to admit the touch;......47. H.131, 5
Whose woollie-bubbles **seem'd** to drowne........167. H.443, 88
Light of the Moon, **seem'd** to comply,..........167. H.443, 98
Where both **seem'd** proud; the Flie to have......185. H.497, 3
She **seem'd** to quench loves fires that there did glow.
251. H.742, 2
Smooth was the Sea, and **seem'd** to call.........294. H.937, 1

So long (it seem'd) as Maries Faith was small,..386. N.192, 1
— — — — — — — — — — — —,..............433. var. H.293, 31
— — — — — — — — — — — —,..............443. var. A.1, 97
Seemingly 'Tis (as S. Bernard saith) but **seemingly**, 385. N.188, 4
Seemly That done; when both of you have **seemly** fed, 124. H.313, 9
— — — — — — — — — — — —,..............439. var. H.443, 29
Seems Now **seems** she to expresse..............55. H.149, 73
To meet it, when it woo's and **seemes** to fold..115. H.283, 116
Every time **seemes** short to be,..............162. H.431, 1
With griefe; **seemes** longer than a yeare........162. H.431, 4
It **seems** a wonder unto me,..................163. H.434, 2
Of the shie Virgin, **seems** to deck............166. H.443, 64
Reapes eyes so rawe are, that (it **seemes**) the flyes 282. H.879, 1
And **seems** halfe ravisht, when he looks upon....295. H.941, 3
And Time **seems** then, not for to flie, but creep;..358. N.77, 2
Seemes like Apollo's when the morne he blesses..404. A.1, 2
throaned in a saffron Evening, **seemes** to chyme 431. ins. H.283, 601
— — — — — — — — — — — —,............440. ins. H.443, 45aa
— — — — — — — — — — — —,..............440. var. H.443, 98
Seen A telling what rare sights h'ad **seen**:........13. H.27, 8
Which being **seen**,..............................30. H.89, 6
When quiet grown sh'ad **seen** them,..............31. H.92, 10
Come, you are faire; and sho'd be **seen**..........49. H.136, 24
Noone-day and Midnight shall at once be **seene**:..59. H.154, 1
Hoping t'ave **seene** of it my fill;..............67. H.175, 20
Rise; and put on your Foliage, and be **seene**.....68. H.178, 15
At Noone of Day, was **seene** a silver Star,......86. H.213, 20
You are a Tulip **seen** to day,..................87. H.216, 1
Had Wolves or Tigers **seen** but thee,............89. H.219, 3
Rare Temples thou hast **seen**, I know,..........90. H.223a, 1
Then say, if one th'ast **seene** more fine..........90. H.223a, 5
Or that ye have not **seen** as yet................104. H.257, 20
Many a sweet-fac't Wood-Nymph here is **seene**,..107. H.265, 5
And **seen** them in a Round:..................110. H.274, 10
W'ave **seen** the past-best Times, and these......133. H.336, 17
Repeat the Times that I have **seen**!..........135. H.336, 116
No more is **seen** the Arch of Peace............139. H.353, 4
Or **seen** rich Rubies blushing through..........164. H.440, 7
I have **seen** many Maidens to have haire;......205. H.571, 1
These **seen**, thou go'st to view thy flocks.......230. H.662, 40
When of thy ragg'd Escutcheons shall be **seene**...231. H.664, 3
Kings must not oft be **seen** by publike eyes;....236. H.682, 1
Deni'd the Mask I wo'd have **seen**..............247. H.729, 8
To be, and not **seen** when and where they will...250. H.737, 2
And Aire-like, leave no pression to be **seen**......250. H.737, 7
Yet he'le be thought or **seen**,..................259. H.772, 21
No, but because he wo'd not have it **seen**,.......275. H.843, 3
T'ave your blushes **seen** by day...............276. H.850, 14
My desp'rate feares, in love, had **seen**..........279. H.863, 15
In depth of silence, heard, and **seene** of none....298. H.954, 3
And let not a man then be **seen** here,..........317. H.1035, 15
As those your Ladies may in time be **seene**,....326. H.1080, 23
Is sober virtue, **seen** to move her sphere.......327. H.1087, 2
What others have with cheapnesse **seene**, and ease, 330. H.1100, 1
Is (and hast **seene**) thy Saviours Sepulcher.....330. H.1100, 14
If **seen**, thou lik'st me, Deb, in none of these,..331. H.1108, 2
Known, or els **seen** to be the emptier:..........341. N.15, 4
Then is the horror of the trespasse **seen**........346. N.37, 2
Had all been poore, who had His Bounty **seen**?..356. N.69, 4
He's **seen**, He's **seen**, why then a Round,......368, N.102, 15
And that His treble Honours may be **seen**,......368. N.102, 23
Seene to the world, Ile giue the skore..........407. A.2, 2
Sees All things decay with Time: The Forrest **sees** 23. H.69, 1
But **sees** these things within thy Map..........36. H.106, 72
And eyes, it neither **sees** or heares...........174. H.465, 22
Whom this Morne **sees** most fortunate,..........208. H.583, 2
The Ev'ning **sees** in poore estate..............208. H.583, 3
None **sees** the fardell of his faults behind......253. H.751, 2
Spokes when he **sees** a rosted Pig, he swears.....305. H.982, 1
She **sees** no teares,..........................314. H.1024, 9
When the artlesse Doctor **sees**..................347. N.41, 13
God crowns our goodnesse, where so ere He **sees**, 356. N.71, 3
That **sees** December turn'd to May..............364. N.96, 10
That **sees** noe setting Sunn.......................413. A.4, 15
which **sees** the body fedd, yet pined..........432. ins. H.283, 70j
See'st Where (though thou see'st not) thou may'st think upon 20. H.55, 5
Seest thou those Diamonds which she weares....130. H.330, 1
See'st, thou that Cloud as silver cleare,..........139. H.348, 1
Then, when Thou see'st thine Age all turn'd to gold, 181. H.483, 9
Thou **seest** a present God-like Power.........230. H.662, 31
Seest thou that Cloud that rides in State.......269. H.815, 1
Burn first thine incense; next, when as thou **see'st** 286. H.898, 5
Thou **seest** me Lucia this year droope,..........303. H.973, 1
And tell us then, when as thou **seest**............365. N.97, 12
Where round about Thou **seest** but all things vaine, 371. N.113, 3
— — — — — — — — — — — —,..........422. var. H. 106, 72
And thinke each man thou **seest** doth doome 441. ins. H.465, 14a
See't See **See**
Thou might'st but onely **see't**, not taste it.......37. H.106, 120
And weep to **see't**; yet this thing doe,..........61. H.159, 20
And open fields, and we not **see't**?..............68. H.178, 38
I **see't** in's puris naturalibus:.................187. H.502, 2
Seeth But he will say, who e'r those Circlets **seeth**, 197. H.543, 3
Seizure To make a **seisure** on the light,........164. H.441, 3
Selden Live thou a **Selden**, that's a Demi-god....143. H.365, 12
Seldom For **seldome** use commends the pleasure. 38. H.106, 140
How we watch, and **seldome** sleep;..............82. H.203, 11
But **seldome** from suspition free:..............118. H.291, 14
Seldome or never, knows a wain,..............143. H.369, 2
Seldome comes Glorie till a man be dead.........218. H.623, 2
'Tis never, or but **seldome** knowne,..............264. H.788, 1
Great Cities **seldome** rest: If there be none...316. H.1030, 1
Rumpe is a Turne-broach, yet he **seldome** can..331. H.1106, 1
Seldome brings order, but confusion..............392. N.230, 8
Selecting **Selecting** here, both Herbs, and Flowers; 289. H.912, 2
Self See **One-self-sweet-conspiring**
Smiles to it **selfe**, and guilds the roofe with mirth; 7. H.8, 6
But so, as that her **self** should be...............8. H.11, 9
Love and my **selfe** (beleeve me) on a day........17. H.44, 1
And did my **selfe** disclose.......................26. H.81, 15
No part besides must of thy **selfe** be known,.....30. H.88, 11
Thy **selfe**, if want comes to endure:...........37. H.106, 104
And the brisk Mouse may feast her **selfe** with crums, 37. H.106, 123
To thine owne **selfe**; and knowne to few.......38. H.106, 136
(Eternall in thy **self**) that canst controule......45. H.128, 20
'Tis her erroneous **self** has made a braine.......46. H.128, 43
As is thy powerful **selfe**. Prethee not smile;....46. H.128, 45
Night now hath watch'd her **self** half blind;...54. H.149, 31
Feels in it **selfe** a fire;.......................57. H.149, 133
And to thy **selfe** be best this sentence knowne,..67. H.177, 3
When thou thy **selfe** dar'st say, thy Iles shall lack 78. H.197, 47
More shak't thy **selfe**, then she is scorch't by thee. 82. H.204. 14
And break thy **self** in shivers on her eye.........87. H.215, 10
And see your **selfe** to beautifie my Book;........94. H.226, 2
And caught'st thy **selfe** the more by twenty fold:..97. H.236, 2
First cur'd thy **selfe**; then come and cure me...97. H.236, 4
But whither, I my **selfe** not know..............111. H.278, 2
Set on your **selfe**, by being nice:..............113. H.283, 54
Or hell it **selfe** a powerfull Bulwarke is?......116. H.283, 146
To make but One (and that's thy **selfe**) admir'd. 121. H.301, 6
(Sweet as your **selfe**, and newly blown)........126. H.318, 8
Crossing thy **selfe**; come thus to sacrifice:.....127. H.320, 2
No, no, that **selfe** same heart, that vow,.......134. H.336, 70
Live in thy peace; as for my **selfe**,............134. H.336, 73
True to your **self**, and sheets, you'l have me swear, 136. H.338, 1
As for my **self**, since time a thousand cares....140. H.355, 5
Sil. Words sweet as Love it **self**. Montano, Hark. 159. H.421, 17
It **selfe** to live or dye........................164. H.441, 12
No, live thee to thy **selfe**, and keep............175. H.465, 47
Had'st power thy **selfe** to keep this vow;......176. H.465, 82
Know vertue taught thee, not thy **selfe**..........176. H.465, 84
And Thrones, thy **selfe** one of Those Senatours: 176. H.466, 4
He Boded good-luck to thy **Selfe** and Spouse...181. H.483, 12
Her **self** i'th' silken Sepulchre.................186. H.497, 14
Of your own **selfe**, a Publick Theater...........187, H.506, 2
To make thy Maids and **selfe** free mirth,.........193. H.521, 49
Dull to my **selfe**, and almost dead to these....214. H.612, 1
Thy **selfe**, which thou put'st other men unto.....214. H.614, 2
To kill her **selfe** for Demophon...............215. H.616, 14
Co'd reade the Intext but my **selfe** alone.......227. H.652, 6
But her **self** held fast by none................232. H.665, 14
Thy servant, not thy own **self**, sweat,........233. H.670, 20
That thou shalt say (thy **selfe**) 'tis rare;.......243. H.716, 33
And by your **self**, the best....................258. H.767, 17
Here I my **selfe** might likewise die,............265. H.794, 1
These I but wish for; but thy **selfe** shall see,....269. H.818, 9
Fortune her **selfe** can lay no claim to it.........272. H.830, 2
Immortall **selfe**, shall boldly trust..............278. H.859, 5
My **selfe** now live: this age best pleaseth mee....292. H.927, 2
My Julia wash her **self** in thee!................294. H.939, 2
Into thy streames my **self** I threw,............294. H.939, 7
Lost to the world; lost to my **selfe**; alone.......298. H.954, 1
Because thy **selfe** art comming to the Presse:..298. H.955, 10
Whether I was my **selfe**, or else did see.......326. H.1080, 1
Out of my **self** that Glorious Hierarchie!.....326. H.1080, 2
Love's of it **self**, too sweet; the best of all.....327. H.1084, 1
Rare is the voice it **self**; but when we sing....331. H.1101, 1
Have soil'd my **selfe**, or cloaths,...............351. N.49, 7
Celerity even it **self** is slow..................378. N.133, 2
Fitted it **self** to ev'ry Feeders tast.............379. N.146, 2
Given by none, but by Thy **selfe**, to me:.........398. N.262, 2
Bares in it **selfe** a gracefull maiestye.............404. A.1, 6
Its humble **selfe** twixt twoe aspiring cloudes,.....406. A.1, 84
Cheifelye my **selfe** to what I must proffess:....412. A.3, 98

Then which, thy **self** ne'er wafted sweeter over...416. A.8, 10
— — — — — — — — — — —,............421. var. H. 106, 55
That as her **selfe**, or Heauen indures.......422. ins. H.106, 92d
Selfsame No, no, that **selfe same** heart, that vow,.134. H.336, 70
Scorch't with the **selfe-same** martyrdome:....169. H.449, 10
One and the **selfe-same** priz'd complexion......209. H.586, 6
And starves with cold the **self-same** part.......290. H.915, 8
Sell **Sell**, and brought hither by the Elves........166. H.443, 62
And weekly Markets for to **sell** his wares:......253. H.753, 2
He'l **sell** her Eyes, and Nose, for Beere and Ale. 272. H.829, 4
For as I will not **sell** ye,....................321. H.1055, 2
Sells, Jove for our labour all things **sells** us.....36. H.106. 62
Center is known weak sighted, and he **sells**.....154. H.401, 1
Rook he **sells** feathers, yet he still doth crie.....163. H.439, 1
The Eggs of Pheasants wrie-nosed Tooly **sells**;..204. H.568, 1
Horne **sells** to others teeth; but has not one....211. H.595, 1
His wife her owne ware **sells** as fast at home....253. H.753, 4
Selves Not only to your **selves** assume.............9. H.15, 5
There to disport your **selves** with golden measure: 38. H.106, 139
Our **selves** to such a height:..................66. H.172, 21
Your **selves** into the mighty over-flow........115. H.283, 118
Cure, cure your **selves**, for I discrie,............157. H.413, 7
Which we to others (from our **selves**).........166. H.443, 61
And smiling at our **selves**, decree,.............216. H.616, 29
As for our **selves** to leave some frankinsence.......295. H.940, 4
Or by our **selves**, or from the Pulpit read.......396. N.249, 8
Into your **selves** like wooll together spunne, 431. ins. H.283, 50h
— — — — — — — — — —,................447. var. A.1, 24
Semblance Puts on the **semblance** here of sorrowing. 214. H.612, 4
Semele As he did once to **Semele**................58. H.152, 4
Senators And Thrones, thy selfe one of Those **Senatours**: 176. H.466, 4
The **Senators** down tumbling with the Roofe,..252. H.745, 14
Send Which I can **send**,........................43. H.123, 16
To **send**, or save;..............................43. H.123, 35
To Glasse, and they will **send**................75. H.193, 26
Ile **send** such Frost, such Haile, such Sleet, and Snow, 82. H.204, 10
And ere long, a Boy Love **send** ye.............125. H.314, 6
We **send** to you; but here a jolly..............126. H.319, 9
We **send** in stead of New-yeares gift...........127. H.319, 26
I **send** my salt, my sacrifice...................146. H.377, 2
But I will go, or **send** a kisse.................156. H.412, 19
A willow Garland thou did'st **send**............161. H.425, 1
Either to **send** me kindly thine,................168. H.446, 7
To thee a Sheep-hook I will **send**,............193. H.521, 43
To **send** your mind...........................198. H.544, 32
The patient Saint, and **send** up vowes for me.....204. H.570, 4
Aske me why I **send** you here..................208. H.580, 1
Aske me why I **send** to you 208. H.580, 3
Can't **send** for a gift.........................256. H.762, 14
Nothing I have (my Crofts) to **send** to Thee....267. H.804, 2
Or **send** to us,...............................289. H.911, 13
Yet **send** no Boules to him?...................290. H.918, 4
But **send** to her a Tearce.......................291. H.918, 8
Ans. Love gifts will **send** ye:................310. H.1001, 10
I **send**, I **send** here my supremest kiss........315. H.1028, 1
It may chance good-luck may **send**...........334. H.1125, 3
All these, and better Thou dost **send**...........351. N.47, 51
Let Balme, and Cassia **send** their scent.........361. N.83, 65
Of Foreskin **send** to me:......................376. N.125, 2
Rich is the Jemme that thou did'st **send**,........376. N.125, 5
Because I **send** Thee all.......................376. N.125, 8
My lipps shall **send** a 1000 back to you...........414. A.5, 16
— — — — — — — — —,..............441. var. H.446, 8
Sending **Sending** them forth, Salute no man by th' way: 378. N.137, 2
Sends Which though it **sends** forth thousand streams, 'tis ne're 341. N.15, 3
Sense To numb the **sence** of Dearth, which sho'd sinne haste it, 37. H.106, 119
To juggle with the **sense**......................76. H.193, 40
Say, have ye **sence**, or do you prove............158. H.420, 7
For why, my Saviour, with the **sense**............354. N.57, 3
If not to'th sound, yet, to the **sense**.............381. N.160, 2
No, No, this scene from Thee takes life and **sense**, 399. N.263, 26
Whose breath is rich perfume, that to the **sence**..404. A.1, 27
Wheare hee may roule, and loose his **sence**.......408. A.2, 45
And In thy **sence**, her Chaster thoughtes Commend 421. ins. H.106, 42a
Senses Bind up his **senses** with your numbers, so,..99. H.244, 3
Your weake **senses** in the night.................117. H.289, 8
Sensible His vertue still is **sensible** of paine:....60. H.158, 2
Sent To me my Julia lately **sent**..................13. H.32, 1
I **sent** my Love a Karkanet:...................14. H.34, 2
Then say, I've **sent** one more..................43. H.123, 13
Many a glance too has been **sent**................69. H.178, 53
Not **sent** ye for to drowne your paine,..........102. H.250, 54
By wretched Wooers **sent**,....................131. H.330, 6
Gifts will be **sent**, and Letters, which..........174. H.465, 23
But more's **sent** in, then was serv'd out........178. H.476, 9
All Flowers **sent** to'is burying.................186. H.497, 10
One more by Thee, Love, and Desert have **sent**, 191. H.516, 1
London my home is: though by hard fate **sent** 242. H.713, 13
A maid (my Prew) by good luck **sent**,........246. H.724, 6
Sent forth by them, our flesh to eate, or bite....278. H.862, 4
Which of Thy kindnesse Thou hast **sent**;........350. N.47, 33
Soe look't the Grecian Oratour when **sent**.........411. A.3, 71
Sentence Which done, thy painfull Thumb this **sentence** tells us, 36. H.106, 61
And to thy selfe be best this **sentence** knowne,...67. H.177, 3
And take this **sentence**, then away;............287. H.899, 8
For truth I may this **sentence** tell,............321. H.1059, 1
For every **sentence**, clause and word,............339. N.2, 3
To heare the Judge give **sentence** on the Throne, 392. N.230, 25
Sentences To change, or call back, His past **Sentences**. 389. N.216, 4
Sentest See **Sent'st**
Sentinel (While Love the **Centinell** doth keep)...35. H.106, 36
Stand for my comming, **Sentinell**...............174. H.465, 14
Sent'st Thou **sent'st** to me a True-love-knot; but I 173. H.464, 1
Sepulchre Her self i'th' silken **Sepulchre**........186. H.497, 14
Die when ye will, your **sepulchre** is knowne,...249. H.734, 3
To my **Sepulcher** now,........................256. H.762, 2
To dress thy silent **sepulchre**..................289. H.912, 4
Is (and hast seene) thy Saviours **Sepulcher**. .330. H.1100, 14
A wing about thy **Sepulcher**!..................361. N.83, 68
Ghost-like, as in my meaner **sepulcher**;..........371. N.115, 4
No one step from this **Sepulcher**..............402. N.269, 19
Gifts to my Saviours **Sepulcher**;...............402. N.270, 2
Sere Trees, at one time, shall be both **sere** and greene: 59. H.154, 2
Sergeant Then Case, as loud as any **Serjant** there, 303. H.975, 5
Servant Who was thy **servant**. Dearest, bury me...20. H.55, 3
Thy **servant**, not thy own self, sweat,..........233. H.670, 20
Thoughe as a **seruant**, yet a Mayde of Honor....412. A.3, 102
Servants When if the **servants** search, they may descry 118. H.292, 4
And leave their **servants**, but the smoak & sweat: 272. H.826, 3
The **servants** thumblesse, yet to eat,............310. H.1004, 3
Let not that Day Gods Friends and **Servants** scare: 376. N.126, 1
God suffers not His Saints, and **Servants** deere, 394. N.236, 1
Servants' With noise, the **servants** eyes from sleep. 179. H.476, 33
Serve Which here I vow to **serve**, doe not remove 79. H.197, 82
Which **serve** for watched Ribbanings...........92. H.223, 73
As it might **serve** me for my skin.............164. H.442, 5
Corrupted wood; **serve** here for shine..........167. H.443, 75
Well will **serve** the Beggars use..............223. H.638, 20
Serve or not **serve**, let Tom doe what he can,...265. H.796, 3
Or see thy injur'd Leaves **serve** well,..........275. H.844, 5
Make hoods of thee to **serve** out Spice..........275. H.884, 8
'Tis liberty to **serve** one Lord; but he.........284. H.887, 1
Serve but for matter to make Paper-kites.......286. H.896, 2
By those who **serve** the Child-bed misteries.....286. H.898, 4
All **serve** to th' Augmentation of his good........349. N.44, 4
God will have all, or none; **serve** Him, or fall....353. N.54, 1
— — — — — — — — — —,..............440. var. H.443, 56
Served **Serv'd**, but as Tapers, for to burne,......109. H.271, 5
But all this while his eye is **serv'd**,...........119. H.293, 13
No Orphans pittance, left him, **serv'd** to set..149. H.377, 123
But more's sent in, then was **serv'd** out.........178. H.476, 9
Serves Then while time **serves**, and we are but decaying; 69. H.178, 69
Where Trouble **serves** the board, we eate.......124. H.312, 3
Serves but for place of Buriall.................197. H.542, 4
Who many **serves**, **serves** base servility.........284. H.887, 2
Gold **serves** for Tribute to the King;...........396. N.254, 1
Service But for True **Service**, worthy of that Gowne, 176. H.466, 7
To grace which **Service**, Julia, there shall be....209. H.584, 3
For shape and **service**, Spaniell like to thee......302. H.967, 2
Bread for our **service**, bread for shew;...........356. N.66, 3
Servile Not for the **servile** feare of punishment...290. H.917, 2
Servility Who many serves, serves base **servility**...284. H.887, 2
Serving But **serving** Courts, and Cities, be.......229. H.662, 3
He is **serving**, who's a Trencher-man..........265. H.796, 4
Serving-man Endure that luke-warme name of **Serving-man**: 265. H.796, 2
Session To the gen'rall **Session**;................373. N.121, 6
Set See **Fair-set, Sunset**
Be her lips ill hung, or **set**,....................11. H.21, 11
(As they were closely **set**).....................18. H.47, 2
By your owne jewels **set** on fire................20. H.54, 6
First, for thy Queen-ship on thy head is **set**......30. H.88, 3
See! see she's yonder **set**,.......................43. H.123, 7
Set on purpose to enthrall.......................53. H.147, 9
Lyd. My heart now **set** on fire is...............70. H.181, 13
Not all thy flushing Sunnes are **set**,..............72. H.185, 1
Sunk is my sight; **set** is my Sun;..............72. H.185, 10
Or **set** it little forth.............................75. H.193, 24
Blush not at all for that; since we have **set**......76. H.194, 5
To teare the world, or **set** it all on fire.........81. H.202, 6

Pillars let some set up,........85, H.211, 21
Yet wither'd, ere you can be set........88. H.216, 17
His Idol-Cricket there is set: 90. H.223, 12
Which one by one here set downe are........91. H.223, 36
To make for others garlands; and to set........94. H.224, 3
And those Meddowes full be set........108. H.266, 15
Set on your selfe, by being nice:........113. H.283, 54
After short prayers, they set on bread;........119. H.293, 8
Set on my Table, (Trouble-free)........124. H.312, 7
But when your own faire print was set........126. H.318, 6
Faire Pearles in order set?........130. H.330, 4
Yet ere ye enter, give us leave to set........140. H.354, 3
Ne'r yet set tooth in stump, or rump of these...142. H.361, 2
Loe, I, the Lyrick Prophet, who have set........142. H.365, 3
Fame, and his Name, both set, and sing his Lyricks.
143. H.366, 4
Sweet virgin, that I do not set........145. H.376, 1
No Orphans pittance, left him, serv'd to set...149. H.377, 123
Where, Amarillis, Thou didst set thy feet........159. H.421, 12
Mont. Set with the Sunne, thy woes: Scil. The day grows old:
160. H.421, 41
Who to the North, or South doth set........162. H.429, 1
What is a Jewell if it be not set........172. H.459, 5
Set up Thine own eternall Images........185. H.496, 10
His Fame's long life, who strives to set up Yours.
188. H.506, 16
Set each Platter in his place:........201. H.556, 2
Water in, ere Sun be set........201. H.556, 4
Of flowers set in comlinesse:........202. H.560, 4
(The Sun once set) all of one colour are........207. H.576, 4
Set you to your Wheele, and wax........221. H.633, 42
And, in the midst, to grace it more, was set....227. H.652, 9
Keep here still, Closet-Gods, 'fore whom I've set 227. H.652, 13
Set the Brush for sprinkling:........258. H.769, 3
Now is your turne (my Dearest) to be set........264. H.789, 1
Wilt thou appear, when thou art set........270. H.819, 7
When the ruffe is set elsewhere?........282. H.878, 8
Set free thy Tresses, let them flow........282. H.881, 7
Lesse set for them, then spred for me........282. H.881, 10
Leave others Beauty, to set up withall........299. H.958, 6
In teeming years, how soon my Sun was set,..304. H.978, 3
And by that One blow set an end to all........310. H.1002, 4
The more on ycie pavements we are set........316. H.1032, 2
And set about with Lillies;........323. H.1068, 6
You set too high a rate upon........324. H.1068, 17
The worke is done: young men, and maidens set
335. H.1128, 1
Fames pillar here, at last, we set,........335, H.1129, 1
Here give me thornes; there, in thy Kingdome, set
343. N.25, 5
Hast set a Guard........349. N.47, 8
So kind, to set me free,........370. N.111, 6
All set about with Lillies........375. N.123, 80
Those Tapers, which we set upon the grave,....384. N.181, 1
And her white teeth which in the gums are sett 405. A.1, 31
Sets Early setts ope to feast, and late:........147. H.377, 46
That sets all eares on fire........151. H.388, 4
Of Wassaile now, or sets the quintell up:........159. H.421, 4
Lungs (as some, say) ne'r sets him down to eate, 223. H.637, 1
Instead of almes, sets dogs upon the poor........238. H.694, 2
He sets his foot, he leaves rich compost there.....259. H.771, 8
Or like vnto Aurora when shee setts........404. A.1, 3
Then nature for a sweet allurement setts........404. A.1, 19
Of Lust, which setts on fier our hartes........408. A.2, 38
Set'st See Settest
Settest Thou set'st their hearts, let chaste desire..174. H.465, 8
Setting And neerer he's to Setting........84. H.208, 8
(Just at the setting of the Sun)........123. H.306, 6
Franck wo'd go scoure her teeth; and setting to't,
247. H.728, 1
That sees noe setting Sunn........413. A.4, 15
Seven That for seven Lusters I did never come....27. H.82, 1
To' th' (almost) sev'n and fortieth yeare........41. H.116, 2
To adde a nobler Planet to the seven?........112. H.283, 6
Having but seven in all; three black, foure white. 195. H.531, 2
Nor is't a life, seven yeares to tell,........233. H.670, 34
But for to live that half seven well:........233. H.670, 35
True, if this Citie seven times rounded was......252. H.745, 11
With rock, and seven times circumflankt with brasse,
252, H.745, 12
Seventh And on the seaventh, he has his Notes to seek.
163. H.435, 2
That on the seaventh, he can nor preach, or pray. 163. H.435, 4
Sever To flaw, or else to sever:........66. H.172, 27
Thou Power that canst sever........95. H.227, 7
Not knowing thus much, when we once do sever,
140. H.355, 3
But though we Sever........162. H.426, 21
And that ty'd to man 'twil sever........209. H.587, 3
And looking back, that look did sever........265. H.798, 11
Lets kiss first, then we'l sever........324. H.1068, 22
Several By dreames, each one, into a sev'rall world. 21. H.57, 2
Sitting, and sorting severall sorts of flowers,......94. H.224, 2
With sev'rall dishes standing by,........101. H.250, 32
Slouch he packs up, and goes to sev'rall Faires,..253. H.753, 1
In sev'rall tills, and boxes keepes 'em safe;....299. H.959, 2
Each one his severall offering;........368. N.102, 21
And when He blest each sev'rall Day, whereon..396. N.249, 3
Thee in Thy severall parts of bitternesse;......399. N.263, 33
Severe The cutting Thumb-naile, or the Brow severe.
212. H.603, 2
One nicely mad, or peevishly severe........234. H.673, 6
Nor Cato the severe........259. H.772, 6
And as time past when Cato the Severe........301. H.962, 1
Be you a Judge; but not a Judge severe........322. H.1062, 6
God in His own Day will be then severe,........381. N.156, 1
Severed And sever'd, joyne in brazen yoke:......70. H.181, 18
Severely God scourgeth some severely, some He spares;
342. N.20, 1
Severest Next, with severest Salvages;........111. H.278, 4
Sew But since It must be done, dispatch, and sowe
116. H.283, 141
Sex Men they shall be, not your sex........177. H.472, 4
Sexton Thou Sexton (Red-brest) for to cover me. 111. H.279, 4
— — — — — — — —,........450. var. A.9, 33
Sextons Though the Sextons truly sweare........418. A.9, 33
Seyd See Said
Shackle Then shackell me........172. H.458, 6
Shackles Farewell my shackles, (though of pearle they be)
17. H.42, 3
From Shackles free:........190. H.515, 20
Nor let the shackles make thee sad;........246. H.725, 3
Dread not the shackles: on with thine intent;..317. H.1034, 1
Sh'ad When quiet grown sh'ad seen them,........31. H.92, 10
Shade See Nightshade
A fable, song, or fleeting shade;........69. H.178, 66
No, here Ile last, and walk (a harmless shade)..73. H.186, 17
They sho'd obey a shade;........76. H.193, 47
And underneath thy cooling shade,........106. H.262, 13
Ere long a fleeting shade: 111. H.280, 6
Ere long, a song, ere long, a shade........133. H.336, 30
Or mournfull Marble; let thy shade........145. H.376, 3
A shade,........178. H.475, 8
Which is His Shade, who can abide His Flame! 237. H.685, 8
His passage through that dreadfull shade:......265. H.798, 8
Spend Harmless shade thy nightly Houres,.....289. H.912, 1
Vnder whose shade twoe starry sparkling eyes....404. A.1, 9
— — — — — — — — — —,........444. var. H.730, 7
Shades Still in the coole, and silent shades of sleep. 9. H.14, 18
Unto the shades have been, or now are due,......27. H.82, 10
By those fine Shades, their Substances:........36. H.106, 80
As if here were those cooler shades of love.....68. H.178, 36
Under your shades, to sleep or die!........158. H.420, 2
Chor. The shades grow great; but greater growes our sorrow,
160. H.421, 43
Yee silent shades, whose each tree here........169. H.449, 1
Let our soules flie to' th' shades, where ever springs
205. H.575, 2
Thou & I'le sing to make these dull Shades merry,
248. H.730, 25
Is He, from hence, gone to the shades beneath, 403. N.271, 5
Vnto the Prince of Shades, whom once his Pen
442. ins. H.575, 28a
Shadow Me, or my shadow thou do'st meet......174. H.465, 16
Whose shadow smels like milder Pomander!......181. H.485, 2
Shadows No shadowes great appeare;........164. H.441, 6
— — — — — — — — — —,........422. var. H.106, 80
Shaft I have a leaden, thou a shaft of gold;.....333. H.1120, 1
Shafts Fight thou with shafts of silver, and o'rcome,
21. H.60, 1
Love will in vain spend shafts on me:........155. H.406, 2
Shag — — — — — — — — —, ...423. var. H.128, 15
Shagged Comets we see by night; whose shagg'd portents
45. H.128, 15
Shake Shake the Thyrse, and bite the Bayes:.....39. H.111, 8
The cold, cold Earth doth shake him;........156. H.412, 18
Can shake a just mans purposes:........215. H.615, 2
I freeze as fast, and shake for cold........290. H.915, 2
Shaked See Shak't
Shakes Shakes the whole Roofe, or ruines all.....153. H.395, 5
Of Corn, when Summer shakes his eares;........340. N.3, 12
Shakespeare — — — — — — — —, ...443. var. H.575, 51
Shaking Shakeing the head, whilst each, to each dothe mourne,
411. A.3, 65
Shak't More shak't thy selfe, then she is scorch't by thee.
82. H.204, 14
Shall (Partial List)
First, I shall decline my head;........38. H.107, 4
She shall: Then my hope is,........43. H.123, 32
What ere enters, out it shall:........116. H.285, 8
Though Granges do not love thee, Cities shall...172. H.456, 10
As Love shall helpe me, I admire........272. H.828, 9
Conquer we shall, but we must first contend;....293. H.933, 1
I'le follow Thee, hap, hap what shall,........399. N.265, 5
how long shall the page, to please........431. ins. H.283, 60g
Shallow Be her cheeks so shallow too,........11. H.21, 9
Shalt (Partial List)
I'm free from thee; and thou no more shalt heare 17. H.42, 1
When thou shalt laugh at my Religious dust;...49. H.138, 3
That thou, within few months, shalt be........63. H.166, 7
Thou shalt have soules for sacrifice........89. H.219, 12
Live, live thou dost, and shalt; for why?........89. H.219, 15
There thou shalt find her lip and cheek........106. H.263, 8

There thou **shalt** have her curious eye:.........107. H.263, 10
Thou **shalt** not All die; for while Love's fire shines
143. H.366, 1
To morrow thou **shalt** see.....................161. H.425, 6
Waking **shalt** find me sleeping there...........175. H.465, 52
Shalt lead, like young Apollo...................184. H.492, 36
Live, live with me, and thou **shalt** see.........192. H.521, 1
Their Milke thy drinke; and thou **shalt** eate....192. H.521, 12
Where thou **shalt** sit, and Red-brest by,.......192. H.521, 17
There thou **shalt** hear Divine Musæus sing....206. H.575, 25
All times unto their frenzies; Thou **shalt** there..206. H.575, 47
Not as a thief, **shalt** Thou ascend the mount,....398. N.263, 15
The Crosse shall be Thy Stage; and Thou **shalt** there
398. N.263, 17
Shambles To lard the **shambles**: Barbels bred...133. H.336, 46
Shame Why wept it? but for **shame**,..............12. H.23, 2
(Love makes me write, what **shame** forbids to speak.)
24. H.74, 2
And **shame** had follow'd long ere this,..........48. H.136, 8
Unbolts the doore, no **shame** comes in...........48. H.136, 13
And 'tis but Native **shame**,....................54. H.149, 23
Get up, get up for **shame**, the Blooming Morne..67. H.178, 1
That's the greatest **shame** of all,...............151. H.386, 5
For **shame** or pitty now encline................168. H.446, 5
Shame is a bad attendant to a State:...........182. H.488, 1
For pitty or **shame**,..........................195. H.534, 7
Ph. Alas for me! Ch. **Shame** on thy witching note,
248. H.730, 11
But weep not, Christall; for the **shame** was meant
249. H.732, 3
By those ignoble Births, which **shame** the stem..251. H.745, 7
From **shame** my face keepe free,..............281. H.874, 10
First, Fear and **Shame** without, then Guilt within.
341. N.11, 3
Shame checks our first attempts; but then 'tis prov'd
362. N.85, 1
The **shame** of mans face is no more...........383. N.170, 1
Shamefaced And **shame-fac't** Plum, (all simp'ring there).
192. H.521, 38
Shamefacedness See **Shamefastness**
(Having resign'd thy **shamefac'tness**:).........287. H.899, 6
Their cheekes unstain'd with **shamefac'tnesse**:..310. H.1004, 8
Shamefastness See **Shamefacedness**
My kisse out-went the bounds of **shamfastnesse**:.294. H.936, 2
Sh'an — — — — — — — — —, ...453. var. H.283, 110
Shapcot **Shapcot**! To thee the Fairy State.......119. H.293, 1
After the Feast (my **Shapcot**) see,.............165, H.443, 1
Shape First, for your **shape**, the curious cannot shew
189. H.511, 1
For **shape** and service, Spaniell like to thee.....302. H.967, 2
Faultless every way for **shape**;...............306. H.984, 27
— — — — — — — — — —,...............449. var. A.3, 93
Shapeless **Shapelesse** the world (as when all Chaos was)
59. H.154, 8
Shapes Present their **shapes**; while fantasie discloses
36. H.106, 47
Ile come to thee in all those **shapes**............58. H.152, 1
Put on all **shapes** to get a Love:.............215. H.616, 16
And **shaps** my Function, for more glorious ends: 411. A.3, 58
Into the Loathsoms < t > **shapps**, thou canst deuise
412. A.3, 93
Share To signifie, in Love my **share**.............28. H.85, 3
And let the Young-men and the Bride-maids **share**
114, H.283, 78
No, no, the utmost **share**.....................231. H.663, 5
Who claim the Fat, and Fleshie for their **share**, 272. H.826, 5
Hog has a place i'th' Kitchen, and his **share**...326. H.1079, 1
I'le take my **share**; or els, my God,...........399. N.265, 9
Shared And Garlands **shar'd**,...................369. N.106, 5
Not **shar'd** alike be unto all..................380. N.149, 2
Shares Last, may your Harrows, **Shares** and Ploughes,
179. H.476, 22
And equall **shares** exclude all murmerings.......318. H.1040, 2
But all in smart have lesse, or greater **shares**.....342. N.20, 2
Shark **Shark**, when he goes to any publick feast,..118. H.292, 1
Sharking Driving these **sharking** trades, is out at heels.
153. H.398, 2
Sharon (Or **Sharon**, where eternall Roses grow.)
326. H.1080, 8
Canst talke to us of **Sharon**; where a spring....330. H.1100, 9
He is the Rose of **Sharon** known:...............354. N.59, 4
Sharp Lust has no eares; He's **sharpe** as thorn;..165. H.443, 13
Sharpen Ile whet my lips, and **sharpen** Love on thee
327. H.1081, 2
Sharp-fanged Then soft Catullus, **sharp-fang'd** Martial,
206. H.575, 43
Sharp-horned — — — — — — — — —, ...442. var. H.465, 78
Sharply That **sharply** trickles from her either eye 178. H.474, 2
Sharply pointed as a thorn:.................306. H.984, 22
Sh'as Two Youths **sha's** known, thrice two, and twice 3. yeares;
180. H.477, 3
Well, when **sh'as** kild, that Pig, Goose, Cock or Hen,
266. H.801, 3
But when again **sh'as** got her healthfull houre,..320. H.1054, 5
Sha't Thou **sha't** have Ribbands, Roses, Rings,..193. H.521, 51
Shave Eggs Ile not **shave**: But yet brave man, if I
202. H.557, 27
She (Partial List)
Yet Jone **she** goes..........................229. H.659, 3
Sheaf Thy **sheaf** of wheat,....................391. N.228, 14
Shear Kings ought to **sheare**, not skin their sheepe.
261. H.780, 2
Shearers See **Sheep-shearers**
Shearing-feast Thy **Sheering-feast**, which never faile.
231. H.662, 55
Shearing-times At **Sheering-times**, and yearely Wakes,
192, H.521, 25
Shears Hang up Hooks, and **Sheers** to scare.....284. H.891, 1
Sheaves Some blesse the Cart; some kisse the **sheaves**;
101. H.250, 19
To strut thy barnes with **sheafs** of Wheat......233. H.670, 21
She'd (Partial List)
She lookt as **she'd** been got with child.........251. H.740, 7
Shed For Health on Julia's cheek hath **shed**........7. H.9, 9
That neither haire was cut, or true teares **shed**....27. H.82, 3
That Lovers tears in life-time **shed**,.............44. H.127, 9
For pitty let a teare be **shed**;..................61. H.159, 23
And then he dons the Silk-worms **shed**,.......93. H.223, 137
By your teares **shed**,.........................105. H.257, 25
Squirrils and childrens teeth late **shed**,.........166. H.443, 55
By all those teares that have been **shed**,........169. H.449, 19
In publique loss to **shed** a Teare:.............203. H.564, 4
Who'l give ye then a sheltring **shed**,...........218. H.626, 3
Cut off thy haires; and let thy Teares be **shed**..219. H.627, 3
If here ye will some few teares **shed**,..........226. H.644, 9
Which, on the white Rose being **shed**,..........241. H.706, 3
As my small stuffe best fits my little **Shed**......249. H.733, 9
With the Wine that must be **shed**.............280. H.870, 9
Since **shed** or Cottage I have none,............321. H.1056, 1
But with this comfort, if my blood be **shed**,...335. H.1128, 5
Then for to **shed** some teares...................352. N.53, 3
And from His sacred Bloud, here **shed**,.........366. N.97, 22
Shed for their Master many a bitter teare:.....384. N.180, 10
— — — — — — — — — —,............437. var. H.336, 117
— — — — — — — — — —,............440. var. H.443, 110
Sheddest Thou **shed'st** one teare, when as I went away;
42. H.122, 10
Shedding See **Silver-shedding**
From her Sonnes Crosse, not **shedding** once a teare:
384. N.180, 2
Shed'st See **Sheddest**
Sheep From rav'ning wolves, the fleecie **sheep**....36. H.106, 52
Chor. Pan pipe to him, and bleats of lambs and **sheep**,
86. H.213, 17
Account of such a flock of **sheep**;...........133. H.336, 44
And **sheep**, grew more sweet, by that breth of Thine.
159. H.421, 14
And when at night, she folded had her **sheep**,..159. H.421, 25
And with my sighs, call home my bleating **sheep**:
159. H.421, 38
Our finer fleeced **sheep**:.......................183. H.492, 14
Lesse for to catch a **sheep**, then me...........193. H.521, 46
Of **sheep**, (safe from the Wolfe and Fox)......230. H.662, 41
Kings ought to sheare, not skin their **sheepe**....261. H.780. 2
But yet harmless as a **sheep**..................306. H.984, 30
From fat of Veales, and **Sheep**?...............391. N.228, 4
Sheep-hook Mirt. And I a **Sheep-hook** will bestow,
86. H.213, 42
To thee a **Sheep-hook** I will send,............193. H.521, 43
Sheep's Passion, but for His **sheeps** dispersion....381. N.159, 2
Sheep-shearers For his **Sheep-shearers**. Mir. True, these are the least.......................................86. H.213, 8
Sheepskin In a **Sheeps-skin** newly flaid,.........209. H.587, 2
Sheepwalk Stirs in our **Sheep-walk**? Amin. None, save that my Ewes,.......................................85. H.213, 4
Sheet See **Winding-sheet**
That done, then wind me in that very **sheet**.......9. H.14, 10
See, here a Maukin, there a **sheet**,..............101. H.250, 9
Up in a **sheet** your Bride, and what if so.....116. H.283, 142
The **sheet** about, like flakes of snow..........116. H.283, 150
For either **sheet**, was spread the Caule........167. H.443, 90
Thee, thee my **sheet**..........................190. H.515, 8
As ere was wrapt in winding **sheet**.............257. H.764, 2
In the next **sheet** Brave Man to follow Thee...329. H.1092, 6
The **sheet** I sleep in, as my Winding-sheet......392. N.230, 18
— — — — — — — — — —, ...453. var. H.283, 21
Sheets Feare to those **sheets**, that know no sin....35. H.106, 40
Have, promis'd to your **sheets**;...............54. H.149, 36
True to your self, and **sheets**, you'l have me swear,
136. H.338, 1
For false Position in his neighbours **sheets**:......195. H.532, 2
The **Sheets**, the Rugs, made by thy hand.......374. N.123, 44
— — — — — — — — — —,...........433. var. H.283, 150
Shelf When I am bruised on the **Shelfe**........134. H.336, 74
But having scapt temptations **shelfe**,..........176. H.465, 83
She'll (Partial List)
I'm sure **she'll** ask no more....................43. H.123, 36
She'l runne to all adulteries.................287. H.899, 10
Shell In Amber, or some Chrystall **shell**..........88. H.216, 14
Hard by, i'th'**shell** of halfe a nut,.............91. H.223, 44
My Palmers hat; my Scallops **shell**;...........123. H.306, 3
Each richly headed with a pearly **shell**.........406. A.1, 102
Shells But ne'r so much as licks the speckled **shells**:
204. H.568, 2

Then, next, to match Tradescant's curious shels,.232. H.668, 3
Sheltering The staffe, the Elme, the prop, the shelt'ring wall 72. H.185, 12
Who'l give ye then a sheltring shed,...........218. H.626, 3
Shephardling See Shepherdling
Shepherd As he is Prince, he's Shepherd too.....86. H.213, 44
A Shepherd piping on a hill.................230. H.662, 45
Shepherdess And all faire Signs lead on our Shepardesse. 85. H.213, 2
Where I may find my Shepardesse..............106. H.263, 4
The Wearer's no meane Shepheardesse.........192. H.521, 24
A Shepheardess so homely;..................324. H.1068, 18
Shepherdling Unto a handsome Shephardling;.......5. H.2, 12
To thee, (my dearest Shepharling)...........192. H.521, 36
Shepherd's Th'art hence removing (like a Shepherds Tent) 188. H.507, 1
Shepherds The feast of Shepheards fail. Sil. None crowns the cup..159. H.421, 3
Where Shepheards sho'd not keep..............183. H.492, 16
Who by the Shepheards, sung (long since)....214. H.611, 5
Shepherds' The Shepherds Fleecie happinesse:........5. H.2, 8
Nor doth the early Shepheards Starre.........164. H.441, 7
We read how Faunus, he the shepheards God,....306. H.986, 1
Sherry To laugh and quaff and drink old sherry. 445. ins. H.730, 26c
She's (Partial List)
She's to me a Paragon........................11. H.21, 14
Say (if she's fretfull) I have bands..............98. H.238, 6
How false, how hollow she's in heart;.........103. H.253, 15
How high she's priz'd, and worth but small;...103. H.253, 17
But when She's up and fully drest,.............154. H.404, 3
Nor courts thou Her because she's well attended 201. H.557, 7
Ch. What's thy request? Ph. That since she's now beneath 248. H.730, 15
She's to me most excellent....................253. H.750, 15
This is my comfort, when she's most unkind,..322. H.1061, 1
Shew See Show
Shewbread Something for Shew-bread, and at hand 92. H.223, 69
Shewed See Showed
Shewest See Showest
Shewing See Showing
Shews See Shows
Shield The House (Love shield her) with her Yea and Nay: 114. H.283, 66
Helpe me so, that I my shield,.................151. H.386, 3
Never since first Bellona us'd a Shield,......170. H.451, 11
Holy-Rood come forth and shield..............177. H.473, 1
To shield the Stranger, and the Poore from wrong: 201. H.557, 12
Shields Resembling sheilds both smooth and christalline. 406. A.1, 80
Shift But this, that I might shift...............100. H.249, 3
Of these, and such like things, for shift,.......127. H.319, 25
Shift now has cast his clothes: got all things new; 144. H.372, 1
For all his shifts, he cannot shift his clothes.....149. H.380, 2
And not by any sordid shift:..................221. H.633, 47
Thus times do shift; each thing his turne do's hold: 285. H.892, 21
If Tythe-pigs faile, then will he shift the scean, 325. H.1076, 3
Shifted See Trans-shifted
Of shifted Snake: enfreez'd throughout.........166. H.443, 67
Then from his Feet, it shifted to his Hand:....207. H.577, 2
Shifting See Trans-shifting
Shifts She shifts and changes like the Moone....103. H.253, 14
Skrew lives by shifts; yet sweares by no small oathes; 149. H.380, 1
For all his shifts, he cannot shift his clothes.....149. H.380, 2
Tom shifts the Trenchers; yet he never can....265. H.796, 1
Shine See Moonshine, Morning-sunshine, Outshine, Sunshine
When the Rose raignes, and locks with ointments shine, 7. H.8, 9
I to my Chimney's shine.......................27. H.81, 21
That scatter'st Spirit and Lust; whose purest shine, 45. H.128, 12
Ne'r shine upon me; May my Numbers all.....79. H.197, 89
Which if it now, or shall hereafter shine..........94. H.226, 7
Blest is the Bride, on whom the Sun doth shine; 113. H.283, 48
Read then, and when your faces shine.........127. H.319, 27
Thus, till we see the fire lesse shine..........136. H.336, 145
Makes the smirk face of each to shine,........147. H.377, 72
Shine like a spangle here....................164. H.441, 8
Lead by the shine of Snails; a way............165. H.443, 22
Corrupted wood; serve here for shine.........167. H.443, 75
Unmixt. I love to have it smirke and shine,....187. H.502, 3
The next, because her Altars did not shine......197. H.539, 9
The while their wreaths and Purple Robes do shine, 234. H.673, 17
Let Me and It shine evermore by you..........264. H.789, 6
So purest Diaper doth shine,...................268. H.811, 7
Flusht was his face; his haires with oyle did shine; 313. H.1017, 3
For thee with richest Jemmes to shine,.......323. H.1068, 15
Let but one beame of Glory on it shine,........371. N.113, 9
To burn, not shine (as learned Basil saith.)....387. N.202, 2
Shines See Sunshines
A golden ring that shines upon thy thumb:......30. H.88, 7
And as it shines, it throwes a scent about,.....131. H.331, 7
Thou shalt not All die; for while Love's fire shines 143. H.366, 1
That shines upon the blewer Plum............166. H.443, 58
Give way, give way, now, now my Charles shines here, 236. H.685, 1
One silver spoon shines in the house of Croot; 332. H.1110, 1
— — — — — — — — — —,............439. var. H.443, 22
Shinest That shin'st thus in thy counterfeit?.....270. H.819, 9
Shining Which shining in her perfect Noone;....49. H.136, 29
Both by a shining Salt-seller;..................133. H.336, 50
The glow-wormes eyes; the shining scales.....166. H.443, 72
A Virgin Taper, ever shining here..............191. H.516, 4
Those crimson clouds i'th'cheeks & lips leave shining. 207. H.576, 2
(As Lamps for everlasting shining here:).......267. H.804, 8
Ship See Babyship, Dictatorship, Dukeship, Heirship, Kingship, Mabship, Queenship.
That my wing'd ship may meet no Remora.......14. H.35, 4
Thus if our ship fails of her Anchor hold,.......266. H.800, 7
My Ship has here one only Anchor-hold;......319. H.1044, 2
And here my ship rides having Anchor cast....334. H.1126, 2
When I a ship see on the Seas,................372. N.118, 1
Ships See Other-saintships, Saintships
Ships have been drown'd, where late they danc't before. 85. H.212, 2
Man knowes where first he ships himselfe; but he 177. H.468, 1
Shipwrack See Shipwreck
Shipwreck He, who has suffer'd Ship-wrack, feares to saile 212. H.601, 1
Shire See Den'-shire, Devonshire
Shirt Made him take up his shirt, lay down his sword. 65. H.171, 6
Put a shirt of sackcloth on:...................183. H.490, 14
His shirt bedangling from his knee,...........295. H.942, 3
Shiver And Wings too, which did shiver;..........27. H.81, 18
Shivers And break thy self in shivers on her eye. 87. H.215, 10
Shoal And the Furies in a shole.................348. N.41, 22
Shock Which tryes, and counter-stands the shock, 148. H.377, 110
Shocks Two, like two ripe shocks of corn.......58. H.149, 170
Sho'd (Partial List) See Shu'd
Cato the Censor, sho'd he scan each here.........28. H.84, 6
Sho'd be a little part..........................28. H.85, 4
That joynt to ashes sho'd be burnt,..............28. H.85, 7
To my content, I never sho'd behold,............29. H.86, 5
For sho'd I not supply..........................32. H.96, 3
Or else desir'st that Maids sho'd tell............34. H.103, 7
Prethee (lest Maids sho'd censure thee) but say..42. H.122, 9
Yet say; sho'd she condemne.....................43. H.123, 25
What next is lookt for? but we all sho'd see.....44. H.124, 3
Come, you are faire; and sho'd be seen.........49. H.136, 24
Promis'd sho'd come to crown your youth........53. H.149, 2
Whom sho'd I feare to write to, if I can........64. H.168, 1
Sho'd wend along his Baby-ship to see?........86. H.213, 26
It sho'd be onely in my Julia's skin:............158. H.416, 2
His eyes and ears strive which sho'd fastest run. 158. H.418, 2
Say, What sho'd Roots do with a Purse in print, 162. H.427, 3
This, this it sho'd be, for to spin,..............164. H.442, 3
What need I care, though some dislike me sho'd, 187. H.506, 5
When to the Temple Love sho'd runne, not go...216. H.618, 6
Sho'd see safe brought to Bed................220. H.633, 17
Shod And shod with silver, prove to be.........239. H.696. 7
Sho'dst See Shouldst
Shoe Anthea bade me tye her shooe;..............14. H.33, 1
That young men have to shooe the Mare:.....126. H.319, 16
How co'd Luke Smeaton weare a shoe, or boot, 240. H.704, 1
Whose Field his foot is, and whose Barn his shooe? 270. H.822, 4
Shoes Dry chips, old shooes, rags, grease, & bones; 93. H.223, 119
Guesse cuts his shooes, and limping, goes about...98. H.239, 1
(Rather than fail) to steal from thence old shoes: 143. H.368, 2
Gloves, Garters, Stockings, Shooes, and Strings 193. H.521, 52
Cob clouts his shoes, and as the story tells,....226. H.648, 1
With Hat and Shooes out-worne................295. H.942, 4
There springs a sope-like-lather in his shoos.....332. H.1113, 2
Rush saves his shooes, in wet and snowie wether; 332. H.1116, 1
Summer and Winter still to save his shooes....332. H.1116, 4
With shoes put off, to tread thy Roome........402. N.269, 3
Shoe-string A carelesse shooe-string, in whose tye..28. H.83, 11
Shole See Shoal
Shook That Earth-quake shook the house, and gave the stout 52. H.146, 15
Till we have wept, kist, sigh't, shook hands, or so. 73. H.186, 6
Shoot To shoot forth Generations like to them. 170. H.451, 4

Of fierce Idolatrie shute into mee, and....424. ins. H.128, 46b
Shooting The Shooting Starres attend thee;....217. H.619, 2
Shooting his Eye-darts 'gainst it, to surprise.....412. A.3, 77
Shoots That nothing shoots, but war and woe....139. H.353, 6
shootes forth his jealous soule, for to surprize
430. ins. H.283, 40b
Shop See Ale-shop
Strut, once a Fore-man of a Shop we knew;.....53. H.148, 1
And work no more; but shut up Shop..........212. H.602, 4
Shopter Old Widow Shopter, when so ere she cryes,
331. H.1107, 1
Shore What though the sea be calme? Trust to the shore:
85. H.212, 1
If so it be I've gain'd the shore.................94. H.225, 3
Then the sand, that makes the shore:...........102. H.253, 6
Wild are Seas, that want a shore...............122. H.304, 2
To shore the Feeble up, against the strong;....201. H.557, 11
To shore up my debilitie.........................303. H.973, 4
Put from, or draw unto the faithfull shore:....315. H.1028, 12
Euc. Charon, O Charon, draw thy Boat to th' Shore,
416. A.8, 1
Shored Shor'd up by you, (Brave Earle of Westmerland.)
40. H.112, 4
Shorn See New-shorn
Short Be my Mistresse short or tall,..............11. H.21, 3
(In my short absence) to unsluce a teare:.......14. H.35, 10
Our life is short; and our dayes run............69. H.178, 61
But borne, and like a short Delight,............69. H.180, 1
That in short time my woes shall cease;........73. H.187, 10
By thy short absence, to desire and love thee?...77. H.197, 24
But (Dearest) of so short a stay;...............87. H.216, 2
A short, but righteous discipline...............92. H.223, 84
Like those short sweets ere knit together.......107. H.263, 22
But yet too short for you: 'tis we,............114. H.283, 73
After short prayers, they set on bread;........119. H.293, 8
May the Bed, and this short night,............124. H.314, 3
We have short time to stay, as you,............125. H.316, 11
We have as short a Spring;.....................125. H.316, 12
Why then, since life to us is short,............133. H.336, 31
Short lot, or not, to be content with all.........153. H.396, 2
Every time seemes short to be,..................162. H.431, 1
This Lady's short, that Mistresse she is tall;....163. H.437, 1
But long or short, I'm well content with all....163. H.437, 2
And say short Prayers; and when we have done so,
168. H.445, 4
In my short absence; yet behold...............174. H.465, 19
The path is but short;..........................195. H.534, 11
What short sweet Prayers shall be said;........216. H.616, 31
Of short sweet grasse, as backs with wool.....230. H.662, 43
Sweet sleep, that makes more short the night...231. H.662, 75
Weak I am grown, and must in short time fall;
242. H.713, 19
Wrongs, if neglected, vanish in short time;....260. H.776, 1
This short but strict condition:................265. H.798, 4
Griefe, if't be great, 'tis short; if long, 'tis light.
268. H.810, 2
One short charme if you but say...............276. H.850, 11
And make short pray'rs to thee:...............281. H.874, 5
Spenke has a strong breath, yet short Prayers saith:
283. H.884, 1
And thence return, (short prayers seyd)......291. H.919, 15
And such as will in short time be,.............297. H.948, 3
I will be short, and having quickly hurl'd......298. H.955, 1
But in short time 'twill please Thee,...........353. N.56, 21
A short and sweet iniquity?....................357. N.72, 4
Nor wo'd I care how short it were, if good:..392. N.230, 10
For, long this work wil be, & very short this Day.
401. N.268, 6
Round short and cleire, like pounded spices sweete
406. A.1, 92
Shorten Cleere Thou my paths, or shorten Thou my miles,
352. N.51, 5
Shortened With Buskins shortned to descrie....51. H.142, 15
Shortest This the short'st day, and this the longest night;
114. H.283, 72
— — — — — — — — —,............432. var. H.283, 72
Short-lived Those possessions short-liv'd are,....241. H.711, 1
Shortly Shortly I shall bid goodnight:..........180. H.482, 2
Shot See Bloodshot, Cup-shot
Shot forth her loving Sorceries:...............135. H.336, 106
Shot's About him, when the Taverns shot's to pay.
173. H.463, 2
Shots Small shots paid often, waste a vast estate...13. H.28, 2
Should (Partial List) See Sho'd, Shu'd
Ther's still more cause, why I the more should love.
10. H.16, 6
Then live we mirthfull, while we should,......233. H.670, 28
Shoulders A Lawne about the shoulders thrown....28. H.83, 3
Down from her comely shoulders hung:........51. H.142, 10
Large shoulders though he has, and well can beare,
60. H.158, 3
Have reference to the shoulders, not the eares...142. H.363, 4
As my weake shoulders cannot beare..........303. H.973, 9
The lovely shoulders now allure the eye.........406. A.1, 95
Shouldst Me thought 'twas strange, that thou so hard sho'dst prove,..................................42. H.122, 7
Or sho'dst thou prize me as a Dish..........321. H.1056, 11

Shout Of Rurall Younglings raise the shout;...101. H.250, 16
Those with a shout, and these with laughter....101. H.250, 18
No clap of hands, or shout, or praises-proofe...150. H.382, 11
And having drunk, we raise a shout...........198. H.544, 10
May fart for joy, as well as shout:............306. H.987, 2
Shoved Shov'd on, by quick succeeding Tides:..244. H.720, 2
Show See Foreshow
As to shew her Tongue wag through:........11. H.21, 10
But forthwith bade my Julia shew................18. H.45, 3
Whose Plantations fully show....................20. H.53, 7
That Roses shew, when misted o're with Lawn...34. H.104, 4
Justice to soone-pleas'd nature; and to show,....35. H.106, 13
My vowes denounc'd in zeale, which thus much show thee,
46. H.128, 47
That shew the womb shall thrive:...............55. H.149, 56
Summer and Winter shall at one time show.....59. H.154, 5
Nor any bed to give the shew..................63. H.164, 10
And by some crosse-line show it;...............64. H.166, 10
And never shew blood-guiltinesse, or feare......64. H.168, 3
To shew at once, both night and day............64. H.169, 8
To shew by this,................................65. H.172, 4
Can shew where you or grew, or stood..........88. H.216, 9
Gold I've none, for use or show,...............88. H.218, 1
And rich for in and outward show:............90. H.223a, 2
Which, gently gleaming, makes a show,.........92. H.223, 66
To make these flowrie Carpets show............104. H.256, 18
Shew thy white feet, and head with Marjoram crown'd:
113. H.283, 32
Shew her how his eyes do turne..............113. H.283, 37
A shew, as if 't 'ad been a snake:..............116. H.284, 4
No fault in women, to make show.............118. H.291, 9
When Julia blushes, she do's show............120. H.295, 1
But to shew thee how in part,.................128. H.322, 4
Of Time, and show..........................134. H.336, 75
For his love then, whose sacred Reliques show 137. H.341, 7
How dull and dead are books, that cannot show
141. H.359, 1
Thy house, well fed and taught, can show......147. H.377, 34
A House-dance neatly, and can'st truly show,..148. H.377, 91
Shew me thy feet: shew me thy legs, thy thighes;
154. H.403, 1
Shew me Those Fleshie Principalities;.........154. H.403, 2
Shew me that Hill (where smiling Love doth sit)
154. H.403, 3
Shew me thy waste; Then let me there withall, 154. H.403, 5
Why! yet to shew that thou art just,...........169. H.446, 11
Not wearing Purple only for the show;.........176. H.466, 5
Meerly to shew your worth,....................176. H.467, 11
And Fading-time do's show,.....................184. H.493, 3
First, for your shape, the curious cannot shew 189. H.511, 1
Rare are thy cheeks Susanna, which do show...193. H.523, 1
Tis worse then barbarous cruelty to show.....199. H.550, 1
Which like a Pinacle doth shew...............202. H.560, 7
And all the shrubs, with sparkling spangles, shew
205. H.575, 11
Looks, shew him truly Bacchanalian like,......206. H.575, 36
And there Ile shew thee that capacious roome..207. H.575, 56
Ask me why this flower do's show............208. H.580, 7
Trust me I will not hurt ye; or once shew.....222. H.634, 7
Ev'n so, those streets and houses do but show..244. H.718, 3
Leaving no shew, where stood the Capitoll....252. H.745, 16
O shew mercy then, and be.....................254. H.757, 7
Shew they are well contented.................260. H.777, 7
If you say (I) Blush-guiltinesse will shew it....274. H.837, 6
The greener Box (for show.)..................285. H.892, 4
To shew thy nakedness to all..................287. H.899, 4
Teach it to blush, to curtsie, lisp, and shew....290. H.914, 5
Lines have, or sho'd have, thou the best canst show.
297. H.947, 10
So plaine and simple cloathes doe show.......311. H.1010, 9
Shew mercy there, where they have power to kill.
321. H.1057, 2
Shew me that world of Starres, and whence......340. N.3, 13
This if thou canst; then shew me Him..........340. N.3, 15
Naked I'le shew a sighing brest;................349. N.46, 6
Bread for our service, bread for shew;..........356. N.66, 3
God is all-sufferance here; here He doth show....357. N.74, 1
Will shew these garments made by thee;.......375. N.123, 82
Or show......................................391. N.228, 11
To shew a heart grief-rent;...................391. N.228, 21
But what God is, we cannot show..............394. N.238, 2
Lesse for to tast, then for to shew,.............400. N.266, 13
Which like a garden manifestly show...........404. A.1, 15
Which makes them shewe like roses vnder lawne...404. A.1, 24
Which ope themselves to shewe an holy shrine....404. A.1, 26
Which headed with twoe rich round rubies showe 405. A.1, 53
To'th shew, but Neuer part w^th^; next..........407. A.2, 31
Bringe to hym next, and in it shew.............408. A.2, 49
Parte wth a hastye kisse; and in that shew........410. A.3, 11
And wth thayr Ceareclothes rotted, not to shew..411. A.3, 37
Encurlld together, and noe difference show.431. ins. H.283, 50f
Showbread See Shewbread
Showed They shew'd me then, how fine 'twas spun; 18. H.47, 9
To part her lips, and shew'd them there..........24. H.75, 7
And pounc't with Stars, it shew'd to me.........67. H.175, 9
Shew'd like to Creame, enspir'd with Strawberries:
81. H.202, 2

They wo'd have **shew'd** civility;................89. H.219, 4
A golden Flie one **shew'd** to me...............185. H.497, 1
Her cloaths held up, she **shew'd** withall..........247. H.729, 3
And **shew'd** me there a Tree,..................278. H.863, 2
He **shew'd**, and told me too,..................346. N.38, 16
— — — — — — — — — —,............437. var. H.336, 106
Shower (After a dew, or dew-like **shower**)........71. H.182, 3
Yet one rude wind, or ruffling **shower**,..........88. H.216, 5
Alas you have not known that **shower**,...........104. H.257, 6
Love in a **showre** of Blossomes came..........283. H.883, 1
Showers First, April, she with mellow **showrs**.......23. H.70, 1
Newly refresh't, both by the Sun, and **showers**....25. H.77, 6
Quickned of late by Pearly **showers**;............25. H.78, 6
And all with **showrs** wet through,..............26. H.81, 11
Said he, with these late **showrs**..............27. H.81, 28
Never was Day so over-sick with **showres**,......52. H.146, 1
Though a thousand **showres** be.................62. H.162, 4
Or like those Maiden **showrs**,..................95. H.227, 24
Instead of common **showers**,..................103. H.255, 6
Nature begets by th' Sun and **showers**,.........103. H.256, 5
Showrs or Sun-shines co'd beget..............108. H.266, 4
The **Shewers** of Roses, lucky-foure-leav'd grasse: 113. H.283, 42
(Nature begets by th' Sun, and **showers**,)......166, H.443, 34
Upon her cheekes she wept, and from those **showers** 204. H.567, 1
Ile sing no more of Frosts, Snowes, Dews and **Showers**; 228. H.658, 3
We pray for **showers** (at our need)............279. H.867, 5
Enspir'd by th' Sun-beams after dews & **showers**. 326. H.1080, 14
Who, with His Sun-shine, and His **showers**,.....364. N.96, 23
Showest And **shew'st** me there much Plate, but little meat; 161. H.424, 2
Showing **Shewing** a heart consenting;...........55. H.149, 75
Shewing me there a fire brand;................153. H.399, 4
Be she **shewing** in her dresse,.................232. H.665, 5
Who **shewing** mercy here, few priz'd, or none...393. N.234, 2
Shown No, no, this sorrow **shown**..............104. H.257, 24
Let but Pink's face i' th' Looking-glasse be **showne**, 110. H.272, 3
And after they have **shown** their pride,........176. H.467, 16
Nor will they leave Thee, till they both have **shown** 181. H.483, 7
Why then (forsooth) a Carcanet is **shown**......232. H.668, 5
To work a wonder, God would have her **shown**,..384. N.183, 1
Faile and scarce leaue to be **showne**............418. A.9, 29
Twixt this and them this Gorgon **showne**..........418. A.9, 57
— — — — — — — — — — —,..............447. var. A.1, 15
— — — — — — — — — — —,...............450. var. A.9, 35
Shows See **Foreshows**
But thou liv'st fearlesse; and thy face ne'r **shewes** 37. H.106, 93
As **shews** the Aire, when with a Rain-bow grac'd; 40. H.114, 1
More radiant then the Summers Sun-beams **shows**; 45. H.128, 13
Her legs were such Diana **shows**,..............51. H.142, 13
But since (me thinks) it **shows**.................51. H.144, 3
Shews you how much is spent of night...........54. H.149, 52
And here, you see, this Lilly **shows**,...........75. H.193, 4
That weares one face (like heaven) and never **showes** 128. H.323, 7
A Strawberry **shewes** halfe drown'd in Creame? 164. H.440, 6
For ropes of pearle, first Madam Ursly **showes**...232. H.668, 1
Nailes from her fingers mew'd, she **shewes**: what els? 232. H.668, 4
And **shewes** his naked flitches;................259. H.772, 20
What is't that wasts a Prince? example **showes**, 331. H.1105, 1
How sweetly **shewes** thy smiling face,........375. N.123, 73
Shewes like the Heavens aboue y[e] Moone,.......413. A.4, 13
— — — — — — — — — — —,..............424, var. H.128, 47
— — — — — — — — — — —,..............447. var. A.1, 2
Shreake — — — — — — — — —, ...452. ins. H.443, 45t
Shreakes Ribbonds and then some silken **shreakes** 440. ins. H.443, 45t
Shredding The while the meat is a **shredding**; 263. H.784, 15
Shreds Onely true in **shreds** and stuffe...........77. H.195, 12
Shrewd Many **shrewd** disasters met,.............209. H.585, 5
Shrill That ere while was heard so **shrill**?......305. H.984, 6
Shrine Enlightned substance; mark how from the **Shrine** 112. H.283, 12
Enclos'd within a christall **shrine**:............135. H.336, 98
For the Saint, we'l keep the **Shrine**............211. H.593, 4
A little Saint best fits a little **Shrine**,..........249. H.733, 1
We offer here, before thy **Shrine**,................360. N.83, 32
Which ope themselves to shewe an holy **shrine**..404. A.1, 26
— — — — — — — — — — —,..............452. var. H.128, 12
Shrined As Lillies **shrin'd** in Christall, so.......271. H.824, 13
Shrink Shall never **shrink**, where making thine abode, 143. H.365, 11
Or depth, these last may yeeld, and yearly **shrinke**, 148. H.377, 105
Shroud Keepe vp those flames, & though you **shroud** 413. A.4, 16
Shrouded Wo'd **shrouded** be, and therewith buried. 332. H.1114, 2
Shrouds Which for the better beawtifying **shrowdes** 406. A.1, 83
Shrubs And all the **shrubs**, with sparkling spangles, shew 205. H.575, 11
Shrugging **Shrugging** as it did move,..........57. H.149, 137
Shu'd See **Sho'd, Should**
And whose the pretty prize **shu'd** be,..............31. H.92, 3
Shun To **shun** the first, and last extreame......38. H.106, 132
O enter then! but see ye **shun**................57. H.149, 141
To **shun**....................................211. H.596, 7
Laugh at my scraps of cloaths, and **shun**......235. H.677, 5
Must **shun** the bad, I, and suspect the best.....305. H.981, 2
Better it is, premonish'd, for to **shun**............349. N.43, 5
Next, that these ills none cowardly may **shun**;..387. N.201, 5
To **shun** the least Temptation to a sin;.......392. N.230, 30
Shut With the Red-capt worme, that's **shut**....120. H.293, 39
Daysies wo'd **shut**, and closing, sigh and weep...159. H.421, 26
Shut not so soon; the dull-ey'd night..........164. H.441, 1
And work no more; but **shut** up Shop..........212. H.602, 4
But now 'tis clos'd; and being **shut**, & seal'd,...227. H.652, 11
Shut every gate; mend every hedge that's torne,.259. H.771, 5
Once **shut**, was never to be open'd more........385. N.190, 4
Shute See **Shoot**
Shuts And as He **shuts**, close up to Maids again. 196. H.537, 4
With the third key He opes and **shuts** the wombe; 390. N.224, 3
Shutting Three dayes before the **shutting** in of May, 86. H.213, 13
Shy To read my Booke the Virgin **shie**..............6. H.4, 1
Of the **shie** Virgin, seems to deck.............166. H.443, 64
Maids nay's are nothing, they are **shie**.........249. H.735, 1
May all **shie** Maids, at wonted hours,..........361. N.83, 73
Obedience, Wise-Distrust, Peace, **shy**............409. A.2, 95
Sibb See **Syb**
Sibb when she saw her face how hard it was,...249. H.732, 1
Sibyl's Like **Sybels** Leaves, throughout the ample world? 172. H.459, 4
Like the **Sybells**, through the world..........242. H.714, 8
Sick See **Lovesick, Over-sick**
Once were Virgins **sick** of love,..................15. H.37, 2
And Leaves did heale, all **sick** of humane seed:..61. H.161, 2
Ease my **sick** head,............................95. H.227, 5
On this **sick** youth work your enchantments here: 99. H.244, 2
Prue, my dearest Maid, is **sick**,................122. H.302, 1
With speed give **sick** men their salvation:......125. H.315, 2
To read by th' Starres, the Kingdoms **sick**:.....126. H.319, 6
I'm **sick** of Love; O let me lie.................158. H.420, 1
His Moon-tann'd Mab, as somewhat **sick**,......167. H.443, 84
Now is **sick**:.................................210. H.591, 9
Sick is the Land to'th' heart; and doth endure..214. H.612, 5
The Rose was **sick**, and smiling di'd;..........237. H.686, 1
A ragd-soust-neats-foot with **sick** vinegar:.....262. H.783, 14
Can make thee **sick**,..........................273. H.833, 5
Sick and surcharg'd with this societie:........297. H.949, 2
Never make **sick** your Banks by surfeiting.....316. H.1028, 24
Sick is Anthea, sickly is the spring,..........320. H.1054, 1
The Primrose **sick**, and sickly every thing:....320. H.1054, 2
And sore without, and **sick** within:............342. N.17, 2
Sick in heart, and **sick** in head,..................347. N.41, 6
While my **sick** heart..........................353. N.56, 16
Sick is my heart; O Saviour! do Thou please.....358. N.77, 8
Sickle To the rough **Sickle**, and crookt Sythe,..102. H.250, 42
Sickly **Sickly** the Prim-rose: Pale the Daffadill:..41. H.118, 2
Next, look thou like a **sickly** Moone;............47. H.132, 3
Sickly Girles, they beare of you................64. H.167, 4
Time-past so fragrant, **sickly** now drawn in....77. H.197, 28
So yellow-green, and **sickly** too?...............208. H.580, 8
No joy to thee their **sickly** Lord..............239. H.696, 12
Sick is Anthea, **sickly** is the spring,..........320. H.1054, 1
The Primrose sick, and **sickly** every thing:....320. H.1054, 2
Sicknesses See **Green-sicknesses**
More then for peevish pining **sicknesses**........245. H.723, 12
After our long, and peevish **sicknesses**..........300. H.961, 4
To make my bed soft in my **sicknesses**:........358. N.77, 9
Side See **Golden-Cheapside, Inside, Outside**
By whose warme **side** thou dost securely sleep..35. H.106, 35
To quick action, or the warme soft **side**........45. H.128, 5
With all luckie Birds to **side**..................57. H.149, 159
Next, then, upon the Chanters **side**...........93. H.223, 125
But gently prest from the soft **side**...........120. H.293, 49
Close to my Beds **side** she did stand...........153. H.399, 3
Come then, and be to my chast **side**...........190. H.515, 9
Come sit we by the fires **side**;................219. H.629, 1
A Pleasing Wife, that by thy **side**.............233. H.670, 13
Apollos Image **side** with Thee to blesse......254. H.756, 11
To **side** with them, the Commons all............282. H.877, 2
She who keeps chastly to her husbands **side**....286. H.898, 13
On either **side** with rich rare Jewells grac'd,......405. A.1, 40
On eyther **side** of theis, quicke Eares...........408. A.2, 39
Sides The **sides**: for 'tis a charme.............55. H.149, 87
Did crack the Play-house **sides**, or cleave her roofe. 150. H.382, 12
Since Fame that **sides** with these, or goes before 329. H.1092, 3

Pardon my trespasse (Silvia) I confesse,........294. H.936, 1
Similitude Wrathfull He may be, by similitude:..397. N.259, 2
Simnel I'le to thee a Simnell bring,............236. H.684, 1
Simper Ye may simper, blush, and smile,........74. H.189, 1
Simpering Like to a Twi-light, or that simpring Dawn, 34. H.104, 3
And shame-fac't Plum, (all simp'ring there)...192. H.521, 38
Simple May take the simple Villages..............6. H.2, 16
So plaine and simple cloathes doe show.......311. H.1010, 9
For 'tis Fee simple, and noe rent................407. A.2, 13
Simplicities Drest in her nak't simplicities:.....154. H.402, 4
Simplicity The Countries sweet simplicity:........35. H.106, 4
Truth by her own simplicity is known,........329. H.1094, 1
Sin Good children kisse the rods, that punish sin...32. H.97, 4
Feare to those sheets, that know no sin........35. H.106, 40
To numb the sence of Dearth, which sho'd sinne haste it, 37. H.106, 119
Suspition now had been the sinne,..............48. H.136, 7
What now is done: since where no sin..........48. H.136, 12
And sung their thankfull Hymnes: 'tis sin,.....68. H.178, 11
And sin no more, as we have done, by staying; 68. H.178, 41
He that may sin, sins least; Leave to transgresse 109. H.270, 1
Sin, in's Nap'rie, not to express his wit;......114. H.283, 68
Artlesse the Sceane was; and that monstrous sin 150. H.382, 13
Thus, though the Rooke do's raile against the sin, 163. H.439, 3
Banish consent, and 'tis no sinne............175. H.465, 56
'Tis sin I know, 'tis sin to throtle Wine.......187. H.502, 4
No man exempted is from Death, or sinne.......199. H.548, 2
Grace with the Gods, who's sorry for his sinne. 329. H.1095, 4
Three fatall Sisters wait upon each sin;.........341. N.11, 1
The sweetest solace is to act no sin.............341. N.13, 2
My God, I'm wounded by my sin,..............342. N.17, 1
God when for sin He makes His Children smart,..343. N.22, 1
If God should punish no sin, here, of men,.......343. N.27, 3
God pardons those, who do through frailty sin;..344. N.32, 1
When once the sin has fully acted been,.........346. N.37, 1
Thou stop'st S. Peter in the midst of sin;........349. N.43, 3
A sin, then fall to weeping when 'tis done........349. N.43, 6
Of sin, we must strive 'gainst the streame of it:..356. N.67, 2
Can I not sin, but thou wilt be.................357. N.72, 1
Sin leads the way, but as it goes, it feels........362. N.86, 1
And be it sin here to be dumb,..................365. N.97, 2
What is corrupt, or sowr'd with sin,............366. N.98, 5
When I shall sin, pardon my trespasse here;....367. N.99, 1
Sin once reacht up to Gods eternall Sphere,....367. N.100, 1
Is that which gives to sin a livelihood...........367. N.101, 2
But that held back by sin......................370. N.111, 4
God had but one Son free from sin; but none...378. N.134, 1
The more occasion still to sin..................379. N.144, 2
He that is hurt seeks help: sin is the wound;..381. N.155, 1
Sin no Existence; Nature none it hath,........383. N.173, 1
As when we sin; God, the great Chymist, thence 386. N.196, 3
Sin never slew a soule, unlesse there went......389. N.217, 1
Sin is an act so free, that if we shall..........389. N.218, 1
Say, 'tis not free, 'tis then no sin at all.........389. N.218, 2
Sin is the cause of death; and sin's alone......390. N.219, 1
And from Gods Prescience of mans sin doth flow 390. N.219, 3
Boldly in sin, shall feel more punishment.......391. N.227, 4
To sterve thy sin,..............................391. N.228, 22
To shun the least Temptation to a sin;.......392. N.230, 30
Though to be tempted be no sin, untill.........392. N.230, 31
The first of sin is, and the next of praise:......395. N.243, 2
It saves the soule, by drowning sin............396. N.253, 2
But where sin swells, there let Thy grace abound. 398. N.261, 6
That for my sin, Thou, Thou must drink,.......400. N.267, 7
Sinne made before..............................401. N.268, 23
I'le not prophane, by soile of sin,..............402. N.269, 4
Thy glaring fires, least in theire sight the sinne 424. ins. H.128, 46a
Sinai Of Sion, Sinai, Nebo, and with them,....330. H.1100, 11
Since Since Coats, and Hamlets, best agree.........5. H.2, 5
Now since my love is tongue-lesse, know me such, 15. H.38, 13
Since which, it festers so, that I can prove.......17. H.44, 5
Since I was born, then here;....................19. H.51, 2
Forgive, forgive me; since I did not know........27. H.82, 5
Or Muse of Roses: since that name does fit......28. H.84, 3
Since I must leave thee; and enforc'd, must say..46. H.128, 39
What now is done: since where no sin..........48. H.136, 12
But since (me thinks) it shows..................51. H.144, 3
Since that Love and Night bid enter...........56. H.149, 100
Since none so good are, but you may condemne;..64. H.168, 5
Above an houre since; yet you not drest,.......68. H.178, 8
Blush not at all for that; since we have set....76. H.194, 5
But since th'art slaine; and in thy fall,.........89. H.219, 7
And since the last is dead, there's hope,.......93. H.223, 111
Co'd never since find any rest..................96. H.229, 6
Since which, though I love many,.............100. H.249, 6
Since which (beleeve the rest)................105. H.258, 7
Since Clouds disperst, Suns guild the Aire again. 105. H.259, 2
But since these Cowslips fading be,...........112. H.281, 3
But since It must be done, dispatch, and sowe 116. H.283, 141
No more shall I, since I am driven hence,......131. H.333, 1
Why then, since life to us is short,............133. H.336, 31
And since I'm free,............................137. H.340, 9
Since you are Lady of this Fairie land.........140. H.354, 10
As for my self, since time a thousand cares....140. H.355, 5
Since now (alas)................................144. H.371, 4
Since neithers height was rais'd by th'ill......149. H.377, 116
Of others; since no Stud, no Stone, no Piece,..149. H.377, 117
Since for thy full deserts (with all the rest.....152. H.392, 1
Since man expos'd is to a world of griefs.......153. H.397, 2
Since which I freeze, but cannot frie..........155. H.406, 4
Since thou art gone, no more I mean to play,..159. H.421, 9
Besides (Ai me!) since she went hence to dwell, 159. H.421, 27
Since so it is; Ile tell thee what,..............161. H.425, 5
Since Jack and Jill both wicked be;...........163. H.434, 1
Never since first Bellona us'd a Shield,........170. H.451, 11
One Cordelion had that Age long since;......170. H.451, 15
Since to th' Country first I came,.............182. H.489, 1
Since you are knowne to be Penelope...........189. H.511, 4
From whom we'l reckon. Wit came in, but since 194. H.526, 5
Since now to the Port.......................195. H.534, 10
Which seals Thy Glorie; since I doe prefer....199. H.545, 9
Which (since here they can't combine).........211. H.593, 3
Who by the Shepheards, sung (long since).....214. H.611, 5
Lost to all Musick now; since every thing.....214. H.612, 3
Since Ghost ther's none to affright thee.........217. H.619, 10
And since it was thy care....................220. H.633, 14
My Threshold, since I see,....................223. H.635, 14
Since Gander did his prettie Youngling wed;...223. H.636, 1
But since I'm cal'd (rare Denham) to be gone,.234. H.673, 13
Yet since cal'd back; henceforward let me be,..242. H.713, 15
Since both have here deserved best.............243. H.716, 36
Since more and more is exacted;..............247. H.727, 9
Ch. What's thy request? Ph. That since she's now beneath 248. H.730, 15
Since that I know, 'mong all the rest..........250. H.739, 3
Break off Delay, since we but read of one.....251. H.744, 1
Stand forth brave man, since Fate has made thee here 251. H.745, 1
Since the Porter he..........................256. H.762, 10
I'le bring a Fever; since thou keep'st no fire...262. H.783, 22
'Twas rich before; but since your Name is downe, 264. H.789, 3
For since I've travail'd all this Realm throughout 267. H.804, 5
Hanch, since he (lately) did interre his wife,...275. H.842, 1
Which ever since has been in thrall,...........281. H.876, 9
Since for one Bad, one Good I know:...........283. H.885, 2
But since th' art Printed, thou dost call........287. H.899, 3
Since we fresh strewings will bring hither,.....289. H.912, 7
Since love so much contents me...............296. H.946, 12
It matters not, since thou art chosen one......305. H.983, 3
Since thence...............................308. H.993, 16
Since when (me thinks) my braines about doe swim, 313. H.1017, 13
Since after death comes glory, Ile not haste....314. H.1022, 2
Nor will hereafter; since I know..............320. H.1052, 3
Since shed or Cottage I have none,............321. H.1056, 1
Since Absolution you can give to them........322. H.1062, 9
My dearest Love, since thou wilt go,..........323. H.1068, 1
With Poesies, since 'tis fitter.................323. H.1068, 14
Since the place wherein ye lye,...............324. H.1070, 2
Since I as yet did never prove,...............327. H.1082, 2
Since longer I can't live,.....................328. H.1091, 5
Since Fame that sides with these, or goes before 329. H.1092, 3
He's double honour'd, since h'as got gay cloathes: 330. H.1099, 2
Since I do sob and crie,......................351. N.49, 2
Since rough the way is, help me when I call,...352. N.51, 7
No more, no more, since thou are dead,........360. N.83, 49
But since...................................363. N.92, 7
To pay Thee that I owe, since what I see.....368. N.103, 3
And, since it fortunes so;....................368. N.104, 5
Since mischiefs neither dare..................373. N.122, 11
Whereas by thee, those, and A Million since....411. A.3, 39
But vnto mee, bee onlye hoarse, since now......411. A.3, 47
Wiser Conclusions in mee, since I knowe........411. A.3, 53
And since you pay............................413. A.4, 21
Since part we must Let's kisse, that done retire...414. A.6, 9
Sincere If her lip, the most sincere..............59. H.155, 3
And in that sincere Christall seek,.............63. H.164, 8
Things are evermore sincere;.................377. N.128, 10
Sincere-silver Wod'st thou to sincere-silver turn thy mold? 144. H.370, 7
Sincerity Part of her leggs sinceritie:.............12. H.27, 4
Part of the nak't sincerity;...................247. H.729, 6
Sinews — — — — — — — —, ...427. var. H.197, 77
Sinful Gods boundlesse mercy is (to sinfull man)..341. N.15, 1
But take no tincture from my sinfull Book:....371. N.113, 8
Gods Prescience makes none sinfull; but th' offence 390. N.220, 1
Sing I sing of Brooks, of Blossomes, Birds, and Bowers: 5. H.1, 1
I sing of May-poles, Hock-carts, Wassails, Wakes,..5. H.1, 3
By these, to sing cleanly-Wantonnesse.............5. H.1,

I **sing** of Dewes, of Raines, and piece by piece......5. H.1, 7
I **sing** of Times trans-shifting; and I write......5. H.1, 9
I write of Groves, of Twilights, and I **sing**........5. H.1, 11
I write of Hell; I **sing** (and ever shall)..........5. H.1, 13
There on a Hillock thou mayst **sing**..............5. H.2, 11
Sing thou my Dirge, sweet-warbling Chorister!....19. H.50, 4
Sing o're Horace; for ere long.................39. H.111, 11
Never **sing**, or play more here...................39. H.111, 14
Castalian sisters, **sing**, if wanting thee.........45. H.128, 30
Of which, sweet Swans must drink, before they **sing**
45. H.128, 34
And the boyes with sweet tunes **sing**,...........54. H.149, 47
Sing I co'd once; and bravely too enspire......84. H.210, 3
While we this Trentall **sing** about thy Grave.....89. H.219, 2
Ye dance, and **sing**, and now clap hands.........94. H.225, 8
So long you did not **sing**, or touch your Lute,....95. H.228, 1
And, to the Pipe, **sing** Harvest home............101. H.250, 6
And Angels will be borne, while thou dost **sing**.
102. H.252, 2
May the thrice-three-Sisters **sing**................108. H.266, 9
Y'ave heard them sweetly **sing**,..................110. H.274, 9
The while the cloud of younglings **sing**,........113. H.283, 43
Maides sho'd say, or Virgins **sing**,............117. H.285, 11
Aske me, why I do not **sing**....................131. H.332, 1
Iülus to **sing** such a song....................135. H.336, 94
When thou do'st play, and sweetly **sing**,.......142. H.362, 1
Fame, and his Name, both set, and **sing** his Lyricks.
143. H.366, 4
Sing me to death; for till thy voice be cleare,..152. H.390, 1
Nor thinke these Ages that do hoarcely **sing**....155. H.405, 5
It is in vain to **sing**, or stay..................179. H.476, 34
Where Poets **sing** the stories of our love.......206. H.575, 24
There thou shalt hear Divine Musæus **sing**......206. H.575, 25
Sing their Evadne; and still more for thee......206. H.575, 53
Meane time we two will **sing** the Dirge of these;
209. H.584, 7
Ile **sing** no more, nor will I longer write......228. H.658, 1
Ile **sing** no more of Frosts, Snowes, Dews and Showers;
228. H.658, 3
Ile write no more, nor will I tell or **sing**........228. H.658, 5
Ile **sing** no more of death, or shall the grave....228. H.658, 7
Let's feast, and frolick, **sing**, and play,..........233. H.670, 30
I have, to **sing** how day drawes on.............246. H.724, 4
Ph. I'le beg a penny, or Ile **sing** so long,......248. H.730, 21
Thou & I'le **sing** to make these dull Shades merry,
248. H.730, 25
Whose restlesse Ghosts shall heare their children **sing**,
252. H.745, 9
I **sing** thy praise Iacchus,.....................259. H.772, 1
When we thy Orgies **sing**,.....................259. H.772, 10
And teach me how to **sing**......................261. H.778, 7
Then while I **sing** your praise,.................261. H.778, 10
Her supreamest Requiem **sing**;.................274. H.838, 6
I heare in thee rare Laniere to **sing**;..........276. H.851, 4
That I may play, and **sing** a Hymne to Love.....280. H.871, 4
So shall I **sing** thy praise.....................281. H.874, 13
With my weake voice Ile **sing**, or say........303. H.973, 13
Here may **sing** the rest of either:................304. H.976, 4
But unamaz'd dares clearely **sing**,..............318. H.1036, 3
I **sing** the more, that thou hast one;..........321. H.1056, 2
Mattens **sing**, or Mattens say:.................324. H.1069, 2
Those Bardes, and I, all in a Chorus **sing**,.......324. H.1071, 3
Rare is the voice it selfe; but when we **sing**....331. H.1101, 1
I **sing** Thy Birth, Oh JESU!....................345. N.33, 2
And as we **sing** thy Dirge, we will.............359. N.83, 9
Then a Caroll, for to **sing**.....................364. N.96, 2
Let's blesse the Babe: And, as we **sing**..........367. N.98, 25
The praises **sing**...............................369. N.106, 12
Or **sing** of mercy, and I'le suit.................393. N.232, 13
And **sing** a Caroll here..........................413. A.4, 5
Singe That ye **singe** no maiden-haire...........315. H.1026, 8
Singer Runs division with the **Singer**............364. N.96, 7
Singing See **Still-sweet-singing**
When I thy **singing** next shall heare,............22. H.68, 1
Of **singing** Crickits by thy fire:.............37. H.106, 122
Sweet **singing** Lark,.............................87. H.214, 5
(As we think) **singing** to the dinne............115. H.283, 103
Broke is my Reed, hoarse is my **singing** too:....205. H.573, 2
And cheer'st them up, by **singing** how..........230. H.662, 27
More curst for **singing** out of tune then he.......266. H.799, 4
Singing about my everlasting fire...............294. H.938, 4
The wounds of love with **singing**...............296. H.946, 18
Now **singing**, homeward let us carrie............366. N.97, 26
Single 'Twas but a **single** Rose,...................51. H.144, 1
And had but **single** grace......................75. H.193, 8
That **single** may have any......................160. H.422, 16
Singleness By how much, neere to **singlenesse**.....254. H.754, 2
Singly As divers strings do **singly** disagree........406. A.1, 107
Sings The Evill is not Yours: my sorrow **sings**,..62. H.161, 15
And as it flyes, it gently **sings**,...............130. H.329, 22
And sweetly **sings**, but yet his breath sayes no..149. H.381, 2
The while the Daulian Minstrell sweetly **sings**,..224. H.642, 7
'Tis still observ'd, that Fame ne're **sings**.......245. H.721, 1
But when he **sings** a Psalme, ther's none can be..266. H.799, 3
Apollo **sings**, his harpe resounds; give roome,....415. A.7, 1
Singular Mirt. And that his birth sho'd be more **singular**,
86. H.213, 19
Pleasing alike; alike both **singular**:............209. H.586, 4
(Amongst the rest) both bright and **singular**;..267. H.804, 10
Sink That done, **sink** down into a silv'rie straine;..67. H.176, 5
Has not whence to **sink** at all...................84. H.209, 8
Sinned With God, then one, that never sin'd 'gainst Him.
388. N.205, 2
Sinners Under the first the **Sinners** ever trust;....340. N.6, 3
Then all the songs of **sinners** are.............379. N.145, 2
Sinners confounded are a twofold way,........388. N.210, 1
Sinners' Teares, though th'are here below the **sinners** brine,
226. H.645, 1
Sin's Sin is the cause of death; and **sin's** alone..390. N.219, 1
Sins He that may sin, **sins** least; Leave to transgresse
109. H.270, 1
Baucis, these were my **sins** of youth...........135. H.336, 120
The body **sins** not, 'tis the Will..............175. H.465, 63
Other mens **sins** wee ever beare in mind;........253. H.751, 1
To load with blessings, and unload from **sins**......341. N.14, 2
And when I my **sins** confesse,....................347. N.41, 3
With the **sins** of all my youth,.................348. N.41, 38
When **sins**, by stripes, to us grow wearisome.....349. N.45, 2
Sins first dislik'd, are after that belov'd..........362. N.85, 2
After true sorrow for our **sinnes**, our strife......362. N.91, 1
My **sinnes**, by gently striking;.................363. N.92, 9
Scores of **sins** w'ave made here many,..........373. N.121, 9
To punish great **sins**, who small faults whipt here.
381. N.156, 2
Mens **sins** destroyed are, when they repent;......388. N.210, 3
Or when, for **sins**, men suffer punishment.......388. N.210, 4
Sion See **Zion**
Sion's See **Zion's**
Sip Of Julia, and began to **sip**;.................71. H.182, 6
Ver. Chor. But I will **sip** a little wine;........400. N.267, 12
Sir Good **Sir**, make no more cuts i'th' outward skin,
44. H.126, 3
And, as **Sir** Thomas Parson tells,..............92. H.223, 79
Who doth both love and feare you Honour'd **Sir**..99. H.245, 8
Who hug our Poems (Honourd **Sir**) and then....141. H.359, 5
Of some rough Groom who (yirkt with corns) sayes, **Sir**
146. H.377, 21
And with our Broth and bread, and bits; **Sir**, friend,
146. H.377, 23
Good morning **Sir** to you:......................156. H.412, 2
For pitty, **Sir**, find out that Bee,..............156. H.412, 11
By you, **Sir**, to awake him...................156. H.412, 20
(Not without glory) Noble **Sir**, you are,........170, H.451, 2
Which may be done, if (**Sir**) you can beget.....170. H.451, 5
For to thanke you (Noble **Sir**)...............182. H.489, 11
If children you have ten, **Sir** John..............208. H.581, 5
If I lye unburied **Sir**,.........................270. H.821, 1
Sire Which crept into each aged **Sire**...........135. H.336, 104
Siren About the Roofe a **Syren** in a Sphere;....115. H.283, 102
Sirens Listen, while they (like **Syrens** in their Spheres)
206. H.575, 52
Or whether Fairies, **Syrens**, Nymphes they were, 326. H.1080, 5
Sires May blaze the vertue of their **Sires**........116. H.283, 160
Our **Sires** betraid their Countrey and their King.
252. H.745, 10
Yet with the bench of aged **sires**,...............303. H.973, 11
Sir-reverence A Fart flew out, or a **Sir-reverence**...200. H.551, 6
Sirs With Water fill'd, (**Sirs**, credit me)..........44. H.127, 2
Tread, **Sirs**, as lightly as ye can..............226. H.644, 1
A Good and Bad. **Sirs** credit me...............283. H.885, 10
Sirup See **Syrup**
Sister A **Sister** (in the stead......................13. H.31, 7
The **sister** to saturitie..........................378. N.138, 2
Sisterhood Or sworn to that sweet **Sister-hood**:........7. H.9, 8
The sweet, and flowrie **Sisterhood**..............237. H.686, 4
And gracefull made, by your neate **Sisterhood**...290. H.914, 10
Sisterhoods Your **Sister-hoods** may stay,........184. H.493, 5
Sisters See **Thrice-three-sisters**
Three lovely **Sisters** working were...............18. H.47, 1
Castalian **sisters**, sing, if wanting thee...........45. H.128, 30
Sisters of Fate appeare to me...................153. H.399, 2
The holy **Sisters** some among...................237. H.686, 9
Three fatall **Sisters** wait upon each sin;..........341. N.11, 1
Sit Where thou mayst **sit**, and piping please.........5. H.2, 3
To meet and **sit** in Parliament:....................8. H.11, 2
Julia and I did lately **sit**.........................19. H.49, 1
Let us **sit**, and quaffe our wine..................39. H.111, 6
But endlesse Peace, **sit** here, and keep..........104. H.256, 15
Part of the way be met; or **sit** stone-still.....113. H.283, 58
Then as ye **sit** about your embers,.............127. H.319, 37
Sit crown'd with Rose-buds, and carouse,......127. H.319, 41
Why nothing now, but lonely **sit**,...............132. H.334, 3
And so we'l **sit**..............................134. H.336, 85
We'l still **sit** up,..............................136. H.336, 147
Nor suffer you the Poets to **sit** cold,...........141. H.359, 7
Of those that **sit** and weep.....................144. H.371, 18
In utter darkenes did, and still will **sit**........150. H.382, 18
And we will, all **sit** mute:......................151. H.388, 2
Shew me that Hill (where smiling Love doth **sit**)
154. H.403, 3
Where thou shalt **sit**, and Red-brest by,......192. H.521, 17
By which we **sit**, and Doe Divine..............198. H.544, 4
Sit smiling in the Meads; where Balme and Oile, 205. H.575, 3
And here we'l **sit** on Primrose-banks, and see...206. H.575, 21

Or let her walk, or stand, or **sit**,..............207. H.579, 3
So, while I thus **sit** crown'd;..................208. H.582, 2
Come **sit** we under yonder Tree,................215. H.616, 1
And as on Primroses we **sit**,.....................215. H.616, 3
Thus we will **sit** and talke; but tell..........215. H.616, 11
Who'l let ye by their fire **sit**?.................218. H.626, 5
Come **sit** we by the fires side;..................219. H.629, 1
Tumble me down, and I will **sit**..................235. H.677, 1
Must **sit** with the losse,..........................256. H.762, 8
Honour to you who **sit**!...........................261. H.778, 1
How thou canst **sit** and smile,...................272. H.828, 10
While others they **sit** wringing...................296. H.946, 15
Close by whose living coale I **sit**,.................350. N.47, 25
While we **sit** by sorrowes streames,...............376. N.128, 2
Because the Law forbad to **sit** and crie.........384. N.180, 3
Beares vp twoe globes where loue and pleasure **sitt**,
405. A.1, 52
Sits Here in green Meddowes **sits** eternall May,..206. H.575, 13
Whom faire Corinna **sits**, and doth comply......206. H.575, 40
From him, who all alone **sits** there,.............263. H.785, 5
Which **sits** as Dew of Roses there:..............328. H.1090, 9
Sits Cupid kissing of his mother Queene,.......405. A.1, 56
— — — — — — — — — —,.................443. var. H.637, 1
Sittest **Sitt'st**, and beleev'st that there be seas,....36. H.106, 70
Sitting And may prevent it, **sitting** still............6. H.2, 26
Sitting alone (as one forsook)....................51. H.142, 1
Sitting, and sorting severall sorts of flowers,.....94. H.224, 2
And **sitting**, see the wiles, wayes, walks of wit,..187. H.506, 3
All **sitting** neer the glitt'ring Hearth...........193. H.521, 50
She by the River sate, and **sitting** there,.........251. H.743, 1
Or Muses, on their mountaine **sitting** there;....326. H.1080, 6
Sate by the Grave; and sadly **sitting** there,......384. N.180, 9
Six **Six** teeth he has, whereof twice two are known 46. H.129, 3
Old Parson Beanes hunts **six** dayes of the week, 163. H.435, 1
Six dayes he hollows so much breath away,....163. H.435, 3
Upon **six** plump Dandillions, high-..............167. H.443, 86
Sixty Made up One State of **Sixtie** Venuses;....326. H.1080, 4
One man has reatch't his **sixty** yeers, but he......328. H.1088, 7
Size Nor is it, that thou keep'st this stricter **size** 37. H.106, 117
Skiagraphy The Painters art in thy **Sciography**?..139. H.347, 2
Skies Under a Lawne, then **skyes** more cleare,....25. H.78, 1
Which Star-like sparkle in their **skies**:..........61. H.160, 2
Faire was the Dawne; and but e'ne now the **Skies**
81. H.202, 1
Like purest **Skies**...............................193. H.524, 2
And trouble the **skies**;.........................225. H.643, 20
Swelling in likenes like twoe Christall **skyes**......406. A.1, 78
Skill For I know you have the **skill**...........204. H.569, 13
And his **skill** runs on the lees;.................347. N.41, 15
Has, or none, or little **skill**,.....................347. N.41, 18
Hath seal'd the promise of her vtmost **skill**.......405. A.1, 64
Lett hym but wth indifferent **skill**..............409. A.2, 105
Skillful Come, **skilfull** Lupo, now, and take........38. H.108, 1
Skilfull i' th' Harpe, and Melodie:..............70. H.181, 10
But to the stout; and those that **skilfull** are.....290. H.916, 2
Skills But it **skills** not; go your way;..........270. H.821, 6
Skin See **Old-skin**, **Sheepskin**, **Silk-soft-skin**, **Smooth-skin**
Smooth Anthea, for a **skin**.......................16. H.39, 5
I put, he pusht, and heedless of my **skin**,........17. H.44, 3
Where the Steletto pierc'd the **skin**:.............18. H.46, 8
Doe they first pill thee, next, pluck off thy **skin**? 32. H.97, 3
Good Sir, make no more cuts i'th' outward **skin**,
44. H.126, 3
Them, from that cleane and subtile **skin**,........75. H.193, 28
Subtile and ductile Codlin's **skin**;...............91. H.223, 61
Skin deepe into the Porke, or lights............147. H.377, 54
It sho'd be onely in my Julia's **skin**:............158. H.416, 2
As it might serve me for my **skin**...............164. H.442, 5
That of my **skin**, I all am stript;...............164. H.442, 7
Unlesse you **skin** again each part...............164. H.442, 10
The roome is hung with the blew **skin**.........166. H.443, 66
Be she rough, or smooth of **skin**;..............253. H.750, 7
Kings ought to sheare, not **skin** their sheepe.....261. H.780, 2
True mirth resides not in the smiling **skin**:.......341. N.13, 1
No crack or Schisme leave i'th subtill **skin**:.......385. N.184, 2
Over the which a meet sweet **skin** is drawne....404. A.1, 23
Skynne and colour, flesh and blood,.............418. A.9, 21
Skinns **Skinns** he din'd well to day; how do you think?
156. H.409, 1
Skin's Her **skins** most smooth, and cleare expansion.
82. H.204, 4
Skirmishing Them to the field, and, there, to **skirmishing**;
370. N.108, 2
Skirts And **skirts** that want their stiches,.......259. H.772, 19
Skoles **Skoles** stinks so deadly, that his Breeches loath
226. H.650, 1
Skrew **Skrew** lives by shifts; yet sweares by no small oathes;
149. H.380, 1
Skulls **Skulls** co'd not well passe through that scum of men.
200. H.551, 2
Skurfe See **Scurf**
Skurffe See **Scurf**
Skurffe by his Nine-bones sweares, and well he may,
180. H.480, 1
Sky Ah! what is then this curious **skie**,..........48. H.133, 16
Whose velome, and whose volumne is the **Skie**,..168. H.444, 7
A Repurgation of the **Skie**:.......................188. H.508, 4
Next, when I see Thee towring in the **skie**,....301. H.966, 3
Slack To **slack** these flames wherein I frie?........40. H.115, 2
That **slack** my pace; but yet not make me stay?..352. N.51, 3
Slackens Back-turning **slackens** Resolution.......252. H.747, 2
Slain But since th'art **slaine**; and in thy fall,......89. H.219, 7
When I behold Thee, almost **slain**,.............400. N.267, 1
To these for sauce the **slaine** stagges teares
435. ins. H.293, p
Slain-stag's Moles eyes; to these, the **slain-Stags** teares:
120. H.293, 44
Slake But if horrour cannot **slake**..............117. H.286, 9
Slakes Either **slakes**, or doth retire;...........242. H.714, 10
Slam At Post and Paire, or **Slam**, Tom Tuck would play
238. H.693, 1
Slave **Slave** to Thrall,...........................12. H.26, 10
And **slave** it in an houre........................100. H.246, 14
A **slave** to state:...............................137. H.340, 8
Who covets more, is evermore a **slave**...........213. H.607, 2
Slaves Here, here the **Slaves** and Pris'ners be..190. H.515, 19
Slay Thus to **slay** me by degrees,................254. H.757, 3
Slays Who smiles, yet **slayes**.....................43. H.123, 4
Sleeded See **Sleided**
Sleek Here thou behold'st thy large **sleek** Neat..230. H.662, 35
Lett itt (in Loues name) bee keept **sleeke**.......409. A.2, 77
Sleep Still in the coole, and silent shades of **sleep**. 9. H.14, 18
Homer himself, in a long work, may **sleep**.........32. H.95, 6
By whose warme side thou dost securely **sleep**....35. H.106, 35
To make **sleep** not so sound, as sweet:..........36. H.106, 54
Because he cannot **sleep** i'th' Church, free-cost..39. H.109, 4
Cooling **sleep** with charming wand.............56. H.149, 110
A **sleep**, untill the act be done.................57. H.149, 142
Into the Brain by easie **sleep**:..................79. H.198, 10
How we watch, and seldome **sleep**;.............82. H.203, 11
Sleepe in thy peace, while we with spice perfume thee,
89. H.219, 13
Lost in the civill Wildernesse of **sleep**:..........99. H.244, 6
My Phill, the time he has to **sleep**,............104. H.256, 16
Is it for want of **sleep**?.........................104. H.257, 18
The Goblin from ye, while ye **sleep**.............121. H.299, 6
Till **sleep** takes place of wearinesse............127. H.319, 48
Sleep, while we hide thee from the light,......146. H. 376, 13
Under your shades, to **sleep** or die!............158. H.420, 2
Our eyes in **sleepe**;.............................160. H.421, 45
Thy thoughts as cold, as is thy **sleep**:..........175. H.465, 48
With noise, the servants eyes from **sleep**........179. H.476, 33
I co'd never breake my **sleepe**,..................182. H.490, 9
Let me **sleep** this night away,...................199. H.549, 1
And Mans Pulse stopt, All Passions **sleep** in Peace.
202. H.558, 4
Sweet **sleep**, that makes more short the night. ..231. H.662, 75
Is this a life, to break thy **sleep**?.............233. H.670, 1
Hags away, while Children **sleep**..............284. H.888, 4
Gods Rod doth watch while men do **sleep**; & then
342. N.21, 1
The Rod doth **sleep**, while vigilant are men.......342. N.21, 2
And the world is drown'd in **sleep**,............347. N.41, 10
Me, while I **sleep**...............................350. N.47, 10
Night hath no wings, to him that cannot **sleep**;..358. N.77, 1
Sleep not for ever in the vaults of death:........358. N.77, 11
Sleep in thy peace, thy bed of Spice;.............361. N.83, 61
Sleep with thy beauties here, while we..........375. N.123, 81
There in calm and cooling **sleep**...............377. N.128, 17
The sheet I **sleep** in, as my Winding-sheet.....392. N.230, 18
When **sleep** shall bath his body in mine eyes,......392. N.230, 19
— — — — — — — — — —,.................448. var. A.3, 19
Sleeping Slept; and thus **sleeping**, thither flew....46. H.130, 3
Sleeping the lucklesse Age out, till that she....150. H.382, 19
Waking shalt find me **sleeping** there...........175. H.465, 52
Keeps the **sleeping** child from harms............284. H.889, 6
And hold'st mine eyes from **sleeping**;............353. N.56, 3
And leave thee **sleeping** in thy Urn.............361. N.83, 78
— — — — — — — — — —,.................448. var. A.3, 10
Sleeps With direful notes to fright your **sleeps**:..56. H.149, 102
That **sleeps** at home; and sayling there at ease,..128. H.323, 3
Tis Julia's Bed, and she **sleeps** there...........139. H.348, 3
His eye in dew of kisses, while he **sleeps**.......206. H.575, 42
Where Venus **sleeps** (halfe smothered.)........269. H.815, 4
Buggins is Drunke all night, all day he **sleepes**; 311. H.1011, 1
Sleeps, laid within some Ark of Flowers,.......367. N.102, 5
Nor dull'd wth Iron **sleeps**; but haue out-worne..410. A.3, 19
Sleepy And troubles thus the **Sleepie**?............26. H.81, 6
By the soone gingling of some **sleepy** keyes,....410. A.3, 10
Sleet Ile send such Frost, such Haile, such **Sleet**, and Snow,
82. H.204, 10
By'th'fire, foretelling snow and **slit**,............134. H.336, 86
Sleeved — — — — — — — — — —,.................447. var. A.1, 57
Sleided <Fingring> the paps that feele like **sleeded** silke
405. A.1, 57
Sleight God He rejects all Prayers that are **sleight**,.342. N.16, 1
Slept **Slept**; and thus sleeping, thither flew........46. H.130, 3
And after sorrowes spent, I **slept**:..............51. H.142, 4
Slew That me unkindly **slew**..................161. H.426, 10
He **slew** the Ammonites, we know,...............360. N.83, 27
Sin never **slew** a soule, unlesse there went......389. N.217, 1
Slide See **Overslide**
Tempting down to **slide** withall:.................15. H.36, 9

Slight None is, **slight** things do lightly please...246. H.724, 32
Slily See Slyly
Slimy I abhor the **slimie** kisse,..................282. H.878, 1
Slip In wayes confus'd, nor **slip** or fall...........33. H.98, 10
If they but **slip**, and never fall................118. H.291, 16
Faith, and Affection: which will never **slip**....252. H.745, 19
That is my hope; which if that **slip**, I'm one....319. H.1044, 3
Slippery Who gripes too hard the dry and **slip'rie** sand.
221. H.633, 52
That **slippery** all Ambition is.................229. H.661, 2
Slips See Bastard-slips, Cowslips
The bastard **Slips** may droop and die.............278. H.859, 3
Slit See Sleet
He'll **slit** her nose; But blubb'ring, she replyes,..44. H.126, 2
Slit's One **slit's** enough to let Adultry in.........44. H.126, 4
Sloth And chose their Priest, ere we can cast off **sloth**:
69. H.178, 50
Slothful Our **slothfull** passage o're the Stygian Lake,
248. H.730, 24
Slothfulness Differs not much from drowzie **slothfullnesse**.
173. H.459, 14
His detestation to all **slothfulnesse**...............384. N.179, 4
Slothfuls Men, but **Slothfulls** most of all...........53. H.147, 10
Slouch **Slouch** he packs up, and goes to sev'rall Faires,
253. H.753, 1
Slow Because y'are **slow**;.......................137. H.340, 4
Fie, Lovely maid! Indeed you are too **slow**,....216. H.618, 5
And then sho'd I in praising thee be **slow**,....298. H.955, 11
Celerity even it self is **slow**...................378. N.133, 2
— — — — — — — — — —,...........431. var. H.283, 59-60
Slowly **Slowly** goes farre: The meane is best: Desire
51. H.143, 3
Bridall-Rites goe on so **slowly**?................53. H.149, 12
On then, and though you **slow**-
ly go, yet, howsoever, go......................113. H.283, 59-60
Why so **slowly** do you move...................276. H.850, 1
Who **slowly** goes, rids (in the end) his way.....352. N.51, 4
Slowly her chariot drives, as if that she........358. N.77, 3
Slowworm Nor Snake. or **Slow-worme** bite thee:..217. H.619, 7
Slug See Sweet-slugabed
Slumber What though the Moon do's **slumber**?..217. H.619, 12
Slumbering See A-slumbering
Like to a **slumbring** Bride, awake againe........99. H.244, 8
Slumbers Thy silken **slumbers** in the night........35. H.106, 38
Away in easie **slumbers**........................95. H.227, 4
Your pleasing **slumbers** in the night:...........121. H.299, 4
Our Peacefull **slumbers** in the night...........200. H.552, 12
Welcome as **slumbers**; or as beds of ease........300. H.961, 3
Sluts **Sluts** are loathsome to the Fairies:........201. H.556, 6
Sluttish Be she **sluttish**, be she cleane,...........253. H.750, 17
Excesse is **sluttish**: keepe the meane; for why?..331. H.1109, 1
Sly Who makes the **slie** Physitian his Heire.......125. H.315, 6
That the Thiefe, though ne'r so **slie**,..........263. H.785, 2
— — — — — — — — —,.............440. var. H.443, 64
Slyly Mark, if her tongue, but **slily**, steale a taste.
100. H.248, 4
Small So three in one **small** plat of ground shall ly, 11, H.22, 9
Small shots paid often, waste. a vast estate.......13. H.28, 2
Small griefs find tongues: Full Casques are ever found
15. H.38, 7
That chiding streams betray **small** depth below...15. H.38, 10
Me thought, her long **small** legs & thighs.........16. H.41, 5
Unlesse thou giv'st my **small** Remains an Urne...19. H.52, 4
Wink at **small** faults, the greater, ne'rthelesse......32. H.95, 3
And from thy Compasse taking **small** advice,..36. H.106, 81
Ordaining that thy **small** stock find no breach,..38. H.106, 133
To see the **small** remainders in mine Urne:........49. H.138, 2
Small Chalice of thy frantick liquor; He........78. H.197, 63
Here burnt, whose **smal** return.................81. H.201, 42
Girt with **small** bones, instead of walls.........90. H.223, 10
In either which a **small** tall bent.............92. H.223, 95
For some **small** fault, to offer sacrifice:.........102, H.251, 2
How high she's priz'd, and worth but **small**;....103. H.253, 17
With some **small** glit'ring gritt, to eate........119. H.293, 10
Where my **small** reliques must for ever rest:....129. H.327, 4
Skrew lives by shifts; yet sweares by no **small** oathes;
149. H.380, 1
But that deni'd, a griefe, though **small**,.........153. H.395, 4
Who can with so **small** charges drive the buck...178. H.474, 4
Great men by **small** meanes oft are overthrown:..181. H.486, 1
When 'twas in's Feet, his Charity was **small**;....207. H.577, 3
Let's live with that **smal** pittance that we have;..213. H.607, 1
Sound Teeth has Lucie, pure as Pearl, and **small**, 226. H.649, 1
Great be my fare, or **small** cheere,..........235. H.674, 17
Her decent legs, cleane, long and **small**.......247. H.729, 4
As my **small** Cruse best fits my little Wine....249. H.733, 3
As my **small** Jarre best fits my little Oyle........249. H.733, 6
As my **small** stuffe best fits my little Shed.........249. H.733, 9
As my **small** Bell best fits my little Spire.......249. H.733, 12
As my **small** Pipe best fits my little note........249. H.733, 15
Beere **small** as Comfort, dead as Charity......262. H.783, 16
With some **small** stock of innocence:..........277. H.854, 2
And Kitchin's **small**:..........................350. N.47, 18
Among Gods Blessings, there is no one **small**.....353. N.55, 2
With that **small** stock, Thy Bounty gave or lent. 368. N.104, 12
Mine's faulty too, and **small**:..................376. N.125, 6
To punish great sins, who **small** faults whipt here.
381. N.156, 2
So long (it seem'd) as Maries Faith was **small**,..386. N.192, 1
In which the tongue, though but a member **small**,..405. A.1, 29
Leaving a distance for the beawtious **small**......406. A.1, 89
With little hands and fingers long and **small**....406. A.1, 99
Smallage And look, what **Smallage**, Night-shade, Cypresse, Yew,
27. H.82, 9
And with **Smallage** dresse my Tomb:..........89. H.220, 2
Smallest Can with the **smallest** cost afford........200. H.552, 2
Smart Little the wound was; greater was the **smart**;
17. H.44, 7
When I did goe from thee, I felt that **smart**,....42. H.122, 1
Insensible of all my **smart**;....................47. H.132, 10
Come tel me then, how great's the **smart**........50. H.139, 14
Let but few **smart**, but strike a feare through all: 132. H.335, 3
With an eternall **smart**:........................161. H.426, 5
Can ease the rawnesse, or the **smart**;...........164. H.442, 9
(But min's the greater **smart**)..................203. H.563, 6
'Tis some solace in our **smart**,..................302. H.968, 3
To ease this **smart**, or cure this wound;..........342. N.17, 6
The utmost **smart**, so Thou wilt cure...........342. N.17, 12
But all in **smart** have lesse, or greater shares......342. N.20, 2
God when for sin He makes His Children **smart**,..343. N.22, 1
With dismall **smart**...........................353. N.56, 17
If thy **smart** Rod..............................363. N.92, 2
That if the twig sho'd chance too much to **smart**, 394. N.241, 3
Smarts May every Ill, that bites, or **smarts**,..........6. H.5, 3
He **smarts** at last, who do's not first take heed...79. H.199, 4
But causelesse whipping **smarts** the most of all...319. H.1050, 2
Smeaton How co'd Luke **Smeaton** weare a shoe, or boot,
240. H.704, 1
Smell And for your breaths too, let them **smell**.....20. H.54, 3
If we the roste have, they the **smell**.............22. H.66, 4
Follow thy Perfumes by the **smell**:................33. H.98, 6
Hereafter, shall **smell** of the Lamp, not thee......46. H.128, 54
Smell, where your soft foot treads;............55. H.149, 64
There I **smell** the Phenix nest:..................59. H.155, 2
Altar of Incense, I **smell** there...................59. H.155, 4
Yet lost ere you transfuse your **smell**...........88. H.216, 15
Which (though sweet unto your **smell**)..........88. H.217, 3
Then we shall **smell** how sweet you be..........112. H.282, 4
See where she comes; and **smell** how all the street
113. H.283, 21
Shall smile and **smell** the better by thy beads...143. H.370, 2
So **smell** those odours that do rise.............145. H.375, 1
So **smell** those neat and woven Bowers,........145. H.375, 11
So **smell** those bracelets, and those bands.....145. H.375, 15
The **smell** of mornings milk, and cream;........145. H.375, 21
Makes guests and fish **smell** strong; pray go....146. H.377, 26
Love may **smell** the Frankincense...............158. H.417, 4
Yet love the **smell** of meat.....................250. H.736, 6
But ther's not one, doth praise the **smell** of thee. 266. H.802, 2
My sight was pleas'd more, or my **smell**:......283. H.883, 6
Or **smell**, like to a Meade new-shorne, ...364. N.96, 16
Smellest And **smell'st** the breath of great-ey'd Kine,
230. H.662, 33
Smell-feast Burr is a **smell-feast**, and a man alone. 296. H.944, 1
Smelling Twoe **smelling** swelling <bashful> Cherrilletts,
404. A.1, 20
Smells So **smels** the flowre of blooming Clove;....145. H.375, 3
So **smells** the Aire of spiced wine;.............145. H.375, 5
So **smells** the Breath about the hives,..........145. H.375, 7
Smells like the maiden-Pomander..............145. H.375, 26
Thus sweet she **smells**, or what can be........145. H.375, 27
These Musks, these Ambers, and those other **smells**
157. H.414, 3
How each thing **smells** divinely redolent!.......159. H.421, 19
Whose shadow **smels** like milder Pomander!....181. H.485, 2
What is the reason Coone so dully **smels**?......210. H.589, 1
Smells like the burnt Sabæan Frankinsense......404. A.1, 28
Smelt Oyle of Roses still **smelt** there...........182. H.490, 8
And **smelt** them, then they **smelt** to me,........203. H.562, 5
But ah! what sweets **smelt** every where,........237. H.686, 11
And in their motion **smelt** much like to flowers 326. H.1080, 13
Smile If good I'le **smile**, if bad I'le sigh for Thee...6. H.3, 8
Where my Julia's lips doe **smile**;...............20. H.53, 5
As is thy powerful selfe. Prethee not **smile**;......46. H.128, 45
Or **smile** more inly; lest thy looks beguile......46. H.128, 46
Ye may simper, blush, and **smile**,..............74. H.189, 1
Wo't thou not **smile**, or tell me what's amisse?....78. H.197, 33
Now let the Rose raigne like a Queene, and **smile**.
105. H.259, 12
Each hieroglyphick of a kisse or **smile**;........115. H.283, 126
To lend the world your scent and **smile**........126. H.318, 5
Shall **smile** and smell the better by thy beads.....143. H.370, 2
Was I fier'd with a **smile**?......................155. H.407, 4
To blush and gently **smile**;....................176. H.467, 5
And **smile** here for your houre;...............184. H.493, 6
Whose **smile** can make a Poet; and your glance..187. H.506, 9
Though then I **smile**, and speake no words at all.
222. H.634, 15
I dare not beg a **smile**;........................231. H.663, 2
Do's she **smile**, or do's she frowne:...........253. H.750, 5
How thou canst sit and **smile**,.................272. H.828, 10
Make her this day **smile** on me,...............313. H.1018, 3
Perilla **smile** on none but me.................313. H.1020, 2

Smile, like a field beset with corne?............364. N.96, 15
Smile, that one smile's full restitution..........371. N.112, 4
His eager Eye, or Smoother **Smyle**,.............413. A.4, 27
Most maye **smile**, beleiue will none,.............418. A.9, 36
Of nature: bidd mee nowe fare well, or **smile** 424. ins. H.128, 46d
Smiled At which she **smil'd**; then with her hairs..50. H.139, 10
I **smil'd**; and bade him once more prove,........64. H.166, 9
At which she **smil'd**; and bade him goe........71. H.182, 27
That **smil'd** in that first-sweet complexion........81. H.202, 4
Then **smil'd**, and sweetly chid her speed;.......187. H.504, 5
She smiling blusht, and blushing **smil'd**,........251. H.740, 5
She **smil'd**; he kist; and kissing, cull'd her too; 313. H.1017, 9
It ever dangling **smil'd** i' th' aire................418. A.9, 26
Smile's Smile, that one **smile's** full restitution....371. N.112, 4
Smiles **Smiles** to it selfe, and guilds the roofe with mirth: 7. H.8, 6
So **smiles** that Riband 'bout my Julia's waste:...40. H.114, 2
Who **smiles**, yet slayes.......................43. H.123, 4
So soft streams meet, so springs with gladder **smiles** 77. H.197, 1
And this same flower that **smiles** to day,........84. H.208, 3
Where spring-time **smiles** throughout the yeare? 103. H.256, 3
That sighs at others death; **smiles** at his own...129. H.323, 13
Juno yet **smiles**; but if she chance to chide,...262. H.781, 11
Her buxom **smiles** from me her worshipper. 426. var. H.197, 26
Smiling I **smiling**, ask'd them what they did?......18. H.47, 5
Then after her comes **smiling** May...............23. H.70, 3
You have beheld a **smiling** Rose................75. H.193, 1
Unto our **smiling**, and our blooming King,.....86. H.213, 34
Shew me that Hill (where **smiling** Love doth sit) 154. H.403, 3
Ripe Cherries **smiling**, while that others blow...193. H.523, 2
Sit **smiling** in the Meads; where Balme and Oile, 205. H.575, 3
And **smiling** at our selves, decree,.............216. H.616, 29
Upon my ruines (**smiling** yet:)................235. H.677, 2
The Rose was sick, and **smiling** di'd;..........237. H.686, 1
A curious Rainbow **smiling** there;..............237. H.687, 6
She **smiling** blusht, and blushing smil'd,........251. H.740, 5
True mirth resides not in the **smiling** skin:......341. N.13, 1
How sweetly shewes thy **smiling** face,.........375. N.123, 73
And such a **smiling** Tulip too.............424. ins. H.164, 11a
Smirk And the **smirk** Butler thinks it..........114. H.283, 67
Makes the **smirk** face of each to shine,........147. H.377, 72
Unmixt. I love to have it **smirke** and shine,......187. H.502, 3
Smirking If **smirking** Wine be wanting here,....101. H.250, 36
— — — — — — — — — —,..............453. var. H.283, 67
Smith Hind, Goderiske, **Smith**............437. var. H.336, 131
Smock See **Lady-smock**, **Wedding-smock**
Smoke Which wanting Lar, and **smoke**, hung weeping wet; 262. H.783, 12
And leave their servants, but the **smoak** & sweat; 272. H.826, 3
Reade acceptance by the **smoake**.............280. H.870, 18
A thousand Altars **smoake**; a thousand thighes..300. H.961, 7
May Sweets grow here! & **smoke** from hence,..361. N.83, 63
The Temple, with a cloud of **smoke**............366. N.98, 17
The **smoake** of his beloued Attica,..............412. A.3, 74
Yor name amidst the sacred **smoke**.............413. A.4, 30
Smoking The fat-fed **smoking** Temple, which in..146. H.377, 6
To see far off the **smoaking** Villages...........352. N.51, 10
— — — — — — — — — — —,............425. var. H.197, 18
Smoky The **smoakie** chimneys of his Ithaca......77. H.197, 18
Smooth See **Soft-smooth**
Some **smooth**, and harmlesse Beucolicks............5. H.2, 10
Which wrapt thy **smooth** limbs when thou didst implore 9. H.14. 11
Smooth Anthea, for a skin.....................16. H.39, 5
So **smooth**, so sweet, so silv'ry is thy voice.......22. H.67, 1
Soft speech, **smooth** touch, the lips, the Maiden-head: 45. H.128, 8
And make me **smooth** as Balme, and Oile againe. 67. H.176, 6
Her skins most **smooth**, and cleare expansion....82. H.204, 4
Smooth, faire, and fat; none better I can tell:...86. H.213, 6
To these **smooth** Lawns, my mirthfull Roundelay. 159. H.421. 10
A pure **smooth** Pearle, and Orient too?........164. H.440, 8
Grow fat and **smooth**: The reason is,..........173. H.461, 3
Each way **smooth** and civilly:..................195. H.530, 4
Make the way **smooth** for me,.................213. H.604, 5
If **smooth** and unperplext the Seasons were,....214. H.612, 9
That **smooth** and silken Columbine.............215. H.616, 24
A Heifer **smooth**, and black as jet,............243. H.716, 8
Unsoft to him who's **smooth** to thee...........252. H.746, 2
Be she rough, or **smooth** of skin;..............253. H.750, 7
As **smooth**, and nak't, as she that was.........271. H.824, 7
Whether **smooth** or not I be,..................277. H.852, 3
Smooth was the Sea, and seem'd to call........294. H.937, 1
Smooth in each limb as a die;................305. H.984, 20
Of this **smooth** Green,.......................360. N.83, 16
Gods Hands are round, & **smooth**, that gifts may fall 380. N.151, 1
Her forehead **smooth** full polish bright and high..404. A.1, 5
For his plumpe white and **smooth** prrogatiue,....405. A.1, 34
Resembling sheilds both **smooth** and christalline...406. A.1, 80
That **smooth** as Oyle, sweet softe and Cleane.....408. A.2, 55
White handes as **smooth**, as Mercies, bring.......408. A.2, 59
Smooth as the Childhood of the yeare.............413. A.4, 4
and the **smooth** Handmaides pay their vowes 431. ins. H.283, 60d
Smoother Adorn'd this **smoother** Mead.........110. H.274, 16
Then being seated in that **smoother** Sphere,....172. H.456, 7
His eager Eye, or **Smoother** Smyle,.............413. A.4, 27
Smoothly Which o're the board is **smoothly** spred, 91. H.223, 62
Each way **smoothly** Musicall:..................122. H.303, 4
And runnes most **smoothly**, when tis well begunne. 128. H.321, 2
Smoothness With sweetness, **smoothness**, softness, be endu'd 290. H.914, 4
Smooth-paced Those **smooth-pac't** Numbers, amble every where; 141. H.359, 10
That done, our **smooth-pac't** Poems all shall be 254. H.756, 15
Smooth-skin Of every straight, and **smooth-skin** tree; 193. H.521, 41
Smother And thus, thus, thus let us **smother**....247. H.727, 3
Smothered Of Roses, almost **smothered**:...........20. H.56, 2
Or Roses **smother'd** in the stove:...............145. H.375, 4
Where Venus sleeps (halfe **smothered**.)........269. H.815, 4
Smutch And dismall Darknesse then doth **smutch** the face. 207. H.576, 6
Snail The unctuous dewlaps of a **Snaile**;.......120. H.293, 45
Snail's Of silv'rie fish; wheat-strawes, the **snailes** 166. H.443, 73
Snails (Hatcht, with the Silver-light of **snails**)..92. H.223, 92
Lead by the shine of **Snails**; a way............165. H.443, 22
Like **snailes** did creep.......................194. H.525, 2
Snake A winged Snake has bitten me,............50. H.139, 8
A shew, as if 't 'ad been a **snake**:.............116. H.284, 4
Of shifted **Snake**: enfreez'd throughout........166. H.443, 67
Nor **Snake**, or Slow-worme bite thee:..........217. H.619, 7
Where most sweets are, there lyes a **Snake**.....283. H.883, 12
Snakes — — — — — — — — —, ...440. var. H.443, 67
Snaky And **Snakie** Perseus, these, and those, whom Rage 206. H.575, 45
Snapped Another **snapt** the Cherry..............142. H.364, 8
Snare For each Ringlet there's a **snare**............52. H.147, 4
None pities him that's in the **snare**,...........219. H.628, 11
Snare, ten i' th' hundred calls his wife; and why? 220. H.631, 1
An Enchantment or a **Snare**,..................232. H.665, 12
Caught my poore soule, as in a **snare**:..........281. H.876, 8
Made by that fetter or that **snare**..............293. H.934, 3
Snares Thy Lime-twigs, **Snares**, and Pit-falls then 231. H 662, 68
Deserve these Mashes and those **snares**.........282. H.881, 6
But to instruct them, to avoid all **snares**........378. N.137, 5
Snarling That are **snarling** now at me:..........329. H.1096, 2
Snatched **Snatcht** off his Crown, and gave the wreath to me: 313. H.1017, 12
Bird **snatcht** away from th' cryinge child, 439. ins. H.443, 45q
Sneap **Sneape** has a face so brittle, that it breaks 124. H.311, 1
Snow In me but **Snow**, and ysicles.................8. H.12, 2
To melt this **snow**, and thaw this ice;..............8. H.13, 4
I'le rather keepe this frost, and **snow**,.............8. H.13, 7
Or **Snow**, or whitest Swans you are:...............34. H.105, 2
O Frost! O **Snow**! O Haile forbid the Banes.....40. H.113, 2
Of the Raine, Frost, Haile, and **Snow**?...........40. H.115, 4
Ripe eares of corne, and up to th'eares in **snow**:..59. H.154, 6
Nor the **Snow** continue pure:..................60. H.159, 14
Such frost and **snow** upon your haire:..........63. H.164, 5
So though y'are white as Swan, or **Snow**,.......76. H.193, 49
To cakes of Ice, or flakes of **Snow**:.............79. H.198, 6
Ile send such Frost, such Haile, such Sleet, and **Snow**, 82. H.204, 10
Like Frost-work glitt'ring on the **Snow**.........92. H.223. 67
Like noyse-lesse **Snow**: or as the dew of night:..100. H.247, 2
The sheet about, like flakes of **snow**..........116. H.283, 150
My locks behung with frost and **snow**:........134. H.336, 76
By'th'fire, foretelling **snow** and slit,............134. H.336, 86
To Frost or **Snow**............................137. H.340, 18
And turn to **snow**,............................171. H.452, 9
Will coole his flames, or quench his fires with **snow**? 187. H.502, 6
And trace the Hare i' th' trecherous **Snow**:....231. H.662, 63
Endlesse Ice, and endlesse **Snow**:...............266. H.803, 3
Here Winter-like, to Frost and Snow............329. H.1093, 4
Like wanton rose buds growing out of **snowe**,....405. A.1, 54
Like a faire mountaine in Riphean **snowe**,........405. A.1, 60
Snows Thaw'd are the **snowes**, and now the lusty Spring 224. H.642, 3
Ile sing no more of Frosts, **Snowes**, Dews and Showers; 228. H.658, 3
Snowy Rush saves his shooes, in wet and **snowie** wether; 332. H.1116, 1
Snug Where we may snug, and close together lye 278. H.860, 7
Snugging And **snugging** there, they seem'd to lye..25. H.78, 3
So (Partial List)
But **so**, as that her self should be.................8. H.11, 9
I'le drink down Flames, but if **so** be..............8. H.13, 5
From this, to that, and **so** Perfume.............9. H.15, 7
So, that the more I look, the more I prove........10. H.16, 5
In thy remembrance (Julia.) So farewell.........14. H.35, 14
So when Love speechlesse is, she doth expresse...15. H.38, 11

So that my Lucia seem'd to me................16. H.41, 12
Since which, it festers so, that I can prove........17. H.44, 5
If so be, you ask me where......................19. H.53, 3
So smooth, so sweet, so silv'ry is thy voice,......22. H.67, 1
A thousand to that hundred: so kisse on,........24. H.74, 5
Ride on with all white Omens; so, that where...25. H.77, 11
So oft, we'll think, we see a King new born........26. H.80, 2
Here I devote; And something more then so;...27. H.82, 11
Which are so cleane, so chast, as none may feare..28. H.84, 5
For that so rich a one;..........................29. H.87, 9
Not so much call'd a tree,.......................30. H.89, 9
So that the path I cannot find:.................32. H.98, 2
So looks Anthea, when in bed she lyes,..........34. H.104, 1
Got, not so beautifull, as chast:................35. H.106, 34
To make sleep not so sound, as sweet:...........36. H.106, 54
Nor can these figures so thy rest endeare,.......36. H.106, 55
Seeing those painted Countries; and so guesse...36. H.106, 79
Be so, bold spirit; Stand Center-like, unmov'd; 37. H.106, 101
So much for want, as exercise:..................37. H.106, 118
Be so one Death, one Grave to both..............38. H.106, 144
If so, we'll think too (when he do's condemne....39. H.110, 3
And Love will swear't, my Dearest did not so...42. H.122, 12
So neare, or deare, as thou wast once to me.....45. H.128, 10
Not so much Rose, as Wreathe....................51. H.144, 4
Never was Day so over-sick with showres,.......52. H.146, 1
This, as I wish for, so I hope to see;..........52. H.146, 17
Love kill'd this man. No more but so..........61. H.159, 31
My longer stay, and so I dy'd...................69. H.180, 4
(So Fate spares her) am well content to die....70. H.181, 12
He drank so much he scarce co'd stir;..........71. H.182, 9
So Julia took the Pilferer.......................71. H.182, 10
When next he came a pilfring so,..............71. H.182, 29
Till we have wept, kist, sigh't, shook hands, or so.
73. H.186, 6
To guard it so, as nothing here shall be........73. H.186, 19
From the first ye were not so:..................74. H.190, 2
So though y'are white as Swan, or Snow,.......76. H.193, 49
So meet stolne kisses, when the Moonie nights...77. H.197, 5
Kisse, and sigh, so part agen....................82. H.203, 14
Mir. Not so, not so. Chor. But if it chance to prove
86. H.213, 27
A neat, though not so great an Offering........86. H.213, 35
With a teare; and so Adieu.......................89. H.220, 4
If so it be I've gain'd the shore.................94. H.225, 3
Now 'tis so full, that when therein I look,.......99. H.245, 3
Yet so it comes to passe,........................100. H.249, 7
That things of greatest, so of meanest worth,..105. H 257, 27
Penance, and standing so, are both but one....106. H.261, 4
And that Apollo shall so touch Your eare,......107. H.264, 2
And't shall doe so for thee......................108. H.267, 12
Of largeness, when th'are nothing so:..........118. H.291, 10
For one so rarely tun'd to fit all parts;........121. H.301, 1
To blow, and seed, and so away;................126. H.318, 2
And so we'l sit...............................134. H.336, 85
Though not so fresh, yet full as merry.......136. H.336, 140
If so, how much more shall I dote thereon.....139. H.347, 3
So smell those neat and woven Bowers,.......145. H 375, 11
But as thy meate, so thy immortall wine......147. H.377, 71
Helpe me so, that I my shield,................151. H.386, 3
Good morrow to the Day so fair;..............156. H.412, 1
Since so it is; Ile tell thee what,.............161. H.425, 5
So like to this, nay all the rest,...............164. H.440, 9
Shut not so soon; the dull-ey'd night..........164. H.441, 1
Your date is not so past;.......................176. H.467, 3
And so to bid goodnight?.......................176. H.467, 9
Who can with so small charges drive the buck. 178. H.474, 4
Your Larders too so hung with meat,..........178. H.476, 5
The food of Poets; so I thought sayes Jill,.....186. H.498, 5
Though ne'r so mean the Viands be,...........200. H.552, 3
Urles had the Gout so, that he co'd not stand;..207. H.577, 1
A kiss to each; and so we'l end..............216. H.616, 36
So as to rise still with an appetite.............220. H 633, 19
Though ne'r so foule be the weather............225. H.643, 6
All scores; and so to end the yeere:...........230. H.662, 14
So little left, as if they ne'r had been:.........231. H.664, 4
Ev'n so, those streets and houses do but show..244. H.718, 3
Times that are ill wo'nt still be so.............247. H 725, 6
None are so harsh, but if they find.............252. H.746, 5
So my fancie be content,......................253. H.750, 14
So good as George-a-Green; 259. H.772, 22
They draw their clothes off both, so draw to bed.
260. H.773, 4
We'l love the Divell, so he lands the gold......266. H.800, 8
So look the mornings when the Sun............268. H 811, 1
When ere I go, or what so ere befalls...........269. H.818, 1
As Lillies shrin'd in Christall, so.............271. H.824, 13
Art so unkind to me;..........................272. H.828, 14
Punchin by Beere and Ale, spreads so..........273. H.832, 4
But nothing so; The Dinner Adam had,........273. H.835, 3
Why so slowly do you move....................276. H.850, 1
Well, or be't or be't not so,....................277. H.852, 5
And so soone stopt my longer living here;......278. H.860, 2
But would to Love I could beleeve 'twas so!...279. H.866, 2
Of his glory. So farewell......................289. H.910, 6
Ponder my words, if so that any be.............290. H.914, 1
He toucht me so, as that I burn,...............295. H.942, 11
Love is a thing so likes me,....................296. H.946, 3
E'ne so my numbers will astonisht be..........301. H.962, 5
Why so lonely on the hill?.....................305. H.984, 4
Why thy pipe by thee so still,..................305. H.984, 5
Live long, Lacon, so adew.....................306. H.984, 41
Nothing's so hard, but search will find it out....311. H.1008, 2
A Shepheardess so homely;......................324. H.1068, 18
Heat and moisture mixt are so,.................324. H.1070, 3
No man so well a Kingdome Rules, as He,....325. H.1074, 1
Old Widow Shopter, when so ere she cryes,....331. H.1107, 1
But if so be that men will not..................334. H.1123, 3
And so away he flew...........................346. N.38, 18
Like as my Parlour, so my Hall................350. N.47, 17
So very-many-meeting hindrances,.............352. N.51, 2
Or strike so as to ease me.....................353. N.56, 24
When thou hast said so, stick it there...........354. N.59, 5
Just so it is with me, who list'ning, pray........358. N.77, 5
Lighten my candle, so that I beneath............358. N.77, 10
His praise; so let us blesse the King:...........367. N.98, 26
Reading Thy Bible, and my Book; so end......371. N.115, 12
Wherewith so many soules were fed...........374. N.123, 16
God, as He's potent, so He's likewise known,...378. N.135, 1
Jacob Gods Beggar was; and so we wait........383. N.171, 1
So she, to keep her mighty woes in awe,........384. N.180, 5
So live in Heaven, in everlasting light..........384. N.181, 5
Christ never did so great a work, but there.....389. N.214, 1
To which the Pesant, so the Prince must come, 392. N.230, 24
And as all-present, so all-filling too............394. N.237, 2
But if Thou wilt so honour me,..................399. N.265, 3
Soe full of clarrett that whoe soe pricks a vine....405. A.1, 49
A Nature, soe well form'd soe wrought...........408. A.2, 65
So long as I haue feares........................414. A.5, 6
And so to Bed: Pray wish us all Good Rest......419. A.10, 8

Soaders See Solders

Soame Seeing thee Soame, I see a Goodly man...176. H.466, 1
Thee sprightly Soame, one of my righteous Tribe:
199. H 545, 2

Soap Be the Seas water, and the Land all Sope,..357. N.73, 3

Soap-like-lather There springs a sope-like-lather in his shoos.
332. H.1113, 2

Soare See Sore

Soaring Soaring them vpp, boue Ruyne, till the doome
410. A.3, 33

Sob Why do you sigh, and sob, and keep........158. H.420, 5
Fold mine Armes, sob, sigh, or weep:.........182. H.490, 10
Since I do sob and crie........................351. N. 49, 2

Sobbed He wept, he sobb'd, he call'd to some.....18. H.46, 5

Sobbing And sobbing deeply, thus he said,........42. H.119, 8

Sober In sober mornings, doe not thou reherse......7. H.8, 1
Your sober Hand-maid; who doth wisely chuse. 99. H.245, 6
Like to a solemne sober Stream...............179. H.476, 13
Trie if this sober streame you can............244. H.720, 3
The sober Sorceresse..........................258. H.767, 12
To th' Temple with the sober Midwife go.......286. H. 898, 2
Is sober virtue, seen to move her sphere.......327. H.1087, 2

Soberly How soberly above the rest.............375. N.123, 64
— — — — — — — — —...............439. var. H.443, 29

Sobriety Vertue's clean Conclave is sobriety.....331. H.1109, 2

Sobs Sighs, and sobs, and sorrowes more.........102. H.253, 5

Sociate For which prevention (Sociate) let there be
287. H.901. 3

Society Two things do make society to stand:...275. H.847, 1

Sock The Sock grew loathsome, and the Buskins pride.
150. H.382, 2

Socrates A poyson too He has for Socrates;....370. N.108, 8

Sodders See Solders

Soft See Silk-soft-skin
By my soft Nerv'lits were embrac'd:............16. H.41, 8
Of soft and dainty Maiden-haire,..............18. H.47, 3
White, warme, and soft to lye with me..........34. H.105, 10
Sweeten, and make soft your dreames:..........35. H.106, 44
While soft Opinion makes thy Genius say,.......37. H.106. 115
To quick action, or the warme soft side..........45. H.128, 5
Soft speech, smooth touch, the lips, the Maiden-head:
45. H.128, 8
Soft and soule-melting murmurings,............46. H.130, 2
All such as are not soft like them..............47. H.132, 14
The soft and am'rous soule;....................54. H.149, 26
Smell, where your soft foot treads;.............55. H.149, 64
Sunk from the tip of your soft eare,............61. H.160, 8
To that soft Charm, that Spell, that Magic Bough,
62. H.161, 9
A weak, a soft, a broken beame;...............75. H.193, 36
So soft streams meet, so springs with gladder smiles
77. H.197, 1
Hence, hence, profane; soft silence let us have;..89. H.219, 1
With thy soft straines;.......................95. H.227, 28
Your soft eare to Discipline....................96. H.232, 2
May his soft foot, where it treads,............108. H.266, 13
A heart as soft, a heart as kind,................108. H.267, 5
But gently prest from the soft side............120. H.293, 49
And makes more soft the Bridall Bed...........130. H.329, 7
Plump, soft, & swelling every where?..........139. H.348, 2
He's soft and tender (Pray take heed).........157. H.412, 25
Soft then the finest Lemster Ore...............165. H.443, 28
Soft Candlelight; the Kitling's eyne;.........167. H.443, 74
Thus soft she lies: and over-head............167. H.443, 100
Though thou beest young, kind, soft, and faire,..174. H.465, 3
The soft sweet Mosse shall be thy bed,........192. H.521, 5

In Cream she bathes her thighs (more soft then silk)
203. H.561, 3
Then soft Catullus, sharp-fang'd Martial,........206. H.575, 43
Sweet words must nourish soft and gentle Love. 222. H.633, 61
The soft, the sweet, the mellow note..........243. H.716, 17
By those soft Tods of wooll...................257. H.767, 1
To be most soft, terce, sweet, and perpolite:....301. H.966, 2
Both soft, and drie;..........................349. N.47, 6
To make my bed soft in my sicknesses:..........358. N.77, 9
Thy soft sweet Earth! but (like a spring).......361. N.83, 71
With plumpe soft flesh of mettle pure and fine....406. A.1, 79
That smooth as Oyle, sweet softe and Cleane.....408. A.2, 55
Comends it to your eares soft tipp..............417. A.9, 14
How long, soft bride, shall your deare C: make
431. ins. H.283, 60a
— — — — — — — — — — — —,.............432. var. H.283, 97
Daffe nuts, soft Jewes eares, and some thin
439. ins. H.443, 45f
— — — — — — — — — — — —,...........440. var. H.443, 108
Soft Saffron Circles to perfume the head. 442. ins. H. 575, 20b
— — — — — — — — — — — —............453. var. H.283, 91
Softer Want is a softer Wax, that takes thereon,
288. H.905, 1
Softest The softest Fire makes the sweetest Mault.
221. H.633, 51
Softly Then weep, and sigh, and softly goe,......47. H.132, 5
Lies softly panting like a Bride...............233. H.670, 14
And softly handle Him: y'ad need,..............366. N.98, 20
Then Parte in name of peace; & softely on......412. A.3, 83
Soft-maidens-blush And soft-Maidens-blush, the Bride
114. H.283, 97
Softness Softnesse in others, will be kind;.......252. H.746, 6
With sweetness, smoothness, softness, be endu'd.
290. H.914, 4
Soft-smooth With soft-smooth Virgins (for our chast disport)
315. H.1028, 9
Soil I! far more welcome then the happy soile,...77. H.197, 15
Shall run, as rivers, all throughout thy soyl.....144. H.370, 6
Roses and Cassia crown the untill'd soyle.......205. H.575, 4
Without extortion, from thy soyle:.............233. H.670, 8
A little Seed best fits a little Soyle,...........249. H.733, 4
And everlasting Harvest crown thy soile!.....269. H.818, 8
I'll not prophane, by soile of sin,..............402. N.269, 4
Soe good a soile bee-stocke and till,.............409. A.2, 106
Soiled Which though well soyl'd, yet thou dost know,
230. H.662, 22
Have soil'd my selfe, or cloaths,...............351. N.49, 7
Looks on the filth, but is not soil'd thereby;....371. N.113, 6
Soils That soiles my land;......................350. N.47, 42
Sojourn See Re-sojourn
Solace 'Tis some solace in our smart,...........302. H.968, 3
The sweetest solace is to act no sin.............341. N.13, 2
Sold But feares not now to see her safety sold...251. H.745, 5
Sold his old Mothers Spectacles for Beere:......272. H.829, 2
And man sold God here for base thirty pence...389. N.213, 2
Solders Which, this night hardned, sodders up her nose.
296. H.945, 2
Soldier Amongst this scumme, the Souldier, with his speare,
398. N.263, 9
Soldiers If ill, then Kings, not Souldiers beare the blame.
260. H.774, 4
The Soldiers leave the Field with equall feare...268. H.813, 4
Sole Prigg bears away the body and the sole....143. H.368, 4
Solecism There is not one least solecisme found; 307. H.992, 4
Solemn My solemne Vowes have here accomplished:
23, H.72, 2
Without a sad looke, or a solemne teare?........73. H.186, 10
Here a solemne Fast we keepe,.................170. H.450, 1
Like to a solemne sober Stream.................179. H.476, 13
But all a solemne Fast there kept..............237. H.686, 8
Come and let's in solemn wise.................280. H.870, 1
Attended thus (in a most solemn wise)........286. H.898, 3
With solemne tears, and with much grief of heart,
300. H.960, 3
With a warm lip, and solemne one:...........402. N.269, 11
Solemnize And so to solemnize..................87. H.214, 15
Some Some smooth, and harmlesse Beucolicks.......5. H.2, 10
Then lastly, let some weekly-strewings be..........9. H.14, 15
To live some few-sad-howers after thee:..........11. H.22, 2
Some would know..............................12. H.26, 1
Turn'd to Flowers. Still in some.................15. H.37, 3
Some sport, to please those Babies in your eyes:..15, H.38, 4
He wept, he sobb'd, he call'd to some............18. H.46, 5
When some shall say, Faire once my Silvia was;..21. H.62, 1
Some ask'd me where the Rubies grew?...........24. H.75, 1
Some ask'd how Pearls did grow, and where?.....24. H.75, 5
Some ruffled Roses nestling were:...............25. H.78, 2
Some Aberrations in my Poetry;.................32. H.95, 2
Led by some light that flows from thee..........33. H.98, 8
Making thy peace with heav'n, for some late fault,
36. H.106, 59
Fore-tell the comming of some dire events:......45. H.128. 16
Or some full flame, which with a pride aspires,..45. H.128. 17
Glasco had none, but now some teeth has got;...46. H.129, 1
And must we part, because some say,...........48. H.136, 1
Know, I have pray'd to Furie, that some wind...49. H.138, 7
To conquer'd men, some comfort 'tis to fall......50. H.141, 1
But that it had some intermitting houres........52. H.146, 2
Or learne some way how to forget............60. H.159, 7
For to quench ye, or some ease.................62. H.162, 8
And by some crosse-line show it;..............64. H.166, 10
A fellon take it, or some Whit-flaw come.......66. H.173, 3
Some numbers prurient are, and some of these...66. H.173, 7
That some conceit did melt me downe,..........67. H.175, 15
Against you come, some Orient Pearls unwept:..68. H.178, 22
Some have dispatcht their Cakes and Creame,....69. H.178, 47
And some have wept, and woo'd, and plighted Troth,
69. H.178, 49
And with some flowrs my grave bestrew,........70. H.180, 7
For some rich flower, he took the lip............71. H.182, 5
For some fresh, fragrant, luscious flowers:.....71. H.182, 16
And told her, (as some tears did fall)..........71. H.182, 25
Comforts you'l afford me some:................74. H.191, 6
Or some fine tincture, like to this,............75. H.193, 12
With some conceal'd delight;...................75. H.193, 19
Without some Scean cast over,.................76. H.193, 39
Some Pearls on Queens, that have been counterfet.
76. H.194, 6
A meere Botch of all and some.................76. H.195, 4
(Some say) for joy, to see those Kitlings drown'd.
80. H.200, 2
Pay when th'art honest; let me have some hope. 83. H.206, 4
Pillars let some set up,.........................85. H.211, 21
While Golden Angels (some have told to me)...86. H.213, 23
In Amber, or some Chrystall shell,.............88. H.216, 14
And some have heard the Elves it call..........91. H.223, 24
Mop-ey'd I am, as some have said,.............97. H.235, 1
Pressing before, some coming after,...........101. H.250, 17
Some blesse the Cart; some kisse the sheaves;..101. H.250, 19
Some prank them up with Oaken leaves:......101. H.250, 20
Some crosse the Fill-horse; some with great....101. H.250, 21
For some small fault, to offer sacrifice:.........102. H.251, 2
Some time in wrangling spent,.................105. H.260, 2
And beat ye so, (as some dare say)............105. H.260, 7
And doe some honour to my Tomb..............111. H.280, 8
Blowne out of April, or some New-..............112. H.283, 3
Some Goddesse, in a cloud of Tiffanie..........112. H.283, 8
'Tis she! 'tis she! or else some more Divine....112. H.283, 11
While some repeat............................113. H.283, 45
Some gin, wherewith to catch your eyes........114. H.283, 70
High in your own conceipt, and some way teach
115. H.283, 128
With some small glit'ring gritt, to eate........119. H.293, 10
Gladding his pallat with some store...........119. H.293, 35
Or some numbers more rehearse;..............122. H.303, 2
Of some rough Groom, who (yirkt with Corns) sayes, Sir
146. H.377, 21
You to some other chimney, and there take....146. H.377, 27
Some private pinch tels danger's nie...........147. H.377, 52
Upon some part of Kid, as if mistooke,........147. H.377, 55
They cling and close, some minutes of the night. 156. H.411, 4
When it is born: (by some enstyl'd............167. H.443, 92
Some Relique of a Saint doth weare:..........169. H.449, 2
Who for some sweet-hearts sake, did prove.....169. H.449, 3
The scrip hath some.........................171. H.455, 14
Forth by a Ring, or some rich Carkanet?......172. H.459, 6
Save but some few Beanes left,................173. H.460, 2
Them like some Picture, or some Mould.......174. H.465, 20
Feacie (some say) doth wash her clothes i'th' Lie
178. H.474, 1
Some Christall of the Spring;..................185. H.495, 2
What need I care, though some dislike me sho'd,
187. H.506, 5
Some parts may perish; dye thou canst not all: 200. H.554, 1
When I love, as some have told,...............204. H.569, 1
Both for their comely need, and some to spare:..205. H.571, 2
Or bring some bane..........................210. H.591, 5
Some storms w'ave past;.....................211. H.596, 13
So spend some minutes of the day:.............215. H.616, 6
What is a Kisse? Why this, as some approve;..218. H.622, 1
Some Race of old humanitie....................218. H.626, 9
Lungs (as some, say) ne'r sets him down to eate.
223. H.637, 1
If here ye will some few teares shed,...........226. H.644, 9
Some mirth, t'adulce mans miseries?...........233. H.670, 6
Although with some, yet little paine:..........233. H.670, 10
Some few sands spent, we hence must go,.....233. H.670, 37
Adopted some; none got by theft..............236. H.681, 4
Some starres were fixt before; but these are dim,
236. H.685, 3
Some hung the head, while some did bring.....237. H.686, 5
Some laid her forth, while other wept,..........237. H.686, 7
The holy Sisters some among..................237. H.686, 9
Too much she gives to some, enough to none...238. H.689, 2
And after that, lay downe some silver pence,...245. H.723, 9
But toyes, to give my heart some ease:........246. H.724, 30
Tygers and Beares (I've heard some say)......252. H.746, 3
And praying, strew some Roses on her,........257. H.764, 9
Wo'd give (some say) her soule unto the Devill.
266. H.801, 2
To seeke, and find some few Immortals out....267. H.804, 6
Nature finds out some place for buriall.........267. H.807, 2
His jawes had tir'd on some large Chine of Beefe.
273. H.835, 2

Some salve to every sore, we may apply;......274. H.841, 1
From thee some raptures of the rare Gotire.....276. H.851, 2
With some small stock of innocence:...........277. H.854, 2
Where some had hang'd themselves for love,...278. H.863, 3
Some have Thee call'd Amphion; some of us,...288. H.907, 7
Some this, some that, but all in this agree,......288. H.907, 9
Eate thou not all, but taste on some:..........288. H.909, 2
Unlesse they have some wanton carriages.......290. H.914, 8
As some plants prosper best by cuts and blowes;
292. H.929, 3
As for our selves to leave some frankinsence....295. H.940, 4
'Tis some solace in our smart,.................302. H.968, 3
Some Odes I made of Lucia:.................303. H.973, 14
Some effusions let me have,...................307. H.991, 5
Princes cure some faults by their patience......309. H.998, 2
Vice doth in some but lodge awhile, not dwell...314. H.1021, 2
Drawn was his tooth; but stanke so, that some say,
323. H.1066, 3
Or some enchanted Place, I do not know......326. H.1080, 7
One Eare tingles; some there be,.............329. H.1096, 1
God scourgeth some severely, some He spares;...342. N.20, 1
Some brittle sticks of Thorne or Briar..........350. N.47, 23
I kenn my home; and it affords some ease,......352. N.51, 9
Then for to shed some teares....................352. N.53, 3
And to repent some crimes,......................352. N.53, 5
He gives not poorly, taking some................356. N.66, 5
That has not bread, and some to spare...........358. N.75, 10
Sleeps, laid within some Ark of Flowers,........367. N.102, 5
Some one poore Almes-house; there to lie, or stir,
371. N.115, 3
Unto temptation God exposeth some;..........380. N.150, 3
The Mountains of the Scriptures are (some say) 381. N.157, 1
Nearer to that place, then to other some:......385. N.186, 2
Puts down some prints of His high Majestie:..385. N.189, 2
But hath th' extraction of some good from it:..386. N.196, 2
As not to know, or feel some Grievances........387. N.199, 2
Therein some beames of His Divinitie:..........389. N.214, 4
Along with it some tempting blandishment........389. N.217, 2
Yawne for Thy coming; some e're this time crie.
398. N.263, 7
But like a Person of some high account:......398. N.263, 16
Some Drops of Wine,.........................401. N.268, 16
Now for some Jewells to supplye...............409. A.2, 89
Some strickter M^ris^ or suspitious other..........410. A.3, 8
By the soone gingling of some sleepy keyes,.....410. A.3, 10
And fowle thy Altar, Charme some into froggs,...412. A.3, 91
Some to bee Ratts, and others to bee hoggs:.....412. A.3, 92
Not soe, but that some Relique In my Harte....412. A.3, 96
When as some kinde...........................414. A.5, 13
Some hours before I should have been his Bride...416. A.8, 16
— — — — — — — — — — —,...............425. var. H.197, 22
— — — — — — — — — — —,...............426. var. H.197, 40
And further of some ort of Peare..........439. ins. H.443, 45a
By the round Urchin, some mixt wheate
439. ins. H.443, 45d
Daffe nuts, soft Jewes eares, and some thin
439. ins. H.443, 45f
Ribbonds and then some silken shreakes
440. ins. H.443, 45t
Some bitts of thimbles seeme to dresse..440. ins. H.443, 45aa

Something Here I devote; And something more then so;
27. H.82, 11
Something made of thred and thrumme;........76. H.195, 3
Something for Shew-bread, and at hand........92. H.223, 69
Though free she be, ther's something yet.........191. H.520, 3
Something there yet remaines for Thee to do;..254. H.756, 7
Doth, here on earth, some thing of novitie:......395. N.244, 2

Sometime Your sometime Poet; but if fates do give
140. H.355, 11
— — — — — — — — — — —,.............439. var. H.443, 20
— — — — — — — — — — —..............439. ins. H.443, 45k

Sometimes Sometimes 'two'd pant, and sigh, and heave.
66. H.175, 5
Sometimes 'two'd blaze, and then abate,........67. H.175, 11
Sometimes away 'two'd wildly fling;............67. H.175, 13
Sometimes freeze, and sometimes frie:..........82. H.203, 6
Sometimes peace, and sometimes strife:..........96. H.232, 4
My sometimes known..........................161. H.426, 7
(Sometimes devoted unto Love)..............165. H.443, 20
Jealous Girles these sometimes were,............187. H.503, 1
Sometimes this, & sometimes that:..............209. H.585, 2
They tread on clouds, and though they sometimes fall,
250. H.737, 3
Sometimes (in mirth) he sayes each whelk's a sparke
273. H.834, 3
At randome, sometimes hit most happily........318. H.1039, 2
All are not ill Plots, that doe sometimes faile;..331. H.1104, 1
Sometimes He strikes us more than flesh can beare;
341. N.10, 3
Out of the which he sometimes sups......439. ins. H.443, 45k

Somewhat And that will please me somewhat: though I know
42. H.122, 11
Yet comming home, but somewhat late, (last night)
65. H.171, 4
His Moon-tann'd Mab, as somewhat sick,......167. H.443, 84
And somewhat give,..........................171. H.455, 2
So, I confesse, 'tis somwhat to do well.........234. H.673, 9
Somwhat for my Thank-Offering...............402. N.270, 4
Somewhat peculiar to each lymm,................408. A.2, 74
guilty of somewhat, ripe the strawberries 430. ins. H.283, 20b.

Son By Ornithes sonne, young Calais;..........70. H.181, 14
Had not *Joves son, that brave Tyrinthian Swain. 78. H.197, 65
Call me The sonne of Beere, and then confine....79. H.197, 87
By thy sonne thus grac't, and thee;..........138. H.346, 2
A course in thy Fames-pledge, thy Sonne.......147, H.377, 44
God had but one Son free from sin; but none....378. N.134, 1
'Twixt God the Father, Holy Ghost, and Sonne:
386. N.191, 4

Song See Even-song
Death will come and mar the song:............39. H.111, 12
A fable, song, or fleeting shade;................69. H.178, 66
As He, the maker of this Song.................88. H.216, 21
Ere long, a song, ere long, a shade.............133, H.336, 30
Iülus to sing such a song.....................135. H.336, 94
And Pipe unto thy Song......................184. H.492, 28
Till thou shalt say, I've paid thee with a song. 248. H.730, 22
The Olive branch, and Victors Song:..........360. N.83, 26
— — — — — — — — — — —,................450. var. A.9, 42

Songs Receive (with Songs) a flowrie Diadem...254. H.756, 18
Prepare for Songs; He's come, He's come;.......365. N.97, 1
Then all the songs of sinners are................379. N.145, 2

Sons Stout sons I had, and those twice three;....41. H.116, 3
Come Sons of Summer, by whose toile,.........101. H.250, 1
High sons of Pith,..........................136. H.336, 131
The Sonnes to suck the milke of Kine,..........310. H.1004, 5
Of all His sonnes free from correction..........378. N.134, 2

Soon I care not now how soone 'tis done,........18. H.47, 11
And soon a Taper lighted;......................26. H.81, 14
She soon wo'd leave her spheare,.................54. H.149, 37
Pity me too, who found so soone a Tomb........58. H.151, 4
Life of my life, take not so soone thy flight,....73. H.186, 1
As soone dispatcht is by the Night, as Day......73. H.186, 4
How crosse, how sullen, and how soone........103. H.253, 13
But turne soone after calme, as Balme, or Oile...105. H.259, 4
That Prince takes soone enough the Victors roome,
109. H.268, 1
Who, as soone, fell fast asleep,................123. H.310, 3
The Platters there, as soone as meat............124. H.312, 4
You haste away so soone:......................125. H.316, 2
Wo'd soon recoile, and not intrude............147. H.377, 32
Doll she so soone began the wanton trade;.....149. H.379, 1
Shut not so soon; the dull-ey'd night..........164. H.441, 1
May read how soon things have...............176. H.467, 14
Did soon draw in agen.......................194. H.525, 5
How soone our life, here,.....................196. H.534, 16
Expecting when to fall: which soon will be;....203. H.565, 3
The world so soon, and in it, you the most......222. H.634, 13
And emptied soon the glasse;...................222. H.635, 6
To rise as soon as day doth peep?..............233. H.670, 2
So soone as Julia I am gon.....................270. H.819, 2
And so soone stopt my longer living here;......278. H.860, 2
Who padling there, the Sea soone frown'd,......294. H.937, 3
In teeming years, how soon my Sun was set,...304. H.978, 3
From the Plough soone free your teame;......315. H.1026, 3
No question but Dols cheeks wo'd soon rost dry,
325. H.1078, 1
Soone after, he for beere so scores his wheat, 327. H.1086, 3
The flesh soone sucks in putrifaction...........332. H.1111, 2
Too soon, too deere did Jephthah buy,........360. N.83, 19
By the soone gingling of some sleepy keyes,.....410. A.3, 10
Of yor beawty death comes soone................418. A.9, 46
— — — — — — — — — — —,...............442, var. H.575, 20

Sooner To grow the sooner innocent:............35. H.106, 6
Me sooner starve, then those can kill...........40. H.115, 16
Sooner, then she, ever yet,.....................57. H.149, 149
Spring, sooner then the Lark, to fetch in May....68. H.178, 14
The sooner will his Race be run,................84. H.208, 7
Sooner the in-side of thy hand shall grow......202. H.557, 23
And sooner play, the sooner win...............243. H.716, 24
That may far sooner speed the poore:..........312. H.1014, 8

Soon-pleased Justice to soone-pleas'd nature; and to show,
35. H.106, 13

Soothing Kissing and glancing, soothing, all make way
24. H.74, 11

Sooty Thy sooty Godhead, I desire.............214. H.613, 1

Sop See Lust-sop
Steale a swolne sop out of the Dripping pan...331. H.1106, 2

Sops See Joy-sops

Sorceress The sober Sorceresse,.................258. H.767, 12

Sorceries Shot forth her loving Sorceries:......135. H.336, 106

Sordid And not by any sordid shift:............221. H.633, 47

Sore Yet I bring Balme and Oile to heal your sore.
52. H.146, 22
Some salve to every sore, we may apply;......274. H.841, 1
To an old soare a long cure must goe on;......312. H.1012, 1
And sore without, and sick within:..............342. N.17, 2
To cure the Sore..............................401. N.268, 22

Sores Nothing but loathsome sores in mee.......344. N.29, 4

Sorrow For to number sorrow by................16. H.39, 13
The Evill is not Yours: my sorrow sings,......62. H.161, 15
This day Ile drowne all sorrow;................65. H.170, 5
No, no, this sorrow shown....................104. H.257, 24
Chor. The shades grow great; but greater growes our sorrow,
160. H.421, 43

Behold them in a spacious Theater............206. H.575, 48
To circumspangle this my spacious Sphere,....267. H.804, 7
The spacious field have for Thy Theater.......398. N.263, 18
Spade With peeps of Harts, of Club and Spade..166. H.443, 49
From the Pickaxe to the spade,..................418. A.9, 43
Spake Whose heart, whose hand, whose ev'ry part spake love.
42. H.122, 8
The voices Daughter nea'r spake syllable.....159. H.421, 28
And as he spake, his mouth ranne ore with wine. 313. H.1017, 4
Spalt Of Pushes Spalt has such a knottie race,....211. H.594, 1
Spangle Shine like a spangle here...............164. H.441, 8
Spangled And spangled too,....................181. H.484, 2
Upon thy cheeke that spangel'd Teare,........328. H.1090, 8
Spangled with deaw-light; thou canst cleere.......367. N.102, 6
Spangles And all the shrubs, with sparkling spangles, shew
205. H.575, 11
Spangle-work Is Spangle-work of trembling dew,..92. H.223, 65
Spangling Fall, like a spangling dew,..........57. H.149, 155
The spangling Dew dreg'd o're the grasse shall be
143. H.370, 3
Spaniell For shape and service, Spaniell like to thee.
302. H.967, 2
Sparables His thumb-nailes-par'd, afford him sperrables.
226. H.648, 2
Spare Love scorch'd my finger, but did spare......28. H.85, 1
As well as spare: still conning o'r this Theame,..38. H.106, 131
Both for their comely need and some to spare:..205, H.571, 2
That has not bread, and some to spare..........358. N.75, 10
Spares (So Fate spares her) am well content to die.
70. H.181, 12
God scourgeth some severely, some He spares;..342. N.20, 1
— — — — — — — — — — —,..............433. var. H.293, 31
Sparing God, the most Wise, is sparing of His talk.
341. N.12, 2
— — — — — — — — — — —,..............421. var. H.106, 23
Spark One drop now deads a spark; but if the same
40. H.113, 3
To testifie the glowing of a spark?............78. H.197, 38
My spark sho'd glow,.........................137. H.340, 14
From whose happy spark here let..............262. H.782, 3
Sometimes (in mirth) he sayes each whelk's a sparke
273. H.834, 3
A sparke neglected makes a mighty fire.........281. H.873, 2
Thou art our candle there, or spark...........372. N.118, 8
Sparkle Which Star-like sparkle in their skies:..61. H.160, 2
Sparkles What Mad-man's he, that when it sparkles so,
187. H.502, 5
It sparkles now like Ariadne's Crowne.........264. H.789, 4
Sparkling You are a sparkling Rose i'th'bud,.....88. H.216, 7
And all the shrubs, with sparkling spangles, shew
205. H.575, 11
Vnder whose shade twoe starry sparkling eyes....404. A.1, 9
— — — — — — — — — — — —,..............439. var. H.443, 29
— — — — — — — — — — — —,..............453. var. H.283, 36
Sparks Like the sparks of fire, befriend thee......217. H.619, 5
Sparrow This Sparrow, she had scorn'd her own: 104. H.256, 12
Spars Under the sparres of which I lie..........349. N.47, 5
Spartaness Was like a slightly Spartanesse.........51. H.142, 8
Spat Two she spat out, a cough forc't out the rest. 158. H.419, 2
For anger spat on thee her Looking-glasse:....249. H.732, 2
Spawned No noise of late spawn'd Tittyries:....126. H.319, 2
Speak Began to speak, and would have been......13. H.27, 7
Who speak but little, 'cause I love so much......15. H.38, 14
(Love makes me write, what shame forbids to speak.)
24. H.74, 2
The rest Ile speak, when we meet both in bed...24. H.74, 14
And for to speak, if possible:.................39. H.108, 12
Gryll eates, but ne're sayes Grace; To speak the troth,
48. H.135, 1
Let but That Mighty Cesar speak, and then,....52. H.146, 13
The Eyes by tears speak, while the Tongue is mute.
58. H.150, 8
Heare all men speak; but credit few or none.....67. H.177, 4
Let them speak by gentle tones,................82. H.203, 9
I co'd not speak the Saints here painted........91. H.223, 27
Speak griefe in you,..........................104. H.257, 2
To speak by Teares, before ye have a Tongue...104. H.257, 14
Speak, whimp'ring Younglings, and make known 104. H.257, 15
Speak but the word, and Ile take you...........112. H.281, 6
But let that speak, the Client gets the suit.....123. H.308, 2
And speak it with the best....................144. H.371, 12
Looke red, and blow, and bluster, but not speake:
150. H.382, 8
I prithee speake: Lyc. I will. End. Say on:....183. H.492, 5
I rather thinke (though they may speake the worst)
219. H.630, 3
Though then I smile, and speake no words at all.
222. H.634, 15
Speak where thou art. Ph. O Charon pittie me!..248. H.730, 6
O Jupiter, sho'd I speake ill...................250. H.739, 1
Speak thou the word, they'l kindle by and by....261. H.781, 4
Speak me faire; for Lovers be.................264. H.790, 3
And what we blush to speake, she bids us write. 275. H.846, 2
That will speake what this can't tell..........289. H.910, 5
For which I might extoll thee, but speake lesse, 298. H.955, 9
If Jove wo'd speake, he wo'd accept of thine...301. H.966, 14
Know when to speake; for many times it brings 318. H.1037, 1
When times are troubled, then forbeare; but speak,
324. H.1072, 1
Speak but the word, and cure me quite.........344. N.29, 10
As to speak, Lord, say and hold..............347. N.40, 4
Speak, did the Bloud of Abel cry...............387. N.203, 1
Speake thou of love and I'le reply............393. N.232, 11
When well we speak, & nothing do that's good,..397. N.256, 1
Doe speake a virgin merry cherry-lip't..........404 A.1, 22
Speak, what art thou? Euc. One, once that had a lover,
416. A.8, 9
— — — — — — — — — — —,..............444. var. H.730, 4
Speakest When e're thou speak'st, look with a lowly eye:
362. N.89, 3
Speaking Ha's it a speaking virtue? 2. Yes;...130. H.329, 16
And in his Raptures speaking Lines of Thine,..206. H.575, 34
How will it drop pure hony, speaking these?....328. H.1089, 4
Speaks Thus speaks the Oke, here; C. and M. shall meet,
26. H.79, 7
Forth into blushes, whensoere he speaks.......124. H.311, 2
How speaks it, say? 2. Do you but this,.......130. H.329, 17
Part your joyn'd lips, then speake your kisse;..130. H.329, 18
Believe, Love speaks it not, but Lust;.......175. H.465, 40
He who commends the vanquisht, speaks the Power,
200. H.553, 1
The Marble speaks it Mary Stone:............257. H.764, 4
And speaks in language keene:................259. H.772, 24
Bice laughs, when no man speaks; and doth protest
265. H.795, 1
Comely Acts well; and when he speaks his part, 266. H.799, 1
Instead of Harts-horne (if he speakes the troth) 299. H.959, 3
What He with laughter speaks, heare thou with tears.
355. N.63, 2
Speak'st See Speakest
Spear Amongst this scumme, the Souldier, with his speare,
398. N.263, 9
The Crosse, the Cords, the Nailes, the Speare,..400. N.266, 8
Spears Tell me the motes, dust, sands, and speares 340. N.3, 11
Speckled But ne'r so much as licks the speckled shells:
204. H.568, 2
Spectacles To others store of helpfull spectacles...154. H.401, 2
Sold his old Mothers Spectacles for Beere:....272. H.829, 2
Sped Say then, how ill sho'd I have sped,......212. H.599, 3
Sped'st Regardlesse whether well thou sped'st, or no. 6. H.3, 6
Speech Soft speech, smooth touch, the lips, the Maiden-head:
45. H.128, 8
Farre hence be all speech, that may anger move: 222, H.633, 60
'Cause my speech is now decaid;...............348. N.41, 31
In speech, in Picture; noe otherwise then when..411. A.3, 61
Prophan'd in Speech, or done an act that's fowle
426. ins. H.197, 29a
Speechless So when Love speechlesse is, she doth expresse
15. H.38, 11
Speed And her loving-lucklesse speed,..............15. H.36, 13
Good speed, for I this day....................87. H.214, 1
With speed give sick men their salvation:.......125. H.315, 2
Then smil'd, and sweetly chid her speed;......187. H.504, 5
With all wise speed for execution..............252. H.749, 2
Wisheth his body, not his soule, good speed.....277. H.855, 2
He wished me all Good speed...................295. H.942, 8
Despaire takes heart, when ther's no hope to speed:
309. H.999, 1
That may far sooner speed the poore:.........312. H.1014, 8
The Birth is fruitlesse: Chor. Then the work God speed.
365. N.97, 19
Speedy Shall I seek (for speedy ease).........40. H.115, 7
Chor. No, or thy zeale so speedy,..............374. N.123, 47
Spell See Care-charming-spell
To that soft Charm, that Spell, that Magick Bough,
62. H.161, 9
Bear up the Magick Bough and spel:........136. H.336, 134
Spells Bring your Magicks, Spels, and Charmes,..10. H.19, 5
The Night-Charme quickly; you have spells,..115. H.283, 133
Spend Nor art thou so close-handed, but can'st spend
38. H.106, 129
Thee spend a sigh, t'accompany my teare.........42. H.122, 6
Or vainly spend,..............................43. H.123, 17
Till passengers shall spend their doome,........104. H.256, 20
She told me too, as that did spend,............153. H.399, 5
Love will in vain spend shafts on me:..........155. H.406, 2
(Unkind to us) to spend thine houres,..........183. H.492, 15
But Ile spend my comming houres,..............191. H.519, 7
Thus, thus, we live, and spend the houres....198. H.544, 19
So spend some minutes of the day:............215. H.616, 6
There will I spend,...........................258. H.770, 5
Lest we that Tallent spend:...................289. H.911, 17
Spend Harmless shade thy nightly Houres,.....289. H.912, 1
Spend on that stock: and when your life must fall,
299. H.958, 5
Ans. Stock ye to spend ye:..................310. H.1001, 12
Spend I my life (that's subject unto change:)..310. H.1003, 2
So, here the remnant of my dayes I'd spend,....371. N.115, 11
Be those few hours, which I have yet to spend, 392. N.230, 1
I'le my Eternitie spend here...................402. N.269, 25
Spending Be ever and ever a spending;...........195. H.534, 9
For good successe in his spending,.............263. H.784, 9
Spends 'Tis flatterie spends a King, more then his foes.
331. H.1105, 2

Spenke Spenke has a strong breath, yet short Prayers saith: 283. H.884, 1
Spent See Here-spent-hours, Love-spent
Though much from out the Cess be **spent**,........33. H.100, 3
And after sorrowes **spent**, I slept:..............51. H.142, 4
Spring up afresh; when all these mists are **spent**, 52. H.146, 11
Shews you how much is **spent** of night.........54. H.149, 52
But being **spent**, the worse, and worst..........84. H.208, 11
My Muse in Meads has **spent** her many houres,..94. H.224, 1
Some time in wrangling **spent**,................105. H.260, 2
Where Maids have **spent** their houres...........110. H.274, 4
Like Unthrifts, having **spent**,.................110. H.274, 17
Which **spent**, one death, bring to ye both one Grave. 124. H.313, 14
The cole once **spent**, we'l then to bed,........136. H.336, 151
Come unto thee for Laurell, having **spent**,......143. H.365, 5
Is it because his money all is **spent**?...........160. H.423, 2
Much I know of Time is **spent**,..................191. H.519, 3
The Morn's farre **spent**; and the immortall Sunne 216. H.618, 3
Some few sands **spent**, we hence must go,......233. H.670, 37
Love is maintain'd by wealth; when all is **spent**, 235. H.676, 1
As Heaven had **spent** all perfumes there.........237. H.686, 12
Chor. Much time is **spent** in prate; begin,.......243. H.716, 23
Of all those times that I in it have **spent**.....334. H.1124, 2
In true repentance **spent**, will be...............388. N.206, 3
Natures, like ours, wee who haue **spent** our tyme 410, A.3, 15
Times, Titles, Trophies, may be lost and **Spent**; 419. A.10, 3
Sperm The silke worms **sperme**, and the delights 435. ins. H.293, dd
Sperrables See Sparables
Spew Abhorre, and **spew** out all Neutralities.......353. N.54, 4
Sphere Vertue had, and mov'd her **Sphere**........37. H.106, 92
Many a lesse and greater **spheare**...............47. H.133, 2
Love makes the cheek, and chin a **sphere**......49. H.136, 21
She soon wo'd leave her **spheare**,..............54. H.149, 37
Charms, that call down the moon from out her **sphere**, 99. H.244, 1
About the Roofe a Syren in a **Sphere**;.........115. H.283, 102
(Binding the wheele of Fortune to his **Sphere**)..137. H.341, 4
Then being seated in that smoother **Sphere**,......172. H.456, 7
And thou then turning in that **Sphere**,..........175. H.465, 51
That turns each **Sphere**,.......................193. H.524, 5
In thy **Sphere**;...............................220. H.633, 8
A Publike Light (in this immensive **Sphere**.)..236. H.685, 2
Blaze by this **Sphere** for ever: Or this doe,....264. H.789, 5
The circumspangle this my spacious **Sphere**,....267. H.804, 7
Love is a Circle, and an Endlesse **Sphere**;......274. H.839, 1
Is sober virtue, seen to move her **sphere**.......327. H.1087, 2
While th' Moone in her **sphere**..............334. H.1122, 16
God is above the **sphere** of our esteem,..........340. N.4, 1
Sin once reacht up to Gods eternall **Sphere**,....367. N.100, 1
And, coveting no higher **sphere**,..............402. N.269, 24
Spheres Drop the fat blessing of the **sphears**.....57. H.149, 152
Fall down, down, down, from those thy chiming **spheres**, 103. H.254, 5
Through heaven, the very **Spheres**...........151. H.388, 7
Their silv'rie **Spheres**, ther's none may doubt,..178. H.476, 8
Listen, while they (like Syrens in their **Spheres**) 206. H.575, 52
— — — — — — — — — —,..............443. var. H.575, 51
Sphering **Sphering** about the wassail cup,......136. H.336, 148
Spice Of Balme, of Oyle, of **Spice**, and Amber-Greece. 5. H.1, 8
Sleepe in thy peace, while we with **spice** perfume thee, 89. H.219, 13
Or **spice**, or fish, or fire, or close-stools here......155. H.405, 2
Shall write in **Spice**, Endimion 'twas..........184. H.492, 39
And for the Bride-Cake ther'l be **Spice**.........267. H.805, 6
Here she lyes (in Bed of **Spice**)...............274. H.838, 1
Make hoods of thee to serve out **Spice**.........275. H.844, 8
With **spice**; that done, Ile leave thee to thy rest. 300. H.960, 6
Sleep in thy peace, thy bed of **Spice**;..........361. N.83, 61
The **Spice** and Spiknard hence is gone,........375. N.123, 55
His soule as to a bedd of **spice**.................408. A.2, 44
Spiced Which sweetly **spic't**, we'l first carouse..135. H.336, 127
So smells the Aire of **spiced** wine;...........145. H.375, 5
Not made of Ale, but **spiced** Wine;.............193. H.521, 48
And Maiden's-blush, for **spiced** wine............216. H.616, 34
Above they are the Angels **spiced** wine.........226. H.645, 2
Spic'd to the brink...........................350. N. 47, 40
Spiceries From out the wealthy **spiceries**:........145. H.375, 2
Spices No **Spices** wanting, when I'm laid by thee....20. H.55, 10
That all the **Spices** of the East.................69. H.179, 3
From Countries far, with Store of **Spices**, (sweet) 86. H.213, 31
All rich **spices** thence will flow...............244. H.719, 6
Or search the beds of **Spices** through,..........367. N.102, 10
And bring our **Spices**, to embalm Thee dead;....399. N.263, 38
Round short and cleire, like pounded **spices** sweete 406. A.1, 92
Spicing And Amber; **Spice-**
ing the Chafte Aire with fumes of Paradise...112. H.283, 15-16
Spicknard See Spikenard
Spied I **spy'd** he had a Quiver..................27. H.81, 20
Will blush to death, if ought be **spi'd**...........366. N.98, 13
But now my muse 'hath **spi'de** a darke descent....405. A.1, 65
Spies Quite through the table, where he **spies**..119. H.293, 25
And vnder it two Chast borne **spyes**...........408. A.2, 35
Spike Oyl of Lillies, and of **Spike**,.............244. H.719, 3
Spikenard This Camphire, Storax, **Spiknard**, Galbanum: 157. H.414, 2
The Storax, **Spiknard**, Myrrhe, and Ladanum.....181. H.485, 4
The Spice and **Spiknard** hence is gone,........375. N.123, 55
Our holy **Spicknard**, & ther's none..............413. A.4, 25
— — — — — — — — — —,..................442. var. H.575, 8
Spill You'l **spil** a tear, or two with theirs:........70. H.180, 6
But not **spill** Wine;................ ....307. H.988, 3
They noiselesse **spill** their Influence:............340. N.3, 14
To board the Magicke bowle, and **spill**....437. var. H.336, 134
Spilt Bloud will be **spilt**;......................401. N.268, 11
Is **spilt** in everlasting night....................413. A.4, 11
— — — — — — — — — —,...............424. var. H.164, 5
allready **spillt**, her rayes must gleame....430. ins. H.283, 20d
Spin This, this it sho'd be, for to **spin**,.........164. H.442, 3
Or else **spin** out the thread of sands,..........215. H.616, 7
To **spin**:....................................221. H.633, 39
The longer thred of life we **spin**,...............379. N.144, 1
Spindles Let bounteous Fate your **spindles** full....58. H.149, 161
Spinner To wrong a **Spinner** or her Loome.......165. H.442, 15
Spinner's A **Spinners** circle is bespread,.......167. H.443, 101
A **Spinners** ham, the beards of mice,........435. ins. H.293, u
Spinning If the Maides a **spinning** goe,.........315. H.1026, 5
Spinster's — — — — — — — — —, ...440. var. H.443, 101
Spire As my small Bell best fits my little **Spire**...249. H.733, 12
Spires As Zephirus when he **'spires**..............55. H.149, 67
Spiring — — — — — — — — —, ...430. var. H.283, 24
Spirit Be so, bold **spirit**; Stand Center-like, unmov'd; 37. H.106, 101
To me, as blood to life and **spirit**: Neare,........45. H.128, 2
That scatter'st **Spirit** and Lust; whose purest shine, 45. H.128, 12
Swell up my nerves with **spirit**; let my blood....79. H.197, 77
As I did, my ravisht **spirit**...................182. H.489, 4
She followes the **Spirit** that guides now.........225. H.643, 12
Ravisht in **spirit**, I come, nay more, I flie....242. H.713, 3
No, but when the **Spirit** fils....................242. H.714, 3
That brave **Spirit** comes agen...................242. H.714, 12
In whom the **spirit** of the Gods do's dwell,....256. H.763, 7
Sweet **Spirit** comfort me!.......................347. N.41, 4
Sweet **Spirit** comfort me!.......................347. N.41, 8
Sweet **Spirit** comfort me!.......................347. N.41, 12
Sweet **Spirit** comfort me!.......................347. N.41, 16
Sweet **Spirit** comfort me!.......................347. N.41, 20
Sweet **Spirit** comfort me!.......................348. N.41, 24
Sweet **Spirit** comfort me!.......................348 N.41, 28
Sweet **Spirit** comfort me!.......................348. N.41, 32
Sweet **Spirit** comfort me!.......................348. N.41, 36
Sweet **Spirit** comfort me!.......................348. N.41, 40
Sweet **Spirit** comfort me!.......................348. N.41, 44
Sweet **Spirit** comfort me!.......................348. N.41, 48
By Faith we all walk here, not by the **Spirit**.....362. N.88, 2
His holy **Spirit**, or doth plant His Grace.........385. N.189, 4
And soule and **spirit** plot, and excellence.......399. N.263, 27
An active **spiritt** full marrow, and what's good: 426. ins. H 197, 48d
— — — — — — — — — — — —,..............427. var. H.197, 49
Spirit's Now the good **Spirit's** gone from me?..132. H.334, 2
Spirits The frost-bound-blood, and **spirits**; and to make 45. H.128, 26
And such **spirits** raise, 'twill then..............52. H.145, 5
And make my **spirits** frantick with the fire.......67. H.176, 4
Of these chaste **spirits**, that are here possest....152. H 392, 2
Great **Spirits** never with their bodies dye.........199. H.547, 2
Those **spirits** rais'd; and with like precepts then 326. H.1080, 17
Whether the world such **Sperritts** had or noe,....411. A.3, 38
Ravish our **spirits**, that entranc't wee see........415. A 7, 17
— — — — — — — — — — —,..............423. var. H.128, 12
Spirting — — — — — — — — —, ...430. var. H.283, 24
Spirting-salt With Holy-meale, and **spirting-salt**...36. H.106, 60
Spirts When Laurell **spirts** 'ith fire, and when the Hearth 7. H.8, 5
Spit Or else because Grill's roste do's burn his **Spit**, 48. H.135, 3
— — — — — — — — — —,..............424. var. H.164, 5
— — — — — — — — — —,..............447. var. H.1106, 1
Spits Where laden **spits**, warp't with large Ribbs of Beefe, 146. H.377, 9
Spittle See Fasting-spittle
Of that we call the Cuckoes **spittle**...........119. H.293, 28
Sacred **Spittle** bring ye hither;................258. H.769, 4
Spleen His **Spleen**, the chirring Grasshopper;....119. H.293, 16
Splendor Phœbean **splendour**! and thou Thespian spring! 45. H.128, 33
Out-shine the **splendour** of his mid-day beams...77. H.197, 12
'Twas by your **splendour** (Lady) not by mine...94. H.226, 8
Split Saile against Rocks, and **split** them too;....31. H.90, 8
Spoil **Spoile** a house to save a town:............21. H.61, 6
So when this War (which tempest-like doth **spoil** 225. H.642, 17
She can but **spoile** me of my Meanes, not Mind. 322. H.1061, 2
To **spoile** the first impression..................354. N.59, 18
But of her owne a **spoile** shee makes.....436. ins. H.336, 48p
Spoils Which precious **spoiles** upon her,........131. H.330, 12
Spoke Then **spoke** I to my Girle,....................24. H.75, 6
And having **spoke** it once, Farewell.............60. H.159, 12

Then a mans frequent Fame, **spoke** out with praise. 241. H.710, 2
Ere a good word can be **spoke**:...............255. H.761, 18
Spoken Which Love fore-fend; but **spoken**......114. H.283, 89
Spokes **Spokes** when he sees a rosted Pig, he swears 305. H.982, 1
Sponge See **Spunge**
His **spunge**, and stick, do ask why Thou dost stay? 398. N.263, 11
Sponge-like Which, **Spunge-like** drinking in the dull- 167. H.443, 97
Spongy **Spungie**, and swelling, and farre more.:165. H.443, 27
— — — — — — — — — —,...............440. var. H.443, 97
Spoon Two Napkins cram'd up, and a silver **Spoone**. 118. H.292, 6
One silver **spoon** shines in the house of Croot;..332. H.1110, 1
Sport Some **sport**, to please those Babies in your eyes: 15. H.38, 4
At childish Push-pin (for our **sport**) did play:..17. H.44, 2
Playing for **sport**, at Cherry-pit:................19. H.49, 2
For **sport** my Julia threw a Lace.............116. H.284, 1
Lets make it full up, by our **sport**............133. H.336, 32
And **sport** it any way;.......................160. H.422, 11
Where the businesse is the **sport**:.............255. H.761, 6
Then bid Christmas **sport** good-night;........315. H.1026, 12
Where Beane's the King of the **sport** here;....317. H.1035, 3
— — — — — — — — — —,..............432. var. H.283, 130
Sports Of Christmas **sports**, the Wassell-boule,..126. H.319, 13
For **Sports**, for Pagentrie, and Playes,.........230. H.662, 46
And Younglings, with such **sports** as these.....231. H.662, 73
And let all **sports** with Christmas dye..........285. H.894, 2
Spot Where nature in a whitenes without **spott**..405. A.1, 61
Spotless Of flowers, was thy **spotlesse** breast:......8. H.11, 4
About her **spotlesse** neck she knit................14. H.34, 3
I saw about her **spotlesse** wrist,................64. H.169, 1
As **spotlesse** pure, as it is sweet:..............101. H.250, 10
Prayers and Praises are those **spotlesse** two......341. N.9, 1
Thy hands (though cold) yet **spotlesse**, white,..375. N.123, 75
Spots All are alike faire, when no **spots** we see...209. H.586, 2
Spouse Welcome, O welcome my illustrious **Spouse**; 77. H.197, 13
And last, when thee (dear **Spouse**) I disavow,....79. H.197, 91
Keepe it till then; and now my **Spouse**,........175. H.465, 73
He Boded good-luck to thy Selfe and **Spouse**....181. H.483, 12
Sprang **Sprang** up a sweet Nativity of Flowres...204. H.567, 2
Spread See **Full-spread, O'erspread, Overspread**
Next, his wilde eares, like Lethern wings full **spread**, 33. H.99, 3
Come thou not neere that Filmne so finely **spred**,..82. H.204, 7
Which o're the board is smoothly **spred**,........91. H.223, 62
A little mushroome table **spred**,................119. H.293, 7
For either sheet, was **spread** the Caule..........167. H.443, 90
With Daisies **spread**, and Daffadils;...........192. H.521, 16
Spread as He **spreads**; wax lesse as He do's wane; 196. H.537, 3
When I behold a Forrest **spread**................202. H.560, 1
They, weeping, **spread** a Lawnie Loome,......237. H.686, 15
Lesse set for them, then **spred** for me..........282. H.881, 10
And no less prais'd, then **spread** throughout the world. 288. H.907, 6
A House **spred** through with Leprosie.........310. H.1004, 12
Over the golden Altar now is **spread**,..........355. N.65, 3
From wch two armies like branches seem to **spread** 406. A.1, 97
Of gold and sylver there is **spread**,......440. ins. H.443, 45w
Spreading Or had I not, I'de stopp the **spreading** itch 411. A.3, 55
Spreads And large she **spreads** by dust, and sweat 148. H.377, 114
Spread as He **Spreads**; wax lesse as He do's wane: 196. H.537, 3
Punchin by Beere and Ale, **spreads** so.........273. H.832, 4
Sprig See **Cypress-sprig**
Take this **sprig** of Eglantine....................88. H.217, 2
That Dress, this **Sprig**, that Leaf, this Vine;...215. H.616, 23
Spright See **Sprite**
Sprightful See **Spriteful**
Sprightly Who a **sprightly** Springall lov'd,........15. H.36, 6
Was like a **sprightly** Spartanesse................51. H.142, 8
Thee **sprightly** Soame, one of my righteous Tribe: 199. H.545, 2
When I drinke my **sprightly** wine:..............309. H.996, 6
— — — — — — — — — —,...............427. var. H.197, 49
Spring See **Offspring**
Part of the creame from that Religious **Spring**;....9. H.14, 8
The seeds of Treason choake up as they **spring**,..10. H.17, 1
When what is lov'd is Present, love doth **spring**;..13. H.30, 1
Which as a warme, and moistned **spring**,........25. H.78, 9
To **spring** from these a sweet Posterity..........44. H.124, 4
Phœbean splendour! and thou Thespian **spring**!..45. H.128, 33
Spring up afresh; when all these mists are spent, 52. H.146, 11
But **spring** from ceremonious feares............54. H.149, 22
Spring, sooner then the Lark, to fetch in May...68. H.178, 14
And with the Christal humour of the **spring**,....78. H.197, 31
In the **Spring**;..............................83. H.205, 3
When as the chosen seed shall **spring**..........89. H.219, 19
But for to make it **spring** againe.............102. H.250, 55
Goddesse of Youth, and Lady of the **Spring**,....107. H.265, 1
Him the Soveraigne of their **Spring**:..........108. H.266, 10
Each Virgin, like a **Spring**,...................110. H.274, 11
What's that we see from far? the **spring** of Day 112. H.283, 1
And drown yee with a flowrie **Spring**:.........113. H.283, 44
We have as short a **Spring**;...................125. H.316, 12
His dayes to see a second **Spring**.............133. H.336, 24
And **spring** fresh Rose-buds, while the salt, the wit 148. H.377, 73
When out of bed my Love doth **spring**,........154. H.404, 1
Some Christall of the **Spring**;................185. H.495, 2
Not Virgils Gnat, to whom the **Spring**.........186. H.497, 9
To **spring** againe another yeare.................189. H.514, 8
Spring with the Larke, most comely Bride, and meet 216. H.618, 1
Thaw'd are the snowes, and now the lusty **Spring** 224. H.642, 3
(To wash her) water from the **Spring**...........237. H.686, 6
To see the day **spring** from the pregnant East,..242. H.713, 2
Streame to the **Spring** from whence it came.....245. H.720, 10
The treasure of the **Spring**....................250. H.740, 4
Others shall **spring** up in their place agen:.....256. H.763, 12
Spring the purple Violet......................262. H.782, 4
Cheerfull day shall **spring** agen................276. H.850, 8
Thee lesse to taste, then to drink up their **spring**; 299. H.956, 2
Tears will **spring**, where woes are deep.........306. H.984, 32
Keep up your state ye streams; and as ye **spring**, 316. H.1028, 23
Sick is Anthea, sickly is the **spring**,...........320. H.1054, 1
Canst talke to us of Sharon; where a **spring**...330. H.1100, 9
Thy soft sweet Earth! but (like a **spring**)......361. N.83, 71
To **spring**; though now a wither'd flower........361. N.84, 8
And our Peace here, like a **Spring**,.............363. N.93, 8
Spring Tulips up through all the yeere;........366. N.97, 21
And our late **spring**...........................375. N.123, 59
Threescore or fourescore **spring** up thence for one 388. N.208, 4
No **spring** of Time, or Times succession........392. N.229, 2
And though all joyes **spring** from the glance....395. N.246, 3
Spring hence thy faith, nor thinke it ill desert....414. A.6, 3
Springal Who a sprightly **Springall** lov'd,..........15. H.36, 6
Springing A sacred Laurel **springing** from my grave: 30. H.89, 5
Springing from two such Fires,...............116. H.283, 159
But in their **springing** blood so play,..........291. H.919, 19
Spring's Of them, the **spring's** once drie;........43. H.123, 20
Sweet Amarillis, by a **Spring's**..................46. H.130, 1
Springs See **Offsprings**
Ope' the fountains and the **springs**,...............21. H.61, 3
A deale of courage in each bosome **springs**.......25. H.77, 9
The Purling **springs**, groves, birds, and well-weav'd Bowrs, 36. H.106, 45
So soft streams meet, so **springs** with gladder smiles 77. H.197, 1
Where the fault **springs**, there let the judgement fall. 132. H.335, 4
Me longer date, and more fresh **springs** to live:..140. H.355, 12
These **Springs** were Maidens once that lov'd,...180. H.478, 1
Turn'd to these **Springs**, which wee see here:..180. H.478, 4
Let our soules flie to' th' shades, where ever **springs** 205. H.575, 2
No more of Groves, Meades, **Springs**, and wreathes of Flowers: 228. H.658, 4
Balm may thy Trees drop, and thy **Springs** runne oyle 269. H.818, 7
Milk stil your Fountains, and your **Springs**, for why? 273. H.831, 1
Teares have their **springs** from joy, as well as woe. 275. H.842, 4
Tel'st when a Verse **springs** high, how understood 297. H.947, 7
Physitians say Repletion **springs**..............298. H.951, 1
There **springs** a sope-like-lather in his shoos.....332. H.1113, 2
Whence beawty **springs**, and thus I kisse thy foot. 406. A.1, 112
— — — — — — — — — —,...............425. var. H.197, 2
Springtime To come forth, like the **Spring-time**, fresh and greene;....................................68. H.178, 16
Where **spring-time** smiles throughout the yeare? 103. H.256, 3
Like to the peeping **spring-time** of the yeare....105. H.259, 8
Strip her of **Spring-time**, tender-whimpring-maids, 114. H.283, 91
Come with the **Spring-time**, forth Fair Maid, and be 140. H.354, 1
Seem like the **Spring-time** of the yeere?........364. N.96, 13
Springtimes And millions of **spring-times** may ye have, 124. H.313, 13
Sprinkled Ev'n as the **sprinkled** bloud cal'd on...387. N.203, 3
Sprinkling Your praise, and bless you, **sprinkling** you with Wheat:..................................113. H.283, 46
Set the Brush for **sprinkling**:..................258. H.769, 3
For the sacred **sprinkling**:......................303. H.974, 2
Sprite Full goblets of thy gen'rous blood; his **spright** 78. H.197, 67
The fouler Fiend, and evill **Spright**............123. H.306, 14
Far from hence the evill **Sp'rite**................258. H.769, 9

So farre keepes the evill **Spright**.............322. H.1064, 6
Spriteful While you are in your **sprightfull** green:
49. H.136, 25
— — — — — — — — — —,............427. var. H.197, 49
Sprout May see it **sprout** forth streames of muscadine.
405. A.1, 50
Sprung Thou art a plant **sprung** up to wither never,
98. H.240, 1
Sprung up a War-like Nation.................297. H.948, 8
Then Night now gone, and yet not **sprung** the Day.
319. H.1046, 2
Where is the Babe but lately **sprung**?..........367. N.102, 2
Spun They shew'd me then, how fine 'twas **spun**;...18. H.47, 9
He'll do no doubt; This flax is **spun**.........168. H.443, 121
Fates revolve no Flax th'ave **spun**.............224. H.639, 4
Into your selves like wooll together **spunne**,
431. ins. H.283, 50h
Spunge See **Sponge**
Spunge makes his boasts that he's the onely man
171. H.454, 1
Spur She takes for a **Spurre**:.................225. H.643, 8
Spur jingles now, and sweares by no meane oathes,
330. H.1099, 1
Spurned Who **spurn'd** at Envie; and co'd bring, with ease,
137. H.341, 5
Spurting See **Spirting**
Spurting-salt See **Spirting-salt**
Spurts See **Spirts**
Square See **Foursquare**
A wise man ev'ry way lies **square**.............37. H.106, 98
Into an Ovall, **square**, or round;.............202. H.560, 10
Squeak Then temper flew from words; and men did **squeake**,
150. H.382, 7
Squeaks Who **squeaks** to all the commers there,..91. H.223, 40
Squint-eyed **Squint'ey'd**, hook-nos'd; and lastly, Kidney-lipt.
62. H.163, 2
Squirrels' A little brush of **Squirrils** haires,......91. H.223, 46
Squirrils and childrens teeth late shed,.........166. H.443, 55
Stable See **Outstable**
To purifie this my Augean **stable**:..............357. N.73, 2
Stabs What needs twenty **stabs**, when one.......254. H.757, 5
Stacks Your **Stacks**, your Stocks, your sweetest Mowes,
179. H.476, 23
Staff See **Buttoned-staff**
The **staffe**, the Elme, the prop, the shelt'ring wall
72. H.185, 12
My Pilgrims **staffe**; my weed of grey:.........123. H.306, 2
Fix here my Button'd **Staffe** and stay..........216. H.617, 4
A **staffe** or a wand............................256. H.762, 4
The **staffe** is now greas'd,....................333. H.1122, 1
Or with thy **staffe**, or with thy rod;.............351. N.48, 2
The one a **Staffe** is, and the next a Rod:.......394. N.241, 2
The **staffe** might come to play the friendly part...394. N.241, 4
Stage The Crosse shall be Thy **Stage**; and Thou shalt there
398. N.263, 17
Stage's Together with the **Stages** glory stood....150. H.382, 3
Stag's See **Slain-stag's**
To these for sauce the slaine **stagges** teares
435. ins. H.293, p
Stain And never **staine** a cheeke for it...............6. H.4, 4
Pure hands bring hither, without **staine**.........91. H.223, 42
Is the beast exempt from **staine**,................280. H.870, 5
Stained **Stain'd** by the Beames of Clarret wine:..268. H.811, 8
Staining See **Swan-staining**
Stairs Hard are the two first **staires** unto a Crowne;
292. H.925, 1
Stake Lay to thy **stake** a lustie Steere,.........243. H.716, 14
Stakes The **stakes** are laid: let's now apply......243. H.716, 19
This Law; that He and I part **stakes**...........376. N.127, 6
Stalk Ask me why the **stalk** is weak............208. H.580, 9
Stall Poore-pittied Child! Who from Thy **Stall**....366. N.98, 22
Stamp But she co'd see each eye to **stamp** a teare:
58. H.150, 4
Stand Thy Watch may **stand**, my minutes fly poste haste;
8. H.10, 3
But with thy equall thoughts, prepar'd dost **stand**,
37. H.106, 95
Be so, bold spirit; **Stand** Center-like, unmov'd;..37. H.106, 101
Weak though it be; long may it grow, and **stand**,
40. H.112, 3
Juno here, far off, doth **stand**................56. H.149, 109
Stand before you, my learn'd Diocesan?.........64. H.168, 2
Which makes me **stand**........................72. H.185, 23
Upon this fetuous board doth **stand**............92. H.223, 68
Here **stand** it stil to dignifie our Muse,.........99. H.245, 5
Let my haire then **stand** an end:...............117. H.286, 6
See how the poore do waiting **stand**,............139. H.350, 1
It is, which builds, 'gainst Fate to **stand**.......148. H.377, 102
Safe **stand** thy Walls, and Thee, and so both will,
149. H.377, 115
Close to my Beds side she did **stand**...........153. H.399, 3
Stand for my comming, Sentinell..............174. H.465, 14
May both with manchet **stand** repleat;.........178. H.476, 4
Stand with thy Graces forth, Brave man, and rise 181. H.483, 1
Is lopt already; and the rest but **stand**.........203. H.565, 2
Thee to the **Stand**, where honour'd Homer reades
206. H.575, 27
Urles had the Gout so, that he co'd not **stand**;..207. H.577, 1
Or let her walk, or **stand**, or sit,..............207. H.579, 3
I am holy, while I **stand**.......................227. H.651, 1
Stand forth brave man, since Fate has made thee here
251. H.745, 1
And the Plums **stand** by......................263. H.784, 17
Two things do make society to **stand**;.........275. H.847, 1
(By his word) the Sun to **stand**:..............276. H.850, 10
Stand by the Magick of my powerfull Rhymes..280. H.869, 1
Of Beeves here ready **stand** for Sacrifice.........300. H.961, 8
To Jove the Mighty for to **stand**...............303. H.973, 16
Attempt the end, and never **stand** to doubt;....311. H.1008, 1
A young Enchantresse close by him did **stand**..313. H.1017, 7
Whereon so many Stately Structures **stand**:....315. H.1028, 4
Stand forth Brave Man, here to the publique sight;
322. H.1062, 10
There did I see the Reverend Rectresse **stand**,..326. H.1080. 15
But **stand** for ever by his owne...............335. H.1129, 13
Here a little child I **stand**,......................364. N.95, 1
Do ravisht **stand**;..............................369. N.106, 10
Which, in full force, did daring **stand**,........370. N.107, 8
Though ills **stand** round about me;............373. N.122, 10
Chor. **Stand** empty here for ever:..............374. N.123, 17
Thy Widdowes **stand** forsaken................374. N.123, 30
If otherwise, I **stand** indifferent:..............392. N.230, 4
As Hell, and Earth, and Heav'n may **stand** amaz'd.
399. N.263, 31
Then lowly yet most lovely **stand** the feete,......406. A.1, 91
The haue their haruest, wch must **stand**..........408. A.2, 51
Shall **stand** for euer, though I doe addresse......412. A.3, 97
Of Youthe <s> swift watch to **stand**.............413. A.4, 7
you, **stand** for to surrender up the keyes..431. ins. H.283, 60h
Standard's Your **Standard's** up, we fix a Conquest there.
25. H77, 12
Standers E'ne all the **standers** by...................9. H.15, 8
Standersby See **Standers**
Standeth May blush, (while Brutus **standeth** by:)....6. H.4, 2
Standing With sev'rall dishes **standing** by,......101. H.250, 32
Penance, and **standing** so, are both but one.....106. H.261, 4
Venus **standing** Vulcan by......................194. H.527, 9
Tha'st got a place here (**standing** candidate)....305. H.983, 2
Of many **standing**, but of fall to none...........389. N.215, 2
Stands See **Counter-stands**, **Stants**
Retires himselfe, or else **stands** still.............68. H.178, 26
There **stands** his Idol-Beetle-flie:...............90. H.223, 14
Stands in the Platter, or close by,...............91. H.223, 48
Neere to the Altar **stands** the Priest,..........91. H.223, 50
The Bason **stands** the board upon...............92. H.223, 85
A little Fuz-ball-pudding **stands**................119. H.293, 29
But fixt it **stands**, by her own power,.........148. H.377, 108
Besides, the most religious Prophet **stands**.....262. H.781, 9
That Stubble **stands**, where once large eares have been.
275. H.843, 4
Thine houre is come; and the Tormentor **stands** 398. N.263, 3
Like purest white **stands** in the middle place......404. A.1, 12
Stands garded with a rosy hilly wall,.............405. A.1, 30
Which with ambitious humblenes **stands** vnder....405. A.1, 45
Which to thy Memorie **stands** as due.............414. A.5, 3
— — — — — — — — — — —,.............443. var. H.575, 40
Stank Drawn was his tooth; but **stanke** so, that some say,
323. H.1066, 3
Stants — — — — — — — — —, ...447. var. A.1, 30
Star See **New-star**
Lyd. Though mine be brighter then the **Star**;...70. H.181, 21
At Noone of Day, was seene a silver **Star**,......86. H.213, 20
Nor doth the early Shepheards **Starre**..........164. H.441, 7
Thy lucky Genius, and thy guiding **Starre**,......181. H.483, 5
Knock at a **Starre** with my exalted Head.......214. H.612, 14
And having fixt Thee in mine Orbe a **Starre**,...267. H.804, 9
What was thy Birth, thy **starre** that makes thee knowne,
299. H.956, 5
Declare to us, bright **Star**, if we shall seek.....367. N.102, 8
Fetcht binding gellye of a **starre**...........434. ins. H.293, 41h
Star-chamber To yond' **Star-chamber**, or do's seale
149. H.377, 128
Star-chamber-bills And all **Star-chamber-Bils** doe cease,
190. H.515, 27
Starches Sudds Launders Bands in pisse; and **starches** them
98. H.237, 1
Stare For men did strut, and stride, and **stare**, not act.
150. H.382, 6
Stares See **Out-stares**
Star-led-birth The **Starre-led-birth** of Charles the Prince.
214. H.611, 6
Star-like And **Star-like**, once more, guild our Firmament.
52. H.146, 12
Which **Star-like** sparkle in their skies:..........61. H.160, 2
Starry Vnder whose shade twoe **starry** sparkling eyes
404. A.1, 9
Stars See **Out-stars**
So all my Morne, and Evening **Stars** from You..3. Ded. H., 7
Whom (**Stars** consenting with thy Fate) thou hast
35. H.106, 33
And pounc't with **Stars**, it shew'd to me........67. H.175, 9
To read by th' **Starres**, the Kingdoms sick:....126. H.319, 6
No, no, thy **Stars** have destin'd Thee to see....155. H.405, 15
And the pure **Starres** the praising Poetrie......168. H.444, 8

As that your kisses must out-vie the **Starres**....216. H.618, 14
The Shooting **Starres** attend thee;.............217. H.619, 2
The **Starres** of the night.......................217. H.619, 13
Some **starres** were fixt before; but these are dim,
236. H.685, 3
But (ah!) by **starres** malignant crost,..........313. H.1020, 3
And like the **Starres** to glitter................323. H.1068, 16
Shew me that world of **Starres**, and whence.....340. N.3, 13
The **Starres**; but she,..........................354. N.58, 10
— — — — — — — — — —,............432. var. H.283, 120
And now y' have wept enough, depart yon **starres**
432. ins. H.283, 140a

Start (As Umber sweares) did make his Lyon **start**.
205. H.572, 4

Started As if they **started** at Bo-peep,...........194. H.525, 4

Starve See **Sterve**
Me sooner **starve**, then those can kill............40. H.115, 16
To **starve**, or wither............................361. N.83, 70

Starved See **Sterved**
And e'en with cold half **starved**.................26. H.81, 12
And leave their subjects but the **starved** ware...272. H.826, 6
Better he **starv'd**, then but to tast one crumme...355. N.65, 10
— — — — — — — — — —,............433. var. H.293, 14

Starves And **starves** with cold the self-same part. 290. H.915, 8
Bestirs his Hand, but **starves** in hand the Suite...303. H.975, 8
Starves, having no companion..................381. N.158, 2

Starving Will storme, or **starving** take here......213. H.609, 6

State See **Mab's-state, Swan-like-state**
Over the which a **State** was drawne...............8. H.11, 5
Shapcot! To thee the Fairy **State**..............119. H.293, 1
No ginne to catch the **State**, or wring..........126. H.319, 7
A slave to **state**:..............................137. H.340, 8
Prithee, when next thou do'st invite, barre **State**,
161. H.424, 3
Shame is a bad attendant to a **State**:..........182. H.488, 1
But I the Courtly **State** wo'd see:.............183. H.492, 19
The yvorie tooke **State** to hold.................185. H.497, 5
State at a distance adds to dignities...........236. H.682, 2
Thy Wife, thy Children, and the **state**.........239. H.696, 9
Trigg having turn'd his sute, he struts in **state**,..240. H.703, 1
Seest thou that Cloud that rides in **State**.......269. H.815, 1
What **State** above, what Symmetrie below,......297. H.947, 9
And that's to love me; in which **state**..........313. H.1020, 7
Keep up your **state** ye streams; and as ye spring,
316. H.1028, 23
The **State** of Poets there attending Thee:......324. H.1071, 2
Made up One **State** of Sixtie Venuses:..........326. H.1080, 4
Mans former Birth is grace-lesse; but the **state** 326. H.1080, 27
Upon Thy Princely **State** here,.................345. N.33, 28
Both void of **state**;...........................350. N.47, 12
In power; or come Thou in that **state**,..........393. N.232, 3
The number here of Heires, shall from the **state** 395. N.248, 3
— — — — — — — — — —,............427. var. H.197, 80

State-like The proud Dictator of the **State-like** wood:
23. H.69, 4

Stately **Stately** Julia, prime of all;................15. H.39, 3
An end to all his **stately** purposes..............137. H.341, 6
And these brave Measures go a **stately** trot;....141. H.359, 11
Stately Goddesse, do thou please,..............141. H.360, 1
Beset with **stately** Figures (every where).......185. H.496, 2
Then **stately** Virgil, witty Ovid, by...........206. H.575, 39
Whereon so many **Stately** Structures stand:....315. H.1028, 4
No, lay thy **stately** terrours by,................393. N.232, 7
Is the swan-stayning faire rare **stately** neck......405. A.1, 44
Bowing my lips vnto y[t] **stately** root............406. A.1, 111

States Fame tell of **States**, of Countries, Courts, and Kings;
36. H.106, 85
— — — — — — — — — —,............422. var. H.106, 87

State-sanctions In our **State-sanctions**, deep, or bottomlesse.
187. H.506, 8

Statues High are These **Statues** here, besides no lesse
185. H.496, 7

Stay Farre safer 'twere to **stay** at home:............5. H.2, 2
Stay then at home, and doe not goe..............6. H.2, 19
From house to house, and never **stay** at home;......6. H.3, 4
Then sweetest Silvia, let's no longer **stay**;.........8. H.10, 5
So you, my Lord, though you have now your **stay**,
52. H.146, 9
On, on devoutly, make no **stay**;................54. H.149, 41
Or by thy love, decree me here to **stay**..........60. H.156, 2
Or so, as Darknesse made a **stay**................64. H.169, 7
As that the **stay**..............................66. H.172, 22
My longer **stay**, and so I dy'd...................69. H.180, 4
But **stay** the time till we have bade Good night...73. H.186, 2
And seeing it, I made a **stay**....................73. H.187, 5
But **stay**; I see a Text,........................81. H.201, 39
Stay while ye will, or goe;.....................83. H.207, 1
That I must **stay**,..............................85. H.211, 6
But (Dearest) of so short a **stay**;...............87. H.216, 2
Bid that heart **stay**, and it will **stay**,..........108. H.267, 9
Stay, **stay**,.....................................125. H.316, 5
We have short time to **stay**, as you,............125. H.316, 11
As Gilly flowers do but **stay**....................126. H.318, 1
Go where I will, thou luckie Larr **stay** here,....132. H.333, 9
Must I here **stay**,..............................137. H.340, 3
Take friendly morsels, and there **stay**..........146. H.377, 16
These Summer-Birds did with thy Master **stay**..151. H.387, 1
Stay but till my Julia close...................164. H.441, 9
But you may **stay** yet here a while,...........176. H.467, 4
It is in vain to sing, or **stay**..................179. H.476, 34
Your Sister-hoods may **stay**,....................184. H.493, 5
When I consider (Dearest) thou dost **stay**......193. H.522, 1
To **stay**.......................................198. H.544, 23
For quick dispatch, Sculls made no longer **stay**, 200. H.551, 3
Fix here my Button'd Staffe and **stay**..........216. H.617, 4
Not making a **stay**,............................217. H.619, 9
Make no long **stay**.............................220. H.633, 6
Behold, for us the Naked Graces **stay**...........261. H.781, 7
Back to come, (and make no **stay**.)..............276. H.848, 3
Will enforce the Moon to **stay**,................276. H.850, 12
Go with thy Faults and Fates; yet **stay**........287. H.899, 7
And by the Law I ought to **stay**...............293. H.934, 7
I prithee **stay**. (Am.) I must away,...........324. H.1068, 21
I can no longer **Stay**;........................328. H.1091, 2
And though a while He makes Requesters **stay**,..344. N.30, 3
Him but a while to **stay**;......................346. N.38, 4
Stay me, by crowing, ere I do begin;............349. N.43, 4
That slack my pace; but yet not make me **stay**?..352. N.51, 3
And I'le no longer **stay**,.......................352. N.53, 2
His spunge, and stick, do ask why Thou dost **stay**?
398. N.263, 11
Vnto the passion, not to **stay**;.................408. A.2, 70
How **stay** thay would, yet forc't thay are to goe...410. A.3, 12
Guesse, soe departe; yett **stay** A while to[o] see
411. A.3, 59
Cha. I cannot **stay**; more souls for waftage wait,..416. A.8, 24

Staying Your joyes, by **staying** long:............53. H.149, 4
And sin no more, as we have done, by **staying**;..68. H.178, 41
Or **staying** there, is scourg'd with taunts.......146. H.377, 20

Stays Stiles, and stops, and **stayes**, that come....355. N.64, 3
The time the Bridegroom **stayes** from hence,....380. N.153, 1
And live in Hell, if that my Christ **stayes** there...403. N.271, 8

Stead See **Instead**
A Sister (in the **stead**.........................13. H.31, 7
We send in **stead** of New-yeares gift...........127. H.319, 26
In **stead** of Holly, now up-raise.................285. H.892, 3
In **stead** of Brine,.............................401. N.268, 17

Steal Me, day by day, to **steale** away from thee?....9. H.14, 2
Mark, if her tongue, but slily, **steale** a taste.....100. H.248, 4
(Rather than fail) to **steal** from thence old shoes:
143. H.368, 2
As colours **steale** into the Peare or Plum,.......250. H.737, 6
Steale a swolne sop out of the Dripping pan.....331. H.1106, 2
Who cannot buie, or **steale** a second to't.......332. H.1110, 2

Stealing And **stealing** still with love, and feare to Bed,
286. H.898, 15

Steals Eeles winds and turnes, and cheats and **steales**; yet Eeles
153. H.398, 1
Time **steals** away like to a stream,.............233. H.670, 22

Stealth How by **stealth** we meet, and then.......82. H.203, 13

Steam If meat the Gods give, I the **steame**........22. H.66, 1
Which rosted, we the **steam**.....................250. H.736, 3

Steel Thy scourge of **steele**,.....................353. N.56, 13
Or lyke as woole meetes **steele**, giue way.........408. A.2, 69
— — — — — — — — — —,............437. var. H.336, 112

Steep But lets go **steepe**.........................160. H.421, 44
We our eyes shall never **steep**;.................377. N.128, 18

Steeps With Yvorie wrists, his Laureat head, and **steeps**
206. H.575, 41

Steer **Steere** Thee to me; and thinke (me gone)..174. H.465, 9
And, as thou look'st, the wanton **Steere**,........230. H.662, 37
Lay to thy stake a lustie **Steere**,...............243. H.716, 14
I have lost my lovely **steere**,..................305. H.984, 15

Steerling To get thy **Steerling**, once again,......244. H.716, 37

Stem That, which may the honour'd **Stem**......57. H.149, 129
Despite of all concussions left the **Stem**........170. H.451, 3
By those ignoble Births, which shame the **stem**..251. H.745, 7
Thou didst deriue from that old **stem**............407. A.2, 21

Stench To **stench** the blood the while...........272. H.828, 12

Step No one **step** from this Sepulcher...........402. N.269, 19

Sterility Untoucht by cold **sterility**;...............291. H.919, 18

Sterner The **sterner** Fates, to cross his purposes; 266. H.800, 4

Sterve See **Starve**
To **sterve** thy sin,............................391. N.228, 22

Sterved See **Starved**
We must not thinke his eare was **sterv'd**:......119. H.293, 14

Stewed But Beards of Mice, a Newt's **stew'd** thigh,
119. H.293, 37

Stick When thou hast said so, **stick** it there.......354. N.59, 5
His spunge, and **stick**, do ask why Thou dost stay?
398. N.263, 11
But brings his **stick** of Cynamon,................413. A.4, 26

Sticks See **Poking-sticks**
Some brittle **sticks** of Thorne or Briar...........350. N.47, 23

Stiff-blue-pig's-feet Two **stiffe-blew-Pigs-feet**, and a sow's cleft eare...................................89. H.221, 4

Stiles Remove the barrs, or lift me o're the **stiles**:..352. N.51, 6
Stiles, and stops, and stayes, that come..........355. N.64, 3

Stiletto Where the **Steletto** pierc'd the skin:.......18. H.46, 8

Still See **Stone-still**
And may prevent it, sitting **still**..................6. H.2, 26
And **still** do'st this, and that verse, reprehend:......7. H.6, 4
Still in the coole, and silent shades of sleep........9. H.14, 18

Stole A **stole** of white, (and Canonized here)....199. H.545, 6
In her white **Stole**; now Victory do's rest......271. H.823, 3
The candid **Stole** thrown ore the Pious Priest;..286. H.898, 6
My sackcloth here; but there my **Stole** of white...343. N.25, 8
In long white **stole**,..........................369. N.106, 8
— — — — — — — — — — —, ...437. var. H.336, 104
Stolen So meet **stolne** kisses, when the Moonie nights
77. H.197, 5
The tempting Mole, **stoln** from the neck........166. H.443, 63
(Hatch't o're with Moone-shine, from their **stolen** delight)
410. A.3, 2
Stomach Keeping the barking **stomach** wisely quiet,
35. H.106, 29
His **Stomach** to a second Meale. No, no,........147. H.377, 33
Which gave his Elveships **stomacke** ease....435. ins. H.293, x
Stomacher Enthralls the Crimson **Stomacher**:......28. H.83, 6
Upon his Bibb, or **Stomacher**:..................354. N.59, 6
Stomachs For want of warmth, and **Stomachs** keepe
179. H.476, 32
Stone **See Cherry-stone, Tombstone**
I got the Pit, and she the **Stone**.................10. H.49, 4
A funerall **stone**,...................................30. H.89, 1
Will last to be a precious **Stone**,................61. H.160, 9
Tomb'd in a Christal **stone**,.....................75. H.193, 5
Behold this living **stone**,......................85. H.211, 17
Without or Lime, or Wood, or **Stone**:..........90. H.223a, 4
Nor made of glasse, or wood, or **stone**,..........91. H.223, 56
As a fir'd Altar, is each **stone**,.................113. H.283, 23
Who formes a Godhead out of Gold or **Stone**,....117. H.288, 1
Congeal'd to Pearle and **stone**;................131. H.330, 11
Day with the white and Luckie **stone**...........133. H.336, 40
Remainder left of Brasse or **stone**,..............146. H.376, 8
Of others; since no Stud, no **Stone**, no Piece,..149. H.377, 117
Then publick praise do's runne upon the **Stone**,..172. H.459, 9
Come thou Brave man! And bring with Thee a **Stone**
185. H.496, 5
Brave Kinsman, markt out with the whiter **stone**:.199. H.545, 8
Write but this upon my **Stone**;................199. H.546, 2
The Dew of griefe upon this **stone**..............203. H.564, 5
Your Grave her Bosome is, the Lawne the **Stone**.
249. H.734, 4
Strikes me dead as any **stone**?.................254. H.757, 6
The Marble speaks it Mary **Stone**:............257. H.764, 4
This **Stone**, for names sake, melts to teares.....257. H.764, 6
For a **Stone**, ha's Heaven his Tombe,............270. H.821, 8
Aske his Story, not this **Stone**..................289. H.910, 4
Here now I rest under this Marble **stone**:........298. H.954, 2
Under which signe we may the former **stone**....300. H.961, 11
Stood as he had been turn'd from flesh to **stone**:..301. H.962, 4
This **Stone** can tell the storie of my life,........304. H.978, 1
(The Altar of our love) thy **Stone**...............359. N.83, 12
Thus, thus I come to kisse Thy **Stone**..........402. N.269, 10
Hence they have born my Lord: Behold! the **Stone**
403. N.271, 1
But deepe mistery, not the **stone**..................417. A.9, 5
Turnes the beholders into **stone**..................418. A.9, 58
— — — — — — — — — —, ...450. var. A.9, 24
Stones **See Tombstones**
More then the **stones** i'th' street by farre:........32. H.98, 4
Draw I co'd once (although not stocks or **stones**,.84. H.210, 5
Lesse in these Marble **stones**, then in thy story...89. H.219, 22
Grudgings turnes bread to **stones**, when to the Poore
220. H.632, 1
As **stones** and salt gloves use to give, even so....248. H.731, 3
Stones, or turfes to cover me....................270. H.821, 4
Instead of Bread, Grubs gives them **stones** to eat.
325. H.1077, 4
His Arrowes flie; and all his **stones** are hurl'd....357. N.74, 3
Stone-still Part of the way be met; or sit **stone-still**.
113. H.283, 58
Stood **See Withstood**
That Timber tall, which three-score lusters **stood**..23. H.69, 3
The Drooping West, which hitherto has **stood**......25. H.77, 3
And as she **stood**, the wanton Aire............51. H.142, 11
When Julia chid, I **stood** as mute the while,......58. H.150, 1
Then if they naked **stood**,........................75. H.193, 29
Can shew where you or grew, or **stood**...........88. H.216, 9
Stood in the Holy-Forum Candidate:...........106. H.261, 2
Together with the Stages glory **stood**............150. H.382, 3
About the Bed, there sighing **stood**..............237. H.686, 3
Who for a long sad time has weeping **stood**,......251. H.745, 3
Leaving no shew, where **stood** the Capitoll......252. H.745, 16
And in a burnisht Flagonet **stood** by...........262. H.783, 15
Stood as he had been turn'd from flesh to stone:..301. H.962, 4
This I am sure; I Ravisht **stood**, as one......326. H.1080, 9
The Virgin-Mother **stood** at distance (there).....384. N.180, 1
Because our flesh **stood** most in need of Him......390. N.222, 4
Stool-ball At **Stool-ball**, Lucia, let us play,........238. H.690, 1
Stools **See Close-stools**
Stoop **Stoop**, mount, passe by to take her eye, then glare
87. H.215, 5
Three Zodiaks fill'd more I shall **stoope**;........303. H.973, 2
The Tulips, Lillies, Daffadills do **stoop**;........320. H.1054, 4
Nor **stoope** to'th Center, but suruiue as Longe....411. A.3, 45
Stop **See Full-stop**
But if you can **stop** the Sive,..................117. H.285, 9
To drye the Widowes teares; and **stop** her Swoones,
201. H.557, 17
The Ev'nings come; here now Ile **stop**,.........212. H.602, 3
And make no one **stop**, till my race be done.....358. N.77, 15
Or had I not, I'de **stopp** the spreading itch........411. A.3, 55
And Hymen call'd to bless the Rites. Cha. **Stop** there.
416. A.8, 20
Stopped At which I **stopt**; Said Love, these be..107. H.263, 17
And Mans Pulse **stopt**, All Passions sleep in Peace.
202. H.558, 4
And so soone **stopt** my longer living here;......278. H.860, 2
The Barber **stopt** his Nose, and ranne away.....323. H.1066, 4
Stoppest Thou **stop'st** S. Peter in the midst of sin;
349. N.43, 3
Stops Stiles, and **stops**, and stayes, that come......355. N.64, 3
Stop'st **See Stoppest**
Stopt **See Stopped**
Storax As Benjamin, and **Storax**, when they meet.
131. H.331, 10
This Camphire, **Storax**, Spiknard, Galbanum:....157. H.414, 2
The **Storax**, Spiknard, Myrrhe, and Ladanum....181. H.485, 4
More sweet, then **Storax** from the hallowed fire:..205. H.575, 8
Our sighs for **Storax**, teares for Wine;..........360. N.83, 33
The **Storax** fries; and ye may see,..............365. N.97, 8
The **Storax** and the Cynamon,.................375. N.123, 56
Store Jem to enrich her **store**;...................43. H.123, 14
From Countries far, with **Store** of Spices, (sweet).86. H.213, 31
Where he of God-heads has such **store**,..........90. H.223, 7
Gladding his pallat with some **store**............119. H.293, 35
Store of courage to me grant,..................151. H.386, 1
To others **store** of helpfull spectacles............154. H.401, 2
But crown'd he is with **store**,..................160. H.422, 15
Please your Grace, from out your **Store**,........223. H.638, 1
Store of diseases, where Physitians flow.........244. H.718, 4
What **store** of Corn has carefull Nodes, thinke you,
270. H.822, 3
That precious stock; the **store**.................289. H.911, 19
Of full provision; such a **store**,...............291. H.919, 3
With **store** of ale too;.......................317. H.1035, 22
But, for our glut, and for our **store**,............356. N.66, 7
And powring still, Thy wealthy **store**,............357. N.75, 3
Or overwhelm'd with **store**.....................368. N.104, 9
I have been gratefull for my **store**:..............376. N.124, 5
The sup'rabundance of my **store**,................376. N.127, 1
Stories With Upper **Stories**, Mutton, Veale......101. H.250, 30
Where Poets sing the **stories** of our love.......206. H.575, 24
What dismall **Stories** will be told..............272. H.828, 15
Storm Your **storme** is over; Lady, now appeare...105. H.259, 7
Will **Storme**, or starving take here..............213. H.609, 6
And look how when a frantick **Storme** doth tear.225. H.642, 13
The **storme** will arise,.........................225. H.643, 19
A mighty **storm** last night.....................373. N.122, 5
Storms And like a surly Oke with **storms** perplext;
37. H.106, 99
Thou that tam'st Tygers, and fierce **storms** (that rise)
103. H.254, 3
Some **storms** w'ave past;......................211. H.596, 13
Of **storms** orebear............................335. H.1129, 8
No boysterous winds, or **stormes**, come hither,..361. N.83, 69
Story Lesse in these Marble stones, then in thy **story**.
89. H.219, 22
To live remembred in your **story**..............170. H.449, 29
My **Story** tells, by Love they were............180. H.478, 3
That's the **Story** of my life....................199. H.546, 4
Cob clouts his shooes, and as the **story** tells,....226. H.648, 1
Aske his **Story**, not this Stone.................289. H.910, 4
This Stone can tell the **storie** of my life,........304. H.978, 1
This known, the rest of thy sad **story** tell,........417. A.8, 35
Stout **Stout** sons I had, and those twice three;....41. H.116, 3
That Earth-quake shook the house, and gave the **stout**
52. H.146, 15
There's that, which drowns all care, **stout** Beere;.101. H.250, 37
But to the **stout**; and those that skilfull are.......290. H.916, 2
Death for **stout** Cato; and besides all these,......370. N.108, 7
Stoutest Of Patience wants. Grief breaks the **stoutest** Heart
169. H.447, 2
Stoutly When we 'gainst Satan **stoutly** fight, the more
372. N.116, 1
Stove Or Roses smother'd in the **stove**:..........145. H.375, 4
Straight Make me the **straight**, and oblique lines;..47. H.133, 3
Or be so **strait** to choak.......................65. H.172, 18
So you be straight, where Virgins **straight** sho'd be.
99. H.242, 2
Or every **straight**, and smooth-skin tree;........193. H.521, 41
One of the five **straight** branches of my hand....203. H.565, 1
Made of a clean **strait** oaten reed,...............354. N.59, 9
And I will **strait**..............................370. N.111, 7
— — — — — — — — — — —, ...439. var. H.443, 38
— — — — — — — — — — —, ...443. var. H.580, 5
Straighter Give unto Love the **straiter** way.....167. H.443, 111
Strain That done, sink down into a silv'rie **straine**;
67. H.176, 5
Strik'st now a Courtly **strain**..................183. H.492, 12
I'le play thee such another **strain**;.............244. H.716, 38
Can'st write the Comick, Tragick **straine**, and fall
298. H.955, 5
Bettering them both, but by a double **straine**,....343. N.24, 3

Strained — — — — — — — —, ...434. var. H.293, 49
Strains With thy soft straines;..................95. H.227, 28
Nor do's it mind the Rustick straines..........184. H.492, 23
While juice she straines, and pith.............258. H.767, 13
Strait See Straight
Straiter See Straighter
Strand No more shall I reiterate thy Strand,.....315. H.1028, 3
Strange Me thought 'twas strange, that thou so hard sho'dst prove,.....................................42. H.122, 7
'Tis strange, ye will not flie....................54. H.149, 33
Who think it strange to see,..................104. H.257, 12
'Tis strange, his Father long time has been ill,..125. H.315, 3
Or tell what strange Tricks Love can do,........215. H.616, 9
And in good faith I'd thought it strange........290. H.915, 3
The fire of Hell this strange condition hath,......387. N.202, 1
Strangely 'Twill strangely make a one of too.....325. H.1075, 4
Stranger See Lank-stranger
To shield the Stranger, and the Poore from wrong: 201. H.557, 12
Thy cradle, Kingly Stranger,..................345. N.33, 13
Strangers Salute we must, nor Strangers, Kin, or Friends. 378. N.137, 8
Straw Not a straw co'd him escape;.............306. H.984, 28
Strawberries Shew'd like to Creame, enspir'd with Strawberries: 81. H.202, 2
I'th'bed of strawburies........................156. H.412, 16
To your Cream, her's Strawberries.............183. H.491, 4
guilty of somewhat, ripe the strawberries...430. ins. H.283, 20b
Strawberry Without a Strawberrie:.............75. H.193, 11
And Straw-berry do stir.......................75. H.193, 34
A Strawberry shewes halfe drown'd in Creame?..164. H.440, 6
Straws See Wheat-straws
Stray Stray, to become lesse circular,............134. H.336, 68
O then, how restlesse do's she stray!..........393. N.233, 2
Streaks Husbands and Wives by streakes to chuse: 127. H.319, 22
— — — — — — — — — — —,............440. ins. H.443, 45t
Stream Like to a solemne sober Stream..........179. H.476, 13
And a sweet concurring stream.................220. H.633, 3
Time steals away like to a stream,..............233. H.670, 22
You see this gentle streame, that glides,..........244. H.720, 1
Trie if this sober streame you can..............244. H.720, 3
Streame to the Spring from whence it came.....245. H.720, 10
A little streame best fits a little Boat;..........249. H.733, 13
Of sin, we must strive 'gainst the streame of it:...356. N.67, 2
Through mid'st thereof a christall stream there flowes 406. A.1, 75
Cha. Those souls which ne'er were drencht in pleasures stream, 417. A.8, 27
Streamer There waves the Streamer of her blood..107. H.263, 12
Streamers — — — — — — — —, ...429. var. H.263, 12
Streaming As Sun-beames pierce the glasse, and streaming in, 385. N.184, 1
Streams That chiding streams betray small depth below. 15. H.38, 10
Like Streams, you are divorc'd; but 't will come, when 26. H.79, 5
Thy rockie bottome, that doth teare thy streams....29. H.86, 3
Were thy streames silver, or thy rocks all gold.....29. H.86, 6
Or Moone-light tinselling the streames:..........34. H.105, 4
The Damaskt medowes, and the peebly streames..35. H.106, 43
Glide, gentle streams, and beare..................43. H.123, 1
You see how Amber through the streams........75. H.193, 17
So soft streams meet, so springs with gladder smiles 77. H.197, 1
Daunc't by the Streames.......................181. H.484, 8
By which the silver-shedding streames...........192. H.521, 7
Into thy streames my self I threw,..............294. H.939, 7
With Swan-like-state, flote up & down thy streams: 316. H.1028, 18
Keep up your state ye streams; and as ye spring, 316. H.1028, 23
Which though it sends forth thousand streams, 'tis ne're 341. N.15, 3
While we sit by sorrowes streames,.............376. N.128, 2
May see it sprout forth streames of muscadine.....405. A.1, 50
— — — — — — — — — —, ...429. var. H.263, 12
like streames which flow.................431. ins. H.283, 50e
— — — — — — — — — —, ...449. var. A.8, 27
Street Or glided through the street).............9. H.15, 10
More then the stones i'th' street by farre:........32. H.98, 4
How each field turns a street! each street a Parke 68. H.178, 30
Can such delights be in the street,..............68. H.178, 37
See where she comes; and smell how all the street 113. H.283, 21
And think (as thou do'st walke the street)....174. H.465, 15
Nor did the street..........................375. N.123, 68
Streets Letcher was Carted first about the streets, 195. H.532, 1
Ev'n so, those streets and houses do but show..244. H.718, 3
Strength Now strength, and newer Purple get,........7. H.9, 3
Who would faine his strength renew,............10. H.19, 13
Her inadult'rate strength: what's done by me...46. H.128, 53
What others can't with all their strength put to...245. H.722, 2
The strength of Baptisme, that's within;........396. H.253, 1
Strengthening Fulfill the Larders, and with strengthning bread 245. H.723, 5
Thy Genius with two strength'ning Buttresses,..252. H.745, 18
Stretch Might stretch the cords of civill comelinesse: 311. H.1006, 2
Stretching — — — — — — — —, ...423. var. H.128, 27
Strew Maids, and here strew Violets...............44. H.125, 6
Feare not; the leaves will strew................68. H.178, 19
Which, by the peepe of day, doe strew..........95. H.227, 25
Witnesse their Homage, when they come and strew 107. H.265, 7
Strew his hopes, and Him with flowers:..........108. H.266, 6
Shall come to strew thy earth with flowers.......145. H.376, 6
Then I'le your Altars strew....................228. H.657, 10
Then maids shall strew Thee, and thy Curles from them 254. H.756, 17
And praying, strew some Roses on her,........257. H.764, 9
With maunds of roses for to strew the way:......261. H.781, 8
Earth afford ye flowers to strew...............306. H.984, 43
Come forth, to strew thy Tombe with flow'rs:..361. N.83, 74
Strewed Rifle the Flowers which the Virgins strew'd: 49. H.138, 6
Strewing And Graces strewing flowers...........54. H.149, 46
Strewings See Strowings, Weekly-strewings
Give her strewings; but not stir................123. H.310, 5
Strewings need none, every flower..............199. H.546, 5
Since we fresh strewings will bring hither,......289. H.912, 7
And bring fresh strewings to thy Tombe..........359. N.83, 6
Strict Or that this Yonker keeps so strict a Lent,..122. H.305, 3
This short but strict condition:.................265. H.798, 4
I turne Apostate to the strict Comande....424. ins. H.128, 46c
Stricter Nor is it, that thou keep'st this stricter size 37. H.106, 117
Some strickter M^rs. or suspitious other............410. A.3, 8
Strictly Close, but not too strictly lac't:..........282. H.878, 4
Stride For men did strut, and stride, and stare, not act. 150. H.382, 6
Strife Woe, woe to them, who (by a ball of strife)..26. H.79, 1
And let it be thy Pensils strife,.................38. H.108, 3
Suspicion, Discontent, and Strife,...............49. H.137, 1
Sometimes peace, and sometimes strife:...........96. H.232, 4
Of her green hopes, we charge ye, that no strife, 114. H.283, 82
A mighty strife 'twixt Forme and Chastitie.......189. H.511, 6
Peacefull by night; my day devoid of strife:.....294. H.938, 2
After true sorrow for our sinnes, our strife........362. N.91, 1
It is to fast from strife,......................391. N.228, 17
Strike To strike him dead, that but usurps a Throne. 32. H.97, 6
May blow my ashes up, and strike thee blind.....49. H.138, 8
Telling the Clock strike Ten, Eleven, Twelve, One. 114. H.283, 76
Let but few smart, but strike a feare through all: 132. H.335, 3
I'le strike thee such a nimble Ayre,............243. H.716, 32
To strike me I will tempt thee:.................296. H.946, 21
In a while it will strike one;...................307. H.991, 3
Ans. Stroake ye to strike ye...................309. H.1001, 4
Thou kil'st with heate, and I strike dead with cold. 333. H.1120, 2
Extreames are fatall, where they once doe strike,.333. H.1120, 5
Then let the Harps inchantments strike mine eare; 343. N.25, 4
And strike it through..........................349. N.46, 9
Or strike so as to ease me......................353. N.56, 24
I stricke thy loues, and greedyly persue.........411. A.3, 69
to stroake not strike: feare you..........431. ins. H.283, 60q
Strikes Love strikes, but 'tis with gentle crueltie.....16. H.40, 4
For thou no Porter keep'st who strikes.........146. H.377, 18
Strikes me dead as any stone?..................254. H.757, 6
Ile kiss the hand that strikes me................296. H.946, 6
Sometimes He strikes us more then flesh can beare; 341. N.10, 3
Men to repent, but when He strikes withall.......342. N.19, 2
God strikes His Church, but 'tis to this intent,....344. N.31, 1
But when He strikes, He quarter-acts His part...394. N.242, 2
Strikest That strik'st a stilnesse into hell:........103. H.254, 2
Strik'st now a Courtly strain..................183. H.492, 12
Striking My sinnes, by gently striking;...........363. N.92, 9
— — — — — — — — —, ...423. var. H.128, 27
String See Purse-string, Shoe-string
And string if they be harm'd,..................27. H.81, 27
And wedded string and arrow,..................27. H.81, 30
Let but thy voice engender with the string,......102. H.252, 1
To the tension of the string,....................131. H.332, 2
Whether it be the voice or string,...............142. H.362, 2
Unto the Lyrick string..........................261. H.778, 8
Then if thy voice commingle with the String....276. H.851, 3
Awake the Voice! Awake the String!............364. N.96, 4
Stringless No Arrow nockt, onely a stringlesse Bow: 357. N.74, 2
Strings See Lyric-strings
And strings my tears as Pearle.................43. H.123, 6
Gloves, Garters, Stockings, Shoes, and Strings..193. H.521, 52
First, crack the strings, and after that,........240. H.705, 11
From the which hung down by strings,........306. H.984, 24

SUCH

Then holding up (there) such religious Things,....11. H.22, 5
My Jet t'enthrall such Ivorie....................14. H.34, 6
Now since my love is tongues-lesse, know me such, 15. H.38, 13
Such fleeting pleasures there I took,.............17. H.41, 20
Such precious thraldome ne'r shall fetter me.......17. H.42, 4
I ne'r invented such.............................19. H.51, 6
Love give me more such nights as these.........20. H.56, 10
To drink in Notes, and Numbers; such...........22. H.68, 3
But, yet though Love likes well such Scenes as these, 24. H.74, 9
True, I confesse; such Whites as these..........34. H.105, 7
With thousand such enchanting dreams, that meet.36. H.106, 53
And beleeve there be such things:..............36. H.106, 86
Till when, in such assurance live, ye may......38. H.106, 145
Such destructive Ysicles;.......................40. H.115, 14
Uncapable of such a Soveraigne,................46. H.128, 44
All such as are not soft like them..............47. H.132, 14
Such a pernicious torment is:..................50. H.139, 13
Her legs were such Diana shows,................51. H.142, 13
And such spirits raise, 'twill then..............52. H.145, 5
Such bashfulnesse at last.......................54 H.149, 28
Praise me, for having such a fruitfull wombe;....58. H.151, 3
Adored Cesar! and my Faith is such,..........62. H.161, 13
Such an one, as will repeat.....................62. H.162, 13
Such frost and snow upon your haire:...........63. H.164, 5
Where such a rare Carnation grew..............63. H.164, 11
Such Freedome in Captivity;....................64. H.169, 10
And be, too, such a yoke,.......................65. H.172, 15
Our selves to such a height:....................66. H.172, 21
Can such delights be in the street,..............68. H.178, 37
All thoughts, but such as aime at getting Princes,.77. H.197, 8
A thought of such like possibilitie?.............78. H.197, 46
In Sack of such a kind,.........................80. H.201, 14
Ile send such Frost, such Haile, such Sleet, and Snow, 82. H.204, 10
Such Flesh-quakes, Palsies, and such fears as shall 82. H.204, 11
To accept such coynes as these;................88. H.218, 8
Where he of God-heads has such store,..........90. H.223, 7
And give me such reposes,......................95. H.227, 18
Not Virgil's Gnat had such a Tomb...........104. H.256, 21
Such pretty flowers, (like to Orphans young)..104. H.257, 13
To passe; but such.............................115. H.283, 135
And of such Torture as no one would grutch..115. H.283, 136
Springing from two such Fires,..............116. H.283, 159
Of these, and such like things, for shift,......127. H.319, 25
Account of such a flock of sheep;............133. H.336, 44
Iülus to sing such a song......................135. H.336, 94
And of her blush at such a feast..............135. H.336, 96
Such as co'd well...............................136. H.336, 133
Henceforth at such a rate,....................137. H.340, 11
Full mirth wait on you; and such mirth as shall 140. H.354, 11
No such crab'd vizard: Thou hast learnt thy Train. 147. H.377, 35
Such is thy house, whose firme foundations trust 148. H.377, 103
Such ignorance as theirs was, who once hist....150. H.382, 15
The passive Aire such odour then assum'd, ...157. H.414, 7
To give an end: Mir. To what? Scil. Such griefs as these. 159. H.421, 32
And multiply; Such is the light,..............167. H.443, 80
Or a sigh of such as bring.....................170. H.450, 5
Such Essences as those Three Brothers; known..170. H.451, 7
Such Three brave Brothers fell in Mars his Field. 170. H.451, 12
My Almnes is such:..............................171. H.455, 6
Triumph in such a Martirdome..............175. H.465, 66
Of such rare Saint-ships, who did here consume..185. H.496, 3
How wo'd he eate, were not his hindrance such? 191. H.518, 6
Such a fire I espie..............................204. H.566, 3
Of Pushes Spalt has such a knottie race,.........211. H.594, 1
With such an arm'd, but such an easie Foe,...216. H.618, 11
The Field is pitcht; but such must be your warres, 216. H.618, 13
Wantons we are; and though our words be such, 218. H.624, 1
To such a height; but never surfeited...........220. H.633, 21
For an Almes; then give me such................223. H.638, 22
Sweet Country life, to such unknown,..........229. H.662, 1
And Younglings, with such sports as these.....231. H.662, 73
Be she such, as neither will....................232. H.665, 17
Where, if such glory flashes from His Name,....237. H.685, 7
Princes, and such like Publike Lights as these,..237. H.685, 9
Adversity hurts none, but onely such..........239. H.697, 1
I'le strike thee such a nimble Ayre,............243. H.716, 32
I'le play thee such another strain;.............244. H.716, 38
Such as the Prince is, will his People be.......255. H.759, 2
Tread ore his gleab, but with such care, that where 259. H.771, 7
Sho'd meet and tire, on such lautitious meat,....262. H.783, 3
No question then, but such a lick is sweet,......269. H.816, 3
When a warm tongue do's with such Ambers meet. 269. H.816, 4
For her beauty it was such....................274. H.838, 3
Less then Apollo, that ursurp'st such Three?..276. H.851, 6
A glorious end by such a Noose,.............279. H.863, 11
And let such curious Net-works be.............282. H.881, 9
But with such sweets commingled,............283. H.883, 4
But such the Drap'ry did betray.............288. H.908, 7
Where we such clusters had,..................289. H.911, 7
Of such a wit the world sho'd have no more.....289. H.911, 20
Of full provision; such a store,................291. H.919, 3
Who, kissing, kill such Saints as these?........294. H.937, 6
Such be our gifts, and such be our expence,..295. H.940, 3
And such as will in short time be,............297. H.948, 3
No man such rare parts hath, that he can swim,..298. H.953, 1
Toucht every where with such diffused grace,..307. H.992, 2
To such a height, as for to tell................369. N.107, 3
But, bastard-slips, and such as He dislikes,....370. N.108, 11
Pleasures, such as shall pursue...............377. N.128, 21
But earth: such vowes nere reach Gods eare.....381. N.158, 8
Of such a rev'rend reckoning,.................388. N.204, 2
Such let my life assure me, when my breath....392. N.230, 33
To such an height, to such a period rais'd,....399. N.263, 30
Loues Cherries from such fyers growe..........408. A.2, 50
That Lookes for such prepared grownd,........409. A.2, 104
Hee may ere longe haue such a wyfe..........409. A.2, 107
A kisse to such a Jewell of the heauen:..........410. A.3, 4
Euen such are wee; and in our parting, doe......410. A.3, 13
Whether the world such Sperritts had or noe,....411. A.3, 38
Such is my parting wth thee; and to proue......412. A.3, 79
With such white vowes as fate can nere dissever..414. A.6, 11
Such rich, such fresh, such sweet varietyes,......415. A.7, 16
But such as have been drown'd in this wilde sea, 417. A.8, 31
There ever lived such a one....................418. A.9, 30
— — — — — — — — — —,...............421. var. H.106, 19
— — — — — — — — — —,.................423. var. H.128, 9
And such a smiling Tulip too...............424. ins. H.164, 11a
For such neglect, have only myrtle rodds..431. ins. H.283. 60p
— — — — — — — — — —,...........437. var. H.336, 96

Suck Woo'd to come suck the milkie Teat:......36. H.106, 50
The Sonnes to suck the milke of Kine,.......310. H.1004, 5
Sucked But when he felt he suckt from thence...71. H.182, 7
Of flowers, ne'r suckt by th' theeving Bee:......86. H.213, 37
And I the Javelin suckt away,..................272. H.828, 3
Suckles See Honey-suckles
Sucks The flesh soone sucks in putrifaction.....332. H.1111, 2
Sudden By sudden death to give me ease:......34. H.103, 14
The sudden danger of a Rape...................37. H.106, 126
Run to a sudden Death, and Funerall...........79. H.197, 90
But on a sudden, all was chang'd and gone......81. H.202, 3
But on a sudden all were gone.................107. H.263, 16
T'ave found in me this sudden change;.........290. H.915, 4
And on a sudden both were drown'd...........294. H.937, 4
Behold a suddaine Metamorphosis.............325. H.1076, 2
Thus, on the sudden? 4. Come and see.........364. N.96, 17
Call'd on the suddayne by the Jealouse Mother,..410. A.3, 7
Suddenness The suddenness did me affright;......116. H.284, 5
Sudds Sudds Launders Bands in pisse; and starches them 98. H.237, 1
Suffer Untaught, to suffer Poverty..............36. H.106, 68
Nor suffer you the Poets to sit cold,..........141. H.359, 7
The wound I suffer, never find a cure.........159. H.421, 34
I cannot suffer; And in this, my part..........169. H.447, 1
Then, while Fates suffer, live thou free,.........233. H.670, 17
I am a free-born Roman; suffer then,.........242. H.713, 11
Lift up thy Sword; next, suffer it to fall,......310. H.1002, 3
To suffer in the Muses Martyrdome:..........335. H.1128, 4
But yet still lesse then Grace can suffer here.....341. N.10, 4
Suffer thy legs, but not thy tongue to walk:......341. N.12, 1
Suffer me to be so bold,........................347. N.40, 3
Or when, for sins, men suffer punishment.......388. N.210, 4
We merit all we suffer, and by far..............393, N.235, 1
Sufferance See All-sufferance
Suffered He, who has suffer'd Ship-wrack, feares to saile 212. H.601, 1
Who hath more suffer'd by us farre, then for us. 388. N.209, 2
Sufferer To the beholder, and the sufferer:........343. N.24, 2
More stripes, then God layes on the sufferer.....393. N.235, 2
Suffering Although our suffering meet with no reliefe, 333. H.1119, 1
Of suffring gives me patience...................354. N.57, 4
And God, as Thou art, comes to suffering.....399. N.263, 25
Sufferings With warbling Notes, her Tyrrean sufferings. 224. H.642, 8
The lesse our sorrowes here and suffrings cease, 372. N.119, 1
— — — — — — — — — —,...................447. var. H.1119, 1
Suffers The drooping Kingdome suffers all.......89. H.219, 8
Who for true glory suffers thus; we grant.....129. H.323, 15
God suffers not His Saints, and Servants deere, 394. N.236, 1
Who suffers not here for mine own,............400. N.266, 5
Suffice Of ashes, scarce suffice...................81. H.201, 43
And if that they will not suffice,...............89. H.219, 11
For punishment in warre, it will suffice,.......132. H.335, 1
Till I shall come again, let this suffice,.........146. H.377, 1
Whom one belov'd will not suffice,.............287. H.899, 9
Farc't with the food, that may themselves suffice. 310. H.1005, 4
Sufficient It is sufficient if we pray...............59. H.153, 1
Christ is the one sufficient Remedie..............390. N.221, 2
Sugar Adde sugar, nutmeg and ginger,.........317. H.1035, 21
Sugar-cakes For Sugar-cakes and Wine;.........238. H.690. 2
Sugared Of sugred Rush, and eates the sagge...119. H.293, 33
Chor. A suger'd note! and sound as sweet....243. H.716, 29

Suit But let that speak, the Client gets the **suit**...123. H.308, 2
Trigg having turn'd his **sute**, he struts in state, 240. H.703, 1
Lupes for the outside of his **suite** has paide;....302. H.969, 1
Bestirs his Hand, but starves in hand the **Suite**. 303. H.975, 8
Most like his **Suite**, and all commend the Trim; 330. H.1099, 3
Or sing of mercy, and I'le **suit**................393. N.232, 13
Suitors And salt, which frets thy **Suters**; fly....174. H.465, 25
Did to her **suitors**) this web done..............174. H.465, 31
Suits Here those long **suits** of Chancery lie....190. H.515, 25
Sullen Frown, and look **sullen** ev'ry where.........72. H.185, 4
How crosse, how **sullen**, and how soone........103. H.253, 13
A **sullen** day will cleere againe.................247. H.725, 8
And **sullen** clouds bound up his head...........393. N.232, 6
Sulphur Ile expiate with **Sulphur**, Haire, and Salt:
77. H.197, 30
Sum Ile cleare the **summe**,......................29. H.87, 10
Who first to the **Summe**........................99. H.243, 4
The order, but the **Sum** of things..............245. H.721, 2
As for the rest, being too great a **summe**......267. H.804, 13
Summer **Summer** and Winter shall at one time show
59. H.154, 5
Come Sons of **Summer**, by whose toile,.........101. H.250, 1
Where ever Nodes do's in the **Summer** come,....270. H.822, 1
And feares in **summer** to weare out the lether:..332. H.1116, 2
Summer and Winter still to save his shooes.....332. H.1116, 4
Of Corn, when **Summer** shakes his eares;........340. N.3, 12
— — — — — — — — —,.....................423. var. H.128, 13
Summer-birds These **Summer-Birds** did with thy Master stay
151. H.387, 1
Summer's More radiant then the **Summers** Sun-beams shows;
45. H.128, 13
As the **Summers** Corne has eares:.............102. H.253, 4
Like to the **Summers** raine;..................125. H.316, 18
As well the Winters, as the **Summers** Tide:....151. H.387, 6
Nor in the **summers** sweeter evenings go,......315. H.1028, 5
Sumpter And thus they praise the **Sumpter**; but not him:
330. H.1099, 4
Sun See **Morning-sunshine**
Light from the **Sun**, that inexhausted Fire:....3. Ded. H., 6
Newly refresh't, both by the **Sun**, and showers..25. H.77, 6
Make me a Chariot, and a Sun;.................47. H.133, 5
But we as fearlesse of the **Sunne**,..............48. H.136, 10
As fast away as do's the **Sunne**:...............69. H.178, 62
Sunk is my sight; set is my **Sun**;...............72. H.185, 10
The glorious Lamp of Heaven, the **Sun**,........84. H.208, 5
Nature begets by th' **Sun** and showers,.........103. H.256, 5
Blest is the Bride, on whom the **Sun** doth shine; 113. H.283, 48
(Just at the setting of the **Sun**)..............123. H.306, 6
As yet the early-rising **Sun**....................125. H.316, 3
To **Sun** his thin-clad members, if he likes,......146. H.377, 17
Mont. Set with the **Sunne**, thy woes: Scil. The day grows old:
160. H.421, 41
Or to seale up the **Sun**.........................164. H.441, 4
(Nature begets by th' **Sun**, and showers,).......166. H.443, 34
Give way, and be ye ravisht by the **Sun**,......196. H.537, 1
Water in, ere **Sun** be set.......................201. H.556, 4
(The **Sun** once set) **all of one colour are........207. H.576, 4**
The Morn's farre spent; and the immortall **Sunne**
216. H.618, 3
With the **Sun** rising he must walk his grounds; 259. H.771, 3
So look the mornings when the **Sun**...........268. H.811, 1
(By his word) the **Sun** to stand:..............276. H.850, 10
Made at the **Sun**,.............................289. H.911, 5
In teeming years, how soon my **Sun** was set,....304. H.978, 3
Or e're dark Clouds do dull, or dead the Mid-dayes **Sun**.
401. N.268, 9
Beames of the **sunn**, the peacefull sea............408. A.2, 58
That sees noe setting **Sunn**......................413. A.4, 15
Doe it like the **Sun** to write......................413. A.4, 18
the creditt from the table of the **Sunne**....432. ins. H.283, 70b
Sunbeam — — — — — — — — —, ...423. var. H.128, 13
Sunbeams More radiant then the Summers **Sun-beams** shows;
45. H.128, 13
And ride the **Sun-beams**. Can there be a thing..78. H.197, 53
Are, by the **Sun-beams**, tickel'd by degrees.....100. H.247, 4
Enspir'd by th' **Sun-beams** after dews & showers.
326. H.1080, 14
As **Sun-beames** pierce the glasse, and streaming in,
385. N.184, 1
Sundays Those **Sundayes** onely, when as Briefs are read.
39. H.109, 2
Sunder — — — — — — — — —, ...427. var. H.197, 71
Sundered We both were lost, if both of us not **sunderd**;
414. A.6, 6
Sundry Crab faces gownes with **sundry** Furres; 'tis known,
232. H.669, 1
With **sundry** precious Jewells,...................345. N.33, 18
Sung Let my Enchantments then be **sung**, or read...7. H.8, 4
And **sung** their thankfull Hymnes: 'tis sin,......68. H.178, 11
Sung out his Birth with Heav'nly Minstralsie...86. H.213, 24
Upon your Boughs, and Requiems **sung**.........169. H.449, 16
Which **sung**, or seyd,.........................198. H.544, 14
One Holy Collect, said or **sung** for Thee......209. H.584, 4
A Tentrall **sung** by Virgins o're thy Grave:....209. H.584, 6
Who by the Shepheards, **sung** (long since)......214. H.611, 5
Sung asleep with Lullabies:..................224. H.640, 2
The sacred Dirge and Trentall **sung**............237. H.686, 10
Sung in the high Doxologie of Thee............254. H.756, 16
Sunk **Sunk** from the tip of your soft eare,........61. H.160, 8
Sunk is my sight; set is my Sun;..............72. H.185, 10
So neatly **sunck**, as that no proof...........167. H.443, 103
Suns Not all thy flushing **Sunnes** are set,........72. H.185, 1
Daies may conclude in nights; and **Suns** may rest, 72. H.185, 5
Since Clouds disperst, **Suns** guild the Aire again. 105. H.259, 2
Sunset Make me a **Sun-set**; and a Night:.........47. H.133, 9
Till **Sunne-set**, let it burne;..................285. H.893, 2
But here's the **Sun-set** of a Tedious day:........419. A.10, 6
Sunshine See **Morning-sunshine**
Who, with His **Sun-shine**, and His showers,....364. N.96, 23
Sunshines Showrs or **Sun-shines** co'd beget.....108. H.266, 4
Sup I did not **sup**, because no friends were there. 197. H.541, 2
Or **Sup**, there wants the Incense and the Wine. 197. H.541, 4
To **sup** with thee thou didst me home invite;....262. H.783, 1
Well I **sup**, and well I dine,..................309. H.996, 7
Superabundance The **sup'rabundance** of my store, 376. N.127, 1
Superabundant So **sup'rabundant** joy shall be....34. H.103, 17
With **sup'rabundant** scorn here:.................345. N.33, 4
But likewise **sup'rabundant** seed;...............356. N.66, 2
Superabundantly There weeping **sup'rabundantly**. 42. H.119, 4
Supercilious Ne'r please the **supercillious** man...279. H.868, 4
Superfine The Romane Language full, and **superfine**,
301. H.966, 13
Superfluous Belongs all gold **superfluous**........394. N.239, 4
Superlast Shall live, and thou not **superlast** all times?
155. H.405, 14
Superstition With **superstition**, (as the Cream of meates.)
204. H.568, 4
Superstitious Let the **superstitious** wife..........284. H.889, 1
That so the **superstitious** find..................304. H.980, 5
Supper Invites to **supper** him who dines,.........146. H.377, 8
At night they draw to **Supper**; then well fed,....260. H.773, 3
Supple Nothing but love can **supple** me;...........8. H.13, 6
Supples When as His grace not **supples** men....396. N.250, 2
Suppliant Denie Thy **suppliant**..................369. N.104, 18
Supplied **Supply'd** the Epithalamie...............109. H.271, 8
Suppling Best and more **suppling** piece he cuts, and by
147. H.377, 51
Suppling and successefull too:................204. H.569, 8
Suppling-healing Of all those **suppling-healing** herbs and flowers.
62. H.161, 8
Supply For sho'd I not **supply**....................32. H.96, 3
Nor will I seek **supply**........................43. H.123, 19
Colours, let Art **supply**........................224. H.641, 2
Now for some Jewells to **supplye**...............409. A.2, 89
Support What Genii **support** thy roofe,..........148, H.377, 98
Suppose To Ovid; and **suppose**,.................80. H.201, 22
Why weres he none? Because we may **suppose**, 154. H. 401, 3
Lulls swears he is all heart; but you'l **suppose** 284. H.886, 1
Parting the paire, as wee may well **suppose**......404 A.1, 13
Supraentity An Ens, but **Supraentitie**..............340. N.5, 2
Supremest That I must give thee the **supremest** kisse;
9. H.14, 6
Give thou my lips but their **supreamest** kiss:....129. H.327, 2
Her **supreamest** Requiem sing;.................274. H.838, 6
I send, I send here my **supremest** kiss..........315. H.1028, 1
Sups Out of the which he sometimes **sups**..439. ins. H.443, 45k
Surcharged Sick and **surcharg'd** with this sacietie:
297. H.949, 2
Sure Who swims with Vertue, he shall still be **sure** 23. H.71, 4
And **sure** his tongue had more exprest,..........42. H.119, 11
I'm **sure** she'll ask no more...................43. H.123, 36
Then **sure** thou't like, or thou wilt envie me......66. H.174, 4
I'm **sure** they'l fashion Roses...................74. H.192, 8
I'm **sure** to find ye there........................83. H.207, 8
As **sure** a Mattins do's to him belong,..........128. H.321, 5
So **sure** he layes claime to the Evensong.......128. H.321, 6
Do not you fall through frailty; Ile be **sure**....136. H.338, 3
As they of freedome may be **sure**:...............153. H.395, 3
Be She too wealthy, or too poore; be **sure**,......185. H.494, 3
(This I am **sure**)...............................211. H.596, 10
The **sure** sweet-Sement, Glue, and Lime of Love.218. H.622, 2
For all our workes, a recompence is **sure**:......276. H.849, 1
And though I saw no Bow, I'm **sure**,..........295. H.942, 15
I have none; but must be **sure**................302. H.968, 5
Next, I'm **sure**, the Nuns will have.............304. H.976, 5
Cold comfort still I'm **sure** lives there........312. H.1014, 10
What's got by Justice is establisht **sure**;........314. H.1023, 1
Die ere long I'm **sure**, I shall;................321. H.1058, 1
Next be **sure** ye have a care,..................322. H.1064, 3
This I am **sure**; I Ravisht stood, as one.......326. H.1080, 9
So where He gives the bitter Pills, be **sure**,......344. N.31, 3
Long, long, I'm **sure**,..........................353. N.56, 19
For, this is **sure**, the Debt is dead..............370. N.107, 14
Bee **sure** thou bringe A Mayden head,............409. A.2, 84
Surer That Princes may possesse a **surer** seat,....163. H.438, 1
The old Hag in. No **surer** thing...............284. H.890, 6
Surfeit That **surfeit** tooke by bread, the worst of all.
286. H.895, 2
to **surfeit** and to hunger.................430. ins. H.283, 20g
Surfeited To such a height; but never **surfeited**...220. H.633, 21
Surfeiting Never make sick your Banks by **surfeiting**.
316. H.1028, 24
Surfeits Bad are all **surfeits**: but Physitians call 286. H.895, 1
Surly And like a **surly** Oke with storms perplext; 37. H.106, 99

Surplices Their curious Copes and **Surplices**.....92. H.223, 98
Put we on pure **Surplices**;....................280. H.870, 14
Surprise I with my Tendrils did **surprize**;..........16. H.41, 6
And all terrors me **surprize**;..................348. N.41, 43
Shooting his Eye-darts 'gainst it, to **surprise**....412. A.3, 77
shootes forth his jealous soule, for to **surprize** 430. ins. H.283, 40b
Surprised And thus **surpriz'd** (as Filchers use)..71. H.182. 11
Surrender Me to **surrender** them;.............43. H.123, 26
Grown old, **surrender** must his place,...........285. H.892, 11
you, stand for to **surrender** up the keyes..431. ins. H.283, 60h
Survey And viewing them with a more safe **survey**, 36. H.106, 73
Survey this Chappell, built, alone,.............90. H.223a, 3
Now loue invites me to **survey** her thighes......406. A.1, 77
Throwing his eye balls backward, to **suruaye**.....411. A.3, 73
And the while yow doe **surveye**..................417. A.9, 15
Survive Nor stoope to'th Center, but **suruiue** as Longe 411. A.3, 45
Susanna Rare are thy cheeks **Susanna**, which do show 193. H.523, 1
Suspect He that doth **suspect**, do's haste........175. H.465, 45
Must shun the bad, I, and **suspect** the best.....305. H.981, 2
Suspected The fairest most **suspected** be..........49. H.136, 17
Suspicion **Suspition** now had been the sinne,......48. H.136, 7
Suspicion questions every haire...................49. H.136, 23
Suspicion, Discontent, and Strife,................49. H.137, 1
With wise **suspicion**:..........................55. H.149, 78
But seldome from **suspition** free:..............118. H.291, 14
Suspicious Men are **suspicious**; prone to discontent: 291. H.921, 1
Some strickter $M^{rls.}$ or **suspitious** other..........410. A.3, 8
Sustain Though a wise man all pressures can **sustaine**; 60. H.158, 1
Swaddling-clout Or one poore **Swadling-clout**, shall be 355. N.60, 5
Swaggers Now **swaggers** in her Leavy gallantry....224. H.642, 6
Swain Had not *Joves son, that brave Tyrinthian **Swain**, 78. H.197, 65
To the lanke-Stranger, and the sowre **Swain**;..146. H.377, 11
And my most luckie **Swain**, when I shall live to see 184. H.492, 41
Swains The Harvest **Swaines**, and Wenches bound 101. H.250, 13
And let the russet **Swaines** the Plough........127. H.319, 45
What ha's the Court to do with **Swaines**,.......184. H.492, 21
Swallow Did seek my soule to **swallow**,.........373. N.122, 6
Swan So though y'are white as **Swan**, or Snow,..76. H.193, 49
Yee see it brusle like a **Swan**,................115. H.283, 114
As now a Satyr, then a **Swan**;.................215. H.616, 17
The Humminge Dorre, the dyinge **Swan**..433. ins. H.293, 17a
Swan-like-state With **Swan-like-state**, flote up & down thy streams:................................316. H.1028, 18
Swans Between thy Breasts (then Doune of **Swans** more white) 30. H.88, 9
Or Snow, or whitest **Swans** you are:............34. H.105, 2
Of which, sweet **Swans** must drink, before they sing 45. H.128, 34
Swans devoted unto thee.......................122. H.303, 6
Beumont and Fletcher, **Swans**, to whom all eares 206. H.575, 51
Swan-staining Is the **swan-stayning** faire rare stately neck 405. A.1, 44
Sway The Gods to Kings the Judgement give to **sway**: 109. H.269, 1
Who now must **sway**........................114. H.283, 65
The saucie Subjects still will beare the **sway**...138. H.345, 2
Where Fortune bears no **sway** o're things.......190. H.515, 35
When Lawes full power have to **sway**, we see..213. H.608, 1
Thou, thou that bear'st the **sway**.............281. H.874, 1
The Holly hitherto did **sway**;.................285. H.892, 5
Where never Moone shall **sway**.................354. N.58, 9
Swear And I dare **sweare**, that I am gray?.......63. H.164, 2
Nay more, Ile deeply **sweare**,...................69. H.179, 2
If that you lye, then I will **sweare** you love.....126. H.317, 2
True to your self, and sheets, you'l have me **swear**, 136. H.338, 1
Others there be, who righteously will **swear**....141. H.359, 9
A thousand times, more **sweare**, then say,.....149. H.377, 132
Hunchs ha's no money (he do's **sweare**, or say) 173. H.463, 1
Never like their lips, to **sweare**...............182. H.490, 7
Marbles will **sweare** that here it lyes...........203. H.564, 2
But by the Muses **sweare**, all here is good,.......212. H.603, 3
That thou shalt **swear**, my Pipe do's raigne...244. H.716, 39
Look upon Sapho's lip, and you will **swear**,....306. H.985, 1
Especially to **sweare** by it.......................388. N.204, 4
Though the Sextons truly **sweare**................418. A.9, 33
— — — — — — — — — —,...............424. var. H.164, 4
— — — — — — — — — —,...............451. var. H.197, 47
Swears Blanch **swears** her Husband's lovely; when a scald 33. H.99, 1
Skrew lives by shifts; yet **sweares** by no small oathes; 149. H.380, 1
Skurffe by his Nine-bones **sweares**, and well he may, 180. H.480, 1
(As Umber **sweares**) did make his Lyon start...205. H.572, 4
Franck ne'r wore silk she **sweares**; but I reply, 207. H.578, 1
Lulls **swears** he is all heart; but you'l suppose..284. H.886, 1
Spokes when he sees a rosted Pig, he **swears**...305. H.982, 1
Spur jingles now, and **sweares** by no meane oathes, 330. H.1099, 1
— — — — — — — — — — —,................450. var. A.9, 33
Swear't And Love will **swear't**, my Dearest did not so. 42. H.122, 12
Sweat Of Roses be your **sweat**. 9. H.15, 4
And large she spreads by dust, and **sweat**....148. H.377, 114
His gifts go from him; if not bought with **sweat**. 177. H.469, 2
Thy servant, not thy own self, **sweat**,........233. H.670, 20
Take it from my Julia's **sweat**:...............244. H.719, 2
Or money? no, but onely deaw and **sweat**.........248. H.731, 2
And leave their servants, but the smoak & **sweat**: 272. H.826, 3
With the mire, and the **sweat**:..................284. H.891, 4
When Pimpes feat **sweat** (as they doe often use) 332. H.1113, 1
Sweating-closet A **Sweating-Closset**, to annoint the silke- 149. H.377, 121
Sweats Fainting swoones, and deadly **sweats**;....102. N.253, 8
Sweep **Sweep** your house: Who doth not so,....201. H.556, 7
Sweepers (I dare not call ye **Sweepers**)........235. H.674, 14
Sweet See **First-sweet, Flowery-sweet, One-self-sweet-conspiring, Still-sweet-singing**
With breath more **sweet** then Violet...............6. H.2, 14
Or sworn to that **sweet** Sister-hood:................7. H.9, 8
And whom she touch't, turne **sweet**................9. H.15, 12
In the same **sweet** eternity of love...............13. H.29, 2
List' **sweet** maids, and you shal know.............14. H.36, 2
Sweet Electra, and the choice.....................16. H.39, 7
But that I heard thy **sweet** breath say,............20. H.56, 5
So smooth, so **sweet**, so silv'ry, is thy voice,.......22. H.67, 1
In a more rich and **sweet** aray:....................23. H.70, 4
A **sweet** disorder in the dresse....................28. H.83, 1
Of flowers a **sweet** commingled Coronet:..........30. H.88, 4
About the **sweet** bag of a Bee,.....................31. H.92, 1
The Countries **sweet** simplicity:.................35. H.106, 4
But that which most makes **sweet** thy country life, 35. H.106, 31
To make sleep not so sound, as **sweet**: 36. H.106, 54
To spring from these a **sweet** Posterity..........44. H.124, 4
Of which, **sweet** Swans must drink, before they sing 45. H.128, 34
Sweet Amarillis, by a Spring's....................46. H.130, 1
Youth, or **sweet** Nature, co'd bring forth,........48. H.134, 2
Is it (**sweet** maid) your fault these holy........53. H.149, 11
To Love's **sweet** mysterie.......................54. H.149, 34
And the boyes with **sweet** tunes sing,............54. H.149, 47
And make, what ere they touch, turn **sweet**.....55. H.149, 62
Or **sweet**, as is that gumme....................57. H.149, 145
Sweet, be not proud of those two eyes,...........61. H.160, 1
And **sweet** as Flora. Take no care...............68. H.178, 17
Sweet Lady-Flower, I never brought...........71. H.182, 13
But (**sweet** things) ye must be gone;...........74. H.189, 3
Why frowns my **Sweet**? Why won't my Saint confer 77. H.197, 25
Then onely Numbers **sweet**,......................81. H.201, 51
More **sweet** then any............................83. H.205, 8
But dear Amintas, and **sweet** Amarillis,..........86. H.213, 9
To Gods **sweet** Babe, when borne at Bethlehem; 86. H.213, 22
From Countries far, with Store of Spices, (**sweet**) 86. H.213, 31
And all most **sweet**; yet all lesse **sweet** then he. 86. H.213, 38
With oaten pipes, as **sweet**, as new..............86. H.213, 41
Sweet singing Lark,............................87. H.214, 5
Which (though **sweet** unto your smell).........88. H.217, 3
Till you (**sweet** Mistresse) came and enterwove..94. H.224, 7
When on her lip, thou hast thy **sweet** dew plac't, 100. H.248, 3
As spotlesse pure, as it is **sweet**:.............101. H.250, 10
Sweet Western Wind, whose luck it is,.........103. H.255, 1
Why doe ye weep, **sweet** Babes? can Tears......104. H.257, 1
Dry your **sweet** cheek, long drown'd with sorrows raine; 105. H.259, 1
In every thing that's **sweet**, she is..............106. H.263, 6
Y'ave laught enough (**sweet**) vary now your Text; 111. H.277, 1
You say y'are **sweet**; how sho'd we know.......112. H.282, 1
Whether that you be **sweet** or no?..............112. H 282, 2
Then we shall smell how **sweet** you be...........112. H.282, 4
Breathes Vine-yards and Pomgranats: O how **sweet**! 113. H.283, 22
And well bestrutted Bees **sweet** bagge:.........119. H.293, 34
Of the most **sweet** and dainty Bride,...........120. H.293, 50
Then those, which come by **sweet** contingences...123. H.307, 2
So you **sweet** Lady (**sweet** as May)...............126. H.318, 3
(**Sweet** as your selfe, and newly blown).......126. H.318, 8
Thy golden Censors fil'd with odours **sweet**,....128. H.320, 7
So vanish hence, but leave a name, as **sweet**,....131. H.331, 9
Say, we must part (**sweet** mercy blesse......134. H.336, 65
Thus **sweet** she smells, or what can be........145. H.375, 27
Sweet virgin, that I do not set................145. H.376, 1
ly that it makes the meate more **sweet**;........148. H 377, 80
(**Sweet** as the Vestrie of the Oracles.)..........157. H.414, 4
Dear Amarillis! Mon. Hark! Sil. Mark: Mir. this earth grew **sweet**..159. H.421, 11
And sheep, grew more **sweet**, by that breth of Thine. 159. H.421, 14

Sil. Words **sweet** as Love it self. Montano, Hark.
159. H.421, 17
Sweet Bents wode bow, to give my Love the day:
159. H.421, 24
Sweet Aires move here; and more divine.....166. H.443, 39
By **sweet** S. Phillis; pitie me:................169. H.449, 23
Who writes **sweet** Numbers well as any can:....172. H.459, 2
Or else **sweet** Nimphs do you but this;........185. H.495, 5
Jill sayes, of what? sayes Jack, on that **sweet** kisse,
186. H.498, 3
I must answer (**Sweet**) thy part...............186. H.500, 3
The soft **sweet** Mosse shall be thy bed,.........192. H.521, 5
'Tis Ev'ning, my **Sweet**,......................195. H.534, 1
What ever comes, content makes **sweet**:........200. H.552, 6
Sweet Bridget blusht, & therewithall,..........203. H.562, 1
Sprang up a **sweet** Nativity of Flowres.........204. H.567, 2
More **sweet**, then Storax from the hallowed fire: 205. H.575, 8
This **sweet** Infanta of the yeere?..............208. H.580, 2
As when the **Sweet** Maria lived here:.........214. H.612, 10
What short **sweet** Prayers shall be said;......216. H 616, 31
And a **sweet** concurring stream.................220. H.633, 3
Sweet words must nourish soft and gentle Love. 222. H.633, 61
Or **sweet** Lady reach to me....................223. H 638, 8
With Roses **sweet** and new;....................228. H.657, 11
Of that **sweet** Lady, or that gallant Knight:....228. H 658, 2
Sweet Country life, to such unknown,..........229. H.662, 1
Of Land makes life, but **sweet** content.........230. H.662, 18
Sweet as the blossomes of the Vine............230. H.662, 34
Of short **sweet** grasse, as backs with wool.....230. H.662, 43
Sweet sleep, that makes more short the night...231. H.662, 75
Order in a **sweet** neglect:......................232. H.665, 8
Of thy brave, bold, and **sweet** Maronian Muse. 234. H 673, 12
Chains of **sweet** bents let us make,.............235. H.678, 5
The **sweet**, and flowrie Sisterhood..............237. H.686, 4
The soft, the **sweet**, the mellow note...........243. H.716, 17
Chor. A suger'd note! and sound as **sweet**.....243. H.716, 29
Ch. What voice so **sweet** and charming do I heare?
248. H.730, 3
Here lies a Virgin, and as **sweet**...............257. H.764, 1
Who doe with **sweet** embraces,..................260. H.777, 6
To you **sweet** Maids (thrice three).............261. H.778, 5
That **sweet** luck may..........................263. H.784, 11
Sweet Oenone, doe but say.....................264. H.790, 1
Thou writes in Prose, how **sweet** all Virgins be; 266. H.802, 1
No question then, but such a lick is **sweet**,.....269. H.816, 3
To **sweet** acquaintance there...................271. H.824, 16
'Tis **sweet** to thinke on what was hard t' endure. 276. H.849, 2
Sweet are my Julia's lips and cleane,............277. H.857, 1
Pardon my feares (**sweet** Sapho,) I desire.......279. H.866, 3
Kisses and Favours are **sweet** things;...........283. H.883, 13
Nam'd thee Terpander, or **sweet** Orpheus:.....288. H.907, 8
More from the **sweet** then sower things.........298. H.951, 2
To be most soft, terce, **sweet**, and perpolite:.....301. H.966, 2
Sweet is.......................................308. H.993, 20
Love's of it self, too **sweet**: the best of all......327. H.1084, 1
Then weepe not **sweet**; but thus much know,...328. H.1090, 12
Here with the **sweet** Pierides..................334. H.1123, 2
Washt with **sweet** ointments; Thus at last I come
335. H.1128, 3
Sweet Babe, for Thee,.........................345. N.33, 22
Without the **sweet** concurrence of the Heart......346. N.35, 2
Sweet Spirit comfort me!......................347. N.41, 4
Sweet Spirit comfort me!......................347. N.41, 8
Sweet Spirit comfort me!......................347. N.41, 12
Sweet Spirit comfort me!......................347. N.41, 16
Sweet Spirit comfort me!......................347. N.41, 20
Sweet Spirit comfort me!......................348. N.41, 24
Sweet Spirit comfort me!......................348. N.41, 28
Sweet Spirit comfort me!......................348. N.41, 32
Sweet Spirit comfort me!......................348. N.41, 36
Sweet Spirit comfort me!......................348, N.41, 40
Sweet Spirit comfort me!......................348. N.41, 44
Sweet Spirit comfort me!......................348. N.41, 48
To be more **sweet**...............................350. N.47, 36
One onely lock of that **sweet** Hay...............355. N.60, 3
Who to that **sweet** Bread unprepar'd doth come..355. N.65, 9
Instead of that, a **sweet** and gentle word:........356. N.71, 2
A short and **sweet** iniquity?....................357. N.72, 4
And all **sweet** Meades; from whence we get.....360. N.83, 17
Thy soft **sweet** Earth! but (like a spring).......361, N.83, 71
To make things **sweet**. Chor. Yet all less **sweet** then He.
365. N.97, 10
That all things **sweet**, and clean may be:........366. N.98, 11
Let's kisse the **sweet** and holy ground;.........368. N.102, 16
The teares of Saints more **sweet** by farre,.......379. N.145, 1
Had no one Beame from Gods **sweet** Majestie...382. N.167, 4
But on our Age most **sweet** Indulgences........383. N.175, 2
How **sweet** this place is! as from hence........402. N.269, 14
Is rowl'd away; and my **sweet** Saviour's gone!..403. N.271, 2
Then nature for a **sweet** allurement setts.........404. A.1, 19
Over the which a meet **sweet** skin is drawne.....404. A.1, 23
Passing the **sweet sweet** of a musky rose.........406. A.1, 76
Round short and cleire, like pounded spices **sweete**
406. A.1, 92
But form'd by number make **sweet** melody.......406. A.1, 108
That smooth as Oyle, **sweet** softe and Cleane.....408. A.2, 55
Distance and **sweet** Vrbanitie,..................409. A.2, 96
Such rich, such fresh, such **sweet** varietyes,......415, A.7, 16
Had a **sweet** complexion........................417. A.9, 20
— — — — — — — — —,..............423. var. H.128, 8
Why then goe forward, **sweet** Auspicious Bride,
431. ins. H.283, 50a
— — — — — — — — — — —,..............432. var. H.283, 71
— — — — — — — — — — —,..............435. var. H.329, 7
— — — — — — — — — — —,..............448. var. A.1, 82
— — — — — — — — — — —,..............452. var. H.128, 19
Sweet-breath While **sweet-breath** Nimphs, attend on you this Day.......................................140. H.354, 8
Sweetbriars, Through Woodbine, and **Sweet-bryers**.
55. H.149, 68
Sweet-cement The sure **sweet**-Sement, Glue, and Lime of Love.
218. H.622, 2
Sweeten **Sweeten**, and make soft your dreames:..35. H.106, 44
Wch **sweeten** Loue, yett ne're come nighe........408. A.2, 41
Sweetened Who **sweet'ned** first,..................401. N.268, 3
— — — — — — — —,..............435. var. H.293, 22f
Sweetens Of that Passion **sweetens** Pleasure......55. H.149, 80
Sweeter Nor can Juno **sweeter** be,.................59. H.155, 9
Sweeter far, then ever yet......................108. H.266, 3
To make my lodging the **sweeter**;..............256. H.762, 3
Nor in the summers **sweeter** evenings go,.......315. H.1028, 5
What **sweeter** musick can we bring,.............364. N.96, 1
Then which, thy self ne'er wafted **sweeter** over....416. A.8, 10
Sweetest Then **sweetest** Silvia, let's no longer stay;..8. H.10, 5
For my Embalming (**Sweetest**) there will be......20. H.55, 9
Or she, in **sweetest** scent.......................105. H.260, 4
The **sweetest** kind of bashfulnesse..............121. H.300, 2
And this loves **sweetest** language is.............130. H.329, 19
Cf **sweetest** Cow-slips filling Them..............179, H.476, 15
Your Stacks, your Stocks, your **sweetest** Mowes,
179, H.476, 23
The softest Fire makes the **sweetest** Mault......221. H.633, 51
Oblations oft, of **sweetest** Marmelet.............227. H.652, 14
But if (my **Sweetest**) I shall get,...............238. H.690, 9
He doth it with the **sweetest** tones of Art:......266. H.799, 2
Green Rushes then, and **sweetest** Bents,........285. H.892, 17
The **sweetest** solace is to act no sin..............341. N.13, 2
Sweet-faced To all our joy, a **sweet-fac't** child was borne,
86. H.213, 15
Many a **sweet-fac't** Wood-Nymph here is seene,..107. H.265, 5
Sweetheart For the lost **sweet-heart** of her youth:..47. H.132, 8
From that **Sweet-heart**, to this?................104. H.257, 23
Still I write a **Sweet-heart** downe...............253. H.750, 6
The Leven of a loving **sweet-heart** is...........298. H.950, 2
Sweetheart's Who for some **sweet-hearts** sake, did prove
169. H.449, 3
Sweethearts Ran for **Sweet-hearts** mad, and dy'd. 152. H.391, 4
Sweetling And (**Sweetling**) marke you, what a Web will come
221. H.633, 40
Sweetly Thou **sweetly** canst convert the same....95. H.227, 12
Y'ave heard them **sweetly** sing,................110. H.274, 9
Do all things **sweetly**, and in comely wise;......124. H.313, 7
Which **sweetly** spic't, we'l first carouse.......135. H.336, 127
When thou do'st play, and **sweetly** sing,........142. H.362, 1
And **sweetly** sings, but yet his breath sayes no...149. H.381, 2
Come forth and **sweetly** dye....................161. H.425, 12
But **sweetly** sounding like a Lute..............179. H.476, 18
Then smil'd, and **sweetly** chid her speed;........187. H.504, 5
The while the Daulian Minstrell **sweetly** sings,..224. H.642, 7
That's **sweetly** touch't, I must confesse:........243. H.716, 25
As **sweetly** Lady, give me leave to tell ye,......249. H.733, 17
And **sweetly** blushing thus,.....................251. H.740, 6
Then, then (me thinks) how **sweetly** flowes......261. H.779, 2
How **sweetly** shewes thy smiling face,..........375. N.123, 73
That done, wee'l see Thee **sweetly** buried.......399. N.263, 39
Which **sweetly** mixed both with white and redd...404. A.1, 17
— — — — — — — — —,..............435. var. H.329, 22
Sweetness The warmth and **sweetnes** had me there..20. H.56, 3
But 'tis **sweetness** that doth please............22. H.65, 3
What times of **sweetnesse** this faire day fore-shows,
44. H.124, 1
Sweetnesse to allay my sowre.................204. H.569, 11
That **sweetness** turnes to Loathsomness.........288. H.909, 4
With **sweetness**, smoothness, softness, be endu'd. 290. H.914, 4
Sweets These **sweets**, but let them fly;.............9. H.15, 6
While other Gums their **sweets** perspire,..........20. H.54, 5
These, and a thousand **sweets**, co'd never be.....45. H.128, 9
Might yon Full-Moon the **sweets**.................54. H.149, 35
He who plucks the **sweets** shall prove............88. H.217, 5
Like those short **sweets** ere knit together.......107. H.263, 22
You, above all Those **Sweets** of Westminster:...137. H.341, 10
Their lives in **sweets**, and left in death perfume...185. H.496, 4
What **sweets** the Country can afford............192. H.521, 3
The **sweets** of Love are mixt with tears.........208. H.580, 6
Besides rare **sweets**, I had a Book which none..227. H.652, 5
But ah! what **sweets** smelt every where,.......237. H.686, 11
By all those **sweets** that be....................257. H.767, 7
A richess of those **sweets** she found,............281. H.876. 3
But with such **sweets** commingled,.............283. H.883, 4
Where most **sweets** are, there lyes a Snake.....283. H.883, 12
Ther's loathsomnesse e'en in the **sweets** of love...297. H.949, 4
May **Sweets** grow here! & smoke from hence,...361. N.83, 63
— — — — — — — — —,..............448. var. A.1, 76
Sweet-sad Mont. A **sweet-sad** passion.——.......159. H.421, 22

Sweet-slugabed Get up, sweet-Slug-a-bed, and see..67. H.178, 5
Sweet-warbling Sing thou my Dirge, sweet-warbling Chorister! 19. H.50, 4
Swell Next, make his cheeks with breath to swell,..39. H.108, 11
Swell up my nerves with spirit; let my blood....79. H.197, 77
A wafer Dol'd by thee, will swell...............139. H.350, 3
Next for Ordaining, that thy words not swell...210. H.590, 7
That swell the Golden Graine:.................257. H.767, 6
Make him thus swell, or windy Cabbages.......327. H.1085, 2
Kindly swell vp with little pretty pride,..........406. A.1, 88
swell, mixe, and loose your soules; implye..431. ins. H.283, 50d
Swelled Of Lyrick Wine, both swell'd and crown'd, 198. H.544, 16
Swel'd with the Lard of others meat...........200. H.552, 16
Swelling The place, where swelling Piles do breed:...6. H.5, 2
Plumpe Bed beare up, and swelling like a cloud, 115. H.283, 112
Pump, soft, & swelling every where?..........139. H.348, 2
Spungie and swelling, and farre more...........165. H.443, 27
Twoe smelling swelling <bashful> Cherriletts,....404. A.1, 20
Swelling in likeness like twoe christall skyes......406. A.1, 78
Swells (When true it is, the out-side swels......118. H.291, 11
But where sin swells, there let Thy grace abound. 398. N.261, 6
Swells with brave rage, yet comely every where,..415. A.7, 12
Swerved By Moonlesse nights have swerved;......26. H.81, 10
Swetnaham Read thou my Lines, my Swetnaham, if there be 328. H.1089, 1
Swift Before thy swift Postilion;...............239. H.696, 4
Of Youthe <s> swift watch to stand...............413. A.4, 7
— — — — — — — — — —,..............425. var. H.197, 1
Swiftest And quickly give, The swiftest Grace is best. 87. H.213, 46
Swim No man such rare parts hath, that he can swim, 298. H.953, 1
Since when (me thinks) my braines about doe swim, 313. H.1017, 13
Swims Who swims with Vertue, he shall still be sure 23. H.71, 4
Swinger To make the wassaile a swinger.......317. H.1035, 24
Swollen Steale a swolne sop out of the Dripping pan. 331. H.1106, 2
Swoon Or like Jocasta in a swoone...............47. H.132, 4
As Lovers fall into a swoone:..................67. H.175, 16
And swowne away to die,.......................351. N.49, 3
I shall lesse swoone, then die for feare.........393. N.232, 10
Young men to swoone, and Maides to dye for love. 415. A.7, 10
Swoons Fainting swoones, and deadly sweats;....102. H.253, 8
To drye the Widowes teares; and stop her Swoones, 201. H.557, 17
Sword Pagget, a School-boy, got a Sword, and then 65. H.171, 1
Made him take up his shirt, lay down his sword. 65. H.171, 6
Lift up thy Sword; next, suffer it to fall,......310. H.1002, 3
The sword of war must trie the Soveraignty.....331. H.1102, 2
Swore For as he breath'd, the People swore from thence 200. H.551, 5
And swore I'de got the ague of the house.......262. H.783, 20
Sworn Or sworn to that sweet Sister-hood:.........7. H.9, 8
That I have sworn, but by thy looks to know thee. 46. H.128, 48
Syb With paste of Almonds, Syb her hands doth scoure; 203. H.561, 1
Sybel's See Sibyl's
Sybell's See Sibyl's
Sylla Then Roman Sylla powr'd out at his feast...262. H.783, 6
Syllable (By many a watrie syllable)..............44. H.127, 8
The voices Daughter nea'r spake syllable.......159. H.421, 28
To any one unsober syllable....................210. H.590, 8
No sillable doth fall here,....................235. H.674, 11
Sylla's Go on with Sylla's Fortune; let thy Fate..254. H.756, 9
Symmetry What State above, what Symmetrie below, 297. H.947, 9
Sympathy In one-self-sweet-conspiring sympathie:..59. H.154, 4
Synod — — — — — — — — —, ...443. var. H.575, 49
Syracusan Chaste Syracusian Cyane............175. H.465, 58
Syrup See Love's-syrup
Where so much sirrop ran at waste.............71. H.182, 18
Craw cracks in sirrop; and do's stinking say,....162. H.428, 1
Love is a sirrup; and who er'e we see...........297. H.949, 1
T' (Partial List)
Like t' a Rose of Jericho:.....................108. H.266, 2
T' enspangle this expansive Firmament..........191. H.516, 2
T' entertain that Deity.......................204. H. 569. 6
And, lying down, have nought t' affright......231. H.662, 74
'T (Partial List)
Like Streams, you are divorc'd; but 't will come, when 26. H.79, 5
A shew, as if 't 'ad been a snake:..............116. H.284, 4
Returning, if 't be mine or no:.................175. H.465, 72
Tabernacle Here shall my endless Tabernacle be:..60. H.156, 4
An Arke a Tabernacle is........................68. H.178, 34
Tabbies Those counter-changed Tabbies in the ayre, 207. H.576, 3
Tissues, or Tabbies manifold:..................355. N.60, 2

Tabitha For Tabitha, who dead lies here,........374. N.123, 11
That reav'd us of thee Tabitha!................374. N.123, 22
Table See Country-table
A little mushroome table spred,................119. H.293, 7
Quite through the table, where he spies........119. H.293, 25
Set on my Table, (Trouble-free)...............124. H.312, 7
But all, who at thy table seated are,............147. H.377, 59
Of thy glad table: not a dish more known......147. H.377, 69
the creditt from the table of the Sunne....432. ins. H.283, 70b
Table's That makes the Tables merriment........124. H.312, 2
Tables See Feasting-tables
Tablets To see two tablets of pure Ivory..........406. A.1, 96
T'abound See Abound
T'accept See Accept
T'accompany See Accompany
Tackling Of any tackling can declare..........167. H.443, 104
Tacks He tacks about, and now he doth profess..266. H.800, 5
T'adulce See Adulce
Tags Blew pinnes, tagges, fescues, beades and thinges 440. ins. H.443, 45r
Tainted Jone is a Girle that's tainted;...........229. H.659, 2
Take May take the simple Villages.................6. H.2, 16
The Extreame Scabbe take thee, and thine, for me..7. H.6, 6
And never take a wife..........................13. H.31, 3
And take a life immortall from my Verse........27. H.82, 16
To take her by the either hand:................37. H.106, 96
Come, skilfull Lupo, now, and take.............38. H.108, 1
These are traps to take fooles in................52. H.147, 6
Take time Lady while ye may..................56. H.149, 120
Made him take up his shirt, lay down his sword...65. H.171, 6
A fellon take it, or some Whit-flaw come........66. H.173, 3
And sweet as Flora. Take no care..............68. H.178, 17
And take the harmlesse follie of the time........69. H.178, 58
I thought I might there take a taste,...........71. H.182, 17
And take his bag; but thus much know,..........71. H.182, 28
Life of my life, take not so soone thy flight,.......73. H.186, 1
When once true-lovers take their last Fare-well...73. H.186, 8
What? shall we two our endlesse leaves take here..73. H.186, 9
He smarts at last, who do's not first take heed....79. H.199, 4
Let it be Doomes-day; nay, take longer scope;...83. H.206, 3
Stoop, mount, passe by to take her eye, then glare 87. H.215, 5
Take this sprig of Eglantine...................88. H.217, 2
To take the Free-Oblation:.....................92. H.223, 86
And take my flight.............................95. H.227, 32
Take thou my blessing, thus, and goe,..........98. H.238, 11
Troth, leave the flowers, and Maids, take me.....112. H.281, 4
Speak but the word, and Ile take you..........112. H.281, 6
But yet take heed;............................113. H.283, 55
Blesse a Sack-posset; Luck go with it; take...115. H.283, 132
Take first the feast; these dishes gone;........119. H.293, 5
Take friendly morsels, and there stay..........146. H.377, 16
You to some other chimney, and there take....146. H.377, 27
Thou had'st the wreath before, now take the Tree; 150. H.383, 1
He's soft and tender (Pray take heed)..........157. H.412, 25
To Take away that Heart from me,.............168. H.446, 3
Take me and mine together...................169. H.446, 12
Take this compression, so by this.............175. H.465, 69
When of the Banks their leave they take;......180. H.478, 6
Take then thy Censer; Put in Fire, and thus,...197. H.539, 13
Take Horse, and come; or be so kind,..........198. H.544, 31
O Sappho! Take...............................210. H.591, 2
Will storme, or starving take here.............213. H.609, 6
And my full thanks take for it.................223. H.638, 14
To take the precious Phesant made:...........231. H.662, 67
Take from thy Herrick this conclusion:.........234. H.673, 14
Their fashion is, but to say no, to take it........235. H.675, 2
Captive one, or both, to take:..................235. H.678, 6
Let us now take time, and play,................238. H.691, 1
Knew'st thou, one moneth wo'd take thy life away, 241. H.709, 1
Take it from my Julia's sweat:................244. H.719, 2
From her moysture take the like:..............244. H.719, 4
Lets now take our time;.......................267. H.806, 1
Take mine advise, and go not neere............279. H.868, 1
To take thine haires when they are knowne......282. H.881, 3
And take this sentence, then away;............287. H.899, 8
If we take it, as they give it..................306. H.987, 4
Still take advice; though counsels when they flye 318. H.1039, 1
Take, if thou do'st distrust, that Vowe;........328. H.1090, 6
After thy labour take thine ease,..............334. H.1123, 1
And take me up; or els prevent the fall...........352. N.51, 8
And next, to take a bit.........................352. N.53, 7
Then never take a second on,...................354. N.59, 17
What God gives, and what we take,.............363. N.93, 1
Take then his Vowes, who, if he had it, would..369. N.105, 5
But take no tincture from my sinfull Book:....371. N.113, 8
We take our leaves now of the Loome,..........374. N.123, 35
To wast, my JESU, I'le take all................377. N.129, 8
I'le take my share; or els, my God,.............399. N.265, 9
For puplike Eyes, take onlye theis..............409. A.2, 91
Take wth my Blessinge; and goe forth..........409. A.2, 101
Take then tribute of my teares,.................414. A.5, 5
And to thy many, take in one soul more.........416. A.8, 2
And take me in, who am in deep Distress;.......416. A.8, 5

Take it then and in a viewe.....................417. A.9, 7
knowne, not thay giue againe, thay take...422. ins. H.106, 92f
But brave soules take illumination:........443. var. H.575, 60
— — — — — — — — — —,...............453. var. H.283, 70
Taken See Ta'ne
Taken in by none but Thee.....................186. H.499, 4
A long-lifes-day I've taken paines...............212. H.602, 1
May baite his hooke, with maggots taken thence...282. H.879, 4
Chor. All's gone, and Death hath taken........374. N.123, 27
Ha's taken wing,..............................375. N.123, 58
When Thou wast taken, Lord, I oft have read,..399. N.264, 1
If Thou beest taken, God forbid,...............399. N.265, 1
Takes To Jove, who gives, and takes away:........59. H.153, 2
That Prince takes soone enough the Victors roome,
109. H.268, 1
Till sleep takes place of wearinesse............127. H.319, 48
That takes and redelivers every stroake........129. H.323, 11
She takes for a Spurre:.........................225. H.643, 8
Coynesse takes us to a measure;................276. H.850, 5
Want is a softer Wax, that takes thereon,.......288. H.905. 1
Despaire takes heart, when ther's no hope to speed:
309. H.999, 1
The Coward then takes Armes, and do's the deed.
309. H.999, 2
Boreman takes tole, cheats, flatters, lyes, yet Boreman,
315. H.1025, 1
Rules but by leave, and takes his Crowne on trust.
331. H.1103, 2
And though it takes all in, 'tis yet no more.......341. N.15, 5
God when He takes my goods and chattels hence..362. N.87, 1
But he takes tole of? all the Griest.............376. N.127, 4
No, No, this Scene from Thee takes life and sense,
399. N.263, 26
Each takes A weeping farwell, rackt in mynde...411. A.3, 63
— — — — — — — — — —,...........435. var. H.293, 41s
But what she gives not, she not takes,....436. ins. H.336, 48o
Takest Or if thou tak'st that bond away,.........293. H.934, 5
Taketh O how that glittering taketh me!........261. H.779, 6
His Death for Love that taketh...............279. H.863, 12
Taking And taking thence from each his flame;....31. H.92, 7
And from thy Compasse taking small advice,....36. H.106, 81
But taking those rare lips of yours.............71. H.182, 15
He gives not poorly, taking some...............356. N.66, 5
Talent Lest we that Tallent spend:............289. H.911, 17
Talents Ten thousand Talents lent me, Thou dost write:
368. N.103, 9
Tales See Telltales
That tels of Winters tales and Mirth,..........126. H.319, 11
Talk To talk with thee familiarly.................58. H.152, 6
Thus we will sit and talke; but tell............215. H.616, 11
And talke of Brides; & who shall make........215. H.616, 21
Ch. Talk not of love, all pray, but few soules pay me.
248. H.730, 18
Canst talke to us of Sharon; where a spring....330. H.1100, 9
God, the most Wise, is sparing of His talk.......341. N.12, 2
To talke with me familiarly;...................393. N.232, 8
Talked Thus, having talkt, we'l next commend...216. H.616, 35
Talking He who with talking can devoure so much,
191. H.518, 5
Talks Talkes most, eates most, of all the Feeders there.
191. H.518, 2
Tall Be my Mistresse short or tall,................11. H.21, 3
That Timber tall, which three-score lusters stood..23. H.69, 3
In either which a small tall bent................92. H.223, 95
This Lady's short, that Mistresse she is tall;....163. H.437, 1
Or low, or tall, she pleaseth me:..............207. H.579, 2
Tally I'le kisse the Tally, and confesse the score. 368. N.103, 8
Talmud The Doctors, in the Talmud, say,.......388. N.206, 1
Tame For to tame, though not to kill............98. H.238, 10
I keep (tame) with my morsells fed,...........246. H.724, 18
Already tame, and all thine owne?..............282. H.881, 4
T'amend See Amend
Tamest Thou that tam'st Tygers, and fierce storms (that rise)
103. H.254, 3
Tan See Moon-tan
Ta'ne (Invited to the Thesbian banquet) ta'ne....78. H.197, 66
When either price, or praise is ta'ne away.......316. H.1033, 2
The Wine Presse now is ta'ne from us,..........375. N.123, 53
Tanned See Moon-tanned
And noses tann'd with Beere...................219. H.629, 4
Tanner The farting Tanner, and familiar King;..155. H.405, 6
Tansy Or for a Tansie let us pay,...............238. H.690, 3
Tap Me to the Tap, the Tost, the Turfe; Let Wine
79. H.197, 88
Tap (better known then trusted) as we heare..272. H.829, 1
Taper And soone a Taper lighted;................26. H.81, 14
A Virgin Taper, ever shining here..............191. H.516, 4
Taper-light Behold! how Hymens Taper-light......54. H.149, 51
By this quaint Taper-light he winds...........167. H.443, 82
Tapers And all his Tapers thus put out:..........42. H.119, 6
And now those Tapers five,.....................55. H.149, 55
To put the Tapers out,........................56. H.149, 104
Serv'd, but as Tapers, for to burne,............109. H.271, 5
To light their Tapers at the Brides bright eye...115. H.283, 108
And with Tapers comes to fright................117. H.289, 7
When the Tapers once are out.................180. H.482, 4
Like Tapers cleare without number............217. H.619, 15
Nor shall the Tapers when I'm there, burn blew. 222. H.634, 9
Give the Tapers here their light,..............258. H.769, 7
Loves thornie Tapers yet neglected lye:........261. H.781, 3
When the tapers now burne blew,..............348, N.41, 25
Those Tapers, which we set upon the grave,....384. N.181, 1
Euc. The hallowed Tapers all prepared were,......416. A.8, 19
T'appear See Appear
T'appease See Appease
Tapping Tapping his plump thighes with a mirtle wand:
313. H.1017, 8
Tardidation Of tardidation in the Lords Affaires...378. N.137, 6
Tares The Seed; so sow'd these Tares throughout my Book.
4. Ap., 4
Tarnished Which renders that quite tarnisht, wch was green;
21. H.62, 3
Tarry Long still doe tarry,.........................12. H.26, 3
If we long tarry.................................31. H.94, 4
You may for ever tarry........................84. H.208, 16
Tarts Tarts and Custards, Creams and Cakes,...255. H.761, 3
Taste To taste boyl'd Nettles, Colworts, Beets, and eate
37. H.106, 113
Thou might'st but onely see't, not taste it.......37. H.106, 120
And love thee; but not taste. Let my Muse.....46. H.128, 51
I thought I might there take a taste,............71. H.182, 17
Mark, if her tongue, but slily, steale a taste....100. H.248, 4
Taste her lips, so over-laid....................138. H.346, 6
Their taste unto the lower end................147. H.377, 68
Eate thou not all, but taste on some:...........288. H.909, 2
Taste it to Temper; then 'twill be.............288. H.909, 5
Thee lesse to taste, then to drink up their spring;
299. H.956, 2
And tast thou them as saltlesse there,.............339. N.3, 5
Better he starv'd, then but to tast one crumme...355. N.65, 10
Fitted it self to ev'ry Feeders tast..............379, N.146, 2
Lesse for to tast, then for to shew,.............400. N.266, 13
Daintye tast for ladyes food..................418. A.9, 22
That which the Aunt did tast, not eate;..439. ins. H.443, 45e
Tasted Thee in thy Vine, or had but tasted one...78. H.197, 62
Tastes He has at home; but who tasts boil'd or rost?
89. H.221, 2
Of which he eates, and tastes a little..........119. H.293, 27
— — — — — — — — — —,.............435. var. H.293, 44o
Tattered The dancing Frier, tatter'd in the bush; 155. H.405, 7
Tatters Teare me to tatters; yet I'le be..........235. H.677, 3
What are our patches, tatters, raggs, and rents,..302, H.970, 1
Taught Subjects are taught by Men; Kings by the Gods.
12. H.25, 2
Thy house, well fed and taught, can show......147. H.377, 34
Know vertue taught thee, not thy selfe.........176. H.465, 84
Not, that He taught His Ministers to be........378. N.137, 3
Taunts Or staying there, is scourg'd with taunts 146. H.377, 20
T'ave T'ave plagu'd, what now unpunisht is.......48. H.136, 9
Hoping t'ave seene of it my fill;................67. H.175, 20
Fashion'd like Thee; which though 'tave eares..174. H.465, 21
T'ave lost the god ye might have had..........179. H.476, 39
Wherein t'ave had an enjoying.................195. H.534, 6
T'ave your blushes seen by day...............276. H.850, 14
T'ave found in me this sudden change;.........290. H.915, 4
T'ave Boyes, and Gyrles too, as they will.......291. H.919, 12
Tavern's About him, when the Taverns shot's to pay.
173. H.463, 2
Teach Who feares to aske, doth teach to be deny'd.
8. H.12, 2
To teach Man to confine desires:..............35. H.106, 16
Teach Nature now to know,....................57, H.149, 147
A Rule, how far to teach,.....................76. H.193, 42
High in your own conceipt, and some way teach
115. H.283, 128
Heare ye Virgins, and Ile teach,................120. H.297, 1
Teach man to keepe a God in man:..........149. H.377, 134
Can teach a man the Art of memory:..........186. H.501, 2
And teach me how to sing.....................261. H.778, 7
But teach us yet..............................289. H.911, 15
Teach it to blush, to curtsie, lisp, and shew.....290. H.914, 5
This rule of manners I will teach my guests,...310. H.1005, 1
Teach me besides, what love wil do;........325. H.1075, 5
But for to teach us, all the grace is there,......346. N.36, 2
Lett Manners teach the <e> whear to bee........407. A.2, 27
To teach the truth of Scenes, and more for thee,
443. var. H.575, 53
— — — — — — — — — —....../.......453. var. H.283, 83
Teacheth When words we want, Love teacheth to endite;
275. H.846, 1
Teage Teage has told lyes so long, that when Teage tells
282, H.880, 1
Teage's Truth, yet Teages truths are untruths, (nothing else.)
282. H.880, 2
Team There at the Plough thou find'st thy Teame,
230. H.662, 25
From the Plough soone free your teame;......315. H.1026, 3
Tear Let fall a Primrose, and with it a teare:......9. H.14, 14
Can make your's bleed a teare:..................11. H.20, 5
A teare at all for that:..........................12. H.23, 6
(In my short absence) to unsluce a teare:.......14. H.35, 10
Thy rockie bottome, that doth teare thy streams...29. H.86, 3
Thee spend a sigh, t'accompany my teare........42. H.122, 6
Thou shed'st one teare, when as I went away;...42. H.122, 10

Along with you my **teare**......................43. H.123, 2
And doe an honour to thy **teare**;...............48. H.134, 6
Unlesse you coole me with a **Teare**:...........50. H.140, 10
But she co'd see each eye to stamp a **teare**:......58. H.150, 4
For pitty let a **teare** be shed;...................61. H.159, 23
You'l spil a **tear**, or two with theirs:...........70. H.180, 6
Without a sad looke, or a solemne **teare**?........73. H.186, 10
To **teare** the world, or set it all on fire..........81. H.202, 6
With a **teare**; and so Adieu....................89. H.220, 4
O! may no eye distill a **Teare**..................104. H.256, 9
And with a **teare** compare these last...........134. H.336, 81
You'l with a **tear** or two, remember me,........140. H.355, 10
But the toning of a **teare**:.....................170. H.450, 4
In publique loss to shed a **Teare**:..............203. H.564, 4
And look how when a frantick Storme doth **tear**.225. H.642, 13
Teare me to tatters; yet I'le be................235. H.677, 3
She wept, and made it deeper by a **teare**........251, H.743, 2
Comes with his Cypresse, and devotes a **teare**?..288. H.907, 2
Teare, that deserves of me a million............302. H.967, 4
He raves, he rends, and while he thus doth **tear**,
325. H.1077, 5
Upon thy cheeke that spangel'd **Teare**,.........328. H.1090, 8
That **Teare** shall scarce be dri'd before.........328. H.1090, 10
Or scourging **teare** me;.........................363. N.92, 14
From her Sonnes Crosse, not shedding once a **teare**:
384. N.180, 2
Shed for their Master many a bitter **teare**:.....384. N.180, 10
But substance, to! receaue this Pearlye **Teare**....412. A.3, 81
One sighe of loue, and coole it with a **teare**;......414. A.6, 8
With a **teare** yow may compare...................417. A.9, 17
— — — — — — — — — —,..............437. var. H.336, 117

Tearce See **Tierce**

Tears And thereupon, in **tears** half drown'd,.......18. H.46, 3
That neither haire was cut, or true **teares** shed....27. H.82, 3
But that his **teares** forbad the rest..............42. H.119, 12
Me turn'd to **tears**; yet did'st not weep for me...42. H.122, 4
And strings my **tears** as Pearle..................43. H.123, 6
For **tears** no more will fall.....................43. H.123, 18
But Lovers **tears** inchristalled,..................44. H.127, 4
That Lovers **tears** in life-time shed,.............44. H.127, 9
And kisses drying up his **tears**:.................50. H.139, 11
These Precious-Pearly-Purling **teares**,...........54. H.149, 21
Her, though she wooe with **teares**...............56. H.149, 98
Teares are the noble language of the eye.........58. H.150, 6
The Eyes by **tears** speak, while the Tongue is mute.
58. H.150, 8
By those true **teares** y'are weeping..............63. H.164, 15
With thy enchantment, melt me into **tears**.......67. H.176, 2
If pittying my sad Parents **Teares**,..............70. H.180, 5
And told her, (as some **tears** did fall)...........71. H.182, 25
Salutes with **tears** of joy; when fires betray.......77. H.197, 17
Flie thou made Bubble of my sighs, and **tears**.....87 .H.215, 2
Washt those thy purple wounds with **tears**.......89. H.219, 6
And offer **Tears** upon thy Tomb:.................89. H.219, 10
Why doe ye weep, sweet Babes? can **Tears**.....104. H.257, 1
To speak by **Teares**, before ye have a Tongue...104. H.257, 14
By your **teares** shed,..........................105. H.257, 25
Conceiv'd with grief are, and with **teares** brought forth.
105. H.257, 28
Bedew'd with **teares**, are worne.................106. H.262, 8
Moles eyes; to these, the slain-Stags **teares**:....120. H.293, 44
Beleeve young man all those were **teares**........131. H.330, 5
She that will weare thy **teares**, wo'd weare thine eyes.
131. H.330, 15
Thus ripe with **tears**,.........................135. H.336, 117
Or in the dampe Jet read their **Teares**.........149. H.377, 126
Love in pitie of their **teares**,..................152. H.391, 5
Time with the **tears**, that I do weep?...........158. H.420, 6
By all those **teares** that have been shed,........169. H.449, 19
To drye the Widowes **teares**; and stop her Swoones,
201. H.557, 17
The sweets of Love are mixt with **tears**.........208. H.580, 6
Cut off thy haires; and let thy **Teares** be shed...219. H.627, 3
If here ye will some few **teares** shed,..........226. H.644, 9
Teares, though th'are here below the sinners brine,
226. H.645, 1
By **tears** and pitie now to come unto mee.......248. H.730, 2
Ph. Ile give thee vows & **tears**. Ch. can **tears** pay skores
248. H.730, 19
Who els with **tears** wo'd doubtles drown my ferry.
248. H.730, 26
This Stone, for names sake, melts to **teares**......257. H.764, 6
In **teares**..258. H.770, 8
That your **teares** may coole her fires...........269. H.814, 6
Was cheese full ripe with **Teares**, with Bread as sad.
273. H.835, 4
Teares have their springs from joy, as well as woe.
275. H.842, 4
Teares most prevaile; with **teares** too thou mayst move
287. H.900, 1
Teares quickly drie: griefes will in time decay:..293. H.930, 1
With solemne **tears**, and with much grief of heart,
300. H.960, 3
Tears will spring, where woes are deep..........306. H.984, 32
She sees no **teares**,...........................314. H.1024, 9
Then for to shed some **teares**...................352. N.53, 3
What He with laughter speaks, heare thou with **tears**.
355. N.63, 2
Our sighs for Storax, **teares** for Wine;..........360. N.83, 33
Receive, for this thy praise, our **teares**:.........360. N.83, 37
With **teares**, distil'd...........................360. N.83, 40
Our present **Teares** here (not our present laughter)
362. N.90, 1
He **teares** and tugs us, then he did before;......372. N.116. 2
And eyes, to pitie Widdowes **teares**............373. N.123, 6
Teares and terrors are our theames............376. N.128, 3
God from our eyes all **teares** hereafter wipes,...379. N.139, 1
The **teares** of Saints more sweet by farre,.......379. N.145, 1
Teares, at that day, shall make but weake defence;
392. N.230, 27
Take then tribute of my **teares**,.................414. A.5, 5
Have pity either on my **tears** or Youth,,..........416. A.8, 4
— — — — — — — — — — —,..............429. var. H.253, 5
— — — — — — — — — — —,..............438. var. H.412, 7

Teaster See **Tester**

Teat Woo'd to come suck the milkie **Teat**:......36. H.106, 50

Teats More then the **teats** of Discipline:........310. H.1004, 6

Tedder's See **Tether's**
— — — — — — — — — —, ...422. var. H.106, 134

Tedious Never was Night so **tedious**, but it knew..52. H.146, 3
How **tedious** they are in their dresse...........118. H.291, 4
The winds, to blow the **tedious** night away;.......358. N.77, 6
But here's the Sun-set of a **Tedious** day:..........419. A.10, 6

Teemed **Teem'd** her refreshing dew?............104. H.257, 5

Teeming By the Brides eyes, and by the **teeming** life
114. H.283, 81
Next may your Duck and **teeming** Hen........179. H.476, 19
In **teeming** years, how soon my Sun was set,....304. H.978, 3
Thou mak'st my **teeming** Hen to lay............350. N.47, 45
From **teeming** eyes; to these we bring,..........360. N.83, 41

Teend See **Tind**

Teending See **Tinding**

Teeth Glasco had none, but now some **teeth** has got;
46. H.129, 1
Six **teeth** he has, whereof twice two are known....46. H.129, 3
He weares all day, and drawes those **teeth** at night.
46. H.129, 6
False in breast, **teeth**, haire, and eyes:..........77. H.195, 10
Of foure **teeth** onely Bridget was possest;......158. H.419, 1
Squirrils and childrens **teeth** late shed,..........166. H.443, 55
You say y'are young; but when your **Teeth** are told
173. H.462, 1
They be but signs of Ursleys hollow **teeth**.......197. H.543, 4
Horne sells to others **teeth**; but has not one......211. H.595, 1
Sound **Teeth** has Lucie, pure as Pearl, and small,
226. H.649, 1
Of **teeth**, as deaf as nuts, and all her own.......232. H.668, 6
Franck wo'd go scoure her **teeth**; and setting to't,
247. H.728, 1
There in your **teeth** much Leprosie..............250. H.738, 4
White as Zenobias **teeth**, the which the Girles....251. H.741, 1
Peapes he do's strut, and pick his **Teeth**, as if....273. H.835, 1
By throwing **teeth** into the ground:............297. H.948, 6
(His **teeth** all out) to rince and wash his gummes.
301. H.965, 2
And her white **teeth** which in the gums are sett.....405. A.1, 31

Tell See **Foretell**
But this I'le **tell** ye too,.........................13. H.31, 5
Next, how I love thee, that my griefe must **tell**,....23. H.72, 3
As any other, this can **tell**;......................24. H.73, 8
Or else desir'st that Maids sho'd **tell**.............34. H.103, 7
The last is but the least; the first doth **tell**........35. H.106, 9
Fame **tell** of States, of Countries, Courts, and Kings;
36. H.106, 85
Do in a trickling manner **tell**,.....................44. H.127, 7
Come **tel** me then, how great's the smart........50. H.139, 14
Tell me, has Strut got ere a title more?..........53. H.148, 3
To **tell** all prosp'rous chance.....................55. H.149, 58
Of Virgins! **Tell** the Maid,.......................56. H.149, 93
Tel them, now they must adventer,...............56. H.149, 99
This to your coynesse I will **tell**;................60. H.159, 11
I **tell** thee, by this score here;..................63. H.166, 6
But Ile **tell** ye...................................74. H.190, 3
Poore pittyed Exile? **Tell** me, did thy Graces....77. H.197, 20
Like a dull Twi-light? **Tell** me; and the fault....77. H.197, 29
Wo't thou not smile, or **tell** me what's amisse?..78. H.197, 33
Too temp'rate in embracing? **Tell** me, ha's desire..78. H.197, 35
Let them **tell** how she doth move................82. H.203, 7
For to **tell**, not publish it........................82. H.203, 16
Smooth, faire, and fat; none better I can **tell**:....86. H.213, 6
Yet the fretfull bryar will **tell**,..................88. H.217, 4
Tell her too, she must not be,....................98. H.238, 3
Tell her, if she struggle still,....................98. H.238, 8
And **tell** her this, but doe not so,...............98. H.238, 12
Love on a day (wise Poets **tell**)................105. H.260, 1
Tell me, said I, in deep distresse,...............106. H.263, 3
I **tell** yee no; but like a.......................116. H.283, 147
So old she was, that none co'd **tell** her yeares...129. H.326, 6
Among thy Fancies, **tell** me this,................130. H.329, 1
Washt o're, to **tell**[1] what change is neare......134. H.336, 90
Untill our tongues shall **tell** our ears,..........136. H.336, 143
And I the truth will **tell**;......................138. H.344, 2

Tell, if thou canst, (and truly) whence doth come 157. H.414, 1
Ile tell thee; while my Julia did unlace........157. H.414, 5
But she is gone. Sil. Mirtillo, tell us whether,....159. H.421, 29
Since so it is; Ile tell thee what,................161. H.425, 5
For a wrought Purse; can any tell wherefore?..162. H.427, 2
Of whom, from Fam's white Trumpet, This Ile Tell, 170. H.451, 9
Never can tell, where shall his Landing be.......177. H.468, 2
Where tell..................................178. H.475, 13
Ah! Lycidas, come tell me why................183. H.492, 1
For Loves-sake, tell me how..................183. H.492, 8
Tell I can't, what's Resident..................191. H.519, 4
Jone wo'd go tel her haires; and well she might,.195. H.531, 1
Can tell by tongue; or true-love tie:..........202. H.560, 12
Will tell thee Pitie thou hast none...............203. H.564, 6
Or tell what strange Tricks Love can do,........215. H.616, 9
Thus we will sit and talke; but tell............215. H.616, 11
I cannot tell; unlesse there be.................218. H.626, 8
Yet, Reader, let me tell thee this...............226. H.644, 7
Ile write no more, nor will I tell or sing........228. H.658, 5
Nor is't a life, seven yeares to tell,...........233. H.670, 34
Or, for revenge, I'le tell thee what.............240. H.705, 9
Chor. And Lallage shall tell by this,............244. H.716, 41
To tell how night drawes hence, I've none,......246. H.724, 2
Her tongue, to tell what danger's neare.........246. H.724, 16
I am a bird, and though no name I tell,.........248. H.730, 7
As sweetly Lady, give me leave to tell ye,......249. H.733, 17
Shall call to Judgment; tell us when the sound..257. H.763, 18
Tell me Anthea, dost thou fondly dread........262. H.781, 13
Orpheus he went (as Poets tell)...............265. H.798, 1
The present Age will tell the world thou art....267. H.804, 11
Shall I go to Love and tell,...................273. H.836, 1
Or curious Wilson: Tell me, canst thou be.....276. H.851, 5
Maidens tell me I am old;......................277. H.852, 1
Tell me, what needs those rich deceits,..........282. H.881, 1
As whether (this) I cannot tell..................283. H.883, 5
That will speake what this can't tell...........289. H.910, 5
Tell me young man, or did the Muses bring......299. H.956, 1
Tell us thy Nation, kindred, or the whence......299. H.956, 7
Tell that Brave Man, fain thou wo'dst have access 301. H.963, 1
Shall not times hereafter tell.................302. H.968, 7
This Stone can tell the storie of my life,......304. H.978, 1
Tell me, do thy kine now fail....................305. H.984, 7
And I'le tell thee what it was:................305. H.984, 12
Tell, and I'le lay down my Pipe...............305. H.984, 14
Now, if you love me, tell me,..................321. H.1055, 1
For truth I may this sentence tell,.............321. H.1059, 1
This Ile tell ye by the way,....................322. H.1063, 1
Tell me, now last, what love will do;..........325. H.1075, 7
Who by his gray Haires, doth his lusters tell,...328. H.1088, 5
Alas I can't, for tell me how..................329. H.1093, 1
Tell me the People that do keep..................340. N.3, 7
Tell me the motes, dust, sands, and speares......340. N.3, 11
And tell Him, by that Bud now blown,..........354. N.59, 3
And tell Him, (for good handsell too)...........354. N.59, 7
Tell Him, for Corall, thou hast none;............354. N.59, 11
But why He did not, let me tell wherefore:......356. N.69, 2
And tell us then, when as thou seest............365. N.97, 12
Tell us, thou cleere and heavenly Tongue,........367. N.102, 1
To such a height, as for to tell................369. N.107, 3
Thus I walk, and this I tell:....................372. N.121, 4
Nor makes it matter, Nestors yeers to tell,.......392. N.230, 5
Tell me rich man, for what intent...............394. N.239, 1
Tell me, white Angell; what is now become......403. N.271, 3
Nay tell the Bell-man of the Night had tould......410. A.3, 17
This known, the rest of thy sad story tell,......417. A.8, 35
— — — — — — — — — —, ...421. var. H.85, 3
— — — — — — — — — — —, ...443. var. H.580, 11
— — — — — — — — — — —, ...449. var. A.8, 9

Tellest Tel'st when a Verse springs high, how understood 297. H.947, 7
And tel'st to us, what once they were, and are...330. H.1100, 6

Telling A telling what rare sights h'ad seen:........13. H.27, 8
Telling the Clock strike Ten, Eleven, Twelve, One. 114. H.283, 76

Tells Which done, thy painfull Thumb this sentence tells us, 36. H.106, 61
And, as Sir Thomas Parson tells...............92. H.223, 79
Look in Prig's purse, the chev'rell there tells you..71. H.183, 3
That tels of Winters Tales and Mirth,........126. H.319, 11
Some private pinch tels danger's nie...........147. H.377, 52
My Story tells, by Love they were............180. H.478, 3
Tels ye but this, they art the same,...........180. H.478, 7
Cob clouts his shooes, and as the story tells,......226. H.648, 1
And tells the world, he's now regenerate........240. H.703, 2
Tells when.................................246. H.724, 11
Teage has told lyes so long, that when Teage tells 282. H.880, 1
As Gospell tells,..............................345. N.33, 14
— — — — — — — — —, ...422. var. H.106, 85

Telltales Tell-tales I wo'd have them be..........82. H.203, 3

ΤΕΛΟΣ God is the ΑΡΧΗ, and the ΤΕΛΟΣ too.....403. N.272, 2

Temper Then temper flew from words; and men did squeake, 150. H.382, 7
Falls to a temper, and doth mildly cast.........225. H.642, 19
Taste it to Temper; then 'twill be.............288. H.909, 5

Temperance Of offending, Temperance, Deare......409. A.2, 98

Temperate Too temp'rate in embracing? Tell me, ha's desire 78. H.197, 35
But temp'rate mirth dealt forth, and so discreet- 148. H.377, 79

Tempest To[o] Calme A tempest, lett bee brought..408. A.2, 66
(As wth a Tempeste) Nature through the worlde 410. A.3, 24

Tempest-like So when this War (which tempest-like doth spoil 225. H.642, 17

Tempests (Ulysses-like) all tempests to endure;....23. H.71, 5
Among these Tempests great and manifold......319. H.1044, 1

Tempestuous In the tempestuous petticote:........28. H.83, 10

Temple His Temple of Idolatry:..................90. H.223, 6
In your Temple, when I pray,...................138. H.346, 8
The fat-fed smoking Temple, which in..........146. H.377, 6
Besides us two, i' th' Temple here's not one......168. H.445, 1
To this white Temple of my Heroes, here........185. H.496, 1
Because with Flowers her Temple was not drest:.197. H.539, 8
When to the Temple Love sho'd runne, not go...216. H.618, 6
From the Temple to your home................220. H.633, 1
To th' Temple with the sober Midwife go.......286. H.898, 2
Unto the Holy Temple ride:..................291. H.919, 14
The Temple, with a cloud of smoke............366. N.98, 17

Temples The leaves) her temples I behung:........16. H.41, 11
Rare Temples thou hast seen, I know,..........90. H.223a, 1
The Candid Temples of her comely face:........197. H.543, 2
Clean my Roomes, as Temples be,...............204. H.569, 5
And crown thy temples too, and let............233. H.670, 19
To whose free knees we may our temples tye....300. H.961, 15

Temporal These temp'rall goods God (the most Wise) commends 387. N.201, 1

Tempt To strike me I will tempt thee:..........296. H.946, 21

Temptation All with temptation doth bewitch.....166. H.443, 38
Demure, but yet, full of temptation too...........290. H.914, 6
Unto temptation God exposeth some;..............380. N.150, 3
To shun the least Temptation to a sin;.........392. N.230, 30
And soe begett lust and temptation........430. ins. H.283, 20f

Temptation's But having scapt temptations shelfe,.176. H.465, 83

Temptations Yet let these glib temptations be.....174. H.465, 5
When temptations me oppresse,.................347. N.41, 2
Temptations hurt not, though they have accesse:..359. N.79, 1

Tempted No man is tempted so, but may o'recome, 389. N.211, 1
Though to be tempted be no sin, untill..........392. N.230, 31

Tempter When the Tempter me pursu'th..........348. N.41, 37

Tempteth God tempteth no one (as S. Aug'stine saith) 380. N.150, 1

Tempting Tempting down to slide withall:..........15. H.36, 9
To kisse that tempting nakednesse:...............51. H.142, 18
And here all tempting Frumentie..............101. H.250, 34
Temptinp the two too modest; can............115. H.283, 113
The tempting Mole, stoln from the neck......166. H.443, 63
Alluring me, and tempting so:...............202. H.560, 16
Tempting all the passers by:................232. H.665, 10
Along with it some tempting blandishment.......389. N.217, 2
More mildlie least thy temptinge lookes beguile 424. ins. H.128, 46e

Tempts That tempts till it be tossed up:........127. H.319, 36
The Devill tempts not least......................344. N.28, 2

Ten Will render ten for this:......................29. H.87, 6
Ten will not pay..............................29. H.87, 8
Telling the Clock strike Ten, Eleven, Twelve, One. 114. H.283, 76
To the ninth number, if not tenne;............127. H.319, 32
And for their two egs render ten.............179. H.476, 21
If children you have ten, Sir John............208. H.581, 5
Snare, ten i' th' hundred calls his wife; and why? 220. H.631, 1
Our trust farre more then ten eare-witnesses.....287. H.904, 2
At twice ten yeares, a prime and publike one?..299. H.956, 6
To do ten Bad, for one Good Action..............339. N.1, 6
Twice ten for one............................350. N.47, 44
Ten thousand Talents lent me, Thou dost write:..368. N.103, 9

Tend But on we must, and thither tend,........133. H.336, 25
— — — — — — — — — —, ...425. var. H.197, 8

Tender More tender then the childhood of the Morne. 86. H.213, 16
He's soft and tender (Pray take heed).........157. H.412, 25
And (Love knowes) tender as a chick..........167. H.443, 85
Ready, to pierce Thy tender Feet, and Hands...398. N.263, 4
With tender ryne and silver coloured,............406. A.1, 98
— — — — — — — — — — —, ...452. var. H.293, 50

Tender-whimpering-maids Strip her of Spring-time, tender-whimpring-maids,.............114. H.283, 91

Tendrils I with my Tendrils did surprize;..........16. H.41, 6
And can with Tendrills love intwine,.............88. H.216, 11
Like to the tendrells of a flattring vine,...........404. A.1, 8

Tends (Farther then Gentlenes tends) gets place..114. H.283, 83

Tenement No Widowes Tenement was rackt to guild 149. H.377, 119
We pay for our poore Tenement:..............200. H.552, 8
To keepe the out-cast in his Tenement:........201. H.557, 14
I'th' Church-yard, made, one Tenement for me...277. H.853, 4
Thou Fortune ow'st for tenement................407. A.2, 14

T'engage See Engage

T'engender See Engender

T'enjoy See Enjoy

Tense Ducking in Mood, and perfect Tense,......91. H.223, 52
Tension To the tension of the string,............131. H.332, 2
Tent To make a Tent, and put it in,..............18. H.46, 7
Th'art hence removing, (like a Shepherds Tent)..188. H.507, 1
Tenth All know a Fellon eate the Tenth away.....180. H.480, 2
The tenth you know the Parsons is...........208. H.581, 2
Won't for his tenth part ask you one.........208. H.581, 6
T'enthrall See Enthrall
Tentrall See Trental
Terce See Terse
Termly When I and they keep tearmly fires;....303. H.973, 12
Terpander Nam'd thee Terpander, or sweet Orpheus:
288. H.907, 8
Terror And that terrour likewise prove,..........117. H.286, 7
Terrors And all terrors me surprize;.........348. N.41, 43
With trialls those, with terrors these He proves,..370. N.108, 3
Teares and terrors are our theames...........376. N.128, 3
In this regard, in those great terrors He........382. N.167, 3
No, lay thy stately terrours by,...............393. N.232, 7
Terse To that Terce Muse of thine...........80. H.201, 28
To be most soft, terce, sweet, and perpolite:....301. H.966, 2
Tersely Thus thou can'st tearcely live to satisfie..35. H.106, 27
T'espy See Espy
Testament You a fore-leader in this Testament...304. H.977, 4
Th' Apostles Mounts of the New Testament,....381. N.157, 4
Testaments Or like old Testaments ingrost,.......190. H.515, 43
Tester Many a Teaster by his game, and bets:....154. H.400, 2
Testify To testifie the glowing of a spark?........78. H.197, 38
Tether's See Tedder's
Or to exceed thy Tether's reach:..............38. H.106, 134
Tettar See Tetter
Tetter Which neither Tettar, Time, or Moth......393. N.231, 3
T'excuse See Excuse
T'express See Express
Text But stay; I see a Text,..................81. H.201, 39
They have their Text for what they doe;......92. H.223, 77
Y'ave laught enough (sweet) vary now your Text;
111. H.277, 1
A piece, then of a higher text:................135. H.336, 100
As In a more Conspicuous Text.................407. A.2, 32
I'th ayre, a greater Text of light..............413. A.4, 19
Texture For to make the Texture lye............195. H.530, 3
Th' (Partial List)
Unto thy Ghost, th' Effused Offering:............27. H.82, 8
Th' industrious Merchant has; who for to find..36. H.106, 65
But lost to one, be th' others death............38. H.106, 142
From th' upper to the under-glasse,............44. H.127, 6
Skilfull i' th' Harpe, and Melodie:..............70. H.181, 10
Rough as th' Adratick sea, yet I..............70. H.181, 23
Illustrious Idoll! co'd th' Ægyptians seek.......78. H.197, 57
Th' Arabian Dew besmears.....................80. H.201, 10
Dead thee to th' most, if not destroy thee all.....82. H.204, 12
Of flowers, ne'r suckt by th' theeving Bee:.......86. H.213, 37
Nature begets by th' Sun and showers,.........103. H.256, 5
To read by th' Starres, the Kingdoms sick:......126. H.319, 6
From th' embers, then the kitlings eyne,......136. H.336, 146
(Nature begets by th' Sun, and showers,)......166. H.443, 34
With Musk-flies, are th' Aromaticks,...........166. H.443, 44
Besides us two, i' th' Temple here's not one....168. H.445, 1
Of all those three-brave-brothers, faln i' th' Warre,
170. H.451, 1
Since to th' Country first I came,..............182. H.489, 1
Then at th' opening of mine eyes,..............199. H.549, 3
Let our soules flie to' th' shades, where ever springs
205. H.575, 2
Snare, ten i' th' hundred calls his wife; and why?.220. H.631, 1
Say, who's the worst, th' exactor, or the whore?..220. H.631, 4
One night i' th' yeare, my dearest Beauties, come.222. H.634, 1
And there to lick th' effused sacrifice:............222. H.634, 4
Th' easie earth that covers her.................224. H.640, 4
To th' number five,.........................227. H.653, 10
For well thou know'st, 'tis not th' extent......230. H.662, 17
This done, then to th' enameld Meads..........230. H.662, 29
That's tost up after Fox i' th' Hole...........231. H.662, 57
And trace the Hare i' th' trecherous Snow:.....231. H.662, 63
Follow to th' wilder Ocean:....................244. H.720, 4
So silently they one to th' other come,..........250. H.737, 5
Th' unequall Pulse to beat, as heretofore.........254. H.756, 6
In th' intrim she desires.......................269. H.814, 5
Bird snatcht away from th' cryinge child,..439. ins. H.443, 45q
Thais Thais in the night, to me................232. H.665, 16
Thamasis To thee my silver-footed Thamasis.....315. H.1028, 2
Than With breath more sweet then Violet..........6. H.2, 14
Then to be thaw'd, or heated so..................8. H.13, 8
The soule, when it doth rather sigh, then sound.....12. H.24, 2
She rather took, then got a fall:...................12. H.27, 2
More like a Stock, then like a Vine............17. H.41, 23
Since I was born, then here;....................19. H.51, 2
Then where I loath'd so much...................19. H.51, 8
Then to live not perfected.....................21. H.59, 6
Then by one, to hazard all.....................21. H.61, 8
Jems, then those two, that went before:..........23. H.70, 6
More wealth brings in, then all those three.........23. H.70, 8
Under a Lawne, then skyes more cleare,...........25. H.78, 1
They blush'd, and look'd more fresh then flowers....25. H.78, 5
Here I devote; And something more then so;....27. H.82, 11
Doe more bewitch me, then when Art.........28. H.83, 13

Between thy Breasts (then Doune of Swans more white)
30. H.88, 9
More then the stones i'th' street by farre:........32. H.98, 4
Beauty, no other thing is, then a Beame..........33. H.102, 1
Me then to make me languish stil!..............34. H.103, 10
More white then whitest Lillies far,..............34. H.105, 1
More white then are the whitest Creames,........34. H.105, 3
More white then Pearls, or Juno's thigh;........34. H.105, 5
More at her nature, then her name:..............35. H.106, 8
Wayes lesse to live, then to live well:............35. H.106, 10
(More blessed in thy Brasse, then Land)........35. H.106, 24
Lesse with a neat, then needfull diet............35. H.106, 30
(Far more with wonder, then with feare)........36. H.106, 84
More in thine eares, then in thine eyes.........37. H.106, 88
Rather then love, let me be ever lost;............40. H.113, 5
Colder yet then any one:......................40. H.115, 12
Me sooner starve, then those can kill...........40. H.115, 16
Nay, thou more neare then kindred, friend, man, wife,
45. H.128, 3
More radiant then the Summers Sun-beams shows;
45. H.128, 13
Work'st more then Wisdome, Art, or Nature can,
45. H.128, 24
And more then well becomes the day?..........48. H.136, 3
Be you more warie, then afraid................49. H.136, 15
No, no, no more then is yond' Moone,..........49. H.136, 28
Sooner, then she, ever yet,....................57. H.149, 149
Be truer to him, then a wise Distrust............67. H.177, 2
Spring, sooner then the Lark, to fetch in May...68. H.178, 14
Then Lydia, far-fam'd Lydia,....................70. H.181, 7
I flourish't more then Roman Ilia...............70. H.181, 8
Lyd. Though mine be brighter then the Star;..70. H.181, 21
Thou lighter then the Cork by far:............70. H.181, 22
Then when it grew alone;.....................75. H.193, 7
Then when the paler hieu.....................75. H.193, 15
Then when he darts his radiant beams..........75. H.193, 20
Then if they naked stood,......................75. H.193, 29
Then if they sho'd discover....................76. H.193, 37
And that, no further, then we see..............76. H.193, 44
I! far more welcome then the happy soile,........77. H.197, 15
God, and far more transcendent then the rest?..78. H.197, 60
More shak't thy selfe, then she is scorch't by thee.
82. H.204, 14
More sweet then any..........................83. H.205, 8
More tender then the childhood of the Morne.....86. H.213, 16
And all most sweet; yet all lesse sweet then he...86. H.213, 38
Lesse in these Marble stones, then in thy story...89. H.219, 22
Then this, the Fairies once, now Thine..........90. H.223a, 6
First, in a Neech, more black than jet,..........90. H.223, 11
More precious, then we prize our gold:.........92. H.223, 88
Rather then mend, put out the light..............97. H.235, 6
To Prayers, then to Merryment,................101. H.250, 24
Then the sand, that makes the shore:...........102. H.253, 6
Sweeter far, then ever yet......................108. H.266, 3
More towring, more disparkling then thy fires:..113. H.283, 36
(Farther then Gentlenes tends) gets place......114. H.283, 83
Play then they ever knew before...............115. H.283, 130
Rather then to which I'le fall,..................117. H.286, 3
They make a feast lesse great then nice........119. H.293, 12
Then those, which come by sweet contingences...123. H.307, 2
More then a Feast contenteth me...............124. H.312, 8
Woman wo'd bring him more then co'd be told,.129. H.326, 4
Then we are now............................134. H.336, 69
Then that insinuating fire,....................135. H.336, 103
From th' embers, then the kitlings eyne,......136. H.336, 146
Farre more then night bewearied..............136. H.336, 152
Free by your fate, then Fortunes mightinesse,..141. H.359, 4
Then beauty turn'd to sowernesse...............143. H.367, 2
(Rather than fail) to steal from thence old shoes:
143. H.368, 2
To thee, then unto any one:...................147. H.377, 70
Do'st rather poure forth, then allow..........148. H.377, 82
Is more in thee, then in her dust,............148. H.377, 104
A thousand times, more sweare, then say,.....149. H.377, 132
He'l turn a Papist, rancker then before.........151. H.385, 6
When one hole wasts more then he gets by Nine..154. H.400, 4
Mon. Bad are the times. Sil. And wors then they are we.
159. H.421, 1
With griefe; seemes longer then a yeare.......162. H.431, 4
Soft then the finest Lemster Ore...............165. H.443, 28
Then to enthrall,............................172. H.458, 10
Jove prospers my meat, more then his...........173. H.461, 4
But more's sent in, then was serv'd out.........178. H.476, 9
More honour had, then this same Flie;.........186. H.497, 17
Lesse is here, then in my heart................186. H.500, 4
For Coronation, then Your onely Praise.........188. H.506, 12
And no one mischief greater then your frown,..188. H.506, 13
Far lesse in number, then our foule dayes are.....189. H.513, 2
Lesse for to catch a sheep, then me............193. H.521, 46
Then to sow Discord 'mongst the Enemies.......196. H.535, 2
Tis worse then barbarous cruelty to show.......199. H.550, 1
Then but to breath, and every one gave way:....200. H.551, 4
Who is his Butcher more then Guardian.........201. H.557, 16
And knit in knots far more then I..............202. H.560, 11
Dotes less on Nature, then on Art.............202. H.560, 18
In Cream she bathes her thighs (more soft then silk)
203. H.561, 3

More sweet, then Storax from the hallowed fire:..205. H.575, 8
There yet remaines to know, then thou can'st see
206. H.575, 54
Then my poore heart,..........................210. H.591, 8
Nothing can be more loathsome, then to see....211. H.597, 1
Then but to read this in my Booke:............214. H.611, 2
Ill us'd, then Babes left fatherless............218. H.626, 15
'Twas better there to toyle, then prove..........219. H.628, 5
The Ravens yeares, go hence more Ripe then old.
222. H.633, 63
Then these, no feares more on your Fancies fall,.222. H.634, 14
Flies no thought higher then a fleece:..........229. H.662, 12
Be she witty, more then wise;..................232. H.665, 3
And thus lesse last, then live our Day...........233. H.670, 31
Kings ought to be more lov'd, then fear'd........234. H.672, 2
Lesse by their own jemms, then those beams of thine.
234. H.673, 18
Then ever, dearest Silvia, yet..................240. H.705, 7
Then a mans frequent Fame, spoke out with praise.
241. H.710, 2
Then to cast off all bashfulnesse...............241. H.712, 2
More then for peevish pining sicknesses.........245. H.723, 12
More pleasing too, then ever was...............251. H.740, 11
Then to want the Wake next Yeare...............255. H.761, 24
Then Roman Sylla powr'd out at his feast.......262. H.783, 6
And for no less then Aromatick Wine...........262. H.783, 9
More curst for singing out of tune then he.....266. H.799, 4
Rather then I once wo'd see,...................266. H.803, 4
It is no other then the Bed....................269. H.815, 3
More rich then Cleopatra's Tombe..............269. H.817, 4
By their wise Counsell, then they be by Warre...271. H.825, 2
Tap (better known then trusted) as we heare....272. H.829, 1
And not unlikely; rather too then fail,..........272. H.829, 3
Less then Apollo, that ursurp'st such Three?....276. H.851, 6
Then the last part of night, and first of day.....278. H.858, 2
Our Crosses are no other then the rods,..........278. H.862, 1
No otherwise, then if he would..................279. H.863, 7
'Tis I am wild, and more then haires...........282. H.881, 5
Lesse set for them, then spred for me...........282. H.881, 10
Then for to murder friendship, by dispute.......287. H.901, 6
Our trust farre more then ten eare-witnesses....287. H.904, 2
And no less prais'd, then spread throughout the world.
288. H.907, 6
Farre faster then the first can wither..........289. H.912, 8
Be lesse anothers Laurell, then thy praise.....297. H.947, 14
More from the sweet then sower things.........298. H.951, 2
Thee lesse to taste, then to drink up their spring;
299. H.956, 2
And no lesse prais'd, then of the maides admir'd.
299. H.956, 10
Then the dead Corps, or carkase of the Wine...301. H.964, 2
In an expansion no less large, then high;........301. H.966, 4
But when all's hush't, Case then a fish more mute,
303. H.975, 7
Then these kine, which I milke here...........305. H.984, 17
To keepe a Citie, then to winne a Towne.......307. H.989, 2
W'ave more to beare our charge, then way to go?.308. H.995, 2
The Genius wastefull, more then free:..........310. H.1004, 2
More then the teats of Discipline:..............310. H.1004, 6
Then Night now gone, and yet not spring the Day.
319. H.1046, 2
Then to thy house be Burdensome;............321. H.1056, 14
The truth of Travails lesse in bookes then Thee..330. H.1100, 18
'Tis flatterie spends a King, more then his foes..331. H.1105, 2
And as our bad, more then our good Works are:
339. N.1, 2
God n'ere afflicts us more then our desert,........341. N.10, 1
Sometimes He strikes us more then flesh can beare;
341. N.10, 3
But yet still lesse then Grace can suffer here.....341. N.10, 4
Full, and fild-full, then when full-fild before.......341. N.15, 6
And more for love, then pittie....................345. N.33, 29
To figure to us, nothing more then this,..........345. N.34, 3
And that number more then true;................348. N.41, 27
A sin, then fall to weeping when 'tis done.........349. N.43, 6
Then for to shed some teares....................352. N.53, 3
Better he starv'd, then but to tast one crumme...355. N.65, 10
To seek of God more then we well can find,......356. N.70, 1
The Cure was worse then the Disease...........360. N.83, 30
Then a Caroll, for to sing.......................364. N.96, 2
To make things sweet. Chor. Yet all less sweet then He.
365. N.97, 10
Ye must not be more pitifull then wise;........365. N.97, 16
Then so t'abound,..............................368. N.104, 7
He teares and tugs us, then he did before;......372. N.116, 2
For, rather then one drop shall fall..............377. N.129, 7
To give us more then Hope can fix upon.......378. N.135, 2
Then all the songs of sinners are...............379. N.145, 2
Then prayers repel'd, (sayes Cassiodore).........383. N.170, 2
No other, then Christs full Affection............383. N.174, 2
Nearer to that place, then to other some:.......385. N.186, 2
God is more here, then in another place,.........387. N.197, 1
With God, then one, that never sin'd 'gainst Him.
388. N.205, 2
More worth, then Heav'ns Eternitie............388. N.206, 4
Who hath more suffer'd by us farre, then for us..388. N.209, 2
I shall lesse swoone, then die for feare.........393. N.232, 10

More stripes, then God layes on the sufferer.....393. N.235, 2
God still rewards us more then our desert:......394. N.242, 1
Then ever, yet, the like was done before.........395. N.244, 4
To Hell I'd rather run, then I..................395. N.245, 5
Lesse for to tast, then for to shew,............400. N.266, 13
Then full affection, enter here.................402. N.269, 9
Richer then that faire pretious virtuos horne....406. A.1, 103
Bondage more Loued then Lybertye..............408. A.2, 64
Vrging diuorcement (worse then death to theis)....410. A.3, 9
Noe otherwise then as those former two..........410. A.3, 14
I've more to beare my Chardge, then way to goe,
411. A.3, 54
In speach, in Picture; noe otherwise then when..411. A.3, 61
Then which, thy self ne'er wafted sweeter over...416. A.8, 10
What more than these can Tombs or Tomb-stones Pay?
419. A.10, 5
Owes more to vertue then too Fate........422. ins. H.106, 92b
Not more, milde nymph, then they would have you doe;
431. ins. H.283, 60r
For that would prove more Heresy then fault
433. ins. H.283, 140h
— — — — — — — — — — — —, ...434. var. H.293, 12b
Then Jove and Chaos them before......437. var. H.336, 136
Thank Love and they'l thank you for't. Adieu.....70. H.180, 8
If not requite, yet thank ye all...............123. H.306, 12
For to thanke you (Noble Sir)..................182. H.489, 11
You say you'l kiss me, and I thanke you for it:
210. H.588, 1
Thanked (God and good friends be thankt for it)..123. H.306, 8
God be thank'd for those, and these:.............363. N.93, 4
Thankful And sung their thankfull Hymnes: 'tis sin,
68. H.178, 11
Thankfull to you, or friends, for me.............111. H.280, 12
A thankfull heart;...............................351. N.47, 54
God make me thankfull still for it.............376. N.124, 4
Thankfulness As men do wane in thankfulnesse...358. N.76, 2
Thank-offering Somwhat for my Thank-Offering..402. N.270, 4
Thanks But with a kisse, or thanks, doe pay......71. H.182, 21
Thanks to the gen'rous Vine;..................72. H.185, 27
Offer'd up, with thanks to thee................129. H.325, 6
And my full thanks take for it.................223. H.638, 14
Paying but common thanks for it...............321. H.1056, 6
I will give them thanks for it.................329. H.1096, 4
I'le call, and cry out, Thanks to Thee..........400. N.267, 5
Least thankes to Nature, most to Art.....421. ins. H.106, 26b
Thanksgiving Thanksgiving is a burden, and a paine;
292. H.923, 3
Thanksgiving for a former, doth invite..........348. N.42, 1
Thare See There
— — — — — — — — — — — —, ...422. var. H.106, 70
Th'are (Partial List)
Of largeness, when th'are nothing so:........118. H.291, 10
Kings though th'are hated, will be fear'd.......165. H.443, 18
Teares, though th'are here below the sinners brine,
226. H.645, 1
The more th'are drawn, the lesse thy wil grow dry.
273. H.831, 2
Th'art Pay when th'art honest; let me have some hope.
83. H.206, 4
But since th'art slaine; and in thy fall,..........89. H.219, 7
Th'art hence removing, (like a Shepherds Tent)..188. H.507, 1
Th'ast Th'ast dar'd too farre; but Furie now forbeare
82. H.204, 1
Then say, if one th'ast seene more fine..........90. H.223a, 5
Tha'st got a place here (standing candidate)....305. H.983, 2
That (Partial List)
Or to a Girle (that keeps the Neat)................6. H.2, 13
That man's unwise will search for Ill,............6. H.2, 25
May every Ill, that bites, or smarts,...............6. H 5, 3
Thinke that of All, that I have writ, the worst:......7. H.6, 2
And still do'st this, and that verse, reprehend:......7. H.6, 4
But when that men have both well drunke, and fed,..7. H.8, 3
But so, as that her self should be..................8. H.11, 9
He Acts the Crime, that gives it Cherishing........10. H.17, 2
Not that I thinke, that any Dart,.................10. H.20, 4
A teare at all for that:..........................12. H.23, 6
Work that to life, and let me ever dwell..........14. H.35, 13
But that I heard thy sweet breath say,............20. H.56, 5
Better tis that one shu'd fall,....................21. H.61, 7
But 'tis sweetness that doth please................22. H.65, 3
Next, how I love thee, that my griefe must tell,....23. H.72, 3
Then to that twenty, adde an hundred more:......24. H.74, 4
Nor can we that a ruine call,.....................25. H 76, 3
Ride no with all white Omens; so, that where....25. H.77, 11
Who's that (said I) beats there,..................26. H.81, 5
And struck me that it went.......................27. H.81, 31
Little I love; but if that he......................28. H.85, 5
Give me that man, that dares bestride............30. H.90, 1
Twilight is yet, till that her Lawnes give way:..34. H.104, 5
With that Heav'n gave thee with a warie hand,..35.-H.106, 23
But that which most makes sweet thy country life,
35. H.106, 31
Nor is it, that thou keep'st this stricter size....37. H.106, 117
As that the Congelation will.....................40. H.115, 15
But that his teares forbad the rest..............42. H.119, 12
Then know, that Nature bids thee goe, not I.....46. H.128, 42
And when, wise Artist, that thou hast,..........48. H.133, 14

With all **that** can be, this heaven grac't;........48. H.133, 15
By me, were you for **that** unchast?...........49. H.136, 27
Know, I have pray'd to Furie, **that** some wind....49. H.138, 7
For **that**, Matrons say, a measure..............55. H.149, 79
Since **that** Love and Night bid enter............56. H.149, 100
If thou wilt say, **that** I shall live with thee;......60. H.156, 3
And **that** is Death, the end of Woe...............60. H.157, 6
And it may chance **that** Love may turn,........61. H.159, 18
Nor be you proud, **that** you can see............61. H.160, 3
I shall be heal'd, if **that** my King but touch....62. H.161, 14
And I dare sweare, **that** I am gray?............63. H.164, 2
I beg of Love, **that** ever I.....................64. H.169, 11
Before **that** we have left to dreame:............69. H.178, 48
That done, the harder Fates deny'd............69. H.180, 3
That, **that** he took, and **that** was all.............71. H.182, 26
He knowes not Love, **that** hath not this truth proved,
73. H.186, 11
Let them prattle how **that** I....................82. H.203, 5
Mirt. And **that** his birth sho'd be more singular, 86. H.213, 19
Yet lost, ere **that** chast flesh and blood.........88. H.216, 8
Whether **that** you be sweet or no?.............112. H.282, 2
What's **that** we see from far? the spring of Day..112. H.283, 1
While **that** others doe divine;..................113. H.283, 47
Crept to **that**, and came to this.................120. H.297, 6
Phoebus! when **that** I a Verse,................122. H.303, 1
Tune my words, **that** they may fall,............122. H.303, 3
Or **that** this Yonker keeps so strict a Lent,.......122. H.305, 3
Sneape has a face so brittle, **that** it breaks......124. H.311, 1
Ye wrong the Threshold-god, **that** keeps peace here:
124. H.313, 4
You say, you love me; **that** I thus must prove;..126. H.317, 1
If **that** you lye, then I will sweare you love.....126. H.317, 2
So old she was, **that** none co'd tell her yeares...129. H.326, 6
That figure discontent;.......................131. H.330, 8
She **that** will weare thy teares, wo'd weare thine eyes.
131. H.330, 15
No, no, **that** selfe same heart, **that** vow,......134. H.336, 70
Give me the Daphne, **that** the world may know it, 143. H.365, 7
She ne'r remembers **that** she was a maide.......149. H.379, 2
Helpe me so, **that** I my shield,..............151. H.386, 3
Pievish doth boast, **that** he's the very first......156. H.410, 1
Those maids **that** never vary;..................160. H.422, 6
And shall dispaire, **that** any art................164. H.442, 8
So neatly sunck, as **that** no proof..............167. H.443, 103
Why! yet to shew **that** thou art just,..........169. H.446, 11
These Springs were Maidens once **that** lov'd,....180. H.478, 1
Let me feed full, till **that** I fart, sayes Jill.......186. H.498, 8
What Mad-man's he, **that** when it sparkles so,..187. H.502, 5
And walk thou must the way **that** others went:..188. H.507, 2
So **that** as either shall expresse................192. H.521, 23
That know'st, my Julia, **that** it is thy turne.....196. H.539, 1
After **that**, in the mould.......................197. H.540, 3
A Prince I'de be, **that** I might Thee preferre....202. H.557, 29
Only, if one prove addled, **that** he eates.........204. H.568, 3
For so decreeing, **that** thy clothes expence......210. H.590, 3
As **that** the Messes ne'r o'r-laid the Lord:......210. H.590, 6
Let's live with **that** smal pittance that we have; 213. H.607, 1
How Herrick beggs, if **that** he can—............214. H.611, 3
This is the height of Justice, **that** to doe.........214. H.614, 1
The turmoiles they endure **that** love............219. H.628, 6
'Tis fit **that** Night, the Paire,.................220. H.633, 16
O happy life! if **that** their good................231. H.662, 70
Not knowing This, **that** Jove decrees............233. H.670, 5
'Tis not ev'ry day, **that** I....................242. H.714, 1
Ch. What's thy request? Ph. **That** since she's now beneath
248. H.730, 15
Ch. And is **that** all? I'm gone. Ph. By love I pray thee,
248. H.730, 17
Since **that** I know, 'mong all the rest..........250. H.739, 3
That done, our smooth-pac't Poems all shall be..254. H.756, 15
Nor art thou lesse esteem'd, **that** I have plac'd 256. H.763, 1
The loss of **that** we call a Maydenhead?........262. H.781, 14
Seest thou **that** Cloud that rides in State........269. H.815, 1
As smooth, and nak't, as she **that** was..........271. H.824, 7
Praise they **that** will Times past, I joy to see....292. H.927, 1
He toucht me so, as **that** I burn,..............295. H.942, 11
Grubs loves his Wife and Children, while **that** they
325. H.1077, 1
So **that** with bold truth, thou canst now relate..330. H.1100, 7
Night hath no wings, to him **that** cannot sleep;..358. N.77, 1
Slowly her chariot drives, as if **that** she..........358. N.77, 3
Bring'st, in Thy Blood, a Balm, **that** shall......366. N.98, 23
To pay Thee **that** I owe, since what I see......368. N.103, 3
But **that**, or this,............................369. N.104, 16
Implies or Essence, or the He **that** Is........385. N.187, 2
Bowing my lips vnto y^t^ stately root.............406. A.1, 111
I give thee this **that** shall withstande...........407. A.2, 10
With holye fier least **that** it dye...............407. A.2, 24
Not soe, but **that** some Relique In my Harte....412. A.3, 96

That's **That's** my Julia's breast; where dwels....40. H.115, 13
A way **that's** best..............................43. H.123, 23
Blast these-like actions, or a thing **that's** worse; 79. H.197, 84
Goes to the Feast **that's** now provided........93. H.223, 142
A heart **that's** free,..........................100. H.246, 13
In every thing **that's** sweet, she is..............106. H.263, 6
Which you must grant; **that's** entrance; with..116. H.283, 153
With the Red-capt worme, **that's** shut......... 120. H.293, 39
To make but One (and **that's** thy selfe) admir'd. 121. H.301, 6
The yeare (your cares) **that's** fled and gon......127. H.319, 44
List of references:...........128. H.323, 5; 143. H.365, 12; 148. H.377, 86; 151. H.386, 5; 158. H.420, 9; 162. H.431, 2; 162. H.431, 3; 168. H.444, 1; 189. H.511, 2; 199. H.546, 4; 201. H.557, 22; 219. H.628, 11; 223. H.638, 2; 223. H.638, 15; 229. H.659, 1; 229. H.659, 2; 229. H.659, 6; 229. H.659, 7; 229. H.659, 10; 231. H.662, 57; 243. H.716, 25; 247. H.727, 12; 259. H.771, 5; 263. H.784, 18; 276. H.851, 8; 292. H.926, 1; 310. H.1003, 2; 313. H.1020, 7; 324. H.1068, 20; 339. N.2, 4; 367. N.98, 29; 391. N.228, 24; 395. N.247, 2; 396. N.253, 1; 397. N.256, 1; 401. N.268, 20; 405. A.1, 55; 426. ins. H.197, 29a; 445. var. H.730, 17

Th'ave See **Have**
Nay, now I think **th'ave** made his grave........156. H.412, 15
Fates revolve no Flax **th'ave** spun..............224. H.639, 4
— — — — — — — — —,..............441. var. H.465, 21

Thaw To melt this snow, and **thaw** this ice;........8. H.13, 4

Thawed Then to be **thaw'd**, or heated so...........8. H.13, 8
Thaw'd are the snowes, and now the lusty Spring 224. H.642, 3

Th'board See **Board**

The (Partial List)
Over **the** which a State was drawne...............8. H.11, 5
So, that **the** more I look, **the** more I prove,........10. H.16, 5
To take her by **the** either hand:..............37. H.106, 96
Nor car'st which comes **the** first, **the** foule or faire;
37. H.106, 97
Growes still **the** stronger, strongly vext.........37. H.106, 100
Rouze Anacreon from **the** dead;.................39. H.111, 9
The which was made a happy Bride,............41. H.116, 5
And **the** evil deads, **the** which..................55. H.149, 89
Out of **the** which, **the** creame of light,............74. H.190, 9
Why are Those Looks, Those Looks **the** which have been
77. H.197, 27
Sho'd I a jot **the** better see?....................97. H.235, 4
And caught'st thy selfe **the** more by twenty fold: 97. H.236, 2
Bestroaking Fate **the** while....................113. H.283, 29
Of Ash-heapes, in **the** which ye use............127. H.319, 21
That keepes his own strong guard, in **the** despight
128. H.323, 9
Shall smile and smell **the** better by thy beads...143. H.370, 2
To be **the** nearer Relative:...................147. H.377, 40
So draw, and paint, as none may do **the** like,....150. H.384, 5
Since for thy full deserts (with all **the** rest.....152. H.392, 1
I know ye do; and that's **the** why,.............158. H.420, 9
The which **the** Elves make to excite.........167. H.443, 114
In **the** dead of dampish night...................177. H.473, 6
All know a Fellon eate **the** Tenth away.........180. H.480, 2
And having danc't ('bove all **the** best)........192. H.521, 33
This begets **the** more delight,.................194. H.527, 6
With daily Fyers: **The** last, neglect of Wine:..197. H.539, 10
The longer here..............................198. H.544, 24
Brave Kinsman, markt out with **the** whiter stone: 199. H.545, 8
And perish at **the** last.......................211. H.596, 16
Left (of **the** large heart, and long hand)........218. H.626, 10
I rather thinke (though they may speake **the** worst)
219. H.630, 3
Say, who's **the** worst, th' exactor, or **the** whore? 220. H.631, 4
This night, and more for **the** wonder,...........225. H.643, 21
And, in **the** midst, to grace it more, was set....227. H.652, 9
The morrowes life too late is. Live to-day.....228. H.655, 2
Who all **the** day themselves doe please,.........231. H.662, 72
The how, where, when, I question not..........236. H.681, 2
Some hung **the** head, while some did bring......237. H.686, 5
That stroke most fear'd is, which is struck **the** last.
237. H.688, 2
And sooner play, **the** sooner win................243. H.716, 24
From her moysture take **the** like:...............244. H.719, 4
The more my rurall privacie:..................246. H.724, 28
Our hope of one for **the** other..................247. H.727, 6
By so much, vertue is **the** lesse,................254. H.754, 1
To make my lodging **the** sweeter;..............256. H.762, 3
Nor Cato **the** severe..........................259. H.772, 6
This not **the** least is, which belongs to Kings.....260. H.774, 2
The listning to my numbers.....................260. H.777, 4
Is not by marriage quencht, but flames **the** higher.
262. H.781, 16
The like not Heliogabalus did eat:.............262. H.783, 4
The more th'are drawn, **the** lesse they wil grow dry.
273. H.831, 2
Mine eyes must wooe you; (though I sigh **the** while)
274. H.837, 7
Vnto **the** Idoll of **y^e^** work divine................406. A.1, 109
T'was braue, t'was braue could we command **y^e^** hand
413. A.4, 6
And lays it gently on **y^e^** Pyle,...................413. A.4, 28

Th'ears See **Ears**

Theatre Or flash about the spacious **Theater**.....150. H.382, 10
Of your own selfe, a Publick **Theater**............187. H.506, 2
Behold them in a spacious **Theater**............206. H.575, 48
Entred the circumspacious **Theater**;............301. H.962, 2
Mixt in that watrie **Theater**;.....................339. N.3, 4
The spacious field have for Thy **Theater**.......398. N.263, 18

Thee (Partial List)
But cry **thee** Mercy: Exercise thy nailes.........66. H.173, 5
I'le strike **thee** such a nimble Ayre,..........243. H.716, 32

Thee-ward To thee-ward dy'd i'th'embers, and no fire
78. H.197, 36
Thee-wards — — — — — — — —, ...426. var. H.197, 36
Th'effect See Effect
Theft Adopted some; none got by theft...........236. H.681, 4
Thefts Night hides our thefts; all faults then pardon'd be:
209. H.586, 1
Their (Partial List)
Beat with their num'rous feet, which by.......165. H.443, 23
Theme As well as spare: still conning o'r this Theame,
38. H.106, 131
Themes Teares and terrors are our theames......376. N.128, 3
Themilis When Themilis his pastime makes,.....192. H.521, 26
Themselves See Selves
That we may praise Them, or themselves prize You.
173. H.459, 12
Who all the day themselves doe please,..........231. H.662, 72
Where some had hang'd themselves for love,....278. H.863, 3
Farc't with the food, that may themselves suffice.
310. H.1005, 4
Studies themselves will languish and decay,.....316. H.1033, 1
Which ope themselves to shewe an holy shrine....404. A.1, 26
Bite of themselves to scape away.........440. ins. H.443, 56b
Then (Partial List)
Stay then at home, and doe not goe...............6. H.2, 19
On with thy fortunes then, what e're they be;......6. H.3, 7
Then sweetest Silvia, let's no longer stay;..........8. H.10, 5
That done, then wind me in that very sheet......9. H.14, 10
Then lastly, let some weekly-strewings be........9. H.14, 15
Then shall my Ghost not walk about, but keep....9. H.14, 17
Then think how wrapt was I to see.............14. H.34, 5
Patient I was: Love pitifull grew then,...........16. H.40, 5
Then melted down, there let me lye..............23. H.68, 5
Then (lastly) July comes, and she...............23. H.70, 7
Then to that twenty, adde an hundred more:......24. H.74, 4
Then laughing loud, he flew.....................27. H.81, 33
Then for an easie fansie; place..................39. H.108, 9
Then say, I've sent one more.....................43. H.123, 13
With weather foule, then faire againe............47. H.133, 13
Then in a Vision I did see.......................51. H.142, 5
Let but That Mighty Cesar speak, and then,....52. H.146, 13
Then away; come, Hymen guide.................53. H.149, 19
O enter then! but see ye shun...............57. H.149, 141
Be ye to the Barn then born,...................58. H.149, 169
When she lyes with Jove, then she..............59. H.155, 10
Ah! then too late, close in your chamber keeping, 63. H.164, 12
If then, (my Lord) to sanctifie my Muse........64. H.168, 7
Then while time serves, and we are but decaying; 69. H.178, 69
Then, even then, I will bequeath my heart........73. H.186, 14
Then, Ah! Then, where is your grace,...........74. H.189, 5
Then be not coy, but use your time;..........84. H.208, 13
'Twas no more you then, but a Cherubin.........95. H.228, 4
Now an Ague, then a Fever,.....................103. H.253, 9
Off then with grave clothes; put fresh colours on;
105. H.259, 9
Dwell, then in lothed Devonshire..............111. H.278, 8
Glide by the banks of Virgins then, and passe..113. H.283, 41
That was too coorse; but then forthwith.......119. H.293, 31
First you, then you, and both for white successe. 124. H.313, 2
Then as ye sit about your embers,.............127. H.319, 37
'Tis now farre off, and then tis nere;...........130. H.329, 14
Ah then consider! What all this implies;......131. H.330, 14
Why then, since life to us is short,...........133. H.336, 31
Well then, on what Seas we are tost,...........134. H.336, 57
Keepe it till then; and now my Spouse,.........175. H.465, 73
Come Virgins then, and see...................184. H.493, 9
Then cause we Horace to be read,.............198. H.544, 13
The Watch once downe, all motions then do cease;
202. H.558, 3
Then unto Dancing forth the learned Round....206. H.575, 19
Of Hero, and Leander; then Ile bring..........206. H.575, 26
To Linus, then to Pindar; and that done,......206. H.575, 31
Then stately Virgil, witty Ovid, by...........206. H.575, 39
Then soft Catullus, sharp-fang'd Martial,......206. H.575, 43
As now a Satyr, then a Swan;.................215. H.616, 17
A Bull but then; and now a man...............215. H.616, 18
I awoke, and then I knew......................219. H.628, 7
Give me then an Ant to eate;..................223. H.638, 5
When I touch, I then begin....................253. H.750, 8
If ill, then Kings, not Souldiers beare the blame. 260. H 774, 4
Then, then (me thinks) how sweetly flowes.....261. H.779, 2
If this can be, say then, what need............297. H.948, 13
Then Biancha, I am gone......................307. H.991, 4
If Tythe-pigs faile, then will he shift the scean, 325. H.1076, 3
First, Fear and Shame without, then Guilt within. 341. N.11, 2
What need there then be of a reckning day:.....343. N.27, 2
O then! for mercies sake, behold...............344. N.29, 5
Come then, come then, and let us bring........368. N.102, 19
What need I then to feare at all,...............371. N.114, 5
O then, how restlesse do's she stray!............393. N.233, 2
God is then said for to descend, when He......395. N.244, 1
Then lowly yet most lovely stand the feete,.......406. A.1, 91
Thence But every Line, and Limb diffused thence, 10. H.16, 3
And taking thence from each his flame;.........31. H.92, 7
But when he felt he suckt from thence..........71. H.182, 7
And reverently departeth thence,.............93. H 223, 139
Gardens thence produce and Meads:..........108. H.266, 14
Next to the Altar humbly kneele, and thence,..128. H.320, 5
(Rather than fail) to steal from thence old shoes:
143. H.368, 2
For as he breath'd, the People swore from thence
200. H.551, 5
Which, done; and thence remov'd the light,......165. H.443, 7
Discovering from thence.......................193. H.524, 3
When thence ye see my reverend Ghost to rise,..222. H.634, 3
Will whirle about, and blow them thence at last. 226. H.650, 4
To bring from thence the scorched Clove.......229. H.662, 8
No return from thence we have...............238. H.691, 6
All rich spices thence will flow..................244. H.719, 6
Command the Roofe great Genius, and from thence
245. H.723, 1
Drive thence what ere encumbers,..............260. H.777, 3
May baite his hooke, with maggots taken thence 282. H 879, 4
But, like full clouds, may they from thence....291. H.919, 7
And thence return, (short prayers seyd)........291. H.919, 15
Since thence................................308. H.993, 16
From thence, to everlasting woe:...............358. N.78, 8
God, who's in Heav'n, will hear from thence;..381. N.160, 1
As when we sin; God, the great Chymist, thence 386. N.196, 3
Threescore or fourescore spring up thence for one 388. N.208, 4
And thence proceed, to act Thy Passion.......399. N.263, 29
There See Thare
There with the Reed, thou mayst expresse.........5. H.2, 7
There on a Hillock thou mayst sing...............5. H.2, 11
There, there, (perhaps) such Lines as These......6. H.2, 15
By no one tongue, there censured.................6. H.2, 24
Follow me weeping to my Turfe, and there.......9. H.14, 13
Is there no way to beget.......................10. H.19, 7
And dropping here, and there:...................10. H 20, 3
No Dislike there is in love:.....................11. H.21, 2
Then holding up (there) such religious Things,..11. H.22, 5
(All parts there made one prisoner.)............16. H.41, 17
Such fleeting pleasures there I took,.............17. H.41, 20
They doe grow? I answer, There...............19. H.53, 4
For my Embalming (Sweetest) there will be......20. H.55, 9
The warmth and sweetnes had me there..........20. H.56, 3
To him that has, there shall be added more;......22. H.64, 3
Then melted down, there let me lye..............23. H.68, 5
Whether in part 'tis here or there...............24. H.73, 5
There is an Act that will more fully please:......24. H.74, 10
To part her lips, and shew'd them there..........24. H.75, 7
Your Standard's up, we fix a Conquest there......25. H.77, 12
And snugging there, they seem'd to lye..........25. H.78, 3
Who's that (said I) beats there,.................26. H.81, 5
An erring Lace, which here and there.............28. H.83, 5
There playes the Saphire with the Chrysolite......30. H.88, 10
Sitt'st, and beleev'st that there be seas,..........36. H.106, 70
And beleeve there be such things:..............36. H.106, 86
Thy pious wishes are, (though thou not there)..37. H.106, 91
There to disport your selves with golden measure:
38. H.106, 139
And as there is one Love, one Faith, one Troth,..38. H.106, 143
Are twigs of Birch, and willow, growing there:..39. H.110, 2
Let there be Patrons; Patrons like to thee,......41. H.117, 1
There weeping sup'rabundantly.................42. H.119, 4
There, there present..........................43. H.123, 10
That Houre-glasse, which there ye see..........44. H.127, 1
But while he, perking, there did prie............46. H.130, 7
Make me a heaven; and make me there...........47. H.133, 1
Next, place me Zones, and Tropicks there;......47. H.133, 7
To dance and play in: (Trust me) there........49. H.136, 22
To be admitted there..........................54. H.149, 38
There was hidden by the Witch................55. H.149, 90
We'll weary all the Fables there................59. H.152, 12
There I smell the Phenix nest:.................59. H.155, 2
Altar of Incense, I smell there.................59. H.155, 4
There, where no language ever yet was known....60. H.156, 6
What is become of me: there I.................60. H.159, 5
To finde Bethesda, and an Angel there,..........61. H.161, 3
Which, circumvolving gently, there.............64. H.169, 3
One[1] fancie more! but if there be................64. H.169, 9
Which erring here, and wandring there,..........66. H.175, 3
And all confus'd, I there did lie...............67. H.175, 17
To safe-guard Man from wrongs, there nothing must
67. H.177, 1
Are circumfused there..........................69. H.179, 4
I thought I might there take a taste,...........71. H.182, 17
Look in Prig's purse, the chev'rell there tells you 71. H.183, 3
Say, if there be 'mongst many jems here; one....76. H.194, 3
But to forsake thee ever, co'd there be..........78. H.197, 45
And ride the Sun-beams. Can there be a thing..78. H.197, 53
Then there is hope that you may see............79. H.198, 11
I'm sure to find ye there.......................83. H.207, 8
Look in his Brine-tub, and you shall find there..89. H.221, 3
There is, that to the Chappel leads:............90. H.223, 2
His Idol-Cricket there is set:..................90. H.223, 12
There stands his Idol-Beetle-flie:................90. H.223, 14
Who squeaks to all the commers there,.........91. H.223, 40
The Holy-water there is put:...................91. H.223, 45
There off'ring up the Holy-Grist:...............91. H.223, 51
There ush'ring Vergers, here likewise,.........92. H.223, 105
We knew 'twas Flesh and Blood, that there sate mute.
95. H.228, 2
'Mongst Roses, I there Cupid found:............96. H.229, 2

Sin never slew a soule, unlesse there went.......389. N.217, 1
Not after one sort, there excruciate all:........391. N.227, 2
To come to Thee, if Christ not there!.........395. N.245, 2
'Tis never read there (as the Fathers say)......396. N.249, 5
But where sin swells, there let Thy grace abound.
398. N.261, 6
The Crosse shall be Thy Stage; and Thou shalt there
398. N.263, 17
And, if I see Thee posted there,................399. N.265, 7
And as I kisse, I'le here and there............402. N.269, 12
And live in Hell, if that my Christ stayes there...403. N.271, 8
At whose faire topp to please the sight there growes
405. A.1, 35
Aboue the entrance there is written this..........405. A.1, 73
Through mid'st thereof a christall stream there flowes
406. A.1, 75
Ther must bee plac'd, for season'd feares........408. A.2, 40
Hee may (a prisoner) ther discrye............408. A.2, 63
And now yf ther A man bee founde.............409. A.2, 103
Ther was not Varnish (only) in my loue......412. A.3, 80
Love lyes a bleeding here, Evadne there.........415. A.7, 11
Here's a mad lover, there that high designe......415. A.7, 13
And Hymen call'd to bless the Rites. Cha. Stop there.
416. A.8, 20
Where, drest with garlands, there they walk the ground,
417. A.8, 29
And there do punish, and are punishèd...........417. A.8, 34
But there to live, where Love shall last for ever...417. A.8, 38
There ever lived such a one...................418. A.9, 30
— — — — — — — — — — —,............437. var. H.336, 125
— — — — — — — — — — —,............439. var. H.443, 36
His hereby broth, and there close by......439. ins. H.443, 451
Of gold and sylver there is spread,......440. ins. H.443, 45w
— — — — — — — — — — —,............449. var. A.3, 43
— — — — — — — — — — —,............452. var. H.443, 75
— — — — — — — — — — —,............453. ins. H.283, 20j

Thereby A Cuffe neglectfull, and thereby..........28. H.83, 7
May think, thereby,..........................95. H.227, 20
What saves the master of the House thereby?...118. H.292, 3
He said, because he got his wealth thereby.....332. H.1114, 4
Looks on the filth, but is not soil'd thereby;....371. N.113, 6
To make them, thereby, mindfull of their own...384. N.178, 3
Like fier-drakes, yett did'st mee no harme therby.
410. A.3, 28

Therefore Gryll will not therefore say a Grace for it.
48. H.135, 4
Therefore now Ile love no more,...............209. H.585, 7
Henceforth therefore I will be.................219. H.628, 9
Forbeare therefore,..........................314. H.1024, 21
It will not be: And, therefore, now,............357. N.72, 15
Alas! I cannot pay a jot; therefore............368. N.103, 7

Therein Now 'tis so full, that when therein I look, 99. H.245, 3
Who therein wo'd not consume.................113. H.283, 27
To live therein for ever: Frie................115. H.283, 137
Either with old, or plant therein new thorne:...259. H.771, 6
Prosper thy Basket, and therein thy Dow.......269. H.818, 4
But yet no end of those therein or me:.........313. H.1019, 2
But never those that persevere therein...........344. N.32, 2
A little Butterie, and therein..................350. N.47, 19
Therein some beames of His Divinitie:.........389. N.214, 4
(Thy fore-head) lett therin bee sign'd..........407. A.2, 33

There'll And for the Bride-Cake ther'l be Spice..267. H.805, 6

Thereof One part thereof left still unfinished:....384. N.178, 2
Through mid'st thereof a christall stream there flowes
406. A.1, 75

Thereon And write thereon, This, Reader, know,..61. H.159, 30
If so, how much more shall I dote thereon,.......139. H.347, 3
Want is a softer Wax, that takes thereon,........288. H.905, 1
And if I chance to wake, and rise thereon,.....392. N.230, 21
gently thereon,..........................430. ins. H.283, 20e

There's Ther's still more cause, why I the more should love.
10. H.16, 6
Twixt Kings and Subjects ther's this mighty odds, 12. H.25, 1
There's the Land, or Cherry-Ile:.................20. H.53, 6
Yet there's a way found (if thou please)........34. H.103, 13
These may coole; but there's a Zone............40. H.115, 11
For each Ringlet there's a snare.................52. H.147, 4
There's not a budding Boy, or Girle, this day,..69. H.178, 43
There's paine in parting; and a kind of hell,......73. H.186, 7
Poore of the Parish, (if there's any)............92. H.223, 90
And since the last is dead, there's hope,........93. H.223, 111
There's that, which drowns all care, stout Beere;
101. H.250, 37
The fat; breathe thou, and there's the rich perfume.
102. H.251, 4
No lust theres like to Poetry.................135. H.336, 112
Ther's in love, no bitterness..................138. H.346, 10
Ther's no vice now, but has his president.........139. H.352, 2
No, know (Blest Maide) when there's not one..146. H.376, 7
But of his gettings there's but little sign;......154. H.400, 3
Their silv'rie Spheres, ther's none may doubt,...178. H.476, 8
And 'gainst your chast behaviour there's no Plea,
189. H.511, 3
Though free she be, ther's something yet.......191. H.520, 3
There's no Carousing..........................197. H.540, 8
Since Ghost ther's none to affright thee.......217. H.619, 10
From whence there's never a return..............233. H.670, 39
In no one Satyre there's a mite of salt.........238. H.692, 2
But when he sings a Psalme, ther's none can be..266. H.799, 3
But ther's not one, doth praise the smell of thee...266. H.802, 2
Only for my wound there's no remedy...........274. H.841, 2
'Twixt Kings & Tyrants there's this difference known;
278. H.861, 1
Ther's loathsomnesse e'en in the sweets of love..297. H.949, 4
Despaire takes heart, when ther's no hope to speed:
309. H.999, 1
Twixt Truth and Errour, there's this difference known,
316. H.1031, 1
Believe it (dearest) ther's not one.............324. H.1068, 19
No plague ther's like to foolishnesse...........332. H.1115, 2
Yet if Thy Bloud not wash me, there's no hope...357. N.73, 4
Let me say grace when there's no more.........376. N.124, 6
In God there's nothing, but 'tis known to be....382. N.165, 1
There's an up-rising but of one for one:........388. N.208, 2
There's no constraint to do amisse,.............390. N.225, 1
That there's a God, we all do know,.............394. N.238, 1
Onely, there's left a little froth,................400. N.266, 2
Our holy Spicknard, & ther's none..............413. A.4, 25
and cherries in her cheekes, there's Creame 430. ins. H.283, 20c
— — — — — — — — — — —,............450. var. A.9, 49

Thereto And I reply'd thereto,...................18. H.47, 10
Which draws the sight thereto,.................75. H.193, 13
Adde a Cypresse-sprig thereto,..................89. H.220, 3

Thereupon And thereupon, in tears half drown'd,.18. H.46, 3
But having got it; thereupon,....................67. H.175, 7
'Tis true, said I, and thereupon................107. H.263, 13
— — — — — — — — — — —,............442. var. H.575, 31

Therewith Wo'd shrouded be, and therewith buried.
332. H.1114, 2
— — — — — — — — — — —,............444. var. H.693, 2

Therewithal And distorted there-withall:...........11. H.21, 4
Therewithall a Holy-cake:......................152. H.393, 4
Sweet Bridget blusht, & therewithall,..........203. H.562, 1
And running therewithall;......................288. H.908, 2
But therewithall I'le bring the Band,...........370. N.107, 7
And therewithall, behold, it hath...............372. N.118, 3

Thesbian (Invited to the Thesbian banquet) ta'ne 78. H.197, 66

These (Partial List)
Full is my Book of Glories; but all These......3. Ded. H., 9
Love give me more such nights as these.........20. H.56, 10
When these Circumstants shall but live to see...79. H.197, 85
To accept such coynes as these;................88. H.218, 8
Those with a shout, and these with laughter....101. H.250, 18
Love those, like these; regard, reward them not. 141. H.359, 12
A place desir'd of all but got by theis............405. A.1, 69
Theis hurte not thyne Inheritance,..............407. A.2, 12
Theis bringe thy husband, like to those..........407. A.2, 29
On eyther side of theis, quicke Eares............408. A.2, 39
Then vnto theis, bee itt thy care...............408. A.2, 53
For puplike Eyes, take onlye theis..............409. A.2, 91
Vrying diuorcement (worse then death to theis)...410. A.3, 9
Looks through the passage of theis lines.........417. A.9, 10

These-like Blast these-like actions, or a thing that's worse;
79. H.197, 84

Thespian Phœbean splendour! and thou Thespian spring!
45. H.128, 33
— — — — — — — — — — —,............427. var. H.197, 66

Th'event See Event

They'll Love and they'l thank you for't. Adieu....70. H.180, 8
I'm sure they'l fashion Roses....................74. H.192, 8
To Bed; or her they'l tire,....................115. H.283, 109
Our eyes they'l blind, or if not blind, they'l bleer.
237. H.685, 12
Speak thou the word, they'l kindle by and by...261. H.781, 4
T'invade from far: They'l finde worse foes at home.
316. H.1030, 2
— — — — — — — — — — —,............436. var. H.336, 20

They're And Harrow, (though they'r hang'd up now.)
102. H.250, 50
Theyre Nobly-home-bread, yett haue price........409. A.2, 93

Th'hand See Hand

Th'have — — — — — — — — —, ...438. var. H.412, 15

Thick Through thick, and through thin,.........225. H.643, 4

Thicket This, that, and ev'ry Thicket doth transpire
205. H.575, 7

Thief That the Thiefe, though ne'r so slie,.......263. H.785, 2
Not as a thief, shalt Thou ascend the mount,...398. N.263, 15

Thieves Not those poor Theeves that act their parts with Thee:
399. N.263, 23

Thieving Hither the least one theeving thought:..71. H.182, 14
Of flowers, ne'r suckt by th' theeving Bee:.....86. H.213, 37
Next, hang'd for Theeving: Now the people say,
195. H.532, 3
Goes theeving from me, I am safe in death;...392. N.230, 34

Thigh More white then Pearls, or Juno's thigh;..34. H.105, 5
The happy dawning of her thigh:...............51. H.142, 16
But Beards of Mice, a Newt's stew'd thigh,....119. H.293, 37

Thighs To enflesh my thighs, and armes:..........10. H.19, 6
Me thought, her long small legs & thighs.........16. H.41, 5
'Tis not a thousand Bullocks thies...............22. H.63, 1
Hands, and thighs, and legs, are all............59. H.155, 5
Then to thy thighs so closely cling,............67. H.175, 14
False in legs, and false in thighes;.............77. H.195, 9
To eate thy Bullocks thighs, thy Veales, thy fat 147. H.377, 63
Shew me thy feet; shew me thy legs, thy thighes;
154. H.403, 1

In Cream she bathes her **thighs** (more soft then silk) 203. H.561, 3
The Gods require the **thighes**................250. H.736, 1
A thousand Altars smoake; a thousand **thighes** 300. H.961, 7
Tapping his plump **thighes** with a mirtle wand: 313. H.1017, 8
Where Rams are wanting, or large Bullocks **thighs**, 369. N.105, 3
Now loue invites me to survey her **thighes**.......406. A.1, 77

Th'ill See **Ill**

Thimbles Some bitts of **thimbles** seeme to dresse 440. ins. H.443, 45aa

Thin Ha's she **thinne** haire, hath she none,........11. H.21, 13
Whose Linnen-Drapery is a **thin**................91. H.223, 60
Wo'd I see Lawn, clear as the Heaven, and **thin**? 158. H.416, 1
A Lawn for me, so fine and **thin**,..............164. H.442, 4
Through thick, and through **thin**,..............225. H.643, 4
Daffe nuts, soft Jewes eares, and some **thin** 439. ins. H.443, 45f

Thin-clad To Sun his **thin-clad** members, if he likes, 146. H.377, 17

Thine (Partial List)
To that Terce Muse of **thine**....................80. H.201, 28
Then this, the Fairies once, now **Thine**.........90. H.223a, 6
And sheep, grew more sweet, by that breth of **Thine**. 159. H.421, 14
Either to send me kindly **thine**,................168. H.446, 7
But walk'st about **thine** own dear bounds,......230. H.662, 15

Thing In Man, Ambition is the common'st **thing**;...21. H.58, 1
Beauty, no other **thing** is, then a Beame........33. H.102, 1
Farewell thou **Thing**, time-past so knowne, so deare 45. H.128, 1
And every **thing** assume.......................55. H.149, 65
And weep to see't; yet this **thing** doe,..........61. H.159, 20
Love is most loth to leave the **thing** beloved....73. H.186, 12
And ride the Sun-beams. Can there be a **thing**...78. H.197, 53
Blast these-like actions, or a **thing** that's worse;..79. H.197, 84
Will no other **thing** imply,....................97. H.232, 16
In every **thing** that's sweet, she is............106. H.263, 6
Love's a **thing**, (as I do heare)...............117. H.286, 1
Then the next **thing** I desire,..................117. H.286, 11
As you, or any **thing**.........................125. H.316, 14
Pure hands, pure habits, pure every **thing**......127. H.320, 4
What is the **thing** we call a kisse?............130. H.329, 2
How each **thing** smells divinely redolent!......159. H.421, 19
Gracefull is ev'ry **thing** from her..............207. H.579, 6
Lost to all Musick now; since every **thing**......214. H.612, 3
Love is a **thing** most nice; and must be fed....220. H.633, 20
Where I have had, what ever **thing** co'd be.....227. H.652, 3
O **Thing** admir'd! there did appeare............237. H.687, 5
Glory no other **thing** is (Tullie sayes)..........241. H.710, 1
Nor Beasts (fond **thing**) but only humane soules. 248. H.730, 10
Whatsoever **thing** I see,......................253. H.750, 1
Nor dreads he any **thing**:.....................259. H.772, 12
The Mean the Musique makes in every **thing**...268. H.812, 2
Twilight, no other **thing** is, Poets say,..........278. H.858, 1
The old Hag in. No surer **thing**................284. H.890, 6
Thus times do shift; each **thing** his turne do's hold; 285. H.892, 21
For Bread, Drinke, Butter, Cheese; for every **thing** 287. H.903, 2
Faith is a **thing** that's four-square; let it fall....292. H.926, 1
Love is a **thing** so likes me,....................296. H.946, 3
The Twi-light is no other **thing** (we say).........319. H.1046, 1
The Primrose sick, and sickly every **thing**:.....320. H.1054, 2
As Inapostate, to the **thing** he heares,........330. H.1100, 16
If any **thing** delight me for to print.............355. N.61, 1
Heart, Eare, and Eye, and every **thing**...........364. N.96, 5
Back, back again; each **thing** is done...........366. N.97, 24
With any **thing** unhallowed, here;..............366. N.98, 2
The bloud of Abel was a **thing**.................388. N.204, 1
Doth, here on earth, some **thing** of novitie;......395. N.244, 2
And whatsoever **thing** they tread vpon...........406. A.1, 93

Things Two of a thousand **things**, are disallow'd,...10. H.18, 1
Then holding up (there) such religious **Things**,....11. H.22, 5
All **things** decay with Time: The Forrest sees.....23. H.69, 1
These **things** thou know'st to th'height, and dost prevent 35. H.106, 21
Jove for our labour all **things** sells us...........36. H.106, 62
But sees these **things** within thy Map...........36. H.106, 72
And beleeve there be such **things**:..............36. H.106, 86
But (sweet **things**) ye must be gone;...........74. H.189, 3
What trust to **things** below, when as we see,.....81. H.202, 7
That **things** of greatest, so of meanest worth,....105. H.257, 27
Though good **things** answer many good intents; 110. H.275, 1
Because thou prizest **things** that are............119. H.293, 3
Good **things**, that come of course, far lesse doe please, 123. H.307, 1
Do all **things** sweetly, and in comely wise;.....124. H.313, 7
Of these, and such like **things**, for shift,........127. H.319, 25
Ile call to mind **things** half forgot:.............135. H.336, 114
Shift now has cast his clothes: got all **things** new; 144. H.372, 1
A curse to Thee, or Thine; but all **things** even.149. H.377, 129
Husht be all **things**; (no noyse here)...........170. H.450, 3
May read how soon **things** have...............176. H.467, 14
In a drie-house all **things** are neere.............179. H.476, 27
All **things** are open to these two events,........182. H.487, 1
Where Fortune bears no sway o're **things**.....190. H.515, 35
When **things** meet most opposite:..............194. H.527, 7
All **things** o'r-rul'd are here by Chance;........197. H.542, 1
All **things** subjected are to Fate;..............208. H.583, 1
All **things** have an ending day:................224. H.639, 2
By the weak'st means **things** mighty are o'rethrown, 240. H.702, 1
The order, but the Sum of **things**..............245. H.721, 2
None is, slight **things** do lightly please........246. H.724, 32
And wonder at Those **Things** that thou dost know. 257. H.763, 22
Time is the Bound of **things**, where e're we go,..257. H.766, 1
Things to perfection:........................258. H.767, 16
In **things** a moderation keepe,..................261. H.780, 1
Two **things** do make society to stand;..........275. H.847, 1
By dainty **things** undo me....................279. H.863, 8
Kisses and Favours are sweet **things**;..........283. H.883, 13
New **things** succeed, as former **things** grow old. 285. H.892, 22
More from the sweet then sower **things**.........298. H.951, 2
For other **things**, my many Children be.........304. H.978, 5
Things are uncertain, and the more we get,.....316. H.1032, 1
Conformity gives comelinesse to **things**.........318. H.1040, 1
Things precious are least num'rous: Men are prone 339. N.1, 5
The why, and wherefore all **things** here.........364. N.96, 12
The cause, why **things** thus fragrant be:........364. N.96, 18
To make **things** sweet. Chor. Yet all less sweet then He. 365. N.97, 10
That all **things** sweet, and clean may be:........366. N.98, 11
For **things** that will not come:................368. N.104, 2
Where round about Thou seest but all **things** vaine, 371. N.113, 3
To hold **things** fitting my necessity;........371. N.115, 6
Things are evermore sincere;..................377. N.128, 10
Great **things** ask for, when thou dost pray,.....381. N.158, 3
God can do all **things**, save but what are known 382. N.166, 1
'Bove all **things** lov'd it, for the puritie:.......390. N.222, 2
Here all **things** ready are, make hast, make hast away; 401. N.268, 5
Of all the good **things** whatsoe're we do,.......403. N.272, 1
— — — — — — — — — —,..............428. var. H.197, 84
Blew pinnes, tagges, fescues, beades and **thinges** 440. ins. H.443, 45r
— — — — — — — — — — —,..............442. var. H.465, 10

Think **Thinke** that of All, that I have writ, the worst: 7 H.6, 2
Not that I **thinke**, that any Dart,................10. H.20, 4
Then **think** how wrapt was I to see..............14. H.34, 5
Where (though thou see'st not) thou may'st **think** upon 20. H.55, 5
So oft, we'll **think**, we see a King new born.....26. H.80, 2
If so, we'll **think** too, (when he do's condemne....39. H.110, 3
Who wo'd not **think** this Yonker fierce to fight?..65. H.171, 3
Made he the pledge, he'd **think**...............80. H.201, 23
And for what use, scarce man wo'd **think** it.....93. H.223, 124
May **think**, thereby,.........................95. H.227, 20
No, I sho'd **think**, that Marriage might,..........97. H.235, 5
To have men **think** he's troubled with the Gout:..98. H.239, 2
Who **think** it strange to see,..................104. H.257, 12
(As we **think**) singing to the dinne............115. H.283, 103
Thinke you that this,.........................116. H.283, 145
We must not **thinke** his eare was sterv'd:.....119. H.293, 14
But **think** on these, that are t'appeare,.........127. H.319, 39
Thou mad'st me **thinke** by this,................142. H.364, 3
Nor **thinke** these Ages that do hoarcely sing....155. H.405, 5
Skinns he din'd well to day; how do you **think**? 156. H.409, 1
Nay, now I **think** th'ave made his grave.......156. H.412, 15
We'll nobly **think**, what's to be done,..........168. H.443, 120
To be but three, Black-ey'd, wee'l **thinke** y'are old. 173. H.462, 2
Steere Thee to me; and **thinke** (me gone)......174. H.465, 9
And **think** (as thou do'st walke the street)....174. H.465, 15
Nor wo'd I have thee **thinke**, that Thou......176. H.465, 81
And I shall **think** I have the heart,...........198. H.544, 34
I rather **thinke** (though they may speake the worst) 219. H.630, 3
Which burnt me so, that I do **thinke**.........222. H.635, 7
Yet, who wo'd **think**,........................229. H.659, 8
In wayes to greatnesse, **think** on this,.........229. H.661, 1
What store of Corn has carefull Nodes, **thinke** you, 270. H.822, 3
'Tis sweet to **thinke** on what was hard t' endure. 276. H.849, 2
For I **thinke** the gods require...............277. H.856, 3
I **think** no other but I see..................311. H.1010, 3
Or **think** on't now,..........................314. H.1024, 14
If ever we **think**.........................320. H.1051, 10
Nor **thinke** that Thou in this my Booke art worst, 329. H.1092, 1
And when we **think** His looks are sowre and grim, 340. N.7, 3
I'le **thinke** I'm going to be buried:..........392. N.230, 14
Co'd I but **think**, He would not be............395. N.245, 3
Vers. But yet it wounds my soule, to **think**,...400. N.267, 6
Spring hence thy faith, nor **thinke** it ill desert.414. A.6, 3
But to this, to **think** 'twas soe...............418. A.9, 38
— — — — — — — — — — —, ...427. var. H.197, 53

Thinking Eates to ones **thinking**, of all there, the least.
118. H.292, 2

Thinks See Methinks
But since (me **thinks**) it shows.................51. H.144, 3
Me **thinks** that onely lustre doth appeare........94. H.226, 3
And the smirk Butler **thinks** it...............114. H.283, 67
Me **thinks** like mine, your pulses beat;.......157. H.413, 5
Ursley, she **thinks** those Velvet Patches grace..197. H.543, 1
Then, then (me **thinks**) how sweetly flowes....261. H.779, 2
Since when (me **thinks**) my braines about doe swim,
313. H.1017, 13
She **thinks** not on..........................314. H.1024, 6
But in His own time, and when He **thinks** fit,.396. N.252, 3

Third Two dayes y'ave larded here; a **third**, yee know,
146. H.377, 25
Which got, the **third**, bids him a King come downe.
292. H.925, 2
Of thrice-boyl'd-worts, or **third** dayes fish;....321. H.1056, 12
With the **third** key He opes and shuts the wombe;
390. N.224, 3

Thirst The Elves present to quench his **thirst**...119. H.293, 20
— — — — — — — — — —, ...426. var. H.197, 40

Thirtieth Unto the **thirtieth** thousand yeere,.....265. H.794, 5

Thirty Just upon five and **thirty** pounds a yeare..151. H.385, 4
Adde to that **thirty** five, but five pounds more,..151. H.385, 5
Who two and **thirty** cornes had on a foot......240. H.704, 2
For **thirty** yeares, Tubbs has been proud and poor;
302. H.972, 1
And man sold God here for base **thirty** pence...389. N.213, 2

This (Partial List)
Twixt Kings and Subjects ther's **this** mighty odds,
12. H.25, 1
And keep one Centre: **This** with that conspires,.35. H.106, 15
Then **this** immensive cup.....................80. H.201, 25
This the lips we will permit.................82. H.203, 15
This if thou dost, woe to thee Furie, woe,......82. H.204, 9
And **this** same flower that smiles to day,......84. H.208, 3
But **this**, that I might shift..................100. H.249, 3
From that Sweet-heart, to **this**?..............104. H.257, 23
As for to make **this**, that, or any one..........107. H.264, 3
Crept to that, and came to **this**...............120. H.297, 6
This way, that way, that way, **this**,...........157. H.415, 3
That doth like me, **this** doth please;...........157. H.415, 5
That richly wrought, and **This** as brave;......192. H.521, 22
This begets the more delight,................194. H.527, 6
Write but **this** upon my Stone;................199. H.546, 2
Sometimes **this**, & sometimes that:............209. H.585, 2
This done, we'l draw lots, who shall buy......215. H.616, 25
This I may do (perhaps) as I glide by,.......222. H.634, 10
Lest having that, or **this**,....................231. H.663, 3
Not knowing **This**, that Jove decrees..........233. H.670, 5
Compar'd (in **this** my ample Orbe) to Him...236. H.685, 4
Make Thee like Him, **this**, that way fortunate,.254. H.756, 10
When **this** or that vast Dinastie must fall.....256. H.763, 9
When **this** or that Horne shall be broke, and when
256. H.763, 11
Of **this** or that great Aprill day shall be,......257. H.763, 19
See **this**, View that, and all the other bounds:...259. H.771, 4
When I am there, **this** then I'le do,...........349. N.46, 3

Thither Which Venus hearing; **thither** came,......31. H.92, 5
Slept; and thus sleeping, **thither** flew.........46. H.130, 3
But on we must, and **thither** tend,............133. H.336, 25
Besmear'd with Grapes; welcome he shall thee **thither**,
206. H.575, 37
Who **thither** come, and freely get............350. N.47, 15
If so; I'le **thither** follow, without feare;.......403. N.271, 7

Thomas And, as Sir **Thomas** Parson tells,........92. H.223, 79

Thorn See White-thorn
Lust ha's no eares; He's sharpe as **thorn**;.....165. H.443, 13
A **Thorn** or a Burr..........................225. H.643, 7
Either with old, or plant therein new **thorne**:..259. H.771, 6
Sharply pointed as a **thorn**:..................306. H.984, 22
Some brittle sticks of **Thorne** or Briar........350. N.47, 23
(S. Ambrose sayes) without the **Thorn**:.......396. N.251, 2
But, for Mans fault, then was the **Thorn**,......396. N.251, 3
But ne're the Rose without the **Thorn**........396. N.251, 5

Thorns Many **thorns** to be in Love..............88. H.217, 6
A thousand **thorns**, and Bryars & Stings,.....272. H.828, 5
But Those have **thorns**, and These have stings..283. H.883, 14
Here give me **thornes**; there, in thy Kingdome, set
343. N.25, 5

Thorny Loves **thornie** Tapers yet neglected lye:.261. H.781, 3

Thorough See Through

Thoroughly For an Ascendent **throughly** Auspicate:
300. H.961, 10
Peruse my Measures **thoroughly**, and where...322. H.1062, 4

Those (Partial List)
And **those** her lips doe now appeare..............7. H.9, 11
Of **those**, thou woundest with thy Dart!.......50. H.139, 15
Why are **Those** Looks, **Those** Looks the which have been
77. H.197, 27
And double my affection on thee; as doe **those**,.78. H.197, 43
(Some say) for joy, to see **those** Kitlings drown'd.
80. H.200, 2
Those with a shout, and these with laughter...101. H.250, 18
You, above all **Those** Sweets of Westminster:..137. H.341, 10
Love **those**, like these; regard, reward them not.
141. H.359, 12

Th'other's See Other's

Thou (Partial List)
Sing **thou** my Dirge, sweet-warbling Chorister!..19. H.50, 4
Goe **thou** afore; and I shall well.............33. H.98, 5
And **thou** a thousand thousand times shalt be...82. H.204, 13
Thou & I'le sing to make these dull Shades merry,
248. H.730, 25
Or kisse it **thou**, but once, or twice,..........267. H.805, 5

Thou'dst **Thou'dst** weep; but laugh, sho'd it not last a day.
241. H.709, 2
Yet sowre and grim **Thou'dst** seem to me;....395. N.246, 5

Though Who gave him forth good Grain, **though** he mistook
4. Ap., 3
Let us (**though** late), at last (my Silvia) wed;......8. H.10, 1
Though you can make........................11. H.20, 10
Farewell my shackles, (**though** of pearle they be)
17. H.42, 3
Where (**though** thou see'st not) thou may'st think upon
20. H.55, 5
But yet, **though** Love likes well such Scenes as these,
24. H.74, 9
Though much from out the Cess be spent,.....33. H.100, 3
Deare, **though** to part it be a Hell,............33. H.103, 1
Thy pious wishes are, (**though** thou not there)..37. H.106, 91
Weak **though** it be; long may it grow, and stand,
40. H.112, 3
Thou did'st not mind it; **though** thou then might'st see
42. H.122, 3
And that will please me somewhat: **though** I know,
42. H.122, 11
Which **though** they furre, will neither ake, or rot.
46. H.129, 2
And what **though** you had been embrac't.......49. H.136, 26
So you, my Lord, **though** you have now your stay,
52. H.146, 9
Though you (my Lord) have been unkind to me:
52. H.146, 18
Well; **though** my griefe by you was gall'd, the more;
52. H.146, 21
Her, **though** she wooe with teares.............56. H.149, 98
Though a wise man all pressures can sustaine;..60. H.158, 1
Large shoulders **though** he has, and well can beare,
60. H.158, 3
Though a thousand showres be..............62. H.162, 4
Gentle friends, **though** I despaire.............62. H.162, 16
And when (**though** long it comes to passe)...63. H.164, 6
Though here the Princely Poet................64. H.166, 12
Close **though** it be,............................65. H.172, 7
Lyd. **Though** mine be brighter then the Star;..70. H.181, 21
White **though** ye be; yet, Lillies, know,..........74. H.190, 1
So **though** y'are white as Swan, or Snow,.........76. H.193, 49
Though thou wert ne'r so blind.................80. H.201, 16
Yet **though** thus respected,......................83. H.205, 13
For payment promis'd, **though** thou never pay:..83. H.206, 2
What **though** the sea be calme? Trust to the shore:
85. H.212, 1
A neat, **though** not so great an Offering.......86. H.213, 35
Which (**though** sweet unto your smell)..........88. H.217, 3
Though thou not kill..........................95. H.227, 10
For to tame, **though** not to kill.................98. H.238, 10
Since which, **though** I love many,...............100. H.249, 6
And Harrow, (**though** they'r hang'd up now.)..102. H.250, 50
Though good things answer many good intents;..110. H.275, 1
Though hourely comforts from the Gods we see, 111. H.276, 1
On then, and **though** you slow-..............113. H.283, 59
But **though** it scar'd, it did not bite............116. H.284, 6
No fault in women, **though** they be..........118. H.291, 13
Though I cannot give thee fires................129. H.324, 1
The Pinnace up; which **though** she erres.......134. H.336, 63
Though not so fresh, yet full as merry........136. H.336, 140
Paske, **though** his debt be due upon the day....142. H.363, 1
Though lost in them, yet found in me...........146. H.376, 10
But that deni'd; a griefe, **though** small,.........153. H.395, 4
The reason is, **though** all the day they fight,....156. H.411, 3
Pray hurt him not; **though** he be dead,......157. H.412, 21
Though I do like to wooe;.....................160. H.422, 2
But **though** we Sever........................162. H.426, 21
Thus, **though** the Rooke do's raile against the sin,
163. H.439, 3
To lye with Mab, **though** all say no.............165. H.443, 12
Kings **though** th'are hated, will be fear'd.......165. H.443, 18
Though Granges do not love thee, Cities shall...172. H.456, 10
Though thou beest young, kind, soft, and faire, 174. H.465, 3
Looke upon; and **though** on fire.................174. H.465, 7
Fashion'd like Thee; which **though** 'tave eares 174. H.465, 21
Though thou art young, thou canst say no,....174. H.465, 34
Their end, **though** ne'r so brave:..............176. H.467, 15
That **though** a thousand, thousand eat;........178. H.476, 6
Yet, **though** now of Muse bereft,...............182. H.489, 9
What need I care, **though** some dislike me sho'd, 187. H.506, 5
What **though** the Heaven be lowring now,......188. H.508, 1
Though free she be, ther's something yet......191. H.520, 3
Fly me not, **though** I be gray,..................194. H.527, 1
Eaten I have; and **though** I had good cheere,..197. H.541, 1
(**Though** but in Numbers few)...................198. H.544, 33

Though ne'r so mean the Viands be,............200. H.552, 3
Vines to prune, though not to kill,..........204. H.569, 14
For my sake next, (though little) be not loud...212. H.600, 2
Upon the Seas, though with a gentle gale........212. H.601, 2
What though the Moon do's slumber?.........217. H.619, 12
Wantons we are; and though our words be such, 218. H.624, 1
I rather thinke (though they may speake the worst)
219. H.630, 3
Though palenes be the Livery that I weare,....222. H.634, 5
Though then I smile, and speake no words at all.
222. H.634, 15
Which, though enchas'd with Pearls, contain..222. H.635, 11
Though ne'r so foule be the weather..........225. H.643, 6
Teares, though th'are here below the sinners brine,
226. H.645, 1
Though long it be, yeeres may repay the debt; 228. H.654, 1
Which though well soyl'd, yet thou dost know,..230. H.662, 22
Pure enough, though not Precise:..............232. H.665, 4
Let's be doing, though we play................235. H.678, 3
Though by well-warding many blowes w'ave past,
237. H.688, 1
Need is no vice at all; though here it be,......239. H.698, 1
London my home is: though by hard fate sent..242. H.713, 13
Though Clock,...................................246. H.724, 1
I am a bird, and though no name I tell,......248. H.730, 7
Who though they do not eat,.................250. H.736, 5
They tread on clouds, and though they sometimes fall,
250. H.737, 3
What though the Lictors threat us,.............259. H.772, 7
And though he doe not rave,...................259. H.772, 13
That the Thiefe, though ne'r so slie,............263. H.785, 2
Dead the Fire, though ye blow................263. H.786, 4
Love thou dost, though Love sayes Nay.........264. H.790, 2
Mine eyes must wooe you; (though I sigh the while)
274. H.837, 7
On your niceness though we wait,.............276. H.850, 3
Though while we living 'bout the world do roame,
278. H.860, 5
Though from without no foes at all we feare;....292. H.928, 1
Though Frankinsense the Deities require,......295. H.940, 1
And though I saw no Bow, I'm sure,..........295. H.942, 15
Welcome to this my Colledge, and though late 305. H.983, 1
Be not dismaide, though crosses cast thee downe;
311. H.1007, 1
On with thy worke, though thou beest hardly prest;
311. H.1009, 1
Grow young with Tydes, and though I see ye never,
316. H.1028, 25
And though with ale ye be whet here;.........317. H.1035, 27
And, though it falls, continues still...........318. H.1036, 5
Still take advice; though counsels when they flye
318. H.1039, 1
I may a Poet come, though poor;.............321. H.1056, 4
And though we bid adieu to day,.............324. H.1068, 23
Goe thou forth my booke, though late;........334. H.1125, 1
Tho Kingdoms fal,...........................335. H.1129, 10
Though He may seem to over-act His part:......341. N.10, 2
Which though it sends forth thousand streams, 'tis ne're
341. N.15, 3
And though it takes all in, 'tis yet no more....341. N.15, 5
In Gilead though no Balme be found,............342. N.17, 5
And though a while He makes Requesters stay,..344. N.30, 3
I'le come, I'le creep, (though Thou dost threat) 349. N.46, 1
Lord, I will kisse it, though it kill:............351. N.48, 4
Temptations hurt not, though they have accesse: 359. N.79, 1
'Tis we are dead, though not i' th grave:.......361. N.83, 57
What though my Harp, and Violl be............361. N.84, 1
What though my bed be now my grave,..........361. N.84, 3
What though my healthfull dayes are fled,........361. N.84, 5
To spring; though now a wither'd flower.........361. N.84, 8
Cold as Paddocks though they be,...............364. N.95, 3
Though ills stand round about me;.............373. N.122, 10
And though thou here li'st dead, we see......375. N.123, 71
Thy hands (though cold) yet spotlesse, white,..375. N.123, 75
(Though ne're so rich) all beggars at His Gate.
383. N.171, 2
And though the Father be the first of Three,.....386. N.191, 5
Though they be few in number, I'm content;....392. N.230, 3
Let me, though late, yet at the last, begin.....392. N.230, 29
Though to be tempted be no sin, untill........392. N.230, 31
Though Thou beest all that Active Love,........395. N.246, 1
And though all joyes spring from the glance....395. N.246, 3
May (though they scorn Thee) praise and pitie Thee.
399. N.263, 35
And tho (Love knows).......................401. N.268, 28
In which the tongue, though but a member small,
405. A.1, 29
Shall stand for euer, though I doe addresse......412. A.3, 97
Thoughe as a seruant, yet a Mayde of Honor...412. A.3, 102
Keepe vp those flames, & though you shroud....413. A.4, 16
Though the Sextons truly sweare...............418. A.9, 33
And though his visage hung i' th' eare.........418. A.9, 47
helpe on her pace; and though she lagg, yet stirre
430. ins. H.283, 20h
What though your laden Altar now has wonne
432. ins. H.283, 70a
— — — — — — — — — — —,..............436. var. H.336, 52
— — — — — — — — — —,..............437. var. H.336, 108
Thought Me thought, (last night) love in an anger came,
16. H.40, 1
Me thought, her long small legs & thighs........16. H.41, 5
And be not onely thought, but prov'd..........37. H.106, 102
Me thought 'twas strange, that thou so hard sho'dst prove,
42. H.122, 7
Hither the least one theeving thought:........71. H.182, 14
I thought I might there take a taste,............71. H.182, 17
A thought of such like possibilitie?...........78. H.197, 46
Of English Poets, and 'tis thought the Worst...156. H.410, 2
The food of Poets; so I thought sayes Jill,......186. H.498, 5
I thought at first 'twas but a dream,............203. H.562, 3
Of which who drank, he said no thought........222. H.635, 3
Flies no thought higher then a fleece:.........229. H.662, 12
Yet he'le be thought or seen,..................259. H.772, 21
Without a thought of hurt, or feare;..........283. H.883, 8
And in good faith I'd thought it strange........290. H.915, 3
That none hereafter sho'd be thought, or be....299. H.956, 3
Me thought I saw (as I did dreame in bed)....313. H.1017, 1
For which (me thought) in prittie anger she...313. H.1017, 11
Me thought I saw them stir, and gently move,..326. H.1080, 11
Me thought, I did Thy bounty chide,..........358. N.75, 5
As that the old World thought it fit,............388. N.204, 3
W'th thought thay goe, whence thay must ner returne.
411. A.3, 66
Or their thought of faith may growe............418. A.9, 37
Thoughts But with thy equall thoughts, prepar'd dost stand,
37. H.106, 95
All thoughts, but such as aime at getting Princes,
77. H.197, 8
That ye could your thoughts remove..........117. H.289, 2
All thoughts of irksome Love:................171. H.452, 8
Thy thoughts as cold, as is thy sleep:........175. H.465, 48
Of harmlesse thoughts, to watch and keep......350. N.47, 9
Possesse my thoughts, next comes my dolefull knell
392. N.230, 12
Them and my thoughts to that sublim'd respecte 411. A.3, 50
And In thy sence, her Chaster thoughtes Commend
421. ins. H.106, 42a
— — — — — — — — — —,..............422. var. H.106, 139
Thy thoughts to say, I backe am come..441. ins. H.465, 14b
Thou'lt Half that blessing thou'lt give me.......236. H.684, 4
Thousand Two of a thousand things, are disallow'd,
10. H.18, 1
'Tis not a thousand Bullocks thies................22. H.63, 1
And 'midst a thousand gulfs to be secure.......23. H.71, 6
A thousand to that hundred: so kisse on,..........24. H.74, 5
To make that thousand up a million.............24. H.74, 6
With thousand such enchanting dreams, that meet
36. H.106, 53
These, and a thousand sweets, co'd never be......45. H.128, 9
Though a thousand showres be................62. H.162, 4
Of a thousand thousand known,................62. H.162, 11
When as a thousand Virgins on this day,......68. H.178, 13
And thou a thousand thousand times shalt be 82. H.204, 13
And thousand Virgins come and weep,..........104. H.256, 17
See, a thousand Cupids flye,..................115. H.283, 107
With thousand rare encolourings:..............130. H.329, 21
As for my self, since time a thousand cares....140. H.355, 5
A thousand times, more sweare, then say,....149. H.377, 132
Thus a thousand Mistresses,...................157. H.415, 6
I know a thousand greedy eyes..............174. H.465, 17
That though a thousand, thousand eat;........178. H.476, 6
Thousand score...............................196. H.538, 8
May a thousand blessings come!...............220. H.633, 2
With thousand blessings by thy Fortune crown'd.
242. H.713, 6
After a thousand Lusters hurld,...............245. H.720, 15
Unto the thirtieth thousand yeere,..............265. H.794, 5
A thousand thorns, and Bryars & Stings,......272. H.828, 5
A thousand Altars smoake; a thousand thighes..300. H.961, 7
To bath in thee (as thousand others doe.)....315. H.1028, 6
Which though it sends forth thousand streams, 'tis ne're
341. N.15, 3
Ten thousand Talents lent me, Thou dost write:
358. N.103, 9
My lipps shall send a 1000 back to you...........414. A.5, 16
Thousands And thousands gladly wish..........113. H.283, 49
Thousands to feed by miracle.................139. H.350, 4
Jove may afford us thousands of reliefs;........153. H.397, 1
And may'st draw thousands with a haire:......174. H.465, 4
Dearest of thousands, now the time drawes neere,
219. H.627, 1
Thousands each day passe by, which wee,........234. H.671, 1
Here we begin new life; while thousands quite..313. H.1019, 3
That makes all æquall. Manye thowsands should
411. A.3, 35
Thy Pompe of Playes which thousands come to see,
415. A.7, 3
— — — — — — — — — — —,............432. var. H.283, 107
Thou't Then sure thou't like, or thou wilt envie me.
66. H.174, 4
Little thou't love, or not at all.................103. H.253, 18
For that once lost, thou't fall to one,..........174. H.465, 27
Thracian Hor. Now Thracian Cloe governs me,..70. H.181, 9

Thraldom Such precious **thraldome** ne'r shall fetter me.
17. H.42, 4
Thrall Slave to **Thrall**,.........................12. H.26, 10
Which ever since has been in **thrall**,..........281. H.876, 9
Thread Who told me, they had drawn a **thred**......18. H.47, 7
Let them not cut the **thred**..................58. H.149, 163
Something made of **thred** and thrumme;.........76. H.195, 3
Knap the **thread**, and thou art free:..........128. H.322, 8
Or else spin out the **thread** of sands,..........215. H.616, 7
Yarne is an Income; and the Huswives **thread** 221. H.633, 44
The woosted **thred**..........................374. N.123, 39
The longer **thred** of life we spin,..............379. N.144, 1
So the Divine Hand work't, and brake no **thred**,
385. N.184, 3
Many a Purse-stringe, many a **thred**,......440. ins. H.443, 45v
Threads The Fringe about this, are those **Threds**
167. H.443, 106
Threat That Towrs high rear'd dread most the lightnings **threat**:...................................181. H.483, 14
That Preternaturall Fever, which did **threat**....254. H.756, 3
What though the Lictors **threat** us,...........259. H.772, 7
I'le come, I'le creep, (though Thou dost **threat**)
349. N.46, 1
Ere Thou dost **threat** me......................351. N.49, 4
Threaten And **threaten** at noone..............333. H.1122, 11
And **threaten** to undo me,......................373. N.122, 2
Threatened **Threatn'd** ruine unto all?...........302. H.968, 10
Threats No **threats** of Tyrants, or the Grim......215. H.615, 3
Say, do's she frown? still countermand her **threats**:
270. H.820, 3
Three See Thrice-three-sacred, Thrice-three-sisters
So **three** in one small plat of ground shall ly,....11. H.22, 9
Three lovely Sisters working were...............18. H.47, 1
(Faire Destinies all **three**)....................18. H.47, 6
More wealth brings in, then all those **three**.......23. H.70, 8
Stout sons I had, and those twice **three**;.........41. H.116, 3
But thrice **three** Moones before she dy'd.........41. H.116, 6
'Tis not Apollo can, or those thrice **three**.......45. H.128, 29
Furze, **three** or foure times with his cheeks did blow
47. H.131, 3
Three dayes before the shutting in of May,....86. H.213, 13
Amint. O rare! But is't a trespasse if we **three** 86. H.213, 25
Who count this night as long as **three**,......114. H.283, 74
By Dream I saw, one of the **three**..............153. H.399, 1
Three quarters were consum'd of it;...........153. H.399, 7
Who having two or **three**,....................160. H.422, 19
Such Essences as those **Three** Brothers; known 170. H.451, 7
Such **Three** brave Brothers fell in Mars his Field.
170. H.451, 12
These were those **Three** Horatii Rome did boast,
170. H.451, 13
Rom's were these **Three** Horatii we have lost...170. H.451, 14
This, **Three**; which **Three**, you make up Foure Brave Prince.
170. H.451, 16
To be but **three**, Black-ey'd, wee'l thinke y'are old.
173. H.462, 2
Two Youths sha's known, thrice two, and twice **3**. yeares:
180. H.477, 3
Having but seven in all; **three** black, foure white.
195. H.531, 2
He by extortion brings in **three** times more:....220. H.631, 3
And thrice **three** weekes) he lived here........226. H.644, 4
Three Formes of Heccate:......................258. H.767, 10
To you sweet Maids (thrice **three**)..............261. H.778, 5
Less then Apollo, that ursurp'st such **Three**?..276. H.851, 6
Three, unto whom the whole world give applause;
276. H.851, 7
Yet their **Three** praises, praise but One; that's Lawes.
276. H.851, 8
Three Zodiaks fill'd more I shall stoope;........303. H.973, 2
After a day, or two, or **three**,................328. H.1090, 4
Three fatall Sisters wait upon each sin;.........341. N.11, 1
I do believe, the One in **Three**,................359. N.78, 13
And **Three** in perfect Unitie:....................359. N.78, 14
Of **Three** in One,..............................369. N.106, 13
God's undivided, One in Persons **Three**;.......386. N.191, 1
And **Three** in Inconfused Unity:.................386. N.191, 2
And though the Father be the first of **Three**,..386. N.191, 5
Three-brave-brothers Of all those **three-brave-brothers**, faln i' th' Warre,.......................................170. H.451, 1
Threefold Sabbaths are **threefold**, (as S. Austine sayes:)
386. N.194, 1
Threescore That Timber tall, which **three-score** lusters stood
23. H.69, 3
Threescore or fourescore spring up thence for one
388. N.208, 4
Threshold For which, before thy **Threshold**, we'll lay downe
41. H.117, 7
Now o're the **threshold** force her in...........55. H.149, 82
To the worn **Threshold**, Porch, Hall, Parlour, Kitchin,
146. H.377, 5
When at the holy **Threshold** of thine house,....181. H.483, 11
My **Threshold**, since I see,...................223. H.635, 14
Finde out a **Threshold** or a doore,............312. H.1014, 7
To whose glad **threshold**, and free door.......321. H.1056, 3
Ile kisse the **Threshold** of thy dore............328. H.1090, 11
And yet the **threshold** of my doore.............350. N.47, 13
Welcome at last unto the **Threshold**, Time 431. ins. H.283, 60k
Threshold-god Ye wrong the **Threshold-god**, that keeps peace here:...124. H.313, 4
Threw She **threw**; I cast; and having thrown,....19. H.49, 3
For sport my Julia **threw** a Lace...............116. H.284, 1
Into thy streames my self I **threw**,............294. H.939, 7
Thrice See Thrice-boiled-worts, Thrice-three-sacred, Thrice-three-sisters
If you prove faithlesse **thrice**,...................32, H.94, 11
Thrice, and above, blest (my soules halfe) art thou,
34. H.106, 1
A heart **thrice** wall'd with Oke, and Brasse, that man
36. H.106, 75
Live, and live blest; **thrice** happy Paire; Let Breath,
38. H.106, 141
But **thrice** three Moones before she dy'd.........41. H.116, 6
'Tis not Apollo can, or those **thrice** three......45. H.128, 29
Thrice I have washt, but feel no cold,..........157. H.413, 3
Two Youths sha's known, **thrice** two, and twice 3. yeares;
180. H.477, 3
And **thrice** three weekes) he lived here..........226. H.644, 4
And **thrice** repeat..............................227. H.653, 6
Thrice happie Roses, so much grac't, to have....249. H.734, 1
To you sweet Maids (**thrice** three)...............261. H.778, 5
Where **thrice** we knock, and none will heare,..312. H.1014, 9
Thrice-boiled-worts Of **thrice-boyl'd-worts**, or third dayes fish;
321. H.1056, 12
Thrice-three-sacred Amongst the **thrice-three-sacred** Virgins, fill
412. A.3, 86
Thrice-three-Sisters May the **thrice-three-Sisters** sing
108. H.266, 9
Thrift See Ding-thrift
Let wealth come in by comely **thrift**,..........221. H.633, 46
This is strong **thrift** that warie Rush doth use 332. H.1116, 3
Thrifty Live with a **thrifty**, not a needy Fate;......13. H.28, 1
Thrive That shew the womb shall **thrive**.........55. H.149, 56
In death I **thrive**:.............................72. H.185, 16
Or nine: but **thrive**...........................227. H.653, 11
That Happines do's still the longest **thrive**,......264. H.792, 1
Thrives When well the work of hony **thrives**;....145. H.375, 8
Throat That rattles i'th' **throat**,................333. H.1122, 5
Throne See Leafy-throne
To strike him dead, that but usurps a **Throne**.....32. H.97, 6
About whose **Throne** the crowd of Poets throng
206. H.575, 29
Power and Peace to keep one **Throne**...........264. H.788, 2
That fill the **Throne**;..........................369. N.106, 14
To heare the Judge give sentence on the **Throne**, 392. N.230, 25
Why then begin, great King! ascend Thy **Throne**,
399. N.263, 28
Her brest (a place for beawtyes **throne** most fitt)
405. A.1, 51
Throned **throaned** in a saffron Evening, seemes to chyme
431. ins. H.283, 60l
Thronelet In thy refulgent **Thronelet**,...........270. H.819, 8
Thrones And **Thrones**, thy selfe one of Those Senatours:
176. H.466, 4
Low, and of **Thrones** the Ancient Majesty.....325. H.1073, 4
Throng About whose Throne the crowd of Poets **throng**
206. H.575, 29
Let's meet in a **throng**.......................320. H.1051, 2
Throttle 'Tis sin I know, 'tis sin to **throtle** Wine. 187. H.502, 4
Through But when He's gone, read **through** what's writ,
6. H.4, 3
Or glided **through** the street)....................9. H.15, 10
As to shew her Tongue wag **through**:............11. H.21, 10
And all with showrs wet **through**,................26. H.81, 11
Quite **through** my heart and marrow.............27. H.81, 32
Through that huge field of waters ride:..........30. H.90, 3
I! and a world of Pikes passe **through**............31. H.90, 9
Them frantick with thy raptures, flashing **through**
45. H.128, 27
And let them **through** a Zodiac run:............47. H.133, 6
Through Woodbine, and Sweet-bryers...............55. H.149, 68
Fresh-quilted colours **through** the aire:..........67. H.178, 4
You see how Amber **through** the streams......75. H.193, 17
Run **through** my veines, like to a hasty flood...79. H.197, 78
When I **through** all my many Poems look,......94. H.226, 1
Through the world, but writ in gold...........108. H.266, 20
Jealousie, and both will **through**:..............116. H.285, 4
Quite **through** the table, where he spies......119. H.293, 25
Quite **through** the young maids and the men,..127. H.319, 31
Through thy watrie-region;......................129. H.325, 4
Let but few smart, but strike a feare **through** all:
132. H.335, 3
Do not you fall **through** frailty; Ile be sure....136. H.338, 3
Through heaven, the very Spheres,.............151. H.388, 7
A red-Rose peeping **through** a white?...........164. H.440, 2
Or seen rich Rubies blushing **through**..........164. H.440, 7
He raves **through** leane, he rages **through** the fat;
191. H.518, 3
Skulls co'd not well passe **through** that scum of men.
200. H.551, 2
Through thick, and **through** thin,...............225. H.643, 4
Through Brakes and **through** Bryars,..........225. H.643, 10

Or did I walk those Pean-Gardens **through**,....234. H.673, 3
Like the Sybells, **through** the world.............242. H.714, 8
That **through** each room a golden pipe may run 245. H.723, 3
Le1 her **through** Hells obscuritie:.............265. H.798, 6
His passage **through** that dreadfull shade:......265. H.798, 8
If blush thou must, then blush thou **through**....271. H.824, 9
When peeping **through** a Brooke...............271. H.824, 12
And thus **through** Woman-kind we see........283. H.885, 9
Then bore me **through** the eare;...............293. H.934, 6
So Lillies **thorough** Christall look:............294. H.939, 3
Who fli'st at all heights: Prose and Verse run'st **through**;
298. H.955, 7
A House spred **through** with Leprosie.........310. H.1004, 12
'Twill hurt and heal a heart pierc'd **through**.....325. H.1075, 8
God pardons those, who do **through** frailty sin;..344. N.32, 1
And strike it **through**.............................349. N.46, 9
No man is blest **through** ev'ry part..............351. N.50, 4
Through all the night.........................353. N.56, 1
Spring Tulips up **through** all the yeere;........366. N.97, 21
Or search the beds of Spices **through**,..........367. N.102, 10
If **through** my Christ I saw not Thee..........395. N.246, 6
Pierc't **through**, and dropping bloud, for me,....400. N.267, 4
Through mid'st thereof a christall stream there flowes
406. A.1, 75
For **through** these Optickes, fly the dartes......408. A.2, 37
(As wth a Tempeste) Nature **through** the worlde
410. A.3, 24
Cast, leading his Euredice **through** hell,..........411. A.3, 68
Looks **through** the passage of theis lines........417. A.9, 10
See how he waves his hand, and **through** his eyes
430. ins. H.283, 40a
— — — — — — — — — — —,...........431. var. H.283, 41
— — — — — — — — — — —,...........442. var. H.575, 8
— — — — — — — — — — —,...........443. var. H.575, 64
— — — — — — — — — — —,...........445. var. H.730, 24
— — — — — — — — — — —,...........450. var. A.9, 47

Throughly See **Thoroughly**

Throughout The Seed; so sow'd these Tares **throughout** my Book..4. Ap., 4
Where spring-time smiles **throughout** the yeare? 103. H.256, 3
And thus, **throughout**, with Christmas playes....127. H.319, 49
Shall run, as rivers, all **throughout** thy soyl....144. H.370, 6
'Tis then broad Day **throughout** the East.........154. H.404, 4
Throughout that Brave Mosaick yard..........166. H.443, 47
Of shifted Snake: enfreez'd **throughout**.........166.H.443, 67
Like Sybels Leaves, **throughout** the ample world?
172. H.459, 4
Throughout.................................198. H.544, 11
For since I've travail'd all this Realm **throughout**
267. H.804, 5
And no less prais'd, then spread **throughout** the world.
288. H.907, 6
This line about, live Thou **throughout** the world;
298. H.955, 2
With charity **throughout**;......................352. N.53, 12
But 'cense the porch, and place **throughout**....365. N.97, 6

Throw The Armes to hugge it? throw, **throw**..115. H.283, 117
And rend the cloud, and **throw**..............116. H.283, 149
Brasse, Leade, or Tinne, **throw** into th' mould; 297. H.948, 10
As when the disagreeing Commons **throw**......303. H.975, 3
— — — — — — — — —,..............421. var. H.49, 3

Throwing **Throwing** about his wild, and active fires.
45. H.128, 18
By **throwing** teeth into the ground:............297. H.948, 6
Throwing his eye balls backward, to suruaye......411. A.3, 73
— — — — — — — — —,..............430. var. H.283, 14

Thrown She threw; I cast; and having **thrown**,....19. H.49, 3
A Lawne about the shoulders **thrown**..........28. H.83, 3
Ne'r to be **thrown**...........................85. H.211, 19
The candid Stole **thrown** ore the Pious Priest;..286. H.898, 6
But for each Graine, that in the ground is **thrown**,
388. N.208, 3

Throws See how Aurora **throwes** her faire........67. H.178, 3
And as it shines, it **throwes** a scent about,....131. H.331, 7

Thrum Something made of thred and **thrumme**;....76. H.195, 3

Thumb See **Long-black-thumb-nail**
A golden ring, that shines upon thy **thumb**:......30. H.88, 7
Which done, thy painfull **Thumb** this sentence tells us,
36. H.106, 61
For to unslate, or to untile that **thumb**!........66. H.173, 4
Into your Chests, drawn by your painfull **Thumb**.
221. H.633, 41
Between the finger, and the **thumb**;..............356. N.66, 6

Thumbless The servants **thumblesse**, yet to eat, 310. H.1004, 3

Thumb-nail The cutting **Thumb-naile**, or the Brow severe.
212. H.603, 2

Thumb-nails-pared His **thumb-nailes-par'd**, afford him sperrables.
226. H.648, 2

Thunder **Thunder** and Lightning Ile lay by,......58. H.152, 5
Bold bolt of **thunder** he will make his way,....116. H.283, 148
Welcome as **thunder** to our beere:...........146. H.377, 30
Cal'd out by the clap of the **Thunder**..........225. H.643, 24
First, peales of **Thunder** we must heare,........247. H.725, 9
Let me (like him) first cracks of **thunder** heare; 343. N.25, 3

Thunder-claps Then **Thunder-claps** and Lightning did conspire
81. H.202, 5
Undreadfull too of courtly **thunderclaps**:......128. H.323, 6
For if Thy **thunder-claps** I heare,..............393. N.232, 9

Thundered But voice of fame, and voice of heauen haue **thunderd**..414. A.6, 5

Thunderer The cleaving Bolt of Jove the **Thunderer**.
181. H.483, 16

Th'unkind See **Unkind**

Thus **Thus** I those..............................12. H.26, 7
And ravish'd **thus**, It came to passe,..............13. H.27, 5
Thus like a Bee, Love-gentle stil doth bring......16. H.40, 7
Thus, and **thus** it now appears....................17. H.43, 9
Thus woe succeeds a woe; as wave a wave........18. H.48, 2
Thus speaks the Oke, here; C. and M. shall meet,
26. H.79, 7
And troubles **thus** the Sleepie?....................26. H.81, 6
And let not Locks **thus** keep ye..................26. H.81, 8
Away, and **thus** said flying,....................27. H.81, 34
Thus held, or led by thee, I shall..............33. H.98, 9
Thus, **thus** to wound, not kill out-right:........34. H.103, 12
And **thus** devis'd, doe thou but this,............34. H.103, 15
Thus thou can'st tearcely live to satisfie........35. H.106, 27
And **thus** thy little-well-kept-stock doth prove, 37. H.106, 127
Thus let thy Rurall Sanctuary be.............38. H.106, 137
And all his Tapers **thus** put out:..............42. H.119, 6
And sobbing deeply, **thus** he said,..............42. H.119, 8
My vowes denounc'd in zeale, which **thus** much show thee,
46. H.128, 47
Slept; and **thus** sleeping, thither flew..........46. H.130, 3
Upon the Custard, and **thus** cooled so:..........47. H.131, 4
Most innocent, and injur'd **thus**..................48. H.136, 5
To his Mother, said **thus** crying;..................50. H.139, 4
By lingring **thus** in doubt:........................53. H.149, 6
But now kisse her, and **thus** say,...............56. H 149, 119
And **thus** surpriz'd (as Filchers use)............71. H.182, 11
He **thus** began himselfe t'excuse:..................71. H.182, 12
And take his bag; but **thus** much know,........71. H.182, 28
Thus Lillie, Rose, Grape, Cherry, Creame,......75. H.193, 33
Thus let this Christal'd Lillie be................76. H.193, 41
Thus Paines and Pleasures turne by turne succeed:
79. H.199, 3
And being ravisht **thus**,..........................81. H.201, 34
Yet though **thus** respected,......................83. H.205, 13
At my death; but **thus** much know,..............88. H.218, 3
And make it **thus** expire........................95. H.227, 15
Let's live merrily, and **thus**....................96. H.231, 5
Take thou my blessing, **thus**, and goe,..........98. H.238, 11
Love and my sighs **thus** intertalkt:..............106. H.263, 2
Thus, thou, that man art, whom the Fates conspir'd
121. H.301, 5
Thus a dew of Graces fall.....................125. H.314, 9
You say, you love me; that I **thus** must prove; 126. H.317, 1
And **thus**, throughout, with Christmas playes..127. H.319, 49
Crossing thy selfe; come **thus** to sacrifice:.......127. H.320, 2
Who for true glory suffers **thus**; we grant......129. H.323, 15
Thus has Infernall Jove decreed;..............133. H.336, 28
Thus frantick crazie man (God wot)........135. H.336, 113
Thus ripe with tears,.........................135. H.336, 117
(Larr **thus** conspiring with our mirth)........135. H.336, 124
Thus, till we see the fire lesse shine..........136. H.336, 145
By thy sonne **thus** grac't, and thee;.............138. H.346, 2
Not knowing **thus** much, when we once do sever,
140. H.355, 3
Thus to en-trance and ravish me:..............142. H.362, 4
When **thus** enkindled they transpire..........145. H.375, 17
Thus sweet she smells, or what can be.........145. H.375, 27
Thus, like a Roman Tribune, thou thy gate..147. H.377, 45
By cruse and measure; **thus** devoting Wine,....148. H.377, 83
Thus a thousand Mistresses,...................157. H.415, 6
Thus, though the Rooke do's raile against the sin.
163. H.439, 3
Wine lead him on. **Thus** to a Grove..........165. H.443, 19
Thus soft she lies: and over-head............167. H.443, 100
Thus I..178. H.475, 1
Have made Thee prosperous in thy wayes, **thus** farre:
181. H.483, 6
Fill me my Wine in Christall; **thus**, and **thus**..187. H.502, 1
Thus faire and cleane you are, although there be
189. H 511, 5
With griefe of heart, methinks, I **thus** doe cry,..193. H.522, 5
Take then thy Censer; Put in Fire, and **thus**,..197. H.539, 13
Thus, **thus**, we live, and spend the houres.......198. H.544, 19
This Primrose, **thus** bepearl'd with dew?.........208. H.580, 4
Pay then your Tythe; and doing **thus**,...........208. H.581, 3
So, while I **thus** sit crown'd;....................208. H.582, 2
Thus we will sit and talke; but tell..........215. H.616, 11
Thus, having talkt, we'l next commend........216. H.616, 35
Thus, **thus** to come unto me:..................217. H.619, 17
And **thus** lesse last, then live our Day.........233. H.670, 31
Soules transfusing **thus**, and die...............235. H.678, 8
And as they **thus** did entertaine................237. H.687, 2
Thus, **thus** with hallowed foot I touch the ground.
242. H.713, 5
Thus inrag'd, my lines are hurl'd,...............242. H.714, 7
And **thus**, **thus**, **thus** let us smother............247. H.727, 3
That made me **thus** hoist saile, and bring my Boat:
248. H.730, 12
And sweetly blushing **thus**,.......................251. H.740, 6
Thus to slay me by degrees,.......................254. H.757, 3

Thus if our ship fails of her Anchor hold,......266. H.800, 7
That shin'st **thus** in thy counterfeit?..........270. H.819, 9
And **thus** through Woman-kind we see..........283. H.885, 9
Thus times do shift; each thing his turne do's hold;
285. H.892, 21
Attended **thus** (in a most solemn wise)........286. H.898, 3
And **thus** ye must doe.......................317. H.1035, 23
When our Beads are **thus** united,.............324. H.1069, 7
He raves, he rends, and while he **thus** doth tear, 325. H.1077, 5
Make him **thus** swell, or windy Cabbages.......327. H.1085, 2
Then weepe not sweet; but **thus** much know,..328. H.1090, 12
And **thus** they praise the Sumpter; but not him: 330. H.1099, 4
Thus have, or have not, all alike is good,......332. H.1112, 5
Washt with sweet ointments; **Thus** at last I come
335. H.1128, 3
God loads, and unloads, (**thus** His work begins) 341. N.14, 1
Thus, thus, and **thus** we compasse round........359. N.83, 7
That **thus** from vices driven,..................363. N.92, 15
Thus, on the sudden? 4. Come and see........364. N.96, 17
The cause, why things **thus** fragrant be:........364. N.96, 18
For Sceva, darts; for Cocles, dangers; **thus**....370. N.108, 5
Thus I walk, and this I tell:...................372. N.121, 4
Our Maundie; **thus,**..........................374. N.123, 29
That, **thus** increast, it might be perfected.......378. N.132, 2
Thus let Thy lips but love distill,............393. N.232, 15
Thus, thus I come to kisse Thy Stone.........402. N.269, 10
Loe! **Thus** I give a Virgin-Flower,.............402. N.270, 5
Thus every part in contrariety.................406. A.1, 105
Whence beawty springs, and **thus** I kisse thy foot.
406. A.1, 112
Thus Crownd with Rose Budds, Sacke, thou mad'st mee flye
410. A.3, 27
Thus wth a kisse of warmth, and loue, I parte...412. A.3, 95
Which **thus** enkindled we invoke...............413. A.4, 29
I finde in thee, that makes me **thus** to part,......414. A.6, 4
Chorus. **Thus, thus** the gods celestial still decree,
416. A.8, 17
That makes grim Charon **thus** to pity thee.......416. A.8, 22
And I must hence. Euc. Yet let me **thus** much know,
416. A.8, 25
— — — — — — — — — — — —,...............422. var. H.106, 61
— — — — — — — — — — — —,...............425. var. H.197, 19
— — — — — — — — — — — —,...............430. var. H.263, 22
— — — — — — — — — — — —,...............432. var. H.283, 99
— — — — — — — — — — — —,...............436. var. H.336, 16
— — — — — — — — — — — —,...............438. var. H.425, 5
— — — — — — — — — — — —,...............451. var. H.336, 85

Th'utmost See Utmost

Thwack Who with thy Thyrse dost **thwack** us:..259. H.772, 2

Thwart **Thwart** all Wizzards, and with these....286. H.897, 7

Thy (Partial List)
In **thy** both Last, and Better Vow:...............34. H.106, 2

Th'year See Year

Thyme Full as a Bee with **Thyme,** and Red,.....165. H.443, 9

Thyrse When up the ***Thyrse** is rais'd, and when the sound
7. H.8, 7
Shake the **Thyrse,** and bite the Bayes:..........39. H.111, 8
Our **Thyrse,** for Scepter; and our Baies for Crown.
41. H.117, 8
Thy **Thyrse,** and bite the Bayes................81. H.201, 32
And dancing 'bout the Mystick **Thyrse,**.......136. H.336, 135
To grace the frantick **Thyrse:**.................198. H.544, 9
Who with thy **Thyrse** dost thwack us:.........259. H.772, 2

Thyrsis And **Thyrsis,** they shall follow.........184. H.492, 34

Thyrsus See Thyrse

Thyself See Self

Tibullus Now, to **Tibullus,** next,................81. H.201, 37
Behold, **Tibullus** lies..........................81. H.201, 41

Tickle Numbers ne'r **tickle,** or but lightly please, 290. H.914, 7

Tickled And **tickled** with Desire,...............57. H.149, 134
Are, by the Sun-beams, **tickel'd** by degrees......100. H.247, 4

Tickling **Tickling** the Citterne with his quill....318. H.1036, 6

Tide See Primrose-tide, Twelfthtide, Whitsuntide
But thou at home without or **tyde** or gale,.......36. H.106, 77
Thou hast both Wind and **Tide** with thee; Thy way
73. H.186, 3
As well the Winters, as the Summers **Tide:**....151. H.387, 6
That at the **tide,** he has not bread to eate.......327. H.1086, 4
and come upon your Bridegroome like a **Tyde**
431. ins. H.283, 50b

Tides Shov'd on, by quick succeeding **Tides:**.....244. H.720, 2
Grow young with **Tydes,** and though I see ye never,
316. H.1028, 25

Tie Anthea bade me **tye** her shooe;...............14. H.33, 1
A carelesse shooe-string, in whose **tye**...........28. H.83, 11
Why I **tye** about thy wrist,...................128. H.322, 1
Thy Love had one knot, mine a triple **tye**.......173. H.464, 3
Can tell by tongue; or true-love **tie**............202. H.560, 12
To whose free knees we may our temples **tye**..300. H.961, 15

Tied See Tongue-tied
Because his Tongue was **ty'd** againe...............13. H.27, 10
And that **ty'd** to man 'twil sever..............209. H.587, 3
And wilt not thou, with gold, be **ti'd**...........357. N.72, 11
Hath in the middle **ty'de** a Gordian knott.........405. A.1, 62

Tierce But send to her a **Tearce**................291. H.918, 8

Tiffanies Orecome, or halfe betray'd by **Tiffanies:**..34. H.104, 2

Tiffany Of **Tiffanie,** or Cob-web Lawne;............8. H.11, 6
Some Goddesse, in a cloud of **Tiffanie**.........112. H.283, 8

Tigers Had Wolves or **Tigers** seen but thee,......89. H.219, 3
Thou that tam'st **Tygers,** and fierce storms (that rise)
103. H.254, 3
Tygers and Beares (I've heard some say)......252. H.746, 3

Till Twilight is yet, **till** that her Lawnes give way;
34. H.104, 5
Till, like Ixion's Cloud you be..................34. H.105, 9
Till that the green-ey'd Kitling comes..........37. H.106, 124
Till when, in such assurance live, ye may......38. H.106, 145
Till you on it did breathe;......................51. H.144, 2
Till you come forth. Wash, dresse, be briefe in praying:
68. H.178, 27
But stay the time **till** we have bade Good night...73. H.186, 2
Till we have wept, kist, sigh't, shook hands, or so.
73. H.186, 6
And **till** I turne Apostate to thy love,..........79. H.197, 81
Till you (sweet Mistresse) came and enterwove..94. H.224, 7
Til I had got the name of Villars here..........99. H.245, 2
Drink frollick boyes, **till** all be blythe..........102. H.250, 43
Till passengers shall spend their doome,........104. H.256, 20
Till they co'd not agree,.......................105. H.258, 2
Weelcome! but yet no entrance, **till** we blesse...124. H.313, 1
That tempts **till** it be tossed up;...............127. H.319, 36
Till Liber Pater twirles the house.............127. H.319, 42
Till sleep takes place of wearinesse............127. H.319, 48
Thus, **till** we see the fire lesse shine..........136. H.336, 145
Till this world shall dissolve as men,..........146. H.376, 12
Till I shall come again, let this suffice,.........146. H.377, 1
Sleeping the lucklesse Age out, **till** that she.....150. H.382, 19
Sing me to death; for **till** thy voice be cleare,...152. H.390, 1
Stay but **till** my Julia close....................164. H.441, 9
Keepe it **till** then; and now my Spouse,........175. H.465, 73
Nor leave the search, and proofe, **till** Thou canst find
181. H.483, 3
Nor will they leave Thee, **till** they both have shown
181. H.483, 7
And **till** thou com'st, thy Lycidas,............184. H.492, 37
Let me feed full, **till** that I fart, sayes Jill......186. H.498, 8
Nor is my Number full, **till** I inscribe.........199. H.545, 1
Till the Dawning of the day:..................199. H.549, 2
Till after I had handled them;................203. H.562, 4
Seldome comes Glorie **till** a man be dead........218. H.623, 2
Till that we see our cheekes Ale-dy'd..........219. H.629, 3
That your plenty last **till** when,...............224. H.638, 27
So the Fancie cooles, **till** when................242. H.714, 11
Till thou shalt say, I've paid thee with a song...248. H.730, 22
Till his Wife licking, so unglews his eyes.......269. H.816, 2
So we keepe **till** her returne...................276. H.848, 4
Till you warn her hence (away)..............276. H.850, 13
Till they be all over wet,.....................284. H.891, 3
Till Sunne-set, let it burne;...................285. H.893, 2
Till Christmas next returne...................285. H.893, 4
Till that the Cooke cries, Bring no more.......291. H.919, 4
And make no one stop, **till** my race be done.....358. N.77, 15
Long may He live, **till** He hath told............367. N.98, 27
Till my Redeemer (on the Tree)..............370. N.107, 9
Till they be hid o're with a wood of darts.......370. N.109, 2
Manners are good: but **till** his errand ends,.....378. N.137, 7
But 'twas not **till** their dearest Lord was dead;..384. N.180, 11
Soe good a soile bee-stocke and **till,**............409. A.2, 106
Soaring them vpp, boue Ruyne, **till** the doome....410. A.3, 33
— — — — — — — — — — —,................448. var. A.3, 17
— — — — — — — — — — —,...............451. var. H.197, 79

Tills In sev'rall **tills,** and boxes keepes 'em safe;..299. H.959, 2

Timber That **Timber** tall, which three-score lusters stood
23. H.69, 3

Time See Fading-time, Lifetime, Springtime
No man at one **time,** can be wise, and love.........8. H.10, 8
I dreamt the Roses one **time** went................8. H.11, 1
As were (**time** past) thy holy Filitings:...........11. H.22, 6
Still with your curles, and kisse the **time** away.....15, H.38, 2
Now is the **time,** when all the lights wax dim;....20. H.55, 1
All things decay with **Time:** The Forrest sees....23. H.69, 1
It seem'd by this **time** to admit the touch;......47. H.131, 5
Now, now's the **time;** so oft by truth............53. H.149, 1
But learn, that **Time** once lost,..................53. H.149, 7
Take **time** Lady while ye may...................56. H.149, 120
And now, both Love and **Time**................56. H.149, 123
Trees, at one **time,** shall be both sere and greene:
59. H.154, 2
Summer and Winter shall at one **time** show.....59. H.154, 5
What will, in **time,** your Fortune be:..........60. H.159, 10
And **time** will come when you shall weare.......63. H.164, 4
And take the harmlesse follie of the **time**.......69. H.178, 58
Then while **time** serves, and we are but decaying;
69. H.178, 69
But stay the **time** till we have bade Good night...73. H.186, 2
That in short **time** my woes shall cease;........73. H.187, 10
Flie discontented hence, and for a **time**.........77. H.197, 21
The **time** that I prevaricate from thee..........79. H.197, 86
Now is the **time** for mirth,......................80. H.201, 1
Old **Time** is still a flying:.......................84. H.208, 2
Then be not coy, but use your **time;**...........84. H.208, 13
O **time** that cut'st down all!....................85. H.211, 9
Downe, envious **Time** by thee..................85. H.211, 20
Time, ere long, will come and plow............97. H.232, 13

My Phill, the time he has to sleep,.............104. H.256, 16
Winds have their time to rage; but when they cease,
105. H.259, 5
Some time in wrangling spent,................105. H.260, 2
By Time, and Counsell, doe the best we can,....120. H.294, 1
Maides (in time) may ravish him..............125. H.314, 8
'Tis strange, his Father long time has been ill,..125. H.315, 3
We have short time to stay, as you,............125. H.316, 11
And my tongue at one time mute..............131. H.332, 6
Of Time, and show..........................134. H.336, 75
In time of life, I grac't ye with my Verse;.....138. H.343, 1
As for my self, since time a thousand cares.....140. H.355, 5
But time (Ai me)...........................144. H.371, 13
The coblers getting time, is at the Last.........144. H.374, 2
And Ramme of time and by vexation growes..148. H.377, 111
Of Life eternall) Time has made thee one,......152. H.392, 3
Time with the tears, that I do weep?...........158. H.420, 6
And time it is our full-fed flocks to fold.......160. H.421, 42
Every time seemes short to be,................162. H.431, 1
Mean time be it.............................171. H.455, 11
Those mites of Time, which yet remain unspent, 171. H.456, 3
By the Time the Cocks first crow..............177. H.473, 8
Let's leave a longer time to wait,..............179. H.476, 28
The time will come, when you'l be sad,........179. H.476, 37
Mean time, let Lycidas have leave to Pipe to thee.
184. H.492, 43
As Time had never known ye.................184. H.493, 12
Or for a little time we'l lye,...................190. H.515, 39
Much I know of Time is spent,................191. H.519, 3
Long time w'ave here been a toying:..........195. H.534, 3
Time flyes away fast;........................196. H.534, 13
Of Day break from the Pregnant East, 'tis time 207. H.575, 64
Meane time we two will sing the Dirge of these;
209. H.584, 7
Lais and Lucrece, in the night time are........209. H.586, 3
Jone, and my Lady have at that time one,......209. H.586, 5
Dearest of thousands, now the time drawes neere,
219. H.627, 1
None loseth that, which he in time may get.....228. H.654, 2
Those minutes, Time has lent us here..........233. H.670, 16
Time steals away like to a stream,............233. H.670, 22
Love at no time idle is:......................235. H.678, 2
Let us now take time, and play,...............238. H.691, 1
Weak I am grown, and must in short time fall; 242. H.713, 19
Chor. Much time is spent in prate; begin,......243. H.716, 23
Grow old with time, but yet keep weather-proofe.
245. H.723, 14
Who for a long sad time has weeping stood,...251, H.745, 3
Meane time that he from place to place do's rome,
253. H.753, 3
What Fate decreed, Time now ha's made us see 254. H.756, 1
Meane time thy Prophets Watch by Watch shall pray;
254. H.756, 13
Meane time like Earth-wormes we will craule below,
257. H.763, 21
Time is the Bound of things, where e're we go,
257. H.766, 1
By time, that hastens on.....................258. H.767, 15
Wrongs, if neglected, vanish in short time;.....260. H.776, 1
Lets now take our time;......................267. H.806, 1
That in little time she be.....................269. H.814, 3
O beware! in time submit;....................273. H.836, 5
Truth is best found out by the time, and eyes;..287. H.902, 1
Teares quickly drie: griefes will in time decay:..293. H.930, 1
Himselfe, at one time, can be wise, and Love....294. H.936, 4
And such as will in short time be,.............297. H.948, 3
And as time past when Cato the Severe........301. H.962, 1
Hence I must, for time doth call..............306. H.984, 38
As those your Ladies may in time be seene,...326. H.1080, 23
Time was upon...............................346. N.38, 1
But in short time 'twill please Thee,...........353. N.56, 21
To charme his cries, (at time of need:)........354. N.59, 10
And Time seems then, not for to flie, but creep;..358. N.77, 2
Which rightly us'd, both in their time and place, 371. N.115, 7
Woe worth the Time, woe worth the day,.......374. N.123, 21
The time the Bridegroom stayes from hence,....380. N.153, 1
Is but the time of penitence..................380. N.153, 2
The first of Time, or Sabbath here of Dayes;...386. N.194, 2
No spring of Time, or Times succession.........392. N.229, 2
Which neither Tettar, time, or Moth...........393. N.231, 3
But in His own time, and when He thinks fit,..396. N.252, 3
Yawne for Thy coming; some e're this time crie, 398. N.263, 7
Att what tyme to say I, or noe,.................407. A.2, 26
Natures, like ours, wee who haue spent our tyme..410. A.3, 15
Know time past this cherrystone................417. A.9, 19
— — — — — — — — — —,..............424. var. H.164, 5
bearing downe Time before you; hye.....431. ins. H.283, 50c
Welcome at last unto the Threshold, Time
431. ins. H.283, 60k
Timely Yet be timely fortunate................334. H.1125, 2
Time-past Farewell thou Thing, time-past so knowne, so deare
45. H.128, 1
Virgins, time-past, known were these,...........64. H.167, 1
Time-past so fragrant, sickly now drawn in......77. H.197, 28
Time's No spring of Time, or Times succession...392. N.229, 2
— — — — — — — — — —,................450. var. A.9, 19
Times See Oft-times, Past-times, Shearing-times, Springtimes

I sing of Times trans-shifting; and I write..........5. H.1, 9
What times of sweetnesse this faire day fore-shows,
44. H.124, 1
Furze, three or foure times with his cheeks did blow
47. H.131, 3
And thou a thousand thousand times shalt be....82. H.204, 13
Times, still succeed the former................ 84. H.208, 12
And Cedar wash thee, that no times consume thee.
89. H.219, 14
And times to come shall, weeping, read thy glory,
89. H.219, 21
How the times away doe goe:..................96. H.231, 2
What the times of old did preach..............120. H.297, 2
W'ave seen the past-best Times, and these.....133. H.336, 17
Lame, and bad times, with those are past,......134. H.336, 82
Repeat the Times that I have seen!..........135. H.336, 116
To all those times,..........................136. H.336, 149
Thou do'st redeeme those times; and what was lost
147. H.377, 41
A thousand times, more sweare, then say,....149. H.377, 132
The times of warmth; but then they flew away; 151. H.387, 2
Shall live, and thou not superlast all times?....155. H.405, 14
Mon. Bad are the times. Sil. And wors then they are we.
159. H.421, 1
All times unto their frenzies; Thou shalt there..206. H.575, 47
If nine times you your Bride-groome kisse;.....208. H.581, 1
O! Times most bad,..........................211. H.596, 1
He by extortion brings in three times more:....220. H.631, 3
To these, thou hast thy times to goe...........231. H.662, 62
Or lookt I back unto the Times hence flown,....234. H.673, 1
Times that are ill wo'nt still be so............247. H.725, 6
True, if this Citie seven times rounded was....252. H.745, 11
With rock, and seven times circumflankt with brasse,
252. H.745, 12
When times and seasons and all yeares must lie 256. H.763, 13
The Blessing fall in mellow times on Thee......269. H.818, 10
'Gainst all the indignation of the Times.........280. H.869, 2
Thus times do shift; each thing his turne do's hold:
285. H.892, 21
Praise they that will Times past, I joy to see..292. H.927, 1
None is discreet at all times; no, not Jove......294. H.936, 3
Shall not times hereafter tell..................302. H.968, 7
Times bad...................................308. H.993, 22
Which wee, and times to come, shall wonder at. 310. H.1002, 2
Know when to speake; for many times it brings
318. H.1037, 1
When times are troubled, then forbeare; but speak,
324. H.1072, 1
Nor those false vows, which oft times don't prevaile.
331. H.1104, 2
Of all those times that I in it have spent.......334. H.1124, 2
Writ in my wild unhallowed Times;..............339. N.2, 2
Afflictions bring us joy in times to come,.........349. N.45, 1
Done in the present times:......................352. N.53, 6
All times, how they............................354. N.58, 6
For times to come, I'le make this Vow,.........357. N.72, 16
Foure times bestrew thee ev'ry yeere............360. N.83, 36
Howeuer after tymes will praise,................407. A.2, 15
When on the Flood that nine times circles Hell...417. A.8, 36
Times, Titles, Trophies, may be lost and Spent;...419. A.10, 3
— — — — — — — — — —,..............426. var. H.197, 28
— — — — — — — — — —,..............437. var. H.336, 114
Tim-Trundell's With all the rabble of Tim-Trundells race,
155. H.405, 12
Tin Brasse, Leade, or Tinne, throw into th' mould;
297. H.948, 10
Tincture For tincture, wonder at..................12. H.23, 8
Or some fine tincture, like to this,.............75. H.193, 12
The tincture of Vermillion:....................118. H.291, 6
But take no tincture from my sinfull Book:......371. N.113, 8
Tinctures, And tinctures naturall.................75. H.193, 32
So, when Death comes, Fresh tinctures lose their place,
207. H.576, 5
By all those Tinctures there,..................257. H.767, 3
Tind Will not teend to your desire;............263. H.786, 2
Part must be kept wherewith to teend..........285. H.893, 5
Tinding Come while the Log is a teending.....263. H.784, 12
Tingles, One Eare tingles; some there be,.......329. H.1096, 1
Tinkers Here of Tinkers;......................320. H.1051, 3
Tinkling And the tinkling of my Bell,...........372. N.121, 3
Tinseled Tinseld with Twilight, He, and They..165. H.443, 21
Tinseling Or Moone-light tinselling the streames:..34. H.105, 4
Like Morning-Sun-shine tinsilling the dew......205. H.575, 12
Tintarret The Palme from Urbin, Titian, Tintarret,
150. H.384, 2
Tintoretto See Tintarret
T'invade See Invade
T'invoke See Invoke
Tip Sunk from the tip of your soft eare,..........61. H.160, 8
Comends it to your eares soft tipp..............417. A.9, 14
Tipped The which with ruby rednes being tipt....404. A.1, 21
Tipple To tipple freely in a flower...............71. H.182, 4
Tippled Tipled he was; and tipling lispt withall; 313. H.1017, 5
Tippling Tipled he was; and tipling lispt withall;
313. H.1017, 5
Tipsy Halfe tipsie to the Fairie Bed,............165. H.443, 4
Tire Grown violent, do's either die, or tire.........51. H.143, 4

Makes the smirk face of each **to** shine,.........147. H.377, 72
Are wanting **to** her exercise, but great........148. H.377, 113
Expos'd **to** all the comming Winters cold.......151. H.387, 4
Sing me **to** death; for till thy voice be cleare,..152. H.390, 1
Which I worke **to** Meale, and make............152. H.393, 3
Skinns he din'd well **to** day; how do you think?..156. H.409, 1
Good morrow **to** the Day so fair;..............156. H.412, 1
Good morning Sir **to** you:.....................156. H.412, 2
Good morrow **to** mine own torn hair...........156. H.412, 3
Good morning **to** this Prim-rose too;..........156. H.412, 5
To morrow.......................................160. H.421, 47
To morrow thou shalt see......................161. H.425, 6
(As Salust saith) co-incident **to** feare...........162. H.430, 2
The worke that I wo'd put ye **to**?..............164. H.442, 2
Are **to** a wilde digestion brought,.............166. H.443, 35
And next **to** these two blankets ore-.........167. H.443, 94
Give way, give way **to** me, who come...........169. H.449, 9
And prayers **to** Venus; if it please............175. H.465, 75
These, or those ends, **to** which Thou wast design'd
181. H.483, 4
He Boded good-luck **to** thy Selfe and Spouse...181. H.483, 12
Shame is a bad attendant **to** a State:...........182. H.488, 1
(Unkind **to** us) **to** spend thine houres,.........183. H.492, 15
What ha's the Court **to** do with Swaines,......184. H.402, 21
Be-pranckt with Ribbands, **to** this end,........193. H.521, 44
And as He shuts, close up **to** Maids again......196. H.537, 4
Let our soules flie **to'** th' shades, where ever springs
205. H.575, 2
I will whisper **to** your eares,..................208. H.580, 5
Dull **to** my selfe, and almost dead **to** these......214. H.612, 1
Lost **to** all Musick now; since every thing......214. H.612, 3
But give thy place **to** night,...................220. H.633, 9
Set you **to** your Wheele, and wax.............221. H.633, 42
When thence ye see my reverend Ghost **to** rise,..222. H.634, 3
But lul'd **to** calmnesse, then succeeds a breeze..225. H.642, 15
To th' number five,..........................227. H.653, 10
Nod **to** this vow of mine:.......................228. H.657, 4
Anathema **to** it, and me......................229. H.660, 4
Time steals away like **to** a stream,.............233. H.670, 22
Like **to** a Deaw, or melted Frost.............233. H.670, 27
Teare me **to** tatters; yet I'le be................235. H.677, 3
Compar'd (in this my ample Orbe) **to** Him......236. H.685, 4
I'le drink **to** the Garlands a-round it:..........239. H.695, 3
O Place! O People! Manners! fram'd **to** please 242. H.713, 9
Lay **to** thy stake a lustie Steere,..............243. H.716, 14
What others can't with all their strength put **to**. 245. H.722, 2
Ch. What's that **to** me, I waft nor fish or fowles,
248. H.730, 9
Meane time that he from place **to** place do's rome,
253. H.753, 3
Then reach those ends that thou wast destin'd **to**.
254. H.756, 8
Green, **to** the end of dayes...................261. H.778, 12
And Genius waits **to** have us both **to** bed.......261. H.781, 6
Ill luck 'twill bode **to** th' Bridegroome and the Bride.
262. H.781, 12
And drink **to** your hearts desiring.............263. H.784, 6
Will not teend **to** your desire;.................263. H.786, 2
Here **to** be paid; Ile pay't i'th'world **to** come...267. H.804, 14
Fortune her selfe can lay no claim **to** it.........272. H.830, 2
I heare in thee rare Laniere **to** sing;...........276. H.851, 4
Or if haire remaines **to** me.....................277. H.852, 4
Neglected there (maids trust **to** me)...........304. H.980, 8
But carve **to** him the fat flanks; and he shall...305. H.982, 3
And lisping reeld, and reeling like **to** fall.......313. H.1017, 6
To his owne vocation..........................315. H.1026, 14
And though we bid adieu **to** day,...............324. H.1068, 23
And in their motion smelt much like **to** flowers 326. H.1080, 13
God has his whips here **to** a twofold end,.........343. N.26, 1
God strikes His Church, but 'tis **to** this intent,...344. N.31, 1
To figure **to** us, nothing more then this,.........345. N.34, 3
His New-yeeres trebled **to** His old:..............367. N.98, 28
To shun the least Temptation **to** a sin;.........392. N.230, 30
But substance, **to**! receaue this Pearlye Teare....412. A.3, 81
Toad If so be a **Toad** be laid.................209. H.587, 1
Toadstones With brownest **Toadstones**, and the Gum
166. H.443, 57
Toast Me to the Tap, the **Tost**, the Turfe; Let Wine
79. H.197, 88
To-day **See Day**
The morrowes life too late is, Live **to-day**.......228. H.655, 2
To-do **See Do**
Tods By those soft **Tods** of wooll...............257. H.767, 1
Toe Mab will pinch her by the **toe**..............201. H.556, 8
Toes A chaine of Cornes, pickt from her eares and **toes**:
232. H.668, 2
Together Wisdome and she **together** goe,.........35. H.106, 14
And keep a Fast, and Funerall **together**,.........41. H.118, 6
Fire and water shall **together** lye...............59. H.154, 3
Like those short sweets ere knit **together**.......107. H.263, 22
And, having pray'd **together**, we..............125. H.316, 9
Together with the Stages glory stood..........150. H.382, 3
Mirt. Where she and I shall never meet **together**.
159. H.421, 30
Take me and mine **together**...................169. H.446, 12
Where both may rage, both drink and dance **together**.
206. H.575, 38
Fall down **together** vanquisht both, and lye....216. H.618, 15
The Devill and shee **together**:..................225. H.643, 3
Chor. And lay we down our Pipes **together**,....244. H.716, 47
Ph. A deale of Love, and much, much Griefe **together**.
248. H.730, 14
So I may but die **together**:....................254. H.757, 2
Meale and it now mix **together**;................258. H.769, 5
Where we may snug, and close **together** lye.....278. H.860. 7
That the Monks and Fryers **together**,..........304. H.976, 3
Let us wash, and pray **together**:...............324. H.1069, 6
Our eyes out all **together**......................373. N.123, 10
Encurlld **together**, and noe difference show
431. ins. H.283, 50f
Into your selves like wooll **together** spunne,
431. ins. H.283, 50h
Toil Come down, and dance ye in the **toyle**..........9. H.15, 1
The Sea-scourg'd Merchant, after all his **toile**,...77. H.197, 16
Come Sons of Summer, by whose **toile**,.........101. H.250, 1
'Twas better there to **toyle**, then prove.........219. H.628, 5
A little Trade best fits a little **Toyle**:...........249. H.733, 5
Reward, we know, is the chiefe end of **toile**.....322. H.1060, 2
Toils Are but **Toiles**, or Manicles................53. H.147, 8
These golden **Toyles**, and Trammel-nets,........282. H.881, 2
To'is All Flowers sent **to'is** burying.............186. H.497, 10
Told And had **told** all; but did refraine,...........13. H.27, 9
Old wives have often **told**, how they............18. H.46, 1
Who **told** me, they had drawn a thred............18. H.47, 7
It will be **told**...................................63. H.164, 13
Many a jest **told** of the Keyes betraying........69. H.178, 55
And **told** her, (as some tears did fall)...........71. H.182, 25
While Golden Angels (some have **told** to me)..86. H.213, 23
Amar. But deare Mirtillo, I have heard it **told**,..86. H.213, 29
And, to these, ye must be **told**,..................97. H.232, 12
And his actions high be **told**...................108. H.266, 19
Woman wo'd bring him more then co'd be **told**,..129. H.326, 4
She **told** me too, as that did spend,.............153. H.399, 5
You say y'are young; but when your Teeth are **told**
173. H.462, 1
When I love, (as some have **told**,..............204. H.569, 1
Live in the Love of Doves, and having **told**....222. H.633, 62
What dismall Stories will be **told**.............272. H.828, 15
And **told** me too, he maketh...................279. H.863, 10
Teage has **told** lyes so long, that when Teage tells
282. H.880, 1
He shew'd, and **told** me too,....................346. N.38, 16
Long may He live, till He hath **told**............367. N.98, 27
Toll **Tole** forth my death; next, to my buryall come.
100. H.248, 6
Boreman takes **tole**, cheats, flatters, lyes, yet Boreman,
315. H.1025, 1
When the passing-bell doth **tole**,.................348. N.41, 21
But he takes **tole** of? all the Griest............376. N.127, 4
Tolled Nay tell the Bell-man of the Night had **tould**
410. A.3, 17
Tom To clense his eyes, **Tom** Brock makes much adoe.
110. H.273, 1
A Vicarige at last **Tom** Glasse got here,........151. H.385, 3
Tom Chipperfeild, and pritty-lisping Ned,.......155. H.405, 9
At Post and Paire, or Slam, **Tom** Tuck would play
238. H.693, 1
Tom shifts the Trenchers; yet he never can.....265. H.796, 1
Serve or not serve, let **Tom** doe what he can,...265. H.796, 3
Tom Blinks his Nose is full of wheales, and these
273. H.834, 1
Tom calls not pimples, but Pimpleides:.........273. H.834, 2
Brown bread **Tom** Pennie eates, and must of right,
309. H.997, 1
Tomasin And be of all admired, **Tomasin**.......304. H.979, 2
Tomb Here, here the **Tomb** of Robin Herrick is...19. H.50, 6
Or for mine honour, lay me in that **Tombe**.......20. H.55, 7
To doe the Rites to thy Religious **Tombe**:.......27. H.82, 2
And with flowers dresse my **Tomb**...............44. H.125, 4
Pity me too, who found so soone a **Tomb**........58. H.151, 4
Next, hollow out a **Tombe** to cover..............61. H.159, 28
And offer Tears upon thy **Tomb**:................89. H.219, 10
And with Smallage dresse my **Tomb**:............89. H.220, 2
Not Virgil's Gnat had such a **Tomb**...........104. H.256, 21
And doe some honour to my **Tomb**..............111. H.280, 8
That will with flowers the **Tomb** bestrew,........156. H.412, 7
And bring those dew-drink-offerings to my **Tomb**.
222. H.634, 2
The ghost from the **Tomb**......................225. H.643, 22
And clos'd her up, as in a **Tombe**...............237. H.686, 16
More rich then Cleopatra's **Tombe**..............269. H.817, 4
For a Stone, ha's Heaven his **Tombe**,..........270. H.821, 8
And bring fresh strewings to thy **Tombe**..........359. N.83, 6
To guild thy **Tombe**; besides, these Caules,......360. N.83, 43
All, all we lay upon thy **Tombe**.................360. N.83, 48
Come forth, to strew thy **Tombe** with flow'rs:...361. N.83, 74
Thy very **Tomb**..................................375. N.123, 89
And with the fourth key He unlocks the **tombe**...390. N.224, 4
Haile holy, and all-honour'd **Tomb**,..............402. N.269, 1
Of Him, we lately seal'd up in this **Tombe**?.....403. N.271, 4
To the **tombe** wher't must be layd...............418. A.9, 44
Tombed **Tomb'd** in a Christal stone,..............75. H.193, 5
With Lillies **Tomb'd** up in a Glasse;............186. H.497, 16
Tombs For I know, in the **Tombs**..................197. H.540, 7

We o're the tombes, and Fates shall flye;......288. H.906, 3
What more than these can Tombs or Tomb-stones Pay? 419. A.10, 5

Tombstone Let not thy Tomb-stone er'e be laid by me: 281. H.875, 1

Tombstones What more than these can Tombs or Tomb-stones Pay?....................................419. A.10, 5

Tomorrow **See Morrow**
To-morrow, Julia, I betimes must rise,..........102. H.251, 1

Tone Or any tone...........................314. H.1024, 10

Tones Let them speak by gentle tones,...........82. H.203, 9
He doth it with the sweetest tones of Art:......266. H.799, 2

Tongue By no one tongue, there, censured..........6. H.2, 24
As to shew her Tongue wag through:............11. H.21, 10
Because his Tongue was ty'd againe.............13. H.27, 10
And sure his tongue had more exprest,..........42. H.119, 11
And (oh!) had it but a tongue,................57. H.149, 139
The Eyes by tears speak, while the Tongue is mute. 58. H.150, 8
To scratch or claw, so that thy tongue not railes: 66. H.173, 6
Nor cheek, or tongue be dumbe:................80. H.201, 2
Wither'd my hand, and palsie-struck my tongue..84. H.210, 10
Mark, if her tongue, but slily, steale a taste......100. H.248, 4
To speak by Teares, before ye have a Tongue...104. H.257, 14
And my tongue at one time mute.............131. H.332, 6
The tongue in peace; but then in warre the hand. 137. H.339, 2
Goes with your mouth, or do's outrun your tongue; 141. H.359, 14
Those silver-pence, that cut the tongue........166. H.443, 70
Get their comportment, and the gliding tongue..172. H.456, 5
Can tell by tongue; or true-love tie:............202. H.560, 12
To heare the incantation of his tongue:........206. H.575, 30
Or let her tongue be still, or stir,..............207. H.579, 5
Her tongue, to tell what danger's neare.........246. H.724, 16
When a warm tongue do's with such Ambers meet. 269. H.816, 4
Not a wimbling Tongue admit:................282. H.878, 6
Suffer thy legs, but not thy tongue to walk:.....341. N.12, 1
Tell us, thou cleere and heavenly Tongue,.......367. N.102, 1
God, in the holy Tongue, they call..............385. N.185, 1
In which the tongue, though but a member small,..405. A.1, 29
As Fame or Rumour, hath or Trumpe or Tongue. 411. A.3, 46

Tongueless Now since my love is tongue-lesse, know me such, 15. H.38, 13
As is the fish, or tonguelesse Crocodile...........58. H.150, 2
True Love is tonguelesse as a Crocodile.........274. H.837, 8
'Twill make a tongless man to wooe............325. H.1075, 2
That in the mirk and tonguelesse night,........357. N.72, 13

Tongues Small griefs find tongues: Full Casques are ever found 15. H.38, 7
If unto me all Tongues were granted,...........91. H.223, 26
Favour your tongues, who enter here............91. H.223, 41
Untill our tongues shall tell our ears,.........136. H.336, 143
The tongues of Kids shall be thy meate;.......192. H.521, 11
Wooers have Tongues of Ice, but burning hearts. 274. H.837, 10

Tongue-tied For those lips, that tongue-ty'd are:..82. H.203, 2

To-night **See Night**

Toning But the toning of a teare:...............170. H.450, 4

Too **See Too-too-kind**
Have their Existence, and their Influence too.....3. Ded.H, 8
Be her cheeks so shallow too,....................11. H.21, 9
But this I'le tell ye too.........................13. H.31, 5
I did; and kist the Instep too:..................14. H.33, 2
You blame me too, because I cann't devise........15. H.38, 3
In her lap too I can lye.........................17. H.43, 5
Yet justly too I must confesse;.................19. H.51, 5
And for your breaths too, let them smell.........20. H.54, 3
As blessed soules cann't heare too much:.........22. H.68, 4
And Wings too, which did shiver;...............27. H.81, 18
Is too precise in every part.....................28. H.83, 14
Who, with his looks too, can appease............31. H.90, 4
Saile against Rocks, and split them too;..........31. H.90, 8
That man loves not, who is not zealous too.........31. H.91, 2
Draw him as like too, as you can,................38. H.108, 5
If so, we'll think too, (when he do's condemne...39. H.110, 3
The Laurell, Mirtle, Oke, and Ivie too..........41. H.117, 10
Say too, She wo'd have this;...................43. H.123, 31
The soule, like lightning, and as active too.......45. H.128, 28
Herrick, thou art too coorse to love............51. H.142, 22
The Last Watch out, and saw the Dawning too...52. H.146, 4
Doves, 'two'd say, yee bill too long...........57. H.149, 140
Pity me too, who found so soone a Tomb.........58. H.151, 4
The Tree, Bethesda, and the Angel too:..........61. H.161, 6
Ah! then too late, close in your chamber keeping, 63. H.164, 12
And be, too, such a yoke,......................65. H.172, 15
As not too wide,...............................65. H.172, 16
Many a glance too has been sent................69. H.178, 53
Where either too much light his worth..........75. H.193, 22
Lest they too far extend.......................76. H.193, 48
Have I been cold to hug thee, too remisse,......78. H.197, 34
Too temp'rate in embracing? Tell me, ha's desire.78. H.197, 35
Too strong for Fate to break us: Look upon....78. H.197, 71

Th'ast dar'd too farre; but Furie now forbeare....82. H.204, 1
Sing I co'd once; and bravely too enspire........84. H.210, 3
As he is Prince, he's Shepherd too..............86. H.213, 44
The Fringe that circumbinds it too,............92. H.223, 64
I, and their Book of Canons too...............92. H.223, 78
I, and their Abby-Lubbers too:................93. H.223, 108
Many a trifle too, and trinket,................93. H.223, 123
Barre close as you can, and bolt fast too your doore, 97. H.233, 1
Tell her too, she must not be,..................98. H.238, 3
But yet too short for you: 'tis we,.............114. H.283, 73
Tempting the two too modest; can............115. H.283, 113
Put in Love, and put in too...................116. H.285, 3
That was too coorse; but then forthwith........119. H.293, 31
The midst is thine; but Joves the Evening too;..128. H.321, 4
Undreadfull too of courtly thunderclaps:.........128. H.323, 6
And stils the Bride too, when she cries........130. H.329, 11
And that, thou lov'dst me too.................142. H.364, 4
Y'ave dipt too long i'th' Vinegar;..............146. H.377, 22
A hand too desp'rate, or a knife that bites......147. H.377, 53
Birds chuse their Mates, and couple too, this day: 149. H.378, 2
Oh fie upon 'em! Lastly too, all witt...........150. H.382, 17
Of Holben, and That mighty Ruben too.........150. H.384, 4
She told me too, as that did spend,............153. H.399, 5
Ile too work, or pray; and then................155. H.407, 5
Good morning to this Prim-rose too;...........156. H.412, 5
Mirt. This way she came, and this way too she went; 159. H.421, 18
Ile beg, and buy it too........................160. H.422, 4
'Tis fit they make no One with them too great...163. H.438, 2
A pure smooth Pearle, and Orient too?..........164. H.440, 8
I call all Maids to witnesse too................165. H.442, 12
And this our life too whirles away,.............172. H.457, 3
The Golden chain too, and the Civick Crown.....176. H.466, 8
Your Larders too so hung with meat,...........178. H.476, 5
And spangled too,............................181. H.484, 2
Be She too wealthy, or too poore; be sure,......185. H.494, 3
And my Enchantments too;....................198. H.544, 27
The top, and the top-gallant too...............202. H.560, 8
Suppling and successefull too:.................204. H.569, 8
Broke is my Reed, hoarse is my singing too:.....205. H.573, 2
Two loving followers too unto the Grove,......206. H.575, 23
So yellow-green, and sickly too?...............208. H.580, 8
Fie, Lovely maid! Indeed you are too slow,....216. H.618, 5
As will if you yeeld, lye down conquer'd too.....216. H.618, 12
What Love said was too too true:..............219. H.628, 8
Who gripes too hard the dry and slip'rie sand,..221. H.633, 52
Floure of Fuz-balls, that's too good...........223. H.638, 15
But if this may seem too much.................223. H.638, 21
The morrowes life too late is, Live to-day.......228. H.655, 2
Thy May-poles too with Garlands grac't:.......230. H.662, 53
And no man payes too deare for it..............231. H.662, 61
And crown thy temples too, and let............233. H.670, 19
To kick the Flow'rs, and scorn their odours too?.234. H.673, 4
For, if we gaze on These brave Lamps too neer, 237. H.685, 11
Too much she gives to some, enough to none.....238. H.689, 2
Whom whitest Fortune dandled has too much....239. H.697, 2
As easie, and els easier too:...................245. H.720, 12
Go on too with this:..........................247. H.727, 2
More pleasing too, then ever was...............251. H.740, 11
Marian too in Pagentrie:......................255. H.761, 8
Besides too, in a brave,.......................259. H.772, 16
As for the rest, being too great a summe......267. H.804, 13
Is both unluckie; I, and foolish too............268. H.813, 2
So many Kings, and Primates too there are,....272. H.826, 4
And not unlikely; rather too then fail,..........272. H.829, 3
And thou do'st languish too:..................273. H.833, 3
Poets co'd not praise too much................274. H.838, 4
And told me too, he maketh...................279. H.863, 10
Close, but not too strictly lac't:...............282. H.878, 4
Teares most prevaile; with teares too thou mayst move 287. H.900, 1
Demure, but yet, full of temptation too.........290. H.914, 6
T'ave Boyes, and Gyrles too, as they will.......291. H.919, 12
By laughing too, and lying downe,..............291. H.919, 21
And strugling there, I kist thee too;...........294. H.939, 8
And meat too, for his need:..................295. H.942, 6
It (Ah!) too late repents me..................296. H.946, 9
Find'st here a fault, and mend'st the trespasse too: 298. H.955, 8
That sho'd you stirre, we and our Altars too....300. H.961, 17
She smil'd; he kist; and kissing, cull'd her too; 313. H.1017, 9
With store of ale too;.......................317. H.1035, 22
Who loves too much, too much the lov'd will hate. 318. H.1038, 2
You set too high a rate upon.................324. H.1068, 17
'Twill quickly mar, & make ye too.............325. H.1075, 6
Love's of it self, too sweet; the best of all......327. H.1084, 1
And all my troubles too......................328. H.1091, 8
I have been wanton, and too bold I feare,......329. H.1095, 1
He shew'd, and told me too,...................346. N.38, 16
Give Thee a Dart, and Dagger too;.............349. N.46, 4
Lord, I confesse too, when I dine,..............350. N.47, 27
And be the blow too what it will,...............351. N.48, 3

And tell Him, (for good handsell too)............354. N.59, 7
Meat for our meales, and fragments too:........356. N.66, 4
Too soon, too deere did Jephthah buy,...........360. N.83, 19
A poyson too He has for Socrates;..............370. N.108, 8
We bid the Creuse and Pannier too:...........374. N.123, 32
Mine's faulty too, and small:..................376. N.125, 6
And fresh joyes, as never too.................377. N.128, 23
And as all-present, so all-filling too............394. N.237, 2
That if the twig sho'd chance too much to smart,
394. N.241, 3
So do the Skurfe and Bran too: Go Thy way,..398. N.263, 12
God is the APXH, and the ΤΕΛΟΣ too...........403. N.272, 2
And such a smiling Tulip too............424. ins. H.164, 11a
— — — — — — — — — — —, ...434. var. H.293, 53
Took She rather took, then got a fall:...............12. H.27, 2
Such fleeting pleasures there I took,..............17. H.41, 20
For some rich flower, he took the lip...........71. H.182, 5
So Julia took the Pilferer......................71. H.182, 10
That, that he took, and that was all.............71. H.182, 26
And took it up, and view'd it; then..............73. H.187, 6
I took him, put him in my cup,..................96. H.229, 3
He tooke her; now the jest in this appeares,....129. H.326, 5
The yvorie tooke State to hold..................185. H.497, 5
A Postern-bribe tooke, or a Forked-Fee........202. H.557, 25
That surfeit tooke by bread, the worst of all.....286. H.895, 2
Rapine has yet tooke nought from me;..........376. N.124, 1
Christ took our Nature on Him, not that He....390. N.222, 1
Tooly The Eggs of Pheasants wrie-nosed Tooly sells;
204. H.568, 1
Too't See To't
Tooth Browne as his Tooth. A little Moth,......120. H.293, 41
Ne'r yet set tooth in stump, or rump of these.....142. H.361, 2
With lawlesse tooth the floure of wheate:......310. H.1004, 4
To have a tooth twitcht out of's native frame....323. H.1066, 2
Drawn was his tooth; but stanke so, that some say,
323. H.1066, 3
— — — — — — — — — — —, ...422. var. H.106, 109
Toothed Rubie-lipt, and tooth'd with Pearl:......136. H.337, 2
Too-too-kind Had Lesbia (too-too-kind) but known
104. H.256, 11
For being too-too-kind?.......................188. H.509, 8
Too-true-report And when thou hear'st by that too-true-Report,
37. H.106, 89
Top The top, and the top-gallant too............202. H.560, 8
At whose faire topp to please the sight there growes
405. A.1, 35
— — — — — — — — — — —, ...427. var. H.197, 52
Topaz But by the Topaz, Opal, Calcedon...........30. H.88, 12
Topgallant The top, and the top-gallant too.......202. H.560, 8
Topic Decree thy everlasting Topick there..........172. H.456, 8
Tops Like Iphyclus, upon the tops of Corn.......78. H.197, 50
— — — — — — — — — — —, ...427. var. H.197, 52
— — — — — — — — — — —,............435. var. H.293, 45y
Torch See, see the Bride-grooms Torch..........54. H.149, 53
Bright as the Wise-men's Torch, which guided them
86. H.213, 21
Mount up thy flames, and let thy Torch........113. H.283, 33
Torment Such a pernicious torment is:...........50. H.139, 13
Tormented To be tormented, or kept Pris'ners here?
33. H.101, 2
And am tormented now.......................295. H.942, 12
Tormenting See Soul-tormenting
Both tormenting Lovers ever...................103. H.253, 10
Tormentor Thine houre is come; and the Tormentor stands
398. N.263, 3
Torments Yet, in torments, I'le commend Thee: 351. N.48, 6
Torments for high Attilius; and, with want,.....370. N.108, 9
Torn Good morrow to mine own torn hair........156. H.412, 3
Turn'd, but not torn:........................190. H.515, 42
Shut every gate; mend every hedge that's torne,.259. H.771, 5
Torn for the use of Pasterie:..................275. H.844, 4
With Hose and Doublet torne:..................295. H.942, 2
Absyrtus-like all torne confusedly:..............300. H.960, 2
And as in meanes, in minde all torne...........312. H.1016, 6
Torrid Runs from his Torrid Zone, to prie, and look,
114. H.283, 62
Torture And of such Torture as no one would grutch
115. H.283, 136
Tortured And back again, (tortur'd with fears) doth fly,
36. H.106, 67
Tortur'd her love, not to transgresse the Law....384. N.180, 6
To's Back must now go to's habitation:..........140. H.355, 2
Tossed That tost up, after Fox-i'th'hole:........126. H.319, 14
That tempts till it be tossed up:...............127. H.319, 36
Well then, on what Seas we are tost,..........134. H.336, 57
That's tost up after Fox i' th' Hole............231. H.662, 57
When (God knowes) I'm tost about,............348. N.41, 33
To't Cock calls his Wife his Hen: when Cock goes too't,
213. H.610, 1
Franck wo'd go scoure her teeth; and setting to't,
247. H.728, 1
Who cannot buie, or steale a second to't........332. H.1110, 2
To'th' (Partial List)
To'th' Glasse your lips incline;...............185. H.495, 6
Sick is the Land to'th' heart; and doth endure..214. H.612, 5
To'th'height See Height
Tottering When as the roof's a tottering:........318. H.1036, 4
Touch The mellow touch of musick most doth wound
12. H.24, 1
Touch not the Tyrant; Let the Gods alone........32. H.97, 5
Soft speech, smooth touch, the lips, the Maiden-head:
45. H.128, 8
To th'board, so hot, as none co'd touch the same:.47. H.131, 2
It seem'd by this time to admit the touch;........47. H.131, 5
And make, what ere they touch, turn sweet.......55. H.149, 62
That ne'r knew Brides, or Bride-grooms touch,. 57. H.149, 132
I shall be heal'd, if that my King but touch.....62. H.161, 14
So long you did not sing, or touch your Lute,....95. H.228, 1
And that Apollo shall so touch Your eare,......107. H.264, 2
Thus, thus with hallowed foot I touch the ground,
242. H.713, 5
When I touch, I then begin.....................253. H.750, 8
Touch but thy Lire (my Harrie) and I heare....276. H.851, 1
And heale me with thy looke, or touch:..........344. N.29, 7
Touch gently, gently touch; and here............366. N.97, 20
Come then, and gently touch the Birth..........366. N.98, 18
Bleeding, that no Blood touch the ground:......377. N.129, 6
Know, to' th' hearing as the touch..............418. A.9, 50
Touched Made all that touch't her with her scent,..9. H.15, 11
And whom she touch't, turne sweet...............9. H.15, 12
But all are toucht (like lawfull plate)...........236. H.681, 5
That's sweetly touch't, I must confesse:........243. H.716, 25
He toucht me so, as that I burn,..............295. H.942, 11
Toucht every where with such diffused grace.....307. H.992, 2
Tough Both with her Husband's, and her own tough fleame.
98. H.237, 2
By whose tough labours, and rough hands,......101. H.250, 3
Tow Burne the flax, and fire the tow:..........315. H.1026, 6
Toward Each Flower has wept, and bow'd toward the East,
68. H.178, 7
Towards See T'wards
With my face towards the East................307. H.991, 8
Towel The sacred Towell, and the holy Eure.........355. N.65, 5
Tower Ye Towre her up, as Danae was;........116. H.283, 144
Kept, as Danae in a Tower:....................120. H.297, 4
Towering See High-towering
More towring, more disparkling then thy fires:..113. H.283, 36
And towring Lucan, Horace, Juvenal,..........206. H.575, 44
Next, when I see Thee towring in the skie,......301. H.966, 3
Towers That Towrs high rear'd dread most the lightnings threat:.....................................181. H.483, 14
Town Spoile a house, to save a towne:.............21. H.61, 6
And cry out, Hey, for our town green..........127. H.319, 20
(While she gossips in the towne).............284. H.889, 4
People a City or a Towne....................291. H.919, 22
To keepe a Citie, then to winne a Towne.......307. H.989, 2
Towns (As other Townes and Cities were) for gold,
251. H.745, 6
Toying Long time w'ave here been a toying:......195. H.534, 3
Toys But toyes, to give my heart some ease:....246. H.724, 30
Trace And trace the Hare i' th' trecherous Snow:
231. H.662, 63
Track See Cross-track
Trade Doll she so soone began the wanton trade;..149. H.379, 1
A little Trade best fits a little Toyle:..........249. H.733, 5
Trades Driving these sharking trades, is out at heels.
153. H.398, 2
Tradescant's Then, next, to match Tradescant's curious shels,
232. H.668, 3
Tradition Noah the first was (as Tradition sayes).386. N.195, 1
Tragedian That must this day act the Tragedian,.398. N.263, 20
Tragic Can'st write the Comick, Tragick straine, and fall
298. H.955, 5
Train See Maiden-train
No such crab'd vizard: Thou hast learnt thy Train,
147. H.377, 35
Trains With eyes of Peacocks Trains, & Trout-..166. H.443, 68
Tramaletts See Trammelets
Trammel See Trammel-net, Trammel-nets
Trammelets Her long disheuel'd rose-crown'd tramaletts:
404. A.1, 4
Trammel-net The Larke into the Trammell net:..231. H.662, 65
Trammel-nets These golden Toyles, and Trammel-nets,
282. H.881, 2
Tramplers A little while from Tramplers free;....123. H.306, 10
Trance See Entrance
Transcendent God, and far more transcendent then the rest?
78. H.197, 60
In me a more transcendant heate,..............135. H.336, 102
Transcending — — — — — — — —, ...427. var. H.197, 60
Transfer Goddesse Isis cann't transfer.............59. H.155, 7
More love, when they transfer..................75. H.193, 35
Transfiguration For all this fair Transfiguration...140. H.356, 4
Transfuse Yet lost ere you transfuse your smell...88. H.216, 15
Or else trans-fuse thy breath into the chest,.......129. H.327, 3
I dreamt, last night, Thou didst transfuse.........357. N.75, 1
Transfusing Soules transfusing thus, and die......235. H.678, 8
Transgress He that may sin, sins least; Leave to transgresse
109. H.270, 1
Man may at first transgress, but next do well: 314. H.1021, 1
Tortur'd her love, not to transgresse the Law....384. N.180, 6
Transgression Pleas'd with transgression ev'ry where:
66. H.175, 4
One chiefe transgression is among the rest,......197. H.539, 7

Who after his **transgression** doth repent,........268. H.809, 1
My delicate **transgression**,......................357. N.72, 6
A mans **transgression** God do's then remit,......359. N.82, 1
But for my friends **transgression**!.............400. N.266, 6
Transgressions For these **Transgressions** which thou here dost see,..4. Ap., 1
If all **transgressions** here should have their pay,..343. N.27, 1
Transgressor But look, how each **transgressor** onward went 391. N.227, 3
Translated Whom gentle fate **translated** hence..226. H.644, 5
Transmit Whose pure-Immortall body doth **transmit** 157. H.414, 9
Transmutation I feele in me, this **transmutation** now. 84. H.210, 8
Transparent More faire in this **transparent** case,..75. H.193, 6
Transpire When thus enkindled they **transpire**...145. H.375, 17
This, that, and ev'ry Thicket doth **transpire**....205. H.575, 7
Trans-shifted When Monarchies **trans-shifted** are, and gone; 210. H.592, 3
Trans-shifting I sing of Times **trans-shifting**; and I write 5. H.1, 9
Transverse But of a little **Transverce** bone;......91. H.223, 57
Trap **Trap**, of a Player turn'd a Priest now is;..325. H.1076, 1
Traps These are **traps** to take fooles in...........52. H.147, 6
Trasy A ***Trasy** I do keep, whereby.............246. H.724, 26
Travail See **Travel**
Travailed See **Traveled**
Travails See **Travels**
Travel Buy'st **Travell** at the lowest price.......36. H.106, 82
And so to **travaile** hence......................352. N.53, 13
Traveled For since I've **travail'd** all this Realm throughout 267. H.804, 5
Ne're **trauylde** for beyonde the seas,............409. A.2, 92
Travels The truth of **Travails** lesse in bookes then Thee. 330. H.1100, 18
Treacherous And trace the Hare i' th' **trecherous** Snow: 231. H.662, 63
Tread See **Cocks-tread**
Whose silv'rie feet did **tread**,..................110. H.274, 14
Himen, O Himen! **Tread** the sacred ground;....113. H.283, 31
And Cock-like Hens Ile **tread**:................160. H.422, 10
Tread, Sirs, as lightly as ye can.............226. H.644, 1
They **tread** on clouds, and though they sometimes fall, 250. H.737, 3
Tread ore his gleab, but with such care, that where 259. H.771, 7
Then depart, but see ye **tread**..................274. H.838, 7
With shoes put off, to **tread** thy Roome.........402. N.269, 3
And whatsoever thing they **tread** vpon...........406. A.1, 93
Treaders Lookes for the **treaders**; every where is wove 115. H.283, 122
Treading **Treading** on Amber, with their silver-feet: 26. H.79, 8
Treading upon Vermilion.....................112. H.283, 14
The following plague still **treading** on his heels..362. N.86, 2
Treads Smell, where your soft foot **treads**;......55. H.149, 64
May his soft foot, where it **treads**,............108. H.266, 13
Cock **treads** his Hen, but treads her under-foot. 213. H.610, 2
Thou go'st; and as thy foot there **treads**,......230. H.662, 30
Treason The seeds of **Treason** choake up as they spring, 10. H.17, 1
Treasure The **treasure** of the Spring............250. H.740, 4
Treasures To the **Treasures**, shall I goe,........40. H.115, 3
And when before him we have laid our **treasures**, 87. H.213, 47
Treaties Know so long **Treaties**; beate the drumme 432. ins. H.283, 140c
Trebius Is not reserv'd for **Trebius** here,........147. H.377, 58
Treble **Treble** that million, and when that is done,..24. H.74, 7
Treble the number of these good I've writ........339. N.1, 4
And that His **treble** Honours may be seen,....368. N.102, 23
Trebled His New-yeeres **trebled** to His old:......367. N.98, 28
Tree See **Crosstree, Gospel-tree, Willow-tree**
Young Bacchus ravisht by his **tree**..............16. H.41, 13
Not so much call'd a **tree**,......................30. H.89, 9
To find that **Tree** of Life, whose Fruits did feed, 61. H.161, 1
The **Tree**, Bethesda, and the Angel too:..........61. H.161, 6
And to that Hand, (the Branch of Heavens faire **Tree**) 62. H.161, 11
The Dew-bespangling Herbe and **Tree**...........67. H.178, 6
The Fruit to grow up, or the **Tree**:............79. H.198, 2
For now each **tree** do's weare....................80. H.201, 6
My Harp hung up, here on the Willow **tree**.......84. H.210, 2
Under that Cypresse **tree**:....................109. H.267, 18
Save only the Curst-Cipresse **tree**:.............132. H.336, 12
Thou had'st the wreath before, now take the **Tree**; 150. H.383, 1
Mon. Troth, bad are both; worse fruit, and ill the **tree**: 159. H.421, 2
And in the Rind of every comely **tree**..........160. H.421, 39
To dye upon the **Tree**.........................161. H.425, 8
Yee silent shades, whose each **tree** here........169. H.449, 1
With Motto's carv'd on every **tree**,............169. H.449, 22
Faire pledges of a fruitfull **Tree**,..............176. H.467, 1
Of every straight, and smooth-skin **tree**;......193. H.521, 41
As Blossomes of the Almond **Tree**.............203. H.562, 6

First dyes the Leafe, the Bough next, next the **Tree**. 203. H.565, 4
My wearied Oat Ile hang upon the **Tree**,......205. H.573, 3
Where ev'ry **tree** & wealthy issue beares........205. H.575, 9
Come sit we under yonder **Tree**,..............215. H.616, 1
The Palms put forth their Gemmes, and every **Tree** 224. H.642, 5
And shew'd me there a **Tree**,...................278. H.863, 2
After leaves, the **tree** must fall................321. H.1058, 2
Till my Redeemer (on the **Tree**)............370. N.107, 9
Or prosper, but by that same **tree**..............371. N.114, 3
But if that **Tree** sho'd fall, and die,............371. N.114, 7
Thou hast, nay more, Thou art the **Tree**,........377. N.129, 3
That those, who see Thee nail'd unto the **Tree**,..399. N.263, 34
Beneath this **Tree**,...........................401. N.268, 37
Nourish in's breast, a **Tree** of Life.............409. A.2, 108
Trees See **Leafy-trees, Mantel-trees**
The growth, and down-fall of her aged **trees**:....23. H.69, 2
Trees, at one time, shall be both sere and greene: 59. H.154, 2
Made green, and trimm'd with **trees**: see how..68. H.178, 31
Not all at once, but gently, as the **trees**......100. H.247, 3
Trees never beare, unlesse they first do blow.....180. H.477, 6
With silken **trees** upon thy head;..............202. H.560, 2
To strip the **Trees**, and Fields, to their distresse, 224. H.642, 11
That scarcely stirs the nodding leaves of **Trees**:.225. H.642, 16
Wassaile the **Trees**, that they may beare......264. H.787, 1
Balm may thy **Trees** drop, and thy Springs runne oyle 269. H.818, 7
Trees this year beare; next, they their wealth with-hold: 292. H.922, 3
Trembling Is Spangle-work of **trembling** dew,..92. H.223, 65
With **trembling** Dew:........................181. H.484, 4
Peepes **trembling** for feare,....................334. H.1122, 17
Trencher-creature The **Trencher-creature** marketh what 147. H.377, 50
Trencher-man He is a serving, who's a **Trencher-man**. 265. H.796, 4
Trenchers Tom shifts the **Trenchers**; yet he never can 265. H.796, 1
Trental While we this **Trentall** sing about thy Grave. 89. H.219, 2
A **Tentrall** sung by Virgins o're thy Grave:....209. H.584, 6
The sacred Dirge and **Trentall** sung............237. H.686, 10
Thou a **Trentall** make for me:..................304. H.976, 2
Trentals No more my Dirges, and my **Trentalls** have. 228. H.658, 8
Trespass Amint. O rare! But is't a **trespasse** if we three 86. H.213, 25
For the least **trespasse**; 'cause the mind......175. H.465, 61
Pardon my **trespasse** (Silvia) I confesse,........294. H.936, 1
Shall by this pleasing **trespasse** quickly prove,..297. H.949, 3
Find'st here a fault, and mend'st the **trespasse** too: 298. H.955, 8
Then is the horror of the **trespasse** seen..........346. N.37, 2
When I shall sin, pardon my **trespasse** here;.....367. N.99, 1
That I shall ne're that **trespasse** recommit,......397. N.255, 3
Trespasses Love for our very-many **Trespasses**...197. H.539, 6
Trespass-free The second is a Conscience **trespasse-free**; 386. N.194, 3
Trespass-offering (For our **Trespasse-offering**....280. H.870, 12
Tresses And dry'd his dropping **Tresses**:..........27. H.81, 24
Then, when I see thy **Tresses** bound............202. H.560, 9
Set free thy **Tresses**, let them flow.............282. H.881, 7
Whose head befringed with bescattered **tresses**....404. A.1, 1
Trials With **trialls** those, with terrors these He proves, 370. N.108, 3
Triangular Nor in a forme **Triangular**;..........91. H.223, 55
Tribe Thee sprightly Soame, one of my righteous **Tribe**: 199. H.545, 2
A **Tribe** of one Lip; Leven, and of One......199. H.545, 3
Tribes Unto which the **Tribes** resort,............255. H.761, 5
Tribune Thus, like a Roman **Tribune**, thou thy gate 147. H.377, 45
Tribute Gold serves for **Tribute** to the King;....396. N.254, 1
Take then **tribute** of my teares,..................414. A.5, 5
(As if it was a **tribute** paid)..............439. ins. H.443, 45c
Trice His choyce bitts with; then in a **trice**....119. H.293, 11
Or see the Grocers in a **trice**,..................275. H.844, 7
Trick 'Twas but a **trick** to poyson me with love:..17. H.44, 6
No new devise, or late found **trick**,............126. H.319, 5
Trickles That sharply **trickles** from her either eye.178. H.474, 2
Trickling Do in a **trickling** manner tell,.........44. H.127, 7
Tricks Or tell what strange **Tricks** Love can do, 215. H.616, 9
Tried Her leggs with twoe cleire calves like siluer **tride** 406. A.1, 87
Tries Which **tryes**, and counter-stands the shock, 148. H.377, 110
Trifle Many a **trifle** too, and trinket,............93. H.223, 123
Trigg **Trigg** having turn'd his sute, he struts in state, 240. H.703, 1
Trim Curld and comely, and so **trimme**,........125. H.314, 7
Put on thy Laurell then; and in that **trimme**..299. H.956, 11
Most like his Suite, and all commend the **Trim**; 330. H.1099, 3
No, but He drest Him with our humane **Trim**,..390. N.222, 3

Trimmed Made green, and **trimm'd** with trees: see how 68. H.178, 31
Trinket Many a trifle too, and **trinket**..........93. H.223, 123
Trinkets Are **trinkets** falne from the Kites nest; 439. ins. H.443, 45o
Trip. Saint Frip, Saint **Trip**, Saint Fill, S. Fillie,.91. H.223, 32
Faire and foule dayes **trip** Crosse and Pile; The faire 189. H.513, 1
Triple Thy Love had one knot, mine a **triple** tye.173. H.464, 3
The Dog, the **triple** Tunne?................289. H.911, 6
Tripping **Tripping** the comely country round,..230. H.662, 50
Triumph **Triumph** in such a Martirdome.......175. H.465, 66
To him, who is the **triumph** of the day,........256. H.763, 4
— — — — — — — — — —,...............442. var. H.465, 79
Triumphant As one **triumphant**; when I find....176. H.465, 79
Enspher'd with Palm on Your **Triumphant** Crest. 271. H.823, 4
I rise **triumphant** in my Funerall..............392. N.230, 36
Triumph's Is this his Glory? then his **Triumph's** Poore; 171. H.454, 3
Triumvir To the **Triumvir**, Love and Wonderment. 79. H.197, 76
Triumviri — — — — — — — —, ...427. var. H.197, 76
Trod Where humane foot, as yet, n'er **trod**:....111. H.278, 6
Trodden No Goose layes good eggs that is **trodden** drye. 223. H.636, 4
Troll With North-down Ale doth **troule** here,....235. H.674, 10
Trophies She weares as **trophees** of her honour. 131. H.330, 13
Times, Titles, **Trophies**, may be lost and Spent; 419. A.10, 3
Tropics Next, place me Zones, and **Tropicks** there; 47. H.133, 7
Trot And these brave Measures go a stately **trot**; 141. H.359, 11
Troth And as there is one Love, one Faith, one **Troth**, 38. H.106, 143
Gryll eates, but ne're sayes Grace; To speak the **troth**, 48. H.135, 1
And some have wept, and woo'd, and plighted **Troth**, 69. H.178, 49
Troth, leave the flowers, and Maids, take me...112. H.281, 4
Troth Lady, no.............................137. H.340, 6
Mon. **Troth**, bad are both; worse fruit, and ill the tree: 159. H.421, 2
Instead of Harts-horne (if he speakes the **troth**) 299. H.959, 3
Troth-breakers **Troth-breakers** ever...............32. H.94, 8
Trouble **Trouble** Death to lay agen.............52. H.145, 6
Ile **trouble** you no more; but goe...............60. H.159, 3
Where **Trouble** serves the board, we eate......124. H.312, 3
Or **Trouble** not..............................190. H.515, 18
As from Love, from **trouble** free............219. H.628, 10
And **trouble** the skies;.......................225. H.643, 20
Troubled **Troubled** with Green-sicknesses,........64. H.167, 2
To have men think he's **troubled** with the Gout: 98. H.239, 2
Megg yesterday was **troubled** with a Pose,......296. H.945, 1
When times are **troubled**, then forbeare; but speak, 324. H.1072, 1
Trouble-free Set on my Table, (**Trouble-free**).....124. H.312, 7
Troubles This **troubles** me: but I as well..........24. H.73, 7
And **troubles** thus the Sleepie?...................26. H.81, 6
This makes Cuffe dull; and **troubles** him the most, 39. H.109, 3
From cares and **troubles** free;................259. H.772, 26
And all my **troubles** too.......................328. H.1091, 8
Troublesome (What's hard to others) nothing's **troublesome**. 298. H.955, 4
Troule See **Troll**
Trout-flies' Grac't with the **Trout-flies** curious wings, 92. H.223, 72
With eyes of Peacocks Trains, & **Trout-flies** curious wings; and these among......166. H.443, 68-69
Truant If I have plaid the **Truant**, or have here 398. N.261, 1
True See **Too-true-report**
True love, we know, precipitates delay............8. H.10, 6
The words found **true**, C. M. remember me.......26. H.79, 10
That neither haire was cut, or **true** teares shed....27. H.82, 3
True, I confesse; such Whites as these..........34. H.105, 7
But to live round, and close, and wisely **true**..38. H.106, 135
'Tis **true**, I kist thee; but I co'd not heare....42. H.122, 5
But turn'd a Ladies Usher now, ('tis **true**:)....53. H.148, 2
And when **true** love of words is destitute,......58. H.150, 7
By those **true** teares y'are weeping..............63. H.164, 15
Onely **true** in shreds and stuffe.................77. H.195, 12
True, I confesse I left thee, and appeale........78. H.197, 41
For his Sheep-shearers. Mir. **True**, these are the least. 86. H.213, 8
Mirt. 'Tis **true** indeed; and each of us will bring.86. H.213, 33
And if Report of them be **true**,................92. H.223, 76
Men say y'are faire; and faire ye are, 'tis **true**;.98. H.241, 1
And, you must know, your Lords word's **true**,..102. H.250, 51
The onely **true** plant found,...................106. H.262, 2
'Tis **true**, said I, and thereupon...............107. H.263, 13
The **true** resemblances of thee;................107. H.263, 18
(When **true** it is, the out-side swels...........118. H.291, 11
Who for **true** glory suffers thus; we grant......129. H.323, 15
True Calenders, as Pusses eare..................134. H.336, 89
True to your self, and sheets, you'l have me swear, 136. H.338, 1
Nor find that **true**, which was foretold.........157. H.413, 4
But for **True** Service, worthy of that Gowne,..176. H.466, 7
Wilt thou my **true** Friend be?.................205. H.574, 1
What Love said was too too **true**:.............219. H.628, 8
And ever live a **true**.........................228. H.657, 12
True, if this Citie seven times rounded was....252. H.745, 11
I came; (tis **true**) and lookt for Fowle of price, 262. H.783, 7
True Love is tonguelesse as a Crocodile.........274. H.837, 8
But **true** it was, as I rowl'd there,............283. H.883, 7
Long I have lasted in this world; (tis **true**)....328. H.1088, 3
True mirth resides not in the smiling skin:......341. N.13, 1
And that number more then **true**;...............348. N.41, 27
After **true** sorrow for our sinnes, our strife......362. N.91, 1
'Tis **true**, my God; but I can't pay one mite...368. N.103, 10
True rev'rence is (as Cassiodore doth prove)....380. N.147, 1
Drawes out th' Elixar of **true** penitence.........386. N.196, 4
God hath this world for many made; 'tis **true**:..387. N.198, 1
In **true** repentance spent, will be..............388. N.206, 3
When I have done **true** Penance here for it.......397. N.255, 4
True heate, whearw^th humanitie doth liue........410. A.3, 30
— — — — — — — — — — —,..............423. var. H.128, 1
— — — — — — — — — — —,..............442. var. H.575, 36
True-love Can tell by tongue; or **true-love** tie:..202. H.560, 12
True-love-knot Thou sent'st to me a **True-love-knot**; but I 173. H.464, 1
True-love-knots By all those **True-love-knots**, that be 169. H.449, 21
True-lovers When once **true-lovers** take their last Fare-well. 73. H.186, 8
True-paced-numbers Their **true-pac'd-Numbers**, and their Holy-Layes,....................................45. H.128, 35
Truer Be **truer** to him, then a wise Distrust......67. H.177, 2
Truest The best and **truest** Chronicles of me.....304. H.978, 6
True-wit Markt for the **True-wit** of a Million:..194. H.526, 4
Truggin **Truggin** a Footman was; but now, growne lame, 283. H.882, 1
Truggin now lives but to belye his name.......283. H.882, 2
Truly A House-dance neatly, and can'st **truly** show, 148. H.377, 91
Tell, if thou canst, (and **truly**) whence doth come 157. H.414, 1
Is mixt with mine; and **truly** know,............175. H.465, 71
Looks, shew him **truly** Bacchanalian like,......206. H.575, 36
Unto those that **truly** love......................240. H.701, 2
Though the Sextons **truly** sweare................418. A.9, 33
Trump See **Funeral-trump**
As Fame or Rumour, hath or **Trumpe** or Tongue..411. A.3, 46
Trumpet Of whom, from Fam's white **Trumpet**, This Ile Tell, 170. H.451, 9
And when the **Trumpet** which thou late hast found 257. H.763, 17
Trundell's See **Tim-Trundell's**
Trundling At **trundling** of the Ball,..............238. H.690, 6
Trunks Ha's none at home, in Coffers, Desks, or **Trunks**. 173. H.463, 4
Truss And then at last to **truss** the Epigram;..301. H.966, 8
Trust But **trust** to this, my noble passenger;......23. H.71, 3
To dance and play in: (**Trust** me) there........49. H.136, 22
And ask, Where's now the colour, forme and **trust** 49. H.138, 4
Trust to good Verses then;....................81. H.201, 45
What **trust** to things below, when as we see,....81. H.202, 7
Yet **trust** me, I shall know....................83. H.207, 3
What though the sea be calme? **Trust** to the shore: 85. H.212, 1
Trust me, I'le not like at all:.................117. H.286, 4
You shall not languish, **trust** me: Virgins here 138. H.343, 3
Such is thy house, whose firme foundations **trust** 148. H.377, 103
If he ha's none in's pockets, **trust** me, Huncks 173. H.463, 3
Trust me Ladies, I will do....................177. H.472, 1
Trust me I will not hurt ye; or once shew.....222. H.634, 7
Thou shalt thy Name have, and thy Fames best **trust**, 231. H.664, 5
Immortall selfe, shall boldly **trust**.............278. H.859, 5
Our **trust** farre more then ten eare-witnesses.....287. H.904, 2
But **trust** me now I dare not say,...............288. H.908, 5
We **Trust** not to the multitude in Warre,......290. H.916, 1
Neglected there (maids **trust** to me)..........304. H.980, 8
Not **trust**...................................308. H.993, 2
In your Pocket for a **trust**,....................323. H.1065, 3
Rules but by leave, and takes his Crowne on **trust**. 331. H.1103, 2
Under the first the Sinners ever **trust**;...........340. N.6, 3
For (**trust** me Girle) shee ouer-does............409. A.2, 81
No **trust** to Metals nor to Marbles, when........419. A.10, 1
Trusted Tap (better known then **trusted**) as we heare 272. H.829, 1
Trusts And credits Physick, yet not **trusts** his Pill: 125. H.315, 4
Truth Mercie and **Truth** live with thee! and forbeare 14. H.35, 9
For to say **truth**, all Garlands are thy due;......41. H.117, 9
Now, now's the time; so oft by **truth**..........53. H.149, 1
He knowes not Love, that hath not this **truth** proved, 73. H.186, 11
Doting, Ile weep and say (in **Truth**).........135. H.336, 119

And I the **truth** will tell;....................138. H.344, 2
Truth, yet Teages **truths** are untruths, (nothing else.) 282. H.880, 2
Truth is best found out by the time, and eyes;..287. H.902, 1
How ere it fortuned; know for **Truth**, I meant 304. H.977, 3
Twixt **Truth** and Errour, there's this difference known, 316. H.1031, 1
Errour is fruitfull, **Truth** is onely one.......316. H.1031, 2
For **truth** I may this sentence tell,............321. H.1059, 1
Truth by her own simplicity is known,........329. H.1094, 1
So that with bold **truth**, thou canst now relate 330. H.1100, 7
The **truth** of Travails lesse in bookes then Thee. 330. H.1100, 18
But **truth** knitt fast; and so farewell for euer. 414. A.6, 12
This lesson you must pearse to' th' **truth**........418. A.9, 39
To teach the **truth** of Scenes, and more for thee, 443. var. H.575, 53

Truths When of these **truths**, thy happyer knowledge lyes, 37. H.106, 87
No cruell **truths** of Philomell,.................215. H.616, 12
Truth, yet Teages **truths** are untruths, (nothing else.) 282. H.880, 2

Try Let's **try** this bow of ours,..................27. H.81, 26
Ah me! I **try**; and trying, prove,...............60. H.157, 3
Let Much-more justly pay his tythes; then **try**..73. H.188, 3
Give me these my (Knight) and **try**...........217. H.620, 7
Trie if this sober streame you can..............244. H.720, 3
The sword of war must **trie** the Soveraignty...331. H.1102, 2
Let's **trie** of us who shall the first expire;....333. H.1120, 3

Trying Ah me! I try; and **trying**, prove,..........60. H.157, 3

Tub See **Brine-tub**

Tubbs For thirty yeares, **Tubbs** has been proud and poor; 302. H.972, 1

Tuck At Post and Paire, or Slam, Tom **Tuck** would play 238. H.693, 1

Tucked When **tuckt** up she a hunting goes;......51. H.142, 14

Tucker He needs a **Tucker** for to burle his face. 211. H.594, 2

Tugs He teares and **tugs** us, then he did before; 372. N.116, 2

Tulip That gallant **Tulip** will hang down his head, 41. H.118, 3
You are a **Tulip** seen to day,..................87. H.216, 1
— — — — — — — — — —,..................429. var. H.263, 7

Tulips Bright **Tulips**, we do know,...............184. H.493, 1
The **Tulips**, Lillies, Daffadills do stoop;......320. H.1054, 4
Spring **Tulips** up through all the yeere;........366. N.97, 21

Tullus Where Anchus and rich **Tullus** blend....133. H.336, 26

Tully Glory no other thing is (**Tullie** sayes).....241. H.710, 1
In's Tusc'lanes, **Tullie** doth confesse,...........332. H.1115, 1
Soe **Tullye** look't, when from the Brest's of Rome 412. A.3, 75

Tumble **Tumble** me down, and I will sit........235. H.677, 1
Tumble shall heav'n, and down will I...........371. N.114, 8

Tumbling The Senators down **tumbling** with the Roofe, 252. H.745, 14

Tun Come, I will drink a **Tun**.................81. H.201, 35
I know the **Tunne** of Hidleberge holds more.....171. H.454, 4
The Dog, the triple **Tunne**?....................289. H.911, 6

Tune **Tune** my words, that they may fall,.......122. H.303, 3
More curst for singing out of **tune** then he.....266. H.799, 4

Tuned For one so rarely **tun'd** to fit all parts;..121. H.301, 1

Tunes And the boyes with sweet **tunes** sing,......54. H.149, 47

Tunny-fish And a **Tunnie-fish** shall be..........129. H.325, 5

Turban (Like a Turks **Turbant** on his head)...93. H.223, 138

Turbant See **Turban**

Turbot With mullet, **Turbot**, guilthead bought 436. ins. H.336, 48g

Turf Follow me weeping to my **Turfe**, and there....9. H.14, 13
Me to the Tap, the Tost, the **Turfe**; Let Wine..79. H.197, 88
Over my **Turfe**, when I am buried............219. H.627, 4

Turfs See **Green-turfs**
I shall, ere long, with green **turfs** cover'd be;....66. H.174, 3
Stones, or **turfes** to cover me..................270. H.821, 4
Present those **Turfs**, which once must cover me: 392. N.230, 16

Turk's (Like a **Turks** Turbant on his head)....93. H.223, 138

Turmoils The **Turmoiles** they endure that love.....219. H.628, 6
The gentle Dove may, when these **turmoils** cease, 225. H.642, 21

Turn And whom she touch't, **turne** sweet...........9. H.15, 12
Ile wish I might **turne** all to eare,...............22. H.68, 2
Rockes **turn** to Rivers, Rivers **turn** to Men.......29. H.86, 14
And make, what ere they touch **turn** sweet......55. H.149, 62
And it may chance that Love may **turn**,........61. H.159, 18
And till I **turne** Apostate to thy love,........79. H.197, 81
Thus Paines and Pleasures **turne** by **turne** succeed: 79. H.199, 3
Yet, quickly you'l see by the **turne** of a pin,....97. H.233, 3
But **turne** soone after calme, as Balme, or Oile. 105. H.259, 4
Shew her how his eyes do **turne**.............113. H.283, 37
And **turne** Apostate: Love will................113. H.283, 57
But warm their wits, and **turn** their lines to gold. 141. H.359, 8
Wod'st thou to sincere-silver **turn** thy mold?..144. H.370, 7
Pray once, twice pray; and **turn** thy ground to gold. 144. H.370, 8
He'l **turn** a Papist, rancker then before.........151. H.385, 6
As men, **turne** all to eares....................151. H.388, 8
The whole world die, and **turn** to dust with thee. 155. H.405, 16
Many a **turn**, and man' a crosse-..............165. H.443, 25
And **turn** to snow,..........................171. H.452, 9
Thou know'st, my Julia, that it is thy **turne**....196. H.539, 1
Untill the roofe **turne** round................208. H.582, 4
And **turn** the iron Age to Gold..............233. H.670, 29
Now is your **turne** (my Dearest) to be set......264. H.789, 1
Thus times do shift; each thing his **turne** do's hold; 285. H.892, 21
To soure the Bread, and **turn** the Beer........321. H.1056, 9
And, from a Priest, **turne** Player once again....325. H.1076, 4
Although we cannot **turne** the fervent fit........356. N.67, 1
I **turne** Apostate to the strict Comande....424. ins. H.128, 46c
— — — — — — — — — —,..............442. var. H.465, 78
— — — — — — — — — —,..............447. var. H.1106, 1

Turnbroach Rumpe is a **Turne-broach**, yet he seldome can 331. H.1106, 1

Turned **Turn'd** her to this Plant, we call..........15. H.36, 14
Turn'd to Flowers. Still in some..................15. H.37, 3
Die, and be **turn'd** into a Lute....................23. H.68, 8
Me **turn'd** to tears; yet did'st not weep for me...42. H.122, 4
But **turn'd** a Ladies Usher now, ('tis true:)......53. H.148, 2
Turn'd to flowers: Stil the hieu,................64. H.167, 3
Then beauty **turn'd** to sowernesse...............143. H.367, 2
Turn'd all to Mell, and Manna there for thee...143. H.370, 4
And **turn'd** my voice.........................144. H.371, 16
Turn'd, from a Papist here, a Predicant.........151. H.385, 2
Now I'm **turn'd** a combatant:....................151. H.386, 2
Gave them Hearts-ease **turn'd** to Flow'rs.......152. H.391, 8
Turn'd to these Springs, which wee see here:....180. H.478, 4
Then, when Thou see'st thine Age all **turn'd** to gold, 181. H.483, 9
The Water **turn'd** to Wine..................185. H.495, 8
Turn'd to Flowers, still they be...............187. H.503, 3
Turn'd, but not torn:........................190. H.515, 42
Trigg having **turn'd** his sute, he struts in state,.240. H.703, 1
To paste of Almonds **turn'd** by thee:..........267. H.805, 4
Thou art all **turn'd** isicle?...................273. H.836, 2
Love **turn'd** himselfe into a Bee...............283. H.883, 9
Away he went, but as he **turn'd**..............295. H.942, 9
Stood as he had been **turn'd** from flesh to stone: 301. H.962, 4
Trap, of a Player **turn'd** a Priest now is;......325. H.1076, 1
That sees December **turn'd** to May............364. N.96, 10
Of mirth is **turn'd** to sadnesse...............375. N.123, 60
— — — — — — — — — —,.................448. var. A.3, 25

Turning See **Back-turning**
And in the **turning** of an eye;.................107. H.263, 20
And thou then **turning** in that Sphere,........175. H.465, 51
Are a **turning**:.............................308. H.993, 24

Turns Which done, that Dawne, **turnes** then to perfect day. 34. H.104, 6
How each field **turns** a street; each street a Parke 68. H.178, 30
A Just man's like a Rock that **turnes** the wroth 152. H.389, 1
Eeles winds and **turnes**, and cheats and steales; yet Eeles 153. H.398, 1
That **turns** each Sphere,.....................193. H.524, 5
Grudgings **turnes** bread to stones, when to the Poore 220. H.632, 1
Where Joyes and Griefs have **Turns** Alternative. 264. H.792, 2
If her patience **turns** to ire,...................273. H.836, 7
That sweetness **turnes** to Loathsomness.........288. H.909, 4
Where War and Peace the Dice by **turns** doe cast. 327. H.1083, 2
Turnes all the patient ground to flowers.........364. N.96, 24
Gives them by **turnes** their grief and jollitie.....394. N.236, 4
Turnes the beholders into stone..................418. A.9, 58
— — — — — — — — — —,..................450. var. A.9, 58

Turtles Home the **Turtles**; Hymen guide........54. H.149, 49
To bed, to bed, kind **Turtles**, now, and write..114. H.283, 71

Tusc'lanes In's **Tusc'lanes**, Tullie doth confesse,.332. H.1115, 1

Tutor My mild, my loving **Tutor**, Lord and God! 398. N.261, 3

Twain — — — — — — — — —, ...427. var. H.197, 66

T'wards See **Towards**
Hanging down his head **t'wards** me;............38. H.107, 2
Shall move **t'wards** you; although I see........49. H.136, 34

'Twas **'Twas** but a trick to poyson me with love: 17. H.44, 6
of Life, and **'twas** for me......................18. H.47, 8
They shew'd me then, how fine **'twas** spun;.......18. H.47, 9
Me thought **'twas** strange, that thou so hard sho'dst prove, 42. H.122, 7
'Twas but a single Rose,......................51. H.144, 1
'Twas done by me, more to confirme my zeale, 78. H.197, 42
'Twas by your splendour (Lady) not by mine...94. H.226, 8
We knew **'twas** Flesh and Blood, that there sate mute 95. H.228, 2
'Twas no more you then, but a Cherubin.........95. H.228, 4
But **'twas**,.................................100. H.246, 4
List of references:..............129. H.326, 3; 152. H.392, 5; 161. H.426, 1; 176. H.467, 10; 184. H.492, 39; 186. H.501, 4; 203. H.562, 3; 207. H.577, 3; 212. H.598, 2; 219. H.628, 5; 219. H.630, 4; 264. H.789, 3; 271. H.825, 1; 279. H.863, 13; 279. H.866, 2; 334. H.1124, 3; 358. N.75, 5; 366. N.97, 25; 384. N.180, 11; 413. A.4, 6; 418. A.9, 38.

Twelfth-day Be **Twelfe-day** Queene for the night here. 317. H.1035, 12
Twelfthtide Of **Twelf-tide** Cakes, of Pease, and Beanes 127. H.319, 17
Thy Mummeries; thy **Twelfe-tide** Kings........231. H.662, 58
Unto our prettie **Twelfth-Tide** King,..........368. N.102, 20
Twelve Telling the Clock strike Ten, Eleven, **Twelve**, One. 114. H.283, 76
Frolick the full **twelve** Holy-dayes............127. H.319, 50
Yet, ere **twelve** Moones shall whirl about......178. H.476, 7
Twenty Then to that **twenty**, adde an hundred more: 24. H.74, 4
And caught'st thy selfe the more by **twenty** fold: 97. H.236, 2
Of **twenty** shall come,..........................99. H.243, 5
And hadst thou wager'd **twenty** Kine,..........244. H.716, 45
What needs **twenty** stabs, when one...........254. H.757, 5
Twice five and **twenty** (bate me but one yeer) 328. H.1088, 2
'Twere Farre safer **'twere** to stay at home:.........5. H.2, 2
Better **'twere** my Book were dead,...............21. H.59, 5
Farre better **'twere** for either to be mute,.......287. H.901, 5
Twice You have broke promise **twice**..............32. H.94, 9
Stout sons I had, and those **twice** three;..........41. H.116, 3
Six teeth he has, whereof **twice** two are known..46. H.129, 3
If **twice** you kisse, you need not feare,..........61. H.159, 26
(To save his life) **twice** am content to die.......70. H.181, 16
That man lives **twice**, that lives the first life well. 121. H.298, 2
Pray once, **twice** pray; and turn thy ground to gold. 144. H.370, 8
Twice has Pudica been a Bride, and led........180. H.477, 1
Two Youths sha's known, thrice two, and **twice** 3. yeares; 180. H.477, 3
Where kissing that, Ile **twice** kisse thee.......193. H.521, 42
Twice fortie (bating but one year,............226. H.644, 3
Twice two fell out, all rotten at the root.......247. H.728, 2
Or kisse it thou, but once, or **twice**,..........267. H.805, 5
At **twice** ten yeares, a prime and publike one?..299. H.956, 6
Twice five and twenty (bate me but one yeer)..328. H.1088, 2
Twice ten for one:...........................350. N.47, 44
Twig That if the **twig** sho'd chance too much to smart, 394. N.241, 3
Twigs See **Lime-twigs**
Mirtle the **twigs** were, meerly to imply;..........16. H.40, 3
Are **twigs** of Birch, and willow, growing there: 39. H.110, 2
Twilight Like to a **Twi-light**, or that simpring Dawn, 34. H.104, 3
Twilight is yet, till that her Lawnes give way; 34. H.104, 5
Into a doubtful **Twi-light**; then,................76. H.193, 54
Like a dull **Twi-light**? Tell me; and the fault....77. H.197, 29
Tinseld with **Twilight**, He, and They..........165. H.443, 21
Twilight, no other thing is, Poets say,..........278. H.858, 1
The **Twi-light** is no other thing (we say)......319. H.1046, 1
Twilights I write of Groves, of **Twilights**, and I sing 5. H.1, 11
'Twill **'Twill** not be long (Perilla) after this,........9. H.14, 5
And such spirits raise, **'twill** then..............52. H.145, 5
Virgins, weep not; **'twill** come, when,..........56. H.149, 111
Are wanton with their itch; scratch, and **'twill** please. 66. H.173, 8
'Twill never please the pallate of mine eare.....152. H.390, 2
For lost like these, **'twill** be,..................184. H.493, 11
And that ty'd to man **'twil** sever..............209. H.587, 3
Ill luck **'twill** bode to th' Bridegroome and the Bride. 262. H.781, 12
Taste it to Temper; then **'twill** be.............288. H.909, 5
In all our high designments, **'twill** appeare,.....292. H.924, 1
'Twill make a tongless man to wooe...........325. H.1075, 2
'Twill strangely make a one of too............325. H.1075, 4
'Twill quickly mar, & make ye too............325. H.1075, 6
'Twill hurt and heal a heart pierc'd through....325. H.1075, 8
But in short time **'twill** please Thee,............353. N.56, 21
Twine I can play, and I can **twine**...............17. H.43, 3
Vnder the which twoe crawling eyebrowes **twine**..404. A.1, 7
Twinkling — — — — — — — — —, ...430. var. H.263, 20
Twins Me **twins** each yeare:...................350. N.47, 48
Twirled And In a Whirl-wynd **twirld** her home, agast 410. A.3, 25
Twirls Till Liber Pater **twirles** the house........127. H.319, 42
Twist But the silken **twist** unty'd,................15. H.36, 10
Of blackest silk, a curious **twist**;...............64. H.169, 2
Julia, this my silken **twist**;....................128. H.322, 2
And gave a **Twist** to me.......................278. H.863, 4
Twisting And **twisting** my Iülus hairs;........135. H.336, 118
Twitched To have a tooth **twitcht** out of's native frame. 323. H.1066, 2
'Twixt **Twixt** Kings and Subjects ther's this mighty odds, 12. H.25, 1
A mighty strife **'twixt** Forme and Chastitie......189. H.511, 6
'Twixt Kings & Tyrants there's this difference known; 278. H.861, 1
Night makes no difference **'twixt** the Priest and Clark; 279. H.864, 1
(**Twixt** the hornes) upon the head............280. H.870, 10
Twixt Truth and Errour, there's this difference known, 316. H.1031, 1
That love **'twixt** men do's ever longest last.....327. H.1083, 1
In the way **'twixt** me, and home:................355. N.64, 4
'Twixt God the Father, Holy Ghost, and Sonne: 386. N.191, 4
Its humble selfe **twixt** twoe aspiring cloudes,.....406. A.1, 84
Twixt this and them this Gorgon showne........418. A.9, 57
Two **Two** of a thousand things, are disallow'd,.....10. H.18, 1
Jems, then those **two**, that went before:..........23. H.70, 6
Two Cupids fell at odds;........................31. H.92, 2
We **two** are last in Hell: what may we feare....33. H.101, 1
Six teeth he has, whereof twice **two** are known..46. H.129, 3
Two, like **two** ripe shocks of corn.............58. H.149, 170
Sweet, be not proud of those **two** eyes,...........61. H.160, 1
You'l spil a tear, or **two** with theirs:............70. H.180, 6
What? shall we **two** our endlesse leaves take here 73. H.186, 9
They were **two** Gelli-flowers....................74. H.192, 4
Two stiffe-blew-Pigs-feet, and a sow's cleft eare...89. H.221, 4
Two pure, and holy Candlesticks:..............92. H.223, 94
But not his mouth (the fouler of the **two**).....110. H.273, 2
Both you **two** have............................111. H.280, 1
Tempting the **two** too modest; can...........115. H.283, 113
Looking upon yee, That **two** Nations.........116. H.283, 158
Springing from **two** such Fires,..............116. H.283, 159
Two Napkins cram'd up, and a silver Spoone....118. H.292, 6
Past one aclock, and almost **two**,..............121. H.299, 7
We **two** are dead,..............................133. H.336, 35
Or ravell so, to make us **two**..................134. H.336, 72
Two parts of us successively command;.........137. H.339, 1
You'l with a tear or **two**, remember me,......140. H.355, 10
Two dayes, y'ave larded here; a third, yee know, 146. H.377, 25
Not **two**, but all the seasons of the yeare.......151. H.387, 8
Two she spat out, a cough forc't out the rest...158. H.419, 2
Who having **two** or three,.....................160. H.422, 19
And next to these **two** blankets ore-...........167. H.443, 94
Besides us **two**, i' th' Temple here's not one....168. H.445, 1
Which joyns **two** souls, remember this;..........174. H.465, 2
Next to which **Two**; among the City-Powers,...176. H.466, 3
And for their **two** egs render ten.............179. H.476, 21
Two Youths sha's known, thrice **two**, and twice 3. yeares; 180. H.477, 3
All things are open to these **two** events,........182. H.487, 1
If I write a Verse, or **two**,....................182. H.489, 5
She brake in **two** the purer Glasse,...........187. H.504, 4
We **two** (as Reliques left) will have..........190. H.515, 11
For that one, **two**..............................196. H.538, 7
As if You **Two**, were one Hermophrodite:......201. H.557, 6
Come then, and like **two** Doves with silv'rie wings, 205. H.575, 1
Two loving followers too unto the Grove,......206. H.575, 23
And flatt'ring Ivie) **Two** recite their Plaies,....206. H.575, 50
Meane time we **two** will sing the Dirge of these; 209. H.584, 7
By quickly making one of **two**.................215. H.616, 10
Or gallant Newark; which brave **two**..........218. H.626, 12
Grow for **two** ends, it matters not at all,.......232. H.667, 1
Who **two** and thirty cornes had on a foot.......240. H.704, 2
Cleave thou my heart in **two**..................240. H.705, 12
Twice **two** fell out, all rotten at the root......247. H.728, 2
Thy Genius with **two** strength'ning Buttresses,..252. H.745, 18
Come Anthea let us **two**.......................255. H.761, 1
Two things do make society to stand;..........275. H.847, 1
To hold us **two**, an endlesse honour have.......281. H.875, 6
Betwixt us **two** no more Logomachie..........287. H.901, 4
Hard are the **two** first staires unto a Crowne:..292. H.925, 1
For a kiss or **two**, confesse,....................305. H.984, 1
'Twill strangely make a one of **too**............325. H.1075, 4
After a day, or **two**, or three,.................328. H.1090, 4
God hath **two** wings, which He doth ever move,...340. N.6, 1
Prayers and Praises are those spotlesse **two**......341. N.9, 1
How am I bound to **Two**! God, who doth give...355. N.62, 1
Two raiments have I: Christ then makes........376. N.127, 5
Or have I **two** loaves; then I use...............376. N.127, 7
To th' good and bad, in common, for **two** ends: 387. N.201, 2
Two instruments belong unto our God;.........394. N.241, 1
Wherefore **two** prayers ought not to be said,....396. N.249, 7
Vnder the which **twoe** crawling eyebrowes twine..404. A.1, 7
Vnder whose shade **twoe** starry sparkling eyes....404. A.1, 9
Twoe smelling swelling <bashful> Cherriletts,.....404. A.1, 20
Her eares, which like **twoe** Laborinths are plac'd..405. A.1, 39
Beares vp **twoe** globes where loue and pleasure sitt, 405. A.1, 52
Which headed with **twoe** rich round rubies showe..405. A.1, 53
Swelling in likenes like **twoe** christall skyes......406. A.1, 78
Hence rise those **twoe** ambitious hills that looke...406. A.1, 81
Its humble selfe twixt **twoe** aspiring cloudes,....406. A.1, 84
Her leggs with **twoe** cleire calves like siluer tride..406. A.1, 87
To see **two** tablets of pure Ivory...............406. A.1, 96
From w^ch^ **two** armes like branches seem to spread 406. A.1, 97
And vnder it **two** Chast borne spyes...........408. A.2, 35
I haue behelde **two** louers in a night.............410. A.3, 1
Noe otherwise then as those former **two**..........410. A.3, 14
These **Two** asleep are: I'll but be Vndrest.......419. A.10, 7
The **two** last fayle, and by experience make 422. ins. H.106, 92e
of **two** makes one Hermaphrodite.........431. ins. H.283, 50j
aloft, and like **two** armies, come.........432. ins. H.283, 140d
'Two'd Doves, **'two'd** say, yee bill too long.....57. H.149, 140

Unmixed Unmixt. I love to have it smirke and shine,
187. H.502, 3
Unmoved Be so, bold spirit; Stand Center-like, unmov'd;
37. H.106, 101
Unperplexed If smooth and unperplext the Seasons were,
214. H.612, 9
Unprepared Who to that sweet Bread unprepar'd doth come
355. N.65, 9
Unpunished T'ave plagu'd, what now unpunisht is. 48. H.136, 9
Unpurged Th' inconstant, and unpurged Multitude
398. N.263, 6
Unpurified Ill-scenting, or unpurifi'd..............366. N.98, 14
Unrighteousness Rich he will be by all unrighteousness:
266. H.800, 6
Unrude Manners knowes distance, and a man unrude
147. H.377, 31
Unsafe Where power is weake, unsafe is Majestie.
302. H.971, 2
Unsealed When the Black Dooms-day Bookes (as yet unseal'd)...................................256. H.763, 15
Unseasoned Uncircumcis'd, unseason'd, and prophane.
371. N.113, 4
Unseen If felt and heard, (unseen) thou dost me please;
331. H.1108, 1
Unshackled Apostles, way (unshackled) to goe out.
52. H.146, 16
Unshorn Upon her wings presents the god unshorne.
67. H.178, 2
Unshorn Apollo, come, and re-inspire..........280. H.871, 2
Or let the Unshorne God lend thee his Lyre,...299. H.956, 13
Unslate For to unslate, or to untile that thumb!..66. H.173, 4
Unsluice (In my short absence) to unsluce a teare:
14. H.35, 10
Unsmooth And unsmooth behaviour.............204. H.569, 12
Unsmooth, or sowre, to all civilitie;............378. N.137, 4
Unsober To any one unsober syllable............210. H.590, 8
Unsoft Unsoft to him who's smooth to thee......252. H.746, 2
Unsound Sound, or unsound, let it be;..........84. H.209, 5
Sound or unsound, be they rent or whole,......143. H.368, 3
So long unsound:..........................401. N.268, 19
Unspent Those mites of Time, which yet remain unspent,
171. H.456, 3
And see, if there it keeps unspent..............245. H.720, 5
Unstained Their cheekes unstain'd with shamefac'tnesse:
310. H.1004, 8
Unstrung Griefe, (my deare friend) has first my Harp unstrung;......................................84. H.210, 9
Untamed The untam'd Heifer, or the Pricket,..136. H.336, 142
Untaught Untaught, to suffer Poverty...........36. H.106, 68
Unthrifts Like Unthrifts, having spent,.........110. H.274, 17
Untied But the silken twist unty'd,..............15. H.36, 10
Knit them with knots (with much adoe unty'd)..291. H.920, 2
Until A sleep, untill the act be done...........57. H.149, 142
Of life, untill ye bid.........................58. H.149, 164
Untill the hasting day.........................125. H.316, 6
Untill the fired Chestnuts leape................127. H.319, 33
We'l drink, my Wickes, untill we be..........136. H.336, 138
Untill our tongues shall tell our ears,..........136. H.336, 143
Untill the roofe turne round...................208. H.582, 4
Untill the dancing Easter-day,..................285. H.892, 7
Though to be tempted be no sin, untill........392. N.230, 31
Untile For to unslate, or to untile that thumb!....66. H.173, 4
Untilled Roses and Cassia crown the untill'd soyle.
205. H.575, 4
Unto (Partial List)
Is despicable unto it.............................6. H.2, 18
But if thou read'st my Booke unto the end,.........7. H.6, 3
A Resurrection unto ye;............................7. H.9, 6
And would have kist unto her knee,...............14. H.33, 3
Unto that watrie Desolation:.....................14. H.35, 2
Submits his neck unto a second yoke............17. H.42, 6
First, for Effusions due unto the dead,............23. H.72, 1
Whose crack gives crushing unto all..............25. H.76, 4
Came one unto my gate,...........................26. H.81, 3
Unto the shades have been, or now are due,.......27. H.82, 10
Unto a Million...................................29. H.87, 12
Mak'st easie Feare unto thee say,................36. H.106, 74
A Divination unto me:............................73. H.187, 9
What Love co'd ne'r be brought unto.............74. H.191, 8
Welcome as are the ends unto my Vowes:......77. H.197, 14
As Queenes, meet Queenes; or come thou unto me,
79. H.197, 73
Which (though sweet unto your smell).........88. H.217, 3
If unto me all Tongues were granted,..........91. H.223, 26
The patient Oxe unto the Yoke,..............102. H.250, 48
And all goe back unto the Plough.............102. H.250, 49
Unto the bed the bashfull Bride;............109. H.271, 4
A savour like unto a blessed field,............112. H.283, 18
Offering Poppy unto thee.......................129. H.324, 4
Unto an almost nothing; then,................134. H.336, 79
Come unto thee for Laureil, having spent,......143. H.365, 5
And adds perfumes unto the Wine, which thou..148. H.377, 81
So drew my life unto an end...................153. H.399, 6
As Beasts unto the Altars go..................161. H.425, 9
It seems a wonder unto me,....................163. H.434, 2
Expose your jewels then unto the view,........173. H.459, 11
And Pipe unto thy Song.......................184. H.492, 28
Thy selfe, which thou put'st other men unto....214. H.614, 2
No man comes late unto that place from whence 228. H.656, 1
Unto the Dew-laps up in meat:...............230. H.662, 36
Or lookt I back unto the Times hence flown,....234. H.673, 1
That gave Progermination unto them:..........251. H.745, 8
'Tis a Mistresse unto mee......................253. H.750, 3
Unto which the Tribes resort,.................255. H.761, 5
Unto the thirtieth thousand yeere,.............265. H.794, 5
Three, unto whom the whole world give applause;
276. H.851, 7
Withstanding entrance unto me................277. H.854, 4
That he reacht forth unto me:..................279. H.863, 6
Unto the end of daies...........................281. H.874, 15
Unto the Holy Temple ride:...................291. H.919, 14
Hard are the two first staires unto a Crowne;..292. H.925, 1
A bondman unto thee.........................293. H.934, 4
Threatn'd ruine unto all?......................302. H.968, 10
Spend I my life (that's subject unto change:)..310. H.1003, 2
Put from, or draw unto the faithfull shore:....315. H.1028, 12
Humbly unto Thy Mercy-seat:...................349. N.46, 2
Unto the prison, I'le say, no;..................370. N.107, 12
If I but call unto Thee.........................373. N.122, 4
My mouth I'le lay unto Thy wound.............377. N.129, 5
To him, who longs unto his Christ to go,........378. N.133, 1
Not shar'd alike be unto all....................380. N.149, 2
Unto temptation God exposeth some;............380. N.150, 3
Much as the ends are to be lookt unto..........387. N.200, 4
Two instruments belong unto our God;.........394. N.241, 1
That those, who see Thee nail'd unto the Tree,..399. N.263, 34
Or like vnto Aurora when shee setts.............404. A.1, 3
Bowing my lips vnto y^t stately root............406. A.1, 111
Thou bring'st vnto his bedd A frost............409. A.2, 86
But vnto mee, bee onlye hoarse, since now.......411. A.3, 47
Welcome at last unto the Threshold, Time 431. ins. H.283, 60k
— — — — — — — — — — —,.............437. var. H.336, 82
Vnto the Prince of Shades, whom once his Pen
442. ins. H.575, 28a
— — — — — — — — — — —,................448. var. A.1, 78
Untouched Untoucht by cold sterility;..........291. H.919, 18
Untruss Untrusse, his Master bade him; and that word
65. H.171, 5
Untruth And halfe damns me with untruth;......348. N.41, 39
Untruths Truth, yet Teages truths are untruths, (nothing else.)
282. H.880, 2
Unurged Can'st, and unurg'd, forsake that Larded fare,
37. H.106, 111
Who unurg'd will not drinke.................317. H.1035, 16
Unwashed Unwasht hands, ye Maidens, know....263. H.786, 3
Unwept Against you come, some Orient Pearls unwept:
68. H.178, 22
Unwise That man's unwise will search for Ill,......6. H.2, 25
Unworn With a neck by yoke unworn..........306. H.984, 23
Up See Raked-up
When up the*Thyrse is rais'd, and when the sound..7. H.8, 7
The seeds of Treason choake up as they spring,..10. H.17, 1
Then holding up (there) such religious Things,....11. H.22, 5
Up she got upon a wall,..........................15. H.36, 8
To be offer'd up by fire:.........................22. H.65, 2
To make that thousand up a million..............24. H.74, 6
Your Standard's up, we fix a Conquest there......25. H.77, 12
Nurse up, great Lord, this my posterity:..........40. H.112, 2
Shor'd up by you, (Brave Earle of Westmerland.).40. H.112, 4
May blow my ashes up, and strike thee blind....49. H.138, 8
And kisses drying up his tears:.................50. H.139, 11
With hands held up to Love, I wept;............51. H.142, 3
When tuckt up she a hunting goes;.............51. H.142, 14
But they left Hope-seed to fill up againe.........52. H.146, 8
Spring up afresh; when all these mists are spent, 52. H.146, 11
Fill, and winde up with whitest wooll.........58. H.149, 162
Ripe eares of corne, and up to th'eares in snow:..59. H.154, 6
Made him take up his shirt, lay down his sword...65. H.171, 6
Get up, get up for shame, the Blooming Morne..67. H.178, 1
Get up, sweet-Slug-a-bed, and see...............67. H.178, 5
Made up of white-thorn neatly enterwove;......68. H.178, 35
But is got up, and gone to bring in May........69. H.178, 44
I'm up, I'm up, and blesse that hand,...........72. H.185, 22
And took it up, and view'd it; then..........73. H.187, 6
Much-more, provides, and hoords up like an Ant;
73. H.188, 1
Swell up my nerves with spirit; let my blood...79. H.197, 77
The Fruit to grow up, or the Tree:.............79. H.198, 2
Catullus, I quaffe up...........................80. H.201, 27
My Harp hung up, here on the Willow tree.....84. H.210, 2
Pillars let some set up,.........................85. H.211, 21
There off'ring up the Holy-Grist:..............91. H.223, 51
An Apples-core is hung up dry'd,..............93. H.223, 126
And drunk with Wine, I drank him up.........96. H.229, 4
And burn thee 'up, as well as I.................98. H.238, 15
Thou art a plant sprung up to wither never,......98. H.240, 1
Bind up his senses with your numbers, so,.......99. H.244, 3
We rip up first, then reap our lands............101. H.250, 4
Drest up with all the Country Art.............101. H.250, 8
Some prank them up with Oaken leaves:........101. H.250, 20
And Harrow, (though they'r hang'd up now.)...102. H.250. 50
And so dresse him up with Love,.............108. H.266, 7
Built up of odours, burneth in her breast.......113. H.283, 26
Mount up thy flames, and let thy Torch........113. H.283, 33

Plumpe Bed beare up, and swelling like a cloud, 115. H.283, 112
Up in a sheet your Bride, and what if so.....116. H.283, 142
Ye Towre her up, as Danae was;.............116. H.283, 144
Two Napkins cram'd up, and a silver Spoone....118. H.292, 6
He fully quaffs up to bewitch.................120. H.293, 52
Be ye lockt up like to these,....................120. H.297, 7
Offer'd up by Her, to Thee.....................122. H.302, 6
I have drank up for to please..................122. H.304, 5
Daffadills g'en up to Thee.......................122. H.304, 8
That tost up, after Fox-i'th'hole..............126. H.319, 14
That tempts till it be tossed up:...............127. H.319, 36
And Harrow hang up resting now;...............127. H.319, 46
Give up thy soule in clouds of frankinsence.....128. H.320, 6
Of Chance, (as made up all of rock, and oake:) 129. H.323, 12
Offer'd up, with thanks to thee...............129. H.325, 6
Their many vertues volum'd up in thee;........131. H.331, 4
But they fill up their Ebbs again:.............133. H.336, 20
Lets make it full up, by our sport.............133. H.336, 32
The Pinnace up; which though she erres.......134. H.336, 63
Bear up the Magick bough, and spel:........136. H.336, 134
Give up the just applause to verse:..........136. H.336, 136
We'l still sit up,..........................136. H.336, 147
Mirtles offer'd up to Thee......................136. H.337, 6
Offerd up by us, to thee.......................141. H.360, 6
The pillars up of weeping Jet,.................145. H.376, 2
Was rear'd up by the Poore-mans fleece:......149. H.377, 118
The Pillars up of lasting Jet,................149. H.377, 124
Offer'd up a Wolfe to thee.....................151. H.386, 8
Which will be burnt up by and by,............153. H.399, 9
But when She's up and fully drest,............154. H.404, 3
Of Wassaile now, or sets the quintell up:.......159. H.421, 4
Ambo. Lets cheer him up. Sil. Behold him weeping ripe. 159. H.421, 7
But one halfe houre, that's made up here.......162. H.431, 3
Or to seale up the Sun........................164. H.441, 4
His Errours up; and now he finds............167. H.443, 83
Arch-like, hold up, Thy Name's Inscription.....168. H.444, 4
To make up now a Congregation...............168. H.445, 2
This, Three; which Three, you make up Foure Brave Prince. 170. H.451, 16
Grow up to be a Roman Citizen................171. H.456, 2
Which sho'd conjure up a line.................182. H.489, 8
That kept his Piping up......................184. H.492, 40
Endimions Moon to fill up full, remember me:..184. H.492, 42
Set up Thine own eternall Images............185. H.496, 10
With Lillies Tomb'd up in a Glasse;...........186. H.497, 16
Dead, and closed up in Yvorie.................186. H.497, 18
Close thou up thy Poets eyes:.................186. H.499, 2
His Fame's long life, who strives to set up Yours. 188. H.506, 16
Lockt up, not lost:.........................190. H.515, 44
Offer'd up with Vows to Thee..................195. H.530, 6
And as He shuts, close up to Maids again......196. H.537, 4
Rake the Fier up, and get.....................201. H.556, 3
To shore the Feeble up, against the strong;....201. H.557, 11
Man is a Watch, wound up at first, but never..202. H.558, 1
Wound up again: Once down, He's down for ever. 202. H.558, 2
Sprang up a sweet Nativity of Flowres.......204. H.567, 2
The patient Saint, and send up vowes for me.....204. H.570, 4
As to bind up her chaps when she is dead......205. H.571, 4
And work no more; but shut up Shop...........212. H.602, 4
Cloy'd they are up with Arse; but hope, one blast 226. H.650, 3
Up to the brim:...........................227. H.653, 2
And cheer'st them up, by singing how.........230. H.662, 27
Unto the Dew-laps up in meat:...............230. H.662, 36
That's tost up after Fox i' th' Hole...........231. H.662, 57
Wrapt up in Seare-cloth with thine Ancestrie:..231. H.664, 2
I'le eat and drink up all here...................235. H.674, 18
And clos'd her up, as in a Tombe............237. H.686, 16
The May-pole is up,.......................239. H.695, 1
Her cloaths held up, she shew'd withall.........247. H.729, 3
Slouch he packs up, and goes to sev'rall Faires,..253. H.753, 1
Others shall spring up in their place agen:.....256. H.763, 12
Must be the first man up, and last in bed:......259. H.771, 2
Kings must not only cherish up the good,.......260. H.775, 1
Seeal'd up with Night-gum, Loach each morning lyes, 269. H.816, 1
Point be up, and Haft be downe;...............284. H.889, 3
Hang up Hooks, and Sheers to scare...........284. H.891, 1
Which quencht, then lay it up agen,...........285. H.893, 3
The Lictors bundl'd up their rods: beside,......291. H.920, 1
Which, this night hardned, sodders up her nose. 296. H.945, 2
Sprung up a War-like Nation..................297. H.948, 8
Rise up of men, a fighting race...............297. H.948, 12
Thee lesse to taste, then to drink up their spring; 299. H.956, 2
Leave others Beauty, to set up withall.........299. H.958, 6
To shore up my debilitie.......................303. H.973, 4
Grow up in Beauty, as thou do'st begin,.......304. H.979, 1
Up with the Quintill, that the Rout,............306. H.987, 1
Drinke up....................................307. H.988, 1
Lift up thy Sword; next, suffer it to fall,......310. H.1002, 3
Labour is held up, by the hope of rest........311. H.1009, 2
With Swan-like-state, flote up & down thy streams: 316. H.1028, 18
Keep up your state ye streams; and as ye spring, 316. H.1028, 23
Whose Peace is made up with a Pardoning.....316. H.1029, 2
And quaffe up a Bowle.......................320. H.1051, 4
Made up One State of Sixtie Venuses;.........326. H.1080, 4
Science puffs up, sayes Gut, when either Pease 327. H.1085, 1
Held up by Fames eternall Pedestall...........329. H.1092, 8
Claspe thou his Book, then close thou up his Eyes. 329. H.1095, 8
And take me up; or els prevent the fall..........352. N.51, 8
When a mans Faith is frozen up, as dead;......359. N.80, 1
Flie up, to dwell...............................363. N.92, 17
Heaving up my either hand;......................364. N.95, 2
Here I lift them up to Thee,.....................364. N.95, 4
Spring Tulips up through all the yeere;......366. N.97, 21
Sin once reacht up to Gods eternall Sphere,....367. N.100, 1
Last night I drew up mine Account,...........369. N.107, 1
Threescore or fourescore spring up thence for one.388. N.208, 4
And sullen clouds bound up his head...........393. N.232, 6
Drunk up the wine of Gods fierce wrath;......400. N.266, 11
Had He not drank them up for you.............400. N.266, 15
Of furie, and of vengeance up.................400. N.267, 9
Of Him, we lately seal'd up in this Tombe?.....403. N.271, 4
Beares vp twoe globes where loue and pleasure sitt, 405. A.1, 52
Kindly swell vp with little pretty pride,..........406. A.1, 88
Cannot deliuer vpp to'th rust,....................407. A.2, 17
Growe vpp wth Mylder Lawes to knowe.........407. A.2, 25
Giue vpp his worth: to the painte;...............409. A.2, 80
Soaring them vpp, boue Ruyne, till the doome....410. A.3, 33
Keepe vp those flames, & though you shroud.....413. A.4, 16
— — — — — — — — — —,..............426. var. H.197, 37
you, stand for to surrender up the keyes..431. ins. H.283, 60h
— — — — — — — — — — —, ...432. var. H.283, 106
— — — — — — — — — — —,.............445. var. H.730, 12
Upon (Partial List)
And look upon our dreadfull passages,...........14. H.35, 6
Up she got upon a wall.........................15. H.36, 8
Where (though thou see'st not (thou may'st think upon 20. H.55, 5
His head upon his hand he laid;.................42. H.119, 7
But why? why longer doe I gaze upon..........45. H.128, 37
Upon her wings presents the god unshorne.......67. H.178, 2
Ne'r shine upon me; May my Numbers all.....79. H.197, 89
And wait upon her...............................83. H.205, 4
Onely this Ile look upon,........................84. H.209, 3
And offer Tears upon thy Tomb:..............89. H.219, 10
Looking upon yee, That two Nations.........116. H.283, 158
About your eares; and lay upon...............127. H.319, 43
Which precious spoiles upon her,..............131. H.330, 12
I made upon my Julia's brest;................135. H.336, 95
Paske, though his debt be due upon the day....142. H.363, 1
Which fain would waste upon thy Cates, but that 147. H.377, 49
Oh fie upon 'em! Lastly too, all witt..........150. H.382, 17
Just upon five and thirty pounds a yeare........151. H.385, 4
Upon six plump Dandillions, high-............167. H.443, 86
Looke upon all; and though on fire............174. H.465, 7
Upon an other Plain:.........................183. H.492, 10
And give a righteous judgement upon it........187. H.506, 4
If full we charme; then call upon.............198. H.544, 7
Instead of almes, sets dogs upon the poor.......238. H.694, 2
Nor let my Herse, be wept upon by thee:......281. H.875, 2
Upon thee many a Benizon....................303. H.973, 18
Three fatall Sisters wait upon each sin;.........341. N.11, 1
To give us more then Hope can fix upon........378. N.135, 2
— — — — — — — — — — —,.............426, var. H.197, 40
and come upon your Bridegroome like a Tyde 431. ins. H.283, 50b
To feed upon the Candid hares...........433. ins. H.293, 31a
Upper From th' upper to the under-glasse,.......44. H.127, 6
With Upper Stories, Mutton, Veale............101. H.250, 30
Up-raise In stead of Holly, now up-raise........285. H.892, 3
Up-rear What we up-rear,......................335. H.1129, 9
Upright To keep cheap Nature even, and upright;.35. H.106, 25
Uprising At my up-rising next, I shall,.........123. H.306, 11
There's an up-rising but of one for one:........388. N.208, 2
Uptails For his Uptailes all;....................247. H.727, 11
Uptails all See Uptails
Urban See Urbin
Urbanity Distance and sweet Vrbanitie,..........409. A.2, 96
Urbin The Palme from Urbin, Titian, Tintarret,..150. H.384, 2
Urchin By the round Urchin, some mixt wheate 439. ins. H.443, 45d
Urge Urge no more; and there shall be..........122. H.304, 7
I will not urge Thee, for I know,............174. H.465, 33
Urgeth When Love (the child of likenesse) urgeth on 77. H.197, 3
Urging Vrging diuorcement (worse then death to theis) 410. A.3, 9
Urles Urles had the Gout so, that he co'd not stand; 207. H.577, 1
Urn And with my Lawrell crown thy Golden Urne...11. H.22, 4
Unlesse thou giv'st my small Remains an Urne...19. H.52, 4
To see the small remainders in mine Urne:........49. H.138, 2

About this **Urne**, wherein thy Dust is laid,.......73. H.186, 18
To fill a little **Urne**............................81. H.201, 44
And light my Reliques to their **Urne**...........109. H.271, 6
Both to be blended in the **Urn**,...............233. H.670, 38
I'le beg of thee first here to have mine **Urn**.....242. H.713, 18
In this little **Urne** is laid......................262. H.782, 1
The **Urne** was little, but the room..............269. H.817, 3
Here, her ashes, or her **Urne**....................276. H.848, 5
And leave thee sleeping in thy **Urn**.............361. N.83, 78
Urns We love to rest in peacefull **Urnes** at home,.278. H.860, 6
Ursley **Ursley**, she thinks those Velvet Patches grace
197. H.543, 1
For ropes of pearle, first Madam **Ursly** showes...232. H.668, 1
Ursley's They be but signs of **Ursleys** hollow teeth.
197. H.543, 4
Use And for the graceful **use** of it:...............16. H.39, 10
For seldome **use** commends the pleasure........38. H.106, 140
Faile of thy former helps; and onely **use**.........46. H.128, 52
Which not for **use**, but meerly for the sight,......46. H.129, 5
And thus surpriz'd (as Filchers **use**)............71. H.182, 11
Then be not coy, but **use** your time;............84. H.208, 13
Gold I've none, for **use** or show,.................88. H.218, 1
And for what **use**, scarce man wo'd think it.....93. H.223, 124
Of Ash-heapes, in the which ye **use**.............127. H.319, 21
Prigg, when he comes to houses, oft doth **use**....143. H.368, 1
Let's live in hast; **use** pleasures while we may:..171. H.453, 1
Go to your banquet then, but **use** delight,......220. H.633, 18
Well will serve the Beggars **use**................223. H.638, 20
As stones and salt gloves **use** to give, even so...248. H.731, 3
Torn for the **use** of Pasterie:....................275. H.844, 4
He bade me then that Neck-lace **use**;..........279. H.863, 9
Then let her **use** the watring pot...............279. H.867, 4
From which mishap this **use** I make,.............283. H.883, 11
Without their **use** we may have men?...........297. H.948, 2
Kings must not **use** the Axe for each offence:..309. H.998, 1
(This night as ye **use**)........................317. H.1035, 8
When Pimpes feat sweat (as they doe often **use**).332. H.1113, 1
This is strong thrift that warie Rush doth **use**..332. H.1116, 3
These Veiles, wherewith we **use** to hide........360. N.83, 45
To my most healthfull **use**,....................368. N.104, 14
Or have I two loaves; then I **use**..............376. N.127, 7
Shall want a Hand-mayde, (as she ofte will **vse**).412. A.3, 100
Used And He, who **us'd** to leade the Country-round,
159. H.421, 5
Never since first Bellona **us'd** a Shield,.........170. H.451, 11
Ill **us'd**, then Babes left fatherless.............218. H.626, 15
Which, rightly **us'd**, both in their time and place,.371. N.115, 7
Usher Nor has the darknesse power to **usher** in..35. H.106, 39
But turn'd a Ladies **Usher** now, ('tis true:)......53. H.148, 2
Ushering There **ush'ring** Vergers, here likewise,..92. H.223, 105
Usurer Moon is an **Usurer**, whose gain,..........143. H.369, 1
The Landlord, or the **Usurer**...................200. H.552, 10
Usurp Base Ballad-mongers, who **vsurpe** thy name..412. A.3, 90
Usurpest Less then Apollo, that **ursurp'st** such Three?
276. H.851, 6
Usurps To strike him dead, that but **usurps** a Throne.
32. H.97, 6
Usury Shee brings in much, by carnall **usury**:....220. H.631, 2
Utmost To th'**utmost** mite,.......................30. H.87, 17
No, no, the **utmost** share........................231. H.663, 5
The **utmost** smart, so Thou wilt cure............342. N.17, 12
Brought at the last to th' **utmost** bit,............376. N.124, 3
Hath seal'd the promise of her **vtmost** skill.......405. A.1, 64
Utter In **utter** darkenes did, and still will sit.....150. H.382, 18
Confus'd in **utter** Admiration.................326. H.1080, 10
So **utter** dark, as that no eye...................357. N.72, 7
Utterly And **utterly** forgotten lye,...............265. H.794, 2
Vaile See **Veil**
Vain Love will in **vain** spend shafts on me:......155. H.406, 2
It is in **vain** to sing, or stay..................179. H.476, 34
Where round about Thou seest but all things **vaine**,
371. N.113, 3
In **vain** our labours are, whatsoe're they be,......379. N.140, 1
Vainly Or **vainly** spend,...........................43. H.123, 17
Valentine Choose me your **Valentine**;..............31. H.94, 1
Who'l be her **Valentine**..........................56. H.149, 116
When I shall couple with my **Valentine**.........149. H.378, 4
Valiant 'Tis still observ'd, those men most **valiant** are,
308. H.994, 1
Necessity makes dastards **valiant** men...........333. H.1118, 2
Valley And in the milky **vally** that's betweene.....405. A.1, 55
Vandyke No, not the glory of the World, **Vandike**.
150. H.384, 6
Vanish So **vanish** hence, but leave a name, as sweet,
131. H.331, 9
I **vanish**; more I had to say;.................207. H.575, 65
Wrongs, if neglected, **vanish** in short time;......260. H.776, 1
Vanished But **vanisht** man,......................133. H.336, 21
Vanishing (Like to a sound that's **vanishing** away)
201. H.557, 22
Vanity Fie on this pride, this Female **vanitie**...163. H.439, 2
He loves the gain that **vanity** brings in.........163. H.439, 4
Vanquish To **vanquish** Hell, as here He conquer'd Death?
403. N.271, 6
Vanquished But being **vanquisht** quite,..........105. H.258, 5
He who commends the **vanquisht**, speaks the Power,
200. H.553, 1
Fall down together **vanquisht** both, and lye....216. H.618, 15
Vapour And as a **vapour**, or a drop of raine......69. H.178, 63
Varieties Such rich, such fresh, such sweet **varietyes**,
415. A.7, 16
Various — — — — — — — — —, ...435. var. H.329, 21
Varnish Falsehood by **Varnish** and Vermillion...329. H.1094, 2
Ther was not **Varnish** (only) in my loue.........412. A.3, 80
Varnished And walks fresh **varnisht** to the publick view.
140. H.356, 2
In **Varnisht** maps; by'th' helpe of Compasses;..330. H.1100, 2
Vary Y'ave laught enough (sweet) **vary** now your Text;
111. H.277, 1
Those maids that never **vary**;..................160. H.422, 6
Must not **vary**,...............................320. H.1051, 15
Vast Small shots paid often, waste a **vast** estate....13. H.28, 2
Here shall endure thy **vast** Dominion............210. H.592, 4
When this or that **vast** Dinastie must fall........256. H.763, 9
Wildred in this **vast** watry Region.............319. H.1044, 4
Of **vast** Eternitie..................................354. N.58, 8
— — — — — — — — — —, ...427. var. H.197, 65
Vats Next to your Flailes, your Fanes, your **Fatts**;
102. H.250, 40
Vault In this little **Vault** she lyes,................52. H.145, 1
Vaults In **Vaults** beneath?........................85. H.211, 14
Drooping, I draw on to the **vaults** of death,....312. H.1013, 3
Sleep not for ever in the **vaults** of death:........358. N.77, 11
Vaunt No more Ile **vaunt**,.........................100. H.246, 8
Veal With Upper Stories, Mutton, **Veale**........101. H.250, 30
Of Mutton, or of **Veale** in it,.....................124. H.312, 6
Veals To eate thy Bullocks thighs, thy **Veales**, thy fat
147. H.377, 63
From fat of **Veales**, and Sheep?.................391. N.228, 4
Veil And now the yellow **Vaile**, at last,............55. H.149, 71
Veils These **Veiles**, wherewith we use to hide....360. N.83, 45
Vein — — — — — — — — —, ...447. var. A.1, 47
Veined — — — — — — — — —, ...448. var. A.1, 98
Veins Run through my **veines**, like to a hasty flood.
79. H.197, 78
In wch the **veynes** ymplanted seeme to lye........405. A.1, 47
Vellum Whose **velome**, and whose volumne is the Skie,
168. H.444, 7
Velvet Ursley, she thinks those **Velvet** Patches grace
197. H.543, 1
Vengeance To God for **vengeance**? yes say I;.....387. N.203, 2
Of furie, and of **vengeance** up...................400. N.267, 9
Vent No closset plot, or open **vent**,..............126. H.319, 3
Venter See **Venture**
Venture We'l **venter** (if we can) at wit:........215. H.616, 4
And no whit further must **venture**;.............256. H.762, 9
Ventures He **ventures** boldly on the pith........119. H.293, 32
Venus Which **Venus** hearing; thither came,........31. H.92, 5
O **Venus**! thou, to whom is known...............56. H.149, 91
But **Venus** having lost the day,...............105. H.260, 5
Emergent **Venus** from the Sea?................112. H.283, 10
And prayers to **Venus**; if it please..............175. H.465, 75
Venus standing Vulcan by.....................194. H.527, 9
Where **Venus** sleeps (halfe smothered.)..........269. H.815, 4
And **Venus**, every way:.........................281. H.874, 3
— — — — — — — — — —, ...429. var. H.260, 2
Venuses Made up One State of Sixtie **Venuses**;..326. H.1080, 4
Verdant Re-cloth'd in fresh and **verdant** Diaper...224. H.642, 2
Vergers There ush'ring **Vergers**, here likewise,..92. H.223, 105
Vergil Next, **Virgil**, Ile call forth,...............80. H.201, 17
Then stately **Virgil**, witty Ovid, by............206. H.575, 39
Vergil's Not **Virgil's** Gnat had such a Tomb.....104. H.256, 21
Not **Virgils** Gnat, to whom the Spring..........186. H.497, 9
Verity Present with just men, to the **veritie**:.....385. N.188, 2
Vermilion And flow, and flame, in your **Vermillion**.
105. H.259, 10
Treading upon **Vermilion**........................112. H.283, 14
The tincture of **Vermillion**:.....................118. H.291, 6
Paints them with fresh **Vermilion**:...............268. H.811, 2
Falsehood by Varnish and **Vermillion**...........329. H.1094, 2
Verse See **Meadow-verse**
And still do'st this, and that **verse**, reprehend:......7. H.6, 4
The holy incantation of a **verse**;....................7. H.8, 2
And take a life immortall from my **Verse**.........27. H.82, 16
Or **Verse** I covet none;..........................30. H.89, 2
That **Verse**, of all the Verses here, shall be.......107. H.264, 5
Phoebus! when that I a **Verse**,.................122. H.303, 1
Verse crown'd with Yvie, and with Holly:......126. H.319, 10
Give up the just applause to **verse**:...........136. H.336, 136
In time of life, I grac't ye with my **Verse**;......138. H.343, 1
A Lyrick **verse**,.................................144. H.371, 11
Besides I give Thee here a **Verse** that shall.....168. H.444, 2
If I write a **Verse**, or two,.....................182. H.489, 5
To praise his **Verse**.........................198. H.544 12
When I a **Verse** shall make,....................212. H.604, 1
Co'd a noble **Verse** beget;.....................217. H.620, 5
And no **Verse** illegitimate......................236. H.681, 6
And yet each **Verse** of thine.....................289. H.911, 9
(That she may flow in **Verse**)...................291. H.918, 6
Tel'st when a **Verse** springs high, how understood
297. H.947, 7
Or mourne, or make a Marble **Verse** for me,....298. H.952, 3
Who fli'st at all heights: Prose and **Verse** run'st through;
298. H.955, 7

And that is this, A verse Instylde................407. A.2, 4
Verses See Virgin-verses
Where others love, and praise my Verses; still....66. H.173, 1
Trust to good Verses then;....................81. H.201, 45
That Verse, of all the Verses here, shall be......107. H.264, 5
If so, why then are not These Verses hurld,....172. H.459, 3
Verses out-live the bravest deeds of men?.......264. H.791, 2
Nis, he makes Verses; but the Lines he writes,...286. H.896, 1
— — — — — — — — — —, ...428. var. H.197, 89
Vertue See Virtue
Vertue's See Virtue's
Vertues See Virtues
Vertuous See Virtuous
Very (Partial List)
That done, then wind me in that very sheet........9. H.14, 10
To be, and is, the very best of Wives:............26. H.79, 4
The very eyes of me:..........................109. H.267, 22
Through heaven, the very Spheres,..............151. H.388, 7
Pievish doth boast, that he's the very first.......156. H.410, 1
'Tis with very much ado;......................182. H.489, 6
To very few, or else to none..................200. H.552, 20
For very little, or no gaines:..................212. H.602, 2
And very well pleas'd,........................333. H.1122, 2
Thy very Tomb................................375. N.123, 89
For, long this work wil be, & very short this Day. 401.N.268, 6
Very-many Love for our very-many Trespasses....197. H.539, 6
Very-many-meeting So very-many-meeting hindrances, 352. N.51, 2
Vessel Ye see the aged Vessell crown'd:.........94. H.225, 6
Wash clean the Vessell, lest ye soure..........320. H.1053, 1
The vessell full, did then run ore:...............357. N.75, 4
Vessels With Bread, and Wine, and Vessells furnished; 355. N.65, 4
Vesta — — — — — — — —,............437. var. H.336, 128
Vestal Come, Ile instruct thee. Know, the vestall fier 262. H.781, 15
Wch like a Vestall Vergine ply..................407. A.2, 23
Vestment More mortall in the vestiment.......311. H.1010, 6
Thou load'st with gold thy vestiment?..........394. N.239, 2
Vestments But the base dregs and lees of vestiments? 302. H.970, 2
Vestry In their Religious Vesterie.............92. H.223, 100
(Sweet as the Vestrie of the Oracles.)..........157. H.414, 4
Vestures With the white Vestures, all attending Thee. 196. H.539, 4
As flowrie vestures doe descrie.................311. H.1010, 7
Chor. Thy vestures were not flowing:..........375. N.123, 67
But, as they walk't here in their vestures white,..384. N.181, 4
Vex If I any fret or vex,........................177. H.472, 3
Vexation Vexation of the mind, and damn'd Despaire. 45. H.128, 22
And Ramme of time and by vexation growes....148. H.377, 111
Vexed Growes still the stronger, strongly vext....37. H.106, 100
Love vext,.......................................172. H.458, 5
Via Ravisht, in that faire Via Lactea.............96. H.230, 4
Vial A Christall Violl Cupid brought,.........222. H.635, 1
Vials Receive these Christall Vialls fil'd..........360. N.83, 39
Viands These, and thy choicest viands do extend.147. H.377, 67
Though ne'r so mean the Viands be,.............200. H.552, 3
Vibration That brave Vibration each way free;....261. H.779, 5
Vicarage. A Vicarige at last Tom Glasse got here, 151. H.385, 3
Vice Vice rules the Most, or All at Court:......37. H.106, 90
Ther's no vice now, but has his president.......139. H.352, 2
Need is no vice at all; though here it be,........239. N.698, 1
Vice doth in some but lodge awhile, not dwell...314. H.1021, 2
Vicegerent — — — — — — — —, ...422. var. H.106, 90
Vices That thus from vices driven,..............363. N.92, 15
Vicious Not to cut off, but cure the vicious part...268. H.808, 2
Victorious Your Fate, and Ours, alike Victorious are. 271. H.823, 2
Victor's That Prince takes soone enough the Victors roome, 109. H.268, 1
The Olive branch, and Victors Song:............360. N.83, 26
Victory In her white Stole; now Victory do's rest 271. H.823, 3
fore this or that hath gott the victory.....433. ins. H.283, 140j
Vie See Out-vie
View A Robin-Red-brest; who at view,............46. H.130, 4
Star fill'd with glory to our view,..............112. H.283, 4
Which when not warmed by her view,...........131. H.330, 9
And walks fresh varnisht to the publick view....140. H.356, 2
Expose your jewels then unto the view,........173. H.459, 11
These seen, thou go'st to view thy flocks......230. H.662, 40
See this, View that, and all the other bounds:..259. H.771, 4
Thee, wth myne Eyes, or in, or out, of View......411. A.3, 70
Take it then and in a viewe.....................417. A.9, 7
— — — — — — — — — — —, ...432. var. H.283, 101
— — — — — — — — — — —, ...450. var. A.9, 51
Viewed And took it up, and view'd it; then.......73. H.187, 6
Viewing And viewing them with a more safe survey, 36. H.106, 73
— — — — — — — — — —, ...422. var. H.106, 79
Vigil For no black-bearded Vigil from thy doore.146. H.377, 13
Vigilant The Rod doth sleep, while vigilant are men. 342. N.21, 2
Villages May take the simple Villages..............6. H.2, 16
The incurious Villages.........................255. H.761, 14
To see far off the smoaking Villages.............352. N.51, 10
Villars Til I had got the name of Villars here.....99. H.254, 2
When I of Villars doe but heare the name,......137. H.341, 1
Vine Was Metamorphoz'd to a Vine;..............16. H.41, 2
More like a Stock, then like a Vine.............17. H.41, 23
'Bout a Virgin like a Vine:......................17. H.43, 4
Crown'd with clusters of the Vine;..............39. H.111, 5
Whereon my Vine did crawle,...................72. H.185, 13
Thanks to the gen'rous Vine;....................72. H.185, 27
Thee in thy Vine, or had but tasted one........78. H.197, 62
You are a full-spread faire-set Vine,..........88. H.216, 10
Ne're ravisht from the flattering Vine,..........120. H.293, 48
That Dress, this Sprig, that Leaf, this Vine;....215. H.616, 23
Sweet as the blossomes of the Vine.............230. H.662, 34
A little prop best fits a little Vine,.............249. H.733, 2
A crawling Vine about Anacreon's head:......313. H.1017, 2
Like to the tendrells of a flattring vine,...........404. A.1, 8
Soe full of clarrett that whoe soe pricks a vine....405. A.1, 49
To Roughnes, Claspe hym lyke a Vine,..........408. A.2, 68
— — — — — — — — — — —, ...426. var. H.197, 47
Vinegar Y'ave dipt too long i'th' Vinegar;......146. H.377, 22
A ragd-soust-neats-foot with sick vineger:.....262. H.783, 14
Those faces (sower as Vineger.)................279. H.868, 2
Vineger is no other I define,...................301. H.964, 1
To an exalted vineger;........................321. H.1056, 10
And that sowre Fellow, with his vineger,.......398. N.263, 10
The Myrrhe, the Gall, the Vineger:.............400. N.266, 9
The Vineger, the Myrrhe, the Gall:.............400. N.267, 11
Vines Vines to prune, though not to kill,........204. H.569, 14
Like loving vines hid vnder Ivorye,..............405. A.1, 48
— — — — — — — — — —, ...426. var. H.197, 47
Vineyard I'th Forum here, or Vineyard.........380. N.152, 2
Vineyards Breathes Vine-yards and Pomgranats: O how sweet! 113. H.283, 22
Wee have noe vinyards which doe beare..436. ins. H.336, 48a
Viol My violl and my lyre.......................228. H.657, 6
Violl, and Voice, is (by thy losse) struck mute?.288. H.907, 4
To'th Lute or Violl, then 'tis ravishing.........331. H.1101, 2
What though my Harp, and Violl be..............361. N.84, 1
To it my Violl and my Lute:...................393. N.232, 14
To grace a Lute, a vyall, Virginall...............406. A.1, 100
Violates Who violates the Customes, hurts the Health, 318. H.1041, 1
Violent Grown violent, do's either die, or tire.......51. H.143, 4
Violet With breath more sweet then Violet...........6. H.2, 14
Each here declining Violet.........................7. H.9, 4
The Rose, the Violet, one day..................61. H.159, 15
You are a dainty Violet,........................88. H.216, 16
The Violet?......................................104. H.257, 21
With the Rose, and Violet.......................108. H.266, 16
And pregnant violet; which done,...............119. H.293, 23
Spring the purple Violet.........................262. H.782, 4
The Primrose, and the Violet...................360. N.83, 18
Healthes to the Rose, the Violet, or Pinke,.........410. A.3, 6
Violets Lillies will languish; Violets look ill;......41. H.118, 1
Maids, and here strew Violets.....................44. H.125, 6
Whether the Violets sho'd excell,..............105. H.260, 3
Of Primroses and Violets.........................192. H.521, 20
— — — — — — — — — — —, ...429. var. H.260, 1
Violl See Vial, Viol
Viols While Harps, and Violls then............369. N.106, 15
Virgil See Vergil
Virgil's See Vergil's
Virgin To read my Booke the Virgin shie.............6. H.4, 1
'Bout a Virgin like a Vine:......................17. H.43, 4
Like to a Virgin newly ravished...................41. H.118, 4
Or like a Virgin full of ruth,.....................47. H.132, 7
Each Virgin, like a Spring,.....................110. H.274, 11
Once in a Virgin Flosculet,.......................126. H.318, 7
When with the Virgin morning thou do'st rise,...127. H.320, 1
Casts forth a light like to a Virgin flame:......131. H.331, 6
Sweet virgin, that I do not set.................145. H.376, 1
Of the shie Virgin, seems to deck..............166. H.443, 64
A Virgin Taper, ever shining here...............191. H.516, 4
Here lies a Virgin, and as sweet................257. H.764, 1
The Virgin Marie was (as I have read)...........385. N.190, 1
Doe speake a virgin merry cherry-lip't...........404. A.1, 22
Wch like a Vestall Vergine ply..................407. A.2, 23
— — — — — — — — — — — —, ...442. var. H.575, 18
— — — — — — — — — — — —, ...449. var. A.8, 5
Virginal To grace a Lute, a vyall, Virginall.......406. A.1, 100
Virgin-altar Before Thy Virgin-Altar I appeare,..368. N.103, 2
Virgin-flower Loe! Thus I give a Virgin-Flower, 402. N.270, 5
Virginities See Feigned-lost-virginities
Virgin-martyr O Virgin-martyr, ever blest.........359. N.83, 3
Virgin-Mother The Virgin-Mother stood at distance (there) 384. N.180, 1
Virgin's A Virgins face she had; her dresse.......51. H.142, 7
Within the Virgins Coronet.......................88. H.216, 18
To chafe o're much the Virgins cheek or eare:..329. H.1095, 2
Virgins Once were Virgins sick of love,.........15. H.37, 2
Virgins promis'd when I dy'd,...................44. H.125, 1
The kisse of Virgins; First-fruits of the bed;......45. H.128, 7
Rifle the Flowers which the Virgins strew'd:...49. H.138, 6
Of Virgins! Tell the Maid,.......................56. H.149, 93
Virgins, weep not; 'twill come, when,..........56. H.149, 111

Virgins, time-past, known were these,............64. H.167, 1
When as a thousand **Virgins** on this day,........68. H.178, 13
She has **Virgins** many,..........................83. H.205, 5
So you be straight, where **Virgins** straight sho'd be.
99. H.242, 2
And thousand **Virgins** come and weep,........104. H.256, 17
Glide by the banks of **Virgins** then, and passe..113. H.283, 41
Maides sho'd say, or **Virgins** sing,............117. H.285, 11
Heare ye **Virgins**, and Ile teach,..............120. H.297, 1
You shall not languish, trust me: **Virgins** here..138. H.343, 3
Virgins coy, but not unkind....................138. H.346, 4
Oft have I heard both Youths and **Virgins** say,..149. H.378, 1
Frollick **Virgins** once these were,..............152. H.391, 1
Come **Virgins** then, and see....................184. H.493, 9
On Holy-dayes, when **Virgins** meet............192. H.521, 29
A Tentrall sung by **Virgins** o're thy Grave:....209. H.584, 6
O! you the **Virgins** nine!......................228. H.657, 1
If fragrant **Virgins** you'l but keep..............257. H.764, 7
Thou writes in Prose, how sweet all **Virgins** be;..266. H.802, 1
Virgins Come, and in a Ring....................274. H.838, 5
With soft-smooth **Virgins** (for our chast disport)
315. H.1028, 9
The eye of **Virgins**; nay, the Queen............360. N.83, 15
May **Virgins**, when they come to mourn,........361. N.83, 75
Amongest the thrice-three-sacred **Virgins**, fill......412. A.3, 86
The **Virgins** lost at Barley-breakes,........440. ins. H.443, 45u
To those **virgins**, whose briske heu..........450. ins. A.9, 52
Virgins' When **Virgins** hands have drawn........75. H.193, 2
By all those **Virgins** Fillets hung..............169. H.449, 15
Their Goales for **Virgins** kisses; which when done,
206. H.575, 18
Virgin-verses Best with those **Virgin-Verses** thou hast writ:
28. H.84, 4
Virgin-vows All prosper by your **Virgin-vowes**...179. H.476, 24
Virtue Who swims with **Vertue**, he shall still be sure.23. H.71, 4
By studying to know **vertue**; and to aime........35. H.106, 7
Vertue had, and mov'd her Sphere..............37. H.106, 92
His **vertue** still is sensible of paine:..............60. H.158, 2
May blaze the **vertue** of their Sires...........116. H.283, 160
Each must, in **vertue**, strive for to excell;......121. H.298, 1
Ha's it a speaking **virtue**? 2. Yes;............130. H.329, 16
The stronger: **Vertue** dies when foes..........148. H.377, 112
Live here: But know 'twas **vertue**, & not chance,.152. H.392, 5
Vertue conceal'd (with Horace you'l confesse)..173. H.459, 13
Know **vertue** taught thee, not thy selfe.........176. H.465, 84
And this remember, **Vertue** keepes the measure..220. H.633, 25
By so much, **vertue** is the lesse,................254. H.754, 1
Vertue best loves those children that she beates...270. H.820, 4
Vertue and pleasure, both to dwell in one.......293. H.935, 2
Where **vertue** walkes, not those that flow.....311. H.1010, 10
Is sober **virtue**, seen to move her sphere.......327. H.1087, 2
He lives, who lives to **virtue**: men who cast....328. H.1088, 9
Is the defensive **vertue**, Abstinence............333. H.1117, 2
But **Vertue** Rears the eternal Monument..........419. A.10, 4
Owes more to **vertue** then too Fate.......422. ins. H.106, 92b
— — — — — — — — — —, ...432. var. H.283, 83
Virtue's To last, but not their ever: **Vertues** Hand
148. H.377, 101
Vertue's clean Conclave is sobriety.............331. H.1109, 2
Virtues Their many **vertues** volum'd up in thee;..131. H.331, 4
The **Vertues** Lesse, or Cardinall,................409. A.2, 100
Virtuous This, this a **virtuous** man can doe,......31. H.90, 7
Vertuous instructions ne'r are delicate...........270. H.820, 2
Richer then that faire pretious **virtuos** horne....406. A.1, 103
(Those wch must growe to **Vertuous** deeds)......407. A.2, 20
— — — — — — — — — — —, ...441. var. H.465, 46
Visage **Visage** of them can alter him;............215. H.615, 4
And though his **visage** hung i' th' eare........418. A.9, 47
— — — — — — — — — — —, ...427. var. H.197, 75
Vision While Faunus in the **Vision** comes to keep,.36. H.106, 51
Then in a **Vision** I did see......................51. H.142, 5
In the **Vision** I askt, why?.....................219. H.628, 3
Visit Ile come and **visit** thee....................271. H.824, 4
Chorus. We sail along, to **visit** mortals never;....417. A.8, 37
Vizard No such crab'd **vizard**: Thou hast learnt thy Train,
147. H.377, 35
Vocation To his owne **vocation**.................315. H.1026, 14
Voice Myrha, for the Lute, and **Voice**............16. H.39, 8
O Earth! Earth! Earth heare thou my **voice**, and be
19. H.52, 1
So smooth, so sweet, so silv'ry is thy **voice**,......22. H.67, 1
But when your Playing, and your **Voice** came in,
95. H.228, 3
Let but thy **voice** engender with the string,......102. H 252, 1
Whether it be the **voice** or string,..............142. H.362, 2
And turn'd my **voice**.........................144. H.371, 16
Sing me to death; for till thy **voice** be cleare,....152. H.390, 1
Cleane in manners, cleere in **voice**:.............232. H.665, 2
Ch. What **voice** so sweet and charming do I heare?
248. H.730, 3
Then if thy **voice** commingle with the String....276. H.851, 3
Violl, and **Voice**, is (by thy losse) struck mute?..288. H.907, 4
With my weake **voice** Ile sing, or say..........303. H.973, 13
Rare is the **voice** it selfe; but when we sing....331. H.1101, 1
Let me Thy **voice** betimes i' th morning heare;..358. N.77, 12
Awake the **Voice**! Awake the String!...........364. N.96, 4
Tis not my **voice**, but heauens, that bidds thee goe;
414. A.6, 2
But **voice** of fame, and **voice** of heauen haue thundered
414. A.6, 5
— — — — — — — — — — —, ...444. var. H.730, 5
— — — — — — — — — — —, ...445. var. H.730, 8
Voiced A fault, tis hid, if it be **voic't** by thee...328. H.1089, 2
Voices To **Voices**, say, Amen...................369. N.106, 16
Voices' The **voices** Daughter nea'r spake syllable.159. H.421, 28
Voicing — — — — — — — — —, ...435. var. H.329, 16
Void Both **void** of state;......................350. N.47, 12
Made **void** for millions, as for me..............370. N.107, 10
Volume The **Volumne** of himselfe, and Name......48. H.134, 4
Whose velome, and whose **volumne** is the Skie,...168. H.444, 7
O **Volume** worthy leafe, by leafe and cover........415. A.7, 5
Volumed Their many vertues **volum'd** up in thee;.131. H.331, 4
Volumes Or reade in **Volumes**, and those Bookes (with all
330. H.1100, 3
Votary — — — — — — —, ...430. var. H.267, 2
Voted **Voted** the Rose; the Queen of flowers.........8. H.11, 8
Vow Or **vow** ye never:..........................32. H.94, 6
In thy both Last, and Better **Vow**:..............34. H.106, 2
False to my **vow**, or fall away from thee......59. H.154, 10
That my last **Vow** commends to you:...........61. H.159, 21
Look, look, by Love I **vow**......................74. H.192, 3
Which here I **vow** to serve, doe not remove......79. H.197, 82
Or prayers, or **vow**............................132. H.336, 3
No, no, that selfe same heart, that **vow**,........134. H.336, 70
If die I must, then my last **vow** shall be,........140. H.355, 9
Had'st power thy selfe to keep this **vow**;......176. H.465, 82
I **vow** by Pan, to come away..................184. H.492, 27
Nod to this **vow** of mine:......................228. H.657, 4
Receive this **vow**, so fare-ye-well for ever.......316. H.1028, 26
Take, if thou do'st distrust, that **Vowe**;........328. H.1090, 6
For times to come, I'le make this **Vow**,..........357. N.72, 16
(Heauen and my soule beare Record of my **Vowe**)
411. A.3, 48
You may **vow** Ile not forgett......................414. A.5, 1
Vowed They **vow'd** to ask the Gods...............31. H.92, 4
He **vow'd** Destruction both to Birch, and Men:..65. H.171, 2
Vower If the **Vower** don't express................22. H.63, 3
Vows See **Virgin-vows**
My solemne **Vowes** have here accomplished:.......23. H.72, 2
Welcome, most welcome to our **Vowes** and us,......25. H.77, 1
Promise, and keep your **vowes**,...................32. H.94, 5
My **vowes** denounc'd in zeale, which thus much show thee,
46. H.128, 47
Pay we our **Vowes**, and goe; yet when we part,..73. H.186, 13
Welcome as are the ends unto my **Vowes**:........77. H.197, 14
And pay no **vowes** to thee? who wast their best..78. H.197, 59
When, after these, h'as paid his **vows**,........93. H.223, 135
For my wisht safety pay thy **vowes**,............175. H.465, 74
Offer'd up with **Vows** to Thee...................195. H.530, 6
The patient Saint, and send up **vowes** for me.....204. H.570, 4
The **vowes** of those, that children beare:........221. H.633, 57
Ph. Ile give thee **vows** & tears. Ch. can tears pay skores
248. H.730, 19
Nor those false **vows**, which oft times don't prevaile.
331. H.1104, 2
Take then his **Vowes**, who, if he had it, would....369. N.105, 5
But earth: such **vowes** nere reach Gods eare.....381. N.158, 8
The **Vowes** of those, who are Petitioners.........382. N.169, 2
Welcome to all o^r^ **vowes**........................413. A.4, 20
With such white **vowes** as fate can nere dissever..414. A.6, 11
— — — — — — — — — — —, ...421. var. H.106, 51
and the smooth Handmaides pay their **vowes**
431. ins. H.283, 60d
Vulcan Venus standing **Vulcan** by...............194. H.527, 9
Vultures And our Diseases, **Vultures** of the Gods:
278. H.862, 2
Wafer A **wafer** Dol'd by thee, will swell......139. H.350, 3
A little **Wafer** or a Cake;.....................284. H.890, 4
Waft Ch. What's that to me, I **waft** nor fish or fowles,
248. H.730, 9
Shall hither **waft** it, and in leiu.................414. A.5, 15
Waftage Cha. I cannot stay; more souls for **waftage** wait,
416. A.8, 24
Wafted Then which, thy self ne'er **wafted** sweeter over.
416. A.8, 10
Wafting — — — — — — — — —, ...449. var. A.8, 24
Wag As to shew her Tongue **wag** through:........11. H.21, 10
Alas! said she, my **Wag**! if this................50. H.139, 12
Wager A **wager**, and let it be this;..............99. H.243, 3
The **wager** thou shalt have, and me,.........238. H.690, 7
A **wager**, who the best shall play,...............243. H.716, 2
Whose now the prize and **wager** is..............244. H.716, 42
Wagered And hadst thou **wager'd** twenty Kine,.244. H.716, 45
Wages To ask our **wages**, e're our work be done..241. H.708, 2
After this life, the **wages** shall.................380. N.149, 1
Wail O modest Matrons, weep and **waile**!......374. N.123, 13
Waist Her Belly, Buttocks, and her **Waste**.........16. H.41, 7
So smiles that Riband 'bout my Julia's **waste**:....40. H.114, 2
Shew me thy **waste**; Then let me there withall,...154. H.403, 5
Wait And **wait** upon her..........................83. H.205, 4
A little-Puppet-Priest doth **wait**,.................91. H.223, 39
I will not **wait**,................................137. H.340, 10
Full mirth **wait** on you; and such mirth as shall.140. H.354, 11

Let's leave a longer time to **wait**,..............179. H.476, 28
Love and the Graces evermore do **wait**..........255. H.760, 1
On your niceness though we **wait**,..............276. H.850, 3
Enter and prosper; while our eyes doe **waite**....300. H.961, 9
Let moderation on thy passions **waite**..........318. H.1038, 1
Jacob Gods Beggar was; and so we **wait**.....383. N.171, 1
Three fatall Sisters **wait** upon each sin;..........341. N.11, 1
Bee readye, thou In mee, to **wayte** vppon her....412. A.3, 101
Cha. I cannot stay; more souls for waftage **wait**,..416. A.8, 24

Waiter Keeping no currish **Waiter** to affright,....147. H.377, 47

Waiting See how the poore do **waiting** stand,....139. H.350, 1
While Reverence, **waiting** at the bashfull board,..148. H.377, 75
— — — — — — — — — —, ...440. var. H.443, 110

Waits And Genius **waits** to have us both to bed..261. H.781, 6
To him, who weeping **waits**,......................370. N.111, 2

Wake Any noise, they both will **wake**,.............52. H.145, 4
Then to want the **Wake** next Yeare............255. H.761, 24
And if I chance to **wake**, and rise thereon,......392. N.230, 21

Wakes I sing of May-poles, Hock-carts, Wassails, **Wakes**, 5. H.1, 3
At Sheering-times, and yearely **Wakes**,........192. H.521, 25
Thy **Wakes**, thy Quintels, here thou hast,.......230. H.662, 52
Are the Junketts still at **Wakes**:................255. H.761, 4

Waking **Waking** shalt find me sleeping there. 175. H.465, 52

Walk See Circumwalk, Sheepwalk
Then shall my Ghost not **walk** about, but keep....9. H.14, 17
No, here Ile last, and **walk** (a harmless shade) 73. H.186, 17
Nothing is New: we **walk** where others went...139. H.352, 1
But **walke** abroad, yet wisely well............174. H.465, 13
And think (as thou do'st **walke** the street)....174. H.465, 15
I co'd never **walke** alone;....................183. H.490, 13
And **walk** thou must the way that others went: 188. H.507, 2
And to **walke** Life's pilgrimage.................191. H.519, 2
Walk in the Groves, and thou shalt find......192. H.521, 39
Or let her **walk**, or stand, or sit,................207. H.579, 3
Or did I **walk** those Pean-Gardens through,....234. H.673, 3
Yet scarre-crow-like I'le **walk**, as one,......235. H.677, 7
With the Sun rising he must **walk** his grounds; 259. H.771, 3
Men must have Bounds how farre to **walke**; for we 307. H.990, 1
Or'e which you'l **walk**, when I am laid beneath. 312. H.1013, 4
Suffer thy legs, but not thy tongue to **walk**:......341. N.12, 1
Cleer the **walk**, and then shall I.................355. N.64, 5
By Faith we all **walk** here, not by the Spirit.....362. N.88, 2
Thus I **walk**, and this I tell:..................372. N.121, 4
Where, drest with garlands, there they **walk** the ground, 417. A.8, 29
— — — — — — — — — — —,..............429. var. H.263, 1

Walked Sadly I **walk't** within the field,..........73. H.187, 1
Among the Mirtles, as I **walkt**,................106. H.263, 1
But, as they **walk't** here in their vestures white, 384. N.181, 4

Walkest But **walk'st** about thine own dear bounds, 230. H.662, 15

Walking But listen to thee, (**walking** in thy chamber) 22. H.67, 3
Walking in and out her eye,...................204. H.566, 4

Walks Your **Walks** with Flowers, and give their Crowns to you. 107. H.265, 8
And ye the **Walks** have been.................110. H.274, 3
And **walks** fresh varnisht to the publick view. 140. H.356, 2
Why **walkes** Nick Flimsey like a Male-content? 160. H.423, 1
And sitting, see the wiles, wayes, **walks** of wit,..187. H.506, 3
But **walks** with dangling breeches,............259. H.772, 18
Where vertue **walkes**, not those that flow.....311. H.1010, 10
Gods wayes and **walks**, which lie still East and West. 386. N.193, 4
Death with it still **walkes** along................418. A.9, 41

Wall Up she got upon a **wall**,.....................15. H.36, 8
Now, The Flower of the **Wall**..................15. H.36, 15
The staffe, the Elme, the prop, the shelt'ring **wall** 72. H.185, 12
Felicitie flies o're the **Wall** and Fence,........257. H.765, 3
Stands garded with a rosy hilly **wall**,...........405. A.1, 30

Walled A heart thrice **wall'd** with Oke, and Brasse, that man '36. H.106, 75

Walls Girt with small bones, instead of **walls**...90. H.223, 10
It be with Rock, or **walles** of Brasse,........116. H.283, 143
Safe stand thy **Walls**, and Thee, and so both will, 149. H.377, 115
'Tis not the **Walls**, or purple, that defends......244. H.717, 1

Wan Looke ye not **wan**, or colourlesse for feare. 222. H.634, 6

Wand But she forbad me, with a **wand**........51. H.142, 19
Cooling sleep with charming **wand**............56. H.149, 110
A staffe or a **wand**..........................256. H.762, 4
Tapping his plump thighes with a mirtle **wand**:..313. H.1017, 8

Wandered A wearied Pilgrim, I have **wandred** here 328. H.1088, 1

Wandering Which erring here, and **wandring** there, 66. H.175, 3

Wane Never did Moone so ebbe, or seas so **wane**, 52. H.146, 7
And Moons to **wain**;..........................133. H.336, 19
Seldome or never, knows a **wain**,..............143. H.369, 2
Not many full-fac't-moons shall **waine**,........176. H.465, 77
I beginne to **waine** in sight;...................180. H.482, 1
Spread as He spreads; wax lesse as He do's **wane**; 196. H.537, 3
As men do **wane** in thankfulnesse..............358. N.76, 2

Want Thy selfe, if **want** comes to endure:......37. H.106, 104
So much for **want**, as exercise:................37. H.106, 118
Yet Much-more still complains he is in **want**.....73. H.188, 2
Is it for **want** of sleep?......................104. H.257, 18
Wild are Seas, that **want** a shore..............122. H.304, 2
Glasse, out of deepe, and out of desp'rate **want**,.151. H.385, 1
Of **want**, or foe,.............................161. H.426, 3
For **want** of warmth, and Stomachs keepe....179. H.476, 32
In regard I **want** that Wine,..................182. H.489, 7
When Jill complaines to Jack for **want** of meate; 186. H.498, 1
I **want** beliefe; O gentle Silvia, be...........204. H.570, 3
Give **Want** her welcome if she comes; we find,..213. H.605, 1
Black I'm grown for **want** of meat;..........223. H.638, 4
This Christmas, but his **want** wherwith, sayes Nay. 238. H.693, 2
Then to **want** the Wake next Yeare..........255. H.761, 24
And skirts that **want** their stiches,..........259. H.772, 19
Man may **want** Land to live in; but for all,....267. H.807, 1
When words we **want**, Love teacheth to endite;..275. H.846, 1
Not out of **want** of breath, but **want** of faith..283. H.884, 2
Want is a softer Wax, that takes thereon,......288. H 905, 1
Nor do thou feare the **want** of these,..........289. H.912, 5
When I **want** my fragrant wine...............309. H.996, 10
Those, who **want** Hearts, and weare a Diadem. 330. H 1097, 2
And **want** their Poise: words ought to have their weight. 342. N.16, 2
If warre, or **want** shall make me grow so poore, 347. N.39, 1
Thou dwel'st aloft, and I **want** wings to flie.....352. N.52, 2
Torments for high Attilius; and, with **want**,....370. N.108, 9
The **Wante** of Eare rings brauerye,.............409. A.2, 90
Shall **want** a Hand-mayde, (as she ofte will vse) 412. A.3, 100

Wanting No Spices **wanting**, when I'm laid by thee. 20. H.55, 10
Brave Porter! Poets ne'r will **wanting** be:......41. H 117, 2
Castalian sisters, sing, if **wanting** thee...........45. H.128, 30
If smirking Wine be **wanting** here,............101. H.250, 36
Are **wanting** to her exercise, but great........148. H.377, 113
Still **wanting** to her Favourite.................191. H.520, 4
Then for effusions, let none **wanting** be,........219. H.627, 5
Must needs wax cold, if **wanting** bread and wine..258. H.768, 4
Which **wanting** Lar, and smoke, hunk weeping wet; 262. H 783, 12
Wanting both Root, and Earth; but thy........278. H.859, 4
On our part, **wanting** all abilities..............356. N.71, 4
Where Rams are **wanting**, or large Bullocks thighs, 369. N.105, 3

Wanton The **wanton** Ambler chanc'd to see........12. H 27, 3
Which done, to still their **wanton** cries,............31. H.92, 9
And as she stood, the **wanton** Aire.............51. H.142, 11
Nor name those **wanton** reaks..................56. H.149, 117
Are **wanton** with their itch; scratch, and 'twill please. 66. H.173, 8
My Weathers, Lambes, and **wanton** Kids are well, 86. H.213, 5
And fan her **wanton** haire.......................103. H.255, 4
Wisely **wanton** (like to me.)..................117. H.289, 4
Doll she so soone began the **wanton** trade;......149. H.379, 1
The **wanton** Satyre did;........................203. H.563, 2
And, as thou look'st, the **wanton** Steere,......230. H.662, 37
And **wanton** as a Kid as yet.................243. H.716, 10
A **wanton** and lascivious eye....................254. H.755, 1
For **wanton** Lais, then we have..............283. H.885, 7
Unlesse they have some **wanton** carriages.......290. H.914, 8
When I drinke my **wanton** wine:.............309. H.996, 4
And I am wilde and **wanton** like to him.......313. H.1017, 14
No drought upon thy **wanton** waters fall......316. H.1028, 19
I have been **wanton**, and too bold I feare,......329. H.1095, 1
Wanton Wenches doe not bring...............330. H.1098, 1
Ev'n so those Lines, pen'd by my **wanton** Wit,....339. N.1, 3
Wanton I may, and thou not write?..............357. N.72, 14
Like **wanton** rose buds growing out of snowe,..405. A.1, 54

Wantoning More by that **wantoning** with it;......75. H.193, 14

Wantonly But when I saw thee **wantonly** to roame.6. H.3, 3

Wantonness See Cleanly-wantonness
Kindles in cloathes a **wantonnesse**:...............28. H.83, 2

Wantons Which **wantons** with the Love-sick aire:.61. H.160, 6
We busse our **Wantons**, but our Wives we kisse. 189. H.512, 2
Wantons we are; and though our words be such, 218. H.624, 1
God makes not good men **wantons**, but doth bring 370. N.108, 1

Wants Prig mony **wants**, either to buy, or brew...71. H.183, 4
No commer to thy Roofe his Guest-rite **wants**; 146. H.377, 19
Where Leaven **wants**, there Levill lies the nose. 154. H.401, 4
Of Patience **wants**. Grief breaks the stoutest Heart 169. H.447, 2
Or Sup, there **wants** the Incense and the Wine. 197. H.541, 4
He that **wants** a buriall roome...............270. H.821, 7
If meate he **wants**, then Grace he sayes to see..332. H.1112, 3
O Thou, that crown'st the will, where **wants** the deed. 369. N.105, 2

War **War**, which before was horrid, now appears..25. H.77, 7
'Tis a known principle in **War**,................118. H 290, 1
For punishment in **warre**, it will suffice,........132. H.335, 1

The tongue in peace; but then in **warre** the hand. 137. H.339, 2
That nothing shoots, but **war** and woe..........139. H.353, 6
Of all those three-brave-brothers, faln i' th' **Warre,** 170. H.451, 1
In this our wasting **Warre**....................211. H.596, 12
So when this **War** (which tempest-like doth spoil 225. H.642, 17
Into the which we come by **warre**............241. H.711, 2
Thy **Warre** (discreetly made) with white successe. 254. H.756, 12
We pray 'gainst **Warre,** yet we enjoy no Peace 264. H.793, 1
Where **War** with rashnesse is attempted, there 268. H.813, 3
This Day is Yours, Great CHARLES! and in this **War** 271. H.823, 1
By their wise Counsell, then they be by **Warre.** 271. H.825, 2
Love is a kind of **warre;** Hence those who feare, 280. H.872, 1
We Trust not to the multitude in **Warre,**........290. H.916, 1
As dearest Peace, after destructive **Warre:**......300. H 961, 2
That are most modest ere they come to **warre**...308. H 994, 2
Those ends in **War** the best contentment bring, 316. H.1029, 1
Where **War** and Peace the Dice by turns doe cast. 327. H.1083, 2
The sword of **war** must trie the Soveraignty...331. H.1102, 2
If **warre,** or want shall make me grow so poore, 347. N.39, 1
Warbling See Sweet-warbling
Of many a **warbling** Cherubim:..............115. H 283, 104
With **warbling** Notes, her Tyrrean sufferings...224. H.642, 8
My **warbling** note will say I m Phylomel.........248. H.730, 8
— — — — — — — — — —,...............445. var. H.730, 11
Ward See Sideward, Thee-ward
Let's doe our best, our Watch and **Ward** to keep.32. H.95, 5
Where Thou my chamber for to **ward**............349. N.47, 7
Warden Of rosted **warden,** or bak'd peare,......145. H.375, 23
Warding See Well-warding
Wards See Me-wards, Thee-wards
Ware His wife her owne **ware** sells as fast at home. 253. H.753, 4
And leave their subjects but the starved **ware**...272. H.826, 6
W'are Here we are all, by day; By night **w'are** hurl'd 21. H.57, 1
This night, and Locks pickt, yet **w'are** not a Maying. 69. H.178, 56
W'are younger by a score of years............136. H.336, 144
And like our living, where **w'are** known........200. H.552, 19
While **w'are** in our Prime;....................267. H.806, 2
Wares And weekly Markets for to sell his **wares:** 253. H.753, 2
Warfare None goes to **warfare,** but with this intent; 42. H.120, 1
That in **warfare** can befall.......................151. H.386, 6
War-like Sprung up a **War-like** Nation...........297. H.948, 8
Warm See Lukewarm
Which as a **warme,** and moistned spring,..........25. H.78, 9
Let me be **warme;** let me be fully fed:............31. H.93, 1
White, **warme,** and soft to lye with me...........34. H.105, 10
By whose **warme** side thou dost securely sleep..35. H.106, 35
To quick action, or the **warme** soft side..........45. H.128, 5
To **warme** my Breast, when thou my Pulse art gone. 73. H.186, 16
From that **warme** kisse of ours?.................74. H.192, 2
By love and **warme** desires fed,.................130. H.329, 6
Warme by a glit'ring chimnie all the yeare........132. H.333, 10
But **warm** their wits, and turn their lines to gold. 141. H.359, 8
For favours here to **warme** me,................234. H.674, 5
When a **warm** tongue do's with such Ambers meet. 269. H 816, 4
To her **warm** bosome, then our Rites are ended...366. N.97, 29
With a **warm** lip, and solemne one:........402. N.269, 11
Warmed But when he felt him **warm'd,**..........27. H.81, 25
Which when not **warmed** by her view..........131. H.330, 9
Warmer When Youth and Blood are **warmer;**....84. H.208, 10
— — — — — — — — — —,...............423. var. H.128, 12
Warm-love-hatching But from thy **warm-love-hatching** gates each may................................146. H.377, 15
Warms W^th^ wch Loue Chafes and **warmes** the soule 408. A.2, 48
Warmth The **warmth** and sweetnes had me there..20. H.56, 3
When ere my heart, Love's **warmth,** but entertaines, 40. H.113, 1
The times of **warmth;** but then they flew away; 151. H.387, 2
For want of **warmth,** and Stomachs keepe......179. H.476, 32
Thus wth a kisse of **warmth,** and loue, I parte..412. A.3, 95
Warn Till you **warn** her hence (away)..........276. H.850, 13
Warned And **warn'd** before, wo'd not beware.....219. H.628, 12
Warning At each **warning** hees as much..........418. A.9, 49
Warns **Warnes** the last Watch; but with the Dawne dost rise 36. H.106, 57
Warped Or **warpt,** as we,......................104. H.257, 11
Where laden spits, **warp't** with large Ribbs of Beefe, 146. H.377, 9
Wars The Field is pitcht; but such must be your **warres,** 216. H.618, 13
If **Wars** goe well; each for a part layes claime: 260. H.774, 3
begin to pinke as weary that the **warres**..432. ins. H.283, 140b

Warts Wise hand enchasing here those **warts,**..166. H.443, 60
Ralph pares his nayles, his **warts,** his cornes, and Ralph 299. H.959, 1
Warty Deane, or thy **warty** incivility...............29. H.86, 2
Wary With that Heav'n gave thee with a **warie** hand, 35. H.106, 23
Be you more **warie,** then afraid.................49. H.136, 15
This is strong thrift that **warie** Rush doth use 332. H.1116, 3
Was (Partial List)
Kept as close as Danae **was:**....................14. H.36, 5
Wash With which (Perilla) **wash** my hands and feet; 9. H.14, 9
Till you come forth. **Wash,** dresse, be briefe in praying: 68. H.178, 27
And Cedar **wash** thee, that no times consume thee. 89. H.219, 14
First **wash** thy heart in innocence, then bring..127. H.320, 3
Feacie (some say) doth **wash** her clothes i'th' Lie 178. H.474, 1
Wash your Pailes, and clense your Dairies;....201. H.556, 5
(To **wash** her) water from the Spring...........237. H.686, 6
Wash your hands or else the fire...............263. H.786, 1
That we **wash** our hearts, and hands...........280. H.870, 4
My Julia **wash** her self in thee!.................294. H.939, 2
(His teeth all out) to rince and **wash** his gummes 301. H.965, 2
Wash our hands in innocence................303. H.974, 6
Wash clean the Vesse'l, lest ye soure.........320. H.1053, 1
Wash your hands, and cleanse your eyes.......322. H.1064, 2
Let us **wash,** and pray together:..............324. H.1069, 6
Yet if Thy Bloud not **wash** me, there's no hope..357. N.73, 4
But no one Jailor there to **wash** the wounds.....372. N. 120, 2
Washed One, onely, worthy to be **washt** by thee:.63. H.165, 2
Washt those thy purple wounds with tears.......89. H.219, 6
Washt o're, to tell[1] what change is neare.......134. H.336, 90
Thrice I have **washt,** but feel no cold,..........157. H.413, 3
As if or'e **washt** in Hippocrene..................277. H.857, 2
And having **washt** thee, close thee in a chest..300. H.960, 5
Washt with sweet ointments; Thus at last I come 335. H.1128, 3
Clean **washt,** and laid out for the Beere;......374. N.123, 12
For I have **washt** both hand and heart,........402. N.269, 6
To be with juice of Cedar **washt** all over;........415. A.7, 6
— — — — — — — — — —,.................443. var. H.580, 6
Washes **Washes** the golden eares of corne.......112. H.283, 20
Waspish Prickles is **Waspish,** and puts forth his sting, 287. H.903. 1
Wasps Of peltish **wasps;** we'l know his Guard..165. H.443, 17
Wassail Sphering about the **wassail** cup,.......136. H.336, 148
Of **Wassaile** now, or sets the quintell up:.......159. H.421, 4
Thy Harvest home; thy **Wassaile** bowle,........231. H.662, 56
That while the **Wassaile** Bowle here...........235. H.674, 9
Wassaile the Trees, that they may beare........264. H.787, 1
To make the **wassaile** a swinger...............317. H.1035, 24
And giv'st me **Wassaile** Bowles to drink,.......350. N.47, 39
Wassail-bowl Of Christmas sports, the **Wassell-boule,** 126. H 319, 13
Wassailing As you doe give them **Wassailing**.....264. H.787, 4
And Queene **wassailing;**.....................317. H.1035, 26
And when night comes, wee'l give Him **wassailing:** 368. N.102, 22
Wassails I sing of May-poles, Hock-carts, **Wassails,** Wakes, 5. H.1, 3
Thou shalt have Possets, **Wassails** fine,.........193. H.521, 47
Wast So neare, or deare, as thou **wast** once to me.45. H.128, 10
And pay no vowes to thee? who **wast** their best 78. H.197, 59
These, or those ends, to which Thou **wast** design'd. 181. H.483, 4
Then reach those ends that thou **wast** destin'd to. 254. H.756, 8
Wast kind...................................314. H.1024, 16
How wise **wast** thou in all thy waies!..........375. N.123, 61
When Thou **wast** taken, Lord, I oft have read,..399. N.264, 1
Was't What **was't** that fell but now............74. H.192, 1
What **was't** (ye Gods!) a dying man to save,....278. H.860, 3
Waste Small shots paid often, **waste** a vast estate. 13. H.28, 2
But yet, Loves fire will **wast**....................54. H 149, 27
Where so much sirrop ran at **waste**..............71. H.182, 18
Or else to ashes he will **waste**.................113. H.283, 40
Which fain would **waste** upon thy Cates, but that 147. H.377, 49
Waste thou in that most Civill Government.....171. H.456, 4
Our houres doe **waste:**........................196. H.534, 14
Makes **waste;**...................................221. H.633, 49
Decline or **waste** at all;......................335. H.1129, 12
To see the **waste;** but 'twas repli'd.............358. N.75, 6
Oft-times for **wast,** as for his need.............358. N.75, 8
To **wast,** my JESU, I'le take all................377. N.129, 8
Wasted Halfe **wasted** in the porch...............54. H.149, 54
Wasteful The Genius **wastefull,** more then free:..310. H.1004, 2
Wastes When one hole **wasts** more then he gets by Nine. 154. H.400, 4
What is't that **wasts** a Prince? example showes,..331. H.1105, 1
Wasting In this our **wasting** Warre............211. H.596, 12
Watch See Gnat's-watchword
Thy **Watch** may stand, my minutes fly poste haste;.8. H.10, 3
Let's doe our best, our **Watch** and Ward to keep 32. H.95, 5

Warnes the last Watch; but with the Dawne dost rise 36. H.106, 57
The Last Watch out, and saw the Dawning too...52. H.146, 4
Watch, or did make the bed:..................56. H.149, 105
How we watch, and seldome sleep;..............82. H.203, 11
Man is a Watch, wound up at first, but never..202. H.558, 1
The Watch once downe, all motions then do cease; 202. H.558, 3
Meane time thy Prophets Watch by Watch shall pray; 254. H.756, 13
To watch it...................................263. H.785, 8
Gods Rod doth watch while men do sleep; & then 342. N.21, 1
Yet mine eyes the watch do keep;..............347. N.41, 11
Of harmlesse thoughts, to watch and keep........350. N.47, 9
But eternall watch shall keep,..................377. N.128, 19
Of Youthe <s> swift watch to stand..............413. A.4, 7
Watched Night now hath watch'd her self half blind; 54. H.149, 31
Which serve for watched Ribbanings............92. H.223, 73
Watchet Watchet the silke was; and did make..116. H.284, 3
Watchword See Gnat's-watchword
Water See Holywater
Water, water I desire,..........................21. H.61, 1
To Bread and Water none is poore;............33. H.100, 1
With Water fill'd, (Sirs, credit me)............44. H.127, 2
Or water; where's the comfort found?..........50. H.140, 8
Fire and water shall together lye...............59. H.154, 3
Water, Water I espie:.........................62. H.162, 1
Prig now drinks Water, who before drank Beere:.71. H.183, 1
If you can see the water grow..................79. H.198, 5
The Water turn'd to Wine.....................185. H.495, 8
Water in, ere Sun be set......................201. H.556, 4
(To wash her) water from the Spring..........237. H.686, 6
Of living water by thy Benizon................245. H.723, 4
Holy Water come and bring;...................258. H.769, 1
Because as Plants by water grow,.............273. H.832, 3
Halfe with a Lawne of water hid,..............294. H.939, 6
Bring in pailes of water then,..................315. H.1026, 9
May all clean Nimphs and curious water Dames, 316. H.1028, 17
To disperse the water farre....................322. H.1064, 4
Be the Seas water, and the Land all Sope,........357. N.73, 3
Cast Holy Water all about,.....................365. N.97, 4
— — — — — — — — — —,..................425. var. H.197, 4
Water-cress Of Water-cresse,...................350. N.47, 32
Water-drinker Had Cassius, that weak Water-drinker, known 78. H.197, 61
Watered — — — — — — — — —, ...435. var. H.293, 26j
Watering See Watering pot
Watering pot Then let her use the watring pot....279. H.867, 4
Waters Deep waters noyse-lesse are; And this we know, 15. H.38, 9
Through that huge field of waters ride:..........30. H.90, 3
Stirring the waters, I am come; and here,........61. H.161, 4
Next, from that world of waters, then..........245. H.720, 7
When the waters by their fall.................302. H.968, 9
Holy waters hither bring......................303. H.974, 1
No drought upon thy wanton waters fall.......316. H.1028, 19
— — — — — — — — — —,..................425. var. H.197, 4
In their silver waters; runne...........431. ins. H.283, 50g
Watery Unto that watrie Desolation:.............14. H.35, 2
And watrie dangers; while thy whiter hap,......36. H.106, 71
(By many a watrie syllable)....................44. H.127, 8
Wildred in this vast watry Region............319. H.1044, 4
Mixt in that watrie Theater;....................339. N.3, 4
Cuft with those watrie savages,.................372. N.118, 2
Watery-region See Watery
Through thy watrie-region;....................129. H.325, 4
Wave Thus woe succeeds a woe; as wave a wave. 18, H.48, 2
A winning wave (deserving Note)................28. H.83, 9
That a Wave, and I will bring..................397. N.258, 3
— — — — — — — — — —,...............429. var. H.263, 12
W'ave W'ave seen the past-best Times, and these 133. H.336, 17
Long time w'ave here been a toying:..........195. H.534, 3
Some storms w'ave past;......................211. H.596, 13
Though by well-warding many blowes w'ave past, 237. H.688, 1
W'ave more to beare our charge, then way to go? 308. H.995, 2
Scores of sins w'ave made here many,...........373. N.121, 9
Wave-offering Give a wave-offring unto Thee.....377. N.130, 4
Waves There waves the Streamer of her blood...107. H.263, 12
Of all the raging Waves, into a froth..........152. H 389, 2
Had not thy waves forbad the rest.............294. H.939, 10
See how he waves his hand, and through his eyes 430. ins. H.283, 40a
Wax Now is the time, when all the lights wax dim; 20. H.55, 1
Their Beads of Nits, Bels, Books, & Wax....93. H.223, 115
Laden with wax and hony home:..............145. H.375, 10
By daily Learning we wax old................187. H.505, 2
Spread as He spreads; wax lesse as He do's wane; 196. H.537, 3
Set you to your Wheele, and wax............221. H.633, 42
Must needs wax cold, if wanting bread and wine. 258. H.768, 4
Want is a softer Wax, that takes thereon,......288. H.905, 1
Continuall reaping makes a land wax old.........292. H.922, 4
Waxen Or ells that she on that white waxen hill.405. A.1, 63
Way When such a Light as You are leads the way: 3. Ded. H., 2
Is there no way to beget.........................10. H.19, 7
Which crawling one and every way,...............16. H.41, 3
Opens the way for early flowers;.................23. H.70, 2
Kissing and glancing, soothing, all make way....24. H.74, 11
Yet there's a way found (if thou please).......34. H.103, 13
Twilight is yet, till that her Lawnes give way;..34. H.104, 5
A wise man ev'ry way lies square...............37. H.106, 98
A way that's best.............................43. H.123, 23
Each way illustrious, brave; and like to those....45. H.128, 14
Apostles, way (unshackled) to goe out.........52. H.146, 16
While Domiduca leads the way:................54. H.149, 42
The best way how to loose the Zone............56. H.149, 92
My way, where you shall never know..........60. H.159, 4
Or learne some way how to forget............60. H.159, 7
Still either way;..............................65. H.172, 14
It chanc't a Bee did flie that way,..............71. H.182, 2
Thou hast both Wind and Tide with thee; Thy way 73. H.186, 3
And as I went my private way,..................73. H.187, 3
A way enchac't with glasse & beads............90. H.223, 1
Part of the way be met; or sit stone-still.......113. H.283, 58
High in your own conceipt, and some way teach 115. H.283, 128
Bold bolt of thunder he will make his way,....116. H.283, 148
Each way smoothly Musicall:.................122. H.303, 4
To which, with silver feet lead you the way,....140. H.354, 7
Demands no money by a craving way;..........142. H.363, 2
And as he leads the way......................151. H.388, 6
Prepares the way for mans docility..............153. H.394, 4
This way, that way, that way, this,............157. H.415, 3
Mirt. This way she came, and this way too she went; 159. H.421, 18
Mirt. In dewie-mornings when she came this way. 159. H.421, 23
And sport it any way;........................160. H.422, 11
Lead by the shine of Snails; a way............165. H.443, 22
Give unto Love the straiter way.............167. H.443, 111
Give way, give way to me, who come..........169. H.449, 9
And if thy fall sho'd this way come,...........175. H.465, 65
Give way, give way ye Gates, and win..........178. H.476, 1
And walk thou must the way that others went:.188. H.507, 2
Each way smooth and civilly:..................195. H.530, 4
And yet our way has no ending..............195. H.534, 12
Give way, and be ye ravisht by the Sun,.......196. H.537, 1
Then but to breath, and every one gave way:..200. H.551, 4
This was the old way; and 'tis yet thy course, 201. H.557, 19
Manners each way musicall:..................204. H.569, 10
Make the way smooth for me,..................213. H.604, 5
So I, now having rid my way;................216. H.617, 3
But on, on thy way..........................217. H.619, 8
Give way, give way, now, now my Charles shines here, 236. H.685, 1
Make Thee like Him, this, that way fortunate, 254. H.756, 10
In great Processions many lead the way.........256. H.763, 3
That brave Vibration each way free;...........261. H.779, 5
With maunds of roses for to strew the way:....261. H.781, 8
But it skills not; go your way;...............270. H.821, 6
Gone she is a long, long way,..................276. H.848, 1
And Venus, every way:.......................281. H.874, 3
A Primrose Banke did cross her way,...........288. H.908, 3
This way or that, it not declines at all.........292. H.926, 2
As Cadmus once a new way found,.............297. H.943, 5
Faultless every way for shape;.................306. H.984, 27
W'ave more to beare our charge, then way to go? 308. H.995, 2
Ah cruell maides! Ile goe my way,.............312. H.1014, 5
But yet a way there doth remaine,...............313. H.1020, 5
Make way to my Beloved Westminster:.......316. H.1028, 14
Is halfe way cured, if the party will............319. H.1048, 2
This Ile tell ye by the way,...................322. H.1063, 1
The way of all Flesh is,.......................328. H.1091, 3
A way to measure out the Wind;...............339. N.3, 2
Who slowly goes, rids (in the end) his way......352. N.51, 4
Since rough the way is, help me when I call,.....352. N.51, 7
For, 'tis no easie way from Earth to Heaven....352. N.52, 4
In the way 'twixt me, and home:...............355. N.64, 4
Sin leads the way, but as it goes, it feels..........362. N.86, 1
In all that way no beaten path;.................372. N.118, 4
Thou art our way i'th wildernesse:............372. N.118, 6
That found a way 374. N.123, 48
God He refuseth no man; but makes way........378. N.131, 1
Sending them forth, Salute no man by th' way:..378. N.137, 2
Sinners confounded are a twofold way,..........388. N.210, 1
By way of Epithalamie,........................393. N.232, 12
When once the Soule has lost her way,..........393. N.233, 1
So do the Skurfe and Bran too: Go Thy way,..398. N.263, 12
Thy way, Thou guiltlesse man, and satisfie....398. N.263, 13
Who passe this way, to pitie me,...............400. N.266, 2
A milky high waye that direction yeilds.............405. A.1, 67
Or lyke as woole meetes steele, giue way......408. A.2, 69
I've more to beare my Chardge, then way to goe,.411. A.3, 54
This Janus looking double waye.................417. A.9, 16
— — — — — — — — — — —,................443. var. H.580, 10

And then to weep they both were licensed......384. N.180, 12
The Lawes of Action, will both sigh, and weep; 399. N.263, 37
Us weepe for Thee..........................401. N.268, 27
And prest a little they will weepe new milke......405. A.1, 58
Cha. Prethee relate, while I give ear and weep...416. A.8, 12

Weeping Follow me weeping to my Turfe, and there
9. H.14, 13
There weeping sup'rabundantly..................42. H.119, 4
By those true teares y'are weeping..............63. H.164, 15
And times to come shall, weeping, read thy glory,
89. H.219, 21
Weeping, shall make ye flourish all the yeere...138. H.343, 4
The pillars up of weeping Jet,..................145. H.376, 2
Ambo. Lets cheer him up. Sil. Behold his weeping ripe.
159. H.421, 7
And weeping Widowes long opprest...........190. H.515, 21
They, weeping, spread a Lawnie Loome,.........237. H.686, 15
She wept upon her cheeks, and weeping so,.....251. H.742, 1
Who for a long sad time has weeping stood,....251. H.745, 3
Which wanting Lar, and smoke, hung weeping wet;
262. H.783, 12
Ile recollect thee (weeping) part by part;.......300. H.960, 4
See mine eyes are weeping ripe.................305. H.984, 13
A sin, then fall to weeping when 'tis done........349. N.43, 6
My wine is mixt with weeping..................353. N.56, 6
To him, who weeping waits,....................370. N.111, 2
Roaring is nothing but a weeping part,.........380. N.154, 1
Each takes A weeping farwell, rackt in mynde...411. A.3, 63

Weeps He weepes and sighs (as weary of his life.)
275. H.842, 2

Weigh Weigh me the Fire; or, canst thou find.....339. N.3, 1

Weight And giv'st our Numbers Euphonie, and weight.
297. H.947, 6
And want their Poise: words ought to have their weight.
342. N.16, 2

Welcome Welcome, most welcome to our Vowes and us,
25. H.77, 1
Welcome, O welcome my illustrious Spouse;.....77. H.197, 13
Welcome as are the ends unto my Vowes:......77. H.197, 14
I! far more welcome then the happy soile,......77. H.197, 15
Welcome Maids of Honour,....................83. H.205, 1
Weelcome! but yet no entrance, till we blesse....124. H.313, 1
Welcome as thunder to our beere:.............146. H.377, 30
Either is welcome; so I have..................158. H.420, 3
Besmear'd with Grapes; welcome he shall thee thither,
206. H.575, 37
Give Want her welcome if she comes; we find,..213. H.605, 1
Welcome, Great Cesar, welcome now you are,...300. H.961, 1
Welcome as slumbers; or as beds of ease.......300. H.961, 3
O Pompe of Glory! Welcome now, and come....300. H.961, 5
Welcome to this my Colledge, and though late..305. H.983, 1
Either's welcome, Stinke or Civt.............306. H.987, 3
To welcome Him. The nobler part.............365. N.96, 27
Welcome to all oʳ vowes......................413. A.4, 20
love to your welcome with the mistick Cake,
431. ins. H.283, 60b
Welcome at last unto the Threshold, Time
431. ins. H.283, 60k

Welcoming For the welcoming of it.............204. H.569, 4

Welfare For my well-fare (Julia)..............277. H.856, 2

Well See Farewell, Fare-ye-well, Little-well-kept-stock, Over-well
Well may my Book come forth like Publique Day
3. Ded. H., 1
Regardlesse whether well thou sped'st, or no.......6. H.3, 6
But when that men have both well drunke, and fed,..7. H.8, 3
Asswag'd, and he was well again................18. H.46, 10
Whose easie natures like it well,.................22. H.66, 3
This troubles me: but I as well..................24. H.73, 7
But yet, though Love likes well such Scenes as these,
24. H.74, 9
Goe thou afore; and I shall well.................33. H.98, 5
Wayes lesse to live, then to live well:...........35. H.106, 10
As well as spare: still conning o'r this Theame, 38. H.106, 131
And more then well becomes the day?...........48. H.136, 3
Well; though my griefe by you was gall'd, the more;
52. H.146, 21
Large shoulders though he has, and well can beare,
60. H.158, 3
And you must fade, as well as they............61. H.159, 17
(So Fate spares her) am well content to die.....70. H.181, 12
My Weathers, Lambes, and wanton Kids are well,
86. H.213, 5
You are like Balme inclosed (well)............88. H.216, 13
And by the glow-worms light wel guided,......93. H.223, 141
As well as I.................................97. H.232, 18
And burn thee 'up, as well as I................98. H.238, 15
Well, on, brave boyes, to your Lords Hearth,...101. H.250, 26
Wept out our heart, as well as eyes...........104. H.256, 14
And well bestrutted Bees sweet bagge:.........119. H.293, 34
That man lives twice, that lives the first life well.
121. H.298, 2
If well thou hast begun, goe on fore-right;.......123. H.309, 1
And runnes most smoothly, when tis well begunne.
128. H.321, 2
Well then, on what Seas we are tost,..........134. H.336, 57
Such as co'd well..........................136. H.336, 133
If thou not read'st them well...................138. H.344, 4
When well the work of hony thrives;............145. H.375, 8
Y'ave farced well, pray make an end;..........146. H.377, 24
Thy house, well fed and taught, can show.......147. H.377, 34
As well the Winters, as the Summers Tide:......151. H.387, 6
Skinns he din'd well to day; how do you think?..156. H.409, 1
He knowes well who do love him,..............157. H.412, 22
Ye boil with Love, as well as I................157. H.413, 8
You sigh for Love, as well as I................158. H.420, 10
But long or short, I'm well content with all.....163. H.437, 2
Who writes sweet Numbers well as any can:....172. H.459, 2
But walke abroad, yet wisely well.............174. H.465, 13
Skurffe by his Nine-bones sweares, and well he may,
180. H.480, 1
Jone wo'd go tel her haires; and well she might, 195. H.531, 1
Skulls co'd not well passe through that scum of men.
200. H.551, 2
They well content my Prew and me.............200. H.552, 4
Nor courts thou Her because she's well attended
201. H.557, 7
If but well read; or ill read, understood........212. H.603, 4
If well the Dice runne, lets applaud the cast:...218. H.621, 1
Well content a craving man...................223. H.638, 18
Well will serve the Beggars use.............223. H.638, 20
Well I can quaffe, I see,.....................227. H.653, 9
For well thou know'st, 'tis not th' extent......230. H.662, 17
Which though well soyl'd, yet thou dost know,..230. H.662, 22
But for to live that half seven well:...........233. H.670, 35
So, I confesse, 'tis somwhat to do well........234. H.673, 9
At night they draw to Supper; then well fed.....260. H.773, 3
If Wars goe well; each for a part layes claime: 260. H.774, 3
Shew they are well contented..................260. H.777, 7
Neere to the well of wit;......................261. H.778, 2
Ready to joyne, as well our hearts as hands.....262. H.781, 10
Well, when to eat thou dost me next desire,....262. H.783, 21
Comely Acts well; and when he speaks his part,..266. H.799, 1
Well, when sh'as kild, that Pig, Goose, Cock or Hen,
266. H.801, 3
He prayes his Harvest may be well brought home.
270. H.822, 2
Teares have their springs from joy, as well as woe.
275. H.842, 4
Or see thy injur'd Leaves serve well,............275. H.844, 5
Well, or be't or be't not so,...................277. H.852, 5
Ready here? Jul. All well prepar'd,............280. H.870, 8
All is well; now next to these................280. H.870, 13
Wo'd I well my worke begin?.................286. H.897, 2
All Rites well ended, with faire Auspice come...286. H.898, 9
How well his nature's fitted to his name!.......287. H.903, 4
Man must do well out of a good intent,.........290. H.917, 1
To heare the worst from men, when they doe well.
293. H.932, 2
May fart for joy, as well as shout:.............306. H.987, 2
Well I sup, and well I dine,...................309. H.996, 7
How well contented in this private Grange.....310. H.1003, 1
Man may at first transgress, but next do well:..314. H.1021, 1
No man dies ill, that liveth well...............321. H.1059, 2
No man so well a Kingdome Rules, as He,.....325. H.1074, 1
Lives not those yeers, but he that lives them well.
328. H.1088, 6
And very well pleas'd,........................333. H.1122, 2
Firme and well fixt foundation...............335. H.1129, 14
That Powres in oyle, as well as wine............342. N.17, 10
To seek of God more then we well can find,.....356. N.70, 1
Well, this I'le do; my mighty score............369. N.107, 5
And fare it well: yet Herrick, if so be..........371. N.112, 2
Paul, he began ill, but he ended well;.........387. N.200, 1
Judas began well, but he foulely fell:..........387. N.200, 2
If man lives long, and if he live not well.......392. N.230, 6
If well, then chant Gods praise with cheerfulnesse.
395. N.243, 4
When well we speak, & nothing do that's good, 397. N.256, 1
Parting the paire, as wee may well suppose........404. A.1, 13
A Nature, soe well form'd, soe wrought..........408. A.2, 65
The Crowne of dutye is our dutye; well........412. A.3, 103
Doing's, the Fruite of Doinge well, Farwell.....412. A.3, 104
Of nature: bidd mee nowe fare well, or smile
424. ins. H.128, 46d
her homewards, well she knowes.........430. ins. H.283, 20i
— — — — — — — — — — —,............434. ins. H.293, 41b
— — — — — — — — — — —,..............439. var. H.443, 17
— — — — — — — — — — —,..............441. var. H.465, 13
— — — — — — — — — — —,..............448. var. A.1, 86

We'll So oft, we'll think, we see a King new born...26. H.80, 2
We'll wish, in Hell we had been Last and First...33. H.101, 4
If so, we'll think too, (when he do's condemne...39. H.110, 3
For which, before thy Threshold, we'll lay downe 41. H.117, 7
Which done, then quickly we'll undresse.........58. H.152, 7
We'll weary all the Fables there................59. H.152, 12
Come, we'll abroad; and let's obay.............68. H.178, 39
We'll blesse the Babe, Then back to Countrie pleasures.
87. H.213, 48
This we will doe; we'll daily come..............89. H.219, 9
At Draw-Gloves we'l play,......................99. H.243, 1
List of references:............ 119. H.293, 6; 124. H.313, 10; 133, H.336, 55; 134, H.336, 85; 135, H.336, 127; 136. H.336, 138; 136. H.336, 147; 136. H.336, 151; 165, H.443, 3; 165. H.443,

8; 165. H.443, 17; 168. H.443, 120; 173. H.462, 2; 179. H.476, 35; 179. H.476, 36; 190. H.515, 37; 190. H.515, 39; 194, H.526, 5; 206. H.575, 21; 206. H.575, 22; 211. H.593, 4; 215. H.616, 2; 215. H.616, 4; 215. H.616, 15; 215. H.616, 25; 216. H.616, 28; 216. H.616, 35; 216. H.616, 36; 233. H.670, 36; 266. H.800, 8; 280. H.870, 15; 300. H.961, 20; 324. H.1068, 22; 345. N.33, 21; 345. N.33, 31; 368. N.102, 22; 368. N.102, 24; 399. N.263, 39; 427. var. H.197, 70; 436. var. H.336, 41; 443. var. H.575, 50; 451. var. H.336, 151.

Welladay Alack and welladay!..................156. H.412, 10

Well-boiled And wel-boyld inkepin of a batt. 434. ins. H.293, 41b

Well-broiled — — — — — — — — —, ...434. ins. H.293, 41b

Well-laid And well-laid bottome, on the iron and rock, 148. H.377, 109

Well-prepared Still with a well-prepared brest:....246. H.725, 2

Well-rated — — — — — — — — —, ...434. ins. H.293, 41b

Well-warding Though by well-warding many blowes w'ave past, 237. H.688, 1

Well-weaved The Purling springs, groves, birds, and well-weav'd Bowrs,............................36. H.106, 45

Wench Was lately whipt for lying with a Wench. 79. H.199, 2
Jone is a wench that's painted;................229. H.659, 1
Jane is a wench that's wittie;.................229. H.659, 7

Wenches The Harvest Swaines, and Wenches bound 101. H.250, 13
Let Country wenches make 'em fine..........323. H.1068, 13
Wanton Wenches doe not bring...............330. H.1098, 1

Wend Sho'd wend along his Baby-ship to see?....86. H.213, 26

Went See Outwent
I dreamt the Roses one time went.................8. H.11, 1
As Goddesse Isis (when she went,................9. H.15, 9
Jems, then those two, that went before:..........23. H.70, 6
And struck me that it went......................27. H.81, 31
Thou shed'st one teare, when as I went away;..42. H.122, 10
And as I went my private way,...................73. H.187, 3
I went to pluck them one by one,.............107. H.263, 14
Nothing is New: we walk where others went....139. H.352, 1
Before I went...............................144. H.371, 7
Mirt. This way she came, and this way too she went; 159. H.421, 18
Besides (Ai me!) since she went hence to dwell, 159. H.421, 27
Roots had no money; yet he went o'th score...162. H.427, 1
To Fetch me Wine my Lucia went,............187. H.504, 1
And walk thou must the way that others went:..188. H.507, 2
And to the Bath went, to be cured there:......201. H.555, 2
But home return'd, as he went forth, halfe blind. 201. H.555, 4
About the Cover of this Book there went.......227. H.652, 7
To gather Flowers Sappha went,...............250. H.740, 1
Orpheus he went (as Poets tell)...............265. H.798, 1
Away he went, but as he turn'd................295. H.942, 9
A Writing as he went;........................346. N.38, 8
That ne're went out by Day or Night:.........374. N.123, 46
Sin never slew a soule, unlesse there went......389. N.217, 1
But look, how each transgressor onward went....391. N.227, 3
The sad soule went, not with his Loue, but doome; 412. A.3, 76
— — — — — — — — — —,..............429. var. H.260, 2

Went'st Or went'st thou to this end, the more to move me, 77. H.197, 23

Wept Why wept it? but for shame,................12. H.23, 2
He wept, he sobb'd, he call'd to some............18. H.46, 5
Wept as he'd drowne the Hellespont,...........42. H.119, 10
With hands held up to Love, I wept;............51. H.142, 3
Each Flower has wept, and bow'd toward the East, 68. H.178, 7
And some have wept, and woo'd, and plighted Troth, 69. H.178, 49
Till we have wept, kist, sigh't, shook hands, or so. 73. H.186, 6
Wept out our heart, as well as eyes..........104. H.256, 14
Upon her cheekes she wept, and from those showers 204. H.567, 1
Some laid her forth, while other wept,.........237. H.686, 7
She wept upon her cheeks, and weeping so,......251. H.742, 1
She wept, and made it deeper by a teare.......251. H.743, 2
Nor let my Herse, be wept upon by thee:......281. H.875, 2
And now y' have wept enough, depart yon starres 432. ins. H.283, 140a

Were (Partial List)
Were it but to pleasure you.....................10. H.19, 14
Were I to give thee Baptime, I wo'd chuse.......28. H.84, 1
Were thy streames silver, or thy rocks all gold.....29. H.86, 6
Of any men that were.........................85. H.211, 12
As we were Lords of all the earth............133. H.336, 56
As the Canary Isles were thine:...............148. H.377, 84
Were there not a Matter known,................163. H.433, 1
How wo'd he eate, were not his hindrance such? 191. H.518, 6
As if You Two, were one Hermophrodite:......201. H.557, 6
If smooth and unperplext the Seasons were,.....214. H.612, 9
— — — — — — — — — —,...............448. var. A.3, 18

We're — — — — — — — — —, ...437. var. H.336, 144

Wert Though thou wert ne'r so blind...........80. H.201, 16
Wert thou a Winckfield onely, not a Brother....210. H.590, 10
Yet if thou wert not, Berkley, loyall proofe,....252. H.745, 13
— — — — — — — — — —,..............423. var. H.128, 10
— — — — — — — — — —,..............451. var. H.197, 59

Wer't (Wert not for thee) haue Crumbled Into Mould, 411. A.3, 36

West The Drooping West, which hitherto has stood 25. H.77, 3
As dead, within the West;.......................72. H.185, 6
Into the loathed West;........................144. H.371, 9
Bring'st home the Ingot from the West........229. H.662, 10
From the dull confines of the drooping West,...242. H.713, 1
For, rather then I'le to the West return,.......242. H.713, 17
A Renovation of the West by Thee.............254. H.756, 2
Gods wayes and walks, which lie still East and West. 386. N.193, 4

Western Gold, runneth to the Western Inde,.....36. H.106, 66
Sweet Western Wind, whose luck it is,........103. H.255, 1

Westmerland See Westmorland

Westminster You, above all Those Sweets of Westminster: 137. H.341, 10
Make way to my Beloved Westminster:.......316. H.1028, 14

Westmorland Shor'd up by you, (Brave Earle of Westmerland.) 40. H.112, 4
Alive, as Noble Westmorland;................218. H.626, 11

Wet And all with showrs wet through,...........26. H.81, 11
Which wanting Lar, and smoke, hung weeping wet; 262. H.783, 12
Till they be all over wet,.......................284. H.891, 3
Rush saves his shooes, in wet and snowie wether; 332. H.1116, 1

Wethers My Weathers, Lambes, and wanton Kids are well, 86. H.213, 5
Weathers, and never grudged at................147. H.377, 64

Wets That wets her Garden when it raines:.....279. H.867, 2

We've — — — — — — — — —, ...436. var. H.336, 17

What (Partial List)
What I fancy, I approve,........................11, H.21, 1
A telling what rare sights h'ad seen:............13. H.27, 8
And look, what Smallage, Night-shade, Cypresse, Yew, 27. H.82, 9
I shall dislike, what once I lov'd before...........31. H.93, 4
And what though you had been embrac't........49. H.136, 26
What? shall we two our endlesse leaves take here..73. H.186, 9
Learne of me what Woman is..................76. H.195, 2
What though the sea be calme? Trust to the shore: 85. H.212, 1
Up in a sheet your Bride, and what if so......116. H.283, 142
What comes in, runnes quickly out:............116. H.285, 6
Of Emits eggs; what wo'd he more?..........119. H.293, 36
I shall resolve ye, what it is.................130. H.329, 3
Can give, and what retract a grace;...........148. H.377, 94
When what is strongly built, no chinke.......148. H.377, 106
To give an end: Mir. To what? Scil. Such griefs as these. 159. H.421, 32
Since so it is; Ile tell thee what,..............161. H.425, 5
What is a Jewell if it be not set...............172. H.459, 5
Means, I shall know what other kisse..........175. H.465, 70
What, were yee borne to be...................176. H.467, 7
What needs she fire and ashes to consume,.....178. H.474, 5
Remember what thy Herrick Thee foretold,....181. H.483, 10
Let Poets feed on aire, or what they will;......186. H.498, 7
What Mad-man's he, that when it sparkles so,..187. H.502, 5
What need I care, though some dislike me sho'd 187. H.506, 5
If Dorset say, what Herrick writes, is good?...187. H.506, 6
Thou art of what I did intend..................189. H.515, 5
And what was made, was made to meet.........190. H.515, 7
(What gets the master of the Meal by that?)..191. H.518, 4
Here, here I live with what my Board,..........200. H.552, 1
I doe love I know not what;....................209. H.585, 1
Fie, (quoth my Lady) what a stink is here?...212. H.598, 1
But what he doth at first entend,..............215. H.615, 5
What Gloves we'l give, and Ribanings:.........216. H.616, 28
What short sweet Prayers shall be said;.......216. H.616, 31
What though the Moon do's slumber?..........217. H.619, 12
What is a Kisse? Why this, as some approve;..218. H.622, 1
What Love said was too too true:..............219. H.628, 8
What made that mirth last night? the neighbours say, 219. H.630, 1
Nailes from her fingers mew'd, she shewes: what els? 232. H.668, 4
Say what thou art. Ph. I prithee first draw neare. 248. H.730, 4
What needs twenty stabs, when one............254. H.757, 5
What though the Lictors threat us,..............259. H.772, 7
Serve or not serve, let Tom doe what he can,...265. H.796, 3
(Not knowing what would come to passe)......281. H.876, 6
What can my Kellam drink his Sack...........290. H.918, 1
What need we marry Women, when.............297. H.948, 1
You aske me what I doe, and how I live?.....312. H.1013, 1
Tell me, now last, what love will do;..........325. H.1075, 7
When we obey, by acting what we heare.........346. N.36, 3
And I nod to what is said,......................348. N.41, 30
What though my Harp, and Violl be............361. N.84, 1
To pay Thee that I owe, since what I see......368. N.103, 3
God can do all things, save but what are known 382. N.166, 1
I'le follow Thee, hap, hap what shall,..........399. N.265, 5

He was——Cha. Say what. Euc. Ay me, my woes are deep. 416. A.8, 11
But what she gives not, she not takes,.....436. ins. H.336, 48o
Whate'er On with thy fortunes then, what e're they be; 6. H.3, 7
And make, what ere they touch, turn sweet..55. H.149, 62
What ere enters, out it shall:................116. H.285, 8
Drive thence what ere encumbers,................260. H.777, 3
God is all-present to what e're we do,.........394. N.237, 1
Whatever What ever comes, content makes sweet: 200. H.552, 6
Where I have had, what ever thing co'd be....227. H.652, 3
What ever Liquor in ye powre..............320. H.1053, 2
What ever men for Loyalty pretend,..........333. H.1121, 1
Whatever comes, let's be content withall:........353. N.55, 1
What's But when He's gone, read through what's writ, 6. H.4, 3
Her inadult'rate strength: what's done by me...46. H.128, 53
What's now the cause? we know the case is cleere: 71. H.183, 2
Wo't thou not smile, or tell me what's amisse?..78. H.197, 33
What's to be done? but on the Sands...........94. H.225, 7
What's that we see from far? the spring of Day..112. H.283, 1
Looks forward, scornes what's left behind:....132. H.336, 14
We'll nobly think, what's to be done,.........168. H.443, 120
Tell I can't, what's Resident..................191. H.519, 4
No man despaires to do what's done before.....236. H.680, 2
Ch. What's that to me, I waft nor fish or fowles, 248. H.730, 9
Ch. What's thy request? Ph. That since she's now beneath 248. H.730, 15
(What's hard to others) nothing's troublesome...298. H.955, 4
What's got by Justice is establisht sure;......314. H.1023, 1
What's said or done..........................314. H.1024, 7
That Prince, who may doe nothing but what's just, 331. H.1103, 1
An active spiritt full marrow, and what's good; 426. ins. H.197, 48d
— — — — — — — — — —,..............436. var. H.336, 14
Whatsoe'er When ere I go, or what so ere befalls 269. H.818, 1
In vain our labours are, whatsoe're they be,....379. N.140, 1
To all our wounds, here, whatsoe're they be,......390. N.221, 1
Of all the good things whatsoe're we do,........403. N.272, 1
Whatosever Whatsoever thing I see,............253. H.750, 1
And whatsoever thing they tread vpon...........406. A.1, 93
Wheals Tom Blinks his Nose is full of wheales, and these 273. H.834, 1
Wheat Devotion, stroak the home-borne wheat:..101. H.250, 22
Your praise, and bless you, sprinkling you with Wheat: 113. H.283, 46
A Moon-parcht grain of purest wheat,..........119. H.293, 9
But curse thy children, they consume thy wheat. 141. H.358, 2
I have there a little wheat;....................152. H.393, 2
To strut thy barnes with sheafs of Wheat......233. H.670, 21
With lawlesse tooth the floure of wheate:......310. H.1004, 4
Aha my boyes! heres wheat for Christmas Pies! 327. H.1086, 2
Soone after, he for beere so scores his wheat,..327. H.1086, 3
Cleane heap of wheat,........................375. N.123, 79
Wheat, Barley, Rie, or Oats; what is't..........376. N.127, 3
Of ours, as is the rising of the wheat..........388. N.208, 6
Thy sheaf of wheat,..........................391. N.228, 14
And stuffed Magazine of wheat;.........436. ins. H.336, 48j
By the round Urchin, some mixt wheate..439. ins. H.443, 45d
Wheaten Then to the Maids with Wheaten Hats: 102. H.250, 41
Wheat-straws Of silv'rie fish; wheat-strawes, the snailes 166. H.443, 73
Wheel (Binding the wheele of Fortune to his Sphere) 137. H.341, 4
Set you to your Wheele, and wax............221. H.633, 42
Had broke her wheele, or crackt her axeltree...358. N.77, 4
Whelk's Sometimes (in mirth) he sayes each whelk's a sparke 273. H.834, 3
Whelmed — — — — — — — — —, ...449. var. A.8, 3
When (Partial List)
But when that men have both well drunke, and fed,.7. H.8, 3
Dead when I am, first cast in salt, and bring......9. H.14, 7
The rest Ile speak, when we meet both in bed...24. H.74, 14
So looks Anthea, when in bed she lyes,..........34. H.104, 1
Fortune when she comes, or goes...............37. H.106, 94
As Zephirus when he 'spires...................55. H.149, 67
Virgins, weep not; 'twill come, when,.........56. H.149, 111
And time will come when you shall weare.......63. H.164, 4
So when or you or I are made..................69. H.178, 65
When Youth and Blood are warmer;...........84. H.208, 10
And know thy when.........................87. H.214, 7
In the wild aire, when thou hast rowl'd about,...87. H.215, 3
Next, when thou dost perceive her fixed sight,...87. H.215, 7
When once the Lovers Rose is dead,..........106. H.262, 5
Shark, when he goes to any publick feast,.......118. H.292, 1
Phoebus! when that I a Verse,................122. H.303, 1
As Benjamin, and Storax, when they meet......131. H.331, 10
When once he gives it incarnation?...........139. H.347, 4
You say y'are young; but when your Teeth are told 173. H.462, 1
The time will come, when you'l be sad,........179. H.476, 37
Then, when I see thy Tresses bound...........202. H.560, 9
Next, when those Lawnie Filmes I see........202. H.560, 13
Expecting when to fall: which soon will be;....203. H.565, 3
So, when Death comes, Fresh tinctures lose their place, 207. H.576, 5
As when the Sweet Maria lived here:........214. H.612, 10
That your plenty last till when,...............224. H.638, 27
When now the Cock (the Plow-mans Horne)....230. H.662, 19
The how, where, when, I question not.........236. H.681, 2
And when that ye wed......................239. H.695, 10
Die when ye will, your sepulchre is knowne,....249. H.734, 3
To be, and not seen when and where they will...250. H.737, 2
When I touch, I then begin..................253. H.750, 8
Shall call to Judgment; tell us when the sound 257. H.763, 18
Next, when I cast mine eyes and see..........261. H.779, 4
Bice laughs, when no man speaks; and doth protest 265. H.795, 1
Go to Bed, and care not when..................276. H.850, 7
When that Death bids come away.............277. H.852, 8
But let that instant when thou dy'st be known,..281. H.875, 3
Say how, or when..........................289. H.911, 2
Tel'st when a Verse springs high, how understood 297. H.947, 7
And as time past when Cato the Severe........301. H.962, 1
Since when (me thinks) my braines about doe swim, 313. H.1017, 13
Then did I live when I did see...............313. H.1020, 1
As when ye innocent met here................317. H.1035, 30
But when again sh'as got her healthfull houre,..320. H.1054, 5
In the morning when ye rise.................322. H.1064, 1
The body's salt, the soule is; which when gon,..332. H.1111, 1
God when for sin He makes His Children smart, 343. N.22, 1
But when by stripes He saves them, then 'tis known, 343. N.22, 3
God heares us when we pray, but yet defers......344. N.30, 1
When I lie within my bed,....................347. N.41, 5
Next, when I have my faults confest,............349. N.46, 5
Since rough the way is, help me when I call,....352. N.51, 7
Call, and I'le come; say Thou, the when, and where: 358. N.77, 13
I do believe, that when I rise,.................358. N.78, 3
When I a ship see on the Seas,................372. N.118, 1
As when, in humane nature He works more....395. N.244, 3
God's wrathfull said to be, when He doth do...397. N.259, 3
Those act without regard, when once a King,..399. N.263, 24
That when thou doest his necke Insnare,..........408. A.2, 61
Whenas (Partial List)
Those Sundayes onely, when as Briefs are read..39. H.109, 2
When as Leander young was drown'd,........42. H.119, 1
Thou shed'st one teare, when as I went away;.42. H.122, 10
When as the Lilly marries with the Rose!......44. H.124, 2
When as that Rubie, which you weare,........61. H.160, 7
When as a thousand Virgins on this day,....68. H.178, 13
When as Cherries come in place?...........74. H.189, 6
What trust to things below, when as we see,...81. H.202, 7
When as the chosen seed shall spring.........89. H.219, 19
When as ye chuse your King and Queen,......127. H.319, 19
When as the meanest part of her............145. H.375, 25
When as a publick ruine bears down All.......155. H.405, 18
When as the humble Cottages not feare......181. H.483, 15
When as your Baby's lull'd asleep?.........189. H.514, 2
(And hang the head when as the Act is done)..196. H.537, 2
When as her Aprill houre drawes neare,........221. H.633, 58
When as in silks my Julia goes,.............261. H.779, 1
Burn first thine incense; next, when as thou see'st 286. H.898, 5
When as his owne still out at elboes is?......295. H.941, 8
Why sho'd we covet much, when as we know,...308. H.995, 1
When as the roof's a tottering:..............318. H.1036, 4
And tell us then, when as thou seest..........365. N.97, 12
When as the Mountains quak'd for dread,......393. N.232, 5
When as the poore crie out, to us............394. N.239, 3
When as His grace not supples men..........396. N.250, 2
When as your Sight..........................413. A.4, 12
When as some kinde.........................414. A.5, 13
Whence Has not whence to sink at all...........84. H.209, 8
The Country has. Amint. From whence? Amar. From whence? Mir. The Court.........................86. H.213, 12
Tell, if thou canst, (and truly) whence doth come 157. H.414, 1
And thy brest the Altar, whence...............158. H.417, 3
How can I chuse but kisse her, whence do's come 181. H.485, 3
No man comes late unto that place from whence 228. H.656, 1
From whence there's never a return...........233. H.670, 39
Streame to the Spring from whence it came....245. H.720, 10
Tell us thy Nation, kindred, or the whence......299. H.956, 7
Shew me that world of Starres, and whence......340. N.3, 13
And all sweet Meades; from whence we get......360. N.83, 17
From whence the house-wives cloth did come:..374. N.123, 36
Whence beawty springs, and thus I kisse thy foot. 406. A.1, 112
W^th thought thay goe, whence thay must ner returne. 411. A.3, 66
Whene'er I'le doe my best to win, when'ere I wooe: 31. H.91, 1

When ere my heart, Love's warmth, but entertaines, 40. H.113, 1
That when ere I wooe, I find..................138. H.346, 3
When ere I go, or what so ere befalls......269. H.818, 1
When e're thou speak'st, look with a lowly eye:..362. N.89, 3
So that when 'ere we circumvolve our Eyes,...415. A.7, 15
Whensoe'er Forth into blushes, whensoere he speaks. 124. H.311, 2
Old Widow Shopter, when so ere she cryes,.....331. H.1107, 1
Where (Partial List) See Anywhere, Everywhere
Hony to salve, where he before did sting......16. H.40, 8
One ask'd me where the Roses grew?............18. H 45, 1
Some ask'd me where the Rubies grew?...........24. H.75, 1
Some ask'd how Pearls did grow, and where?.....24. H.75, 5
That's my Julia's brest; where dwels..........40. H.115, 13
There, where no language ever yet was known...60. H.156, 6
He feeles when Packs do pinch him; and the where. 60. H.158, 4
Where hast thou been so long from my embraces, 77. H.197, 19
The place, where I may find ye..................83. H.207, 4
Ships have been drown'd, where late they danc't before. 85. H.212, 2
Can shew where you or grew, or stood......88. H.216, 9
So you be straight, where Virgins straight sho'd be. 99. H.242, 2
Where Maids have spent their houres........110. H.274, 4
See where she comes; and smell how all the street 113. H.283, 21
Quite through the table, where he spies........119. H.293, 25
Where Trouble serves the board, we eate........124. H.312, 3
Go where I will, thou luckie Larr stay here,....132. H.333, 9
Where the fault springs, there let the judgement fall. 132. H.335, 4
Nothing is New: we walk where others went.....139. H.352, 1
And knowes not where i'th world to borrow more. 160. H.423, 4
Man knowes where first he ships himselfe; but he 177. H.468, 1
Or where else shall we find....................188. H.509, 6
Let our soules flie to' th' shades, where ever springs 205. H.575, 2
Where shall I goe...............................211. H.596, 5
Where merry as the Maids we'l be...........215. H.616, 2
(Where I have cause to burn perfumes to it:)..234. H.673, 8
The how, where, when, I question not..........236. H.681, 2
Speak where thou art. Ph. O Charon pittie me! 248. H.730, 6
To be, and not seen when and where they will....250. H.737, 2
Leaving no shew, where stood the Capitoll......252. H.745, 16
Where the Northern Winds do blow............266. H.803, 2
Where War with rashnesse is attempted, there...268. H 813, 3
Where he will kisse (next drunk) conjecture ye...295. H.943, 2
That (where meat is) will be a hanger on........296. H.944, 2
Tears will spring, where woes are deep.........306. H.984, 32
Shew mercy there, where they have power to kill. 321. H.1057, 2
(Or Sharon, where eternall Roses grow.).......326. H.1080, 8
So where He gives the bitter Pills, be sure,......344. N.31, 3
Where never Moone shall sway...............354. N.58, 9
Had all been rich, where then had Patience been? 356. N.69, 3
Call, and I'le come; say Thou, the when, and where: 358. N.77, 13
Where is the Babe but lately sprung?............367. N.102, 2
All doubts, and manifest the where..............367. N.102, 7
O Thou, that crown'st the will, where wants the deed. 369. N.105, 2
Where round about Thou seest but all things vaine, 371. N.113, 3
Beares vp twoe globes where loue and pleasure sitt, 405. A.1, 52
Lett Manners teach the <e> whear to bee........407. A.2, 27
Departing hence, where Good and Bad souls go...416. A.8, 26
Where, drest with garlands, there they walk the ground, 417. A.8, 29
To be of that High Hyrarchy, where none..443. var. H.575, 59
Whereas Whereas (perchance) my fortunes may..312. H.1014, 6
Whereas but one enforcement is.................390. N.225, 2
Whearas by thee, those, and A Million since......411. A.3, 39
Whereby A *Trasy I do keep, whereby..........246. H.724, 26
A stock of Goods, whereby he lives.............351. N.50, 2
The mind; the King, the meanes whereby I live...355. N.62, 2
— — — — — — — — — —, ...453. var. H.283, 70
Where'er So that where ere ye look, ye see,....90. H.223, 19
Learn this of me, where e'r thy Lot doth fall;..153. H.396, 1
Where ere the luckie Lot doth fall,............197. H.542, 3
Where e're they met, or parting place has been..250. H.737, 8
Time is the Bound of things, where e're we go,.257. H.766, 1
— — — — — ← — — — —,..............453. ins. H.283, 20j
Wherefore For a wrought Purse; can any tell wherefore? 162. H.427, 2
If thou aske me (Deare) wherefore............186. H.500, 1
But why He did not, let me tell wherefore:.......356. N.69, 2
The why, and wherefore all things here..........364. N.96, 12
Wherefore two prayers ought not to be said,....396. N.249, 7
Wherein Wherein thou liv'st for ever. Deare farewell, 23. H.72, 4
Wherein all pleasures of the world are wove.....40. H.114, 4
To slack these flames wherein I frie?............40. H.115, 2
Wherein or Light, or Day, did never peep.........52. H.146, 6
About this Urne, wherein thy Dust is laid,......73. H.186, 18
Wherein my Love is laid.......................156. H.412, 8
Wherein t'ave had an enjoying.................195. H.534, 6
Wherein I dwell;.............................198. H.544, 26
Wherein we rest, and never feare..............200. H.552, 9
Since the place wherein ye lye,................324. H.1070, 2
Wherein to dwell..................................349. N.47, 2
Whereof Six teeth he has, whereof twice two are known 46. H.129, 3
Whereof (at last) to make.....................173. H.460, 3
Whereon Whereon my Vine did crawle,..........72. H.185, 13
Whereon so many Stately Structures stand:....315. H.1028, 4
Whereon the blessed Babie lay..................355. N.60, 4
And when He blest each sev'rall Day, whereon..396. N.249, 3
Where's And ask, Where's now the colour, forme and trust 49. H.138, 4
Or water; where's the comfort found?............50. H.140, 8
God, He is there, where's nothing else (Schooles say) 388. N.207, 3
Wheresoe'er Christ, He requires still, wheresoere He comes, 356. N.68, 1
God crowns our goodnesse, where so ere He sees,.356. N.71, 3
Wheresoever God's said to dwell there, wheresoever He 385. N.189, 1
Where't To the tombe wher't must be layd.........418. A.9, 44
Whereupon Whereupon in anger flying.............50. H.139, 3
Wherever Where ever Nodes do's in the Summer come, 270. H.822, 1
Wherewith Wherewith young men and maids distrest, 106. H.262, 3
Those holy lights, wherewith they guide........109. H.271, 3
Some gin, wherewith to catch your eyes.........114. H.283, 70
Wherewith ye make those merry Sceanes,.......127. H.319, 18
Give me words wherewith to wooe,..............204. H.569, 7
This Christmas, but his want wherwith, sayes Nay. 238. H.693, 2
Part must be kept wherewith to teend...........285. H.893, 5
Wherewith ye drest the Christmas Hall:........304. H.980, 4
These Veiles, wherewith we use to hide..........360. N.83, 45
Wherewith so many soules were fed............374. N.123, 16
True heate, whearwth humanitie doth liue........410. A.3, 30
your eyes are they, wherewith you draw the pure 432. ins. H.283, 70h
Wherry — — — — — — — —, ...445. var. H.730, 26
Whet And though with ale ye be whet here;....317. H.1035, 27
Ile whet my lips, and sharpen Love on thee.....327. H.1081, 2
Whether Regardlesse whether well thou sped'st, or no. 6. H.3, 6
Whether by th' eye, or eare, or no:..............24. H.73, 2
Or whether with the soule it came...............24. H.73, 3
Whether in part 'tis here or there,...............24. H.73, 5
Whether thy bones had here their Rest, or no.......27. H.82, 6
Not curious whether Appetite be fed,...........37. H.106, 107
Whether by choice, or common flame:.............50. H.140, 6
Whether high he builds or no:...................84. H.209, 2
Whether I wo'd; but (ah!) I know not how,.....84. H.210, 7
Whether my Sapho's breast,....................105. H.258, 3
Whether the Violets sho'd excell,...............105. H.260, 3
Whether that you be sweet or no?..............112. H.282, 2
Whether or no, that we shall meet here ever......140. H.355, 4
'Tis to be doubted whether I next yeer,..........140. H.355, 7
Whether it be the voice or string,..............142. H.362, 2
But she is gone. Sil. Mirtillo, tell us whether,...159. H.421, 29
Burne, or drowne me, choose ye whether,........254. H.757, 1
Whether smooth or not I be,....................277. H.852, 3
As whether (this) I cannot tell...................283. H.883, 5
Whether I was my selfe, or else did see........326. H.1080, 1
Or whether those (in orders rare) or these......326. H.1080, 3
Or whether Fairies, Syrens, Nymphes they were,.326. H.1080, 5
Mooving a question whether that by them........405. A.1, 41
Whether the world such Sperritts had or noe,....411. A.3, 38
Whether in the morne or noone....................418. A.9, 45
Which (Partial List)
Which Rubies, Corralls, Scarlets, all.............12. H.23, 7
Those Deities which circum-walk the Seas,........14. H.35, 5
Which being done, the fretfull paine..............18. H.46, 9
The Drooping West, which hitherto has stood......25. H.77, 3
War, which before was horrid, now appears........25. H.77, 7
Which being seen,...............................30. H.89, 6
Which Venus hearing; thither came,..............31. H.92, 5
Which done, to still their wanton cries,............31. H.92, 9
But that which most makes sweet thy country life, 35. H.106, 31
Which done, thy painfull Thumb this sentence tells us, 36. H.106, 61
The which was made a happy Bride,...............41. H.116, 5
That Houre-glasse, which there ye see........44. H.127, 1
That, which subverts whole nature, grief and care; 45. H.128, 21
Which when I saw, I made accesse...............51. H.142, 17
By which, mine angry Mistresse might descry,....58. H.150, 5
Which done, then quickly we'll undresse..........58. H.152, 7
Which, circumvolving gently, there...............64. H.169, 3
At which she smil'd; and bade him goe..........71. H.182, 27
Out of the which, the creame of light,............74. H.190, 9

Which draws the sight thereto,.................75. H.193, 13
That Age is best, which is the first,..............84. H.208, 9
Into the which who looks shall see.................90. H.223, 5
Which one by one here set downe are...........91. H.223, 36
In either which a small tall bent.................92. H.223, 95
Which if it now, or shall hereafter shine,.........94. H.226, 7
Since which, though I love many,..............100. H.249, 6
Which freely drink to your Lords health,......102. H.250, 38
Since which (beleeve the rest)..................105. H.258, 7
Which spent, one death, bring to ye both one Grave.
124. H.313, 14
Seest thou those Diamonds which she weares....130. H.330, 1
Which when not warmed by her view,...........131. H.330, 9
Mease brags of Pullets which he eats: but Mease.142. H.361, 1
Part of which I give to Larr,...................152. H.393, 5
His eyes and ears strive which sho'd fastest run...158. H.418, 2
Which mercy if you will but do,................165. H.442, 11
This, Three; which Three, you make up Foure Brave Prince.
170. H.451, 16
Which eaten, they and I.......................173. H.460, 5
Next to which Two; among the City-Powers,....176. H.466, 3
Turn'd to these Springs, which wee see here:.....180. H.478, 4
Like to these Garden-glories, which here be......193. H.522, 3
Rare are thy cheeks Susanna, which do show....193. H.523, 1
For which, her wrath is gone forth to consume..197. H.539, 11
By which we sit, and doe Divine................198. H.544, 4
Which Love and noble freedome is;...........198. H.544, 28
To grace which Service, Julia, there shall be....209. H.584, 3
Is yours, in which you challeng'd are to fight..216. H.618, 10
Or gallant Newark; which brave two...........218. H.626, 12
Of which who drank, he said no thought........222. H.635, 3
None loseth that, which he in time may get......228. H.654, 2
On which the young men and maids meet,......230. H.662, 48
That stroke most fear'd is, which is struck the last.
237. H.688, 2
That flow of Gallants which approach...........239. H.696, 1
That fleet of Lackeyes, which do run............239. H.696, 3
Into the which we come by warre...............241. H.711, 2
That Preternaturall Fever, which did threat.....254. H.756, 3
From which mishap this use I make,...........283. H.883, 11
(From which poore seed, and rudely sown)......297. H.948, 7
Which knowne, let us make..................317. H.1035, 13
That is my hope; which if that slip, I'm one..319. H.1044, 3
At which the hounds fall a bounding;.........334. H.1122, 15
Those Saints, which God loves best,............344. N.28, 1
For which obedient zeale of thine,..............360. N.83, 31
Which, rightly us'd, both in their time and place,.371. N.115, 7
And those great are, which ne're decay...........381. N.158, 4
Ask not for gold, which metall is:...............381. N.158, 6
Those Tapers, which we set upon the grave,.....384. N.181, 1
Which to effect, let ev'ry passing Bell..........392. N.230, 11
That without wrath, which wrath doth force us to.
397. N.259, 4
Which like a garden manifestly show............404. A.1, 15
Which to the knees by nature fastned on.........406. A.1, 85
Ore which the hand.....................436. ins. H.336, 48m
Out of the which he sometimes sups....439. ins. H.443, 45k

While While thou didst keep thy Candor undefil'd,....6. H.3, 1
May blush, (while Brutus standeth by:)............6. H.4, 2
And while the Wood-nimphs my cold corps inter,..19. H.50, 3
While other Gums their sweets perspire,........20. H.54, 5
Charls the best Husband, while Maria strives....26. H.79, 3
(While Love the Centinell doth keep)..........35. H.106, 36
Present their shapes; while fantasie discloses....36. H.106, 47
While Faunus in the Vision comes to keep,......36. H.106, 51
And watrie dangers; while thy whiter hap,....36. H.106, 71
While soft Opinion makes thy Genius say,......37. H.106, 115
While the milder Fates consent,.................39. H.111, 1
Thee and their lips espous'd; while I admire,....46. H.128, 50
But while he, perking, there did prie..............46. H.130, 7
While you are in your sprightfull green:........49. H.136, 25
And may a while controule......................54. H.149, 25
While Domiduca leads the way:..................54. H.149, 42
Take time Lady while ye may..................56. H.149, 120
When Julia chid, I stood as mute the while,....58. H.150, 1
The Eyes by tears speak, while the Tongue is mute.
58. H.150, 8
Come, and receive them while the light..........68. H.178, 23
Come, let us goe, while we are in our prime;....69. H.178, 57
Then while time serves, and we are but decaying;.69. H.178, 69
Hor. While, Lydia, I was lov'd of thee,..........70. H.181, 1
Lyd. While thou no other didst affect,...........70. H.181, 5
Yet, Porter, while thou keep'st alive,............72. H.185, 15
And perfume the aire a while:..................74. H.189, 2
In a Cloud; while both did play,..............77. H.190, 6
While leanest Beasts in Pastures feed,............77. H.196, 1
Stay while ye will, or goe;......................83. H.207, 1
Gather ye Rose-buds while ye may,..............84. H.208, 1
And while ye may, goe marry:.................84. H.208, 14
Rest but a while here, by this bank of Lillies,...86. H.213, 10
While Golden Angels (some have told to me)....86. H.213, 23
While we this Trentall sing about thy Grave.......89. H.219, 2
Sleepe in thy peace, while we with spice perfume thee,
89. H.219, 13
Fall gently, gently, and a while him keep........99. H.244, 5
While other Rusticks, lesse attent..............101. H.250, 23
And Angels will be borne, while thou dost sing...102. H.252, 2
While I have eyes to see:.....................109. H.267, 14
Bestroaking Fate the while....................113. H.283, 29
The while the cloud of younglings sing,........113. H.283, 43
While some repeat..........................113. H.283, 45
While that others doe divine;.................113. H.283, 47
While you wring your hands and weep.........118. H.289, 14
But all this while his eye is serv'd,...........119. H.293, 13
The Goblin from ye, while ye sleep............121. H.299, 6
A little while from Tramplers free;............123. H.306, 10
Meane while, the Holy-Rood hence fright......123. H.306, 13
The gardens-glory liv'd a while,...............126. H.318, 4
Let's live, my Wickes, then, while we may,....132. H.336, 15
While Baucis by,...........................134. H.336, 83
While sweet-breath Nimphs, attend on you this Day.
140. H.354, 8
Thou shalt not All die; for while Love's fire shines
143. H.366, 1
Sleep, while we hide thee from the light,........146. H.376, 13
And spring fresh Rose-buds, while the salt, the wit
148. H.377, 73
While Reverence, waiting at the bashfull board,.148. H.377, 75
Was I idle, and that while...................155. H.407, 3
Ile tell thee; while my Julia did unlace.........157. H.414, 5
And all the while my part shall be to weepe;....159. H.421, 37
While all beauty lyes asleep....................170. H.450, 2
Let's live in hast; use pleasures while we may:..171. H.453, 1
While Fates permits us, let's be merry;..........172. H.457, 1
But you may stay yet here a while,............176. H.467, 4
Like you a while: They glide..................176. H.467, 17
With all the rest; while thou alone............184. H.492, 35
While they liv'd, or lasted here:................187. H.503, 2
I held Love's head while it did ake;............188. H.509, 1
And for a while lye here conceal'd,............190. H.515, 45
Ripe Cherries smiling, while that others blow....193. H.523, 2
The while we never remember,.................196. H.534, 15
Purfling the Margents, while perpetuall Day....206. H.575, 14
His eye in dew of kisses, while he sleeps.......206. H.575, 42
Listen, while they (like Syrens in their Spheres).206. H.575, 52
So, while I thus sit crown'd;..................208. H.582, 2
Let's be jocund while we may;.................224. H.639, 1
The while the Daulian Minstrell sweetly sings,...224. H.642, 7
While mischeifs, by these,......................225. H.643, 16
I am holy, while I stand.......................227. H.651, 1
Drink Wine, and live here blithefull, while ye may:
228. H.655, 1
I might grow proud the while.................231. H.663, 4
Then, while Fates suffer, live thou free,.........233. H.670, 17
Then live we mirthfull, while we should,.....233. H.670, 28
The while their wreaths and Purple Robes do shine,
234. H.673, 17
That while the Wassaile Bowle here.............235. H.674, 9
Draw in your feeble fiers, while that He........236. H.685, 5
Some hung the head, while some did bring......237. H.686, 5
Some laid her forth, while other wept,...........237. H.686, 7
Love, and live here while we may;..............238. H.691, 2
While we have our being here:.................238. H.691, 4
Chor. Lay by a while your Pipes, and rest,.....243. H.716, 35
Our lips for a while,........................247. H.727, 4
Ch. Why then begin, and all the while we make.248. H.730, 23
While young Charles fights, and fighting wins the day.
254. H.756, 14
Princes and Fav'rites are most deere, while they.255. H.758, 1
A Fast, while Jets and Marbles weep,..........257. H.764, 8
While misery keeps in with patience............257. H.765, 4
While juice she straines, and pith..............258. H.767, 13
Then while I sing your praise,................261. H.778, 10
While my good Dame, she...................263. H.784, 4
Come while the Log is a teending..............263. H.784, 12
The while the meat is a shredding;............263. H.784, 15
Backward he should not looke while he..........265. H.798, 5
While w'are in our Prime;....................267. H.806, 2
To stench the blood the while...................272. H.828, 12
Mine eyes must wooe you; (though I sigh the while)
274. H.837, 7
But while he met with his Paternall grave;......278. H.860, 4
Though while we living 'bout the world do roame,.278. H.860, 5
While others perish, here's thy life decreed......280. H.869, 5
And (while we the gods invoke)..............280. H.870, 17
Hags away, while Children sleep.................284. H.888, 4
(While she gossips in the towne).............284. H.889, 4
While other generations dye..................288. H.906, 4
Lay by the good a while; a resting field......292. H.922, 1
While others they sit wringing.................296. H.946, 15
Enter and prosper; while our eyes doe waite.....300. H.961, 9
Then while thou laugh'st; Ile, sighing, crie,......303. H.973, 5
That ere while was heard so shrill?............305. H.984, 6
In a while it will strike one;................307. H.991, 3
Here we begin new life; while thousands quite..313. H.1019, 3
The while my deer Anthea do's but droop,......320. H.1054, 3
Grubs loves his Wife and Children, while that they
325. H.1077, 1
He raves, he rends, and while he thus doth tear,.325. H.1077, 5
While th' Moone in her sphere..............334. H.1122, 16
Gods Rod doth watch while men do sleep; & then.342. N.21, 1
The Rod doth sleep, while vigilant are men.......342. N.21, 2
And though a while He makes Requesters stay,...344. N.30, 3
Him but a while to stay;......................346. N.38, 4

Me, **while** I sleep............................350. N.47, 10
The **while** the conduits of my Kine............350. N.47, 49
While my sick heart............................353. N.56, 16
Awake! the **while** the active Finger............364. N.96, 6
Heaven to come down, the **while** we choke......366. N.98, 16
While Harps, and Violls then..................369. N.106, 15
And **while** we blunder in the dark,.............372. N.118, 7
To make paiment, **while** I call.................373. N.121, 12
Sleep with thy beauties here, **while** we..........375. N.123, 81
While we sit by sorrowes streames,.............376. N.128, 2
And we (Thy Lovers) **while** we see Thee keep..399. N.263, 36
Meane **while**, let mee,..........................401. N.268, 36
Or **while** that each from other's breath did drincke
410. A.3, 5
Guesse, soe departe; yett stay A **while** to[o] see...411. A.3, 59
A **while** yo[r] forehead in a Cloude................413. A.4, 17
Cha. Prethee relate **while** I give ear and weep.....416. A.8, 12
And the **while** yow doe surveye..................417. A.9, 15
— — — — — — — — — —, ...428. var. H.208, 10
Lead on faire paranymphs, the **while** her eyes,
430. ins. H.283, 20a
— — — — — — — — — — — —, ...449. var. A.3, 52
— — — — — — — — — — — —, ...449. var. A.3, 65
Whiles For these, and marbles have their **whiles**
148. H.377, 100
Whilom Thy **whilome** merry Oate...............183. H.492, 2
Whilst Shakeing the head, **whilst** each, to each dothe mourne,
411. A.3, 65
— — — — — — — — — — — —, ...428. var. H.208, 1
— — — — — — — — — — — —, ...436. var. H.336, 15
— — — — — — — — — — — —, ...453. ins. H.283, 20a
Whimpering See Tender-whimpering-maids
But if thy **whimpring** looks doe ask me why?....46. H.128, 41
Speak, **whimp'ring** Younglings, and make known.104. H.257, 15
The pretty **whimpering** that they make,........180. H.478, 5
And hear'st His **whimp'ring**, and His cries;......365. N.97, 14
— — — — — — — — — — —, ...453. var. H.283, 91
Whip Boyes to the lash) that he do's **whip** with them.
39. H.110, 4
Whipped And brought a rod, so **whipt** me with the same:
16. H.40, 2
With rods of Mirtle **whipt** them..................31. H.92, 8
Was lately **whipt** for lying with a Wench.........79. H.199, 2
For cruell Love ha's me so **whipt**,..............164. H.442, 6
His wife to death **whipt** with a Mirtle Rod.......306. H.986, 2
To punish great sins, who small faults **whipt** here.
381. N.156, 2
Whipping But causelesse **whipping** smarts the most of all.
319. H.1050, 2
Whipping-cheer Hell is the place where **whipping-cheer** abounds,
372. N.120, 1
To be all-flayd with **whipping-cheere**,............399. N.265, 8
Whips Scobble for Whoredome **whips** his wife; and cryes,
44. H.126, 1
God has his **whips** here to a twofold end,........343. N.26, 1
Whirl Yet, ere twelve Moones shall **whirl** about..178. H.476, 7
Will **whirle** about, and blow them thence at last..226. H.650, 4
Whirls And this our life too **whirles** away,......172. H.457, 3
Whirlwind And In a **Whirl-wynd** twirld her home, agast
410. A.3, 25
Whirry See Whorry
Whiskers Fone sayes, those mighty **whiskers** he do's weare,
39. H.110, 1
Whisper I will **whisper** to your eares,............208. H.580, 5
— — — — — — — — — — — —, ...453. var. H.283, 64
Whistle That thou hast brought a **Whistle** new,....354. N.59, 8
Whistling With a Hind **whistling** there to them:.230. H.662, 26
Whit And no **whit** further must venture;........256. H.762, 9
White How Roses first come Red, and Lillies **White**.
5. H.1, 10
White, and Heaven-like Chrystalline:..............16. H.39, 6
Ride on with all **white** Omens; so, that where....25. H.77, 11
Between thy Breasts (then Doune of Swans more **white**)
30. H.88, 9
More **white** then whitest Lillies far,...............34. H.105, 1
More **white** then are the whitest Creames,.........34. H.105, 3
More **white** then Pearls, or Juno's thigh;..........34. H.105, 5
White, warme, and soft to lye with me..........34. H.105, 10
White though ye be; yet, Lillies, know,..........74. H.190, 1
And made ye **white**..............................74. H.190, 12
So though y'are **white** as Swan, or Snow,.......76. H.193, 49
And that **white** cloud divide....................76. H.193, 53
Amar. With all **white** luck to you. Mirt. But say, What news
85. H.213, 3
(Clad, all, in Linnen, **white** as Lillies.).........101. H.250, 12
Roses at first were **white**,.......................105. H.258, 1
Or they more **white** sho'd be....................105. H.258, 4
Shew thy **white** feet, and head with Marjoram crown'd:
113. H.283, 32
Of that **white** Pride, and Drowne...............115. H.283, 119
Of **white**, where nature doth deny...............118. H.291, 8
First you, then you, and both for **white** successe..124. H.313, 2
Day with the **white** and Luckie stone...........133. H.336, 40
Which is as **white** and hair-less as an egge.........139. H.349, 2
With thy most **white** Predestination........ ....155. H.405, 4
A red-Rose peeping through a **white**?...... ....164. H.440, 2
Of whom, from Fam's **white** Trumpet, This Ile Tell,
170. H.451, 9
To this **white** Temple of my Heroes, here.......185. H.496, 1
When with **white** commingled....................194. H.527, 4
Black your haires are; mine are **white**;.........194. H.527, 5
Having but seven in all; three black, foure **white**.
195. H.531, 2
With the **white** Vestures, all attending Thee.....196. H.539, 4
A stole of **white**, (and Canonized here)..........199. H.545, 6
Which, on the **white** Rose being shed,...........241. H.706, 3
She goes her long **white** egg to lay.............246. H.724, 12
White as Zenobias teeth, the which the Girles....251. H.741, 1
Thy Warre (discreetly made) with **white** successe.
254. H.756, 12
Cut the **white** loafe here,.......................263. H.784, 14
In her **white** Stole; now Victory do's rest.......271. H.823, 3
The Blooms that fell were **white** and red;.......283. H.883, 3
Because his stock will not hold out for **white**.....309. H.997, 2
Gray or **white**, all's one to me.................330. H.1098, 4
My sackcloth here; but there my Stole of **white**...343. N.25, 8
In long **white** stole,..........................369. N.106, 8
Thy hands (though cold) yet spotlesse, **white**,...375. N.123, 75
But, as they walk't here in their vestures **white**,..384. N.181, 4
Tell me, **white** Angell; what is now become.......403. N.271, 3
Like purest **white** stands in the middle place......404. A.1, 12
Which sweetly mixed both with **white** and redd....404. A.1, 17
Like rose leaves, **white** and redd seeme mingled..404. A.1, 18
And her **white** teeth which in the gums are sett...405. A.1, 31
For his plumpe **white** and smooth p[r]rogatiue,......405. A.1, 34
Or ells that she on that **white** waxen hill.........405. A.1, 63
White handes as smooth, as Mercies, bring........408. A.2, 59
(**White** Fame) and Resurrection to the Good,....410. A.3, 32
With such **white** vowes as fate can nere dissever..414. A.6, 11
— — — — — — — — — —, ...447. var. A.1, 35
White-loaf End now the **White-loafe**, & the Pye,..285. H.894, 1
Whiteness Where nature in a **whitenes** without spott
405. A.1, 61
Whiter And watrie dangers; while thy **whiter** hap,.36. H.106, 71
Reach, with your **whiter** hands, to me,..........185. H.495, 1
Brave Kinsman, markt out with the **whiter** stone:
199. H.545, 8
In that **whiter** Island, where...................377. N.128, 9
— — — — — — — — — —, ...440. var. H.443, 93
Whites True, I confesse; such **Whites** as these....34. H.105, 7
Whitest More white then **whitest** Lillies far,.....34. H.105, 1
Or Snow, or **whitest** Swans you are:.............34. H.105, 2
More white then are the **whitest** Creames,.......34. H.105, 3
Fill, and winde up with **whitest** wooll.........58. H.149, 162
To hug thy **whitest** neck: Then I,................70. H.181, 3
(With **whitest** Wool be ever crown'd that day!)..86. H.213, 14
Whom **whitest** Fortune dandled has too much...239. H.697, 2
— — — — — — — — — — — —, ...436. var. H.336, 40
White-thorn Made up of **white-thorn** neatly enterwove;
68. H.178, 35
Back, and with **White-thorn** laden home.........69. H.178, 46
Whitflaw A fellon take it, or some **Whit-flaw** come.66. H.173, 3
Whitflaws The nails faln off by **Whit-flawes**: Art's.166. H.443, 59
Whither **Whither**, Mad maiden wilt thou roame?......5. H.2, 1
But **whither**, onely Grief do's know..............33. H.103, 4
Whither? Say, **whither** shall I fly,...............40. H.115, 1
But **whither**, I my selfe not know...............111. H.278, 2
Whither dost thou whorry me,..................157. H.415, 1
Or **whither** run.................................211. H.596, 6
Whitlow See Whitflaw
Whitlows See Whitflaws
Whitsun-ale Thy Morris-dance; thy **Whitsun-ale**;.230. H.662, 54
Whitsuntide To honour **Whitsontide**............285. H.892, 16
Who (Partial List)
Who a sprightly Springall lov'd,.................15. H.36, 6
Who is penurious, he shall still be poore...........22. H.64, 4
For I a Boy am, **who**...........................26. H.81, 9
That man loves not, **who** is not zealous too.......31. H.91, 2
And can'st instruct, that those **who** have the itch.35. H.106, 19
By th hand of him **who** is the Generall...........50. H.141, 2
Pity me too, **who** found so soone a Tomb.........58. H.151, 4
Come, and coole ye; all **who** frie................62. H.162, 2
Who wo'd not think this Yonker fierce to fight?..65. H.171, 3
Prig now drinks Water, **who** before drank Beere:..71. H.183, 1
Thou **who** wilt not love, doe this;...............76. H.195, 1
Into the which **who** looks shall see...............90. H.223, 5
Favour your tongues, **who** enter here.............91. H.223, 41
I call, I call, **who** doe ye call?.................112. H.281, 1
Let him come, **who** dares undo her...........114. H.283, 100
I could wish you all, **who** love,.................117. H.289, 1
But yet Love (**who** subtile is)..................120. H.297, 5
Who, as soone, fell fast asleep,................123. H.310, 3
Others there be, **who** righteously will swear....141. H.359, 9
I **who** have favour'd many, come to be......142. H.365, 1
Loe, I, the Lyrick Prophet, **who** have set........142. H.365, 3
For thou no Porter keep'st **who** strikes...........146. H.377, 18
This is that Princely Pemberton, **who** can......149. H.377, 133
Such ignorance as theirs was, **who** once hist..150. H.382, 15
He knowes well **who** do love him,..............157. H.412, 22
Who hath but one of many;....................160. H.422, 14
Give way, give way to me, **who** come..........169. H.449, 9

My old leane wife, shall kisse it dry:..........134. H.336, 84
Or for Widow, Maid, or Wife.................182. H.490, 4
To find a Wife, that is most fit for Thee.......185. H.494, 2
Chaste I liv'd, without a wife,................199. H.546, 3
Cock calls his Wife his Hen: when Cock goes too't, 213. H.610, 1
Snare, ten i' th' hundred calls his wife; and why? 220. H.631, 1
A Pleasing Wife, that by thy side............233. H.670, 13
Thy Wife, thy Children, and the state..........239. H.696, 9
His wife her owne ware sells as fast at home,..253. H.753, 4
Till his Wife licking, so unglews his eyes......269. H.816, 2
Hanch, since he (lately) did interre his wife,....275 H.842, 1
Chaste Lucrece, or a wife as grave:............283. H.885, 8
Let the superstitious wife 284. H.889, 1
A wife most richly married......................291. H.919, 16
Fat be my Hinde; unlearned be my wife;......294. H.938, 1
What was my Birth, to whom I was a Wife:..304. H.978, 2
His wife to death whipt with a Mirtle Rod.....306. H.986, 2
Kisse my Brown wife, and black Posterity......310. H.1003, 4
The Husband drunke, the Wife to be..........310. H.1004, 9
Is, that I never yet had wife;................320. H.1052, 2
Grubs loves his Wife and Children, while that they 325. H.1077, 1
His Wife and Children fast to death for fear....325. H.1077, 6
Hee may ere longe haue such a wyfe...........409. A.2, 107
Wild I see a wilde civility:.....................28. H.83, 12
Next, his wilde eares, like Lethern wings full spread, 33. H.99, 3
Throwing about his wild, and active fires.......45. H.128, 18
Lost in the wild sea, once againe:...............79. H.198, 8
Wild I am now with heat;......................81. H.201, 29
In the wild aire, when thou hast rowl'd about,..87. H.215, 3
Wild are Seas, that want a shore..............122. H.304, 2
(If a wild Apple can be had).................135. H.336, 122
Are to a wilde digestion brought,............166. H.443, 35
Play with a wild civility:.....................202. H.560, 14
Drown'd in the Sea of wild Eternitie:..........256. H.763, 14
'Tis I am wild, and more then haires..........282. H.881, 5
As made us nobly wild, not mad;...............289. H.911, 8
The Daughters wild and loose in dresse;........310. H.1004, 7
And I am wilde and wanton like to him.......313. H.1017, 14
Writ in my wild unhallowed Times;..............339. N.2, 2
But such as have been drown'd in this wilde sea, 417. A.8, 31
As Butter'd bred, the which the wild......439. ins. H.443, 45p
Wilder When Kings obey the wilder Multitude...196. H.536, 2
Follow to th' wilder Ocean:....................244. H.720, 4
The Plague of wilder Jelousie................408. A.2, 42
Wildered Wildred in this vast watry Region.....319. H.1044, 4
Wilderness Lost in the civill Wildernesse of sleep: 99. H.244, 6
Us both i'th' Sea, Camp, Wildernesse)..........134. H.336, 66
Like a civill Wilderness;......................232. H.665, 6
Has made me like a wilderness:..............312. H.1016, 2
Thou art our way i'th wildernesse:..............372. N.118, 6
Wildfire Then like a Globe, or Ball of Wild-fire, flie, 87. H.215, 9
Wildly Sometimes away 'two'd wildly fling;......67. H.175, 13
And wildly force a passage in,.................175. H.465, 55
Wile And know each wile,....................115. H.283, 125
Wiles And sitting, see the wiles, wayes, walks of wit, 187. H.506, 3
Thy witty wiles to draw, and get.............231. H.662, 64
Will (Partial List of Verb)
As with a will repenting.......................55. H.149, 76
Stay while ye will, or goe;....................83. H.207, 1
Saint Will o'th' Wispe (of no great bignes)....91. H.223, 30
I have Mirtle rods, (at will)....................98. H.238, 9
Go where I will, thou luckie Larr stay here,....132. H.333, 9
Will ye heare, what I can say..................138. H.342, 1
Safe stand thy Walls, and Thee, and so both will, 149. H.377, 115
Love he that will; it best likes me,............155. H.408, 1
Will, with my Willow-wreath also,............161. H.425, 11
Who can hold that (my friends) that will away? 162. H.428, 2
The body sins not, 'tis the Will................175. H.465, 63
Nor will; for why, Pudica, this may know,......180. H.477, 5
I prithee speake: Lyc. I will. End. Say on:....183. H.492, 5
Let Poets feed on aire, or what they will;......186. H.498, 7
I brake thy Bracelet 'gainst my will;..........240. H.705, 1
T'ave Boyes, and Gyrles too, as they will.......291. H.919, 12
Praise they that will Times past, I joy to see..292. H.927, 1
Like will to like, each Creature loves his kinde; 319. H.1043, 1
Is halfe way cured, if the party will..........319. H.1048, 2
O Thou, that crown'st the will, where wants the deed. 369. N.105, 2
Not for the fault of Nature, but of will.........370. N.110, 2
If that he has a will to Masterdome...........389. N.211, 2
Man to th' alluring object gives his will.......392. N.230, 32
God, who me gives a will for to repent,........397. N.255, 1
Willingness A bashfull willingnesse:............55. H.149, 74
No other, but the doers willingnesse...........275. H.845, 2
Satan o'recomes none, but by willingnesse.....359. N.79, 2
Will-o'-the-wisp Saint Will o'th' Wispe (of no great bignes) 91. H.223, 30
No Will-o'th'-Wispe mis-light thee;...........217. H.619, 6

Willow Are twigs of Birch, and willow, growing there: 39. H.110, 2
Me weare the Willow; after that,..............161. H.425, 7
Willow garland A willow Garland thou did'st send.161. H.425, 1
Willow garlands Then Willow-garlands, 'bout the head, 106. H.262, 7
Willows How by Willowes we doe weep:........82. H.203, 12
Willow-tree My Harp hung up, here on the Willow tree 84. H.210, 2
Both hung upon the Willow-tree?...............361. N.84, 2
Our Harps hung on the Willow-tree:..........373. N.123, 2
Willow-wreath Will, with my Willow-wreath, also, 161. H.425, 11
Wilson Then shall Wilson and Gotiere..........39. H.111, 13
Or curious Wilson: Tell me, canst thou be....276. H.851, 5
Wilt Whither, Mad maiden wilt thou roame?.........5. H.2, 1
Thou wilt complaine, False now's thy Looking-glasse 21. H.62, 2
Nor wil't be long, ere this accomplish'd be;......26. H.79, 9
If thou wilt say,................................29. H.87, 7
If, Reader, then thou wilt draw neere,..........48. H.134, 5
If thou wilt say, that I shall live with thee;...60. H.156, 3
Then sure thou't like, or thou wilt envie me.....66. H.174, 4
Thou who wilt not love, doe this;..............76. H.195, 1
How long, Perenna, wilt thou see..............177. H.471, 1
If thou wilt love, and live with me...........193. H.521, 56
Wilt thou my true Friend be?.................205. H.574, 1
Thou still wilt cozen me.......................223. H.635, 16
Wilt thou appear, when thou art set...........270. H.819, 7
My dearest Love, since thou wilt go,...........323. H.1068, 1
The utmost smart, so Thou wilt cure...........342. N.17, 12
But if thou wilt not deigne so much,............344. N.29, 8
Can I not sin, but thou wilt be..................357. N.72, 1
And wilt not thou, with gold, be ti'd...........357. N.72, 11
But yet this Gift Thou wilt commend,..........376. N.125, 7
But if Thou wilt so honour me,................399. N.265, 3
Act when Thou wilt,.........................401. N.268, 10
— — — — — — — —,................426. var. H.197, 33
Wimbling Not a wimbling Tongue admit:.........282. H.878, 6
Win I'le doe my best to win, when'ere I wooe:....31. H.91, 1
Notwithstanding Love will win,...............121. H.297, 11
Give way, give way ye Gates, and win.........178. H.476, 1
And sooner play, the sooner win...............243. H.716, 24
Now for to win thy Heifer faire,..............243. H.716, 31
Wo'd I wooe, and wo'd I winne,..............286. H 897, 1
To keepe a Citie, then to winne a Towne.......307. H.989, 2
Beg for my Pardon Julia; He doth winne......329. H.1095, 3
Lastly, if thou canst win a kisse..............354. N.59, 15
Winckfield Wert thou a Winckfield onely, not a Brother. 210. H.590, 10
Wind See Whirlwind
That done, then wind me in that very sheet......9. H.14, 10
Know, I have pray'd to Furie, that some wind....49. H.138, 7
Fill, and winde up with whitest wooll.........58. H.149, 162
Thou hast both Wind and Tide with thee; Thy way 73. H.186, 3
Yet one rude wind, or ruffling shower,.........88. H.216, 5
Sweet Western Wind, whose luck it is,.........103. H.255, 1
Breath of a blasting wind;....................104. H.257, 9
Our own fair wind, and mark each one......133. H.336, 39
A way to measure out the Wind;................339. N.3, 2
And winde all other witnesses:..................357. N.72, 10
Winde...414. A.5, 14
Winding See Winding-sheet
Winding-sheet As ere was wrapt in winding sheet..257. H.764, 2
Wrapt in the winding-sheet with thee:.........361. N.83, 56
The sheet I sleep in, as my Winding-sheet.....392. N.230, 18
Winds The ruffling winds and raging Seas,.........31. H.90, 5
Winds have their time to rage; but when they cease, 105. H.259, 5
Let the winds drive.........................134. H.336, 59
Eeles winds and turnes, and cheats and steales; yet Eeles 153. H.398, 1
By this quaint Taper-light he winds............167. H.443, 82
What gentle Winds perspire? As if here........224. H.642, 9
By ruffling winds, about the world............245. H.720, 16
Where the Northern Winds do blow............266. H.803, 2
As aires doe breathe, or winds doe blow:......282. H.881, 8
No ruffling winds come hither to discease....316. H.1028, 21
The winds, to blow the tedious night away;......358. N.77, 6
No boysterous winds, or stormes, come hither,..361. N.83, 69
When Winds and Seas do rage,................373. N.122, 1
— — — — — — — — — —,...............436. var. H.336, 39
Windy Make him thus swell, or windy Cabbages. 327. H.1085, 2
Wine Let us sit, and quaffe our wine............39. H.111, 6
O thou the drink of Gods, and Angels! Wine..45. H.128, 11
With Wine and Oile besmear'd.................65. H.170, 4
Invites fresh Grapes to fill his Presse with Wine. 72. H.185, 28
In hot Adult'ry with another Wine?............78. H.197, 40
Me to the Tap, the Tost, the Turfe; Let Wine 79. H.197, 88
In Wine, whose each cup's worth..............80. H.201, 19
Of Aromatike wine,...........................80. H.201, 26
Yet dry'd, ere you distill your Wine............88. H.216, 12
And drunk with Wine, I drank him up........96. H.229, 4
We are the Lords of Wine and Oile:............101. H.250, 2

If smirking Wine be wanting here,............101. H.250, 36
Ore-come in musicke; with a wine,............120. H.293, 47
With bucksome meat and capring Wine:......127. H.319, 28
(Loving the brave Burgundian wine)..........135. H.336, 130
Butter of Amber, Cream, and Wine, and Oile..144. H.370, 5
So smells the Aire of spiced wine;...........145. H.375, 5
The wine of cherries, and to these,.............145. H.375, 19
No, no, thy bread, thy wine, thy jocund Beere..147. H.377, 57
But as thy meate, so thy immortall wine......147. H.377, 71
Flowes from the Wine, and graces it:.........148.. H.377, 74
And adds perfumes unto the Wine, which thou..148. H.377, 81
By cruse and measure; thus devoting Wine,..148. H.377, 83
Wine lead him on. Thus to a Grove............165. H.443, 19
In regard I want that Wine,.................182. H.489, 7
The Water turn'd to Wine.....................185. H.495, 8
Fill me my Wine in Christall; thus, and thus..187. H.502, 1
'Tis sin I know, 'tis sin to throtle Wine.........187. H.502, 4
To Fetch me Wine my Lucia went,............187. H.504, 1
Come thou, who art the Wine, and wit.........189. H.515, 1
Drinking wine, & crown'd with flowres..........191. H.519, 8
Not made of Ale, but spiced Wine;............193. H.521, 48
With daily Fyers: The last neglect of Wine:....197. H.539, 10
Or Sup, there wants the Incense and the Wine. 197. H.541, 4
As Wine.......................................198. H.544, 5
Of Lyrick Wine, both swell'd and crown'd,....198. H.544, 16
In Wine and Flowers:........................198. H.544, 20
Quaffing his full-crown'd bowles of burning Wine, 206. H.575, 33
And Maiden's-blush, for spiced wine............216. H.616, 34
Give me wine, and give me meate,............217. H. 620, 1
Our salt, our Corn, our Honie, Wine, and Oile) 225. H.642, 18
Above they are the Angels spiced wine.........226. H.645, 2
Drink Wine, and live here blithefull, while ye may: 228. H.655, 1
For Sugar-cakes and Wine;...................238. H.690, 2
Drink rich wine; and make good cheere,.......238. H.691, 3
As my small Cruse best fits my little Wine.....249. H.733, 3
Must needs wax cold, if wanting bread and wine. 258. H.768, 4
And richer Wine wo'dst give to me (thy guest) 262. H.783, 5
And for no less then Aromatick Wine..........262. H.783, 9
Stain'd by the Beames of Clarret wine:........268. H.811, 8
With the Wine that must be shed............280. H.870, 9
Out-did the meate, out-did the frolick wine.....289. H.911, 10
A drought of wine, ale, beere (at all).........291. H.919, 6
With Flowers and Wine,.....................296. H.946, 19
Then the dead Corps, or carkase of the Wine. 301. H.964, 2
But not spill Wine;..........................307. H.988, 3
When I drinke my capring wine:..............309. H.996, 2
When I drinke my wanton wine:..............309. H.996, 4
When I drinke my sprightly wine:............309. H.996, 6
When I drinke my frolick wine:...............309. H.996, 8
When I want my fragrant wine..............309. H.996, 10
And as he spake, his mouth ranne ore with wine. 313. H.1017, 4
That powres in oyle, as well as wine..........342. N.17, 10
Run Creame, (for Wine.).....................350. N.47, 50
Of Bread, and Wine with it:.................352. N.53, 8
My wine is mixt with weeping................353. N.56, 6
With Bread, and Wine, and Vessells furnished; 355. N.65, 4
Our sighs for Storax, teares for Wine;........360. N.83, 33
For now the Corne and Wine must faile:.......374. N.123, 14
The Wine Presse now is ta'ne from us,.........375. N.123, 53
Drunk up the wine of Gods fierce wrath;......400. N.266, 11
Ver. Chor. But I will sip a little wine;.......400. N.267, 12
Some Drops of Wine,........................401. N.268, 16
with oyle and wine,.....................431. ins. H.283, 60e
— — — — — — — — — —,................448. var. A.3, 22
Wine press See Wine
Wing The wing, to flie away;...................346. N.38, 2
A wing about thy Sepulcher!................361. N.83, 68
Ha's taken wing,............................375. N.123, 58
— — — — — — — — — —,..............448. var. A.3, 22
Winged That my wing'd ship may meet no Remora. 14. H.35, 4
A winged Snake has bitten me,.................50. H.139, 8
Thou mak'st me nimble, as the winged howers, 78. H.197, 51
Wings And Wings too, which did shiver;........27. H.81, 18
Next, his wilde eares, like Lethern wings full spread, 33. H.99, 3
Upon her wings presents the god unshorne......67. H.178, 2
Grac't with the Trout-flies curious wings,.......92. H.223, 72
Thy wings shall be embalm'd by me,...........103. H.255, 7
Has it a body? 2. I, and wings................130. H.329, 20
flies curious wings; and these among.........166. H.443, 69
Come then, and like two Doves with silv'rie wings, 205. H.575, 1
Hold but her hands; You hold both hands and wings. 271. H.823, 6
God hath two wings, which He doth ever move,..340. N.6, 1
Thou dwel'st aloft, and I want wings to flie.....352. N.52, 2
Night hath no wings, to him that cannot sleep; 358. N.77, 1
Wink Wink at small faults, the greater, ne'rthelesse 32. H.95, 3
Winner If thou, my Deere, a winner be.........238. H.690, 5
Winning A winning wave (deserving Note).......28. H.83, 9
Shall have for his winning a kisse...............99. H.243, 6
Of winning Colours, that shall move..........193. H.521, 53
Winning postures; and withall,................204. H.569, 9
In Prayer the Lips ne're act the winning part, 346. N.35, 1
Of Thy most winning countenance;...........395. N.246, 4
Wins While young Charles fights, and fighting wins the day. 254. H.756, 14
Falsehood winnes credit by uncertainties........287. H.902, 2
Winter Summer and Winter shall at one time show 59. H.154, 5
At last, i' th' noone of winter, did appeare......262. H.783, 13
Summer and Winter still to save his shooes.......332. H.116, 4
— — — — — — — —,...................443. var. H.580, 2
Winter-like Here Winter-like, to Frost and Snow. 329. H.1093, 4
Winter's That tels of Winters Tales and Mirth,..126. H.319, 11
Expos'd to all the comming Winters cold.......151. H.387, 4
As well the Winters, as the Summers Tide:....151. H.387, 6
But a Winters face in thee,....................266. H.803, 5
Why do's the chilling Winters morne...........364. N.96, 14
Wipe Who with thy leaves shall wipe (at need)......6. H.5, 1
Wiped She kist, and wip'd thir dove-like eyes;....31. H.92, 11
Wip't out few, (God knowes) if any...........373. N.121, 10
Wipes God from our eyes all teares hereafter wipes, 379. N.139, 1
Wisdom Wisdome and she together goe,.........35. H.106, 14
Work'st more then Wisdome, Art, or Nature can, 45. H.128, 24
What Wisdome, Learning, Wit, or Worth,.....48. H.134, 1
In her wisdome co'd beget....................57. H.149, 150
But with that wisdome, and that method, as..148. H.377, 85
Wisdom's 'Tis Wisdomes part to doubt a faithfull friend. 333. H.1121, 2
Wise No man at one time, can be wise, and love...8. H.10, 8
A wise man ev'ry way lies square..............37. H.106, 98
And when, wise Artist, that thou hast,.........48. H.133, 14
With wise suspicion:..........................55. H.149, 78
Though a wise man all pressures can sustaine:..60. H.158, 1
Be truer to him, then a wise Distrust............67. H.177, 2
By Arts wise hand, but to this end............76. H.193, 46
As the wise Cato had approv'd of thee..........78. H.197, 64
Love on a day (wise Poets tell)...............105. H.260, 1
And beautious Bride we do confess y'are wise,..113. H.283, 51
Do all things sweetly, and in comely wise;......124. H.313, 7
And when wise Poets shall search out to see..149. H.377, 135
Wise hand enchasing here those warts,........166. H.443, 60
All wise; all equall; and all just.............190. H.515, 31
To imply your Love is wise....................221. H.633, 31
Is the wise Masters Feet, and Hands..........230. H.662, 24
Be she witty, more then wise;................232. H.665, 3
With all wise speed for execution............252. H.749, 2
By their wise Counsell, then they be by Warre. 271. H.825, 2
Come and let's in solem wise.................280. H.870, 1
Attended thus (in a most solemn wise).........286. H.898, 3
Himselfe, at one time, can be wise, and Love...294. H.936, 4
God, the most Wise, is sparing of His talk......341. N.12, 2
Gifts blind the wise, and bribes do please,......357. N.72, 9
Ye must not be more pitifull then wise;........365. N.97, 16
How wise wast thou in all thy waies!.........375. N.123, 61
Mercy, the wise Athenians held to be..........380. N.148, 1
These temp'rall goods God (the most Wise) commends 387. N.201, 1
Wise-distrust Obedience, Wise-Distrust, Peace, shy.409. A.2, 95
Wisely Keeping the barking stomach wisely quiet, 35. H.106, 29
But to live round, and close, and wisely true..38. H.106, 135
But for us, who wisely see.......................96. H.231, 3
Your sober Hand-maid; who doth wisely chuse, 99. H.245, 6
Wisely wanton (like to me.)...................117. H.289, 4
But walke abroad, yet wisely well.............174. H.465, 13
Wisely to husband it;.........................289. H.911, 16
Wisemen's Bright as the Wise-men's Torch, which guided them 86. H.213, 21
Wiser Wiser Conclusions in mee, since I knowe..411. A.3, 53
Wish Ile wish I might turne all to eare,..........22. H.68, 2
We'll wish, in Hell we had been Last and First. 33. H.101, 4
Nor feare, or wish your dying day..............38. H.106, 146
As faultlesse; will not wish undone,............48. H.136, 11
This, as I wish for, so I hope to see;.........52. H.146, 17
And thousands gladly wish..................113. H.283, 49
I could wish you all, who love,................117. H.289, 1
I could wish you dispossest....................117. H.289, 5
I co'd wish, ye all, who frie.................117. H.289, 9
To kisse our hands, nor do we wish............133. H.336, 47
We'l wish both Them and Thee, good night.....165. H.443, 8
These I but wish for; but thy selfe shall see,..269. H.818, 9
And I wish all maidens mine,.................309. H.996, 5
Ile write no more of life; but wish twas ended, 334. H.1124, 3
And so to Bed: Pray wish us all Good Rest...419. A.10, 8
Wished Call forth fierce Lovers to their wisht Delights: 77. H.197, 6
For my wisht safety pay thy vowes,............175. H.465, 74
He wished me all Good speed.................295. H.942, 8
— — — — — — — —,...................452. var. H.128, 40
Wishes Thy pious wishes are, (though thou not there) 37. H.106. 91
Or Lords be, (granting my wishes)............239. H.695, 9
Neer to the wishes of his heart:................351. N.50, 3

No, no, (my God) Thou know'st my wishes be..352. N.51, 13
Wisheth Wisheth his body, not his soule, good speed. 277. H.855, 2
Wisp See Will-o'-the-wisp
Wit See True-wit
But for the Court, the Country wit..............6. H.2, 17
Next, Corinna, for her wit,........................16. H.39, 9
Not onely subject-matter for our wit,............41. H.117, 5
What Wisdome, Learning, Wit, or Worth,........48. H.134, 1
Sin, in's Nap'rie, not to express his wit;.......114. H.283, 68
Wit and new misterie; read, and..............115. H.283, 123
Paying before you praise; and cockring wit,..141. H.359, 15
And spring fresh Rose-buds, while the salt, the wit 148. H.377, 73
Oh fie upon 'em! Lastly too, all witt.......150. H.382, 17
And sitting, see the wiles, wayes, walks of wit,..187. H.506, 3
Come thou, who art the Wine, and wit........189. H.515, 1
There thou shalt be; and be the wit,..........192. H.521, 27
For civill, cleane, and circumcised wit,.........194. H.526, 1
From whom we'l reckon. Wit came in, but since 194. H.526, 5
We'l venter (if we can) at wit:................215. H.616, 4
Although ye have a stock of wit,..............218. H.626, 6
Thy Nut-browne mirth; thy Russet wit;......231. H.662, 60
But by Apollo! as I worship wit,..............234. H.673, 7
Neere to the well of wit;......................261. H.778, 2
All has been plundered from me, but my wit;..272. H.830, 1
Of such a wit the world sho'd have no more...289. H.911, 20
For brave comportment, wit without offence,....297. H.947, 1
Ev'n so those Lines, pen'd by my wanton Wit, 339. N.1, 3
Witch There was hidden by the Witch.........55. H.149, 90
— — — — — — — — —,.............434. var. H.293, 52
Witchcrafts To my pretty Witchcrafts all:........10. H.19, 2
Witching To all thy witching beauties, Goe, Away. 46. H.128, 40
Ph. Alas for me! Ch. Shame on thy witching note, 248. H.730, 11
With (Partial List)
There with the Reed, thou mayst expresse..........5. H.2, 7
And with thy Eclogues intermixe....................5. H.2, 9
On with thy fortunes then, what e're they be;....6. H.3, 7
Away with doubts, all scruples hence remove;....8. H.10, 7
All things decay with Time: The Forrest sees....23. H.69, 1
There playes the Saphire with the Chrysolite.....30. H.88, 10
Blest with perpetuall greene,......................30. H.89, 7
They must be borne with, and in rev'rence had...32. H.97, 2
Nature with little is content...................33. H.100, 4
That Roses shew, when misted o're with Lawn...34. H.104, 4
White, warme, and soft to lye with me.........34. H.105, 10
Whom (Stars consenting with thy Fate) thou hast 35. H.106, 33
Warnes the last Watch; but with the Dawne dost rise 36. H.106, 57
Making thy peace with heav'n, for some late fault, 36. H.106, 59
Attended with those desp'rate cares,............36. H.106, 64
But thou at home, blest with securest ease,....36. H.106, 69
Or let me 'gender with eternall frost...........40. H.113, 6
Contented with the bed of one...................41. H.116, 8
When as the Lilly marries with the Rose!......44. H.124, 2
Play not with the maiden-haire;...............52. H.147, 3
When she lyes with Jove, then she.............59. H.155, 10
If thou wilt say, that I shall live with thee;....60. H.156, 3
Here, with all her jealousies:...................61. H.160, 6
Troubled with Green-sicknesses,................64. H.167, 2
Had met t'engender with the night;............64. H.169, 6
Are wanton with their itch; scratch, and 'twill please. 66. H.173, 8
Pleas'd with transgression ev'ry where:........66. H.175, 4
And pounc't with Stars, it shew'd to me........67. H.175, 9
Thou hast both Wind and Tide with thee; Thy way 73. H.186, 3
To juggle with the sense........................76. H.193, 40
Was lately whipt for lying with a Wench.......79. H.199, 2
For with the flowrie earth,......................80. H.201, 3
Shew'd like to Creame, enspir'd with Strawberries: 81. H.202, 2
Amint. And I will beare along with you........86. H.213, 39
Wither'd with yeeres, and bed-rid Mumma lyes..90. H.222, 1
Girt with small bones, instead of walls.........90. H.223, 10
To have men think he's troubled with the Gout: 98. H.239, 2
Let but thy voice engender with the string,....102. H 252, 1
(Made rivall with the aire).....................103. H.255, 2
Off then with grave clothes; put fresh colours on; 105. H.259, 9
Gladding his pallat with some store..........119. H.293, 35
But 'tis otherwise with me;....................128. H.322, 9
(Larr thus conspiring with our mirth)......135. H.336, 124
Whose fortunes I have frolickt with:.........136. H.336, 132
Rubie-lipt, and tooth'd with Pearl:............136. H.337, 2
Where laden spits, warp't with large Ribbs of Beefe, 146. H.377, 9
When I shall couple with my Valentine.........149. H.378, 4
Keepe it for ever; grounded with the good,....152. H.392, 7
That will with flowers the Tomb bestrew,......156. H.412, 7
Now Patrick with his footmanship has done,.....158. H.418, 1
Tinseld with Twilight, He, and They..........165. H.443, 21
What ha's the Court to do with Swaines,......184. H.492, 21
Shall pranke thy Hooke with Lillies...........184. H.492, 32
Beset with stately Figures (every where)....185. H.496, 2
Growes old with the yeere,......................196. H.534, 17
That dyes with the next December.............196. H.534, 18
Cloy'd they are up with Arse; but hope, one blast 226. H.650, 3
Thy May-poles too with Garlands grac't:......230. H.662, 53
Art discontent with me.........................240. H.705, 4
She lookt as she'd been got with child.........251. H.740, 7
While misery keeps in with patience...........257. H.765, 4
To make her Philters with:...................258. H.767, 14
Cloth'd all with incorrupted light;.............270. H.819, 5
Yet ere thou counsel'st with thy Glasse,........271. H.824, 5
Then if thy voice commingle with the String..276. H.851, 3
Down with the Rosemary and Bayes,..........285. H.892, 1
Down with the Misleto;.........................285. H.892, 2
What others have with cheapnesse seene, and ease, 330. H.1100, 1
God when He's angry here with any one,........340. N.7, 1
Withal See Therewithal
Down dead for griefe, and end my woes withall: 11. H.22, 8
Julia was carelesse, and withall,...................12. H.27, 1
Tempting down to slide withall:.................15. H.36, 9
Put in secrecies withall,........................116. H.285, 7
Shew me thy waste; Then let me there withall,..154. H.403, 5
Winning postures; and withall,.................204. H.569, 9
With mellow Lips, and luscious there withall....226. H.649, 2
Her cloathes held up, she shew'd withall.......247. H.729, 3
Yet freedome, shee enjoyes withall.............281. H.876, 10
To prettie girles to play withall:...............294. H.937, 2
Leave others Beauty, to set up withall..........299. H.958, 6
Tipled he was; and tipling lispt withall;........313. H.1017, 5
Men to repent, but when He strikes withall.....342. N.19, 2
Whatever comes, let's be content withall:.......353. N.55, 1
To beawtify the legg and foote withall..........406. A.1, 90
Withdraw And thou (Anthea) must withdraw from him 20. H.55, 2
Withdrew Nero commanded; but withdrew his eyes 236. H.679, 1
Wither Pansies will weep; and Marygolds will wither; 41. H.118, 5
Thou art a plant sprung up to wither never,......98. H.240, 1
And all thy hopes of her must wither,.........107. H.263, 21
That Ye must quickly wither..................184. H.493, 4
Farre faster then the first can wither...........289. H.912, 8
To starve, or wither..........................361. N.83, 70
But all we wither and our Light................413. A.4, 10
Withered Ye Roses almost withered;................7. H.9, 2
Like to a Lillie withered:......................47. H.132, 2
Wither'd my hand, and palsie-struck my tongue...84. H.210, 10
Yet wither'd, ere you can be set..............88. H.216, 17
Wither'd with yeeres, and bed-rid Mumma lyes; 90. H.222, 1
With withered cherries; Mandrakes eares;.....120. H.293, 43
Or Roses, being withered:....................233. H.670, 25
Then will I heave my wither'd hand...........303. H.973, 15
To spring; though now a wither'd flower.........361. N.84, 8
And Olive Branch is wither'd now..............375. N.123, 52
Kernells, and wither'd hawes: the rest....439. ins. H.443, 45n
Withhold Trees this year beare; next, they their wealth with-hold:................................292. H.922, 3
Within But sees these things within thy Map.....36. H.106, 72
Had we kept close, or play'd within,...........48. H.136, 6
Within the Chamber here.....................56. H.149, 108
That thou, within few months, shalt be..........63. H.166, 7
As dead, within the West;.......................72. H.185, 6
Sadly I walk't within the field,..................73. H.187, 1
Within my Lucia's cheek,......................83. H.207, 5
Within the Virgins Coronet....................88. H.216, 18
Within the concave of a Nut,..................120. H.293, 40
Enclos'd within a christall shrine:............135. H.336, 98
Within a Lillie? Center plac't?.................164. H.440, 4
The holy Entrance; where within..............166. H.443, 65
Within your Greenie-Kalendar.................169. H.449, 14
Keepes still within a just circumference........210. H.590, 4
Within the Bosome of my Love your grave......249. H.734, 2
Within her Lawnie Continent,..................250. H.740, 3
I saw a Flie within a Beade...................269. H.817, 1
Within the Kingdomes of the Deep;..............340. N.3, 8
First, Fear and Shame without, then Guilt within. 341. N.11, 2
And sore without, and sick within:..............342. N.17, 2
When I lie within my bed,.......................347. N.41, 5
Sleeps, laid within some Ark of Flowers,.........367. N.102, 5
The strength of Baptisme, that's within;.........396. N.253, 1
Now they the Elves within a trice,........434. ins. H.293, a
— — — — — — — — — —,............437. var. H.336, 112
Without Droops, dies, and falls without the cleavers stroke. 23. H.69, 6
But thou at home without or tyde or gale,......36. H.106, 77
Without a sad looke, or a solemne teare?........73. H.186, 10
Without a Strawberrie:..........................75. H.193, 11
Without some Scean cast over,.................76. H.193, 39
Without a fame in death?.......................85. H.211, 16
Without or Lime, or Wood, or Stone:..........90. H.223a, 4
Pure hands bring hither, without staine........91. H.223, 42
Not without mickle majesty....................165. H.443, 6

To those, who crave............................171. H.455, 4
Who can scoure Linnens with her own salt reeume?
178. H.474, 6
Of such rare Saint-ships, who did here consume..185. H.496, 3
Being drunke, who 'twas that Can'd his Ribs last night.
186. H.501, 4
Come thou, who are the Wine, and wit........189. H.515, 1
Out of the world he must, who once comes in:..199. H.548, 1
As in our clothes, so likewise he who lookes,....202. H.559, 1
Who dead, deserve our best remembrances.......209. H.584, 8
Who covets more, is evermore a slave..........213. H.607, 2
And talke of Brides; & who shall make.......215. H.616, 21
This done, we'l draw lots, who shall buy.......215. H.616, 25
Who then the joyning Priest shall be..........216. H.616, 30
Of which who drank, he said no thought........222. H.635, 3
Yet, who wo'd think,..........................229. H.659, 8
A wager, who the best shall play,.............243. H.716, 2
As these have done to Thee, who art the one,....256. H.763, 5
Who claim the Fat, and Fleshie for their share,...272. H.826, 5
Who violates the Customes, hurts the Health,..318. H.1041, 1
Who Weds, ore-buyes his weal with woe.......320. H.1052, 4
Who may do most, do's least: The bravest will..321. H.1057, 1
Who plants an Olive, but to eate the Oile?....322. H.1060, 1
Let's trie of us who shall the first expire;.....333. H.1120, 3
How am I bound to Two! God, who doth give....355. N.62, 1
Take then his Vowes, who, if he had it, would...369. N.105, 5
For Tabitha, who dead lies here,..............374. N.123, 11
For those, who did as malefactors die..........384. N.180, 4
Natures, like ours, wee who haue spent our tyme..410. A.3, 15
But tis the god of Nature, who Intends.........411. A.3, 57
Cha. Who calls? who calls? Euc. One overwhelm'd with ruth;
416. A.8, 3
Whoe'er But he will say, who e'r those Circlets seeth,
197. H.543, 3
Love is a sirrup; and who er'e we see......297. H.949, 1
Whole And stroak'd the stripes, and I was whole agen.
16. H.40, 6
Or, like the soule, whole every where: 24. H.73, 6
That, which subverts whole nature, grief and care;
45. H.123, 21
As in the whole world thou canst find,..........108. H.267, 7
Sound or unsound, be they rent or whole,......143. H.368, 3
Shakes the whole Roofe, or ruines all..........153. H.395, 5
The whole world die, and turn to dust with thee.
155. H.405, 16
And let the whole world then dispose..........164. H.441, 11
Neither broke i'th whole, or part.............183. H.490, 20
Be she whole, or be she rent,..................253. H.750, 13
If not to th' whole, yet satisfy'd in part.........267. H.804, 12
Three, unto whom the whole world give applause;
276. H.851, 7
Part, or the whole of Thee......................369. N.106, 2
Meets in the whole and maks a harmony........406. A.1, 106
Wholesome The wholsome savour of thy mighty Chines
146. H.377, 7
If wholsome Diet can re-cure a man,...........319. H.1049, 1
Who'll Who'l be her Valentine.................56. H.149, 116
Who'l give ye then a sheltring shed,...........218. H.626, 3
Who'l let ye by their fire sit?..................218. H.626, 5
Who'l hear, and so judge righteously..........243. H.716, 22
Wholly As wholly Thine;.......................351. N.47, 56
Whom (Partial List)
And whom she touch't, turne sweet..............9. H.15, 12
Blest is the Bride, on whom the Sun doth shine;
113. H 283, 48
For one to whom espous'd are all the Arts;....121. H.301, 2
Whom they neglected, thou hast crown'd a Poet. 143. H.365, 8
Not Virgils Gnat, to whom the Spring........186. H.497, 9
To gaine her whom I wo'd get..................209. H.585, 6
Or Phyllis, whom hard Fate forc't on,........215. H.616, 13
Keep here still, Closet-Gods, 'fore whom I've set 227. H.652, 13
And hazards those most, whom the most He loves;
370 N.108, 4
Whome love admitts to this Hesperides...........405. A.1, 70
Whore To keep out the Letcher, and keep in the whore:
97. H.233, 2
The Whore to come out, or the Letcher come in..97. H.233, 4
Say, who's the worst, th' exactor, or the whore?.220. H.631, 4
Whoredom Scobble for Whoredome whips his wife; and cryes,
44. H.126, 1
Whorry Whither dost thou whorry me;..........157. H.415, 1
Who's Who's that (said I) beats there,.........26. H.81, 5
Say, who's the worst, th' exactor, or the whore? 220. H.631, 4
Unsoft to him who's smooth to thee............252. H.746, 2
He is a serving, who's a Trencher-man.........265. H.796, 4
Grace with the Gods, who's sorry for his sinne. 329. H.1095, 4
To do Him honour; who's our King,............365. N.96, 31
Of Him, who's Lord of Heav'n and Earth;.....366. N.98, 19
God, who's in Heav'n, will hear from thence;..381. N.160, 1
Whose (Partial List)
When that day comes, whose evening sayes I'm gone
14. H.35, 1
And whose the pretty prize shu'd be,............31. H.92, 3
Whose heart, whose hand, whose ev'ry part spake love.
42. H.122, 8
In Wine, whose each cup's worth..............80. H.201, 19
Feed him ye must, whose food fils you.......102. H.250, 52
Sweet Western Wind, whose luck it is,..........103. H.255, 1
Beset with Mirtles; whose each leafe drops Love.
107. H.265, 4
For his love then, whose sacred Reliques show..137. H.341, 7
But you, my Lord, are One, whose hand along 141. H.359, 13
Such is thy house, whose firme foundations trust
148. H.377, 103
But pitie those, whose flanks grow great,......200. H 552, 15
Whose now the prize and wager is............244. H.716, 42
Whose Field his foot is, and whose Barn his shooe?
270. H.822, 4
A little house, whose humble Roof..............349. N.47, 3
'Tis he is borne, whose quickning Birth....364. N.96, 19
To those virgins, whose briske heu..........450. ins. A.9, 52
Whoso Soe full of clarrett that whoe soe pricks a vine
405. A.1, 49
Why (Partial List)
Ther's still more cause, why I the more should love.
10. H.16, 6
I saw a Cherry weep, and why?..................12. H.23, 1
But why? why longer doe I gaze upon..........45. H.128, 37
And why, my pretty Lad, said she?............50. H.139, 6
Why doe not all fresh maids appeare............103. H.256, 1
Why doe ye weep, sweet Babes? can Tears....104. H.257, 1
The reason, why..............................104. H.257, 16
Why nothing now, but lonely sit,.............132. H.334, 3
Why then, since life to us is short,............133. H.336, 31
For why sayes he, all debts and their arreares, 142. H.363, 3
I know ye do; and that's the why,.............158. H.420, 9
Why then, say, what is he.....................160. H.422, 17
Why! yet to shew that thou art just,..........169. H.446, 11
If so, why then art not These Verses hurld,....172. H.459, 3
Why do yee fall so fast?.......................176. H.467, 2
Nor will; for why, Pudica, this may know,.....180. H.477, 5
Ah! Lycidas, come tell me why...............183. H.492, 1
Aske me why I send you here................208. H.580, 1
Ask me why the stalk is weak.................208. H.580, 9
What is a Kisse? Why this, as some approve;..218. H.622, 1
In the Vision I askt, why?..................219. H.628, 3
Snare, ten i' th' hundred calls his wife; and why?
220. H.631, 1
What is the cause? Why Gander will reply,....223. H.636, 3
Why so lonely on the hill?...................305. H.984, 4
But why He did not, let me tell wherefore:......356. N.69, 2
The why, and wherefore all things here........364. N.96, 12
The cause, why things thus fragrant be:........364. N.96, 18
— — — — — — — — — —,................425. var. H.197, 20
Wicked Since Jack and Jill both wicked be;......163. H.434, 1
Against the wicked, in another world............357. N.74, 4
But with the wicked if He doth comply,........385, N.188, 3
Because the wicked do partake of them:......387. N.201, 4
Wickedness Enfeebles much the seeds of wickednesse.
109. H.270, 2
Wicker With Wicker Arks did come............110. H.274, 6
Wicker-baskets In Wicker-baskets Maids shal bring
192. H.521, 35
Wickes Let's live, my Wickes, then, while we may,
132. H.336, 15
'Tis constancy (my Wickes) which keepes......134. H.336, 62
We'l drink, my Wickes, untill we be..........136. H.336, 138
Yet sho'd I chance, (my Wicks) to see.........321. H.1056, 7
Wicks See Wickes
Wide As not too wide,.........................65. H.172, 16
In his wide Codpiece, (dinner being done)......118. H.292, 5
Widow See Long-lamented-widowhood
Like to a widdow drown'd in woe:..............47. H.132, 6
An old, old widow Greedy needs wo'd wed,.....129. H.326, 1
Or for Widow, Maid, or Wife..................182. H.490, 4
Old Widdow Prouse to do her neighbours evill 266. H.801, 1
Old Widow Shopter, when so ere she cryes,....331. H.1107, 1
Widowhood See Long-lamented-widowhood
Each like a poore and pitied widowhood.........150. H.382, 4
Like a poore Lady lost in Widdowhood:.........251. H.745, 4
Widow's No Widowes Tenement was rackt to guild
149. H.377, 118
To drye the Widowes teares; and stop her Swoones,
201. H.557, 17
Widows And weeping Widowes long opprest....190. H.515, 21
Who see, or heare poor Widdowes crie:........373. N.123, 4
That Thou on Widdowes didst bestow.........374. N.123, 26
Thy Widdowes stand forsaken.................374. N.123, 30
Widows' And eyes, to pitie Widdowes teares...373. N.123, 6
Wife And never take a wife......................13. H.31, 3
Of Wife) about I'le lead;......................13. H.31, 8
Doe, and have parted here a Man and Wife:......26. H.79, 2
Is, the fruition of a wife:......................35. H.106, 32
But still thy wife, by chast intentions led,......35. H.106, 41
Elizium to thy wife and thee;.................38. H.108, 138
Scobble for Whoredome whips his wife; and cryes,
44. H.126, 1
Nay, thou more neare then kindred, friend, man, wife,
45. H.128, 3
Come in for Dowrie with a Wife.................49. H.137, 2
Of the good man and the wife..................55. H.149, 60
First, Jollies wife is lame; then next, loose-hipt: 62. H.163, 1
But out of hope his wife might die to beare 'em..72. H.184, 2
The pleasing wife, the house, the ground........132. H.336, 9

Half rotten, and without an eye,...............166. H.443, 52
(Not without glory) Noble Sir, you are,.......170. H.451, 2
Fully, without exception;......................191. H.520, 2
Chaste I liv'd, without a wife,................199. H.546, 3
Without the scope..............................211. H.596, 2
Like Tapers cleare without number.............217. H.619, 15
Without extortion, from thy soyle:............233. H.670, 8
And title me without compare..................243. H.716, 34
Without a thought of hurt, or feare;..........283. H.883, 8
Though from without no foes at all we feare;...292. H.928, 1
For brave comportment, wit without offence,....297. H 947, 1
Without their use we may have men?..........297. H.948, 2
Him, as He is, is labour without end.............340. N.8, 2
First, Fear and Shame without, then Guilt within.
341. N.11, 2
And sore without, and sick within:.............342. N.17, 2
The calfe without meale n'ere was offered;.......345. N.34, 2
Without the heart, lip-labour nothing is.........345. N.34, 4
Without the sweet concurrence of the Heart.......346. N.35, 2
Without due reverence, playes the cheaters game...347. N.39, 6
Leave that without, then enter in;..............366. N.98, 6
In, or without; all, all belongs to Thee:.......368. N.103, 4
Whom ease makes his, without the help of blowes.
372. N.116, 4
To bark, or bite, without Thee?...............373. N.122, 12
The Good without the Bad are here plac'd never.
383. N.172, 2
Without the least hope of affection...........392. N.230, 26
(S. Ambrose sayes) without the Thorn:........396. N.251, 2
Without the fragrant Rose-bud, born;..........396. N.251, 4
But ne're the Rose without the Thorn.........396. N.251, 5
That without wrath, which wrath doth force us to.
397. N.259, 4
Those act without regard, when once a King,...399. N.263, 24
If so; I'le thither follow, without feare;........403. N.271, 7
Where nature in a whiteness without spott........405. A.1, 61
Withstand As to withstand the blow............335. H.1129, 4
I give thee this that shall withstande............407. A.2, 10
Withstanding Withstanding entrance unto me....277. H.854, 4
Withstood Be he oppos'd, or be he not withstood,..349. N.44, 3
Might I make choice, long life sho'd be with-stood;
392. N.230, 9
Witness Witnesse their Homage, when they come and strew
107. H.265, 7
I call all Maids to witnesse too...............165. H.442, 12
Witnessed The Ev'ning witnest that I dy'd......109. H.271, 2
Witnesses See Ear-witnesses
Markt in thy Book for faithfull Witnesses.......188. H.507, 4
And winde all other witnesses:.................357. N.72, 10
Wit's Thy wits great over-plus;.................289. H.911, 14
Wits But warm their wits, and turn their lines to gold.
141. H.359, 8
Good wits get more fame by their punishment...317. H.1034, 2
Witty Then stately Virgil, witty Ovid, by......206. H.575, 39
Of Cupid, and his wittie coozning:.............228. H.658, 6
Jane is a wench that's wittie;..................229. H.659, 7
Thy witty wiles to draw, and get..............231. H.662, 64
Be she witty, more then wise;.................232. H.665, 3
Our witty appetites to please,...........436. ins. H.336, 48f
Wives See Housewives
Old wives have often told, how they.............18. H.46, 1
To be, and is, the very best of Wives:............26. H.79, 4
Husbands and Wives by streakes to chuse:....127. H.319, 22
We busse our Wantons, but our Wives we kisse.
189. H.512, 2
Wives' See Housewives'
Wizards Thwart all Wizzards, and with these....286. H.897, 7
Wo'd (Partial List)
Ere I wo'd love at all...........................28. H.85, 8
Say too, She wo'd have this;.....................43. H.123, 31
That they wo'd each Primrose-tide,.............44. H.125, 2
She soon wo'd leave her spheare,...............54. H.149, 37
Who wo'd not think this Yonker fierce to fight?..65. H.171, 3
To see what comfort it wo'd yeeld:.............73. H.187, 2
Gubbs call's his children Kitlings: and wo'd bound
80. H.200, 1
That it wo'd make thee see,....................80. H.201, 16
Tell-tales I wo'd have them be..................82. H.203, 3
Whether I wo'd; but (ah!) I know not how,....84. H.210, 7
They wo'd have shew'd civility;................89. H.219, 4
Now this the Fairies wo'd have known,.........91. H.223, 22
And for what use, scarce man wo'd think it......93. H.223, 124
Wo'd have this Lecture read,.................105. H.257, 26
Of Emits eggs; what wo'd he more?..........119. H.293, 36
If I co'd, I wo'd not so.......................128. H.322, 12
An old, old widow Greedy needs wo'd wed,......129. H.326, 1
Woman wo'd bring him more then co'd be told, 129. H.326, 4
She that will weare thy teares, wo'd weare thine eyes.
131. H.330, 15
Wo'd I see Lawn, clear as the Heaven, and thin?
158. H.416, 1
Daysies wo'd shut, and closing, sigh and weep...159. H.421, 26
There wo'd be no Passion.....................163. H.433, 2
Yee pretty Huswives, wo'd ye know............164. H.442, 1
The worke that I wo'd put ye to?..............164. H.442, 2
Wo'dst Wods't thou know, besides all these,......103. H.253, 11
Wod'st thou to sincere-silver turn thy mold?....144. H.370, 7
And richer Wine wo'dst give to me (thy guest).262. H.783, 5
Reader, wo'dst thou more have known?........289. H.910, 3
Tell that Brave Man, fain thou wo'dst have access
301. H.963, 1
Woe Or flie abroad to seeke for woe...............6. H.2, 20
Thus woe succeeds a woe; as wave a wave........18. H.48, 2
Woe, woe to them, who (by a ball of strife).......26. H.79, 1
Like to a widdow drown'd in woe..........47. H.132, 6
And that is Death, the end of Woe.............60. H.157, 6
This if thou dost, woe to thee Furie, woe,.......82. H.204, 9
As to entrance his paine, or cure his woe.........99. H.244, 4
That nothing shoots, but war and woe..........139. H.353, 6
Ah woe is me, woe, woe is me,................156. H.412, 9
Fate gives a meeting. Death's the end of woe...257. H.766, 2
Teares have their springs from joy, as well as woe.
275. H.842, 4
Who Weds, ore-buyes his weal with woe.......320. H.1052, 4
From thence, to everlasting woe:................358. N.78, 8
Crosses we must have; or, hereafter woe.........359. N.81, 2
But to thy woe;..............................360. N.83, 28
Wealth brings much woe:......................368. N.104, 4
Woe worth the Time, woe worth the day,......374, N.123, 21
Our Destination to eternall woe.............390. N.219, 4
Woes See Wooes
Down dead for grief, and end my woes withall:..11. H.22, 8
That in short time my woes shall cease;........73. H.187, 10
Mont. Set with the Sunne, thy woes: Scil. The day grows old:
160. H.421, 41
Tears will spring, where woes are deep.........306. H.984, 32
Thy woes and weep...........................314. H.1024, 23
So she, to keep her mighty woes in awe,........384. N.180, 5
Thy dreadfull Woes..........................401. N.268, 29
He was——Cha. Say what. Euc. Ay me, my woes are deep.
416. A.8, 11
Euc. Great are my woes. Cha. And great must that Grief be,
416. A.8, 21
Wolf Offer'd up a Wolfe to thee. 151. H.386, 8
Of sheep, (safe from the Wolfe and Fox)....230. H.662, 41
May no Wolfe howle, or Screech-Owle stir......361. N.83, 67
— — — — — — — — —,.............421. var. H.106, 52
Wolf-like-man To free the Orphan from that Wolfe-like-man,
201. H.557, 15
Wolves From rav'ning wolves, the fleecie sheep...36. H.106, 52
Had Wolves or Tigers seen but thee,............89. H.219, 3
Woman Learne of me what Woman is............76. H.195, 2
How hard a woman 'tis to please?.............103. H.253, 12
Woman wo'd bring him more then co'd be told,..129. H.326, 4
Of creatures, woman is the best...............250. H.739, 4
Christ did her Woman, not her Mary call:......386. N.192, 2
But no more Woman, being strong in Faith;....386. N.192, 3
— — — — — — — — — —,.............442. var. H.465, 39
Womankind No fault in womankind, at all,......118. H.291, 15
In thee, all faith of Woman-kind.............176. H.465, 80
Of woman-kind, first die I will;................250. H.739, 2
And thus through Woman-kind we see.........283. H.885, 9
All Pleasures meet in Woman-kind............327. H.1082, 4
Woman's Of Womans beauty? and with hand more rude
49. H.138, 5
Little you are; for Womans sake be proud;......212. H.600, 1
Womb That shew the womb shall thrive:........55. H.149, 56
Praise me, for having such a fruitfull wombe;....58. H.151, 3
With the third key He opes and shuts the wombe;
390. N.224, 3
Women No fault in women to refuse............118. H.291, 1
No fault in women, to confesse.................118. H.291, 3
No fault in women, to lay on...................118. H.291, 5
No fault in women, to make show..............118. H.291, 9
No fault in women, though they be............118. H.291, 13
Women, although they ne're so goodly make it,..235. H.675, 1
Naught are all Women: I say no,..............283. H.885, 1
What need we marry Women, when............297. H.948, 1
Have we of Women or their seed?............297. H.948, 14
— — — — — — — — — — — —,.............441. var. H.465, 38
— — — — — — — — — — — —,.............442. var. H.465, 80
Women's — — — — — — — — —, ...443. var. H.600, 1
Won Is wone with flesh, not Drapery...........154. H.402, 6
(Undone as oft as done) I'm wonne;...........174. H.465, 32
Lamented Maid! he won the day,..............360. N.83, 23
What though your laden Altar now has wonne
432. ins. H.283, 70a
Wonder For tincture, wonder at...................12. H.23, 8
(Far more with wonder, then with feare).......36. H.106, 84
It seems a wonder unto me,....................163. H.434, 2
This night, and more for the wonder,..........225. H.643, 21
This with a wonder when ye do,...............245. H.720, 11
And wonder at Those Things that thou dost know.
257. H.763, 22
Which wee, and times to come, shall wonder at. 310. H.1002, 2
O Thou, the wonder of all dayes!..............359. N.83, 1
Thou wonder of all Maids, li'st here,..........360. N.83, 13
To work a wonder, God would have her shown,..384. N.183, 1
Then, with a wonder, I confesse,..............372. N.118, 5
So that the wonder is not halfe so great,........388. N.208, 5
To wonder and affrightment: Thou art He,....398. N.263, 21
Bearing aloft this rich round world of wonder.....405. A.1, 46
Wonderment To the Triumvir, Love and Wonderment.
79. H.197, 76
Wonderous — — — — — — — —,........441. var. H.465, 37

Wonders Why then, go on to act: Here's **wonders** to be done, 401. N.268, 7
Wont I cannot pipe as I was **wont** to do,........205. H.573, 1
Won't Why frowns my Sweet? Why **won't** my Saint confer 77. H.197, 25
Won't for his tenth part ask you one..........208. H.581, 6
Times that are ill **wo'nt** still be so............247. H.725, 6
Wonted Who hither at her **wonted** howers.......145. H.376, 5
May all shie Maids, at **wonted** hours,...........361. N.83, 73
But first cast off thy **wonted** Churlishness........416. A.8, 6
Woo I'le doe my best to win, when'ere I **wooe**:....31. H.91, 1
None then will **wooe** you.......................32. H.94, 12
Her, though she **wooe** with teares...............56. H.149, 98
Begin to **wooe**:...............................87. H.214, 4
That when ere I **wooe**, I find..................138. H.346, 3
Thou gav'st me leave to **wooe**;................142. H.364, 2
Though I do like to **wooe**;.....................160. H.422, 2
But if they **wooe** thee, do thou say,............174. H.465, 29
Never beg, or humbly **wooe**.....................182. H.490, 11
Give me words wherewith to **wooe**,.............204. H.569, 7
Go **wooe** young Charles no more to looke,........214. H.611, 1
Next we will act, how young men **wooe**;......215. H.616, 19
Then Julia let me **wooe** thee,...................217. H.619, 16
Ph. Charon! O gentle Charon! let me **wooe** thee, 248. H.730, 1
The nimble howers **wooe** us on to wed,.........261. H.781, 5
Mine eyes must **wooe** you; (though I sigh the while) 274. H.837, 7
This day I goe to **wooe**;......................281. H.874, 7
Wo'd I **wooe**, and wo'd I winne,...............286. H.897, 1
'Twill make a tongless man to **wooe**............325. H.1075, 2
Which if that can't Thy pittie **wooe**,.............349. N.46, 7
Can I not **wooe** thee to passe by................357. N.72, 3
Wood The proud Dictator of the State-like **wood**:...23. H.69, 4
Without or Lime, or **Wood**, or Stone:..........90. H.223a, 4
Nor made of glasse, or **wood**, or stone,.........91. H.223, 56
Corrupted **wood**; serve here for shine...........167. H.443, 75
And of any **wood** ye see,......................204. H.569, 15
Dares now range the **wood**;....................225. H.643, 14
Till they be hid o're with a **wood** of darts.......370. N.109, 2
Woodbine Through **Woodbine**, and Sweet-bryers...55. H.149, 68
With crawling **Woodbine** over-spread:...........192. H.521, 6
Wood-nymph Many a sweet-fac't **Wood-Nymph** here is seene, 107. H.265, 5
Wood-nymphs And while the **Wood-nimphs** my cold corps inter, 19. H.50, 3
Wooed **Woo'd** to come suck the milkie Teat:.....36. H.106, 50
And some have wept, and **woo'd**, and plighted Troth, 69. H.178, 49
Wooer Who both your **wooer**, and your Poet is...274. H.837, 2
Wooers By wretched **Wooers** sent,..............131. H.330, 6
Wooers have Tongues of Ice, but burning hearts. 274. H.837, 10
— — — — — — — — — —,.............441. var. H.465, 4
Wooes To meet it, when it **woo's** and seemes to fold 115. H.283, 116
Who by a double Proxie **woes**...................409. A.2, 82
Wooing's My **wooing's** ended: now my wedding's neere; 180. H.479, 1
Wool See **Lamb's-wool**
Fill, and winde up with whitest **wooll**.........58. H.149, 162
(With whitest **Wool** be ever crown'd that day!) 86. H.213, 14
This flock of **wooll**, and this rich lock of hair,..159. H.421, 15
And then a Rug of carded **wooll**,..............167. H.443, 96
Rich, by the Ductile **Wool** and Flax...........221. H.633, 43
Of short sweet grasse, as backs with **wool**.....230. H.662, 43
By those soft Tods of **wooll**...................257. H.767, 1
Farewell the Flax and Reaming **wooll**,.........374. N.123, 41
Or lyke as **woole** meetes steele, giue way.........408. A.2, 69
Into your selves like **wooll** together spunne, 431. ins. H.283, 50h
Woolly — — — — — — — — —, ...421. var. H.106, 52
Woolly-bubbles Whose **woollie-bubbles** seem'd to drowne 167. H.443, 88
Woosted See **Worsted**
Word See **Gnat's-watchword**
Untrusse, his Master bade him; and that **word**..65. H.171, 5
The **word** is Roman; but in English knowne:...106. H.261, 3
Speak but the **word**, and Ile take you...........112. H.281, 6
Is in this **word**, Batchelour...................199. H.546, 6
Modest I will be; but one **word** Ile say........201. H.557, 21
Ere a good **word** can be spoke:...............255. H.761, 18
Speak thou the **word**, they'l kindle by and by....261. H.781, 4
One **word** more I had to say;...................270. H.821, 5
(By his **word**) the Sun to stand:...............276. H.850, 10
For every sentence, clause and **word**,............339. N.2, 3
Speak but the **word**, and cure me quite.........344. N.29, 10
Instead of that, a sweet and gentle **word**:........356. N.71, 2
God, is His Name of Nature; but that **word**....379. N.141, 1
Word's The **words** found true, C. M. remember me. 26. H.79, 10
And, you must know, your Lords **word's** true,..102. H.250, 51
Words Melting melodious **words**, to Lutes of Amber. 22. H.67, 4
Aire coyn'd to **words**, my Julia co'd not heare;....58. H.150, 3
And when true love of **words** is destitute,........58. H.150, 7
Tune my **words**, that they may fall,............122. H.303, 3
Then temper flew from **words**; and men did squeake, 150. H.382, 7
Sil. **Words** sweet as Love itself. Montano, Hark. 159. H.421, 17
Give me **words** wherewith to wooe,............204. H.569, 7
Next for Ordaining, that thy **words** not swell....210. H.590, 7
Wantons we are; and though our **words** be such, 218. H.624, 1
Sweet **words** must nourish soft and gentle Love..222. H.633, 61
Though then I smile, and speake no **words** at all. 222. H.634, 15
When **words** we want, Love teacheth to endite;..275. H.846, 1
Place my **words**, and all works else...........286. H.897, 9
Words beget Anger: Anger brings forth blowes: 287. H.901, 1
Ponder my **words**, if so that any be...........290. H.914, 1
Words fully flowing, yet of influence:.........297. H.947, 2
Chaste **words** proceed still from a bashfull minde. 319. H.1043, 2
And want their Poise: **words** ought to have their weight. 342. N.16, 2
Good **words**, or meat:.........................350. N.47, 16
But when good **words**, by good works, have their proof. 397. N 256, 3
To cloath thy **words** in gentle Ayre.............408. A.2, 54
Here's **words** with lines, and lines with Scenes consent, 415. A.7, 7
Here melting numbers, **words** of power to move...415. A.7, 9
Wore Franck ne'r **wore** silk she sweares; but I reply, 207. H.578, 1
Why **wore** th' Egyptians Jewells in the Eare?....346. N.36 1
Work See **Frost-work, Lily-work, Moss-work, Seal-work, Spangle-work**
Work that to life, and let me ever dwell..........14. H.35, 13
Homer himself, in a long **work**, may sleep.........32. H.95, 6
To **work**, but first to sacrifice;................36. H.106, 58
Of the Fryar, (of **work** an odde-piece.)........93. H.223, 122
On this sick youth **work** your enchantments here: 99. H.244, 2
To **work** Love's Sampler onely here...........103. H.256, 2
Beginne with Jove; then is the **worke** halfe done; 128. H.321, 1
When well the **work** of hony thrives;..........145. H.375, 8
Which I **worke** to Meale, and make............152 H 393, 3
Ile too **work**, or pray; and then...............155. H.407, 5
The **worke** that I wo'd put ye to?..............164. H.442, 2
And **work** no more; but shut up Shop..........212. H.602, 4
And when once the **Work** is done;..............224. H.639, 3
To ask our wages, e're our **work** be done.......241. H.708, 2
This **worke** thou put'st me too.................281. H.874, 9
Wo'd I well my **worke** begin?...................286. H.897, 2
On with thy **worke**, though thou beest hardly prest; 311. H.1009, 1
Partly **worke** and partly play.................315. H.1026, 1
Part of the **worke** remaines; one part is past:..334. H.1126, 1
The **worke** is done: young men, and maidens set 335. H.1128, 1
The Glory of my **Work**, and Me...............339. N.2, 10
God loads, and unloads, (thus His **work** begins)..341. N.14, 1
And let it **work**, for I'le endure................342. N.17, 11
Adverse and prosperous Fortunes both **work** on..349. N.44, 1
The Birth is fruitlesse: Chor. Then the **work** God speed. 365. N.97. 19
And that will make me, and my **Work** divine....371. N.113, 10
To **work** a wonder, God would have her shown,..384. N.183, 1
Christ never did so great a **work**, but there.....389. N.214, 1
God blest His **work** done on the second day:...396. N.249 6
The **work** is done; now let my Lawrell be......398. N.262, 1
For, long this **work** wil be, & very short this Day. 401. N.268, 6
Vnto the Idoll of y^e **work** devine...............406. A.1, 109
I consecrate this loving **work** of mine,...........406. A.1, 110
The brave cheape **worke**, and for to pave 440. ins. H.443, 45bb
Worked So the Divine Hand **work't**, and brake no thred. 385. N.184, 3
Workest **Work'st** more then Wisdome, Art, or Nature can, 45. H.128, 24
Working Three lovely Sisters **working** were........18. H.47, 1
And **working** it, by chance from Umbers Erse..205. H.572, 2
At noone of Night are a **working**..............225. H.643, 18
Work's Who are my **Works** Creator, and alone..3. Ded. H., 3
Works See **Networks**
Brugel and Coxu, and the **workes** out-doe,......150. H.384, 3
For all our **workes**, a recompence is sure:......276. H.849, 1
Place my words, and all **works** else.........286. H.897, 9
And as our bad, more then our good **Works** are:..339. N.1, 2
Heaven is not given for our good **works** here:..390. N.223, 1
Are **works** of mercy to the poore,..............393. N.231, 2
As when, in humane nature He **works** more....395. N.244, 3
But when good words, by good **works**, have their proof. 397. N.256, 3
— — — — — — — — — — —,............452. ins. H.443, 45bb
World By dreames, each one, into a sev'rall **world**..21. H.57, 2
Goes the **world** now, it will with thee goe hard:...22. H.64, 1
I! and a **world** of Pikes passe through..........31. H.90, 9
Wherein all pleasures of the **world** are wove.....40. H.114, 4
Shapelesse the **world** (as when all Chaos was)...59. H.154, 8

When all your world of Beautie's gone.........61. H.160, 10
A world of men to love:.......................76. H.193, 51
The world had all one Nose.....................80. H.201, 24
To teare the world, or set it all on fire..........81. H.202, 6
And bid the world Good-night..................85. H.211, 4
Through the world, but writ in gold...........108. H.266, 20
As in the whole world thou canst find,..........108. H.267, 7
To lend the world your scent and smile........126. H 318, 5
The world with us is buried...................133. H.336, 36
Give me the Daphne, that the world may know it,
143. H.365, 7
Till this world shall dissolve as men,..........146. H.376, 12
No, not the glory of the World, Vandike.......150. H.384, 6
Since man expos'd is to a world of griefs.......15?. H.397, 2
The whole world die, and turn to dust with thee.
155. H.405, 16
And knowes not where i'th world to borrow more.
160. H.423, 4
And let the whole world then dispose..........164. H.441, 11
Like Sybels Leaves, throughout the ample world?
172. H.459, 4
Thee to the World a Prime and Publique One...181. H.483, 8
Out of the world he must, who once comes in:..199. H.548, 1
I, and all the world shall rise.................199. H.549, 4
When I must leave the World (and you)......218. H.626, 2
The world so soon, and in it, you the most...222. H.634. 13
And tells the world, he's now regenerate........240. H.703, 2
Like the Sybells, through the world............242. H.714, 8
Next, from that world of waters. then..........245. H.720, 7
By ruffling winds, about the world.............245. H.720, 16
The present Age will tell the world thou art....267. H.804, 11
Here to be paid; Ile pay't i'th'world to come.....267. H.804, 14
Three, unto whom the whole world give applause;
276. H.851, 7
Though while we living 'bout the world do roame,
278. H.860, 5
And no less prais'd, then spread throughout the world.
288. H.907. 6
Of such a wit the world sho'd have no more....289. H.911, 20
Lost to the world; lost to my selfe; alone......298. H.954, 1
This line about, live Thou throughout the world;
298. H.955, 2
Of a world to drowne but One.................302. H.968, 12
When all the world with rifts is full:..........318. H.1036, 2
Tis no discomfort in the world to fall,.........319. H.1045, 1
Long I have lasted in this world; (tis true)....328. H.1088, 3
Shew me that world of Starres, and whence.....340. N.3, 13
And the world is drown'd in sleep,.............347. N.41, 10
Against the wicked, in another world............357. N.74, 4
The Darling of the world is come,..............365. N.96, 25
In this world (the Isle of Dreames)...........376. N.128, 1
God hath this world for many made; 'tis true:..387. N.198, 1
But He hath made the world to come for few...387. N.198, 2
As that the old World thought it fit,...........388. N.204, 3
That in this world, one onely day.............388. N.206, 2
Bearing aloft this rich round world of wonder.....405. A.1, 46
Seene to the world, Ile giue the skore...........407. A.2, 2
(As wth a Tempeste) Nature through the worlde 410. A3, 24
(The generall Aprill of the worlde) dothe Come,..410. A.3, 34
Whether the world such Sperritts had or noe,.....411. A.3, 38
None writes lov's passion in the world, like Thee. 415. A.7, 18
— — — — — — — — — —,..............426. var. H.197, 47
Worlds Search worlds of Ice; and rather there...111. H.278, 7
Worm See Glowworm, Slowworm
With the Red-capt worme, that's shut..........120. H.293, 39
Nor that fine Worme that do's interre........186. H.497, 13
Worm's See Glowworm's, Silkworm's
Worms See Earthworms
Worn See Outworn, Reworn
Nor are ye worne with yeares;...............104. H.257, 10
Bedew'd with teares, are worne...............106. H.262, 8
To the worn Threshold, Porch, Hall, Parlour, Kitchin,
146. H.377, 5
Out of my comely manners worne;...........312. H.1016, 5
Is worn by'th poore,..........................350. N.47, 14
At thy worne Doore,...........................374. N.123, 19
This livery wch the *greeke hath worne..........418. A.9, 54
Worse Blast these-like actions, or a thing that's worse;
79. H.197, 84
But being spent, the worse, and worst..........84. H.208, 11
His mouth worse furr'd with oathes and blasphemies.
110. H.273, 4
Mon. Bad are the times. Sil. And wors then they are we.
159. H.421, 1
Mon. Troth, bad are both; worse fruit, and ill the tree:
159. H.421, 2
Tis worse then barbarous cruelty to show.......199. H.550, 1
Are made farre worse, by lawless liberty........307. H.990, 2
T'invade from far: They l finde worse foes at home.
316. H.1030, 2
The Cure was worse then the Disease..........360. N.83, 30
Vrging diuorcement (worse then death to theis)..410. A.3, 9
Worship But by Apollo! as I worship wit,......234. H.673, 7
To worship ye, the Lares,.....................234. H.674, 2
Worship be to the Graces!....................260. H.777, 9
Glory and worship be!........................261. H.778, 4
Worship, and not to'th' Asse that carried her...330. H.1099, 6
Not to adore that, but to worship Thee.........371. N.115, 10
Worshiper Her buxom smiles from me her worshipper.
426. var. H.197, 26
Worst Thinke that of All, that I have writ, the worst:
7. H.6, 2
Alas! If kissing be of plagues the worst,........33. H.101, 3
But to avert the worst;........................55. H.149, 83
But being spent, the worse, and worst..........84. H.208, 11
Of English Poets, and 'tis thought the worst....156. H.410, 2
I rather thinke (though they may speake the worst)
219. H.630, 3
Say, who's the worst, th' exactor, or the whore?
220. H.631, 4
That surfeit tooke by bread, the worst of all....286. H.895, 2
To heare the worst from men, when they doe well.
293. H.932, 2
Nor thinke that Thou in this my Booke art worst,
329. H.1092, 1
Worsted The woosted thred....................374. N.123, 39
Wort Or Pea, or Bean, or Wort, or Beet,......200. H.552, 5
Worth What Wisdome, Learning, Wit, or Worth,..48. H.134, 1
Where either too much light his worth.........75. H.193, 22
In Wine, whose each cup's worth..............80. H.201, 19
How high she's priz'd, and worth but small;...103. H.253, 17
That things of greatest, so of meanest worth,..105. H.257, 27
Meerly to shew your worth,...................176. H.467, 11
Woe worth the Time, woe worth the day,......374. N.123, 21
More worth, then Heav'ns Eternitie............388. N.206, 4
Giue vpp his worth: to the painte;.............409. A.2, 80
Injewelld wth thy Natiue worthe,..............409. A.2, 102
Worthiness Thou are a man of worthinesse:......243. H.716, 26
Worth's — — — — — — — —,...........429. var. H.253, 17
Worthy Which makes them worthy Cedar, and the Bayes.
45. H.128, 36
One, onely, worthy to be washt by thee:.........63. H.165, 2
Worthy their everlasting Chronicle,...........170. H.451, 10
But for True Service, worthy of that Gowne,...176. H.466, 7
And glorifies the worthy Conquerer............200. H.553, 2
Worthy the Publique Admiration:..............297. H.947, 4
Worthy thy Benediction;.......................339. N.2, 8
How worthy of respect and praise!............375. N.123, 62
O Volume worthy leafe, by leafe and cover.......415. A.7, 5
Worts See Thrice-boiled-worts
The Worts, the Purslain, and the Messe........350. N.47, 31
Wot Thus frantick crazie man (God wot)......135. H.336, 113
Wo't Wo't thou not smile, or tell me what's amisse?
78. H.197, 33
Would (Partial List) See Wo'd
Who would faine his strength renew,............10. H.19, 13
Some would know................................12. H.26, 1
What man would be here,........................12. H.26, 9
Began to speak, and would have been............13. H.27, 7
And would have kist unto her knee,...............14. H.33, 3
Name it I would; but being blushing red,........24. H.74, 13
Sweet Bents wode bow, to give my Love the day:
159. H.421, 24
But would to Love I could beleeve 'twas so!...279. H.866, 2
His Providence who would not question then?....343. N.27, 4
I would to God, that mine old age might have..371. N.115, 1
Wouldst See Wo'dst
Wound The mellow touch of musick most doth wound
12. H.24, 1
Little the wound was; greater was the smart;....17. H 44, 7
He cry'd aloud, Help, help the wound:..........18. H.46, 4
Thus, thus to wound, not kill out-right:.........34. H.103, 12
No heart by love receiv'd a wound;.............42. H.119, 2
To wound my heart, and never to apply,.........52. H.146, 19
The wound I suffer, never find a cure...........159. H.421, 34
Did wound my heart...........................161. H.426, 4
Man is a Watch, wound up at first, but never....202. H.558, 1
Wound up again: Once down, He's down for ever.
202. H.558, 2
And heal'd the wound in thee..................272. H.828, 4
Only for my wound there's no remedy...........274. H.841, 2
Why do'st thou wound, & break my heart?......328. H.1090, 1
To ease this smart, or cure this wound;..........342. N.17, 6
Nor shalt thou give so deep a wound,..............351. N.48, 9
My mouth I'le lay unto Thy wound.............377. N.129, 5
He that is hurt seeks help: sin is the wound;....381. N.155, 1
To search the Wound,..........................401. N.268, 18
Wounded Draw in't a wounded Heart:.............10. H.20, 2
Their wounded hearts; and names we find.......169. H.449, 7
And with his Javelin wounded me:...............283. H.883, 10
We shall be wounded by the cloathes we weare...292. H.928, 2
My God, I'm wounded by my sin,................342. N.17, 1
Woundest Of these, thou woundest with thy Dart!.50. H.139, 15
Wounds Washt those thy purple wounds with tears.
89. H.219, 6
If wounds in clothes, Cuts calls his rags, 'tis cleere,
144, H.373, 1
By pouring Balme and Oyle into her wounds...201. H.557, 18
For to delight in wounds and murderings.........292. H.929, 2
The wounds of love with singing...............296. H.946, 18
But no one Jailor there to wash the wounds......372. N.120, 2
To all our wounds, here, whatsoe're they be,.....390. N.221, 1
Vers. But yet it wounds my soule, to think,....400. N.267, 6

Wove Wherein all pleasures of the world are wove.
40. H.114, 4
Lookes for the treaders; every where is wove..115. H.283, 122
Woven See Inter-woven
So smell those neat and woven Bowers,........145. H.375, 11
Wrack See Shipwreck
Nor wrack, or Bulging thou hast cause to feare:...23. H.71, 2
Wracked — — — — — — — —,..............449. var. A.3, 63
Wrangling Some time in wrangling spent,........105. H.260, 2
Wrapt See Rapt
Which wrapt thy smooth limbs (when thou didst implore
9. H.14, 11
Our mortall parts may wrapt in Seare-cloths lye:.199. H.547, 1
Wrapt up in Seare-cloth with thine Ancestrie:...231. H.664, 2
As ere was wrapt in winding sheet..............257. H.764, 2
Wrapt in the winding-sheet, with thee:..........361. N.83, 56
Wrath For which, her wrath is gone forth to consume
197. H.539, 11
No wrath of Men, or rage of Seas..............215. H.615, 1
His wrath is free from peturbation;............340. N.7, 2
Thou dost their wrath asswage..................373. N.122, 3
That without wrath, which wrath doth force us to.
397. N.259, 4
Drunk up the wine of Gods fierce wrath;.......400. N.266, 11
Wrath yf resisted ouer boyles...................408. A.2, 71
Wrathful Not wrathfull seem, or fright the Maide,
145. H.376, 4
Love has yet no wrathfull fit:..................273. H.836, 6
God can't be wrathfull; but we may conclude,...397. N.259, 1
Wrathfull He may be, by similitude............397. N.259, 2
God's wrathfull said to be, when He doth do.....397. N.259, 3
Wreath See Willow-wreath
Not so much Rose, as Wreathe..................51. H.144, 4
Your Name to be a Laureat Wreathe to Hir,....99. H.245, 7
Is but a Wreathe from thee...................106. H.262, 12
Thou had'st the wreath before, now take the Tree;
150. H.383, 1
Long may I live so, and my wreath of Bayes,...297. H.947, 13
Snatcht off his Crown, and gave the wreath to me:
313. H.1017, 12
This Hollie, and this Ivie Wreath,..............365. N.96, 30
Wreaths My wreaths on those, who little gave or lent.
143. H.365, 6
No more of Groves, Meades, Springs, and wreaths of Flowers:
228. H.658, 4
The while their wreaths and Purple Robes do shine,
234. H.673, 17
Wretched By wretched Wooers sent,.............131. H.330, 6
And, wretched, I did see.......................240. H.705, 2
Wring See Ring
While you wring your hands and weep........118. H.289, 14
Wringing While others they sit wringing........296. H.946, 15
Wrinkle Can keepe the wrinkle from the brow:..132. H.336, 4
Wrinkles Upon thy Forme more wrinkles yet will fall,
21. H.62, 5
Wrinkles no more are, or no lesse,..............143. H.367, 1
Wrist About thy wrist, the rich *Dardanium....30. H.88, 8
I saw about her spotlesse wrist,.................64. H.169, 1
Why I tye about thy wrist,.....................128. H.322, 1
Or wth thy wrist or flattering Hayre,...........408. A.2, 62
Wristed See Lily-wristed, Silver-wristed
Wrists With Yvorie wrists, his Laureat head, and steeps
206. H.575, 41
Writ But when He's gone, read through what's writ,.6. H.4, 3
Thinke that of All, that I have writ, the worst:......7. H.6, 2
Best with those Virgin-Verses thou hast writ:......28. H.84, 4
And mark it for a Rapture nobly writ,............64. H.168, 9
Through the world, but writ in gold...........108. H.266, 20
And over-read what I have writ................132. H.334, 4
Writ in the Poets Endlesse-Kalendar:..........168. H.444, 6
Among your Mirtles to be writ:................170. H.449, 27
Of all I've writ:................................189. H.515, 2
Writ in my Psalter.............................213. H.604, 12
Who read'st this Book that I have writ,..........229. H.660, 1
Who writ for many. Benedicite.................298. H.952, 4
Treble the number of these good I've writ.........339. N.1, 4
Writ in my wild unhallowed Times;..............339. N.2, 2
(Who writ that heavenly Revelation).............343. N.25, 2
Write I write of Youth, of Love, and have Accesse...5. H.1, 5
I sing of Times trans-shifting; and I write..........5. H.1, 9
I write of Groves, of Twilights, and I sing.........5. H.1, 11
I write of Hell; I sing (and ever shall)............5. H.1, 13
For Epitaph, in Foliage, next write this,..........19. H.50, 5
(Love makes me write, what shame forbids to speak.)
24. H.74, 2
Ile write, because Ile give......................32. H.96, 1
And write thereon, This, Reader, known,........61. H.159, 30
Whom sho'd I feare to write to, if I can........64. H.168, 1
I have to write,..................................85. H.211, 2
To bed, to bed, kind Turtles, now and write.....114. H.283, 71
If I write a Verse, or two,......................182. H.489, 5
Shall write in Spice, Endimion 'twas.............184. H.492, 39
I do write of thee no more:....................186. H.500, 2
If I dare write to You, my Lord, who are,......187. H.506, 1
Write but this upon my Stone;..................199. H.546, 2
Ile sing no more, nor will I longer write........228. H.658, 1
Ile write no more, nor will I tell or sing........228. H.658, 5
Full of fier; then I write......................242. H.714, 5
Still I write a Sweet-heart downe..............253. H.750, 6
And what we blush to speake, she bids us write.
275. H.846, 2
Who with thine owne eyes read'st what we doe write,
297. H.947, 5
Can'st write the Comick, Tragick straine, and fall
298. H.955, 5
When first I find those Numbers thou do'st write;
301. H.966, 1
Il'e write no more of Love; but now repent....334. H.1124, 1
Ile write nor more of life; but wish twas ended,.334. H.1124, 3
Where God is merry, there write down thy fears:.355. N.63, 1
Wanton I may, and thou not write?............357. N.72, 14
Ten thousand Talents lent me, Thou dost write:
368. N.103, 9
God (as the learned Damascen doth write)......381. N.161, 1
Doe it like the Sun to write...................413. A.4, 18
Writes Who writes sweet Numbers well as any can:
172. H.459, 2
If Dorset say, what Herrick writes, is good?....187. H.506, 6
Prat He writes Satyres; but herein's the fault,..238. H.692, 1
Thou writes in Prose, how sweet all Virgins be;..266. H.802, 1
Nis, he makes Verses; but the Lines he writes,...286. H.896, 1
None writes lov's passion in the world, like Thee..415. A.7, 18
Writhing About her head I writhing hung,........16. H.41, 9
Or writhing Brides; when, (panting) they....167. H.443, 110
Writing A Writing, as he went;..................346. N.38, 8
— — — — — — — — — — —, ...440. var. H.443, 110
Written Whose deeds, and deaths here written are.169. H.449, 13
Aboue the entrance there is written this..........406. A.1, 73
Wrong Then Faire ones, doe not wrong..........53. H.149, 3
Ye wrong the Threshold-god, that keeps peace here:
124. H.313, 4
To wrong a Spinner or her Loome..............165. H.442, 15
To shield the Stranger, and the Poore from wrong:
201. H.557, 12
Age shall not wrong thee; or one jot abate.......280. H.869, 3
Wronged The wronged Client ends his Lawes....190. H.515, 23
Wrongs To safe-guard Man from wrongs, there nothing must
67. H.177, 1
Wrongs, if neglected, vanish in short time;....260. H.776, 1
Wroth A Just man's like a Rock that turnes the wroth
152. H.389, 1
Wrought For a wrought Purse; can any tell wherefore?
162. H.427, 2
As if Loves Sampler here was wrought:........166. H.443, 36
That richly wrought, and This as brave;........192. H.521, 22
Under whose Roofe with Mosse-worke wrought, there I
310. H.1003, 3
A Nature, soe well form'd, soe wrought..........408. A.2, 65
Wry-nosed The Eggs of Pheasants wrie-nosed Tooly sells:
204. H.568, 1
Y' (Partial List)
And now y' have wept enough, depart yon starres
432. ins. H.283, 140a
Y'ad And softly handle Him: y'ad need,.........366. N.98, 20
Yard See Churchyard
Throughout that Brave Mosaick yard......... 166. H.443, 47
Yards See Vineyards
Y'are By those true teares y'are weeping.........63. H.164, 15
So though y'are white as Swan, or Snow,.........76. H.193, 49
Y'are the Maiden Posies,.......................83. H.205, 9
Men say y'are faire; and faire ye are, 'tis true;..98. H.241, 1
Y'are left here to lament......................110. H.274, 19
You say y'are sweet; how sho'd we know......112. H.282, 1
And beautious Bride we do confess y'are wise,..113. H.283, 51
And now y'are enter'd; see the Codled Cook...114. H.283, 61
Because y'are slow;..........................137. H.340, 4
Merry at anothers hearth; y'are here..........146. H.377, 29
You say y'are young; but when your Teeth are told
173. H.462, 1
To be but three, Black-ey'd, wee'l thinke y'are old.
173. H.462, 2
We know y'are learn'd i'th' Muses, and no lesse.187. H.506, 7
— — — — — — — — — — —, ...431. var. H.283, 59-60
Yarn Yarne is an Income; and the Huswives thread
221. H.633, 44
— — — — — — — — — — —, ...440. var. H.443, 121
Y'ave Y'ave had at Barly-breaks................56. H.149, 118
Y'ave heard them sweetly sing,.................110. H.274, 9
Y'ave laught enough (sweet) vary now your Text;
111. H.277, 1
Y'ave dipt too long i'th' Vinegar;............146. H.377, 22
Y'ave farced well, pray make an end;..........146. H.377, 24
Two dayes y'ave larded here; a third, yee know,.146. H.377, 25
Yawn Yawne for Thy coming; some e're this time crie.
398. N.263, 7
Yawning Or yawning rupture can the same devoure.
148. H.377, 107
Ye (Partial List) See Fare-ye-well
Come down, and dance ye in the toyle............9. H.15, 1
Gather ye Rose-buds while ye may,...............84. H.208, 1
I co'd wish, ye all, who fric....................117. H.289, 9
Heare ye Virgins, and Ile teach,.................120. H.297, 1
Be ye lockt up like to these,....................120. H.297, 7
Mercie secure ye all, and keep..................121. H.299, 5

If not requite, yet thank **ye** all..................123. H.306, 12
Burne, or drowne me, choose **ye** whether,........254. H.757, 1
What was't (**ye** Gods!) a dying man to save.....278. H.860, 3
Yea The House (Love shield her) with her **Yea** and Nay:
114. H.283, 66
By **yea** and by nay,..........................256. H.762, 17
— — — — — — — — — — — —, ...425. var. H.197, 15
— — — — — — — — — — — —, ...433. var. H.283, 144
Year No sound calls back the **yeere** that once is past..8. H.10, 4
All the **yeere**, where Cherries grow..............20. H.53, 8
To, th' (almost) sev'n and fortieth **yeare**.......41. H.116, 2
With all the Seasons of the **Yeare**..............47. H.133, 8
Where spring-time smiles throughout the **yeare**?.103. H.256, 3
Like to the peeping spring-time of the **yeare**......105. H.259, 8
He keeps not one, but many Lents i' th **yeare**....122. H.305, 6
As Daughters to the instant **yeare**:............127. H.319, 40
The **yeare** (your cares) that's fled and gon.....127. H.319, 44
Warme by a glit'ring chimnie all the **yeare**.....132. H.333, 10
Weeping, shall make ye flourish all the **yeere**.....138. H.343, 4
This **year** again, the medows Deity..............140. H.354, 2
'Tis to be doubted whether I next **year**,.........140. H.355, 7
Just upon five and thirty pounds a **yeare**.........151. H.385, 4
Nor two, but all the seasons of the **yeare**.........151. H.387, 8
With griefe; seemes longer then a **yeare**.........162. H.431, 4
To spring againe another **yeare**................189. H.514, 8
Next, at that great Platonick **yeere**,............190. H.515, 47
The Queen of Roses for that **yeere**.............192. H.521, 32
Growes old with the **yeere**,.....................196. H.534, 17
And make the frollick **yeere**,...................198. H.544, 21
This sweet Infanta of the **yeere**?................208. H.580, 2
One night i' th' **yeare**, my dearest Beauties, come
222. H.634, 1
Twice fortie (bating but one **year**,..............226. H.644, 3
All scores; and so to end the **yeere**:.............230. H.662, 14
An everlasting plenty, **yeere** by **yeere**...........242. H.713, 8
Then to want the Wake next **Yeare**.............255. H.761, 24
Unto the thirtieth thousand **yeere**,...............265. H.794, 5
If that my Fate has now fulfill'd my **yeere**,.......278. H.860, 1
The Christmas Log next **yeare**;.................285. H.893, 6
Enjoy a Christning **yeare** by **yeare**;............291. H.919, 10
Trees this **year** beare; next, they their wealth with-hold:
292. H.922, 3
Thou seest me Lucia this **year** droope,..........303. H.973, 1
Twice five and twenty (bate me but one **yeer**)..328. H.1088, 2
From **yeere** to **yeere**...........................345. N.33, 30
Me twins each **yeare**:...........................350. N.47, 48
Foure times bestrew thee ev'ry **yeere**,...........360. N.83, 36
Seem like the Spring-time of the **yeere**?..........364. N.96, 13
Spring Tulips up through all the **yeere**;.........366. N.97, 21
Smooth as the Childhood of the **yeare**............413. A.4, 4
Their lustfull Clusters all the **yeare**,......436. ins. H.336, 48b
Listen, while they call backe the former **yeare**,
443. var. H.575, 52
Yearly Me, when thou **yeerly** go'st Procession:....20. H.55, 6
Or depth, these last may yeild, and **yearly** shrinke,
148. H.377, 105
At Sheering-times, and **yearely** Wakes,.........192. H.521, 25
No more, at **yeerly** Festivalls.....................361. N.83, 51
Year's See New Year's
With the last **yeeres** brand.....................263. H.784, 7
Years See New Years
That our love out-lasts our **yeeres**.............17. H.43, 10
On your minutes, hours, dayes, months, **years**,..57. H.149, 151
And in compassion of thy **yeeres**,........ ....89. H.219, 5
Wither'd with **yeeres**, and bed-rid Mumma lyes;..90. H.222, 1
Nor are ye worne with **yeares**;................104. H.257, 10
So old she was, that none co'd tell her **yeares**....129. H.326, 6
Ah Posthumus! Our **yeares** hence flye,..........132. H.336, 1
W'are younger by a score of **years**...........136. H.336, 144
And their losse in blooming **yeares**;...........152. H.391, 6
Two Youths sha's known, thrice two, and twice 3. **yeares**;
180. H.477, 3
The Ravens **yeares**, go hence more Ripe then old.
222. H.633, 63
Though long it be, **yeeres** may repay the debt;...228. H.654, 1
Nor is't a life, seven **yeares** to tell,............233. H.670, 34
When times and seasons and all **yeares** must lie..256. H.763, 13
Who dying in her blooming **yeares**,.............257. H.764, 5
My wearied **yeares**.............................258. H.770, 7
And Apricocks, in youthfull **yeares**:............268. H.811, 4
At twice ten **yeares**, a prime and publike one?...299. H.956, 6
We'l from our owne, adde far more **years** to his..300. H.961, 20
For thirty **yeares**, Tubbs has been proud and poor;
302. H.972, 1
In teeming **years**, how soon my Sun was set,....304. H.978, 3
But yet those **yeers** that I have liv'd but few...328. H.1088, 4
Lives not those **yeers**, but he that lives them well.
328. H.1088, 6
One man has reatch't his sixty **yeers**, but he....328. H.1088, 7
For faults of former **yeares**;....................352. N.53, 4
O **Yeares**! and Age! Farewell:..................354. N.58, 1
Nor makes it matter, Nestors **yeers** to tell,.......392. N.230, 5
Yellow And now the **yellow** Vaile, at last,........55. H.149, 71
Yellow, markt for Jealousie.....................187. H.503, 4
— — — — — — — — — — — —,..................433. var. H.293, 9
— — — — — — — — — — — —, ...443. var. H.580, 8
Yellow-green So **yellow-green**, and sickly too?....208. H.580, 8

Yerk Stripes justly given **yerk** us (with their fall)
319. H.1050, 1
Yerked Of some rough Groom, who (**yirkt** with Corns) sayes,
Sir..146. H.377, 21
Yes Ha's it a speaking virtue? 2. **Yes**;.........130. H.329, 16
To God for vengeance? **yes** say I;..............387. N.203, 2
Yesterday I co'd but see thee **yesterday**.........272. H.828, 1
Megg **yesterday** was troubled with a Pose,......296. H.945, 1
Yet **Yet** doe it to this end: that I,................11. H.20, 7
And kisse, but **yet** be chaste....................13. H.31, 10
But **yet** for Loves-sake, let thy lips doe this,......14. H.35, 11
To give (if any, **yet**) but little sound.............15. H.38, 8
But I am not **yet** grown cold;....................17. H.43, 2
Yet justly too I must confesse;..................19. H.51, 5
Upon thy Forme more wrinkles **yet** will fall........21. H.62, 5
But **yet**, though Love likes well such Scenes as these,
24. H.74, 9
Yet Dianeme now farewell:.....................33. H.103, 2
Yet there's a way found (if thou please)........34. H.103, 13
Twilight is **yet**, till that her Lawnes give way;....34. H.104, 5
Yet can thy humble roofe maintaine a Quire....37. H.106, 121
Colder **yet** then any one:........................40. H.115, 12
Me turn'd to tears; **yet** did'st not weep for me.....42. H.122, 4
Who smiles, **yet** slayes..........................43. H.123, 4
Yet say; sho'd she condemne....................43. H.123, 25
A poore, **yet** loving heart.......................43. H.123, 30
Of the resigning, **yet** resisting Bride.............45. H.128, 6
Quiet **yet**; but if ye make.......................52. H.145, 3
Yet I bring Balme and Oile to heal your sore....52. H.146, 22
But **yet**, Loves fire will wast...................54. H.149, 27
Yet not a Maiden-head resign'd!...............54. H.149, 32
Sooner, then she, ever **yet**,.....................57. H.149, 149
May Death **yet** come at last;...................58. H.149, 165
There where no language ever **yet** was known.....60. H.156, 6
You, and your name, for ever: **yet**................60. H.159, 8
And weep to see't; **yet** this thing doe.............61. H.159, 20
All hearts your captives; yours, **yet** free:........61. H.160, 4
Still a falling, **yet** I see.......................62. H.162, 5
Yet comming home, but somewhat late, (last night)
65. H.171, 4
Above an houre since; **yet** you not drest,........68. H.178, 8
This night, and Locks pickt, **yet** w'are not a Maying.
69. H.178, 56
Rough as th' Adratick sea, **yet** I...............70. H.181, 23
Herrick, as **yet**:...............................72. H.185, 2
Yet the next Morne, re-guild the fragrant East...72. H.185, 7
Yet, Porter, while thou keep'st alive,...........72. H.185, 15
Pay we our Vowes, and goe; **yet** when we part,..73. H.186, 13
Yet Much-more still complains he is in want......73. H.188, 2
White though ye be; **yet**, Lillies, know,..........74. H.190, 1
Yet, when your Lawns & Silks shal flow;......76. H.193, 52
'Tis like a Lawnie-Firmament as **yet**...........82. H.204, 5
Where no one piece is **yet** unlevelled.............82. H.204, 8
Yet you are...................................83. H.205, 7
Yet though thus respected,.....................83. H.205, 13
Yet trust me, I shall know......................83. H.207, 3
And all most sweet; **yet** all lesse sweet then he...86. H.213, 38
Yet one rude wind, or ruffling shower............88. H.216, 5
Yet lost, ere that chast flesh and blood...........88. H.216, 8
Yet dry'd, ere you distill your Wine............88. H.216, 12
Yet lost ere you transfuse your smell............88. H.216, 15
Yet wither'd, ere you can be set................88. H.216, 17
Yet the fretfull bryar will tell,................88. H.217, 4
Dry-rosted all, but raw **yet** in her eyes...........90. H.222, 2
The Oile was yours; and that I owe for **yet**:......94. H.226, 9
Yet, quickly you I see by the turne of a pin,.....97. H.233, 3
Yet so it comes to passe,......................100. H.249, 7
Or that ye have not seen as **yet**................104. H.257, 20
Sweeter far, then ever **yet**......................108. H.266, 3
And having none, **yet** I will keep...............109. H.267, 15
No life is **yet** life-proofe from miserie...........111. H.276, 2
Where humane foot, as **yet**, n'er trod:..........111. H.278, 6
Yet, if that neither you will doe,................112. H.281, 5
But **yet** take heed;...........................113. H.283, 55
ly go, **yet**, howsoever, go......................113. H.283, 60
But **yet** too short for you: 'tis we,.............114. H.283, 73
By, **yet** not blessed by his hands,...............119. H.293, 30
But **yet** Love (who subtile is)..................120. H.297, 5
If not requite, **yet** thank ye all.................123. H.306, 12
Weelcome! but **yet** no entrance, till we blesse...124. H.313, 1
And credits Physick, **yet** not trusts his Pill:....125. H.315, 4
As **yet** the early-rising Sun.....................125. H.316, 3
Although not archt, **yet** weather proofe,........133. H.336, 52
Our Barke; **yet** she will keepe alive............134. H.336, 60
Though not so fresh, **yet** as merry..............136. H.336, 140
Yet ere ye enter, give us leave to set...........140. H.354, 3
Loth to depart, but **yet** at last, each one........140. H.355, 1
Ne'r **yet** set tooth in stump, or rump of these.....142. H.361, 2
Thou mad'st me chop, but **yet**,..................142. H.364, 7
Though lost in them, **yet** found in me...........146. H.376, 10
Skrew lives by shifts; **yet** sweares by no small oathes;
149. H.380, 1
And sweetly sings, but **yet** his breath sayes no...149. H.381, 2
Eeles winds and turnes, and cheats and steales; **yet** Eeles
153. H.398, 1
Yet out alas! the deaths the same,..............155. H.406, 5
But **yet** get chilren (as the neighbours say.)....156. H.411, 2

I have now; yet I alone,......................157. H.415, 7
But yet I would not marry.....................160. H.422, 8
Roots had no money; yet he went o'th score....162. H.427, 1
Rook he sells feathers, yet he still doth crie.......163. H.439, 1
Ha's not as yet begunne.......................164. H.441, 2
No Marigolds yet closed are;..................164. H.441, 5
Why! yet to shew that thou art just,..........169. H.446, 11
Those mites of Time, which yet remain unspent,..171. H.456, 3
'Tis better yet...............................172. H.458, 7
One feeds on Lard, and yet is leane;..........173. H.461, 1
Yet let these glib temptations be.............174. H.465, 5
But walke abroad, yet wisely well.............174. H.465, 13
In my short absence; yet behold...............174. H.465, 19
The Pearle of Princes, yet despaire...........175. H.465, 38
But yet if boundlesse Lust must skaile.........175. H.465, 53
So Medullina fell, yet none...................175. H.465, 59
But you may stay yet here a while,............176. H.467, 4
Many we are, and yet but few possesse.........177. H.470, 1
Yet, ere twelve Moones shall whirl about.......178. H.476, 7
Yet to the Lares this we'l say,...............179. H.476, 36
Yet not a Lillie from the Bed appeares;........180. H.477, 4
Yet, though now of Muse bereft,...............182. H.489, 9
Your Child lyes still, yet is not dead:.........189. H.514, 6
Though free she be, ther's something yet........191. H.520, 3
And never, as yet,............................195. H.534, 4
And yet our way has no ending.................195. H.534, 12
This was the old way; and 'tis yet thy course,..201. H.557, 19
Eggs Ile not shave: But yet brave man, if I....202. H.557, 27
He ever pickt (as yet) of any one..............204. H.568, 6
There yet remaines to know, then thou can'st see 206. H.575, 54
And bending, (yet it doth not break?).........208. H.580, 10
But, as lucklesse, I have yet.................209. H.585, 4
Yet we must all...............................211. H.596, 14
And once more yet (ere I am laid out dead)....214. H.612, 13
Cold and hunger never yet.....................217. H.620, 4
Yet, Reader, let me tell thee this.............226. H.644, 7
Never man yet had a regredience...............228. H.656, 2
Yet Jone she goes.............................229. H.659, 3
Yet, who wo'd think,..........................229. H.659, 8
Which though well soyl'd, yet thou dost know,..230. H.662, 22
Although with some, yet little paine:..........233. H.670, 10
Crown'd Poets; yet live Princes under thee:....234. H.673, 16
Upon my ruines (smiling yet:).................235. H.677, 2
Teare me to tatters; yet I'le be...............235. H.677, 3
Yet scarre-crow-like I'le walk, as one,........235. H.677, 7
Then ever, dearest Silvia, yet.................240. H.705, 7
Yet since cal'd back; henceforward let me be,..242. H.713, 15
And wanton as a Kid as yet....................243. H.716, 10
Grow old with time, but yet keep weather-proofe. 245. H.723, 14
Ch. A sound I heare, but nothing yet can see,..248. H.730, 5
Yet love the smell of meat....................250. H.736, 6
Yet if thou wert not, Berkley, loyall proofe,.......252. H.745, 13
Something there yet remaines for Thee to do;..254. H.756, 7
Yet with strutting they will please...........255. H.761, 13
When the Black Dooms-day Bookes (as yet unseal'd) 256. H.763, 15
And yet thou so dost back us..................259. H.772, 3
Yet he'l the courage have.....................259. H.772, 14
Yet he'le be thought or seen,.................259. H.772, 21
Loves thornie Tapers yet neglected lye:.......261. H.781, 3
Juno yet smiles; but if she chance to chide,....262. H.781, 11
We pray 'gainst Warre, yet we enjoy no Peace..264. H.793, 1
Tom shifts the Trenchers; yet he never can......265. H.796, 1
If not to th' whole, yet satisfy'd in part.......267. H.804, 12
But yet how more admir'dly bright.............270. H.819, 6
Yet ere thou counsel'st with thy Glasse,.......271. H.824, 5
Yet ne'r can see that salve which brings.......272. H.828, 7
Love has yet no wrathfull fit:................273. H.836, 6
Yet if my Julia kisse me, there will be.........274. H.841, 3
Yet the houres say 'tis late:..................276. H.850, 4
Yet their Three praises, praise but One; that's Lawes. 276. H.851, 8
But yet those blessed gates I see..............277. H.854, 3
Yet freedome, shee enjoyes withall.............281. H.876, 10
Yeilding I wo'd have them; yet.................282. H.878, 5
Truth, yet Teages truths are untruths, (nothing else.) 282. H.880, 2
Spenke has a strong breath, yet short Prayers saith: 283. H.884, 1
Go with thy Faults and Fates; yet stay.........287. H.899, 7
And yet each Verse of thine...................289. H.911, 9
But teach us yet..............................289. H.911, 15
Demure, but yet, full of temptation too..........290. H.914, 6
Yet send no Boules to him?....................290. H.918, 4
That if (unknitting) men wo'd yet repent,.......291. H.920, 3
Words fully flowing, yet of influence:...........297. H.947, 2
Live long and lovely, but yet grow no lesse......299. H.958, 3
Yet the deluge here was known,................302. H.968, 11
The inward carbage for his cloathes as yet.....302. H.969, 4
Yet with the bench of aged sires,...............303. H.973, 11
Last, yet to be with These a Principa'l.........304. H.977, 2
But yet harmless as a sheep...................306. H.984, 30
Yet still.....................................308. H.993, 13
The servants thumblesse, yet to eat,............310. H.1004, 3
But yet no end of those therein or me:........313. H.1019, 2
But yet a way there doth remaine,.............313. H.1020, 5
Boreman takes tole, cheats, flatters, lyes, yet Boreman, 315. H.1025, 1
Yet part ye from hence,.......................317. H.1035, 28
Then Night now gone, and yet not sprung the Day. 319. H.1046, 2
Is, that I never yet had wife;.................320. H.1052, 2
Yet sho'd I chance, (my Wicks) to see..........321. H.1056, 7
Yet, in my depth of grief, I'de be.............321. H.1056, 15
Since I as yet did never prove,................327. H.1082, 2
But yet those yeers that I have liv'd, but few...328. H.1088, 4
Rumpe is a Turne-broach, yet he seldome can..331. H.1106, 1
To this our poore, yet ever patient Flood.......332. H.1112, 6
Be yet assur'd, thou shalt have one............334. H.1123, 5
Yet be timely fortunate.......................334. H.1125, 2
But yet still lesse then Grace can suffer here.....341. N.10, 4
And though it takes all in, 'tis yet no more.....341. N.15, 5
Yet, Lord, I know there is with Thee............342. N.17, 7
God heares us when we pray, but yet defers......344. N.30, 1
Yet mine eyes the watch do keep;...............347. N.41, 11
Yet before the glasse be out,..................348. N.41, 35
And yet the threshold of my doore..............350. N.47, 13
Yet, in torments, I'le commend Thee:............351. N.48, 6
To the full, yet I will love Thee:..............351. N.48, 8
That slack my pace; but yet not make me stay?...352. N.51, 3
Fain would I rest; yet covet not to die,.........352. N.51, 11
Yet none of these have made me sad:............354. N.57, 2
Let's go (my Alma) yet e're we receive,.........355. N.65, 7
Yet if Thy Bloud not wash me, there's no hope..357. N.73, 4
His was the Bond and Cov'nant, yet.............360. N.83, 21
Yet I have hope, by Thy great power,............361. N.84, 7
To make things sweet. Chor. Yet all less sweet then He. 365. N.97, 10
And fare it well: yet Herrick, if so be..........371. N.112, 2
A deale of beauty yet in thee..................375. N.123, 72
Thy hands (though cold) yet spotlesse, white,..375. N.123, 75
Rapine has yet tooke nought from me;...........376. N.124, 1
But yet this Gift Thou wilt commend,............376. N.125, 7
Angells are called Gods; yet of them, none......379. N.143, 1
As just Men are intitled Gods, yet none.........379. N.143, 3
Nor yet for houses, which are here.............381. N.158, 7
If not to'th sound, yet, to the sense...........381. N.160, 2
One Birth our Saviour had; the like none yet....384. N.182, 1
At once, a Bud, and yet a Rose full-blowne.....384. N.183, 2
Yet it is given to the Labourer.................390. N.223, 2
One onely fire has Hell; but yet it shall,........391. N.227, 1
Of Flesh, yet still............................391. N.228, 6
Be those few hours, which I have yet to spend,..392. N.230, 1
Let me, though late, yet at the last, begin......392. N.230, 29
Then ever, yet, the like was done before.........395. N.244, 4
Yet sowre and grim Thou'dst seem to me;.........395. N.246, 5
Vers. But yet it wounds my soule, to think,......400. N.267, 6
Yet doe Thou please,..........................401. N.268, 31
Then lowly yet most lovely stand the feete,......406. A.1, 91
Yett I keepe peacefull in my dust...............407. A.2, 18
Wch sweeten Loue, yett ne're come nighe........408. A.2, 41
Yett to bee found when hee shall seeke..........409. A.2, 78
Theyre Nobly-home-bread, yett haue price........409. A.2, 93
How stay thay would, yet forc't thay are to goe...410. A.3, 12
Past Noone of night, yett weare the howers not old 410. A.3, 18
Like fier-drakes, yett did'st mee no harme therby..410. A.3, 28
Guesse, soe departe; yett stay A while to[o] see..411. A.3, 59
Knowe yet, (rare soule,) when my diuiner Muse...412. A.3, 99
Thoughe as a seruant, yet a Mayde of Honor....412. A.3, 102
Swells with brave rage, yet comely every where,..415. A.7, 12
But now come in. Euc. More let me yet relate....416. A.8, 23
And I must hence. Euc. Yet let me thus much know, 416. A.8, 25
— — — — — — — — — — —, ...424. var. H.128, 51
helpe on her pace; and though she lagg, yet stirre 430. ins. H.283, 20h
for your approach, yet see their Altars pine? 431. ins. H.283, 60f
which sees the body fedd, yet pined....432. ins. H.283, 70j
Of all that ever yet hath blest............435. ins. H.293, ee
— — — — — — — — — — —, ...436. var. H.336, 64
— — — — — — — — — — —, ...441. var. H.465, 22
— — — — — — — — — — —, ...444. var. H.666, 1

Yew And look, what Smallage, Night-shade, Cypresse, Yew, 27. H.82, 9
Unto the crisped Yew.........................285. H.892, 12
When Yew is out, then Birch comes in,..........285. H.892, 13

Yield To see what comfort it wo'd yeeld:..........73. H.187, 2
Then come on, come on, and yeeld............112. H.283, 17
Or depth, these last may yeeld, and yearly shrinke, 148. H.377, 105
As will if you yeeld, lye down conquer'd too....216. H.618, 12
Thy faithfull fields to yeeld thee Graine..........233. H.670, 9
Will, after ease, a richer harvest yeild:.........292. H.922, 2
Fight bravely for the flame of mankinde, yeeld 433. ins. H.283, 140f
— — — — — — — — — — —,..................448. var. A.1, 67

Yielding Yeilding I wo'd have them; yet..........282. H.878, 5
Of gentle Paste, and yeelding Dow,............374. N.123, 25
— — — — — — — — — — —,..................443. var. H.580, 10

Yields Love, honie yeelds; but never stings.....130. H.329, 23

A milky high waye that direction yeilds..........405. A.1, 67
Cha. I will be gentle as that Air which yeelds....416. A.8, 7
Yirkt See Yerked
Yoke Submits his neck unto a second yoke.........17. H.42, 6
So when Love's yoke is on,......................65. H.172, 9
And be, too, such a yoke,......................65. H.172, 15
And sever'd, joyne in brazen yoke:..............70. H.181, 18
The patient Oxe unto the Yoke,................102. H.250, 48
To have my neck from Loves yoke-free...........155. H.408, 2
Thy yoke;.....................................172. H.458, 2
With a neck by yoke unworn.................306. H.984, 23
— — — — — — — — — —,..............438. var. H. 408, 2
Yon Might yon Full-Moon the sweets..........54. H.149, 35
— — — — — — — — — —,................429. var. H.263, 9
And now y' have wept enough, depart yon starres
432. ins. H.283, 140a
Yond' No, no, no more then is yond' Moone,....49. H.136, 28
In yond' Carnation goe and seek,.............106. H.263, 7
To yond' Star-chamber, or do's seale........149. H.377, 128
Yonder See! see she's yonder set,................43. H.123, 7
Come sit we under yonder Tree,................215. H.616, 1
— — — — — — — — — —,..............429. var. H.263, 7
Yonker Who wo'd not think this Yonker fierce to fight?
65. H.171, 3
Or that this Yonker keeps so strict a Lent,....122. H.305, 3
You (Partial List)
Be pleas'd to rest you in This Sacred Grove,....107. H.265, 3
Thinke you that this,........................116. H.283, 145
I could wish you all, who love,................117. H.289, 1
First you, then you, and both for white successe. 124. H.313, 2
You'll As she, so you'l be ripe for men.........56. H.149, 112
One onely Poem out of all you'l chuse;.........64. H.168, 8
You'l spil a tear, or two with theirs:..........70. H.180, 6
Comforts you'l afford me some:................74. H.191, 6
Yet, quickly you'l see by the turne of a pin,....97. H.233, 3
True to your self, and sheets, you'l have me swear,
136. H.338, 1
You'l with a tear or two, remember me,........140. H.355, 10
Vertue conceal'd (with Horace you'l confesse)..173. H.459, 13
The time will come, when you'l be sad,........179. H.476, 37
Lady, this I know you'l say;..................194. H.527, 2
You say you'l kiss me, and I thanke you for it: 210. H.588, 1
If fragrant Virgins you'l but keep............257. H.764, 7
You'l do my Neice abundant honour..........257. H.764, 10
Lulls swears he is all heart; but you'l suppose..284. H.886, 1
Or'e which you'l walk, when I am laid beneath. 312. H.1013, 4
Young Baths that made him young againe:......10. H.19, 10
Young Bacchus ravisht by his tree...............16. H.41, 13
Young I was, but now am old,...................17. H.43, 1
When as Leander young was drown'd,..........42. H.119, 1
By Ornithes sonne, young Calais;.............70. H.181, 14
A Laurel for her, (ever young as love)..........94. H.224, 8
You are young, but must be old,..............97. H.232, 11
Such pretty flowers, (like to Orphans young)..104. H.257, 13
Wherewith young men and maids distrest,......106. H.262, 3
Profane no Porch young man and maid, for fear 124. H.313, 3
That young men have to shooe the Mare:......126. H.319, 16
Quite through the young maids and the men,..127. H.319, 31
Beleeve young man all those were teares......131. H.330, 5
I'le call my young...........................135. H.336, 93
You say y'are young; but when your Teeth are told
173. H.462, 1
Though thou beest young, kind, soft, and faire, 174. H.465, 3
Though thou art young, thou canst say no,....174. H.465, 34
Shalt lead, like young Apollo..................184. H.492, 36
Go wooe young Charles no more to looke,......214. H.611, 1
Next we will act, how young men wooe;.......215. H.616, 19
On which the young men and maids meet,......230. H.662, 48
By young Favonius...........................251. H.740, 8
While young Charles fights, and fighting wins the day.
254. H.756, 14
Tell me young man, or did the Muses bring....299. H.956, 1
A young Enchantresse close by him did stand..313. H.1017, 7
Grow young with Tydes, and though I see ye never,
316. H.1028, 25
The worke is done: young men, and maidens set
335. H.1128, 1
Unto young Eternitie.........................377. N.128, 7
Young men to swoone, and Maides to dye for love.
415. A.7, 10
— — — — — — — — — —,...............437. var. H.336, 111
Younger W'are younger by a score of years.....136. H.336, 144
Youngling Since Gander did his prettie Youngling wed;
223. H.636, 1
Younglings Of Rurall Younglings raise the shout;
101. H.250, 16
Speak, whimp'ring Younglings, and make known
104. H.257, 15
The while the cloud of younglings sing,........113. H.283, 43
To Thee, thy Lady, younglings, and as farre....146. H.377, 3
Here, naked Younglings, handsome Striplings run
206. H.575, 17
To see the Younglings wed;..................220. H.633, 15
And Younglings, with such sports as these.....231. H.662, 73
Young-men And let the Young-men and the Bride-maids share
114. H.283, 78
Your (Partial List)
By your teares shed,........................105. H.257, 25
You're — — — — — — — — — —, ...431. var. H.283, 51
— — — — — — — — — —,..............431. var. H.283, 61
Yours (Partial List)
From scaring you or yours this night.........123. H.306, 15
His Fame's long life, who strives to set up Yours.
188. H.506, 16
Yourself See Self
Youth I write of Youth, of Love, and have Accesse...5. H.1, 5
For the lost sweet-heart of her youth:..........47. H.132, 8
Youth, or sweet Nature, co'd bring forth,........48. H.134, 2
Promis'd sho'd come to crown your youth........53. H.149, 2
And bid the Youth apply......................56. H.149, 95
A deale of Youth, ere this, is come............69. H.178, 45
And as I prune my feather'd youth, so I........72. H.185, 19
When Youth and Blood are warmer;...........84. H.208, 10
On this sick youth work your enchantments here:
99. H.244, 2
The love-spent Youth, and love-sick Maid,....106. H.262, 15
Goddesse of Youth, and Lady of the Spring,......107. H.265, 1
Baucis, these were my sins of youth..........135. H.336, 120
On, as thou hast begunne, brave youth, and get..150. H.384, 1
Ambo. Poor pittied youth! Mir. And here the breth of kine
159. H.421, 13
Youth (I confess) hath me mis-led;.............216. H.617, 5
Goddesse of Pleasure, Youth and Peace,........221. H.633, 54
Our heat of youth can hardly keep the mean...318. H.1042, 2
With the sins of all my youth,..................348. N.41, 38
God on our Youth bestowes but little ease;....383. N.175, 1
Have pity either on my tears or Youth,..........416. A.8, 4
Whose blessèd Youth with endless flow'rs is crown'd.
417. A.8, 30
And know (faire mistris) of yoʳ youth.........418. A.9, 40
Youthful The youthfull Prince D'Amour here.....63. H.166, 8
The youthfull Bride-groom, and the fragrant Bride:
114. H.283, 88
Youthfull Mirtillo, Here he comes, Griefdrownd. 159. H.421, 6
And Apricocks, in youthfull yeares:...........268. H.811, 4
Then youthfull Box which now hath grace,....285. H.892, 9
Or with thy youthfull houres?................323. H.1068, 10
Youth's Of Youthe <s> swift watch to stand....413. A.4, 7
Youths Oft have I heard both Youths and Virgins say,
149. H.378, 1
Two Youths sha's known, thrice two, and twice 3. yeares;
180. H.477, 3
My frolick Youths adieu;.....................328. H.1091, 6
Zeal My vowes denounc'd in zeale, which thus much show thee,
46. H.128, 47
'Twas done by me, more to confirme my zeale,..78. H.197, 42
The first foundation of that zeale sho'd be......201. H.557, 3
For which obedient zeale of thine,.............360. N.83, 31
With zeale alike, as 'twas begun;..............366. N.97, 25
Chor. No, or thy zeale so speedy,.............374. N.123, 47
Zealless I am zeallesse, prethee pray.............277. H.856, 1
Zealot See Zelot
Long Locks of late our Zelot Peason weares,..275. H.843, 1
Zealous That man loves not, who is not zealous too...31. H.91, 2
Zelot See Zealot
Is Zelot pure? he is: ye see he weares........232. H.666, 1
Zenobia's White as Zenobias teeth, the which the Girles
251. H.741, 1
Zephirus As Zephirus when he 'spires...........55. H.149, 67
Zion Of Sion, Sinai, Nebo, and with them,....330. H.1100, 11
Zion's Ah! Sions Daughters, do not feare......400. N.266, 7
Zodiac And let them through a Zodiac run:......47. H.133, 6
Zodiacs Three Zodiaks fill'd more I shall stoope; 303. H.973, 2
Zone These may coole; but there's a Zone......40. H.115, 11
The best way how to loose the Zone.............56. H.149, 92
Runs from his Torrid Zone, to prie, and look,..114. H.283, 62
Zones Next, place me Zones, and Tropicks there; 47. H.133, 7
Zonulet Or like——Nay 'tis that Zonulet of love,.40. H.114, 3

85